THE
LUTHERAN LITURGY

by

Luther D. Reed

A Study of the Common Liturgy of the
Lutheran Church in America

FORTRESS PRESS   PHILADELPHIA

THE

LUTHERAN LITURGY

"Any one who is to find Christ must first find the church. For how can one know where Christ is, and where faith in him is, unless he knew where his believers are? Whoever wishes to know something about Christ must not trust to himself, nor by the help of his own reason build a bridge of his own to heaven, but must go to the church, must visit it, and make inquiry. Now the church is not wood and stone, but the company of people who believe in Christ; he must keep in company with them, and see how they believe, and teach, and live."

MARTIN LUTHER

"Früh-Christmess" sermon, 1522

v

FOREWORD

This second edition of *The Lutheran Liturgy* is a thoroughgoing revision of the earlier work. In the past twelve years, new treatises by liturgical scholars have appeared in Europe and in this country. Significant changes have affected the organization and life of the church in America. The book itself has won general acceptance as a text and reference work. These facts, if there were no other, make a new edition desirable.

The real reason for revision, however, is that the Lutheran churches in America have jointly prepared and adopted a Common Liturgy. This new work, while based squarely upon the earlier Common Service as expanded in the *Common Service Book,* is a further development with significant changes and additional features. It includes a common hymnal and twenty-five newly prepared occasional services (baptism, confirmation, marriage, burial, etc.). It thus, and for the first time, provides the whole Lutheran church with a single liturgy and hymnal in place of the several service books and hymnals previously in use in eight major Lutheran church bodies operating in all parts of the United States and Canada.

The developments which led to this co-operative achievement are described in later pages. A brief statement, however, may be helpful at this point. Henry Melchior Muhlenberg, sent from Germany in 1742 to shepherd the scattered Lutheran congregations in the American colonies, founded the first Lutheran synod, the Ministerium of Pennsylvania, in 1748. Nearly forty years later, in 1786, he proclaimed the ideal of "One church, one book," for the entire church in the country. Many years passed before this could be attempted.

The reasons were the same as those which prevented the Lutheran Church in Europe from having a common liturgy or a common hymnal. In addition to liturgical ignorance and poverty, the inevitable fruits of Pietism and Rationalism, there were powerful factors of nationalism and language, the self-sufficiency of provincial state churches, and the failure to visualize the possibility of a continent-wide Lutheran Church except as a vague and ineffective theological abstraction.

Early Lutherans in America redrew the map of Europe on American soil. Linguistic groups established separate synods and general bodies, founded colleges and seminaries, and published separate liturgies and hymnals, each after its kind. It took long years, the restriction of immigration, the birth of new generations, the influence of the public schools, and the impact of two world wars to accelerate the process of Anglicization and Americanization, to erase the old European map lines, and to lift the Lutheran *churches* in America to a common conception of a Lutheran *Church* in America.

Conditions improved gradually. Mergers and regroupings simplified and strengthened the church's organizational structure. The first important co-operative effort in the liturgical field produced the Common Service in 1888. This liturgy, though limited to the Office of Holy Communion with proper appointments, and without a common hymnal or occasional services, met with universal acclaim. In more or less complete form, it was included in practically all the service books and hymnals issued by the different Lutheran churches in the country. When the United Lutheran Church in America was formed in 1918 by the merger of three independent churches, the Common Service, in materially expanded form, was incorporated in the official *Common Service Book* of the new organization.

The *Service Book and Hymnal* of 1958 is a work of greater range and content than its precursors. Prepared by two separate but co-operating joint commissions, on the liturgy and on the hymnal respectively, and over a period of nearly fourteen years, it witnesses to inner spiritual unity, cultural maturity, and the sense of common mission of a church which is growing with the country, a church whose separate groupings are no longer loosely tied together in federations but are now being welded together by strong bonds in unity of faith and worship. The thirty-four officially appointed commissioners who prepared the new book were a representative group of scholars and church musicians. Among them were ten presidents or professors in colleges and seminaries, presidents of synods, editors, and prominent pastors.

The present volume discusses only the Service of Holy Communion, with its Propers and its musical settings; Matins and Vespers; the Litany and other general prayers. It makes but brief reference to the hymnal and to the extensive collection of occasional services (baptism, marriage, burial, ordination, etc.) which the commissions also prepared. Important new features of the Common Liturgy are listed in Chapter XI, and discussed in later pages. In addition to comment upon the new texts, the bibliography has been revised with sixty-five new entries of important or relevant books and articles.

The inclusion of this new material, and the necessity of holding the book within reasonable limits, have made it necessary to omit or condense certain passages in the earlier edition.

There remains but the pleasant duty of ackowledging with gratitude the special help given the author by Drs. Edward T. Horn, III, George R. Seltzer, William R. Seaman, and Conrad Bergendoff, his colleagues and friends on the Joint Commissions; by his colleague Dr. John H. P. Reumann of the Philadelphia Seminary faculty; and particularly by Mr. James P. Berg, candidate of theology, who not only verified all bibliographical references in the first edition but also made valuable suggestions and, particularly, undertook the extensive research involved in the revision of Chapter XXIX (Collects and Prayers.) The Rev. Paul H. Feil, missionary in Japan presently on furlough in the United States, gave help in checking references in the chapters on the Propers (Chapters XXVII and XXVIII). Sincere appreciation must also be expressed of the constant courtesies extended by Miss Margaret J. Hort, librarian, and by the staff of the Krauth Memorial Library of the Philadelphia Seminary. To them, to the publishers who have encouraged and assisted in this work, and to all whose counsel and help have lightened the task, the author gives his heartiest thanks.

LUTHER D. REED

Mt. Airy, Philadelphia
St. Andrew's Day, 1959

FOREWORD TO THE FIRST EDITION

This book offers an interpretation of the Lutheran Liturgy and its music as set forth in the *Common Service Book* of the United Lutheran Church. Its practical suggestions constitute a directory for ministers, organists, and choirmasters.

The perfect observance of every one of its directions would not in itself realize the author's purpose. More important than mastery of details is the development of an attitude, an understanding, a spirit with respect to corporate worship and the Liturgy as a whole.

The church's characteristic forms and ceremonies of worship are meaningful, beautiful, and unique. The inspiration behind them is not primarily that of art, but rather of faith. Common appreciations of God's greatness and goodness, and appropriations of his grace in Christ Jesus, have prompted common expressions of thanksgiving and petition. Drawing upon the rich experiences of faith and devotion in many lands and times. the church has fashioned its Liturgy, and empowered and enriched it with the fullest resources of architecture, music, and other arts.

The Lutheran Church, as one of the historic liturgical communions, more than shares in this devotional inheritance. Its strong grasp of the heart of the gospel and the peculiar gifts of its people have enabled it to simplify and purify the historic services of the church and enrich them with noble contributions of its own in prayers, hymns, and liturgical music. To impress upon ministers, organists, and choirmasters the scope and meaning, the unity and harmonious beauty, of these liturgical and musical forms, and to arouse in them the will to study and interpret them in services of ordered reverence, dignity, and beauty, are the chief purposes of this book.

A further hope is that this work may help scholars of other communions, singularly uninformed on this point, to know something of the historic development and rich content of the Lutheran Liturgy, whose distinction it is to have been the first complete liturgy in the language of the people, antedating by several decades—as it did in Germany, Sweden, and Denmark—the fine achievement of the Church of England in its *Book of Common Prayer*. As one of the three great liturgies of the Western Church, the Lutheran Liturgy merits close comparison with the other two, and this book employs a comparative method of study throughout. Such study shows the Lutheran Rite to be purer than the Roman, simpler and yet more complete and unified than the Anglican, and as truly in the historic churchly tradition as either. Its distinctive qualities, in addition to historical continuity and simplicity, are doctrinal clarity and consistency, objective emphasis, encouragement of congregational participation, and complete liturgical texts (Introits, Graduals, antiphons, responsories) for choir use.

The church's worship must be conducted in the church's way. A service is more than a meeting; the Liturgy more than a program; liturgical practice more than the observance of practical rules of order. The forms which the church has perfected through the centuries should be conducted devoutly and intelligently, with the use of a moderate, universally recognized ceremonial.

Extreme practices, whether individualistic or ritualistic, fail to provide a representative exposition of the church's worship and life. Uninformed individualism ignores the experience of the whole church, brings personal preference and peculiarities into prominence, and offends by crude and incongruous experiments. Fussy ceremonialism, though grounded in love of the Liturgy and appreciations of dignity, reverence, and beauty, externalizes worship and, by excessive emphasis upon visible detail, absorbs strength which should be devoted to larger affairs. Between these two extremes the great body of the church lives and moves and has its being. This body is edified and unified by an informed and reasonable observance of approved usages. It is in the interest of this larger group, and of a normal representative type of service, simple in form and spirit but beautiful and correct in every detail, that this study is issued.

Even within this middle group there is ample room for differences in practice. Every effort should be made to use the complete text of the Liturgy (the Rite of the church) throughout the church. In matters of ceremonial detail there will be degrees of appreciation and use. Congregations which follow the suggestions in this treatise will have a moderately rich type of service. Congregations which follow a simpler procedure will have a plain service. Such differences in the manner of worship will not impair the essential unity of content and spirit which the Liturgy itself guarantees if—and this is important—if the text of the Liturgy is used in its entirety and if each detail, whether simple or elaborate, is correctly carried out.

The *Common Service Book* gives practically no directions concerning tempo, volume, shading, or other details of musical expression. Its compilers knew that choirs differ greatly in numbers, ability, and training. They supplied the text with music, but left large liberty in the matter of interpretation. There is now evident a general desire for more specific directions in order that expressive and spiritually edifying services may be promoted with a reasonable measure of uniformity.

Organists and choirmasters can achieve excellence in their special work only if they understand liturgical values. We must understand what is to be sung before we can know how it should be sung. This treatise seeks first of all to present ideas drawn from the best liturgical and musical tradition of the church, and then to give directions concerning interpretation and expression. Historical discussion thus has a considerable place in the book. Those familiar with the complexities of the subject, however, will know that the effort has been to present results rather than processes of investigation.

The directions and suggestions given are not put forth in any dogmatic spirit as though offering in every detail the only possible interpretation. It is hoped that they may be a contribution to the development of an important subject. As long as Christian worship is a living science, there can be no final word. As an aid to those who would extend their studies in this field, frequent references to authorities and other bibliographical details are given.

General discussion is given in large type; historical and other details which may not interest the general reader are printed in smaller type; reference to sources and bibliographical details are confined to still smaller type in footnotes and section endings.

The plan of this book has grown out of the experience of the author. Participating in the preparation of the *Common Service Book,* he has also taught liturgics and church music in a theological seminary for many years and has conducted conferences on worship and church music in many parts of the country. His observation has been that ministers and theological students are generally interested in the Liturgy, less so in the hymnal, and, with few exceptions, not particularly concerned at all with the music of the church. Also that organists and choirmasters, while deeply interested in the music of the church, know very little about the Liturgy or the history and theory of worship.

A further personal word may be in place. Shortly after I came to the Philadelphia Seminary, Dr. Edward T. Horn, then pastor of Trinity Church, Reading, Pa., remarked to me that Dr. Henry E. Jacobs had once proposed that they collaborate in the preparation of a historical introduction and commentary on the Common Service. Preoccupation with other matters, however, made it impossible for Dr. Jacobs to undertake the task.

Dr. Horn, who had never relinquished the idea, then suggested that he and I might attempt the work, though expressing fear that the time required for investigation and compression of material would be greater than he could command. This proved to be the case, and the project again languished.

Time has increasingly made clear the desirability of such a work. In attempting it alone after so many years, and in carrying it to completion amid the pressure of other duties, I have been encouraged by the hope that my efforts might, in part at least, fulfil the purpose and plan of those two great Christians to whose friendship and guidance I owed so much when I became their colleague in the seminary faculty and their close associate in the work of the joint committee which prepared the *Common Service Book* of the United Lutheran Church in America.

My indebtedness to many scholars has, I hope, been fully acknowledged in references throughout the book. In addition, I wish to acknowledge the valued assistance of my colleague, Dr. George R. Seltzer, who has seen most of the manuscript in various stages of its development, and who, in addition to preparing the Glossary, has given many helpful suggestions. Dr. Theodore G. Tappert, also of the Philadelphia Seminary faculty, read the historical section (Part I) and gave me valuable suggestions with respect to content and bibliography. Prof. Charles M. Cooper kindly shared with me some of the fruits of his study of the Introit Psalms and the Trinitytide lessons. President Conrad Bergendoff of Augustana College and Theological Seminary read the first draft of the chapter on "The Liturgy in Sweden" and gave me helpful comments and valuable clues. William T. Timmings, Mus.Doc., choirmaster of St. Michael's Church, Germantown, has reviewed the directions for the musical rendition of the services, and his experience and taste have contributed much to their value for organists and choirmasters. I also wish to express my appreciation of the willingness of the publishers to sponsor a work as technical and extended as this.

It will be understood, of course, that this valued co-operation in no sense commits these friends to any statement that I have made.

I am also indebted to Miss Winifred V. Eisenberg and to Miss Helen E. Pfatteicher, of the staff of the Philadelphia Seminary Library, for help in verifying references, comparing texts, and completing technical details of the bibliography.

To all these friends and associates I tender my warmest thanks for valuable assistance so freely given.

The Liturgy of the church and the music of the church in the service book of the church challenge the best thought and endeavor of every congregation. Every minister, organist, choirmaster, choir member, and intelligent layman should seek to know the structure, meaning, and spirit of the church's service. Religious earnestness and artistic endeavor can lift our worship to new heights of spiritual reality, beauty, and power.

LUTHER D. REED

Mt. Airy, Philadelphia
All Saints' Day, 1946

CONTENTS

INTRODUCTION

PART I: HISTORY

CHAPTER I

CHAPTER II

—Dr. Charles M. Jacobs' statement—Other aspects of Eucharistic faith and practice—Bishop Brilioth's five points: thanksgiving; communion-fellowship; commemoration; sacrifice; mystery—The classic Lutheran tradition—The structure of the Service—The music of the Service.

scheme—A significant liturgical inheritance of the universal church. The Epistle: The word of Christian law—Directions.

The Gradual: A choral response and introduction—Significance of the Alleluia—Luther's appreciation—Omitted in the *Book of Common Prayer*—The historic series restored in the *Common Service Book*—Directions.

The Gospel: The summit of the office of the Word—The living Word in the written Word—Accompanying customs and ceremonies—Lutheran usage—Congregational response—Directions.

The Preface: Antiquity and exalted character—Structure—Jewish and other antecedents—Western development of the proper prefaces—The Preface in the historic liturgies—The preface melodies —Directions.

The Sanctus: Climax and conclusion of the Preface—An act of awesome adoration and thanksgiving—A balance to the Gloria in Excelsis—Significance of the Hosanna—Historic details—The Swedish use—Directions.

The Pax: The ancient blessing of the people and the kiss of peace
—Luther's appreciation—Relation to the Verba and to the Agnus
Dei—Historical details—Directions.

The Agnus Dei: A communion hymn of A.D. 700—Of Roman
origin—The Lutheran conception—Usage of the church orders and
of the *Book of Common Prayer*—Early connection with the fraction—Medieval farsing—The traditional melody—Directions.

The Distribution: The officiant receives first—Question of self·
communion—Preparation by fasting, devotional reading and spiritual concentration—The approach to the altar—Kneeling or
standing—The formula of distribution—The ministration of the
bread—The sacramental blessing—Music or silence.

The hymn.

The Psalm—Significance of the Gloria Patri.

The Lesson.

The Responsory: Character and significance—Capable of rich development.

The Sermon: Its place.

The Te Deum: The confession of faith in song—Content and structure—Its historic melody—Polyphonic settings.

The Benedictus: Text and content.

The prayer: Kyrie, Lord's Prayer, Collect for the day, Collect for Grace—Directions.

The Benedicamus.

The Benediction.

CHAPTER XXV

Name, significance and origin—Lutheran use—The Church of England—Structure of the office.

The versicles: Significance—Directions.

The Psalm—Significance of the Gloria Patri.

The Lesson.

The Responsory: Character and influence—Capable of rich development.

The Sermon: Its place.

The hymn.

The Magnificat: Text and content—Musical settings—Anglican vacillation.

The Nunc Dimittis: Significance and content.

The prayer: Kyrie, Lord's Prayer, collect for the day, Collect for Peace—Directions.

The Benedicamus.

The Benediction.

CHAPTER XXVI

A comparative study of the introits, collects, lessons, epistles, graduals, and gospels of the church year as observed in the

Roman, the Lutheran, and the Anglican churches—Sources of the introits, collects, and graduals—Brief comment on distinctive features of the Lutheran system.

THE MIND OF THE CHURCH

Private devotion is the duty and privilege of the individual. It may well be artless, that is, spontaneous and free. Public worship, on the other hand, is the privilege and responsibility of the church. It must be ordered and administered. It is not an abstraction; it is a solemn transaction. It is faith in action. Times, places, forms, and musical settings must be provided. Reverence, dignity, beauty, and efficiency can best be attained by appropriate formality.

The church has thought much about these matters. It has pondered over principles and details of worship as deeply as over points of doctrine. Centuries of striving to fulfil its mission and of experience with people and conditions have matured convictions, perfected ideals, and developed an impressive body of rites and ceremonies.

Before discussing details we should seek to understand the mind of the church with respect to worship and liturgy in general. We begin by noting the present high interest in everything pertaining to public worship. The rising flood of materialism, godlessness, and selfish brutality in the world threatens all moral and spiritual values. Yet it increases the longing of Christians for spiritual reality in the house of God. Christian believers everywhere are determined to preserve the things of the spirit in the church and to develop the church's distinctive life.

Communions which until recently gave but scant attention to the subject of worship are now deeply concerned. Books and pamphlets abound. Courses of instruction are being introduced in theological seminaries. Church music schools are being established. In many instances this is a positive reaction from an overemphasis upon purely intellectual or emotional aspects of religion. There is today a real desire to recover lost or impaired qualities of dignity, reverence, and beauty in worship, and to promote a definite "awareness of the presence of God." Men are seeking to rise above the uncertainty and mediocrity of individualism in an appreciation of forms of dignity and beauty.

The church also shares in the cultural developments of America to-day, with the increasing understanding of art and music. Courses in the history and appreciation of the arts, museums, collections, and exhibitions, symphony orchestras, choral groups, and, amid the soap operas and cowboy shows, many radio and television performances elevate standards of taste. These and similar activities bring into the smallest communities and the humblest homes the cultural resources formerly found only in great cities. Pioneer conditions for the most part no longer obtain. Men and women are conscious of crudity and ugliness and are determined to eliminate them.

For the historic liturgical communions liturgical study is not a matter of recent or temporary interest, but a continuous endeavor. The current liturgical movement in these churches has theological foundations, historic perspective, and the promise of permanence. The subject will never lose its importance for those who regularly find spiritual refreshment and strength in ordered, meaningful, and beautiful services.

CORPORATE WORSHIP ESSENTIAL, UNIVERSAL, UNIQUE

Christian worship is distinctive because the church itself differs from every other human society. It is the one universal and permanent institution in a world of change. Its divine Founder stamped upon it his conception of a spiritual brotherhood spread throughout all lands and speaking many tongues, yet acknowledging the same heavenly Father, the same Redeemer, and the same Holy Spirit, and following a common rule of faith and life.

The church received at the beginning certain spiritual gifts which are by their very nature perpetual—the revelation of God's will and grace, the sacraments, and the promise of the Holy Spirit to abide with it forever. The Christian ministry was established as an institution of responsible leadership, an organ of the entire fellowship with particular responsibility for the administration of the means of grace and the exercise of the "spiritual authority" which the church as a whole possesses.

Unique in character and ideals, the church seeks that which is "spiritually discerned." As a visible or empirical organization, its ordered purpose is to live in constant fellowship with God through Christ, and to bring Christ and his salvation to individuals, communities, and the whole world. This double purpose is realized chiefly by the maintenance of services of worship, by the exercise of moral and spiritual self-discipline, and by acts of serving love. Because of the Word which "dwelleth in them richly" and the enlightenment and power of the Holy Spirit, its members strive to realize in their own experience the fruits of the Spirit—love, joy, peace, meekness, long-suffering, holiness. Amid complexity and confusion their faith finds a simple, divine plan for humanity. Their hope looks beyond the veil for a glory yet to be revealed.

No matter what other activities the church may engage in, public worship is essential to its life and mission. Common assembly and worship foster spiritual development and perpetuate the common faith. Christian believers everywhere recognize a deep, inner compulsion to "give unto the Lord the honor due unto his Name." Because of God's greatness and goodness revealed in Jesus Christ, our Lord, "it is truly meet, right, and salutary, that we should at all times and in all places give thanks" unto him and praise his holy Name. Intellectual and moral elements are ever present. Supplication and intercession have their place. The mainsprings of common worship, however, are a compelling sense of adoration, praise, and thanksgiving; the desire to hear the truth of God and to be strengthened by the Sacrament; and the joy of spiritual fellowship. The early Christians risked their lives to assemble for common worship. Throughout the centuries since, the church has lifted up its voice in unending song, and we may well believe that even today without common worship the church in any given community would inevitably perish.

In the world men are physicians, lawyers, engineers, mechanics, farmers, businessmen. These distinctions fall away in the house of God. Men are spiritual brothers, children of a common Father, equal before the living God, and equally in need of his grace. The rich and the strong lose the consciousness of secular place and power; the poor and the humble are lifted to levels of comfort and hope; the rich and the poor, the strong and the weak, are of equal stature as they unite in a common service which has greater scale and significance than the private devotions of any in the group could attain. Individuals are raised above the plane of the personal and selfish. Their sympathies, desires, and resolves attain breadth and power as they become conscious of a fellowship with fellow believers in all lands and times, with just men made perfect, and with all the company of heaven. In spite of great and obvious weaknesses here and there—defects of individual character and ability, indifferent preaching, limited understanding, crudities of one kind or another—the experiences of common worship compel men to give their loyalty to the community which, as the mystical Body of Christ, carries his gospel and his sacraments as living means of grace throughout all lands and times.

Corporate worship is essential, universal, and yet unique. The church building is different from the office or the home. The chancel and the altar speak of God and holy things. The liturgy is unlike the books and the periodicals we read during the week. The Lord's house, the Lord's Day, the Lord's Service, occupy a place apart. Because believers remember his promise, "Where two or three are gathered together in my name, there am I in the midst of them," every assembly of worship is pervaded with solemnity and reverence.

Such an experience is realized nowhere else. The church in its worship has a virtual monopoly upon a whole range of powers, emotions, and experiences which profoundly affect life. The messages of Holy Scripture and the weight of Christian experience, the celebration and administration of the sacraments, the sense of common gifts combined with personal responsibility, and the thrill of participation in a solemn and inspiring transaction—these are factors in the equation of life which the church alone possesses and controls. No other organization or institution can compete in this field. It would be well if these unique privileges and powers were more generally recognized and cultivated.

Of all the Reformers, Cranmer probably had the keenest appreciation of the central importance of worship, and *The Book of Common Prayer* has always been a tower of strength in the Anglican communion. Luther and his associates also, while stressing the essentially individual assurance of pardon and peace inherent in the idea of justification by faith, had high appreciation of the values to be found in corporate worship. The Lutheran Reformation was marked by the triumphant restoration of popular participation in the services, by a great increase in the number of communicants, and by an outburst of liturgical prayer, congregational song, and choral music of astonishing quality and extent. The reform of the liturgy and of liturgical worship released newly awakened powers of individuals and of the church as a whole.

Public worship in exercising and developing the spiritual powers of the Body of Christ, appeals to the best in all men. Individuals who could not be interested in doctrinal discussion or even in practical Christian activities are impressed by sincere acts of corporate worship. For as Loehe says, "As the planets go about the sun, so the congregation in her services, full of loveliness and dignity, moves about her Lord . . . pure confession has no lovelier form, no more attractive manner, than when it is engaged in adoration and praise."[1]

Religious conviction is not produced by preaching a code of ethics or by crusading for social and moral reforms. Christianity impresses its

[1] Wilhelm Loehe, *Three Books Concerning the Church*, trans. Edward T. Horn (Reading, Pa.: Pilger, 1908), pp. 196-97.

claims upon the non-Christian world by its public worship of God and its proclamation of a gospel that begets a new life. Self-interest and sordid thoughts disappear when the church in common assembly exalts Christ as the Lord who has loved us and saved us from our sins, and to whom glory and dominion are due. The common man is profoundly affected by such common worship if it possesses reality, strength, and beauty. All these aspects of worship may influence him, but he must feel the power of at least one of them.

REALITY IN WORSHIP IS ATTAINED BY FAITH

Many people today regard religion as a refuge from reality. They believe that we Christians leave the real world behind us when we enter the church to pray. Realism of this sort, particularly as expressed in much modern art, inadequately interprets life because it fails to appreciate spiritual values. Impressed by incandescent bulbs and neon lights, it forgets the stars. Overwhelmed by vastness and complexity, surrounded by wretchedness and need, and convinced of the failure of most human endeavors, realism of this sort believes that only the material, and all too frequently the sordid, can be real. Skeptical even of human achievement, it has no appreciation of divine creation and inspiration, of the supernatural and the spiritual.

The Christian believes in a reality which includes the spiritual. He believes in a great objective Reality, a "wholly other" apart from himself, a divine Being who in Jesus Christ has revealed himself as the eternal God and Father of mankind.

Faith presupposes revelation. It is not mere aspiration, pious wish, or beautiful ideal. It rests upon something objective. Christianity is essentially a revealed religion. Faith is an adventure, but an adventure with map in hand, compass in heart, and a voice to guide. God lives and loves and speaks first of all. Because he is, we are; because he first loved us, we love him; because he has spoken, we believe. "In the beginning God . . ."—whether in creation, redemption, or sanctification. His revelation of himself through the Old Testament prophets is completed in Jesus Christ. In this Christ we behold the divine glory, full of grace and truth, loving, merciful, spending itself, suffering and dying for our eternal good. Such a revelation—recorded for all generations in the Scriptures and brought to human souls through the power of the Holy Spirit in and through the church—such a revelation undergirds our faith and empowers our life.

We are apt to minimize the importance of the Holy Spirit in our worship. Back of all that I can think or do is the divine person, the

5

divine energy, the eternal God. Not by my own reason or strength can I even "believe in Jesus Christ my Lord or come to him; but the Holy Ghost has called me through the gospel, enlightened me by his gifts, and sanctified and preserved me in the true faith; in like manner as he calls, gathers, enlightens, and sanctifies the whole Christian church on earth and preserves it in union with Jesus Christ in the true faith."[2]

Faith which calls forth worship, therefore, is more than philosophic speculation. Its certainties begin where the hypotheses of philosophy end. It rests upon a revelation whose truthfulness it accepts and whose power it demonstrates in its own experience. Back of all common prayer is the common faith of believers; back of the common faith is the revelation of God in Jesus Christ. We begin our collects and prayers not only with a reverent address to God, but with a definite reference to some word or quality of his. Upon such an "antecedent reason" we build our petitions. On Christmas Day we say: "O God, who hast made this most holy night to shine with the brightness of the true Light: Grant, we beseech thee . . ." On Ash Wednesday we pray for forgiveness only after we have said: "Almighty and everlasting God, who hatest nothing that thou hast made and dost forgive the sins of all those who are penitent: Create and make in us new and contrite hearts." We first say: "O God, who hast prepared for them that love thee such good things as pass man's understanding"; before we pray: "pour into our hearts such love towards thee."

Similarly in the great and ringing ascription which builds to a climax in the Sanctus, the Proper Prefaces ground our thanksgiving and praise upon specific facts of revelation: "It is truly meet, right, and salutary . . . *for* in the mystery of the Word made flesh, thou hast given us a new revelation of thy glory"; . . . "Who on the Tree of the Cross didst give salvation unto mankind." Because of these accepted facts we can say: *"Therefore* with Angels and Archangels . . . ." Before any administration of the Lord's Supper we must say that our Lord Jesus Christ "in the night in which he was betrayed, took bread; . . . this do in remembrance of me." Only after this recitation of the words of our Lord's institution can we say: "The Body of Christ, given for thee."

Luther calls this faith, which rests upon revelation and centers in Christ, "a divine work in us" which "changes us and makes us to be born anew of God. . . . Faith is a living, daring confidence in God's grace, so sure and certain that a man would stake his life on it a thousand times. This confidence in God's grace and knowledge of it makes

[2] Martin Luther, *Small Catechism,* Explanation of the Third Article of the Creed.

men glad and bold and happy in dealing with God and with all His creatures."[3]

Faith of this living, active sort believes that back of all the manifold phenomena of life there are eternal values—truth, beauty, goodness—and that back of all the power there is a Person. This person is to be adored, loved, and obeyed as the heavenly Father of us all who invites our worship and trust.

Doubt builds no cathedrals, sings no Te Deums, frames no liturgies. Faith builds and prays and sings. It fills the house of God with melody and beauty. It carries the inspiration of the sanctuary into the home, the community, and everyday life. For essentially faith is life, in its finest, fullest, most harmonious and spiritual development.

Reality in worship, therefore, is attained by the faith which accepts the essential truthfulness and sincerity of the Christian tradition. Without this faith Christian worship would be simply fantasy or pageantry or some other form of make-believe.

REALITY IN WORSHIP IS MAINTAINED BY COMMUNION

Corporate worship is the expression of a belief in the existence of God, and conviction that men may unitedly commune with him. No matter what separate ideas may be involved in the act of worship—adoration, confession, commemoration, thanksgiving and praise, sacrifice and offering, supplication and intercession—all are but parts of the larger idea of corporate communion. William Adams Brown has said: "In the last analysis it comes to this: either there is a God or there is not; either we are alone in the universe, facing its unsolved mysteries and its appalling tragedies with only the help that comes from other mortals as ignorant and as helpless as we, or there is Someone who hears us when we speak and can answer when we call. . . . The man who has learned to pray is no longer alone in the universe. He is living in his Father's house."[4]

This essential idea of communion is particularly stressed in the Lutheran system. It is fundamental to the church's doctrine of the Person of Christ and to its conception of Baptism and of the Lord's Supper. It is inherent in its doctrine of the church and in its teaching concerning the inseparableness of the Holy Spirit and the Word of God. Similarly in the sphere of worship Lutheranism requires something more than mere aspiration or mystical contemplation. It recognizes

[3] "Introduction to the Epistle to the Romans," *PE* VI, 451-52. Cf. *WA* DB 5, 623.
[4] *The Life of Prayer in a World of Science* (New York: Scribner's, 1927), pp. 179-80.

a two-way street. It builds its worship forms around the thought of spiritual contact and exchange of spiritual force.

With naive directness Luther put the matter thus: "These are the two priestly offices, viz., to hear God speak and to speak to God who hears us. Through the benediction, through the sermon and the distribution of the Holy Sacraments, God comes down to us and talks with me; there I listen to him and again I go up to him and speak in the ears of God who hears my prayer."

At another time he declared the nature and aim of worship to be: "That we assemble together at one time and place; that we hear God's Word and lay before God our own needs and those of other groups; and that we lift to heaven strong, earnest prayer, and together celebrate and praise God's blessing with thanksgiving."[5]

Melanchthon in the twenty-fourth article of the *Apology* ("Of the Mass") developed this conception of worship, distinguishing fully between the sacramental and the sacrificial elements; the former being God's gift and signs to us of his will, and the latter our responses of prayer, praise, and thanksgiving.

Dr. Von Ogden Vogt characterizes this Lutheran emphasis upon communion as "a balanced pattern of initiation and response" which comprehends the grace of God and the offering of man. He says, "It is possible that this account of worship is true and that no more valid pattern of worship than this can be discovered."[6] At all events it is a corrective of the subjectivism which characterizes much Protestant worship today, and which exaggerated interest in the psychology of religion is likely to intensify. It represents a positive affirmation as to the objective reality of God and to our belief in his love for us and his revelation to us. Standing upon this objective foundation, the Lutheran Church has developed a rich and joyous response in hymns, prayers, sermons, and music—a literature of devotion unsurpassed in quality and extent.

Communion in its larger sense includes not only personal contact

[5] "Sermon at the Dedication of the Castle Church at Torgau" (1544), *WA* 49, 594.

[6] *Modern Worship* (New Haven: Yale Univ. Pr., 1927), p. 42. Dr. Vogt discusses (p. 53) several "patterns of worship" and expands one which he first proposed in *Art and Religion* (1921) into a seven fold psychological program. This includes vision, humility, vitality, recollection, illumination, dedication, and peace. It is not accurate to contrast with this "the simple pattern" of initiation and response as if that were all there is to the Lutheran system. The Lutheran Liturgy, too, may properly be analyzed into various elements, such as confession, aspiration, praise, instruction, supplication, intercession, commemoration, adoration, reception, thanksgiving, etc. The point is that in the experience of the Lutheran worshiper the thought of communion as an active interchange between God and man pervades all these elements, not mechanically or programatically, but generally.

with God but also fellowship with other believers. Public worship witnesses to the belief that spiritual experience of the highest value can be realized when a group representing the "communion of saints" unitedly enters into communion with God.

Our Lord gave his disciples a form of prayer intended for group use. His words, "Where two or three are gathered together, there am I in the midst of them," assure his special presence with the church as an assembly. Paul exhorted his hearers, "Forsake not the assembling of yourselves together," and developed the thought of sacramental fellowship into the doctrine of the body of Christ: "We being many, are one bread and one body; for we are all partakers of that one bread" (I Cor. 10:17). Luther rediscovered and re-emphasized the significance of Christian fellowship in connection with worship and the Sacrament. In his "Sermon on the Sacrament" (1519) he says: "Christ with all his saints is one spiritual body just as the people in a city are a community and a body, and every citizen is related to his neighbor and to the city. So are all saints members in Christ and in the church, which is a spiritual eternal city of God. . . . Thus to receive the Sacrament in bread and wine is naught else than to receive a sign of this fellowship and incorporation with Christ and all his saints. . . . When we rightly use this Sacrament, Christ with all saints takes our form through his great love, and fights with us against sin, death, and all evil. By this we too are enkindled in love to take his form, to trust in his righteousness, life and salvation; and so through fellowship between his blessedness and our woe, to become one cake, one bread, one body, one cup, and all is shared in common."[7]

Modern leaders stress this point. Wilhelm Loehe says: "We are born for fellowship. . . . The Lord did not make the earth for one man . . . nor heaven for one man. . . . The divine fellowship is the Church of God, the communion of saints. . . . In my pilgrimage through this dark vale I am not alone. . . . The Church is an eternal fellowship here and hereafter."[8] Friedrich Heiler urges the necessity of "group devotion," and in the final sentence of a chapter on "Prayer in Public Worship" says: "The spiritual adoration of God by an assembly of spiritually mature personalities is the highest and purest form of worship, the true divine service."[9] Emil Brunner fights individualism as "the disease of our times" and calls for that identity of personality and community

---

[7] "A Sermon Concerning the Sacrament of the Body of Christ and of the Brotherhoods (1519), *WA* 2, 743-48.

[8] *Op. cit.*, pp. 3-13.

[9] *Prayer, A Study in the History and Psychology of Religion* (New York: Oxford, 1932), p. 346.

which is "the Christian conception of personality and society." He says: "In order that man might realize what is truth and what is lie, in order that he might cease to conceive of all truth as his private possession, immanent in himself, God in His wisdom has so ordered things that this truth cannot be found by the individual man. He must enter into fellowship or communion in order to obtain it. The Word of God can be found only in the message of the Church."[10] Professor Robert Will of Strasbourg in his monumental work, *Le Culte,* elaborates the idea that in public worship individual religious experience and aspiration are intensified in an atmosphere of religious collectivity possessing spiritual unity and universality.[11]

The church is more than the aggregate of its members. As a fellowship, a living body, it possesses functions and powers not found in the experience of individuals apart from the group. Corporate worship is something different from and stronger than the sum total of the personal devotions of individual worshipers. Even where but half a dozen say their prayers together quietly in a fellowship of silence, a distinctive corporate sense is experienced.

Public worship thus has supreme spiritual values for all sorts and conditions of men. A few scholars may project their thinking into the realm of pure theology, the philosophy of religion and biblical criticism. But even such men cannot find their highest satisfactions in these subjects alone. They must join their fellow believers in the temple courts if they would keep their souls alive. For the great body of believers, corporate worship is more significant and constructive than any other single factor in their Christian experience. The liturgy and the liturgical year, with their regular unfolding and offering of means of grace, maintain a weekly and seasonal rhythm which keeps the church in spiritual health. They discipline, direct, and enlarge the individual religious experience of all individual Christians.[12]

POWER IN WORSHIP IS CONDITIONED ON PURITY

If reality in worship is attained by faith and maintained by communion with God in fellowship with other believers, power in worship is realized through purity.

Science holds it a truism that power is in direct proportion to purity

[10] Emil Brunner, *The Word and the World* (New York: Scribner's, 1931), pp. 118-19.

[11] For extracts quoted from these writers in translation, see Bernard E. Meland, *Modern Man's Worship* (New York: Harper, 1934), chaps. 4-6.

[12] For fuller discussion of social values in worship, see A. G. Hebert, *Liturgy and Society* (London: Faber & Faber, 1935).

in chemicals, drugs, and food. Health and strength depend upon cleanliness and freedom from infection. Electrical energy is sapped by short circuits, corrosion, and impurities in contacts. Telescopes and microscopes are effective only when lenses are clean. In a similar way power in worship is conditioned on purity.

First of all, worship must have a great and holy objective. Nothing less than the eternal, holy God and eternal and holy things will suffice. Fellowship and common assembly for lesser ends are important, of course. But fellowship and assembly for the purpose of communing with God in his transcendent holiness, might, and love have the power to appeal to all men because of the elevation and purity of their motive. The vigor inherent in this pure and lofty purpose has built churches and cathedrals everywhere, created liturgies and hymns, composed cantatas and anthems, and inspired the noblest art in the history of the race.

We today know vastly more about the universe than did King David. Yet we find the deepest experiences of our souls anticipated in the story of the psalmist who called upon the creator of the universe: "Create in me a clean heart, O God, and renew a right spirit within me." In the inner sanctuary of our souls we find the same kind of world as that which David knew—the same moral disorder and dishonor. We, too, know that impurity is impotence, that sin ends in suffering. We, too, know that real satisfaction comes only from communion and harmony with God, and that only the pure in heart may see him. These convictions enable Christian worshipers to cast away unworthy motives, and with hearts purified by the knowledge of God's forgiveness to invoke the divine blessing. It is not accidental that for a thousand years or more the minister's private preparation for public service regularly began with an office of confession and absolution, and that the public worship of our congregations so begins today.

In addition to having a high and holy objective, worship must be pure in content and form. And there is no greater impurity than heresy. Impure doctrine may be taught in sermons, in phrases in the liturgy or the hymnal and even by improper ceremonial and decoration. Because of this, the historic liturgical churches have seen to it that in the preparation of their liturgies and hymnals able scholars have weighed every sentence, studied every phrase, and considered the finest points of capitalization and punctuation in the effort to secure not only all possible literary grace but a clear and consistent expression of doctrinal truth as well.

We must also refer to secular influences which frequently confuse and

11

blur Christian thought and worship. When religion is reduced to little more than cheap sentiment, there can be no clear appreciation of premises or principles. Similarities are emphasized and differences minimized. The church itself is thought of as being simply a social-welfare agency concerned with the study of environment and the promotion of reformatory programs. The Christian ministry is scarcely differentiated from the Y.M.C.A. secretariat or social service personnel.

Where such ideas prevail it is inevitable that conceptions of worship and its conduct should sink to low levels. Church buildings of the auditorium and platform type suggest secular places and occasions of assembly. "Worship programs" built around topics of current interest provide novel and ever changing exercises for different days. Cheap and noisy greetings and nervous conversation before, during, and after services, intended as a "friendly welcome" for the stranger, embarrass and distract the serious worshiper. Sermons which explore the remotest boundaries of history, literature, philosophy, art, and international relations make all too infrequent reference to Christ and his gospel. Crudities and positive imperfections in speech and manner mar the reading of the service as well as the delivery of the sermon. Prayers of limited and selfish scope, lacking reverence and nobility of thought, leave the worshiper on the dead level of mediocrity and spiritual apathy. Music of concertistic or sentimental character beguiles or offends the ear, and leaves the spirit untouched. Announcements of social and secular character ranging from church dinners to trivial community affairs chain the thoughts of worshipers to earth.

Is it too much to say that these and similar practices are impurities which dilute, distort, and impair the fabric of worship and short-circuit its spiritual effectiveness? Anything less than the finest and purest we have is unworthy as an offering to Almighty God. Anything less than sustained spirituality in an atmosphere of reverence will fail to satisfy soul-hunger or send worshipers from the house of God refreshed and rededicated to high endeavor. Worship must be lifted above the levels of the secular and the commonplace. The liturgy must never look like the daily newspaper; the music of the church must not sound like that of the concert hall or the opera. Worshipers must come to the altar of God with uplifted hearts and a sense of holy mystery and joy. Purity and nobility will exalt their souls and powerfully impress the world as well.

SCIENCE AND ART AS AIDS TO WORSHIP

Reality and power in worship have to do with its inner essentials, its spiritual factors. In its external manifestations corporate worship achieves beauty and effectiveness by the aid of science and art.

The contributions of science, numerous and important, have to do with physical and practical requirements concerning the times, places, and manner of worship. The calendar, with its calculations concerning the dates of Easter and related days and festivals, is determined by astronomy. The hours of service are determined by clocks and watches, regulated with astronomical precision. Our church buildings, particularly those employing modern materials and methods, require for their construction the science of engineering as well as the art of architecture. Many of the crafts employed—masonry, carpentry, glass-making, metal work, etc.—involve a knowledge of chemistry. Science is now an important factor in matters of heating, illumination, and acoustics.

The elements of public worship are also scientifically organized. The liturgy achieves intellectual strength and consistency because it has been prepared not by literati but by theologians with literary appreciations. The hymnal has been critically edited with the use of scientific apparatus and method. Organ music is an art built upon scientific foundations involving the production and regulation of tone, the composition of pipes, pneumatic and electric action, etc. Earphones, microphones, and loud speakers are all within the field of scientific study and production.

Science establishes conditions and promotes effectiveness, and many matters having to do with the convenience and comfort of worship, as well as its beauty, depend upon the aid which science affords. The living form of worship, with its powers of growth and development, however, is created chiefly by the aid of art.

The association of art with religion has ever been close. As soon as Christianity was firmly established in centers of Graeco-Roman culture, it made a discriminating use of the art of the time in spite of the ascetic ideals of some of its leaders. The earliest decorations in the catacombs were designed to veil Christian truth from pagan eyes while conveying a cryptic symbolism to the initiated. When persecution ceased and imperial patronage made large undertakings possible, the church built her basilicas, decorated them with mosaics, and boldly employed the monograms of the Saviour's Name and other symbols of the new faith.

Christianity rejected the pagan temple along with paganism itself. Paganism was an outdoor religion. Its temples were monuments, not houses of worship. They lavished their architectural detail and decorative beauty on the exterior. Christianity concerned itself with the interior of its church edifices, giving particular attention to the requirements of worshiping congregations.

13

The church grew to strength amid strong currents of political and intellectual life in centers like Antioch, Alexandria, Corinth, Carthage, and Rome. When the empire fell and civilization tottered under the inroads of barbarian hordes, the church became the stabilizing and unifying factor in society. With the passing of the pagan influences of the classic era, art became Christian in spirit. The church, with its teachings, sacraments, ceremonies, and discipline, bound peoples of diverse origins, languages, and traditions into a great moral commonwealth.

The monastic orders, too, became a power in the shaping of art to the needs of the church. Letters, learning, and the arts were sheltered by them and later repaid the debt a thousand fold. Eventually art had practically no field outside the walls of the church and her institutions. Monks labored unknown in their monasteries, beginning works of transcription and illumination in the freshness of youth and completing them in old age or bequeathing this duty to the next generation. Art was not yet commercialized. Even the lay craftsmen outside the monasteries, associated in powerful guilds, strove to exalt the church and her worship.

Thus church art swept on majestically into the Gothic centuries. The power of faith, under the direction of the church, had in a few hundred years transformed barbarians into artists, engineers, builders, and men of science. Princely, episcopal, and civic pride were factors, but religious conviction and poetic inspiration pervaded all achievements. The cathedrals and ministers that raised columned aisles, buttressed walls, and pierced spires to heaven were wonderful indeed, but the buildings themselves were but the heavy settings for unnumbered jewels within. Windows, beautiful in design and aflame with color, revealed wonderful carvings in wood and stone; great altars and reredoses, rood screens and choir stalls; marvelous paintings on walls, wood, and canvas; fonts and ciboria; creations in gold and silver, enamelware, bronze, brass, iron, and lead; superb reliquaries, altar crosses, croziers, censers, incense-boats, crucifixes, cruets, basins, and chalices; and countless service books beautifully bound and encrusted with jewels. Nor may we forget the vestments and embroideries; the innumerable chasubles, copes, albs, stoles, and mitres; the equally notable frontals and superfrontals for the altar. Men of talent designed them and women of skill and patience toiled to produce them.

The church encouraged this mighty effort. She furnished the inspiration and the themes for it, and her liturgical life determined its forms. She bent all art to her will and made it bear her message. Emile Mâle, perhaps more clearly and fully than anyone else, has shown how Christian history and belief were portrayed in the sculptured fronts of

14

medieval cathedrals, and how art became a teacher and preacher of the gospel through the use of Christian symbolism.[13]

Poetry found enduring expression in the liturgy, hymns, and sequences of the church. Music, under the tutelage of the church, had a belated but marvelous development which paralleled that of architecture. Building upon the earlier Greek modes and recitative, the Gregorian system clothed the liturgy in melody. Unfolding in forms of harmony and counterpoint, it blossomed forth into the loveliness of the Netherlands school in the fifteenth century and the spiritual beauty of the Palestrina school in the sixteenth. The quantity and the technical elaboration of these compositions were amazing. Edward Dickinson is not far from the truth when he says, "The world has never seen, and is never likely to see, anything fairer or more majestic than that sublime structure, compounded of architecture, sculpture, and painting, and informed by poetry and music, which the church created in the Middle Age, and fixed in enduring mould for the wondering admiration of all succeeding time."[14]

The Renaissance stirred the whole social fabric to its foundations. It profoundly influenced art and the church. Humanism and the classic revival uncovered forgotten elements and promoted intellectual and artistic endeavor outside the ecclesiastical field. Art became professionalized with a desire for personal expression, recognition, and remuneration. As it became less dependent upon church teaching and tradition it developed a freer appreciation of nature. It thus lost much of its spiritual heritage while developing to the full its technical powers in the spirit of individualism.

The Reformation, broadly speaking, emphasized doctrinal and ecclesiastical reform and gave comparatively little thought to art. The spirit of Zwinglianism and of Calvinism was definitely hostile. This negative attitude prevailed in Switzerland and Holland and permeated the dissenting elements of Scotland and England. Though in time it spent its force, it demonstrated the fact that where the liturgy was destroyed liturgical art, always collective in spirit, perished and with it all power to re-create it. Zeal for doctrine alone, without appreciation of other values, is so purely intellectual and individual that the spirit of worship languishes and the art of worship decays in the dry atmosphere it creates.

Luther and his followers appreciated art and its place in worship. Luther kept the liturgy and the liturgical principle. He preserved much

---

[13] *Religious Art in France, XIII Century* (New York: Dutton, 1913).

[14] *Music in the History of the Western Church* (New York: Scribner, 1902), p. 74.

ancient plain song; he dignified the popular element in worship and gave it a position which it had not enjoyed since the post-apostolic age; he translated the Service into the vernacular and enabled the people to sing it. While at work on the translation of the Psalms "the spirit of the psalmist and the prophets came over him," as Koch says, and he wrote his earliest hymns as a sincere, spontaneous outburst of devotion. He thus laid the foundations of the German chorale, which became more popular and influential than the ancient plain song, and like the latter, supplied inspiration and suggestion for later polyphonic compositions of Protestant composers for choruses and organ. Luther also knew and appreciated the best motet music and vigorously advocated choral singing. His service to church art was immeasurable and the church that bears his name has ever welcomed and employed art of many kinds in its worship.

Formal worship and church art both languished in the days of Pietism and Rationalism. The liturgical revival of the nineteenth century, aided by contemporary romanticism, reawakened interest in the liturgy and uncovered the great treasures of the church in architecture, music, painting, and the minor arts. Church consciousness and a deepened sense of devotion led to the determination that the house of God should again become beautiful. The arts and crafts were welcomed, and they made significant contributions to the revival of worship. Renewed interest in Gothic architecture, and the work of the Pre-Raphaelites and associated craftsmen in England had a parallel, if less extensive, manifestation on the continent. Hymnology, particularly in England, received its greatest impulse since the Reformation. Church music flourished under new inspiration and encouragement in the Roman as well as the Lutheran and the Anglican communions.

This survey shows that art and the church cannot be separated. The radical objections of the Zwinglians and Puritans only emphasized the strength of the union between the two, and the spiritual descendants of these objectors are today zealous advocates of the use of art in worship. It is generally recognized that, quite apart from practical or utilitarian considerations, art employs interpretative and suggestive powers which clothe the forms of worship with propriety, dignity, and beauty.[15]

Art has maintained its long and intimate association with worship because of certain qualities which true worship possesses. Religion, as the experience of the highest values in life, comprehends goodness, truth, and beauty. These three are manifestations of God himself. They

---

[15] For fuller discussion see the author's article on "Church Art," *Lutheran Church Review*, XXIX (October, 1910), 765-88.

are constituent ideals of his kingdom which cannot be dissociated from each other without injury to the whole. They all have their place in worship. To suppress or distort any one of the three impairs the other two. Art belongs to the completeness, the wholeness of life. Life itself, if it is to be fully rounded and wholesome, must be beautiful as well as true and good. Similarly worship without beauty, however sincere, is imperfect because it is incomplete.

Truth, goodness, and beauty are vital qualities which constantly create new and significant forms expressive of their nature. Some of these are intellectual (philosophical or systematic); some are practical (social and benevolent); others are worshipful (liturgical). In the liturgical field it is art which enables the truth and the goodness of the Christian faith to express themselves significantly and beautifully.

Art has supreme powers of expression. Science, by way of contrast. is essentially statistical. It assembles, states, and explains facts. It has to do primarily with the extent, the quantity of things. Art, like religion itself, is concerned primarily with the inner spirit, with relationships, with moral and spiritual values. It is descriptive, representational, interpretative. It perceives and interprets quality in life.

Philosophy and science discuss universal truth impersonally. Great art is objective too, but, perceiving quality in persons and things, it expresses truth with feeling and discerns aesthetic and human values even in specific truths. Liturgical art derives its inspiration from the Christian faith. Its emotional power, quickened by that faith, heightens its spiritual perceptions and intensifies and ennobles its formal expressions. It believes certain things, it ascribes certain qualities to persons and acts, and its expressions of what it believes and feels are not only beautiful but vital.

Art, by its supreme power of expression, impresses, suggests, evokes. Professor Hans Preuss shows how clearly Luther understood this suggestive, evocative power in music.[16] It and all art not only objectify and emotionalize our own conceptions, but awaken and call forth in others an appreciative response of corresponding qualitative character.

Canon Streeter, in an illuminating discussion, speaks of art as, par excellence, the method by which we are made to feel quality beyond the limits of our own experience, by entering into an experience finer, deeper, or wider than our own. He explains how the quantitative power of science can produce an exact map of Venice with its canals, bridges, and buildings; but also how the qualitative power of art can produce a wonderful painting like Turner's, which recreates in everyone who

---

[16] *Martin Luther, der Künstler* (Gütersloh: Bertelsmann, 1931).

17

has seen Venice, and suggests to everyone who has not, the very character and life and atmosphere of the city.[17]

Liturgical art, particularly, has this dynamic, evocative quality. The Nicene Creed is a theological formula which clearly states the divinity of our Lord. The Te Deum is a great hymn which expresses precisely the same truths in a worshipful, vital, and dynamic way. The beauty of its text, enhanced by the power of music, gives it wings. It soars above the high plateaus of intellectual definition and scales the loftier heights of objective, corporate experience, not sentimental but solidly emotional.

The Augsburg Confession and the decrees of Trent give theological conceptions and definitions concerning the Lord's Supper. The Mass and the Holy Communion, as actually celebrated both by Roman and Protestant congregations, give the picture of our Lord's breaking, blessing, and distributing the bread and the wine to his disciples, and vividly suggest significant meanings of the Sacrament for all believers. The historic liturgies afford one of the best approaches to an understanding of the most important doctrines of the church. Students of Christian doctrine might profitably study them as representing dogma emotionalized and expressed in forms of living devotion.

It is this power to impress and suggest that makes liturgical art so valuable a servant in the temple. Mindful of this fact, Wilhelm Loehe said: "The Church remains what she is even without a Liturgy, she remains a queen even in beggars' rags. It is better to give up everything else and to hold only the pure doctrine than to go about in the pomp and glory of splendid services which are without light and life because the doctrine has become impure. Yet it is not necessary to let the Church go in beggars' rags. Much better is it that her prayers, her hymns, her sacred order, the holy thoughts of her Liturgy, should be impressed upon the people."[18]

Should not realization of the unique and positive values in public worship lead the church to concentrate more of its effort on this field and cultivate, with all the resources at its command, the art of worship? The great majority of believers are fundamentally sincere and spiritually minded. They desire and respect solemnity, dignity, and beauty in the formal services of the church. This is the type of religion and religious activity which men and women of the world also can understand and respect.

[17] Burnett H. Streeter, *Reality: A New Correlation of Science and Religion* (New York: Macmillan, 1926), pp. 23-48.
[18] *Op. cit.*, pp. 198-99.

THE SIGNIFICANCE OF THE LITURGY

With relatively few and brief exceptions, Christian worship in general has been and is liturgical. This means that it is ordered, prescribed as to general outline and contents by authority, and accepted and used by congregations widely distributed geographically but united in some general church body. The historic churches—Eastern, Roman, Lutheran, Anglican and some smaller communities—all have their historic liturgies. The so-called "free churches," definitely a minority group in Christendom, all have developed more or less stereotyped forms for local and limited use. These vary from severe simplicity to elaborately developed "programs" built up largely by means of extensive borrowings of responses, canticles, prayers, etc., from the historic liturgies and from other devotional literature of the universal church.

"The liturgy" is a general designation for the officially prescribed services of a church body. The name is derived from the Greek word *leitourgia,* a public act or duty performed by individual citizens for the benefit of the state. Specifically the term is applied to the approved formulary for the celebration of the Eucharist. In a less restricted sense, and as used generally, the liturgy denotes the whole system of formal, prescribed services, including the text, the seasons and festivals of the church year, the prescribed ceremonial, etc.

In either sense, the liturgy is a work of large dimensions and universal significance. It is not a "worship program" or a collection of such programs. The latter, usually prepared by an individual pastor for the use of a particular congregation at a single service, develops a topic or theme in accordance with some "psychological pattern." Lessons, responsive readings and other liturgical extracts, hymns, litanies, and prayers are chosen from various sources and interspersed with organ and choral numbers. This "program" is usually designed as "preliminary" to the sermon in which the topic chosen by the minister is specifically discussed. Such a worship program, however balanced, beautiful, and edifying in itself, is necessarily of local and temporary significance. Privately prepared and locally used, it has no connection with the services of other congregations and usually no close relationship with other services in the same congregation. Any such connection or any continuity with the past is soon broken and forgotten.

The liturgy, particularly in the restricted sense of the historic service of the Holy Communion, is quite different. It is not a sheaf of pretty autumn leaves but a noble, living tree. It is the work and possession of the whole church. It has been carefully prepared and authorized by a general church body. It is used by thousands of congregations over continental areas. Its plan encompasses the cycle of a year. It includes a certain fixed framework for every service throughout the year but inserts in this rich selections of variable material appropriate for particular festivals and days. The beliefs, needs, and desires of all men find expression in its unchanging order for Confession, its Kyrie, its Gloria and other canticles of praise, its Creed, Preface, Sanctus, the Prayer of Thanksgiving, the formula of distribution, the Post-Communion Collect, and the Benediction. The so-called "propers" unfold the theme of the particular day or season in varying Lessons, Introits, Graduals, Collects and prayers, Proper Prefaces, the sermon, and appropriate congregational hymns and choral music.

Each service is a balanced order complete in itself, but each service is related to the other services in its season and to the cycle of the year. Like spokes in a wheel, each service is a polished and perfected part of a larger whole, while the wheel is something in itself, something greater than the sum of all its spokes. Ever revolving, this great cycle of the liturgical year carries the church onward and upward in its experiences of public worship from century to century, from shore to shore, in unbroken historic and corporate continuity. Grounded upon the older and deeper foundations of historic Christianity, the liturgy has the dimension of depth. Its comprehensive quality and the extent of its use testify to its breadth. Its polished and perfected forms, to the completion of which highly endowed spirits throughout the centuries have contributed, give it the inspiration, life, and power which exalt and lift the common devotions of Christians everywhere to the throne of God in the heavenly heights.

It is important, however, that we should not regard perfection of form as the chief quality in the liturgy. Many doubtless regard the liturgy simply as a "fair form of words." It is this—a perfectly balanced form of worship, monumental in proportions and beautiful in detail. Its essential significance, however, lies in its content rather than in its form. It presents a complete and well-organized summary of Christian faith and life as a basis for common meditation, prayer, and thanksgiving. It is an exposition of the Creed and the catechism in devotional form. In the full round of the liturgical year it unfolds God's eternal plan of salvation in the life, teaching, death, and resurrection of Jesus Christ our Lord. It regularly reviews the "things most surely believed among us." It reminds us of the history of the church and of the purifying and enabling power of the Holy Spirit in the lives of believers. Unlike many privately ordered worship programs, it omits no essential part of the gospel. It includes nothing insignificant or unworthy. Because of its confessional character and its careful preparation, it is a living, truthful expression of the church's fundamental beliefs.

The scriptural content and tone of the liturgy is one of its greatest distinctions. Gems from the Psalms, the Prophets, the Four Gospels, and many other books of the Bible are set in the golden fabric of its text surrounded by pure pearls of devotion in confessions and thanksgivings, canticles and collects. These too are scriptural in tone and feeling. "The Word of the Lord endureth forever." Embodied in letter and spirit in the historic and beautiful services of the universal church, it glows with glory unquenchable and gives spiritual grace and power to all who hear and heed it.

In addition to this rich and devotionally satisfying exposition of the Word, the liturgy provides for the regular observance of the great memorial in the celebration and administration of the Holy Sacrament. Its supreme function is to present and administer with all possible dignity, beauty, and holy joy the divine gifts of grace in Word and Sacrament and to call forth reverent and thankful response in the united prayer, praise and thanksgiving of the faithful. It is thus a means, which experience has approved, of establishing communion and fellowship between the Lord and the church. Or, to accept Abbot Herwegen's stronger statement, it is "the medium of a transforming, life-embracing communication of the grace of Christ in his Church."

The liturgy is the product and possession of the universal church. It enshrines the faith and the experience of every age and continent. Traces of Jewish worship are preserved not only in the use of material from the Old Testament but in the posture of standing in prayer and in the distinction between sacrificial and sacramental made by the minister when he faces the altar in prayer and turns to the people in blessing. The gentile Christians established Sunday as the day for common worship and led in the development of the Christian year. The Eastern church framed the Gloria in Excelsis, the Prayer of the Church, the Preface, and the Sanctus, and established the custom of standing during the reading of the Gospel. The Western church developed the Confiteor (greatly modified at the Reformation), the series of Introits, Graduals, Collects, and Proper Prefaces, with the liturgical lessons as we have them and their responses. The Reformation simplified and purified the text of the liturgy, established the use of the vernacular, developed the active participation of the congregation, restored the sermon to its rightful place in the service, and evoked a flood of congregational song, a wealth of collects and prayers, and a glorious body of artistic choral music. The Church of England provided the English-speaking world with noble translations of the historic collects and other liturgical texts. The liturgical scholarship, taste, and practical ability of leaders in America restored the historic services of the Lutheran church in representative and full-bodied form in the Common Service and *The Common Service Book,* and brought forth an even more refined liturgy in the present *Service Book and Hymnal.*

Thus, much like a noble cathedral in some Old World city, the liturgy of the church has been fashioned by the church of all ages— prayer upon prayer, canticle upon collect, invitation and admonition, supplications and thanksgivings in alternate order, the Word of God and the response of man together woven into a living spiritual fabric. If we lived in an Old World city and worshiped in its cathedral, we would know every nook and corner of it, every bay and pillar, the length of the nave and the height of the vaults, the story of its carved portals and the figures in every window. We would wish to know who began the choir, who carved the stalls, who completed the spire, and when and by whom each part was restored.

Similarly, history and biography are written in the liturgy. It, too, bears the marks of centuries and, in places, the scars of battle. The Word and the Sacrament it enshrines have nourished and still keep alive all faith on the earth. Its Te Deums and Magnificats praise the Almighty throughout the centuries; its collects, litanies, and spiritual songs have brought human souls close to God for ages; its creeds and Glorias ring out unceasingly as battle cries against falsehood and error; its atmosphere of devotion is the purest known to man. If such be in truth the high character and function of the liturgy, is it not natural that the church should wish its sons and daughters to know its plan, study its parts, and learn its spirit?

A final important conviction of the church concerning its liturgy is that it is ever youthful though age-old. It is something more than a heritage. It is a living, flexible, powerful instrument for today.

The liturgy indeed comes to us, as it will come to every generation, as a gift from the past; as something possessing the weight and worth of a high heritage. It is a treasure which we have and hold and seek to transmit unimpaired and even enriched to those who come after us. We admire its beauty and appreciate its worth as a representative expression of historic Christianity and of our common faith today. It is a monumental and glorious work of art. Understanding of God's gracious will and mastery of universal Christian experience have given it perfect proportion. A work of art and beautiful in itself, it is the mother of all liturgical art. Noble architecture has built a home for it. Music has borne its text aloft on wings of melody. Preaching has personalized its message. Vestments and ceremonial have clothed it in dignity and grace. Thus, honored and enhanced by all the arts, the liturgy is a gift of the Christian centuries to our own time. The church of today, however, as it studies and uses these beautiful forms, finds them intact with life and power.

The liturgy represents the objective, the universal, and the eternal rather than the individualistic and the temporal. It has, however, great value for the individual worshiper. It gives his personal and disarranged thoughts adequate expression in forms richer and more satisfying than he himself could likely fashion. It unites him in spiritual intimacy and endeavor with his fellow believers in the awesome yet warmly spiritual experience of communion with almighty God. This power of incorporation and unification is one of its great functions. More fully than any other instrument the church possesses, the liturgy promotes general church consciousness and appreciation of the church as "the communion of saints." It makes the individual worshiper conscious of his fellow worshipers and of his own part and place in the Christian community. It lifts the congregation above parochial and local levels to an understanding of the whole church with all its needs and work. It brings the church of today into conscious fellowship with our Lord, with the prophets and apostles, the confessors and martyrs of old. It lifts the Church Militant on earth in confident faith and hope into spiritual communion with the Church Triumphant, with the saints in heaven, and with Christ himself, our heavenly King.

The liturgy acquaints youth with the most important truths of God's Word and impresses upon them the duty and privilege of corporate worship. The liturgy with its power of suggestion enforces the truths which education labors to implant more directly. At the same time, its forms satisfy the devotional needs and aspirations of mature Christians of whatever station or intellectual qualification. It is a flexible and powerful instrument for promoting unity and loyalty in a broad program of intelligent churchmanship and common endeavor. Nor is its influence limited to its own special field. Its constant and intelligent use strengthens and uplifts every phase of the church's thought and life.

With these preliminary observations concerning the thought and the experience of the church in this field we are prepared to trace the development of the liturgy and liturgical worship from the earliest times to our own day.

CHAPTER I

WORSHIP AND THE LITURGY IN THE EARLY CHURCH

The meaning of historic institutions is often best understood by penetrating later adhesions and discovering earliest principles and forms. Such is the case with the liturgy. Our present services contain elements from many parts and periods of the church. The relative simplicity of early forms was soon obscured by elaborations and additions. Some were true developments, others were accretions, and some were perversions. Many find in the medieval church the ultimate expression of worship. Its rich forms in liturgy, architecture, ceremonial, and decoration were impressive. We find simplicity, purity, strength, and conviction, most clearly revealed in formative and reformative periods. The first to the third centuries mark the heroic age. Christianity was a minority religion surrounded by a sea of paganism and enduring hostility and persecution. To be a Christian meant much. Faith and worship possessed urgency and reality, and the forms which come to us from this early time bear the stamp of inspiration and sincerity. Similarly in the Reformation century there was a rebirth of spiritual perception and power which enabled the church, in certain groups at least, to purify its doctrine and worship by reforming the old and developing the new in significant confessions and services.

THE EARLIEST CHRISTIAN WORSHIP

In thinking of the beginnings of Christian worship we must first consider the highly significant period of fifty days between the first Easter and Pentecost. Then, as never again, the little company of believers had the awesome privilege of communing with their risen Lord, whose actual presence was manifested to them in their common assembly. Out of this unique and intense experience came definite conceptions which determined the future of public worship.

24

Unity of Christian thought and life early developed a corporate personality, the "one body" of which Paul speaks (Eph. 4:4, I Cor. 10:17).[1] Regular assemblies and services kept alive the memory of Christ's death and resurrection and the promise of his continued presence with believers. This public worship with the use of some form of eucharistic service became from the beginning the most expressive feature of Christian faith and life wherever it was found.

The New Testament reveals two types of early worship. In the Jerusalem type, older of the two, the faithful continued "with one accord" to frequent the temple and the synagogue. They also held private daily assemblies of their own. At these there was a common meal, prayer, psalms or hymns, an exhortation, and, in some form, the Eucharist (Acts 2:42, 46; 4:24; 5:42; 6:2-4, etc.). Certain Jewish forms persisted but a new spirit is apparent in the interpretation of the Scriptures, the recognition of the presence of Jesus and the power of the Spirit, the expectation of the Second Coming, and a heightened appreciation of the ministry of serving love.

The gentile-Christian type developed twenty years later in Corinth and Asia Minor. Antioch and the churches organized by Paul were quite separate from Judaism. The Jewish year as such soon lost its force. There was an entirely new conception of the *ecclesia* and a definite invocation and confession of "Christ the Lord." Instead of a daily gathering, the Lord's Day was emphasized as the time for assembly and worship (Acts 20:7; I Cor. 16:2). The Lord's Day and the Lord's Supper were new features universally observed before any books of the New Testament were written. In addition to the Lord's Supper (I Cor. 11:20), other names for the Eucharist were the "breaking of bread" (Acts 2:42) and possibly the Communion (I Cor. 10:16).[2]

The first part of the service was general in character and non-Christians were admitted. The second part was for believers only. The elements of worship included readings from the Old Testament and the letters of the apostles, psalmody (including "hymns and spiritual songs" [Col. 3:16]), prayer (I Tim. 2:1), teaching, and prophecy. The *charismata,* or gifts and power bestowed by the Holy Spirit upon individuals for the edification of the church, were a unique feature. Baptism was regularly observed. Offerings for the poor were also received.

[1] On the importance of this concept, see John A. T. Robinson, *The Body, A Study in Pauline Theology* ("Studies in Biblical Theology," Vol. V [Chicago: Regnery, 1952]).

[2] On these two types see Hans Lietzmann, *Messe und Herrenmahl* (Bonn: Marcus, 1926) pp. 249ff. (English trans. by D. H. G. Reeve: *Mass and Lord's Supper* [Leiden: Brill, 1953]). For criticism of Lietzmann's theory see Oscar Cullmann, *Early Christian Worship* ("Studies in Biblical Theology," Vol. X [1953]).

The Agape, an ordinary meal of semireligious character, preceded the Eucharist. This fellowship meal was a continuation in Christian circles of the custom of Jewish fellowships which regularly partook of a meal of social and religious character in connection with their assemblies. As Christian thinking gradually grasped the sacrificial significance of our Lord's death and its redemptive purpose, emphasis shifted from recollections of the Last Supper to observance of the Lord's Supper as an institution of formal and ceremonial character and universal import. In the early decades, however, men and women brought their own provisions and ate them in company with their fellow believers. The wealthy brought much and presumably ate much; the poor brought little and were satisfied with that. Paul in his first letter to the Corinthians (Chaps. 11-14), seeks to correct abuses which had arisen in connection with the Agape and the more or less spontaneous devotional exercises which followed the Eucharist.[3]

The services of the Hellenistic synagogues included, in addition to the Psalter, hymns and other material of psalmlike character. Several passages in Paul's epistles and the Book of Revelation are probably fragments of such hymns, prayers, and other liturgical forms based upon synagogue models, but undoubtedly of Christian composition.[4]

Following are a few examples:

And that, knowing the time, that now it is high time to awake out of sleep: for now is our salvation nearer than when we believed. The night is far spent, the day is at hand: let us therefore cast off the works of darkness, and let us put on the armour of light (Rom. 13:11-12).

Wherefore he saith, Awake, thou that sleepest, and arise from the dead, and Christ shall give thee light (Eph. 5:14).

And without controversy great is the mystery of godliness: God was manifest in the flesh, justified in the Spirit, seen of angels, preached unto

---

[3] On the Agape see Lietzmann, *op. cit.*, Chap. 12. An extensive literature in English has appeared since Lietzmann's time, confirming some of his findings, disputing others. Among the most significant works are Cullmann, *Early Christian Worship;* J. Jeremias, *The Eucharistic Words of Jesus* (New York: Macmillan, 1955); A. B. J. Higgins, *The Lord's Supper in the New Testament* ("Studies in Biblical Theology," Vol. VI [1952]); and, with some significant corrections of the varying views expressed in these earlier volumes, N. Clarke, *An Approach to the Theology of the Sacraments* ("Studies in Biblical Theology," Vol. XVII [1956]).

[4] On the interesting question of liturgical quotations see John Mason Neale, *Essays on Liturgiology and Church History* (London: Saunders, 1863), Chap. 15; and Warren, *Liturgy and Ritual of the Ante-Nicene Church* (2d ed; New York: Gorham, 1912), pp. 30ff. Also comprehensive collection with Greek and Latin texts in Cabrol and Leclercq, *Reliquiae Liturgicae Vetustissimae* (Paris: 1900), I, 1-51. These represent the earliest studies.

the Gentiles, believed on in the world, received up into glory (I Tim. 3:16).

But as it is written, Eye hath not seen, nor ear heard, neither have entered into the heart of man, the things which God hath prepared for them that love him (I Cor. 2:9).

It is a faithful saying: For if we be dead with him, we shall also live with him: if we suffer, we shall also reign with him: if we deny him, he also will deny us: if we believe not, yet he abideth faithful: he cannot deny himself (II Tim. 2:11-13).

And they sung a new song, saying, Thou art worthy to take the book, and to open the seals thereof: for thou wast slain, and hast redeemed us to God by thy blood out of every kindred, and tongue, and people, and nation; and hast made us unto our God kings and priests: and we shall reign on the earth. . . . Saying with a loud voice, Worthy is the Lamb that was slain to receive power, and riches, and wisdom, and strength, and honour, and glory, and blessing (Rev. 5:9-10, 12).

Also Phil. 2:5-11; and Col. 1:15-20.

These liturgical and creedal fragments reflected the practical needs of the primitive Christian community. In particular, the discipline of form criticism *(Formgeschichte)* has been responsible for recognizing the role which the primitive Christian community played in shaping materials during the period from the resurrection to the appearance of the first written documents, like the letters of Paul or the earliest gospels.

Some insight is given in most modern introductions to New Testament study. Community needs from the very beginning were met by adopting materials from both Judaism and the pagan world, adapting them in the spirit of the new faith, and creating new forms to express the experience of the church in the resurrection and exaltation of her Lord. Theology determines and informs liturgy. What men believed about God they confessed in worship and life. It is also true that over the years worship practice colors the theology of the church. Worship practices, which sometimes came into Christianity from outside sources, as in the medieval period, reshaped the formal confessions of the church. In the beginning, however, the experience of the risen Lord overshadowed all else. Both theology and worship were reflections of the living fellowship men enjoyed with God through Christ. Thus in the earliest period references to both theology and worship—belief about what God has done and response of men's hearts to him in praise—appear in New Testament literature. The experience of the living Lord led to belief and worship which set patterns for the development of the church.

27

The author is indebted to his colleague, Prof. John H. P. Reumann, for recent information on studies in liturgical and creedal fragments in New Testament literature. A brief survey is found in A. M. Perry's article, "The Growth of the Gospels" in *The Interpreter's Bible* (New York: Abingdon-Cokesbury, 1951), VII, 60ff. Oscar Cullmann's monograph, *The Earliest Christian Confessions* (London: 1949), suggests reasons why such creed-like, semiliturgical formulas developed, citing the needs of worship, preaching, baptism, catechization, and other situations. Noteworthy examples of analysis of such fragments include E. Lohmeyer's treatment of Philippians 2:5-11 in *Die Briefe an die Philipper, an die Kollosser, und an Philemon* (Göttingen, 1930), which sees the verses as pre-Pauline "Christ-psalm," going back perhaps to the Aramaic-speaking church, and James M. Robinson's article, "A Formal Analysis of Colossians 1:15-20" in *Journal of Biblical Literature,* LXXVI, Part IV (December, 1957), 270-88.

THE SECOND CENTURY

In the second century there are many references to public worship. The Lord's Day was the time for assembly and the Eucharist. The latter, as most intimately related to the final and all-important days of our Lord's life, was the central and distinctive feature.

The past, the present, and the future were woven into one devotional concept as the worshipers recalled the days when the Master had blessed and broken the bread for his disciples; as they became convinced of his continued presence with them; and as they meditated upon his words concerning the heavenly feast to be spread at his return and the consummation of the kingdom. Their services included the singing of hymns and a lengthy prayer of thanksgiving for the blessings of creation and redemption. This prayer introduced the Words of Institution. Greek, the language of the New Testament and the educated classes, was the liturgical language, even in Rome, where it maintained its supremacy until the close of the fourth century. Even as late as the eighth century the lessons were read in Greek and some psalms were sung in Greek at Rome.

Clement's *First Letter to the Corinthians,* A.D. 97, assumes the existence of common ideas concerning ordered worship in Rome and Corinth. This epistle does not refer specifically to the Eucharist. It does include a prayer of exalted character and sustained solemnity, traces of which are found in the later *Apostolic Constitutions* and other liturgical formularies. Following is a brief extract:

> Thou hast opened the eyes of our hearts that they may know Thee, Thou the sole Highest among the highest, the Holy One who rests in the midst of the holy ones. . . . Thou who art our help in danger, Thou who savest us from despair, Creator and Overseer of all spirits; Thou who has multiplied

the nations upon earth, and chosen from among them those who love Thee through Jesus Christ, Thy well-beloved Servant, by whom Thou has instructed, sanctified, and honoured us. We beseech Thee, O Master, be our help and succour. Be the Salvation of those of us who are in tribulation; take pity on the lowly, raise up them that fall, reveal Thyself to those who are in need, heal the ungodly, and restore those who have gone out of the way. Appease the hunger of the needy, deliver those among us who suffer in prison, heal the sick, comfort the faint-hearted . . . remember not the sins of Thy servants and Thy handmaids, but cleanse us by Thy truth and direct our steps, that we may walk in holiness of heart. . . . It is Thou, Lord, who hast given to our princes, to those who rule over us upon earth, the power of royalty. . . . Grant them, Lord, health, peace, concord, and stability, that they may exercise unhindered the authority with which Thou has entrusted them.[5]

A letter of Pliny, governor of Bithynia, to the Emperor Trajan, *c.* A.D. 110, reports that it was the custom of Christians in his province to meet on a fixed day (Sunday?) before dawn and to sing antiphonally a hymn (or psalm) to Christ as to a God.

The *Didache,* a manual of instruction which probably dates from the very beginning of the second century,[6] and which is one of the most important documents of the early church, describes a Jewish-Christian type of worship in which the Agape and the Eucharist were combined, and in which the cup was blessed before the bread. The "Lord's Day of the Lord" is indicated as the day of assembly when the faithful were "to break bread and give thanks, after having confessed your sins, so that your sacrifice may be pure." Forms of thanksgiving over the cup and the bread are given. Wednesday and Friday are set as fast days.

This document also contains a prayer which, in addition to its eschatological ideas, shows a conception of the church remarkable for that early time. The thought of this prayer is constantly repeated in later collects and prayers in every age. It reads as follows:

We thank Thee, our Father, for the life and knowledge which Thou hast made known to us through Jesus, Thy servant: to Thee be glory for ever. As this broken bread was scattered [in grains] upon the mountains, and

---

[5] Translation in L. Duchesne, *Christian Worship* (5th ed.; New York: Macmillan, 1931), pp. 51-52. Duchesne properly calls attention to "the spirit in which the Christians at Rome prayed for the Emperor on the morrow of the fury of Domitian."

[6] More recently certain scholars—Armitage Robinson, J. Muilenburg, Dom R. H. Connolly, etc.—have suggested considerably later dates for the *Didache.* Canon B. H. Streeter, J. M. Creed, and others have ably defended the earlier and generally accepted date. For reference to discussions see E. C. Ratcliff's article, "Christian Worship and Liturgy," in Kenneth E. Kirk, *The Study of Theology* (New York: Harper, 1939), pp. 407ff., especially pp. 425-26.

being gathered together became one, so let Thy Church be gathered together from the ends of the earth into Thy Kingdom; for Thine is the glory and the power through Jesus Christ for ever.[7]

Here also we find a post-communion prayer of excellent and comprehensive character.

And after being filled, give thanks in this manner: We thank Thee, O Holy Father, for Thy holy name, which Thou hast enshrined in our hearts, and for the knowledge, and faith, and immortality which Thou madest known to us through Jesus, Thy Servant: to Thee be the glory forever. . . . Remember, O Lord, Thy Church, to deliver her from every evil, and to make her perfect in Thy love; and do Thou gather her together from the four winds [the church] sanctified for Thy Kingdom, which Thou didst prepare for her: for Thine is the power and the glory for ever.[8]

Justin Martyr, a philosopher who embraced Christianity and later suffered martyrdom, c. A.D. 165, addressed his *Apologia* to the emperor, defending the practices of the Christians. Writing from Rome about seventy years after the death of Paul, his description gives a vivid account of the assemblies and worship of the time. It also shows clearly, and for the first time, an unbroken connection between the Service of the Holy Supper and the Service of the Word in Christian worship. The Service of the Word included readings from the Old Testament and the "memoirs of the apostles" (the various epistles and gospels which circulated up until the closing of the canon), a homily by the president, common prayers said by all standing, and the Kiss of Peace. In the Communion Service proper the solemn Prayer of Thanksgiving and Consecration (with the Words of Institution) was said "at length" and "according to the ability of the celebrant."

The marked emphasis upon prayer and thanksgiving is reminiscent of the central action of the Jewish synagogue service. The conception of the Christian community as "one body" was so strong that provision was made even for the absent to receive portions of the bread and wine which were blessed at the service.

Following are extracts from the brief chapters in Justin's *First Apology* (LXV-LXVII) which deal with worship.

On the day called Sunday, all who live in cities or in the country gather together in one place, and the memoirs of the Apostles or the writings of the prophets are read, as long as time permits; then, when the reader has

[7] Translation by Philip Schaff in *The Teaching of the Twelve Apostles* (3d ed.; New York: Funk & Wagnalls, 1885), Greek text in Lietzmann, *op. cit.,* p. 231.
[8] Schaff, *op. cit.,* p. 58; and Lietzmann, *op. cit.,* p. 231.

ceased, the president verbally instructs, and exhorts to the imitation of these good things. Then we all rise together and pray. . . . But Sunday is the day on which we all hold our common assembly, because it is the first day on which God, having wrought a change in the darkness and matter, made the world; and Jesus Christ our Saviour on the same day rose from the dead. . . . (LXVII)

After describing a baptismal service Justin says:

Having ended the prayers, we salute one another with a kiss. There is then brought to the president of the brethren bread and a cup of wine mixed with water; and he taking them, gives praise and glory to the Father of the universe, through the name of the Son and of the Holy Ghost, and offers thanks at considerable length for our being counted worthy to receive these things at His hands. And when he has concluded the prayers and thanksgivings, all the people present express their assent by saying Amen. This word Amen answers in the Hebrew language to *genoito* [so be it]. And when the president has given thanks, and all the people have expressed their assent, those who are called by us deacons give to each of those present to partake of the bread and wine mixed with water over which the thanksgiving was pronounced, and to those who are absent they carry away a portion.

And this food is called among us *Eucharistia* [the Eucharist], of which no one is allowed to partake but the man who believes that the things which we teach are true, and who has been washed with the washing that is for the remission of sins, and unto regeneration, and who is so living as Christ has enjoined. For not as common bread and common drink do we receive these; but in like manner as Jesus Christ our Saviour, having been made flesh by the Word of God, had both flesh and blood for our salvation, so likewise have we been taught that the food which is blessed by the prayer of His word, and from which our blood and flesh by transmutation are nourished, is the flesh and blood of that Jesus who was made flesh. For the Apostles, in the memoirs composed by them, which are called Gospels, have thus delivered unto us what was enjoined upon them; that Jesus took bread, and when He had given thanks, said, "This do ye in remembrance of Me, this is My body"; and that, after the same manner, having taken the cup and given thanks, He said, "This is My blood"; and gave it to them alone. Which the wicked devils have imitated in the mysteries of Mithras, commanding the same thing to be done. For, that bread and a cup of water are placed with certain incantations in the mystic rites of one who is being initiated, you either know or can learn. (LXV-LXVI).[9]

During the first two centuries Christian worship was essentially congregational, with hymns and liturgical responses. The congregation was a universal priesthood. Under the direction of recognized leaders, it offered its spiritual sacrifices of prayer, praise, and thanksgiving and brought its gifts of bread and wine for the Eucharist and for distribu-

[9] Alexander Roberts & James Donaldson (eds.), *The Ante-Nicene Fathers* (New York: Christian Literature Co., 1885-96), I, 185-86.

tion to the poor. When the term "priest" was used it signified an office, not an order. Up to the middle of the second century at least, the services were characterized by spontaneity and fervor, particularly because of the activities of the "prophets" and others specially endowed with the "gifts" of the Spirit, who were allowed great freedom in leading worship.

At the principal celebration on Sunday, when "the solemnities of the Lord" were observed, there was a general prayer of the litany type. The people prayed standing, with hands uplifted, facing the east. Confession preceded the Eucharist. The lessons included selections from the Prophets, the Epistles, and the Gospels, with alternate chanting of psalms between. The Preface and the Invocation of the Holy Spirit (*epiclesis*) were found everywhere. The Lord's Supper was thought of not only as a thank offering of the people (Eucharist), but also as a means through which the life of Christ was imparted to the believer. Bishops, regularly elected, rapidly took the place of the earlier "prophets." After the death of Polycarp (155), veneration of the martyrs received new impetus. By the fourth century the observance of the anniversaries of martyrs' deaths (their "birthdays") became an important factor in the development of the church's calendar.

The Holy Scriptures naturally were the first written portions of the Service. The short exclamations of the people, Amen. Alleluia, Kyrie eleison, etc., were more or less spontaneous. Habit and memory established a common order long before service books were prepared. Certain liturgical responses and simple litany forms came into early use. These, like the psalms and the Lord's Prayer, were said by heart. The longer prayers were extemporaneous. The second century saw the disappearance of the Agape and of prophecy ("speaking with tongues," etc.) and the development of a somewhat more formal type of worship.

In concluding this section we call attention to a fresh and satisfying account of Christian worship in the first two centuries by the late Canon Percy Dearmer. The following summary is particularly interesting.

> Christian worship began then in a table-fellowship, consecrated by the very presence of the Lord, a devout and joyful love-feast which was at once a domestic meal and a communion, as S. Paul said, of the body and blood of the Christ; its prayers were mainly thanksgivings, its object the offering of praise and love to God and the reception of his Spirit in a new kind of divine fellowship; it culminated at first in ecstatic spiritual exercises. As time went on and numbers increased, it necessarily lost something of this domestic intimate character; by the end of the second century the Agape had been separated from the Eucharist, during the third it survived as a funeral feast, and then gradually disappeared. Meanwhile, during the sec-

ond century, the Eucharist had of necessity developed into a stately service, in which congregations, increasingly numerous, stood before the Lord's table, round which the ministers officiated under the bishop, who left his seat at the end of the church during the service and came forward, still facing the congregation, to offer the Great Thanksgiving which was the consecration of the elements. Because these things had to be done (as S. Paul had said) decently and in order, a ceremonial developed, a ceremonial of action, broad and stately, free from petty details, containing still many elements of improvisation, and varying freely in different parts of the Church. The development had been necessary and legitimate, the principles of Christian worship had not been lost. To us of the twentieth century the position then reached seems to be almost ideal.[10]

THE THIRD CENTURY

Formerly scholars regarded the Leonine Sacramentary, (*c.* A.D. 530) as the oldest liturgical book of the Western church. The picture changed when, in 1916, Hugh Connolly, an English Benedictine, revealed the true significance of the *Apostolic Tradition* of Hippolytus. This Roman bishop of the first quarter of the third century wrote extensively on exegetical, doctrinal, and practical subjects. His *Tradition,* which was widely accepted, particularly in Syria and Egypt, consists chiefly of laws for church organization and directions for the conduct of worship. As his purpose was to perpetuate accepted uses, rejecting all innovations, this document presumably portrays conditions in the church considerably earlier than his own time. It marks the close of the freer and more spontaneous period and the recognition of a formal ritual pattern at least for the central action of the Eucharist.

The Eucharistic Prayer (*Anaphora*) of Hippolytus gives us the earliest form of what later developed into the Canon of the Mass. It contains not only a prayer of consecration of the bread and wine, but also a summary of the Christian faith. After prescribing the use of the Salutation and the Sursum Corda ("Lift up your hearts")—the latter in extended form and in both Greek and Latin—the prayer continues as follows:

THANKSGIVING: We give thee thanks, O God, through thy beloved Servant Jesus Christ, whom at the end of time thou didst send to us a Saviour and Redeemer and the Messenger of thy counsel. Who is thy Word, inseparable from thee; through whom thou didst make all things and in whom thou art well pleased. Whom thou didst send from heaven into the womb of the Virgin, and who, dwelling within her, was made flesh, and was manifested as thy Son, being born of [the] Holy Spirit and the Virgin.

[10] Percy Dearmer, *The Church at Prayer and the World Outside* (London: Clarke, 1923), pp. 88f., see also pp. 103-20.

Who, fulfilling thy will, and winning for himself a holy people, spread out his hands when he came to suffer, that by his death he might set free them who believed on thee. Who, when he was betrayed to his willing death, that he might bring to nought death, and break the bonds of the devil, and tread hell under foot, and give light to the righteous, and set up a boundary post, and manifest his resurrection,

NARRATIVE OF THE INSTITUTION: taking bread and giving thanks to thee said: Take, eat: this is my body, which is broken for you. And likewise also the cup, saying: This is my blood, which is shed for you. As often as ye perform this, perform my memorial.

ANAMNESIS: Having in memory, therefore, his death and resurrection, we offer to thee the bread and the cup, yielding thee thanks, because thou hast counted us worthy to stand before thee and to minister to thee.

EPICLESIS: And we pray thee that thou wouldest send thy Holy Spirit upon the offerings of thy holy church; that thou, gathering them into one, wouldest grant to all thy saints who partake to be filled with [the] Holy Spirit, that their faith may be confirmed in truth, that we may praise and glorify thee. Through thy Servant Jesus Christ, through whom be to thee glory and honour, with [the] Holy Spirit in the holy church, both now and always and world without end.[11]

Rather fragmentary notices in the writings of Tertullian and Cyprian (and later Optatus and Augustine) inform us concerning liturgical developments in the Church of North Africa. Tertullian describes the Agape or evening social meal, and refers to the Eucharist as being celebrated early in the morning. He speaks of readings from the Law, the Prophets, Gospels, and the Letters of the Apostles; and of prayers by the assembly for the emperor and all in authority, and for the peace and good estate of the world. The prayers on Sundays and on all days from Easter to Pentecost were said standing.

Cyprian, bishop of Carthage, who suffered martyrdom A.D. 258, was the original "high churchman." He conceives the church as established upon the unity of the bishops, and declares that outside of the church there is no salvation. He also testifies that the Eucharist was celebrated in the morning. He mentions the Sursum Corda which, after this date, introduces the Prayer of Consecration in every liturgy. He also mentions the Kyrie Eleison, the exclamation "Thanks be to God," and the Lord's Prayer following the consecration. His account also refers to the so-called "mixed chalice," the mingling of the water with the wine. The people stood when the Gospel was read. The celebrant received the elements first, after him the other clergy, then the laity,

---

[11] Translation from Burton Scott Easton, *The Apostolic Tradition of Hippolytus* (London: Cambridge Univ. Pr., 1934), pp. 35-36. On the *Tradition* see also G. Dix, *The Treatise on the Apostolic Tradition of St. Hippolytus of Rome* (London: S.P.C.K., 1937). Lietzmann regarded this prayer as an elaboration of a type of eucharistic prayer in use in congregations established by Paul.

first the men and then the women. About this time additional cere-monial developed in connection with the bringing of the Gospel book from the holy table to a place from which the Lesson was read and in connection with bringing the elements to the holy table.

The so-called "Prayer of the Faithful" was an important element in the services of this period. Its petitions included not only the needs of the church, but also prayers for catechumens, penitents, those in affliction, travelers, prisoners, etc., as well as for the emperor and magistrates. It dropped out of the liturgy proper during the medieval centuries, but was retained in part in the Prone. The Reformation restored it in the form of the Prayer of the Church (General Prayer) after the sermon. By Cyprian's time also the Lord's Day was freed from the restraints of the Jewish Sabbath and established as a joyous festival. The thought of the unity of the church and the expectation of our Lord's early re-turn overtoned the theological conception of the atonement, which later became so important.

While Christian worship in these first three centuries was character-ized by relative simplicity and freedom of expression, we are able to trace in it the outlines and many of the details which later flowered into the great liturgical systems of the Eastern and the Western churches.

POST-NICENE DEVELOPMENTS

The so-called "Edict of Milan" of Constantine and Licinius, A.D. 313, brought peace to the church and inaugurated a liturgical development of great significance. The church expanded rapidly. It spread eastward more quickly than westward, and found its most congenial soil in the great cities. By the year 325 it was possible to call a great council of the church, and there were probably several million Christians in the empire.

It is difficult to comprehend the enrichment of worship and the new features which were then introduced. Probably no period of the church's history ever witnessed such great changes in so brief a time. The Council of Nicaea was held amid high liturgical solemnities. The Spanish abbess Etheria has described the great festivals as observed at Jerusalem in the middle of the century.[12] In Constantinople, Rome, and elsewhere great basilicas were erected and endowed with lavish gifts by the emperor. Processions, pilgrimages, and pageants were undertaken on an elaborate scale. Within a generation or two the church had invested public worship, and particularly the administration of the sacraments,

[12] M. L. McClure and C. L. Feltoe, *The Pilgrimage of Etheria* (New York: Macmillan, n.d.).

with a dignity and beauty which not only brought spiritual satisfaction to believers but also impressed the pagan world. Chateaubriand describes the introduction of many of these features in striking, even grandiloquent, phrase: "Incense, flowers, vessels of gold and silver, lamps, crowns, lights, linen, silk, music, processions, festival days, passed from the altars of the vanquished to the altar of the victor. Paganism attempted to borrow from christianity its dogmas and its ethics; christianity despoiled paganism of its ornaments."[13]

These features, however, were largely external. If we examine the whole field carefully we shall find something like the following:

First of all, the destruction of Jerusalem, A.D. 70, and the dispersion of the Jewish people shattered the Mosaic institutions and prepared the way for a freer development of Christian forms and life. The persistence of Jewish influence, however, particularly that of the synagogue, is seen in the full development of the first part of the Christian Service—the Service of the Word—with its continued reading and exposition of the Old Testament, the use of Hebrew words and phrases, and the devotional use of psalms, hymns, and prayers. The psalms were read (probably chanted) at vigils, funerals, gatherings of ascetics, etc, as well as in the liturgy proper, between the Old and the New Testament lessons.

It should be noted that the Christians were discriminating in their use of Jewish elements. They retained the Old Testament teaching concerning the one true God and whatever else was not antagonistic to the Christian faith. In addition to Hebrew formulas, such as Amen, Alleluia, Hosanna, Peace be with you, and doxologies, they took over the observance of the week and of the great festivals, Easter and Pentecost, though with different meanings. Minor details, such as ablutions, the use of oil and incense, the imposition of hands, standing in prayer, were also retained. On the other hand, Jewish features irreconcilable with the Christian faith were definitely rejected—the observance of the Sabbath, the new moon, national festivals, circumcision, bloody sacrifices, temple ceremonial, etc. In fact, the early Christians, coming out of Judaism, applied the same conservative and discriminating principle which the Lutheran Reformers later applied in dealing with details of medieval worship.

The second important influence was exerted by the Hellenistic civilization in which Christianity grew to strength. Paganism as such did not exert the formative influence upon Christian worship which Hatch, Bousset, Reinach, and others have suggested. Certain general ideas such

---

[13] Quoted in F. Cabrol, *The Prayer of the Early Christians,* trans. Ernest Graf (London: Burns, Oates, and Washbourne, 1930), p. xiii.

as sacrifice, expiation, redemption, purification, etc., were common to all religions and a few terms and ritualistic details may have been contributed to the general development particularly by the mystery religions. But the early church held paganism and all its works in abhorrence. It rejected everything connected with idolatry. Its catechumens were called upon to renounce Satan and false systems of religion; it exorcised all elements associated with pagan worship; it offered continual prayer for the conversion of pagans. After the fourth century, however, when it was felt that paganism had lost its hold upon men's souls, there were borrowings and adaptations, such as the divisions of the civil year, the names of months and days of the week, the choice of the dates of pagan holidays for Christian festivals, and various domestic customs which remained in marriage and funeral rites.

The broader elements of Greek culture also materially affected early Christian life and worship. As the church entered upon its world mission and spread to Antioch, Corinth, Athens, Ephesus, Alexandria, and Rome, it carried with it what was to become the Greek New Testament. Its services were conducted in Greek. Many of its influential leaders wrote in Greek. Greek expressions become a lasting part of its liturgical terminology, e.g., such words as eucharist, epiclesis, exorcism, acolyte, deacon, and doxology. Greek rhetoric influenced the sermon. The increasing use of symbolism may also be credited to this source.

The third and really creative force in the development of early Christian worship was Christian faith and life. Whatever features were carried over from Judaism were filled with the new faith in Christ as the Son of God, the Redeemer of the world, the Lord of men. He took the first and central place in all Christian worship. The old Jewish emphasis upon the books of the Law gave way to more frequent reading of the Prophets. The New Testament Epistles and Gospels—the latter called by Origen "the crown of all Scripture"—soon came to have the highest place.

Christian worship at its very beginning also instituted new and unique features drawn from experiences in the Upper Room. The "breaking of bread" re-enacted the scene of the Last Supper. Firm belief in the continued presence of the Lord in the assemblies of the faithful, as he had promised, and particularly in the observance of the memorial he had enjoined, gave a sublime and unique character to the Holy Communion and compelled every worshiper to exclaim with Thomas, "My Lord and my God." Here was something not found in Judaism or any other religion of the time. Here is something still unique and inexpressibly precious in Christian experience today.

37

The choice of Sunday instead of Saturday as the day of worship; the observance of baptism as the rite of initiation and regeneration in accordance with Christ's command and in his Name; the recognition of a ministry set apart and ordained for spiritual functions by prayer and the imposition of hands; the composition of new canticles and hymns in praise of Christ, etc.—all of these were the outworking of Christian ideas. The life and teaching of our Lord controlled the thought and worship of the church. His example and commandments were fundamental for the continued use of the sacraments. The gradual formation of the canon of Scripture was a stabilizing influence. The observance of festivals and days in addition to the Lord's Day and Easter testified to the power of love and remembrance and laid the foundations for the later Christian year.

With the growth of the church, public worship was increasingly recognized as the one corporate and significant expression of devotion to Christ and as the means of manifesting and administering his gifts of grace. Leaving out of consideration the unusual activities of exceptional men such as Paul and others of missionary spirit, it may be said that the purpose of the normal Christian community was primarily to promote the edification and well-being of the company of believers; and secondarily to treat the services of the community as a means of bringing the gospel message and the Christian way of life to the attention of those still without the church.

LITURGICAL UNITY

A remarkable feature of early Christian worship is its high degree of unity. Notwithstanding fluidity of form in different places, there was substantial agreement in essentials. Services of the same kind were held everywhere. The Eucharist was the distinctive service which united Christians with one another and with their Lord. Augustine (d. 430), the greatest spiritual leader the church had produced since Paul, stated the universal belief when he said: "Without baptism and partaking of the Supper of the Lord it is impossible for any man to attain either to the kingdom of God or to salvation and everlasting life."[14] In the Holy Communion, Augustine, among the first, also saw the community of believers offering itself to God as a whole in unity with Christ's sacrifice.

The faithful everywhere assembled on the Lord's Day for their principal service. Wednesdays and Fridays were thought of as penitential days. Certain formulas, usages, and prayers gained general currency. Everywhere a eucharistic prayer, containing lengthy thanksgivings, led

---

[14] For satisfactory discussion of these and related factors see Cabrol, *op. cit.*

up to the narrative of the Institution. This prayer was known in the East as the *anaphora* (offering) and in the West as the Canon (rule). It always concluded with an *epiclesis*, or invocation of the Holy Spirit. This disappeared from the Western liturgy when the Latin language was substituted for the Greek. After the consecration the bread and wine were distributed. The communicants stood to receive the elements; each responding "Amen" as the minister repeated the simple words: "The Body of Christ" and "The Blood of Christ." The bishop or presbyter administered the bread and the deacon the chalice.

Everywhere admission to church membership was by baptism, and only after extended periods of instruction and oversight by sponsors. Water was always employed and the Trinity invoked. With this was combined quite early the imposition of hands and anointing by chrism with prayers by the bishop and the congregation. Baptism, with its accompanying rites, generally followed the first part of the Eucharistic Service. After the baptism the second part of the Eucharistic Service continued and the newly baptized received the Sacrament. Certain local rites required them also to partake of milk and honey after receiving the consecrated bread and before receiving the wine. This represented their entrance into the Promised Land. Details of Baptism and the Lord's Supper were regularly guarded from pagan eyes and ears. This "secret discipline" *(disciplina arcani)* was established everywhere during the fourth century. The Creed and the Lord's Prayer were not taught to catechumens until the time of baptism. Non-Christians were rigidly excluded from the second part of the Communion service.

With all its freshness and spontaneity, the public worship of the early church was characterized by dignity, simplicity, and restrained fervor. Neither persecution nor the lack of institutional strength gave it a gloomy countenance. Rather its forms were pervaded by a spirit of peace, consolation, joy, and thanksgiving. Grave and moderate, the early church also possessed a richness and warmth not found in later Puritanism. A common spirit determined what should be done and what should not be done. The authority of leaders, and their agreement upon essential principles, undoubtedly account for liturgical unity as well as the larger unity of the church which confessed "One Lord, one faith, one baptism" (Eph. 4:5). It is interesting to recall similar unity of principle and form in the church orders of the Reformation century. Then, too, regardless of local variations as to detail, there was common agreement over widely scattered areas as to general outline and content. This also represented the common acceptance of essential principles by the recognized leaders of the church in that era.

The liturgical unity of the early church was first broken when in the West the Latin language was substituted for the Greek in the fourth century. A further break came with the adoption by the Western rites of the principle of liturgical variables. This made the Latin service something more than a mere translation of the earlier Greek. This Latin service with its series of lessons, collects, introits, etc., and its omission of the ancient *epiclesis,* became the distinctive Service of the Western church. Henceforth there was a definite liturgical cleavage between East and West. Liturgical diversity became more and more pronounced as events led up to the final separation of the churches, A.D. 1054.

WORSHIP IN THE EASTERN CHURCHES

The scope of this book limits discussion to the Lutheran line of liturgical descent, which is clearly that of the Western church. We may only sketch, in briefest fashion, the distinctive and very different type of liturgical development in the East.

The earliest extended presentation of Eastern services is found in the eighth book of the *Apostolic Constitutions.* This dates from approximately A.D. 380 and in all probability sets forth the use of the city of Antioch and possibly of the Syrian church in general.

Antioch and Alexandria were early important centers. By the third century their respective local uses in matters of worship were well established. In the fourth century the influence of these metropolitan centers expanded. Missionary activity established new congregations in neighboring areas. The daughter churches looked to the mother church in their own provinces for guidance in worship as in other matters. Thus, ecclesiastical and liturgical expansion went hand in hand and the local "use" of a great center was followed as closely as conditions permitted throughout an entire province and even beyond.

In the fourth century Constantinople became the seat of what would develop into a new Eastern empire. Here Byzantine culture, with occasional bursts of splendor and long periods of quiescence, flourished for a more than a thousand years. From these centers, Antioch and Alexandria in the earliest times and Constantinople somewhat later, different families of Eastern liturgies developed.

Most Eastern Christians today belong to the Greek Orthodox Church or to national churches which, if they are not immediately under the jurisdiction of Constantinople, are not affiliated with Rome. A minority of the Eastern churches—the so-called Uniates—profess obedience to Rome and are permitted to retain their own liturgies, to use their own vernaculars in worship, to administer the Sacrament in both kinds, etc.

The Eastern liturgies are of two main types, the Syrian and the Egyptian. The Egyptian, developing from Alexandria, includes the Coptic and the Abyssinian liturgies. The Syrian type, developing from Antioch, includes three groups of families: the western Syrian (Antioch and Jerusalem); the eastern Syrian (Persia and Mesopotamia); and the Cappadocian-Byzantine (Armenian and Byzantine). From these families certain "derived rites" developed, each with its own peculiar features, usually of minor character.

The purest form of the Antiochene Rite is preserved in the Greek Liturgy in the *Apostolic Constitutions*. The Jerusalem form of the western Syrian Rite is found in the Liturgy of St. James. This is used in Greek once a year in Jerusalem and in Cyprus and Zante. It is also used in Syriac by the Syrian Jacobites and Uniates. The eastern Syrian Rite is used in Syriac forms in Persia and Mesopotamia by the Nestorians.

The Byzantine Rite gradually extended its influence from Constantinople (Byzantium) throughout the provinces of the Eastern empire and eventually supplanted all the later rites in the Balkans, Russia, and other areas controlled by the Eastern Orthodox church. It thus became the second most widespread Christian rite, being followed by (nominally) nearly one hundred and fifty million people. Unlike the Roman, its great rival, the Byzantine Rite is celebrated in many vernaculars, particularly in Greek, Old Slavonic (used by Russians, Serbs, Bulgarians and Slavs), Georgian, Romanian, and Arabic. The missionary activities of the Russian church during the past hundred years have led to the translation and use of the Byzantine Rite in whole or in part in Estonian, German, and Lettish in the Baltic provinces, in Chinese, Japanese, and English, and even in Eskimo and Indian dialects in Alaska and neighboring areas. Not infrequently different languages are used in the same city. In Palestine, where the higher Orthodox clergy are Greek, the liturgy is said in Greek and in Arabic. In the Church of the Nativity in Bethlehem, there is a Greek choir and an Arabic choir. In Jerusalem where pilgrims come from all countries at the great feasts, we are told that it is not uncommon for certain chants to be heard in several languages at the same service.

The Eastern liturgical books constitute a veritable library. Twelve are recognized as authoritative in the Byzantine Rite. The most important are the following: The *Typikon* includes rubrical details and directions for all services (Liturgy and Office) throughout the year; the *Leitourgikon* contains the ordinaries of the liturgies (masses) of St. John Chrysostom, St. Basil, and the Mass of the Presanctified, and an abridgment of the Ritual (orders for baptism, marriage, confession, etc.); the *Euchologion* contains the complete texts of the sacraments and the sacramentals (blessings for various occasions); the *Apostolos* is the book of the subdeacon and contains liturgical extracts from the Four Gospels; the *Psalterion*, the *Horologion*, the *Octoekhos* and the *Menaia* provide material for the Divine Office.

The music of the Byzantine Rite in most countries is a form, more or less pure, of the traditional Greek liturgical chant. This contains quarter-tones and other intervals not found in Western music. In Russia, a work of significance was undertaken in the nineteenth century by Rimsky-Korsakov, ably seconded by Gretchoninov, Rachmaninoff, Chesnokov, Katalsky, and others. These able composers successfully harmonized the old Muscovite chants and developed a type of church polyphony for men's and boys' voices which enriched the stately services of the Orthodox church and added a glowing chapter to the ever expanding volume of music of the universal church.

Without entering upon an extended discussion of worship in the Eastern churches, we may say that in comparison with Western services all Eastern liturgies are characterized by great objectivity. They breathe the spirit of the Patristic period in which they were first composed. They manifest a sustained quality of meditation and praise. In contrast to the relatively brief and simple affirmations in the Western services, the Eastern liturgies amplify and develop doctrinal ideas in wearisome repetition. They express glowing appreciation of the glory of the natural creation and celebrate it in lofty phrase. They have developed a distinctive form of the Christian year with marked veneration for Old Testament saints, patriarchs, and prophets. In the liturgy they maintain a clear distinction between the Service of the Word and the Service of the Faithful. They emphasize in many ways the office and functions of the deacon. They have never developed variables in the sense of the "propers" in the Western liturgies. They insist upon a theory of consecration in the Eucharist by invocation of the Holy Spirit and not by repetition of a formula (the Words of Institution) as in the Roman Mass. They provide for administration of the Sacrament in both kinds. Their lengthy prayers are characterized by richness of imagination and poetic fervor. In connection with the recitation of the Office, particularly, they have developed an enormous body of hymnody, much of indifferent quality but much also of real merit. These and other features—particularly colorful accessories, such as dramatic action, vestments, lights, and ceremonial which court popular interest by means of external splendor—distinguish the Eastern rites from the Western from the earliest times to the present.

While rich in devotional content and suggestiveness, the Eastern liturgies, so far as doctrine is concerned, reveal substantial agreement with many beliefs and practices which we condemn in the Roman church—transubstantiation, excessive veneration of Mary, appeals to the saints, intercession for the departed, etc. Their practical value for Western minds is also reduced by inordinate length, literary and musical repetitions, unrestrained exuberance of expression, excessive use of symbolism, and exaggerated emphasis upon dramatic and spectacular effect.

On the other hand, their emphasis upon the revelation of the transcendent God by the incarnation of the eternal Word, and upon the importance of our Lord's resurrection as setting the seal of authority and hope upon all his life and promise, is a living reminder of dominant thoughts in the mind of the early church. The responsive character of

Eastern worship, its sustained note of joyous adoration, its Johannine mysticism, its recognition of the power of the supernatural in the natural, its breadth of intercession for men of every station, its administration of the Sacrament in both kinds, and its great use, in the Office particularly, of hymnody—all these are features reminiscent of the corporate character of early Christian worship, recaptured in the West by the evangelical services of the Reformation and incorporated in simpler forms in Lutheran services today.

Unfortunately the average worshiper in any communion—Greek, Roman, Lutheran, or Anglican—is unable to understand the wealth of historical, theological, and devotional material contained in the liturgy of his own church. Even the most highly endowed and educated worshiper cannot grasp all its meaning. Just as in the public reading of the Holy Scriptures, some are prepared with large understanding and insight to receive great benefit while others with smaller capacity receive a smaller, though it may be a filled, measure—so many worshipers in all communions "assist" rather than fully participate in a developed liturgical service. The simpler and the clearer the liturgical structure and the higher the intelligence and spiritual abilities of the worshipers, the more fully will devotional satisfaction and benefit be realized. These conditions, we may say as a broad observation, are most fully met in the Protestant churches. The more complicated and mystical the liturgy and the less developed the worshipers, the less likely are the latter to participate actively or to receive actually the blessings inherent in their services. In the Roman church, and to an even greater degree in the Eastern churches, the liturgy has lost its congregational character and is conducted on behalf of the congregation by the priest, the deacon or other assistant, and the choir, who are trained to carry through their respective parts, the faithful meanwhile accompanying this "sacred dialogue" with private devotions of varied character. The present liturgical movement in the Roman church is seeking to enable all groups in the church from the clergy to the humblest layman to understand the theological and spiritual implications of their liturgy, and to participate in it with deeper devotion and spiritual satisfaction. Liturgical study and endeavor in the Anglican communion and in the Lutheran church in this country during the past three-quarters of a century have had the same objectives and have realized them progressively to the good of many individuals and of the whole church.

THE LEADERSHIP OF ROME IN THE WEST

In the West successive hordes of barbarians invaded the empire, sacked Rome, and drove out the imperial armies. They ceased even to need a puppet Roman government, and quietly deposed the last emperor in 476. Islam became a power in Arabia after the flight of the Prophet from Mecca to Medina in 622, and soon spread along the southern shores of the Mediterranean. Amid these political and social upheavals with their destruction of classical culture, the church not only survived but grew to power through sheer force of conviction and character. The bishops of Rome secured primacy for their see. In the absence of imperial power they administered affairs throughout ever expanding areas in a vast program of endeavor which included the definition and defense of doctrine, the development of worship and liturgical art, the prosecution of missionary activity, the stabilization of government and the extension of episcopal authority. All of this involved them in ceaseless conflicts with rulers and states.

In the fourth, fifth, and sixth centuries the Roman church displayed constructive and inventive gifts which profoundly affected the Western liturgy. Odo Casel, the Benedictine scholar of Maria Laach, in a conjecture now regarded as proven, claimed that Ambrose, bishop of Milan, 374-97, was responsible for the transition from Greek to Latin as the language of the liturgy, an innovation promptly accepted at Rome. Pope Damasus is usually credited with being the first to adopt the principle of variable prayers in the Canon in recognition of festivals and seasons in the calendar. The Prefaces and collects prepared about this time are remarkable for their literary grace, dogmatic significance, and terseness of expression. But the Roman and Gallican idea that formulas in the Mass and the Office might vary according to feasts was never adopted in the East, nor did it apply to baptism and other rites in the West.

In the fourth and fifth centuries the sermon was a prominent feature. Athanasius, Ephraim the Syrian, John Chrysostom, Basil, Cyril of Jerusalem, Gregory of Nazianzus in the East, and Ambrose, Augustine, Jerome, and Pope Leo in the West, were among the great preachers. The observance of annual festivals, and days commemorating apostles, martyrs, etc., gave definite form to the church year by the fifth century. The *epiclesis* had dropped from the Roman Rite, and the Verba, perhaps because of stern conflict with heresy, was recognized as the consecratory formula. By the sixth century some of the festivals of Mary were generally observed, and a refined polytheism was built up by the invocation of saints as patrons and intercessors.

The first five centuries saw the development of the great outlines and much material of the liturgy and the church year. The next ten centuries overelaborated detail and developed evils whose beginnings can be traced at a surprisingly early period. Worship became less congregational. The Prayer of Oblation assumed great importance. A realistic conception of a change of the elements into the body and blood of Christ supplanted the earlier more spiritual representation.

By the seventh century the Roman Canon differed entirely from corresponding parts in the Eastern rites and in the later Gallican rites of the West. The influence of Gregory the Great (pope, 590-604) was important here, as in other liturgical and musical matters. In addition to codifying material and extending uniformity he made at least three changes in the liturgy—the use of the Kyrie without its accompanying litany; the addition of the second half of a much-discussed prayer in the Canon; and the insertion of the Lord's Prayer before the Communion instead of after it.[15] Rome was crystallizing and impressing upon the whole Western world its ideas of priesthood and sacrifice and its program of centralized authority. The functions of the deacons were limited by the omission of all litanies, and the priests' powers were correspondingly enhanced. The Kiss of Peace, instead of being at the beginning of the Mass of the Faithful, as in all other liturgies, was put later in the service in close connection with the act of oblation and sacrifice. Intercessions are scattered in fragments throughout the Canon, and the ancient Prayer of the Faithful disappeared from its original place after the sermon. Roman scholars admit that the present Roman Canon is not in its original form, but that it is a "rearrangement and almost certainly a fragment.[16]

Some of the most important and constructive suggestions concerning this problem have been made by Protestant scholars, among others Baron Bunsen, the Prussian ambassador at London, 1841-54, and particularly Professor Paul Drews of the University of Halle. Fortescue presents theories of various scholars (pp. 110-71). F. D. Brightman in the appendices to his *Liturgies Eastern and Western* gives suggested reconstructions.

OTHER DEVELOPMENTS IN THE WEST

Many churches were founded in Gaul in the fourth century during the time of Constantine and his sons. Close commercial connections existed between Asia Minor and Gaul, and Syriac was spoken in some Gallic cities. Christians in southern Gaul were in close contact with Christians in Asia and Phrygia. Thus the worship of these Western churches in the fourth century was influenced by the East, though how much is not clear. Duchesne demolished the thesis of older Anglican scholars who regarded Lyons as the center through which liturgical influences from Ephesus in Asia Minor penetrated the West. He believes that Milan was this center. We know that in the fourth century Milan was a city of outstanding importance. It controlled the north Italian cities and was in constant communication with Constantinople and Asia Minor. It was the seat of an exceptionally able line of bishops whose influence penetrated to Antioch, Africa, and Spain. Assemblies of oriental

---

[15] On the position of the Lord's Prayer, see Archdale A. King, *Notes on the Catholic Liturgies* (New York: Longman's, 1930), pp. 48ff.

[16] Adrian Fortescue, *The Mass* (New York: Longmans, 1937), p. 170.

bishops met within its gates, and the bishops of Gaul and Spain frequently visited it.

When Augustine came to England in 597, the ancient British church had long existed in the Celtic communities of Wales, Scotland, and Ireland. Even after this its virtual independence from Rome was continued for centuries. The Celtic Liturgy was Gallican in derivation and character, with certain features peculiar to itself. The Anglo-Saxon church in southern and eastern England was influenced much more by Rome, since it had been established among the pagan Anglo-Saxons by Roman missionaries. It too, however, maintained some independent characteristics. The Leofric Missal is one of the important early liturgies. After the thirteenth century the Use of Salisbury (Sarum) supplanted the other diocesan uses of Hereford, Bangor, York, Lincoln, Exeter, etc.

After the fifth century monasticism developed into an institution of great importance. In every land the celibate communities became centers of faith and activity. Perhaps the outstanding achievement of the system was the perfecting and extension of Christian culture and the maintenance of an elaborate program of daily worship in the hour services of the Divine Office.

While Christian worship from the beginning had its center in the unique corporate celebration of the Eucharist, the daily observance of the hour services came to have great meaning for members of monastic communities and eventually for all the clergy. The earliest beginnings of the Divine Office are found in the custom of private prayer and in the assemblies or vigils held in preparation for the eucharistic services on Sundays and martyrs' anniversaries. These all-night watches soon developed into services at the hour of lamplighting and again, after a period of rest, at cockcrow. Wednesdays and Fridays were thought of as "station days" observed with fasting and prayer as the faithful "stood guard" against evil. Monasticism, especially as organized by Benedict of Nursia (d. 543) in his community at Monte Cassino, encouraged the extension of these daily prayer services which Benedict called "God's work" (*opus Dei*).

After the fifth century also, in the West, bishops, priests, and deacons were required to remain unmarried. By the next century all orders adopted the tonsure. The continued use of the old Roman dress by the clergy, after the laity had accepted new styles introduced by the barbarian invaders, gave heightened significance to the ancient garments as official vestments of the church.

EARLY SACRAMENTARIES AND CHURCH ORDERS

Written liturgies, as such, date from the middle of the fourth century. The desire to protect the sacramental mysteries from pagan ridicule and irreverence had previously restrained the clergy from committing liturgical forms to writing. Nor had the church yet assimilated the various elements which it had taken over from Jewish, Greek, and Roman sources. When the prayers used in the Eucharist were committed to writing, an early arrangement gave all the material required by the bishop (or priest) in collections called "sacramentaries." Three of these are of particular importance; the Leonine, the Gelasian, and the Gregorian. In these sacramentaries we find not only the complete outline of the Western Liturgy, but also much of the actual text which we use today, and which thus has an unbroken history of nearly twelve hundred years. Of our collects *de tempore* alone, no less than seven appear in the best texts of the Leonine, twenty-five in the Gelasian, and thirty-seven more in the Gregorian Sacramentary.

Renaudot dates the earliest liturgical books from the fourth century. The prayers in the *Didache* and other early sources do not prove the existence of liturgical collections. The Synod of Hippo, A.D. 393, forbade anyone to use the written prayers of other churches until he had shown his copy to the more learned brethren.

Diptychs were among the earliest written portions of the Service. These were tablets hinged and folded like a book, containing the names of those for whom prayers were to be offered. The early custom of reading from the Scriptures until the bishop made a sign to stop developed into the reading of a fixed selection (*pericope*). An index gave the first and last words of these passages (*capitulare*). A complete index including references to homilies, lives of saints, etc., was supplied in the *comes*. Finally entire texts were provided in the Gospel-book, Epistle-book, and Lectionary.

The Leonine Sacramentary was found and published by Bianchini in 1735. He arbitrarily attributed it to Leo I (pope, 440-61). Duchesne places it about 538. It is a fragmentary collection of prayers which omits the Ordinary and the Canon of the Mass. It is a purely Roman use without a trace of later Gallican influence. The complete text is given with critical notes in Charles L. Feltoe, *Sacramentarium Leonianum* (London: Cambridge Univ. Pr., 1896). Edward Burbidge, in *Liturgies and Offices of the Church,* gives extracts tending to establish the connection of portions of the sacramentary with the age of Leo.

The Gelasian Sacramentary is a later and more complete collection. An early tradition ascribes to Gelasius I (pope, 492-96) the composition of a sacramentary. This collection has long borne his name, though his connection with it cannot be established. Duchesne and Buchwald agree in dating it between 628 and 731. It was the Roman Rite prepared for use in Gaul and it contains numerous Gallican additions. The standard edition, based upon a collation of numerous manuscripts, is by H. A. Wilson, *The Gelasian Sacramentary* (Oxford: Clarendon, 1896).

The Gregorian Sacramentary is of still later date and also represents the Roman use with Gallican additions. Many copies of this book were made by Charlemagne. It apparently became the basis for the liturgical use of all the churches.[17] The clergy and people were so attached to their local uses, however, that when they copied the book the most popular of these local forms were added as supplements. In later manuscripts these appear incorporated with the original book. This last represents the "Gregorian Sacramentary" as finally used. Some of the local additions found their way back

[17] Text in H. A. Wilson, *The Gregorian Sacramentary* (London: Harrison, 1915).

to Rome and were incorporated in the Roman Liturgy. The complete sacramentary as thus developed finally formed the foundation for the later Roman Missal. No modern edition of the Roman sacramentary has been published. The standard text is still that of Muratori, in the second volume of his *Liturgia Romana Vetus* (Venice: Pasquale, 1748).

The sacramentaries contained only the fewest and briefest directions. An effort to remove uncertainty and confusion of practice was made in the so-called *Ordines Romani,* which were directions prescribing functions and procedure. The earliest of these dates from the eighth century. The *Ordo Romanus Primus* has been edited with introduction and notes by E. G. C. F. Atchley (London: Moring, 1905). The sacramentaries eventually gave way to a more complete collection called the Missal (*Missale plenarium*). This included the lessons and the chants of the choir (Introit, Gradual, etc.) as well as the prayers of the priest. The Missal replaced the sacramentary for altar use by the twelfth century, though lectionaries and Gradual (grail, grayle) were still printed separately.

Many details of worship and church life in the first five centuries may be gathered from writings which Bishop Maclean has collectively termed "the ancient church orders."[18] To some of these reference has already been made. They were privately prepared manuals of instruction and worship. Among those to be noted, in addition to the *Didache,* are the *Apostolic Tradition of Hippolytus,* the *Didascalia,* the *Canons of Hippolytus,* the *Apostolic Church Order,* the *Testament of Our Lord,* and the *Apostolic Constitutions.* The *Pilgrimage of Sylvia (Etheria),* and the *Prayer of Serapion* are also important sources of information. These writings discuss church buildings; details of worship, particularly the Eucharist; the ministry; the ordination of bishops, presbyters, and deacons; baptism and confirmation with their ceremonies; festivals, fasts, seasons, etc.

CHURCH MUSIC AND CHURCH ARCHITECTURE

All too little is known about the music of the early church. We do know that the earliest responses were made by the congregation in answer to an officiant or other leader. Antioch adopted the practice of antiphonal singing, with one group answering another group. This was introduced into Milan by Ambrose, who also wrote hymns and encouraged hymn-singing, which until that time had been a distinctive feature of Eastern Christianity. Ambrose also established a choir school at Milan and undertook the systematization of the church's musical forms. Instrumental music, while forbidden in the East, was encouraged in the West. A simple form of organ was introduced late in the fifth century.

Gregory the Great continued and extended this work. He reorganized the choir school which Pope Sylvester had founded early in the fourth century. He also edited the growing body of plain song, a form

[18] A. J. MacLean, *The Ancient Church Orders* (Cambridge: The Univ. Press, 1910).

of unaccompanied unisonal singing of psalms, canticles, hymns, and liturgical responses. The earliest chant forms and melodies were probably developed from Jewish and Hellenistic musical forms. Gregory's efforts transferred liturgical and musical leadership to Rome at the end of the sixth century.

Before the decree of Constantine and Licinius which established the Peace of the Church (313), few church buildings had been erected. However, during the periods which were comparatively free from persecution some churches had been built in Rome and elsewhere. These were confiscated, but later were restored to the church by Constantine. For the most part the early Christians assembled in the large upper rooms of Syrian-type houses; or in the inner courts of other private houses—the atrium of a Roman house or the peristyle of a Greek home. In times of persecution small groups resorted to funeral halls at the cemeteries or to underground chambers in the catacombs.

When free to worship publicly, the church erected imposing edifices for its own use. It could not use pagan temples, even if it so desired, because they had not been designed for congregational worship. They simply sheltered the statue of a pagan deity. Paganism was an outdoor religion with sacrifices held in the open. Hence its architectural interest centered on the exterior of its temples. The church required a building where believers could assemble in large numbers for instruction and edification and the administration of the sacraments. The imposing basilicas used by the law courts—rectangular buildings with side aisles—provided satisfactory models. The early church buildings were often plain and unattractive on the outside, but impressive and richly decorated inside. The men were placed on one side in the nave and the women on the other. The clergy occupied the bema, or platform, and the apse. The choir was placed in a low screened enclosure in the center of the nave near the apse, in front of which was the altar. Provision was made for baptism in separate places called baptistries, one such building of considerable size usually being provided in each city.

The literature for this early period is extensive. Only a few outstanding and easily accessible works can be mentioned.

L. Duchesne, *Christian Worship; its Origin and Evolution* (trans. from the third French ed. by M. L. McClure, second English ed.), is indispensable for the period until the time of Charlemagne. Two articles by Charles M. Jacobs in the *Memoirs of the Lutheran Liturgical Association* (VI-VII), cover the apostolic and the first post-apostolic age. Canon F. E. Warren, *Liturgy and Ritual of the Ante-Nicene Church* (second ed.) assembles a striking amount of material known to have been used in this early period. Hans Lietzmann, *Messe und Herrenmahl; eine Studie zur Geschichte der Liturgie*

(English trans. *Mass and Lord's Supper*), is a valuable study. Georg Rietschel, *Lehrbuch der Liturgik* (Berlin, 1900-09), available in a second edition by Paul Graff (Göttingen: Vandenhoeck, 1951-52), gives an excellent summary, as does Oscar Hardman in his smaller work, *A History of Christian Worship,* and also William D. Maxwell in his *Outline of Christian Worship.*

Bishop A. J. Maclean, *The Ancient Church Orders,* is useful. J. H. Srawley, *The Early History of the Liturgy,* is valuable even if dry. Adrian Fortescue, *The Mass; a Study of the Roman Liturgy,* is filled with accurate information in readable form, as is Abbot Fernand Cabrol, *The Prayer of the Early Christians* (trans. by Ernest Graf), and also his *Liturgical Prayer; its History and Spirit,* (trans. by a Benedictine of Stanbrook). Evelyn Underhill in *Worship* offers a fresh and satisfying approach.

More recent works of importance are: Oscar Cullmann, *Early Christian Worship;* A. J. Higgins, *The Lord's Supper in the New Testament;* Joachim Jeremias, *The Eucharistic Words of Jesus;* Joseph A. Jungmann, *The Mass of the Roman Rite;* Archdale A. King, *Liturgies of the Primatial Sees.* (For publishers and dates, see bibliography, p —).

CHAPTER II

IN THE MEDIEVAL CHURCH

As we have seen, the Eastern liturgies stem from the parent rites of Antioch and Alexandria. The later Western liturgies are different in character and of two sorts. Rome and Carthage developed a common type which we call "Roman." A second type, more or less influenced by Eastern forms and spirit, probably through Milan, appeared in various centers throughout France, Spain, southwestern Germany, Britain, Sweden, etc. The liturgies of this second type are collectively called "Gallican."

It is not easy to unravel the tangled skeins of medieval history in the West. Rome was steadily extending its influence. The mission of Boniface (d. 755), the apostle of Germany and reformer of the Frankish church, was designed to create a German church connected with Rome.[1] Boniface labored in Bavaria, Thuringia, Hesse, and northern France. About the time he died, Pope Stephen crossed the Alps to visit the court of Pepin the Short, and secured the king's promise to introduce the Roman Rite throughout his kingdom.

Less than half a century later Charlemagne emerged as the outstanding figure. Crowned emperor in Rome in the year 800, he proved to be not only a great conqueror but also a great administrator. Pepin before him, by royal decree in the year 754, had introduced the Gregorian liturgy into his empire, but it was Charlemagne who made it stick. Securing the aid of scholars, churchmen, musicians, architects, and other leaders, he attempted to mold diverse peoples and lands into an empire. He encouraged preaching and had collections of sermons prepared for his clergy. Believing that the order and discipline of the Roman church might be helpful in unifying his domain, he appealed to Pope Adrian I for help in regulating liturgical and musical matters throughout his lands. Adrian sent him, by John, abbot of Ravenna, a copy of the service book used in Rome at that time. This was probably the so-called

---

[1] Albert Hauck, *Kirchengeschichte Deutschlands* (3. Aufl.), I, 420, 484-94.

51

Gregorian Sacramentary, the nucleus of which may have been edited by Pope Gregory two centuries before. It was copied and widely circulated. Thus the Roman Rite, originally only the use of the city of Rome, entered the field in competition with the local liturgies of western Europe.

CONFLICT OF GALLICAN AND ROMAN RITES

The origin of the Gallican rites, and their relationship to the Eastern liturgies and to the Roman Liturgy, present a difficult problem. Various theories have been proposed and defended with great learning.

The liturgy assumed definite form in the West much later than in the East. Worship in the West was concrete and dynamic, less contemplative, less pervaded by mystery than in the East. Its sacred actions for the most part were in the open and called for proper and perfect performance.

Both the Gallican and the Roman rites differed from the Eastern liturgies in the important matter of the *propria,* or liturgical variables for the days and festivals of the church year. These "propers," unknown (except for variable lessons and certain chants) in the Eastern liturgies, provided a rich variety of liturgical material, and emphasized the historic and commemorative features of public worship. It has been suggested that they may represent a survival of the ancient liberty of the celebrant to improvise. At all events, some Gallican rites carry the principle of liturgical variables to great length. The fixed part of the liturgy is definitely limited, and occasionally even the parts corresponding to the Roman Canon appear in a variety of forms. Many of the collects, Proper Prefaces, and other prayers are lengthy, highly imaginative, and even exuberant in style. The consecration prayers contain lengthy and varying introductions.[2]

While the variableness of parts and the number of proper prefaces definitely align the Gallican liturgies with the Western groups, these liturgies contain traces of earlier oriental influence. They often have a third lesson (from the Old Testament) preceding the Epistle, as had also the early Roman Rite. Occasionally they contain groups of brief intercessions (*preces*) similar to the Deacon's Litany in the Greek liturgies. They place the Kiss of Peace before the Communion and not after the Consecration as in the Roman order. There are traces in services for certain days of the ancient *epiclesis* following the Verba. They also contain prayers at the Offertory and the Communion, conclud-

[2] Examples of different forms of consecration prayers from all sections are given in Arthur Linton, *Twenty-five Consecration Prayers* (New York: Macmillan, 1921).

ing devotions, and special observances for Palm Sunday and Holy Saturday not found in the pure Roman Rite.[3]

The responses and certain variable musical elements gave the people a larger part in the Gallican services than in the Roman. The deacons, as in the East, were important. They read the litanies, proclaimed "Silence" before the Epistle, and administered the cup (withdrawn in the twelfth century). The Lord's Prayer in the Communion Office was probably said by all. Many of the more elaborate and sensuous features of the Mass, such as the elevation of the host with its accompanying ceremonies, genuflections, the use of lights, incense, and certain parts of the ritual for Holy Week, developed first of all in the Gallican church and later were fused with the simpler Roman Rite. These exuberant and decorative additions strengthened the aesthetic appeal of the service.

The original Roman Rite, while recognizing the common Western idea of variables, had definitely limited these in quality and style. The Proper Prefaces were few and all prayers were brief. The polished, balanced collects of the Roman sacramentaries are excellent examples of Roman objectivity and severity of expression. These pithy prayers are never diffuse. They ask simply and clearly for but one thing. That one thing may be very great—the forgiveness of sins, to be governed and preserved evermore, to be defended against all adversity, to have a right judgment in all things, or the gift of peace which the world cannot give. This terseness of expression is generally credited to the influence of Leo the Great. At all events, the Roman Rite of the sixth century, in comparison with the contemporary Gallican rites, was quite simple. It gave evidence of what Brilioth has called "stylistic pruning." In addition to other reasons which may be advanced, one important reason for the triumph of the Roman Rite in the West is to be found in its comparative simplicity and strength.

In outline and essential content the Roman liturgical system was practically complete by the close of the eighth century. About this time the Canon began to be said inaudibly. Unleavened bread was used in the Sacrament. The custom, which began in Gaul, of placing this in the mouth instead of in the hands of communicants became general. In this century also, throughout Gaul and Germany, a brief vernacular office called the Prone followed the sermon. This was not part of the prescribed text of the Mass, and its content varied in different districts.

[3] A. Ebner, *Quellen und Forschungen zur Geschichte und Kunstgeschichte des Missale Romanum im Mittelalter, Iter Italicum* (St. Louis: Herder, 1896), gives a painstaking account of these addditions. See also Evelyn Underhill's *Eucharistic Prayers from the Ancient Liturgies* (New York: Longmans, 1939).

It frequently included biddings to prayer, a confession and absolution, the Creed, Lord's Prayer, and Ten Commandments. The use of the Prone later aided the Reformers in their reintroduction of the General Prayer (Prayer of the Church) into the Service.

Fortescue mentions, as the only important changes in the liturgy of the Mass since the eighth century, the insertion of the Creed, the Offertory prayers, the elevation, the blessing, and the last Gospel, together with incensing, bell ringing, and similar minor details. (*The Mass,* p. 177). Batiffol asserts that there was no appreciable modification of the Divine Office at Rome from the time of Charlemagne to the close of the twelfth century. Bäumer endeavors to show some development and alteration which he ascribes chiefly to Gregory VII.[4]

More recent scholarship materially modifies these earlier views. Theodor Klauser in *The Western Liturgy and Its History* (pp. 36ff) attaches much greater importance to the period from Gregory the Great to Gregory VII (590-1073). He calls it "The epoch of Franco-German leadership," and shows that while chaotic conditions prevailed in Rome where creative liturgical activity had ceased, the zeal of the Cluniac monks and the creative activity of the Franco-German church in general "at this critical juncture saved the Roman liturgy for Rome itself, and for the world," and, more important, "gave the Roman liturgy real enrichment."

For discussion of the Prone see F. E. Brightman, *The English Rite,* II, 1020-45; also I, cxlvi ff. Brightman's contention that the Reformed services at Strasbourg and Geneva, and later in Scotland, were definitely built upon the Prone, is vigorously refuted by W. D. Maxwell, *John Knox's Genevan Service Book, 1556* (London: Oliver, 1931), pp. 17-47; 66-76.

SUPREMACY OF THE ROMAN RITE

The final supremacy of the Roman Rite over the more ornate and even florid Gallican forms followed as a natural result of Roman influence in general and from the desire to end confusion. The rite which finally prevailed everywhere except in Milan and Toledo was really a "fused" rite. Its core, which included the essential features, was definitely Roman. About this were gathered elements more or less Gallican, survivals of local forms and customs beloved by the clergy and the people—forms which had first been introduced as supplementary material and later incorporated within the services proper. Thus developed the text which was finally accepted generally throughout France, Spain, Germany, and England. By the eleventh century it prevailed in Scandi-

[4] Cf. Baudot, *The Roman Breviary, its Sources and History,* pp. 93-101).

navia, Moravia, Bohemia, Poland, Pomerania, and Hungary. The Crusades for a time established it in the Near East, even in Constantinople. Franciscan missionaries carried it to central Asia and China in the thirteenth and fourteenth centuries. It came to the American continent with the Spanish and the Portuguese, and the latter carried it to India. St. Francis Xavier took it to the Malay Peninsula, and three years after the death of Martin Luther he introduced it into Japan.[5]

With the typical features which thus became a part of the Mass in every land—collects, graduals, the Offertory, the Canon, etc.—went Roman ideas of propitiatory sacrifice, good works, and belief in a materialistic localizing of the eucharistic mystery in a precise moment of time and at the command of a particular priestly caste. This realistic view triumphed over more spiritual conceptions and finally resulted in the formal acceptance of the doctrine of transubstantiation by the Fourth Lateran Council in the year 1215. This action, so far as popular religion was concerned, sanctioned a crude conception of the miraculous element in the Mass and led to reservation and adoration of the host and other abuses.

Meanwhile, due to the influence of Gregory VII (Hildebrand) and subsequent popes, the power of the papacy had been greatly extended. In the early thirteenth century Innocent III (pope, 1198-1216) brought the temporal power of the papacy to its highest point. The Crusades and the establishment of mendicant orders—particularly the Franciscans— also increased the influence of Rome. Thomas Aquinas formulated the doctrine of the church in a system which is authoritative to the present day. An enormous development of church building during the five centuries from 1000 to 1500 carried architecture and the minor arts through the Romanesque period (Norman period in England) and the glorious achievements of the Gothic.

We have referred to Duchesne's theory which explains the difference between the Gallican and the Roman rites by the suggestion that the former were strongly influenced by the Eastern liturgies through Milan in the fourth century. Fortescue and most recent scholars accept the view of the French Benedictines (Cabrol, Cagin, etc.), and of Professor Drews, who trace the Gallican rites directly to an early liturgical tradition in the West, which supplied the basis for the later forms, both Gallican and Roman. According to this view the Gallican rites remained more faithful to the common early tradition which had spread throughout northern Italy, Spain, Gaul, the British Isles, etc., than did the Roman Rite. This latter, in its earlier development at least, was a local simplification and rearrangment of the more florid forms which western Europe, with its ruder peoples and less advanced culture, pro-

[5] F. E. Brightman, *The English Rite,* I, vi-vii.

duced. For further discussion of this subject see, in addition to Duchesne, *Christian Worship,* and Fortescue, *The Mass,* Dom Fernand Cabrol, *The Mass of the Western Rites;* Archdale A. King, *Notes on the Catholic Liturgies;* Brilioth, *Eucharistic Faith and Practice,* pp. 70-78. An admirable analysis of the spirit of both the Roman and Gallican rites with illustrative material is given by Edmund Bishop in the opening chapter of his scholarly work, *Liturgica Historica.* See also the recent brief, though able, summary by Theodor Klauser, of the University of Bonn, in his *The Western Liturgy and its History* (trans. by F. L. Cross [London: Mowbray, 1952]).

PERSISTENCE OF LOCAL USES

Liturgical order, however, was still not uniform. There was a broad Gregorian basis common to all. The parts of the Mass were the same in number and order. There was a standard text of the Canon and other fixed parts as well as of many prayers and other variables. Local episcopal influence, however, was still strong. Every bishop, after consultation with his chapter, was at liberty to exercise his *jus liturgicum* and decree various rites and ceremonies within his own diocese. Local feasts developed special prayers and other *propria.* The influence of strong diocesan centers extended throughout adjoining bishoprics. The minor variations thus arising in the texts of introits, graduals, lessons, prayers, Prefaces, and blessings and in local ceremonies, the use of colors, etc., were endless.

Absolute uniformity did not become an ideal until the sixteenth century. The Lutheran Liturgy of Sweden (1531), which superseded the old local uses of Strengnas, Lund, Uppsala, Abo, etc., was perhaps the first really national rite. In 1549 the *Book of Common Prayer* of the Church of England became a national use. The Council of Trent, called to reform and solidify the Roman church in opposition to the growing power of Protestantism, issued the *Missale Romanum* in 1570. This eliminated many of the florid Gallican features and provided a text more in agreement with earlier Roman forms. The bull of Pope Pius V which accompanied it commanded that all other rites be abandoned with the exception of those which could show an unbroken use for at least two centuries. The Dominicans, Carmelites, and Carthusians among the "regulars" and the churches in Milan and Toledo were thus enabled to keep their own peculiar forms.

The text of the Roman Mass today is practically that of the Missal of Pope Pius V. Subsequent revisions in 1604, 1634, and 1884 made no important changes beyond simplifying the calendar, clarifying the rubrics and providing additional propers for new feasts.

The most recent change is the reform of the Holy Week observances declared by Pope Pius XII in 1955 and first observed in 1956. Other important developments in our own time include: permission to hold evening masses (originally a wartime provision); permission for most of the *Rituale* (order for baptism, marriage, burial, etc.) to be used in the vernacular: and the promotion in many countries of quasi-official "liturgical weeks" held annually in the interest of serious liturgical study and improved practice.

During the medieval period the Benedictine and the Roman breviaries entered into a strong rivalry which has continued to the present day. The Mozarabic Breviary was characterized by an unusual number and length of hymns and by an unusual type of collect. Most of these were addressed to the second Person of the Trinity. The Ambrosian Breviary also had its distinctive features.

The Celtic Liturgy, at least in important details, lingered in Scotland and Ireland until the eleventh and twelfth centuries.

The Ambrosian or Milanese Rite is the most important surviving member of the Gallican group, though in its present form many of its distinctive features have been lost in the process of gradual assimilation of Roman forms. Early manuscripts of the rite published by Pamelius and Muratori show these features, many of which are traceable to Eastern influence. Among these— in addition to an Old Testament lesson from the Prophets, the Deacon's Proclamation of Silence before the Epistle, varying forms of introduction to the Lord's Prayer, and other items already mentioned as characteristic of the Gallican liturgies in general—we may note a prayer after the spreading of the corporal, the litanies said after the Introit during Lent, the position of the Fraction before the Lord's Prayer, the lay offering of the oblations with accompanying formulas, etc.

Charlemagne in his effort to unify worship and life throughout his domain endeavored to eradicate the Ambrosian Rite and to substitute the Roman Order as he did in France. He ordered the Milanese liturgical books destroyed or removed. His efforts were only partially successful. The Lombards were deeply attached to their own use and their cause was vigorously championed by a Gallican bishop named Eugenius. The importance of the See of Milan and the determination of the Milanese compelled Pope Alexander VI in 1495 formally to approve the continued use of the Ambrosian Rite throughout the province of Milan. This approval was continued in the papal bull *Quo primum* of 1570, previously referred to, which permitted the use of non-Roman rites which could be proven to have been in continuous use for at least two hundred years.

There are interesting traces of the use of the Ambrosian Rite in Germany during the Middle Ages at Regensburg and at Augsburg (as late as 1584). When Luther on his journey to Rome desired to celebrate Mass in Milan, he was denied the privilege by the local priests, who said: *"Nos sumus Ambrosiani, non poteritis hic celebrare."*[6]

The so-called Mozarabic Rite was the national liturgy of Spain until the end of the eleventh century. The Synod of Burgos in 1085 imposed the

Roman Rite upon the entire Spanish peninsula except in Toledo, where the ancient use was permitted. This, however, lapsed into partial neglect until the sixteenth century, when Cardinal Ximenes reprinted its liturgical books and founded a college of priests to perpetuate its use. The Mozarabic Rite is now restricted to a chapel of the cathedral and six parish churches in the city and to a chapel at Salamanca.

Other important "uses" of the Gallican group were those of Lyons, Paris, and Rouen in France; Treves, Cologne, Mainz, Bamberg, and Nuremberg in Germany; Lund and Uppsala in Sweden; York, Lincoln, and Salisbury in England. The latter, known as the Sarum Use, was generally adopted throughout southern England after the twelfth century. These and many other local uses are not to be regarded as different rites, like the Ambrosian or the Mozarabic, but rather as local varieties of the Roman Rite, which agree with the Roman in essentials, and differ from it in nonessentials. Each important monastic community had its own breviary and its distinctive features in the Liturgy of the Mass. Before Luther's death in 1546 fully 125 local centers had printed their missals, often in sumptuous editions. Scarcely two of these agreed in all details.

Much of the strength of liturgical scholarship in recent years has been given to the investigation of these different uses, republishing their texts, classifying their details and relationships, etc. The Benedictines in France have been particularly active as well as Milanese scholars in Italy and Anglican scholars in England. The Lutheran reform of worship was based upon local diocesan "uses" which differed materially from the present Roman use. Among the more important of these were Bamberg and Mainz in Germany, and Uppsala, Lund, Strengnas, etc., in Sweden. Similarly the later *Book of Common Prayer* in England was based principally upon the Salisbury (Sarum) Use. A complete list of printed pre-Tridentine missals is given in W. H. J. Weale, *Bibliographica Liturgica, Catalogus Missalium Ritus Latini.*

THE SUPREMACY OF THE MASS

A survey of the field just before the Reformation reveals the cathedral, with its mighty proportions and infinite detail, and the Mass, enhanced by all the resources of art—light and color, music, vestments, ceremony, and elaborate symbolism—as the two most imposing structures of medieval worship.[7] The ordered worship of the church also included the Divine Office, the Occasional Services, and certain lay devotions. All of these were involved in the later reforms.

[6] See Henry Jenner's article, "Ambrosian Liturgy and Rite," in *The Catholic Encyclopedia,* I, 394-403. The Ambrosian Mass is described in Duchesne, *Christian Worship,* Chap. VII, and Georg Rietschel, *Lehrbuch der Liturgik,* I, 303-8. An English translation with introduction is provided by E.G.C.F. Atchley, *The Ambrosian Liturgy* (London: Cope, 1909). For the Gallican liturgies in general, see Archdale A. King, *Liturgies of the Primatial Sees* (London: Longmans, 1957).

[7] Henry Osborn Taylor groups these two in one chapter in his book, *The Mediaeval Mind.* Henry Adams, in *Mont-Saint-Michel and Chartres,* carries his penetrating analysis of medieval thought and life through both the services of the church and the great edifices in which they were held.

The dominant place which the Mass held in the medieval church can only be appreciated if we understand the theory of the Mass which prevailed then and still obtains today. According to this the Eucharist is a propitiatory sacrifice which the whole church constantly offers to God through the order of the priesthood, and which may be efficacious for the absent and even for the departed. In the Mass the bread and the wine are miraculously changed to the very body and blood of Christ by divine power, which the priest alone can invoke. The Oblation and Consecration renew in a bloodless manner the sacrifice of our Lord on Calvary. The consecrated host on the altar must be reverenced as if it were the body of Christ on the cross. It has the properties of Christ's body and is in fact a sacrifice. At his ordination every priest receives a paten and a chalice with the words: "Receive the power to offer sacrifice to God and to celebrate mass both for the living and for the dead." The fine rhythm of oblation, thanksgiving, and communion found in the Sunday services of the early church has been lost in a conception of the Mass which is entirely propitiatory and sacrificial.[8]

With such a theory the Lord's Supper ceased to be a sacrament to be administered and became a sacrifice to be celebrated with all the dramatic and symbolical elaboration possible. The cup was gradually withdrawn from all but the celebrant. Because of this, and of the idea that the Service was complete even if only the priest communicated, popular superstition centered upon the Consecration and particularly upon the elevation of the host as the supreme moment in the service. It was felt to be more important to witness the elevation than to receive Holy Communion itself. Miraculous effects were attributed to the mere sight of the sacred body. With most of the Service said inaudibly, the Mass became more and more a spectacle. Ceremonial, much of which had its origin in Eastern sources, gained increasing importance as popular interest was directed toward visible action.[9]

The name "Mass" comes from the Latin *missa,* a late form for *missio,* meaning "dismissal." Its first use was in connection with the dismissal of catechumens at the conclusion of the first part of the Service (called the *missa catechumenorum*). Later it marked the end of the Service of the Faithful, which concluded with the words *Ite missa est,* "Go, it is the dismissal." After the disappearance of the catechumenate, it came to mean the entire Eucharistic Service in the Roman and the Gallican churches. It thus forms a part of such English words as "Christ*mas*," "Candle*mas*," etc.

[8] For complete text of the Ordinary and the Canon of the Mass, see pp. 693ff in the appendix.

[9] For discussion of the elevation, which was introduced in the thirteenth century, see Fortescue, *The Mass,* pp. 337-45. Also T. W. Drury, *Elevation in the Eucharist.*

The normal kind of mass was the *missa solemnis* (the so-called "Solemn High Mass"), with celebrant, deacon, and subdeacon. Low mass was a shortened form said by a priest with one server. If the choir was present and the liturgy was sung and not said, it was a *missa cantata*.

The Eastern church still provides only one altar in a church and requires that the celebrant have assistants. Only one service may be said each day. In the West in the early Middle Ages, speculation urged that if one mass had a definite value as a propitiatory sacrifice, two masses would have twice this value. Separate masses were thus required to be said by each priest and the so-called *missa privata* (a form of low mass) was introduced. In this the celebrant alone partook of the Sacrament, though he was generally assisted in the liturgy by a server. The custom spread for priests to celebrate daily, until now it is mandatory.

The spread of low mass increased the number of altars in the churches and led to the formation of the missal. This book contains the complete texts of every mass, not only the parts said by the priest but the texts normally sung by the choir at high mass. At low mass the priest was required to repeat the choir texts as well as the priest's parts. This practice eventually reacted upon high mass itself and in this the priest is now required to say the choir texts quietly (*secreta*) even though they are sung by the choir.

The propitiatory theory led to the practice of having a definite "intention" for each mass. The more general ideas of the earlier periods, such as masses for good weather and fruitfulness, soon gave way to specific masses for prisoners, for safety from epidemics, the Turk, etc.; masses for the repose of a particular soul; even masses to secure the death of an individual! (Condemned by the synod of 694 at Toledo.) Gifts of money for such masses naturally multiplied their number and demanded that many altars and "chantries" be erected in the greater churches and monastery chapels. Here "solitary masses" were frequently said with no one present except the priest.

While only one solemn high mass might be celebrated in a church at any one time, private masses might be said by priests at other altars at the same time. Pontifical and papal masses prescribed special formulas and ceremonies for bishops and the pope respectively. Chapter masses were said daily in the cathedral and collegiate churches. Nuptial masses contained special prayers for the newly married; and requiem masses, prayers for the dead.[10]

During the medieval period the host came to be "reserved" on the altar for future adoration as well as for carrying to the sick. In pre-Reformation times it was generally kept in a cup (*pyx*) suspended in a dove-shaped vessel over the altar or in a tower-like sacrament-house with metal lattice-work doors near the altar and on the north side. About the time of the Reformation the practice developed of locking it in the tabernacle above the altar.

Allegory and symbolism ran riot in elaborating mystical ideas. One of the most influential expositions of the Mass with allegorical explanations of its parts was by Amalarius of Metz, a pupil of Alcuin. His ideas were repeated in sermons and popularizations throughout the following centuries. Another important work was the *Rationale Divinorum Officiorum* by William Duran-

---

[10] For a full account of the ceremonial at all celebrations of the Mass see Adrian Fortescue, *The Ceremonies of the Roman Rite Described*, Part II. Also O'Connell, *The Celebration of Mass* (3 vols.; [Milwaukee: Bruce, 1940-41]).

dus, bishop of Mende. According to these authorities the Mass represents Christ's life on earth. The antiphonal chanting of the Introit signifies the voice of the patriarchs and prophets. The bishop appearing from the sacristy suggests Christ the expected Savior emerging from the womb of the Virgin and entering the world. The Gloria in Excelsis reflects the joy in heaven after the Lord's resurrection. The session of the risen Christ at the right hand of the Father is indicated when the bishop is seated on his throne. The Epistle represents the preaching of John the Baptist, and the Gospel the beginning of Christ's preaching. The twelve parts of the Creed (Nicene) refer to the calling of the twelve apostles. When the oblation is offered the faithful think of Christ as entering the temple to offer himself to the Father. As the Service proceeds the symbolism increases in intricacy. It includes all the details of the Saviour's passion and death, the deposition, burial, resurrection, and the ascension. Thus the medieval conception of the Eucharist was a vastly different one from that of the early church and of the later Reformers.[11]

THE DIVINE OFFICE

The second great body of medieval liturgical material is that connected with the Divine Office, the name given the series of daily services held in monastic communities. All monks and friars, and all priests, whether "secular" (parish priests) or "regular" (members of a monastic order), were bound by their ordination to observe the "canonical hours" and read the appointed services daily. These hours were Matins, Lauds, Prime, Terce, Sext, Nones, Vespers, and Compline. The liturgical provisions for so many services, with their variations throughout the year, soon became very great. After the eleventh century all the material was gathered into office books called breviaries. The Benedictine Breviary finally gained recognition as the monastic use; and the Roman Breviary became popular among the secular clergy.

The purely devotional idea which underlay this series of daily services merged with the later ideas of "merit" and "good works." The monks, clergy, and all "religious" were supposed to win a store of merit for themselves and also for the church by deeds not demanded by God, yet pleasing to him. Such deeds were called "works of supererogation." Thus the obligations steadily became heavier and the services more complicated. The days in the calendar differed as to rank or degree. This determined the manner of recitation. Homilies, legends, and lives of the saints practically supplanted Scripture in certain of the hours.

The Office was a colossal system of daily devotions for monks and clergy which paralleled the people's Service of the Mass. Every priest was obliged to celebrate the latter on Sundays and festivals, and daily

[11] A summary of the Expositions of Amalarius is given in Yngve Brilioth. *Eucharistic Faith and Practice*, p. 83. Henry Osborn Taylor, *The Mediaeval Mind*, gives a summary of both Amalarius and Durandus (II, 76ff).

if possible. The faithful also were obliged to attend Mass at least on Sundays and other "days of obligation." But in addition to this, everyone in orders, from subdeacon to pope, was bound to spend an average of nearly two hours every day in reciting the canonical hours which composed the Office. It thus became a chief duty of the clergy to see that the daily sacrifice was offered in the Mass and that the "prayer wheel" of the church was kept revolving in the daily Office.[12]

A third type of liturgical material is represented by the Occasional Services. Some of these services, such as baptism, marriage, burial, etc., were provided in the *Rituale* or manual of the parish priest. Others— dedication of churches, ordination, etc.—which could be performed only by a bishop, were included in the *Pontificale*.

Other books known as "primers" provided vernacular prayers and other simple devotions which people commonly said while the priest was reading the Latin Service. These primers also generally contained the "little hours of the Blessed Virgin," a series of devotions, intercessions, etc., somewhat on the plan of the canonical hours for the clergy.

MEDIEVAL MUSIC

Music throughout the medieval centuries was priestly and choral. The eighth century witnessed a great development of liturgical hymns for the Office in the East; in the West, Gregorian music (plain song) spread everywhere. It was cultivated particularly in music schools connected with monastic communities.

Plain song, unlike modern music, was without harmony or parts. The melodies were free in form without bars or measures. Instead of our modern major and minor scales there were eight modes—the so-called "church modes"—which in some respects gave greater variety than we know today. The objectives of this music were liturgical rather than artistic. The supreme purpose was to clothe the text in dignified melodic form. All parts of the liturgy, whether intoned by the priest or sung by the choir, were set to these melodies, many of which have been included in the *Service Book and Hymnal.*

The ninth century marks the beginning of musical notation as we understand it today. The first marking was a single red line (F) drawn across the page to assist the singer in reading the neumes, a system of musical shorthand placed above the text. Later a yellow line (C) was added, and still later two additional lines. Thus the four-line staff was produced which continued in universal use for seven centuries and is still employed in plain song, while modern music uses a five-line staff.

[12] For fuller discussion of the Divine Office see Chapter XXIII, pp. 388ff.

The liturgical chants were finally classified into collections known as the *Graduale* and the *Troperium*. The *Graduale* contained the music sung by the choir during the Mass—including particularly the variable introits, graduals with Alleluia, offertories, and communions. The *Troperium* contained parts interpolated ("farsed") between the regular texts of the Kyrie, Gloria in Excelsis, Sanctus, Agnus Dei, etc. It also contained sequences and proses. In cathedral and monastic communities these melodies by the thousand were continually transcribed in the office books of the church. The Psalms were chanted antiphonally in the hour services to a fixed body of chant forms known as the Gregorian or psalm Tones. Hymn melodies of freer form were also sung to Latin texts.

Church music had a wonderful development paralleling that of architecture. It was slower in maturing and was perhaps more truly a child of the church than was architecture. It also remained longer under her care. The entire Gregorian system was influenced by the earlier Greek modes and Greek recitative. But once within the church it developed its own spirit and forms. Melody and a worshipful spirit were its gifts to the church and to the world.

After the twelfth century, the time in which architecture was approaching its great expansion and culmination, music began its modern development. The influence exerted by the troubadours and the minnesingers was due largely to the active co-operation of the wealthy classes in France and Germany. The church, however, led in the new development of harmony and counterpoint, and this, after architecture had passed its proudest moment, blossomed forth into the loveliness of the Netherlands school of the fifteenth century and culminated in the spiritual beauty of the Palestrina school in Rome.

The world is familiar with the great monuments of medieval architecture. It knows little of the vast store of liturgical music of the fifteenth and sixteenth centuries or of the intellectual vigor and force which characterized these compositions. Their quantity and technical mastery are amazing. Counterpoint was carried on through single and double, augmented and diminished, direct, inverted, and retrograde, until it obscured the rhythm and the words and almost broke under its own weight. Edward Dickinson is well within the truth when he says: "The world has never witnessed a more absorbed devotion to a single artistic idea, neither has there existed since the golden age of Greek sculpture another art form so lofty in expression and so perfect in workmanship as the polyphonic church chorus in the years of its maturity.[13]

[13] *Music in the History of the Western Church,* p. 133.

The best of this music was characterized by melodic beauty and liturgical objectivity. It never compromised with the world nor sought to establish itself outside the church. Its worth and distinctive qualities, however, gained for it a permanent place within the church, where it is zealously cultivated in many centers today.

After an unchallenged sway of a thousand years, this unisonous plain song provided the basis for a development which progressed through organum and descant to contrapuntal polyphony. The latter included many voice parts developed according to established rules. This music, purely vocal, was carried to its early perfection in a series of masses and motets by composers of the Netherlands school, Josquin des Prés, Orlando di Lasso, and their contemporaries. Palestrina (1526-94), Allegri, and other composers of the Roman school in the sixteenth century brought contrapuntal music to its culmination in compositions of high technical interest and spiritual effectiveness. The Venetian School led to a freer treatment of the old church modes and the introduction of instrumental accompaniment. Vienna, Munich, Paris, and the Royal Chapel in England were other important centers of development. Instrumental music, which included the psaltery, harp, and other stringed instruments, trumpets, and the organ, was increasingly found throughout the West. The organ, however, was prohibited in Rome.

THE GOOD AND THE EVIL

As we survey the medieval centuries we find much in them that was good. The Word of God and the Christian faith were preserved, though mixed with much that was false and evil. Communion with God, the ideas of devotion and reverence, and the spirit of selfless sacrifice were kept alive. The best of the age was in the church—the greatest personalities and intellects. Great theologians, architects, artists, and administrators built up a complex civilization which maintained the honor and dignity of Christianity and exercised a mighty sway over all peoples. The Crusades, the spread of the monastic orders, great missionary activity, intellectual speculation, the erection of the great cathedrals, and the development of the Christian liturgy all testify to vigor and capacity. Fine examples of contrapuntal music, religious painting, and Latin hymnody give ample evidence of refinement and power of expression. The thirteenth century and the later period just before the Reformation were interesting and vigorous times. The thirteenth century particularly, with its abstract scholasticism and its popular romanticism, stamped its own character indelibly upon all future times. The revival of learning quickened intellectual forces. The Copernican discoveries, the finding of America, and a new way to India extended all horizons. The invention of printing supplied new elements of power.

Notwithstanding its spectacular and emotional features, medieval worship was not a shallow or vain thing. It rested solidly upon theological principles and reflected a deep understanding of human nature. Logic and sympathy combined to build up a vast system with definite but varied requirements for the several groups within the church. Heavy duties were exacted of the clergy and other "religious"; a few definite obligations were laid upon the laity; all shared in the sum total of the church's devotional activities and the rewards they secured. From the humblest to the highest each felt that he had a place in a vast "system of grace" and that by the co-operation of all something far greater could be achieved than by individual effort alone.

The medieval system of worship was impressive in its unity and universality. The one liturgy and the one liturgical language crossed all frontiers. In every village church as well as in the great cathedrals, among the peoples of every land and language, the same services and ceremonies were daily observed. This testified to the unquestioned authority of the church, the key to our understanding of medieval thought and life in general. Any fair and well-informed view of this expanse of history—longer in point of time than the centuries since the Reformation—must recognize its vigorous achievements.

But admiration for these achievements must not blind us to the faults of the medieval church. Intermingled with good and great things were grievous errors and abuses. Some of these were serious and fundamental. The church had become something more than the "communion of saints." It was a powerful, visible organization animated by sacerdotal, hierarchical, and imperialistic principles. Decrees of councils and popes were regarded as of equal authority with Scripture itself. The external features of worship, like the details of the Gothic cathedrals of the time, were overweighted with ornament. The whole fabric of worship was weakened by impurity in doctrine and practice.

The Word of God with its clear and simple plan of salvation was obscured by the lack of vernacular Scriptures and services and the decline of preaching and instruction. Tradition, legends, and stories of saints supplanted the Scriptures themselves among the illiterate masses. Allegory and symbolism carried the thought of the sophisticated to absurd lengths. The idea of salvation by works ruled all minds. The peace and assurance which came with the later emphasis upon the doctrine of justification by faith were little known. The Mass was a propitiatory sacrifice instead of a true sacrament and gift of grace. Its celebration was a good work which merited favor. The doctrine of transubstantiation led to the withdrawal of the cup from communicants and to other unscriptural and superstitious practices. Mariolatry and hagiolatry clouded the honor and worship due God alone, while the teaching concerning purgatory robbed souls of the certainty of salvation. The worship of images and the granting of indulgences were additional abuses.

The individual conscience was overridden by the exaggerated authority of the church. The priesthood of believers was submerged under the terrifying power of priests, bishops, and popes, who multiplied exactions, imposed obligations, and wrested wealth from the people. All services were in a foreign tongue. Morality and spirituality were rarely attained among the people and were often lacking in the clergy. The calendar was crowded with feasts in honor of the saints, the traffic in whose relics enormously increased after the Crusades. Among later feasts must also be mentioned Corpus Christi. A multitude of popular devotions, such as the reserved Sacrament, Benediction and Exposition, the Holy Name, the Rosary, the Stations of the Cross, and the cult of the Blessed Virgin Mary, with their proper appointments, obscured the original design of early Roman worship with its restrained objectives and severe beauty.

Celibacy of the clergy and monasticism withdrew thousands of the finest spirits from family and social life. The religious orders, with their compact organization, attained great wealth and power. They taught the people in a rude way and dispensed the charity of the church. Gifts and bequests, exemptions, and privileges enriched them. Yet they sheltered the arts, which knew practically no field outside the church's walls. Great works of transcription and illumination were begun in the writing rooms of monasteries and marvelous embroideries in the sewing rooms of nunneries, only to be finished by later generations. The crown and the nobility poured great gifts into the church's treasury, thinking to atone for oppression, injustice, and deeds of violence. Toilers and workers had their guilds and craft organizations, but they were not yet commercialized. Most of them were religious as well as craft organizations, each having its own particular patron saint. The craftsmen freely gave their best efforts to the church, satisfied with slender wages and the other returns which appreciation, pride in their work, guild and civic prestige, and the approval of the church afforded.

The two sacraments instituted by our Lord had long since been increased to seven (confirmation, ordination, penance, marriage, and extreme unction having been added), and elaborate services were built about them all. Faith in what Christ had done was obscured by the necessity of doing all that the church required. Tradition crowded Scripture to the wall. The people came to Holy Communion, that is, actually to receive it, less and less often. Once a year, probably, was the usual practice, while many received it even less frequently, often out of sheer dread.

Though receiving rudimentary education in the monasteries, the clergy as a whole were ignorant. Only the few attained any breadth of learning. Before the days of printing, illiteracy prevailed generally among the masses, who were oppressed politically, socially, and ecclesiastically. All active participation in worship had been withdrawn from them, and superstition and legend supplied the lack of fundamental truth.

The cathedral or church building was school, library, museum, music hall, and meeting-place as well as church. Allegorical and symbolical ideas filled every part of the edifice. The foundations were said to be faith, which was not seen; the four walls were the evangelists; the roof was charity, which covers a multitude of sins; the towers were the preachers and the prelates; the door was Christ; the pillars were the bishops and the doctors. The statuary, carvings, and stained glass depicted scenes from biblical history, the parables and the miracles, or legendary attributes of birds and animals.

One important fact remains to be stated. As we study these medieval centuries, we must remember that they form part of the history of our own church. The Lutheran church is not a creation of the sixteenth century. It is a reformation and purification of the historic church. We are Lutherans, but first of all—and more important—we are Christians. We owe many of our finest possessions in matters of faith, worship, and life to the protecting care and creative enrichment of the medieval centuries. The things which were good in them and the things which were bad belonged to our own spiritual fathers. We cannot disown them if we would, for we must trace the history of our own faith and of our own church back through these medieval centuries to the early church, and through that to the apostolic age, and beyond that to our Lord himself, the Founder and Head of the church.

We must look upon these centuries as our Reformers looked upon them. The radical Reformers saw nothing but evil in them. They thought to ignore them and to build a new Christianity upon the basis of Scripture and apostolic precedent. The conservative Reformers saw the good as well as the evil. They recognized the fact that no age has been entirely without the presence of the Holy Spirit, and that fifteen hundred years of Christian experience and expression could not be ignored. What was needed was reformation, not re-creation. The problem was to up-root the evil, to save the good, and to find true principles upon which to establish a new and healthier development. This they accomplished. We honor them today because they did not break with the church universal but purified its form of worship, quickened its spirit of devotion, and brought new offerings of their own for the services of the sanctuary.

CHAPTER III

REFORM AND DEVELOPMENT IN GERMANY

Liturgical reform was part of the program of the Reformation in all lands. Discussion and clarification of doctrine were the first step. The reform of worship was reached only as the movement worked outward from its inner center and as the leaders and the people themselves became convinced of its necessity.

EARLY EFFORTS

As early as 1516 Luther in preaching on the Third Commandment stressed the necessity of "hearing the Word of God" as over against the idea of "hearing Mass."[1] In 1520 he advocated communion in both kinds, "for the sake of the completeness of the sign"; objected to the Verba being said secretly; and indicated a distinction between sacramental and sacrificial elements in the Service which has ever since been recognized as important in theoretical discussions. Declaring that man cannot "begin and lay the first stone" he says that God "must first come and give man a promise. This Word of God is the beginning, the foundation, the rock upon which afterward all works, words and thoughts of man must build."[2] A few months later, in his *Babylonian Captivity of the Church,* he vigorously attacked the withholding of the cup, the doctrine of transubstantiation, and the conception of the Mass as a good work and a sacrifice.[3]

In these writings, as in his later activities, Luther protested against unevangelical features but never sought to abolish the historic order and substitute a new service built upon evangelical principles. He reverenced the forms which faith had built and which enshrined the Lord's institution. He recognized the fact that the whole devotional and ceremonial system of the church was deeply impressed upon popular

---

[1] *WA* 1, 443.
[2] *A Treatise on the New Testament, that is the Holy Mass.* In *PE* 1, 294ff. German text in *WA* 6, 349ff.
[3] *PE* 2, 170ff (*WA* 6, 497ff).

imagination. He was convinced that purification and not destruction was needed. The programs of Karlstadt, the Anabaptists, and other radicals with their different spirit strengthened him in this conviction.[4]

These radical procedures impelled Luther to leave the Wartburg secretly in March, 1522, and preach eight sermons in the parish church at Wittenberg. He counseled moderation and a conservative reform of worship. He insisted that ministers omit the parts of the Mass which referred to the Sacrament as a propitiatory sacrifice. But the Service itself, with vestments, he restored, together with the singing of the Latin chants.

In Whitsuntide, 1523, in fulfilment of a promise made to the congregation at Leisnig,[5] Luther published an eight-page pamphlet, *Von Ordnung Gottesdiensts in der Gemeinde.*[6] This went through at least eight editions in the first year. In it Luther objected to the silencing of God's Word, the introduction of unscriptural material, and the conception of the Service as a meritorious work. He criticized the multiplicity of saints' days, legends, etc., and emphasized the importance of the sermon as a particular form of the Word of God. "One thing is needful," he concludes, viz., "that Mary should sit at Christ's feet and hear his word daily . . . There is one eternal Word; all else must pass away, no matter how much concern it may cost Martha." He did not as yet make the sermon a regular part of the Mass but provided separate daily preaching services.

These early efforts were educational. They stated principles rather than proposed reforms. Luther did not undertake a reconstruction of the Mass until the end of 1523 when the logic of events drove him to prepare his Latin Service. He and the conservative Reformers in general hesitated to embark upon extensive practical reforms until thorough discussion of principles had cleared the air. They appreciated the fact that the Mass was everywhere regarded as a supreme form of devotion perfected by centuries of thought and enhanced by all the resources of art. Luther, particularly, dreaded the possibility that a new type of service might be regarded as the symbol of a party or of a personal following. A strain of mysticism also led him to feel that if Christians were sufficiently spiritual, they could "worship in spirit"; and that forms and ceremonies were chiefly of value for the young, the unlearned, and imperfect Christians. These facts, together with his preoccupation with

[4] For a summary of these activities and of the entire development, see "Luther on the Principles and Order of Christian Worship," by Edward T. Horn, in *Lutheran Church Review,* X (1891), 217-56.

[5] Enders, *Dr. Martin Luthers Briefwechsel,* IV, 70.

[6] *WA* 12, 31-37. English translation with notes in *PE* 6, 51-64.

other matters, explain why Luther waited nearly six years before attempting a serious liturgical reconstruction.

In the meantime others had entered the field. In 1522 Prior Kantz of Nordlingen in southern Germany prepared a revision of the Mass. Karlstadt attempted radical changes in Wittenberg. New orders of worship appeared in Basel. Many priests omitted objectionable parts of the Canon, substituted evangelical prayers, and read the Words of Institution in the vernacular. Confusion and uncertainty reigned everywhere. Demands upon Luther to outline a program became insistent. The most importunate among the pastors was Nicholas Haussmann in Zwickau, to whom Luther addressed his first important liturgical work.

It would have been easy to prepare a simple order to be used instead of the historic Mass, as Zwingli and others did. Luther, however, chose to reform the Mass and not to substitute a new service for it. He realized that if the good were destroyed with the bad, much of the devotional, artistic, and spiritual inheritance of the church would be lost, also that substitution of a new order would leave the most expressive and significant feature of the medieval system undisturbed. So while conscious of the difficulties, he determined to take the historic Mass, regarded by all as a perfect and finished product, and make it express the thought of the New Testament and primitive Christianity. He determined to make it the servant of the gospel instead of the master in the church. Laying aside his unfinished translation of the Old Testament, he labored on the liturgy for two months and then issued his *Formula Missae et Communionis* in December, 1523.[7]

The fundamental character of the radical opposition must be understood. It involved more than an assertion of taste or objections to incidental or unimportant details. It was rooted in convictions concerning the nature of worship and the sacraments according to which objective (sacramental) values were denied or minimized and subjective (sacrificial) values magnified.

Zwingli in his *Fidei Ratio,* dated Zurich, July 3, 1530, and laid before the emperor at Augsburg a few days later, says: "I believe, yea I know, that all the sacraments are so far from conferring grace that they do not even convey or distribute it . . . a channel or vehicle is not necessary to the Spirit."[8] Lutheran influences modified this view somewhat among the Zwinglians in Germany. Calvin's position was not so extreme, but he failed to appreciate the highest objective sacramental values in worship or the Eucharist. For both the sermon became the principal feature. Even this was thought of chiefly as a personal, subjective utterance in the nature of testimony and exhortation. The Sacrament was a memorial and thanksgiving, nothing more.[9]

[7] Text in *WA* 12, 205-20. English translation with notes in *PE* 6, 67-117.

[8] H. E. Jacobs, *Book of Concord,* II, 168ff. See also Samuel M. Jackson, William J. Hinke, *et al., The Latin Works of Huldreich Zwingli,* II, 35ff.

[9] For discussion of Luther's psychology with extensive quotations, see Leonhard Fendt, *Der lutherische Gottesdienst des 16. Jahrhunderts.*

THE FORMULA MISSAE

In this pamphlet, after stating his purpose to "purify that which is in use," Luther sketches the historical development of the Mass and mentions the portions which are good and cannot be censured. Then he turns to the objectionable part and denounces the Canon, "that mangled and abominable thing,"[10] the "sacedotal monopoly" of the Mass, and states, "We will prove all things and hold fast that which is good."

In discussing the order of the Service, he approves the Introits for the Lord's Day, and the festivals of Easter, Pentecost, and Christmas. He does not object to other festivals based upon Scripture but proposes that festivals of saints not so mentioned be abolished. He approves the Kyrie; the Gloria in Excelsis; the Collect ("provided it be godly, as those appointed for Sundays usually are"); the Epistle; the Gradual (though suggesting that those which exceed two verses might well "be sung at home"); the Gospel (with the usual ceremonies); the Nicene Creed; the sermon (at this point, or, if preferred, before the Introit); the Preface; Words of Institution (recited aloud); the Sanctus and Hosanna (a location which later became a characteristic feature of the Swedish liturgy); the Elevation ("on account of the weak"); the Lord's Prayer; the Pax and its response; administration; Agnus Dei, or communion hymn sung by the choir; Collect, the Benedicamus, and the Aaronic benediction.

Then follow sixteen paragraphs on such matters as Christian liberty, vestments (permitted if pomp and luxury be absent), participation of the people, examination for communion, communion in both kinds, vernacular hymns, and Matins and Vespers.

The *Formula Missae* was Luther's greatest liturgical writing. It was his objective criticism of a historic and vital institution. He was not concerned, as he was later in his German Service, with introducing a new liturgical language or with paraphrasing portions of the historic order in German verse for immediate use by congregations of limited capacity and unaccustomed to active participation in the service. Luther was not a special student of the liturgy, as was Cranmer. He took the local use, probably his Augustinian missal, and prepared his reconstruction without going further afield. His *Formula* was intended as a local program and not a general order for the whole church. It proved to be, however, of all his many works his greatest contribution to general liturgical reform.

---

[10] The word "canon" means a rule. The complete term is *canon actionis,* "the rule of procedure," according to which the thanksgiving, consecration, oblation, and intercession are to be conducted.

If we would understand some of Luther's sharpest criticisms, we must study the missals of his time. The Augustinian missals contained not only the usual Offertory and Canon, but features peculiar to local or monastic uses. Fendt[11] quotes some of the effusive Introits, Graduals, and Prefaces for saints' days found in the Augustinian Missal of 1501. Many of these objectionable features were later corrected by Tridentine reform.

Apart from this, however, the Offertory and Canon in all missals of that time and of today reveal the principal ground for Luther's attitude. Luther himself translated the Canon of the Mass into German and quoted it in a pamphlet, *Vom Greuel der Stillmesse,* of the year 1525.[12]

The Canon follows the Sanctus and extends to the Lord's Prayer. The text is invariable and contains ten paragraphs. It must be said secretly by the priest without the variation of a syllable. It contains intercessions for the living, a commemoration of apostles and martyrs, prayers for acceptance and consecration of the Offering about to be made, recital of the Words of Institution, the Oblation or Offering, and Invocation (in place of the ancient *epiclesis*), intercessions for the dead, and the Lord's Prayer. The last has a brief introduction and an expansion of the last petition (*embolismus*). This is followed by the Fraction, the ceremonial breaking of the host into three parts to symbolize the suffering and death of Christ; and the commixture, the placing of a small portion of the Host in the chalice to symbolize the reunion of our Lord's body and spirit at the Resurrection. Elaborate ceremonial—genuflections, osculations, the use of lights, incense, etc.—accompanies the reading of the text by the priest.[13]

Following is a brief outline of the text of the *Formula.*

Introit (sung to customary tones)	Sanctus
Kyrie (ninefold)	Elevation (during *Benedictus qui*
Gloria in Excelsis	*venit*)
Collect (one only)	Lord's Prayer
Epistle	Pax
Gradual (but not long Lenten tracts)	Communion (of priest, then people)
Sequence (for Nativity and Pentecost only)	Agnus Dei (during communion)
	Communio (permissive)
Gospel	Final Collect (one or two only)
Nicene Creed (sung)	Salutation
Sermon (here or before the Mass)	Benedicamus
Preface	Benediction
Verba (sung to Paternoster tone, read aloud, or read silently)	

The critical nature of the *Formula* is shown in its rejection of medieval corruptions, together with all ideas of obligation, sacrifice, and good works, as well as in the fact that, while seeking to preserve the historic

[11] *Op. cit.,* p. 375.
[12] Text in *WA* 18, 22-36. English translation with notes and Latin original in *PE* 6, 121-32.
[13] The complete text of the Ordinary and the Canon of the Mass is given in pp. 695-735 in the appendix.

order and much material of the Mass, the principle of freedom is stressed. It also distinguishes sharply between essential and nonessential features. Vestments, lights, incense may be used or not; but the Offertory and the Canon must be discarded without compromise.

While critical, the *Formula* is conservative. It breathes the spirit of the gospel as opposed to Roman and also to radical extremes. It counsels moderation and patience. Its conservatism is not that of timidity, but of courageous conviction. The Service is kept in Latin except for the Sermon and a few hymns, largely because Luther appreciated much of the liturgical material in its Latin form, recognized its cultural value for schools and colleges, and wanted to retain the fine music traditionally associated with it.

The *Formula* is also constructive. This is evident in its presentation of principles, in its suggestions concerning a vernacular sermon and vernacular hymns, and in its effort to approach worship from the congregational rather than from the priestly side. With respect to method, it presents a pedogogical point of view. The first thought is to express faith; the final purpose is, perhaps too restrictedly, to create more faith.

The *Formula* is but an outline. If filled in with the proper Introits, Collects, Epistles, Graduals, Gospels, etc., for the church year, and with the Psalms, antiphons, responsories, and similar material referred to approvingly in its pages, it would make a book almost as large as the *Service Book* and strikingly like it in content and arrangement.[14]

THE FIRST VERNACULAR SERVICES

Though Luther repeatedly expressed a desire for services in German, he was not the first to provide them. Before he published his *German Mass* in 1526, vernacular forms had appeared in twenty or more widely scattered districts. Many of these simply omitted the Canon and kept the greater part of the service in Latin. The Sermon, the Words of Institution, and occasionally the lessons were the only parts in German.

The orders of Kantz, the Strasbourg masses, and the Reformed services in Nuremberg, Zurich, and Basel were quite free in form and of considerable interest. The evangelical Mass of Kaspar Kantz, prior of the convent at Nördlingen (1522) probably had little more than literary significance. Among other features it contained, in German, a confession of sins, an absolution, an exhortation and sermon, the Preface and a brief prayer of consecration leading to the Words of Institution—"O most gracious Father, merciful

[14] For critical study of the *Formula,* see particularly the introduction and notes by Paul Zeller Strodach in *PE* 6, 67-81, 101-17.

eternal God, grant (*hilf*) that this bread and wine may become and be for us the true Body, the innocent Blood of thy beloved Son, our Lord Jesus Christ, who in the day . . . ."[15]

In 1523 Thomas Münzer introduced a German Service in Alstädt which had many excellent qualities. It was built upon five series of propers from the Roman Missal (Advent, Christmas, Passiontide, Easter, and Pentecost). It preserved practically the entire historic outline. The Gloria in Excelsis was given in prose translation. This Service was widely used in Brunswick and after being slightly modified became known as the "Erfurt *Kirchenampt.*" In 1525 Duke Albrecht of Prussia approved for his duchy a service which adhered closely to the order of the *Formula Missae.* The greater part of the service, however, was in German.

The first complete German mass was held in St. John's Chapel of the Münster in Strasbourg on Tuesday, February 16, 1524. It was read by Theobald Schwartz (Nigri). The influence of Luther is apparent, although there are important independent provisions. The Confession of Sins and the Collects are new evangelical prayers, congregational in character. In the Confession there is a phrase or two which appears twenty-eight years later in the *Book of Common Prayer.* The historic order is followed until after the Creed (all in German). After this there is a brief exhortation to the communicants and an invocation for the sanctification of the congregation. The Invocation of the Holy Spirit and the General Prayer (Prayer of the Church) are significant substitutes for the Offertory and the Canon. The Nunc Dimittis is substituted for the Post-Communion.

In Nuremberg one group sought the translation of the entire Service into German, while another endeavored to retain the Latin forms as fully as possible. Volprecht, the Augustinian prior, and Döber, chaplain of the convent at the hospital, representing the first group, formulated services somewhat similar to those of Kantz and the Strasbourgers. The beautiful exhortation to communicants taken from these services spread throughout Germany and is embedded in an abbreviated form in our Order for Public Confession. German hymns were substituted for the Introit and the Gradual; and paraphrases and translations of the Creed, Sanctus, and Agnus Dei were used. These German services, however, were only introduced in limited circles.

The Nuremberg spirit was more generally expressed by the type of reform which kept the Latin services after the general plan of the *Formula Missae,* but with German lessons (*lectio continua*) and a German exhortation to the communicants, as in Döber. The administration was in both kinds. A Sunday preaching service was held in connection with Matins. This service was read after the first mass and was in Latin except the lessons. After the use of the Prone and the sermon, the second mass was held. The city council was loath to sanction the introduction of German services. Only Osiander contended for these, desiring to restrict the Latin services to the schools. But even he was satisfied to continue the Latin in the church for a time, "until we are furnished with more music." This type of service, Latin except for German lessons, hymns, and sermon, remained essentially the Nuremberg use for centuries.

Fendt credits all of these attempts at vernacular services to the spirit of

---

[15] Fendt, *op. cit.* p. 90.

Luther working through many minds in different places. He discusses them all under the suggestive heading, "The Echo."[16]

Even Julius Smend, overzealous in stressing the independence of others from Luther, acknowledges the all-determining influence of Luther's *Babylonian Captivity*. The situation paralleled that of German translations of the Bible, fully twenty of which had been printed before Luther's German New Testament appeared in 1522. In both instances Luther's work was so superior and his personal influence so great that his Service and his Bible, like his hymns and his catechisms, finally determined in a broad way the future development of the Lutheran church and of a large part of Protestantism.[17]

This survey indicates how general was the movement in the direction of vernacular worship, and yet how strong was the conviction that this must be done with the greatest care lest the wheat be destroyed with the tares and the precious inheritance of the past be sacrificed for a less noble and adequate substitute. The general attitude and development was the direct outworking of the spirit of Luther and his Wittenberg associates. The Reformed groups in Zurich and Geneva were of a different spirit.

LUTHER'S GERMAN MASS

While opposing the idea that services must be entirely in the vernacular and dreading in principle absolute uniformity, Luther was practically forced to prepare a German Service. In approaching this task he had an appreciation of the difficulties involved which few, if any others, shared. For him the music and the text must have *"eine rechte deutsche art."*

The times and the tides of popular feeling would not wait for a gradual solution of the problem. Luther was impressed by the growing confusion, but he also was unable to approve what others had attempted. This was not because of wounded vanity, as Smend intimates, but more probably, as Edward T. Horn suggests, because he feared that radical action might go too fast and too far. He distrusted the spirit which produced hasty and immature forms. His taste and sense of fitness could not approve inartistic and impossible phrases, harsh, wooden versions of fine Latin texts, or sentimental terms of endearment and (as particularly in Münzer) intimations of pantheistic mysticism. The Strasbourg masses also, in their overemphasis upon instruction and their undervaluation of the church year and the historic scheme of lessons, seemed to be seeking novelty at the expense of stability.[18]

---

[16] *Op. cit.,* pp. 82-178.

[17] The most extended discussion of these attempts to introduce vernacular services is to be found in the scholarly works of Smend, *Die evangelischen deutschen Messen bis zu Luthers deutscher Messe* and *Der evangelische Gottesdienst* . . . .

[18] See Dr. Horn's article, "Remarks on Some of our Liturgical Classics," *Memoirs of the Lutheran Liturgical Association,* VI, 17-22.

Yielding to the situation, Luther called Bugenhagen and Jonas to his aid and began the preparation of a German Service. This was introduced in the parish church in Wittenberg, October 29, 1525. The next Sunday Luther said to the congregation: "Since so many from all countries beseech me with letters, and writings, and even bring worldly force to bear upon me, we can no longer excuse ourselves and protest, but must believe that it is God's wish."[19] Beginning with Christmas this Service was used, at least in parts, in the parish church on Sunday mornings "on account of the uneducated lay folk." The Latin Service (Luther's *Formula Missae*) was used on weekdays as before.

The German Mass[20] begins with a preface in which Luther recognizes the value of a German Service "on account of the simple and the young who are to be and must be exercised daily and educated in the Scriptures and God's Word." Concerning the Latin order Luther says: "I do not wish to have this abrogated or changed; but as we have hitherto observed it among us, so we shall be free to use the same where and when we please or occasion requires."

The pedagogical point of view is further emphasized in the discussion concerning worship. After this follows a chapter on Sunday for the laity. "We allow Mass vestments, altar, and lights to remain, until they are no longer serviceable or it pleases us to change. Whoever wishes to do otherwise we allow it to be done."

Following is a brief outline of the *Deutsche Messe:*

Hymn or German Psalm in Tone I (A substitute for the Latin Introit)
Kyrie (threefold only)
Collect (sung without inflection, facing the altar)
Epistle (intoned facing the people)
Hymn (in German, but by choir)
Gospel
Nicene Creed (German versification sung by congregation)
Sermon (on the Gospel)
Lord's Prayer (paraphrase)
Exhortation to communicants
Consecration (by Verba) of bread, and administration
Sanctus (versified) or hymn
Consecration (by Verba) of wine, and administration
Hymn or German Agnus Dei, during administration of chalice
Post-Communion collect
Benediction (Numbers VI)

As can be seen, the Gloria in Excelsis is not mentioned. Rietschel surmises that Luther took it for granted as belonging to the Kyrie. A German hymn takes the place of the Gradual. The Gospel is intoned in the fifth tone. There is a German translation of the Nicene Creed, *Wir glauben all an einen Gott,* to be sung by the congregation. All the

---

[19] *WA* 19, 50f.
[20] *Deutsche Messe und Ordnung Gottesdiensts.* Text with critical notes in *WA* 19, 44-113. English translation with notes in *PE* 6, 153-89.

usual prayers of the Mass are omitted. The Words of Institution are sung aloud by the minister to a melody which Luther provides. He suggests that the bread be administered immediately after the consecration "before one blesses the cup." The elevation was retained (until 1542, when it was dropped by Bugenhagen).

This German Service, even more than Luther's Latin Service, is a treatise rather than a formula. Its outstanding features are the use of German throughout and its emphasis upon congregational hymns. Every part of the Service is in the vernacular except the Kyrie. Certain elements, formerly sung in Latin—Introit, Gradual, Creed, Sanctus—are translated into German verse and sung as congregational hymns. The Preface is omitted and the Lord's Prayer is placed before the Verba and expanded into a paraphrase. The latter feature is all the more remarkable in view of Luther's vehement opposition to any but the precise words of Scripture in connection with the Verba. The collects and prayers are fixed forms and not left to the inspiration of the pastor. The pedagogical spirit is evident throughout.

It is clear that in Luther's own mind this Service possessed limited rather than universal significance. When the Elector desired to introduce the German Mass everywhere by authority, Luther objected. Luther never abandoned the type of service outlined in his *Formula Missae*. The German Service was largely for the uneducated laity, a simplification of the historic order adapted to the needs and abilities of a part of the people. Luther's mature ideas on worship are reflected in the later orders for Wittenberg (1533) (prepared chiefly by Bugenhagen), and Saxony (1539) (chiefly by Jonas). The German Mass sought to promote congregational participation and to retain as much as possible of the historic Service for use in the villages and where there were no capable choirs. It took advantage of a popular movement and turned to churchly account the recently awakened enthusiasm for German hymns.

The Lutheran church as a whole approved certain features of Luther's German Mass, particularly the principle of a vernacular service, the historic outline of worship, congregational hymns, and active congregational participation in the Service. With occasional exceptions, chiefly in south and southwest Germany, however, the church finally rejected many features. Among these were the omission of the Gloria in Excelsis, the substitution of an exhortation to communicants for the noble and ancient Preface, the paraphrasing of the Lord's Prayer (which opened the way to grave abuses in the period of Rationalism), the impractical division of the Verba, the twofold administration of the elements, and the retention of the elevation. The transfer of the Lord's

Prayer to a place before the Verba unfortunately gained wide acceptance, though some orders of the first rank never adopted it. It created permanent confusion in all subsequent Lutheran orders and its wisdom on other accounts is questionable. The introduction of rhymed paraphrases of the Creed, Sanctus, Te Deum, etc., was a regrettable feature, all too frequently adopted, which deprived congregations of the full and historic texts and gave them a poor type of hymn as a substitute.

It was unfortunate that certain districts fastened upon their churches by legal enactment the type of service outlined in the *Deutsche Messe*. In doing this they failed to appreciate Luther's own view of the German Mass as intended only for the uneducated laity. By making it general features binding, they perpetuated an abnormal and temporary situation and restricted future development. These districts dropped to the level of the simplest and easiest forms of vernacular worship and stayed there. They were not following their leader—though they thought they were— for they ignored the limitations which he recognized and did not study his preference as exemplified in the use at Wittenberg and throughout Saxony during Luther's lifetime. This latter provided a fuller type of worship than is generally recognized, in some details richer than the services provided in the Common Service or *The Common Service Book*.

SCOPE AND SIGNIFICANCE OF LUTHER'S LITURGICAL REFORM

Luther's other liturgical reforms included an order of baptism (*Taufbuchlein*) (1523, extensively revised in 1526); an order for marriage (1529); an order for ordination (1535); the Litany, in Latin and German (1529); numerous collects and prayers with introductory versicles; thirty-eight hymns and various hymnbook prefaces. His great work of translating the Bible also cannot be considered entirely apart from its significance and use in public worship.

Luther's appreciation of historic continuity and of classic and accepted forms of expression led him to retain as much of the historic order and content of the services as possible, together with music, vestments, lights, and the usual ceremonies not contrary to the spirit of the gospel. This spirit of the gospel was made active and powerful in and through the old forms, which were purified and simplified. The ancient balance of the Word and Sacrament was thus restored.

Believing with all his soul in the "given-ness" of the gospel, Luther attached an almost sacramental authority to the uttered word which proclaimed God's will and mercy. At the same time veneration for the Sacrament as the seal of forgiveness and a means of grace in which "Christ and his saints come unto thee," kept him in accord with the historic church in concluding the chief service of every Lord's Day and festival with the Lord's Supper. The custom which became general in Lutheran churches two centuries later of reducing the Sunday morning service to a preaching service and only infrequently celebrating Holy Communion, as in the Zwinglian and Calvinistic churches, must not be laid at Luther's door. He would be stirred to indignation by the infrequent observance of the Sacrament in many Lutheran churches today.

All this was more than mere conservatism. It was keen value-judgment. Luther fearlessly cut out errors and impurities and with equal earnestness sought to preserve the good. In addition, he distinguished sharply between essentials and nonessentials, permitting great liberty with respect to the latter. This point is important. The principle of discrimination pervades the entire Lutheran system of doctrine and life, often in sharp contrast with the greater traditionalism of Romanism and Anglicanism on the one side and the scriptural literalness and indiscriminating subjectivism of extreme Protestant groups on the other.

Luther's constructive efforts also definitely promoted vernacular services and active congregational participation in worship. He gave the sermon great importance, restored the chalice to all communicants, and greatly increased frequency of communion. New forces which he released enriched the services of the church with hymns, chorales, and choir music of high devotional and artistic importance. A new era in Christian worship was inaugurated, an era which as it expanded enriched all European lands and all Protestant communions for a century or more and which still, after long periods of decline and neglect, gives inspiration to students and leaders in this field.

Luther's emphasis shifted sharply from appreciation of the action of the whole church to a concept of individual experience in the reception of the Sacrament. His most radical action, and the most questionable, was his omission from the heart of the communion service of all prayers of commemoration and thanksgiving and the limiting of liturgical material at this point to the Lord's Prayer and the Words of Institution. No other Christian liturgy had ever done this. In later years none but Lutherans—and not all of them—followed Luther in this drastic procedure.

The influence of Luther's liturgical work was far greater than he anticipated and greater than many historians realize. His exegetical and doctrinal studies—preaching, teaching, writing, his books and discussions—formed his mightiest contribution to the inner spiritual development of Protestantism. In their immediate influence, however, they were limited to the learned classes. Luther brought the meaning and power of the Reformation home to the common man by his translation of the Bible, his catechisms, his hymns, and his reconstruction of the liturgy. His principles of worship became all-powerful and his suggested forms guided other students and Reformers on their way. His orders were mere outlines. He did not, like Cranmer, provide a complete book with full appointments for the liturgical year. He enunciated principles and indicated approved material within the traditional use of the church. His outlines had to be filled in from the old liturgical books.

Nevertheless, Luther's two liturgical pamphlets established the foundation upon which Lutheran services throughout Germany, Austria, Denmark, Sweden, the Baltic lands, the Slovak districts, etc., were constructed. On the basis of extensive study, the entire liturgical system of the church was purified and simplified. Not only was the historic liturgy retained with its chief outlines and most of its propers, but a new spirit was breathed into the ancient forms and new and important features were developed. The Lutheran program also strongly influenced later liturgical reforms in England.[21]

The keen interest recently displayed by European theologians in worship, and particularly in Luther's theology of worship, is well exhibited in the Hungarian Vilmos Vajta's *Die Theologie des Gottesdienstes bei Luther* (Stockholm: 1952). This work, originally written in German and published in Sweden, has recently become available in an English translation and condensation by Ulrich S. Leupold under the title *Luther on Worship* (Philadelphia: Muhlenberg, 1958). In its English dress the book suffers because of its omissions of important material in the original German work.

Vajta's chief constructive contribution is his development of a suggestion first offered, but not elaborated, by Professor Georg Rietschel of Leipzig. According to this, Luther regarded worship as primarily a work of God, and only secondarily a work of man. As a divine institution it provides an occasion for the presentation of the Word and the administration of the sacraments, and for the acceptance of these gifts by the faith of the assembled believers. This conception permits Vajta to harmonize Luther's frequently divergent expressions concerning worship, and to reconcile the "pedagogical" and the "re-presentative" principles which scholars have often considered mutually exclusive.

Liturgics cannot be fitted narrowly into a Procrustean bed of theology. Theology is but one of many formative factors in the development of worship and the liturgy. The liturgical communions particularly submit their

---

[21] Dr. Edward T. Horn, with characteristic crispness, thus described Luther's work: Luther "was a practical liturgist—as was Cranmer in his own age, and Cosin in a later. He put his hand to the very central sanctuary of the Roman Mass, and cut the Canon out of it; he put the Gospels into the vernacular; he passed every prayer in review; he criticized the feast-days; and he put an end to the awkward transference of Epiphany Sundays to the end of the Christian year, supplying an appropriate finial to the whole year." ("The Significance of Liturgical Reform," *Memoirs of the Lutheran Liturgical Association*, I, 36).

worship form to the final arbitrament of doctrine, but they also fill them with free and full expressions of faith and devotion. Our praise and our petitions soar in poetic flights high above the levels of dogmatic definition. We recite the Creed, but our Te Deum is a song. Luther was a theologian. He was also a poet, a musician, a lover of beauty, a master of language, a scholar who respected the common man and the traditions and limitations of the uneducated. His passion for freedom was as strong as his passion for truth. All of these things reveal themselves at one place or another in his liturgical pronouncements. In the heat of controversy he frequently ignored consistency. It is impossible to prove that every single item in his liturgical practice and pronouncements was consistently fashioned and theologically inspired.

Luther's orders were private, unofficial works which established principles rather than elaborated forms. The actual reform of the church in organization, life, and worship was carried out under the authority of the rulers of the different states and free cities by means of official "church orders" (*Kirchenordnungen*). These will be discussed in the following chapter.

OTHER PROTESTANT REFORMS

The liturgical reforms of Zwingli and Calvin cannot be discussed at length. In a word it may be said that they were radical, particularly those of Zwingli. While agreeing with the Lutheran program in certain respects, such as the restoration of congregational worship, the use of the vernacular, the rejection of propitiatory sacrificial ideas and priestly domination, etc., they were in sharp disagreement in other respects.

The corruptions and abuses of the time led the Reformed leaders to break with the historic church and all historic development and to attempt a revival of certain aspects of primitive Christianity. They ran counter, however, to primitive practice in subordinating eucharistic worship to a new type of service which consisted chiefly of preaching, exhortation, psalm-singing, and prayer. Discarding the objective character of worship together with its historic expressions, they made of it a subjective exercise which stressed fellowship, prayer, exhortation, and instruction, and which centered chiefly in preaching and other personal activities (prayers, etc.) by the minister.

Zwingli, essentially a humanist, published his *De Canone Missae Epicheiresis* ("Attack upon the Canon of the Mass") in 1523. This retained quite a few features of the liturgy in Latin with lessons and sermon in the vernacular. Four original prayers were substituted for the Canon. His *Action, oder, Bruch des Nachtmals* (Use of the Lord's Supper) of 1523 is more radical. This became the real pattern for his

followers. The Service became a preaching service with Scripture readings and lengthy prayers. The regular Sunday morning service seems
modeled upon the Divine Office of the monastery rather than upon the
Eucharistic Service. The Lord's Supper was restricted to four times a
year and was thought of as a mere memorial feast. The altar became a
table, and the elements were received sitting. All music was forbidden.

Calvin's reforms were less revolutionary but still radical in a broad
sense. Expelled from Geneva in 1530, Calvin took charge of the French
Reformed congregation in Strasbourg. Here he found a revision of a
rather full German Mass of 1524 in use. He adopted this in modified
form for his congregation. Upon his return to Geneva he established
there in 1542 a form of service built upon a combination of the Strasbourg Rite with the forms used by Farel in Geneva. This order was
called *La forme de prieres et chantz ecclesiastiques avec la maniere
d'administrer les sacramens* (the Form of Church Prayers with the
Manner of Administering the Sacraments). It was richer in content
than the Zwinglian Rite, being based upon the Eucharistic Service rather
than the Choir Office. Its debt to the German Service of Strasbourg is
great. As Calvin could not read German, a friend had to help him
translate this and prepare his final French form.

The demand for extreme simplicity by the Genevan magistrates led
Calvin to abbreviate the Strasbourg Order considerably. He personally
did not seek to dethrone the Eucharist from its historic place as the culmination of the Lord's Day worship. To the end of his life he desired a
weekly communion. The civil magistracy overruled him, however, and
imposed a quarterly communion upon the city of Geneva. This eventually
became the practice of most Calvinistic churches in Scotland, France,
south Germany, and Holland. The English congregation in Geneva,
under the leadership of John Knox, administered communion monthly.
This practice was enjoined in the later Scottish liturgies, though the
custom of quarterly communion finally became general in Scotland.

The usual Sunday morning service according to the Calvinistic orders
thus became practically a preaching service with opening Scripture sentences, a confession, metrical psalms, collect, lesson, sermon, and intercessions. The variable parts of the Service were reduced to a minimum.
Music was restricted to the singing of metrical Psalms. In the quarterly
communion service the Sacrament was received standing, the people
coming forward to the holy table. After the administration the Nunc
Dimittis was sung. [22]

[22] For further account of Zwingli's services, the Strasbourg Rite, and Calvin's
reforms, see particularly William D. Maxwell, *An Outline of Christian Worship*,
pp. 81-119.

In summation it may be said that the practices and general spirit promoted by Zwingli, and to a lesser degree by Calvin and Knox, eventually destroyed the historic liturgical system of the church for their followers. Not only the liturgy itself, with its texts, ceremonies, and vestments, but the church year, church music, and the accepted appointments of church architecture were abrogated and displaced by substitute forms. In Switzerland, Scotland, and England extreme opposition to all historic worship manifested itself. Beautiful buildings were demolished, choirs disrupted, organs wrecked, music destroyed, stained glass smashed, and vestments and ornaments profaned.

CHURCH MUSIC

Luther was a son of the church and a man of culture. His appreciation of historic expressions and his recognition of the fact that the liturgical and musical system of the church was deeply engraved upon popular imagination kept him well within the limits of selection, translation, and adaptation. His own original compositions were limited to a small but important number of collects and hymns. His command of language and idiomatic expression was remarkable. In all that he did, however, conviction rather than taste was the ruling principle. He attempted few substitutes for the historic forms his age inherited. He sought above all things to purify the liturgy of doctrinal error; to simplify and strengthen its structure; to breathe into it a new spirit; and to make worship congregational and choral rather than priestly in character.

For his Latin Service Luther expected the traditional music to be used. For his German Service he himself spent weeks, with the aid of the musicians Johann Walther and Conrad Rupff, in arranging musical settings for the German text.

The church orders frequently gave a mere outline of the services. Complete texts with music, particularly for the parts to be sung by the choir and congregation, were provided in so-called cantionales prepared by Spangenberg (1545), Lucas Lossius (1553), Eler (1588), Keuchenthal (1572), Ludecus (1589), and others.

These are notable works of great compass and worth which combine features of the medieval Gradual, Psalter, and Antiphonary. They supply the text as well as the music of the propers for the church year (Introits, Collects, Epistles, Graduals, Gospels, antiphons, responsories, etc.) approved by the Reformers but only indicated in a general way in most of the church orders. These Lutheran choir books with their ample liturgical and musical provisions contrast sharply with the single comparable work of the period produced by the Church of England, the small and musically emasculated *Bookè of Common Praier Noted* of 140 pages by John Merbecke (1550). This provided only the simplest plain chant setting for the responses of the liturgy, as Archbishop Cranmer's instructions had forbidden the musician to set more than a single note of music to a syllable of text. This arbitrary and inartistic procedure robbed even the few ancient melodies which were included of all character and beauty. The work made no pretense whatever of providing choral elements such as Introits, Graduals, antiphons, or responsories, as these had vanished completely from the *Book of Common Prayer* itself.

Spangenberg's book (*Cantiones Ecclesiasticae*), a magnificent folio volume of 750 pages with Latin and German texts, was directly inspired by Luther, who urged its preparation. Melanchthon wrote the preface to the *Psalmodia* of Lossius which was an octavo volume of more than 800 pages and which ran through many editions. All of these works incorporated melodies of the old rite, where pure Latin texts were to be found, and adapted hundreds of the ancient Introits, Graduals, antiphons, responsories, and canticles to the new vernacular. Taken together, and with the musical features incorporated in the church orders, they testify impressively to the German love of music and the endeavor of Lutheran churchmen to promote it. They also make it evident that the Lutheran Church in Germany in the sixteenth century regarded itself as the legitimate heir to the liturgical and musical culture of the medieval centuries and the conserver of all that was good and pure and beautiful in the great tradition of faith, worship, and life of Western Christendom.

In addition to his interest in hymnody, both Latin and German, and his knowledge of the ancient plain song and the music of the liturgy, Luther was familiar with the vast literature of complicated, artistically interesting music found in motets and other polyphonic compositions. He thoroughly enjoyed music of this character and encouraged its composition and the perpetuation of choir schools and trained choirs. He appealed to men of means and to the civil authorities to support such schools and institutions. He urged the Elector John not to permit choral groups to perish, for "Kings, princes, and lords must support music."[23]

Luther regarded music as one of the greatest gifts of God. It was an essential part of his own personal piety and of his churchly program. In this respect he stands in sharp contrast to other Reformers.

Zwingli was an admirable musician, far surpassing Luther in his attainments. He not only sang, but played the lute, harp, viol, flute, clarinet, and

[23] W. M. L. de Wette, *Dr. Martin Luthers Briefe*, III, 102.

horn. Yet he prohibited instrumental and vocal music in the church. Calvin inaugurated a movement of great importance when he introduced psalm-singing among his followers. But because his literalistic views of Scripture permitted nothing but metrical versions of the Psalms in worship, church music received from him a very limited development. Cranmer endowed the Church of England with a superb liturgy. He did nothing, however, to encourage church music, though fortunately after the first shock of the Reformation this was kept alive in cathedrals and chapels by local churchmen and musicians and eventually regained much of its vigor.

Luther, on the contrary, regarded music as having inspiring, creative power and desired to see it, with all the arts, "in the service of him who has given and created them."[24]

Thus, while the Reformation dealt with the fundamental and central things first—doctrine and life—the broad movement soon released forces which reformed and developed many fields. Luther's pioneering, creative work opened a new era in Christian hymnody. In a sense which often involved loss as well as gain, the Lutheran hymnbook came to be the people's prayer book. The collection of vernacular hymns, breathing robust faith and gratitude combined with humility, was given a recognized place in the principal service of the congregation, and formed one of the greatest contributions of Lutheranism to the common stock of worship in all communions.

Luther not only taught the German nation to sing in church but led the way in a significant development of German culture and expression. His work eventually made possible congregational participation and worship in every land and established hymn-singing by the people as a characteristic and important feature of Protestantism. His efforts and encouragement led to such general cultivation of church music in the first two centuries after the Reformation that musical leadership was transferred from Italy to Germany. Heinrich Schütz was the pioneer in a development which finally culminated in the mighty works of Johann Sebastian Bach. Hundreds of chorale melodies were produced by Crüger, Hassler, Nicolai, Franck, Teschner, Albert, Neumark, and many others. Their strength, dignity, and beauty made them ideal forms for unisonous congregational singing. They also served, together with older plain-song melodies, as thematic material for choral motets, cantatas, and organ compositions. The German chorale thus gained an importance historically and musically never realized by the Calvinistic psalm tunes or later English hymn tunes. Oswald Spengler finds Roman Catholicism's greatest contribution to art in the field of painting and

[24] Preface to Walther's hymnbook (*Geystliche Gesangk Buchleyn* [1524]) (PE 6, 284). On this subject see also the author's "Luther and Congregational Song" in the *Papers of the Hymn Society of America* (New York; 1947).

Protestantism's in the field of choral music. "We may say that the Catholic faith is to the Protestant as an altar piece is to an oratorio."[25] Walther, Eccard, Schroeter, Calvisius, and Ahle in the sixteenth century; Praetorius and Keiser in the seventeenth century, and Bach, Telemann, Graun, and Hiller in the eighteenth were among the many composers who enriched this field of artistic choral composition.[26]

[25] *The Decline of the West,* trans. C. F. Atkinson. (New York: Knopf, 1926-28), I, 187.

[26] For full discussion of these liturgical and musical features, see particularly Ludwig Schoeberlein, *Schatz des liturgischen Chor- und Gemeindegesangs* . . . (Göttingen: Vandenhoeck, 1865-72); Rochus Liliencron, *Liturgisch-musikalische Geschichte der evangelischen Gottesdienste von 1523 bis 1700* (Schleswig: Bergas, 1893); Hans Preuss, *Martin Luther, der Künstler; The Choral Service Book* and *The Psalter and Canticles,* ed. by Harry G. Archer and Luther D. Reed; and an interesting work by a Roman Catholic scholar, Theobald Schrems, *Die Geschichte des Gregorianischen Gesanges in den protestantischen Gottesdiensten* (Freiburg: St. Paulusdruckerei, 1930).

CHAPTER IV

THE LUTHERAN CHURCH ORDERS

In England and Sweden the entire nation accepted the Reformation. The majority of the bishops and clergy co-operated with the crown in reorganizing the church and in enforcing the use of the new service books. In Germany the problem was more complicated. There were many independent states and cities. Some accepted the Reformation while others did not, and the bishops for the most part remained with the old organization.

Luther himself was opposed to centralization of authority and rigid uniformity, but something had to be done to meet the disorganization of church life and the school system. There was no oversight or control. Priests and monks, cut loose from the old organization, had no definite relation to each other, to the church as a whole, or to the state. After the Diet of Spires in 1526, by which time it was evident that the bishops would not institute reforms, a territorial form of church government was constituted. In accordance with this the Protestant princes and the civil authorities in the Protestant free cities determined to reorganize the church in their territories and put into effect the principles and spirit of the Reformation.

PREPARATION

Luther exhorted the Elector of Saxony to institute a formal visitation of the churches in his domain. For this visitation the territory was divided into four parts. Among the visitors sent out was Melanchthon, who spent a month in Thuringia interviewing priests. He later prepared the Visitation Articles which Luther and Bugenhagen approved and which were issued in 1528. Luther prepared a preface to these instructions. As a result churches and schools were reorganized, competent priests installed, supervisors appointed, and Luther's catechisms introduced. Similar surveys were conducted in other territories.

Commissions of eminent theologians, with the occasional addition of jurists and educators, were now appointed by the rulers. These commissioners prepared church orders which usually included lengthy statements of doctrine, regulations concerning church administration, organization of the schools, care of the poor, preservation of church property, and detailed directions for worship. Discussion of this last subject was usually confined to a section called the "agenda" which was often issued separately.

It is noteworthy that the most eminent Reformers were as greatly concerned about the reform of worship as they were about the restatement of doctrine and the correction of other abuses. The men who wrote the confessions helped prepare the church orders. The closest associates of Luther were actively engaged in this work—Melanchthon, Bugenhagen, Jonas, Brenz, Osiander, Spalatin, Cruciger, Myconius, Bucer, Aurifaber, and many others. Bugenhagen reorganized the church in Brunswick, Hamburg, Lübeck, and Pomerania, prepared the liturgy for the Church of Denmark, and had a large part in the preparation of the Wittenberg order of 1533.

Between 1523 and 1555 no fewer than 135 church orders appeared. Though differing greatly in minor details, they were pervaded by an inner unity of purpose and plan. This was due to the far-reaching influence of Luther and also to the fact that the most important of the orders were prepared by theologians who had a common understanding as to general principles of procedure. Since most of the Reformers helped to prepare several orders each (Bugenhagen seven, Brenz five, Jonas four, etc.), it is possible to group the orders in families and trace the influence which the most impotrant ones exerted upon others.

CLASSIFICATION

Certain orders, such as Brandenburg-Nuremberg (1533), lay particular emphasis upon doctrine and the details of the services, especially the Holy Communion. Bugenhagen's orders make detailed provision for the church schools and community chests and pay particular attention to Matins and Vespers. The generally accepted classification of all the orders, however, recognizes three groups or types: the central Saxo-Lutheran, the ultra-conservative, and the mediating or radical. The first group, by far the largest and most important, represents chiefly the orders of central and northern Germany. It includes Luther's two orders and the orders of Bugenhagen (Brunswick [1528]; Hamburg [1529]; Lübeck [1531]; Pomerania [1535]; Denmark [1537]; Schleswig-Holstein [1542]; and Hildesheim [1544]). In this group are also the following: Wittenberg (1533) (partly by Jonas, but introducing Bugenhagen's influence anew in the Saxon group); Duke Henry of Saxony (1539) (by Jonas); Mecklenburg (1540 and 1552) (by Aurifaber, Riebling, and Melanchthon); Hannover (1536) (by Urbanus Rhegius); Brandenburg-Nuremberg (1533) (by Brenz and Osiander); and the important Swedish Mass of 1531 (by Olavus Petri). These orders may be thought of as those "of greatest weight."

The ultra-conservative group, limited to three or four orders, retained as many as possible of the pre-Reformation forms and ceremonies. Representative of this group were Brandenburg (1540); Pfalz-Neuburg (1543); Austria (1571) (prepared by Chyträus); and possibly Riga (1530).

The third group, called radical or mediating, included orders in south and west Germany where Zwinglian and Calvinistic influences were strong. The most important of these were Brenz's orders of Württemberg (1553 and 1559). Others were Bucer's orders for Strasbourg; the orders for Baden (1556); Worms (1560); Rhein-Pfalz (1557), etc. The Württemberg orders are characterized by liturgical poverty. Brenz's order for Schwäbisch-Hall (1526), though in this same territory, is of a more positive and fuller type.

The orders of Hesse (1532), Cassel (1539), Marburg (1574), and Nassau (1576), show Reformed influence but possess strong individuality. Another unique and important order is Archbishop Hermann's Reformation of Cologne (1543), prepared chiefly by Bucer and Melanchthon. This strongly influenced later liturgical developments in England. Gasquet and Bishop[1] regard the first Prayer Book (1549) as a Lutheran liturgy.

The orders are related to one another through political and ecclesiastical connections; through the influence of active personalities (often difficult to determine because of the large number of collaborators); or through the use of identical liturgical material. This latter relationship reveals itself in the precise order of parts of the service or the use of identical addresses, exhortations, collects, prayers, versicles, etc. A. L. Richter[2] mentions the most important liturgical connections, and Horn has indicated them more graphically by a diagram in his "Lutheran Sources of the Common Service,"[3] which is repeated in Jacobs and Haas, *The Lutheran Cyclopedia* (New York: Scribner, 1899), p. 4.

With this as a basis and adding items from similar diagrams in Fendt[4] and from Althaus' discussion of collect borrowings we attempt a grouping of selected orders according to liturgical relationships. The importance and influence of certain orders are at once apparent. Particularly significant are

[1] *Edward VI and the Book of Common Prayer* (3d. ed.), pp. 224ff.
[2] *Die evangelischen Kirchenordnungen des sechszehnten Jahrhunderts* (Weimar: Land-industrie comptoir, 1846), II, 509ff.
[3] *The Lutheran Quarterly* (1891), pp. 239-68.
[4] *Der lutherische Gottesdienst des 16. Jahrhunderts*, pp. 360ff.

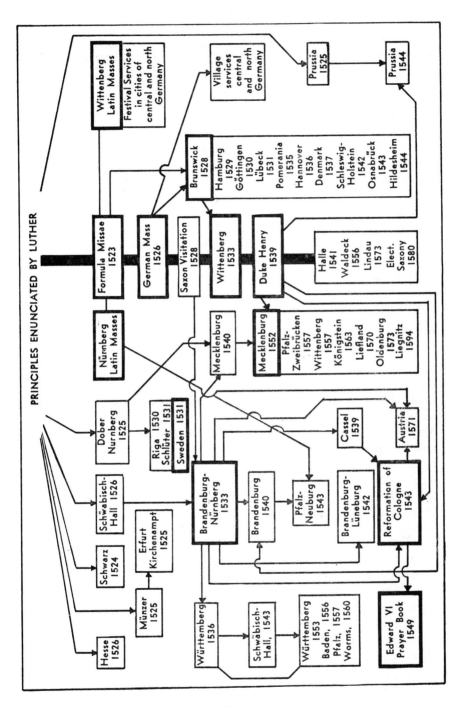

PRINCIPLES ENUNCIATED BY LUTHER

Wittenberg Latin Masses

Festival Services in cities of central and north Germany

Village services central and north Germany

Prussia 1525

Prussia 1544

Formula Missae 1523

German Mass 1526

Saxon Visitation 1528

Wittenberg 1533

Duke Henry 1539

Brunswick 1528

Hamburg 1529
Göttingen 1530
Lübeck 1531
Pomerania 1535
Hannover 1536
Denmark 1537
Schleswig-Holstein 1542
Osnabrück 1543
Hildesheim 1544

Halle 1541
Waldeck 1556
Lindau 1573
Elect. Saxony 1580

Nürnberg Latin Masses

Mecklenburg 1540

Mecklenburg 1552

Pfalz-Zweibrücken 1557
Wittenberg 1557
Königstein 1563
Liefland 1570
Oldenburg 1573
Liegnitz 1594

Dober Nurnberg 1525

Riga 1530
Schlüter 1531
Sweden 1531

Cassel 1539

Austria 1571

Schwäbisch-Hall 1526

Schwarz 1524

Erfurt Kirchenampt 1525

Münzer 1525

Hesse 1526

Brandenburg-Nürnberg 1533

Brandenburg 1540

Pfalz-Neuburg 1543

Brandenburg-Lüneburg 1542

Reformation of Cologne 1543

Württemberg 1536

Schwäbisch-Hall, 1543

Württemberg 1553
Baden, 1556
Pfalz, 1557
Worms, 1560

Edward VI Prayer Book 1549

Luther's *Formula Missae* and his German Mass, the orders of Bugenhagen, Duke Henry (1539), Brandenburg-Nuremberg (1533), Mecklenberg (1552), and the Reformation of Cologne (1543).

TYPICAL ORDERS

Luther's orders have already been discussed (pp. 72ff). The Swedish liturgies will be considered in a separate chapter (pp. 111ff). A brief description of several typical church orders may help the reader to understand the preparation, contents, and influence of the orders themselves and also the general character of Lutheran worship in different parts of Germany in the Reformation period.

It must be remembered that the directions for worship in the orders were outlines which left the texts largely to be supplied by the ministers and choirmasters from the ancient office books. The following summary is based upon a study of the original orders themselves, of the critical comments by Richter, Sehling, and Brightman, and of the reconstructions by Fendt of texts and other details briefly indicated in the order themselves.

Brunswick, 1528.[5]

This is the first of a series of church orders prepared by Johan Bugenhagen, Luther's pastor and colleague in the University of Wittenberg, for cities and territories in north Germany and for the Kingdom of Denmark. These were alike in providing practically complete vernacular services with the Latin portions restricted to the texts sung by the choir. They all reveal the strong influence of Luther's German Mass of 1526, and thus provide a simpler type of service than was known in Wittenberg, Nuremberg, and many other German cities where services were regularly held in Latin as well as German.

The Brunswick Order was authorized by the city council and the church authorities in September, 1528. Bugenhagen, himself a Pomeranian or *Plattdeutscher,* prepared the order in Low German. A High German translation appeared in Nuremberg in 1531 and a revised edition in 1563. The latter contained an appendix which included the Augsburg Confession, the Apology, and the Schmalkald Articles. Because of its early date and the prominence of its author, the Brunswick Order exerted considerable influence.

The High German edition is an octavo volume of 370 pages, devoted to the discussion of church order itself, baptism, the school system (Latin and German schools), the duties of superintendents (bishops),

[5] Sehling, *Die evangelischer Kirchenordnungen des XVI. Jahrhunderts,* VI, Part I, 348ff; Richter, *op. cit.,* I, 106ff; Fendt, *op. cit.,* pp. 210ff.

pastors, and organists, marriage, care of the sick, the Mass in German, the common chest for the care of the poor, etc.

Bugenhagen contrasts the Evangelical Mass with the Roman Mass and claims that the essentials of the traditional service must be retained and that novelties should not be introduced needlessly. He objects to the great variety of masses for saints' days and other occasions and urges the use of the one Sunday mass in the German language, so that the people may truly "hear Mass." The traditional vestments are approved, though not commanded by Christ, as not contrary to his command. The order reveals vigorous reformatory spirit but checks disorder and individualism with the assertion that the new provisions for worship are an *order* and must be accepted and observed as faithfully as was the old.

As an illustration of the brevity of the actual directions for the services in many orders as well as of the peculiar form of German which prevailed in a large part of northern Germany before Luther's translation of the Bible established a modern literary (High) German, we give in its entirety the *Ordeninge der misse* of the Brunswick order:

Int erste singet me eynen düdeschen psalm. Darna Kyrie eleyson unde dat Gloria in excelsis, welk me ock to tiden mach nalaten. Darup leset de prester eyne dudesche collecta unde dat volk antwerdet: Amen. Denne keret sick de prester tome volke unde lest de epistele also: So scrifft Sunte Pauel to den Romeren imme teynden capitele: Leven brodere etc. edder anders, wo sick dat wol schickende wert. Darup singen de kynde eyn Haleluja sine caudis cum versu. Darna eynen düdeschen sank uth der scrift. Wor neyne schölere synt, dar darf me des Haleluja nicht. Up de dre hoge feste wert me na deme Haleluja singen latinische sequentien unde düdesch dartusschen, alse nagescreven schal werden.

Denne keret sick de prester wedder umme tome volke unde lest dat evangelion also: So scrifft Sunte Joannes amme sosten capitele: De Here Jesus gink, sprack etc. Item: Id is geschehn etc. Darup singet de prester na deme altare gewendet: Ick love an eynen Got, so singet dat volk vortan dat ganze symbolum nicenum uth unde darto: Wy gelöven al an eynan Got etc. Id were wol gut, dat de prester vor der predige stunde, dar me de collecta, epistele unde evangelion over de ganze kerk wol hören konde, doch late wy dat geschehn, wo me dat maken wil. Overs de communicatio mit alleme togehöre na der predige schal geschehn imme chore.

Darna geschut de wönlike predige des evangelii. Wen de uthe is, so vorkundiget me nötlike saken. Darna vormanet me up deme predickstole, to beden vor de overicheit etc., alse Paulus bevelet 1. Timo. 2, welke vormaninge edder exhortatio schal nagescreven werden. Wen de predicante affstiget, so singet me eynen düdeschen psalm edder led, dewile gan de communicanten int chor, de frauen unde de junkfrauen an de luchter side besundergen, unde de mans unde knechte an de rechter side besundergen, unde de prester bereydet bröt und wyn, wes darto nöt is. Na deme lede keret he sick umme unde deyt eyne exhortatio vamme sacramente, welke nagescreven schal werden.

Darnä keret he sick tome altare unde in den groten festen, de sunderge prefatien hebben, unde sus, wen he wil, up etlike Sundage mit der prefatie trinitatis (de wedder de Arrhianer alse ock dat symbolum nicenum gemaket is), schal he anheven latinisch de prefatie Dominus vobiscum unde singen se bet an dat ende, darup singe dat chör eyn latinisch Sanctus. Sus mach wol totiden sulke prefatie unde Sanctus nabliven, wente de exhortatie vamme sacramente is de rechte prefatie, dat is eyne vohrrede. Wor neyne scholere synt, dar mach sulke prefatie unde Sanctus wol stedes nabliven, me wolde denne sus se gerne singen.

Darna edder (wen me de prefatie unde Sanctus singet) balde na der exhortatie schal dat bevehl Christi vamme sacramente unde danksegginge bet in dat ende der missen stedes also gehölden werden. Dar höret nicht vele wunders in, wy möten dar up syn bevehl sehn.

De prester hefft also an slicht to singen dat bet, van Christo bevalen:

Vader unse, de du bust im hemmele, gehilget werde dyn name, tokame dyn rike, dyn wille gescheh alse im hemmele ock up der erden, unse dagelike brot giff uns hüden, unde vorgif uns unse schulde, alse wy vorgeven unsen schuldigern, und vohr uns nicht in vorsökinge, sonder erlose uns van dem bösen.

Dat volk antwordet:

Amen.

Balde nympt he dat bröt in de hand unde bringet up den bevehl Christi also:

Unse Here Jesus Christus in der nacht, dön he vorraden wärt, nam dat bröt, dankede und brackt und gaf synen jungeren und sprack: Nemet hen und etet, dit is myn lyff, dat vor ju gegeven wert. Solk doht to myner gedechtnisse.

Balde gan hento de communicanten, de mans und knechte vohr, de frauen unde junkfrauen na, unde nemen den licham des Heren, unde eyn jewelick geyt wedder up syne stede. Dewile singet dat volk: Jesus Christus, unse heyland etc. edder: Got sy gelavet unde gebenedyet etc., wen overs de communicanten synt togegangen, so schal de sank uphören unde de prester neme den kelk unde drege den bevehl Christi vortan vohr also:

Desgeliken nam he ock den kelk na deme aventmale, dankede, gaff en und sprak: Drinket alle daruth. Disse kelk is eyn nye testament in myneme blude, dat vor ju uthgegaten wert to vorgevinge der sunden. Sulk doht, so vaken gy drinken, to myner gedechtnisse.

Balde entfangen de communicanten den kelk des Heren unde gän wedder up öre steden, sitten up den knehn edder stän bet to der letsten segeninge, dewile singet me, wat overich is vamme lede edder me hevet mehr an, wen vele communicanten synt. Wen se overs alle communiceret hebben unde synt up ören steden, so singen se unde alle volk to Christo imme hemmele dat düdesche Agnus Dei dremäl also:

Christe, du lam Gades, de du drechst de sünd der werlt, erberm dick unser.

Tom drudden male:
Giff uns dynen frede. Amen.
Lat uns beden.
Darto danket de prester vor alle also:
Wy danken dy, almechtige Here Got, dat du uns dorch disse heylsame gave hest erquicket, unde bidden dyne bermherticheit, dat du uns sulks gedyen latest to sterkeme loven jegen dy unde to berniger leve mank uns allen.

Dorch unsen Heren Jesum Christum. Amen.
Denne keret he sick umme unde gifft den communicanten unde deme volke vorlöff mit disser segeninge, bescreven Numeri 6:
De Here segene dy unde behöde dy. De Here erluchte syn angesichte över dy unde sy dy gnedich. De Here heve syn angesichte up dy und geve dy frede. Amen.

(Sehling, *op. cit.*, VI, H.I, 440-42.)

The following somewhat fuller reconstruction of the service in English follows Fendt's text rather closely and shows what the clergy and choirmasters of the time were expected to do in filling out these outlines on the basis of their intimate knowledge of the liturgical and musical material in the old books, the missal, breviary, antiphonary, etc., of the medieval church:

In place of the Introit, the choir sings Psalm 34 or another psalm, which is followed by the Kyrie. The minister intones *Gloria in excelsis Deo* and the choir chants the *et in terra* (this was often omitted). The minister: Let us pray, followed by the Collect for the Day, facing the altar.

The minister faces the people and reads the Epistle; the choir boys (*kinder*) sing the Gradual (*Ein Hallelujah sine caudis, aber cum versu*) as, for example, on Whitsunday: *Emitte Spiritum tuum,* etc. Provision is also made for the singing on the great festivals (Christmas, Easter, Whitsunday) of the traditional sequences, the choir singing the first strophe in Latin and the congregation responding with a German translation, and thus to the end.

The minister meanwhile faces the altar. Turning to the people he reads the Gospel. Facing the altar again, he intones: *"Ich glaube an einen Gott";* the congregation responds: *"Wir glauben all an einen Gott,"* and continues to the end of the Nicene Creed.

The minister's sermon on the Gospel is followed by announcements and an exhortation to prayer for the state (*die Obrigkeit*) with the use of a fixed formulary. Then follows a German hymn or Psalm; the communicants enter the choir (chancel), the men and boys on the right and the women and girls on the left. The minister prepares the bread and the wine, faces the people and gives them an exhortation according to a fixed form.

Then follows the historic Preface in Latin, with Proper Prefaces for festivals and the Trinity Preface for ordinary Sundays. The choir sings the *Sanctus* in Latin and the minister chants the Lord's Prayer in German with the Amen sung by the congregation. Taking the bread in his hands, the minister uses the Words of Institution and communicates the people. Meanwhile the congregation sings a German hymn. The minister then consecrates the wine and gives the cup to the communicants while the congregation sings the remaining stanzas of the hymn. The communicants who return to their seats kneel or remain standing until the final Blessing. All sing the *Agnus Dei* in German and the minister offers Luther's Thanksgiving Collect and gives the Old Testament benediction.

If no communicants present themselves, the minister nevertheless wears the customary vestments and the service concludes with the Preface, Sanctus, Lord's Prayer, and Benediction. The only changes are the omission of the Words of Institution and the administration, and the substitution of a collect of the Sunday for the Post-Communion Collect.

Bugenhagen's orders for Hamburg and Lübeck differ from the Brunswick Order only in minor details.

Brandenburg-Nuremberg, 1533.[6]

Following the example of Electoral Saxony, a visitation of the churches in the territory of Margrave George the Pious of Brandenburg and in the prosperous and art-loving city of Nuremberg was conducted as early as 1528. The margrave had succeeded to his title in 1527. He was an intelligent and zealous supporter of the Reformation, and his influence extended to Bohemia and throughout the territories which later constituted the Kingdom of Prussia.

The first of a series of articles adopted at a preliminary conference at Schwabach had declared: "The church has been born of the Word of God; and God's Word must not be judged according to the church, but the church must be judged by the Word of God." This sounded the keynote of the church order which finally appeared in 1533 and which laid special emphasis upon pure doctrine, in the first place, and then upon correct rite and ceremonial as illustrating the pure doctrine.

Andreas Osiander, pastor of St. Sebaldus' Church in Nuremberg and Johann Brenz, pastor in Schwäbisch-Hall, were the principal authors. Osiander himself records how he sketched the first material. This was enlarged and improved by other theologians of the district and was then sent to Wittenberg for the criticism of the theologians there. Following this, Brenz spent six weeks in Osiander's home, unifying the literary form of the book.

The order appeared in many different editions and probably was more influential in Lutheran circles than any other document of the period, excepting the Saxon Visitation Articles. Its collection of twenty-six collects was incorporated and expanded in many other orders, and its whole content and spirit strongly influenced Brandenburg (1540), Brandenburg-Lüneburg (1542), Mecklenburg (1540 and 1552), Cassel

---

[6] Richter, *op. cit.*, I, 176ff; Fendt, *op. cit.*, pp. 216ff; Brightman, *The English Rite*, I, xxxviiiff.

(1539), Cologne (1543), Austria (1571), and other important orders. (Cf. diagram, p. 91.) Archbishop Cranmer, political emissary of King Henry VIII in negotiations with the German princes, lived more than a year in Osiander's home. He was familiar with the details of this Lutheran order which materially influenced the Reformation of Cologne (1543), an order which Cranmer himself used extensively in his preparation of the first *Book of Common Prayer* (1549).

The Brandenburg-Nuremberg Order took high ground in regarding liturgical worship with its accompanying details of music and ceremonial as all important, not because of human considerations of piety or art, but because of our Lord's promise to be present with believers whenever they gathered themselves together. Its framers, to use a modern phrase, had a keen "awareness of the presence of God in worship." Everything in word and ceremony must be worthy of his presence, and character- ized not only by formal correctness but by exceptional dignity, reverence, and sincerity.

The doctrinal sections of the order express Lutheran convictions un- equivocally in lengthy discussions of church order, Christian doctrine, the Old and the New Testaments, the law and the gospel, suffering, prayer, Baptism, and the Lord's Supper. The liturgical provisions show high appreciation of traditional but purified forms and ceremonies and of the musical inheritance of the historic church. Perhaps chiefly be- cause of the music, Latin services were retained in Nuremberg for many years side by side with services in German. The traditional vestments were retained until the beginning of the nineteenth century.

The Order of the Mass is partly in Latin and partly in German. It shows the influence of both the *Formula Missae* and the *Deutsche Messe* of Luther. Both the Latin and the German masses may be intoned by the minister. When there are no communicants (on weekdays) a special office is to be used. This consists of two or three Psalms (instead of the last Psalm, espe- cially on Sundays, the *Quicunque vult* may be sung), the Epistle, a hymn, the Gospel, the Te Deum or a hymn, three collects, the Benedicamus and the final Blessing.

The Latin service, with propers for Ascension Day by way of example, is as follows:

The minister recites the Confiteor, or whatever his devotion suggests, at the altar. He then quietly reads the Introit for the day (*Viri Galilaei,* etc.) while the same is sung by a choir of boys and men.

The minister reads the Kyrie and the following Gloria in Excelsis, while these are sung by the choir. Then follows the usual Salutation and Oremus (either in Latin or in German) and a German collect or collects; the Epistle in German (*lectio continua* and not the historic pericopes); the Gradual sung in Latin by the choir; and the Gospel (*lectio continua*).

Following the Creed, sung in Latin, comes the Sermon and then an exhortation to communicants, spoken in German from the altar. This is followed by the Words of Institution in German; the Sanctus and the Lord's Prayer in Latin, the latter introduced by the traditional *Praeceptis salutaribus moniti et divina institutione formati audemus dicere.* The Pax then leads into the distribution. The latter is accompanied by the words: "Nyme hyn und iss, das ist der leib Christi, der für dich geben ist; nyme hin und trinck, das ist das blut des newen testaments das für dein sünde vergossen ist." The officiant administers the bread and the deacon the cup. Meanwhile the choir sings the Agnus Dei in Latin. If there are many communicants, the choir may also sing a Latin responsory, or some other appropriate text.

Following the administration, there is a thanksgiving collect in German, somewhat fuller than Luther's collect, which indeed may be used instead. The Benedicamus and the Old Testament benediction conclude the service. Alternate forms of benediction are indicated, among them, "Der segen gott des vaters und des sons and des heyligen gaystes sey mit euch unnd bleybe allzeyt mit uns allen. Amen."

The German Service begins with a German hymn, or the Introit in German, sung while the minister says the Confiteor or some other devotion. The minister reads the Kyrie and the Gloria in Latin while the congregation sings the same in German. Then follow the Salutation, a German collect, a chapter from an Epistle as above; the minister reads the Gradual in Latin, if the choir boys do not sing it; a chapter from the Gospels or the Acts; the minister says the Credo in Latin while the congregation says it in German; the Exhortation; the Words of Institution; the Sanctus; the Lord's Prayer; the Pax; the distribution as above, during which the congregation sings a German hymn; the Post-Communion Collect and Benediction as above.[7]

Mark Brandenburg, 1540.[8]

Joachim I, elector of Brandenburg, was personally hostile to the Reformation, but did not oppose it vigorously. When he died in 1535, his domains were divided between his two sons. Johann, the younger, introduced the Reformation in his territories in 1538. Joachim, the elder son, known as Joachim II, succeeded to the dignity of elector. He appreciated the popular strength of the Reformation and the fact that it was welcomed by the nobles and the towns within his realm. He also did not disdain the material advantages which might accrue to him and to his state by a secularization of the bishoprics and monasteries.

---

[7] On the Nuremberg services, see also Max Herold, *Alt Nürnberg in seinen Gottesdiensten,* and an article by Edward T. Horn, "The Reformation in Nürnberg," in *The Lutheran Church Review,* X, 123-45.

[8] Sehling, *op. cit.,* III, 39ff; Richter, *op. cit.,* II, 122ff; Fendt, *op. cit.,* pp. 273ff; Brightman, *op. cit.,* I, xli.

His personal inclinations sought the retention of the fullest form and ceremonial in the worship of the church. Personal as well as princely pride led him to strive for an ecclesiastical organization that would be independent of the papacy and at the same time not too subservient to Wittenberg. At one time he said, "Just as little as I am willing to be bound by the Roman church, just so little am I willing to be bound by the Wittenberg church. I do not say, 'I believe in the Holy Roman or the Wittenberg but the Catholic Church, and my church here in Berlin and Cologne (a. Spree) is just as true a Christian church as the church of Wittenberg.' "[9] In all these matters we may note a certain resemblance to his more famous contemporary, King Henry VIII of England.

Luther shrewdly estimated this "problem child of the Reformation" and said that he was "a man who contends for the pure gospel but who has many extravagances." When Buchholzer, the elector's chaplain, informed Luther of his prince's concern for the retention of the alb and chasuble, with processions, etc., Luther wrote (December 4, 1539):

> As to the matter that worries you . . . this is my advice: If your lord, the margrave and elector, will allow the gospel of Jesus Christ to be preached openly, clearly, and without admixture—and the two sacraments of baptism and the flesh and blood of Jesus Christ to be administered and given according to his institution, and will let the invocation of the saints fall away, so that they are not patrons, mediators, and intercessors, and the sacrament be not carried about in procession, and will let the daily masses and the vigils and the requiems for the dead fall, and not have the water, salt, and herbs consecrated, and will sing pure responsories and songs in both Latin and German during the march or procession; then in God's Name, go along in the procession, and carry a silver or golden cross, and a chasuble or an alb of velvet, silk, or linen. And if one chasuble or alb is not enough for your lord the elector, put on three of them, as Aaron the high priest put on three, one over the other . . . and if his Electoral Grace is not satisfied with one circuit or procession, in which you go about and ring and sing, go around with him seven times, as Joshua and the children of Israel went around Jericho shouting and blowing with trumpets. . . . For such matters, if free from abuses, take from or give to the gospel nothing: only they must not be thought necessary to salvation, and the conscience dare not be bound to them. . . . And if the pope would let these matters be free, and [the gospel] be preached, and commanded me to hang my breeches about my neck, I'd do his pleasure.[10]

Joachim appointed a commission which included Stratner, Buchholzer, and Matthias von Jagow, bishop of Brandenburg, who favored the Reformation. A letter of Luther's also mentions Georg Witzel, a friend of Melanchthon. This commission prepared a very conservative church

[9] Fendt, *op. cit.*, p. 274.
[10] Enders, *Martin Luthers Briefwechsel*, XII, 316f.

order, the draft of which had been approved by Luther, Melanchthon, and Jonas, and which the nobles and the towns accepted March 1, 1540. The preface was by the Elector Joachim himself. The doctrinal sections are largely taken from the Brandenburg-Nuremberg Order of 1533 and the Saxon Order of Duke Henry (1539). The agenda contains an unusually rich provision with respect to ceremonial and external usages. The order concludes with a formal approval by Bishop von Jagow "until further Christian agreement can be secured."

This order, in spite of its positively Lutheran dogmatic section, is frequently called "catholicizing," a criticism which is undoubtedly extreme. The order contends that just as man is not spirit only but body, so in worship we need not only the Word but external forms and ceremonies, which latter are justified on the ground of necessity, dignity, the honoring of the sacraments, and as an aid in bringing the Word to the common people. It professes to keep all the old ceremonies that do not actually conflict with the gospel. It places an unusually high value upon confession. It appoints the Holy Communion for every day in the cities and once a week in the towns and villages.

The Order of the Mass is as follows:
The minister and his assistants go to the altar in customary vestments and the traditional lights are used. The Confiteor is recited; the choir sings the proper Introit and the Kyrie, followed by the Gloria in Excelsis. After the Salutation and the Oremus, there follow the Collect for the Day (in Latin) and the Epistle in German. The Epistle concludes with the statement, "This is the Epistle which you, my beloved, have heard sung in Latin." Then follow the German hymn by the people and a Latin Gradual, *"mit Sequenz oder Traktus,"* sung by the choir. Following another Salutation, the minister reads the Gospel in German with a reference to its having been chanted in Latin. Then follows the Nicene Creed sung by the choir in Latin or in village churches by the congregation in a German versification (*Wir glauben all an Einen Gott*).

The choir sings the customary Offertorium but all reference to the Offertory as such is omitted. Then follow the Preface and the Sanctus in Latin. While the Sanctus is being sung, the minister quietly offers four German prayers, for the emperor and civil rulers, for the clergy, for unity, and for forgiveness of sins, this last the collect from the Brandenburg-Nuremberg Order. Then follows the Consecration in German with the use of a form similar to that of the Brandenburg-Nuremberg Order, but with inclination and elevation. This is followed by a Latin respond by the choir or a German hymn. The Lord's Prayer and the Pax are intoned by the minister. While the minister prays the choir sings the Agnus Dei in Latin. Following these communion prayers the Exhortation to communicants from the Brandenburg-Nuremberg Order is given. The choir sings a Latin verse and the communicants approach the altar. The minister gives the bread, the deacon the cup, according to the form found in most orders. Following the administration the congregation sings a German hymn and the Thanksgiving Collect, in German, followed by several prayers from the Missal said quietly by the minister in Latin.

When there are no communicants, as on weekdays, the Order of the Mass is to be used up to the sermon, after which the German Litany was recited or a metrical version of the Lord's Prayer followed by collects and the Blessing. The Litany was appointed in towns on Wednesdays or Fridays and in villages on every other Sunday.

A sick person, unable to be present at the Mass, may be communicated in church at another hour if notice has been previously given; or if he be quite ill, the minister, wearing a surplice and preceded by the sacristan with lantern and bell, shall take the sacrament to him directly from the altar at the conclusion of the congregational service and communicate him at home, after receiving his confession.

The burial of the dead included a procession to the grave with cross and lights, while Luther's paraphrase of the *Media vita* and his *De profundis* are sung. The office in church includes Luther's *Nunc dimittis,* one or more lessons, with responds or German hymns between them; the Benedictus with its antiphon, a collect, a Latin respond, the Epistle (I Thess. 4:13-18), and the Gospel (John 11:21-28).

Saxony (Duke Henry) 1539.[11]

In Albertine Saxony Duke George opposed the Lutheran Reformation. In Ernestine Saxony the Elector John vigorously supported it. Duke George died in 1539. His brother Henry succeeded him and, notwithstanding the opposition of the bishops, he immediately instituted a visitation. The articles for this were prepared by the faculty at Wittenberg. Justus Jonas, professor of canon law in the university, and George Spalatin, friend of Luther and intimate counselor of three Saxon electors, were among the commissioners.

The church order which was introduced by ducal authorization at the time of the visitation was most likely prepared chiefly by Jonas. The order appeared September 19, 1539, in provisional form (*zum Anfang*). The next year (1540), an enlarged edition appeared under the title: *Agenda das ist kirchenordnung fur die diener der kirchen in herzog Heinrich zu Sachsen fürstenthum gestellet.* Sehling's text includes the material in both editions. The order was printed by Hans Lufft in Wittenberg. The approval and co-operation of the Wittenberg faculty gave it immediate recognition and influence far beyond Saxon boundaries.

The preface calls the Evangelical service "the true, apostolic, Christian service," and exalts the ministry as the custodians of spiritual and heavenly treasures and as the leaders of the people's devotions before God. The order begins with Luther's revised order of baptism (1526),

---

[11] Sehling, *op. cit.,* I, 264ff; Richter, *op. cit.,* I, 307ff; Fendt, *op. cit.,* pp. 270ff; Brightman, *op. cit.,* I, xxxix ff).

to which three exhortations are added. It further includes a discussion of penance with a form of absolution; an order for the visitation and communion of the sick; an order of Divine Service; Luther's German Litany, which is prescribed in towns on Wednesdays or Fridays in Ember weeks and in villages on alternate Sundays; an order of marriage (Luther's form with slight changes), and an order of burial. A table of holy days, a collection of fifty-six collects, and extensive musical settings are given in the 1540 edition.

The Order of Divine Service begins with the singing of the Introit for the Day or Festival by the choir of boys and men. Then follows the Kyrie (nine-fold); the minister intones *Gloria in Excelsis* and the choir responds *Et in terra*, etc.; the minister intones a German or Latin collect; he then intones the Epistle and the Gospel in German, facing the people; the choir singing a sequence or a German psalm (omitted in 1540) between the lessons; the congregation sings *Wir glauben all an Einen Gott* or the choir sings the Latin *Credo* (1540). Then follows the sermon on the Gospel for the Day.

Following the sermon the minister (presumably at the altar) gives a para-phrase of the Lord's Prayer and an exhortation to communicants after which he intones the Words of Institution in German. The congregation sings *"Jesus Christus unser Heiland"* or *"Gott sei gelobet"* during the administration. Collects and the Benediction conclude the service. On feast days, however, the minister intones the Latin Prefaces, using the traditional plain-song melodies (fully given, 1540). These conclude with the Sanctus. The Lord's Prayer and the Words of Institution are in German. The Agnus Dei is sung in Latin or the hymn *"Jesus Christus unser Heiland"* or Psalm 111 is sung in German during the distribution. The service is concluded with collects and the Old Testament benediction.

In villages the Service is a simple one with hymns, collects, the Epistle and the Gospel, the Creed, sermon, paraphrase of the Lord's Prayer, and Exhorta-tion, Verba, Sanctus, collects, and Benediction—all in German.

In cities where there are Latin schools the order of Vespers is as follows: The boys chant one to three Psalms, using the antiphon of the Sunday or festival; a Latin responsory or hymn; a New Testament lesson intoned by one of the boys (a deacon, 1580); the Magnificat with an appropriate antiphon, collects and the Benedicamus. Confessions were heard after Saturday Vespers and catechetical instruction was given after Sunday Vespers.

At Sunday Matins the boys sang one to three Psalms with antiphon; these were followed by an Old Testament lesson; the Benedictus with an antiphon or the Te Deum sung in German by the congregation. The service concluded with collects.

Reformation of Cologne, 1543.[12]

Hermann von Wied, archbishop-elector of the important diocese of Cologne, numbering twenty-two deaneries and 875 parishes, at first sup-ported the papacy in its conflict with Lutheranism. He attended the Diet

---

[12] Richter, *op. cit.*, II, 30ff; Fendt, *op. cit.*, p. 293; Brightman, *op. cit.*, I, xlv ff.

of Augsburg and was sufficiently impressed to advocate concessions to the Lutherans. In the years immediately following his efforts to secure moderate reform in his diocese were supported by his clergy. When he determined to institute real reforms he met strong opposition.

In 1542, notwithstanding the protests of the chapter of Cologne and of the university, Hermann invited Martin Bucer of Strasbourg and Caspar Hedio of the same city to set up a program of reform and prepare a church order. Early the next year Hermann implored Melanchthon to aid in this undertaking. The latter was at first quite willing, writing to the archbishop that "our aid ought not to be denied good princes." Later he sought to withdraw from the project, stating that the university needed him, that he was taking important matters through the press, and that "you would be moved with pity if you could see the constancy of our labors. This is the tenth letter I am writing today, and it is the shortest of all."[13]

Luther encouraged Melanchthon to go to the aid of the archbishop and he journeyed to Bonn in the beginning of May, accompanied by Justus Jonas, junior. Bucer had completed the first draft of a large portion of the doctrinal and liturgical sections of the order. Melanchthon revised this work and with the aid of Hedio and Becker added several doctrinal articles, as did Bucer also. By the express wish of the archbishop, the order of Brandenburg-Nuremberg (1533) was used as the basis. The orders of Cassel (1539), Duke Henry (1539), and Schwäbisch-Hall (1543) were also used. Others, too, may have been consulted.

(Brightman suggests Brandenburg, [1540].)

Luther saw Bucer's hand in the treatment of the doctrine of the Lord's Supper, which he denounced without having read the entire order. Bucer's verbosity is also evident in the didactic and hortatory character of large portions of the liturgical sections of the book.[14] Bucer was attacked as a radical by the Cologne clergy and was defended by Melanchthon. The archbishop and a select group of his advisors participated in the final reading of the manuscript. The order was adopted by the lay estates in July and published sometime before October, 1543.

Hermann had reached his decision too late and the reforms he planned were not inaugurated. His ultraconservative chapter protested violently in a document under the title *Antididagma* put forth in 1544. The emperor, Charles V, whom Hermann had helped to elect, interposed and prevented the introduction of the order in the diocese. April 16, 1546,

[13] C. G. Bretschneider (ed.), *Corpus Reformatorum*, V, 56.
[14] Melanchthon called Bucer *copiosus* and Luther referred to his *Klappermaul* (M. Decker, *Hermann von Wied, Erzbischof und Kurfürst von Köln*, p. 109).

Hermann was excommunicated by Pope Paul III, and he died, deprived of his bishopric, in 1552. While never introduced in the diocese of Cologne, Hermann's Order was nevertheless used in Hesse, Nassau-Saarbrücken, and in parts of Alsace, and its material influence upon the First Prayer Book of King Edward VI (1549) is generally recognized.

The German edition of Hermann's *Einfaltigs bedencken,* printed in Bonn, is a handsome folio volume of 310 pages in black and red Gothic letter. This was followed by a Latin edition with modifications (*Simplex ac pia deliberatio*) in 1545, and by two English editions, further modified, in 1547 and 1548 ("A Simple and Religious Consultation," etc.).[15]

Hermann's order provides an office of preparation the day before communion. This includes a German psalm, a lesson, an exhortation (one form provided from the Cassel Order and another from the Brandenburg-Nuremberg Order); silent prayer, concluding with a collect.

The Order of the Holy Communion is as follows: The minister reads a confession before the altar "in the name of the whole church." In the German order this confession is preceded by the versicle, Psalm 32:6-7. The confession is followed by one of the Comfortable Words and the Absolution. The form of the confession, one of the earliest in any of the German church orders, is as follows:

Almechtiger ewiger Gott und Vatter, wir bekennen und veriehen, dass wir leider in sunden entpfangen, und geboren seind, und daher voll unwissens und unglaubens deines Göttlichen worts, und immer geneigt zu allem argen, und treg zu allem guten, ubertrette deine H[eiligen] gebot on underlass, Dardurch wir in ewigen todt falle, und uns selbst immer mer und mehr verderben. Das ist uns aber leidt, und begeren deiner gnaden unnd hilff. Erbarm dich über uns aller gutigster, barmhertzigster Gott unnd Vatter, durch deinem Son unseren Herren Jesum Christum, verleihe und mehre uns deine H. Geist der uns lehre unsere sunde, vn ungerechtigkeit recht gründlich erkennen, unnd bereuwen, auch dem gnad und verzeyhung unser sunden inn Christo unserem Herren deinem liebem Son, mit warem glauben ergreiffen, und annemen. Also, das wir den sunden immer mer absterben, und dir in einem neuwen leben, zu deinem preyss vn besserug deiner gemein dienen unnd wolgefallen mögen.[16]

The choir begins the service proper with the Introit in Latin; the Kyrie

---

[15] On the Cologne Reformation, see Konrad Varrentrapp, *Hermann von Wied und sein Reformations versuch in Köln* (Leipzig: Duncker and Humblot, 1878); Henry E. Jacobs, *The Lutheran Movement in England* (Philadelphia: Frederick, 1890); and his article, "Archbishop Hermann of Cologne and His 'Consultation.'" in the *Lutheran Church Review,* XI, 301-44; and John Dowden, *Workmanship of the Prayer Book* (London: Methuen, 1902) and *Further Studies in the Prayer Book* (London: Methuen, 1908).

[16] From the Bonn edition of 1544: *Von Gottes genade unser Hermans Ertzbischoffs zu Cöln . . . einfaltigs bedencken, warauff ein Christliche, inn dem wort Gottes gegrünte Reformation, an Lehr, brauch der Heiligen Sacramenten und Ceremonien, Seelsorge, und anderem Kirchen dienst . . . anzurichten seye,* fol. CLIII.

and Gloria in Latin (*Das Volk soll aber Kyrie und Gloria auch deutsch singen lernen*); a German collect (intoned or clearly spoken). The Collect is to be concluded "according to common usage." The Epistle and the Gospel are read facing the people with a Latin Gradual and sequence and a German hymn between. Then follows the Sermon and after that the General Prayer for all estates of men and the needs of the church, two forms being given from the Cassel Order. The congregation sings the Creed (*Wir glauben all an Einen Gott*) during which the offerings are received. After an admonition to those unprepared to communicate, the communicants approach the altar, the men on one side, the women on the other.

Then follow the Salutation with its response and the Preface with a lengthy form of the *Vere dignum* which concludes with the Sanctus and Benedictus sung alternately in Latin by the choir and in German by the people. The minister intones the Words of Institution followed by an Amen by the congregation and the Lord's Prayer with congregational Amen. After the Pax the Sacrament is administered first to the men and then to the women while the choir sings the Agnus Dei in Latin and then the German *"Gott sei gelobet"* and *"Jesus Christus unser Heiland."* The formula of distribution is "Take and eat to thy salvation the Body of the Lord which was given for thee," and "Take and drink to thy salvation the Blood of the Lord which was shed for thee." The service concludes with the Salutation with response and the Thanksgiving Collect (either that of the Brandenburg-Nuremberg Order or Luther's collect) and the Benediction, four different forms of which are provided.

In villages where there are no capable choirs, the Service is to be said or sung in German. There is to be no reservation or exposition of the Sacrament.

It should be noted that the extended form of the Preface in the Cologne Order indicates more than a Gallican tendency. It in all probability reveals familiarity with the ancient Greek liturgies.

Brightman, *The English Rite,* gives interesting details of the Cologne Order's provisions for baptism, confirmation, marriage, communion of the sick, and burial.

SIGNIFICANCE OF THE CHURCH ORDERS

Study of these typical orders will convince the reader that there was substantial agreement among them as to content and order of parts and similar agreement between the orders themselves and the age-old liturgical tradition of the church. The Lutheran Reformation was not a radical revolt; it was a conservative reform. There was no thought of withdrawing from the historic church or of establishing new forms of worship. In liturgical and musical fields all effort was concentrated upon simplifying and purifying existing forms, upon conserving that which was significant, pure, and beautiful, and upon developing latent powers and gifts in the composition of new prayers, hymns, and choral music to enrich the historic services of the church.

In the preparation of the orders great care was taken to secure pure texts. Only a limited number of rubrical directions was included. It was taken for granted that the ministers of the time knew the ceremonial and the other liturgical traditions of the church and that whatever historic usages were retained would be properly performed. The principle of freedom in nonessentials was carefully guarded. Rigid uniformity was not sought, while a decent regard for tradition was everywhere encouraged.

Luther characteristically expressed his general attitude and that of his followers in his tract of 1525, *Wider die himmlischen Propheten.* "We take the middle path . . . we are neither popish nor Karlstadtish, but free and Christian. We elevate the Sacrament or we do not, as, when, if, so long as it pleases us, as God has given us the liberty to do. Just as we are free to remain unmarried or married, to eat meat or not, to wear a chasuble or not, to be cowled or tonsured or not. Here we are masters, and allow no law, commandment, doctrine, or prohibition." He states that in the monastery at Wittenberg the Mass was held with the utmost simplicity, without chasuble or elevation, while in the parish church traditional usages were observed in alb, chasuble, etc. He further says, "The pope and Dr. Karlstadt are of one family in their teaching, for they both teach, the one to do, the other to omit. But we teach neither and do both."[17]

This broad program of discrimination and simplification eventually resulted in the dropping of many usages that were either unnecessary or of doubtful value. Because, however, of a free rather than a legalistic approach to the whole subject, a fuller ceremonial persisted in Germany than in England for quite some time. In conservative districts like Saxony, Nuremberg, and Mecklenburg, vestments, lights, colors, plain song, ministerial intonations, etc., survived the disintegrating influences of war and of individualistic conceptions of worship well into the eighteenth and even the beginning of the nineteenth century. By this time Rationalism had effectively destroyed liturgical life and feeling throughout Germany and Scandinavia as well as England.[18]

The church orders had an importance for their own time and beyond. Prepared by representative leaders of the church and issued by the civil authorities, they had the force of law. They checked discord, made

[17] *WA* 18, 112-13. (Cf. also 37-214.)

[18] See particularly Paul Graff, *Geschichte der Auflösung der alten gottesdienstlichen Formen in der evangelischen Kirche Deutschlands* (2nd ed.; Gottingen: Vandenhoeck, 1937-39), I (*Bis zum Eintritt der Aufklärung und des Rationalismus*). Also article by P. G. Bronisch: "A Lutheran Service from the Second Half of the Seventeenth Century," *Lutheran Church Review*, XVIII, 107-10 (trans. Edward T. Horn). Also Max Herold, *Alt-Nürnberg in seinen Gottesdiensten.*

possible the permanent organization and development of the church, and created a new educational system. Their principles and forms determined subsequent developments in the field of worship. Their liturgical provisions were fundamentally in such substantial agreement that a "consensus" of them made three and a half centuries later, with necessary adaptations to modern conditions, established the complete and typical form of the Lutheran liturgy in the Common Service of the church in America.

Thus the Lutherans, in Germany and Scandinavia particularly, found in worship a new and significant possession in which all might share and rejoice.[19] L. Fendt says: "Nowhere does the pulse [Blutwelle] of the Reformation beat so warmly as in its worship. Worship is the body in which Luther's spirit entered into the life of the people."[20] When we understand worship as including within its framework not only the liturgy but extensive readings from Scripture, effective preaching, and a great development of congregational song and artistic choral music, we know that this is not an overstatement.

No new rite had been prepared for the people. The old Roman Rite had been simplified and purified. The historic liturgy of the church had become evangelical and had been made once more the property of the common folk. It was not merely that the people had been given a voice and that they were now able to sing the service and newly composed hymns in their own language. There was a new content, a new spirit in worship. Worship had found its soul and that soul was the Word of God. God himself spoke; he was present in his Word. Worship comprehended the Word and the Sacrament. These gifts of God which strengthened faith and made men really Christian were centralized in worship. Worship therefore became the means by which divine grace and power were mediated. This idea gave it strong sacramental character. Its sacrificial elements—hymns, prayers—were in the nature of reverent and thankful response to these divine gifts of grace. All propitiatory sacrificial ideas were rejected. The matter of ceremonies, lights, vestments, forms, became a secondary consideration. There was no Puritan idea that spirituality could be attained only by austerity and plainness. All emphasis was laid upon the essential spirit and purpose—a purpose which could be expressed either simply or richly so far as form was concerned. Because of this there was no attempt to secure absolute uniformity.[21]

[19] For discussion of the Lutheran Liturgy in Sweden see Chapter V (pp. 111ff).
[20] Fendt, *op. cit.*, p. v.
[21] For fuller discussion of this, see Fendt, *op. cit.*, pp. 196, 245, etc., and, more extensively, Theodor Kliefoth, *Liturgische Abhandlungen*, VII.

For exhaustive study of the church orders reference must be made particularly to the works of Richter, Sehling, and Fendt. Ludwig Richter, *Die evangelischen Kirchenordnungen des sechszehnten Jahrhundert*s . . . , two volumes in one, was prepared as source material for his work on ecclesiastical law. His arrangement of material is purely chronological, but indexes show the relationship of orders (II, 509). Many important features of the orders are omitted or abbreviated. Emil Sehling, *Die evangelischen Kirchenordnungen des XVI. Jahrhunderts,* 6 vols. to date, is an exhaustive work complete so far as it goes, but it was interrupted by both world wars. The orders discussed are arranged territorially and are given entire with important introductions. Fendt, *Der lutherische Gottesdienst des 16. Jahrhunderts,* presents a comprehensive view of the theological and philosophical principles which underlay the appearance of the church orders. He stressed the point that the contents of the Lutheran orders are not to be judged primarily by fidelity to traditional forms or by freedom from them, but by their own significant worth as expressions of pure Christian faith and devotion. His discussion includes not only the Lutheran orders but similar work in this field by other Reformers to the end of the century. Significant orders are discussed in detail with valuable summaries of their preparation, content, and essential features. Paul Althaus, *Zur Einführung in die Quellengeschichte der kirchlichen Kollekten in den lutherischen Agenden des 16. Jahrhunderts,* establishes the relationship of many orders through the use of common collects.

In addition to the authorities just mentioned attention should be called to three articles by Paul Schmieder in the *Lutheran Church Review,* XXXII (1913), 361ff; XXXVII (1918), 195ff, 450ff; also to summary accounts by Edward T. Horn in *Outlines of Liturgics,* pp. 119-32; and in the articles on "Agenda, Consensus of" and "Liturgy" in *The Lutheran Cyclopedia* (Jacobs and Haas).

A CREATIVE CENTURY AND ITS SIGNIFICANCE

The sixteenth century practically brought to a close the long and unbroken development which worship, the liturgy, and the church year received at the hands of the Christian church. This development began in the early centuries during which the great outlines were fashioned. It continued throughout the medieval centuries by way of enrichment and overelaboration and all too frequently in the direction of doctrinal impurity. It continued, in the liturgical churches, throughout the Reformation century. Even the Roman church attained a higher degree of liturgical uniformity through the official missal and breviary authorized by the Council of Trent.

In the Lutheran and the Anglican churches this development included not only purification and simplification, but expansions of spirit and activity which once again secured congregational participation and also led to creative efforts in the matter of the sermon, congregational hymnody, and artistic choral music. These features, of great significance and worth, justify the inclusion of the sixteenth century in the cycle of creative liturgical development. Some of these constructive activities carried over into the following century or later. Generally speaking, however, as far as Lutheranism is concerned, the period of sustained liturgical development closed with the end of the sixteenth century. The next two centuries witnessed a great decline in church life and worship. The nineteenth century was marked by a slow but real recovery, and the present century, in this country, is witnessing a heightened appreciation of the Lutheran inheritance in the liturgical field and an earnest endeavor to develop the fabric of corporate worship constructively upon the historic foundations.

The Lutheran church in America is in close spiritual kinship with the historic Lutheran churches of Europe. There is, however, no organic connection. The church in America is increasingly conscious of the fact that it is in America and that it shares with all others this country's youthful energy, undeveloped resources, and freedom of opportunity. It thankfully and loyally accepts the leading positions which Luther as prophet and reformer proclaimed and which the church in Europe has, for the most part, maintained. It freely recognizes, however, the limitations which Luther and his associates could not overcome, and the mistakes which the judgment of history inevitably records with respect to every crisis.

Separated by wide distances from Europe and from the sixteenth century, we in America today recognize the conditions in Germany at the time of the Reformation which made it necessary for the Protestant rulers to step in and assume an authority which the church itself should never have relinquished. The territorial system of church government thus inaugurated brought with it inevitable control by the civil authorities in crises and a multiplicity of church orders and agenda. As a result, Lutheranism in Europe, while strongly represented in all parts of Germany, Sweden, Finland, Denmark, Norway, Hungary, Slovakia, Russia, and other countries, has not had continent-wide vision or grasp in organization, worship, and practical activities. Its inner unity has been real, particularly in the sphere of doctrinal formulation and theological scholarship. In these fields it has shown an impressive solidarity and has made its influence felt. In the sphere of worship and practical church life, however, it has been provincial.[22]

One indeed may conjecture what the Lutheran church in Europe might have been and what it might have accomplished if Luther had

[22] Some idea of the confusion in modern German church life may be gained from the article, "Church Services in German Lutheranism," by H. H. Kramm, in the *Church Quarterly Review* (London), July-September, 1942, pp. 192-219.

retained even a normal appreciation of the positive values in organization, authority, and uniformity; if he had done more than proclaim principles and prepare outlines of worship; if, like Archbishop Cranmer and his associates in England, he had provided a complete service book for use in German-speaking Protestant lands. His Bible translation, his catechisms, his Litany, and his hymns were used everywhere, and his outlines of worship were very influential. However, he gave the church no complete book of worship, and to the end of his life he remained opposed to uniformity and all centralization of authority.

The Lutheran church in this country today knows that it has lost a full century in potential development, and incalculable resources in human souls and material wealth, by the perpetuation in America of European provincialism with its lack of church consciousness and effective co-operation. It believes that proper organization and authority and reasonable uniformity in worship promote church consciousness and loyalty and Christian benevolence and endeavor. The elimination of linguistic and nationalistic barriers, the consolidation of synods and general bodies, the preparation and wide acceptance, first of the Common Service, and now of the Common Liturgy, and efforts toward practical co-operation in ever widening fields—all of these testify to the strength and sincerity of this conviction.

CHAPTER V

THE LITURGY IN SWEDEN

Liturgical reform in Sweden paralleled developments in Germany. The Swedish Reformation was part of a movement which involved the entire nation and resulted in the establishment of the modern Swedish state. Gustav Vasa headed a revolt against the Danish king in 1521 and two years later was proclaimed king of Sweden. Some of the bishops promptly allied themselves with the national movement. Death, exile, royal pressure played a part in completing the task. The leaders in the Reformation were able to preserve the historic episcopate, and the succession of the archbishops of Uppsala from 1164 to the present was unbroken.

Theological trends during the period of the Reformation were definitely Lutheran. Zwinglianism was practically unknown in Sweden and Calvinism exerted only a sporadic influence. These factors combined to produce liturgical reforms of a conservative Lutheran type. The text of the liturgy was freed from Romanizing taint. Evangelical preaching was promoted. The ancient churchly appointments—altars, altar-pieces, vestments, and usages—were generally retained along with the historic episcopate.

OLAVUS PETRI AND HIS LITURGICAL REFORMS

The great Swedish Reformer was Olavus Petri. He had been a student at Wittenberg from 1516 to 1518. Though he was only a deacon on his return to Sweden, his preaching attracted attention and he soon became the recognized spiritual leader of the reformation movement. Archdeacon Laurentius Andreae of Strengnas was an influential adviser of the king in ecclesiastical matters. Laurentius Petri, younger brother of Olavus, and also a student at Wittenberg for a time, was consecrated the first Lutheran archbishop of Uppsala in 1531. He held the liturgical development within conservative lines throughout his long administration of forty-two years.

Olavus Petri published his Swedish New Testament in 1526; a little hymnbook (lost); and a manual (*Een Handbock påå Swensko, Ther doopet och annat mera vthi ståår*). This work, which appeared in 1529, was the first Protestant handbook for the clergy in all Europe, with forms for baptism, marriage, visitation and communion of the sick, burial, etc. His *Swedish Mass* appeared in Stockholm in 1531, five years after Luther's German Mass. It was one of the most complete early ver-nacular liturgies in any Lutheran land. While it is in general of the type of Luther's *Formula Missae,* Conrad Bergendoff has revealed its indebt-edness to Döber's *Evangelische Messe.* This latter was a translation of a Latin Service used in the hospital chapel in Nuremberg as early as 1524, published in German in 1525, and included in a hymnbook issued by Slüter in Rostock in 1531. It undoubtedly influenced Petri in his preparation of the Swedish Mass of the same year.[1]

Petri's service, like Luther's, retained the traditional order of the medieval Mass, which, in Sweden as throughout Europe, represented a fusion of Gallican and Roman elements.[2] Most of the parts in the service are in Swedish. Since it seems intended to be said instead of sung and since there is no reference to a sermon, Brilioth suggests that it was designed not as a substitute for high mass, but for the low mass at which the people made their communion. For quite some time both Latin and Swedish services were used in Sweden, thus following the usual procedure in Germany.[3]

In his introduction, Petri criticizes the use of the Latin language and the Roman Canon, though in terms less vehement than those employed by Luther. He justifies a vernacular Mass by the history of the early church, by the fact that earlier attempts at using Swedish have succeeded, and by the variety of liturgical use in other parts of the universal church. The Service itself begins with a Call to Confession by the minister and a poignant Confession recited by the congregation, followed by a Prayer for Forgiveness and Grace by the minister. The congregational character of the service is indicated by the plural form: "Forgive *us* all *our* sins and give *us* grace." These features, all by Petri himself, con-stitute one of the first attempts in Lutheran services to provide a general confession in the vernacular by the congregation in place of the Latin Confiteor of the priest at the altar. Luther had made no such attempt.

[1] Bergendoff, *Olavus Petri and the Ecclesiastical Transformation in Sweden* (1521-1552), pp. 151ff.
[2] The principal extant medieval missals in Sweden are: Uppsala (1484), Streng-nas (1487), The Finnish diocese of Abo (1488), and Lund (1514). Cf. Gustaf Lindberg, *Die Schwedischen Missalien des Mittelalters* (Uppsala: Almquist, 1923), I, 27.
[3] Brilioth, *Eucharistic Faith and Practice,* p. 243.

The brief forms suggested in Strasbourg and Nuremberg were probably intended for the officiant rather than for the congregation and were none too satisfactory. It was years before an adequate vernacular congregational form developed and gained general acceptance in Germany. Petri's Confession (in the first person singular), is still found, with unimportant changes, in Swedish services today.

The Confession is followed by an Introit (which may be an entire psalm), the Kyrie, Gloria in Excelsis, Salutation, Collect, Epistle, Gradual, and Gospel. The Apostle's Creed is given in the text, with the historic form of the article on the church: "I believe in the Holy Catholic [almennligha, or universal] Church." Permission is given to use the Nicene Creed as an alternate. The celebrant is given freedom in selection of collects and lessons, and preference is expressed for a consecutive reading of lections from the Epistles and Gospels. A selection of seventeen collects, translated from the Missal, is supplied. One is fixed. The other sixteen were to be used "sometimes the one, sometimes the other, until more shall be set forth."[4] The Gradual may be a hymn on the Ten Commandments. There is no mention of a sermon, which, in Sweden as elsewhere, often preceded Mass.

A fuller series of propers (five Epistles and nine Gospels) appeared in the edition of 1535. The Liturgy of 1557 permitted the use of Latin introits and graduals, and supplied additional translations of collects for the church year from the medieval missals. The collects from the Third Sunday after Trinity are one Sunday ahead of the Roman Missal, an arrangement which agrees with the plan of the Common Liturgy of the Lutheran church in America.

THE SWEDISH MASS OF 1531

In the Petri Mass of 1531 everything relating to the Roman Offertory and Canon was excluded. The Sursum Corda was followed immediately by a lengthy and, in part, original Vere Dignum of strongly penitential character, probably based, as Brilioth suggests, on the Latin Paschal Preface. Petri also followed the unfortunate order of Luther's Formula Missae in placing the Sanctus after the Verba instead of at the end of the Preface, an order which—it has been argued—emphasizes the Lutheran doctrine that the presence of Christ is effected by the consecration and reception, linked together as an indivisible whole. The Words of Institution are accompanied by the Elevation. Following the Sanctus

---

[4] These collects are the ancient collect for Whitsunday, for the mass Pro Pace, Pro Statu Ecclesiae, and for Sundays after Trinity (1-6, 8-10, 13, 14, and 17) and one De Sanctis, adapted from the Roman collect for St. Felix, Confessor. Cf. Eric E. Yelverton, The Mass in Sweden (London: Harrison, 1920), pp. 35, 44ff.

are the Lord's Prayer, the Pax, and the Agnus Dei. The Lord's Prayer is said by all, which is still the Swedish use. Then, following the Nuremberg pattern, a lengthy Exhortation to communicants is introduced, "if the priest think it necessary and the time permit." Possibly, as Yelverton suggests, Petri had some misgivings as to the appropriateness of the Exhortation at this point.

A psalm or the Nunc Dimittis (as at Nuremberg) are indicated as a communion hymn. The Salutation and a fixed post-communion collect, the Benedicamus, and the Aaronic benediction followed by the New Testament invocation conclude the Service. The benediction is introduced by a phrase which has ever since that time remained in Swedish services: "Bow your *hearts* [not heads] to God and receive the Blessing."

The features which distinguished the first Swedish Mass from the majority of the church orders in Germany (location of the Sanctus, the Exhortation, etc.) were greatly prized by Swedish churchmen a generation or two ago. Recent Swedish liturgical scholars, however, do not defend them, but agree that the real significance of the Swedish Mass is not to be found in these peculiarities, but in the fact that it so early and so thoroughly grounded the Swedish reform of worship upon the same historical and theological principles which determined the preparation of the important orders in Germany, many of which appeared considerably later. The most recent liturgy of the Church of Sweden (1942) restores the Sanctus to its historic location immediately after the Preface.

The Swedish liturgy is the historic order of worship of the Western church purified and simplified and in the vernacular. Its further agreement with the general Lutheran program of liturgical reform is indicated by its omission of the entire Offertory and Canon, its rejection of everything pertaining to propitiatory sacrifice and its emphasis upon eucharistic sacrifice of prayer, praise, and thanksgiving; its insertion of homiletical features such as the Invitation to Confession and the Exhortation to communicants; and by its provision for congregational responses and hymnody.

The Swedish service, like Luther's German service, was not intended to displace the Latin high mass. It took the place of the Latin low mass at which the people received the sacrament at a side altar. For decades the Latin and the Swedish services continued side by side. Eventually the vernacular supplanted the Latin, though in the process it added some of the liturgical and ceremonial features of the latter. The revisions by Laurentius Petri resulted in what was practically a Swedish high mass.

The explanation of the difference in the collects in the different communions lies in the fact that Uppsala, Abo, Strengnas, etc., in Sweden, like Bamberg, Mainz, and other German dioceses, were remote from Rome. Their medieval missals frequently retained the earlier Latin order and texts after changes had been made in Rome itself. The medieval Swedish missals differed from the later Roman missals in the text of the Confiteor, mentioning only God the Father, the Blessed Virgin, and St. Dominic. Petri's Mass reverted to the older Gregorian order of collects even though another order had been introduced in the Uppsala Missal of 1513.[5] An extended study of the medieval missals of Sweden is given in Gustaf Lindberg, *Die schwedischen Missalien des Mittelalters,* Vol. I.

The following extracts from Olavus Petri's Service of 1531 may be of interest:

Confession

I, poor sinful man, who am both conceived and born in sin, and ever afterwards have led a sinful life all my days, heartily confess before thee, almighty and eternal god, my dear heavenly father, that I have not loved thee above all things nor my neighbour as myself: I have (alas!) sinned against thee and thy holy commandments in manifold ways both in thoughts, words and deeds, and know that for that cause I am worthy of hell and everlasting damnation, if thou shouldest judge me, as thy stern justice requires and my sins have deserved. But now hast thou promised, dear heavenly father, that thou wilt deal graciously and pitifully with all poor sinners who will turn themselves and with a steadfast faith fly to thine incomprehensible mercy; with them thou wilt overlook whatsover they have offended against thee, and nevermore impute to them their sins; in this I miserable sinner put my faith, and pray thee trustfully that thou wilt after thy same promise vouchsafe to be merciful and gracious to me and forgive me all my sins, to the praise and honour of thy holy name.

Absolution

The almightiest eternal god of his great incomprehensible mercy forgive us all our sins and give us grace that we may amend our sinful life and attain with him eternal life. Amen.

The Preface and the Canon

Verily it is meet right and blessed that we should in all places give thanks and praise to thee, holy lord, almighty father, everlasting god, for all thy benefits, and especially for that one that thou didst unto us, when we all by reason of sins were in so bad a case that nought but damnation and eternal death awaited us, and no creature in heaven or earth could help us, then thou didst send forth thine only-begotten son Jesus Christ, who was of the same divine nature as thyself, didst suffer him to become a man for our sake, didst lay our sins upon him, and didst suffer him to undergo death instead of our all dying eternally, and as he hath overcome death and risen again into life, and now dieth nevermore, so likewise shall all they who put their trust therein overcome sins and death and through him attain to everlasting life, and for our admonition that we should bear in mind and never forget such his benefit, in the night that he was betrayed celebrated a supper, in which he took the bread in his holy hands, gave thanks to his heavenly father, blessed it, brake it, and gave to his disciples,

[5] Dr. Bergendoff believes that Laurentius Petri in the main followed the order of the Strengnas collects and that variations in the Uppsala order may stem from an old English source.

and said: Take ye and eat, this is my body which is given for you, do this in remembrance of me.

Likewise also he took the cup in his holy hands, gave thanks to his heavenly father, blessed it and gave to his disciples and said: Take and drink ye all of this, this is the cup of the new testament in my blood, which for you and for many is shed for the remission of sins; as oft as ye do this, do this in remembrance of me.

Post-Communion Collect and Benediction

O lord almighty god, who hast suffered us to be partakers of thy sacrament, we beseech thee that thou wilt likewise suffer us to partake of thine eternal honour and glory together with thee and all thine elect saints, through our lord Jesus Christ, thy son, who liveth and reigneth with thee and the holy spirit in one godhead from everlasting to everlasting. Amen.

Bow your hearts to god and receive the blessing.

The lord bless us and keep us, make his countenance to shine upon us and be gracious unto us, the Lord turn his countenance toward us, and give us an eternal peace; In the name of father and son and the holy spirit. Amen.[6]

LAURENTIUS PETRI AND HIS CHURCH ORDER

Archbishop Laurentius Petri, the younger brother of Olavus, was head of the Swedish church for a full generation, 1541-73. Bishop Wordsworth refers to Laurentius as "the Cranmer of Sweden, as Olavus was its Luther."[7] The archbishop's conservative yet concilatory attitude is disclosed in his *Dialogue Concerning the Changes in the Mass,* which he wrote in 1542. Laurentius had a part in all the revisions, five in number, of the Mass of Olavus, which were carried through before Laurentius published his own church order in 1571. One of these revisions, that of 1541, was fairly important, and in this George Norman, the king's ordinary, was also influential. This revision permitted Latin at various places in the Service including the Preparation, and sung Introits, Graduals, and Apostles' Creed. The Epistle and Gospel "which belong to the Day" were also allowed. In addition, the order combined the Confession and the Kyrie. The revision of 1548 reintroduced the Nicene Creed, placed a Swedish hymn after the Agnus Dei, and introduced a Latin Communio and four additional thanksgiving collects. The revision of 1557 supplied collects for all the Sundays in the church year and so practically restored the ancient system which Olavus Petri had disregarded.

During the reign of Erik, Gustav's son, Calvinism became aggressive in Sweden. Seeking to buttress the Lutheran position, Laurentius Petri

---

[6] Yelverton, *op. cit.,* pp. 33, 39, 42.

[7] John Wordsworth, *National Church of Sweden* (London: Mowbray, 1911), p. 218.

in 1567 wrote a tract only recently published: *Concerning Church Ordinances and Ceremonies*. His great work, however, was his Church Order of 1571. This was the result of thirty years' study and experience and, according to Brilioth, was the summation of "the positive results of the whole Swedish Reformation."

An extended Preface introduced this church order. The Service itself was normally supposed to be sung and not said, indicating that by this time Swedish was replacing Latin, not only in the "low" communion masses, but also in the "high" sung masses. A hymn is permitted instead of the Introit (as in Luther's German Mass); Latin Graduals are permitted on festivals and the Tract during Lent "in towns where there are schools." The Collect *de tempore* or *de festo* and the Gospel for the Day are assumed; a Swedish confession and absolution is given after the Sermon instead of after the Introit "if desired"; a general intercession in which the Litany might be included is provided before the Preface. The "customary vestments" are ordered. "Elevation, mass vestments, altars, altar cloths, lights, and whatsoever of these ceremonies there are, such as have been adopted here in the kingdom since God's pure Word hath been preached, may we freely retain as optional matters, albeit such things in other countries have been set aside through the same freedom." In case there are no communicants, the officiant is instructed simply to use hymns, the Sermon, and the Litany. The work also contains an important section on church discipline and pastoral care.

In concluding his study of this church order of 1571, Yelverton says, "Laurentius Petri's work was a different kind from that of Olavus Petri. It extended for thirty years, and is marked by greater patience and deliberation." He restored the ancient system of pericopes; introduced the sermon in the Mass proper, and revived the Latin language in certain parts, particularly parts for which there was traditional music. "He attempted to combine the medieval tradition with the evangelical principles of Lutheranism" or, as Quensel says, "to pour the new wine of the Reformation into the old bottles of the Middle Ages."[8] Many years later his Church Order of 1571 was reverted to as the basis of a new manual.

The first stages of liturgical reform in Sweden reversed the order of the corresponding procedure in Germany. Luther began with his revision of the Latin service and followed this after three years with a simplified vernacular service. Olavus Petri inaugurated the Swedish reform with a simple vernacular service and Laurentius Petri followed this forty years

[8] *Bidrag till Svenska Liturgiens Historia* (Uppsala: Berling, 1890), II, 75.

later with a much more developed service which included certain Latin features and in other respects also quite closely resembled Luther's *Formula Missae* of 1523, as well as the Württemberg Order of 1553.[9]

THE RED BOOK OF KING JOHN III

An interesting episode in Swedish liturgical history was the revision of the services in the so-called "Red Book" of 1576. (The title refers to the binding of the earliest copies.) This was chiefly the work of King John III, an earnest student of patristics and of the liturgy. Petrus Fecht, a former pupil of Melanchthon and later the king's secretary, collaborated with him. Fecht's ideal was a return to primitive catholicism, and both he and the king desired to enhance the appeal and power of eucharistic worship, which they felt was being weakened everywhere by Calvinism.

The Liturgy of 1576 contained Latin and Swedish texts in parallel columns, with Latin rubrics and marginal notes, chiefly quotations from the fathers. The framework is that of the Petri Service of 1531, but the text is much altered in places to bring it into closer agreement with medieval forms and spirit. The opening Preparation, which includes the priest's private devotions, the vesting prayers (all the medieval vestments), and the Confession, is greatly expanded. The use of Latin Introits and Graduals is permitted. Two collects are given, the first being Petri's of 1531, and the second the one for the Twenty-second Sunday after Trinity. The ancient system of pericopes is restored. Both the Apostles' and the Nicene Creeds are given in full. The Offertory chant is restored, to be sung "sometimes" while the elements are brought to the altar. The Lavabo is also re-introduced. The Intercession is followed by the Preface. A version of the medieval Te Igitur follows. This leads into a prayer which contains a passage recalling the ancient prayers of consecration—"which Supper, we, according to his command and ordinance desire to celebrate, bless with his Word (the) bread and wine, the gifts, which are set before (thee) that they in a right use may become thy Son's (true) body and blood."

Eight Proper Prefaces are given. Strangely enough, the unfortunate dislocation of the Sanctus from its historic location is retained as in Petri's Mass of 1531. While the Sanctus is sung, the celebrant reads a prayer which is an ingenious reconstruction of the final paragraphs of the Roman Canon with the opening words of each section reproduced. There is no reference to propitiatory sacrifice or to the memorial of the departed. A

[9] Cf. Brilioth, *op. cit.*, p. 250. Also the recently published volume by Eric E. Yelverton, *An Archbishop of the Reformation* (London: Epworth, 1958), a valuable study of the liturgical projects of Laurentius Petri.

brief sentence from the Liturgy of St. John Chrysostom is incorporated in the text. In the administration, the priest's communion follows instead of preceding that of the people, a feature peculiar to Swedish rites in general. The Benediction is said facing the altar.

The Red Book met vigorous opposition and was rejected by the Swedish church at the Uppsala Möte of 1593. Yelverton regards it sympathetically as "an organised attempt to return to the better things of medievalism, which has no parallel in English liturgical history." He says of its rejection, "so there passed on to the bookshelf a liturgical masterpiece, whose beauty would henceforth be lost to all but a few antiquarians treading the by ways of liturgiology."[10]

Quensel regards its spirit and trend as definitely "un-Lutheran"— "whether it be the bowings, the consignations, the lavabo, or the silent repetition of the intercessions in the Canon of the Action, all these things must have alienated the sympathies of the people who were daily growing more and more attached to the grand, simple, manly, ardent spirit of Luther" (*Op. cit.*, I, 122).

Brilioth gives a careful analysis of King John's Liturgy and of the *Nova Ordinantia Ecclesiastica,* an extended document which prepared the way for it in 1575. He believes the latter "nowhere exceeds the limits of what is permissible according to Lutheran tradition, although its spirit is very different from that of the orthodox tradition of German theology." The king earnestly desired to lift the church out of confusion and disorder, but "at a time when there was no adequate clerical education, and no real university in the country, and the treasures and valuables of the church had to a large extent been pillaged and wasted, his refined and intellectual piety was like an exotic plant, lacking roots in the native soil." His good intentions were frustrated by the compulsory measures by which he sought to enforce the use of the Red Book, and by the latter's too-close correspondence with Roman forms, a defect which might have been avoided by a return to pre-Roman tradition and a use of primitive materials in the creation of an evangelical liturgy.[11] Dr. Bergendoff believes that "neither the Red Book nor Charles IX's revision [which followed it] had any great influence in Sweden, except as indices of the strength of the Church to resist them."

When the church assembly rejected the Liturgy of King John in 1593, it re-established the Church Order of 1571 and the Manual of 1529. Charles IX, King John's successor, however, was a Calvinist and eager to introduce his own ideas. Thinking to take advantage of the general

[10] Yelverton, *op. cit.* pp. 73-74.
[11] Brilioth, *op. cit.*, p. 254-59.

opposition to the medieval tone of the repudiated Red Book, King Charles, with the aid of his chaplain Micronius, proposed a revision of the liturgy—even less successful—in quite the opposite direction.

King Charles' suggested Communion Office of 1600 had several unusual features: the Verba were repeated five times—four times in succession in the introductory Exhortation and once again in the Preface. They were treated purely as the record of a historical event. The communion address included the Ten Commandments with a running commentary and again gave no hint of an objective presence of Christ in the Sacrament.

When the clergy declined to accept this office, Charles published a new proposal in 1602 which Yelverton characterizes as "a glaring example of liturgical impropriety," and which Brilioth more complacently regards as "an almost unique compromise between Lutheran and Reformed usage."

In this revised service the title "Mass" is abandoned in favor of "the Lord's Supper"; the word "altar" is retained, but the word "priest" gives way to "preacher." The Introit is placed before the Preparation and Confession. Olavus Petri's Exhortation is used, but "His worthy body and blood *in* bread and *in* wine" becomes "the sacrament of his worthy body and blood *with* bread and wine." The confession is followed by a lengthy prayer; the Collect for the Day is omitted. The single lesson contains the account of the Institution from I Corinthians 11. There is no liturgical Gospel, and no real recognition of the liturgical year. There are several changes in the Preface and the Canon. The Exhortation before Communion is omitted and in the words of administration the medieval and primitive reference to the "body" as well as the soul restored.

This office met with no approval and Charles withdrew his proposals. The net result of the matter seemed to be that the clergy were led by its emptiness and un-Lutheran character to new appreciations of the earlier liturgies and of the type of worship established by the Reformation, a type which royal proposals in opposite directions had threatened.

LATER DEVELOPMENTS

We have seen that worship in the sixteenth century was influenced in turn by strong personalities—Olavus Petri, Laurentius Petri, King John, and King Charles. Since the beginning of the seventeenth century, however, church committees and not individuals have been responsible for liturgical revision and development, both of which have been rather limited.

The revision of 1614 incorporated the Mass Book in the Manual and substituted the title "church service" for the word "Mass," though the term *Högmässa* (high mass) is still in general use. The entire Collect, Epistle, and Gospel system was restored. The medieval Prone, which attached vernacular devotions and instructions to the sermon, was revived. As early as 1530 Olavus Petri had given directions for prayers before and after a sermon in his *Postilla*. This preaching service evidently preceded mass—or followed—until in 1541 the sermon was incorporated in the Mass. As revised the Prone consisted of a hymn, the Lord's Prayer, a Confession and Absolution, a general Intercession, and a hymn. In the Apostles' Creed the word "universal" was changed to "Christian" in the article on the church, an alteration in line with German precedent which remained in force for two hundred years. Directions are given for the officiant in case there are no communicants.[12]

The Liturgy of 1811 provides a striking introduction which survives in greatly abbreviated form in modern Swedish services. The opening section of this so-called "Allocution" is a combination of the Sanctus and the Te Deum: "Holy, holy, holy, Lord God almighty! The heavens and the earth are full of thy glory! We praise thee: We worship thee," etc. This rhetorical form, so different in spirit from the traditional invocation, "In the name of the Father . . . ," is in keeping with other products of the rationalistic era, though we may recall the statement of Duchesne that Gallican masses in the sixth century frequently began with the use of the *Trisagion*.[13] The allocution is followed by a prayer of great dignity addressed to God, and introducing the Confession. The Liturgy of 1811 also placed the Exhortation before the Preface and omitted the Nicene Creed as an alternative to the Apostles' Creed. The liturgical Gospel was lost, the Gospel itself being read in the pulpit as a text. The double confession of 1614 was made mandatory. The Preface and the Sanctus were considerably altered. Altogether, this liturgy marked a low point in Swedish liturgical history, though Bishop Rodhe claims that it is superior to contemporary German services and in some respects an improvement over the 1614 Swedish service.

An unfortunate action in 1861 permitted the holding of communion services in the evening or at other times apart from the chief Sunday service with the omission of the first half of the traditional liturgy by

---

[12] Dr. Bergendoff remarks that "the history of the Swedish Mass is closely connected with the problem of communicants. Swedish congregations soon expressed dissatisfaction with the poverty of the service when there was no Communion. Gradually throughout the seventeenth century elements from the Mass were added to the Non-Communion Service, until the normal service became practically the full Mass without the canon. Even today in the Augustana Manual there is a Service and a Service with Communion, though originally the Mass was a Communion service."

[13] *Christian Worship*, p. 171.

passing immediately from the Confession to the Sursum Corda. This innovation marked a Reformed influence by way of Germany which robbed the Sacrament of its central place in the church's worship. Though only permissive and not normal, it is a defect which the Swedish church has not yet removed, and one which has become engrained in the practice of a number of Scandinavian churches in America today.

In the 1894 revision the Allocution was modified in the direction of an Introit, the Laudamus being dropped. The form for Confession also was shortened and the Gloria in Excelsis was appointed for high festivals.[14] A commendable feature was the restoration of the word "universal" *(allmännelig)* in the Apostles' Creed. There is a reference to the departed in the church notices. The Exhortation, which had had four different locations in previous services, is finally dropped.

The revision of 1917 restored the Nicene Creed, included Introit antiphons for the high festivals, slightly altered certain prayers, and added in an appendix the musical notation of the sung parts of the service. The new liturgy authorized by the king in 1942 and later approved by the Church Assembly retains the opening "Holy, holy, holy," as an Introit but appoints special Introits for the major festivals. Three alternative forms of Confession and a positive absolution are given. Proper Prefaces are introduced, and these conclude with the Sanctus. This agrees with the historic and universal order and marks the abandonment of a peculiar Swedish use which obtained since 1531 when Olavus Petri's Mass placed the Sanctus after the Verba instead of at the end of the Preface. A noteworthy feature is the inclusion of a brief Eucharistic Prayer with an *epiclesis.*

SIGNIFICANCE OF THE SWEDISH LITURGY

The Swedish Liturgy has been discussed at length because of its importance as one of the earliest Lutheran liturgies, and one with an unbroken use, and also because the facts of its history are little known to English readers.

Its doctrinal and formal affinities with the German Lutheran church orders are evident. Its mature development established it definitely as of the *Formula Missae* rather than of the *Deutsche Messe* type. From the beginning it provided adequate vernacular translations of the great liturgical texts (the Gloria in Excelsis, Creed, Sanctus, etc.) and only later, and then only in the case of the Gloria, fell into the unhappy *Deutsche Messe* expedient of substituting weak hymn versions for these

[14] In modern Swedish use, however, Decius' hymn, "All glory be to thee" still usurps the place of the Gloria in Excelsis, except in the Augustana Liturgy which properly gives the Gloria text in full.

texts. In other respects also its development has shown a certain freedom from that close adherence to Luther's experimental vernacular forms which has limited so many German liturgies.

The reactionary proposals of King John swung further to the right than did the equivalent German orders of Mark Brandenburg, Pfalz-Neuburg or Austria. The compromise service of King Charles betrays a stronger feeling for Calvinism than one is able to sense in the simpler forms of Württemberg or Baden. Eventually the liturgical compass settled definitely in the direction of positive Lutheranism, though some revisions, particularly the one of 1811, too strongly emphasized those penitential features which appear to be inherent in Lutheran worship.

While close spiritual relationship with the German Lutheran liturgies is evident, Swedish liturgical development in several respects found closer parallels in England than in Germany. The Swedish Reformation like the English was a national movement rather than a grouping of provincial and local efforts. There was one nation, one national church, and one national use for all the Swedish people, while in Germany there were many states (Saxony, Bavaria, Prussia, etc.) and many state churches (some Lutheran, some Roman, some Reformed) and many orders of worship. The Swedish Liturgy, like the *Book of Common Prayer,* was a separate publication, and not combined with cumbersome doctrinal and administrative materials in bulky church orders. In Sweden, as in England, most of the bishops supported the national movement, broke with Rome, and continued the episcopal system under the new order. This assured a stable ecclesiastical organization, and the retention of many of the ancient church usages—vestments, lights, a pure ceremonial, etc. The episcopate has consistently exerted its independence over against the royal state whenever its religious interests are concerned.

These facts enabled the Swedish Liturgy, again like the English *Book of Common Prayer,* to withstand the inroads of Pietism and Rationalism more successfully than did most of the German services. There was more to build upon in Sweden than in Germany when the liturgical movement of the nineteenth century under the leadership of Kliefoth, Loehe, Schoeberlein, and others swept across to Sweden and enlisted the energies of members of the Lund school, chief among them E. G. Bring, and others in that country. The introduction of a Eucharistic Prayer—brief though it is—in the Communion Office of the recent (1942) liturgy testifies to the initiative and scholarship of the leaders of the Swedish church today.

Similarity to the contemporary Oxford Movement in England breaks at one point—the importance attached to the eucharistic revival and the necessity of more frequent reception of the Sacrament. Strong emphasis upon this developed from the narrower Tractarian position, and carried the Anglican movement to great and sustained achievements in a revival of public worship and church life in general. In Sweden, a certain somberness and sense of holy fearfulness has always been associated with the Sacrament. Strong emphasis upon the necessity of penitence and confession, and upon guarding the Sacrament from those who would treat it lightly, have resulted in a low percentage of communicants. This gives the current liturgical movement in Sweden a more or less academic character, remote from popular understanding and experience.

Gustaf Aulén, retired bishop of Strengnas, regards this "liturgical renaissance" as "a period of renewal and transformation in respect to liturgy and church music, the like of which our church has not experienced since the time of the Reformation." He and the late Bishop Brilioth have been powerful leaders in a movement which emphasizes evangelical preaching and eucharistic worship. The Brotherhood of the Apostolic Confession, organized at Malmö in 1919, is an association devoted to the churchly revival and the deepening of the spiritual life. Another society with similar aims is Pro Ecclesia.

Important books and articles by Dr. Gunnar Rosendal, Lindberg, Bishop Eduard Rodhe, and others have awakened the church and aroused great interest, particularly among theological students and the younger clergy. The Sigtuna Foundation, a remarkable work established in 1915 by Manfred Björkquist, then a lay leader in the Young Church Movement and later bishop of Stockholm, has provided a center for conferences and discussions of these and other matters. Beginning at Uppsala University with the active co-operation of such outstanding leaders as Söderblom, Aulén, Billing, and Eklund, and with the later aid of students from Lund University, the foundation has developed in the town of Sigtuna, between Stockholm and Uppsala, a great institution which includes a folk high school, a humanistic gymnasium, a library, chapel, hospice, etc., and which over a period of years has inspired many workers "to bring the church to the people" and "to revive the immanent catholicity of the Swedish church."

Among other encouraging results of this national and churchly movement is a gratifying increase in the number of students preparing for the ministry, these having more than doubled at Uppsala and more than trebled at Lund during the past forty years.

A word should be said concerning the importance of the Swedish church and the Swedish Liturgy in the general development of the Lutheran church in America. The Swedish settlements along the Delaware were well established a generation before German immigrants began to arrive in Pennsylvania. Old Swedes' in Wilmington and Gloria

124

Dei in Philadelphia are two of the four church buildings along the Atlantic seaboard which were dedicated before 1700 and are still standing and in use. The First Lutheran clergyman ordained in America, Justus Falckner, a German, was ordained according to the Swedish Rite in Gloria Dei Church, Philadelphia, in 1703.

Swedish solidarity expressed in the single state and the one established Church of Sweden finds its counterpart in America with the Augustana Church, the single ecclesiastical organization which includes American Lutherans of Swedish descent and maintains but one theological seminary (at Rock Island, Illinois).

It is greatly to be regretted that the growth of the free-church movement in Sweden and the failure of the established church to hold many of its most spiritual and earnest members in the homeland should have led American Lutherans of Swedish descent to reject or ignore important features of their birthright. An important contribution which they could well make to American Lutheran liturgical development would be an heightened appreciation and use of institutions and practices preserved by the Church of Sweden and lightly esteemed by its descendants in this country—the historic episcopate, the use of historic vestments and pure ceremonial, and the feeling for ordered and beautiful liturgical worship.

With respect to the liturgy proper, the Common Liturgy provides English Lutherans in America, of all backgrounds and bodies, with a liturgy fuller and richer and in closer agreement with the type of service found in the cities of Germany and Sweden for half a century after the Reformation than is provided in any other Lutheran liturgy in Europe or America today. The essential content and order of almost the entire Swedish service is found in the Common Service of 1888. The features peculiar to the text of the Swedish Liturgy—with possibly three exceptions—would not have improved the Common Service if they could have been grafted upon it. On exception is the unique Swedish Benediction at the conclusion of the Service. This impressive combination of the Aaronic and the New Testament forms, adopted by Muhlenberg in his first American Lutheran Liturgy of 1748, has been taken over again in the Common Liturgy of our own time.

The Swedish Confession at the beginning of the Service, while unfortunately placed after instead of before the Introit, might claim consideration as the earliest (1531) important Lutheran form produced in the Reformation era, though it is not better than the Confession in the Common Service, which comes from a later German source (Mecklenburg, 1552).

The inclusion of a Eucharistic Prayer in the recent Liturgy of the Church of Sweden (1942)—though this particular form is perhaps inadequate—is a third feature which was favorably considered in the formation of the Common Liturgy, with the result that a better (though perhaps not perfect) prayer has brought the American Lutheran church into the forefront in the attempt to provide a distinctively Lutheran consecration which is at the same time free from the *opus operatum* appearance of the simple Verba.

American Lutherans of Swedish descent have well preserved their fine musical inheritance. This includes intonations for the minister in chanting the Service as well as melodic forms for the congregation. Such intonations are in common use in other European Lutheran lands and in many congregations in America where languages other than English are still used. Their adaptation to the English text of the Common Liturgy was a comparatively simple task. From an esthetic point of view important parts of the Service should be sung by all or said by all, not partly sung by some and partly said by others.

Dr. Gustaf Lizell, dean of Uppsala Cathedral, writing in Ekklesia,[15] emphasizes the essentially conservative spirit which has kept the Swedish church and its worship close to ancient tradition. Discussing the current liturgical movement in the Church of Sweden, he distinguishes four tendencies. The first is represented by a group which in general is satisfied with the present liturgy but desires stylistic changes, new forms for confession and baptism, development of Matins and Vespers, etc., all in line with proposals originally made by the late Archbishop Söderblom. A much smaller group, with little popular support, under the leadership of Professor Emmanuel Linderholm (Uppsala) and in general sympathy with the work of Professor Rudolf Otto of Marburg, has proposed new and experimental forms which include antitrinitarian formularies and many departures from historic uses. The third group, more liberal than the first and less radical than the second, would use the traditional liturgy and the proposals of 1926 as a starting point for new developments, especially richer *de tempore* provisions, alternate texts to satisfy different points of view, additional lessons within the framework of the historic church year, the reintroduction of ancient symbolism, etc. A fourth group, smaller in numbers and influence, desires freer liturgical forms throughout.

Dr. Bergendoff points out that the emphasis has shifted somewhat since Dean Lizell wrote the above (1935), and that the first and the third groups appear to have coalesced into a moderate reform group, while another group has more definitely assumed form as a High Church, almost Romanizing, party.

Efforts for revision, coming to at least partial fruition in the Liturgy of 1942, date from 1917 and the appointment by the Crown of a commission on revision in 1925. The commission presented proposals in 1926. Convoca-

[15] Vcl. II (*Die Kirche in Schweden*), pp. 91-100.

tion in 1932 adopted new forms for baptism and an order for the combination of morning service and communion, which the government approved and issued the next year. Archbishop Eidem was appointed to continue the revision, and in 1938 he submitted further proposals. Upon recommendation by Convocation the Crown authorized Bishop Tor Andrae, with the assistance of Bishops Aulén and Brilioth, to review and rework the proposals of Archbishop Eidem. In 1942 the new liturgy was approved by the Crown and the Church Assembly.

A significant feature of the current developments is the greatly increased interest in church music, especially in plain song and other strict church forms. Excellent church choirs are being organized and diocesan and national choral associations foster their development throughout the entire church and country.

Bishop Eduard Rodhe's *Svenkst gudstjänstliv: Historisk Belysning av den Svenska Kyrkohandboken* (Stockholm: Daikonistyr, 1925) is probably the best work on the history of the Swedish services. English readers, however, will depend largely upon two Anglican and two Lutheran guides for their introduction to Swedish liturgical history and life. Eric E. Yelverton in his *The Mass in Sweden* has given an excellent study of historical development with excerpts from the liturgies of different periods. His *The Swedish Rite* (New York: Macmillan, 1921), supplies a good translation of the *Handbook för svenska kyrkan* of 1917. John Wordsworth, late bishop of Salisbury, has endeavored to interpret the Swedish church as seen through Church of England eyes in his *The National Church of Sweden*. Bishop Yngve Brilioth of the Swedish church has embedded a valuable and discriminating study of Swedish liturgical development in his larger work, *Eucharistic Faith and Practice, Evangelical and Catholic*, Chap. VII. Dr. Conrad Bergendoff, president of Augustana College, Rock Island, Illinois, in his *Olavus Petri and the Ecclesiastical Transformation in Sweden*, has brought new facts to light and has supplied an excellent bibliography, particularly of Swedish and German authorities. Recent liturgical trends and the Sigtuna Foundation are discussed in separate chapters in *Ekklesia*, Bd. II. Note also the recent book by Eric E. Yelverton, *An Archbishop of the Reformation*.

O. V. Anderson, *The Church Manual of Olavus Petri* (Rock Island: Augustana Book Concern), is useful. *The Hymnal and Order of Service of the Evangelical Lutheran Augustana Synod* (Rock Island: Augustana Book Concern, 1927) contains an English translation of the liturgy as used in Sweden, with significant changes. Among magazine articles, the following may be mentioned: G. Aulén, "Liturgy and Church Music in the Church of Sweden," *American Church Monthly*, September, 1934; Clifford A. Nelson, "The Renewal of the Church," *The Lutheran Companion*, January 20, 1938; M. Lindquist, "Sigtuna, a Modern Spiritual Center," *The American Scandinavian Review*, XXIII (1934), No. 1. See also an article by Prof. N. Forsander, "The Swedish Liturgies," in the *Memoirs of the Lutheran Liturgical Association*, II, 15-27; and "The Music of the Augustana Service" in *The Augustana Quarterly*, April, 1944, pp. 127-45.

Limitations of space prevent consideration of liturgical developments in the national Lutheran churches of Denmark, Norway, Finland, Russia, France, Czechoslovakia, Hungary, and other European countries.

CHAPTER VI

ANGLICAN AND LUTHERAN LITURGIES

A quarter of a century after Luther's pioneering activities, the Church of England embarked upon a program of liturgical reform similar in many respects to the Lutheran, and yet quite different. The medieval office books of the church were revised, simplified, and combined with new material in a single service book in the language of the people called the *Book of Common Prayer*. This work is probably the most important and enduring monument of the English Reformation. It has been for centuries a factor second only to episcopacy itself in unifying and perpetuating the Church of England and the Anglican communion. Everything considered, it is probably the most influential single book of corporate devotion in the English language.

The Anglican communion, which was greatly extended during the last century, now consists of the mother Church of England, and daughter churches in Ireland, Wales, Scotland, the United States, the Dominions of Canada, South Africa, Australia, and New Zealand, together with the newly autonomous nations of Central and West Africa, India, Burma, Ceylon, and others. The first six of these independent churches have their own prayer books, which differ from each other in details. The Anglican churches in China and Japan combine features of the English and the American books in their vernacular uses. The Prayer Book has appeared, in whole or in part, in at least one hundred sixty-five different languages and is in use in about half that number today.[1]

Archbishop Cranmer was the leading spirit of the commission which prepared the *Book of Common Prayer*. Bishops Ridley, Holbeach, Thirlby, and Goodrich, and Drs. May, Haynes, Robertson, and Redman are supposed to have collaborated, but the archbishop was the master-

---

[1] Figures are from S.P.C.K. as of November, 1956. Undoubtedly there are additional translations issued from mission presses of which S.P.C.K. has no knowledge For full account of translations to 1913, see William Muss-Arnolt, *The Book of Common Prayer Among the Nations of the World* (New York: Gorham, 1914).

craftsman of the group. He had great gifts, and his work in this field has placed him in the company of Shakespeare, Bacon, Milton, the translators of the Authorized Version, and other great writers who made the hundred years after 1550 the great century in English literature.

The genius of the English people themselves and their appreciation of dignity, order, and beauty of literary expression are revealed in the Prayer Book. Within the Anglican communion it is an instrument and symbol of unity and strength, universally used and beloved. Enshrining, as it does, jeweled quotations from the Scripture in the golden settings of its text, it endears itself to devout worshipers in many other communions by its devotional quality and the lyrical beauty of its prose.

RECIPROCAL INFLUENCES

Relations between the *Book of Common Prayer* and the Lutheran Liturgy have been close and consequential. Lutheran influence upon the first Prayer Book was very important. It had to do with essential matters of content and arrangement which have persisted in subsequent revisions and translations. The English Litany followed closely Luther's revision through Hermann of Cologne, incorporating at least fourteen petitions or extensive phrases from this source. The construction of the new order for Morning Prayer from material in pre-Reformation Matins and Lauds, and of Evensong from similar material in Vespers and Compline, had been anticipated by Luther's suggestions, by the church orders of Bugenhagen, and quite definitely by the Calenberg and Göttingen Order of 1542. In the Communion service the first Prayer Book's prescription of entire psalms to be used as introits instead of the historic texts of the Roman use may be traced to Luther's expressed preference (*Formula Missae*), though his suggestion was not generally followed by Lutheran orders. Expressions in the exhortations, the Confession and Absolution, the prayer "for the whole state of Christes churche," the beginning of the Prayer of Consecration and the second half of the Benediction are from Hermann's Reformation of Cologne. The introduction of the Ten Commandments in the second Prayer Book may have been influenced by Pullain's service for the foreign congregation at Glastonbury (1551), but this had been anticipated by the orders for Frankfort (1530), Bremen (1534), etc. The Comfortable Words are unquestionably from the German text of Hermann's Reformation of Cologne (1543).[2] The recital of the Institution is a harmony of the New Testament accounts quite as in Brandenburg-Nuremberg (1533). The orders for baptism,

[2] Archbishop Cranmer's copy of the Latin edition of this work contains his own autograph and is preserved in the library of Chichester Cathedral.

confirmation, marriage, and burial reveal extensive indebtedness to Lutheran sources. Baptism and marriage conform closely in general structure and numerous details to the suggestions made by Luther, with certain features in baptism drawn from Bucer. Expressions in the confirmation service and the use of the old sequence "in the midst of life" in the burial service are examples of a general following of Lutheran precedents fully established in German and Scandinavian church orders before 1549.

Prayer Book influence upon the Lutheran Liturgy was much later. Lutherans in London in the eighteenth century used the orders for baptism and marriage in the Prayer Book for their English services. These same English orders were incorporated in the German manuscript liturgies used in America by Lutheran ministers of Muhlenberg's day. Lutherans in Nova Scotia in 1864, "feeling the necessity of having a liturgy of our church suitable for a British congregation," prepared an abbreviated edition of the Anglican Prayer Book for their own use.[3] Later English Lutherans in the United States, drawing upon their inheritance of English literature and culture, incorporated in their Common Service the Authorized Version of the Scriptures and the Prayer Book translation of collects and other liturgical texts (Gloria in Excelsis, Creed, Te Deum, etc.). The wisdom of this decision, placing American Lutheranism in the stream of English cultural tradition, was recognized by the framers of the Common Liturgy, who decided to keep these translations. Influences less easily discernible were equally important. Original English Lutheran material in addresses, collects, prayers, etc., has been cast in forms for liturgical expression fixed for all English-speaking people in the Prayer Books of the sixteenth century.

English Lutheranism in America, while firmly rooted doctrinally in Lutheran backgrounds in Europe, has also been materially influenced in other respects by British church life, Nonconformist as well as Anglican. In its development of the Sunday school, and in matters of church organization and finance, it has profited greatly by the experience of the English free churches. Its popular appreciation of liturgical worship, its forms of church architecture and churchly appointments in general, its hymnody and church music have felt the powerful influence of forces and forms originating within the established Church of England.

For details of Lutheran influence see particularly: H. E. Jacobs, *The Lutheran Movement in England;* Francis Gasquet and Edmund Bishop,

[3] This curious volume also includes the Augsburg Confession and a selection of forty-eight hymns from the General Synod hymnal. It was published at Halifax under the title, *The Book of Common Prayer and Administration of the Sacraments . . . according to the use of the Lutheran Church of Nova Scotia.*

Edward VI and the Book of Common Prayer (3rd ed.; London: Hodges, 1891); Dowden's two books, *Workmanship of the Prayer Book* and *Further Studies in the Prayer Book,* and his article, "Foreign Influences on the First Book" in G. Harford, *et al., Prayer Book Dictionary* (New York: Longmans, 1912); F. E. Brightman, *The English Rite,* Vol. I (Introduction); the article, "Prayer, Book of Common," by Canon F. E. Warren in the *Encyclopedia Britannica* (11th ed.), XXII, 258-62; W. K. L. Clarke and C. Harris, *Liturgy and Worship* (New York: Macmillan, 1933); and Messenger, *The Reformation, the Mass and the Priesthood* (New York: Longmans, 1936-37).

IMPORTANT DIFFERENCES

While Anglican and Lutheran liturgies are in close agreement in basic principle and content, important differences show that they are expressions of two different types of organized Christianity.

Lutheran liturgical reform was clear-cut and definite where matters of doctrine were concerned; the language of the Prayer Book is frequently capable of various interpretations. The church orders contained lengthy doctrinal discussions; the Prayer Book is definitely a service book and nothing else. Outlines of services were given in the church orders and were to be filled in with the texts of lessons, introits, collects, etc., from the old office books and with new material provided in the orders themselves. The text of the Prayer Book was complete in itself. The church orders contained few rubrical directions; they were of local or provincial authority; it was left largely to individual discretion whether traditional vestments and ceremonies should be retained, simplified, or abandoned. The Prayer Book was a national use; its rubrical directions concerning vestments and ceremonies were specific; there was a parliamentary law of uniformity which enforced its observance in all details and all churches. In Germany particularly, and to a lesser degree in Sweden, the Lutherans retained parts of the Service in Latin, particularly Introits, Graduals, responsories, canticles, and similar choral elements. This practice continued in some places for centuries. The Anglicans after a brief period of experimentation dropped the Latin language completely.

Lutheran unity has always been sought in the sphere of faith rather than in matters of order or externals. The Prayer Book was a more complete and practical liturgy than that in any of the church orders. All parts of the service were in English, and there was no need to refer to any other book for texts or directions. Thus, paradoxically, the Lutherans who emphasized faith produced a series of church orders, and the Anglicans who emphasized order produced a great Prayer Book. The Lutheran orders were administered in a spirit of evangelical freedom, while the use of the Prayer Book was enforced by governmental authority.

The achievement of the Prayer Book in rendering the entire series of Latin collects for Sundays and festivals, the Gloria in Excelsis, Creed, Sanctus, Te Deum, and other great liturgical texts into English of singular nobility, restraint, and beauty, cannot be praised too highly. As indicated above, the Lutheran orders retained many of these texts in Latin with their traditional music. For their vernacular services they provided a few collects in German translation for each season and reduced the canticles, etc., to rhymed German paraphrases devoid of literary merit. On the other hand, the Lutheran orders retained important choral elements of the historic liturgy which were entirely lost to the English church.

Luther and his followers purified and simplified the local Roman services, incorporating new prayers and hymns of evangelical character. Beyond this they did not go. Cranmer, with broader liturgical interest and information, and more eclectic spirit, freely incorporated in the English liturgy features from the Lutheran orders and material from Greek and Mozarabic sources. He also accepted numerous suggestions originally proposed by Cardinal Quignon in his Reformed Breviary of 1535. Luther and his followers rejected as doctrinally impure the entire Canon of the Mass, retaining only the Verba and the Lord's Prayer. Cranmer and his associates composed a new and lengthy prayer of consecration, evangelical in character, but closely modeled upon features of the Roman Canon.

English liturgical reform supplied the people fully with the Holy Scriptures in the vernacular. Compared with the Lutheran reform, however, it was less consciously directed by appreciation of the significance of the Word of God as the animating principle of worship. Instead we find a sacrificial conception of worship stressed in the Prayer Book. Its Morning and Evening Prayer are reminiscent of monastic ideals in their strong emphasis upon daily service and the use of the entire Psalter as an offering of prayer and praise to God. In the Holy Communion the emphasis is upon the offering of the consecrated elements to God, and the presenting of "ourselves, our bodies and souls a reasonable service" rather than upon the sacramental gift of the body and blood of our Lord, and the divine assurance of forgiveness and peace. The Anglican and the Lutheran services both provide didactic as well as devotional material in their liturgical forms.

There is one other important difference in the midst of general agreement. Both churches preserve fully the historic structure of the Western

Liturgy and the church year. They frequently agree in differing from the present Roman arrangement of Collects, Epistles, and Gospels. There is a difference, however, in the measure in which the two communions in their normal Sunday services share in the historic liturgical provisions of the universal church.

The normal Lutheran services are richer in content and more definitely in harmony with liturgical tradition than are the corresponding services of the Anglican communion, first, because the Lutheran Church has a fuller series of liturgical propers. In retaining the Introit and the Gradual for each Sunday the Lutheran Liturgy is not only more complete but contains basic liturgical texts for the development of appropriate choral compositions for the musical enrichment of its services. In the second place, the normal Lutheran service, without the Holy Communion, is the so-called ante-communion, the first part of the ancient Mass of the Day. The normal service, with sermon, of Anglican congregations is Morning Prayer. Comparatively few attend the early services of Holy Communion which most parishes provide. Morning Prayer, while providing in the course of the year a rich series of lessons from Scripture, does not include the historic Epistles and Gospels which give each day its distinctive character. The Lutheran Liturgy is better furnished to establish for worshipers the mood of each season and the meaning of each Sunday or festival. In a normal Sunday service, the Lutheran still "goes to Mass" while the Anglican attends Matins. Even if Holy Communion is not administered, the Lutheran has the full propers of the really significant congregational service of the day. The Anglican enjoys a beautifully constructed service of praise and prayer, fashioned from material in two of the monastic hour services. The Collect is the only variable feature from the day's Mass included in this service.

THE ENGLISH REFORMATION

The Reformation in England was related to earlier reforms on the continent. Thomas Bilney, Robert Barnes, Hugh Latimer, Miles Coverdale, Nicholas Ridley, and other young scholars at the University of Cambridge eagerly discussed evangelical developments. They frequented a house contemptuously called "Germany" and were ridiculed by their fellow-students as "Lutherans." Twenty books or pamphlets by or concerning Luther, and works by Melanchthon, Bugenhagen, Bucer, and others were included in an "Index of Prohibited Books" as early as 1529. Tyndale leaned heavily upon Luther, as did Cranmer in his catechism, and Coverdale in his English Bible. By the middle of the century there was a definitely "Lutheran movement" in England. The end of the century saw no less than sixty-five English Lutheran books in print.

Political maneuvers and ecclesiastical developments were mingled. King Henry VIII broke with the papacy and established himself as head of the English church in 1534. This had national support, but neither the king nor his people were prepared to renounce Roman doctrine.

One of the ambassadors sent by King Henry to Germany to arrange a political alliance with Protestant princes was Thomas Cranmer. He spent the year 1532 in Regensburg and in Nuremberg, where he met many influential German Reformers—Camerarius, Osiander, Brenz, and probably Bucer. He himself lived at the home of Andreas Osiander, pastor of the historic Church of St. Lawrence; and after a few months he married Osiander's niece. During this very summer of 1532, Osiander and Brenz were at work in Osiander's home preparing the important Brandenburg-Nuremberg Church Order, which, after approval by the Wittenberg faculty, was published the following year. Cranmer's familiarity with the principles and results of liturgical reform in Germany strongly influenced his later procedure in England.

King Henry's efforts to form alliances failed. Cranmer was recalled and was made Archbishop of Canterbury. To this the pope consented, in spite of the fact that Cranmer was married and in sympathy with Protestant reform. With the aid of Fox and others Cranmer published the Bishops' Book in 1537. This owed much in plan and content to Luther's catechisms, the Augsburg Confession, and the Apology. In 1544 Cranmer issued his English Litany, a work based directly upon the Reformation of Cologne (1543), which in turn was derived from Luther's Litany of 1529. In 1543 it was decreed that a chapter should be read from the English Bible after the Te Deum in Matins and after the Magnificat in Vespers. Four years later the Gospel and Epistle were ordered read in English at high mass, and the Gloria in Excelsis, the Creed, and the Agnus Dei were to be sung in English, though the rest of the service was in Latin.

King Henry died January 28, 1547, eleven months after the death of Luther. The boy king, Edward VI, ascended the English throne. His uncle the Duke of Somerset was an ardent Protestant, and became "Protector." Archbishop Cranmer was now free to inaugurate further reforms. An experimental measure provided an English Service to supplement the Latin Mass. This contained an exhortation to communicants, a confession, absolution, and the Comfortable Words, all based upon earlier German forms, particularly those of Cologne, Cassel, Volprecht of Nuremberg, and the order of Schwäbisch Hall. Though only a partial and temporary form, this order of March, 1548, became the nucleus of the full English communion service in the Prayer Book authorized for use the following year.

THE FIRST PRAYER BOOK

The first Prayer Book was introduced in the churches on Whitsunday, June 9, 1549. Fundamentally it was a revision of the diocesan use of Salisbury (Sarum), which in the centuries preceding the Reformation had been adopted in whole or in part by other dioceses—Wells, Exeter, Lichfield, Lincoln, etc.—and by various collegiate churches and other large foundations.

The book was definitely anti-Roman in its rejection of transubstantiation and the idea of propitiatory sacrifice, and in its prohibition of celebration without communicants. Yet in some places its language was equivocal. There were so many evidences of Lutheran influence in the work that some scholars regard this first Book as a Lutheran liturgy. Several medieval features, however, were retained which would be unacceptable to most Lutherans today. Among these were the mixed chalice, the commemoration of the Blessed Virgin, prayers for the dead, and reservation for the sick.

Dr. Henry E. Jacobs uncovered a new field of historical research and fully demonstrated the strength of Lutheran influence upon the first Book of Common Prayer in his book *The Lutheran Movement in England*. The Benedictine, Francis A. Gasquet, and the equally eminent liturgical scholar Edmund Bishop, declared that after comparing the new Anglican Service "on the one hand with the ancient missal and on the other with the Lutheran liturgies, there can be no hesitation whatever in classing it with the latter, not with the former."[4] Dr. Edward T. Horn always regarded the first Prayer Book as a Lutheran book. Apart from the revelations of Dr. Jacobs and the frank admissions of Edmund Bishop and John Dowden, a comparison of the Communion Service in the Prayer Book of 1549 with the Roman Mass and a group of Lutheran orders as given by the eminent Anglican scholar F. E. Brightman in *The English Rite* (I, xcviii-ciii, and introduction), seems to justify this claim.

It must never be forgotten that the Lutheran orders in Germany and Sweden were the first complete vernacular services in Europe, and that many of them were regularly in use a decade or two before the Prayer Book was prepared in England. The fact that there was no space given in the Prayer Book to doctrinal discussions similar to those which bulked so large in the Lutheran orders does not prove that "there is no Lutheranism in the Prayer Book." For the Lutheran point of view is evident in the retention and simplification of certain parts of the Service, the rejection of other medieval features (e.g., the Offertory, the invocation of saints, the benediction of things, etc.); and in the general tone of the book. Definite Lutheran influence is, of course, also evident in the actual texts of parts of the Holy Communion, the Litany, baptism, confirmation, marriage, burial, etc., as well as in the retention or introduction of various other liturgical practices.

The Act of Uniformity which authorized the use of the Prayer Book in all the churches of the realm instead of unifying the church divided it into two parties which have continued to the present day. The Book of 1549 was too radical to suit the moderates and too conservative to suit the extremists. The radicals were greatly encouraged in their opposition by foreign Reformers. Calvin, Peter Martyr the Italian, Pollanus, and John à Lasco all urged extensive changes. Bucer of Strasbourg, who could not speak English, was invited to give a formal criticism of the Book. This he did in twenty-eight chapters in his *Censura,* delivered to the Bishop of Ely a month before Bucer's death.

THE SECOND PRAYER BOOK AND PURITAN INFLUENCE

The entire country was in confusion following the death of King Henry. The nobles who had come into power were not religious reformers. Many of them encouraged the extremists, and in many places confiscated the treasures

---

[4] Gasquet and Bishop, *Edward VI and the Book of Common Prayer,* p. 224.

of the churches as ruthlessly as did later Puritans, though not always because of religious conviction. Archbishop Cranmer yielded to the pressure of the radicals and prepared a second Book, which contained drastic changes and many features definitely Calvinistic in tone.

The second Book was approved by Parliament on April 14, 1552. In this, a group of introductory sentences led to an Exhortation, Confession, and Absolution which gave a strong penitential character to Morning and Evening Prayer. In the Communion Office the Kyrie was expanded and made a response to the sections of an inserted Decalogue. The Introit and the Agnus Dei disappeared entirely and the Gloria in Excelsis was transferred to the end of the service. The Eucharistic Prayer was divided into five parts, separated by exhortations. Thanksgivings and commemorations were omitted, together with the sign of the cross, the mixed chalice, and the invocation of the Word and the Holy Ghost in the consecration. Vestments approved in 1549 were forbidden (alb, chasuble, cope), and priests were permitted only surplices and bishops rochets. The new text restricted consecration to persons and not to the elements, and encouraged the idea that the "presence of Christ was not in the sacrament, but only in the heart of the believer."

The second Book represented the widest swing from conservative and historical positions. Nevertheless, it did not satisfy the extreme Protestant group. It greatly offended the conservatives, whose strength was largely in the west of England. This Book had a brief life of eight months.

King Edward VI died in 1553. The accession of Queen Mary, an ardent Roman Catholic, swept aside all evangelical efforts, and reintroduced the entire series of medieval Latin services. Cranmer's stand against this reactionary program led to his martyrdom along with Latimer, Ridley, Hooper, and three hundred others. The scholars whom the archbishop had brought to England fled back to the Continent, and many active English Protestants went with them to Frankfort or Strasbourg. The English exiles in Frankfort soon split into two factions. The radical group finally settled in Switzerland, where its leader, John Knox, became closely associated with Calvin.

After more than five years of terror and bloodshed, Queen Mary's reign ended, and Queen Elizabeth came to the throne in 1558. She succeeded, though with great difficulty, in carrying out a program of moderate reform, based upon a policy of comprehensiveness. Parliament, by a majority of only three votes, re-established the second Edwardian Book with important modifications in the spirit of the first Book. Permission was given to restore the traditional altar and chancel, and to use the vestments and ornaments which had been authorized in the second year of King Edward's reign. A few prayers were added, and minor changes made in the Litany. Church music was again encouraged.

The power of the Puritan party, however, was increasing. The Marian exiles who now returned from Geneva became the leaders of the English middle classes, whose thinking was largely colored by Calvinistic ideas. They fought the established church and the Prayer Book on every front. They objected to the sign of the cross in baptism, kneeling at communion, the use of all vestments, even the black gown, the use of the wedding ring and all prescribed ceremonial, as well as organs in the church. The Queen's strong hand enforced conformity and held the opposition in check during her long reign, and the Prayer Book remained unaltered for nearly half a century.

Puritan opposition broke out with new violence when King James I came to the throne in 1603. A petition signed by more than one thousand ministers urged changes in the Prayer Book. The king called a conference at Hampton Court in January, 1604. A number of minor changes were agreed upon, several prayers were introduced, and all lessons from the Apocrypha were omitted. In this form the fourth *Book of Common Prayer* appeared in 1604.

The Puritan power increased, and finally prevailed. The Puritans had just grievances against the tyranny of the crown and the intolerance of the bishops. Their bitterness, however, led them to oppose indiscriminately all established order in church and state. The Long Parliament, convened in 1640, drove King Charles into exile, abolished episcopacy, imprisoned many bishops, executed Archbishop Laud, and in 1645 outlawed the Prayer Book. The "Directory for the Public Worship of God," which was substituted for it, was largely an abridgment of a scheme prepared for the Genevan exiles. The use of the Prayer Book "in any public place of worship or in any private place or family" was forbidden under a penalty of a year's imprisonment. The suppression of the Prayer Book carried with it, of course, nonobservance of the church year. These radical changes were accompanied by acts of violence and the destruction of church property on a scale which had no parallel in Lutheran reform on the Continent.

After nearly sixteen years of this revolutionary regime, the Restoration in 1660 brought Charles II to the throne, the bishops to their sees, and the Prayer Book to the churches. The Savoy Conference, April to July, 1661, considered a long list of Puritan demands, which included the elimination of all responsive reading, the combination of collects into longer prayer forms, the facing of the people by the minister at all times, etc. About the only important concession made, however, was the use of the Authorized Version for the Epistles and Gospels. Bishop John Cosin of Durham was the principal author of new prayers and thanksgivings, and Bishop Sanderson of Lincoln wrote a preface to this fifth Prayer Book which was authorized May 19, 1662. The whole tendency of this Book was away from the Puritan position, and two thousand ministers of that party relinquished their parishes rather than accept it. This led to the withdrawal from the established church of many Nonconformists who now became "Dissenters" and organized free churches in many communities.

LATER DEVELOPMENTS

The English *Book of Common Prayer* remained practically unchanged for the next 250 years. Meanwhile variant forms of the Book were issued by different branches of the Anglican communion in Scotland, Ireland, the United States, South Africa, Canada, etc. The very considerable differences between the texts of these books give the Anglican Liturgy almost as great diversity of form as the Lutheran Liturgy displays.

The Scottish bishops with the aid of Archbishop Laud modified the English Prayer Book in the direction of Puritan desires. Their Book of 1637 was not accepted. It did, however, lay the foundation for liturgical interest and scholarship in Scotland which later proved significant. It was reprinted in the eighteenth century by the Nonjurors, a group of eight bishops and four hundred ministers who refused to take the oath of allegiance to William of Orange and who, after being ejected, mantained a separate organization for a century, ordained new bishops and clergy, and issued a complete Prayer Book of their own in 1734. This reverted in its communion office to features of the first Prayer Book of 1549. It also incorporated material drawn from the early Greek liturgies. The Scottish Book was thoroughly revised in 1928 with the addition of new collects and prayers, and the office of Compline. This book has been an important and influential member of the Anglican family of liturgies. Its consecration prayer definitely influenced the American Prayer Book of 1789 and subsequent revisions, and also was incorporated in the Proposed Book of the Church of England in 1928.

The Church of Ireland accepted the revised English Book of 1662, which it slightly altered in later editions. A final revision of considerable scope was made in 1727. The Church in South Africa issued its revised Prayer Book in 1954. A conservative revision of the Canadian Book appeared in 1921. The *Book of Common Prayer* of the Church of England in India has some interesting and unusual features.

The intensive studies which precipitated decades of discussion and finally resulted in revisions of the Prayer Book in practically all areas of the Anglican communion began about a third of a century ago. Various desires, each expressive of a particular group within the church, motivated the movement. One of these sought to bring formal worship into closer touch with modern life by altering archaic expressions, and by adding new prayers and offices. A second sought brevity and flexibility by permitting omissions and alternate forms. A third purpose was represented by the Anglo-Catholic party which was united and increasing in strength. This group desired to rid the Book of distinctively Protestant features, to make changes sanctioning sacrificial conceptions of the Sacrament, and to restore medieval practices. Tacitly each party agreed to accept points in the programs of the other parties in order to secure its own desires.[5]

The greatest interest attached to the proposals of the English bishops in 1927. Because of the relationship between the established church and the state it is necessary for alterations in the Prayer Book to be authorized by Parliament. After securing approval of revisions by the Church Assembly, the bishops requested Parliament to authorize a new Book which would include a body of general rubrics permitting flexibility (abbreviated services, omission of portions of the Psalter, etc.), and which added new services, thanksgivings, collects, etc., inserted as alternate forms the memorial (anamnesis) and the epiclesis in the Prayer of Consecration, and permitted reservation of the consecrated bread and wine to be taken to the sick on the day of communion. Parliament, which consists of members of many communions and of no church connection, and which in its legislative functions represents the entire country, followed the debate on the Book with closest attention. Sentiment throughout the country was opposed to reservation as

---

[5] For discussion of the Oxford Movement and its influence upon English liturgical development, see below, Chap. VII, pp. 155ff. For a convenient collection of all collects appearing in the current Prayer Books of the Anglican communion (England, Scotland, Ireland, Canada, South Africa, and the United States of America), see John Wallace Suter, Jr., *The Book of English Collects* (New York: Harper, 1940).

likely to lead to adoration, and to any extension of episcopal power in the determining of rules. The epiclesis was also viewed with suspicion. The proposed Book finally passed the House of Lords, but was rejected by Commons by a vote of 238 to 205. Revised proposals met the same fate in 1928 by a vote of 266 to 220. While these proposals failed of legal authorization, many Anglican bishops now tacitly permit the use of material from the so-called "Deposited Book" by indicating that they will not initiate proceedings against ministers who, with the consent of their church councils, substitute forms from this Book for the text of the Prayer Book of 1662.

The first American *Book of Common Prayer* dates from 1789. The English Prayer Book was used in Jamestown in the colony of Virginia as early as 1607, and later in Pennsylvania, New York, and most of the other colonies. The Independents and Congregationalists fought its introduction in New England. At the time of the Declaration of Independence there were only a few scattered congregations of the Church of England in that whole area. There were no bishops in the entire country, and there had been no general convention. The Scottish bishops finally consecrated Samuel Seabury as bishop of Connecticut in 1785. The first General Convention met in Philadelphia that same year, but without representatives from the New England states. A proposed book based upon the English Prayer Book, but with alterations, was rejected by the congregations in all states represented. Bishop Seabury postponed final action. Two years later, the English archbishops consecrated William White bishop of Pennsylvania and Samuel Provost bishop of New York, and in 1789 a General Convention approved an American Prayer Book. This, in the communion office particularly, closely followed the first Prayer Book of 1549 and the Scottish Book, influenced by the nonjuring tradition. Prayers for the president and for Congress were substituted for the English forms, and there were other alterations. The American Book was unchanged until 1892, when a conservative revision was authorized. In 1928 a much more thorough revision was made in the interest of simplification on the one hand and enrichment on the other. This book contains many features of the English Deposited Book. There are additional canticles, new collects and thanksgivings, three new proper prefaces, definite intercessions for the departed, etc. English liturgical scholars regard the American Book as an improvement upon their own.

139

CHAPTER VII

DECLINE AND RECOVERY

The spiritual and intellectual vigor which produced the confessions and liturgies of the Reformation period suffered an immediate decline. Disintegrating forces of many kinds brought church life throughout Europe to low ebb in the seventeenth and eighteenth centuries. These adversely affected the liturgy, the observance of the church year, frequency of the celebration of Holy Communion, standards of hymnody, and many other features connected with public worship. The first of these destructive factors was the Thirty Years' War, 1618-48.

THE THIRTY YEARS' WAR

The bitter theological debates of the sixteenth century between Romanists and Protestants and later between Lutherans and Calvinists finally emerged in the national and political arena in a series of wars in which political quarrels were interwoven with religious issues. The Counter-Reformation, under Jesuit leadership in Cologne and Vienna, strengthened and disciplined the inner forces of Roman Catholicism. The Hapsburg rulers crushed the Protestant nobles in Bohemia and Hungary and closed their churches and schools. All non-Catholics were required to renounce their faith or leave the country.

The time seemed ripe for a concerted drive upon Protestantism in general. King Maximilian of Bavaria became the head of a Catholic league which sought to restore Roman Catholic power in Europe through the military leadership of the able General Tilly. When the Spaniards joined Austria and Bavaria and occupied the German Palatinate, Richelieu, though persecuting the Huguenots at home, threw the power of France against the Hapsburgs, whose ambitions he feared. France was thus allied with the Protestant princes of Germany and with the Swedes. The latter were aroused when Wallenstein invaded northern Germany, subdued every Baltic city except Stralsund, and proclaimed himself Duke of Mecklenburg and Admiral of the Baltic. Gustavus

140

Adolphus, a wise ruler of men, master of eight languages, a great general and statesman, yielded to the plea of the German princes. With an army superior in moral character and discipline to the forces of the imperial allies he entered Germany and by a series of brilliant victories swept on to occupy Munich in the heart of Bavaria.

The magnitude, length, and bitterness of this struggle stagger the imagination. Though the conflict swept at times into Austria, Italy, Spain, and Belgium, the real battleground was Germany. Here Frenchmen, Spaniards, Austrians, Germans, and Swedes contended for the mastery. A series of marches, countermarches, invasions, occupations, evacuations, reoccupations, sieges, reliefs, and other military maneuvers converted whole districts into deserts. Famine and disease took a terrible toll, while complicated diplomacy sought for solutions acceptable to a dozen nations.

The church suffered irreparable losses. Protestant pastors who were not slain were driven into poverty and exile. Those permitted to stay ministered to their people in barns or in the forests. Ordered church life was disrupted, churches were closed, wrecked, or defiled. Liturgical books, music, and sacred vessels were destroyed, together with vernacular translations of the Scriptures. Yet even here roses blossomed in the desert. The hymns of Johann Heermann and Martin Rinkart have permanently enriched all later worship, and Paul Gerhardt learned in young manhood from the distress about him how to sing of patient trust and triumphant faith.

The war ended in compromise, but actually it was a victory for Protestantism. Though driven out of eastern Europe, the Protestants retained possession of all lands in western Europe which had been Protestant in the year 1624. The religious settlement was practically permanent despite the pope's rage. Germany's material wealth, however, had been destroyed, and France became dominant on the continent. The church in Germany was reduced to pitiful poverty, not only in material possessions, but in the loss of spiritual effectiveness and the traditions of liturgical and musical culture.

Dr. A. W. Ward gives a sober judgment of the material and moral effects of the conflagration and characterizes them as "perhaps the most appalling demonstrations of the consequences of war to be found in history. The mighty impulses which the great movements of the Renaissance and the Reformation had imparted to the aspirations and efforts of contemporary German life were quenched. . . . The mainspring of the national life was broken."[1] One-third of all the cultivated land in northern Germany was

---

[1] *Cambridge Modern History,* IV, 417.

reduced to barrenness. Wolves and other wild beasts took the place of the horses and cattle which had been consumed or destroyed. Cities, rich in all that the Middle Ages and the Reformation had bequeathed to the modern world, were reduced to ashes. In Württemberg less than one-fifth of the inhabitants survived. Germany's total population of 16,000,000 was reduced by armed conflict, murder, famine, disease, and emigration to less than 6,000,000.

Friedrich Schiller, historian as well as poet and philosopher, brilliantly described this "desolating war of thirty years, which, from the interior of Bohemia to the mouth of Scheldt, and from the banks of the Po to the coasts of the Baltic, devastated whole countries, destroyed harvests, and reduced towns and villages to ashes; which opened a grave for many thousand combatants, and for half a century smothered the glimmering sparks of civilization in Germany, and threw back the improving manners of the country into their pristine barbarity and wildness."[2]

Rapine and murder accompanied the sack of cities. The horrors connected with the fall of Magdeburg in 1631 were revolting even to the Catholics. Tilly reported to the emperor that nothing equal to this massacre had happened since the capture of Jerusalem. Wallenstein's army of 60,000, consisting largely of mercenaries without home or national sympathies, plundered and burned their way through Saxony until they were checked at Lützen. When the Bavarian army of 30,000 was finally defeated in 1648, it was estimated that no less than 130,000 hangers-on had accompanied them, living off the land and the people.

The war had lasted longer than the average expectancy of life in those times. Even when peace was signed the agony was not over. A whole generation of youth, familiar only with violence and brutality, had grown to maturity without either secular or religious education. The population sank into ignorance and superstition from which even some of the highest among them were not free. The bishop of Würzburg, for example, is charged by responsible historians with having put to death 9,000 "witches" and "wizards" within a period of two years.

Richard C. Trench, in his *Gustavus Adolphus in Germany* (London: Kegan Paul, 1892), gives a concise but admirable account of the war. The best extended discussion is to be found in the thousand pages devoted to The Thirty Years' War in *The Cambridge Modern History,* Vol. IV. The more recent work by C. V. Wedgwood, *The Thirty Years' War* (New Haven: Yale Univ. Pr., 1939), is well written but cynical. There are good summary statements in Williston Walker, *A History of the Christian Church* (New York: Scribner, 1918), pp. 446-51; Charles M. Jacobs, *The Story of the Church* (Philadelphia, Muhlenberg, 1947) and K. S. Latourette, *A History of Christianity* (New York: Harper, 1953), pp. 884-89.

ORTHODOXY AND ITS LEGALISTIC PROGRAM

Efforts were promptly made to restore orderly church life. Many church orders were reissued, but with modifications and additions. The

[2] *History of the Thirty Years' War,* trans. A. J. W. Morrison (New York: Alden, 1885), p. 9.

people, demoralized by war and its effects, were not as responsive to the gospel as they had been in the days of the Reformation. The effort to lead the church out of disaster produced a new scholasticism among the clergy. Throughout this time of "orthodoxy" great emphasis was laid on rigid formulation and precise definition of belief, the objective efficacy of the Sacraments, and a legalistic conception of worship. The practical development of Christian life and character was pushed into the background. Clerical scholasticism and governmental bureaucracy reduced church life and worship to mechanical levels.

Practical difficulties arose from the destruction not only of the church orders, but of the missals, breviaries, graduals, and other pre-Reformation books which had been kept in the churches before the war. Many of the church orders, though prescribing the Introit, Collect, Gradual, etc., had not included the complete texts of these propers. The clergy and the choirmasters were expected to find them in the older liturgical books. In addition to losing these books, the new generation was untrained in liturgical and musical tradition and understanding.

So far as the people were concerned, attendance at the services and the Holy Communion was insisted upon. Fines were imposed for non-attendance. Civil offenders were sentenced by the courts to come to confession and receive the Sacrament. The church became more and more a department of the civil government. With the hardening and narrowing of its intellectual life went externalization of worship and neglect of spiritual quality in everyday life and conduct. Thus, while the earlier forms of worship were partially restored, the spirit which had characterized faith and worship in the sixteenth century was not recaptured.

One must not overlook constructive achievements. The leaders in church and state faced a colossal task. Their work checked the sway of ignorance and lawlessness. In the field of theology the reconstituted universities enabled the work of great dogmaticians like Chemnitz, Hutter, and John Gerhard to inspire men entering the ministry with a clear conception of religious truth. In point of mastery of biblical and historical material and in the power of organization and logical presentation the dogmatic treatises of these theologians compare favorably with the systematic works of Thomas Aquinas and John Calvin. We must also remember mystics like Jacob Böhme as well as the healthier piety of the earlier John Arndt. The hymns of Paul Gerhardt effectively promoted real spirituality in wide circles. But generally speaking, theology had become scholastic again. It pursued its objective in a heightened spirit of controversy. The people were drilled in the catechism and driven to church, but the influence of religion upon moral and spiritual life became less and less potent.

PIETISM

The necessary reaction came in the movement known as Pietism. While some of its origins are obscure, the first man to give it direction was Philip Jacob Spener, an Alsatian born thirteen years before the end of the Thirty Years' War. In 1666 he became senior pastor at Frankfort. His sermons assailed as pharisaical the current emphasis upon doctrinal definition and mechanical subscription to orthodox confessions without personal spirituality and morality. In 1675 he published his *pia Desideria* with six major proposals for reform. He inaugurated private devotional assemblies in his house twice a week (*collegia pietatis*) with common discussions of Scripture and life. He also developed a new type of catechization and instituted strict ecclesiastical discipline while stressing gentleness and love.

These private assemblies or conventicles, composed largely of laymen, led to an undervaluation of the regular church services, of the sacraments, and of the clergy. Some of Spener's adherents definitely broke with the church and emigrated to Pennsylvania. After accepting a call to Dresden as chaplain to the Elector, Spener himself ran into further difficulties. He chided his prince for intemperance and criticized the universities of Leipzig and Wittenberg for their training of theological students. Reactions soon made him uncomfortable and forced him to remove to Berlin (1691), where he remained until his death in 1705.

One of Spener's pupils was August Hermann Francke. He had been expelled from Leipzig because of a controversy with the old orthodoxy, but in 1698 was called to the faculty of the new (1694) university at Halle where, thanks to the influence of Spener at the Prussian court, he had already helped to shape the theological curriculum. This university soon became a powerful center of the movement which was dividing Lutheranism into two camps. A flood of pamphlet literature discussed the issues. Francke exerted a great influence as a professor in the university which presently attracted a thousand students of theology. He was aided by Thomasius, an able professor of law and an exponent of religious toleration.

In the field of practical religion and missions Francke's establishment of an orphans' asylum with associated schools, a publishing house, a hospital, etc., was equally significant. Halle sent the first Lutheran missionaries to India—Ziegenbalg and Plütschau, and later Christian Friedrich Schwartz. Henry Melchior Muhlenberg, the patriarch of the Lutheran

Church in America, was greatly influenced by this institution and its spirit. When Francke died in 1727, there were 2,200 children under instruction in his schools, and his institutions have continued to the present day.

Pietism met a real need in its insistence upon "vital godliness." It was not a separatist movement such as Moravianism became after 1727 under the guidance of Zinzendorf, the godson of Spener. As a movement within the established church it awakened the latter from coldness and institutionalism. The clergy were made to recognize the importance of personal character and conviction as a prerequisite for official service. They were also won to a new type of biblical interpretation and to more practical and effective preaching. Bible reading, personal devotion, and prayer were widely promoted. The privilege and responsibility of lay activity were stressed, and the entire church was given a new conception of missionary endeavor.

The movement became particularly strong in Württemberg where the effort to infuse the Pietistic spirit into scientific theology reached pronounced success in the work of Johann Albrecht Bengel and his New Testament studies. Contemporary influences in England, Holland, and Switzerland were important. In its promotion of higher morality among clergy and laity, its encouragement of biblical study and distribution, its improved methods of education, and the development of streams of practical benevolence, Pietism bequeathed vital and permanent influences to the whole Christian world. Though often intensely subjective and even sentimental, many hymns of Schmolck, Bogatsky, Tersteegen, and Zinzendorf have won a permanent place in Protestant worship.

There is another side to the shield. In opposing the institutionalism of the established church, Pietism produced an unbalanced type of Christianity which overemphasized personal experience and relatively minor details of life and conduct. By its violent opposition to dancing, cardplaying, the theater, etc., it encouraged a new type of asceticism and justification by works which led to self-complacency and severe criticism of the "unawakened." The masses of the people were given up as lost. The movement radiated gloom and austerity and narrowed and hardened the Christian spirit. Its methods encouraged all manner of individual and subjective expressions. Sectarians and fanatics flourished on its congenial soil. While some of its best features have become the permanent possession of contemporary Lutheranism, Pietism's worst features continue to plague the church.

So far as ordered public worship was concerned, Pietism's influence was unfavorable. Beginning with the attempt to supplement the regular services and usages of the church, it soon supplanted these by meetings in private homes which included religious discussions and administration of the Sacrament. As its spirit entered into the established church, the services of the latter became more and more subjective and emotional. The struggle for personal consciousness of conversion and regeneration led to an undervaluation of the objective means of grace. The historical and the formal in liturgical worship gave way to expressions of individual ideas and emotions. The liturgy and the church year were too objective and constraining. The formal common prayer of the church gradually disappeared under a flood of extempore utterances by ministers and laymen. Hymns based upon objective facts of redemption were discarded for others expressive of immediate, personal experience. New and emotional tunes displaced the more vigorous chorales. Operatic arias and sentimental solos supplanted the impersonal polyphonic chorus music of the choir. Orthodoxy, though cold and intellectual, had respected objectivity and preserved formal dignity and reverence. Pietism with its intensely personal limitations neither understood nor long used what remained of the restrained and polished forms of the church's historic liturgical system.

Hans Schubert's judgment is that "German Pietism is certainly to be regarded as an overflow of the Calvinistic spirit into the territory of Lutheranism." The movement which Spener started "towards piety, towards a living religion amongst the people, had the effect of a deliverance and a popular reformation which supplemented and completed the work of Luther on the side of active life. . . . [It] religiously fertilized the whole of Middle and North Germany, and by doing charitable works and beginning the task of foreign missions, showed its love in a broad way and opened up a whole world of duties. Rejected, however, by the leaders of Lutheranism, and brought into the warmest conflict with a dictatorial orthodoxy, it reproduced and developed those slumbering and thinly disguised propensities which so lowered the gospel, a form of duty consisting in avoidance of the world, a subjective exercise of the feelings—the reverse side of the picture being a contempt of learning —an unhealthy practice of probing and schematizing inward experiences, an indifference to the great associations of church and confession, a fanatical cultus of communal life in select circles. In Württemberg alone, where confessional opposition was not nearly so strong, it made a sound alliance with church and theology."[3]

For good summary discussions see Williston Walker, *History of the Christian Church,* and C. M. Jacobs, *The Story of the Church.* For the

[3] Hans Schubert, *Outlines of Church History,* pp. 292ff.

effect of Pietism upon public worship see Heinrich Alt, *Der christliche Cultus* (2. Aufl.; Berlin: Müller, 1851-60); Kliefoth, *Liturgische Abhandlungen;* and particularly the miscroscopic studies of Paul Graff, *Geschichte der Auflösung der alten gottesdienstlichen Formen in der evangelischen Kirche Deutschlands.* An interesting account by Dr. C. W. Schaeffer, "Mühlenberg's Defense of Pietism," written in 1741, the year before he left for America, may be found in the *Lutheran Church Review,* XII (July, 1893), 349-75.

RATIONALISM

One reason for the brevity of Pietism's rule was its lack of intellectual strength. This left the field vacant for a movement generally known as Rationalism and in Germany as the "Enlightenment." The establishment of magazines which discussed literary, philosophical, and theological subjects promoted exchange of thought between scholars in different European countries. Influences of this sort, particularly from England and France, furthered the movement in Germany.

Broadly speaking, Rationalism was a child of the Renaissance, even though it developed late. Its dignification of human nature and its emphasis upon the supremacy of the mind and the freedom of the will marked it as an expression of humanism. Leibnitz and Wolff prepared the way for it in the field of philosophy. Descartes with his critical examination of all knowledge and Bacon with his inductive method laid the foundations for a scientific era. The knowledge of God and the pursuit of virtue which did not require divine revelation but could be attained by rational reflection were regarded as the essentials of religion. Christianity was regarded as superior to other religions because of its greater reasonableness. The church was thought of as without divine authority —more superfluous than evil.

Thus Rationalism sought to derive religious essentials from reason. It opposed supernaturalism and the idea of a positive revelation from God. Authority was the primary question at issue. Supernaturalism found it in revelation, while rationalism found it in reason. Both stressed the intellectual approach as over against Pietism, and Kant endeavored to prove that the two systems were not mutually exclusive but could exist together.

Some features of the movement were constructive. De Wette introduced the historical method in the study of biblical theology, and Mosheim an objective and critical method in church history. The teaching and preaching of the church, however, were soon affected unfavorably. An ideal of happiness was substituted for the divine plan of redemption. Practical interests rather than orthodox doctrines or high spirituality were stressed in the pulpit. The stream of hymnody which had continued to flow through the Pietistic era now dried up completely. Toleration and the practice of virtue in ordinary life and civil service were cherished ideals. Scriptural inspiration was minimized, miracles explained by natural causes, original sin repudiated or defined as a limitation of nature. The moral aspects of the life of our Lord were emphasized and theories of satisfaction and forgiveness rejected. In the matter of justification, Rationalism moved toward Catholicism; on the doctrine of the sacraments it approximated the Reformed. In the theological field its logical development was Unitarianism; in the political field, the French Revolution.

Within the sphere of worship, Rationalism was wholly destructive. Pietism had rejected or neglected many of the ancient forms but had not denied their content. Rationalism rejected content and form alike. The church year with its annual festivals and seasons had no meaning for those who disbelieved the resurrection and other historically recorded facts. The altered views of the Word and sacraments made the liturgy and the great hymns of the church unintelligible. The Service was mutilated beyond recognition. The church building became a mere place of assembly, and the pulpit a lecture platform from which the minister gave moral instructions. The Sacrament was reduced to an empty form and was observed in Reformed fashion four times a year. Influences from Geneva thus allied themselves with the spirit of the age. Lengthy, verbose moralizings replaced the ancient collects and prayers. Hymns were modernized to meet current ideology. Sturdy churchly music was displaced by frivolous compositions which encouraged the exhibition of personal skill.

Permission was granted pastors by the consistory in Hannover and elsewhere to make "alterations and improvements" in the Service after careful consideration and "consultation with the more cultured members of their congregations." Soon a flood of private orders and liturgical forms appeared and supplanted the historic services. Among these were collections by Adler, Seiler, Koester, Gutbier, Sintenis, Zollikofer, Busch, and others. They ranged in character from empty sentimentality to moralizing soliloquy and verbosity.

Christian F. Sintenis, whose sermons display the wordy weakness of the period, issued such an agenda in 1808. In his order for public confession we find the following exhortation:

"Let us do as the Apostles did, and not come to the altar to receive a sacrament, but to bring our sacrament [!] thither," viz., "the obligation to hold fast His teachings, which bring us so much happiness, and always and everywhere to show public spirit, as He did."

His exhortation to communicants is as follows: "At this Table, consecrated to the Lord, let all eat and drink with profoundest emotion! Let this bread and wine typify to you the death of Jesus on the cross . . . . May you be deeply moved by the surpassing greatness and beauty of soul of which this Divine One gave evidence, when for your salvation He permitted His body to be broken and His blood to be shed, and died upon the cross! Come to Him then, as it is natural for good people to do [!], with ardent gratitude . . . ."

His reconstruction of the Lord's Prayer is as follows: "Most High Father; Let it be our supreme purpose to glorify Thee; Let truth thrive among us; Let virtue already dwell here as it does in heaven; Reward our industry with bread; And our forgiving disposition with grace; From severe conflicts preserve us; And finally let all evil cease. That Thou art powerful, wise and good over all—let this forever be our confidence."

A form of distribution of this time was the following: "Eat this bread; may the spirit of devotion rest upon you with all its blessings. Drink a little wine; moral power does not reside in this wine, but in you, in the teachings of God, and in God."

In an Order for Baptism in the agenda of von J. F. Schlez, published as late as 1834, the baptism is followed by a lengthy address from which the following is an extract:

"Water, an element required by the whole of nature, has thus been the emblem of thy Christian consecration, dear child. May the religion of Jesus become the element of thy entire moral life! . . .

"Water is the common property of the rich and the poor, the high and the low. Thus also the religion of Jesus is intended for all: and to thee, dear child, as we hope to God, it will come to purer quality and in larger measure than to countless others. . . .

"Water, the best means for cleansing the body, is the most fitting emblem of soul-purity. May thy heart remain pure and thy life unspotted, thou still innocent angel! . . .

"Water contains great and refreshing potencies for our bodies. Still greater healing-powers for the soul are contained in the genuine Christian belief. May the religion of Jesus prove to thee, dear child, a never-failing source of moral health! . . .

"Water is related to heaven and earth, rises from the latter to the former, and falls down from the former upon the latter. May thy whole life, dear child, be directed toward the higher, heavenly things! Mayest thou often lift thy heart toward heaven and bring down for thyself the heavenly into the earthly! . . .

"Water, so often scorned by those in health, is generally the last physical refreshment of the dying. May the religion of Jesus be and remain throughout thy entire life thy daily refreshment! May it be to thee and to us all a quickening draught in life's sufferings, until we reach that better land, where we shall hunger and thirst no more! Amen."[4]

Rationalism was a possible system of philosophy but an impossible religion. Its weakness was not its intellectuality but its lack of historical

---

[4] Quoted from J. F. Ohl, "The Liturgical Deterioration of the Seventeenth and Eighteenth Centuries," *Memoirs of the Lutheran Liturgical Association,* IV, 75-77.

foundations and its spiritual emptiness. It had nothing in common with the fundamental teachings of Paul, Augustine, or the most eminent of the Reformers. Its constructive value lay largely in driving its opponents to a critical examination of problems of historicity and authority. All conservative thinkers, Lutheran, Calvinistic, and Roman, engaged in a common warfare against it. Claus Harms rallied the supernaturalists by his new Ninety-five Theses. Schleiermacher, though opening up an enlarged view of man's social obligations, insisted upon religion as an absolute and necessary dependence upon God. Romanticism, with its awakening of the historical sense and its appeal to a lofty emotionalism, strengthened the opposition.

In England the Rationalist movement took the form of deism. Here it was overthrown by the combined efforts of Wesleyanism, the Evangelical forces led by Wilberforce, and the later Tractarian movement in the established church.

Considerable space has been given to the destructive influences of the Thirty Years' War, bureaucratic orthodoxy, subjective pietism, and earth-bound rationalism. The cumulative effects of more than two centuries of internal disintegration, with which were allied unfavorable influences from the Reformed tradition, are not generally appreciated. The Lutheran Church was transplanted to America during this time of spiritual and liturgical poverty in Europe. The revival of faith and church life here, as in Europe, has had to make its way against powerful odds. Had these destructive forces not been so strong, so pervasive, or so long continued, the church would be further along today in the recovery of its ancient heritage in worship, church music, and liturgical art of every kind.

MOVEMENTS TOWARD RECOVERY IN GERMANY

At the beginning of the nineteenth century public worship and church life in general were at low ebb throughout Europe. In some respects conditions in Germany were not as bad as in England, in others they were worse. Nuremberg, parts of Saxony, Mecklenburg, and a few other places still retained much of the historic Service with the ancient vestments and customs and with much of the old music sung to Latin texts. But the spirit was gone, and the churches were empty.[5]

In most districts the rich responsive forms had long given place to a bare order conducted by the minister alone. The whole purpose and direction of public worship had been changed. Instead of lifting com-

---

[5] See particularly Max Herold, *Alt-Nürnberg in seinen Gottesdiensten;* Paul Graff, *Geschichte der Auflösung der alten gottesdienstlichen Formen in der evangelischen Kirche Deutschlands.*

mon devotions Godward, the Service was directed manward in the hope of appealing to the minds and emotions of the hearers. Man's ability to achieve moral perfection was exalted above the grace of God. The sacraments and the sacramental idea in worship were minimized and, since the liturgy with its responsive features had collapsed, the congregation had little to do but listen to the sermon and the prayers. Many of the prayers were lengthy and homiletical in character. Hymns, sometimes a series of them, reflecting the spirit of the time, served to introduce the sermon. The historic prayers of the church gave way to new forms breathing the spirit of the age. All of this represented not so much a loss of ancient forms as the destruction of the essential content and spirit of worship. There was no presence to adore, no divine Person with whom to commune, no divine gift to receive. Faith in the Redeemer and the divine plan of salvation had given way to reason. Man by his own efforts attempted to realize ethical standards of conduct and to solve the problems of life. The church was spiritually cold, if not dead. Its ideals were little more than those of ancient paganism in its best estate.

The clarion call of Claus Harms, archdeacon of St. Michael's Church in Kiel, awakened the church. Harms had been won back to faith from a skeptical position after studying Schleiermacher's *Reden über die Religion* (1799). He brooded over Rationalism and indifferentism, and as the date for celebrating the three hundredth anniversary of the Reformation approached in 1817 he conceived the idea of reissuing Luther's Ninety-Five Theses and of publishing with them ninety-five theses of his own. Thus by reminding German Christians of Luther's fight against the errors of the papacy at Rome, he sought to arouse them to the dangers of the "papacy of reason" which ruled the church of his time.

Harms's theses, which were set forth "to the honor of God and the welfare of the church, and in grateful memory of Luther," were fundamental, searching, and powerful. They swept across the country like a whirlwind, awakening support in some quarters and arousing opposition in others. An idea of their general tenor may be gathered from the following extracts.

Thesis 1: When our Master and Lord Jesus Christ says: "Repent," he wills that men shall be conformed to his doctrine, but he does not conform the doctrine to men, as is now done, in accordance with the altered time-spirit [Zeitgeist] (II Tim. 4:3).

Thesis 27: According to the old faith, God created man; according to the new faith, man creates God, and when he has finished him he says Aha! (Isa. 44:12-20).

Thesis 32: The so-called religion of reason is without reason, or without religion, or without both.

Thesis 43: When reason touches religion it casts the pearls away, and plays with the shells, the empty words.

Thesis 71: Reason runs mad in the Lutheran church, tears Christ from the altar, throws God's Word down from the pulpit, casts mud into the baptismal water, mixes all kinds of people in sponsorship, erases the inscription from the confessional, hisses the priests out and all the people after them . . . .

Thesis 78: If at the Colloquy at Marburg, 1529, the body and blood of Christ was in the bread and wine, it is still so in 1817.[6]

A return to the historic type of worship was started by the Prussian king, Frederick William III, in his Agenda of 1822. More than a century before, his predecessor Frederick I had proposed that the liturgy of the Church of England be used by both the Lutheran and Reformed churches throughout his kingdom, a proposal which was not adopted. King Frederick William began his study of liturgical conditions as early as 1798 when he appointed two commissions, one for the Lutheran and another for the Reformed Church. With the general strengthening of the sense of authority in state and church which followed the Napoleonic wars, the king resumed his efforts to end liturgical confusion and the arbitrary individualism of pastors and to improve the bare and inartistic services which prevailed. Eylert was commissioned to prepare a new agenda, but his efforts failed to meet the king's approval. The king said: "You have fallen into the error of all who have written new liturgies and agenda. You have forsaken the historic ground . . . . All the liturgies and agenda which have appeared in our time seem to have been shot out of a pistol . . . . If anything is to come out of this matter at all we must return to Father Luther."[7]

The king studied diligently the orders of the sixteenth century. His advisers were men like Borowsky and Baron Bunsen. He himself now led in the effort to reconstruct Christian worship upon historic foundations and to recover an understanding of the liturgy. His Service for the court church at Potsdam and the garrison church in Berlin, first published in 1816, was revised, and in 1822 introduced in the Dom Kirche in Berlin. It met with criticism and opposition by Schleiermacher and others, but during the next fifteen years it was widely introduced throughout the provines of Prussia. Its connection with the historic liturgy of the church was through the Lutheran orders of the sixteenth century. Briefly, it contained the following elements: Hymn, Invocation, Versicle, Confession of Sins, Declaration of Grace, Gloria Patri (by the choir), Kyrie (choir), Gloria in Excelsis, Salutation and Collect, Epistle,

---

[6] Translated by William A. Lambert in "Theses," in Jacobs and Haas, *The Lutheran Cyclopedia*, pp. 513f. See also *Lutheran Church Review*, XXXV (1916), 357-72.

[7] Rietschel, *Lehrbuch der Liturgik*, I, 448.

Hallelujah, Gospel, Apostles' Creed, Preface, Sanctus, General Prayer, Lord's Prayer, Benediction. The Sermon followed the Creed or the Lord's Prayer.

When communion was held in connection with the Service, the order included: Exhortation, Words of Institution, Pax, a prayer leading up to the distribution, during which the choir sang the Agnus Dei. This was followed by the Post-Communion Collects and the Benediction.

This agenda met criticism chiefly because it was a part of the movement to unite the Lutheran and the Reformed churches throughout Prussia. There were other individual features also, such as the formula of distribution, which were unsatisfactory. When we view it against the liturgical deficiencies of its period, however, we must recognize it as a great step forward and as a strong impulse to the entire movement of liturgical study and reform which now set in.[8]

Outside of Prussia we first note new developments in Bavaria in 1823. Privately prepared services on historic models were issued by Edelmann, Boeckh, and other Munich clergy in 1836. An even earlier writing by Kapp was influential. The most important work, however, was the *Agende für christliche Gemeinden* of Wilhelm Loehe (1844).

Loehe was one of the most forceful Lutheran preachers and leaders of the century. After studies at Erlangen and Berlin he became pastor at Neuendettelsau. His personality was dynamic, yet he was a beloved pastor. Men and women of all classes came to hear him preach and to seek his spiritual counsel. His literary activity was considerable; his work *Drei Bücher von der Kirche* (1845), was particularly important.

Loehe's labors raised the obscure village of Neuendettelsau to world prominence. He founded there a deaconess motherhouse with affiliated homes, hospitals, and educational institutions. Impressed with the need for Lutheran pastors in the midwest American states, he also conducted a theological seminary and trained missionaries for the work. The Iowa Synod was the direct result of the labors of these missionaries, some of whom had also aided in the establishment of the Missouri Synod. In the midst of all these practical activities Loehe's deeply spiritual nature was evident. His agenda, the fruit of much scholarly research as well as spiritual insight, inspired many others. It was brought to America by his students and greatly influenced the liturgical studies of Drs. Krauth, Schmucker, Henry E. Jacobs, and others who prepared the *Church Book* of the General Council and the later Common Service.

The ablest leader in north Germany was Theodor Kliefoth of Meck-

[8] See Edward T. Horn, "Agenda Controversy," in Jacobs and Haas, *The Lutheran Cyclopedia*, p. 5.

lenburg (1810-1895). His *Theorie des Kultus der evangelischen Kirche* (1844); *Die ursprüngliche Gottesdienstordnung in den deutschen Kirchen lutherischen Bekenntnisses* . . . (1847); and *Liturgische Abhandlungen* (1854-61) were works of great erudition. The last-named, in eight volumes, discussed the history of Christian worship with particular reference to the Lutheran church and gave extended comment on the occasional services. With the aid of Otto Kade, the musician, Kliefoth brought out the liturgically rich and sumptuously printed *Cantionale* of the Duchy of Mecklenburg in four folio volumes (1868-87).[9]

Revised liturgies and hymnals appeared in the state churches of Saxony, Hannover, Württemberg, Baden, Brunswick, and other districts. The Eisenach Conference of the German state churches gave attention to details of worship and published a series of lessons, regulations concerning church building, etc. Most of the new liturgies were restorations, with revision, of the sixteenth-century orders in their respective lands. Similar activities were carried out in the Lutheran church in Austria, Bohemia, Poland, Russia, as well as in Denmark, Norway, and Sweden.

This Lutheran liturgical movement in Germany was furthered by an extensive literature. Heinrich Alt, J. W. F. Höfling, H. A. Köstlin, H. A. Daniel, Edward D. Koch, Theodosius Harnack, Philip Wackernagel, J. W. Lyra, Rochus W. von Liliencron wrote exhaustively upon the liturgy, the church year, and the hymns of the Latin and the German churches. In the field of church music there was a real revival. Ludwig Schoeberlein, professor in Heidelberg and later in Göttingen, issued, with the aid of Fr. Riegel, a most important work in three large volumes—*Schatz des liturgischen Chor- und Gemeindegesangs* (1865-72). This explored the musical as well as the liturgical treasures of the church of the sixteenth century and adapted them to modern use. He also established the liturgical monthly *Siona* later edited by Max Herold of Nuremberg. Another liturgical-musical periodical of influence was the *Monatschrift für Gottesdienst und kirchliche Kunst* founded in 1896 by Professors Friedrich Spitta and Julius Smend of the University of Strasbourg. Kraussold had published a *Musicalische Altaragende* as early as 1853. In the field of hymnology, in addition to the great collections by Daniel and the special studies of Fischer, Nelle, etc., Johannes Zahn published his monumental work in six volumes, *Die Melodien der deutschen evangelischen Kirchenlieder* (1889-93). This discussed nearly eight thousand chorale melodies and gave their variant forms. Another important work was the four-volume *Encyklopädie der evangelischen Kirchenmusik* by S. Kümmerle (1888-95).

[9] Kliefoth's work, particularly his establishment of critical standards by which to test and date the different manuscripts of historical texts, influenced the distinguished English scholar, Edmund Bishop, in his investigation of medieval manuscripts in connection with his studies in the history of the Roman missal (Stanley Morison, *English Prayer Books*, pp. 84ff).

Meanwhile Felix Mendelssohn had rediscovered the forgotten works or Johann Sebastian Bach and brought forth the mighty St. Matthew's Passion in 1828, on the one hundredth anniversary of its first performance. The compositions of the sixteenth- and seventeenth-century composers were studied again, and interest in choral music was greatly increased. Bach societies and *Kirchengesangvereine* were founded everywhere. The latter were organized into provincial church music societies in all German-speaking lands, including Switzerland, Austria, Russia, etc., as well as throughout Germany itself. Annual conferences lasting several days were given to the study of the best forms of church music and the works of important composers and choirs. Standards were advanced, works of artistic merit and churchly character promoted, and the entire church life quickened by this liturgical and musical revival.

This summary account should include some reference to the work of the last few decades in this field. The beginning of the twentieth century saw the appearance of the fine two-volume *Lehrbuch der Liturgik* by Professor Georg Rietschel of the University of Leipzig. This work organized the material brought to light by earlier scholars, and is still outstanding, though limited by the viewpoint from which it was written, viz., that of the state churches of Europe. Professor Emil Sehling of Erlangen published five volumes of *Die evangelischen Kirchenordnungen des XVI. Jahrhunderts* (more accurate and complete than Richter's) before the first world war interrupted the work, which has only recently been resumed. Professor Paul Drews explored the important field of German collect literature (carried much farther by the researches of Professor Paul Althaus of Erlangen) and advanced theories concerning the early history of the Canon of the Mass which Roman scholars accept as important. Dr. Hans Lietzmann published his critically edited reprints of classical liturgical texts, sixteenth-century orders, etc. The ecumenically minded works of Professor Friedrich Heiler (*Prayer, The Spirit of Worship*, etc.) and the special studies of Leonhard Fendt (*Der lutherische Gottesdienst des 16. Jahrhunderts*, etc.) were also important.

LITURGICAL REVIVAL IN ENGLAND

The so-called Oxford Movement in England was part of the general nineteenth-century revival of church life and worship. This revival, like the Reformation in the sixteenth century, entered England several decades after its beginnings in Germany. The Lutheran church in America is deeply indebted to developments in both countries. The revival in Germany has influenced us directly through our common faith. The revival in England has influenced us through our common language, literature, and art.

Conditions in England at the beginning of the nineteenth century were little if any better than in Germany. The established church had not lost its Prayer Book, except during the sixteen-year reign of the Commonwealth. It had never known anything comparable to the beggarly forms, privately prepared, which had flooded the church in Germany. Its Prayer Book services, however, were frequently abbreviated and more often slovenly performed. Exceptions to this were to be found chiefly in the cathedral foundations which generally maintained some sort of liturgical and musical tradition even in an age of religious indifference and neglect.

It is easy to recount the evils of the time. In general the ideology of the French Revolution and of English deism had broken down the old church tradition. The historic parliamentary structure of the nation had been altered by the liberal program of political reform. The relation of church and state had profoundly changed. The spirit of secular politics had entered the sphere of the established church, and reforming politicians were undertaking to legislate for the established church. Churchmen themselves were divided in council. The Evangelicals lacked intellectual power. The High Churchmen maintained some traditions, but rather from a sense of duty than from a sense of vocation. The liberals were indifferent to creed and liturgy alike, and were willing to recognize Nonconformity on the one hand and to accept the rule of the state on the other.

There were many abuses beyond the mutilation of the services, the deplorable conditions of church buildings, and the small percentage of communicants. Bishops received enormous salaries while curates lived in poverty. The revenues of the Archbishop of Canterbury were in excess of $150,000 a year; the Bishop of Durham received $100,000. Influential clergy frequently held as many as a dozen benefices at one time. The Black Book published in 1820 by the Church Reform party showed that of twenty-seven bishoprics eleven were held by members of noble families, and fourteen by men connected in one way or another with royal or noble houses. Youths of favored families were provided with church livings up to $50,000 a year, and this in a day of extremely low prices and wages. They delegated their duties to curates at two or three pounds a week. In 1811 it was stated that there were 3,611 non-resident incumbents. Pluralism—the holding of several offices, including several parishes, at one time—was prevalent. The parish clergy took over civil duties to eke out an existence. Thus emerged the figure of the "squarson," a combination of squire and parson whose secular duties during the week considerably overbalanced his spiritual activities on Sunday.

Mr. Gladstone, speaking in Parliament on the Public Worship Regulation Act in July, 1874, said: "I wish every man in this House was as old as I am—for the purpose of knowing what was the condition of the Church of England forty to fifty years ago. At that time it was the scandal of Christendom. Its congregations were the most cold, dead, and irreverent; its music was offensive to anyone with a respect for the House of God, its clergy, with exceptions, somewhat numerous, chiefly, though not exclusively, belonging to what was then called the Evangelical School—its clergy with that exception were in numbers I should not like to mention worldly-minded men, not conforming by their practice to the standard of their high office, seeking to accumulate preferments with a reckless indifference, and careless of the cure of the souls of the people committed to their charge, and upon the whole declining in moral influence. This is the state of things from which we have escaped."[10]

In spite of all this there was a spiritual vitality beneath the surface. The activities of the Wesleys, George Whitefield, and others after the middle of the eighteenth century had profoundly stirred Christian forces in Britain and softened the full effect of the French Revolution upon English society. Though John Wesley had asserted in 1787, four years before his death, that "when the Methodists leave the Church of England, God will leave them," he had laid foundations for a new church body by allowing laymen to administer the Sacrament and by his own ordinations. The hostility of the established church finally made the new organization inevitable.

The earnestness of the Nonconformists was matched by an evangelical group within the established church—John Newton, William Wilberforce, Henry Thornton Scott, and others. This common revival of Christian spirit and endeavor set notable reforms in motion a generation before the Oxford Movement was inaugurated. The Sunday school experiment had been launched by Robert Raikes at Gloucester in 1780. The slave trade had been abolished in 1807 and slavery itself in 1833. The Church Missionary Society was founded in 1799 and the British and Foreign Bible Society in 1804. Prison reforms were inaugurated. The Christian point of view was asserting itself again in Britain.

Within the established church a crisis was reached when Earl Grey's reform ministry introduced a bill in Parliament in 1833 suppressing ten bishoprics and two archbishoprics in England. The challenge was met by John Keble, a gifted and deeply spiritual country parson who was also professor of poetry at Oxford. His book of devotional verse, *The Christian Year,* had been published in 1827 and went through 158 printings in the next four decades. In a sermon of July 14, 1833, in the University pulpit at Oxford, Keble denounced the "national apostasy" of the English state in withholding support from the established church and encroaching upon that church's own field of administration and discipline. The instant response testified to the substantial body of Christian thought in the country. Seven thousand clergy, and later 23,000 heads of families, addressed the Archbishop of Canterbury professing their loyalty to the doctrine and discipline of the church. Richard Hurrell Froude, William Palmer, John Henry Newman, and Edward B. Pusey, professor of history at Oxford, stepped to the side of Keble and became leaders in a movement which stirred the church and the country to the depths. At Newman's suggestion a series of "Tracts for the Times"

---

[10] Quoted in N. P. Williams and Charles Harris, *Northern Catholicism (Centenary Studies in the Oxford and Parallel Movements* [London: S.P.C.K., 1933]), p. 1.

was issued, and his own vigorous, deeply spiritual preaching kindled many minds. Ninety "Tracts" appeared between 1833 and 1841.

These early leaders of the so-called Oxford Movement did more than arouse the church to recognition of abuses and the necessity for action. They exalted the divine nature of the church, the sacramental means of grace, and the importance of historic continuity and church tradition as over against the *Zeitgeist* which dominated Protestantism at the time. Their doctrinal and historic studies led the movement into higher appreciation of the episcopal office and recognition of unique values in corporate worship. There was a great revival of church life. Ancient church buildings were restored; new edifices were erected, particularly in the cities and industrial centers; daily services and frequent communions were encouraged and earnest efforts made to relieve the spiritual destitution of slum districts and to care for the aged and neglected.

Keble's *Christian Year* brought Anglican piety into immediate contact with the broad movement of Romanticism. Even closer connections, through Wordsworth and others, awakened immediate interest in the medieval backgrounds of the liturgy and in church architecture. The Cambridge-Camden Society, founded in 1839, became the Ecclesiological Society in 1845, and for nearly twenty-five years more, with the aid of John Mason Neale and many others, promoted studies in historic types of church buildings and furnishings, ceremonial, etc. There was a great revival of Gothic architecture and of stained glass, embroidery, and other ecclesiastical arts and crafts.

Hymnology received its greatest impulse since the days of the Reformation. Some of the finest hymns and translations of any age in the church's history were produced. *Hymns Ancient and Modern* (1861) opened a new era in hymnbook making. Church music in all its forms—plain song, choral music, hymn tunes, etc.—received extensive cultivation and enrichment. In the field of painting William Dyce and Holman Hunt were strongly influenced by the movement, as were Christina Rossetti and Charlotte Yonge in the field of literature. Among architects the names of John N. Pearson, Sir Charles Barry, A. W. N. Pugin, Sir Gilbert Scott, G. F. Bodley, John Bentley, J. D. Sedding, and Sir Giles Gilbert Scott are particularly to be remembered. Incredible wealth and endeavor went into the restoration of churches and cathedrals; the installation of beautifully appointed altars; church furniture, organs, etc.; the establishment of choirs and choir schools upon solid foundations; and the publication of an extensive literature.

Many of these achievements were at least under way by October 9, 1845, when Newman, wearied with controversy and hoping to find spiritual peace under an authority and catholicity which he felt the Anglican church could not supply, knelt before the Passionist Father Dominic and made his obedience to Rome—that Rome which during his travels in Italy in 1832 he had characterized as "polytheistic, disgusting, idolatrous." Ward, Oakley, and Faber preceded him and Manning and others followed him into the Roman communion. Thus the Church of England, which in the preceding century had lost some of its finest spirits to Nonconformity, was now depleted by the defection of a large and spiritually minded group to Rome.

The early leaders of the Oxford Movement—the Tractarians—were reformers concerned with fundamentals. The later leaders—the Ritualists —were generally men of lesser mold and perhaps may be thought of as decorators. Keble and his early associates were not interested in ritualistic practices. One has but to visit Keble's parish church at Hursley to see how simple are its appointments even at the present day. Newman did not have even a cross upon his altar, and he celebrated the Holy Communion standing at the north end of the communion table. After 1872, the progress of the movement was embittered by ritualistic controversies with resulting suits, imprisonments, etc. Such matters as vestments, lights, and incense, the mixed chalice, eastward position, and similar details were projected into the foreground and the unity of the church was seriously threatened. The movement is now in its third phase, the Tractarians and the Ritualists having been succeeded by the Anglo-Catholics.

While extremists have gone to indefensible lengths, the Oxford Movement as a whole restored to the Anglican church the general type and spirit of worship which both the Lutheran and the Anglican churches had known in the sixteenth century. Churchly standards and taste were elevated by a program whose influence eventually reached to all other Christian groups in the English-speaking world. Thus the distinguished Congregationalist, Principal Fairbairn of Mansfield College, says: "Its ideal of worship has modified the practice of all the churches, even of those most hostile to its ideal of Religion. The religious spirit of England is, in all its sections and varieties, sweeter today than it was forty years ago, more open to the ministeries of art and the graciousness of order, possessed of a larger sense of 'the community of the saints,' the kinship and continuity of the Christian society in all ages. Even Scotland has been touched with a strange softness, Presbyterian worship has grown less bald, organs and liturgies have found a home in the land and church of Knox."[11]

Thus in their own very different ways the early Wesleyan and Evangelical revival and the later Oxford revival quickened Christianity in Britain and throughout the English-speaking world. Between them these

---

[11] A. M. Fairbairn, *Catholicism Roman and Anglican*, p. 73.

several movements lifted the church to new levels of thought and action. Religion was vitalized, not only emotionally and experimentally, but also intellectually and institutionally. The Lutheran church in America, with theological foundations solidly in continental Europe, has been aided greatly in its devotional and practical life by the comprehensive and sustained liturgical movement within the established Church of England in the nineteenth century.

A few of the most important published works of the period should be mentioned. William Palmer's *Origines Liturgicae* of 1832 led the way. Charles Wheatly's *A Rational Illustration of the Book of Common Prayer* and Matthew Hole's four-volume work, *Practical Discourses on the Liturgy,* followed in 1837. After these came Philip Freeman's *The Principles of Divine Service,* Dean E. M. Goulburn's *The Collects of the Day,* and Edward Burbidge's *Liturgies and Offies of the Church,* to mention but a few. John Mason Neale's translations of Eastern liturgies and of Greek and Latin hymns were important. Later followed critical editions of the ancient sacramentaries by H. A. Wilson and C. A. Feltoe; the scholarly works of F. E. Brightman (*Liturgies Eastern and Western, The English Rite,* etc.); W. H. Frere's authoritative *New History of the Book of Common Prayer* (1901), based on the 1855 work of Francis Procter; John Dowden's interesting studies; J. Wickham Legg's *The Sarum Missal* (1916); and *The Prayer Book Dictionary,* by G. Harford, Morley Stevenson, and J. W. Tyrer; Julian's *Dictionary of Hymnology* (1891); *Liturgy and Worship* by W. K. Lowther Clarke and Charles Harris; Dean Church, *The Oxford Movement, Twelve Years, 1833-1845;* Brilioth, *The Anglican Revival;* Williams and Harris, *Northern Catholicism.*

CHAPTER VIII

EARLY AMERICAN LITURGIES

The earliest Lutherans in America were Hollanders and Swedes. Some of the former came to North America with the early settlers in 1623 and 1625, settling in the Dutch colonies on the Hudson. A clergyman was sent from Holland to New Amsterdam in 1657 to minister to the Lutherans there. He met with such opposition from the Dutch Reformed that he was compelled to return after two years. Religious tolerance came with English control in 1664. The Lutherans along the Hudson from Long Island to Albany, however, received only indifferent pastoral care until Justus Falckner, the first Lutheran minister ordained in America (1703), began his ministry among them.

Swedish settlements in Delaware and Pennsylvania date from 1638. Campanius built the first Lutheran church in America on Tinicum Island, nine miles southwest of Philadelphia, in 1646. When the Swedish Lutherans dedicated their Gloria Dei Church in Philadelphia in 1700, it was the largest and finest church building in the city. About this same date there was a German congregation at New Hanover (Falckner's Swamp). Other congregations were organized at Germantown (1728), Trappe (1730), and elsewhere.

In 1734, one year after the founding of Georgia, fifty Lutheran families settled the town of Ebenezer near Savannah. They were part of the twenty thousand or more Lutherans who had been expelled from Salzburg in Austria by the Roman archbishop of that province. The English people provided transportation as part of General Oglethorpe's plan for the establishment of his new colony.

PIONEER CONDITIONS

The Lutheran communities in the New World were scattered over a wide and sparsely settled territory. Their numbers were greatly increased by the German immigration of the first half of the eighteenth century.

Conditions at that time in Württemberg, the Rhineland, and the valley of the Neckar were deplorable. Incessant wars ravaged the country. The inhabitants listened eagerly to William Penn who, on his three visits to the Palatinate, spoke fluently in their own language concerning his colony and held out the promise of civil and religious liberty. Queen Anne's liberal policy aided thousands who decided to seek a new home. Most of these immigrants finally reached America by way of Rotterdam and London. In the year 1709 no less than 13,500 Palatines arrived in London alone.[1]

Conditions were still primitive in Pennsylvania, the center of this immigration. Lancaster, founded in 1728, had less than one thousand inhabitants in 1742. Lebanon was laid out in 1740, and the sons of William Penn surveyed Reading in 1748. Philadelphia at this time was a substantially built, poorly paved trading town of less than 15,000. In 1752 the entire colony had less than 200,000 souls, of whom at least 90,000 were Germans. These included Reformed as well as Lutheran, along with many sectarian groups—Mennonites, Schwenkfelders, Moravians, etc. The Lutherans had built a few churches but were without general organization or oversight. There was dissension in the congregations and the people were constantly imposed upon by irregulars who claimed to be ordained ministers. The presence on the field of the Moravian Count Zinzendorf added to the confusion.

To meet these conditions the three congregations at Philadelphia, New Hanover, and Trappe united in sending a commission to the Lutheran church authorities in London and Halle asking that a pastor be sent to America to take charge of the situation. In long-delayed response Henry Melchior Muhlenberg, a graduate of Göttingen University, thirty-one years of age, was sent out by Dr. Francke of Halle and Dr. Ziegenhagen of London to labor among the scattered Lutherans in Pennsylvania and the other colonies.

Muhlenberg, after a visit in London, arrived in Charleston September 23, 1742. He spent a week with the Salzburgers and then left for Philadelphia, where he arrived November 25. His authority was promptly recognized by the German-speaking churches and the Swedish pastors co-operated with him to the fullest extent. His advent marked a new era. He spent most of his life in Philadelphia and Trappe. His travels, however, extended from northern New York to Georgia, and his correspondence and influence reached throughout the colonies and to Nova Scotia. He married the daughter of Conrad Weiser, the colonial Indian agent, and his three sons became dis-

---

[1] The generosity of the English people and the difficulties encountered in caring for the wholly unexpected number of immigrants are described by Walter Allen Knittle, *Early Eighteenth Century Palatine Emigration* (Philadelphia: Dorrance, 1937), pp. 65ff.

tinguished leaders in public life. He was a man of spiritual power and apostolic zeal, indefatigable energy, and unusual gifts of administration. Six years after his arrival he organized the Ministerium of Pennsylvania, the first Lutheran synod in America. For this he had no models in Germany. The synod, however, became a model for similar organizations in the New World. In character and achievements Muhlenberg well deserves the title, Patriarch of the Lutheran Church in America.

The name Muhlenberg is one of the most highly honored in the early history of our nation. By the beginning of the Revolutionary War the German population constituted one-third of the total in the colonies. Muhlenberg and his sons were personal acquaintances of Washington, Franklin, and other leaders. Their influence in holding the German elements in Pennsylvania, New York, New Jersey, Maryland, and Virginia loyal to the colonies and their later programs of ratification of the Constitution were most important. Muhlenberg himself was honored with the degree of Doctor of Divinity by the University of Pennsylvania. John Peter Gabriel, while pastor of the Lutheran church at Woodstock, Virginia, was the close friend of George Washington, Patrick Henry, and Richard Henry Lee. He answered the call to arms, recruited a regiment, and later became one of Washington's ablest and most trusted generals. Frederick Augustus responded to the call of the German element to represent it and become a member of the Continental Congress and eventually the first Speaker of the national House of Representatives. Henry Ernst remained in the ministry. He was pastor of Trinity Church, Lancaster, the first president of Franklin College, and one of the most eminent of early American botanists.

The important and scholarly work in three volumes, *The Journals of Henry Melchior Muhlenberg,* edited and translated by Theodore G. Tappert and John W. Doberstein (Philadelphia: Muhlenberg, 1942-57), gives the fullest information concerning the life, work, and times of the patriarch. The original manuscripts upon which their work is based are mostly in the archives of the Ministerium of Pennsylvania in the library of the Lutheran Theological Seminary, Mt. Airy, Philadelphia. A few are in the archives of the Francke Institutions at Halle, and microfilm copies of most of these are in the Library of Congress at Washington. More limited accounts are given in William J. Mann, *Life and Times of Henry Melchior Muhlenberg.* (2nd ed.; Philadelphia: Frederick, 1888), and William Keller Frick, *Henry Melchior Muhlenberg* (Philadelphia: Lutheran Publication Society, 1902). The *Nachrichten,* edited by Drs. Mann and B. M. Schmucker and W. Germann (Philadelphia, 1886-95), give material from Muhlenberg's reports to the authorities at Halle.

FIRST AMERICAN LUTHERAN LITURGY

When we remember Muhlenberg's association with the Pietists at Halle and the fact that he labored in America under primitive conditions with groups on the frontiers of civilization, it is astonishing that he should have concerned himself greatly about the preparation of a liturgy. His sense of historical and devotional values, his appreciation of church order, and his statesmanlike insight led him there almost at once.

His diaries, correspondence, and catechetical methods all indicate Pietistic strains and influences. His substantial personal endowment of intellect and character, however, lifted him to levels of appreciation and achievement far above the average. The influence of his early home environment was also a steadying factor. His native Hanover, and Saxony where he had lived, were still very conservative, and their church life for the most part preserved the traditional character of early Lutheranism. Halle was less than twenty miles from Leipzig. While Muhlenberg was a schoolmaster in Halle and for almost a decade after he came to America, Johann Sebastian Bach in Leipzig continued to exemplify the Lutheran church year and to proclaim with unexampled force and beauty the typical Lutheran doctrines of sin and grace and personal communion with Christ in a golden flood of cantatas, Passions, and compositions for the organ.

While planning for the organization of the Ministerium of Pennsylvania, Muhlenberg, with the aid of his assistants Brunnholz and Handschuh, prepared the liturgy which was adopted by the Ministerium at its first convention in 1748. Much later he aided in the selection of hymns for the hymnal of 1786 and wrote the preface. He constantly expressed the hope that the day would come when all Lutheran congregations in America would be united and use the same liturgy and hymnal. The organization of the United Lutheran Church by the union of the synods which had developed upon the foundations he had laid and the adoption of the *Common Service Book* were at least a partial realization of Muhlenberg's ideas. The adoption of the Common Liturgy by a much larger proportion of American Lutheranism, and recent efforts toward the consolidation of synods and general bodies, bring us even closer to the goal.

The first American Lutheran liturgy is important not only because of its early date but because of its character and influence. Muhlenberg's manuscript *Journal* under the date of April 28, 1748, has the following entry:

> April 28. We consulted together in Providence with regard to a suitable liturgy [*Agende*] which we could introduce for use in our congregations. True, we had been using a small formulary heretofore, but had nothing definite and harmonious in all its parts, since we had thought it best to wait for the arrival of more laborers and also until we had acquired a better knowledge of conditions in this country. To adopt the Swedish liturgy did not appear either suitable or necessary since most of our congregations came from the districts on the Rhine and the Main and considered the singing of collects to be papistical. Nor yet could we select a liturgy with regard to every individual's accustomed use, since

almost every country town and village has its own. We therefore took the liturgy of the Savoy Church in London as the basis, cut out parts and added to it according to what seemed to us to be profitable and edifying in these circumstances. This we adopted tentatively until we had a better understanding of the matter in order that the same ceremonies, forms, and words might be used in all our congregations. But, notwithstanding this, Pastors Wagner, Stöver, and other contrary-minded men took occasion to instigate some simple-hearted people against us under the pretext that we ought to introduce the liturgy of Württemberg or of Zweibrücken, and they also tried to make the people believe that we intended to lead them away from Lutheran doctrine and church order, etc., etc. For example: We thought of using at the distribution of the consecrated bread and wine the words of the Lord Jesus: "Take and eat, this is the body of Jesus Christ," etc.; "Take and drink, this cup is the new testament in the blood of Jesus Christ," etc. At the Baptism of children we intended to ask the sponsors or godparents: "Do you in the name of this child renounce," etc.? On these points our opponents tried to stir up agitation even before we had finished our work. We consequently made the changes at once and put in the words which the troubled consciences wanted, saying, "This is the true body," etc., "This is the true blood," etc., and in the forms of Baptism, "Peter, Paul, or Mary, dost thou renounce," etc.?[2]

Sunday, August 14, 1748, the pastors and delegates from nine congregations in the colony assisted at the dedication of St. Michael's Church, Philadelphia, and the ordination of the catechist, J. N. Kurtz. The next day, August 15, the synod was organized by six pastors, twenty-four lay delegates, and a further group of laymen from Philadelphia. The pastors, in addition to Muhlenberg and the Swedish provost Sandin, included Brunnholz, Handschuh, Hartwig, and Kurtz. The lay delegates, including one Swedish layman, represented congregations in Philadelphia, Germantown, Providence, New Hanover, Upper Milford, Lancaster, Tulpehocken, and Saccum.

Among other matters this first convention of the Ministerium ratified the liturgy which had been prepared and already introduced in some congregations. It resolved to use it and no other forms in every congregation, though the fear was expressed by one delegate that "during the cold winter days the service might be somewhat too long."

The first American Lutheran liturgy was the only one authorized for nearly forty years. It was never printed, but was circulated in possibly forty manuscript copies. It was to be strictly adhered to in the interest of good order and uniformity. Every candidate for ordination and every minister received into the synod promised to introduce no

[2] Theodore G. Tappert and John W. Doberstein (eds.), *The Journals of Henry Melchior Muhlenberg*, I, 193.

formulary or ceremonies in public worship and administration of the sacraments other than those prescribed by the *Collegium Pastorum*. Thus the first synod in America at its first meeting pledged its pastors and congregations to a form of the historic Lutheran liturgy, as its first constitution thirty years later accepted the church's historic Confessions.

SOURCES AND CONTENT

Muhlenberg recorded in his diary, and in a letter to the Halle authorities, that in preparing this liturgy the printed church order of the German Lutheran congregation (St. Mary's) in the Savoy district in the Strand, London, had been used as a basis "because we had no other one at hand." This congregation had been established in 1692 and had adopted a liturgy prepared by translation and adaptation from the liturgy of the Lutheran churches in Holland, the so-called Antwerp Agenda of 1567.

Dr. Beale M. Schmucker, after an exhaustive study of the Muhlenberg liturgy and comparison with the Service of the Savoy congregation in London, was positive that "the London Agenda is to a very small extent the original source of the Pennsylvania Liturgy." He believed that while this London Agenda was "the only printed one at hand," Muhlenberg and Brunnholz reproduced from memory much of the material in the liturgies with which they had been familiar in Europe, specifically Lüneburg (1643); Calenberg (1569); Brandenburg (1739); Saxony (1712).

These were all typical Lutheran orders of the purest type which had been changed but little since the Reformation. Melanchthon, Bugenhagen, Jonas, Myconius, Spalatin, Chemnitz, and John Arndt had assisted in their preparation or later revision. They all provided two forms of the communion service, one a complete form for use in cities and whenever there was a capable choir, the other a simpler service for use in towns and villages.

Dr. Schmucker's comparative study of these agenda shows that they are practically the same in outline and content and that the Muhlenberg liturgy is in almost complete agreement with them. The only changes noted are the Confession of Sins, the place for announcements and the collection of alms, the Votum, the Invitation to Communion, and the use of the trinitarian formula "In the Name of the Father, and of the Son," etc. following the Aaronic benediction.

The Muhlenberg Liturgy in parts was little more than an outline. It lacked complete texts of the Collects, Epistles, and Gospels. The pastors were directed to use these *propria* as given in the Marburg hymnal which, in various European editions, was widely used by the Germans throughout the colonies. Christopher Sauer printed an American edition in Germantown in 1762. The hymnal contained the historic Gospels and Epistles of the church year and the series of Collects published by Veit Dietrich in his Nuremberg *Agend-büchlein* (1543).

The liturgy in general represented the historic, conservative type of service found in the Saxon, north German, and Scandinavian Lutheran churches. It contained five chapters: I, The Order of Public Worship; II, Baptism; III, Marriage; IV, Confession and the Lord's Supper; V, Burial. The order of regular services and Holy Communion was:

A hymn of invocation of the Holy Spirit.

Confession of Sins—Exhortation, Confession, Kyrie (farsed). The text of the Confession is taken in part from the Calenberg Order. A public confession at this place in the Service, however, is not found in any of the four agenda nor in the London Service. Saxony and Calenberg give a similar confession after the sermon before the general prayer.

There is precedent for a public confession at this place in the early Nuremberg and Strasbourg services, Sweden (1531), Mecklenburg (1552) (revised by Melanchthon), Wittenberg (1559), etc. Brunnholz may also have been familiar with the Confession in this place in the Schleswig-Holstein Order of 1542 and later editions. It is also possible that Muhlenberg was familiar with the Confession at the beginning of Morning Prayer in the English Prayer Book and that this led him to introduce it at this point.

Gloria in Excelsis, in metrical form.

Collect—Salutation and Response with Collect for the Day from the Marburg book.

Epistle for the Day (from the Marburg hymnbook).

Hymn. The insertion of the principal hymn at this place was a Reformation substitute for the Gradual.

Gospel for the Day.

Nicene Creed. In Luther's metrical version, *Wir glauben all an Einen Gott*. The Gospel and Creed were to be omitted if there were baptisms in the service.

Hymn.

Sermon. The Gospel which formed the text for the sermon was read a second time, the people standing.

The General Prayer, with special intercessions. "Nothing else shall be read than the appointed church-prayer, or the Litany instead of it, by way of change; and nothing but necessity shall occasion its omission."

The prayer concluded with the Lord's Prayer.

Announcements.

Votum: "The peace of God which passeth all understanding," etc.

Hymn.

Salutation, responses, and closing collect.

Aaronic benediction, and the invocation: "In the Name of the Father," etc.

The Holy Communion was definitely appointed for Christmas, Easter, and Pentecost. When the Sacrament was administered the order was as follows:

> Preface—Salutation and response; Sursum Corda; abbreviated Sanctus.
> Exhortation: Luther's form from the *Deutsche Messe* (1526) beginning with a paraphrase of the Lord's Prayer.
> The Lord's Prayer.
> Words of Institution.
> Invitation to communion (a form taken from the London Liturgy).
> Distribution.
> Versicle and Thanksgiving Collect (Luther's).
> Old Testament Benediction followed by: "In the Name of the Father," etc.

The unusual use at this place of the trinitarian invocation, Dr. Schmucker regarded as "without warrant either of use or of fitness." It is a characteristic feature, however, of the Swedish Liturgy, and Muhlenberg undoubtedly introduced it from this source, as did the framers of the Common Liturgy.

> Dr. B. M. Schmucker collated two manuscript copies of the first American liturgy. One of these was made by Jacob Van Buskirk in 1763, and has the sections numbered with titles and rubrics in full. The other copy was made by Peter Muhlenberg in 1769. Dr. Schmucker's analysis of this liturgy with comparative study of the London Service and the four German church orders, which he suggests as printed sources of the Muhlenberg Liturgy, are given in two articles in *The Lutheran Church Review* under the heading, "The First Pennsylvania Liturgy" (I [1882], 16-27 and 161-72). An English translation of the liturgy by Dr. C. W. Schaeffer is given in Henry E. Jacobs, *A History of the Evangelical Lutheran Church in the United States,* pp. 269ff.

In addition to the German texts for the Service and the Holy Communion, English forms for baptism and marriage were included in the manuscript copies of this first American liturgy. These were taken from the Book of Common Prayer.

Comparison with the Common Liturgy shows how close is the agreement in parts and arrangement between the present Service and the one of 1748. The chief differences are the use in the Muhlenberg Service of the collects of Veit Dietrich, the omission of the Introit, the combining of the Kyrie with the confession, the use of a metrical Gloria in Excelsis and a metrical Creed, a shortened form of the Sanctus, and the lack of a Eucharistic Prayer.

This first American liturgy, therefore, was the historic Lutheran order with minor features which show Muhlenberg's own taste and judgment.

Our appraisal of it must take account of the conditions under which it was prepared. The church got its start in this country during a period of low vitality in Europe. It was established here by ministers and laymen who knew only subnormal conditions in the homeland. The circumstances of the people limited public worship to the simplest essentials. The strongest Lutheran settlements were made in soil thoroughly uncongenial to liturgical worship—among the Quakers and Pietistic sectarians of Pennsylvania and the Dutch Reformed of New York. The steadfastness of Muhlenberg and his associates in preparing and upholding a very creditable liturgy under such circumstances is remarkable.

It would have been a blessing if this liturgy could have remained in use. Later departures from it introduced confusion and weakness. The first definite program of anglicization was colored by Calvinistic and other nonliturgical influences from the dominant English-speaking groups on the territory. The privations and poverty of pioneer days and the influences of these relatively stronger communions fastened mixed and impure practices upon Lutheran congregations. The already weak liturgical tradition was further diluted. The church was confused in practice as well as doctrine, and the abnormal came to be thought of as the normal. The *Church Book* of the General Council, the Common Service, and the *Common Service Book* marked successive steps in the effort to return to the historic Lutheran Liturgy as represented quite fully by the Muhlenberg Service and more completely by the church orders of the sixteenth century. Careful, scholarly work of this character, though often imitative rather than creative, laid the solid foundations upon which the Common Liturgy of today is built.

OTHER EARLY LITURGIES

Liturgical development is always closely connected with doctrinal development. The four decades after the adoption by the Ministerium of its first liturgy witnessed great changes in theological thinking in the Old World and the expansion of religious bodies in the new. The deteriorating influences of rationalism described in a previous chapter were repeated, after an interval, in America. The leaders were conscious of something they could not check. Helmuth, then a man of forty, voiced his concern in a letter to Muhlenberg. The latter replied that conditions must drive the faithful to prayer, but that truth would ultimately prevail.[3] As doctrinal definiteness declined, the expression of Lutheran principles in worship was clouded. The thought of possible

[3] Original in the archives of the Ministerium at Mt. Airy, Philadelphia, dated September 29, 1785.

union with other religious bodies also gained ground—with the Episcopalians in New York and with the Reformed in Pennsylvania. All this was reflected in the liturgy which the Ministerium at its thirty-fifth convention in 1782 resolved to print.

The only addition proposed was the confirmation formula from the Württemberg Church Order. It was also decided to publish a new hymnbook to supplant the Marburg book. In addition to Dr. Muhlenberg, Kunze, Helmuth, and Dr. Muhlenberg's son were appointed a committee. It was resolved not to omit any of the old standard hymns, especially those by Luther and Gerhardt. The Gospels and Epistles for apostles' days, etc., however, and the catechism were to be omitted. Dr. Helmuth was to prepare a series of new prayers. In 1785 Mr. Schmidt was added to the committee authorized to "make some changes in the *Agende.*"[4]

The liturgy and hymnbook which appeared from the press in 1786 contained fifty-eight pages. The rubrics directing the minister to face the altar or the people respectively were omitted, as were the Gloria in Excelsis, the Collect for the Day, and the Creed. One of Dr. Helmuth's prayers was substituted for the Collect, with permission also for a prayer by the minister *aus dem Herzen.* A lengthy General Prayer was substituted for the earlier form. There were minute directions for instruction and confirmation, with highly emotional emphasis. There also were many changes in the content and character of the hymnal. The omission of the catechism, the Gospels, Epistles, and Collects was evidently regretted by many and an appendix (*Anhang*) printed by Billmeyer in Germantown in 1790 included this material, which was reintroduced into the 1795 edition of the *Kirchen-Agende.*

The next liturgy, a German *Liturgie oder Kirchen Agende,* published in Baltimore in 1818, marked a further decline. A committee appointed in 1817 had failed to function, but the agenda was finally prepared by a few interested pastors and authorized by the synod. In this scarcely a trace of responsive service remained. There was a confession of sins with a prayer ending with the Kyrie as a substitute for the Absolution. This led immediately to the Salutation, the reading of "the Gospel, Epistle, or any other suitable selection from the Scriptures," a hymn, sermon, General Prayer, closing verse, and Benediction. An alternate form of service, though very sketchy, seems to have been built on the Matin order, with use of the opening versicles, part of the Venite, etc.

---

[4] A. Spaeth, H. E. Jacobs, and G. F. Spieker (eds.), *Documentary History of the Evangelical Lutheran Ministerium of Pennsylvania and Adjacent States* (1898), pp. 183, 196, 200, 205. The title of the book which appeared in 1786 was *Kirchen-Agende der evangelisch-lutherischen vereinigten Gemeinen in Nord-America.*

There were three different forms for the administration of the Lord's Supper, including the objectionable one, "Jesus says, take, eat, etc." Candidates for ordination were not required to subscribe to the Lutheran Confessions.

This agenda was accompanied by a hymnal prepared for joint use by the Lutheran and the Reformed congregations with the hope of "breaking down the partition wall between the Lutherans and the Reformed which is only based on prejudice." The incapacity of the editors was revealed not only in the omission of the classic hymns of the church and the insertion of weak and frivolous hymns, but also in frequent errors in crediting authorship, etc. Only one of Luther's hymns was included and eleven by Gerhardt, while Gellert, leading writer of the Rationalistic period, was represented by forty. It should be gratefully noted that sixteen years later a committee of the General Synod— J. G. Schmucker, F. Heyer, A. Lochmann—brought out a hymnal published at Gettysburg in 1834 which restored many of the fine old hymns and was a vast improvement upon the book of 1818.

In the early decades of the nineteenth century the liturgy was thought of simply as a minor feature of the hymnal. Dr. F. H. Quitman appended one to the New York Synod hymnbook of 1814. This English liturgy, in the preparation of which the Ministerium of Pennsylvania had no part whatever, was recommended for use by the Ministerium in 1835. Rationalistic tendencies were evident throughout the book. The Ministerium turned to it presumably as a help in its English work. Both the liturgy and the hymnal were a sorry deterioration from proper Lutheran standards and represent the low point in an unhistorical and un-Lutheran type of worship in this country. The General Synod in 1837 also appended this English liturgy of the New York Synod to its own hymnbook.

In 1839 the Ministerium of Pennsylvania and the Ministerium of New York co-operated in the appointment of a joint committee to revise the liturgy "in an approved and more complete form." This German Service was adopted in 1842, and the General Synod the following year also recommended it "as suitable for adoption among our German churches." This liturgy differed very little from the one of 1818, the responsive elements being negligible.

In 1843 the General Synod appointed a committee to prepare an English liturgy to be based on the German liturgy of the Ministerium of Pennsylvania. Two years later the committee proposed to add some features of a historical nature. Drs. Charles Philip Krauth, Benjamin Kurtz, Ezra Keller, J. G. Morris, W. M. Reynolds, and C. A. Smith carried out this work which appeared in print in 1847. The next year the Ministerium expressed satisfaction with this translation of its liturgy into English; but the liturgy itself, whether in German or in English, was most unsatisfactory. No responsive features were included, and there was no evidence of familiarity with the pure, restrained liturgical material of the Lutheran church of the sixteenth century. Cheap sentiment and bombastic phrases in the manner of the Rationalistic era abounded. They appeared in the forms for Baptism as well as those for Holy Communion.

In 1855 came the first promise of improvement. By this time constructive developments in Germany were being reflected in America, and there was evidence of growth in confessional and churchly consciousness. In 1850 the Ministerium of Pennsylvania resolved to seek the co-operation of the synods of New York and Ohio and the General Synod in the preparation of a revised agenda. Dr. Demme took the lead in this matter. A definite effort was made to return to confessional clarity and a responsive type of service. With reference to the latter the committee said, "If we succeed in restoring this right to the congregations so that they become accustomed to exercising it regularly, we will have contributed essentially toward a true revival of well ordered services in the house of God, and in doing so we will have acted in the spirit of the fathers of our church, who never approved of keeping the congregation in silence." In the Service which this committee prepared, the principal parts of the old Lutheran Liturgy were restored, generally in proper order. A form of invocation, addressed to the Lord Jesus Christ, was given before the Verba. Definite reference was made to the Lutheran confessions, and the text of the Augsburg Confession was included.

In spite of the merits of this liturgy it was far from satisfactory. The Confiteor and the Kyrie were still combined; the Sursum Corda was introduced at the beginning of the Service; the Introit was read by the minister after the Gloria in Excelsis and before the Collect; and the Communion Office was separated from the preaching service and placed among the occasional services. The material described as "introits and collects" was not, generally speaking, historical. The Epistle was an optional feature which might be read after the Gospel, and after this the minister if he desired might read the Creed. An extempore prayer followed the Sermon. Alternate forms, unhistorical and in poor taste, were given equal importance with the regular order.

With all its imperfections this Liturgy of 1855 was a distinct advance. One important fact is to be noted—there was a definite effort to secure co-operation among several synods and general bodies in the hope of promoting unity in the church and of creating a greater degree of uniformity in worship.

This breadth of purpose was an American feature which contrasted sharply with the local or provincial character of Lutheran liturgies in Germany, in both the sixteenth and the nineteenth centuries.

The Ministerium of Pennsylvania took steps at once to translate this German Liturgy of 1855 into English. A committee consisting of Drs. C. F. Schaeffer, C. W. Schaeffer, C. F. Welden, G. F. Krotel, and B. M. Schmucker was appointed. Since these men possessed high literary culture and were students of the liturgy, their work soon became much more than mere translation. The influence of recent liturgical reform in Germany and England was definitely felt. The Rev. A. T. Geissenhainer, F. W. Conrad and J. Kohler were subsequently added to the committee. Various features of the German Liturgy of 1855 were omitted; other features were introduced, all—as the preface states— "for the purpose of securing a stricter conformity to the general usage of the ancient and purest liturgies of the Lutheran Church." A selection of introits, chiefly from the Bavarian agenda, was included; the Nicene Creed was introduced "for occasional use"; and the General Prayer was placed after the Sermon. A condensation of Loehe's preface to his liturgy of 1844 was included. Dr. Schmucker and Mr. Geissenhainer were largely responsible for the final form. The book was published by Lindsay and Blakiston of Philadelphia in 1860 under the title: *A Liturgy for the Use of the Evangelical Lutheran Church.*[5]

Two years later the Ministerium authorized its committee to consider a new English hymnbook. The aid of the Rev. F. M. Bird, a member of the New York Ministerium, was secured, and Drs. Charles Porterfield Krauth and Joseph A. Seiss were added to the committee, which now attacked its task with vigor. In 1866 the Ministerium withdrew from the General Synod and further official action was postponed, though the committee industriously continued its work. As a result the General Council at its organization meeting in 1867 was able to "accept and authorize the publication of the English Church Book prepared by the Ministerium of Pennsylvania."[6]

Leadership in liturgical and hymnological matters had now been definitely assumed by the English part of the church. The historic Service of the Lutheran church, at least in its essential features, had been restored. This was a return in principle and form to the general

---

[5] An interesting feature of the proof copy of this liturgy of 1860 was the inclusion of a prayer for the sanctification of believers by the Holy Spirit, inserted before the Lord's Prayer in the Communion Office.

[6] For fuller discussion of these early liturgies see A. Spaeth, "History of the Liturgical Development of the Ministerium of Pennsylvania," *Lutheran Church Review,* XVII (1898), 93-119.

type of the Muhlenberg Liturgy of 1748 and the more fully developed classic liturgies of the sixteenth century. Doctrinal reform and liturgical reform, as always, were moving together and in the same direction.

OTHER SYNODS AND GENERAL BODIES

The main stream of liturgical development under the leadership of the Ministerium of Pennsylvania had been sketched. Brief reference should be made to the course of events in other parts of the church. The Ministerium of New York, organized less than thirty years after the Ministerium of Pennsylvania, at first probably used the Muhlenberg Liturgy in manuscript and later the printed form of 1786. The synod, however, was affected by the English movement earlier than was the Ministerium of Pennsylvania. Dr. J. C. Kunze published a *Hymn and Prayer Book* in 1795, which contained an English translation of the Liturgy of 1786 and a considerable number (144) of very unsatisfactory translations of hymns from the German. Later books by Strebeck (1797) and Williston (1806) have different selections of hymns and an altered liturgy. In 1814, as we have seen, the devastating effects of rationalism became evident in the liturgy prepared by Dr. Frederick H. Quitman, president, and Augustus Wackerhagen, secretary of the New York Ministerium, and authorized by the synod. Some of its forms were highly objectionable, and its entire tone reflected the low doctrinal and liturgical spirit of the time. The hymnal was, if possible, even worse than the liturgy. The enlarged liturgy published in 1833 was no improvement.

The Joint Synod of Ohio, nine years after its organization in 1818, undertook the preparation of an English liturgy. This liturgy, published at Lancaster, Ohio, in 1830, contained two forms of worship, including an order for the Lord's Supper. In general it approximated the contemporary developments in the Ministerium of Pennsylvania. The Synod of Ohio continued its liturgical efforts by co-operating with the Pennsylvania and New York synods in the preparation of the Liturgy of 1842 and in the later studies of 1862. A revised German agenda was published in 1884; and after a recommendation that the synod "adopt the Common Service and co-operate with the other Lutheran bodies in preparing a good hymnal" had been defeated, a revised English liturgy appeared in 1894. In 1909 the German and the English liturgies of the synod were unified. In addition the Communion Office was restored to its historic place as the conclusion of the regular Sunday service, instead of a distinct form among the occasional services. In general these forms developed by the Ohio Synod gave evidence of the same general im-

174

provement in liturgical character as those which marked the developments in the Ministerium of Pennsylvania. The Ohio Liturgy contains a prayer of consecration in which the Verba and the Lord's Prayer are imbedded. After 1902 an evening service, substantially the same as the Vespers of the Common Service, was included.

The General Synod, organized in 1820 at Hagerstown, Maryland, never displayed constructive ability in liturgical and hymnological matters. It was satisfied to recognize the leadership of the Ministerium of Pennsylvania in these fields. In 1825 it appointed a committee to prepare an English liturgy and hymnbook upon the basis of the German liturgy of Pennsylvania and the New York hymnbook. Nothing, however, was accomplished until 1832, when a liturgy "prepared by the Rev. Mr. G. Lintner" and "perused by the book committee and sanctioned by them" was offered to the synod. In accordance with the general developments of the time, there was no provision for responsive worship. In 1835 and 1837 committees were appointed to amend forms in the liturgy (1832) then in use and to prepare prayers to be appended to the hymnbook. This committee reported progress in 1839, and in 1841 was instructed to continue its work. In 1847 a liturgy appeared, which, however, was not regarded as satisfactory. The committee, despairing of meeting the apparently "irreconcilable differences," begged to be excused. It was continued, however, and in 1856 produced the so-called "Pocket edition of the German Synod's English Liturgy." This edition reintroduced the Apostles' Creed (including the phrase, "The Holy Catholic Church").

In 1862 the Rev. B. M. Schmucker presented the English liturgy of the Ministerium of Pennsylvania (1860) to the convention of the General Synod at Lancaster, Pennsylvania. It was referred to a special committee which failed to approve it. In 1868 Drs. L. E. Albert, T. Stork, and J. G. Butler were appointed to revise the liturgy. When the General Synod met the following year at Washington, D. C., the report of this committee was adopted and gave the synod its so-called "Washington Service." This was in most respects dependent upon the "provisional liturgy" which Dr. Schmucker had proposed, though there were numerous changes. This Liturgy of 1869 may be regarded as "the first approximation of anything resembling a historical order of service since the organization of the General Synod." The next step was taken when the General Synod co-operated with the General Council and the United Synod in the South in the preparation of the Common Service.[7]

[7] See a summary characterization of all these developments in, "Liturgical Development within the Evangelical Lutheran Church in the United States," *Lutheran Church Review*, XXXVI (1917), 469-500.

Before the Civil War the Lutheran synods in the South depended largely upon developments in the North, particularly within the General Synod. The Tennessee Synod was an exception. In 1840 it published its own liturgy. This was used until the synod adopted the *Church Book* of the General Council in 1872. The withdrawal of the Southern synods from the General Synod and the formation of a new General Synod South in 1863 were accompanied by renewed activity in liturgical matters. A *Book of Worship* influenced by the provisional service of the Pennsylvania Ministerium was published in 1867. This book also incorporated some features from the Danish liturgy. It was used throughout the synod until the Common Service appeared in 1888.

The Augustana Church in its earlier history in this country used the Liturgy of the Church of Sweden of 1811. Some parts of this liturgy were so unsatisfactory that the services were frequently altered by individual pastors. The synod in 1870 adopted various changes, and in 1895 a complete liturgy, modeled upon the revised liturgy of the Church of Sweden (1894), was adopted. In 1898 a revised edition of the Swedish church book and an English translation of the liturgy were adopted, and this work was brought to completion in 1905. These forms followed developments in Sweden and represented a return to the historic Lutheran service, particularly the Swedish Liturgy of 1531 of Olavus Petri. In 1924 the English liturgy of the Common Service was included in the *Hymnal* of the Augustana Church as an alternate form. In 1936 a Commission on Liturgical Theory and Practice was established to give authoritative pronouncements.[8]

The Synodical Conference in its early years adopted no single liturgy. Its pastors generally used either the Saxon Agenda or Loehe's Agenda, which had been specially prepared for the use of German Lutheran congregations in the Middle West. In 1856 a revision of the Saxon Agenda was approved and published by the Missouri Synod. Dr. Friedrich Lochner published *Der Hauptgottesdienst* in 1895. This was a worthy plea for a fuller and better form of liturgical service similar to the Common Service, and the Missouri Agenda was later revised along these general lines. In 1899 the English Synod of Missouri (later the English District of the Missouri Synod) adopted the Common Service. A separate musical setting of it was issued in 1906.[9] A new edition, including both the Common Service and a translation of the German

---

[8] A. D. Mattson, *Polity of the Augustana Synod* (Rock Island: Augustana Book Concern, 1941), pp. 121-40.

[9] This, so far as melodies, adaptation to text, and even ornamental details of printing are concerned, was borrowed by the editor, Louis Kahmer of Baltimore, from Archer and Reed, *Choral Service Book* (1901), without permission or credit.

agenda, appeared in 1917 as *Liturgy and Agenda.* And of this a second, corrected edition was issued in 1921.[10]

The next notable effort was the *Lutheran Hymnal,* published in 1941 under the joint sponsorship of all bodies in the Synodical Conference. This completed the transition to the official use of the English language and the Common Service. Its deficiencies, especially in its musical settings, were the result of the heavily Germanic culture of the church for which the book was intended. In recognition of this, the book was supplemented by a full musical setting (including intonations for the minister) which appeared in 1944, and by a book of occasional services, *The Lutheran Agenda* (1951).[11]

CHURCH BOOK OF THE GENERAL COUNCIL

The decade 1860-70 witnessed important developments in the country and in the church. The nation was torn by a great civil war, and the body of the church likewise was rent. Political conditions caused the Southern Lutherans to withdraw from the General Synod to form the United Synod in the South. Doctrinal differences led the Ministerium of Pennsylvania also to withdraw and assume leadership in a movement which in 1868 resulted in the organization of the General Council, a union of synods definitely committed to historic confessional and liturgical principles. As part of this general movement the Ministerium established the Philadelphia Seminary in 1864 and Muhlenberg College in 1867.

Before the break with the General Synod, Dr. William J. Mann in his president's report to the Ministerium of Pennsylvania at Allentown in 1862 called attention to the need of "an improved English Hymn Book .... more fully in harmony with the spirit of our Church." The synod referred this subject to its standing liturgical committee, which had prepared the English Liturgy of 1860.

The English hymnbooks in general use at the time were the General Synod's hymnal of 1828, with an appendix of 1852, and the New York hymnbook of 1814, with an appendix of 1834. The first of these was thoroughly impregnated with Calvinistic and Arminian material of highly subjective character. It was arranged in accordance with a dogmatic scheme which practically ignored the church year. The New York book, while of higher literary and intellectual quality, had a strong infusion of Rationalistic

---

[10] The situation prior to 1935 is discussed by Theodore Graebner in *The Problem of Lutheran Union and Other Essays* (St. Louis: Concordia, 1935), Chap. III, "Our Liturgical Chaos," pp. 135-66.

[11] For a discussion of the response of the Missouri Synod to an invitation to co-operate in the Joint Commissions on the Liturgy and Hymnal, see p. 208.

thought. Its emphasis upon the ethical rather than the devotional was in agreement with the point of view and the practice of New England Unitarianism. To meet the needs of a more evangelical and yet objective type of hymnal, Dr. Joseph A. Seiss, aided by Dr. W. A. Passavant of Pittsburgh and Dr. McCron of Baltimore, published a hymnal with music called *The Evangelical Psalmist* in 1860. This hymnal contained nearly one thousand hymns, approximately 250 of which came from the pens of Watts and Charles Wesley. Dr. Seiss in his manuscript, "Notes of My Life," says that practically the only assistance he received from his associates in preparing this work was financial help to meet the cost of the printing plates.[12]

In 1863 the committee of the Ministerium recommended the preparation of a new hymnal as part of a new church book to include "such portions of our liturgy as are necessary for the regular Sunday services, Luther's Catechism, and the Augsburg Confession." Ten years before a similar plan had been presented to the Virginia Synod by Drs. Charles Porterfield Krauth and Beale M. Schmucker. After Dr. Schmucker had become a member of the Ministerium of Pennsylvania and the recognized leader of its liturgical committee, his plan was accepted by the Ministerium. The Rev. Frederick Mayer Bird was invited to co-operate in the preparation of the hymnal.[13]

To understand the liturgical portion of this book we must realize the strong reaction of leaders within the Ministerium of Pennsylvania against the unhistorical and un-Lutheran type of service which had reached its extreme form in the New York Liturgy of 1818. We must also remember the intense interest of Drs. Charles P. Krauth and Beale M. Schmucker in liturgical study. This had begun as early as 1847 while these future leaders were members of the Virginia Synod. Dr. Seiss at this time lived at Martinsburg, Virginia (subsequently Martinsburg, West Virginia), and later made his home at Cumberland, Maryland. He, too, was genuinely interested in the liturgical revival of the Lutheran church in Germany and in the possibility of accomplishing something of a similar nature for the church in America. When these men became members of the Ministerium of Pennsylvania, they threw the weight of their scholarship and general influence into the effort to give the church a liturgy and a hymnal superior to anything it had known.

[12] For more extended characterization of these early hymnals as well as for important details connected with the preparation of the *Church Book,* see a published address by Dr. Henry E. Jacobs, "The Making of the Church Book" (1912: privately printed). Also available in *Lutheran Church Review,* XXXI, 597-622.

[13] The course of Mr. Bird's studies is reflected in a series of three aricles on Lutheran hymnology which he contributed in 1865 to the *Evangelical Review.* These contain material of great interest to the student of American hymnody.

The first great improvement, as already noted, was the Liturgy of 1860. The addition of Drs. Krauth and Seiss to the committee in 1865 aided materially in the final preparation of the *Church Book*. The plan of the book was approved by the General Council at its first convention in 1867, and the book itself was printed in time for the second convention in 1868.

The intense interest of representative leaders of the Ministerium in this project is noteworthy. A call was extended to all ministers "using or expecting to use the English Liturgy" to assemble in Philadelphia to discuss the question. Meetings of this group were held January 30 and 31, February 1, 1865, and February 13 and 14, 1866. Dr. Charles P. Krauth was chosen chairman, and, in association with Drs. Seiss and Krotel, published a pamphlet embodying the discussions of these five days and proposing fifty-eight emendations of the liturgy which it petitioned the Ministerium to incorporate in the next edition. Important items included preparation of an Introit for each Sunday and festival of the church year "upon the basis of the ancient Introits"; the sentence, "the Holy Catholic Church" instead of "the Holy Christian Church" in the Creed; the substitution of a series of collects for the festivals and Sundays; the addition of collects for "particular necessities and circumstances"; preparation of additional forms of the General Prayer; the insertion of a form of blessing after the reception of the elements; the omission of the Nunc Dimittis, etc.

As Dr. Krauth's influence on the floor of the Council had effected certain changes in the interest of historical order, the council compromised by including in the new book's first edition alternate forms to meet the desires of some pastors and congregations. These, however, were withdrawn from later editions. The edition of 1870 included a considerable number of additional translations of the historic Introits and Collects. In order to meet the needs of its German congregations the General Council instructed a committee consisting of Drs. Spaeth, S. Fritschel, and Schmucker to prepare the *Kirchenbuch,* which was published in 1877. This for the first time restored the full Matin and Vesper orders to the Lutheran church in this country. In 1883 a committee consisting of Drs. Schmucker, Spaeth, Mohldenke, Jacobs, and Fritschel, prepared a series of occasional services (orders for ministerial acts) which the General Council adopted and inserted in the *Church Book.*

The *Church Book* of the General Council was unquestionably the best liturgy and hymnal which the Lutheran church in America had yet produced. In nearly every particular the liturgy marked a return to the type of service represented by the Muhlenberg Liturgy in 1748. In various details, however (proper Introits, Collects, etc.), it was much more fully elaborated, being based upon a broader study of the Lutheran liturgies of the sixteenth century. In this respect it anticipated the principle more specifically carried out in the preparation of the Common Service twenty years later and of *The Service Book* of 1958.

In preparing the hymnal the committee availed itself of latest developments in England, where, as a by-product of the Oxford Movement, a new era in English hymnology had opened. Bishop Heber, John Keble, Christopher Wordsworth, William Walsham How, Anne Steele, Charlotte Elliott, and many others had written original hymns of merit. John Mason Neale, Edward Caswall, John Chandler, John Henry Newman, Richard Chenevix Trench, and others unlocked the storehouses of Greek and Latin hymnody and provided the English-speaking world with many noble translations. Catherine Winkworth, Jane Borthwick, Frances Elizabeth Cox, Mrs. Charles, Mrs. Bevan, Richard Massie, and others explored the treasures of German Lutheran hymnody and supplied the church with admirable English translations of many of the finest German Lutheran hymns. Many of these English hymns and translations appeared in England in the first edition of *Hymns Ancient and Modern* in 1861. All of this work was available to the committee, and material from this source immeasurably enriched the *Church Book*.

In addition to this the committee made every effort to secure the utmost accuracy in texts. Mr. Bird's own fine hymnological library and the collection of Mr. David Creamer of Baltimore were constantly drawn upon. Dr. Schmucker and Mr. Bird, with the aid of their associates, finally prepared a proof copy which was published by the Ministerium in 1865. This was circulated widely and sent to every living author represented in the collection. The services of Daniel Sedgwick of London, a recognized specialist, were also secured for textual revision. Constructive criticism by Drs. Krauth and Seiss, recently added to the committee, was an important factor. Dr. Seiss's influence in particular reduced the number of hymns by Charles Wesley. The merit of the hymnal as finally published is indicated in the objective statement of Dr. Louis Fitzgerald Benson, the eminent American hymnologist, who in his scholarly work wrote: "English-speaking Lutheranism had at last expressed itself in a hymnal worthy of its own traditions, and on a plane where no other American denomination could hope to meet it. Beside this Lutheran Hymnal of 1868 the Protestant Episcopal *Hymnal* of 1872 seems like an amateur performance."[14]

Frederick Mayer Bird (1838-1908) was a grandson of Dr. Philip Mayer, pastor of St. John's Church, Philadelphia. He was a graduate of the Uni-

[14] *The English Hymn* (New York: Doran, 1915), p. 561.

versity of Pennsylvania and of Union Theological Seminary and served as chaplain in the U.S. Army 1862-63. In 1868 he left the Lutheran Church and entered the ministry of the Episcopal Church. Later (1881-86) he became a professor in Lehigh University, and after that (1893-98) editor of *Lippincott's Magazine.* He contributed articles to Julian's *Dictionary of Hymnology* and to various encyclopedias. His hymnological library of 3,000 volumes is now at Union Seminary.

Joseph Augustus Seiss (1823-1904) was outstanding among Lutheran leaders. His principal pastorates were in Baltimore and Philadelphia. He was a founder and later a president of the General Council; president of the Board of Directors of the Philadelphia Seminary from 1865 to his death; editor of *The Lutheran,* 1869-79; an eloquent preacher and prolific author. His contribution to the making of the *Church Book* was considerable. His manuscript autobiography (Krauth Memorial Library, Mt. Airy) claims credit for securing the separation of the Kyrie from the Confiteor and the preparation of a complete series of Introits and Collects for each Sunday and festival. He translated and published these in *The Lutheran and Missionary,* of which he was editor. He also translated several of the general prayers and composed all the additional prayers for festivals in the so-called "pulpit edition" of the *Church Book.*

Dr. Henry E. Jacobs, who was appointed a member of the Church Book Committee following the death of Dr. C. F. Schaeffer in 1879, has recorded his impressions of the men who collaborated in the preparation of the several editions of the *Church Book.* In a letter to Mr. Horn he states that there were many collaborators; that Dr. Schmucker painstakingly gathered most of the material; that Dr. Krauth was the "happy translator" of some of it; that the services of the Rev. A. T. Geissenhainer were important; and that Dr. Seiss, though much of his work was not "based on mastery of principles," had a great deal to do with final shaping of the material and editing it for the press.

In his as yet unpublished memoirs, Dr. Jacobs writes: "The foundation work for the *Church Book* was laid in the Ministerium of Pennsylvania before Dr. Seiss entered it. How much was accomplished may be learned from an examination of the English Liturgy of the Ministerium of Pennsylvania published in 1860. Dr. Beale M. Schmucker, as one of the few English pastors in the Ministerium, at once gained prominence in the efforts to provide an English Liturgy with his entrance into the Ministerium in 1853. He became secretary of the committee and diligently collected the literary apparatus . . . . Dr. Seiss's strength never lay in that study of sources and mastery of the literature of the subject that belonged to Dr. Schmucker. The one was guided more by his personal tastes; the other by close adherence to rule and the weight of historical testimony. Dr. Seiss's strength lay in putting into the very best English such material as was finally decided upon, and in this department he spared himself no pains, writing and re-writing, amending, condensing, polishing, until he was satisfied." (Chap. XXXV.)

CHAPTER IX

THE COMMON SERVICE
AND THE COMMON SERVICE BOOK

Henry Melchior Muhlenberg clearly had in mind a "common Service" for use by all Lutheran congregations in the country. In a letter of November 5, 1783, four years before his death, he wrote, "It would be a most delightful and advantageous thing if all the Evangelical Lutheran congregations in North America were united with one another, if they all used the same order of service." During the century after Muhlenberg's death the expansion of the church led to a multiplication of synods and liturgies. His ideal, however, remained a cherished hope.[1]

FIRST STEPS

The first echo of Muhlenberg's thought is to be noted forty years later in the preliminary correspondence connected with the founding of the General Synod, specifically in letters addressed to leaders in the Ministerium of Pennsylvania by Gottlieb Schober, a minister of the Evangelical Lutheran Synod of North Carolina. In 1870 the venerable Dr. John Bachman, for fifty-six years pastor of St. John's Church, Charleston, South Carolina, eminent alike as a leader in the church and in the world of science, and then in his eightieth year, revived the idea of "one church, one book" in a letter which he sent to the General Synod (later the United Synod in the South), meeting in Winchester, Virginia.

> We cannot fail in the course of time to become one of the largest denominations, in point of membership, on this Continent . . . . We have, however, too many Synods and the shades of difference that are formed in

[1] Some of the material in this chapter first appeared in an article by the author, "Historical Sketch of the Common Service," *Lutheran Church Review*, XXXVI (October, 1917), 501-19. See also Luther D. Reed, "The Common Service in the Life of the Church," *Lutheran Church Quarterly*, XII (January, 1939), 3-25, an address commemorating the fiftieth anniversary of the Common Service delivered at the convention of the United Lutheran Church in Baltimore, Maryland, on October 10, 1938.

our doctrines have prevented such a union as ought to exist in the Church of the Reformation.

I have ventured to suggest to our Synod the appointment of delegates to meet those of other Synods in consultation, for the purpose of promoting a greater uniformity in our Books of Worship, than at present exists . . . . If this object could be accomplished, our Church would, in my opinion, be more respected at home and abroad, and would accomplish a far greater amount of good.[2]

The synod expressed its approval of the idea, but declined to act because such a proposal would "not be likely to meet with a favorable response from other Lutheran Bodies." In 1876, however, this synod, in session at Staunton, Virginia, considering a report on the revision of its own liturgy, adopted a resolution offered by the Rev. Junius B. Remensnyder, then of Savannah, Georgia, which prepared the way for conference with other bodies on the subject. (*Minutes,* 1876, p. 29.) :

Resolved, That, with the view to promote uniformity in worship and strengthening the bonds of unity throughout all our churches, the committee on the Revision of the Book of Worship, be instructed to confer with the Evangelical Lutheran General Synod in the United States, and with the Evangelical Lutheran General Council in America, in regard to the feasibility of adopting but one Book containing the same hymns and the same order of services and Liturgic forms to be used in the public Worship of God in all the English-speaking Evang. Lutheran Churches of the United States.

In 1878 the synod instructed its delegates to the General Council and to the General Synod North "to inquire whether these Bodies will be willing to appoint a committee to co-operate with a similar committee appointed by this Synod for the purpose of preparing a Service Book."

The General Council in 1879, at Zanesville, Ohio, "consented to co-operate provided that the Rule which shall decide all questions arising in its preparation shall be: The common consent of the pure Lutheran liturgies of the sixteenth century, and when there is not an entire agreement among them the consent of the largest number of greatest weight." The Church Book Committee was also authorized to propose any changes in the *Church Book* or the *Kirchenbuch* which might be deemed necessary to conform more perfectly to this rule.

In 1881 the General Synod adopted the following committee report: "As this Synod has but recently adopted its own Book of Worship, and is in doubt as to the acceptability of any basis which it might suggest for a Common 'Service Book,'

[2] *Minutes of the Sixth Convention of the Evangelical Lutheran General Synod in N. A., 1870,* p. 8.

"*Resolved,* That a committee be appointed to confer with the General Synod South and with any other committee appointed for this purpose in order to ascertain whether an agreement upon any common basis is practicable."

Earlier in this same year the Rev. Edward T. Horn had published an article in the *Lutheran Quarterly Review* (N.S., XI, 163-78) entitled "Feasibility of a Service for all English-speaking Lutherans." Taking the rule proposed by the General Council as a text, the article contended that there is a normal Lutheran service common to the best liturgies of the sixteenth century and that the time was propitious for its restoration. This article informed the church and helped crystallize sentiment. Incidentally it probably first employed the term "Common Service."

In 1882 the General Synod South accepted the rule and authorized "the prosecution of this important work with all the speed compatible with the care and research which its thoroughness and accuracy will require." The synod also accepted important suggestions made by the Rev. Edward T. Horn involving changes in its own liturgy which would bring it more into harmony with the proposed rule.

In May, 1883, the General Synod North considered the petition of fifty-five ministers, expressing a desire for a liturgy "more in harmony with the historic Books of Worship and enunciating more clearly the doctrines of the Church." In view of negotiations with other bodies, it declined to revise its own liturgy, but advised its publishing committee to keep on hand only a limited number of copies of the latter and suggested "to the ministers possessing a liturgic spirit and gifted with a style of writing characterized by scholarly excellence the propriety of a thorough study of the whole liturgical subject and the outlining of well matured forms," etc. What was more to the point, the synod at this same session adopted the following with reference to the common project reported by a committee of which Dr. J. B. Remensnyder, then of New York City, was chairman: "*Resolved,* That we hail as one of the most auspicious outlooks of our Church in America the prospects of securing a 'Common Service for all English-speaking Lutherans.' Believing such a Service to be feasible upon the generic and well-defined basis of 'the common consent of the pure Lutheran liturgies of the sixteenth century,' we hereby declare our readiness to labor to this end."

THE JOINT COMMITTEE AND ITS WORK

Actual work began April 17-22, 1884, when Drs. Schmucker, E. J. Wolf, S. A. Repass, and the Rev. T. W. Dosh, George U. Wenner, and

Edward T. Horn met in Mr. Horn's study in Charleston, South Carolina. Dr. Schmucker was chosen chairman and Mr. Horn secretary, and these two with Mr. Wenner constituted the subcommittee which prepared the first draft of the Service as reported to the joint committee in the spring of the following year. This same subcommittee later worked out the countless details.

The first conference in Charleston continued five days. The rule proposed by the General Council was adopted as the basis for the work. The following principles were also adopted:

"1. It is the understanding of the whole Joint Committee that the result of our labors must be referred to the Bodies we represent.

"2. We dare make no service binding on the Congregation, and no part of a service should be used any longer than it serves to edification.

"3. We agree to furnish the full Lutheran service, with all its provisions, for all who wish to use it."[3]

The "constituent parts and order of the full normal Lutheran Service" were fully discussed and unanimously agreed upon. The only difference of opinion arose in connection with the relative position of the Lord's Prayer and the Words of Institution in the Communion Service.

The first meeting of "The Joint Committee on a Common Service Book" was held in Philadelphia in the library of the theological seminary, May 12-14, 1885. Present were: From the General Synod, Rev. G. U. Wenner, F. W. Conrad, A. C. Wedekind, M. Valentine, and possibly E. J. Wolf. From the General Council, Rev. B. M. Schmucker, J. A. Seiss, Samuel Laird, John Kohler, H. E. Jacobs, A. Spaeth. From the General Synod South, Rev. S. A. Repass and Edward T. Horn.

Dr. Schmucker was called to the chair and Mr. Horn was elected secretary. The committee considered the report of the subcommittee's work and unanimously adopted the three general principles and the order and outline of the Service substantially as offered. The matter was then referred to the three general bodies, each of which approved the procedure.

Dr. Henry E. Jacobs in his memoirs, written in 1906 but still in manuscript, comments interestingly upon this meeting which he says was "the first real effort at co-operation since the break at Fort Wayne twenty years before." Considerable anxiety was felt "as to the possibility of harmonious action in a committee composed of men so widely different." He describes Dr. Wenner as "a man of cultivated tastes, gentlemanly bearing, and high appreciation of German church life, but testy, petulant, captious." Dr. Conrad was not personally familiar with the authorities, but his sympathies were undoubtedly with the preparation of a full liturgical Service. Dr. Valentine was "an intense partisan" who "had no sympathy with the move-

---

[3] *Protocol of the Conferences of the Joint Committee on a Common Service Book for All English Speaking Lutherans, Philadelphia, Pa., May 12-14, 1885* (Charleston, S. C.: Lucas and Richardson, 1885), p. 4.

ment" and who was likely to follow "an obstructionist policy." Dr. Wede-kind "was a blunt, outspoken German, of moderate attainments but liturgical sympathies."

Dr. Wolf's sympathies "were for a free Service" but he "grew in depth of conviction, grasp of principles, and liturgical scholarship as the work pro-gressed," and "he did not flinch when he saw that the observance of the rule adopted was carrying his committee toward the General Council." Dr. Repass, one of the Southern representatives, only recorded his presence and left. Of the General Council's committee, Dr. C. W. Schaeffer "had a very cultivated liturgical taste. His translation of Bogatsky's *Golden Treasury*, his volume of *Family Prayers* and his work as a translator of German hymns gave him influence wherever the language of devotion was under considera-tion. Drs. Laird, Kohler and Welden seemed deeply interested but had very little to say in the discussions. Drs. Schmucker, Spaeth, Horn, and Wenner were the liturgical experts, followed by Dr. Seiss and C. W. Schaeffer, as well as by Dr. Wolf."

Dr. Jacobs records the skilful manner in which Dr. Schmucker led the discussions. In enumerating the parts of the Service "he referred to the Col-lects not as such, but to 'prayer before the reading of the Epistle and Gospel,' etc. By carefully avoiding the technical liturgical terms, he suggested to the General Synod men a manner of meeting opposition that was entirely feasible and at the same time endorsed their order as in its main features in harmony with the best traditions of the Church. . . . The *Church Book* of the General Council was never referred to or even mentioned. . . . There was no dissent to the position that the Service proper began with the Introit, or 'Psalmody' as Dr. Schmucker first called it, and if the rule were rigidly enforced the Confiteor and the Declaration of Grace would have to be omitted. But all were equally desirous that these be retained, and good sixteenth century authority for this was found. . . . There was some slight discussion on the position of the Kyrie." Dr. Jacobs' account concludes with the remark that "the meetings of the Committee were held in an atmosphere heavily laden with smoke. Dr. Valentine and I were the only members of the Committee who did not participate in this custom so inconsistent with sixteenth-century Lutherans. I was proof against the effect from association with other committees where the practice prevailed, but Dr. Valentine was generally disabled by the time evening arrived."

The order of service, without details, but with several preliminary pages containing a statement of principles and historical notes, was printed in a sixteen-page pamphlet, and presented to the General Synod at Harrisburg, Pennsylvania, in 1885. The minutes of the General Synod record an ex-tended additional report by the synod's committee which was in effect an argument for historical liturgical forms in general and for the Common Service in particular, and urged the adoption of the work of the joint com-mittee in the belief that "after so many anxious years of waiting and effort the time has come, when, forgetting the prejudices of the past, we should make a determined and faithful effort to demonstrate to the world the substantial unity of our church." The report was unanimously adopted by the synod and the committee instructed to complete details and to publish the Service when finally adopted by the other bodies.[4]

[4] *Proceedings of the General Synod, 1885*, pp. 15-22.

The General Council, meeting in Philadelphia in October of the same year, received the report of its Church Book Committee, which stated that "for the General Council the acceptance of the Common English Service propsed presents no serious difficulties. Our Church Books were prepared under the operation of the same Rule which controlled in this. The result in most cases must necessarily be substantially the same. Indeed, no changes of any serious or noticeable character would be made in our *Church Book* except such as have already been approved by the Council in its action on the German *Kirchenbuch.*" The report further suggested that each body in its own edition of the Service might "allow some concessions to its own usages in minor, unessential matters." The Council thereupon adopted the Common Service and instructed the committee to continue its work.

Dr. Schmucker, writing to Mr. Horn, October 23, 1885, reported this "hearty and unanimous" action by the General Council and said, "I must congratulate the Committee of your Synod and especially yourself on this prosperous progress of your proposal. I had not the least hope of such achievement when it was proposed and only entered into the preliminary work under the rule of my official life to do in any case what is the right thing without regard to the result. But no one can more highly estimate the importance of the result. If the coming generations of Lutherans have put in their mouths and hearts the pure, strong, moving words of our Church's Service, from week to week and year to year, they will be brought up in the pure teaching of the Church, and the Church of the future will be a genuine Lutheran Church." After referring to the adoption by the Council of the orders for baptism and expressing the hope that Mr. Horn might meet with the Council's committee to assist it in correcting the English translation, Dr. Schmucker suggested a meeting with Mr. Horn and Mr. Wenner for continuance of the work on the Common Service. He said, "it can only be wrought out by a small subcommittee. If we three can spend a week or two in my study, where all the books are, we can do very much. We cannot work without the books and they are nowhere else."

The General Synod South, which had separated from the northern church in 1863 because of war conditions, met in its last convention in Roanoke, Virginia, June 23, 1886, and in accordance with its own previous action and with that of the Evangelical Lutheran Diet, organized on June 26 "The United Synod of the Evangelical Lutheran Church in the South." Dr. Schmucker and Mr. Wenner were present as delegates from the General Council and the General Synod respectively. Dr. Schmucker expressed his gratification at the prospect of securing a Common Service Book and presented a communication from Dr. A. Spaeth, president of the General Council, voicing his congratulations and his prayers for the progress of the work. Mr. Horn's report to the synod, which asked its approval of this work "so wonderfully blessed of God," was adopted by a resolution which specifically thanked Mr. Horn for his important part in the undertaking.

Mr. Horn, as secretary, now prepared a manuscript text of the Service which was submitted to the liturgical committee of each body. The General Synod's committee met December 7-10, 1886, and proposed a list of forty-five emendations in the text. Most of these were very minor matters dealing with rubrics, etc. Others were more important. The Church Book Committee of the General Council met January 13, 1887, and passed upon the manuscript and the changes proposed by the General Synod's committee. Their report contained thirty items. Perhaps more than half of the emendations proposed by the General Synod were accepted. Others, e.g., alternate forms in the Confiteor, the permissive use of other prayers instead of the Collect for the Day, omission of the Proper Prefaces, omission of nearly all the minor responsive connections in Matins and Vespers, etc., were rejected.

A second meeting of the joint committee was called to consider the points of difference. The committee met March 22 and 23, 1887, in Philadelphia. It had before it the manuscript of 125 pages prepared by Mr. Horn and the formal arguments presented in the reports of the three separate committees. Agreement was reached on practically every point at issue except the relative position of the Lord's Prayer and the Verba, a question which had been debated for two full years. The following resolution was finally adopted with Mr. Wenner recording his vote in the negative.

"Resolved, that we acknowledge that the authorities adduced for the placing of the Verba before the Lord's Prayer are of great worth; but the authorities for the opposite arrangement seem to us of greater weight."

The subcommittee of three was empowered to prepare the book for publication. Mr. Wenner, writing April 20, 1887, reported for the General Synod's committee suggesting twelve emendations, the only serious point being insistence upon a different position of the Lord's Prayer in the Communion Office, but stating that "if we can agree to disagree just as they did in the sixteenth century, we may be able to go on with the work." The result was that different forms of the Service were incorporated in the separate service books of each body.[5]

THE SERVICE IN THREE DIFFERENT EDITIONS

The edition published by the United Synod appeared in Holy Week, 1888; that of the General Synod in Whitsuntide, 1888. Dr. Schmucker read the proof of the Southern edition and reported to the General Council that "the text of the Common Service as settled for the use of the General Council and United Synod South agrees in all respects." He again reported to the General Council at Minneapolis, September 14, 1888, the exact agreement between this edition of the United Synod and

[5] This manuscript of approximately 130 pages, with copious marginal notes, as well as other manuscripts, reports, correspondence, and the minutes of the joint committee, is preserved in the library of the Philadelphia Seminary at Mt. Airy.

the form adopted for the Council and explained that the delay in the appearance of the Council's edition was due to the effort to include the Ministerial Acts adopted by the Council. He had also made an analysis of the difference between the General Synod edition on the one hand and the United Synod and proposed General Council editions on the other.[6] Upon the adjournment of the Council, Dr. Schmucker began preparation of the copy for the new and enlarged edition of the *Church Book* which was to contain the Common Service. On October 15, 1888, he ran, with his completed manuscript in his handbag, to take a train from Pottstown to Philadelphia, and from overexertion died on the train.

The appearance of the General Council edition was greatly delayed and the copy for the printer which Dr. Schmucker carried with him on the day of his death "was never published in the form in which he had left it. The committee [General Council Church Book Committee] was paralyzed for a time by his death. When at last it was reorganized, it devoted its attention to the remaining orders for Ministerial Acts, in order to include them also in the new book. The disability of Dr. Spaeth and his absence in Europe during the winter of 1891-92 deprived it of a most important member."[7] The revised *Church Book* issued from the press in 1892. In preparing its text the Church Book Committee "was persuaded in a few instances by several of its older members not to make changes in the text of 1868 until it was certain that the Common Service would actually have wide use in the other bodies."[8]

Thus the ideal of a "Common Service Book for all English Speaking Lutherans," held aloft by the joint committee in the beginning of the work, was partially realized. The Common Service as such appeared in three editions with decided variations in text. It was incorporated in the several books of the three bodies, each of which retained its separate Ministerial Acts, hymnal, and other material as before. But even this was a solid achievement upon which later the fuller ideal was to be realized. The differences in text, though regrettable, were probably less numerous and important than the differences to be found among the English, Scottish, and American versions of the *Book of Common Prayer*. They did not materially affect the real character of the Service as a whole.

The variations from the standard text in the two other editions are about ninety in number. Some are "permissive uses," e.g., differences in tables of festivals and lessons, and in rubrics. Important variations are additional

[6] Cf. *The Lutheran*, August 9, 1888, p. 9.
[7] Henry E. Jacobs, "The Making of the Church Book," *Lutheran Church Review*, XXXI (October, 1912), 618.
[8] *Ibid.*, p. 615.

forms for the Declaration of Grace, rubrics permitting the substitution of another collect for the Collect for the Day, different texts in the Exhortation, Verba, and Thanksgiving Collect, different relative position of the Lord's Prayer and Verba, omission of certain propria, addition of six responsories, twenty-one psalms, eight canticles, and one general prayer, etc. All the variations have been noted and discussed in an article by the author entitled "The Standard Manuscript of the Common Service and Variata Editions," *Lutheran Church Review,* XX (July, 1901), 459-73.

Because of these discrepancies in the several editions, however, the joint committee was called together for its third meeting in Philadelphia, November 30, 1888. The entire work was reviewed and the edition of the United Synod in the South was formally recognized and adopted as the correct exhibit of the standard text.

THREE HONORED NAMES

The church should ever hold in high honor the three whose eminent services made the Common Service possible. There were but two meetings of the joint committee before the Service was published. While this larger committee was responsible to the church, discussed principles, and determined many details presented from a single manuscript copy, the actual selection and arrangement of the material and the critical attention to details which gave it final character were still in the hands of the smaller group.

All of them were American born. They knew the history of the church in Europe, but were free from provincial preferences or prejudices often found in those coming from any one of the Lutheran states in the Old World. They knew the American church and American conditions and possibilities. They moved freely and confidently among the Latin and German originals with which they had to work, but they were also masters of English expression.

Beale Melanchthon Schmucker had contributed more than anyone else to the preparation of the *Church Book.* He was fifty-seven years of age when the subcommittee began its work in 1884. He brought to his new task a mastery of principles and a maturity of judgment that carried great weight. The strength of his life's work had gone into the *Church Book* and he was not as actively or constructively engaged in the collection of the new material except as a critic; yet he was far more than a critic.

Dr. Schmucker came of a distinguished ministerial line. His father, Dr. Samuel Simon Schmucker, was a graduate of the University of Pennsylvania and of Princeton Theological Seminary. For many years he was president of the Lutheran Theological Seminary at Gettysburg. Dr. Beale M. Schmucker was a graduate of Pennsylvania College and of Gettysburg Seminary and was ordained by the Virginia Synod in 1849. He served pastorates in Martinsburg, West Virginia; Allentown, Easton, Reading, and Pottstown, Pennsylvania. A keen parliamentarian, he exerted great influence in the Ministerium of Pennsylvania and the General Council, particularly in the fields of education, missions, and Christian worship. The Preface to the Common Service stood as he wrote it throughout that Service's history, an admirable example of his scholarship and his literary ability.

In addition to his work on the English *Church Book* of the General Council and the Common Service, Dr. Schmucker played a constructive role in the preparation of the *Kirchenbuch* (1877). He contributed articles on liturgical and hymnological subjects to church periodicals. He collaborated with Dr. William J. Mann and the Rev. W. Germann in the preparation of an annotated edition of the *Hallesche Nachrichten,* and prepared a number of historical and biographical sketches. The Ministerial Acts of the *Church Book* were based upon his exhaustive studies, and the burial service which he had completed two weeks before was used for the first time at his funeral. His young colleague in the subcommittee on the Common Service later wrote of the "earnest, thorough labor that stretched over twelve years," and of the extensive correspondence which this involved. Referring to Dr. Schmucker's letters, Dr. Horn says: "They awakened my old wonder at the readiness with which he [Dr. Schmucker] gave into our hands the notes of lifelong studies and made ours what no one of the Committee could have got with equal devotion. And I remembered that his fairness and unselfishness in the Committee and out of it revealed a beauty in his character that we had overlooked before in our regard for the scholar and admiration of the Churchman."[9]

George Unangst Wenner (1844-1934) was born in Bethlehem, Pennsylvania, in the heart of the Ministerium of Pennsylvania. He was a graduate of Yale University and of Union Theological Seminary. He brought to the work of this committee a keen mind, familiarity with the sources, and a highly developed critical spirit. His liturgical preferences may be said to have been of the *Deutsche Messe* rather than of the *Formula Missae* type. His position as a leader of the General Synod, his earnest and able advocacy of the Common Service, and his refutation of hostile criticism by scholarly articles in the church periodicals secured and held the support of the General Synod for the enterprise in the face of bitter opposition.

Dr. Wenner was chairman of the liturgical committee of the General Synod for more than twenty years. His efforts also contributed greatly to the establishment of deaconess' work in that body. He was recognized as a pioneer in the field of weekday religious education in the United States. Though a conservative Lutheran, he was active in inter-church affairs, being secretary of the Evangelical Alliance, and a founder of the Federal Council of the Churches of Christ in America. He was genial, devout, sympathetic, and scholarly, and his pastorate of Christ Church, New York City, for sixty-six years established a record for length of service.

Dr. Wenner was always quite unpredictable as to mood or speech. He lived to be more than ninety years of age, and his later years witnessed a reaction from some of the positions which he had previously defended. He registered

[9] Edward T. Horn, "The Lutheran Sources of the Common Service," *Lutheran Quarterly Review,* XXI (April, 1891), 268.

his opposition to the adoption of the *Common Service Book* then in preparation, objecting particularly to the Confiteor and the Introit, the insertion of definite rubrics, the relative positions of the Lord's Prayer and the Words of Institution, the use of the Nunc Dimittis after the Communion, etc. At his death he left manuscripts containing fragmentary studies for a book on liturgics. Some of these notes are interesting, if not convincing. Of the Confiteor he says: "Behind the Lutheran minister stands the shadow of a Roman priest." Of the Introit, which he had helped secure in complete series for the Common Service, he now writes: "For lovers of art and musical content, it would be a pity to lose it . . . but, as the Scotchman said of a liturgical service in a cathedral: 'It is all very fine, but a dreadful thing to have on the Sabbath.' "

In addition to numerous articles Dr. Wenner was the author of *Religious Education and the Public School* (1907); *The Lutherans of New York* (1918); *Sixty Years in One Pulpit* (1928).

Edward Traill Horn (1850-1915) was the youngest of the three, being but thirty-four years of age when he began this work. He was a graduate of Pennsylvania College and of the Philadelphia Seminary (1872). After making a careful study of the *Church Book* and the principles and material underlying it, he published in 1876 his little book on *The Christian Year*. The same year he became Dr. Bachman's successor as pastor of St. John's Church, Charleston, South Carolina, and was soon recognized as a leader in the Southern church. His liturgical studies were exhaustive and thorough, as manuscripts and other remains preserved in the archives at Mt. Airy, as well as many solid articles in the *Lutheran Quarterly, The Lutheran Church Review,* and other church periodicals, clearly show.[10] As secretary of the subcommittee the first and final preparation of material was in his hands. He held the balance of power in the committee and used it with rare judgment and effectiveness. His initiative and energy pushed the project to completion and his taste and judgment determined many of its important details. His ability and leadership were promptly recognized by his brethren and at thirty-eight he received the degree of Doctor of Divinity from both Roanoke and Newberry Colleges in 1888, the year the Common Service appeared from the press. In 1897 he became pastor of Trinity Church, Reading, Pennsylvania. In 1911 Dr. Horn was called to the Philadelphia Seminary (Mt. Airy) as professor of ethics and missions. His grasp of liturgical principles, history, and forms was fortified by a scholarship which encompassed the full round of theology. His powers of clear and concise literary expression were unequalled.

Dr. Horn helped prepare the way for common action by his article on "Feasibility of a Service for all English-speaking Lutherans" in the *Lutheran Quarterly* (XI [April, 1881], 163-78). This article, which was republished separately as a sixteen-page pamphlet, discusses the situation in the church at the time, with comparative study of the services in use in different bodies, and asks whether among the great variety and number of church orders a

---

[10] These archives contain many manuscript studies and notes of all kinds by Drs. Horn and Schmucker and also considerable material by Drs. Krauth and Seiss—comparative studies, first drafts with marginal notes, correspondence, notes on the introits and the collects, etc.

normal type of Lutheran Service is to be distinguished. This question he answered affirmatively upon the basis of a comparative study of eight orders.

In addition to his books, *The Christian Year, Outlines of Liturgics,* and important articles in *The Lutheran Cyclopedia* (especially the fine article on "The Liturgy"), his other strictly liturgical articles included: "Liturgical Work of John Brenz," *Lutheran Church Review,* I (Oct., 1882), 271-91; "Luther on the Principles and Order of Christian Worship," *Ibid.,* X (July, 1891), 217-56; "The Lutheran Sources of the Common Service," *Lutheran Quarterly,* XXI (April, 1891), 239-68; "Notes on the Translation of the Collects . . . ," *Lutheran Church Review,* XIX (April, 1900), 256-73; "The Reformation of Worship in the City of Nürnberg," *Ibid.* XI (April, 1892), 123-45; "Significance of Liturgical Reform," *Memoirs of the Lutheran Liturgical Association,* I, 19-39; "Liturgical Development in the Period of the Reformation," *Ibid.* IV, 63-66; "Remarks on Some of our Liturgical Classics," *Ibid.* VI, 17-22; "The Old Matin and Vesper Service of the Lutheran Church," *Lutheran Quarterly Review,* October, 1882, pp. 514-25.

A REPRESENTATIVE WORK

The movement which produced the Common Service was part of the doctrinal and historical revival which was lifting the church in Germany and in England out of spiritual depression and liturgical poverty. The claim of the Common Service itself to representative character is strengthened when we recall the kind and quality of service books which the church, in America and in Europe, possessed in the period before 1888.

The *Book of Worship* of the General Synod (eighth edition, 1880), contained only sixteen pages of liturgical material. This was overshadowed by a lengthy collection of family prayers for morning and evening of each day of the week. The morning service included a confession lifted bodily from the Prayer Book of the Episcopal Church. It contained some historical elements, but they were at times in unhistorical order. There was no provision whatever for the historical Introits, Collects, Epistles, and Gospels of the church year, nor was any liturgical order provided for the Holy Communion. The hymns were largely subjective and frequently Calvinistic in character. The only recognition accorded the church year was the inclusion of twenty hymns for church festivals.

The *Book of Worship* of the United Synod in the South contained a fuller liturgical service with definite recognition of the historic Gospels and Epistles and a few Introits of mixed character. The church festivals were provided with lengthy prayers. The Holy Communion contained historic liturgical elements but was separated from the usual morning service and placed among the Ministerial Acts. The naive way in which historical material was occasionally introduced may be illustrated by what, it must be admitted, is an extreme example. One of the so-called introits reads: "Let us commence our religious exercises in the Name of the Lord, who made heaven and earth," to which the congregation responded by singing the Gloria Patri. The Te Deum, the Litany, the penitential psalms, and a form of Passion history were included in the book. Subjective and Calvinistic elements preponderated in the hymnal.

The General Council, while homogenous doctrinally, was diverse linguistically, with services in German, Swedish, and English. Its English *Church Book* of 1868, as has been stated, first exhibited in this country with fulness and clarity the historical, liturgical, and hymnological ideals of the Lutheran church. Nonetheless, it lacked completeness. It contained a morning service and Holy Communion developed upon the structure of the church year with historic Gospels and Epistles, Proper Prefaces, etc. Only a selection of introits and collects in season groups was given. The Litany, Suffrages, and the Bidding Prayer were included, as was a collection of collects and prayers from ancient sources. The edition of 1870, in which the influence of Dr. Seiss and Dr. Krauth was felt, included a more complete series of Introits and Collects. There was no provision for Matins or Vespers. Its hymnal was the best which the church had produced up to that time, and subsequent editions improved the book in every particular.

It is only necessary to study the first draft of the Common Service prepared by Dr. Horn (130 pages or more) to see how much material previously provided in the *Church Book* could be used in the Common Service. This does not indicate the influence of any one personality or of any one general body—for example, the *Church Book* was not once mentioned in committee—but testifies to the fact that the studies which resulted in the *Church Book* had been directed by the same historical and liturgical principles which later prevailed in the preparation of the Common Service, and that in matters of translation and literary expression the *Church Book* text could not be generally improved upon.

The services of the Lutheran state churches in Germany presented a varied pattern, more or less complete, of recovered historical elements. The Common Service rose above the provincialism and nationalism which characterized developments in Europe. It provided a liturgy— later supplemented by the occasional services and the hymnal of the *Common Service Book*—of universal scope and influence. It was not an outline, only partially developed, as were most of the Reformation orders, but was complete. It was thoroughly American in breadth of view and provision for practical use by the people, and yet it was not merely American in any provincial or exclusive sense. It remained in fact the typical historic Lutheran Liturgy in the English language for over sixty years, more fully representative of Lutheranism in its best estate than any other order of service that could be named.

The representative character of the Common Service is shown not only by its fidelity to history and its completeness, but also by its literary excellence. In all these respects, though not in extent of use, the *Common Service Book* well sustained comparison with a similar work whose merits have been acclaimed for fully four centuries—the English *Book of Common Prayer*.

The *Book of Common Prayer* and the Common Service stem from the same tree — the historic liturgy of the Western church. While the specialist will recognize great differences, they have practically the same lessons for the parts of the church year which they have in common, and many of their responses, canticles, prayers, and propers are identical. The material included in the Common Service is completely justified by Lutheran precedent and agreeable to Lutheran doctrine, but the literary form in which much of it appears is that first given to the English-speaking world in the Prayer Book of 1549. Yet the borrowing is not slavish. Certain features, such as the Psalms, a number of independent translations, original collects, etc., are entirely different from the forms in the Prayer Book.

It will readily be understood why the Gospels and the Epistles should appear in the Authorized Version and why such liturgical commonplaces as the Lord's Prayer, the Creeds, the great canticles, and many of the collects should be given in the Prayer Book forms hallowed by centuries of use and association. In supplying the English dress for much of the material common to both communions, the Prayer Book repaid in the nineteenth century the debt which its framers owed to the Lutheran church orders of the sixteenth century. Apart from this, however, a point specially to be noted is that the independent translations, the original material, the rubrical directions, and the general spirit and tone of the Common Service and the *Common Service Book* were definitely influenced by the character and quality of the older English liturgy. They expressed the same churchly feeling in forms of comparable literary value.

The Common Service met with a most gratifying reception. Some synods and congregations were better prepared to introduce it than were others. There was bitter opposition to it in a few quarters, but its opponents waged a losing battle. Back of it was the momentum of centuries. Accompanying it was the vigorous energy of a church now well established in American life and eager for common forms of devotion which might adequately express faith and feeling in the spirit of the fathers, yet in the language of the land, and which might serve as a bond and a basis for common churchly development.

RESULTS OF IMPORTANCE

The rule under which the Service was prepared was not only historically correct but practically wise. It lifted the entire work above individual preference or taste, or the mere effort to reconcile imperfect and conflicting uses in different parts of the church. Common understanding, agreement, and use were possible only because of this wise principle of procedure, a principle which later pointed the way to further co-operation and helped attain at least a measure of organic union. This principle grounded the work upon recognition of a common heritage in the confessions and liturgies formulated by the Reformers in the classic period of the sixteenth century. Upon this historic foundation the European forefathers of all Lutheran groups in America had stood. To it their spiritual descendants could return with confidence and pride.

The church in every century must gain direction and inspiration from the periods in its history when forms of faith and worship are purified and restated. The sixteenth century is as important as it is because it was the crucial, creative period in which, under the leadership of eminent theologians and churchmen, principles were clarified and classic confessions and fundamental orders of worship produced. During that century the church also was still conscious of the solid achievements of historic Christianity and of a universal Christian tradition. New comprehensions of the gospel set all hearts aglow and released a creative spiritual energy which later war, scholasticism, state control, subjectivism, intellectualism, and the undue influence of Calvinism successively reduced or destroyed.

Muhlenberg had established the church in this country upon positive doctrinal and liturgical foundations, but pioneer conditions here and disintegrating church life abroad held liturgical practice and development in this country to levels far beneath the normal type of worship which had prevailed in Lutheran lands in the Reformation era. The framers of the Common Service went beyond Muhlenberg to the Reformers themselves for their principles and their models.

The rule of the Common Service specified "the consensus of the pure Lutheran liturgies of the sixteenth century," which reminds us that certain liturgies of that time, while nominally Lutheran, were not truly representative, but reflected influences from non-Lutheran sources. Those particularly in mind in all probability were liturgies of southern and southwestern Germany whose character was strongly influenced by the program of Calvin in Geneva and the mediating procedure of Martin Bucer in Strasbourg.

The Common Service distilled the devotional experiences of the Western church from the days of the apostles to its own times in clear canticles of praise and well-constructed prayers. As presented in the *Common Service Book* it contained features seldom found in other Lutheran liturgies of today and not found in Anglican services at all. Luther was a musician; Archbishop Cranmer was not. The Lutheran Reformers did everything possible to preserve the choral elements in the liturgy with their musical settings. Consequently the Common Service had proper Introits for every Sunday and special service and a complete series of Graduals, antiphons, and responsories.

These provisions were as complete as they were because the "consensus of the pure Lutheran liturgies of the sixteenth century" includes the Latin as well as the German, Swedish, and other vernaculars. Luther's Latin Service and the Latin portions of many sixteenth-century orders and choir books supplied forms which were eventually dropped from Lutheran services in many districts when the vernacular was fully introduced. These features were unobjectionable in themselves. Their omission was occasioned by difficulties of translation and musical adaptation, and the necessity of simplification to meet local conditions. The Common Service, taking an objective view of the entire field, restored the full order of the church, and, in the words of its own preface, presented "the complete Lutheran Service with all its provisions for all who desire to use it." The church had never produced in any land or time another vernacular liturgy so full-bodied and completely developed. Lutheran services in the sixteenth century in German and Swedish cities were as complete, but they were only partly in the vernacular, with choral and other features in Latin.

CHURCHLY AND SCHOLARLY INFLUENCE

The Common Service immediately drew the constituencies of the three general bodies closer together. Appreciation of a common birthright quickened a common spirit and endeavor. All sections began to study it. Other synods and general bodies, appreciative of the impersonal and objective principles which controlled its preparation, secured permission to use it. The Iowa Synod, the Joint Synod of Ohio, the Missouri Synod, the Norwegian synods, and later the Augustana Synod and the Icelandic

Synod provided it for their English services. Its prompt acceptance by these bodies which had not participated in its preparation was a generous and statesmanlike action which not only testified to the worth and representative character of the Common Service itself, but also affirmed the desire of the entire Lutheran church in America to employ again the rich forms which their fathers had used in the formative periods of the church's history and which later developments had obscured or destroyed. A church which had been confused in its thinking, unfamiliar with its own history, uncertain of its objectives, and weak in its organization was brought to self-respect and united endeavor. Translations, in whole or in part, in Telugu, Japanese, Spanish, and Italian carried it into the mission fields and helped make widely separated brethren in many lands conscious of their unity with the church in America. When we also remember the extensive literature and the many musical works it called forth, we may ask whether any other single achievement did as much in its time to elevate and unify the Lutheran Church in this country.

We recall the general promotion of liturgical study; the organization of the Lutheran Liturgical Association in Pittsburgh in 1898, the establishment in 1911 of a chair of liturgics and church art in the Philadelphia Seminary, and the founding of various local liturgical societies in more recent years. The Liturgical Association enrolled more than four hundred members in twenty-two states and four provinces of Canada. It published its collected papers in 1907 in a substantial volume of more than eight hundred pages (*The Memoirs of The Lutheran Liturgical Association,* ed. Luther D. Reed).

The constructive work of standing committees of the United Lutheran Church is also to be noted—the Common Service Book Committee, the Committee on Church Music, and the Committee on Church Architecture. The volumes prepared by the Common Service Book Committee—particularly the *Family Service Book, Hymns and Prayers for Church Societies,* the *Parish School Hymnal,* additional *Occasional Services, Collects and Prayers for Use in Church,* etc.—were a direct extension of the spirit and work of the framers of the Common Service.

The periodical literature of the decade 1880-90 has been referred to. Dr. Horn, in addition to his important articles in the church reviews, issued his *Outlines of Liturgics* in 1890. Henry E. Jacobs' *The Lutheran Movement in England,* so rich in important liturgical material, appeared the same year. *An Explanation of the Common Service,* which ran through several editions, was prepared in 1903 by Drs. E. F. Keever, J. C. Seegers, Joseph Stump, and Rev. F. E. Cooper, G. A. Bruegel, and P. Z. Strodach.

Musical settings of the Service were printed for the use of choirs and congregations. Among these were: Seiss and Engelmann, *Church Song;* Spaeth, *Church Book with Music;* J. F. Ohl, *School and Parish Hymnal;* the *Book of Worship* of the General Synod; the several publications of Emanuel Schmauk, etc. The historical melodies of the liturgy were adapted and arranged for the Common Service and were first brought out in the several publications of Archer and Reed, particularly *The Choral Service Book, The Psalter and Canticles,* and *Season Vespers.*

The Common Service was a purely literary effort. The text of the historic liturgy of the Lutheran Church was set forth completely and in admirable English. The work which was completed in 1888, however, did not include proper music, a hymnal, or occasional services.

The success of the Common Service, the desire to harmonize the texts in the several editions, and the growing demand for a complete book to include occasional services and a hymnal led to the further joint labor of years which resulted in the preparation of the *Common Service Book* a generation later. Though comprising only one-fourth or less of the content of the *Common Service Book,* the Common Service determined the principles, the spirit, and the fundamental material upon which the later and more comprehensive work was built.

FURTHER WORK OF THE JOINT COMMITTEE

By action of the three bodies the joint committee was continued. During the years 1889-1906 this committee held no less than seventeen meetings. It brought out a new English translation of the Augsburg Confession and a new translation of Luther's *Small Catechism.* Considerable work was also done in the matter of a common hymnal.[11] Preliminary studies in the orders for occasional services were also made.

While it had been relatively easy to agree upon the liturgy, once a historical principle or rule had been determined, there was greater difficulty in the matter of a hymnal and of occasional services. There was not the same consensus of historic usage upon which to build. Individual preferences and tastes, reflecting the divisions and backgrounds of the church in different parts of the country, asserted themselves and progress was slow. The association of representative leaders in the meetings of the committee, however, was valuable, and appreciation of higher standards of churchly practice was steadily growing. The Common Service was extending its use and influence, and a strong doctrinal consciousness was developing. The desire naturally increased to give this expression in a common liturgical, hymnological, and musical system which would bear testimony to the inner and essential unity of the church.

Definite work along these lines was inaugurated by the General

[11] As part of this undertaking, Dr. Seiss in 1899 published at his own expense a *Proof Copy of a Proposed New Hymnal* containing 541 hymns.

Council in Minneapolis in 1909, when it resolved to conform its text of the Common Service to that of the standard edition and to invite the co-operation of the General Synod and the United Synod in the South in an effort to arrive at a full and perfect agreement which would permit the Common Service henceforth to be published and used in the three bodies without a single variation; also to enter upon a final revision of the proposed common hymnal; to prepare a common authorized musical setting for the same; and to print the common book when prepared from a standard set of plates. The General Synod and the United Synod in the South cordially and promptly accepted this invitation and these objectives.

The way was prepared for this action by the publication of an article by Luther D. Reed in the *Lutheran Church Review,* XX (July, 1901), 459-73, on "The Standard Manuscript of the Common Service and Variata Editions." This was followed by a resolution proposed by Dr. Strodach and adopted by the Ministerium of Pennsylvania in 1905, which memorialized the General Council "to publish the Common Service as it was adopted by the Joint Committee." After the three bodies had agreed to enter upon this larger work the Church Book Committee prepared for the work by undertaking a serious study by its own members of the whole subject of a common book, part by part. This included the text of the liturgy and preliminary studies of hymns and music. (For fuller account of the progress of the subsequent joint work until the completion of the *Common Service Book* in 1918 see extended reports of the Church Book Committee in the Minutes of the General Council, 1905-18.)

A GREAT WORK BEGUN

The first meeting of the joint committee was held in Philadelphia, November 1, 1910. The challenge of the project was presented in a paper prepared by the secretary of the Church Book Committee, in which it was stated that "Never before in any land or in any century of its history has the Lutheran Church attempted to prepare a Service Book and Hymnal of such comprehensive character to meet the devotional needs of its congregations and homes throughout such a vast extent of territory as is contemplated in the task immediately before us."

The joint committee of 1910-17 consisted of thirty-eight members, among whom were five heads of theological seminaries and three presidents of general bodies. Eight others were professors of theology. The remainder were pastors, editors, and executives in all parts of the church.

Four major problems were involved: the unification of the text of the Common Service itself with revision of minor provisions; the preparation of a hymnal; the adoption of musical settings for the liturgy and the hymnal; and the preparation of orders for occasional services.

Five subcommittees were appointed, each of which designated a small group of its active members to make preliminary studies. The assembled material was thoroughly considered and final recommendations in printed form were forwarded to all members of the joint committee well in advance of its meetings. The extent of the task and the thoroughness of method employed carried the work over a period of eight years (1909-17). The impatience of the church at large was appreciated, but those laboring upon the project also realized the importance and far-reaching influence of the undertaking and the necessity of thorough work which would stand the test of time.

Each subcommittee made exhaustive studies. Unity and balance were secured by having the secretary of the joint committee (Luther D. Reed) also serve as a member of each subcommittee and act as its secretary. The committee on the hymnal had the advantage of preliminary studies and recommendations by the Church Book Committee of the General Council embodied in a manuscript volume of 243 pages. It further explored the entire field of English hymnody, including translations from Greek, Latin, German, Swedish, Danish, and Icelandic originals. The idea of a consensus of the use of particular hymns throughout the English-speaking world led to the tabulation of the contents of some twenty representative hymnals. Attention was thus directed to certain hymns whose wide usage demanded recognition; and to others whose limited use suggested possible omission. Every hymn was tested for purity of doctrinal content and excellence of literary form. Hymns which met these standards were welcomed from many sources. A number of new hymns and translations by members of the committee and others were included. The content and arrangement of the collection as finally completed exhibited a positive Lutheran emphasis.

The one regret of the committee was that it could not secure a larger number of acceptable translations of Swedish, Danish, and Norwegian hymns. Every available source was investigated, but only a few English translations of Scandinavian hymns met the literary requirements of the work, a difficulty which returned to plague the Joint Commission when they prepared our present hymnal forty years later. Some Scandinavian hymns which might have been considered proved to be translations or adaptations of German hymns which were already represented in the collection in acceptable English translation. The final recommendations of the subcommittee were presented to the joint committee in a printed proof copy containing 629 hymns. After final selection by the joint committee of hymns to be included, the subcommittee made a critical study of the text of each. The original text, whenever accessible, was compared with the texts given in a dozen or more representative hymnals and final decisions concerning text and punctuation made.[12]

In similar fashion the committee on music investigated the traditional settings to the liturgical texts and the freer work of individual editors and com-

[12] To meet the objection voiced in the Middle West that the hymnal of the *Common Service Book* contained too small a proportion of hymns by Lutheran authors, Henry E. Jacobs published an interesting article, "What is a Real Lutheran Hymn?" in the *Lutheran Church Review*, XLI (July, 1922), 210-19.

posers in Europe and America. It studied the comparative usage of tunes and the consensus of editorial judgment as shown in sixteen of the best-edited hymnals in England, Scotland, Canada, and the United States. A number of original tunes were also contributed, particularly by Dr. J. F. Ohl, chairman of the subcommittee, whose other services in arranging the first musical setting for the liturgy and in general editorial supervision of the music throughout the book were invaluable. A plain-song setting for the liturgy, based on Archer and Reed, *The Choral Service Book,* was also included in the first edition. This proved to be in advance of the times and was omitted from the book after 1919.

The committee on the liturgy harmonized all differences in text and prepared a number of additional Introits, Collects, and Lessons to complete the appointments for certain days in the calendar. It also provided new collects for missions, the nation, etc. Collect terminations were carefully revised and harmonized; the selection of psalms was modified. A new arrangement of the History of the Passion (the work of John C. Mattes) and new tables of daily lessons were adopted. One of the most difficult, and also most important, of its achievements was its study of the occasional services (baptism, confirmation, public confession, ordination, etc.). Agreement was reached in the text of fourteen of these. In acting finally upon them the joint committee officially recognized "the unparalleled contributions of labor and learning made by Dr. Henry E. Jacobs in his investigations and preparation of material."

A committee on rubrics with Dr. Paul Z. Strodach as chairman prepared and harmonized all rubrical directions.

Printed copies of the music edition of the *Common Service Book with Hymnal* were available in 1917, the quadricentennial year of the Protestant Reformation. Work on the plates of the text editions was well under way, though hampered by war conditions, when the first convention of the United Lutheran Church met in New York City in 1918. The editorial committee, appointed April 9, 1915, consisted of Luther D. Reed (chairman), P. Z. Strodach (secretary), Charles M. Jacobs, T. E. Schmauk, J. F. Ohl, J. A. Singmaster, F. H. Knubel, E. K. Bell, and E. C. Cronk. A dozen or more meetings were held over a period of less than two years. The minutes of the committee (now in the Krauth Memorial Library, Mt. Airy) record the difficulties confronted and the necessity of going beyond the preparation of the manuscript to assumption of the actual responsibility for manufacture of the key plates of the book. By an agreement finally reached between the editorial committee and the boards of publication of the three bodies, it was decided that "The two Boards (of the General Synod and the General Council) shall co-operate with the Joint Committee in the supervision, control, and preparation of the key plates. In cases of irreconcilable difference the Editorial Committee shall have the final decision. The Boards, together with the Publication Board of the United Synod of the South, shall have the sole privilege of making printing plates at any time."

A NEW CHURCH BODY

The United Lutheran Church was organized in New York City on November 14-18, 1918, at a merger convention of the three general bodies whose representatives had prepared the Common Service of 1888 and the *Common Service Book* of 1918. The union drew together the oldest Lutheran elements in American life, which had been transplanted from European soil. They were thoroughly rooted in this continent for generations and had helped found the American nation. By this time they were thoroughly anglicized. Forty-five synods (now merged to thirty-two) covering the territory from the Atlantic to the Pacific and from Nova Scotia to Florida, were included.[13]

The organization of the United Lutheran Church was intimately related to the quadricentennial celebration of the Protestant Reformation. In 1914 Dr. E. Clarence Miller and other representative laymen of the church urged that the quadricentennial should be marked, among other things, by a merger of the General Council, the General Synod, and the United Synod in the South. The proposition was considered premature. Sentiment grew rapidly, however, and was accelerated by conditions resulting from the first world war which made it necessary for the church to deal in a united way with the government. On April 18, 1917, resolutions signed by John L. Zimmerman, chairman of a group of laymen, were presented which requested the joint committee on the quadricentennial celebration "to arrange a general meeting of Lutherans to formulate plans for the unification of the Lutheran Church in America." After earnest discussion the following resolution offered by Dr. Henry E. Jacobs was adopted: "Believing that the time has come for the more complete organization of the Lutheran Church in this country, we propose that the General Synod, the General Council, and the United Synod of the South, together with all other bodies one with us in our Lutheran Faith, be united as soon as possible in one general organization, to be known as the United Lutheran Church in America."[14]

The presidents of the three bodies, Drs. T. E. Schmauk, V. G. Tressler, and M. G. G. Scherer, undertook preliminary studies and appointed a Committee on Constitution. The constitution itself and a set of merger resolutions offered by Dr. J. A. Singmaster were adopted by the three bodies at their conventions in 1917. A Ways and Means Committee

[13] The United Lutheran Church maintains twelve theological seminaries (including one in India and one in Japan); fourteen colleges and numerous hospitals, homes, asylums, deaconess institutions, etc. Its home mission activities are conducted in thirty-five states, Puerto Rico, the Virgin Islands, and seven provinces of Canada. This work is largely in English, but is also conducted in German, Swedish, Slovak, Hungarian, Italian, Spanish, Finnish, Estonian, Lettish, Icelandic, Polish, and Cree Indian, in addition to work among the Jews. Foreign mission operations are conducted in India, Japan, Malaya, Liberia, Argentina, and British Guiana.

[14] *Minutes of the First Convention of the United Lutheran Church in America* (1918), p. 39.

prepared plans for consolidating the boards and important committees and effecting transfer of property and vested interests to the new body. The United Lutheran Church itself was organized in the fall of 1918 by the election of Dr. Knubel as president; Dr. Scherer as secretary; and Dr. Clarence Miller as treasurer.

It was quite remarkable that when the new body was organized it had ready for immediate use a complete and carefully prepared service book and hymnal. The fact that such a work, whose preparation had required many years of labor, should have been brought to completion just when the new body was formed, can only be understood when we recognize that identical principles were working out separately in different fields.

Representative laymen of the church are rightly accorded special recognition for the initiative and energy which finally brought the different parts of the church together. They were anticipated, however, both as to vision and work, by the clerical leaders who labored steadily toward the same end for many years in the development of a common doctrinal consciousness and the preparation of a common liturgical, hymnological, and musical system.

THE BOOK AND THE CHURCH

The *Common Service Book* furnished the United Lutheran Church at its organization with a complete liturgy and hymnal, a series of occasional services, and musical settings for the liturgy and the hymns. It also supplied an important body of general rubrics with detailed directions concerning simple ceremonial, altar vestments, the use of colors, etc. This was an extension and application of the principles which had determined the preparation of the Common Service itself, which now constituted only approximately one-fourth of the material in the *Common Service Book*.

The church orders of the sixteenth century in Germany and Scandinavia were provincial or local in character and use. This is true even of the best modern Lutheran service books in Europe today, whether we consider those of Saxony, Bavaria, Hannover, Mecklenberg, France, Sweden, or Norway. The organization of the United Lutheran Church and the preparation of the *Common Service Book and Hymnal* were expressions of the American spirit. It spoke in comprehensiveness of plan, catholicity of outlook, compact and practical arrangement, and in the extensive use of the book by the people and clergy throughout the continent.

CHAPTER X

THE COMMON LITURGY, 1958

A generation passed before the next significant step was taken. The Lutheran church in America had to face unusual problems. No other church except the Roman Catholic has had such a variety of national backgrounds, with so many different linguistic and cultural strains represented in its hymnody and its forms of worship. In earlier years these European influences were obvious, with Lutheran services conducted in German, Dutch, Swedish, Norwegian, Danish, Finnish, Slovak, Hungarian and other languages. The transition to the language of the land was a long and difficult process which resulted in a variety of English orders of service, different musical settings, and different collections of hymns.

However, strong unifying forces were at work. Among these were the gradual Americanization and anglicization of all groups, the potent influence of the public schools, the restriction of immigration, the catastrophic effects of two world wars, etc. Above all, there was a growing recognition of essential Lutheran unity in doctrine, and the necessity for closer co-operation in Christian endeavor. These factors eventually led to simplification and unification in organizational structure and greater uniformity in worship.

SURVEY OF DEVELOPMENTS

The organization of the National Lutheran Council was one of the first steps, followed closely by mergers of synods and general bodies, and finally by the decision to prepare a new *Service Book and Hymnal* for the use of all Lutherans in the United States and Canada who would co-operate in this undertaking.

The year 1944 found the different linguistic groups still separated by services in other languages. Each was entrenched within the solid walls of its own organization, whether of synods, general bodies, colleges, seminaries, publication houses, etc. There were roughly three major, nearly equal groups: The United Lutheran Church in America; The Lutheran Church—Missouri Synod; and a constellation of smaller independent church bodies with Danish, Swedish, German, Norwegian, and Finnish backgrounds. The first and the third of these major groups had already established the National Lutheran Council. They are the churches which united in the preparation of the new *Service Book and Hymnal.* The second group—the Missouri Synod and its associates in the Synodical Conference—declined to participate.

The mounting desire for simplification, unification, and greater uniformity in worship found expression in pious resolutions recorded through the years in the minutes of the American Lutheran Church, the Augustana Church, and the United Lutheran Church. Nothing of consequence, however, was accomplished. The Common Service was included in all English service books and hymnals, even in the *Hymnal* of the Missouri Synod, though often with different musical settings. Nor was there uniformity in text in this professedly "Common Service." There were differences in Introits, Collects, Lessons, Graduals, rubrics, etc. Each church continued to publish and use its own hymnal and its own series of occasional services (baptism, confirmation, marriage, burial, etc.). However, while the United Lutheran Church, the Augustana Church, and the American Lutheran Church were all actively engaged in revising their own hymnals, a resolution that sparked a whole new enterprise was introduced to the United Lutheran Church meeting in Central Lutheran Church (ELC), Minneapolis, October 17, 1944.

THE ENABLING RESOLUTION

The Common Service Book Committee had presented its final report on a revision of the church's hymnal. A motion approving the report and authorizing publication was before the house when Dr. Oscar Blackwelder of Washington, D. C., introduced an additional clause instructing the committee "to seek the fullest possible co-operation with other Lutheran bodies, in the hope of preparing, as nearly as proves feasible, a Common Lutheran Hymnal in America." This proposal was enthusiastically adopted, and events proved that the churches were ready for further and concerted action. The long and successful administration of Dr. Frederick H. Knubel as president of the United Lutheran Church was drawing to a close. Dr. Franklin Clark Fry was elected president at this meeting.

At the author's request Dr. Fry met with him in Philadelphia December 16. They discussed a plan of procedure which Dr. Reed had prepared. Dr. Fry approved it in general and suggested that it might be best to report it to the next meeting of the Executive Board. On January 12 Dr. Fry informed Dr. Reed of the board's hearty approval of the program. He also instructed the Common Service Book Committee, to whom the church's mandate had originally been given, to write directly to the authorities of the other churches, explaining the possibilities and inviting their participation in the project.

It thus fell to the lot of the officers, Drs. Reed and Hoover, chairman and secretary respectively of the committee, to extend a formal invitation to the presidents of the churches to appoint representatives on a joint committee to study possibilities. The Lutheran Church—Missouri Synod was not invited at this point since—as was explained in a later letter to the president of that synod—"it so recently published its own new hymnal and could not be expected immediately to sponsor a new and different work of the same kind."

There were delays and misgivings. Eventually, however, the presidents of all the other churches appointed representatives. At a meeting in the First English Lutheran Church in Pittsburgh on June 23, 1945, the Joint Commission on the Hymnal was organized. At a subsequent meeting, Dr. Reed was elected permanent chairman and Dr. E. E. Ryden secretary.

The work proceeded so auspiciously that representatives of the Augustana Church suggested the possibility of constituting a joint commission on the liturgy. The presidents of the churches felt that it would be more difficult to reach agreement in the liturgy, but eventually authorized a small exploratory conference which met in Chicago on February 26, 1946, with the following present: Prof. H. C. Leupold, The American Lutheran Church; President Conrad Bergendoff, the Augustana Church; the Rev. C. M. Videbeck, the United Evangelical Lutheran Church; Prof. Luther D. Reed and Dr. Paul Z. Strodach, the United Lutheran Church. Dr. Selmar Berge of the Evangelical Lutheran Church, who had been appointed to the study, was unable to attend.

This conference reported its findings as follows: (1) Lutheran services in all bodies are now conducted almost entirely in the English language; (2) several bodies publish English translations and adaptations of liturgies used in Europe; (3) the Common Service is officially recognized and appears in all service books and hymnals; (4) the great majority of Lutherans in this country use only the Common Service, though in slightly variant forms; (5) each general body had its own hymnal.

The following resolutions were adopted:

1. We agree unanimously that a Common Liturgy for our Church in America is desirable and possible.
2. We agree that the Common Service shall be the basis and that other current uses in our Church shall be considered.
3. We request each of the Presidents of our General Bodies to appoint not more than three or four representatives to form a Joint Commission which shall seek to achieve this goal.
4. We believe that it is highly desirable that all Lutheran Bodies in this country co-operate in this undertaking and we therefore ask authority to issue the necessary invitations.

APPROVAL OF PRELIMINARY FINDINGS

The presidents approved these findings and authorized the five conferees to request the presidents of all Lutheran churches in the country to appoint representatives to attend a conference in Pittsburgh on June 26-28, 1946. A communication signed by all who had attended the February 25 conference was sent. This communication included the original resolution of the Joint Commission on the Hymnal (October 22, 1945) and the findings of the exploratory committee which had met in Chicago, and concluded by inviting the presidents "to appoint a representative or representatives to join with us in studying this subject, which is of such great importance for the entire Lutheran Church in America . . ." and "to set up a Joint Commission on the Liturgy if this seems feasible."

The chairman, Dr. Reed, under date of July 22, reported the results of this conference to President Behnken, and said, "Believing that the shortness of the notice may have made it impossible for the Missouri Synod to be represented at the Pittsburgh meeting, we wish to inform you of the Chicago meeting well in advance and to say again that we shall be glad to have representatives of the Missouri Synod participate with us in this joint project."

President Behnken replied as follows:

Our Synod recently published a new hymnal. It was a joint effort with the constituent members of the Synodical Conference. The new hymnal contains the liturgy which is now used quite extensively in our circles and is being introduced in many places where very little liturgy formerly was in use. Our Synod would not be interested now in effecting another change.[1]

[1] This correspondence ended with a letter from Dr. Reed to President Behnken which reads as follows:
"We shall all be sorry not to have representatives of the Missouri Synod co-operate with representatives of all the other major Lutheran bodies in this proposed study.
"It is nearly sixty years since the Common Service was adopted (1888). The experience gained during those years suggests a few changes; certain deeply cher-

The uncertainty and timidity with which this enterprise was begun is reflected in a letter (January 20, 1952) from Dr. H. C. Leupold to Dr. Reed recalling the circumstances of the February 25, 1946, meeting. This meeting, says Dr. Leupold, "was exploratory in character . . . since we merely discussed things, no motions were passed. We scarcely dared to hope to organize . . . so there was no secretary. No minutes were kept. The second time, when we met in Pittsburgh, we finally concluded that a Commission should be organized . . . That is when I was chosen [secretary]. . . ."

ORGANIZATION AND METHODS

Dr. Leupold continued to record the voluminous notes of the commission to the end. Fifteen regular meetings of the commission were held. Several of these continued for three or four days. Several joint meetings were held with the Commission on the Hymnal.

Though only Drs. Berge, Bergendoff, Leupold, Reed, and Strodach were present at the second meeting, the problem was attacked with vigor. The decision to use the Common Service as the basis for discussion was re-affirmed, with two explanations: "that we interpret the term 'basis' as the equivalent of 'starting point'; and that we continually refer to, and faithfully consider, all uses current in American Lutheran Churches." Dr. Bergendoff was appointed to study collects in German, Scandinavian, and other historic sources; Dr. Leupold to draft a series of Old Testament Lessons for possible introduction before the Epistle. Dr. Seltzer, though not yet appointed to the commission, was asked to give special attention to the General Prayer and the Offertory. Proper prefaces for Advent and All Saints' Day, prepared by Dr. Strodach, were accepted for future consideration. The group approved the preparation of a Eucharistic Prayer, and asked Drs. Reed and Strodach to propose separate forms. It also approved the form of administration in the Swedish use, with its response "Amen." Dr. Strodach was asked to propose additional post-communion collects.

Thus the work began. As it proceeded (and this was the case with the Commission on the Hymnal as well) the horizons widened, and the commissioners learned as they labored. Conviction deepened that it would be impossible simply to pool resources and prepare a superficial assortment of features in current use. Thoroughgoing study of the entire field was required—American and European Lutheran uses, the Re-

ished uses of some Lutheran groups require examination; and the results of inten-sive study of liturgical matter in all communions during the last half century should be considered; so that in the light of all these factors, we may be able to improve the already fine Liturgy we have. Such a careful, critical study is now getting well under way; and its results will, I am certain, be of very great importance for the entire Lutheran Church in America.

"It was with the hope that all of our groups might have part in this work and together accomplish something significant for all American Lutheranism that an invitation was extended to the Missouri Synod."

formation era, the Roman and the Anglican rites, and particular investigation of the researches of modern scholarship in the worship of the
early church.

It was also realized that the commissioners had greater freedom than
the framers of the Common Service had possessed under the rule which
was then necessary. The "common consent of the pure Lutheran liturgies
of the sixteenth century" provided an objective, historic principle,
which at that time made agreement possible. Coming to grips with the
major problem again, the commission recognized that it not only had
to provide material not found at all in the Common Service, but that in
all its work it needed not be strictly bound by the rule which had proved
so useful sixty or more years ago, but which had not the same significance today. The church orders of four centuries ago were local reforms,
intended for a single kingdom, duchy, or city (Nürnberg, Strasbourg,
Cologne), or even a town like Wittenberg or Göttingen. These church
orders were prepared by theologians and jurists who knew little if anything about the worship of the early church, or of liturgical forms in
general beyond the local Roman rites. Moreover, we are not living in
the sixteenth century which produced these orders, or in the nineteenth
century which rediscovered them. We must do in our time precisely
what these scholars did in their time—prepare, with all the resources
at our command, the best possible liturgy for our own time and place.
Historic principles and confessional conformity must ever prevail, but
we must be free to profit by practical experience in the use of the
Common Service. We must be sensitive to contemporary conditions and
needs. We must encourage an ecumenical outlook with appreciation of
valuable features in the formal worship of other communions. And we
must study with an open mind the results of modern scholarship, particularly in the field of early Christian worship.

Basic, of course, was work upon the Service with Holy Communion,
Matins, and Vespers together with their great body of proper Introits,
Collects, liturgical Lessons, Graduals, antiphons, responsories, etc. The
Common Service had established the foundations for this, and common
acceptance of its provisions presented no difficulties. Awareness of
recent studies of these features in the Lutheran churches of Germany
and Scandinavia, in the Roman and Anglican communions, and in the
Church of Scotland and other independent churches led to exhaustive
comparative studies and to changes in the appointed Epistles and Gospels. There were other major problems, such as musical settings for the
liturgy, a series of occasional services, and an entirely new selection of
collects and prayers. In addition, special studies were made of such

difficult questions as a Eucharistic Prayer, versions of the Scriptures, etc., which will all be discussed later. The immediate question is one of method. How were these matters cared for, how did the commission work?

It fell to the lot of the chairman, as in the case of the Commission on the Hymnal, to call and preside at meetings, to appoint committees, and to make assignments. He had to keep the work moving, confer with the presidents of the churches, and conduct a general correspondence which eventually ranged over twenty-three states and half a dozen foreign countries. He also drafted reports to the churches and took his share of study and conference in the work of the "study group" in the East (Seltzer, Horn, Seaman, and Reed). However consequential this may or may not have been, the chairman felt that much of the time he was simply handling the wheel while the power that drove the machine came largely from others. How true this was, and how definitely the resulting liturgy was a work of the entire commission, is indicated by the following list of assignments.

Committee appointments:

Text of the liturgy—Dr. Seltzer (chairman)

Old Testament lessons for Matins and Vespers—Drs. Leupold and Bostrom.

Changes in archaic expressions in the Authorized Version, text of Epistles and Gospels—Drs. Strodach, Hoover, and Salzmann.

Changes in the Authorized Version text of the Psalms—Drs. Leupold, Seltzer, and Bostrom.

The occasional services—Drs. Seltzer (chairman), Salzmann, Field, Horn (later Preus or Tweet), and Kloth.

Music of the liturgy—Drs. Horn (chairman), Bostrom (later Bergendoff), Leupold, Reed, and Seltzer.

Rubrics—Drs. Seltzer, Horn, and Fisher.

The Litany, Suffrages, and Bidding Prayer—Drs. Horn and Seltzer.

Joint Editorial Committee—Drs. Seltzer (chairman), Bergendoff, Field, Hansen, Leupold, and Reed, together with Drs. Jagnow, Ryden, and Seaman (secretary) from the Commission on the Hymnal.

Individual assignments:

Beginning of the Service (Confession, Kyrie, etc.)—Dr. Bergendoff.

Eucharistic Prayer—Drs. Strodach (died 1947) and Reed.

Prayer of the Church—Dr. Seltzer.

Collects and prayers—Dr. Strodach, later Dr. Seltzer.

Old Testament Lessons in the Service—Dr. Leupold.

Lectionary for Matins and Vespers—Dr. Strodach, later Dr. Horn.

All details of text and music were reported to the entire commission, which acted upon every sentence and syllable and upon every note of music. Mimeographing of all reports was required to facilitate study and action. Major decisions were reported in full to the co-operating churches and approved by them. In a few instances—the text of the Eucharistic Prayer, the choice of Scripture versions, etc.—individual churches presented comments and requests which were carefully considered. The complete program envisioned by the commission includes, besides the music edition of the *Service Book* and *Hymnal,* a word edition to contain orders not included in the music edition, an altar book, a book of occasional services for pastors, and, eventually a popular companion to the liturgy and a handbook on the hymnal.

DISTINCTIVE FEATURES

If it be asked what are the distinctive features, old and new, of the Common Liturgy, and what, particularly, are the new features not found previously in Lutheran liturgies in America or in present liturgies in Europe—features which will establish the Common Liturgy as a distinctly American use—one may answer:

The Common Liturgy is a new work on foundations laid centuries ago. It conforms closely to the ideas expressed by Luther in his classic *Formula Missae* of 1523, which was a purified form of the historic rite of the Western church. Inasmuch as some sixteenth-century revisions and adaptations are inadequate or even impossible to use today, modifications were necessary. Also a few historic features, chiefly from the worship of the early church, have been introduced. In spirit and form the Common Liturgy is historic and not individual or sentimental; its tone is devotional and not dogmatic; its outlook is ecumenical rather than narrowly confessional or provincial; its total impact is that of a contemporary form well adapted to the requirements of a continent-wide constituency.

With respect to content, the Common Liturgy presents the historic Lutheran service in fullest form for all who wish to use it. Simplifications may be made by observance of the "may" rubrics, of which there are many. There is a preliminary service of confession with a Declaration of Grace. The Service of the Day begins with the Introit for the Day. Main divisions are the Service of the Word and the Service of the Sacrament. The latter includes the Preface and the Sanctus, the Prayer of Thanksgiving with the Words of Institution and the Lord's Prayer, the administration, Post-Communion and Benediction.

Material revisions of previous parts:

> The liturgical lessons, with three new Epistles, four new Gospels, and several optional alternate Gospels.
> Insertion of the Festival of the Holy Innocents, Martyrs, in the calendar.
> A few changes in archaic expressions in the Authorized Version of the Scriptures.
> A simplified formula of distribution of the Sacrament.
> A new text of the Prayer of the Church (General Prayer).
> Sixty-five new collects and prayers.

New features:

"A Brief Order of Public Confession."

An alternate Declaration of Grace, based upon a Compline text.

Additional historic Introits, Collects and Graduals.

A new and expanded text of the Kyrie, a restoration of a historic form of the early church.

A complete series of Old Testament lessons, for optional use before the Epistle.

Original music settings for ten "season graduals."

Propers for an early service on Easter.

A change in the order of parts following the Sermon.

Permissive use of the historic word "catholic" instead of "Christian" in the Creeds.

Restoration of the ancient Prayer of Thanksgiving (Eucharistic Prayer).

Proper Prefaces for Advent and All Saints' Day.

Additional post-communion collects.

A new series of lessons for Matins and Vespers, and a series of daily lessons.

Three complete musical settings for the Liturgy, Matins, Vespers, and the Litany, including ministerial intonations.

A new system of pointing ("speech-rhythm") for chants.

A modern free type of harmonization for the plain-song setting.

Twenty-five occasional services, some material revisions, others entirely new.

SPECIAL PROBLEMS

Much of the work went forward normally, with agreement readily reached. Other items presented difficulties, some of which may be mentioned, though further discussion will be found in subsequent chapters.

In the Service proper, problems, large and small, were: the very beginning from the confession to the Kyrie; the order of parts in the offertory; the Prayer of Thanksgiving (Eucharistic Prayer); and the word "catholic" in the Creeds. In the first of these items an attempt was made to reconcile the texts of the Common Service with the use of the Swedish church in Europe and America, which connected the Confession of Sins with the Kyrie. This arrangement was also found in some German orders as well. It was finally decided to abide by the order of the Common Service—Confession, Introit, Gloria, Kyrie— and thus preserve intact the historic sequence of the Mass following a separate preliminary confession and absolution. Dr. Bergendoff's researches, however, uncovered the early complete form of the Kyrie ʊr Ektene of the Greek liturgies. The commission, after lengthy discussion at several sessions, accepted a portion of this as a "valid form of the Kyrie," and proposed this fuller litany-type text as a substitute for the simple threefold Kyrie.

The change in the order of parts in the Offertory was made by unanimous action in an effort to correct the popular misunderstanding of the Offertory sentences, "Create in me a clean heart," etc., as a response to the Sermon. The Service of the Word ends with the Votum after the sermon, and the Offertory as a whole, with its features of the Offering, Offertory sentences, and Prayer of the Church, actually begins a new major section of the liturgy. It looks forward to the Sacrament.

With respect to the text of the Creeds, the commission unanimously agreed to restore the historic word "catholic" in place of "Christian," a peculiarity of the German Lutheran church no longer found in Swedish, Danish, Norwegian, Finnish, or French Lutheran liturgies, and which indeed is never found in the Latin confessions of the church. They always gave the original and universally accepted form: "Credo in sanctam ecclesiam catholicam." Uninformed opinion may accept this return to the historic text with reluctance. What is right and true, however, must prevail over what is inaccurate. As a concession to popular prejudice it was decided to print the text of the Creeds as heretofore, but to supply footnotes to the word "Christian" permitting the use of the word "catholic" at this place.

The liturgical lessons (Epistle and Gospel) of the Common Service were at first accepted without question. Later it was realized that thoroughgoing studies of this subject had been made within the past few years with important revisions in the lectionaries of European and American churches. The chairman of the commission made a preliminary study of these lectionaries in comparison with the appointments in the Common Service. This study included the Roman Missal, the *Book of Common Prayer* (English, American, Scottish and the *Proposed Book* of 1928), the Church of Sweden, German Lutheran groups (VEKD, ELKD, Rhineland, etc.), the proposals of Bishop Stählin, and the *Book of Common Order* of the Church of Scotland. Studies were made independently by Drs. Seltzer, Horn, and Seaman, with results and recommendations presented to the Joint Editorial Committee in an extended mimeographed report prepared by Dr. Horn.

This committee devoted days to consideration of this report, and submitted its findings to the entire commission. Final action, in addition to changes in the selection of lessons, included a number of abbreviations or extensions of lessons, particularly in the case of certain Epistles. The commissioners were aware of the fundamental character of this work and changes in the accustomed use were made only after careful consideration. It was also decided to include a number of "liturgical introductions," (as for example: "At that time Jesus said," etc.), and to substitute different words or phrases for archaic or difficult expressions in the Authorized Version text. There were probably not more than twenty substitutions. In retrospect it may be said that the commission regards this revision of the liturgical lessons as one of its most important and constructive achievements. Of similar importance was the adoption of Old Testament Lessons for optional use in the Service, of a lectionary for Matins and Vespers, and of a daily lectionary for the year. Consideration of these items was based upon preliminary studies of Old Testament Lessons by Dr. Leupold and of two other series by Dr. Horn.

The Prayer of Thanksgiving (Eucharistic Prayer) is the restoration of a feature from the early church and the ecumenical church which, with a few notable exceptions, is not generally found in Lutheran liturgies. Many liturgical scholars in Germany and Scandinavia during the last century have pleaded for the restoration of this central feature of the "Eucharist" ("Thanksgiving," one of the earliest names given the celebration of the Lord's Supper). There was no agreement in the matter of a suggested text, and these appeals received limited consideration. Dr. Strodach, a student of the early liturgies, proposed a text in his *Manual on Worship* which the Lutheran Church in India adopted practically unchanged. The author of the present volume suggested a somewhat similar form in the first edition of THE LUTHERAN LITURGY (1947), p. 336. The commission requested Drs. Strodach and Reed to propose separate texts. As presented the two texts resembled each other quite closely, since both authors, instead of fashioning original forms, had prepared literary mosaics of phrases appearing repeatedly in eucharistic prayers in the ancient liturgies. The commission devoted hours of discussion to this subject. It finally agreed, quite harmoniously, on a text which was reported in full to the churches, of which several debated the subject at length. The insertion of a Prayer of Thanksgiving was finally approved by all the churches, but with comments and requests which were carefully considered by the commission. Several significant changes in the original text were made, and the resulting form was finally approved by the churches.[2]

Another serious problem was the question of Scripture versions in the liturgical lessons—whether to use the Authorized Version or the Revised Standard Version. Solution was difficult not only because of

---

[2] In this connection it is gratifying to note the inclusion of a similar Prayer of Thanksgiving in the recently published *Agende für evangelisch-lutherische Kirchen und Gemeinden* (Berlin: Lutherisches Verlagshaus, 1955).

the texts themselves but because of a sharply divided opinion in nearly all the co-operating churches. There was no disagreement among the commissioners themselves. All believed that for a book of corporate devotion the Authorized Version was greatly to be preferred. It was agreed that more precise expressions should be substituted in a number of instances, including such words as "love" for "charity"; "strewed" for "strawed"; "precede" for "prevent"; "heart" for "bowels"; "citizenship" for "conversation"; "shun" for "eschew," etc. With these amendments the commission reaffirmed its decision to use the Authorized Version and so reported in 1948, which report was approved by all the churches. Subsequently, however, the massive commercially inspired advertising program of the publishers of the Revised Standard Version and the awakened interest of pastors and of representatives of educational interests led to a challenge of the commission's decision. The Augustana Church, the only church which used the American Revised text of 1901 in its service books, and the United Lutheran Church both requested the Revised Standard Version text.

The commission considered this entire question again, reviewing a report submitted by a special committee (Drs. Horn, Leupold, and Preus) which summarized the debate. The commission expressed its appreciation of the value of other versions, including the Revised Standard Version, for educational and homiletical use, but reaffirmed its united opinion that for liturgical use the Authorized Version should remain because of its literary excellence and its deep-rooted position in our English-speaking culture. The commission also called attention to the fact that the entire liturgy is in the language of the Authorized Version, and to the further fact that at that time the Revised Standard Version was available only for the New Testament, while the Old Testament translation would not appear from the press for several years. It was also felt that the appearance of two different versions on every page of the propers would be inharmonious, inartistic, and indefensible. In addition the commission realized that no matter which version was adopted a large section of the church would be displeased. In view of these facts it decided to print no Epistles and Gospels in the *Service Book,* but only to indicate Scripture references, and then to issue two supplementary lectionaries: one in the Authorized Version, the other in the Revised Standard Version, affording pastors and congregations an option.

DIFFICULTIES SURMOUNTED

The Augustana Church in June, 1952, directed its book concern "to make necessary arrangements to publish a special edition of the Common Hymnal and Service Book, with the pericopes in the text of the RSV." The chairman of the commission expressed the distress all felt "in the situation that has been created and in facing the possibility that the one area which held such a bright promise of Lutheran unity and endeavor may now be blighted by friction and disunity again." When it became clear that the other churches had accepted the decision of the commission; that the publishers were opposed to printing two editions of the Service Book; and that if Augustana should withdraw, the book would undergo thorough revision and be copyrighted by the seven other churches, wiser counsels prevailed and the final decision of the commission was accepted.

The early request of the Evangelical Lutheran Church for a supplement to the *Service Book and Hymnal* to contain the current liturgy of that church and a selection of additional hymns from its *Hymnary,* to be bound into copies introduced in their congregations, gave the commission real concern. At the very beginning the commission was informed that the co-operation of this church could be secured only if permission were granted, and it was reluctantly given. Representatives of this church worked faithfully and constructively with the commission throughout the years, and strove earnestly to secure the repeal by their church of their request for special consideration. To the deep satisfaction of all, the Evangelical Lutheran Church on June 26, 1956, withdrew its request and thus came into final and complete agreement with the other churches in the common enterprise.

Another problem confronting the commission was the question of the Psalter. The original Common Service provided a selection of only 69 psalms. The *Common Service Book* increased the number to 101. The commission at one time approved the insertion of all 150 psalms. Subsequent action, recognizing the fact that the principle of selection had always prevailed, resulted in the preparation of a "liturgical Psalter" instead of a complete Psalter. The imprecatory psalms and others regarded as too lengthy, as containing unattractve descriptions of human suffering, or as otherwise inappropriate for public worship were omitted. This left 134 psalms in the selection. Eventually the necessity of compressing material to keep within the agreed-upon number of pages led to further excision which left 114 psalms or portions of psalms as the actual number in the Service Book.

The preparation of the occasional services presented difficulties because of the volume of material and also because of the diversity of uses in the different churches. While there had been substantial agreement in the structure of the Service, including the Holy Communion, there was no agreement in the number or the character of the ministerial acts. Many of these were translations and transplants of widely different forms in the service books of Lutheran state churches in Europe. It seemed impossible to reach an agreement. The subcommittee on this subject, however, held many meetings, labored patiently and through several sessions laid copies of voluminous mimeographed pages before the commission. Mutual respect and understanding, and an indomitable will to agree, finally led to the adoption of the orders listed below. This material is extensive. Only the most necessary and generally used services are included in the music edition of the *Service Book*. Other orders will be printed in the altar book, and still others in the complete collection for the use of pastors. The importance of this body of material, now for the first time in common form and use, cannot be overestimated, perhaps not even fully understood at the moment.

Following is the list of orders adopted:

Baptism of Infants	Ordination
Baptism of Adults	Setting Apart of a Deaconess
Adult Baptism and Confirmation at the Same Service	Laying the Cornerstone of a Church
Brief Order for Public Confession	Blessing of a Cemetery
Public Confession	Installation of a Pastor
Private Confession and Absolution	Sending Forth of a Missionary
Burial of the Dead	Induction of a President
Marriage	Installation of a Church Council
Visitation of the Sick	Opening of Synods
Communion of the Sick	Closing of Synods
Commendation of the Dying	Induction of Office-Bearers

MUSICAL SETTINGS

The musical settings of the liturgy demanded close and prolonged attention. A beginning was made late in 1948 when a committee consisting of Drs. Bostrom, Horn, Seltzer, Saltzmann, and Reed was appointed "to determine principles and policies." This committee recommended that three settings be prepared for the liturgy proper, that ministerial intonations be provided, and that a single setting be given for Matins and Vespers, the Litany, and the burial office. The music committee as finally organized consisted of Drs. Horn (chairman), Bergendoff, Field, Preus, Reed, and Seltzer.

The commission decided that in order to secure richness and quality in all settings expert professional advice should be secured. For the first or Anglican chant setting, the services of Dr. Harold Wells Gilbert, organist and choirmaster of St. Peter's Episcopal Church in Philadelphia and headmaster of its nationally known choir school, were secured. Dr. Gilbert studied organ with

Charles Courboin and theory with Dr. Hugh A. Clarke. He later studied church music and choir training with Sir Charles MacPherson of St. Paul's Cathedral and with Sir Sydney H. Nicholson of the School of English Church Music in London. In Philadelphia, Dr. Gilbert also gained high recognition as the musical director of the Mendelssohn Club for twenty years, conductor of the Fortnightly Club, head of the music department of the Philadelphia Divinity School, and as an author and editor as well.

For the second or "continental" setting the Augustana Church offered the services of Regina Holmen (Mrs. F. M.) Fryxell. She is a graduate of Augustana College and of the Juilliard School of Music in New York City, an organist, teacher, and composer of distinguished choral and instrumental music and a discerning student of church music in Europe through her travels in England, France, Denmark, Sweden, and Norway.

The third or plain-song setting was prepared by Ernest White, for many years music director of the Church of St. Mary the Virgin (Episcopal) in New York City, distinguished teacher, organist, music editor, and authority on Gregorian music. A pupil of Healey Willan and of Sir Ernest Macmillan at the University of Toronto and later of Lynwood Farnum in New York, Mr. White gained national reputation as an organ recitalist, playing more than one thousand programs in all parts of the country. He taught Gregorian music at the Pius X School of Liturgical Music in New York City, made frequent broadcasts from his own studio, published much choir and organ music from his own press, and at present is chief consultant on tonal design and research for the M. P. Moller Organ Company.

An earnest effort was made to combine the first and second settings, but this was found impractical because of the different character of the music in the settings and the number of alternate items that would have been required.

The first setting is called "Anglican chant" but really is a mixed form. It does, though, contain Anglican chants and is the only one of the three settings which uses them. It also includes several Gregorian, chorale, and even more modern forms. The text of Matins and Vespers is set throughout to Anglican chants. There are no less than twenty-five of them in the *Service Book*.

This chant form developed within the Church of England, particularly in the cathedrals and larger parish churches where the chanting of the Psalter is a regular feature of Morning Prayer and Evensong. During the Reformation era the use of the unisonous Gregorian psalm tones was continued. The fury of the Puritan rebellion suppressed the Prayer Book and drove liturgical music out of the churches. The restoration of the monarchy in 1660 reintroduced liturgical worship, but musical traditions had been broken, and the religious and social climate was different. Musicians returning to their posts attempted adaptations of plain-song melodies, but as it proved difficult to adjust melodies associated with the Latin text to English words, they experimented with simpler and lighter chant forms. The influence of the psalm tones was felt, but four-part harmonies were added and a great variety of melodic inflections developed.[3]

The next two centuries witnessed the composition and use of an incredible number of these chants. With awakened interest in congregational singing in the mid-nineteenth century various systems of pointing —setting the text to the inflections of the chant—were employed. One of these gained general ascendency with the publication of the *Cathedral Psalter* in 1874 and formed the basis for the Anglican chant forms in the *Common Service Book*. This "cathedral system" had first regard for the music. It required the chants to be sung in strict time, and the text was subordinated to the measured rhythm of the chant. Under this system many words received false accents, syllables were unduly abbreviated or prolonged, and the natural meaning of the text itself was frequently obscured.

Early in the present century English church musicians, influenced by studies in plain song, focused attention upon the natural rhythm and accent of the texts. New systems of pointing appeared which gave primary consideration to the words and their meaning.[4] The inflexible metrical form of the chant was modified in favor of a flexible form accommodating itself to the rhythmic flow and accents of the text. Thus developed the so-called speech-rhythm system of chanting employed in English, Scotch and American Psalters for the past thirty years and more. This system is now generally recognized as the best yet devised. It is this system which the commission, after thorough study and discussion, adopted for the *Service Book*.

The introduction of this system of pointing in congregations accustomed to another system will occasion some difficulties. In a choice, however, between the easier way and the better way there was little question as to what should be done. The late Sir Sydney H. Nicholson, who resigned his important post as organist of Westminster Abbey chiefly to promote the development of speech-rhythm chanting, has made this pertinent observation: "the older stiff system still lingers on in many places, for church people and church choirs are conservative and take

---

[3] See articles "Chant, Anglican" and "Chanting" in the *Prayer Book Dictionary*, and in Groves' *Dictionary of Music and Musicians* (5th ed.; New York, 1954).

[4] See *The Psalter Newly Pointed* (London: S.P.C.K., 1925), the *English Psalter* (London: Novello, 1925), *The St. Paul's Cathedral Psalter* (London: Novello, 1934), *The Parish Psalter* (Faith Press, 1932), *The Oxford Psalter* (London: Oxford Univ. Pr., 1929), *The Scottish Psalter* (Authorized Version; London: Oxford Univ. Pr., 1939). In America we have *Songs of Praise for America* (New York: Oxford, 1938), and Ray F. Brown's *The Oxford American Psalter* (New York: Oxford, 1949).

slowly to new ideas; but it is certainly doomed, for it is founded on false principles. . . . When it comes to a choice between the claims of the words and of the music, the words are bound in the end to prevail, for it is for them that the chants exist."[5]

The second setting is called "continental" because it represents the type of liturgical music used in the Reformation era and to the present day in Lutheran churches in Germany, Scandinavia, and elsewhere on the European continent. Anglican chant forms are unknown, with much less use of the Psalter and less popular participation in Matins and Vespers than in England. Even Gregorian psalm tones are rarely heard. Church musicians, however, have preserved the distinctive modal character and church associations of plain song in all their adaptations and original compositions for the text of the liturgy. In the matter of measured rhythm the influence of the chorale is also evident. This combination of plain song, chorale, and motet features has given liturgical music in European Lutheran churches a somewhat heavy and solemn character, but one with unquestioned depth, quality, and richness as well. The second setting, ably edited as noted above by Mrs. Fryxell, well represents historic and current European musical tradition, particularly that of the Church of Sweden and of provincial churches in Germany. English congregations in America are better acquainted with the lighter Anglican chant and other forms of liturgical music universally found in the English-speaking world. The solemnity and richness of European Lutheran music, however, is quite worthy of presentation in the *Service Book* and of use in our American churches. As a general statement it may be said that the continental setting provides a *sung* service; the Anglican chant setting a *chanted* service. The latter, particularly with speech-rhythm pointing, flows more lightly and speedily. It gives primary consideration to the words, while the continental setting, with its fuller melodic forms, focuses primary attention upon the music.

The third or plain-song setting, edited by the Gregorian authority Ernest White, exhibits the traditional type of music for the liturgy developed in the early Middle Ages. It was carried over, with some necessary adaptations to vernacular texts, into the cantionales of Spangenberg, Keuchenthal, Lossius, Eler, and many other Lutheran church orders of the sixteenth century. The unison melodies are those of the popular and beautiful *Missa Orbis Factor* (Mass XI in the Roman *Kyriale*). Some of these melodies have been identified as tenth century in origin; others as belonging to the fourteenth and sixteenth centuries. Their ageold history is testimony to their rare beauty and quality. To

[5] *Quires and Places Where They Sing* (London: Bell, 1932).

the regret of the commission, considerations of size, weight, and cost of the book as well as established arrangements with the publishers, whose contracts with manufacturers and printers were based upon a book of 1024 pages, made it impossible to include the plain-song setting in the service book. Arrangements were made for its separate publication.

THE EDITORIAL COMMITTEE

In this brief sketch of activities particular mention must be made of the Joint Editorial Committee. This consisted of ten members appointed from the two Joint Commissions in 1950; Drs. Field, Hansen, Horn, Reed, and Seltzer, all members of both commissions; Drs. Bergendoff, and H. C. Leupold, of the Commission on the Liturgy; and Drs. Jagnow, Ryden, and Seaman of the Commission on the Hymnal. Dr. Seltzer and Dr. Seaman were the efficient chairman and secretary, respectively, of this committee, which had to consider a vast amount of material, both in preliminary studies and in final checking of the actions of both commissions. It edited the final manuscript for capitalization, punctuation, and harmonization of rubrics. It read all proofs; it co-operated with the publishers in matters of style, format, etc., and in the preparation of contractual agreements. It secured permissions for the use of liturgical texts, hymns, and music from publishers and other copyright owners. In addition to many meetings of the entire committee in Philadelphia and Chicago, a special responsibility rested on the officers, Drs. Seltzer and Seaman. They gave hundreds of hours to countless details: the preparation and checking of indexes; the collation of corrected proofs; conferences with the publishers, the book designer, etc. Occasionally Dr. Horn, chairman of the music committees, and Dr. Reed, chairman of the commissions, assisted these officers, but they bore the heaviest burdens. In this selfless and time-consuming service they earned the deep gratitude of their fellow commissioners.

THE PROMISE OF THE FUTURE

The *Service Book and Hymnal* is a flexible and powerful instrument for the promotion of church consciousness, unity, and loyalty. Intelligent and general use of it will harmonize and unify the church in a constructive development which has the promise of permanence because it is doctrinally and historically grounded, comprehensive and consistent. Individualism and provincialism must give way before an informed church consciousness of significant dimensions. Close and constant familiarity with these beautiful forms, as with fine models in art and literature will elevate standards of churchly appreciation and taste and train coming generations in practical churchmanship. Officially prepared and authorized by eight churches, which together enroll more than two-thirds of all the Lutherans in the United States and Canada, the *Service Book* will be as important an instrument for these churches as the Anglican Prayer Book and the Roman Missal are in their respective communions. Muhlenberg's ideal of "one church, one book" must still be held aloft to inspire us to further united endeavor.

While primarily intended for public worship, the rich provisions of the *Service Book* offer countless possibilities for private devotional use. Intimate familiarity with its details will encourage effective use of many of the proper collects, lessons, etc., on occasions other than the stated ones. Many of the collects, for example, have a wealth of petition and, like the Lord's Prayer, can be used in connection with a great variety of need. The same is true of the selections from Scripture. As these classic prayers and passages become the possession of pastors and people they will enrich the spiritual life of the church. Next to the Holy Scriptures themselves and the church's historic confessions, the *Service Book* will be the most important and influential book the church possesses.

The movement which produced the Common Service, the *Common Service Book,* and the Common Liturgy is not a spent force. Church life in the Lutheran communion in Europe today is sadly confused. But even there active minorities are pursuing liturgical studies and calling the church to renewed appreciations of common worship and a deepened spiritual life. The Anglican communion has recently revised its liturgies in England, Scotland, and America. The Oxford Movement, after a full century, has restored the general type of worship which was the common possession of the Church of England and of the Lutheran Church in Europe in the sixteenth century, and there is no diminution of interest in the subject.

In the Roman church there is widespread activity, particularly in the effort to make the traditional usages of the church more generally understood and participated in by the laity, and also to promote cultivation of historic and churchly types of liturgical music. In the free churches there is a movement which recognizes the fact that overemphasis upon the sermon often leaves worship itself without form and void. This movement seeks to recover lost qualities of dignity, reverence, and beauty and "an awareness of the presence of God."

The Lutheran communion has the purpose and unity which doctrinal definiteness and historical continuity assure. Its people share in the cultural developments of our land and time. But beyond all this, which is more or less on the surface, the Lutheran Church has always cherished a theory of worship based upon the objective principle of the supremacy of the Word of God and the efficacy of the means of grace as proclaimed and administered in public services in which popular participation is systematically developed. This means liturgical worship. In the Lutheran communion there will always be a liturgical movement, for liturgical practice, development, and reform are all expressions of the living church.

The resolve to make the fullest use of our recovered inheritance will mean earnest study of a large field—the liturgy itself, the church year, church music, church architecture, and liturgical art. It will mean awakening interest among pastors, organists, choir members, and intelligent laymen. It will mean programs of education, study courses, addresses, and discussions in seminaries, colleges, and congregations. A much more adequate literature, both scientific and popular, will be required. The whole church should strive to bring its churchmanship up to standards maintained by the Reformers and reaffirmed in the Common Service, which, indeed, was far ahead of the church itself in 1888. It was no compromise product designed to meet average ideas or practices. In its complete provisions it held aloft a type of service once usual but by then long forgotten. In many particulars the Common Service is still ahead of the church. With all our progress, our average liturgical and musical practice today does not approach in richness, correctness, and consistency the average attained by Lutheran congregations in the cities of Germany and Sweden during the lifetime of the Reformers—which was the standard, textually at least, of the Common Service of 1888.

The Common Service and the new Common Liturgy are not reactionary works. Theirs was and is the spirit of progressive conservatism. Their framers were able churchmen, resourceful, forceful leaders of their own time. They had, and they have, unbounded faith in the future. In endeavoring to recover and make serviceable the finest liturgical expressions of the past, they were, and are, conservative; in studying and providing for the requirements and the possibilities of the church in America today, they were progressive. Some of our congregations have not yet caught up with or understood the spirit even of the Common Service. None of us have completely realized the possibilities contained in the logical completion of that work, of which the creation of the Common Liturgy is but a single step.

We frequently do not realize that Pietism, Rationalism, and the Calvinistic influences which weakened and destroyed the church's doctrinal and liturgical foundations in the eighteenth and nineteenth centuries also practically erased all liturgical understanding and feeling. We rejoice in the restoration of the church's confessional position and of its historical liturgical services and texts, but we do not realize how much we have to learn if we would recapture the "liturgical sense" which our sixteenth-century churchmen possessed. The facts should challenge us in our own time. Our church life today should rise to a better understanding and use of all that is best and most distinctive in our inheritance—not by way of mechanical imitation or in the spirit of mere repristination, but with an informed appreciation of churchly devotional life and the ability to distinguish elements of universal and permanent significance and to exercise responsible freedom in matters of secondary importance.

The Common Service was a purely literary effort without adequate study of proper music or ceremonial or of the liturgical requirements of the church building. Nor did the *Common Service Book,* thirty years later, attempt to cover all areas in this field. It supplied only the simplest musical forms for congregational use. It provided no music whatever for choral parts, such as chants for the Psalms or settings for the Introits, Graduals, antiphons and responsories. It made no pronouncements upon proper architectural appointments. Its rubrical directions were limited to the simplest and most necessary observances.

The wisdom of this procedure, whether understood at the time or not, has been fully justified. The church has been won to an appreciation of essential values without having to engage in endless controversies over nonessentials. Now with the text and its traditional music well established, greater attention may be given to accuracy, consistency, and refinement of rendition. The Common Liturgy and its musical settings represent a great forward stride in this direction.

THE BEST USE OF A RECOVERED INHERITANCE

The genius of Lutheranism reacts not only against a casual or irreverent approach to God, but also against externality and display in public worship. We seek to approach God directly, simply, sincerely. The simplicity and forthrightness of our liturgy require corresponding qualities in its setting and rendition. Overelaboration, fussy decoration, excessive ceremonial, concertistic music are all out of harmony with the Lutheran understanding. A strong sense of historic values and of what is inherently worshipful, distinctive, and beautiful, however, is entirely in the Lutheran spirit.

Creative activity, controlled by established principles, should be encouraged. We must expect the liturgy itself to receive minor revisions from time to time—and possibly some development. Use and criticism will lead to compression and elimination, particularly perhaps in some of the occasional services. New collects and prayers will meet new needs. In the hymnal there will be subtractions and additions.

The entire field of plain song, as yet invaded by only a few explorers, lies before our musicians. No church in Christendom has a clearer right than the Lutheran to enter this and take possession. It gave the congregational chorale to the Christian world, but few American Lutheran choirs and congregations have an intimate acquaintance with this great body of church song. Organists and composers will also find admirable texts in the liturgy for new settings to Introits, Graduals, Antiphons, and responsories. No other Protestant communion offers in its liturgy so rich and wide an opportunity for musical enrichment and development. Our hope is that this dignified, objective, yet rich and warm, type of worship which was the common possession of the church centuries ago, together with its wonderful music, may again become the prized possession of all our people in our own land and time.

A word of caution should temper this zeal. True development will be a balanced effort. We can expect good practice and progress only from those who study and love the liturgy, its music, and its proper architecture. We should encourage interest and endeavor in all these fields. We should also have patience with the enthusiasm and the zeal of youth as some of our juniors strive to lift the services of their congregations to higher levels. This will only balance the patience we frequently must extend to the indifference and immobility of age and its frequent refusal to abandon slovenly, incorrect, and individualistic practices.

We realize how far all of us have come when we now find responsive services, chancels, altars, crosses, vested choirs, and clerical gowns in many churches of the so-called nonliturgical communions. These features have long since been established in Lutheran congregations. We should now understand that some congregations, particularly in the larger cities, because of unusual musical and artistic attainments, may desire and be prepared to maintain services of a fuller and more ornate type than others. None should be too greatly disturbed if pastors prefer the ancient surplice and stole of the church to the later black gown of the academic world; if on festivals an occasional altar glows with many lights or a processional cross be carried before the choir; if a choirmaster revives interest in plain song and *a cappella* compositions of our old masters; or if efforts be made to have more frequent administrations of the Holy Communion. With respect to the last we all must know that Luther and other eminent leaders of the sixteenth century would be stirred to the depths by the casual consideration given the Sacrament in congregations scheduling only four, or fewer, celebrations a year. They would never approve the "half mass" (the Service without the Sacrament), an inheritance from Rationalism and close association with Zwinglians, which is so often found among us today. Luther himself, according to Veit Dietrich's reminiscences, used to receive the Sacrament every fourteen days or at least every three weeks.[6]

With this understood, it is also true that too aggressive an emphasis upon externalities, such as vestments, lights, ceremonial, etc., disturbs the balanced order of congregational life and threatens the peace and unity of the whole church. Minor matters which seem very important to extremists today are often meaningless after the lapse of centuries, or else are filled with a meaning which we cannot accept.

Worship is a means to an end. It must establish men and women in communion with God and in the fellowship of the saints. If the strongest impression that remains after a service is one of liturgical technique, that service has been a failure. Exaggerated concern for precise and perfect observance of traditional detail cannot satisfy the spiritual hunger of souls seeking God. Ritualism which magnifies detail, and individualism which ignores common usage, are the extremes. Good churchmen will demonstrate a healthy interest in a well-rounded program of church life and work. They will seek to consolidate the gains of previous liturgical development, to conduct the church's service in the church's way, and to unite and elevate the entire church in a broad advance rather than to bring individual congregations to extremely "high" and spectacular performance.

Thankful for our great inheritance, let us diligently study the principles, history, and literature of Christian worship and strive to maintain our services in a manner representative of our best traditions and ideals. Let us develop our musical and artistic resources to the limit of our ability though subordinating art to the liturgy. And whatever the service —whether simple or ornate—let every part be correctly and devoutly rendered.

A program of such breadth, depth, and sincerity will enable the art of worship to flower naturally and beautifully among us in an atmosphere of spiritual reality.

[6] *WA* 48, 326. Also Hans Preuss, "Luther as Communicant," *Lutheran Church Quarterly*, XIV (1941), 199.

CHAPTER XI

THE SERVICE

The Service, in Lutheran use, corresponds to the Divine Liturgy of the Eastern church and the Mass of the Roman church. The German name for it is *Hauptgottesdienst*. Its unique character and importance are indicated in the English title by the significant word "The." More than any other form of worship, it roots itself in our Lord's own example and command. In its complete form it enshrines both Word and Sacrament.

What we call the Service is not a nondescript collection of devotional forms. It has but one theme and that is the loftiest. It lives to proclaim the gospel of Jesus Christ, and through it to reveal God to the world. It lives to offer the Holy Sacrament for the spiritual comfort and strengthening of believers. It lives to express the faith, gratitude, and joy of Christian communities. As the church's normal order of worship on the Lord's Day it is unique, purposeful, powerful. In its several parts and in its totality it builds up a towering majesty of thought and expression, which exceeds that of any other liturgical form in the church's use.

SIGNIFICANCE OF FORM AND DEVELOPMENT

Sooner or later every important and constantly repeated action takes on definite and significant form. Even the highest spiritual values are best expressed and grasped when embodied in appropriate form. God's holy Son became incarnate and took upon himself the form of a servant in order to serve man. His gifts of heavenly grace continue to reach down through the media of written and spoken words and the earthly elements of water, bread, and wine. Similarly the spirit of man employs language and music and art, and even more material things, to express his reverent thanksgiving, hopes, and prayers, and to set forth and preserve the faith by which his own soul lives. The liturgy, through a long and natural process of development, finally came to be the corporate expression of the church's faith and fellowship, and to provide the normal opportunity for the effective administration of the means of grace.

This process was entirely different from the way in which "worship programs" are assembled today. The Service of the church was not privately prepared. No man or group of men set out to analyze and arrange in order the emotions and acts which should enter into a well-balanced program, and then prepare appropriate forms to express these emotions and intentions in acts of worship. The liturgy is a work of the whole church. It grew naturally, as did the Creeds, the Confessions, the great hymns of the church, and even as the Holy Scriptures themselves. It was born not of philosophy but of faith. Psychology may analyze its elements, and logic may arrange its parts, but neither had much to do with its origin and development.

The earliest forms of the liturgy developed from the efforts of groups of believers to do a few simple things. They desired to perpetuate in a vital manner the communion with Christ which the first disciples had known in the flesh, and through Christ unitedly to commune with the Father in heaven. Obedience to our Lord's commands with reference to baptism and the Holy Supper and the endeavor to provide opportunities for instructing the catechumens and the faithful led to readings from Scripture, hymns, prayers, and actions which presently assumed more or less permanent form. Word and Sacrament were the core about which expressions of adoration, confession, petition, intercession, and thanksgiving gradually developed. As the church year evolved, the objective facts of faith were rehearsed and celebrated. Forms which persisted and gained general currency were assembled and arranged, and thus the liturgy grew.

Fragments of Jewish worship persisted in such words as "Amen," "Alleluia," "Hosanna," etc., in the extensive use of the Psalms in introits, graduals, versicles, etc., and in the text of the Sanctus. Greek influence is to be noted in the use of lights and ceremonial, and in the modal system underlying medieval music. Local and provincial history colored the development of the ecclesiastical year. The Scriptures of the New Testament and the institution of the Lord's Supper, however, were the fundamental and positively Christian elements which determined development.

Attention has been called (pp. 52-56) to two types of services in the West during the early Middle Ages: the Roman, which finally prevailed nearly everywhere, and the Gallican. While the later Lutheran liturgy was fundamentally a reform of the Roman Mass, certain features peculiar to the Gallican liturgies have persisted in it to this day. Among these are the rich development of the first part of the Service (the Mass of the Catechumens), the singing of hymns during Communion, the approach of the laity to the altar instead of only to the chancel rail for the Sacrament, the use of the Nunc Dimittis, the Aaronic benediction, etc.

THE REFORMATION'S REDISCOVERY OF THE SACRAMENT

The medieval errors and abuses which called for reform and the program and processes of that reform have already been discussed (pp. 64-110). In rediscovering the gospel the Lutheran Reformation rediscovered the Sacrament. In rediscovering the gospel and the Sacrament it rediscovered the purpose of the liturgy. These discoveries resulted in the development of a liturgical movement which purified, enriched, and empowered the worship of the church.

The teaching of the Lutheran Church with respect to the Sacrament developed on an avenue of discussion with the Roman Catholics on the one side and the Zwinglians and the Calvinists on the other. Some of Luther's personal intensity of conviction and expression are evident in the great emphasis laid by the church on penitence and confession, upon the individualization of the gift of grace, and the personal assurance of salvation enjoyed by the individual communicant.[1]

The Lutheran doctrine, however, has a broader base than this. It rests upon the Lutheran conception of the gospel as comprehending both the audible and the visible Word. In the audible Word of Scripture, the liturgical services, the sermons, etc., the love, the mercy, and the goodness of God are proclaimed to all men. In the visible Word of the Sacrament these are applied individually in the forgiveness and grace given the worshiper through the gift of the body and blood of Christ received in faith.

The doctrine of the Sacrament also involves the doctrine of the church and of the ministry. The conception of the Real Presence rests upon the

---

[1] Seeberg claims that overemphasis upon forgiveness of sins tends to narrow the meaning of the Sacrament and to make of it simply another form of penance. Robert M. Adamson, a Scotch theologian, says: "It is only natural that one who magnified justification by faith as almost the sum and substance of the Gospel should view the central Christian rite in the dazzling light of that glorious doctrine. ... The nature and the greatness of that gift can only be expressed by saying that it consists of Christ Himself." (*The Christian Doctrine of the Lord's Supper*, pp. 152 ff.) While recognizing the force of these judgments, we should also remember that Luther's idea of "the forgiveness of sins" was broadly inclusive and that in his *Small Catechism* he explains the benefits of the Sacrament as "the remission of sins, life and salvation . . . for where there is remission of sins there are also life and salvation" (Part V). For an interesting summary of Luther's view, see Einar Billing, *Our Calling*, trans. Conrad Bergendoff (Rock Island: Augustana Book Concern, 1947), pp. 8ff.

doctrine of the person of Christ, and this again upon the doctrine of the Incarnation. By the Real Presence is understood the presence of the whole Christ in the Sacrament—the human as well as the divine Christ. The Lutheran denies as strongly as does the Calvinist the teaching of transubstantiation, but he believes as strongly as does the Roman Catholic in the Real Presence itself.

The Lutheran church regards the Lord's Supper as the *missa fidelium*. Participation in other services or in the first or general part of the Service is a matter of general privilege. The Sacrament itself is offered only to those who have been instructed as to its meaning and who desire to receive it and come forward to the altar. The church will not administer it promiscuously in the pews or treat it as a semisocial function, or as an expression of unity which does not exist. No Lutheran would desire to commune at a Roman altar even if permitted; nor will he find spiritual satisfaction in communing in churches which profess a merely memorial or symbolical view of the Sacrament. Church members are encouraged to receive the Sacrament in other Lutheran churches as freely as in their own congregations. The significance of the Sacrament as an expression of Christian unity is thus recognized. But since real unity is a matter of faith rather than of organization or emotion, and since unity does not exist among Christian groups in general, intercommunion or open communion is not encouraged.

The Lord's Supper, like baptism, is an act of the church in obedience to Christ's command, "This do," and in reliance upon his assurance, "This is my body which is given for you; this is the blood of the New Testament shed for you and for many for the remission of sins." Its historical recollections point directly to the Upper Room and to the cross on Calvary. Its beneficiaries are all the faithful in the communion of saints. Its hopes encompass greater spiritual powers and deeper consecrations in this present life, and the completion of Christ's work of redemption in the eternal kingdom which he will usher in.

All this centers in the reality of the Presence. If Christ is truly present, all this is true; if he is not present all is vain and false. This is why the Lutheran attaches so much importance to the doctrine of the Real Presence. The late Charles M. Jacobs has happily separated these teachings "from the controversial matrix in which they are historically embedded," and has expressed them simply and beautifully in a glowing passage:

> . . . This Sacrament gathers into itself all the elements of the Christian Gospel. No other act of worship contains them so completely. The work of Christ for the salvation of the world, the gracious will of God in which

231

the work of Jesus had its source, the forgiveness of sin, the hope of the life to come, the reality of the Christian fellowship that has grown out of Christ's work—all of these things come to expression in this Sacrament, and all of them are offered to the communicant. In the Lord's Supper he may hear God saying to him, "All this is yours, if you will but claim it as your own." . . .

The Real Presence of Christ with the bread and wine of the Eucharist presents no difficulties to faith. If we believe that Jesus died and rose again and is our living Lord and Saviour, why should we not believe that He can be really present, where and as He will? If we believe that the Christ who now lives is the same Jesus who endured the suffering of the Cross, why should we doubt that His humanity, as well as His deity, is present in and with the Sacrament? If we believe that, in the Resurrection, Christ's human body was transformed, and became, in St. Paul's phrase, "a spiritual body," why should we stumble at the thought of a "bodily presence"? . . .

That in the Lord's Supper Christ comes to us, not only in a word that He spoke nineteen hundred years ago, but in His very Person; that this Christ is the same Jesus who was with the Twelve in the Upper Room "on the night in which He was betrayed," who died upon a Roman cross and rose from the grave in Joseph's garden; that we may know Him close to us, "closer to us than breathing and nearer than hands or feet"; that our souls can feel His nearness, our hearts go out to Him in adoration, our lives be renewed by contact with His own—that is the meaning of the Real Presence. That we, of times far distant from His own, might be thus keenly conscious that He is with us, Jesus said, "This is My body; this is My blood."

We who believe in this Presence are sure that it is "real." It is not contingent upon the faith of those who receive or those who administer the Sacrament, but is for all alike, for believers and unbelievers, for the godly and the ungodly. It depends in no way upon our perception of it. But to those who are conscious of it, it becomes an additional assurance of the promise, which the Sacrament confers, "of forgiveness of sins, life and salvation." It belongs to the "sign" by which our faith is strengthened and increased.[2]

OTHER ASPECTS OF EUCHARISTIC FAITH AND PRACTICE

Apostolic hands briefly sketched three types of eucharistic thought in the Synoptic, Johannine, and Pauline accounts. Later liturgies and doctrinal formularies have stressed different approaches to and interpretations of the subject. Bishop Brilioth of Sweden in an important contribution to the study of doctrine and the liturgy, speaks of the Eucharist as a jewel which "shows endless changes of light and colour as it is regarded from different angles" though "the light which it refracts is one and the same: The holy Presence, the Mystery."[3] Examining his-

[2] Charles M. Jacobs, *The Ministry and the Sacraments* (London: S.C.M. Pr., 1937), pp. 142-44.
[3] Brilioth, *Eucharistic Faith and Practice*, p. 288.

torically important beliefs and practices, he reveals their relationships and pleads for a fuller and more harmonious expression of all true aspects of "the great Christian sacrament in the wholeness of its many-sided glory." He enumerates five elements or aspects of the Eucharist found with varying emphasis and proportion in all communities. These are: thanksgiving, communion-fellowship, commemoration, sacrifice, and mystery. Bishop Brilioth's thesis calls for the balance of these elements and for the recognition of the Eucharist as the church's chief service of worship and praise.

In agreement with this line of thought, one may say that the Lutheran Service, particularly the Common Liturgy, gives good representation to each of these five elements except the one of sacrifice.

1. *Thanksgiving* was the dominant note in the Lord's Supper of the early church. Justin's *Apology* expressly calls the Sacrament the Eucharist, or Thanksgiving. The lengthy anaphoras of many liturgies testified to "gladness of heart" for the blessings of the natural creation and came to majestic heights in thanksgiving for the objective facts of redemption. But in time Paul's commemoration of the Passion and the later idea of sacrifice were magnified by the medieval church at the expense of this earlier note of thanksgiving, which dwindled to insignificance.

Luther recognized the importance of "the sacrifice of praise." The choral portions of the Mass (Gloria in Excelsis, Alleluia, Creed, Preface, Sanctus, etc.), which he labored to preserve, had their chief significance as acts of praise and thanksgiving. His leadership and encouragement led to a great development of hymnody which struck the same lofty notes in more personal and individualistic fashion than did the medieval Latin hymns. Melanchthon also appreciated the Eucharist as an act of thanksgiving. In the twenty-fourth article of his *Apology* he expanded this thought and developed the sharp distinction between the sacramental and the sacrificial elements in worship which Kliefoth and other nineteenth-century Lutherans carried to undue lengths.

Brilioth laments the fact that "Lutheran individualism has tended to deprive the Eucharist of its robes of thanksgiving" and has given an air of "penitential gloom" to its services. This criticism may apply particularly to the Swedish Liturgy, in which penitential features are unusually prominent. The Common Liturgy, however, with its abundant provision of historic choral elements and its encouragement of congregational participation in the responses gives generous recognition to the thought of thanksgiving. This is evident in the Introit, Gloria in Excelsis, Gradual, the responses at the Gospel, the Prayer of the Church, the Preface and especially the Proper Prefaces, the Sanctus, the Prayer of

Thanksgiving, the Post-Communion Collect, and the Benedicamus. The note of thanksgiving also sounds in the hymns and the Sermon.

2. The Reformation greatly increased the frequency of communion by the people and strengthened the idea of *communion-fellowship*. The mystery of the faithful as "the Body of Christ" is little more than a theological abstraction until we see the body living and functioning in worship and work. The more material aspects of the early Agape were heightened and refined in the restrictions of the *missa fidelium,* which made the Sacrament an expression of unity in the faith on the part of believers in all times and places.

The medieval church destroyed the earlier unity and the sense of corporate worship by emphasizing the priestly class and by relieving the laity of active participation. The Reformation corrected this and re-emphasized the priesthood of believers and the congregational character of worship. Masses without communicants were forbidden and actual communion by the people was promoted. The use of the vernacular, together with the development of hymnody and of popular preaching, were significant factors. The world-wide liturgical movement in the Roman church today is a belated effort to develop intelligent active lay participation in the Mass so that the people may think of themselves as "co-celebrants" with the priest.

The Reformed churches have always stressed the idea of Christian fellowship, some at times seeming to emphasize aspects of the Agape rather than the deeper thought of the *missa fidelium*. Luther's controversy with Zwingli, which centered on the Real Presence, led him to stress the personal assurance of salvation in the Sacrament. His earlier writings, however, reveal a deep appreciation of the fellowship of the faithful. In his *Treatise on the Blessed Sacrament* of 1519, he expands in an original way the attractive idea first expressed in the *Didache* and recurring in the Liturgy of St. Mark, in the Clementine Liturgy, and in various Gallican liturgies:

"Just as the bread is made from many little grains kneaded together, and the bodies of the many grains become the body of the one bread, each single grain losing its body and form and taking to itself the common body of the bread; and similarly the little grapes, losing their separate form, become one common body of wine—so should it be, and so it is, with us when we use this Sacrament aright."[4]

And again: "Whoever is troubled on account of his sins . . . let him go joyously to the Sacrament of the Altar and lay his sorrow upon the congregation, and seek help from the whole multitude of the spiritual body."[5]

[4] *WA* 2, 748. Also *PE* 2, 17.
[5] *WA* 2, 745.

And again, in the Treatise on *Winkelmesse und Pfaffenweihe* (1533): "God be praised, in our churches we can show to Christians a proper Christian mass . . . our minister, bishop or servant in the pastoral office goes to the altar . . . he chants publicly and distinctly Christ's words of institution . . . and we, especially those who wish to receive the Sacrament, kneel behind and around him, man, woman, young, old, master, servant, wife, maid, parents, children, as God brings us together . . . and we do not let our minister speak the words of Christ for himself, as for his own person. On the contrary he is the mouth of us all and we all say them with him from the heart, and with faith uplifted to the Lamb of God who is there for us and with us, and according to his appointment feeds us with his body and blood. That is our mass, and the right mass, which does not fail us."[6]

Later doctrinal formulations emphasized objective considerations, but the Lutheran Liturgy preserves quite fully the thought of communion-fellowship. Its whole spirit tends to make worshipers conscious of their membership in the Christian society. Individuals unite with others in expressing common beliefs in the Creed and common petitions in the *"Our* Father"; together they sing: *"We* lift up our hearts unto the Lord" and *"We* laud and magnify thy glorious Name." As they do this, they realize that they are part of a Body which is alive and working. The individual's own confession and praise mingle with the confession and praise of the Body; his own reception of the sacrificial gift gains higher meaning as he kneels with others at the altar; his own sense of blessing is deepened as the entire service impresses upon him the idea of participation in the life of the universal church, a body which by reason of its relation to Christ has a character and quality above the human and temporal.

The Lutheran Liturgy contains recognition of a still larger fellowship—that of the Church Militant with the Church Triumphant, the union of the whole body of believers here on earth with those who have gone before us in the faith. To be sure, there is no reference to any individual saint in this connection, such as may be found in abundance in the Latin and Greek rites. Nor would we desire their invocation as in the Roman Canon, even in the indirect terms used there. The Lutheran church has limited its recognition of the eternal community of heaven to the grand phrases of the Preface: "Therefore with Angels and Archangels, and with all the company of heaven, we laud and magnify thy glorious Name . . ." This is not much; many would prefer a more direct reference. But the reference is there. We do remember before God's altar the great company whose love and example have given us strength, and we join our praise with theirs. We remember them in a place most exalted—in the Preface of the *missa fidelium,* and in a manner thoroughly evangelical. We have not forgotten our ancestors in the faith—but neither have we set them up as intermediaries between ourselves and God.

[6] *WA* 38, 247. See also Hans Preuss, "Luther as Communicant," *Lutheran Church Quarterly,* XIV (1941), 199.

3. The idea of *commemoration* is satisfactorily represented in the Lutheran Liturgy, particularly because of Lutheran fidelity to the church year. The Evangelists record the Lord's Supper, but Paul specifically connects it with Christ's Passion and death. Justin relates it to the Incarnation. The early liturgies elaborate the entire story of redemption as the ultimate reason for the church's thanksgiving. They also include in diptychs and prayers historic commemorations drawn from the life of the church.

The Lutheran Liturgy by its omission of the entire Canon and its emphasis upon the Words of Institution narrowed the broader outlook of the early church and focused thought upon our Lord's Passion and the idea of atonement. Lutheran conservatism, however, retained the cycle and propers of the church year, and thus provided a historical setting of breadth and variety, and brought new reasons for thanksgiving into every celebration. Thus, while not specifically referring, as does the *Book of Common Prayer,* to "the memorial thy Son has commanded us to make," the Lutheran Liturgy is much fuller in its commemorative features than are the Zwinglian and Calvinistic services. The liturgical Gospels extend the commemorative thought far beyond the limits of the Upper Room and the mount of Calvary. The Proper Prefaces (in which the Common Liturgy is richer than other present-day Lutheran liturgies) definitely fix the thought of the day or season in the very center of the eucharistic thanksgiving. And once again in the Prayer of Thanksgiving itself our attention is called to the central events of our Lord's life on earth. It is to be noted, however, that when in any place the Sacrament is celebrated infrequently, these commemorative values are largely lost so far as the Eucharist itself is concerned.

4. The idea of *sacrifice* cannot be dissociated from the Sacrament, for the memorial which our Lord commanded his disciples to make centers in the thought of his body given and his blood shed for the salvation of men. All Christians recognize Christ's sacrifice on the cross as the only and all-sufficient sacrifice for sin. Where they differ is in their views concerning subjective aspects of sacrifice, and the manner and extent to which believers share in the sacrifice of Christ.

We cannot compromise with pagan or Roman (rather than earlier Gallican) conceptions of the offering of material things and of our own human action as a propitiatory sacrifice. We do, however, recognize the eucharistic sacrifice of praise and thanksgiving. There are other ideas of sacrifice too, which, though valid, fell under suspicion in the violence of Reformation debate and the necessity of opposing the massive medieval belief in propitiatory sacrifice.

What these valid but forgotten ideas of sacrifice are may be disclosed by a study of liturgical texts of various periods and of Luther's writings before he became deeply involved in controversy.

From the Clementine Liturgy in Book VIII of the *Apostolic Constitutions:* "Remembering, therefore, His passion and death and resurrection . . . we offer to Thee, Our King and our God, according to His institution, this bread and this cup; giving thanks to Thee through Him . . . that all who shall partake thereof may be confirmed in piety, may receive remission of their sins, may be delivered from the devil and his wiles, may be filled with the Holy Ghost, may become worthy of Thy Christ and may obtain eternal life."[7]

From the Liturgy of St. James (Jerusalem): ". . . that they may be to all those who partake of them for the remission of sins and for eternal life, for the sanctification of souls and of bodies, for the bringing forth of good works, for the confirmation of Thy Holy Church. . . ."[8]

From the Gallican Liturgy: "Fed with Heavenly Food, we pray the Father, and the Son and the Holy Ghost, that all carnal desires being mortified we may in all things live holy and spiritual lives."[9]

From the first Prayer Book of Edward VI (1549): "Wherefore, O Lorde and heauenly father . . . we thy humble seruauntes do celebrate, and make here before thy diuine Maiestie, with these thy holy giftes, the memoryall whyche thy sonne hath wylled vs to make . . . . And here wee offre and present vnto thee (O Lorde) oure selfe, oure soules, and bodies, to be a reasonable, holy and liuely sacrifice vnto thee: humbly besechyng thee, that whosoeuer shalbee partakers of thys holy Communion, maye worthely receiue the moste precious body and bloude of thy sonne Jesus Christe: and bee fulfilled with thy grace and heauenly benediccion, and made one bodye with thy sonne Jesu Christe, that he maye dwell in them, and they in hym. . . ."[10]

From the *Book of Worship* of the Lutheran churches in India (1938): "We bring before Thee, according to His institution, these Thy gifts of bread and wine, giving thanks to Thee through Him. . . . And we beseech Thee: . . . that in true faith and with contrite hearts we may eat and drink thereof to the remission of sins, and be sanctified in soul and body; that we may be one body and one spirit, and may have our portion with all Thy saints who have been well pleasing unto Thee. . . ."

Luther's *Treatise on the New Testament, that is, the Holy Mass* (1520): "What shall we offer then? Ourselves and all that we have with unending

---

[7] Linton, *Twenty-five Consecration Prayers*, p. 38.

[8] *Ibid.,* p. 43.

[9] J. Comper, *A Popular Handbook on the Origin, History and Structure of Liturgies* (Edinburgh: R. Grant, 1898), Part 2, pp. 141-42.

[10] The thought of this fine prayer of oblation in the Anglican Liturgy is anticipated by expressions in the Strasbourg Mass (1525) (Friedrich Hubert, *Die Strassburger liturgischen Ordnungen im Zeitalter der Reformation* [Göttingen, 1900], p. 85), and specifically in the discussion "Of Holie Oblations" in Archbishop Hermann's Reformation of Cologne, in English as, *A Simple and Religious Consultation . . .* (London: Daye, 1548), folio CXXIVff, especially CXXXV *recto.*

prayer; as we say, Thy will be done on earth as it is in heaven. Herewith must we dedicate ourselves to the divine will that he may do with us as he wills, according to his divine pleasure. And so also we offer him our thanks and praise with our whole heart for his unspeakable sweet grace and mercy which he has promised and given unto us in this sacrament."

Recalling the figure in the Epistle to the Hebrews (Chap. 13) of our Lord as the great High Priest, Luther speaks of our participation in his oblation: "This is indeed true, we must not offer such prayer, praise, thanks, and ourselves before God's eyes through our own selves, but lay them on Christ and let him present them."[11]

Luther's *Treatise concerning the Blessed Sacrament* (1519): "There are those, indeed, who would share the benefits but not the cost, that is, who gladly hear in this sacrament that the help, fellowship and assistance of all the saints are promised and given to them but who, because they fear the world, are unwilling in their turn to contribute to this fellowship, to help the poor, to endure sins, to care for the sick, to suffer with the suffering, to intercede for others, to defend the truth, to seek the reformation of the Church . . . they are self-seeking persons, whom this sacrament does not benefit. . . . We could not endure a citizen who wanted to be helped, protected and made free by the community, and yet in his turn would do nothing for it nor serve it . . . . For the sacrament has no blessing and significance unless love grows daily and so changes a man that he is made one with all others.

"There your heart must go out in love and devotion and learn that this sacrament is a sacrament of love, and that love and service are given you and you again must render love and service to Christ and His needy ones. . . . You must fight, work, pray, and, if you cannot do more, have heartfelt sympathy.

"When they have done this [fear and honor Christ in the sacrament with their prayers and devotion] they think they have done their whole duty, although Christ has given His body for this purpose, that the significance of the sacrament, that is, fellowship and mutual love, may be put into practice . . . that faith in the fellowship with Him and with His saints may be rightly exercised and become strong in us, and that we, in accordance with it, may rightly exercise our fellowship with one another."[12]

"In this sense it is permissible and right to call the Mass a sacrifice, not needed in itself, but as a means whereby we offer up ourselves together with Christ; that is to say, that we cast ourselves upon Christ with a sure faith in His testament, to come before God with our prayer, our praise, and our oblation, only through Him and His meditation, believing firmly that He is our Shepherd and our Priest in heaven before the face of God."[13]

These passages, which might be greatly multiplied, bring two thoughts into the clear. First, God takes earthly things and uses them as vehicles of divine grace and power. Our divine Lord assumed a human body in the Incarnation. In the Eucharist he commands his church to provide

[11] *WA* 6, 368.
[12] *PE* 2, 17, 14, 21-22.
[13] Brilioth, *op. cit.*, pp. 99f. Cf. also H. Jacoby, *Die Liturgik der Reformatoren* (Gotha: Perthes, 1871-76), I, 205.

earthly elements, to give thanks and to distribute them in order that the faithful may receive his divine gift. The point to be observed is that the faithful are required to *do* something, to bring something before God and to show forth Christ's death before the world.

The liturgy is more than a literary composition. It is a sacred action in response to our Lord's injunction. "This do." In the "enacted prayer" of the liturgy the church pleads the merits of Christ and his all-sufficient sacrifice and sums up with dramatic impressiveness all that we have in mind when we conclude our prayers with the familiar words, "And this we ask for Jesus' sake." Here is corporate action which includes praise and thanksgiving, but embraces more than that—an act, an offering, a sacrifice of faith and obedience and dedication. This sacrifice is in no sense propitiatory. It is commemorative and eucharistic. And it is necessary for the realization of Christ's promises to his disciples of every time and clime. In the high solemnity of this corporate action, the church proclaims before God and men its faith and obedience, and brings the Christ of Galilee and Calvary into the midst of the disciples of today. The substitution of mere edification for this sense of corporate experience of God definitely weakens the church's worship.

In addition to this objective, ceremonial sacrifice, we also recognize a subjective, personal sacrifice. We must bring more than bread and wine to the altar. We must offer ourselves in love and devotion, in self-denial and consecrated service, in an action which is the fruit and the proof of our faith. We may not all understand or accept the idea that spiritual union with the crucified and risen Christ gives the faithful a share in his sacrifice. We may not realize fully what Augustine meant when he said that only as we are incorporated through communion with Christ and his oblation can we truly render thanks and praise to God. We know, however, that we must "present our bodies a living sacrifice, holy, acceptable unto God" and that we must not "be conformed to this world" but be "transformed by the renewing of our minds" so that we may henceforth live before God in righteousness and true holiness. Unless we bring this self-oblation, this sacrifice of moral obedience and spiritual earnestness with all its ethical implications for daily living, we are weak and unprofitable servants, and the holy Sacrament is for us a hollow mockery. Justification by faith may lead us in all confidence to the altar. Sanctification of spirit and life must follow us as we leave the holy table. Both are embraced in the one great transaction.

There is little of this sense of self-oblation in the Lutheran liturgy except as it enters by way of hymns and the Sermon. The consciousness of our people transcends the poverty of our forms, and they realize that we all must bring to the altar of God a sacrifice more worthy of the name than the mere act of praise and thanksgiving. They cannot forget the Savior's words in John's Gospel, "He that abideth in me and I in him, the same bringeth forth much fruit . . ." or Paul's words, "I can do all things through Christ which strengtheneth me." We visit Calvary's hill in all reverence; but we also learn humility and service in the Upper Room, and obedience in the Garden. Our commitment to the divine will involves the sacrifice of our own wills, and the consecration of all that we are and have. As individuals and as members of Christ's mystical Body we offer ourselves to God in love and a renewed sense of unity and service. All of us are aware of the practical place of this sacrifice in Christian life. The difficulties in such a discussion as this arise because of improper and unspiritual conceptions of sacrifice.

5. *Mystery* is a convenient term which includes all the things which pass understanding, the manifestations of divinity and infinity which defy explanation and excite our wonder, awe, and reverence.

Even the exact sciences recognize the factor of the unknown. Real scientists approach their study of the universe with reverent minds. The reverence which springs from recognition of the majesty of the almighty, all-merciful God is never absent from true worship. One should not, however, think of mystery such as this apart from other elements, but rather as something present in them all.

Programmatic students of worship name this as the first element in the psychological patterns they discover or invent. Rudolph Otto built up the transcendence of God to overpowering proportions in his idea of the *Mysterium Tremendum,* the Wholly Other, whose purity and power we finite, sinful creatures confess and adore.[14]

Dean Sperry and Dr. Von Ogden Vogt[15] recall the magnificent passage of Job 38, "Where wast thou when I laid the foundations of the earth? . . . Hast thou entered into the springs of the sea? . . . Have the gates of death been opened unto thee?" and the vision of Isaiah (6), "I saw also the Lord sitting upon a throne, high and lifted up. . . . Above it stood seraphims . . . and one cried unto another, and said, Holy, holy, holy, is the Lord of hosts: the whole earth is full of his glory." They place the vision and the adoration of God as foundation stones in the temple of worship.

There is truth and logic in this, particularly as applied to the building of isolated "programs" of worship. The purely psychological approach to worship, however, undervalues objective reality and historical con-

---

[14] Rudolph Otto, *The Idea of the Holy* (rev. ed.; New York: Milford, 1928).
[15] In *Reality in Worship* and *Art and Religion,* respectively.

tinuity. It is for the most part subjective and eclectic and its search for illustrative and appropriate material soon carries its advocates beyond the limits of any single historical order.[16]

The student of liturgy, too, appreciates the holiness and majesty of the divine and qualities of awe and wonder, of reverence and adoration in worship. He does not locate these, however, in a single block in a logically prepared program. Rather he finds them mingling with other elements and permeating the whole fabric of the living liturgy in its rich provision of ever changing appointments for the liturgical year. The revelation of God in Christ Jesus and personal experience of the riches of his grace temper the austere thought of the Old Testament prophets; but still the sense of mystery and the quality of reverence pervade every part of the Christian liturgy. We find them in hymns, in sermons, and in the quiet moments of worshipers in the pew as well as in the Confiteor, the Sanctus, or the moment of reception at the holy table.

The worship of the early church was heavily charged with mystery. The arrangement of the church building, with its outer court for catechumens and inner room for the baptized, the screening of the altar, the distinctive vestments and ceremonies of the priests, as well as worshipful expressions in the liturgy with its ascriptions of honor and praise, are ample evidence of an attitude and an atmosphere which was heightened in the medieval centuries by the glory of Gothic cathedrals, the splendor of lights and color and elaborate ceremonial, and the practices which centered in the miracle of the Mass and illustrated the doctrine of transubstantiation.

The Reformers repudiated this doctrine, magnified edification and instruction, and promoted active congregational participation in worship. They nevertheless retained a high appreciation of mystery. It remained for pietism with its intense preoccupation with self, and for rationalism with its exaltation of reason, to discard mystery and thus pave the way for Puritan and later Protestant impoverishment of worship. Calvin was still big enough to humble himself before the transcendent God. Luther held in contempt the aberrations of the religious fanatics of his own time, but gave ample evidence of a deep vein of genuine, wholesome mysticism in his own nature. Thoroughly versed in Johannine and Pauline thought, and with vivid recollections of Augustine and St. Bernard, Luther could reject the rationalism of Karlstadt and Zwingli,

---

[16] Beginning with Rudolf Otto's *Idea of the Holy,* the psychological approach has been carried on by Dean Sperry in his *Reality in Worship* (an able work), and in the writings of Von Ogden Vogt, George W. Fiske, Bernard E. Meland, and others. The comprehensive work of Robert Will, *Le Culte,* is a particularly fine blend of the historical and the philosophical.

and the visionary superficialities of Münzer and the Anabaptists, and yet revel in the mystery of an almighty, all-holy, all-merciful God who "over-brims with pure goodness" and deigns to dwell in the hearts and souls of men.

Lutheran hymnody reached some of its loftiest flights in extolling the mystery of the Holy Communion. The high objectivity of Greek devotion exemplified in John Brownlie's hymn, "Let Thy blood in mercy poured," and the cool sincerity of Thomas Aquinas in his "With all the powers my poor heart hath," were surpassed in warm and intimately personal expressions of the mystery of the Sacrament in the glowing lines of Johann Franck's "Deck thyself with joy and gladness, Dwell no more, my soul, in sadness."

There was more than liturgical conservatism in the retention by the Lutherans of medieval church buildings, with their appointments, and of the historic liturgy and its music. Beyond the sense of historic continuity and high appreciation of aesthetic values was the conviction that the church's sense of reverence and honor due the Almighty were truly expressed by the inner spirit and purified forms of the historic service culminating in the Sacrament. Not only the Preface with its exalted phrases, and the Sanctus with its praise to the Holiest, but the reverence before the altar and the kneeling communion—all expressed the sense of mystery which centered in the Real Presence and which declared with Augustine and Paul and John that in some mystic but real way we are incorporated in Christ and Christ in us. This sacramental presence and sacramental power are indescribable because they are incomprehensible. Because of this, the Presence, though patently focused in the elements, must not be too definitely limited or too sharply localized. Our thought must expand to include Christ's presence as high priest throughout the entire transaction, and the further mystery of Christ's presence in his body, the church. In every part of the Service the faithful are conscious of his living presence and power, glowing with spiritual radiance and beauty, and bringing to every heart the assurance of remission of sins, life, and salvation.

Two thoughts emerge from this discussion. The first is that any attempt to analyze such a living and spiritual thing as worship and the Eucharist and to separate their component parts is necessarily imperfect, and can at best be but suggestive. The botanist tears petals and stamens apart and examines each with microscopic care. He knows, however, that the flower is greater than the sum of all its parts, that its glory is its life and that this glory has been destroyed by his analysis. Theology and philosophy give us an analysis of worship. The liturgy and its action provide more than a synthesis, for worship and the liturgy are more than a mechanical assembly of parts. Their reality, their power, and their beauty are in their life, which unites the highest aspirations and holiest beliefs of men with the ineffable love and eternal power of God.

The second thought is that the Eucharist is the church's supreme act of worship, its highest, holiest endeavor to realize actual communion with God. Here as nowhere else is the Christian conscious of the presence of his Lord and Savior, the Jesus of the Judean hills, the Christ of history and the Lord of all eternity. Here as nowhere else is there such concentration of all Christ's words and works in the realization of his completed act of redemption. Here as nowhere else is there such conviction of our actual participation in the salvation he has won for us—participation through incorporation with his own true body in the Sacrament, and in fellowship with his mystical body, the church.

This fulness of thought concerning the Sacrament was recaptured by the Reformers in the sixteenth century. In this classic period the Lutheran Church restated the faith of the church in noble confessions. In this classic period it recognized the Eucharist as the supreme act of corporate worship and celebrated it every Lord's Day and festival with rich form and ceremony, beautiful music, and vital preaching. We have much to learn today from the faith and life of our own best moment in history.

THE CLASSIC LUTHERAN TRADITION

The appreciation and unbroken use of the Service by the Lutheran Church in all lands is noteworthy. While failing at times to appreciate and use the orders of Matins and Vespers, the church has everywhere retained the Service—at times in simplified form—for its normal Sunday service. Other Protestant churches promptly abandoned the historic liturgy and established a type of preaching service separate from the Holy Communion. The Anglican church lost important elements of the ancient Service (Introits, Graduals, Agnus Dei, etc.), and transferred the Sermon to Morning Prayer (Matins). This made the latter the principal service on most Sundays, with the Holy Communion celebrated at a separate hour. The Matin order thus received an emphasis unknown in the Lutheran system. Most worshipers in the Anglican communion are still deprived of the regular Gospels and Epistles of the church year and they know nothing whatever of the historic Introits and Graduals.

The Lutheran Church restored the "primitive synthesis" of the early church by including in balanced proportion the preaching of the Word and the administration of the Sacrament in the principal service of the day. This service was held in its entirety on appointed Sundays and all great festivals.

Some orders recognized that on certain days in towns and villages there might be no communicants. Permission was given in this event to conclude the Service with appropriate prayers and the Benediction. This exceptional provision later became the regular use. In the beginning, however, it was part of a plan to maintain the historic order of the Mass and to encourage the faithful to communicate. So successful was the effort that it was emulated by the leaders of the Counter-Reformation. Thus, the practice of frequent communions in the church of Rome today owes much to Reformation inspiration.

This was the Service as Luther and the conservative Reformers knew it. Great preachers themselves, they made the Sermon a significant part of the Service. They did not mutilate the liturgy to do this, however, or banish the Sacrament to a separate service. In fact, in the major confession of the church they vigorously defended their practice: "Falsely are our churches accused of abolishing the Mass; for the Mass is retained on our part and celebrated with the highest reverence." Luther and his associates never would have approved of the "half-mass" commonly found amoung us today as the normal Sunday worship of our congregations. For two hundred years, or nearly half the time from the Reformation to the present, the normal Sunday service in Lutheran lands was the purified Mass, or *Hauptgottesdienst,* with its twin peaks of Sermon and Sacrament. There were weekly celebrations and the people in general received the Sacrament much more frequently than before. The ravages of war, the example of Calvinism, the later subjective practices of Pietistic groups in a domestic type of worship, and the unbelief of rationalism, however, finally broke the genuine Lutheran tradition.

Two factors in the late seventeenth and eighteenth centuries worked against frequent communion by the people and made the liturgy more and more a "preaching service." The first affected the lay folk particularly. The Sacrament was surrounded with an atmosphere of awe and fear; excessive emphasis was placed upon personal and intensely introspective preparation; and there grew up in the people's minds a dread of possibly being unworthy and of "being guilty" of the body and blood of Christ. These morbid and exaggerated emphases upon preparation for the Sacrament, rather than upon the Sacrament itself, are still

244

occasionally in evidence. The second factor, which affected the clergy and the educated classes primarily, was intense emphasis upon doctrinal discussion and formulation. The net result was dogmatic definition rather than common devotion. Argument took the place of adoration and it was not long before the pulpit was elevated above the altar.

Thus the fine balance between Word and Sacrament was lost. There was no decline in the field of doctrine. The Lutheran Confessions which had held the Sacrament on lofty levels were still accepted. Lutheran services in general, however, after centuries of proper use, came to consist of a truncated liturgy with the first half (the Office of the Word) existing apart from its crown and completion in the Holy Communion. The Communion in most districts was administered quarterly, in conformity with the Calvinistic and Zwinglian program.

In some large city congregations in Europe the ancient agreement between doctrine and practice still obtains, and the church offers the Sacrament as well as the Word every Lord's Day. A thousand may come for the Office of the Word and only half a hundred remain for the Sacrament. But the church at least does its part and provides a weekly administration for those who desire to commune. In our own country many congregations have monthly or even weekly administrations, and the desire for more frequent communions is genuine and growing.

The use of the Service in its entirety, with more frequent opportunities for communion, is to be encouraged because of its spiritual values and because of its agreement with genuine Lutheran tradition and with the practice of the early church. From the very beginning the Lord's Supper was the central feature of Christian worship. Albert Schweitzer is well within the truth when he says of the early church: "All the praying, prophesying, preaching and taching took place within the framework of the Thanksgiving at the celebration of the Lord's Supper." The so-called "Word of God services" are a later development.

The medieval church regarded the Mass as the highest expression of its doctrinal system and the strongest bond among its members. The Reformation simplified and purified the Service, but it is still the greatest single edifying, inspiring, and unifying factor in the church's life. Either with the Holy Communion, or with the Office of the Word alone, it is the regular and significant service of the Lutheran Church in all lands on all Sundays and festivals. Whether there be a communion or not, the proper appointments give the Service of each day a historical completeness surpassing that of the Anglican Liturgy, and a richness and distinctive quality not found at all in the miscellaneous unhistorical orders of worship of non-liturgical churches.

THE STRUCTURE OF THE SERVICE

The proclamation of the Word and the administration of the Sacrament determine the structure of the Service. Devotional introductions and conclusions, and a preliminary service of confession, are built into the liturgical framework. Each service is complete in itself. Each, however, is also a part of the cycle of services comprising the Christian year.

Each service consists of the ordinary and the propers (*propria*). The ordinary comprises the invariable elements and forms which represent the great unchanging beliefs, needs, aspirations, and consolations of believers. Such elements are the Confession of Sins, Kyrie, Creed, Lord's Prayer, Preface, Sanctus, Prayer of Thanksgiving, Benediction, etc. Within this fixed framework are grouped variable parts called the Propers. These are the particular liturgical appointments for each day—Introit, Collect, Lesson, Epistle, Gradual, Gospel, Proper Preface, etc. The Sermon and the hymns should also be thought of as "propers." Together the ordinary and the propers build up a harmonious and beautiful service for each day or festival. The many services combine to form the fully rounded liturgical year.

The Gospel for the Day usually presents the central objective thought. The Epistle expands or impresses this in a practical way, while the Lesson may provide analogy or contrast from the Old Testament. The Collect sums up the whole in a brief but pertinent prayer. The Introit strikes the keynote and indicates the mood and spirit of the day. The Gradual provides a transition from the Epistle to the Gospel or links the thought of the two. This harmony of the propers, however, is not always apparent in the Sundays after Trinity which celebrate no particular festival and merely provide devotional settings for a particular Gospel.

The late medieval centuries produced many commentators on the liturgy, among others Amalarius of Metz, Walafried Strabo, Honorius of Autun, William Durandus of Mende, etc. Their attempts to explain its parts in accordance with the allegorical and symbolical method of the time were naïve and whimsical, and often absurd.

Perhaps the first attempt to develop a general principle of worship is to be found in Luther's *Von Ordnung Gottesdiensts* of 1523, which clearly distinguishes between the sacramental or objective and the sacrificial or subjective. This discussion was limited to historic material and stressed objective values as fundamental. The idea was elaborated by Melanchthon in the *Apology of the Augsburg Confession* (Chap. 12). It was later developed, often rather mechanically, in the writings of Kliefoth, Schoeberlein, and other Lutherans of the nineteenth century.

Following is an outline of the Service of the Lutheran Church as in practical use today, with an indication of the major divisions observed by the early church.

The Invocation

I. THE PREPARATORY CONFESSION

The Address
The Versicles
The Confession of Sins
The Prayer for Grace
The Declaration of Grace

II. THE OFFICE OF THE WORD
(The ancient *missa catechumenorum*)

Psalmody

The Introit for the day,
with the Gloria Patri
The Kyrie
The Gloria in Excelsis

Word

Salutation and response
The Collect for the day
The Lesson for the day and **hymn**
(optional)
The Epistle for the day
The Gradual (for the day or season)
The Gospel for the day
The Creed
The Hymn
The Sermon
(The ancient *missa fidelium*)

Offering

The Gifts
The Offertory
The Prayer of the Church
The hymn

III. THE OFFICE OF THE HOLY COMMUNION

Preface

The Salutation and response
The Sursum Corda
The Vere Dignum
The Proper Preface
The Sanctus and Benedictus

Consecration and Administration

The Prayer of Thanksgiving,
with the Words of Institution.

247

The Lord's Prayer
The Pax
The Agnus Dei
The Communion
The Blessing

Post-Communion
The Nunc Dimittis
The Post-Communion Collect
The Salutation and response
The Benedicamus
The Benediction

THE MUSIC OF THE SERVICE

The music of the Service is of fundamental importance. It should receive careful and constant consideration at the hands of organists, choirmasters, and choirs. Like the liturgy itself, this music is largely historic. Its melodies, like the melodies of many of the hymns of the church, have long been associated with the text. There is a "proper music" of the liturgy, at least of large parts of it, just as there are "proper tunes" for hymns. The melodies of *Ein' Feste Burg,* of *Veni, Veni Emmanuel,* or of Holy, Holy, Holy (Nicaea) are as well known and as widely used as these hymns themselves. This is true of many of the responses of the liturgy, the preface melodies, and other forms. Most obvious in the case of the plain-song melodies of the third setting, some of which have been sung to these words for more than a thousand years, this close wedding of text and tune is no less true of the other settings to the liturgy in the *Service Book and Hymnal.*

The definitely congregational character of its service music is a marked feature of Lutheran worship. Both the Roman and the Anglican churches have the choral service as their ideal. The Roman church has a wealth of musical "masses," and the Anglican church a wealth of musical "services." In each case these more or less elaborate settings are designed primarily for choir use than for congregational participation.

The latest official hymnal of the Protestant Episcopal Church (1940) gives four relatively simple settings to the liturgy. This provision indicates a strong desire for greater congregational participation in the musical responses. The Lutheran Church especially seeks to encourage congregational singing in the responses of the liturgy as well as in the hymns. The *Common Service Book,* for this very reason, after 1918 provided but one musical setting for the greater part of the liturgy, and this in such simple form that the average congregation could readily learn to use it. The Commission on the Liturgy, recognizing the varied backgrounds of those who would use the Common Liturgy, and at the same time aware of the developing taste and ability of the church, provided three settings for use in the *Service Book and Hymnal*. Each of the three, however, has been carefully edited, and is well within the limits of congregational ability. The emphasis on full participation remains.

The gifts and possibilities of the choir are fully recognized, however. Certain parts of the liturgy (the Introit and the Gradual in the Service; the Antiphon, Psalm, and Responsory in Matins and Vespers) definitely are choir numbers. In addition to these, opportunity is given for the use of anthems and similar choral pieces. The responses of the invariable portions (the ordinary) of the liturgy itself, however, like the hymns, are to be sung by choir and congregation together, and not by the choir alone.

The music of the liturgy is simple and strong in melodic structure with broad and sustaining harmonies. It is devotional in feeling and not concertistic. In spirit as well as form it furthers the corporate expression of successive moods of reverence, adoration, aspiration, praise, and prayer.

The music in all three settings, like the liturgy itself, is distinctive, unique. It has its own definite character which is of the church and not of the world. Departures from this churchly type in the direction of secular feeling and form are always disastrous. They result in weakness, commonplaceness, and loss of spiritual values. Organists and choirmasters should appreciate the opportunity, as well as the responsibility which is theirs, of developing a type of service music artistically adequate but churchly and spiritual. The music should share with the liturgy itself this quality of distinction.

Fundamentally the music of the Service in the *Service Book and Hymnal* is rooted in the plain-song tradition of the church. The melodies to the Preface are the same in all three settings. They are plain-song melodies carried over into the Lutheran church orders and cantionales. These service books of the sixteenth century contain hundreds of plain-song melodies and establish the historic right of the Lutheran Church to the fullest use of Gregorian music. The versicle forms and the sentence for Lent in the first setting are plain-song adapted to English texts in the cathedral services of the Church of England in the Reformation century. The first settings of the Sanctus and of the Angus Dei are modifications of Gregorian melodies. Other forms are set to simple Anglican chants, as are Matins and Vespers. The second setting is almost completely based upon plain song. The third setting is plain song, pure and simple.

The musical settings to the liturgy in *The Common Service Book* were mixed in character and uneven in merit. The *Service Book and Hymnal* provides improved and more unified settings which more nearly approximate the ideal. But even these are not perfect in every respect. For the present, however, we may well study what we have and endeavor to render it intelligently and artistically.

The attention of ministers, organists, and choirmasters is particularly directed to the important body of general rubrics (pp. 274-84) in the Service Book and Hymnal. All who share the responsibility of leadership must be thoroughly familiar with these technical details.

The primary purpose of this book is to interpret the text of the liturgy thoughtfully, spiritually, and artistically. The brief suggestions concerning the music which are given here and later are intended to express ideas and suggest meaning and mood rather than mere details of tempo and volume. Frequently they also seek to guard against common faults.

The chant settings to the liturgy are different from our usual "measured" music. Many of the chants have no time signature and no fixed bars or measures. The text is sung to these settings in free rhythm. Time values are *not* to be taken literally. The whole rendition must be in the nature of a dignified musical declamation of the text without precise values for individual notes. The importance of maintaining this free flowing quality in all settings cannot be overemphasized.

Broadly speaking, it is well to sing the traditional plain-song melodies in unison and the Anglican chants in parts. Taste will largely determine the treatment to be given the chants which are not purely Gregorian or purely Anglican. No one procedure is absolutely right and every other wrong. The beginning of a chant may be taken in unison so as to establish a strong lead, the singers breaking into parts after the opening section. Or unison passages may be effective in the middle of a chant by way of contrast. These are matters for individual choirmasters to determine. Several suggestions of this character are given in later pages.

CHAPTER XII

THE SERVICE IN DETAIL: INVOCATION; CONFESSION

On festivals and special occasions an opening hymn may be sung in procession. The custom is much to be preferred, however, of having the choir regularly enter the church in reverent, silent procession and go to the choir stalls before the hymn is sung. The congregation should rise as the choir enters the church.

The organist plays softly until the choir is in its place and the minister is in the chancel. He then leads into the hymn in which minister, choir, and congregation unite.

A hymn of invocation of the Holy Spirit is prescribed in Spangenburg and in many church orders. Austria (1571) requires: "At the beginning of every spiritual office earnest prayer must be offered to God for grace, enlightenment, and help, and the *Veni Sancte Spiritus* must be sung."

The minister may follow the choir or he may enter the chancel separately from the sacristy. He goes to the front of the altar on the chancel level, where he will reverently offer his personal devotions and remain facing the altar until the conclusion of the hymn.

If the key of the hymn is different from that of the Service the organist will modulate into the latter before the minister begins the Invocation. Valuable in any case, this is especially important if the minister is to chant the liturgy.

Sufficient time should be allowed between the opening hymn and the invocation for an adjustment of mood or spirit which may be required, particularly if the final stanza of the hymn rises to a climax. Impatience, thoughtlessness, or nervousness on the minister's part should not interfere with his giving the organist ample time to improvise an appropriate modulation. A well-constructed phrase of four or eight measures based upon a fragment of the hymn tune itself is not too much, and this should conclude with a gradual diminuendo.

The preparation of such "improvisations" and modulations in advance is an important part of the organist's work. So far as devotional and churchly effects are concerned, the mastery by the organist of these details of the Service itself is more important than the playing of a fifteen-minute recital beforehand, however brilliant that performance might be.

THE INVOCATION

¶ The Congregation shall rise. The Minister shall sing or say:

In the Name of the Father, and of the Son, and of the Holy Ghost.

¶ The Congregation shall sing or say:

Amen.

Paul admonishes the faithful: "Whatsoever ye do in word or deed, do all in the name of the Lord Jesus, giving thanks to God and the Father by him." (Col. 3:17. Cf. also Eph. 2:18, I Cor. 12:3.) The liturgy thus fittingly begins with the Invocation, as an act of corporate devotion.

This formula sums up all that we know of the divine Being in a brief scriptural phrase which has long been used in devotional and liturgical acts of many kinds throughout the universal church. It is used sacramentally as a solemn formula of benediction in baptism, marriage, ordination, church dedication, and various "blessings." As used here at the beginning of the Service, however, it has the value of an "invocative blessing." As the name indicates, it is addressed to God and not to the congregation. It is an affirmation of faith, a prayer of profession—an approach similar in character to a hymn of invocation, or to the words "Our Father" at the beginning of the Lord's Prayer. We formally express our "awareness" of the presence of God, we place ourselves in that presence, and invoke the divine blessing upon the service which is to follow. We confess our faith in the Holy Trinity, for whose worship we are assembled. We solemnly call God to witness that we are "gathered together" in his name (Matt. 18:20) and in that name offer all our prayer, praise, and thanksgiving (John 16:23).

The invocation is not found in the early liturgies nor in the services of the Greek or the Anglican churches. In the Roman church it begins the priest's office of preparation before mass and other offices (occasional services), and is said at the beginning of sermons. The Lutheran church orders give the invocation or take it for granted. The Swedish Liturgy is an exception and does not have it at this place, though it does give it as the final benediction.

Historically these words accompanied the sign of the cross, which began every act of devotion, including the confession of sins said by the priest and his associates privately at the foot of the altar before mass. The church orders retained the Confession at the beginning of the Service, but purified the form and made it a congregational act. The fact that it became a congregational act and the further fact that the sign of the cross later dropped from general use have not changed the Invocation's real character. The entire Confiteor, with the single exception of the Declaration of Grace which concludes it, is sacrificial in character. Its spirit is the spirit of preparation and purification.

The sign of the cross, now generally omitted in America, added the note of self-blessing. Anciently the sign of the cross was more important than the formula. It was in general use long before the cross itself was used in worship or in church building. The formula "In the Name," etc., was a verbal accompaniment to the action.

It is difficult to realize the hold which the sign of the cross has had upon popular imagination and life. Cyprian, Tetullian and many others are witnesses to its use among Christians as early as the end of the second century. Tertullian says: "In all our travels and movements, in all our coming in and going out, in putting on our shoes, at the bath, at the table, in lighting our candles, in lying down, in sitting down, whatever employment occupieth us, we mark our forehead with the sign of the cross. For these and suchlike rules, if thou requirest a law in the Scriptures thou shalt find none. Tradition will be pleaded to thee as originating them, custom as confirming them, and faith as observing them. That reason will support tradition, and custom and faith, thou wilt either thyself perceive, or learn from someone who hath perceived it. Meanwhile thou wilt believe that some reason there is, to which due submission is due."[1]

Chrysostom concludes a glowing passage concerning the sign of the cross by saying: "When, therefore, thou signest thyself, think of the purpose of the cross, and quench anger and all other passions. Consider the price that hath been paid for thee, and then wilt thou be a slave to no man. Since not merely by the fingers ought one to engrave it, but before this by the purpose of the heart with much faith."[2]

As a reminder of the saving passion and death of Christ and an emblem of the mercy of God, the sign of the cross from the earliest times was accompanied by various formulas, such as "The sign of Christ," "In the Name of Jesus," "Our help is in the Name of the Lord," and "In the Name of the Father, and of the Son, and of the Holy Ghost." Eventually the last came into universal use and supplanted all others. These words and the sign became a summary of the Christian faith, a simple yet comprehensive recognition of the Unity and the Trinity in the Godhead, and of the central significance of the sacrificial death of Christ.

[1] Tertullian, *Of the Crown* (Oxford Trans.), p. 165.
[2] Chrysostom on St. Matt. *Hom. liv.* (Oxford Trans.), pp. 735-37.

The church at the time of the Reformation reacted against the excessive and superstitious use of the sign of the cross which had characterized the late Middle Ages. It did not abolish it, but endeavored to restrict its use to significant occasions, such as baptism, the Lord's Supper, the benediction at the end of the service, etc. Luther kept it, together with a form of the invocation, in his directions for morning and evening prayer in the *Small Catechism.* Thus he says: "In the morning when thou risest, thou shalt make the sign of the cross and say: May God, the Father, the Son, and the Holy Ghost, grant it"—a paraphrase which breathes the spirit of prayer even more definitely than does the original *In Nomine,* etc.[3]

The church orders took for granted the use of the sign of the cross with the Invocation by the minister at the altar as part of his private devotion before the Service. When this became a public congregational act, the sign of the cross was gradually dropped. The formula which had accompanied it for so many centuries, however, remained as an invocation, that is, a solemn recognition of the Holy Trinity, and a petition for the divine presence and blessing. Thus the Lutheran Liturgy, at least in its German development, gave the Invocation a prominence and importance not found in the Roman Mass or in any other liturgy.

This discussion reveals the difficulties which arise in attempting to classify parts of the liturgy too mechanically. Some are not wholly sacramental, others are not entirely sacrificial. There is a blending of these elements in some parts of the Service. Since, however, the minister by his position at the altar interprets the Service, and as there are only two positions he can take, it is necessary to determine the prevailing character of each part. In the case of the invocation it is better to take the words as Luther, the Reformers, and the ancient church used them in this connection, that is, as primarily devotional in character and not as a proclamation addressed to the congregation.

Some nineteenth-century scholars ignored the devotional significance of these words at this place and interpreted them as legitimatizing, or at least as establishing, a sacramental basis for the entire service (even Loehe). Some altered the text itself in clumsy fashion to agree with the new interpretation and made it read "Unser Anfang sei im Namen des Vaters, des Sohns und des Heiligen Geistes." The Common Liturgy has done well to retain the historic text, and we give it its ancient and generally accepted meaning.[4]

The minister leads the devotions of the congregation in this act and faces the altar.

[3] "Das walt Gott, Vater, Sohn, Heiliger Geist, Amen." Luther apparently combined in this form references to both the usual *In Nomine* and the other formula, *Deus in adjutorium,* also frequently used with the sign of the cross. Cf. *WA* 30[1], 392-93.

[4] The principle underlying the orientation of the minister was affirmed for the

The rubrics at the beginning of the musical settings of the Service should be noted. They state that "Intonations provided for the Minister's parts of the Services represent a permissive use. They are not to be considered directive. The preparatory office up to the Introit may be said."

The Amen is sung promptly and firmly, though with devotional spirit and moderate volume of tone.

It is questionable whether it is wise to suggest exact tempos. The author would certainly not desire to do this throughout the work. Local conditions differ greatly with respect to the size of church buildings and of congregations, and other details. There also are very real differences in the "moods" of the settings. We must also allow for proper differences in judgment and taste, and not attempt to regiment our worship severely.

It may be helpful, however, to suggest a metronome tempo of M.M.♩ =84 for the first Amen of the service, at least in the first setting. Most later Amens, such as those following the collects, etc., may be taken more rapidly. "Percussive" and similar thoughtless and undevotional effects are absolutely to be avoided. The final Amen of the Service should again have significant breadth and solemnity and be held to a slower tempo.

THE CONFESSION OF SINS

¶ *The Minister shall say:*

Beloved in the Lord! Let us draw near with a true heart, and confess our sins unto God our Father, beseeching him, in the Name of our Lord Jesus Christ, to grant us forgiveness.

¶ *The Minister and Congregation may kneel.*
¶ *They shall sing or say:*

Our help is in the Name of the Lord.
℟. Who made heaven and earth.

I said, I will confess my transgressions unto the Lord.
℟. And thou forgavest the iniquity of my sin.

Anglican communion at the Savoy Conference in 1661, in the reply of the bishops to the proposals of the Puritans. The latter desired that the minister should face the people throughout the service, as this was "most convenient." The bishops replied: "The minister's turning to the people is not most convenient throughout the whole ministration. When he speaks to them, as in Lessons, Absolution, and Benedictions, it is convenient that he turn to them. When he speaks for them to God, it is fit that they should all turn another way, as the ancient church ever did" (Edward Cardwell, *A History of Conferences and other Proceedings Connected with the Revision of the Book of Common Prayer* [2nd ed.; London: Oxford Univ. Pr., 1891], p. 353).

¶ *Then shall the Minister say:*

Almighty God, our Maker and Redeemer, we poor sinners confess unto thee, that we are by nature sinful and unclean, and that we have sinned against thee by thought, word, and deed. Wherefore we flee for refuge to thine infinite mercy, seeking and imploring thy grace, for the sake of our Lord Jesus Christ.

¶ *The Congregation shall say with the Minister:*

O most merciful God, who hast given thine only-begotten Son to die for us, have mercy upon us, and for his sake grant us remission of all our sins; and by thy Holy Spirit increase in us true knowledge of thee and of thy will, and true obedience to thy Word, that by thy grace we may come to everlasting life; through Jesus Christ our Lord. Amen.

¶ *Then the Minister, standing, and facing the Congregation, shall say:*

Almighty God, our heavenly Father, hath had mercy upon us, and hath given his only Son to die for us, and for his sake forgiveth us all our sins. To them that believe on his name, he giveth power to become the sons of God, and bestoweth upon them his Holy Spirit. He that believeth, and is baptized, shall be saved. Grant this, O Lord, unto us all.

¶ *Or, he may say:*

The Almighty and merciful God grant unto you, being penitent, pardon and remission of all your sins, time for amendment of life, and the grace and comfort of his Holy Spirit.

¶ *The Congregation shall sing or say:*

Amen.

The Confession of Sins is an invariable introductory office which provides a helpful preparation for each day's worship. "We lay down our burdens at the doorway before entering upon the praises of God" (Dowden). The Service of the day properly begins with the Introit, but before this it is fitting to seek a purification of spirit, turn from ourselves to God in penitence and prayer and receive his assurance of mercy and grace.

The Confiteor, as it is called from the Latin word meaning "I confess," developed from the prayers originally said by the minister in the sacristy in connection with putting on his vestments. It is a late feature in the liturgy. No special prayers of this sort were appointed in the early centuries, though the *Didache* admonishes the early Christians, "Assemble on the day of the Lord, break bread and celebrate the Eucharist; but first confess your sins, that your sacrifice may be holy." Dr. Parsch, the learned Augustinian of Klosterneuburg, calls attention to the fact that nothing is said about the rite of contrition in later descriptions of the Lord's Supper. He makes the further interesting observation that "the primitive Church considered itself 'a holy people'; nor did it possess the clearly defined consciousness of sin of medieval and modern times It did not, therefore, see the need for a special rite of purification."[5]

As emphasis was laid increasingly upon private confession and absolution of the people before reception of the Sacrament, the practice developed of the priest's also making a personal confession before beginning the Service. About the eleventh century certain so-called apologies of the time were fashioned into prayers which were said by the priest at the foot of the altar as part of his private preparation for the Service. They were not said by or for the congregation. The text of the Roman Confiteor in its present form was adopted by the Synod of Ravenna in 1314 and finally authorized in the Missal of Pius V (1570).

The text begins with the responsive reading by the priest and his attendants of Psalm 43, "Judge me, O God . . . send out thy light and thy truth . . . then will I go unto the altar of God. . . ." This was originally in the Milan liturgy, the baptismal hymn the neophytes chanted in procession. The psalm is followed by a lengthy confession with enumeration of many saints, a form of absolution, and the Collect for Purity ("Almighty God, unto whom all hearts are open, all desires known," etc.). The choir sings the Introit while the priest says the Confiteor.[6]

The Reformers appreciated the spiritual values in a preparatory confession. They could not use existing forms because of their doctrinal impurity. In parts of Germany, in Sweden, and later in England, entirely new forms were developed which well illustrate the principles and methods of conservative liturgical reform in the sixteenth century. Recognizing the principle of the priesthood of all believers, the Confession was made a congregational instead of a priestly act. It was addressed to God alone, and all references to intercessions by the Virgin and the saints were omitted. A thoroughly scriptural text was provided for the entire office which did more than enumerate known transgressions, and included an acknowledgment of our sinful nature. The phrase "thought, word and deed," the first versicle, "Our help is in the Name of the Lord," and the first portion of the alternate declaration: "The Almighty . . . grant . . . pardon and remission of . . . sins," are the only parts of the pre-Reformation service retained in the Common Liturgy. The church in this introductory act, by its positive declaration of forgiveness to all who "believe on his Name," grounds all its worship upon the atoning sacrifice of Jesus Christ.

The Common Liturgy has rightly kept the introductory act of confession separate from the Service proper, which begins with the Introit for the

[5] Pius Parsch, *The Liturgy of the Mass,* trans. F. C. Eckhoff (St. Louis: Herder, 1936), pp. 65f.

[6] (For complete text, see Appendix II, p. 695).

Day. The combination of the Confession with the Kyrie rests upon an imperfect understanding of the nature and the history of the Kyrie and an inadequate appreciation of the integrity of the Mass order. This regrettable arrangement is found in Sweden (1541), and later (though not in Petri's Mass [1531]), in Muhlenberg's liturgy (1748), in several nineteenth-century German liturgies (Baden, Bavaria, etc.) and in the Ministerium of Pennsylvania Liturgy of 1860. Dr. Krauth and Dr. Seiss led the movement which restored the Confession to its proper place before the Introit in the *Church Book* (1868), and the Common Service (1888).[7]

Providing an evangelical form of confession was a slow and uneven procedure. Luther in his orders omitted all reference to the Confiteor. Experimental forms were found as early as the Nuremberg Missal (1525). The Confiteor was retained as the private prayer of the minister in Brandenburg-Nuremberg (1533), Schleswig-Holstein (1542), Pfalz-Neuburg (1543), Hildesheim (1544), and in Pomerania as late as 1563. One of the earliest and most extended congregational forms is that of Sweden (1531). Others are Hamburg (1537), Reformation of Cologne (1543), Hesse-Cassel (1566), Austria (1571). Dr. E. T. Horn's *Outlines of Liturgics,* p. 107 (2d ed., p. 110), lists orders which give forms of confession and those which do not.

The text of the first three paragraphs, also used in the Common Service of 1888, is derived chiefly from Melanchthon's order for Mecklenburg (1552), as later adopted in Wittenberg (1559). Richter finds germs of this in John Riebling (1534).

In one respect at least the Lutheran form of confession is unique. The expression "we are by nature sinful and unclean" is found only in Lutheran services. The Roman church provides no public service of confession because it requires private confession of all its members. The priest's confession in the office of preparation contains no reference to original sin. The *Book of Common Prayer,* though prepared with full knowledge of Lutheran forms, passes over this idea also and simply says, "We acknowledge and bewail our manifold sins and wickedness, which we, from time to time, most grievously have committed." Similarly in the General Confession of Morning Prayer it says, "We have erred, and strayed from thy ways . . . we have offended . . . we have left undone . . . there is no health in us."

Versicles and their responses are passages from the Psalms used throughout the liturgy in many connections, particularly to introduce collects, canticles, prayers, and other features. They have been aptly described as "eloquent in their laconic brevity . . . an appeal darted swiftly forth to God, a cry from the heart . . . in which the faithful join by making the response" (Cabrol). They penetrate directly to the heart of the matter of the moment. They also strengthen the congregational

---

[7] For further discussion, see under the Kyrie, p. 269.

and social element in the liturgy and lift it above the level monotony of a monologue.

The first versicle in the office of confession is given in Nuremberg (1525), Mecklenburg (1552), and Wittenberg (1559). The second versicle is found in Strasbourg (1525), Reformation of Cologne (1543), and Austria (1571).

✠

The essentially preparatory character of this office of Confession is indicated by the short line or rule which separates it from the Introit, and by suggestions concerning the place and manner of conducting the office—the chancel level, kneeling, saying instead of singing, etc. This shortest form of confession is omitted when the fuller "Brief Order for Public Confession" is used preceding the Holy Communion, or when there has been an earlier service of public confession.

The minister in conducting the Confession stands at the foot of the altar on the chancel level.

The address, "Beloved in the Lord" (based on Heb. 10:22), should be read clearly and freely, facing the congregation. The *Service Book* should not be followed too closely. It may be held in the hand or laid upon the altar rail or sanctuary step.

At the versicles the minister faces the altar. At this point the minister and the congregation may kneel (prescribed in Austria [1571]). The minister kneels at the sanctuary rail or the lowest altar step. He rises and faces the congregation throughout the Declaration of Grace.

The Declaration of Grace as a sacramental act should be pronounced in a firm tone of assurance. The final sentence, "Grant this, O Lord, unto us all," is in effect a prayer, but it contains an element of admonition, and the minister should not turn to the altar at this point. The entire declaration should be regarded as a unit and be said facing the congregation.

The alternate declaration: "The Almighty and merciful God grant unto you," etc., is a more prayerful form based upon a text first found in the ancient office of Compline in the Sarum Breviary, and given in our own time in the Scottish *Book of Common Prayer* (Episcopal Church in Scotland) (1929), and in the American *Book of Common Prayer* (1928).[8]

---

[8] The original text is as follows: "*Absolutionem et remissionem omnium peccatorum nostrorum, spatium verae poenitentiae, emendationem vitae, gratiam et consolationem Sancti Spiritus: Tribuat nobis omnipotens et misericors Dominus. Amen*" (Proctor & Wordsworth [eds.], *Breviarium ad usum Sarum* [Cambridge; 1882], col. XIII.)

The versicles may be said instead of sung. It would be well if this were done generally as it would emphasize the invariable and preparatory character of the confessional office as distinguished from the actual Service of the day which properly begins with the Introit.

If sung, the versicle responses should be held to moderate volume and tempo so as to express the devotional and searching character of the act of confession. In the second response the word "of" should be passed over lightly with stronger emphasis upon "my" and "sin." The organ accompaniment should be in subdued tone, with a soft diapason chorus and upper work of great refinement. Heavy diapasons alone are likely to be "tubby," and upper work of too great strength may be hard and shrill.

¶ *A brief silence may be kept before the Introit for the Day.*

The first natural break in the Service comes at the end of the confessional office. A brief pause may be made before the actual Service of the Day. The minister may go to the clergy stalls and stand until the Introit is begun by the choir, when he will return to the altar, this time going up to it, not just to the rail. Or he may pause a few moments before going to the altar to read the Introit. Latecomers, who have remained quietly in the rear, now go to their seats. The organist will extemporize softly and lead with increasing volume into the tonality and mood of the Introit.

¶ *The Congregation shall stand until the close of the Collect.*

¶ *The Introit for the Day with the Gloria Patri shall be sung or said.*

CHAPTER XIII

THE INTROIT; THE KYRIE; THE GLORIA IN EXCELSIS

INTROIT

(First Sunday in Advent)

Unto thee, O Lord, do I lift up my soul: O my God, I trust in thee;
Let me not be ashamed: let not mine enemies triumph over me;
Yea, let none that wait on thee: be ashamed.

Psalm. Show me thy ways, O Lord: teach me thy paths.

Glory be to the Father, and to the Son, and to the Holy Ghost: as it was in the beginning, is now, and ever shall be, world without end. Amen.

The Introit marks the actual beginning of the Service. It strikes the keynote of the day or season in objective and exalted fashion by the use of pertinent verses from the Psalms, and calls the congregation to united consideration of the central thought or theme of the paricular service. It is the first variable part of the Service, different texts being employed on different days. The use of such "propers" is a characteristic of the Western church. The Eastern rites have no Introits, Collects, Graduals, of similar variable material.

The word *introit* means "entrance" or "beginning." In the early church the service began with a litany. After persecution ended and the church was recognized and large basilicas were built, it became possible to invest the details of public worship with special dignity.

In the early fifth century Pope Celestine I (d. 432) decreed that an entire psalm should be sung antiphonally by a double choir as the clergy came from the sacristy to the altar. This was intended to add solemnity to the entrance of the clergy and to establish the thought or mood appropriate for the particular service. Later a single verse was chosen for its appropriateness, and was sung as an antiphon before and after the psalm, and on festivals after each verse of the psalm. As the melodies which developed with these processional psalms became more and more elaborate, and as other features also lengthened the service, Gregory the Great abbreviated the psalm and established the introit form much as we have it.

The Introit is an important and meaningful element in the liturgy. Because it is something of a torso or fragment of an earlier use, its full significance is often not understood. A historic reconstruction of its full body and earliest use would help to a better understanding of its function and value in our services today.

In its present form the Introit consists of one or more Versicles called the antiphon, followed by a versicle called the psalm (representing the entire psalm originally used), and the Gloria Patri, after which, if the Introit is sung, the antiphon should be repeated. The versicles are generally chosen with fine propriety. On festivals and other important days the antiphon announces the tone or theme of the day with special definiteness. Frequently this is trumpeted as by a herald in the very first words, as on Easter Day: "He is risen, alleluia"; or on Pentecost: "The spirit of the Lord filleth the world, alleluia." Occasionally the scene or setting is pictured, as on Ascension Day: "Ye men of Galilee," etc. Again, a simple devotional appropriateness is indicated, as in the text above for the first Sunday in Advent and the beginning of the church year. "Unto thee, O Lord, do I lift up my soul . . . show me thy ways." Much as in a symphony or great choral composition, this theme is sounded again after shorter or longer intervals in all the later variable parts of the Service. In this rich and varied way the liturgy carries the thought of the day in significant fundamental tone throughout the entire Service.

Introits entirely from the Psalms are called "regular"; those whose texts are taken from other parts of Scripture are "irregular." A study of the complete texts of all the introits would show their content to be as full and varied as the church year itself. There are at least twenty-eight "irregular" introits in the Common Liturgy. Of these, ten contain passages from Isaiah, and twelve have passages from the New Testament.

The names of many Sundays, particularly those in Lent and Eastertide, are derived from the first words of the Latin introits, e.g., Invocabit, Judica, Jubilate, etc.

Luther retained the Introit in the Service but expressed his preference for the custom of the early church in using an entire psalm. Only one or two Lutheran orders followed his suggestion (Schwäbisch-Hall [1526]). The great majority retained the historic Gregorian series whenever there were choirs competent to sing the Latin texts. As vernacular services were introduced, the difficulties of translating the texts and of adapting the music led to the choice of a single introit for each season. This reduced the historic series of introits to a smaller number of selected texts. In towns and villages where there were no adequate choirs, vernacular hymns of the season were substituted.

It is to be regretted that modern Lutheran services in Germany and Scandinavia know only a fragmentary use of a few psalm verses at the beginning of the Service, instead of the rich and complete series of historic introits retained in their sixteenth-century services. The Common Service restored the entire series of historic Introits to the English Lutheran liturgy in 1888, and the editors of the Common Liturgy of 1958 carefully retained it.

The first *Book of Common Prayer* (1549), followed Luther's suggestion and the use of the early church and appointed an entire psalm for the Introit for each Sunday and festival. The second Book of 1552 omitted the Introit entirely. The reason for this is not altogether clear. "It is not improbable . . . that the debased state of ecclesiastical music at that time might induce the Revisers of 1552 to reduce yet further the occasions of musical display."[1] Perhaps a better explanation might be the lack of musical interest and ability which characterized the whole program of English liturgical reform in the sixteenth century. Cramner and his associates were masters of devotional literary composition and their achievements in this field have not been surpassed. They were not musicians and they made no effort to retain choral elements in the Service or even to encourage congregational song. The Introit, Gradual, antiphon, and responsory soon were all lost and little interest was shown in translating Latin hymns or in promoting a vernacular hymnody. Luther's efforts in this field and the wealth of choral music in the church orders and cantionales and of congregational chorales in the hymnals testify to an entirely different attitude and capacity in musical matters on the part of Lutheran Reformers and people in all lands.

The Introit is a choral element in the Service and should be sung by the choir, which may be thought of as "the voice of the church universal, specifically of the Old Testament church."[2] Like the Gradual, the

[1] W. E. Scudamore, *Notitia Eucharistica* (2nd ed.; London: Rivingtons, 1876), p. 215. Some of the older commentators on the *Book of Common Prayer* deplore the loss of the Introit. (Cf. Charles Wheatly, *Rational Illustration of the Book of Common Prayer* [London: Bell, 1877], pp. 204-5, where the entire series of psalms used in the first Prayer Book is given.) In many Anglican churches today, under Anglo-Catholic leadership, the historic introits are sung as extra choral numbers to settings in *The English Hymnal* or other chant forms.

[2] Schoeberlein, *Ueber den liturgischen Ausbau des Gemeindegottesdienstes* (Gotha: Perthes, 1859), p. 247.

Offertory, and the responsory, the Introit consists almost entirely of psalm verses. All of these, however, are built up in characteristic formal patterns, which, in structure and in relation to other elements in the Service, are distinctive. It is well to think of them as liturgical anthems. As such they are specifically intended for choral rendition and not for the use of the minister alone, and certainly not for responsive use by the minister and the congregation as in an ordinary psalm. Solemnity is added by repeating the antiphon immediately after the Gloria Patri.

The Gloria Patri or Little Doxology (as distinguished from the Gloria in Excelsis) has doctrinal as well as devotional values. It distinguishes the Christian use of the Psalter and connects the Old Testament texts with the later and fuller revelation of the New Testament. Thus it is regularly added to every psalm, canticle, or portion thereof. Its use in the early church affirmed the orthodox belief in the divinity, equality, and eternity of the three Persons, in opposition to Arian and other heresies. Yet the continued use of the Gloria Patri in the liturgy today is more than a memorial of ancient controversies. It is a brief but clear profession of faith in the Holy Trinity and particularly in the divinity of our Lord.

In old Lutheran circles the custom has been maintained to the present time of bowing the head in "due and lowly reverence" at the Gloria Patri and at the Name of Jesus throughout the Service.

The scriptural basis for the Gloria Patri is found in such passages as Romans 16:27; Ephesians 3:21; Philippians 4:20; Revelation 1:6. The Roman missal and most pre-Reformation missals (Sarum excepted), omit the Gloria Patri after the Introit from Judica Sunday until Easter. Lossius, *Psalmodia Sacra* gives it for Palm Sunday. Spangenberg, the Nuremberg *Officium Sacrum,* and the first Prayer Book of Edward VI retain it.

The ancient Mass had four chants sung by the choir during the progress of some other liturgical action: the Introit, while the priest went to the altar; the Gradual, after the Epistle while preparing to read the Gospel; the Offertory, while the faithful presented their offerings; and the Communio, when they received the Holy Communion.

In the present Roman missal, the text of all these chants is not from the Vulgate but from an earlier Latin translation called the Italia. Gihr[3] says the older version has been retained "because the original and unaltered mode of thought has always been intimately connected with it." Fondness for the text itself and for the melodies associated with it were probably additional reasons. Similarly the *Book of Common Prayer* retains its Psalter in the version of the Great Bible of 1539, and the Common Liturgy uses the Authorized Version for all texts instead of later revised versions. We are fortunate in having the greater part of this wealth of devotion preserved in our liturgy.

[3] *The Holy Sacrifice of the Mass* (St. Louis: Herder, 1902), p. 382.

Many of the church orders simply refer to the Introits, leaving the texts and music to be supplied from the old choir books (*Graduale*) or the later evangelical cantionales. The full series with Latin texts and music is given in Spangenberg, *Kirchengesänge lateinisch und deutsch* (1545), Lucas Lossius, *Psalmodia Sacra* (1553), Eler, *Cantica sacra* (1588), and the Nuremberg *Officium Sacrum* (1664).

Some of the orders reveal the difficulties encountered in introducing a vernacular service. Brandenburg-Nuremberg (1533) directed the pastor to read the Introit when there are no choir boys; Hoya (1573) permits the pastor to sing it; Osnabrück (1652) was probably the first to omit it.

In the restoration of the Lutheran liturgy in the nineteenth century, Schoeberlein opposed the attempt to reintroduce the full series. The Mecklenburg *Cantionale* (1868) kept only nine introits for the entire year. The *Church Book* (1868) led the way in attempting an almost complete series. The Common Service (1888) restored the entire series, correcting a few variations from the historic texts which the *Church Book*, following Loehe, had made. The *Common Service Book* (1918) provided a few additional introits for special services. The Common Liturgy added the Introit for the Festival of the Holy Innocents, Martyrs. (For scriptural sources of the Introit texts see Chaps. 26-28.)

✠

When the Introit is sung the minister goes from the chancel level to the altar and, as one of the congregation, faces the altar. Reading the Introit is about as uninspiring a performance as reading a hymn. If it should be necessary for the minister to read the Introit he does so facing the altar, a position which represents the ancient view of the Introit as an entrance psalm, therefore devotional in character.

A late Lutheran interpretation emphasizes sacramental values in the Introit as proclaiming the theme of the particular service. Schoeberlein, who stressed this in the late nineteenth century, probably never had the opportunity of hearing a sung Introit and in consequence was led to a pedagogical treatment of this proper.

In turning to the congregation, the minister always turns by the right (Epistle) side. He turns back to the altar by the same side, completing only a semicircle. The reason for this is to be found in pre-Reformation ceremonial. When the celebrant was assisted by a deacon, the latter stood at the celebrant's right as they faced the altar. In turning to and from the altar the celebrant was careful not to ignore the presence of the deacon or turn his back upon him.[4]

✠

[4] Fortescue, *Ceremonies of the Roman Rite Described*, p. 46; O'Connell, *The Celebration of Mass*, II, 67; Gihr, *The Holy Sacrifice of the Mass*, p. 411; Percy Dearmer, *The Parson's Handbook* (11th ed.; 1928), p. 332.

The Introits may be chanted to the psalm tones, the simplest and most ancient way (General Rubrics, p. 274). Or they may be sung to more elaborate settings. In every case, the objective, declamatory character of the text must be remembered and first attention given to clear, forceful enunciation of the words.[5] Here, as in all chanting, it is well in learning first to recite the text without music and then to sing it in a manner as closely resembling speech as possible without loss of dignity.

The antiphon of the Introit may be given by a solo voice. The full choir sings the psalm verse and the Gloria Patri. Especially on festivals, the antiphon may be repeated after the Gloria Patri by the full choir.

When the Introit is read by the minister, the choir and congregation unite in the Gloria Patri.

The Gloria Patri should be sung in the spirit of praise and with fair volume, but not with as full a tone as the later Gloria in Excelsis. Smoother rendition can be secured by "carrying through" without pause at some points (commas) in the punctuation. The average congregation finds it difficult to sing short phrases with confidence or to start with full volume again after sudden pauses.

In the responses throughout the Service a whole note is used to mark the syllable which receives the natural accent of the sentence. It has no precise time value—that is to say, it is not to be held just twice as long as the other notes. Its length is determined entirely by the time values in the text as recited naturally to musical tone.

¶ *Then shall be sung or said the Kyrie.*

KYRIE

In peace let us pray to the Lord.
℟. Lord, have mercy.

---

[5] Settings to psalm tones are provided in Archer and Reed, *The Choral Service Book*. Another psalm tone series is provided in W. E. Buszin (ed.), *The Introits for the Church Year* (St. Louis: Concordia, 1942). H. Alexander Matthews has composed a series for mixed voices, *Introits and Graduals of the Church Year* (2 vols.) (Philadelphia: U.L.P.H., 1924). These are well adapted to the abilities of the average choir as are the introits in another anthem-type series by Ralph P. Lewars, *Musical Settings for the Introits and Graduals of the Church Year*, 2 vols. (Philadelphia: U.L.P.H., 1948). The H. W. Gray Co. publishes Christensen and Schuneman (eds.), *The Proper of the Service*, with introits, graduals, and offertories set to very full forms of the Gregorian psalm tones. 2 vols. (New York: 1947.) The same firm also publishes Christensen and Mayer (eds.), *Introits for the Lutheran Church* (New York: 1939). Another Gregorian series is by Ernest White (New York: St. Mary's Pr., 1958). Emmanuel Schmauk also published the introits in anthem style.

For the peace that is from above, and for the salvation of our souls, let us pray to the Lord.
℟. Lord, have mercy.

For the peace of the whole world, for the well-being of the churches of God, and for the unity of all, let us pray to the Lord.
℟. Lord, have mercy.

For this holy house, and for them that in faith, piety and fear of God offer here their worship and praise, let us pray to the Lord.
℟. Lord, have mercy.

Help, save, pity, and defend us, O God, by thy grace.
℟. Amen.

The fabric of the liturgy is not woven only by the alternation of sacramental and sacrificial elements. It is also colored by contrasting moods and by an almost rhythmic succession of adoration, praise, and petition. In the Introit we have an announcement of God's grace. This is celebrated in bright tones in the Gloria Patri. The Kyrie in more somber shades expresses our humility and appreciation of our own weakness and need. The Gloria in Excelsis lifts us again into the clear light of exalted joy and praise, though even in its heart there is embedded a tender Agnus. Hebrews 4:16, "Let us therefore come boldly unto the throne of grace, that we may obtain mercy, and find grace to help in time of need," expresses conscious need no less than boldness. Upon these two wings of humility and confidence all liturgical prayer rises to the throne of grace.

The word "Kyrie" is the first part of a Greek phrase which in its full form (*Kyrie eleison*—"Lord, have mercy") is the surviving fragment of a brief litany-type prayer of the early church. The Greek language was the language of culture in the Mediterranean area. It was the language used in worship by Christians, even in Rome, during the first three centuries. The Kyrie, however, is not found in the liturgy proper in any Christian rite, East or West, before the middle of the fourth century. It is not mentioned by Cyprian, Hippolytus, Tertullian, Origen, Clement of Alexandria or any of the early church fathers.

The phrase might have passed into Christian use from Jewish sources. The petition "Lord, have mercy upon us"—or "upon me"—is found in many psalms (25:16, 26:11; 41:4; 51:1; 123:3, etc.) as well as in the Gospels of Matthew (9:27; 15:22) and Luke (17:13; 18:38). It is always a cry for help in distress—blindness, leprosy, sickness—and only in two instances (Psalms 41 and 51) is it a plea for forgiveness. Christian scholars, familiar with the Greek of the New Testament and with the Greek-language Septuagint translation of the Old Testament, knew this phrase. It is clear, however, that the shorter phrase, "Lord, have mercy," came into Christian use from a different source.

Modern scholarship has discovered the pre-Christian origin of the phrase and established the fact of its relatively late incorporation in the liturgy. The early Christians were a simple folk. They had no printed or written liturgies. Their participation in the services was real and hearty. But it consisted, for the most part, of simple responses such as: Amen; Hosanna; And with thy spirit; Lord, have mercy. As an acclamation and invocation the last phrase was known throughout the Greek-speaking world. Persian and Egyptian sun-worshipers had first used it. Later it passed into popular use in connection with emperor worship and finally came into Christian worship in Asia Minor as a response to petitions in a litany-type prayer at the close of Vespers. Subsequently it appeared in the Greek Clementine Liturgy in the form of a deacon's litany (*ektene*) at the beginning of the service of Holy Communion. Finally, at some period before the time of Gregory the Great (A.D. 590), and probably through the powerful influence of the great church of Constantinople, it became part of the Latin Mass as a Greek response to Latin petitions of general character in a short litany following the Introit. It travelled into Gaul via Arles sometime before the Synod of Vaison, A.D. 529.

Originally an acclamation or praise-shout, the Kyrie resembled the Hebrew Hosanna ("Save now"). It had within it a plea for favor or help, but not for forgiveness. The Liturgical Commission of the Protestant Episcopal Church states that an adequate rendering of the Kyrie as used by the primitive church might be "Thou art the Lord, the fount of all mercy."[6] During those centuries the phrase took different forms and was used on secular as well as religious occasions. Sun-worshipers cried, "O Helios (Sun), have mercy." Pagan emperor-worshipers cried, "O Lord (Emperor), have mercy." Epictetus, a highly respected Stoic philosopher who died in A.D. 125, wrote: "In our invocations to God we entreat him 'Lord, have mercy upon me, suffer me to come off safe.' "[7] Franz Dölger in his learned work cites this and many other examples of similar acclamations and petitions in secular and religious use in the early Christian centuries. Religious forms are persistent and as late as the fifth century a preacher in Alexandria is on record as denouncing the custom still observed by some Christians of bowing to the rising sun and crying, "Kyrie eleison."[8] This widespread popular use of the Kyrie in Mediterranean lands at that time, and its character as an acclamation and petition, probably explains the unique retention by the Roman church of the Greek phrase in its Latin liturgy.

The earliest reference to the use of the Kyrie in Christian worship is found in a description by Etheria, a Spanish abbess, of her "pilgrimage" to holy places in the East, about the middle of the fourth century. She states that she heard it in Jerusalem as a people's response to suffrages or petitions said at the close of Vespers. As we have stated, it later came into the Divine Liturgy of the Greek church and into the

---

[6] *Prayer Book Studies* (New York: Church Pension Fund, 1950), IV, 17 ff.

[7] *Discourses* II:7.

[8] *Sol Salutis, Gebet und Gesang im Christlichen Altertum* (Münster in Westf.: 1920), pp. 60-105.

Latin Mass of the Western church. Gregory the Great speaks of it as a comparatively recent item in the liturgy and defends the Roman manner of using it in a form differing from that of the Greeks. In his final reconstruction of the liturgy he transferred some of the petitions in this litany-prayer to a later place in the service. He retained only the simple response of the people in ninefold form and changed the three middle petitions to *Christie, eleison,* thus giving the entire text the character of an invocation of the Holy Trinity.

The Western Kyrie now became a liturgical remnant, its early litany form and its broad, objective petitions completely forgotten. The fragment that remained came to be thought of simply as a cry of penitence and a plea for forgiveness. In this mutilated form, and with this penitential meaning, it received a marvelously rich musical development in the medieval trope, whose interpolated texts have given us the titles of many well-known masses—*Orbis factor, Rex genitor, Fons bonitatis,* etc. Great masters of music, including Johann Sebastian Bach, with the same penitential interpretation of the text, have composed choral works of great compass and complexity upon this theme.

Originally the Kyrie was sung by alternate choirs until the celebrant gave the sign to cease. Later the number of petitions was fixed at nine. Luther's orders established the simpler threefold use. From the simplest, oft-repeated liturgical acclamation of the early church, it developed into lengthy litanies and elaborate choral compositions. Within the liturgy proper the Kyrie is one of the five texts comprising the musical masses of Palestrina, Mozart, Bach (B minor), Gounod, and countless other masters, the other four texts being the Gloria in Excelsis, Creed, Sanctus, and Agnus Dei.

The use of the Kyrie in the earliest Christian liturgies clearly shows that no special pentitential character was attached to it. The liturgies of St. James (Jerusalem), St. Mark (Alexandria), St. Clement (*Apostolic Constitutions*) and St. John Chrysostom (Constantinople) all use *Kyrie eleison* as a choral or a congregational response to intercessions of great breadth and objectivity. In St. James and St. John Chrysostom the deacon begins with an exhortation: "In peace let us make our supplications to the Lord," and follows with "bids" for "the peace that is from above and the loving-kindness of God and the salvation of our souls . . . for the peace of the whole world and the union of all the holy Church of God . . . for the forgiveness of our sins and the remission of our transgressions that we may be preserved from all afflictions, wrath, danger and necessity . . . for the king . . . for the archbishop . . . for the whole city and country . . . for healthfulness of air, plenty of the fruits of the earth and peaceful times . . . for them that voyage, that journey, that are sick, that labor, that are in bonds," etc. The choir, or the people, respond at the end of each petition: "Lord, have mercy."

The Common Liturgy restores the Kyrie to its original form and seeks to invest it with its original significance as a congregational acclaim of the Lord as he comes to meet with his people as they begin their worship, and as an objective, unselfish intercession for peace and the good estate of the church, the state, and the world. As the first prayer of the Service, this restored and valid form lifts the service to high levels at its very beginning. Its petitions have spiritual dimensions of breadth, depth, and height. They reverently recognize the presence of the Lord and invoke his blessing and peace, not only for themselves but for others. Upon such an unselfish and exalted plane of thought and concern the people of God build their fabric of worship in liturgical forms which begin with the great canticle of praise—the Gloria in Excelsis.

If anyone should be disturbed by the pre-Christian origin and use of the phrase, "Lord, have mercy," let him recall that the early Christians, like missionaries in pagan lands today, observed non-Christian festivals, customs, and days, giving them a Christian content and meaning. December 25, the birthday of the sun-god throughout the pagan world, became the day on which Christians celebrated the birth of Jesus Christ, the Sun of Righteousness. January 6, another pagan festival, became the Feast of the Epiphany in Christian observance. We have already referred to the incorporation of Jewish words and features in the early Christian liturgies.[9]

The standard English form of the Kyrie response contains two extra words, "upon us," not found in the original. The Episcopal Liturgical Commission makes this comment: "Cranmer's translation, 'Lord, have mercy *upon us,*' is unfortunate in the last two words, which are not in the Greek, and which have some tendency to underscore the medieval understanding of the phrase as penitential in quality . . . Bishop Dowden proposed that the last two words be dropped in order to restore what he called 'the large indefiniteness of the original.' "[10] The Scottish Liturgy of 1912 accepted Dowden's amendment, and was followed in this by the English *Proposed Book* of 1928. We are glad to note this approval of the ancient text given in the Common Liturgy. This commission's further statement, however, though interesting, seems naive. It opines that Cranmer "appended the two extra words . . . to fill out seven syllables, the same number as the original Kyrie eleison, so that the new English version could be sung to the inherited plainsong music."[11] It is questionable whether the archbishop, whose knowledge of or interest in the music of the church was so limited that he omitted all choral parts from the English liturgy—introits, graduals, antiphons, respon-

[9] The best summary discussion of the origin and development of the Kyrie is to be found in Dölger, *op. cit.;* in *Leiturgia, Handbuch des evangelischen Gottesdienstes* (Kassel: Johann Stauda Verlag, 1952), II, 14ff.; Joseph A. Jungmann, S.J., *The Mass of the Roman Rite* (New York: Benziger, 1950), I, 333ff.; and in Edmund Bishop, *Liturgica Historica* (Oxford: 1918.)
[10] Dowden, *The Workmanship of the Prayer Book.*
[11] *Prayer Book Studies,* IV, 172 ff.

sories, etc. — was particularly concerned about the musical forms of the Kyrie. He most likely carried over the words "upon us" from current Latin and German forms.

As far as is known, the Common Liturgy is the first official Lutheran Service to restore the original and fuller form of the Kyrie to its historic place in the Communion Office. The material is given in a litany form of general prayer in the 1948 liturgy for the Rhineland and Westphalia. Similarly it appears in certain Anglican service books and in some other recent European Lutheran works. It is found, of course, in much fuller form, in current office books of the Eastern Orthodox churches.

For those who prefer to continue the simple threefold form the traditional text is provided as an alternate.

¶ *In place of the foregoing, the following Kyrie may be sung or said.*

KYRIE

Lord, have mercy upon us.
℟. Lord, have mercy upon us.

Christ, have mercy upon us.
℟. Christ, have mercy upon us.

Lord, have mercy upon us.
℟. Lord, have mercy upon us.

In extraliturgical use the popularity of the Kyrie found expression not only in litanies, but in a type of vernacular hymn sung on pilgrimages, in processions, etc., and called *"Leisen* hymns" because each stanza concluded with the phrase *"Kyrie Eleis."* The refrain after each commandment in the Communion service of *Book of Common Prayer* may be a not-so-distant relative of this medieval type of hymn. Even in liturgical use within the framework of the Mass, medieval devotion elaborated the text with *tropes,* or "farsed" Kyries. A popular German form was the "Kyrie, ach Vater, allerhöchster Gott, etc.," of Michael Weise.

The German church orders generally retained the Kyrie in the Service in its simple Greek form. Frequently, however, they alternated the Greek and the German texts. The minister intoned (or said) *Kyrie eleison* and the congregation responded *Herr, erbarme dich unser. A* few orders prescribe that it shall be sung in Greek, Latin, and German (Prussia [1525]; Riga [1531]; Brandenburg [1540]; Pomerania [1563]). The more elaborate ninefold musical settings long continued in use in many places, particularly on festivals (Wittenberg [1533], etc.). Occasionally the independent value of the Kyrie was not appreciated, and it was combined with the Confiteor (Naumburg [1537]; Sweden [1541]), or was supplanted by the General Confession (*Offene Schuld*) (Strasbourg [1598]).

The first *Book of Common Prayer* kept the traditional ninefold Kyrie. The second Book (1552) developed a unique feature to which reference has already been made, and which has characterized Anglican services ever since.

271

An expanded form of the Kyrie was inserted in the nature of a refrain after each commandment in the Decalogue, brought into the Prayer Book at this time: "Lord, have mercy upon us, and incline our hearts to keep this law." This insertion, together with the loss of the Introit and the Gradual, and the transfer of the Gloria in Excelsis to the end of the Service, not only represented a great change from the text of the historic liturgy, but also gave a strong penitential character to the first part of the Anglican Service. The Roman and the Lutheran liturgies introduce the elements of worship and praise early in their services, and sustain this mood. The Anglican liturgy scarcely reaches these more joyous notes before the Preface to the Holy Communion.

The responses in the first musical setting are beautiful melodic forms, readily learned by the congregation, and with richly harmonized parts for the choir. They should be sung devotionally and freely with close attention to the natural rhythm of the text. Originally by Arnold Richardson, they have been adapted by Harold W. Gilbert. Dr. Gilbert's simple alternate in C-minor has been inserted by request. Unhappily its feeling of heaviness suggests the erroneous conception of the Kyrie as a penitential text. The two series of responses in the second setting have been adapted by Mrs. Fryxell from tenth-century plain song and sixteenth-century Bohemian Brethren forms respectively. These also must be chanted in free rhythm.

The Kyrie is a sacrificial element, and the minister faces the altar.

¶ Then shall be sung or said the Gloria in Excelsis.

GLORIA IN EXCELSIS

¶ The Minister shall sing or say:

Glory be to God on high!

¶ Congregation

And on earth peace, good will toward men. We praise thee, we bless thee, we worship thee, we glorify thee, we give thanks to thee for thy great glory, O Lord God, heavenly King, God the Father Almighty.

O Lord, the only-begotten Son, Jesus Christ; O Lord God, Lamb of God, Son of the Father, that takest away the sin of the world, have mercy upon us. Thou that takest away the sin of the world, receive our prayer. Thou that sittest at the right hand of God the Father, have mercy upon us.
For thou only art holy; thou only art the Lord; thou only, O Christ, with the Holy Ghost, art most high in the glory of God the Father. Amen.

This is a hymn of praise which in this place represents the final chorus of responding voices with which the early church concluded its litanies. Coming immediately after the Kyrie, without a single word between, it is a response to the Kyrie itself which proclaims the glory of God and voices the joy of believers in his merciful goodness in sending his Son to be the Savior of the world.

The Gloria in Excelsis follows the Kyrie immediately in swift change of mood. Its outburst of joy and praise to the Holy Trinity lifts the worshipers from thought of self to contemplation of the divine and from consciousness of human need to glorification of God's majesty, power, and holiness. Its opening address is to "God the Father Almighty." Its middle section, like the great Western hymn, the Te Deum of Matins, is a glorious confession of the divinity of Jesus Christ, the "only-begotten Son . . . the Lamb of God."

Competent scholars believe that this middle part was the earliest form of the Gloria—that it at first consisted of a series of acclamations addressed to Christ, and that the addresses to the Father were added later, and the opening phrase, "Glory be to God on high, and on earth peace, good will toward men" last of all.[12]

However this may be, the Gloria in Excelsis is not merely a hymn of praise to the Father, but a "jubilant anthem of redemption." Thus early in the Service it grounds our faith and worship again on the incarnation, the atonement, and the perpetual intercession of our Lord. For a moment it stops in its flight to invoke mercy and help. Then swiftly and objectively, as though having glimpsed the glory of the Almighty, it rises to its final outburst of worship and praise to Christ and the Holy Ghost as "most high in the glory of God the Father." Through its coming to us from the early centuries, we should sense something of the grave dignity, strong faith, and devotional fervor of the early Christians as we sing these simple but profound sentences in our services today.

Like the Kyrie, the Gloria in Excelsis has inspired many notable musical compositions. In the period from the tenth to the sixteenth centuries many farsed forms of the Gloria as well as the Kyrie were developed, appropriate to particular seasons or occasions, and set to elaborate melodies. These *tropes* or interpolated texts were forbidden by the Tridentine Missal of Pius V.

Luther said the Gloria "did not grow, nor was it made on earth, but it came down from heaven." He gave it in its usual place in his Latin Service, but omitted all reference to it in his German Mass. Olavus Petri shows his preference for the *Formula Missae* type of service rather than the order of the German Mass by including the Gloria in his Swedish Mass of 1531.

[12] See Parsch, *The Liturgy of the Mass,* p. 99, where comparison of early texts is given.

The Common Service restored the full text of the Gloria, and the Common Liturgy prescribes its use on festivals and whenever there is a communion. At other times another canticle or hymn of praise is permitted in the interest of variety and wider acquaintance with the liturgical material of the church. It will be well, however, to restrict the use of other canticles to the seasons of Advent and Lent, when their use can give a more subdued tone to this part of the service.

The earliest known form of the Gloria in Excelsis dates from the fourth century, though it is probably older. It is found in the *Apostolic Constitutions* (VII:47), and is mentioned by Athanasius (d. 373). Cabrol says (*Liturgical Prayer,* p. 101), "It contains no expression but what might have been written in the first or second century." It is in three parts, the middle portion anticipating the phraseology of the Agnus Dei, which did not come into the liturgy until centuries later.

In its original form the Gloria in Excelsis was a "private psalm" sung in Greek in the morning office but not as a part of the Mass. It is undoubtedly of Eastern origin. We may see in it possibly the only surviving complete example of the eloquent compositions improvised in the early Christian assemblies as expressions of fervid devotion. In spirit it is akin to the Magnificat and the Benedictus. Three principal versions of the early text are to be distinguished: (1) the Syrian (Nestorian); (2) the Greek, from the *Apostolic Constitutions;* and (3) the Greek, from the Byzantine Liturgy, which is closest to our Western text.[13]

The Gloria in Excelsis was most likely introduced into the eucharistic service in the Western church in connection with the Christmas Vigil. This was particularly appropriate because of the reference to the song of the angels at the time of our Lord's nativity. The Incarnation and the Holy Communion are both manifestations of the real presence of Christ among men.

Pope Symmachus (A.D. 498-514) ordered the Gloria to be sung every Lord's Day and on the feasts of martyrs. For centuries the Gloria was the exclusive privilege of bishops, priests being permitted to chant it only on Easter. Since the eleventh century the opening phrase has been chanted by celebrants of whatever degree and the rest sung by the choir. Honorius (A.D. 1130) quaintly says this is done "because the angel also began this alone, and the whole army of the heavenly host sang it all together." The Gloria is omitted entirely in the Roman use during Advent and from Septuagesima to Easter Eve.

Some Lutheran orders (Prussia [1544]) direct the minister to sing the Gloria in Excelsis in Latin, and the congregation to sing it in German. Occasionally it was restricted to festivals, which agrees with the universal medieval practice which regarded both the Gloria and the Creed as festal features which might be omitted on work days. Schoeberlein gives many settings of the complete German text to be sung by the congregation, or by choir and congregation. Difficulties of translation and musical adaptation which were not promptly overcome led to the substitution, in many church orders, of

---

[13] J. A. Jungmann, *op. cit.,* I, 347 ff.

vernacular versifications such as Luther's "All Ehr und Preis soll Gottes sein" or the "Allein Gott in der Höh' sei Ehr" of Decius. The result is that German services of the present day rarely give the actual text of the Gloria in complete prose form. Usually the minister intones the opening phrase: "Ehre sei Gott in der Höhe"; the choir responds: "Und auf Erden Fried, den Menschen ein Wohlgefallen!" and the congregation sings a metrical version of the Gloria or another hymn of praise.

The Gloria in Excelsis concludes the first section of the Service of the Word. This part has been preparatory and largely sacrificial in character. From this point the sacramental element is dominant.

✠

The Gloria in Excelsis is sacrificial in character, and the minister faces the altar throughout, even when he recites the opening phrase.

The responsive use of the pre-Reformation church is continued in many German and Scandinavian churches, and has been accepted in the Common Liturgy. According to this the minister says or intones the first phase and the choir and congregation begin singing with "and on earth peace," etc. The reintroduction of this practice eliminates awkward repetition of the opening phrase.

✠

Some of the traditional plain song melodies of the Gloria in Excelsis are of surpassing beauty. One of these has been well adapted to the English text by Ernest White in his Gregorian setting of the Common Liturgy. Another is given in Archer and Reed, *The Choral Service Book,* p. 7.

The Old Scottish Chant (*Service Book,* p. 20) was chosen as a setting for the Gloria not only because its simplicity would encourage congregational participation, but particularly because of its widespread use in all parts of the country. Being found in one or another of the official books of all the co-operating churches, it was an item upon which common agreement could immediately be reached.

A much more sophisticated and very beautiful setting of the Gloria is provided in the alternate chant by Leo Sowerby. The unusual harmonies of this brilliant composition may at first seem to distract attention from the text. The melody, however, is simple and can readily be learned by the congregation. The total effect, while "modern" in feeling, is genuine and good.

The music of the Gloria in the second (Continental) setting is a skilful adaptation by Regina H. Fryxell of forms in the tenth-century plain-song Latin mass *Lux et Origo* and the German chorale *Allein Gott in der Höh' sei Ehr* by Nikolaus Decius. The strong melody must be sung in unison.

The musical rendition must definitely express the real character of the Gloria as a canticle of praise. It must be sung brightly and in good tempo, even in the contrasting middle portion.

In a choir of some size, the male voices, if effective, may sing the phrase "and on earth peace, good will towards men," in vigorous unison. The entire choir may then continue the chant in parts.

The second part, "O Lord, the only-begotten Son," begins with diminished volume. Each of the three petitions in this part is to be sung softly but without change of tempo.

The third part, "For thou only art holy," is sung with breadth and vigor. In order to give strong leadership the choir may sing this opening phrase in unison, and then continue in parts with gradual crescendo to a strong climax at the very end.

Careful attention must be given to clear enunciation throughout, as well as to proper phrasing and breathing, in order to secure the fine legato quality which characterizes good choral work. All chant forms must preserve a free rhythm and a natural declamation of the text. The accents of the latter determine the relative length of musical tone. For example, in the phrase, "receive our prayer," the first three notes are all quarters, but the first syllable "re" is passed over lightly, while the second syllable "ceive," as having the natural accent, will be slightly stressed.

CHAPTER XIV

THE SALUTATION AND THE COLLECT

THE SALUTATION AND RESPONSE

¶ *Then shall the Minister sing or say:*

The Lord be with you.
℞. And with thy spirit.

The first division of the Office of the Word ends with the Gloria in Excelsis. A new and predominantly sacramental division begins with the Salutation.

This essentially Hebrew form of greeting and response expresses the thought contained in the Hebrew word *Emmanuel,* "God with us." In the book of Ruth (2:4) we read that when Boaz came from Bethlehem he said to the reapers, "The Lord be with you" and they answered, "The Lord bless thee." The angel of the Lord appeared to Gideon and said, "The Lord is with thee" (Judg. 6:12). Also in the New Testament, when the Archangel Gabriel appeared to Mary, he greeted her with the exclamation, "Hail, thou that art highly favored, the Lord is with thee" (Luke 1:28). Paul expanded the thought somewhat in his benedictions (II Thess. 3:16, Tim. 4:22, etc.). And so, particularly before sacramental acts such as the reading of the Word or the administration of the Holy Communion, we have the Salutation and response. The phrase finally became imbedded in the early Christian liturgies as a significant responsive introduction to new and different parts of the Service. Thus it precedes the Collect, the Preface, the Benediction, etc., and introduces the use of collects and prayers generally as in Matins and Vespers.

The Salutation and its response are not addressed to God but to man. They constitute a reciprocal prayer of the minister for his people and of the congregation for its pastor before they unitedly offer their petitions to God. As such they serve as constant reminders of the pastoral relationship while renewing the ties of faith and common purpose in further acts of prayer. Cabrol somewhere suggests that the people answer 'And with thy spirit' as though commissioning him (the priest) to speak for all. Loehe says: "The bonds of love and unity between pastor and people are tied anew." The Oremus, "Let us pray," is a clear indication of the corporate character of the act. It is the prayer of the congregation, and indeed of the whole church for a particular day or festival.

✠

The minister turns by his right (Epistle) side and faces the congregation. The *Service Book* is left on the missal stand. According to ancient usage he may extend his parted hands as he says, "The Lord be with you." Joining his hands again, he acknowledges the response of the people by a slight inclination of his head. Gihr explains this conventional practice as follows: "The extending of the hands expresses the ardent longing and the earnest desire of the priest that the blessing he invokes may be bestowed; the joining of the hands signifies that the priest humbly mistrusts his own strength and confidently abandons himself to the Lord."[1] After the response, "And with thy spirit," the minister turns to the altar again by the Epistle side for the Collect. (See p. 265.)

✠

The response should be sung in moderate volume and without dragging.

¶ *The minister shall say:*

Let us pray.

¶ *Then shall the Minister say the Collect for the Day.*

THE COLLECT

(First Sunday in Advent)

Stir up, we beseech thee, thy power, O Lord, and come; that by thy protection we may be rescued from the threatening perils of our sins, and saved by thy mighty deliverance; who livest and reignest with the Father and the Holy Ghost, one God, world without end.

¶ *The Collect ended, the Congregation shall sing or say:*

Amen.

The Collect is a brief but significant prayer which the church appoints in this place for each Sunday or festival. The minister, expressing the thought of the entire congregation, reads it aloud at the altar. The Collect for the Day is the second "proper" or variable part of the

[1] Gihr, *The Holy Sacrifice of the Mass*, p. 411.

liturgy. It is usually related in thought to the Gospel or the Epistle for the Day, and its chief function is to prepare the mind for the liturgical lessons.

Many of the ancient collects are general in character and reflect the thought of a season rather than of a particular day. The vitality and stability of this prayer form, in spite of controversies, revolutions, and reformations, constitute one of the remarkable facts in the history of Christian worship.

With an unbroken use of nearly fifteen centuries by multitudes of believers in all lands, the collects constitute an important part of the liturgical inheritance of the church. They are regularly used in Roman, Lutheran, and Anglican services throughout the world today. Their humility of spirit is more than balanced by certainty of faith, and their brevity of form by breadth of thought. Contributing to the liturgical unity and harmony of each service, they also span the full breadth of human need. They are pervaded by the spirit of the gospel and by a constant feeling for the communion of saints. We prize them for their antiquity, universality, excellence, and beauty.

Terse, significant prayers such as these, though probably improvised at first, were carefully pruned and later compositions were prepared in accordance with a definite pattern. The finest, those excelling in devotional content, doctrinal expression, or formal beauty, gained wide usage and finally were preserved in the sacramentaries, breviaries, and other prayer collections. The prayers in the Roman collections were usually general in character and were distinguished by what Edmund Bishop has called "soberness and sense" as well as by terseness, even severity, in style. The prayers of Gallican (western European) authorship were often diffuse, even ornate. The collects composed in the Reformation period and later were specific in thought and frequently extended in form.[2]

The perfect collect is an art form the poetic values of which are expressed not in rhymed words but in rhymed thoughts, arranged in definite patterns of rhythmic prose. The essential merit of the collect is its spiritual content, its forthrightness, fervor, and sincerity. Many collects possess these qualities without being especially distinguished otherwise. Others compel our admiration by combining weight of content with excellence of form. Many of the Latin as well as the finer English collects reveal an appreciation of this principle.[3]

[2] For comparison of the Roman and the Gallican collects see the admirable discussion by Edmund Bishop in *Liturgica Historica*, pp. 1-19.

[3] Cf. Clarke and Harris, *Liturgy and Worship,* pp. 806-12. Also Dowden, *Workmanship of the Prayer Book.*

The individual character and excellence of the collects have been highly praised by many scholars. Macaulay in his "Essay on Milton," (*Critical and Miscellaneous Essays*) lauds their "unity of sentiment and severity of style" and says that they have "soothed the griefs of twenty generations of Christians."

Cardinal Wiseman says: "Nothing can be more perfect in structure, more solid in substance, more elegant in conception, or more terse in diction than the Collects, especially those of the Sundays and of Lent. They belong essentially to the traditional depositories of the Church." Dr. Edward T. Horn says that as a body the collects are a monument to the piety of the fathers and "a treasury of sound theology and ethics."

Canon Goulburn has the following striking paragraph: "One has seen at the root of a decaying tree tufts of wild hyacinths or primroses, engendered by that decay, bred of corruption. And there are correspondences in the moral world with this natural phenomenon. When the old Roman Empire was in its last stage of decay, when all old landmarks were being removed, and old institutions were going to pieces, then appeared for the first time these bunches of fragrant beautiful prayers, giving token of a spiritual vitality below the surface of society, a sure evidence that all was not corrupt, that the antiseptic salt of God's grace in the hearts of His elect endured still, and had not lost its savour."[4]

Loehe, who led the way in a reawakened appreciation of the collects in the middle of the last century, spoke of them as "the breath of a soul, sprinkled with the blood of Jesus, brought to the eternal Father in the Name of his Son." The passages in the fifth and the eighth chapters of Revelation also come to mind—"golden vials full of odors which are the prayers of the saints."

The earliest name for the Collect was simply *Oratio*—"the prayer." Perhaps the earliest intimation of its appearance in the liturgy is in Bishop Serapion's prayer book where mention is made of "the First Prayer of the Lord's Day."[5] Its use in the church from that time to the present has been continuous.

The name "collect" is most probably derived from the early custom in Rome where an early gathering for worship (*ecclesia collecta*) was held, at which a prayer like this was used. This prayer was repeated after the Litany and a hymn in the later service at the stational (appointed) church. (So Bona, Duchesne, Thalhofer, and others.) According to another explanation (favored by Walafried Strabo, Hugo of St.

---

[4] E. M. Goulburn, *The Collects of the Day* (London: Rivingtons, 1880), I, 38.
[5] John Wordsworth, *Bishop Serapion's Prayer Book* (2d ed.; London: S.P.C.K., 1923), pp. 30, 80.

Victor, and others), it may come from the practice in the Gallican church where, particularly in monastic services, after the psalms had been recited and the lessons read, the officiant called upon all to pray. A period of silent prayer followed. This was concluded by the officiant, who offered a prayer (*collectio*), which summed up the thought of all.

Though brief, the collects are models of form, and are constructed in accordance with a definite prose pattern. The complete collect contains five parts: 1. an invocation; 2. a basis for the petition; 3. the petition; 4. the purpose or benefit desired; 5. the ending, which is in effect a doxology. Frequently part two, or part four, is missing, and occasionally both. The first three parts are found in the prayer of the disciples after the ascension: "Thou, Lord, which knowest the hearts of all men, shew whether of these two thou hast chosen" (Acts 1:24). The basis for the petition (often called the "antecedent reason") recalls some quality or promise or command of God. It thus contributes a sacramental quality and makes the normal collect "a word of man to God based upon a word of God to man" (Goulburn).

Most collects are addressed to God the Father. A few ancient collects (none earlier than the Gregorian) are addressed to our Lord. A very few later ones (chiefly Mozarabic) are addressed to the Holy Spirit. All collects conclude with the words "through Jesus Christ our Lord," or "through *the same* Jesus Christ our Lord," in case reference to Christ has been made in the body of the prayer. The immediate explanation for this conclusion is to be found in our Lord's words: "That whatsoever ye shall ask the Father in my name, he may give it you." Archbishop Temple has a further comment upon the termination in the collect pattern: "You cannot see God, but you can remember Jesus Christ who is 'the Image of the Invisible God, the effulgence of His glory, the express image of His Person.' There you see God. In your prayers act on His words, 'He that hath seen Me hath seen the Father.' Only pray to God as you have come to understand Him in Christ . . . The throne of God for this world is, after all, the Cross, and it must be to Jesus that our minds are turned when we want to speak to God."[6]

The Collect for the Day and the final collect in a series always have the complete ending: "Through Jesus Christ our Lord, who liveth and reigneth with thee and the Holy Ghost, one God, world without end." F. R. Webber earnestly urges the importance of using this ancient trinitarian form as a constant testimony against the modernists who address the Savior simply as "Master" and avoid all reference to the Trinity as such.[7]

[6] William Temple, *Basic Convictions* (New York: Harper, 1936), p. 51.
[7] F. R. Webber, *Studies in the Liturgy* (Erie, Pa.: Ashby, 1938), p. 49ff.

The following examples illustrate the collect structure.

	First Sunday in Advent	Christmas Early	Collect for Purity
Invocation	O Lord,	O God,	Almighty God,
Basis for petition		who hast made this most holy night to shine with the brightness of the true Light:	unto whom all hearts are open, all desires known, and from whom no secrets are hid:
Petition	Stir up, we beseech thee, thy power . . . and come;	Grant, we beseech thee, that as we have known on earth the mysteries of that Light, we may also come to the fulness of his joys in heaven;	Cleanse the thoughts of our hearts by the inspiration of thy Holy Spirit,
Purpose	that by thy protection we may be rescued from the threatening perils of our sins, and saved by thy mighty deliverance;		that we may perfectly love thee, and worthily magnify thy holy Name;
Ending	who livest and reignest with the Father and the Holy Ghost, one God, world without end. *Amen.*	who liveth, etc.	through Jesus Christ, thy Son, our Lord. *Amen.*

The sacramentaries are the earliest known collections of prayers used by the priest at the Holy Communion. The most ancient, the Leonine, bears the name of Pope Leo the Great (A.D. 440-61). Later revised and enlarged collections, the Gelasian and the Gregorian, are named after Popes Gelasius I (492-96) and Gregory I (590-604), respectively. The earliest collects may have been condensations of still earlier and longer prayers, but their definite pattern, no less than their brevity, immediately established a Roman type of liturgical prayer.

Of the *Service Book* collects for Sundays and festivals, forty-one are found first in the Gregorian Sacramentary, twenty-four in the Gelasian and seven in the earliest or Leonine Sacramentary.[8] The collects in the sacramentaries were later incorporated into the missal, the service book of the Mass. This, like all the other service books of the church, was produced and circulated in manuscript for a thousand years, the first

[8] Cf. the critical editions by C. L. Feltoe and by H. A. Wilson.

printed missal appearing only a few years before Luther's birth.

The breviaries contained the liturgical material used in the hour services (Matins, Lauds, Vespers, Compline, etc.), which together comprised the Divine Office. The collect received an exceedingly rich development in western Europe during the Middle Ages in connection with the office. Each psalm and each lesson frequently had its own collect. Many of these Gallican or Western collects were diffuse in style and lacked the clarity and sententious brevity of the typically Roman prayer.

About the eleventh century it became customary, particularly in western Europe, to recite more than one collect before the Epistle in every mass. In the thirteenth century the number of collects was definitely prescribed according to the rank and solemnity of the feasts. For the highest rank (duplex), only one collect was appointed. On a semi-double feast other commemorations and petitions were permitted to a total of three collects. A simple (simplex) may have five or seven. Mystical commentators explained that the reason the number seven may never be exceeded is not only because of weariness but also because our Lord comprised all that we require for soul and body in seven petitions. Luther restricted the number of collects before the Epistle to one, the actual Collect for the Day.

The Lutheran Reformers translated and adapted a number of the historic collects for use in vernacular services. Many of the finest ancient collects of the Latin church were used in German and Swedish Lutheran services before they appeared in English translation in 1549. In addition to regular collects for Sundays and festivals, the Lutheran collections included general collects for the church seasons, for peace, fruitful seasons, etc. Many new collects were also composed, definitely evangelical in tone, and, for the most part, in the Gallican rather than the Roman tradition as to form and length.

Luther translated many collects, sometimes combining two or three in one German collect, or using part of an ancient collect as a basis for a new one. These appeared in his hymnbooks, *Deutsche Messe, Taufbüchlein,* Litany, marriage service, etc. Prof. Paul Drews and Dr. Strodach have severally traced all of Luther's collects to pre-Reformation sources (missals, breviaries, etc.), except his post-communion prayer, and Dr. Strodach suggests several possible foundations for that.

The framers of the *Book of Common Prayer* in 1549 provided a matchless series of English translations and adaptations. Two-thirds of the collects in the first Edwardian Book are close translations of the terse Latin originals. Most of the remainder were original compositions (fourteen for saints' days alone), by Cranmer in 1549. Bishop Cosin added a number of his own in the revision of 1662. In most of these original compositions the English Reformers, like their German and Swedish colleagues, departed from the severity of the Roman collect form, and approached the exuberance of the Gallican type. The English and the continental Reformers were also at one in seeking to relate the Collect specifically to the liturgical Lessons.

Many of the collects for the day in the *Service Book* are in the Prayer Book version. This is because it was felt desirable to employ classic English translations whenever possible rather than to provide new and original renderings. In many cases, however, where the Prayer Book discarded the historic collects or gave an unsatisfactory translation, the commission, or the Common Service Book Committee before it, provided translations of its own (Advent I, II, III, etc.). It should also be noted that beginning with the Fourth Sunday after Trinity the Anglican collects fall one Sunday behind the Lutheran series.

Many of the church orders permitted the Collect for the Day to be intoned in Latin or in German. Difficulties of translation led to the use in many orders of one or two German collects throughout a season. In addition to this partial series of translated collects, new German collects were composed and used. The Brunswick-Lüneburg Order of 1564, for example, contains twenty-three translations of Latin collects and thirty-four new German ones. The Oldenburg Order (1573) contains thirty-four translations and forty-seven new collects.

In southern and southwestern Germany the reader was required "to sing or to say" the Collect. Mecklenburg (1552) and Austria (1571) specify that it shall be in German and so said as to be clearly understood *(verständlich)*: "With loud voice so that the whole congregation *(Kirch)* can say Amen and, as well as the pastor, cry to God." This effort to provide audible reading of the Collect by the minister and a hearty response by the congregation was typical of the Reformation. It elevated the Collect again to the dignity of a congregational prayer, turned a secret, priestly act into an open, representative function, established the choir as a part of the congregation, and roused the latter to attention and active participation in the Service.

Professor Althaus has given us the valuable results of his exhaustive studies of the collect literature of the sixteenth century. He describes the process of assimilation and expansion of inherited material, and the emergence of new collects in more than one hundred church orders, whose relationship to one another can frequently best be traced by the identity or similarity of collect material. There is every evidence of theological and literary discrimination, and of critical appreciation on the part of editors of the desirable qualities of clarity, pithiness, and power. A relative fact is the unanimity with which the Lutheran orders excluded all mystical and catholicizing influences. Prayers reflecting the spirit of Schwenkfeld, or of the Jesuits, or even of Erasmus, are not found. In addition to Luther's collects and those in the catechism of Andreas Altamer (1528), perhaps the most important collections are in Prussia (1525) (67 translations of Roman collects); Brandenburg-Nuremberg (1533) (27 collects, 11 new translations); Duke Henry of Saxony (1539-55); Spangenberg (1545) (87 Latin and 35 German); Mecklenburg (1552) (edited by Melanchthon); Pomerania (1568) (63 collects); and Austria (1571) (a rich collection of nearly 200 collects).

Professor Althaus shows how, at the very beginning of the Reformation, the mystic-Augustinian type of prayer, which had prevailed throughout the Middle Ages, stopped at one stroke. In its place entered a type of prayer based entirely upon Scripture. The historic collects took on a new meaning as a preparation of the spirit for hearing the Word of God and a request for the blessing and the wholesome fruit of the Word. New prayers in the collect form, some dependent upon inherited material, and others freely composed, were also produced in great numbers, as were longer prayers of the "general prayer" type. While numerous prayer books of private preparation contained prayers reflecting the spirit of contemporary mystical or subjective groups, the prayers of the sixteenth-century agenda are noteworthy for their scriptural and objective character. Friedrich Heiler in his great work on prayer gives examples of Lutheran collects which stress the thoughts and emphases of the Reformation period.[9]

In addition to translations of many historic collects for the festivals and Sundays, collects of somewhat fuller form and related to the Epistles and Gospels were composed by various authors. Foremost among these were Veit Dietrich, intimate friend of Luther and Melanchthon and pastor of St. Sebaldus' Church, Nuremberg (1543); and Johan Mathesius, the first biographer of Luther and the outstanding leader of the Lutheran church in Bohemia (1563). These compositions were called "text collects," to be used in the pulpit before or after the Sermon. The Dietrich series was limited in content and stereotyped in form. Of his ninety-one collects no less than seventy-seven have the same address: *"Herr Gott, himmlischer Vater,"* while the collects for the day in the *Service Book* have at least twenty different invocations. Nevertheless, the Dietrich series attained great popularity. It finally supplanted the historic collects said before the Epistle in the Danish church, and came into the Swedish service books for use in the pulpit after the Sermon.[10] The more extensive and varied Mathesius series of 147 collects was incorporated almost in full (111 collects) in the Austrian Church Order of 1571.

The collects in Lutheran services of the sixteenth century were generally intoned by the minister at the altar, in accordance with simple inflections published by Luther in his German Mass or by others in the church orders and cantionales. These all were based upon centuries of "choral reading" in the pre-Reformation Latin services.[11]

English scholars have led in thoroughgoing study of the Latin and English

---

[9] Friedrich Heiler, *Prayer.*

[10] Cf. Otto Dietz, *Die Evangelien-Kollekten des Veit Dietrich* (Leipzig: Wallmann, 1930). Also in an English translation by Sigfrid Estborn, *A Church Year in Prayers—The Gospel Collects of Veit Dietrich* (Guntur: Bd. of Pub. of the Federation of Evangelical Lutheran Churches in India, 1937).

[11] *WA* 19, 70ff.

collects. Outstanding works are: E. M. Goulburn, *The Collects of the Day*, 2 vols. (London: Rivingtons, 1880; Amer. ed. New York: Young, 1883); William Bright, *Ancient Collects* (London: Oxford Univ. Pr., 1887), and his important article in the *Prayer Book Commentary* (London: S.P.C.K., 1905); Charles L. Feltoe's article "Collects" in the *Prayer Book Dictionary* (New York: Longmans, 1912); Percy Dearmer, *The Art of Public Worship* (Milwaukee: Morehouse, 1919); F. Armitage, *History of the Collects* (London: Weare, n.d.); and various commentaries on the Prayer Book by Palmer, Procter and Frere, Brightman, Blunt, etc. Other excellent comments on the collects in the American Prayer Book are in Massey Hamilton Shepherd, Jr., *The Oxford American Prayer Book Commentary* (New York: Oxford, 1950.)

The field was neglected by German scholars until rather recently. Richter's work on the church orders was incomplete, and Sehling's exhaustive collection omits many collects. Loehe, who was a pioneer in reawakening interest in the historic collect, was not precise as to sources. Professor Drews made an important contribution in his study of Luther's collects in *Studien zur Geschichte des Gottesdienstes und des gottesdienstlichen Lebens* (Leipzig: Mohr, 1902-10). Paul Althaus has mastered a complex problem and clarified many obscurities in his *Zur Einführung in die Quellengeschichte der kirchlichen Kollekten in den lutherischen Agenden des 16. Jahrhunderts* (Leipzig: Edelmann, 1919).

Outstanding work in this field characterized by breadth of information and minuteness of investigation has been done by the American Lutheran scholar, Paul Z. Strodach, in his *The Collect for the Day* (Philadelphia: U. L. P. H., 1935), and particularly in a series of articles on the collects of the church year in *The Lutheran Church Review*, Vols. XXXV and XXXVI (1916, 1917). These articles give not only the Latin originals with sources, etc., of the Collects from Advent to Easter, but all available English and German translations, with enumeration of textual abbreviations and devotional commentary.

✠

The Collect is introduced by the Oremus—"Let us pray." This liturgical phrase is related to the Collect rather than to the Salutation and response. There may well be a slight pause after "And with thy spirit." The Oremus should then lead very promptly into the Collect.

The minister faces the altar during the Collect. The Collect should be recited deliberately and clearly. Otherwise, instead of being a significant feature of the Service, it will be insignificant. The minister may recite the Collect with hands parted and extended slightly over the altar, the palms facing each other, and the arms held close to the body. This ancient liturgical custom is traced to the posture in prayer of the early Christians. Our usual practice of folding the hands symbolizes earnestness, concentration, and freedom from secular things. The open and extended hands express appreciation of the fact that every good and perfect gift is of God, and readiness on our part to open our hearts and minds to divine grace.

At the end of the prayer proper, a brief pause may be made before the liturgical conclusion, "Through Jesus Christ," etc. (Detailed directions concerning the use of the Collects are given in the general rubrics, p. 274.)

When there is an "occurrence," with a lesser festival falling on a Sunday, not a festival, the Collect for the Sunday is said after the Collect for the Day as a "memorial." The Oremus may be repeated, the minister continuing to face the altar, before the second collect. This will inform the people and keep them from sitting down too soon. Where the Sunday is itself a festival (as, for example, the First Sunday in Advent), the lesser festivals (as, for example, St. Andrew) will be put off until the next free day.

✠

The Amen should be sung promptly, though devotionally, and in moderate volume. After the Amen the organist may continue playing softly until the people are entirely seated and the minister is ready to read the Old Testament Lesson or, if this is not used, the Epistle.

CHAPTER XV

THE LITURGICAL LESSONS
The Old Testament Lesson:
The Epistle: The Gradual: The Gospel

In the Service so far, there has been a gradual approach to the altar of God. Our spirits have been purified and elevated as we ascended the four steps of contrition, longing, praise, and petition. In all of this we have spoken. We now pause in reverent silence while God speaks. The thought that nothing we say or do can compare in importance with his Word invests the reading of the liturgical lessons with special solemnity and dignity.

The synagogue service regularly had readings from the Law and the Prophets. Luke (4:16-21) tells how our Lord himself one Sabbath entered the synagogue at Nazareth, chose a passage from the Book of Isaiah, and expounded it to his fellow-townsmen. The twofold lesson of the synagogue was continued in the early services of the Christians. Soon selections from the Epistles were added, and a little later passages from the various Gospels. The next step reduced the lessons from the Old Testament to one which, with the New Testament Epistle and Gospel, gave a threefold Lesson. This is still the use in the Ambrosian and the Mozarabic liturgies. Eventually the Old Testament lesson was dropped from general use in the Roman service, while the Epistle and the Gospel remained. In some cases, however, (as in the weekdays of Lent), it was in fact the Epistle that was dropped, which led to the reading of selections from the Prophets as Epistles in our own church. The rubrics of the Common Service permitted the reading of an Old Testament lesson, if desired, before the Epistle, "but the Epistle and the Gospel for the Day shall always be read."

The Common Liturgy has taken a further step in the direction of the restoration of an Old Testament lesson by providing more than simply a permissive rubric. It presents a complete, carefully chosen series of

Old Testament lessons, each of which is definitely related to the thought of the festival or day for which it is appointed. Like other constructive features of the Common Liturgy, this is a return to a practice of the early church, long before Gregory the Great put a definite Roman stamp upon the Western liturgy. Liturgical scholars have often expressed regret that, with the exception of the psalms and occasional lessons in Matins and Vespers, and a very few Epistles, the Old Testament Scriptures have passed out of the regular services of the Christian church. The restoration of an Old Testament lesson before the Epistle will help to correct this failure, and will enrich our worship with valuable historical, poetical, and prophetic material from these ancient canonical sources. (On the entire subject of the lessons, see the lengthy discussion "Die Lesungen" by Gerhard Kunze in *Leiturgia,* I, 88ff.)

From apostolic times the reading of carefully chosen lessons from Holy Scripture has been an important feature, and indeed the high point, of the first part of the Christian liturgy. At first sections from the letters of the apostles and from Gospels were read consecutively, "as long as time permits," as Justin Martyr says. There were no fixed selections. The development of the church year with its observance of festivals led to the selection of particularly appropriate lessons and other "proper" material. The three great festivals were the first to have definite lessons. Specific assignments were next made for the "octaves" of these feasts, and then for associated seasons, and thus the scheme developed. Traces of the early *lectio continua* method are still to be found in the Gospels for the Third to the Sixth Sundays after the Epiphany (from Matthew), and in the Epistles for the Sixth to the Twenty-third Sundays after Trinity (excepting the Eighteenth). Traces of Gallican uses, earlier than the present Roman use, seem to indicate that John was read in the spring, Luke in the summer, and Matthew in the autumn. No one seems to know why so few lessons have been chosen from Mark.[1]

As time went on the lessons to be read were indicated by marginal signs in the manuscripts. Later indexes to lessons, called *capitularia,* were given at the beginning or the end of manuscripts of the Scripture. Finally the complete capitularia, with the full texts of the lessons, were provided separately and used at the altar. This manuscript was called a *Comes* ("companion") and the lessons themselves came to be known as the pericopes, from the Greek word meaning a portion "cut out."

---

[1] See W. H. Frere, *Studies in Early Roman Liturgy,* 3 vols. (Oxford: Clarendon, 1930-35.) For a summary statement, see Parsons and Jones, *The American Prayer Book* (New York: Scribner's, 1937), pp. 81-85.

Tradition credits Jerome (d. 420) with having selected most of the lessons, though it is improbable. By the time of Charlemagne (A.D. 800), the entire series of propers was elaborated and authorized in the diocesan missals of western Europe. Charlemagne secured the preparation of homilies upon the lessons by leading ecclesiastics of the time. Minor differences in lessons, however, characterized the medieval missals until Pope Pius V in 1570 prescribed a single order for the Roman church.

The Reformation emphasis upon the gospel as recorded in the Scriptures increased the relative importance of this part of the Service in the practical life of the church. Liturgically this was expressed in general recognition of the controlling power of the lessons in establishing the theme and tone of each day's Service; in the development of a sermon as interpreting and enforcing this central usage; and in a rich outpouring of congregational hymns (and melodies) based upon the thought of the lessons as appointed for particular Sundays and festivals in the church year.

Luther was at first disposed to criticize some of the selections, particularly those from the "straw epistle" of James. In general, however, he approved the retention of the historic series. He himself published homilies ("Postils") upon these lessons, and Melanchthon, Bugenhagen, and other Reformers did the same. Similar publications appeared in England during the sixteenth century. The Lutheran orders, with a few important exceptions, retained the historic lessons, while the Zwinglian and Calvinistic churches abandoned them, together with the church year itself.

Though continuing the historic series, the Lutherans made a few characteristic changes. They appointed eschatological texts (selected by Luther from Veit Dietrich) for the twenty-fifth to twenty-seventh Sundays after Trinity. They also followed Luther's suggestion in appointing the story of the Transfiguration for the sixth Sunday after Epiphany as a fitting climax to Epiphanytide which celebrates the manifestation of the glory of Christ. The Common Service gave the historic series of liturgical lessons as modified by the church orders, and provided additional tables of lessons for comparative study and homiletical use. The *Common Service Book* appointed the Transfiguration for the last Sunday in Epiphany each year (rarely the sixth Sunday). The Common Liturgy, too, follows the historic series, but provides no alternate lections. Returning to Luther's usage, it approves the use of the Transfiguration propers on the sixth Sunday after Epiphany only, though still permitting the *Common Service Book* usage as an alternate. The festival itself has been moved to August 6, when it is celebrated by the rest of Western Christendom.[2]

While exceptions may be taken to particular lessons and desire felt for the inclusion of passages of Scripture omitted in the series, the general plan and essential content of the historic pericopes are admirable. The mature judgment of the church has retained them because their use is a guarantee of sound and complete teaching of fundamental Christian truth. Altogether they constitute a solid block of fundamental material about which the services of a particular day or season are constructed. They are a most important part of the common liturgical inheritance of the universal church, with a continuous history of nearly fifteen hundred years, and current use in the Roman, Lutheran, and Anglican communions. The recent effort of the free churches to reconstruct a church year approximating the historic scheme of the liturgical churches is a remarkable recognition of the essential worth of a system which the radicals repudiated in the sixteenth century and later.[3]

The historic series of Epistles and Gospels as given in the Common Service was at first accepted by the Joint Commission with few changes. The commission later came to appreciate the exhaustive study of this subject by contemporary scholars, and the fact that important changes had been made by many churches in Europe and America. It finally adopted a number of new Epistles and Gospels, appointed several optional Gospels, and lengthened or shortened a number of lessons. Equally careful study was given to the optional series of Old Testament lessons and to the preparation of a complete series of lessons from both Testaments for Matins and Vespers, and a daily lectionary for the year for private devotional use.

In general the Gospels for the first half of the church year (*semester Domini*, the half-year of our Lord) give the steps in the development of our Lord's life on earth. The second half (*semester ecclesiae*, the half-year of the church) presents a selection of his parables, miracles, and teachings.

The original scheme probably included appointments for Wednesdays and

[2] Study of a table showing the Epistles and Gospels of the liturgical year in the Roman, Lutheran, and Anglican liturgies will be rewarding. The so-called "Eisenach series" and the three-year arrangement of lessons in the Swedish Liturgy introduce important scriptural passages not included in the historic series, but on the whole these selections do not equal the ancient choices, particularly from the standpoint of devotional values. Recent revisions of the *Book of Common Prayer* in England, Scotland, and America have introduced several important changes in the lessons of the Anglican communion.

[3] See the *Christian Year* of the Federal Council of the Churches of Christ in America, and in revised form, the program of the Department of Worship and the Arts of the National Council of Churches. The Church of Scotland (Presbyterian) has also given careful and scholarly attention to this subject. See also *Leiturgia*, particularly Lieferung 9.

Fridays as well as Sundays. This may account for the fact that some important passages of Scripture are not included in the Sunday series. There is usually a real connection between the Gospel and the Epistle for the great days and seasons. Attempts to establish similar relationships or connections with the Collect for the Day in the second half of the year are usually inconclusive. Suggestions of a logical scheme for all the lessons after Trinity are likewise not entirely satisfactory.

The lessons were regularly sung (intoned) by the minister in the Lutheran services of the sixteenth century in solemn festal manner (*fein laut, deutlich und langsam*)—so particularly in Mark Brandenburg (1540), Herzogin Elizabeth (1542), Pomerania (1563), Hoya (1581), etc. This was a continuation of pre-Reformation usage. Luther in his German Mass (1526) indicated in detail a method for the choral reading of the lessons in the vernacular. The church orders occasionally permitted reading the lessons instead of intoning them "if the minister is unable to sing." Sometimes the Epistle was read and the Gospel chanted. The later influence of Pietism and Rationalism led to the omission of the liturgical lessons in many parts of Germany, the Epistle or the Gospel being read in the pulpit as a text for the sermon. Full recovery from this regrettable procedure has not yet been made.

Scholarly discussions may be found in *Leiturgia, Handbuch des evangelischen Gottesdienstes* (Lieferungen 8 and 9); Gregory Dix, *The Shape of the Liturgy;* Joseph A. Jungmann, *The Mass of the Roman Rite,* I, 301-421. For ready reference, see W. K. Lowther Clarke and Charles Harris, *Liturgy and Worship,* pp. 378-409. The specialist will find valuable, though highly technical, material in Walter Howard Frere's *Studies in Early Roman Liturgy* (London: Oxford Univ. Pr., 1934-35.) This covers the period A.D. 700-1000. Also see "The Liturgical Lectionary" in *Prayer Book Studies* by the Standing Liturgical Commission of the Protestant Episcopal Church. The question of principle or plan in the selection of the lessons is fully discussed in S. Beissel, *Entstehung der Perikopen* (Freiburg: Herder, 1907); and Leonhard Fendt, *Die Alten Perikopen* (Tübingen: Mohr, 1931). Summaries are in Rietschel, *Lehrbuch der Liturgik,* pp. 223ff, and Fortescue, *The Mass,* pp. 257ff.

THE LESSON

¶ *Here the Minister may read the appointed Lesson from the Old Testament, saying:* The Lesson is written in the............Chapter of............, beginning at the............Verse. *The Lesson ended, he shall say,* Here endeth the Lesson.

(First Sunday in Advent)
Jer. 31:31-34.

Behold, the days come, saith the LORD, that I will make a new covenant with the house of Israel, and with the house of Judah: not according to the covenant that I made with their fathers in the day that I took them by the hand to bring them out of the land of Egypt; which my covenant they brake, although I was an husband unto them, saith the LORD: but this shall be the covenant that I will make with the house of Israel; After those days, saith the LORD, I will put my law in their inward parts, and write it in their hearts; and will be their God, and they shall be my people. And they shall teach no more every man his neighbor, and every man his brother, saying, Know the LORD: for they shall all know me, from the least of them unto the greatest of them, saith the LORD: for I will forgive their iniquity, and I will remember their sin no more.

¶ *Then may be sung a Psalm or a hymn version of a Psalm.*

As previously stated, a lesson from the Old Testament was regularly read before selections from the Epistles and Gospels in the services of the early church. This custom is still observed in the Ambrosian and the Mozarabic rites, though now absent from Roman, Lutheran, and Anglican services. Believing that there will be rich values in restoring this feature, at least for optional observance, the Joint Commission provided a complete series of Old Testament lessons, closely related to the thought of the epistle or of the gospel for the day. The selection from the Old Testament is technically known as "The Lesson," while the selections from the New Testament are designated as the Epistle or the Gospel respectively. The two latter selections are collectively known as the liturgical lessons.

In accordance with the universal practice in both Jewish and Christian services of singing psalms between Scripture readings, the rubric in the Common Liturgy suggests that a psalm or a hymn version of a psalm may be sung between the Lesson and the Epistle. A table of hymn versions of psalms is provided on p. 284.

When two or more ministers have part in the Service, one, the officiant, conducts the entire liturgy. Another, however, may read the lessons.

It is important that ample time be given the congregation to be comfortably settled in their seats before the Lesson or the Epistle is announced. Deliberation at such places as this, that is to say, between major portions of the Service, adds dignity and permits thoughtful participation by the people. At other places there should be no break, and the effort should be made to secure smooth continuity.

In announcing the lessons the minister should follow the form in the rubrics precisely.

THE EPISTLE

¶ *Then shall the Minister announce the Epistle for the Day, saying:* The Epistle for *(here he shall name the Festival or Day)* is written in the............

Chapter of............, beginning at the............Verse.

(First Sunday in Advent)
Romans 13:11-14.

Brethren, ye know the time, that now it is high time to awake out of sleep: for now is our salvation nearer than when we believed. The night is far spent, the day is at hand: let us therefore cast off the works of darkness, and let us put on the armor of light. Let us walk honestly, as in the day; not in rioting and drunkenness, not in chambering and wantonness, not in strife and envying. But put ye on the Lord Jesus Christ, and make not provision for the flesh, to fulfil the lusts thereof.

¶ *The Epistle ended, the Minister shall say:* Here endeth the Epistle for the Day.

The Epistle is the word of Christian law, but law with the breadth and elevation of the New Testament in it. Augustine said, "We have heard the apostle, we have heard the psalm, we have heard the gospel." In some of the early service books the Epistle was called the "apostle," and was a distinctive feature of the Sunday services as distinguished from weekday services. It precedes the Gospel in the Service as the lesser precedes the greater. Medieval commentators thought of it as representing the ministry of John the Baptist, who "went before the face of the Lord to prepare his ways." While usually taken from the letters of the apostles, a few Epistles have been chosen from the Acts, Revelation, etc.

In the case of the Epistle printed above as in other instances where abrupt or unintelligible beginnings are found in the appointed lessons, the commission has followed traditional liturgical practice in providing so-called liturgical introductions, such as "At that time Jesus said," etc. In this particular instance (First Sunday in Advent) the text begins with the words, "Brethren, ye know," instead of "And that, knowing . . . ."

In accordance with ancient universal custom, the liturgical lessons may be read from the altar. When this is done, the minister may read the Epistle from the south (right) side of the altar and the Gospel from the north side. Or, he may stand before the center of the altar. In either case he will face the congregation.

The lessons may also be read from the lectern.

The Epistle should be read deliberately and distinctly. The text should be set apart from everything else. A brief pause may be made after the announcement and at the end before the words, "Here endeth the Epistle for the Day."

THE GRADUAL

¶ *Then may the Gradual for the Day be sung.*

¶ *When the Gradual for the Day is omitted, the Alleluia or the Gradual for the Season may be sung.*

(First Sunday in Advent)

Let none that wait on thee: be ashamed.

Verse.　Show me thy ways, O Lord: teach me thy paths.

Alleluia, alleluia. *V.* Show us thy mercy, O Lord: and grant us thy salvation. Alleluia.

THE ALLELUIA

Alleluia

¶ *In Lent this Sentence shall be sung instead of the Alleluia:*

Christ hath humbled himself, and become obedient unto death: even the death of the Cross.

The Gradual, like the Introit, is a distinctively choir element, a choral response to the Epistle and introduction to the Gospel. It has been called "a song of passage" from the words of the servants of Jesus to the words of our Lord himself.

Public worship from the days of the synagogue to the present has always provided a chant form of some sort, choral or congregational, as an interlude between liturgical readings. This is not only a refreshing variation in the Service, but provides a musical echo to the passage already read and a transition to the next. In the synagogue a psalm was sung between the readings. The hour services developed the responsory; The Service has the Gradual, which is probably as ancient as the lessons themselves. Augustine at the beginning of the fifth century refers to it as an established custom.

The Gradual is a liturgical arrangement of portions of psalms originally sung entire and from a step (*gradus*) of the altar. The first part constitutes the Gradual proper and reflects the thought of the Epistle. The second part is known as the Alleluia and serves as a prelude to the Gospel. Originally, as we have noted, three lessons were read. The Gradual proper was sung after the prophetic lesson and the Alleluia after the Epistle. With the disappearance of the Old Testament Lesson during the course of the Middle Ages, the Gradual and the Alleluia were united.

The Hebrew word "alleluia" is a song of joy and triumph in four syllables. It is found in many psalms, especially in the section (Ps. 113-118) called the "Great Alleluia," the latter part of which our Lord likely chanted with his disciples at the last Passover. John in his heavenly vision heard "as it were the voice of a great multitude, and as the voice of many waters, and as the voice of mighty thunderings, saying, Alleluia: for the Lord God omnipotent reigneth" (Rev. 19:6). The early Christians used "alleluia" as an acclamation of faith and joy while at their daily work. Together with the other Hebrew word, "amen," it came into the earliest services. Meaning "Praise ye the Lord" it is appropriate in the liturgy as an expression of joy at hearing the Word of God. The Common Liturgy has wisely chosen the more musical form "alleluia," as found in the Greek and Latin liturgies, and in English hymnody, instead of the earlier but rougher form "hallelujah."

Luther, with his appreciation of the festal note in worship as well as his love of music, retained the Gradual in his Latin Service. In his German Mass he suggested a vernacular hymn between the Epistle and the Gospel. This became general both because of the difficulties of translation from Latin into German, and also because of the zeal for hymn singing which had been awakened. Later appropriate choral music was frequently substituted for the historic Gradual. The cantatas of Bach and other composers were generally sung at this point in the service.[4]

The English *Book of Common Prayer* (1549) omitted the Gradual, as the next edition (1552) also omitted the Introit. The *English Hymnal* (Part XII), however, provides settings of the historic texts for choir use. Modern European Lutheran liturgies do not have the historic series of gradual texts. The Common Service did not supply them, but included a series of brief "sentences for the season" first given in the *Church Book* (1868) and based upon Schoeberlein. The *Common Service Book* (1918) restored the entire historic series of Graduals.

In the Eastern Liturgy, and in the Gallican and Mozarabic rites as well, the Alleluia is a part of the procession with the elements following the Gospel. In the Roman Rite it immediately precedes the Gospel. An account preserved in Migne tells of a tragic experience in a church in North Africa in the fifth century, when a member of an invading band of Vandals entered the church, drew his bow, and shot an arrow into the very throat of the cantor who was "singing the alleluia."[5] In the Roman use during the somber time from Septuagesima to Easter Eve the jubilant Alleluia is replaced by the tract *(psalmus tractus),* which derives its meaning from the unbroken manner in which it was anciently sung by a cantor without choral response.[6]

In the ninth and tenth centuries lengthy continuations of the final vowel of the Alleluia developed into free "jubilee" melodies. As these were without text, prose compositions known as "proses" were supplied for them. In the

---

[4] Full discussion in Schoeberlein, *Schatz des liturgischen Chor- und Gemeindegesangs.*

[5] *Patrol. lat.,* t. LVIII, p. 197. See also Cabrol, *Liturgical Prayer,* p. 45.

[6] This suppression of the Alleluia led to the introduction in some liturgies of a "farewell to the Alleluia." Cabrol gives an interesting example of an antiphon in the Ambrosian Rite for the first Sunday in Lent: "Alleluia, enclose and seal up the word, alleluia; let it remain in the secret of your heart, alleluia, until the appointed time: you shall say it with great joy when that day comes, alleluia, alleluia, alleluia" (*Liturgical Prayer,* p. 45).

twelfth century these developed into metrical hymns called sequences. The melodies sung to these lengthy compositions were of freer form than the plain-song chants for the psalms. Adam of St. Victor (d. 1192) composed many sequences, and melodies in great number were produced in Germany and France. Rome, with characteristic restraint, did not favor this innovation, and the authoritative Roman Missal of today retains only five of the more than 900 known sequences. Some of our finest translations of Latin hymns are from the medieval sequences.

The Gradual was a more restricted form than the sequence, but its texts received high musical elaboration. It was sung by a solo voice with a refrain verse by the choir. Such importance was attached to the artistic music of the Gradual that the celebrant paused in his prayers at the altar to give it full attention.

✠

If the minister reads the lessons from the altar he will face it during the Gradual. If he reads the lessons from the sides of the altar he will move the *Service Book* from the Epistle side to the Gospel side during the singing of the Gradual. If he reads the lessons from the lectern he need not change his position.

✠

Excellent musical settings for the Graduals are now available, and choirs will do well to give their first thought to preparing the proper Introit and Gradual for each Sunday.[7] When the choir is not prepared to sing the Gradual, a simple "alleluia" or the "Seasonal Gradual" may be sung as a substitute.

The music for the threefold Alleluia in the first setting is a simple arrangement from Palestrina by Monk. It should be sung with promptness and vigor. The form of the melody well expresses a progression of praise from forte to double forte. The music in the second setting consists of fuller forms from plain-song originals.

When the choir desires to sing two anthems in the Service, one will follow the Offertory and the other may be sung as a substitute for the Gradual immediately after the simple Alleluia. In this significant location, between the Epistle and Gospel for the day, care should be taken to have the text and the music of the anthem strictly liturgical, that is, in harmony with the lessons and the mood of the day or season.

If the Gradual is not used, the Alleluia is omitted during Lent, and the sentence, "Christ hath humbled himself . . . ," an adaptation from Merbecke (1550), is sung softly but without dragging. The phrases

---

[7] H. Alexander Matthews, *The Introits and Graduals of the Church Year.* (U.L.P.H.) The introduction to this work by Dr. Reed gives an extended account of the history and function of the Gradual. There is another anthem-like series by Ralph P. Lewars (*op. cit.*), and two plain-song settings by Christensen and Schuneman (*op. cit.*), and by Ernest White (*op. cit.*).

should not be broken except at the punctuation marks and the conclusion should be rallentando and double piano.

THE GOSPEL

¶ *Then shall the Minister announce the Gospel for the Day, saying:* The Holy Gospel is written in the.............Chapter of St.............., beginning at the.............Verse.

¶ *The Congregation shall rise and sing or say:*

Glory be to thee, O Lord.

¶ *Then shall the Minister read the Gospel for the Day.*

(The First Sunday in Advent)
Matt. 21:1-9.

And when they drew nigh unto Jerusalem, and were come to Bethphage, unto the mount of Olives, then sent Jesus two disciples, saying unto them, Go into the village over against you, and straightway ye shall find an ass tied, and a colt with her: loose them, and bring them unto me. And if any man say ought unto you, ye shall say, The Lord hath need of them; and straightway he will send them. All this was done, that it might be fulfilled which was spoken by the prophet, saying, Tell ye the daughter of Sion, Behold, thy King cometh unto thee, meek, and sitting upon an ass, and a colt the foal of an ass. And the disciples went, and did as Jesus commanded them, and brought the ass, and the colt, and put on them their clothes, and they set him thereon. And a very great multitude spread their garments in the way; others cut down branches from the trees, and strawed them in the way. And the multitudes that went before, and that followed, cried, saying, Hosanna to the Son of David: Blessed is he that cometh in the name of the Lord; Hosanna in the highest.

(*Or,* Luke 3:1-6.)

¶ *The Gospel ended, the Minister shall say:* Here endeth the Gospel for the Day.

¶ *The Congregation shall sing or say:*

Praise be to thee, O Christ.

The Gospel is the liturgical summit of the first half of the Service, the "Office of the Word." It usually presents the central, objective thought of the day. Origen called the Gospel "the crown of all Holy Scriptures." Cyprian ordained a lector that he might "read the Gospel which forms martyrs."

The Four Gospels from which the liturgical Gospel is chosen have always stood apart from the rest of Holy Scripture as giving a clear and living picture of the divine person of our Lord. These inspired records of eyewitnesses, convincing in their simplicity, sincerity, and power, reveal to us the Christ of God in the lowliness of his humanity and the majesty of his divinity. They tell us the incidents of his daily life. They record his actions, conversations, and teaching. They lead us through the unfolding drama of his suffering, death, and resurrection to the sure foundations upon which the Christian church is built—the message of salvation, the commissioning of the apostles, and the institution of the Sacrament.

The reading in public worship of selections from the Gospels was early accompanied by appropriate liturgical action. Special honor was accorded the liturgical Gospel as revealing the divine nature of our Lord as the living Word ever present in the written Word. Veneration of the Word of God in this double sense expressed itself in significant customs and ceremonies, which, like a garden of fragrant flowers, surrounded the actual reading and indicated both the supremacy of the liturgical Gospel in the Service and the homage rendered the person of Christ in his Word.

In addition to giving vital significance to the readings from Holy Scripture by providing them in the vernacular, Lutheran services retained at least three of the most ancient and universal ceremonies: the standing of the people in reverence and willing obedience; the ascription of praise at the announcements; and less generally, the reading from the liturgical "north side" of the altar.

The brief congregational responses are full of meaning. "Thanks be to God" as a terse profession of faith, was a watchword or sign used by the early Christians and accepted by the doorkeepers as worshipers sought admission to the assemblies of the faithful in days of persecution. These words soon found a place alongside readings from the Gospel.

Together with the response after the Gospel, "Praise be to thee, O Christ," they express our recognition of the real presence of Christ in our worship. We address him as one actually present. We acknowledge the fact that the Christ of the Gospels and the Christ of the Sacrament are one and the same. Like Thomas of old we believe and cry, "My Lord and my God." The Scottish *Book of Common Prayer* (1764 and later) sacrifices broader poetic associations by the precise and more prosaic, "Thanks be to thee, O Lord, for thy glorious Gospel."

In medieval times the "Book of the Gospels" was often written in letters of gold on purple vellum, sumptuously bound and encrusted with jewels. It was borne in formal procession to the ambo, later to the north side of the altar from which it was to be read (the lesser entrance in the Greek Liturgy). Incense and lighted tapers added fragrance and splendor to the action. The lights recalled his word: "I am the Light of the world."[8] Silence and atten-

---

[8] For full discussion of the ceremonial use of lights with its symbolism see article *"Kerze"* in Wetzer and Welter's *Kirchenlexicon;* V. Thalhofer, *Handbuch der katholischen Liturgik* (3rd ed. rev. by L. Eisenhofer; Freiburg: Herder, 1932-33), I, 666ff; article "Lights, ceremonial use of" in *Encyclopedia Britannica* (11th ed.); and Staley, *Studies in Ceremonial,* pp. 169-94.

tion were proclaimed. Clergy and people rose respectfully as servants rise to receive the words of their Lord, and stood bareheaded. Bishops removed their mitres, kings took off their crowns, and soldiers laid down their weapons.

The reading of the Gospel, at least after the fifth century, was a privilege accorded the deacon, or highest assistant to the officiant. At his ordination the deacon received a copy of the Gospels, and ancient mosaics show him with book in hand. Occasionally the bishop would read the Gospel, and on Christmas night the emperor would read it.

The custom of reading the Gospel from the north side of the altar is associated with medieval symbolism which regarded the warm sunny south and its rich profusion in nature as representing the higher life of grace, while the dark and frigid north represented the kingdom of the evil one to which inhabitants particularly the Gospel must be proclaimed.

✠

The congregation should rise immediately after the announcement of the Gospel.

The Gospel should be announced and read impressively. The importance of this is often not realized, and as a result the lessons become insignificant. A brief pause before the words, "Here endeth the Gospel for the Day," will help give the liturgical text its distinctive character and full value.

If the lessons are read from the altar, the minister turns to the altar by the Epistle side, and places the book from which he has read the Gospel on the missal stand while the choir and congregation sing the response.

✠

The responses before and after the Gospel should be sung promptly with breadth and volume. The words "glory," "praise," and "thee" should be made significant but not unduly stressed.

CHAPTER XVI

THE CREED; THE HYMN; THE SERMON

¶ Then shall be said or sung the Creed.

THE CREED

¶ The Nicene Creed shall be said or sung on all Festivals and whenever there is a Communion.

THE NICENE CREED

I believe in one God, the Father Almighty, Maker of heaven and earth, And of all things visible and invisible.

And in one Lord Jesus Christ, the only-begotten Son of God, Begotten of his Father before all worlds, God of God, Light of Light, Very God of very God, Begotten, not made, Being of one substance with the Father, By whom all things were made: Who, for us men, and for our salvation, came down from heaven, And was incarnate by the Holy Ghost of the Virgin Mary, And was made man; And was crucified also for us under Pontius Pilate. He suffered and was buried; And the third day he rose again, according to the Scriptures, And ascended into heaven, And sitteth on the right hand of the Father. And he shall come again with glory to judge both the quick and the dead: Whose kingdom have no end.

And I believe in the Holy Ghost, The Lord and Giver of Life, Who proceedeth from the Father and the Son, Who with the Father and the Son together is worshipped and glorified, Who spake by the Prophets. And I believe one Holy Christian* and Apostolic Church. I acknowledge one Baptism for the remission of sins. And I look for the Resurrection of the dead, And the Life of the world to come. Amen.

* *Or,* "And I believe one Holy catholic and Apostolic Church," *the original and generally accepted text.*

THE APOSTLES' CREED

I believe in God the Father Almighty, Maker of heaven and earth:

And in Jesus Christ his only Son, our Lord, Who was conceived by the Holy Ghost, Born of the Virgin Mary, Suffered under Pontius Pilate, Was crucified, dead, and buried: He descended into hell; The third day he rose again from the dead; He ascended into heaven, And sitteth on the right hand of God the Father Almighty; From thence he shall come to judge the quick and the dead.

I believe in the Holy Ghost; The Holy Christian* Church, the Communion of Saints; The Forgiveness of sins; The Resurrection of the body, And the Life everlasting. Amen.

* *Or,* "The Holy catholic Church," *the original and generally accepted text.*

The Creed is again—after the variable Collect, Epistle, Gradual and Gospel—a fixed element in the service. It is the church's reply to God's Word, the public acceptance and confession in summary form of the faith of the whole church. Every use of it is in a sense a renewal of our baptismal covenant. Its brief but comprehensive statements encompass "the whole dispensation of God." It outlines and preserves, in balanced proportion, Christianity's fundamental beliefs; it witnesses to the perpetuity, unity, and universality of the Christian faith; it binds Christians to one another and to the faithful of all centuries. As used in this place in the Service it enables the congregation to view and review the whole horizon of the church's belief before giving attention to the exposition of a particular doctrine or idea. From a somewhat different point of view it may be thought of as a corporate expression of praise and thanks, reciting what God has done for our salvation.

The Creed is not found in the earliest known liturgies, particularly in the East. Its later insertion may be ascribed to the appreciation for precise doctrinal statement characteristic of the Western church. In the Roman Rite its use in the liturgy is restricted to Sundays and festivals. It is thus regarded as a festal addition rather than an absolute essential.

Historically the two Creeds correspond to the two sacraments. The Lutheran liturgies generally retained the Nicene Creed in the Service either in Latin or in German. A few orders (Nuremberg [1525], Strasbourg [1525], Sweden [1531], Austria [1571]), permitted the Apostles' Creed as an alternative. Pomerania appointed the Apostles' Creed for Sundays and the Nicene Creed for festivals. In many places (Liegnitz [1534], Brandenburg [1540], Reformation of Cologne [1543]), the Creed was sung after the Sermon. The Common Liturgy prescribes the Nicene Creed "on all Festivals and whenever there is a Communion."

It is to be regretted that the German Lutheran liturgies, and the Common Service, which followed them in this respect, departed in the Creeds from the ancient and generally accepted phraseology, "one Holy catholic and Apostolic Church," "the Holy catholic Church," and substituted the word "Christian" for "catholic." This change was not a Reformation, but a pre-Reformation German alteration. (See below, p. 303). The Creed is a historical pronouncement and the possession

302

of the entire church. It is not to be altered at will. The Swedish, Danish, Norwegian, and French Lutheran liturgies use the historic word "catholic," and the Common Liturgy also gives this as "the original and generally accepted text."

In the early church individual bishops or councils framed creeds which had local authority and use (thus Irenaeus, Origen, Tertullian, and others).[1] These creeds were useful as a concise formula in connection with baptism or with preparation for it.[2] They also served as a standard by which to test loose or heretical teachings. The Apostles' Creed, while much of it is earlier than the Nicene, did not assume its present precise form until about A.D. 750.

The Creed generally incorporated in the liturgy was the one adopted by the Council of Nicaea (A.D. 325) and somewhat extended in the regular use of the churches of Constantinople during the next century. After the Council of Constantinople (A.D. 553) the Eastern churches generally recited this creed between the reading of the Gospel and the Diptychs (tablets on which the names of martyrs and saints were recorded.) The third synod of Toledo in 589 introduced the Creed into the Mass in all Spanish churches as part of an effort to confirm the people in their conversion to Christianity and to combat the Arian heresy. The custom spread throughout the Frankish territory. The *filioque* clause ("and the Son") was added to the article on the Holy Spirit, an addition which the Eastern churches never accepted.[3]

The Creed is wanting in the sacramentaries and appears to have been introduced into the Roman Mass upon the insistence of the German Emperor Henry II while he was in Rome in the year 1014. Its absence in Rome was justified by the claim that Rome was not bothered with heretics. The persistence of the king, however, finally secured a decree from Pope Benedict VIII, sanctioning the use of the Creed in the Mass. All liturgies now contain a creed.

The word *christliche* was in common vernacular use in Germany before the Reformation. Luther accepted this in his catechism. The church orders followed him and established a phraseology peculiar to the German Lutheran church. In following this unfortunate national use the English Lutheran liturgy lost the thought of "universality" or "wholeness" in its definition of the church, broke with the primitive and the modern universal church, and established a variant form inconsistent with its own confessions. The latter everywhere accept the historic phraseology. (On

[1] See Cabrol, *Liturgical Prayer*, pp. 108-10.

[2] The Apostles' Creed is everywhere recognized as primarily a baptismal formula. It is surprising that the 1928 *Book of Common Prayer* of the Protestant Episcopal Church should omit this creed in its order for baptism, thus dropping the historic symbol from the service which produced it.

[3] The development of creedal statements in the New Testament itself is given in Canon Maclear, *An Introduction to the Creeds* (2d ed.; London: Macmillan, 1921). For the various stages in the development of the Creeds during the early centuries, see Philip Schaff, *Creeds of Christendom* (New York: Harper, 1877), I, 1-42; II, 1-76; or, H. Denzinger, *Enchiridion symbolorum,* etc. (30th ed.; Freiburg: Herder, 1955), pp. 1-18.

Luther's use of *"christliche"* see *WA* 30[1], 130; also Wilhelm Walther, *Lehrbuch der Symbolik*, p. 329.)[4]

Anciently the Service of the Word ended with the sermon following the Gospel. The Creed began the Service of the Faithful. In the present Roman use, the sermon, when there is one, is placed before the Creed. In the Lutheran and Anglican liturgies, the Creed immediately follows the Gospel. Parsons and Jones (*The American Prayer Book,* p. 203) are in error when they state that "the use of the Creed in immediate sequence with the Gospel is an Anglican peculiarity."

✠

The Creed, as used in the Service, is a response to the liturgical lessons and an act of worship. The minister goes to the middle of the altar, whether he has read the lessons from the altar or the lectern. He faces the altar and joins his hands.

Anciently the minister intoned the opening phrase, "I believe in one God," and the choir and congregation continued with "the Father Almighty."

The people stand in reciting the Creed in token of readiness to profess and of resolution to defend the Christian faith. In accord with ancient and universal custom, still observed in many places, the choir joins the minister and the congregation in facing the altar (presumably in the east), during the recitation or chanting of the Creed. The usual explanation is that paradise is in the east. Basil says, "We are seeking our ancient country." The custom also is a reminder of baptism and of the early church's requirements that all candidates for baptism, when making their profession of faith, should face the east from whence the Sun of Righteousness appears.

✠

The rubrics state that the Creed may be sung or said. In France, Germany, and Italy it was customary for the people (not the choir only) to sing the Creed to a simple plain-song chant. The custom still survives in places and is being revived generally in connection with the current liturgical movement within the Roman church. Luther in his German Mass prepared a versification of the Creed to be sung by congregations.

[4] Creeds of the thirteenth, fourteenth and fifteenth centuries in England do not have either "catholic" or "Christian," but simply say "I believe in Holy Church." See Maskell, *Monumenta Ritualia Ecclesiae Anglicanae* (2d ed.; Oxford: Clarendon, 1882), III, 251 ff. Also Dowden, *The Workmanship of the Prayer Book,* Chap. VIII. The Germans apparently could not assimilate a word like *catholica.* There was no real objection to the idea of catholicity as such. Even German Roman Catholics after the Reformation continued to speak of *eine heilige christliche Kirche.* We must recognize this as a German idiomatic expression. Only after the Council of Trent did the Roman church succeed in monopolizing the term "Catholic." Like many other good things it should not be left to them but restored to our use.

At the present time we are so accustomed to saying the Creed that the singing of it might seem strange. There is much to be said for this method, however, where proper leadership is available.[5]

There should be no soft organ playing during the recitation of the Creed. This practice, in some instances borrowed from the movie theatre, in other instances may be based upon Anglican usage. Stainer and others published accompaniments to the Creed and Lord's Prayer for the intoned services. The use of soft organ accompaniment at this place, however, is sentimental and clouds what should be a clear confession of faith.

¶ *Then shall be sung the Hymn.*

THE HYMN

This is the principal hymn of the Service *(Hauptlied)*. Following the lessons and the Creed and immediately preceding the Sermon, it has practically the significance of an additional proper, and must be chosen with care.

The congregational hymn was one of the great contributions of the Reformation to public worship. For a century or more later the church year and the liturgy determined the general character both of the Sermon and of this hymn. The church orders indicated particular hymns to be sung during the different seasons. The melodies to these were developed by eminent composers in elaborate "figurated chorales" for choir use. Bach richly harmonized many of these in his church cantatas.

The idea of choosing the hymn entirely with reference to the Sermon dates from the early eighteenth century. After this time the Sermon more and more dominated the service. During the next hundred years, with increasing indifference to the church year, it ruled the liturgy and the hymns.

The hymn should be accorded its own proper dignity. Its text should not be abbreviated or mutilated any more than should the texts of other parts of the Service.

✠

The minister should be seated in the chancel during the singing of the hymn and join in the singing, or at least follow the text. Retirement to the sacristy breaks the unity of the Service and the continuity of leadership. The conception of a "common service" is best expressed when minister, choir, and congregation unite in all parts throughout.

The Sermon developed from the early homily which followed the

[5] The Creed is set by Ernest White for unison singing to a fine plain-song melody in the third setting of the Common Liturgy. Another fine plain-song setting is given in Archer and Reed, *The Choral Service Book*, p. 14.

THE SERMON

¶ *Then shall follow the Sermon.*

¶ *The Sermon being ended, the Congregation shall rise and the Minister shall then say:*

The Peace of God, which passeth all understanding, keep your hearts and minds through Christ Jesus.

¶ *The Congregation shall sing or say.*

Amen.

Gospel. With the introduction of the Creed into the Service, the Sermon, when there was one, followed the Creed. This was particularly the case in Germany, and Durandus recognizes it as the general custom in the thirteenth century.

All the Reformers castigated the church of their day for its neglect of preaching. The restoration of the Sermon to its ancient place and power became one of the marks of the Reformation. Luther in his Latin Mass suggested that the Sermon be placed at the very beginning of the Service so as not to break its liturgical continuity. In his German Mass, however, he favored the place it now occupies following the Creed. The Missal of Pope Pius V (1570) placed the Sermon before the Creed. Lutheran and Anglican services place the Sermon after the Creed.

The Sermon follows the Creed as the Creed follows the Gospel. It must be true to the common faith as the expression of this faith must be true to the everlasting gospel. It has no value in itself. Its only effectiveness is as a means of preaching the Word of God. This Word is also proclaimed in the administration of the sacraments and in other elements of testimony and edification in the liturgy. But the Sermon is the voice of the living church lifted in instruction, testimony and exhortation.

The liturgy in its normal form needs the Sermon. The Sermon, to realize its fullest power, must never be merely personal or independent of the liturgy. Like the rest of the Service it must breathe the spirit of worship. Otherwise, no matter what its intellectual or moral strength, it differs little from the platform utterances of secular speakers on serious things. Only as it delivers the word of prophecy or of the positive Christian testimony is it really powerful.

Liturgical unity requires that the Sermon should bear a definite relationship to the liturgical lessons, or at least to the thought of the day or season. By building upon the thought of the lessons the Sermon becomes the climax of the Office of the Word. By relating the Sermon and the Service of any one day to the cycle of the church's year, completeness and strength are gained. "Not that which for the moment is nearest the heart of the minister, nor that which is nearest the heart of the individual members, but that which is so arranged that the entire contents of the divine Word are unfolded and communicated in a complete cycle, will afford most permanent edification, and maintain the interest of devout people."[6]

These limits are wide enough to include all but the most exceptional occasions. Conformity to this principle insures a harmonious service with all parts impressing one definite message. The Sermon gains effectiveness because it is *in* the service. The liturgy with its varied and harmonious structure supports and strengthens the Sermon. Only as it is filled with a thoroughly worshipful quality can the Sermon gain its spiritual dynamic.[7]

When, nearly three centuries after the Reformation, a rationalistic theology exalted the preacher and the Sermon to undue prominence and made them the center and sum of all worship, the church lost all sense of reverence and mystery, of order and beauty, and of historic continuity. The church soon languished in spiritual poverty and impotence.

The Sermon combines sacramental and sacrificial elements. It is an interpretation and expansion of the Word. It is also an expression of personal Christian conviction; a testimony to the experience of God's people in accepting his Word as the rule of faith and life.

Before entering the pulpit the minister may offer silent prayer at the altar while the congregation concludes the hymn.

While the liturgy does not prescribe it, the minister, after entering the pulpit and before beginning the Sermon, may conform to the general custom in Lutheran churches abroad, and give the apostolic greeting: "Grace be unto you, and peace, from God our Father and from our Lord Jesus Christ" (Eph. 1:2). Or, in place of this he may say: "In the Name of the Father, and of the Son, and of the Holy Ghost, Amen."

The Sermon ended, the minister pronounces the Votum—"The Peace of God," etc.,—with uplifted hands. Anciently it was customary to end the homily with an ascription of praise. The Votum, as we use it today, is a benediction (Phil. 4:7), invoking the promised blessing of peace upon all who stand fast in the Lord and worship him. It fittingly concludes the second part of the Office of the Word and leads into the Offertory.

[6] H. E. Jacobs, *The Lutheran Movement in England*, p. 302.
[7] Cf. the interesting article by Yngve Brilioth, "Preaching as Worship," in *Christendom*, VI (1941), 14-21.

CHAPTER XVII

THE OFFERING; THE OFFERTORY;
THE PRAYER OF THE CHURCH

Up to this point the Common Liturgy conforms closely to the structure
of the historic pre-Reformation service. The first important break occurs
immediately after the Sermon, and for this there are doctrinal reasons.
An earlier edition of this present work suggested that the historical
structure of the liturgy would be better exhibited if a more definite
break could be made in the Service between the Sermon and the Offertory. This has been accomplished by the rearrangement of parts in
the Common Liturgy.

The Service of the Word ends with the Votum after the Sermon. The
Offertory as a whole includes the Offering, the Offertory sentences and
the Prayer of the Church; as such it begins a new and prevailingly sacrificial part of the Service. In a broad and comprehensive view of the
liturgy we may think of the Offertory and all that follows it as a
response to the sacramental reading and preaching of the Word. But
actually it looks forward and not backward; with it a new division of
the liturgy begins.

The Common Service placed the Offertory sentences before the
Offering, and popular misunderstanding came to regard these sentences as a response to the sermon. In an effort to correct this the
Common Liturgy gives the order: Offering, Offertory sentences, Prayer
of the Church. We do indeed look back upon the message and meaning
of the Gospel, but more specifically at this point do we direct our
thoughts forward to the celebration and reception of the Sacrament.
In an act of corporate thanksgiving and of personal reception and dedication we anticipate the gracious gift of God and bring before him our
substance (II Cor. 8:2-4), our praise (Heb. 13:15, 18) and our very
selves (II Cor. 8:5).

The offering of gifts and the chanting are reminders of the ancient

308

offertory procession. The resemblance is more than a suggestion in Lutheran services in Scandinavia and elsewhere, where the people themselves come forward with their gifts and leave them on the altar. The Prayer of the Church is essentially a restoration of the ancient "prayers of the faithful," though the Reformers in all probability developed it from the vernacular devotions called the prone, as we shall see later, and which now became a part of the Service proper.

Reformation developments thus restored to the Communion Service two important features of early Christian worship—the people's offering of gifts and the people's offering of praise and intercession.

✠

The organist may play some measures in the key and spirit of the Offertory sentences while the minister goes from the pulpit to the altar. This momentary delay in the liturgical action by quiet extemporization at the conclusion of the sermon will impress upon the congregation the fact that the Offertory is not a conclusion to the sermon but the beginning of a new part of the liturgy. The musical rendition should be in keeping with the devotional and prayerful character of the moment. The organist may play softly a selection of churchly character while the offering is being taken. The selection should be terminated promptly when all have made their offering. The choral preludes of Bach and his contemporaries, based for the most part on chorale melodies, generally provide good "organ offertories."

The offering and the anthem, as we know them today, are two relatively modern features in the Service. Neither should prolong the Service unduly, though each should have its own proper dignity. The anthem should not be sung while the offering is being taken unless the matter of time makes this necessary. It may be sung before the offering is received or after the Prayer of the Church.

¶ *Then shall the Offering be received and presented at the Altar.*

THE OFFERING

This is an act of worship and an acknowledgment of our stewardship. The congregation offers to God the gifts of its substance, as the outward sign of its inner, spiritual dedication to the Lord.

The offering should be received and brought forward by the responsible officers of the congregation, the people standing. The people's gifts, which support the church and the objects of Christian benevolence, should be gathered and offered to God, as they are administered, by the proper officials.

The deacons may leave the altar before the Prayer of the Church. They should retire quietly and not in military step. The essential unity of the offering and the Prayer of the Church as a common act of worship is emphasized, however, if the deacons remain in the chancel, facing the altar while the prayer is said. Particularly should this be done when the offering is presented by the responsible officers of the congregation. It should not be done if youthful "ushers" present the offering.

✠

If there is to be a communion, the minister now prepares for the administration. Reverently and unhurriedly he offers silent prayer. If the elements have been placed on a credence table, they are now brought to the altar. The corporal is taken from the burse and spread upon the altar, and the vessels are properly arranged. The cover is removed from the ciborium and wafers placed on the paten. The pall is removed from the chalice, and the chalice filled with wine from the cruet flagon. If the sacramental vessels have been on the altar throughout the Service, the veil is now removed, folded, and laid on the altar, and other preparations made as just described.

The minister, after receiving the offering plates and turning to the altar, may elevate the gifts slightly before placing the plates upon the altar, or, which is preferable, upon the credence table or shelf.

The injection of prayers of blessing by the minister, or of verses sung by the choir and congregation, impairs rather than enhances the impressiveness of the offering as an act of worship. Nothing is more impressive than the simple procedure of the officials of the congregation presenting the gifts of the people, and the minister offering them at the altar in quiet dignity, while the congregation stands in reverent silence.

✠

¶ *Then shall follow the Offertory, the Congregation standing meanwhile. One of the Offertories here following, or any other suitable Offertory, may be sung or said.*

¶ *When there is a Communion, the Minister, after Silent Prayer, and during the singing of the Offertory, shall uncover the Vessels and reverently prepare for the Administration of the Holy Sacrament.*

THE OFFERTORY

I

The sacrifices of God are a broken spirit: a broken and a contrite heart, O God, thou wilt not despise.

Do good in thy good pleasure unto Zion: build thou the walls of Jerusalem.
Then shalt thou be pleased with the sacrifices of righteousness: with burnt-offering and whole burnt-offering.

II

What shall I render unto the Lord: for all his benefits toward me?
I will offer to thee the sacrifice of thanksgiving: and will call upon the Name of the Lord.
I will take the cup of salvation: and call upon the Name of the Lord.
I will pay my vows unto the Lord now in the presence of all his people: in the courts of the Lord's house, in the midst of thee, O Jerusalem.

III

Create in me a clean heart, O God: and renew a right spirit within me.
Cast me not away from thy presence: and take not thy Holy Spirit from me.
Restore unto me the joy of thy salvation: and uphold me with thy free Spirit.

The Offertory as we have it includes a selection of psalm verses or other permitted sentences. It is a substitute for the ancient custom, generally dropped before medieval times, of the offertory procession, as well as a substitute for a later medieval feature which the Reformers deliberately rejected: the Offertory prayers.

The Offertory sentences originally varied with the day or season, and the Offertory is properly a variable element in the Service. Only three texts are supplied, though the rubric provides that "any other suitable Offertory" may be used.

In the primitive church at this point in the Service the people brought food and other gifts for the poor and for the support of the clergy. They came in an offertory procession and placed their gifts on a table *(prothesis)* near the altar. In agreement with the custom of dedicating to God everything used in his service, these gifts came to be offered before their consecration in a prayer of thanksgiving much like an extended grace at meat. Later this formal act expanded into elaborate prayers and ceremonies.

Bread and wine sufficient for the communion were selected by the ministers, and the other gifts were set aside for later distribution. These often included fruit, wool, oil, milk, honey, olives, and cheese, and also silver and gold. The famous mosaics in the clerestory walls of San Vitale in Ravenna depict the Emperor Justinian and the Empress Theodora walking in an offertory procession. During the procession the choir sang a psalm. The Offertory chant in the present Roman Mass is the surviving antiphon of this psalm.[1] A reminder of the old offertory per-

[1] The church order of Hippolytus (*c.* 218) contains prayers of singular beauty for the blessing of the "first fruits of the field." It distinguishes between fruits. Grapes, apples, figs, olives, pears, pomegranates, peaches, cherries, and almonds are to be blessed; lotus, onions, garlic, pumpkins, and cucumbers are not. Roses and lilies are acceptable as gifts, but other flowers are to be rejected.

sists in the Milanese Mass, at which special ministers bring in bread and wine. In foreign mission fields today the people frequently bring their gifts in kind to the altar, a practice which is being revived in many parts of the world.

The offertory procession was continued in many localities until late in the Middle Ages. When it finally ceased its place was taken by a series of ceremonies and prayers of entirely different character. These developed as a sacerdotal function instead of an action of the people. They anticipated the consecration and the "miracle of the Mass" and invoked the divine blessing in view of the eucharistic sacrifice to be offered.

By the fourteenth century this so-called "little canon" included, besides the prayers, the mingling of the water with the wine, the offering of the host and of the chalice, the incensing of the altar and the elements, and the washing of hands. The Offertory prayers were of mixed origin, chiefly Gallican. They were admittedly of poorer quality than the prayers of the Canon which followed. The central prayer of the offertory, *Suscipe sancte Pater,* is a perfect exposition of the Roman dictrine of the sacrifice of the Mass: "Receive, O holy Father, almighty and eternal God, this spotless host which I, thy unworthy servant, offer unto Thee, my living and true God, for mine own countless sins, offences and negligences, and for all here present; as also for all faithful Christians living and dead, that it may avail for my own and their salvation unto life eternal." (Appendix II, pp. 703-04.)

All the Reformers rejected the Roman Offertory and its idea of a sin offering by the priest instead of a thank offering by the people. Luther, with his conviction of the Sacrament as a gift of God to man and not an offering of man to God, called the Roman Offertory an "abomination" which made "everything sound and smell of oblation." "Repudiating all things which reek of sacrifice and of the Offertory, together with the entire Canon, let us retain those things which are pure and holy, and thus order our Mass" *(Formula Missae* [1523]).

Following Luther's example the church orders, with probably the single exception of Mark Brandenburg (1540), omitted the Roman Offertory prayers. Various substitutes were proposed to occupy the time while the communicants came forward and stood in the choir (chancel) and the celebrant ordered the bread and wine at the altar. Eventually the chanting of appropriate psalm verses became the general practice.

THE PRAYER OF THE CHURCH

¶ *Then shall follow the Prayer of the Church.*

¶ *The indented paragraphs in the Prayer of the Church may be omitted, at the discretion of the Minister.*

¶ *If special prayers are desired by or for members of the Church, the Minister may make mention of them before beginning the Prayer of the Church, as occasion may require, or as follows:*

Intercessions: The prayers of the Church are asked for the following brethren who are sick (*or*, in adversity, *or*, in suffering, *or*, in need): N. N.

Thanksgivings: N. N. desires to return thanks to God, for special blessings (*or*, for restoration from illness, *or*, for gifts of grace), and asks the prayers of the Church.

Commemorations: Let us remember with thanksgiving before God our brethren who have departed this life with the sign of faith, N. N. (*or*, our brother N. N., who has departed this life).

Let us pray.

Almighty God, the Father of our Lord Jesus Christ: We give thee praise and hearty thanks for all thy goodness and tender mercies. We bless thee for the love which hath created and doth sustain us from day to day. We praise thee for the gift of thy Son, our Saviour, through whom thou has made known thy will and grace. We thank thee for the Holy Ghost, the Comforter; for thy holy Church, for the Means of Grace, for the lives of all faithful and godly men, and for the hope of the life to come. Help us to treasure in our hearts all that our Lord hath done for us; and enable us to show our thankfulness by lives that are given wholly to thy service;

℟. We beseech thee to hear us, good Lord.

Save and defend thy Church Universal, purchased with the precious Blood of Christ. Give it pastors and ministers according to thy Spirit, and strengthen it through the Word and the holy Sacraments. Make it perfect in love and in all good works, and establish it in the faith delivered to the saints. Sanctify and unite thy people in all the world, that one holy Church may bear witness to thee, the God and Father of all;

℟. We beseech thee to hear us, good Lord.

Upon all in any holy office in thy Church bestow thy wisdom and heavenly grace, and enable them to fulfill their duties in thy fear and in purity of heart. Let thy gracious benediction rest upon our clergy and people, and upon all who are set over us in the Lord; that faith may abound, and thy kingdom increase;

℟. We beseech thee to hear us, good Lord.

Send forth thy light and thy truth into all the earth, O Lord. Raise up, we pray thee, faithful servants of Christ to labor in the Gospel at home and in distant lands;

℟. We beseech thee to hear us, good Lord.

According to thy merciful goodness, O God, extend thy saving health and strength to the younger Churches. Grant that they may rejoice in a rich harvest of souls for thy kingdom. Support them in times of trial and weakness, and make them steadfast, abounding in the work of the Lord;

℟. We beseech thee to hear us, good Lord.

Preserve our Nation in righteousness and honor, and continue thy blessings to us as a people, that we may lead a quiet and peaceable life, in all godliness and honesty. Grant health and favor to all who bear office in our land (especially to the President and the Congress, the Governor and Legislature of this State)*, and help them to acknowledge and obey thy holy will;

℟. We beseech thee to hear us, good Lord.

Give to all men the mind of Christ, and dispose our days in thy peace, O God. Take from us all hatred and prejudice, and whatever may hinder unity of spirit and concord. Prosper the labors of those who take counsel for the nations of the world, that mutual understanding and common endeavor may be increased among all peoples;

℟. We beseech thee to hear us, good Lord.

Bless, we pray thee, the schools of the Church, universities and centers of research, all institutions of learning, and those who exercise the care of souls therein. Withhold not, we pray thee, thy Word and Wisdom, but bestow it in such measure that men may serve thee in Church and State, and our common life be brought under the rule of thy truth and righteousness;

℟. We beseech thee to hear us, good Lord.

We pray thee especially, heavenly Father, to sanctify our homes with thy light and joy. Keep our children in the covenant of their baptism, and enable their parents to rear them in a life of faith and godliness. By the spirit of affection and service unite the members of all Christian families, that they may show forth thy praise in our land and in all the world;

℟. We beseech thee to hear us, good Lord.

God of mercies, we pray thee to comfort with the grace of thy Holy Spirit all who are in sorrow or need, sickness or adversity. Remember those who suffer persecution for the faith. Have mercy upon those to whom death draws near. Bring consolation to those in sorrow or mourning. And to all grant a measure of thy love, taking them into thy tender care;

℟. We beseech thee to hear us, good Lord.

Let thy blessing rest upon the seed-time and harvest, the commerce and industry, the leisure and rest, and the arts and culture of our people. Take under thy special protection those whose toil is difficult or dangerous, and be with all who lay their hands to any useful task. Give them just rewards for their labor, and the knowledge that their work is good in thy sight, who art the Maker and Sustainer of all things;

℟. We beseech thee to hear us, good Lord.

We remember with thanksgiving those who have loved and served thee in thy Church on earth, who now rest from their labors (especially those most dear to us, whom we name in our hearts before thee). Keep us in fellowship with all thy saints, and bring us at length to the joy of thy heavenly kingdom;

℟. We beseech thee to hear us, good Lord.

¶ *Here special Supplications, Intercessions, and Thanksgivings may be made.*
All these things, and whatever else thou seest that we need, grant us, O Father, for his sake who died and rose again, and now liveth and reigneth with thee in the unity of the Holy Ghost, one God, world without end.

℟. Amen.

────────────

¶ *If there be no Communion the Minister and Congregation shall say the Lord's Prayer.*

* *In Canadian Churches, the following may be said:* especially to Her Gracious Majesty the Queen, the Prime Minister and the Parliament, and all Provincial Authorities.

Our Father, who art in heaven, Hallowed be thy Name, Thy kingdom come, Thy will be done, on earth as it is in heaven. Give us this day our daily bread; And forgive us our trespasses, as we forgive those who trespass against us; And lead us not into temptation, But deliver us from evil. For thine is the kingdom, and the power, and the glory, for ever and ever. Amen.

¶ *A Hymn may then be sung.*

¶ *Then the Minister, standing at the Altar, shall sing or say the Benediction.*
The Lord bless thee, and keep thee.
The Lord make His face shine upon thee, and be gracious unto thee.
The Lord lift up His countenance upon thee, and give thee peace:
In the Name of the Father, and of the Son, and of the Holy Ghost.

¶ *The Congregation shall sing or say:*
Amen.

The Prayer of the Church is a part of the Offertory in a larger sense, the three parts of which—the offering of gifts, the Offertory sentences, and the Prayer of the Church—must be thought of as a unit. The prayer is the liturgical counterpart of the offering of alms and oblations. "The gifts and prayers are the offering of the worshipers, presented in union with the intercessions of Christ, 'the high priest of our offerings' (Clement of Rome), as an expression of gratitude and love."[2] Dr. Henry E. Jacobs states that "the office of the General Prayer [Prayer of the Church] is to present most forcefully the Church as the Communion of Saints, where the end of all our prayers for men is that they may be brought to repentance and faith and through repentance and faith experience the fullness of the divine blessing, both temporal and eternal."[3]

This prayer includes the fundamentals and the universals in its grasp. Like the Creed it lifts the individual and the local congregation out of personal and parochial consideration. It is a "prayer for all sorts and conditions of men." Understandingly and unselfishly it reveals true concern for the church in all its operations, the state and its governance, and the home and its welfare, while it remembers before God all men in their several callings and necessities. It is one of the outstanding elements in the liturgy and probably the one above all others which illustrates the congregation's active exercise of its functions as a priesthood of believers. We instinctively feel that the principal service of the Lord's Day or festival could not be complete without some such lofty, pure, and acceptable form of prayer, the scriptural inspiration for which is Paul's admonition (I Tim. 2:1-2), "I exhort therefore, that, first of all, supplications, prayers, intercessions, and giving of thanks, be made for all men; For kings, and for all that are in authority;

[2] J. H. Srawley, in Clarke and Harris (eds.), *Liturgy and Worship*, p. 323.
[3] *The Lutheran Movement in England*, p. 303.

315

that we may lead a quiet and peaceable life in all godliness and honesty."

In rising above small, local, and selfish considerations, the Prayer of the Church reveals the true mind of the church. There is in it no mere repetition of the thought of the day or of the sermon, no narrow expression of individual needs or desires. It is directed to God in humility and trust and its sincere purpose is to be heard of him. There is no attempt to touch, please, or instruct the congregation nor to seek other improper objectives which mar many free prayers and actually take God's Name in vain. Nor do we find in it developed forms of adoration, confession, or even thanksgiving which are prominent features of the usual "long prayer" of non-liturgical churches. The Lutheran Liturgy has provided for these necessary features in the earlier parts of the Service.

The Prayer of the Church corresponds to the Deacon's Litany or Great Intercession, which begins the Mass of the Faithful in all Greek rites, and to the Prayer of the Faithful which had the same place and office in the early Roman and Gallican rites. The Reformation restored this general church prayer to the Lutheran and the Anglican liturgies after it had degenerated in medieval times into a series of commemorations of the departed, invocation of the saints, etc., scattered through the Offertory and Canon. Following Luther's suggestion of a model form in his German Mass of 1526, and drawing upon the material in the extraliturgical vernacular devotions called the prone, the Lutheran church orders developed the *Allgemeine Kirchengebet*. The idea of a general church prayer, and even its place after the Sermon, is advanced in the Wittenberg Reformation of 1545.[4] In 1549 the English *Book of Common Prayer* provided a corresponding form in the prayer for "the whole state of Christes churche." The text in the Common Service was comprised of material approved in the classic century of the Reformation. The first part was from Hesse Cassel (1657) (also partly in Austria [1571]). Much of the remainder was from Baden (1556), Pfalz Zweibrücken (1557), and Strasbourg (1598). The *Common Service Book* (1918) inserted new paragraphs referring to missions, Christian education, and the home. The entire text was heavy and not in the best English idiom.

The Common Liturgy provides an entirely new text which in simpler and more modern speech includes many of the earlier ideas, but which also more definitely expresses the thoughts and needs of our time.

The response, "We beseech thee to hear us, good Lord," secures

---

[4] Sehling, *Die evangelischen Kirchenordnungen*, I, 213. See also Jacoby, *Die Liturgik des Reformatoren*, II, 246.

the attention and participation of the congregation and relieves the tedium of an unbroken form. It is not intended that every paragraph of the comprehensive text should be used at any one time. The first rubric expressly states that "indented paragraphs . . . may be omitted, at the discretion of the Minister."

For discussion of the alternate general prayers, see pp. 661-62.

As alternates to any of these forms, the Litany or the Suffrages may be used (General Rubrics, p. 275).

Anciently the Office of the Word (*missa catechumenorum*) ended with the sermon after the Gospel. A few brief prayers for the catechumens, penitents, etc., were offered and these groups wre dismissed. The baptized Christians who remained then began the second division of the Service, the *missa fidelium*, which culminated in the Holy Communion. Their first act was to offer the "prayers of the faithful" for all men, the church and the ministry, the state, the poor, prisoners, etc.

When the catechumenate and its discipline came to an end, the prayers relating to the catechumens dropped from the liturgy. Eventually the ancient "prayers of the faithful" also disappeared. As a substitute for this true "general prayer," a new group of commemorations and intercessions for the departed and the living, etc., was introduced. Hierarchical tendencies placed this material farther back in the Service, combining it with the prayers of the Offertory and the Canon.

The churches north of the Alps, however, retained something of the idea of a Prayer of the Church in the form of the prone with its "bidding of the bedes," usually after the sermon. This survived on Sundays and festivals in Germany, France, and England, until the Reformation. The prone included some or all of the following devotions in the vernacular; a collect, recitation of the Creed, the Lord's Prayer (occasionally the Decalogue), intercessions for the living and departed, in addition to miscellaneous instructions, announcement of banns, etc. The names of notables of the church and the parish who were commemorated in the "common prayers" were recorded in the "bede-roll."[5]

[5] For full discussion of the prone see Brightman, *The English Rite*, Appendix, II, 1020-45. Among other interesting material Dr. Brightman gives a translation of a German fourteenth-century prone (p. 1023) and also an English example (p. 1050). The German form is as follows: "Next pray ye almighty God for the holy catholic Church, that God for all his saints' sake uphold and establish the Christian faith in its integrity even unto the end of the world, as it hath come down to us. Pray ye for all Christian princes: first for the spirituality, our pope, our bishop, our priests, our parsons, our readers, our vicars, all priests, all clerks, all spiritual folk and all Christian orders, that God impart to all of them his spiritual light for the help and support of Christendom. Next pray ye for the secular princes, whether king or duke or barons or counts, that God give them victory and welfare and all fidelity towards their subjects. Pray ye for all true knights, for all true burghers, for all true peasants, all upright judges, all upright counsellors, that God preserve every one of them in truth. Pray ye God for all true craftsmen, for all common labourers, that God provide them with such labour as that thereby soul and body be sustained. Pray ye God with true devotion to grant peace and grace to the holy catholic Church. Pray ye God for seasonable and clement weather, whereby land and people are gladdened. Pray ye touching every ill wherewith this world is beset, that God remove it according to his grace. Pray ye for all afflicted folk, for all

Thus the general character of the Lutheran Prayer of the Church or Great Intercession, and its close proximity to the Sermon and the Offertory, are definitely in agreement with the original Gallican rite. The earliest Roman rite also most probably had intercessions of this character at this place.

At the time of the Reformation, then, the church was without a true general prayer in the liturgy proper. Luther made no reference to such a prayer in his *Formula Missae*. In his German Mass of 1526, however, he introduced at this place the Lord's Prayer in the form of a paraphrase which expanded its petitions and which concluded with the recitation of the Lord's Prayer itself by the congregation. The Calvinistic and Zwinglian churches promptly developed free prayers. The Lutheran church orders, with Luther's suggestion and the prone in mind, gradually developed a form of *Allgemeine Kirchengebet* which consisted in some instances of a series of collects and in others of one or more complete prayers of comprehensive scope (thus Mecklenburg [1540], Pomerania [1542], Brunswick-Lüneburg [1564], Austria [1571], etc.). Baden (1556) supplies five prayers, one of which is to be used after the sermon and concluded with the Lord's Prayer. Calenberg (1569) and others gave the Litany as revised by Luther. Reformation of Cologne (1543) gives the Litany.

In developing and incorporating such a general intercession in the liturgy proper, the Reformation actually—though perhaps not consciously—restored the essential features of the ancient "prayers of the faithful." By broadening petitions it gave new emphasis and importance to the idea of a general prayer as such. By introducing new thanksgivings and petitions concerning the Word and its fruitfulness, it stressed Lutheran ideas. By inserting brief responses at the end of the sections it gave the whole prayer a distinct congregational character. The reintroduction of the responses as a prescribed form should strengthen our worship still more at this point and overcome the powerful tendency of the mind to wander.

A few of the ultraconservative orders (Mark Brandenburg [1540], Rhein-Pfalz [1543]) kept the prayer in close connection with the consecration. Austria (1571) placed it at the beginning of the Service. Frequently, however, the Prayer of the Church found its place in Lutheran services in connection with the lessons or the Sermon, and thus became a part of the Office of the Word rather than an introductory feature of the Office of the Supper.

The "Prayer for the Church" in the English *Book of Common Prayer* corresponds, as its name implies, to the Prayer of the Church in the Lutheran

---

sick folk, for all poor folk, for all imprisoned folk, that God succour them according to his grace and according to their needs. Pray ye for all them that are living aright, that God confirm them. Pray ye for all them that are in deadly sins, that God convert them and help them to a true repentance before their end. Next pray ye for the needy souls which are in the pains of purgatory, for all souls that are buried here and have belonged to this church, or are written in the bede-roll and are mentioned in the mass, for all the souls that have been commended to me and to you, and for the souls that have departed from this world in the right faith, that God honour all his saints in them and all priests' prayers and all good folk's devotion, that they be delivered from their pains and come to eternal joy. Next pray ye the holy prayer, that God grant us all we need in soul and in body. God, our Father, which art in heaven, etc."

Liturgy. Archbishop Cranmer assembled and consolidated the intercessory material for the living and the dead which was scattered through the medieval Canon and developed from this a prayer "for the whole state of christes churche." This was placed after the Sanctus, thus still keeping the intercessions of this character in close proximity to the consecration. Since 1552, however, the Prayer Books have included the "Prayer for the Church" in the ante-communion service. Specific intercessions for the departed and the limiting phrase "militant on earth" as descriptive of the church, have been in and out of the Prayer Book, according to the ascendency of party power in the "church militant" in the centuries since the Reformation. Thus the intercessions were in the Prayer Book of 1549, out in 1552, in again in 1637, and they are in the recent American Book of 1928.

The Prayer Book has had one unchanging Prayer for the Church. The Lutheran Liturgy has manifested its Gallican affinities at this point, and the Common Liturgy provides alternate texts and permits the use of the Litany and other general prayers in place of the form appointed. The wisdom of the Lutheran provision of alternate forms may be questioned. There is probably some value in sharpening attention and aiding concentration, for, as has been remarked, its constant emphasis upon a few broad essentials make the prayer seem like "an old coin that has passed through many hands and been abraded by the attrition of the ages."[6]

An interesting fact may be noted, viz., that while the early church included the names of martyrs, etc., in the "prayers of the faithful," the Reformation in Germany and in England produced general prayers which mentioned rulers by name (Duke Albrecht, King Edward, etc.), but omitted all names of martyrs or saints. This may have been due to the intimate relation of the state to the church in Protestant lands.

Eighteenth-century Pietism failed to distinguish between the personal, subjective prayer of the individual Christian and the objective common prayer of the assembled worshipers, or church prayer proper. Rationalism lost all right conceptions of the church and of prayer alike. Modern German liturgies give a complete series of general prayers for seasons and festivals. (Thus Saxony [1906]; Bavaria [1879], etc.) Mecklenburg (1868) is probably unique in permitting only the Litany or the Te Deum.

The first American Lutheran Liturgy (Muhlenberg [1748]) gives a lengthy form of Prayer of the Church, and the synod ordered that "nothing else shall be read but the appointed church prayer or the Litany instead of it by way of change, and nothing but necessity shall occasion its omission." This same rubric appears in the printed liturgy of 1786. This is remarkable when we consider the unchurchly practices which generally prevailed at that time.

The United Lutheran Church, in addition to the alternate forms of general prayer provided in the *Common Service Book*, authorized a series for seasons and festivals (published in *Collects and Prayers*, pp. 177-216). These, plus the four alternates in the *Service Book* (pp. 238-41), provide material suitable to almost every situation and taste.

✠

---

[6] Parsons and Jones, *The American Prayer Book*, p. 138.

The Prayer of the Church is a sacrificial act and the minister faces the altar. The general rubrics (p. 275) direct that "The Prayer of the Church, or one of the General Prayers . . . shall be used on Festivals and whenever there is a Communion. At other times the Litany or a selection from the Collects and Prayers . . . or any other suitable Prayer, may be said." The final alternative permits free prayer. This type, at best, breaks the structure of a formal service and usually suffers by comparison with the high standards set by the prayers and other liturgical texts of the liturgy. But apart from this consideration, free prayer is apt to miss the real objectives of true church prayer.

There are occasions, however, which clearly call for special commemoration or intercession in the common worship of the congregation. Material specially prepared for such occasions should not supplant the Prayer of the Church itself, but rather should become a part of it. Appropriate petitions carefully prepared in advance can usually be inserted at the designated place in the Prayer of the Church. Or the minister may compose an entirely new prayer in good liturgical form expressing the comprehensive ideas of a general prayer with petitions appropriate to the occasion. Or an entirely separate prayer, in addition to the Prayer of the Church, may be inserted after the sermon or after the announcements. The appointed forms in the liturgy should be regarded as the normal use. Our practice as a rule should aim at relative permanence of form with possible flexibility of adjustment.

The rubrics instruct the minister to "make mention of" special petitions, intercessions, or thanksgivings which may have been requested, before the Prayer of the Church, so that the congregation may have these in mind as the prayer is offered.

When there is a communion the rubrics require the omission of the Lord's Prayer at this place in order to avoid repeating it too frequently in the same service.

If one of the occasional services—baptism, confirmation, etc.—is used in the Service the Lord's Prayer is omitted at this place.

"Needful announcements" after the Prayer of the Church should be limited to items which cannot be brought to the attention of the congregation by means of a parish paper or a bulletin board in the vestibule. As a direct and personal message of the pastor to his people, these may have a value all their own. They can be given so as not to destroy the spirit of worship, but indeed to further it. They should be as brief as possible.

CHAPTER XVIII

THE HOLY COMMUNION:
The Preface; The Sanctus

THE HYMN

¶ *A hymn shall be sung.*

This leads into the second great division of the Service, the Office of the Holy Communion. It should prepare the hearts and minds of the people for the spiritual blessings which are to be received.

If there be no communion, the Service ends at this point with the Benediction. The hymn should be appropriate to the season or message of the day. It should be sung standing. The Benediction is given by the minister at the altar and facing the congregation.

(For notes on the Benediction and the conclusion of the Service, see pp. 384-87.)

THE HOLY COMMUNION

The Holy Communion is not a separate service (as it became in the reforms of Zwingli and Calvin). It is the culmination and completion of the Service of the Word. As in the church building the chancel is not a separate structure, but the head and crown of the entire edifice, so in the liturgy the Service of the Word finds its crown and completion in the celebration and reception of the Sacrament. As Dr. Horn expresses it: "There is now a transition by means of the Salutation and Response to the Holy Communion, in which our Lord gives to each, personally, His grace, the grace promised and offered in the Lessons of the day, and prayed for in the Collect, especially the forgiveness of sins."[1]

The holy Supper is an institution of our Lord, a memorial of his death and resurrection, a bond of fellowship, and a means of grace. As a unique institution of Christ the Holy Communion conveys unique

[1] Article "Liturgy" in the *Lutheran Cyclopedia* (Jacobs and Haas), p. 278.

321

sacramental gifts. It is different in kind and degree from all other services. As no other service does, it individualizes the gifts of God's grace and promotes conscious fellowship with the communion of saints. In it all the elements of ordinary worship are heightened, the spiritual factors strengthened and the human factors subordinated. In the Real Presence of the Christ, the personality of the minister and the peculiarities of the people fade into obscurity, and the believer is united with his Lord as at no other time.

The Office of the Word is general, and all who desire may have part in it. Worship and instruction are its outstanding features. Its special character is that of Christian fellowship, common praise and prayer, and general spiritual edification, all in accordance with the general plan of the Christian year. Upon this broad, general foundation rises the structure of the Holy Eucharist, a service of thanksgiving and of Holy Communion. Participation in this, with its deeper spiritual meanings and intimate personal relationships, is reserved for mature Christians who have been baptized and have received the instruction of the church.

The church has been established in the world to administer the Word and the sacraments. These are its true marks. It fails in its privilege and its duty if it neglects either. One great failure of the medieval church was the neglect of the Word. The church today frequently fails in adequate appreciation and administration of the sacraments.

In the Holy Communion particularly, the church possesses something unique. Mohammedans and Jews worship God; philosophers and theorists of all kinds preach and teach; scientists promote education; social and moral welfare agencies combat crime and foster an ethical culture; the state maintains institutions for the sick and helpless. Fraternal and altruistic societies develop religious and charitable activities. But none of them, however much they may quote from Holy Scripture, include the Holy Sacrament in their ritual. Instinctively this is recognized and respected as a divine institution committed to the church and to the church alone. Why should not the church more generally appreciate and use the one divinely appointed means of grace which is its own distinctive possession? All too frequently it spends its energies upon activities which it shares with secular organizations and neglects the one supreme spiritual and distinctive gift which God has entrusted to it and to it alone.

The Word gives the Sacrament its power. The Sacrament, however, is the most exalted, the most spiritual way in which the Word comes to us. There is less of the human element—less of the man—at the altar than in the pulpit.

The unifying power of the Sacrament has always been appreciated. One of the prayers of the *Didache,* in the beginning of the second century, expresses this appreciation, though with obvious eschatological reference, in these words: "Even as this broken bread was scattered over the hills and, being gathered together became one, so let thy church be gathered together from the ends of the earth into thy kingdom." The Mass in the Roman church is the visible bond of the faithful in all lands. The Lord's Supper, to all who understand its real significance, is the loftiest commemoration of Christ's redemptive work, the purest means of fellowship with the divine, and the highest expression of inner spiritual unity among believers.[2]

The Holy Communion is one great eucharistic action. It may, however, be divided into three parts: the Preface (Salutation to the Sanctus); the consecration and administration (Prayer of Thanksgiving to the Blessing); and the post-communion (Nunc Dimittis to the Benediction).

✠

The rubrics require that a hymn be sung at this point. If the hymn is in a key unrelated, it will be necessary for the organist to modulate into the key of the liturgy. This should be done softly and the new tonality fully established before the minister begins the Preface.

THE THANKSGIVING

¶ *The Congregation shall rise at the beginning of the Preface.*

THE PREFACE

¶ *The Minister and Congregation shall sing or say:*

The Lord be with you.
℟.   And with thy spirit.
Lift up your hearts.
℟.   We lift them up unto the Lord.
Let us give thanks unto the Lord our God.
℟.   It is meet and right so to do.

¶ *Then shall the Minister turn to the Altar and sing or say:*

It is truly meet, right, and salutary, that we should at all times, and in all places, give thanks unto thee, O Lord, Holy Father, Almighty, Everlasting God: ¶ *Here shall follow the Proper Preface for the Day or Season. If there be none especially appointed, then shall follow immediately,* Therefore with Angels, *etc.*

PROPER PREFACES

For Advent
Who didst comfort thy people with the promise of the Redeemer, through whom

[2] See fuller discussion in Chap. XI, "The Service."

thou wilt also make all things new in the day when he shall come again to judge the world in righteousness. Therefore with Angels, *etc.*

For Christmas

For in the mystery of the Word made flesh, thou hast given us a new revelation of thy glory; that seeing thee in the person of thy Son, we may be drawn to the love of those things which are not seen. Therefore with Angels, *etc.*

For Epiphany

And now do we praise thee, that thou didst send unto us thine only-begotten Son, and that in him, being found in fashion as a man, thou didst reveal the fullness of thy glory. Therefore with Angels, *etc.*

For Lent

Who on the Tree of the Cross didst give salvation unto mankind; that whence death arose, thence life also might rise again; and that he who by a tree once overcame, might likewise by a Tree be overcome, through Christ our Lord; through whom with Angels, *etc.*

For Easter

But chiefly are we bound to praise thee for the glorious Resurrection of thy Son, Jesus Christ our Lord: for he is the very Paschal Lamb, which was offered for us, and hath taken away the sin of the world; who by his death hath destroyed death, and by his rising to life again, hath restored to us everlasting life. Therefore with Angels, *etc.*

For the Ascension of our Lord

Through Jesus Christ our Lord, who, after his Resurrection, appeared openly to all his disciples, and in their sight was taken up into heaven, that he might make us partakers of his divine Nature. Therefore with Angels, *etc.*

For the Day of Pentecost

Through Jesus Christ our Lord, who, ascending above the heavens and sitting at thy right hand, poured out on this day the Holy Spirit as he had promised, upon the chosen disciples; whereat the whole earth rejoices with exceeding joy. Therefore with Angels, *etc.*

For Trinity Sunday

Who with thine only-begotten Son, and the Holy Ghost, art one God, one Lord. And in the confession of the only true God, we worship the Trinity in Person, and the Unity in Substance, of Majesty co-equal. Therefore with Angels, *etc.*

For All Saints' Day
(or at any time when the faithful departed are remembered)

Through Jesus Christ our Lord, who in the blessedness of thy saints hath given us a glorious pledge of the hope of our calling; that, following their example and being strengthened by their fellowship, we may exult in thee for thy mercy, even as they rejoice with thee in glory. Therefore with Angels, *etc.*

¶ *After the Preface shall follow immediately:*

Therefore with Angels and Archangels, and with all the company of heaven, we laud and magnify thy glorious Name; evermore praising thee and saying:

This is a liturgical introduction which leads into the heart of the communion office. In its exalted sentences we have the oldest and least changed part of the liturgy. The thought is simple, strong, majestic; the form one of great dignity, beauty, and power. Hippolytus (A.D. 220) and Cyprian in the third century used some of its phrases. It is found in practically every ancient rite. Augustine says, "Daily throughout the whole world the human race, with almost one voice, responds that it lifts up its heart unto the Lord."

Reverence, adoration, joy, and thanksgiving surge through these brief but lofty sentences. The strongly marked note of thanksgiving reminds us of our Savior's action when he took bread and wine and "gave thanks" (Luke 22:19; I Cor. 11:24). There is an evident connection with the Jewish grace before meat: "Let us give thanks to *Adonai* our God," and particularly with the prayer said by the head of the family at the paschal meal. The action of our Lord and the character of the Communion Service from the beginning gave the name "Eucharist" (thanksgiving) to the entire service. Thus the Preface gives us the key to one meaning of the Sacrament which refutes medieval misconceptions and some modern Protestant ones as well. It teaches us that the Lord's Supper is a "thanksgiving" for the divine gifts of grace which flow to us from the sacrificial life and death of our Lord Jesus Christ.

The plural form "you," "your," "we," etc., is significant as indicating the common united action of the whole body of believers. In a spirit of mutual exhortation, these sentences lift the transaction which follows to a plane of high solemnity. They strongly suggest the idea of "communion" in the sense of fellowship among the faithful, and of united commemoration and thanksgiving in the worship of God the Father. They seem the native and free expression of the original spirit of Christianity. It is significant that they have come down to us unchanged by the hierarchical tendencies which suppressed so many common elements during the medieval centuries.

The lofty tone of the Latin text and its crisp "lapidary" style are noteworthy features which are well preserved in the English translations. The Proper Prefaces are charged with historical commemoration and doctrinal significance. Cast in pure devotional phrase, they give no suggestion of didactic, homiletical, or hortatory tone which frequently characterized the liturgical productions of later times, especially the Reformation era. There is no thought of making or of instructing believers. The voice is not that of the church *in Werden* but that of the church *in esse*. The church as the actual body of believers pours out its love and gratitude in reverent commemoration and exalted praise.

The Preface is a liturgical structure whose invariable framework (prefatory sentences, thanksgiving, and ascription) permits the insertion of changing Proper Prefaces as commemorations. These Proper Prefaces, as Brilioth reminds us, "serve to set the day's commemoration at the center of the eucharistic thanksgivings, and thereby widen and enrich the act of thanksgiving itself."[3] The Preface includes the prefatory sentences (with the Proper Preface) and concludes with the Sanctus.

The prefatory sentences are found in responsive form in all liturgies. The Salutation, as always, invites attention, imparts a blessing, and introduces a sacramental element. "Lift up your hearts" is a strong note, calling for the elevation of the soul above all earthly things. (See Lam. 3:41 and Ps. 86:4.) Origen says that a man must "lift up his soul before lifting up his hands; lift up his mind to God before lifting his eyes, and, before standing to pray, lift up his spirit from the things of earth and direct it to the Lord of all."[4] The *Missale mixtum* begins the Preface with a versicle, "Lift up your ears," with the response, "We lift them up," etc. Then follows, "Lift up your hearts," with the response. "Let us give thanks" points to the character of the prayer which follows. The phraseology here and in the response, "It is meet and right to do," suggests Semitic poetry as a source.[5]

The words, "It is truly meet, right and salutary," are an invariable thanksgiving. "Holy Father" recalls John 17:22. They conclude with the ascription, "Therefore with Angels and Archangels," etc. This unites the Church Militant and the Church Triumphant with the angelic host in an ascription of praise which magnifies the holy Name and introduces the Sanctus (cf. Eph. 3:14-15).

The thanksgiving and the ascription together are known as the Common Preface. Between these two portions of the Common Preface there is inserted a feature peculiar to the Western church, the variable Proper Preface. This connects the particular service with the thought of the day or season. It emphasizes a particular phase of our Lord's redemptive work as the especial occasion for thanksgiving, quite as in the Litany specific acts of redemption are called to remembrance as a ground for petitions of mercy.

The Proper Prefaces give liturgical expression to deep devotional feeling. In their office as a solemn prayer said by the minister in the name of the congregation, and in the poetic inspiration of their stately phrases, they bear a strong resemblance to the finest collects. Note the striking antithesis of Lent with the tree of Eden and the "Tree of the Cross"; the fulness of thought in the acclaim of the Easter Preface; and the religious enthusiasm of Pentecost, "whereat the whole earth rejoices with ex-

[3] *Eucharistic Faith and Practice,* p. 136.
[4] Origen, *Prayer; Exhortation to Martyrdom* (Ancient Christian Writers, No. 19) (Westminster, Md.: Newman, 1954), p. 131.
[5] Fortescue, *The Mass,* p. 320.

ceeding joy." In contrast to these earlier and happier texts one cannot but be impressed by the heaviness and lack of inspiration of the later Preface for the Festival of the Holy Trinity with its pompous procession of dogmatic precisions.

The brief thanksgiving immediately following the Proper Preface has Jewish antecedents in the great Hallel which was chanted at the paschal supper. It was introduced by the words, "Therefore it is our bounden duty to thank, praise, exalt, glorify, praise and celebrate Him who has done all these things for our fathers, and for us. He has led us out of bondage to freedom, etc. . . . Therefore let us sing before Him a new song, Hallelujah."[6]

In the early liturgies, as still in the Eastern church, the Preface is very lengthy. It recounts all the benefits for which we should thank God, with mention of the wonders of the natural creation, an outline of God's progressive revelation, and a commemoration of our Lord's life upon earth, which leads to an account of the institution of the Supper. The Western liturgies omitted these details, retaining only the phrase, "We should at all times and in all places," etc., as a terse summary of the early elaborate expressions. In addition to achieving brevity, the Western liturgies gained variety by the introduction of the variable proper prefaces. These also had the important office of concentrating thought upon the theme of redemption rather than upon the works of creation.[7]

We have noted above the Jewish antecedents of the first part of the Preface. The lengthy Preface of the *Apostolic Constitutions* (Books VIII and XII) gives an extended recital of God's dealings with worthies in the Old Testament which leads to the Sanctus. Thus, if we look behind the simplified text of our liturgy and study its background, we see that the first half of our Communion Office (Preface to Sanctus inclusive) represents the Old Covenant. The second part, beginning with the Prayer of Thanksgiving, consists of New Testament material. The entire office fittingly represents a fusion of the Old and the New.

Luther in his Latin Service retained the entire Preface, as did most of the church orders. These frequently gave the Preface and the Sanctus in Latin. Spangenberg (1545) set German proper prefaces to music. In his German Mass, which emphasized homiletical features, Luther substituted an exhortation to communicants, and a number of south German orders followed his example. Some orders inserted an exhortation on ordinary Sundays but kept the Preface on the great festivals. The entire Bugenhagen series and many other orders kept both the Preface and the Exhortation. The Common

[6] F. E. Warren, *Liturgy and Ritual of the Ante-Nicene Church*, pp. 200f.
[7] See article "Preface" in the *Catholic Encyclopedia*, XII, 384-86.

Service of 1888 included an exhortation as well as the Preface, but placed the former after the Sanctus. The framers of the *Common Service Book,* believing the exhortation to have been called forth by the peculiar conditions of the Reformation period, omitted it from the Service proper and placed it where it more properly belongs—in an order for public confession. The Common Liturgy follows its example. Modern Lutheran liturgies almost without exception give the historic Preface. Kliefoth expresses the universal appreciation of it in his praise of its "great antiquity, doctrinal purity, earnest Christian import and inimitable liturgical beauty."

The Greek Rite has one lengthy invariable Preface. Hermann's Reformation of Cologne (1543) (German edition, fol. CIX) is also unusual in providing one invariable preface. This contains an expansion of the Vere Dignum along doctrinal lines, quite as we find in Petri's Swedish Mass.[8] Variety is secured in the Greek church by the use of different liturgies instead of by variable parts in a common framework. Proper prefaces were introduced in the Western church perhaps as early as the fourth century. Great liberty of improvisation was permitted in the early period. Hundreds of prefaces were composed for every conceivable occasion or situation. The earliest extant service book (the Leonine Sacramentary) has no less than 267 proper prefaces. The Gelasian Sacramentary reduced the number to fifty-three and the Gregorian Sacramentary to ten. Many Gallican rites have a preface for every Sunday and festival.

The modern Roman missal has eleven Proper Prefaces, nearly all of which are given, or referred to, in some Lutheran orders. The *Common Service Book* had seven, all of which were historical except the one for the Epiphany. This was prepared by Dr. P. Z. Strodach. The translation of the Proper Preface for Lent is taken from Orby Shipley, *The Ritual of the Altar* (London: Longmans, Green, 1870). The commendable increase in frequency of celebration of the Sacrament led the Commission on the Liturgy to provide two additional proper prefaces for the Common Liturgy for Advent and for All Saints' Day.

The *Book of Common Prayer,* influenced particularly by Hermann's Reformation of Cologne (1543) has at this point a series of brief exhortations (only one in the American Book), an invitation to communicants, a form of confession and absolution, and the Comfortable Words. This last item, with its quaint but liturgically questionable title, is a beautiful and unique feature taken directly from Hermann. The historic Preface follows with the omission of the Salutation and a few other variations from the original Latin. The First Book of 1549 had five Proper Prefaces, two of which were entirely new compositions. In reducing the number to five the Prayer Book departed from the Sarum Use, being influenced in all probability by the Saxon Order of 1539.

The texts of the Preface and of the Proper Prefaces in the Common Liturgy and in the *Book of Common Prayer* (American) differ greatly, the Easter Proper Preface being the only one in which there is entire agreement. The Lutheran use is in closer agreement with the historic Latin text than is the Prayer Book, though Prayer Book departures from the pre-Reformation text were in all probability chiefly influenced by the Reformation of

---

[8] Quoted in full in Brilioth, *op. cit.,* pp. 141-43.

Cologne (1543).[9] The 1928 Prayer Book still has no Proper Preface for Lent, though it has them for Purification, Annunciation, Transfiguration, and All Saints. Additional proper prefaces are given in recent Prayer Books of the South African and Scottish churches and in the Deposited Book of 1928.

The discrepancies between the Lutheran and the Anglican uses at this point are interesting, particularly in view of the fact that the Common Service whenever possible took the Prayer Book translations of classic expressions of historic elements in the liturgy.

The table in the appendix (pp. 691ff) permits comparison between the texts of the Preface in the three Western liturgies. (For discussion of textual variations in the Prayer Book see Clarke and Harris, *Liturgy and Worship*, pp. 335-57; also the article "Preface" in the *Prayer Book Dictionary*, pp 559f.)

☩

The prefatory sentences are recited by the minister from memory, facing the congregation. The service book remains on the missal stand. The minister may extend his parted hands, holding his arms close to his body, in giving the Salutation. He may slightly incline his head in recognition of the response ("And with thy spirit"). He turns to the altar to say, "It is truly meet," etc., at which point the text is addressed to God. All that follows to the distribution is read from the service book on the missal stand to the left of the sacramental vessels.

The minister may keep his hands joined throughout, or, as a mark of special solemnity, he may raise his separated hands to shoulder height, the palms facing each other, and extend them straight forward a few inches from his body during the recitation from the Vere Dignum to the Sanctus. This was the ancient attitude of prayer among the Jews and also in the early Christian church (as witness the so-called *Orantes* in the catacombs). The practice has been traditionally associated with the Preface in liturgical churches ever since.

The Proper Preface for a festival is used throughout the festival season, except that the Proper Preface for the Festival of the Holy Trinity is used only on Trinity Sunday and its octave.

☩

The music, like the text, belongs to the most ancient and universal tradition of the church, and is used in all settings of the Common Liturgy. No one knows the origin of these beautiful preface melodies, which include not only the prefatory sentences but the proper prefaces as well. They have been in general use for a thousand years or more.

---

[9] Clarke and Harris, *Liturgy and Worship*, p. 335. As an illustration, note the Lutheran use of "It is *truly* meet and right" which is closer to the Latin *"Vere dignum et justum est"* than is the Prayer Book's, "It is *very* meet." Brightman suggests that "very" may have been chosen for the sake of rhythm.

With all their beauty they employ but four notes. Practically all the Lutheran church orders and cantionales of the sixteenth century give them in slightly varied forms. They may be heard in the services of practically all the liturgical communions throughout the world today. It is said that Mozart had such a high appreciation of their beauty that he declared that he would gladly forgo his reputation won in other ways if he could claim to have been the composer of these simple but beautiful melodies.

With an origin long antedating the invention of harmony, these melodies should be sung in unison and in the free rhythm suggested by the words themselves. To facilitate this freedom, no bars or measures are indicated. Solemn dignity and deep devotion should characterize the rendition. The musical tone, however, should flow freely and not drag. Each sentence should be sung through in unbroken phrase.

The organ accompaniment should be very simple, nothing more than foundation stops, with possible upper work of utmost delicacy. It should be used only with the congregational responses.

THE SANCTUS

¶ Then shall be sung or said the Sanctus.

Holy, holy, holy, Lord God of Sabaoth; Heaven and earth are full of thy glory; Hosanna in the highest.

Blessed is he that cometh in the Name of the Lord; Hosanna in the highest.

The Sanctus, which derives its name from the Latin word for "holy," is the climax and conclusion of the Preface. In it the congregation dramatically joins in the song of the angels. It is a solemn act of adoration and thanksgiving in the spirit of holy awe. It has been called "the most ancient, the most celebrated, and the most universal of Christian hymns."

Roman scholars are apt to regard it as an interpolation which in effect cuts in two the Canon, which originally began with the Preface. From our point of view it is the great hymn of praise of the Communion Service, balancing the Gloria in Excelsis in the ante-communion. Its full liturgical and aesthetic effect is realized when every part of the Service from the Sursum Corda to the Sanctus is chanted and not said.

The text in the Common Liturgy, which conforms to the traditional Latin, proclaims the glory of God the Father in the first paragraph, and the praise of Christ as God in the second (see John 12:41). "Heaven and earth are full of thy glory" is but a brief suggestion of the rich commemoration of the glory of God which characterized the Greek services at this point. Its references to Isaiah's vision with its praise of the Creator (Isa. 6:2-3) and to the Hosanna to Christ by the multitude at the triumphal entry into Jerusalem (Matt. 21:9), span the Old and New Testaments. (See also Ps. 117 and Rev. 4:8.) Dr. Parsch suggests that the picture is that of our Lord upon the cross, with all creation gathered about; the Sanctus proper brings in the angels, the Benedictus the disciples. The entire composition takes the character of a drama.[10]

"Hosanna in the highest" means "Save now, I beseech thee in high heaven." Psalm 118 (vss. 25-26), which our Lord undoubtedly chanted with his disciples at the Last Supper, contains these words. In our Lord's time they were used as a triumphant acclaim, similar to the modern "God save the king." They appear in Christian use as early as the *Didache*. "Blessed is he that cometh" may possibly be construed as anticipating the thought of the administration. In the Roman church the "Sanctus bell" is rung at this point in the Service to apprise the worshipers of the approaching consecration and elevation.

The earliest church fathers refer to the Sanctus, and it is found in various forms in the earliest liturgies. It probably originated in North Africa about A.D. 200, with the Benedictus added in Syria at the beginning of the fifth century. The frequent use of Isaiah 6:2-3 in Jewish rituals, particularly in the *Kedushah* (Sanctification) of the daily synagogue service, may have influenced this addition to the Christian liturgy.[11] Lietzmann[12] regards the omission of the Sanctus in Hippolytus as indicative of a primitive Pauline type of liturgy, non-eucharistic in character, but with a mystical commemoration of the Passion. Brilioth disputes this and believes that Hippolytus reacted against Jewish elements in Christian worship and deviated from the use of his time. Under the influence of Pauline theology he developed the Passion and the atonement as dominant ideas.[13]

A very full form of the Sanctus is given in Serapion's *anaphora* and in the *Apostolic Constitutions*. The Sanctus is not to be confused with the Trisagion of the Greek liturgy, which is as follows: "Holy God, holy Mighty, holy Immortal, have mercy upon us."

The early church gave eschatological meaning to the words, "Blessed is he that cometh in the Name of the Lord," by placing them after the Communion in a closing prayer which carried the thought forward to the return of our Lord (the Parousia).

[10] Pius Parsch, *The Liturgy of the Mass*, p. 212.
[11] V. Thalhofer, *Handbuch der Katholischen Liturgik*, II, 161.
[12] *Messe und Herrenmahl*, pp. 164-67, English ed. pp. 134-35.
[13] Brilioth, *op. cit.*, pp. 23-26.

Luther in his Latin service (1523) placed the entire Sanctus after the Words of Institution, and Brandenburg-Nuremberg (1533), the Swedish liturgy of 1531 (and subsequent editions), and Riga (1530) did likewise. This was probably not altogether an innovation. Fortescue in *The Mass* (p. 323) speaks of the practice of waiting until after the consecration and then singing the *Benedictus qui venit,* etc. as "once common" but no longer tolerated. Whether this was particularly intended to heighten the emphasis upon the thought of the Real Presence is debatable.[14] Luther's direction that the bread and the cup should be elevated while the Benedictus was sung lends some substance to this opinion. Some Swedish liturgical scholars still defend the former practice of the Swedish church in maintaining this unusual location of the Sanctus by asserting that this position best accords with Lutheran doctrine in associating the Real Presence with the administration rather than with the consecration. Others (Brilioth, etc.), admit that the change was a "false step." Unquestionably this unhistorical arrangement loses the original force of the Sanctus as a natural and beautiful climax to the Preface, disorganizes the historic framework of the liturgy to reinforce a particular doctrine, and breaks with the order of other Lutheran churches and with that of the church universal to establish a provincial use. The Common Service retained the order given in the great majority of the liturgies of the Lutheran Church and of the church universal, and the recent liturgy of the Church of Sweden (1942) has also accepted this arrangement.

Luther in his German Mass (1526) with a sense of hymnological rather than of liturgical values, paraphrased the Sanctus in the form of a German hymn, to be sung by the congregation during the distribution. Unfortunately, in point of literary and poetic values, this was the least happy of Luther's liturgical and hymnological endeavors. Apart from that, it gives only the story of Isaiah 6:1 and does not include the praise of the congregation.

The Reformation of Cologne (1543) has a curious combination of Latin and German texts. In the quaint form of the English translation we have the direction: "After these thinges, Sanctus shall be songe, where clearkes be in latine, but of the people in douche, one syde answeringe the other, thyrse of boeth partes. As for that, that is wont to be added The Lorde God of hostes, and Benedictus shall be songe communely of the whol congregacion, and therefore in douche."[15] Many other orders (Pomerania [1535]; Mecklenburg [1540]; Prussia

[14] Cf. Kliefoth, *Liturgische Abhandlungen,* VIII, 84.
[15] *Simple and Religious Consultation,* fol. CCX recto.

[1544]; Rhein Pfalz [1557]) permit either Latin or German texts.

The Anglican Prayer Book of 1549 retained the Sanctus in part. It paraphrased the Hosanna and omitted the Benedictus. Comparison of the texts of the Lutheran and the Anglican versions further reveals that both omit reference to the cherubim and the seraphim of the earlier liturgies. The Lutheran form, "Lord God of Sabaoth . . . Hosanna in the highest," is represented in the Prayer Book by "Lord God of Hosts . . . Glory be to thee, O Lord most high." The Scottish Prayer Book of 1929 and the English Deposited Book of 1928 have restored the Benedictus as "an anthem" which may be sung after the Sanctus proper.

✠

The Sanctus is an act of adoration, and the minister continues to face the altar.

✠

The musical settings for the Sanctus in the *Service Book* are varied and beautiful. The first is a chorale-like number usually "ascribed to J. S. Bach" and found in Steinau (1726) and in many other German and Swedish service books. The melody is a simplification of plain song and set to the Latin Sanctus (*Minus summum*) appointed for the First Sunday in Advent and Lent in Spangenberg, Keuchenthal, and other Lutheran sixteenth-century cantionales. Bach, or someone before him, treated this melody, much simplified, as a chorale. Bach's rich four-part harmonies are given in the Bach Gesellschaft edition, LIX, 212. Later editors further simplified it.

The alternate setting in the *Service Book* is an original and very beautiful composition by Healey Willan, eminent church musician of Toronto, Canada. The melody in its free rhythmic form has much of the character of plain song, and its sustained effect is that of deep solemnity and reverence. In the second (continental) setting the Sanctus is set to tenth-century plain song given in the Swedish *Mässbok* of 1942 and adapted to the English text by Mrs. Fryxell.

CHAPTER XIX

THE RECENSION OF THE CANON

The most radical reform of the liturgy made by Luther and his followers was the omission of the Offertory and Canon. Up to this point the outline of the medieval Mass was followed closely, and, except for the Confiteor, comparatively few changes were made in the text. The treatment of the Offertory has already been discussed (pp. 311ff). We now consider the recension of the Canon.

The Canon is the consecration prayer of the Roman Liturgy. It includes the section which begins immediately after the Sanctus and ends just before the Lord's Prayer. Alternate Latin names for this part of the Service are *Prex* and *Actio*. The corresponding name in the Greek Liturgy is *anaphora*. In the Common Liturgy it is called the Prayer of Thanksgiving.

The Greek word from which the name "canon" is derived means a fixed standard or rule. Thus we have the canon of Scripture, the canon of saints, etc. The Canon of the Mass is that central and vital part of the liturgy which, in the mind of the Roman church, contains the essential features for the holding of a true mass. Its text has been practically unchanged for more than a thousand years, but is clearly a collection of fragmentary material which gives evidence of early transpositions and omissions.

Every Christian liturgy seems to have experienced difficulties at this point. No other part of the service has been so thoroughly worked over and in no other part have there been such diversity and confusion. The thought of the early church focused upon the offering of the gifts by the faithful in a great prayer of thanksgiving. These gifts were hallowed by the Word of God and prayer. With the post-Nicene era there came a growing perception of the work of the Holy Spirit and the church specifically invoked his presence and power at this point in the Service. This action soon came to be regarded as the true consecration of the elements. These features of offering, thanksgiving, and invocation of the Holy Spirit (epiclesis) have been preserved in all the anaphoras of the Greek Orthodox rites.

The Roman church shifted the emphasis from the offering and the thanksgiving to the consecration, and limited this latter to a precise moment. The epiclesis was dropped in the early part of the fourth century, and the consecration gradually came to be regarded throughout the Western church as being effected by the recitation of the Words of Institution.

The Reformation again shifted the emphasis from the consecration to the reception. This was accomplished in different ways and degrees by independent recensions of the Roman Canon by the different Protestant churches. Luther rejected the entire Canon and retained only the scriptural narrative of the institution and the Lord's Prayer. The Verba thus received a new and significant emphasis as proclaiming the heart of the gospel. The Lutheran church orders generally followed this procedure and the classic Lutheran Liturgy at this point became unique in liturgical literature. All other liturgies, ancient or modern, Greek, Roman or Protestant, developed, simply or elaborately, formal expressions of the spirit of commemoration, thanksgiving, self-dedication, and supplication in immediate connection with the Words of Institution. The Lutheran Liturgy, as generally found, provided nothing but the simple words of Holy Scripture. The few Lutheran liturgies which introduce additional material are exceptions to the general rule.

Archbishop Cranmer in 1549 reconstructed the Canon on evangelical principles and reintroduced the epiclesis of the ancient church in a form which the Scottish (1637) and the American Episcopal (1789) liturgies expanded. The *John Knox Liturgy* (1564) and the *Common Directory* (1644) outlined full forms of prayer, thanksgiving, and blessing, and the *Book of Common Order* of 1940 contains a lengthy and excellent canon. Other Presbyterian services have rich forms of thanksgiving and supplication in immediate connection with the recitation of the Words of Institution.

Great interest has been shown during the past fifty years in this central part of the liturgy. A flood of books and pamphlets has carried the discussion throughout the Anglican and Lutheran communions. Anglican interest has centered in the rearrangement of the text of the Eucharistic Prayer, and in argument between the "Roman" groups in the church, which stress the importance of the Dominical Words, and others who emphasize the importance of the epiclesis as related to the consecration. Most Lutheran scholars, bearing in mind Chrysostom's statement concerning consecration, which the framers of the Formula of Concord

335

later approved and expanded,[1] are not primarily interested in the restoration of the epiclesis (though the Common Liturgy includes this, as do the liturgy of the Church of Sweden [1942], and the liturgy of the church in India), and particularly not as something essential to the consecration. Their chief concern is to comply fully with the Savior's command: "This do," remembering that he gave a thanksgiving or blessing before he broke the bread and gave it to the disciples. Secondly, they wish by the restoration of such a prayer or blessing to retrieve the Lutheran Liturgy from its isolation and to incorporate it again within the universal Christian tradition. And, finally, they seek to clear their church's liturgy of Romanizing conceptions which may arise in the minds of worshipers who regard the use of the Verba alone as a mechanistic formula precisely determining the moment of consecration. This point is stressed by most writers, but the other two points are equally worthy of serious consideration. Practically all who discussed the subject believed that the desired objectives could be attained by providing a worthy evangelical eucharistic prayer in all respects harmonious with the other parts of the Lutheran Rite. Practically all modern Lutheran liturgical scholars agree that this is desirable. The framers of the Common Liturgy undertook to provide such a prayer, agreeable to Lutheran doctrine and the needs of the American church.

IN THE EARLY CHURCH

The accounts of the Last Supper by three of the Evangelists tell us what our Lord did. We learn the practice of the apostolic church from Paul. Matthew (26:26) tells us, "And as they were eating, Jesus took bread, and blessed it, and brake it, and gave it to the disciples, and said, Take, eat; this is my body." Mark (14:22) uses almost the same words. Luke (22:19) varies slightly: "And he took bread, and gave thanks, and brake it, and gave unto them." In other words, our Lord *gave thanks* over, or *blessed*, the bread and the cup and then said the Words of Institution as he gave the bread and the cup to the disciples, or, as Mark tells us in the case of the cup, not until *after* his disciples had received the wine (14:24). Paul's statement (I

---

[1] "Christ is present, and it is he who has prepared this table, and he who now blesses it. For no man makes what is set before us to become the body and blood of Christ; but Christ himself, who was crucified for us. The priest standing at the altar fulfils the form, speaking the words; but the power and the grace are God's. It is he who says, 'This is my Body.' These words transform what is set out. And just as the words, 'Be fruitful and multiply and replenish the earth,' were spoken only once, yet through all time empower nature so that it produces offspring; so also these words, spoken but once, work a perfect sacrifice at every table in the churches, from that time until this, and even to his coming again." Chrysostom, "Homily I on the Betrayal by Judas," in *Opera Omnia quae Extant* (2nd ed.; Paris: Gaumé, 1839), II, 453A. For additional reference to the thought of the fathers, with abundant quotations, see Darwell Stone, *A History of the Doctrine of the Holy Eucharist* (London: Longmans, Green, 1909), I, especially 70-123).

Cor. 10:16) is the only other specific reference we have in the New Testament, and is in entire agreement: "the cup of blessing which we bless, is it not a communion of the blood of Christ?"

The *Didache,* one of the earliest Christian documents apart from the New Testament, refers to the Lord's Supper as the Eucharist or Thanksgiving, and the Sacrifice. Justin Martyr (A.D. 100-165) speaks of the Prayer of Thanksgiving as containing "praise and glory to the Father" for creation, providence, and redemption. He mentions the Incarnation and institution, the "moment of the Passion," the oblation of "the food made Eucharist by the word of prayer from him." Irenaeus (d. *c.* A.D. 190) refers to "the bread receiving the invocation of God" and to the elements being consecrated by the "Word of the invocation." Clement of Alexandria and Tertullian refer, respectively, to our Lord's "blessing the wine" and using the Words of Institution.

Hippolytus (*c.* A.D. 150-235) was in all probability a disciple of Irenaeus. Students of the Roman Rite recognize the great importance of his *Apostolic Tradition.* Hippolytus was a schismatic bishop of Rome but is included by the Roman church among the fathers and martyrs. His treatise was written to oppose radical innovations and to perpetuate usages of early times. Harnack says of it, "Here is the richest source that we in any form possess for our knowledge of the polity of the Roman church in the oldest time." The service he gives is for the consecration of a bishop. The Canon is really an expanded Preface, which, strangely enough, lacks the Sanctus. It includes an extended thanksgiving, a narrative of the institution, a memorial and oblation, an invocation of the Holy Spirit, an intercession for "all the saints who partake . . . unto the strengthening of faith in truth," and a doxology which specifically recognizes the church as a divine society most intimately related to the Holy Trinity.[2] This earliest Roman form probably influenced the later forms of the *Apostolic Constitutions* and through these the liturgies of St. James and St. John Chrysostom.

Origen (*c.* A. D. 240) refers to the eucharistic thanksgiving and prayer and in three places to the Words of Institution. He connects Paul's words, "it is sanctified by the word of God and prayer" (I Tim. 4:5) with the Eucharist; he also speaks of the "loaves on which has been invoked the name of God and of Christ and of the Holy Ghost" and says further: "it is not the substance of the bread but the Word which has been said over it which benefits." In the fourth century, Cyril of Jerusalem, Basil, Gregory of Nyssa, and Chrysostom refer to the invocation of the Holy Ghost and to the Words of Institution. Ambrose, like Chrysostom, seems to regard our Lord's Words of Institution at the Last Supper as effecting consecration once for all, but he also emphasizes the necessity of prayer. The references in Justin and in Irenaeus to the operative power of the Word (Logos) in the Lord's Supper and similar ideas in the writings of the Alexandrians, Clement, Origen, and Athanasius come to clear expression in the Liturgy of Serapion (*c.* 350),

---

[2] For extracts from this remarkable treatise, see the Appendix, pp. 751-52. For complete text and discussion, see Burton Scott Easton, *The Apostolic Tradition of Hippolytus,* and Gregory Dix, *The Treatise on the Apostolic Tradition of St. Hippolytus* (pp. 75ff). Dix surmises that the epiclesis is a later interpolation in the Hippolytan text, but others do not share this view. There is an admirable summary in Clarke and Harris, *Liturgy and Worship,* particularly pp. 97-105.

bishop of Thmuis in Lower Egypt. His unique invocation reads: "O God of truth, let thy holy Word come upon this bread, that the bread may become the body of the Word, etc."

Thus patristic evidence shows that the early church everywhere and always thought of a prayer of blessing as an integral part of the eucharistic service, whether they regarded this as necessary to consecration or not. Examination of the liturgies fully confirms this fact. From Hippolytus to Serapion, and on to the Clementine Liturgy of the late fourth century and the diverging services of the fifth century in the East, we find a practically identical pattern.

The ancient liturgies in developing a eucharistic prayer placed it immediately after the adoration and praise of the Preface and the Sanctus. The introductory invitation in the Preface, "Let us give thanks unto the Lord," reminds us of our Savior's act in giving thanks before distributing the broken bread, and indicates the fundamental character of the entire prayer which follows. This includes lengthy thanksgiving for the fruits of the earth, of which the bread and wine were tokens, for all the works of creation and for the completed plan of redemption. This commemoration of divine benefits follows the order of the Creed and recounts the successive steps of God's revelation. It finds its climax in reference to the Holy Spirit and in an invocation of his presence and power. Solemn and dramatic action accompanies the text. This prayer really explains the meaning of the entire Service.

The principal parts of the Eucharistic Prayer as found universally, though not everywhere in the same order, are: first, the Offertory or Oblation, in which the faithful brought their gifts to the altar with thanksgiving for the benefits of creation and redemption, and in many liturgies brought their self-offering in symbolic sacrifice with their gifts; second, the great Intercession which included supplications for every human necessity and intercessions for "the whole family of man"; third, the Anamnesis or "remembrance," which grounds the entire action upon our Lord's command, "this do in remembrance of me," and recalls the incidents of our Lord's passion and the institution of the Supper; fourth, the Epiclesis, or invocation of the Holy Spirit, whose power and blessing were sought for the worshipers as well as for their gifts. The Lord's Prayer immediately followed and led to the communion or reception.

The whole prayer constituted a single exalted act of remembrance, obedience, worship, thanksgiving, and supplication. The theological speculation which finally attributed special efficacy to the invocation of the Holy Spirit and indicated a precise moment for the consecration was a later development. (See texts in the Appendix, pp. 751-58).

DEVELOPMENTS IN THE WEST

In the West, other views gradually came to prevail, and the invocation of the Holy Spirit disappeared from the Roman Liturgy some time in the fourth century. The Gallican liturgies throughout western Europe (the Mozarabic Rite in Spain, etc.), provided varying forms of eucharistic prayer for the different days and festivals. These also contained a definite invocation of the Holy Spirit. Isidore of Seville, and other representatives of Gallican thought well into the eighth century and even later, clearly regarded this as the consecratory feature of the prayer. In Rome in the meantime, however, the

Canon had undergone many changes from the simple Hippolytan form. There were omissions and transpositions of text and insertions of compilations chiefly from Gallican sources. The principle of variable texts for other parts of the liturgy was recognized, but the Canon was established as a fixed invariable form. The controversy with the Donatists, who claimed that the validity of the consecration was dependent upon the character of the celebrant, may have led to an increasing recognition of the idea of consecration by a specific formula rather than by a more or less indefinite prayer of invocation. This focused attention upon the Dominical Words which now were no longer regarded simply as the warrant for the service, but came progressively to be thought of as a consecratory formula. Augustine and Chrysostom had sought to preserve the balance between the Verba and the invocation, but the whole trend in the Roman area exalted Christ and his work and minimized the work of the Holy Spirit. Some time near the middle of the fourth century, specific reference to the Holy Spirit disappeared from the Roman Canon, which attained its present form about the time of Gregory the Great (A.D. 590-604). Subsequent developments in ceremonial reflected the gradual hardening of theological thought. This culminated in the promulgation of the dogma of transubstantiation by the fourth Lateran Council in 1215, and the spread of popular superstitions and abuses in connection with the Sacrament (text of Roman Canon in Appendix II, pp. 721ff).[3]

THE REFORMERS AND THE CANON

The lengthy prayers of the Roman Canon definitely interpret the Eucharist as a propitiatory sacrifice. They also include commemorations of the living and the dead, venerations of the Virgin, the apostles and the saints, prayers for the departed, etc. These all lead to an embellished form of the Words of Institution, of which recitation by the priest is supposed to secure the miraculous change of the elements into the very body and blood of Christ. Because of its special solemnity and importance, every portion of the Canon must be said by the priest without

---

[3] Henry Riley Gummey contends that Roman scholars definitely held to the theory of consecration by the operation of the Holy Spirit well into the Middle Ages, and even after the scholastic and mechanistic idea of consecration by recitation of the Verba with its resulting elevations and ceremonies had fully captured popular thought (*The Consecration of the Eucharist* [Philadelphia: Anners, 1908], Chap. 4). For excellent summary of discussion concerning the Canon see Fortescue (*The Mass*, pp. 110-71; 323-60), who practically accepts the theory of the Protestant Paul Drews, first advanced in his *Zur Entstehungsgeschichte des Kanons* (Tübingen: Mohr, 1902), and further developed in his *Untersuchungen . . .* (1906). This theory attempts a reconstruction of the original Roman Canon upon the basis of the material and order in the Greek Liturgy of St. James of the Jerusalem-Antioch family of liturgies. Edmund Bishop in his *Liturgica Historica* gives a learned account: "Early Texts of the Roman Canon" (pp. 77-115). Lietzmann believes that the Canon comes from the sixth century, based on earlier forms found in the Ambrosian Canon, and that the Hippolytan text is the unabbreviated ancient Roman formula (*Messe und Herrenmahl*, p. 167, English ed., p. 134; *Liturgy and Worship*, p. 124). All recent authorities stress the importance of the Hippolytan form.

the variation of a syllable. Anciently it was said aloud, but since the tenth century it has been said in silence.[4]

Because the prayers of the Roman Canon, with their ceremonies (see pp. 721ff) were such truthful expositions of corrupt medieval doctrine, all the Reformers denounced them. Many attempts were made to revise them in an evangelical sense. Kaspar Kantz, in his revised order of 1522, used a paraphrase of one of the prayers to introduce the Words of Institution. Oecolampadius (1523) prepared a form of canon which featured the self-oblation of the worshipers. Other agenda gave a prayer of humble access for the communicants (Nuremberg [1525]; Strasbourg [1525]; Nördlingen [1538]; Waldeck [1556]; Austria [1571]; Hesse [1574]).

Zwingli replaced the Canon by four prayers which led to the Verba. Calvin at Geneva developed an elaborate and heavily didactic Preface and omitted practically everything of the ancient Canon. Archbishop Cranmer in the English *Book of Common Prayer* (1549) reached out constructively in an extended prayer of consecration which recast much of the Canon in an evangelical sense and combined with it certain features from the Eastern and other Western liturgies.

Luther was the most vehement of all the Reformers in denunciation of the Canon. He characterized it as the "mangled and abominable Canon gathered from every source of filth and corruption," and declared that it changed the very nature of the Sacrament into "cursed idolatry and sacrilege." He said that by the silent repetition of the Verba "the devil has in a masterly manner stolen from us the chief thing in the Mass and put it to silence." Taking advantage of the fact that the Canon was said secretly, he suggested that all that sounded of sacrifice could be omitted without offense to the people inasmuch as they did not hear it. His *Formula Missae* cut out everything in the Canon except the Verba, which the minister was ordered to chant aloud. The Lord's Prayer and the Pax followed immediately. In his German Mass he placed a paraphrase of the Lord's Prayer first and followed this by the Verba.

This was Luther's most radical liturgical reform. Thomas Münzer in his *Deutsche Evangelische Messe* had anticipated Luther in the elimination of the Canon. It was Luther's powerful leadership, however, which established this procedure in Lutheran circles. With a single bold stroke he completely changed the character of the liturgy at this point. The Holy Communion became again a sacrament, or gift from God,

[4] Silence may have been imposed at first as a means of shortening the service. Mystic reasons were advanced later in justification of it. See Cardinal Bona, *Rerum liturgicarum* (Turin: Typog. Regia, 1747-53), II, Chap. 13, § 1.

instead of a sacrifice offered to God. This was an immense gain. Something was lost, however, of the richness and warmth of the spiritual satisfactions which a fuller liturgical form at this place might have conserved. With the few exceptions noted above (p. 340) and later (p. 351) the church orders generally followed Luther's procedure and gave only the Verba and the Lord's Prayer. Fortunately they did not adopt Luther's paraphrase of the latter.

Luther's inconsistency in placing the Verba first in his Latin Service and the Lord's Prayer first in his German Mass threw the later practice of the church into confusion. Important orders, including the Nuremberg family of liturgies, Reformation of Cologne (1543), etc., followed the *Formula Missae,* placing the Verba first. The majority, however, followed the *Deutsche Messe* and Bugenhagen's orders and placed the Lord's Prayer first. This may have been because the Reformers recognized the desirability of a prayer at this place, and, having rejected all the prayers in the old Canon, turned to the Lord's Prayer with its immemorial association with the Communion Office as a substitute, an arrangement which also brought the distribution into close connection with the Words of Institution.

THE DEVELOPMENT OF LUTHER'S THOUGHT

Luther's decision concerning the Canon was the culmination of years of reflection and effort to restate the doctrine of the Lord's Supper and to bring the practice of the church into harmony with pure teaching. The violent change he made in the liturgy at this point reveals the corresponding change in his own thinking, from the day when he said his first mass (Cantate Sunday, 1507), to the time of the publication of his *Formula Missae* in 1523. In 1507 he so thoroughly believed the medieval doctrine that he trembled at the thought of the miracle which his secret recitation of the Verba would produce, and only the reassurance of his spiritual advisor restrained him from fleeing from the altar. The progress of his thought to evangelical certainty, and the problem of liturgical reform, of which he was very conscious, can be traced in his published sermons, lectures, and other writings.

In his three great treatises of 1520, and in the equally important *Treatise on the New Testament, that is, The Holy Mass,* of the same year, Luther declaims against the secret reading of the Verba by the priest as a suppression of the gospel; against the erroneous conception of the Mass as a good work; and against belief in the Mass as a sacrifice. He made no effort, however, to alter the text of the Canon, but sought to give an evangelical and spiritual interpretation to its words. There is dignity of utterance as well as appreciation of the magnitude of the problem in his statement: "I am attacking a difficult matter, and one perhaps impossible to abate, since it has become so firmly entrenched through century-long custom and the common consent of men that it would be necessary to abolish most of the books now in vogue, to alter well-nigh the whole external form of the churches, and to introduce, or rather re-introduce, a totally different kind of ceremonies. But my Christ lives; and we must be careful to give more heed to the Word of God than to all the thoughts of men and of angels . . . let the priest bear in mind that the Gospel is to be set above all canons and collects devised by men."[5]

In his "Sermon on the Worthy Reception of the Holy and True Body of Christ" (1521), Luther emphasized again the character of the Lord's Supper as a testament. He repeated his desire that the Verba be said aloud and suggested that the elevation be regarded as a dramatic proclamation of the gospel.[6]

Late in the same year he addressed the brethren of the Augustinian cloister at Wittenberg concerning the abrogation of private masses. Here he revealed how often his own heart had been oppressed by the "one strongest argument" of his adversaries: "Do you know it all, have all others gone astray, have so many centuries been wrong?"[7] This treatise contains an important discussion of the Canon and argues that the Verba are to be considered as words of a testament and not primarily as a formula of consecration. He suggests the possibility of replacing the Offertory and the Canon with material of evangelical character, but actually proposes no form.

In this discussion, Luther contends that the florid expressions of the Canon seek "to draw us every time from the Word of God to the word of men, by what the fathers, the fathers, the fathers, the decretals, the decretals, the church, the church traditionally says. . . . we also can talk this way and cry ever more loudly; the gospel, the gospel, Christ, Christ. . . . we shall triumph and say; yield, Canon, to the gospel, and give place to the Holy Ghost, since thou are but the word of men . . . Sir Canon, thou hast been invited to the wedding feast and hast taken the highest place. But lo, one more honorable has been invited, yea, the Lord himself is present as a guest. Therefore, make him room and be you seated in the lowest place."[8]

When he wrote this Luther was at the Wartburg. Spalatin, hoping to restrain public discussion of Luther's affairs, withheld this work from publication. The disorders resulting from Karlstadt's radical procedure brought Luther back to Wittenberg, where he preached his eight sermons and prepared a treatise on "The Reception of Both Kinds in the Sacrament." Up to this point, however, so far as Luther was concerned, everything was still in the sphere of theological discussion. The chapter of the Castle church did not accept his suggestions, but pastors in Strasbourg and other places began to administer the Sacrament in both kinds, to omit portions of the Canon, and to introduce private prayers in German as substitutes.

Two factors delayed material change in the Canon. One was the force of tradition and the veneration which the universal church had given this part of the Mass. The other was the fact that the Canon included the Verba, the very heart of the gospel. Prior Kaspar Kantz in Nördlingen substituted a series of private German prayers before and after reception for the Canon.[9] These included the Verba and the petition that God the Father's power would cause "this bread and wine to become and to be for us, the true

[5] "The Babylonian Captivity of the Church," *PE* 2, 194, 215 (*WA* 6, 512, 525).
[6] *WA* 7, 689ff.
[7] *WA* 8, 411f.
[8] *WA* 8, 448-49.
[9] Julius Smend, *Die evangelischen deutschen Messen . . .* , pp. 73 ff.

body," etc. Oecolampadius in 1523 proposed a substitute for the Canon which included the following: "Almighty and merciful Father, we humbly beseech thee in the name of thine own Son, Jesus Christ, that thou wouldst accept our gifts, which are our bodies and souls, which we have received from thee. Sanctify them through thy heavenly grace." This was followed by the narrative of the institution according to St. Luke, the Verba as in the missal, and two collects.[10] The prayers of Kantz were intended for the pastor; those of Oecolampadius for the laity. Both were suggestions for private devotion and looked forward to the time when the liturgy as a whole would be used in German.

The first attempt at a German canon was made by Anton Firm and others in Strasbourg in 1523. There the Service, which was published the following year, attempted to do in German, though on a smaller scale, what Archbishop Cranmer later accomplished in the English *Book of Common Prayer*. This was to recast, in evangelical mold and in the language of the people, at least some of the prayers of the medieval Canon. After the Preface and the Sanctus in German, the order continues: "All-kind Father, merciful and eternal God, grant (*hilf*) that this bread and wine may become and be for us the true body and the innocent blood of thy beloved Son, Our Lord, Jesus Christ, who on the day before his passion, took bread," etc. The Verba is followed by the Lord's Prayer, the Agnus Dei, and a prayer to Christ imploring salvation from our sins "through this thy holy body and precious blood. Grant that we may accomplish thy will at all times and that we may never be separated from thee in eternity."[11]

At the Easter service in 1523 Thomas Münzer of Alstädt introduced a vernacular Mass which provides lengthy explanations of parts of the Service and a good order beginning with the Confiteor and including the Preface, Sanctus, and Verba, all sung aloud in German.[12]

Luther had always desired the Verba in the vernacular, but he never attempted a German substitute for the Canon. His only solution for its unevangelical character was omission. His *Formula Missae* in 1523, a Latin treatise intended for the clergy, attacked and omitted the Offertory and the Canon, except that the Verba was retained. By this very procedure, supreme attention was focused upon the Verba as the heart of the gospel and the real Mass. They were followed by the Sanctus and the bread and the chalice were elevated "according to the rite now in use." Previously the Verba had been said quietly by the priest, and the Benedictus, the concluding part of the Sanctus, had been sung by the choir during the consecration and elevation. Luther directed the Verba to be said "in moderate voice," and the choir continued to sing the Sanctus and Benedictus while the Verba were being read. Later when provision was made for chanting the Verba aloud, this, except in the case of a few orders, was held back until the completion of the Sanctus. So, in all probability, there was no intentional "displacement" of the Sanctus as has frequently been thought. The elevation was retained at Wittenberg as late as 1533 and together with the use of the sacring bell was continued sporadically in Lutheran circles throughout the sixteenth

[10] *Ibid.*, pp. 51 ff., especially pp. 54-55.
[11] *Ibid.*, pp. 131 ff.
[12] *Ibid.*, pp. 94 ff. See also Sehling, *Die evangelischen Kirchenordnungen des 16. Jahrhunderts*, I, 504 ff.

century. Eventually it was abandoned. After the Lord's Prayer and the Pax, the administration followed, and during this the Agnus was sung. The Service concluded with the usual prayers from the missal.

In his German Mass three years later, Luther also omitted the Offertory and the prayers of the Canon. He extended the text of the Verba by combining the New Testament accounts in Matthew and First Corinthians. He made one significant change which must have impresssed clergy and laity alike. He set the Verba to a chant form and directed that these words of the institution should be sung aloud for all to hear.

Another change had to do with the Lord's Prayer, which previously had followed the Canon immediately. The Lord's Prayer was now advanced to a point following the sermon. Its text was expanded in a paraphrase. Luther may not have thought of this as a revival of the Prayer of the Faithful of the early church, but he certainly was familiar with the medieval prone or bidding of the bedes and its vernacular petitions.[13] By the transference of the Lord's Prayer and the expansion of its text, Luther laid the foundation for one of the significant and characteristic features of the later Lutheran Liturgy, namely, the General Prayer (Prayer of the Church), with the Lord's Prayer as its proper summary and conclusion.

Thus, nearly ten years after the posting of his Theses, and after violent attacks on the Canon in his several writings, Luther's practical suggestions for the reform of the latter called for nothing except omission, the Words of the Institution from the Scriptures alone being retained and sung aloud. This seemingly negative action, however, must be recognized as a very positive procedure. Not only did it eliminate erroneous and extraneous material, with resulting simplification and concentration, but it invested the public proclamation of the all-important Dominical Words with an altogether new and solemn dignity. Luther's solution was thus eminently suited to the need of the German Reformation.[14]

THE ANGLICAN RECONSTRUCTION

Archbishop Cranmer's reconstruction of the ancient Latin Canon in the Prayer Book of the Church of England ranks, with his translation of the collects and his litany, as one of his notable accomplishments. He was fully conscious of the unevangelical character of the Roman Canon. He was also familiar with the solutions of the problem proposed by Luther, Zwingli, Calvin, the Strasbourg Reformers, and others. Lacking Luther's intensity of emphasis upon the supremacy of the Word, but having a much higher regard for historic continuity and liturgical tradition than did Zwingli or Calvin, he sought to retain as much as possible of the ancient Canon, recast in an evangelical mold.

Cranmer's reconstruction of the Canon in the Prayer Book of 1549

---

[13] Duchesne, *Christian Worship,* p. 172. Brightman, *The English Rite,* II, 1020, 1045.

[14] An able discussion of Luther's thought is given in an unpublished thesis by Charles Muhlenberg Cooper. (Krauth Memorial Library, Philadelphia Seminary.)

included the Prayer for the Church, a prayer of consecration, the memorial and oblation and the truly spiritual and beautiful Prayer of Humble Access. He developed elements from the *Te igitur memento* and *Communicantes* section of the Canon into the Prayer for the Church. In this he retained a prayer for the departed but omitted all reference to oblation and sacrifice, and freely adapted, paraphrased, and expanded all material. The Prayer for the Church formed the introduction to the new English canon. In the second Book of 1552, however, this prayer was considerably altered, partly in deference to Bucer's criticisms. The prayers for the departed and the commemoration of saints were omitted, and the prayer for the church was definitely limited to the living by the addition of the words, "Militant here in earth."

In this form the prayer was moved forward to its present position before the Preface. This position, which corresponds to that of the Lutheran General Prayer and the ancient bidding of the bedes, has been retained in practically all the Anglican rites to the present. More recent Scottish, South African, English, and American revisions of the Prayer Book have returned to Cranmer's original thought and now omit the words, "Militant here in earth," and insert explicit prayers for the departed, giving "high praise and hearty thanks for the wonderful grace and virtue declared in all thy Saints whose good example is to be followed."

Cranmer retained and recast other portions of the Roman Canon (*Ut nobis corpus et sanguis, Unde et memores,* etc.), in a prayer of consecration. This now begins with the words, "All glory be to thee, Almighty God." It first received its title, "Prayer of Consecration," in the Scottish Liturgy in 1637. In this prayer the Words of Institution were prominent, but they did not stand apart as a simple narrative as in the Lutheran orders. In Cranmer's Service these words became part of a prayer specifically addressed to God the Father and beseeching him that "whosoeuer shalbee partakers of thys holy Communion, maye worthely receuve the moste precious body and bloude of thy sonne Jesus Christe." Eastern and Western views of consecration are combined in this prayer which contains a direct invocation of the Holy Spirit and also includes the Word as an agent ("with thy holy spirite and worde vouchsafe to blesse and sanctifie these thy gyftes, and creatures of bread and wyne"). Bucer's objections secured an altered form of the invocation in 1552, but the Scottish and American Prayer Books and the English Proposed Book of 1928 restored Cranmer's reference to the Holy Spirit.

The account of the institution incorporated in the prayer of consecration definitely follows the Brandenburg-Nuremberg Order of 1533 in providing a harmony of four New Testament passages. Unlike the Lutheran orders, however, Cranmer's prayer expresssed the sacrificial or Godward aspect of the Eucharist as the church's memorial of the sacrifice of Christ, and as an act of self-oblation on the part of the worshipers. This was in line with Augustine's repeated injunction to offer "ourselves, our souls and bodies" in union with the sacrifice of Christ. It was also reminiscent of certain passages in the old Latin Canon, which were skilfully paraphrased to admit of evangelical interpretation.

As indicated above, Cranmer's reconstructed canon was considerably altered in the second Prayer Book of 1552. Other changes and distributions of parts were made in 1661 and in later editions of the English, Scottish, South African, and American books. The nonjurors' liturgy of 1718 rewrote much of the Canon in line with the early liturgies and introduced a definite epiclesis. The American *Book of Common Prayer* has been strongly influenced by the Scottish liturgies, as has the South African liturgy of 1919 and Prayer Book of 1954. Each of these, however, has features peculiar to itself.

The chief interest of Anglican liturgical scholars in recent years has been in securing the reintroduction of the epiclesis and other features of Cranmer's first Prayer Book. The trend in this direction is shown by a comparative study of the prayers of consecration in the latest Anglican prayer books. These reveal extensive differences in text within the common framework. Notwithstanding the variations there is an essential unity in them all. Everything considered, the Prayer Book texts provide a successful reconstruction of the ancient Latin Canon.[15]

THE USUAL LUTHERAN FORM

Luther's drastic action in cutting into the Canon like a surgeon and removing everything except the Verba was motivated by two factors. The first was his violent reaction against the doctrinal impurities of the Roman text. The second was his desire to feature the Word of God in this part of the Service rather than "the words of men." In general, he appreciated the value of hymns, psalms, canticles, and prayers as expressing in variant form the truths of the gospel. At one time he said of his own efforts, "Our opponents cannot claim ignorance of the doctrine

[15] For critical discussion of the Anglican forms and a table showing the variations see Clarke and Harris, *Liturgy and Worship*, pp. 341-56, and the article "Eucharistic Consecration" by J. W. Tyrer in *The Prayer Book Dictionary*. Mention should also be made of other noteworthy reconstructions of the ancient Canon. The outlines of the Scottish *Directory* have been filled in briefly with forms from the ancient liturgies in *Euchologion, A Book of Common Order*, issued by the Church Service Society for use in the Church of Scotland, and now in its eleventh edition. *The Book of Common Order*, issued by authority of the General Assembly of the Church of Scotland (London: Oxford Univ. Pr., 1940; 2nd ed., 1952), contains an excellent canon. The Liturgy of the Catholic Apostolic Church (Irvingite) also contains a very full canon, as does the recent *Book of Worship* of the Evangelical and Reformed Church (now United Church of Christ). The new liturgy of the Church of Sweden (1942) is also noteworthy.

of the gospel, since we have preached, written, painted, and sung it." But here, in the very heart of the Communion Office, where we expect richness and warmth of liturgical expression, he will have nothing but the bare recital of the institution in the words of Holy Scripture. This is the more inconsistent when we recall his own unhappy efforts, in the German Mass, to expand the text of the Lord's Prayer in paraphrase!

Whether or not we believe that circumstances justified Luther's unusual procedure, his decision determined the content and form of the classical Lutheran Liturgy. The order he proposed became a characteristic and unique feature of Lutheran worship. Lutheran services in every land since Luther's time, with a few exceptions, have recognized the Reformer's leadership and have omitted extended prayers at this place. The Verba followed by the Lord's Prayer, or the Lord's Prayer followed by the Verba, stand alone. Yet the Lord's Prayer in either position is not a valid substitute for a eucharistic prayer.

Whatever else may be said concerning this unique feature of the traditional Lutheran Liturgy, with its sharp break with the universal church before and since the Reformation, we must recognize the humble faith which achieves grandeur by the simple expedient of restraining all human speech and giving spaciousness and solemnity to the words of our Lord at the original institution. Exponents of the traditional Lutheran use believe that this reverent, unadorned use of the Words of Institution accomplishes two things. It focuses all thought upon the action and the words of Christ, who was himself the very Word of God. In doing this it demonstrates the Lutheran conception of the Sacrament as a particular form of the Word, the *verbum visibile* of Augustine, which proclaims to the world and seals to believers the assurances of the gospel concerning God's gracious will, the forgiveness of sins, and the ultimate satisfaction which the soul of man finds in the redemptive work of Christ. The strongly objective character of the Lutheran Liturgy is expressed by this simple narration of the historic institution. It commemorates the experiences of the disciples in the Upper Room and on Calvary, and at the same time provides a means whereby the grace of Christ is communicated to us here and now. For every Holy Communion is at once a celebration of the facts and the mystery of our redemption and an administration of the heavenly grace by which believers are nourished in this mortal life.

In the second place, this reverent, unadorned use of the Words of Institution, if rightly understood, serves to express the Lutheran view of the consecration. The *Formula of Concord,* Part II, Chapter VII, approves and amplifies the well-known statement of John Chrysostom:

Christ himself prepares this table and blesses it; for no man makes the bread and wine set before us the body and blood of Christ, but Christ himself who was crucified for us. The words are spoken by the mouth of the priest, but, by God's power and grace, the elements presented are consecrated in the Supper by the Word, where he speaks: "This is my body." And just as the declaration (Gen. 1:28): "Be fruitful, and multiply, and replenish the earth," was spoken only once, but is ever efficacious in nature, so that it is fruitful and multiplies; so also this declaration [This is my body; this is my blood] was once spoken, but even to his advent it is efficacious, and works so that in the Supper of the churches his true body and blood are present.[16]

According to this the consecration is not effected mechanically and at a precise moment and place by the recitation of the Dominical Words as the Romanists teach; nor by the invocation of the Holy Spirit whose special presence and power the modern Greek churches beseech. The effective consecration is the original institution. The creative words of Christ in the Upper Room potentially included every subsequent celebration and administration. A formal setting apart of the elements for their sacred use is fitting at every subsequent administration, and the use of the words of the original institution illustrates Augustine's statement, first applied to baptism: "The Word is added to the element and it becomes a sacrament." But we dare not limit the thought of consecration to the precise moment of recitation of the Verba. The local and particular "setting apart" finds its completion and value not at the end of the Verba, but in connection with the administration, for apart from the administration there is no sacrament. Many centuries and continents separate us from the experiences of the Upper Room, but as we reverently obey our Lord's command today and observe this great tradition of discipleship we believe that our living Lord himself is present throughout the entire Service, that his creative word consecrates the earthly elements anew, and that he imparts to all believers his grace and benediction.

A EUCHARISTIC PRAYER DESIRABLE

Notwithstanding the force of this position, many Lutherans have long desired something richer, warmer, and emotionally more expressive— something less likely to foster erroneous conceptions and something more in harmony with the New Testament account and with the thought and practice of the universal church. We have seen the scriptural statement that first of all our Lord blessed the bread and the wine and then gave them to his disciples with the Words of Institution, as we call them.

[16] Henry E. Jacobs (ed.), *Book of Concord*, I, 615. It is interesting to compare the Reformer's text with modern editions.

The admonition "this do" comprehends the entire action, which, so far as we are concerned, may well include a prayer of thanksgiving and blessing, reminiscent of our Lord's blessing, and such as is found in every early Christian liturgy. An invocation of the Holy Spirit may also be included, as this was the normal and universal use of the church in the fourth century and the well-established custom in many parts of the church at a much earlier period. Bishop Brilioth's comment is: "The pruning knife of the Reformation" had to clear away "the disfiguring outgrowths of the Roman Mass," but "the richer treasures of the older liturgies were not recovered. Thus the operation left a gaping void . . . a central problem of the Lutheran Rite still awaits its solution."[17]

All other Christian liturgies, no matter what their doctrinal position—Greek, Roman, Anglican, Protestant of many kinds—provide some extended form of eucharistic prayer. Luther's reform at this point was drastic, and completely unlike his usual conservative procedure. His amputation of all prayer forms—good as well as bad—surrounding the Words of Institution robbed the liturgy of its historical and ecumenical character and fastened a strange and unique use upon subsequent Lutheran history. Overwhelmed at the moment by his realization of the supreme importance of the Word of God, he discarded all other considerations and made the Sacrament at this point illustrate his own powerful concentration upon a single idea, the thought that here and now we must do away with all "words of men and angels" and listen only to the words of Christ as they reveal the heart of the gospel message. However necessary in 1523, this excessive emphasis upon the Verba alone mars the ageless and universal quality which otherwise characterizes the Lutheran liturgy. It dates this central and significant part of it as of the third decade of the sixteenth century. It reveals too sharply the preoccupation of a single reformer with a single idea.

It has been felt also that the bare use of the Verba, divorced from all prayer forms of remembrance and thanksgiving, and particularly when accompanied by the sign of the cross—as in most Lutheran liturgies since the seventeenth century[18] encourages in the popular mind

---

[17] *Eucharistic Faith and Practice*, p. 125.

[18] Thomas Münzer's order for Alstädt (1523) is the only sixteenth-century liturgy which retained the sign of the cross in connection with the Verba in the Holy Communion, though this was universally retained in the baptismal service. Hannover (1536) directly forbade it. The pastor is frequently directed to take the paten or the cup in his hand, to hold them on a level with his hearts, etc., but no mention is made of the sign of the cross. The first reference to it appears to be by John Gerhard (LL. CC. XXI, 13-156), who calls it an external sign of blessing and consecration, recalling the memory of the cross of Christ. The first church order to introduce it was Coburg (1626) where it is indicated twice in connection with the word "took." The supposition is that its later general introduction into Lutheran liturgies was part of a movement against crypto-Calvinism.

a mechanistic and Roman conception of consecration, in spite of the doctrine *extra usum nullum sacramentum*. The simple worshiper, unfamiliar with subtle theological distinctions but devoutly following the liturgy at this point, is easily led to believe, "now it has happened!"—quite as the Romanists believe in the "miracle of the Mass." In fact, liturgical scholars in other communions seem to think that at this point the Lutherans are "more Roman than the Romans."

In the original institution of the Lord's Supper the "consecration" in all probability was an unrecorded prayer. The Verba, as such, were connected with the distribution. There was little in the Lutheran Church's order, before the Common Liturgy, to help the worshiper to realize this or to understand that we used these words in the spirit of commemoration and prayer and as a warrant for all that we did, and not as a formula for a magical act. We rejected the "category of space" inherent in the doctrine of transubstantiation. We dare not retain the "category of time" inherent in the same false doctrine. As we do not limit the divine presence to wafer or wine, so we should not even seem to restrict divine power to a single moment.[19]

A final objection is that the Verba alone, without any accompanying thanksgiving, intercession, or petitions, leaves the spirit of devotion unsatisfied. To borrow Bishop Brilioth's characterization, there is a "void" at this point. Even the most literal appeal to scriptural authority must recognize the fact that our Lord, and later the disciples, "gave thanks" in connection with the Supper. And in our worship today, after the rich forms of the Preface and the Sanctus, some fuller expression is required at this place, as the testimony of the universal church clearly shows.

The use of the Verba alone is elemental and strong, but it lacks the richness, warmth, and spiritual satisfaction which liturgical maturity demands. It attains high dignity and solemnity, but it also has the coldness and austerity of unrelieved objectivity. Our spirit of devotion longs to incorporate these divine words in some expression of our own which might reveal the gratitude, love, sense of fellowship, and self-dedication which they inspire. The Common Liturgy supplies just such an expression.

The fact that Luther employed the Verba alone and that the great majority of Lutheran liturgies in the past four centuries have followed him in this procedure determined the text of the Common Service of 1888. The scholars at work on the Common Liturgy of 1958 were conscious of the dissatisfaction of Lutheran students of the liturgy in all periods with this

[19] See Rietschel, *Lehrbuch der Liturgik*, I, 435 ff.

Lutheran peculiarity. They believed that historical, doctrinal, and devotional aspects of the problem would find their natural solution in the restoration of a carefully framed eucharistic prayer which would continue the exuberant strains of the Preface and the Sanctus, and encompass our Savior's life-giving words with solemn thoughts of remembrance and exalted expressions of thanksgiving. Believing this, they prepared the Prayer of Thanksgiving.

The early church developed a pattern for such a prayer. This almost universally included a post-Sanctus, with its continuing notes of adoration; a recitation of the Words of Institution; a solemn reference to our Lord's incarnation, sufferings and death, resurrection and ascension (anamnesis); an invocation of the Holy Spirit (epiclesis); and petitions for the spiritual blessing of the Sacrament upon all who partake of it. Several Lutheran church orders of the sixteenth century attempted, though not too successfully, to surround the Verba with pure prayer forms.

The very first German liturgy (Kantz, [1522]), the Strasbourg Order (1525), and Pfalz Neuburg (1543) had some form of eucharistic prayer. The last order invoked the grace and blessing of the Christ, as did the early Liturgy of Serapion and the later Mozarabic.[20] The Bavarian Liturgy (1879), and the Russian (1898), give fuller forms of eucharistic prayer. The German liturgy of the Ministerium of Pennsylvania (1855) followed the Pfalz Neuburg form and provides the first American Lutheran precedent. The liturgy of the Joint Synod of Ohio gave the Bavarian form. The recent liturgy of the Federation of Lutheran Churches in India (1936) provides a eucharistic prayer based chiefly upon the early Greek liturgies and containing an epiclesis. The liturgy of the Church of Sweden (1942) also has a brief eucharistic prayer with epiclesis (see p. 758). The *Agenda für evangelisch-lutherische Kirchen und Gemeinden* prepared by the Lutherische liturgische Konferenz Deutschlands (Berlin: Lutherisches Verlagshaus, 1955), reflects present-day scholarship and the general desire in Germany for a eucharistic prayer. It provides a longer and somewhat different form (see p. 758). Some of these forms are extremely subjective and some are inadequate on other counts. Taken as a group, however, they testify to a general desire for a eucharistic prayer in the Lutheran Service.

Luther at first regarded the Verba as an announcement to the congregation. This idea is also frequently expressed in the *Formula of Concord* and the writings of later dogmaticians. After 1523, however, Luther certainly viewed the Verba as words of consecration, referring to them as *Benedictio* (Blessing) in the *Formula Missae* of that year and as *das Amt und Dermung* (Consecration) in the German Mass of 1526. In a letter to Karlstadt in 1528 Luther expresses his belief that the recitation of the Verba over the elements marks the consummation of the sacramental union.[21] This view, which Rietschel in giving additional references to sources does not hesitate to characterize as "essentially catholicizing," gained wide acceptance in Lutheran circles particularly in the seventeenth century.[22]

---

[20] Brightman, *op. cit.*, xliv, comments on this prayer and consecration as "abnormal" in being addressed to Christ, but calls attention to the prayer *"Adeste"* in the Mozarabic Mass (Migne, *Patrologia latina*, LXXXV, 550).

[21] De Wette. *Dr. Martin Luthers Briefe,* III, 231 ff. Also *WA* Br. 4, 363ff.

[22] Rietschel, *op cit.,* I, 434.

The confusion resulting from the differing positions expressed by Luther was partially resolved by later theologians. Chemnitz in his *Sana doctrina* (1560) says: "The Words of Institution are a word of invocation, that is a prayer that Christ will be present according to his promise, in a sacramental manner, and will give his body to be eaten with the bread," etc. John Gerhard in his "Complete Explanation of the Articles Concerning Baptism and the Holy Supper" (1610), makes a similar statement.[23] Among moderns, von Zezschwitz calls the recitation of the Verba "an act of prayer in which his own word is held up before the exalted Head of the congregation, that it may be applied to these elements."[24]

This conception is a departure from Luther's original idea of rejecting all prayer forms and disentangling the simple words of Christ from every priestly act. It also involves an improper use of our Lord's words, which as he uttered them were neither a prayer form nor consecratory. They were definitely related to the distribution and the reception. If a prayer form is desired, something additional to the Verba is necessary. We could accept and justify the isolated use of the Verba only if we were willing to accept either Luther's first expressed position with its definite limitations, or his second with its unsatisfactory but logical conclusions. The first of these positions would satisfy the Calvinists completely, while the second in itself would not offend the Romanists. Mature Lutheran consciousness in the interest of truth and devotion hopes for something more expansive, expressive, and spiritually satisfying.[25]

In the first edition of THE LUTHERAN LITURGY (1947), the author offered a "constructive contribution to the study" of this subject and proposed a form of eucharistic prayer "in the spirit of the early liturgies and in agreement with Lutheran teaching" (pp. 336-37). On the basis of this and a text previously proposed by Paul Zeller Strodach in his *Manual on Worship* (rev. ed.; Philadelphia: Muhlenberg, 1946), pp. 253-54, the Commission on the Liturgy composed the prayer of thanksgiving which now appears in the Common Liturgy, and which is given, with annotation of sources, in the pages following (Chap. XX).

---

[23] *Ausführliche schriftmässige Erklärung der beiden Artikel von der heiligen Taufe und von dem heiligen Abendmahl* (Jena:1610; reproduced Berlin:1868), Chap. XIII, pp. 236 ff.

[24] *System der Praktischen Theologie* (Leipzig: Hinrichs, 1818), p. 280.

[25] Julius Muethel of St. Petersburg brought this whole question into sharp focus at the time of the preparation of the agenda for the Lutheran church in Russia in 1898. His treatise, *Ein wunder Punkt in der luth. Liturgie* (1895), and his later *Nochmals Sätze über unsere luth. Konsekrations-Liturgie im Abendmahlsakt* (1895), assailed the traditional isolated use of the Verba as catholicizing and proposed a none-too-satisfactory prayer of thanksgiving within which the Verba were incorporated. In the numerous articles and pamphlets which appeared during the ensuing controversy Muethel was supported by Kawerau, Beck, Praeger, M. Bär, Smend, and Rietschel. Caspari, Herold, Haussleiter, and others were sympathetic. The synods of Liefland and Estonia approved Meuthel's proposal; Kurland did not. (Discussion in Rietschel, *op. cit.*, I, 436, 542ff.)

On this entire subject, and in addition to the writing of Julius Muethel (note 20), see Walter Howard Frere, *The Anaphora* (New York: Macmillan, 1938); Gregory Dix, *The Shape of the Liturgy* (Westminster: Dacre Pr., 1945); J. W. Tryer, *The Eucharistic Epiclesis* (New York: Longmans, 1917); Henry Riley Gummey, *The Consecration of the Eucharist* (Philadelphia: Anners, 1908); and the lengthy discussion by Peter Brunner of Heidelberg in his "Zur Lehre vom Gottesdienst," in *Leiturgia*, I, 340-61. Note the text of the prayer proposed there. Also worth noting are the reports of the Lutheran World Federation's Commission on Liturgy (Hanover: 1952, and Minneapolis: 1957), both of which approve of a eucharistic prayer.

THE PRESENT SITUATION

It may be said that Lutherans in general have been satisfied with the classic confessional statement which speaks approvingly of John Chrysostom's idea of consecration (see p. 348). Current Roman thought, though of course not denying the doctrine of transubstantiation, veers away from spatial considerations to conceptions of action. The Eucharist is regarded primarily as a "re-presentation" of our Lord and of his actions in the Upper Room. Protestant scholars in general, with renewed appreciations of the doctrine of the Real Presence, and with fuller knowledge of the thought and liturgical expressions of the early church than they possessed a half-century ago, are emphasizing Christ's living Presence in the Supper as Creator Lord.

Confusion at this point results from the ambiguity which surrounds the term "The Word." This expression occurs frequently not only in theological discussions, but also in the liturgy and in our hymnody. We understand John's reference to "the Word" (the Logos) as meaning our Lord Jesus Christ ("In the beginning was the Word"). In another sense the "Word of God" means the Holy Scriptures. Even this is capable of several interpretations. Literalists think particularly of the actual words of the Bible, though no one can be certain that every word as we have it in the Scriptures today is a precise rendering of the words originally uttered or written in Hebrew, Aramaic, or Greek. Lutheran understanding of these matters regards the Word of God in a broader sense as meaning the gracious thought and will of God, his loving purpose for man—in other words, the gospel as revealed by our Lord who was and is the Word of God himself.

Medieval and modern Roman thought has concerned itself with words (the Verba) rather than with the Word. The early church thought much about the Logos and, in the East at least, about the work of the Holy Spirit. The author's colleague, Professor George R. Seltzer of the Philadelphia Seminary, reminds us that Augustine, in his famous statement, "the Word is added to the element and it becomes a sacrament," said "accedit *Verbum*" (singular) and not "verba" (plural). It is He, the Word, working in the church by the Holy Spirit, who makes himself known in the breaking of bread.

We have previously (pp. 336-38) referred to passages in Justin Martyr, Irenaeus, Clement of Alexandria, Origen, and Athanasius, as well as to the Liturgy of Serapion (*c.* 350 A.D.) which acknowledges the operative power of the Word, in the sense of the Logos, in the Lord's Supper. We recall particularly the unusual invocation of Serapion: "O God of truth, let the holy Word come upon this bread, that this bread may become the body of the Word, etc." This conception, together with ever increasing appreciation of the function of the Holy Spirit, colored the thought of the entire early church and the Eastern church, while the church in the West progressively limited and hardened its ideas of consecration by placing all emphasis upon a single action: the recitation of the Words of Institution as a formula repeated by a priest whose ordination conferred upon him the duty and the sole privilege of invoking divine power in a transubstantiation of the elements.

Luther's powerful conception of the Word of God as the gospel, his mighty emphasis upon justification by faith and not by works, and his controversies with Zwingli and the Anabaptists carried his inherited ideas of the importance of the Verba to new heights and to new meanings as he rejected the doctrine of transubstantiation but proclaimed the fact not only of the Real Presence of Christ in the Sacrament but also the reality of the true Body and Blood "in, with and under" the bread and wine. But in this connection we may well note the comment of Philip S. Watson, a Methodist theologian of Cambridge, England, who came to a keen understanding of Luther's theology during the course of his studies in Sweden. In his recent book, *The Concept of Grace,* he says: "It is . . . through the Word alone that the sacraments have their significance. . . . Here, however, it is important to remember that the Word, as Luther understands it, is always ultimately the Word that became flesh in the person of Jesus Christ . . . . It is this same Word that forms the essential content of the sacraments. If the Word 'added to the element' is primarily the dominical 'words of institution', it must not be forgotten that these are spoken by the incarnate Word, and are a concentrated expression of the Good News of God that He brings to us in His own person."[26]

Luther's elimination, in his liturgical orders, of all surrounding prayer forms left the Verba standing alone in stark, if strong, simplicity. It

[26]Philip S. Watson, *The Concept of Grace* (Philadelphia: Muhlenberg, 1959), 92-93.

intensified the medieval conception of consecration by a fixed formula, and in a single moment of time, even though the idea of a change of substance was vigorously rejected.

In the restoration of a form of Eucharistic Prayer in the Common Liturgy, we return to the earlier pre-Roman conception, according to which the church sets apart the elements in a blessing or thanksgiving which includes four actions in imitation of our Lord's actions at the Last Supper. These actions are: taking, blessing (or giving thanks), breaking, and distributing. This is indeed all one action. Its comprehensive character helps free us from the erroneous conception of consecration limited to a moment and effected by a formula.

Our Prayer of Thanksgiving follows the order and in all its parts the thought of the prayers in the early Christian church. We address our prayer to the Father. We recognize the Word (the Logos) who is present in the Sacrament, according to his promise, as Creator Lord. We invoke his blessing (consecration), and that of the Holy Spirit, upon ourselves and upon the elements of bread and wine. We conclude our prayer with an ascription of honor and glory to the same three Persons of the Holy Trinity.

The Prayer of Thanksgiving in the Common Liturgy is a pure text which follows the order of the Creed. It is based throughout upon historic models in the early church and is entirely pre-Roman in character. In addition to its historic and devotional features, this prayer makes manifest, as no other single part of the Service does, the real meaning of the Sacrament we celebrate and its relation to the Last Supper and to the entire redemptive work of Christ. It should be understood as a prayer of thanksgiving and an act of self-dedication and not as a prayer of consecration of the elements in the usual sense. Our Lord has consecrated and ever will consecrate them. Our part is faith, obedience, thanksgiving.

An invocation of the Holy Spirit in this connection refers specifically to the worshipers. The presence of the Holy Spirit in our hearts assures a worthy reception of the Sacrament and a renewed consecration of ourselves to God's will and service. References to the elements must be carefully phrased or they will cloud the issue. But we certainly may ask divine blessing on them, quite as in our "grace before meat" we seek a blessing on our daily food.

CHAPTER XX

THE PRAYER OF THANKSGIVING:
The Words of Institution;
The Invocation of the Holy Spirit

¶ *Then may the Congregation kneel.*

¶ *The Minister standing before the Altar, and facing it, shall say the Prayer of Thanksgiving.*

THE PRAYER OF THANKSGIVING

HOLY art thou, Almighty and Merciful God. Holy art thou,[a] and great is the Majesty of thy glory.[b]

Thou didst so love the world as to give thine only-begotten Son, that whosoever believeth in him might not perish, but have everlasting life;[c] Who, having come into the world to fulfill for us thy holy will[b] and to accomplish all things for our salvation,[d] IN THE NIGHT IN WHICH HE WAS BETRAYED,[a] TOOK BREAD; AND WHEN HE HAD GIVEN THANKS, HE BRAKE IT AND GAVE IT TO HIS DISCIPLES, SAYING, TAKE, EAT: THIS IS MY BODY, WHICH IS GIVEN FOR YOU; THIS DO IN REMEMBRANCE OF ME.

(*a*) *Here he shall take the* BREAD *in his hand.*

AFTER THE SAME MANNER, HE[b] TOOK THE CUP, WHEN HE HAD SUPPED, AND, WHEN HE HAD GIVEN THANKS, HE GAVE IT TO THEM, SAYING, DRINK YE ALL OF IT; THIS CUP IS THE NEW TESTAMENT IN MY BLOOD, WHICH IS SHED FOR YOU, AND FOR MANY, FOR THE REMISSION OF SINS; THIS DO, AS OFT AS YE DRINK IT, IN REMEMBRANCE OF ME.[e]

(*b*) *Here he shall take the* CUP *in his hand.*

Remembering, therefore, his salutary precept, his life-giving Passion and Death, his glorious Resurrection and Ascension and the promise of his coming again,[f] we give thanks to thee, O Lord God Almighty, not as we ought, but as we are able;[g] and we beseech thee mercifully to accept our praise and thanksgiving, and with thy Word and Holy Spirit to bless us, thy servants, and these thine own gifts of bread and wine,[h] so that we and all who partake thereof may be filled with heavenly benediction and grace,[i] and, receiving the remission of sins, be sanctified in soul and body,[f] and have our portion with all thy saints.[j]

And unto thee, O God, Father, Son, and Holy Spirit, be all honor and glory in thy holy Church, world without end. Amen.

¶ *Then shall the Minister sing or say:*

Our Father, who art in heaven, Hallowed be thy Name, Thy kingdom come, Thy will be done, on earth as it is in heaven. Give us this day our daily bread; And forgive us our trespasses, as we forgive those who trespass against us; And lead us not into temptation, But deliver from evil.

¶ *The Congregation shall sing or say:*

For thine is the kingdom, and the power, and the glory, for ever and ever. Amen.[1]

Two items in the Prayer of Thanksgiving call for special comment —the Words of Institution (Verba) and the invocation of the Holy Spirit (epiclesis). The importance of this particular project may justify some repetition of material.

Bishop Frere in his important work *The Anaphora* traces the Jewish antecedents of the occurrences in the Upper Room, particularly certain similarities between the Kiddush of the Passover and the institution of the Lord's Supper. The later Christian sacrifice of thanksgiving and re-membrance or memorial had its foreshadowing in the ancient Jewish custom of "offering a sacrifice in thankful remembrance of any great event or mercy—a specialized form of Peace-Offering." The blessings invoked had a parallel in the Jewish blessings said over the cup and the bread. These, it should be remembered, were blessings of God and not of any creature, yet "said over the things."[2]

The triple form of Christian worship began to build up early in formulas, creeds, and prayers. Clement and Ignatius speak of the offer-ing of the gifts, the sacrifices of thanksgiving, prayers of intercession, and commemorations. Justin Martyr, speaking for Palestine, Asia, and Rome, says: "Over all our offerings we bless the Maker of all things through his Son Jesus Christ and through the Holy Ghost." Cyprian,

---

[1] Portions of this prayer appear again and again in variant forms in many liturgies, ancient and modern. The reference marks a-j indicate the earliest known appearance of a passage:

    a. Liturgy of St. James, Jerusalem
    b. Liturgy of St. John Chrysostom
    c. John 3:16
    d. John 19:28
    e. Narrative of the institution, the Common Service
    f. St. James, Jerusalem, amplified by Scottish Presbyterian *Book of Common Order* (1940)
    g. *Apostolic Constitutions*
    h. First Prayer Book of Edward VI (1549)
    i. Roman missal
    j. Liturgy of St. Basil

[2] For more recent discussion of the nature of the Last Supper, see Lietzmann, *Mass and Lord's Supper;* Jeremias, *The Eucharistic Words of Jesus;* and Cullmann, *Early Christian Worship.*

357

bishop of Carthage (A.D. 248-58), speaking for the Latin world, inaugurated a trend of thought which centered upon consecration rather than upon remembrance and thanksgiving, upon the recitation of the Dominical Words rather than upon a form of prayer. The Syrian *Didascalia* of the middle of the third century testifies to the developing understanding of the work of the Holy Spirit. "Prayer is heard by the Holy Spirit, and the Eucharist through the Holy Spirit is accepted and sanctified."

We have already referred to the discovery and publication (in 1900) of the *Apostolic Tradition* of the Graeco-Roman theologian Hippolytus (martyred A.D. 235). This work gives us the earliest known instance of an invocation of the Holy Spirit in an anaphora: "And we pray thee to send thy Holy Spirit on the oblation of holy Church." This represents a use in Rome before the middle of the third century, when Greek was still the language of worship there as in the East and in much of the Mediterranean area. Among other interesting features is the fact that the invocation of the Holy Spirit is upon the gifts (the oblation of holy church) and not upon the worshipers. Also the note of atonement and redemption is strongly stressed for the first time. Important derivatives of the Hippolytan text later appeared in Latin, Greek *(Apostolic Constitutions),* Syriac, and Ethiopic anaphoras.[3]

It was not long before many and varying anaphoras appeared in the plethora of "Eastern liturgies" which soon developed, and which F. E. Brightman (in *Liturgies Eastern and Western*) has classified as Syrian, Egyptian, Persian, and Byzantine. Most of these adhered to a common pattern with variety in details. They all included, in some form, a recitation of the Verba and an invocation of the Holy Spirit.

There is evidence that an *anaphora* in Greek, and in Latin translation, was current in Rome in the second half of the fourth century. About that time, however, the invocation disappeared entirely from the Roman Rite, at least locally, as theological thinking in the West attached more and more importance to consecration by recitation of the Dominical Words rather than by invocation of the Holy Spirit. Augustine, bishop of Hippo in Africa A.D. 395-430, regarded the divine Word, as originally spoken, as still operative and effective, and he simply attaches the consecration to the "Word of God." However he also writes: "the Sacrament is not sanctified but by the invisible operation of the Holy Spirit." From other sources we can be certain that an invocation of the Holy

[3] Text and comment in Walter H. Frere, *The Anaphora* (London: S.P.C.K., 1938); Easton, *The Apostolic Tradition of Hippolytus;* E. G. Cuthbert and F. Atchley, *On the Epiclesis of the Eucharistic Liturgy* (London: Oxford, 1935); Dix, *The Treatise on the Apostolic Tradition of St. Hippolytus.*

Spirit was still part of the anaphora of the African Rite at that time. The church in Rome decided against the freer Gallican system of variety in lessons, psalms, prayers, etc. It desired a stable type of service, particularly in the central part of the rite. This decision finally became stereotyped in the inflexible though mixed Roman Canon. By its elimination of the trinitarian feature of the invocation of the Holy Spirit, the Canon left Rome standing alone and apart from the practice of all other churches in the Christian world.

The Eastern liturgies retained both the Verba and the Epiclesis in one great prayer. The Gallican liturgies, from Milan in northern Italy to Toledo in Spain, frequently gave a series of variable and closely linked prayers instead of the simple continuous forms of the Greek anaphoras or the more terse fixed form of the Rome Canon. Some of them contain vestiges or suggestions of consecration prayers of the Eastern rather than the Roman type. The liturgical services of Milan continued to show Eastern and Gallican influences until the middle of the seventh century, when they yielded much to Roman influence. In the West, Isidore of Seville, speaking for the Spanish Rite, stoutly defends the balanced view which recognized the Dominical Words as essential but also required the trinitarian form with its recognition of the Holy Spirit. In France also, well into the ninth century, theologians continued to protest against surrender to the Roman view of the Word which sought to banish the Holy Spirit from the Latin Canon.

THE WORDS OF INSTITUTION

OUR LORD JESUS CHRIST, IN THE NIGHT IN WHICH HE WAS BETRAYED,[a] TOOK BREAD; AND, WHEN HE HAD GIVEN THANKS, HE BRAKE IT AND GAVE IT TO HIS DISCIPLES, SAYING, TAKE, EAT; THIS IS MY BODY, WHICH IS GIVEN FOR YOU; THIS DO IN REMEMBRANCE OF ME.

([a]) *Here he shall take the* BREAD *in his hand.*

AFTER THE SAME MANNER ALSO, HE[b] TOOK THE CUP, WHEN HE HAD SUPPED, AND, WHEN HE HAD GIVEN THANKS, HE GAVE IT TO THEM, SAYING, DRINK YE ALL OF IT; THIS CUP IS THE NEW TESTAMENT IN MY BLOOD, WHICH IS SHED FOR YOU, AND FOR MANY, FOR THE REMISSION OF SINS; THIS DO, AS OFT AS YE DRINK IT, IN REMEMBRANCE OF ME.

([b]) *Here he shall take the* CUP *in his hand.*

As the record of our Lord's original institution, these words, whether alone or within the context of a eucharistic prayer, give objective validity to every subsequent administration, and set apart the earthly elements for their holy use. They are found in all liturgies, though not precisely in the same form. The text is a harmony of the four New Testament accounts in Matthew 26, Mark 14, Luke 22, and I Corinthians 11. Many early liturgies omit the phrases, "this do . . . in remembrance of me." Luther in his Latin Service (1523), omitted several medieval embellishments and added the scriptural phrase, "which is given for you" (also in the Mozarabic), after the words "This is my Body." The English *Book of Common Prayer* followed the Lutheran form as found in Brandenburg-Nuremberg (1533), reproduced in the Nuremberg catechism of Justus Jonas and incorporated in translation in Cranmer's catechism of 1548.[4]

The use of the Verba at this point is more than the recital of a historic event or the citation of authority to engage in this holy proceeding. It is a solemn, corporate act of prayer, an exalted liturgical celebration, in which the worshiping congregation apprehends and holds aloft the divine promises, claims the divine warrant and invokes the divine blessing. It becomes a vivid and exalted rite as the minister not only repeats our Lord's own words, but in a measure imitates his actions. In the scriptural narrative the actions are given importance equal to that of the words.

Dr. Horn says: "The Words of Institution are addressed to God. They are the warrant of the act in which we are engaged, and of the faith nourished by the Sacrament, and they ask and receive from the risen Lord the grace by which the bread and wine become, to those who receive them, His Body and His Blood."[5]

The actual consecration is to be found in the original institution of our Lord. The actual reception of the elements, which also is implied in the command "This do," completes the transaction. As John Gerhard says: "The consecration consists not merely in the repetition of those four words, 'This is my body,' but in that we do what Christ did, i.e., that we take, bless, distribute, and eat the bread according to Christ's institution and commandments." The consecration is completed by the administration, apart from which there is no sacrament.

The Verba, whether used alone or in the Prayer of Thanksgiving, are to be read, or intoned, clearly and with solemn dignity (see *Choral Service Book*, p. xxviii). At the words "took bread" the minister lifts the paten (or ciborium) with the bread in both hands and holds it before him. At the words "this is my Body," he may raise the paten to shoulder height, a "moderate elevation" enjoined by Luther. Similarly

---

[4] For discussion of this see Parsons and Jones, *The American Prayer Book*, pp. 208ff, and Gasquet and Bishop, *Edward VI and the Book of Common Prayer*, p. 207.
[5] *Lutheran Cyclopedia*, p. 282.

at the words "he took the cup" the minister takes the filled chalice in both hands and holds it before him. At the words "The New Testament in my Blood" he may raise the chalice to shoulder height.

Even if individual cups are used by the congregation, the minister uses the common chalice in the consecration and later in the administration, pouring the wine from the chalice into the individual cups in the hands of the communicants. In order to permit this the chalice must be provided with a pouring lip. Trays of individual cups should not be placed on the altar or used in connection with the recitation of the Words of Institution.

In the Anglican church the "manual acts" include, in addition to the taking of the paten and the chalice into the hands, the fraction or breaking of the bread, and the laying of the minister's hands upon all the bread and upon every vessel in which there is any wine to be consecrated. The latter action takes the place of signings with the cross in the Roman Rite. Luther rejected the sign of the cross in connection with the consecration and no church order of the sixteenth century except Münzer (Alstädt [1523]) expressly indicates it at this place, though traditional usage probably continued it in many places. John Gerhard reintroduced it and Coburg (1626) gives it (cf. Rietschel, *Lehrbuch der Liturgik,* I, 436). Modern German and Swedish liturgies have it universally. In spite of this general consensus in Lutheran services in other than the English language today, the propriety of using the sign of the cross at this point is to be questioned. It can only be justified upon the broadest possible grounds as an expression of the general idea of blessing which might be made elsewhere in the service, but which is liable to be completely misinterpreted at this precise point.

Some authorities (Theodore Harnack, Höfling, H. E. Jacobs, E. T. Horn) reject the so-called *Nach Konsekration,* or repetition of the Words of Institution in setting apart additional elements which has been a Lutheran custom, and the rubrics of the Common Liturgy make no provision for this action. If the Verba are said as a declaration there is no sense in repeating them. If they be taken as a prayer, the repetition would be superfluous, just as no housefather would think of repeating the grace every time a new dish was brought to the table.

THE INVOCATION OF THE HOLY SPIRIT

The sixteenth-century Reformers on the continent were more interested in purifying the existing Roman Rite of false doctrine and superstitious practices than in constructing new formulas. None of them had the advantages we have today by way of discoveries and study of early

Christian liturgies. None of them could have known of the great body of liturgical discussions by early scholars which has only recently become available. They had a practical problem to face, and they had to make prompt decisions. Luther, as we have seen, eliminated all the Offertory prayers and the entire Canon except the simple recitation of the Words of Institution. Others attempted simplifications and adaptations, none of which gained general acceptance.

Luther and Cranmer were at one in recapturing the early "prayers of the faithful," which had lingered in somewhat unliturgical form in the vernacular prone. Luther expanded the petitions of the Lord's Prayer and thus opened the way for a generally accepted type of general prayer (Prayer of the Church). Cranmer provided a prayer "for the whole estate of christes churche" to follow the Sanctus. Luther, under the prevailing scholastic and Roman view that consecration was effected solely by the recitation of the Verba, and possessed by his dynamic conception of the supremacy of the Word (whether this meant the whole gospel, the Holy Scriptures, or the second person of the Trinity), cut out everything except the Dominical Words. Cranmer also, under the weight of scholastic tradition, placed the invocation, which he reintroduced, before the recital of the Verba, thus destroying the trinitarian and creedal form of the prayer. He stressed the note of thanksgiving, which Luther and his followers failed to do. Cranmer also emphasized the "offering of ourselves, our souls and bodies," in union with the holy sacrifice, which had been so strongly emphasized by Augustine.

The Second Prayer Book of 1552 made radical changes. It omitted the anamnesis and the invocation entirely and transferred the Lord's Prayer to a point after the Communion. It remained for the leadership of the Scottish (Anglican) church in 1637 to recover and revise the best features of the first Prayer Book of 1549, and to restore the invocation to its original place after the recital of the Verba. All of which served as a model for the later Anglican "prayers of consecration" in the Prayer Books of the American Episcopal church and the Church of South Africa. The Proposed Book of 1928 also restored the main features of the first Prayer Book and placed the invocation of the Holy Spirit after the anamnesis and Verba, thus restoring the creedal form of the prayer.

We have already referred to the admirable prayer of thanksgiving (with an epiclesis) of the *Book of Common Order* of the Church of Scotland (1940), which is what we might expect from the enlarging group of able liturgical scholars in that communion. Also we should call attention to the equally fine prayer in the *Book of Common Wor-*

ship of the Presbyterian Church in the United States of America (1946).

The location of the Epiclesis within the structure of the Prayer of Thanksgiving—whether the invocation of the Holy Spirit should be before or after the Words of Institution—remains a point of discussion, in both Anglican and Lutheran communions. The Common Liturgy gives the recital of the Verba first, and in the closing sentences of the prayer beseeches God "with the Word and Holy Spirit, to bless us, thy servants, and these thine own gifts of bread and wine." This is in line with the universal non-Roman tradition. A relatively few scholars, unable to free themselves from the domination of scholastic theology and the continuing force of medieval tradition, which asserts that consecration is effected at a precise moment by the recital of the Verba, and by this alone, insist that the Epiclesis should precede the Verba. We rejoice that the Common Liturgy has rejected this mechanistic view, has recovered the ancient and universal prayer of thanksgiving with its invocation of the Holy Spirit, and that it has given the invocation its proper location in the prayer. We believe that in the original Words of Institution we have an unending consecration. We may also believe that, in the words of Paul, "the Spirit giveth life."

The minister does not turn to the people when he says, "Let us pray," before the Prayer of Thanksgiving, but continues to face the altar. The prayer is read from the service book on the missal stand. The minister's hands are kept in the posture of prayer and free for the manual acts later required by the rubrics.

CHAPTER XXI

THE LORD'S PRAYER; THE PAX;
THE AGNUS DEI; THE DISTRIBUTION

THE LORD'S PRAYER

¶ *Then shall the Minister sing or say:*

Our Father, who are in heaven, Hallowed be thy Name, Thy kingdom come, Thy will be done, on earth as it is in heaven; Give us this day our daily bread; And forgive us our trespasses, as we forgive those who trespass against us; And lead us not into temptation, But deliver us from evil.

¶ *The Congregation shall sing or say:*

For thine is the kingdom, and the power, and the glory, for ever and ever. Amen.

The Lord's Prayer is found in every liturgy in close connection with the Holy Communion. It is not in any sense consecratory of the elements. It would be improper so far as the prayer itself is concerned, and inadequate so far as consecration is concerned. The fourth petition cannot be spiritualized and made to refer to the Sacrament. It is the distinctive prayer of the children of God, who, conscious of their fellowship and unity as brethren and of their part in the communion of saints, are about to come to the table of the Lord. As such we may think of it as consecratory of believers. Its proper place, as in the Common Liturgy, is immediately before the distribution.

In the early church only believers were permitted to use the Lord's Prayer, its use being confined to the Mass of the Faithful. The medieval liturgical introduction, preserved in many early Lutheran orders, indicates its real character: "Admonished by thy saving precepts and instructed by thy divine ordinance, we make bold to say, 'Our Father,'" etc. It is definitely a prayer of sonship and of brotherhood, and in this particular place may be thought of as a prayer of humble access. In the Greek liturgies it concludes with the doxology. The Roman Mass gives the seventh petition as a response.

Our rubrics, following the Roman use, direct the minister to say the prayer alone. This conforms to a general principle which obtains throughout the liturgy, according to which the minister alone voices the prayer of the people (as in the collects, Prayer of the Church, etc.), the congregation responding at the end. It also expresses the classic severity and restraint of the Roman tradition which invests parts of the liturgy with high solemnity by giving them to the priest alone. The Eastern, Gallican, and Anglican churches have the congregation unite in the Lord's Prayer. A few Lutheran orders in southern Germany directed the congregation to sing it in German. Congregational participation is less formal, and it avoids the possibility of erroneous conceptions concerning the Lord's Prayer at this place; as though it were in any sense consecratory of the elements.[1]

The Common Liturgy has followed the German Lutheran orders (Mark Brandenburg, Herzogin Elizabeth, Pomerania, Hoya, Saxony) which assign the liturgical doxology (fourth century) and the Amen— "For thine is the kingdom," etc.—to the congregation as a fitting corporate conclusion to the petitions of the prayer.

Luther in his German Mass provided a musical setting for the minister to chant both the Lord's Prayer and the Verba. This became a distinctive use of the Lutheran church in all lands. Musical settings are given in practically all the sixteenth-century orders. In many congregations today, even though the rest of the Service is not chanted by the minister, it is still the custom for him solemnly to intone the Words of Institution and the Lord's Prayer. Whether intoned or recited, these parts of the Service must be given with the greatest clearness, reverence, and dignity.

✠

The organist may accompany the minister softly if he intones the prayer, as an aid in maintaining the pitch. If these parts are said and not intoned, no organ accompaniment should cloud their solemn recitation.

THE PAX

¶ Then shall the Minister turn to the Congregation and sing or say:

The Peace of the Lord be with you alway.

¶ The Congregation shall sing or say:

And with thy spirit.

---

[1] See F. E. Brightman, *Liturgies Eastern and Western* (London: Oxford, 1896), for examples. The Mozarabic Liturgy has an impressive use according to which the celebrant says the prayer alone, but the people respond "Amen" after each clause.

This is a short benediction which is the remaining fragment in the liturgy of two observances of the early church: a solemn blessing of the people by the celebrant immediately before the communion, according to the Eastern, Mozarabic, and Gallican liturgies; and the Kiss of Peace, which as a mark of fellowship and unity is found in all early liturgies at the beginning of the Mass of the Faithful.

As retained in the Roman services, the Pax is one of the private prayers of the priest which accompany such ritual actions as the Offertory, the commixture, the ablutions, etc. In this case, the Pax is connected with the first part of the fraction, or ceremonial breaking of the bread which immediately follows the silent recitation of the Lord's Prayer.

Luther appreciated this brief blessing very highly. He lifted it out of relative obscurity and gave it something more than its original dignity and significance as a blessing of the people, and, indeed, a form of absolution. In his *Formula Missae* (1523), he says: "It (the Pax) is the voice of the gospel announcing the forgiveness of sins, the only and most worthy preparation for the Lord's table . . . hence I wish it announced with face toward the people as the bishops were accustomed to do." Strangely enough Luther omitted the Pax from his German Mass (1526). Many church orders directed the Pax to be sung (intoned) by the minister; others ordered it to be said. Some placed it as we have it, before the Agnus; others after the Agnus; and Brandenburg (1540) gave it after the distribution.

Brilioth says that Luther's interpretation involved a "violent importation of his favorite idea into a phrase which was originally intended to convey a different meaning." This is a true observation. It is probable that the emptiness of the Roman form at this place invited it, and Luther's insight and directness enabled him to relate this brief sentence in a living way to the deepest thought of the liturgy at this moment. The response to the Pax has been variously given. The Joint Commission followed the Latin Rite and the early Lutheran orders (Erfurt [1526], Prussia [1525], Riga [1530], Reformation of Cologne [1544]) in giving the usual response after the Salutation: "And with thy spirit."

We may well note the significance of the Pax in relation to the Prayer of Thanksgiving which precedes and the Agnus Dei which follows it. Dr. Parsch suggests that, in the Gallican churches at least, the Pax may have been intended as "a blessing and a dismissal of those who did not receive the Communion."[2] The highest meaning that can be attached to it in the Roman Liturgy is that of an exhortation to a mutual act of

---

[2] Parsch, *The Liturgy of the Mass,* p. 294.

forgiveness and charity among the faithful, though the latter are not likely to understand this esoteric thought. We may follow Luther and regard the Pax as a blessing, a sacramental announcement of the gift of peace promised by our Lord to his disciples before his death (John 20:19-21).

The Pax originally introduced the blessing of the communicants which followed the dismissal of the catechumens. This blessing dropped from the Roman Rite, but survived for centuries in the Gallican. In the Roman use the Pax eventually attracted to itself the Kiss of Peace, which anciently had been given earlier in the Service. In his *Apologia* (*c.* 150), Justin Martyr wrote that before the Offertory "We salute one another with a kiss, when we have concluded the prayers." Coming before the offertory procession, this expression of fellowship and unity recalled our Lord's admonition: "If therefore thou offer thy gift at the altar and there remember," etc. (Matt. 5:23). Augustine in the fourth century records that in the African church the Kiss of Peace was given after the Lord's Prayer and before the Communion: "After that [the Lord's Prayer] is said 'Peace be with you,' and Christians kiss one another in a holy kiss which is the sign of peace."

The Kiss of Peace is referred to in the New Testament by Paul no less than four times (Rom. 16:16, I Cor. 16:20, II Cor. 13:12, I Thess. 5:26), and by Peter once (I Pet. 5:14). During the next centuries there are constant references to it. In the early church the men sat on one side of the church and the women on the other, and this familiar oriental greeting, cheek to cheek, was given regularly in the assemblies of the faithful as a mark of Christian fellowship and unity, the men saluting the men and the women the women. The practice continued in many parts until the thirteenth century, when a substitute was introduced in the form of a "Pax-board" or *osculatorium*. The celebrant kissed the deacon at this point in the Mass and gave him a little tablet or other object to be kissed by him and passed to others in turn.

In the Armenian Church the deacon still says, "Salute one another with a holy kiss" and the people bow to one another saying, "Christ is in the midst of us." In the Roman use the only survival of the Kiss of Peace is in high mass, when the celebrant ceremonially salutes the deacon. The brief text of the Pax, however, is still said by the priest in every mass in connection with the fraction. Holding the host with both hands over the chalice, the priest breaks it in half, places one portion on the paten, and after breaking a particle from the other half, unites the larger fragments again on the paten. Then, taking the smallest particle in his right hand, he makes the sign of the cross three times over the chalice, saying aloud: *Pax Domini sit semper vobiscum.* After the acolyte has responded with the words: *Et cum spiritu tuo,* the priest drops the particle of the host into the chalice and silently recites another prayer.

The Anglican Prayer Book of 1549 retained the Pax, but it was omitted in the Second Book of 1552. It has been restored again in the English Proposed Book of 1928 and in the Scottish Liturgy of 1929, which has added the exhortation, "Brethren, let us love one another, for love is of God." The duty symbolized by the ancient Kiss of Peace and the Pax as related to it is emphasized in the Anglican Liturgy by the words in the priest's invitation to communicants: "Ye who . . . are in love and charity with your neighbors . . . draw near," etc.

✠

The minister turns from the altar by his right and faces the congregation as he says the Pax.

✠

The response should be sung softly. There should be no delay at this point. The organist should proceed at once to the Agnus Dei. The choir should begin with prompt attack.

¶ Then, the Congregation standing, shall be sung or said the Agnus Dei.

THE AGNUS DEI

O Christ, thou Lamb of God, that takest away the sin of the world, have mercy upon us.

O Christ, thou Lamb of God, that takest away the sin of the world, have mercy upon us.

O Christ, thou Lamb of God, that takest away the sin of the world, grant us thy peace. Amen.

This beautiful communion hymn was introduced into the liturgy by Pope Sergius I, about A.D. 700, as a eucharistic devotion sung during the fraction. This was in line with the usual liturgical procedure which introduced chant forms to occupy the time required by ceremonies performed by the priest at the altar.

The scriptural source of the Agnus is John 1:29, "Behold the Lamb of God which taketh away the sin of the world," which harks back to the prophetic utterance in Isaiah 53. We also recall more than thirty references to Christ as a lamb in John's Revelation.

Absent from the earliest Christian services and from the Mozarabic and other Gallican liturgies as well, the Agnus may be thought of as part of the Roman emphasis upon moral duty, evident also in the Confiteor, the Offertory prayers, the Lavabo psalm, and other parts of the Roman Mass. This view is supported by similarities in ceremonial between the Confiteor and the Agnus. In reciting the former, the priest smites his breast at the words *mea culpa;* in the Agnus Dei he also strikes his breast at the words *miserere nobis* and at the final *dona nobis pacem.*

In the Lutheran conception the Agnus is closely connected with the distribution and has a strongly sacramental interpretation. It is not so much a renewed confession of sin as a means of spiritual communion with the Christ who is directly addressed, not the Father. The text contains a threefold confession of Christ's vicarious atonement in fulfilment of prophecy (Isa. 53:7, 12; I Pet. 1:19-20), and a prayer for the mercy and peace which his death on the cross has won for us (Eph. 2:13-17). Its address reverently recognizes Christ as the Savior of the world. Its petitions embrace all the blessings which his sacrificial death has procured for believers. The reference to Christ as a lamb recalls to the worshiper not only the sacrificial character of his death, but also his freedom from guilt, his patience and gentleness, and his voluntary submission to sufferings and death. Thus, reception of the elements in the Holy Communion is intimately connected with our Lord's sacrifice on Calvary and its fruits, which are forgiveness and peace.

The Agnus Dei is found in practically all the Lutheran church orders. Erfurt (1525) and Bayreuth (1755) place it between the Verba and the Lord's Prayer. Brunswick (1528), Hamburg (1529), Wittenberg (1533), and Oldenburg (1573) give it after the distribution and before the thanksgiving collect. Generally, however, it had its historic place, though frequently it was drawn back and made a hymn to be sung during the distribution. This weakened its position and value as a distinctive part of the liturgy as such. Occasionally it was sung in versified form in the arrangement of Decius' *"O Lamm Gottes unschuldig."*

The Anglican Prayer Book of 1549 followed Lutheran precedent and appointed the Agnus Dei to be sung "in the communion time." The Second Book (1552) omitted it entirely. A proposal to restore it to the English Book in 1661 was not adopted, and a similar effort in 1928 was narrowly defeated. It has been restored in the Scottish Liturgy of 1929, but not in the American Book of 1928. It is frequently sung in Anglican services by choirs, however, under the broad interpretation of its text as a "hymn," which was the ruling of Archbishop Benson in the famous Lincoln judgment of 1887.

In the earliest times, when one loaf was consecrated and all received a portion, a "breaking of the bread" was necessary, and this became one of the names for the Holy Communion (Acts 2:42; 20:7). Even in medieval times the hosts for the laity were of large size, and time was required for breaking these before distribution. Later, with the decline of communicants, the fraction became chiefly a symbolical and ceremonial act, and was regarded as one of the climaxes of the liturgy.

Durandus and other symbolists regarded the breaking of the consecrated host as signifying the passion and death of our Lord at the hands of his executioners. The Eastern churches frequently speak of the host as "the Lamb," and in the Eastern liturgies (as well as in the Mozarabic), the fraction and disposition of the broken parts of the host are a complicated action.

Sergius was a Syrian by birth, and the Greek Liturgy may have influenced him in his choice of a liturgical text at this point in the Service. In the Liturgy of Antioch the celebrant uses the Baptist's greeting (John 1:29).

In the Liturgy of St. John Chrysostom the priest divides the host into four parts and says, "The Lamb of God, the Son of the Father, is broken and divided, broken and yet not divided, eaten at all times and yet not consumed, but sanctifying all those who receive him."

Anciently the Agnus Dei was repeated as long as the fraction lasted. By the twelfth century the Roman ceremony of the fraction was simplified and the repetitions were limited to three. Since the early twelfth century the Agnus Dei has had its present threefold form, with "Grant us thy peace" at the end. Pope Innocent III informs us that this petition came into the liturgy because of the wars and general disorder of that time.

The Agnus, like the Kyrie, was often farsed in the Middle Ages, additions called "tropes" being interpolated within the text itself. Following is an interesting example given by Cardinal Bona:

> Agnus Dei, qui tollis peccata amundi,
> Crimina tollis, aspera mollis, Agnus honoris,
>
> Miserere nobis.
>
> Agnus Dei, qui tollis peccata mundi,
> Vulnera sanas, ardua planas, Agnus amoris,
>
> Miserere nobis.
>
> Agnus Dei, qui tollis peccata mundi,
> Sordida mundas, cuncta foecundas, Agnus odoris,
>
> Dona nobis pacem.

The text of the Agnus bears a close resemblance to the second part of the earlier Christian hymn, the Gloria in Excelsis. It is one of the five texts of the musical masses of Mozart, Hadyn, Gounod, and other composers (Kyrie, Gloria, Creed, Sanctus, and Agnus). It also concludes the Litany.

Fortescue calls attention to the fact that "Agnus" as a vocative is unusual, and suggests that in all probability this form was employed to reproduce exactly the original text of Scripture. The word "Christ" at the beginning of each of the three parts is a unique Lutheran interpolation, found nowhere else. Its first appearance in Lutheran use was in the Brunswick Order (1528).

It is difficult to understand the strength of the opposition to the Agnus in the Anglican communion. It has been said that the effort to make the Prayer Book of 1552 as different as possible from that of 1549 swept the Agnus out, along with the Introit, Gradual, and many minor choral features of the historic Service. Scudamore thinks it was done "to promote a habit of communicating among the clerks by freeing them from the necessity of singing the Agnus during the Administration."[3] Parsons and Jones suggest that the transfer of the Gloria in Excelsis from before to after the communion may have made Cranmer willing to drop the Agnus, since the latter was practically found in the Gloria.[4] The real reason probably was the conviction of ultra-Protestant groups that the use of the Agnus at this particular moment in the liturgy might foster erroneous notions concerning the adoration of the

---

[3] *Notitia Eucharistica*, p. 757.
[4] *The American Prayer Book*, p. 190.

host. Four centuries of experience have shown this fear to be groundless, in the Lutheran communion at least, where the thought is of confessing and adoring the Christ of the Gospels as truly present not only in the bread and the wine or in the moment of consecration, but in the entire service of worship and communion.

The first melody in the *Service Book* originated in one of the earliest church orders of the Reformation period (Brunswick [1528]), where it is set to the German text, *"Christe du Lamm Gottes."* It unquestionably derives from an earlier plain-song source. The second melody dates from the thirteenth century in Scandinavia. Traditionally in the plain-song period the Agnus and the invariable parts of the liturgy in general were sung to simple melodies. The Creed, for example, was sung in all countries to a single well-known melody down to the time of the Reformation. This contrasted sharply with the high development given the melodies of the Introit, the Gradual, and other propers of the liturgy. The text of these parts changed with the days and festivals, and the musical settings frequently taxed the vocal and artistic powers of skilled singers.

✠

As an act of adoration and petition, the Agnus Dei is a sacrificial element, and the minister faces the altar while it is sung. It should be accorded its full liturgical value. The minister, the choir, and the congregation should give it undivided attention and endeavor to realize its deeply devotional spirit.

✠

The music of the Agnus should be sung softly with deep devotion. The phrasing in both settings must be carefully rendered so as not to break either the thought or the musical effect. The final petition should be sung pianissimo. The Amen in the Brunswick melody is taken softly but in more rapid tempo. Special care must be taken to observe the unusual syncopation in the next to the last measure.

¶ *Then shall the Communicants present themselves before the*
Altar and receive the Holy Sacrament.

THE COMMUNION

¶ *When the Minister giveth the* BREAD *he shall say:*

The Body of Christ, given for thee.

¶ *When he giveth the* CUP *he shall say:*

The Blood of Christ, shed for thee.

¶ *The Communicant may say* Amen *after each Element has been received.*

¶ *After he hath given the* BREAD *and the* CUP, *or after all have been*
communicated, the Minister shall say:

The Body of our Lord Jesus Christ and his precious Blood strengthen and preserve you unto eternal life.

This marks the individual application and reception of all that has been celebrated and invoked by the entire congregation in the preceding part of the service. While this is true, it is at the altar as nowhere else that the individual communicants realize their common fellowship as members of the mystical Body of Christ.

The ministers at the altar make their communion first. When there is an assistant minister (deacon), he may administer to the officiant, whose reception of the elements is essential to the formal, if not the actual, completion of the ceremony. After his own reception the officiant communicates the assistant.

Self-communion of the minister has always been an open question in Lutheran liturgics. Luther himself approved it and repeatedly defended it (*deinde communicet tum sese, tum populum* [*Formula Missae*]). It is quite certain that for a generation or two this liturgical action, which belongs to the integrity of the rite, was usual in Lutheran services. Later when liturgical knowledge and feeling had declined, dogmatic biblicism and pietistic subjectivism brought about its disuse. The dogmaticians, however, generally allow it, though advising that if another minister be present he should administer to the officiant. The Schmalkald Articles forbid self-communion only when this involves reception apart from the congregation (Part II, Art. II). Chemnitz says the minister includes himself in the confession and the absolution and he may include himself in the Communion. He should not be required to participate at all times, nor should he be prevented from communing if he desires.[5] Seventeenth-century orders frequently forbade self-communion. Nineteenth-century agenda generally permit it.

Those who object to self-communion base their objections upon the sacramental conception of the Holy Communion (as a divine gift) which dominates Lutheran history and, with its "disintegrating individualism" (Brilioth), emphasizes the personal benefit in the Sacrament almost to the exclusion of other objective and corporate values (such as liturgical completeness, commemoration, fellowship, incorporation with the church as the Body of Christ in eucharistic sacrifice to God, etc.). Putting all other considerations aside, the objectors feel that to receive the highest personal values the minister should make his personal confession and receive absolution from another, and that in the Sacrament itself he should hear the assurance of forgiveness pronounced by lips other than his own.

[5] *Examinis decretorum concilii Tridentini* (Frankfurt: Fabricius, 1578), Part II, sect. 4, canon 9, p. 112. Also *passim*.

Those who believe that when there is no other minister present the officiant should commune himself urge this as the natural and fitting completion of a liturgical action which has other than purely personal values. They also believe that participation by the minister in the reception is essential to the idea of fellowship inherent in the very nature of communion. They regard a communion in which the officiant does not receive as an anomaly, unknown in the Greek, Roman, Anglican, or other Protestant churches, and practically limited to instances in the Lutheran communion. They believe that the difficulty of reconciling the sacramental function of the minister with his sacrificial attitude as a man is but an intensification of the problem constantly in evidence in the interplay of sacramental and sacrificial elements throughout the entire service. According to their view the officiant should always receive, whether from his own or another's hand, and he should always receive before others.

Proper preparation by recipients is most important. The church has ever insisted upon freedom from gross sin and upon confession. The Reformation strongly stressed the necessity of faith and repentance. On the other hand, Pietism so magnified self-examination and the fear of unworthy reception as to surround the Sacrament at times with almost impassible barriers. The Sacrament is greater than any preparation for it. Communicants should be encouraged to approach it in love and not in fear.

Fasting before reception has the sanction of early and universal usage. This first developed as a matter of reverence. Most Protestants today give little thought to this ancient Christian custom, but those who in different communions do observe it find spiritual values in the discipline.

The use of proper devotional literature at home and in church before and after going to the altar is most helpful. Quiet minds and bodies, as well as clean hearts, are essential. Talking or idle gazing is intolerable. Worshipers should at least accord the Sacrament the serious concentration they would give a sermon or a symphony. Above all, they should not leave after they have received before the conclusion of the service, any more than they would leave a friend's dinner without thanking their host.

In the Roman church the laity receive at the rail outside the chancel. In churches of the Presbyterian system the people receive in their pews. The Lutheran and the Anglican churches, in agreement with ancient Gallican custom, direct communicants to enter the chancel and come to the altar. In fact in Lutheran confessional literature the Lord's Supper is called "The Sacrament of the Altar."

The church officers may direct the communicants' approach, though this need not be done. If the deacons do this, they should begin with the front pews and proceed in order to the rear. They should see that there is always a proper group, neither too large nor too small. waiting its turn in or near the chancel. Such direction will avoid unseemly crowding and save time, and will also enable the communicants in the pews to engage quietly in prayer without concern as to their turn.

In the interest of good order and promptness, twice as many communicants as can find place at the altar may come forward at the very beginning. Half of these will kneel or stand at the rail; the other half will wait in the chancel, or before it, facing the altar. After receiving the Sacrament the first group will return to their pews by side exits at the end of the altar rail, or by passing through an open lane in the center of the group which stands in the chancel. This second group then comes to the rail and the distribution continues immediately. Meanwhile a third group large enough to fill the communion rail comes forward and stands in or near the chancel.

In the early church the Sacrament was received standing, which is still the custom in the Eastern church and in many Lutheran congregations. After the twelfth century kneeling became general throughout the West, particularly on fast days.[6] The first Prayer Book of the Church of England gave no directions, but the second Book (1552) specified kneeling probably to meet the agitation for sitting which came from Scotland. The Lutheran church prescribes no particular posture. Either kneeling or standing is proper, but not sitting. Kneeling more fittingly expresses the right spirit of the moment, born of reverence and humility. Practical considerations sometimes favor standing. Luther approved kneeling, though he refers to standing.[7]

The traditional use of the liturgical churches calls for the common chalice. This is an impressive symbol of the Christian fellowship and unity of which Paul speaks and to which reference is made in the Order for Public Confession: "For as we are all partakers of this one Bread and drink of this one Cup, so are we all one body in him." If individual cups are used the common chalice should be retained for the consecration and the administration. The individual cups should *not* be filled beforehand in the sacristy and placed in trays upon the altar. Each communicant should receive his individual cup, taking it from a rack in his pew or from a cabinet at the entrance to the chancel, and bring it with him to the altar. The chalice should be provided with

[6] Joseph Bingham, *The Antiquities of the Christian Church* (London: Bohn, 1880), Vol. II, Book XV, ch. 5, sect. 3, pp. 812ff.
[7] Luther, *Sämtliche Schriften*, ed. J. G. Walch, Bd. II, col. 2709.

a pouring lip. Thus the minister will have the consecration in the traditional form with the common chalice and from this administer the wine, each communicant receiving it in his individual cup. Upon leaving the altar the communicants deposit their empty cups at the entrance to the chancel or in the pew racks.

In distributing the elements the minister begins at the south (epistle) end of the communion rail and proceeds to the north end.[8] If there be no assisting minister, the celebrant returns to the altar and places the paten (or the ciborium) on the corporal. He then removes the pall from the chalice and proceeds with the latter to the south end again, and administers the wine. When all at the rail have communed he returns to the altar, deposits the chalice upon the corporal, and turning to the communicants, pronounces the sacramental blessing. A new rubric in the Common Liturgy permits the blessing to be said "after all have been communicated," that is, at the conclusion of the whole administration, and not after each "table" or group.

If there be an assisting minister (deacon), the celebrant (officiant) distributes the bread; the deacon follows immediately and administers the wine; and the officiant pronounces the blessing. The celebrant has complete charge of all details at the altar. He renews the supplies of bread and wine, he delivers the chalice to the deacon, and he receives the same from him again.

✠

The formula of distribution in the early church was simply "The body of Christ," "The blood of Christ," to each of which the communicant responded "Amen." By the time of Gregory the Great this had expanded into the prayer, "The body of Christ preserve thy soul."[9]

Luther in his *Formula Missae* (1523) kept the Mass formula. He gave no formula in his German Mass (1526) and there is none in Duke Henry (1539), Wittenberg (1533), and Mecklenburg (1552). Bugenhagen rejected all formulas, saying: "When one gives the Sacrament let him say nothing to the communicants, for the words and commandments of Christ already have been said in the ears of all, and he cannot improve upon them" (Schleswig Holstein [1546]). Lübeck, one of the Bugenhagen cities, however, introduced a formula in 1647. Many of the sixteenth-century orders and practically all of the later agenda prescribe formulas of distribution.

The formula in the Common Liturgy is a return to the simple form of the early church, which is also in the liturgy of the Church of

[8] Fortescue, *The Ceremonies of the Roman Rite Described*, p. 61; Dearmer, *Parson's Handbook* (11th ed.; 1928), p. 346.
[9] For medieval forms see Gihr, *The Holy Sacrifice of the Mass*, p. 737.

Sweden and in that of the Augustana Church. Its brevity permits individual application. It should be used precisely. "Given for thee" is an addition made by Luther, though there is precedent for it in some Eastern liturgies. The use of miscellaneous Scripture passages or other unaccustomed phrases is disconcerting and destructive to devout concentration.

The words should be spoken distinctly and solemnly, though in a quiet tone, as an assurance of significant value for each individual. The entire sentence should be spoken to each communicant. The communicant may quietly respond, "Amen."

✠

In the early centuries the minister placed the bread in the communicant's hand. Tertullian in the second century and Cyril of Jerusalem in the fourth testify to this. The latter describes the communicants as "making the left hand a throne for the right, and hollowing the palm of the right to receive the Body of Christ."[10] Medieval practice required the priest to place the wafer directly on the communicant's tongue. This was to guard against breaking off particles of bread, and also to make impossible the practice to which the first English Prayer Book refers when it speaks of some who superstitiously "conveyed the same secretly away." Cardinal Bona suggests that probably the introduction of thin altar breads also furthered the practice of administering directly in the mouth.

Bucer suggested that the English church should return to the earlier custom and give the bread "in their hands." This was prescribed in the second Prayer Book (1552) and has remained the general practice of the Anglican communion.

The Lutheran church has generally retained the late Western custom of receiving the bread directly in the mouth. When it is received in the hand, women communicants must be instructed to receive the wafer in bare, ungloved hands. The right hand rests upon the left, both palms held open. If the communicant brings an individual cup to the altar the procedure will be modified. He will hold the cup in one hand and receive the bread between the thumb and the forefinger of his other hand.

The laity seldom receive the wine in the Roman Church, unless it be in the Uniate churches. The Church of England requires the minister to give the chalice entirely into the communicant's hands. In Lutheran practice the minister retains a firm grasp of the chalice while the communicant determines its inclination by touching its base.[11]

---

[10] Scudamore, *op. cit.*, p. 721.
[11] For suggestions concerning the use of individual cups see pp. 374-75.

After administering the wine to all at the altar rail, or at the conclusion of the distribution, "after all have been communicated," the minister gives the sacramental blessing: "The Body of our Lord Jesus Christ and his precious Blood strengthen and preserve you unto eternal life," and the group at the altar returns to the pews.

This blessing is an adaptation of the pre-Reformation formula used in distributing the bread to each communicant. The sign of the cross, which should not be used in connection with the recitation of the Verba, may be used, if desired, with the blessing. At this place it corresponds to the sign of the cross which anciently accompanied each individual administration.

☩

Immediately upon returning to the pew, each communicant kneels and offers a prayer of thanksgiving and self-dedication. Only necessity should lead him to leave the church before the entire Service is ended. Rich spiritual values accrue from remaining quietly in the pew and engaging in personal devotions as a member of the communion of saints, conscious of intimate fellowship with Christ and his believers. As an aid in these devotions the communicant may read collects, psalms, and hymns in the *Service Book,* or appropriate prayers, etc., in booklets provided for this purpose.

☩

During the administration the congregation may sing stanzas of appropriate hymns. This is an ancient custom of the Western church, distinct from the use of Rome, and found in the Celtic, Mozarabic, and other Gallican services centuries before the Reformation. Luther's German Mass and Bugenhagen's orders also prescribe it.[12]

Or—and this is less mechanical and preferable in many cases—a capable and spiritually discerning organist may be trusted to play softly during the distribution. Only churchly selections—plain song, chorales, or other church melodies with deep spiritual associations—should be used. The playing must be of the utmost refinement and not attract attention to itself.

Or again, the distribution may well take place in complete silence. Reverent silence may be an effective element in worship.

As soon as the last communicants have left the altar the minister unfolds the veil and covers the sacramental vessels and the elements which remain.

[12] Rietschel, *Lehrbuch der Liturgik,* I, 329.

CHAPTER XXII

THE POST-COMMUNION

The moments immediately following the reception of the Sacrament should be rich in grace in realization of communion with our Lord, fellowship with all believers, and assurance of God's forgiveness and blessing. Our natural impulse is to adore and thank him and to seek his further grace and strength in our daily lives.

The formal liturgical post-communion is relatively brief in all liturgies. Augustine said: "When that great Sacrament has been partaken, a thanksgiving concludes all." The Lutheran Liturgy is particularly restrained, as if conscious of the fact that any extended expressions after receiving the communion would be an anticlimax. It provides the permissive use of the Nunc Dimittis, a variable Thanksgiving Collect, the Salutation, the Benedicamus, and the Benediction. The Common Liturgy provides five historic collects, any one of which may be used. This is in line with the provisions of the Latin rite and also of the liturgy of the Church of Sweden (1940). In the mood of deep and reverent devotion, this continues the fundamental eucharistic note of grateful thanksgiving and finally comes to rest in the blessedness of peace.

The earliest Roman use had only a brief variable collect for grace and perseverance which was followed at once by the dismissal. The modern Roman rite, after the ablutions with the accompanying prayers, has several collects which are followed on non-penitential days by the sentence, *Ite missa est,* "Go, this is the dismissal," which has given the name "Mass" to the entire service. Then follows a further prayer, a brief benediction, and the Last Gospel (John 1:1-14). This latter is recited silently by the priest and is intended to focus thought upon the mystery of the Incarnation as related to the Eucharist. At the very end is a group of prayers (the Leonine prayers; dating from 1884) recited by the priest at the altar steps. These features are all late additions to the public service brought in from the private devotions of the priest, precisely as the Confiteor came into the liturgy at the very beginning of the service. In an effort to shorten the service the late Pope Pius XII ordered the shortening of certain of these texts.

The English Prayer Book of 1549 has a Post-Communion which was definitely influenced by the Reformation of Cologne (1543), prepared by Melanchthon and Bucer. The 1552 revision developed fresh acts of thanksgiving and adoration. It provided the Lord's Prayer; a prayer of oblation or an alternate prayer of thanksgiving; the Gloria in Excelsis (transferred from its ancient place at the beginning of the Service); and the blessing. The Scottish, American, and South African Books omit the Lord's Prayer at this place. The American Book of 1929 simply provides the Thanksgiving Prayer of 1549 with its petitions for grace and perseverance, the Gloria in Excelsis, and the Blessing.

¶ *Then shall the Congregation rise, and the Nunc Dimittis may be sung or said.*

NUNC DIMITTIS

Lord, now lettest thou thy servant depart in peace: according to thy word;

For mine eyes have seen thy salvation: which thou hast prepared before the face of all people;

A light to lighten the Gentiles: and the glory of thy people Israel.

Glory be to the Father, and to the Son, and to the Holy Ghost:

As it was in the beginning, is now, and ever shall be, world without end. Amen.

The Nunc Dimittis is a canticle which properly belongs to Compline, from which office it came into the Lutheran Vespers. It is found in the Greek church at the close of the liturgy, but is not given in the Roman or Anglican services of Holy Communion. It is appointed, however, at this place in the ancient Spanish (Mozarabic) Liturgy. Luther's orders for the Holy Communion do not mention it, but it is given in the Swedish liturgy (1531) and in some of the earliest German orders of the sixteenth century (Nuremberg [1525], Strasbourg [1525]).

The Nunc Dimittis forms an appropriate and beautiful conclusion to the Service, relating the mystery of the Holy Communion to that of the Incarnation. It expresses fulness of spiritual satisfaction and realization in personal appropriation of God's promises and in appreciation of the world significance of the "salvation prepared before the face of all people." As sung at this place it also reminds us of the conclusion of the first Supper—"when they had sung a hymn they went out into the Mount of Olives."

Being a permissive use, the Nunc Dimittis may be omitted when circumstances make it desirable to shorten the service.

Most of the Lutheran orders of the sixteenth century followed the traditional Roman structure of the liturgy and did not include the Nunc Dimittis. It could not, therefore, become a part of the Service under a strict application of the rule which determined the preparation of the Common Service.

In response to general desire, however, and on the basis of good if limited precedent, it was inserted as a permissive use.

(For fuller discussion of the Nunc Dimittis see pp. 440-41.)

✠

This canticle is a sacrificial element and the minister faces the altar while it is sung.

The organist must observe carefully when the last group of communicants leaves the altar. While the minister covers the vessels the organist builds up the volume of organ tone and leads into the Nunc Dimittis.

The chant should be begun in moderate volume and built up in the latter part. The Gloria Patri is given with breadth and strong organ support. This leads into the prayer and the brighter note on which the service concludes.

¶ *Then shall be said The Prayer.*

THE PRAYER

¶ *The Minister shall say one of the following Prayers; or he may say the Collect for Thursday in Holy Week.*

O give thanks unto the Lord, for he is good.

℞.   And his mercy endureth for ever.

We give thanks to thee, Almighty God, that thou hast refreshed us with this thy salutary gift; and we beseech thee, of thy mercy, to strengthen us through the same gift, in faith toward thee and in fervent love toward one another; through Jesus Christ, thy dear Son, our Lord, who liveth and reigneth with thee and the Holy Ghost, one God, world without end.

Or,

Pour forth upon us, O Lord, the spirit of thy love that by thy mercy thou mayest make of one will those whom thou hast fed with one heavenly food; through thy Son, Jesus Christ our Lord, who liveth and reigneth with thee and the Holy Ghost, one God, world without end.

Or,

Almighty God, who givest the true Bread which cometh down from heaven, even thy Son, Jesus Christ our Lord: Grant, we beseech thee, that we who have received the Sacrament of his Body and Blood may abide in him, and he in us, that we may be filled with the power of his endless life; who liveth and reigneth with thee and the Holy Ghost, one God, world without end.

Or,

Almighty God, who hast given thine only Son to be unto us both a sacrifice for sin and also an ensample of godly life: Give us grace that we may always most thankfully receive that his inestimable benefit, and also daily endeavor ourselves to follow the blessed steps of his most holy life; through the same Jesus Christ our Lord, who liveth and reigneth with thee and the Holy Ghost, one God, world without end.

¶ *The Congregation shall sing or say:*

Amen.

The Nunc Dimittis sounded a definitely individual note. The call to congregational thanksgiving comes in the versicle which introduces the Thanksgiving Collect. The first collect is from Luther's German Mass (1526) and is found in practically every Lutheran liturgy.[1] This collect was long thought to be entirely original with the Reformer, but earlier texts have been uncovered which contain similar expressions. These tend to show that in this, as in all his other collects, Luther did not strive for originality, but endeavored to ground his own forms for public prayer upon the broad liturgical tradition of the church. In its final form, the collect is definitely Luther's and expresses his emphasis and spirit.

Essential thoughts are presented in briefest form, and yet with characteristic warmth. The first is that of thanksgiving. The next is an emphasis upon the fact that the Sacrament is God's gift to man, not an offering of man to God. The Sacrament is recognized as a means of grace, and we pray that we may be strengthened by its use. The goals sought are stronger faith toward God and fervent love among Christians.

These ideas stand out cameo-like, clear-cut, and concisely expressed after the manner of many of the ancient collects. Comparison with the variable post-communion prayers of the Roman Mass, with the thanksgiving of the *Book of Common Prayer,* and even with Thomas Aquinas' fine collect on the Blessed Sacrament (appointed for Holy Thursday), reveals the excellence of Luther's prayer.

There is no one invariable collect of thanksgiving in the Roman Rite. There are proper appointments for every Sunday or festival quite as in the case of introits, collects, lessons, etc. In proposing the use of a single invariable collect, Luther, though probably unaware of the fact, reverted to the custom of the early Eastern churches as distinguished from the Roman. Early Roman post-communion collects, which varied with each day or festival like the Introit and the Gradual, generally contained petitions for grace and perseverance. The Gallican collects first brought in the definite note of thanksgiving, with the added thought of communion fellowship and right living. Scudamore gives several examples of French and Spanish forms including the following: "Let us give thanks to Almighty God, for that He hath refreshed us with the Bread of Heaven and with the spiritual Cup."[2]

[1] Many variant and expanded forms in the church orders are listed in Höfling, *Liturgisches Urkundenbuch* (Leipzig: Teubner, 1854), pp. 126-30.

[2] W. E. Scudamore, *Notitia Eucharistica,* p. 780.

Gasquet and Bishop in their discussion of the thanksgiving prayer of the first Prayer Book of Edward VI refer to a prayer in the Sarum Missal said by the priest immediately after communion which begins: "Gratias tibi ago sancte Pater omnipotens eterne Deus qui me refecisti de sacratissimo corpore et sanguine filii tui Domini nostri Ihesu Christi." There are several points of similarity here with Luther's collect.[3] The Latin prayer suggested by Paul Drews as a possible inspiration for Luther's collect is not convincing.[4]

Attention may be called to the forthrightness and vigor of Luther's original, which is not so evident in our excellent but refined translation:

Wir danken dir Almechtiger Herr Gott, das du uns durch diese heilsame gabe hast erquicket, und bitten diene barmhertzigkeit, das du uns solches gedeien lassest, zu starkem glauben gegen dir, und zu brünstiger liebe unter uns allen, durch Jhesum Christ, dienen Son unsern herrn, Amen.

Luther's method in collect composition had its parallel in his treatment of hymn tunes. Scraps of the melody of *Ein' Feste Burg* are to be found in the pre-Reformation music of the church.[5] Both this collect and the melody of *Ein' Feste Burg* in their final forms, however, are definitely to be ascribed to Luther.

The *American Book of Common Prayer* (1928) gives the Thanksgiving Prayer composed for the First Book of 1549, which offers thanks for "the spirituall foode of the moste precious body and bloude of thy sonne, our sauiour Jesus Christ," and for the assurance "that we be very membres incorporate in thy Misticall bodye." The final petition is one for grace "that we may continue in that holy felowship, and doe all suche good woorkes, as thou has prepared for vs to walke in." This prayer, Clarke and Harris admit, "exhibits some parallels to Hermann's form."[6] Hermann's Cologne Order also gives Luther's collect as an alternate thanksgiving, and the English version of Hermann's order under the title *A Simple and Religious Consultation* (1548) gives the earliest English translation of Luther's collect in quaint form. The present translation in the Common Liturgy first appeared in the later editions of the *Church Book* of the General Council.

The next collect, "Pour forth upon us, O Lord," is a free translation of the Post-Communion for Easter in the Roman Missal. The original Leonine text is as follows:

Spm nobis Dñe tuae caritatis infunde ut quos uno caelesti pane satiasti una facias pietate concordes per.[7]

The third collect: "Almighty God, who givest the true Bread" is a

---

[3] For complete text of this collect and illuminating discussion, see Paul Zeller Strodach in *PE*, 6, 329-32.

[4] *Beiträge zu Luthers liturgischen Reformen*, p. 95.

[5] Wilhelm Bäumker, *Das katholische deutsche Kirchenlied in seinen Singweisen* (Freiburg: Herder, 1886-1911), I, 30; IV, 692.

[6] *Liturgy and Worship*, p. 358.

[7] Charles L. Feltoe (ed.), *Sacramentarium Leonianum* (Cambridge: The Univ. Pr., 1896), p. 134.

text prepared by the Commission on the Liturgy, but based upon a prayer in *The Kingdom, the Power and the Glory*.[8]

The fourth collect, "Almighty God, who hast given thine only Son" is the collect for the Second Sunday after Easter in the first *Book of Common Prayer* (1549).[9]

The collect for Thursday in Holy Week, referred to in the rubric, "O Lord God, who hast left unto us in a wonderful Sacrament," is discussed in the chapter on the Propers under that day (pp. 502-03).

✠

The minister faces the altar, even during the versicle. The latter, as always, is introductory to the collect, from which it takes its character. This versicle is peculiarly appropriate, recurring frequently in the Psalms. Its use at this place in the Service comes from the Coburg order of 1626.

✠

The music of the response should be sung in moderate volume, but with confidence and in the spirit of thanksgiving.

THE SALUTATION AND BENEDICAMUS

¶ *Then may be sung or said the Salutation and the Benedicamus.*

The Lord be with you.

℟. And with thy spirit.

Bless we the Lord.

℟. Thanks be to God.

The Salutation and Benedicamus introduce the final sacramental feature, the Benediction. The Benedicamus was regularly used in pre-Reformation times to conclude masses which were followed immediately by other prayers, at which times the usual *Ite missa est* ("Go, it is the dismissal") was omitted. The sentence "Bless we the Lord" is a doxology which concludes each of the five books of the Psalter (Pss. 41, 72, 89, 106, 150). As such it forms an appropriate conclusion to the Christian liturgy. The response leaves the word "thanks" as the final expression of the congregation at every Eucharist.

Paul says, "Thanks be to God, which giveth us the victory through our Lord Jesus Christ" (I Cor. 15:57.). Augustine thought highly of this brief phrase. He wrote: "Can our minds conceive, or our lips utter,

---

[8] *The Grey Book,* Part III (3d ed.; London: 1925), p. 69.
[9] See No. 107 in the chapter on collects and prayers, p. 613.

or our pen write anything better than *Deo gratias?* No words could be shorter to say, more joyful to the ear, more sublime to the understanding, and more profitable to act upon."[10]

✠

The minister faces the congregation during the Salutation and the Benedicamus.

✠

The prayerful response "And with thy spirit" should be given softly. "Thanks be to God" should have fuller volume and an impressive, stately rendition.

¶ *Then the Minister, standing at the Altar, shall sing or say the Benediction.*

THE BENEDICTION

The Lord bless thee, and keep thee.
The Lord make his face shine upon thee, and be gracious unto thee.
The Lord lift up his countenance upon thee, and give thee peace:
In the Name of the Father, and of the Son, and of the Holy Ghost.

¶ *The Congregation shall sing or say:*

Amen.

The Benediction is the final sacramental feature of the Service. It is more than a prayer for blessing. It imparts a blessing in God's Name, giving positive assurance of the grace and peace of God to all who receive it in faith.

God's command to Moses (Num. 6:22-27) and our Lord's final act in taking leave of his disciples on the Mount of Olives (Luke 24:50) strongly support this conviction. Aaron and his sons are directed to use the words now embedded in the Lutheran Liturgy, and God says, "They shall put my name upon the children of Israel: and I will bless them." When our Lord's earthly ministry was ended and his bodily presence was about to be withdrawn, he led his disciples out "as far as to Bethany and he lifted up his hands, and blessed them" (Luke 24:50) and then ascended into heaven. In the Holy Sacrament, his presence has again been a reality for us, and he now gives us his blessing through the word of his servant as our worship ends.

No finer or more spiritual word in the vocabulary of devotion could be found with which to conclude the Service than the word "peace." We begin our worship by confessing our sin. The Kyrie, the first prayer of the Service of the day, says: "In peace let us pray to the Lord." We conclude with the assurance of forgiveness and peace. Upon this note,

---

[10] Cabrol, *Liturgical Prayer*, p. 51.

which has been sounded again and again in the Pax, the Agnus Dei, and the Nunc Dimittis, the entire service of thanksgiving and communion comes to rest.

The Aaronic benediction (Num. 6:24-26) is a unique Lutheran use. We would naturally expect the Pauline benediction as a conclusion to the service which features the New Testament Sacrament. The Old Testament form, however, has an impressive dignity all its own. It is the only benediction commanded by God.

The Mozarabic Liturgy gives the Aaronic benediction as a blessing before the reception. Luther evidently desired a stronger and more positive form than the brief phrase which, after the manner of a prayer, concludes the Roman Mass. In his Latin Mass of 1523 he suggested the use of the words from Numbers, or of a passage from the Psalms, saying simply, "I believe Christ used something of this kind when he blessed his disciples as he ascended into the heavens." He definitely incorporated the Aaronic form in his German Mass (1526) and the church orders generally employed it. It may well be, as Brilioth suggests, that Luther's simple, strong statement concerning this blessing "is the origin of the extraordinary popularity of this form in the Lutheran part of Christendom."

Brandenburg-Nuremberg (1553), Mecklenburg (1540), Württemberg (1553), Worms (1560), etc., give the Mass form in conjunction with the Aaronic. The Swedish Liturgy immediately follows the Aaronic benediction with "In the Name of the Father, and of the Son, and of the Holy Ghost." Thus the Old Testament form is impressively concluded with the trinitarian formula. The latter is used in this place as a benediction and not as an invocation. It has sacramental character, quite as when used in other blessings in marriage, ordination, church dedications, etc. Its earliest use was as the accompaniment to the sign of the cross. Henry Melchior Muhlenberg, in his liturgy for the Ministerium of Pennsylvania (1748), followed the Swedish use, and the Common Liturgy of 1958 has done the same.

In the early church the Holy Communion was concluded very simply with the words, "Depart in peace" (also the Ulm Church Order, [1747]). The Greek and the oriental rites generally soon introduced final blessings. The Roman Liturgy, however, was without a final benediction for a thousand years. The thought seemed to be that the reception of the Sacrament was the high point and that any extended formula after this would be an anticlimax. However, with the increasing number of persons at mass who did not communicate, it was thought desirable to dismiss them with a formal blessing. In the eleventh century the sentence, "May God Almighty bless you, Father, Son, and Holy Ghost," with which bishops were wont to bless the people in processions, was made a part of the liturgy. More extended forms first appeared in German (though not French or English) missals of the thirteenth and fourteenth centuries. It remained for the German church orders of the sixteenth century and the Prayer Book of 1549 in England to give this final blessing the dignity and significance it now has.

The quaint form of the Aaronic benediction, as found in the English translation of Archbishop Hermann's Order for Cologne (1543) is interesting: "The Lorde blesse the, and keepe the, the Lorde lighten his countenaunce upon the and have mercye on the, the Lorde lyfte up hys face upon the and settle the in peace."

The final blessing in the Anglican Prayer Books is impressive. The first part (based on Phil. 4:7), "The Peace of God, which passeth all understanding, keep your hearts and minds in the knowledge and love of God, and of his Son, Jesus Christ our Lord," is from Hermann's Order for Cologne (1543). The concluding sentence, "And the blessing of God Almighty, the Father, the Son, and the Holy Ghost be amongst you, and remain with you always," an amplification of the traditional episcopal blessing, was added in 1549.

Throughout middle and northern Germany the Benediction was sung (intoned) impressively by the minister. The church orders and cantionales contain many musical settings for it. Frequently the sign of the cross accompanied the concluding words. Schoeberlein comments that uplifted hands convey the idea of blessing, and that the sign of the cross gives a specific Christian character to the use of the Old Testament text. The threefold form of the final "Amen" corresponds to the threefold character of the Benediction itself.

✠

The minister faces the congregation with uplifted hands. He may make the sign of the cross—never ostentatiously or extravagantly—at the words "and of the Son, and of the Holy Ghost."

After the Amen the minister turns to the altar for his final devotions while the congregation bows or kneels in silent prayer. First of all he should close the service book on the missal stand. The traditional method is to leave the open edge farthest from the cross.[11]

✠

The organist may play very softly during the Benediction. This will continue the musical tone of the Amen after the hymn and blend it with the final Amen of the service which, developing naturally out of the sustained musical tone, will be without the hard effect of a new tonal attack.

The Amen after the Benediction is sung in moderate volume, but with

[11] This is the easiest way to close the book with the right hand. An additional mystical reason is supplied by medieval commentators who suggest that the book should be closed toward the cross because the latter represents Christ, the Lamb, who alone "is worthy to open the book and loose the seals thereof."

breadth and an impressive sense of finality. The last note may be pro-longed in diminished volume.

The organist should continue playing softly, giving ample time for the silent prayer of the minister and the congregation. If a hymn is sung he will finally modulate into its key, building up the organ tone and giving out at least a portion of the melody, perhaps the opening and the concluding phrases. It will usually not be necessary to play through the entire tune.

The choir may remain in the stalls to the end of the hymn and then leave in silent procession. The congregation stands while the choir and the minister leave the church.

The minister, however, may go directly to the sacristy. On festival or special occasions the choir may sing the hymn as it leaves the church.

The final organ music should be in harmony with the solemnity of the service itself. The vulgar intrusion of fortissimo postludes and noisy marches at this point encourages talking and wrecks the mood of worship beyond hope of recovery.

CHAPTER XXIII

MATINS AND VESPERS

These orders are historic and beautiful forms of worship supplementary to the Service. Their origin may be traced to the observance by the Jews of the third, sixth, and ninth hours of the day (counting from sunrise) as hours of prayer. The daily morning and evening sacrifices in the temple were rich in formal character. The early Christians continued to observe these hours in their private devotions (Acts 3:1; 10:9). Hippolytus in the early third century gave direction for private prayer at specific hours as a daily discipline and obligation of the faithful.

When Christianity was recognized by the state, the bishops were exhorted "to charge the people to come regularly to church in the early morning and evening of each day."[1] Thus in the fourth century public services were held, at least in certain centers, at times which corresponded to the hours enjoined for private prayer. The secular clergy and the laity therefore developed daily congregational services long before the complete system of offices was perfected by the ascetics.

Cabrol connects the origin of the Office—as the complete cycle of daily services is called—with the Mass of the Catechumens. "The *Synaxis* for which the early Christians assembled by night, consisted of the 'breaking of bread,' preceded by the singing of psalms and hymns, litanies and collects, readings, homilies, invocations and canticles. This was at one time the whole of the official liturgical prayer. From this somewhat crowded celebration . . . the Night Office (Matins, Lauds, and perhaps Vespers) came into existence, and afterward threw out, like stars of the second magnitude, Prime, Compline, and the Little Hours of the Day."[2]

The monastic communities increased the number of these services and elaborated their forms. The men and women who had withdrawn from

---

[1] *Apostolic Constitutions,* II, 59.

[2] Introduction to *The Day Hours of the Church* (London: Burns, Oates & Washbourne, 1921), p. xvi. See also Michel, *The Liturgy of the Church* (New York: Macmillan, 1927), p. 290.

the world to lead a life of fasting, prayer, and self-denial, remembered the words of the psalmist, "Seven times a day do I praise thee" (Ps. 119:164), and developed a series of seven hours of prayer. For these seven hours eight services were provided, Matins and Lauds being combined in one hour. These became known as the "canonical hours," because they were prescribed in the canon or "rule" of St. Benedict about A.D. 530, and were promptly adopted by monastic communities throughout the West. Benedict's scheme was probably a rearrangement and adaptation to monastic requirements of the plan of daily services observed in Rome, to which he added the offices of Prime and Compline. Gregory the Great, himself a monk, further unified the system. Roman singers later sent throughout the West carried the Roman tradition of liturgical music and the Roman observance of these offices throughout the monastic communities of France, England, and Germany, especially in the time of Charlemagne (A.D. 768-814).

The central feature in each office was the recitation of a portion of the Psalter. To this were added the reading of Scripture, homilies, hymns, canticles, and prayers. Additional elements such as antiphons, versicles, responsories, etc., later enriched the services.

Each hour had its own distinctive character. Matins, originally read at midnight or later, was thought of as a night office. Meditation on the divine Word is its chief characteristic, and full provision is made for Scripture reading. Lauds, at dawn when all nature wakes and the birds begin their song, is marked by the thought of praise to God the Creator and Redeemer. Prime, at the beginning of the day's work, is characterized by supplication. Terce, Sext, and None, at 9, 12, and 3 o'clock, respectively, hallow the forenoon, noon, and afternoon, and have the same structure and general character of petition. They share with Prime the reading of Psalm 119 as if to direct the soul again and again during the work of the day to the eternal law of God of which the psalm speaks. Vespers at the close of the day reviews God's mercies and lifts the grateful hearts of men, free from the toil and cares of earlier hours, in praise and thanksgiving. Compline, before rest at night, is the hour in which the Christian commends himself into the safe hands of his Lord.

The observance of these hours spread from the religious communities to cathedrals and collegiate chapels where groups of clergy assembled daily for worship. Collectively the services came to be known as the Divine Office or the choir offices, as by that time they belonged almost entirely to the monks and the clergy and were generally sung in the choir (chancel) of cathedrals and monastic churches. The laity occasionally attended the morning and evening hours. About the eleventh century the liturgical material employed in these offices was collected in a single work called the breviary. This was issued in four parts corresponding to the seasons of the year. Each monastic order had its own edition which was known as its "use."

The early simplicity of psalter, lessons, hymns, and prayers eventually became overloaded with an intricate mass of detail which required different observances according to the rank and degree of festivals and days in the calendar. This artificial complexity robbed these hour services of much of their spiritual value. The lessons from Scripture were abbreviated to a simple verse. Long passages from the lives of the saints were inserted in some of the hours. The recitation of the complete office, with its eight orders of service, required an average of two hours every day. The mechanical burden of this as a daily obligation was felt by many earnest minds before the Reformation. Various reforms were attempted, but the Roman church with its theory of the "meritorious work" of its clergy in these daily devotions, has never permitted any great change.[3]

The reformers appreciated the valuable features in these offices. They sought to retain morning and evening hours, particularly in the churches' schools. They also used them in simplified form for supplementary congregational services—thus reviving the practice of the early church. Luther refers approvingly to the outline of Matins, Vespers, and Compline as containing "nothing but the words of Holy Scripture." Bugenhagen in his church orders in north Germany and Denmark provided for daily Matins and Vespers in the principal churches where there were schools and choirs, and for congregational Vespers on Saturdays, Sundays, and days before great festivals. Brandenburg-Nuremberg (1533) prescribes Vespers "at the usual time and in the usual manner."

Nearly all the church orders retained Matins and Vespers, and occasionally the other hour services were referred to with approval (Brandenburg [1540], etc.). Scripture readings were greatly extended, and homilies and explanations generally followed. Frequently these services were conducted by laymen, the minister not being present. The observance of these orders, with their rich provision of psalms, Scripture readings,

---

[3] The English translation of the Roman Breviary by John, Marquess of Bute, is a work of more than three thousand pages, double column. The complexity of the Pye (general rubrics, 40 pages), well justifies the quaint statement in the preface to the first *Book of Common Prayer* (1549): "Moreouer, the nõbre and hardnes of the rules called the pie, and the manifolde chaunginges of the seruice, was the cause, yᵗ to turne the boke onlye, was so hard and intricate a matter that many times, there was more busines to fynd out what should be read, then to read it when it was founde out." *The First Prayer Book of King Edward VI*. Reprint. (London: De La More Press, 1903), p. 3.

expositions, hymns, and prayers, in the schools was an important factor in the religious development of a generation from which came many great writers, dogmaticians, and defenders of the faith.

The fact, however, that the orders remained chiefly the possession of the schools, with large portions sung in Latin, eventually resulted in their being almost lost to the congregations, particularly after the disorganization caused by the Thirty Years' War. Vespers lingered here and there in occasional afternoon and evening services, in some form of catechetical service, and in services of confession preparatory to the Holy Communion (*Beicht-Vesper*).

Pietism and Rationalism made no attempt to revive these orders. The churchly revival of the nineteenth century restored Matins and Vespers to deaconess motherhouses and similar religious communities. They were, however, only occasionally reinstated in congregational use throughout Europe. The Common Service of 1888 incorporated Matins and Vespers in a form well adapted to congregational requirements and thus restored these historic services to the Lutheran church in America.[4]

The Church of England in its first Prayer Book (1549) abandoned several earlier schemes of Archbishop Cranmer for new Latin services based upon Quignon's proposed revision of the breviary. Following the simpler plan of several church orders in Germany, the Prayer Book combined elements from Matins and Lauds in a service of Morning Prayer and elements from Vespers and Compline in a service of Evening Prayer or Evensong.[5] The Anglican effort introduced considerable new material while it omitted antiphons, responsories, and other musical elements retained in Lutheran services. It provided complete texts for both the Morning and the Evening offices in English and it was quite successful in adapting the new services to congregational requirements. It changed the place of the canticles. It prescribed the regular recitation of the entire Psalter once a month. It promptly enlisted the aid of English composers in providing original musical settings. Later it added much new material such as the opening "scripture sentences," the General Confession and Absolution (1552), the prayer for the royal family, the clergy and people, etc. (1662).

While the first concentration of interest upon these services may have been due to the strength of monastic tradition, ever powerful in England,

---

[4] The Mecklenburg cantionale (1867) is notable for the complete liturgical and musical provisions which it makes for both Matins and Vespers. The *Kirchenbuch* of the General Council (1877) anticipated the Common Service in providing Matins and Vespers for German Lutheran congregations in America.

[5] The order for Calenberg-Göttingen (1542) is thought to have been the particular model followed. See Leighton Pullan, *History of the Book of Common Prayer* (3d ed.; London: Longmans, Green, 1901), pp. 160ff.

the permanent result was the conferring of a new dignity and a definitely congregational character upon these ancient orders. The Anglican church has ever since succeeded in maintaining daily Morning Prayer and daily Evensong in its cathedrals and important parish churches, and indeed these two services have popularly come to be regarded as the principal congregational services of the Lord's Day. The Sermon became attached to them instead of to the Holy Communion, and they have been enriched by a wealth of musical material—choral settings, chants, anthems, hymns, etc.—by eminent composers.[6]

Thus the Anglican *Book of Common Prayer* and the Lutheran Common Liturgy represent two—and possibly the only two—successful attempts to master the essential content of certain of the hour services of the pre-Reformation church and to make full liturgical and musical provision for their use in English-speaking congregations. In the matter of relative importance and emphasis, however, the points of view in these two communions differ widely.

The Lutheran church recognizes the fact that Matins and Vespers are not grounded in any institution of our Lord or of the earliest church; that they are later developments; that they make provision only for the Word and not for the Sacrament. The Eucharistic Service retains its primacy as founded upon a definite institution of our Lord and the practice of the church from the beginning. The Service represents powerfully and objectively the grace of God in the salvation offered by Jesus Christ. Matins and Vespers are additional minor offices of prayer and praise which stress the subjective rather than the objective side of worship. The Service may be thought of as a cathedral; Matins and Vespers as chapels which cluster around the apse of the greater building.

These orders, however, have real value and a character all their own. Their simple outlines are capable of rich liturgical and musical elaboration. There is a flexibility about them which makes them adaptable to unusual circumstances and occasions. They provide an edifying devotional order even if an address is not included. This, if used, may find its place immediately following the lesson, or it may come at the end of the entire office. It is difficult to conceive of a finer order of worship for the congregation's second service on Sundays, for early services on

---

[6] "The intention and spirit of the new Offices are summed up not by the verse 'Seven times a day do I praise Thee,' but by 'Thy Word is a lantern unto my feet.' The Offices, as occasions of the ministering of the Word of God, became by a process natural within Reformed circles, the central religious observances of English Church Life." (E. C. Ratcliff in article, "The Choir Offices," in *Liturgy and Worship*, pp. 257ff, esp. pp. 266ff.) On the entire Anglican development see especially Leighton Pullan, *History of the Book of Common Prayer*, pp. ix, 139-67; Brightman, *The English Rite*, pp. lxxxv ff., and Jacobs, *The Lutheran Movement in England*, pp. 245 ff.

festivals, or for the daily worship of church schools, colleges, seminaries, etc.

When used in the corporate worship of such institutions, day by day, these services in their simpler forms take on something of the intimate character of worship in the Christian family. When used as a framework for important festival services of the congregation, they are capable of great enrichment. The use of seasonal antiphons and responsories, as well as appropriate anthems, provides unlimited opportunity for musical elaboration. The church in the twentieth century has not yet realized the possibilities in these services either as a medium for the simple devotions of a group, or as a pattern for an elaborate art work richly built up with chanting, responsories, and other choral features and an enlarged selection of lessons, hymns, and prayers. The texts of the choral elements provided in the Common Liturgy are a challenge to our musical editors and composers offered by the services of no other Protestant communion.

Before considering the orders of Matins and Vespers in detail, attention may be directed to the six principal features found in both offices. These are Psalmody, hymnody, Scripture lessons, the responsory, prayer, and the canticle.

PSALMODY

The common recitation of the Psalter united the Jews scattered throughout many lands in their synagogue worship and in the temple services in Jerusalem upon the great feasts. The early church incorporated the Psalter bodily into its worship. It became the first hymn book of the Christians. The medieval church used large portions of the Psalter in its liturgical and musical enrichment of the Mass. As it developed the hour services into a great system it arranged that the Psalter be recited in its entirety once a week, because it regarded the book of Psalms an inexhaustible mine of devotion. Priests and monks soon came to know the Psalter by heart. An early council at Toledo ordered that no one "should be promoted to any ecclesiastical dignity who does not perfectly know the whole Psalter," and similar statements can be found in the Eastern churches.

The musical rendition of the Psalter in monasteries, cathedrals, and college churches became a noteworthy feature. The entire Psalter was chanted antiphonally during the course of the week to nine psalm tones, or melodies, eight regular and one irregular (*Tonus Peregrinus*). These were called the Gregorian Tones. They differed widely in character, being in different modes or scales and having different inflections or cadences at the end of their respective reciting notes. Each tone also had a variety of "finals," some for ferial (daily) and others for festival use. An antiphon, consisting of a separate psalm verse sung to a proper melody of its own, introduced and concluded the chanting of each Psalm on festivals. To render adequately the hundred and fifty psalms in this fashion every week required trained singers and constant application. The chanting of the Latin Psalter to these fine melodies for a millennium or more is one of the most impressive features in the liturgical and musical history of the church.[7]

The Lutheran Reformers made every effort to retain the chanting of the psalms and their historic melodies. Where Matins and Vespers were continued as daily services, Psalms 1-109 were assigned to Matins and Psalms 110-150 to Vespers. Many of the church orders printed the psalm tones. They are found complete in the cantionales (choir books) edited by Lossius, Eler, Ludecus, etc. The great development of vernacular hymnody, however, the dissolution of monastic communities, and the discontinuance of corporate clerical worship, eventually caused the chanting of the psalms and the use of the traditional psalm tones to disappear almost entirely from Lutheran worship. The Anglican church, with its greater emphasis upon Morning Prayer and Evening Prayer and its continuance of the ancient choir system in cathedrals and college chapels, retained the chanting of the psalms much more generally. The Prayer Book provided for the chanting or the reading of the entire Psalter once every month. After the Restoration a new type of chanting was introduced, and hundreds of so-called "Anglican chants" supplemented the ancient Gregorian tones.

In recent times many organists and choirmasters have turned again to the plain-song chants. The chanting of the psalms has been revived in the Lutheran deaconess institutions in Germany and Scandinavia. The Common Liturgy of the Lutheran church in America provides for the reading or chanting of psalms in Matins and Vespers. A selection of psalms is provided, containing those of marked devotional character and especially appropriate for congregational use. No attempt is made to cover the entire Psalter once a week or once a month. One, two, or three psalms are used at each service as propriety may suggest.[8]

[7] For discussion of methods of psalmody, see Bäumer, *Geschichte des Breviers* (Freiburg: Herder, 1895), pp. 119 ff. Brief summary in Procter and Frere, *A New History of the Book of Common Prayer*, p. 345.

[8] The setting generally used in Germany is that found in *Der Psalter* by Friedrich Hommel (Stuttgart: Liesching, 1859). Archer and Reed in their *Psalter and Canticles Pointed for Chanting to the Gregorian Psalm Tones* (Philadelphia, 1901), were the first to give a plain-song setting to the entire Psalter in the Authorized Version. This book is now out of print. A later able work is Herbert Lindemann's *The Psalter of the Authorized Version of the Scriptures* (Minneapolis: Augsburg, 1940).

A table of proper psalms for festivals and seasons gives suggestions for particular services (*Service Book,* pp. 282f). Where Matins and Vespers are said daily as in church schools, seminaries, etc., it is customary to read from the selection of psalms in numerical order. In general practice the antiphons are not used; the psalm is said, and the Gloria Patri alone is sung to a simple chant which the congregation can readily learn.

Whenever it is possible to chant the psalms beautifully and impressively this should be done. Good reading, however, is to be preferred to poor chanting, and by reason of its corporate and responsive character it, too, may be very impressive. Reading antiphonally is an excellent method—with half (or the choir) leading and the rest responding, rather than having the minister lead with all responding.

The antiphons are a minor and distinctive feature which the Lutheran church retained in its sixteenth-century services while they were dropped entirely from the Anglican *Book of Common Prayer.* The antiphon is a psalm verse, or other sentence from Holy Scripture, recited or sung immediately before each psalm, or each group of psalms, and before the canticles, except the Te Deum. On festivals ("double" feasts), the antiphon is repeated after the psalm and after the canticle. In the Roman Breviary, throughout the whole Divine Office, the psalms are never said without antiphons. Antiphons are supposed to have been introduced from the East by Ambrose. Originally sung as a refrain after each verse of the psalms, they were later generally restricted to the beginning and the end. Liturgically the antiphon gives the key to the meaning of the psalm as related to the particular service; musically it aids by providing the keynote for the psalm tone.

The traditional melodies of the antiphons are rather simple, though more elaborate than a monotone with inflections. As a preparation for the psalm tone they are in the same mode as the latter and lead easily into it. The psalm tone in turn leads into the antiphon again, when the psalm is finished, by means of different "finals." The antiphon is first given out by a solo voice; the psalm or the canticle is chanted antiphonally, that is, responsively, by two choirs or by the choir and the congregation; and the antiphon is repeated in unison by the entire choir.

The Introits in the Service in their present form consist of an antiphon, followed usually by a single psalm verse instead of by the entire psalm as originally. The antiphon is thus the most significant part of the text. In the ancient breviary use a notable feature of the Advent office was the use of seven "Greater Antiphons" in connection with the Magnificat at Vespers on the seven days preceding the Vigil of Christmas. These were known as the "O" antiphons (*O sapientia, O Adonai,* etc.). The hymn *Veni veni Emmanuel* (O come, O come, Emmanuel) developed out of a paraphrase of these antiphons.

A few antiphons originally used with the Psalms later came to be sung as "detached chants." Some of these addressed to the Blessed Virgin Mary were sung at the close of Compline. The melodies were of great beauty and were used as themes for elaborate figurated choral settings by many composers. In England this paved the way for the development of the anthem, which thus is historically descended from the antiphon. As far as the antiphon proper is concerned, however, the Anglican Reformers, as we have seen, omitted all of them, together with responsories, from the first *Book of Common Prayer,* and they have never been restored to any of the Prayer Books of the Anglican communion.

The Lutheran Reformation in retaining the antiphons carefully selected "pure" texts. Hundreds of these with their traditional melodies are given in the church orders and cantionales. The *Psalmodia* of Lossius (1553), to which Melanchthon wrote a preface, contains no less than 206 antiphons. In many church orders and cantionales their use was prescribed without text or melody being given, familiarity with both being taken for granted.[9]

The Common Service restored the antiphons and gave a careful selection of texts. Their use, at least on festivals, would add liturgical and musical interest to our services. The chief difficulty is a lack of proper music to the English texts and of an established tradition in the English-speaking world. Here is a fine opportunity for editors and composers who will master the spirit of the liturgy and its ancient music, and provide the church of today with forms equal in merit to those of pre-Reformation origin.[10]

HYMNODY

The use of hymns, as distinct from psalms, Scripture, canticles, etc., has been associated with the hour offices from the earliest times. Ambrose, the "father of Latin hymnody," probably first introduced the hymn into the Office. The Benedictine Rule gave it universal recognition and secured its development by appointing one hymn or more for every hour, and by building up cycles of weekly and annual hymns. Prudentius, Fortunatus, Theodulf of Orleans, Hrabanus Maurus, and others were among the earlier known hymn writers. Some fine hymns, e.g., the *Te Deum,* the *Veni Creator Spiritus,* etc., came into universal use anonymously.

[9] On this procedure, so characteristic of the church orders, see Kliefoth, *Liturgische Abhandlungen,* VIII, 32; Schoeberlein, *Schatz des liturgischen Chor- und Gemeindegesangs,* I, 553, 555, etc. Also E. T. Horn, "Lutheran Sources of the Common Service," pp. 27-29, also in *The Lutheran Quarterly, XXI* (1891), 265 ff.

[10] Schoeberlein in his *Schatz* adapted many old Latin melodies to German texts. This influenced Harriet Reynolds Krauth (Mrs. Adolph Spaeth) in her preparation of settings for the English antiphons in her *Church Book with Music* (1893). A similar though smaller collection of traditional melodies, more fully preserving the feeling of the Latin originals, is given in Archer and Reed, *Season Vespers,* (Philadelphia: General Council Pub. House, 1905).

The highest point of development was reached during the eleventh, twelfth, and thirteenth centuries. The seasonal themes suggested by the church year gave way to meditations upon the mystery of the cross, the glories of the heavenly world, the life and blessedness of the Virgin, etc. Bernard of Cluny, Bernard of Clairvaux, Adam of St. Victor, and many others wrote hymns which expressed deep religious feeling in verse of highest excellence. The Franciscans and others later gave peculiar intensity to these devotional expressions. Then for a time the rise of humanism checked the development of Latin hymnody. A fresh impulse was given by the preparation of local breviaries, especially in France in the late seventeenth and eighteenth centuries. The brothers de Santeuil and Charles Coffin contributed hymns characterized by more modern feeling and polished latinity to the Cluniac and the Paris breviaries respectively.

Altogether, Latin hymnody is impressive in quantity and quality. Possibly ten thousand texts have been edited, chiefly by German scholars —Daniel, Mone, Wackernagel, Königsfeld, etc. In many cases plain-song melodies were composed for these hymns and gained currency with them. The Mozarabic, Ambrosian, Roman, Sarum, and Paris breviaries probably had the greatest influence upon modern hymnody. The modern Roman Breviary contains 155 hymns, nearly all of which have been in use for centuries. These, because of their Latin texts, are to all intents and purposes the property of only the clergy and monks. Generally speaking, the only opportunity for vernacular hymn singing in parish churches is in the use of a limited number of hymns to the Virgin at Vespers. As a rule, especially here in America, no hymns are sung at Mass. This absence of hymn-singing is one of the striking differences between Roman and Protestant worship. Here and there in Germany, Austria, and America, sporadic efforts are now being made to encourage popular hymn singing. But the movement is not yet widespread.[11]

Except for the Lutheran church, Protestantism deliberately threw away this fine inheritance. Zwingli, Calvin, and Knox ignored the whole body of Latin hymnody and made a new and all-too-crude start with vernacular paraphrases of the Psalms. Luther was not willing to surrender the fine Latin hymns of the church to the Romanists, or to let

[11] For discussions of Latin hymnody see John Julian's articles, "Latin Hymnody" and "Breviary," in his *A Dictionary of Hymnology* (rev. ed.; London, Murray, 1925); F. J. E. Raby, *A History of Christian Latin Poetry* (Oxford: Clarendon, 1927); Matthew Britt, *The Hymns of the Breviary and the Missal* (New York: Benziger, 1922); Samuel W. Duffield, *The Latin Hymn Writers, and Their Hymns* (New York: Funk and Wagnalls, 1889), especially chapter 31, "Latin Hymnody and Protestantism," by Robert Ellis Thompson. Also Ruth Ellis Messenger, *The Medieval Latin Hymn* (Washington, D. C.: Capital Pr., 1953), with an excellent bibliography.

the world and the devil have the music. While leading the way in the movement for popular hymn-singing in the vernacular, he based it solidly upon achievements of the past. Of his thirty-eight German hymns, no less than fifteen are translations and expansions of Latin originals. The church orders incorporated many of the best hymns of the pre-Reformation church either in Latin or in German translations. Lutheran authors—Heermann, Arndt, Gerhardt, etc.—while composing new German hymns, also translated many Latin ones. Lutheran scholars—Spangenberg, Lossius, Eler, etc.—edited important collections of Latin hymns and adapted them and their plain-song melodies for use not only in the offices, but for all the services of the Lutheran church. Thus the spirit and forms of Latin hymnody and its music largely determined the type and standards of the new vernacular hymnody which swept through the Lutheran churches in Germany and Scandinavia during the next three centuries in such volume and value as to constitute one of the greatest religious expressions of all time.

In England these centuries were barren in the field of hymnody. Reformers who had accomplished a marvelous work in their revision of liturgical portions of the ancient offices, strangely neglected the whole body of Latin hymnody and its music. The *Book of Common Prayer* (1549) contained only one hymn, the *Veni Creator Spiritus* in the ordination service. This appeared in a version which expanded the 105 words of the Latin original to 357 words in English. The Church of England skilfully and beautifully preserved the thread of historic continuity in its liturgy. It broke with all historical achievement and development in hymnody.

It remained for the dissenting bodies two centuries later, under the leadership of Watts and the Wesleys, to introduce hymn-singing among the English-speaking people. They retained leadership in this field until the nineteenth century, when the Oxford Movement gave the established church a new realization of the beauty and value of hymnody. Interestingly enough, this awakening came when the leaders of the movement rediscovered the pre-Reformation backgrounds of the *Book of Common Prayer*. Their study of the breviary and other ancient service books revealed the fact that hymnody had been an integral and important part of the medieval services and that there were rich mines of spiritual beauty and power in Latin hymnody. Once they became convinced that it was historically and liturgically proper for hymns to be used in formal liturgical worship, a new development of great significance began. Neale, Caswall, Chandler, Mant, Newman and a host of others produced fine translations of the old Latin breviary hymns. This work inspired the writing of original English hymns similar in spirit and form. Thus, long after the stream of Latin hymnody had ceased to flow, and many decades after inspiration in German hymnody had failed, the Church of England enriched the modern English-speaking world with a dower of fine liturgical hymnody. In extent and importance this later accomplishment is second only to the achievements of the Lutheran Reformation.

Modern standard hymnals draw from all these sources and include translations of great Latin and German hymns as well as original English hymns by English, Scotch, Welsh, and American writers of all communions. The present Lutheran hymnal (1958) is particularly rich in all this material.

READINGS FROM SCRIPTURE

The ancient Jewish synagogue services followed the chanting of the psalms with readings from the Law and the Prophets. This practice was continued in the earliest Christian services and selections from the Old and the New Testaments constituted an important part of the later hour services.

With reference to the choice of Scripture, two principles were followed. For the ferial (daily) offices consecutive readings from different books of the Bible were appointed (*lectio continua*). For greater festivals and the feasts of the saints the most appropriate selections from Scripture were chosen. A universally accepted scheme of consecutive readings appointed Isaiah for Advent, Genesis for Lent, the Acts of the Apostles for Eastertide, etc. Matins, the night office, was particularly given over to lengthy readings of Scripture. Sunday Matins had three lessons for each nocturn, or nine for the entire office (in monastic use, twelve). Not all of these, however, were from Holy Scripture. The second lesson was from one of the homilies of the fathers, and the third from the lives of the saints. The extensive use of these homilies led Charlemagne to authorize a collection for use throughout his kingdom, and he himself wrote the preface to it. Most of the other hours contained brief lessons, and in time these were reduced to a single verse (*capitulum*). The multiplicity of festivals and special observances with their appointments so interrupted the course of even these lessons that the actual reading of Scripture itself was crowded into the background.

Many of the legends connected with the lives of the saints were so absurd that the broad margins of the ancient breviaries sometimes record the contemptuous regard of the monks themselves for "an old wives' fable," and "to lie like a second nocturn" became a proverb. The reformers swept these features away and restored extensive and connected reading of Holy Scripture to its place of central dignity and importance.

It was natural that the new ideas concerning the Bible—its authority, importance for the average man, etc.—should dominate every sphere of reform. The leaders in Germany and in England, in their effort to adapt the hour services to congregational use, emphasized the reading of Scripture and edification rather than worship as such. Luther in his *Formula Missae* (1523) approves the continuing of "Matins of three lessons, and the hours, including Vespers and Compline *de tempore,* [excluding the *feriae* of the saints] . . . Let the entire Psalter divided into parts remain in use and the entire Scriptures, divided into lections, let this be preserved in the ears of the Church." He directs that "daily lessons be appointed," one for the morning, another for Vespers, "with vernacular exposition."

In his German Mass (1526) Luther outlined a complete scheme as follows:

Since the chief and greatest aim of any Service is to preach and teach God's Word, we have arranged for sermons and lessons as follows: On Monday and Tuesday, early, we have a German lesson on the Ten Commandments, the Creed and the Lord's Prayer, Baptism and the Sacrament, so that these two days shall preserve the Catechism and deepen its understanding. On Wednesday, early, again a German lesson for which the Evangelist Matthew has been appointed, so that the day shall be his very own, especially since he is an excellent evangelist for the instruction of the congregation, reports the great sermon of Christ on the mount, and strongly urges the exercise of love and good works. The Evangelist John, who is so mighty in teaching faith, has his own day, too, on Saturday afternoon at Vespers. In this way we have a daily study of two evangelists. Thursday and Friday bring us, early in the morning, the weekday lessons from the Epistles of the Apostles and the rest of the New Testament. Thus enough lessons and sermons are appointed to give the Word of God free course among us. . . .

To exercise the boys and pupils in the Bible, this is done. Every day of the week they chant a few Psalms in Latin, before the Lesson, as customary at Matins hitherto. For we want to keep the youth in the knowledge and use of the Latin Bible, as was said above. After the Psalms a chapter from the New Testament is read in Latin by two or three of the boys in succession, depending on its length. Another boy then reads the same chapter in German, for the exercise, and for the benefit of any layman who might be present. Thereupon they proceed with an antiphon to the German lesson mentioned above. After the lesson the whole assembly sings a German hymn, the Lord's Prayer is said secretly (*heimlich*), the pastor or chaplain reads a collect, closing with the *Benedicamus Domino* as usual.

Similar directions are given for Vespers, and this section of the writing closes with the sentence, "This is the daily weekday service in the cities where there are schools."[12]

The church orders made similar provisions for Scripture reading and exposition in the vernacular.

In England Cranmer followed the general plan of the German Reformers. As early as 1541 he directed that chapters from the New Testament should be read in English on Sundays and holy days after the Te Deum and the Magnificat, and that when the New Testament was finished the Old was to be started. The Prayer Book arrangement of 1549 shows the influence of Quignon's reformed breviary which had provided for the reading of the whole Bible in the course of the year under the plan of three lessons daily. The Prayer Book began the secular year with lessons from Genesis, appointing Isaiah for Lent. The New Testament, with the exception of Revelation, was to be read through twice in one year. The recent revised lectionary in England (1922) and the subsequent Canadian, Irish, Scottish, and American lectionaries are based on the ecclesiastical year with numerous variations between themselves. The Prayer Book of the Anglican communion thus provides extensive readings from Scripture for daily Morning Prayer and Evening Prayer. Because of the emphasis upon the idea of daily services, the lessons appointed for Sundays, particularly the first lesson, taken from the Old Testament, often seem without relation to the day and quite mechanical.

One of the noteworthy features of the Common Liturgy is the unique provision of a complete series of Old Testament lessons for optional reading before the Epistle in the Service. Provision for daily services in seminaries, schools, etc., includes a table of daily lessons (omitted from the music edition). These are generally shorter than the Anglican series. For Sunday Matins and Vespers, however, all effort to conform to a *lectio continua* arrangement has been abandoned in favor of appropriate lessons for each particular service (*Service Book,* pp. 280f).

THE RESPONSORY

The responsory is an ancient and characteristic chant form originally sung after each lesson at Matins. With the development of the Divine Office, the responsory assumed a unique liturgical pattern which combined verses and responses from the Scriptures appropriate to the feast or the season. The name may have been derived from the arrangement of the text or from the method of its musical rendition. Amalarius

[12] *PE* 4, 177ff. Cf. *WA* 19, 78-80.

of Metz in the ninth century first describes the characteristic form which developed in the Gallican church and which later was adopted by Rome.

The first part, the responsory proper, consists of a series of verses and responses. The second part, called "the verse," is so constructed that its conclusion could be used as a response to each part of the responsory proper. Then follows the first part of the Gloria Patri (without the *et in terra*), after which the concluding part of the verse is repeated. In Lent the Gloria Patri is omitted.

The breviary contains an enormous number of responsories. On an ordinary Sunday or festival when there were nine lessons, eight responsories were required, the Te Deum being sung after the last lesson. On weekdays not festivals there were three lessons and three responsories.

Many of the texts were of great merit and interest because of their appropriateness to particular lessons or to the feasts or seasons. Batiffol regards the responsories of the church year proper and the graduals in the Mass among the oldest and finest liturgical texts of the church. He compares them favorably, with respect to function and literary value, with the chorus dialogues of classical Greek tragedy.[13] The music of the responsories, also, like that of the Gradual in the Mass, ranked among the highest achievements of the ancient plain-song system. Unfortunately in the late Middle Ages many texts included questionable material not derived from the Scriptures. The Paris Breviary (1735), on the other hand, developed a new and thoroughly scriptural series of high excellence which combined texts from both Old and New Testaments in admirable fashion.

The extent and elaborateness of these texts and melodies made their use in vernacular worship difficult. Bishop Frere, speaking for the Anglican communion, says: "The whole of this rich treasure had to be sacrificed and excluded from the Prayer Book."[14]

The Lutheran Reformers, on the contrary, made every effort to retain at least a limited number of responsories with their music. Their revisions of the Office provided for a "pure responsory" to be sung, not after each lesson, but after the last lesson at Matins and also at Vespers. Thus they simplified the breviary requirement for a responsory after each lesson, but provided for its use at Vespers as well as at Matins. The *Psalmodia* of Lucas Lossius contains texts and melodies to forty-seven responsories. A proportionate number are included in the cantionales of Eler, Ludecus, etc.

[13] Pierre Batiffol, *History of the Roman Breviary,* tr. A.M.Y. Baylay (London: Longmans, Green, 1912), pp. 79f, 242, n. 3.
[14] *A New History of the Book of Common Prayer,* p. 380.

With the general neglect of Matins and Vespers as a form of congregational worship during the periods of Pietism and Rationalism, the Lutheran state churches of Europe lost the responsory and the antiphons. The Common Service restored both to the English Lutheran Liturgy in America. Texts were given for the greater festivals and seasons. Directions for their use followed the Reformation custom, and they were appointed to follow the last lesson in Matins and in Vespers. The texts pertinently introduce the thought of the season or day, and are individual in their structure.

Choirs will do well to master the responsories and use them as choral responses to the lessons in Matins and Vespers. Adequate musical settings are available, and the texts themselves are a constant challenge to church musicians to provide new compositions of merit for the enrichment of our worship.[15]

THE PRAYERS

The use of variant forms of prayer has always characterized the hour services. Originally collects or prayers followed each psalm or canticle. Quite early the Collect for the day was borrowed from the Mass and used to close the devotions, at least on Sundays and festivals. Later a number of shorter prayers were assembled at the end of the office in the form of versicles and responses. In the Gallican services these assumed the character of a litany with which were combined the Kyrie, the Lord's Prayer, and, after the ninth century, the creed. A triple form was commonly employed containing a bid, a versicle, and a response. The following may serve as an example.

Let us pray for every condition in the Church.

℣. Let thy priests be clothed with righteousness.

℟. And let thy saints shout for joy.

This plan of including prayers (in the form of Kyrie, Lord's Prayer, versicles, responses, and collects) eventually became a part of the Roman Rite and was called "suffrages." Abbot Cabrol comments upon these responsive prayer forms as follows: "They may be described as an appeal darted swiftly forth to God, a cry from the heart uttered by the cantor or lector, in which the faithful join by making the response.

---

[15] A complete series of settings to the texts of all the responsories in the Common Service was composed by Max Reger, the eminent German musician, shortly before his death. Arrangements for this were made with the composer by Harry G. Archer and Luther D. Reed, who published Reger's sixteen responsories as one of their series of service books in 1914. The title is *Twenty Short Anthems or Responses* (New York: H. W. Gray, 1914). These compositions are of great merit and will well repay serious study by capable choirs. Another complete and simpler series is by J. F. Ohl, *The Responsories of Matins and Vespers, Set to Music* (Philadelphia: General Council Pub. House, 1909).

The versicle is often truly eloquent in its laconic brevity. . . . This brief and concise dialog between the cantor and the choir attains a high degree of liturgical beauty." In illustration of the latter statement he quotes the series of versicles said at Prime. The suffrages at Compline were similar in outline and use.[16]

The Book of Common Prayer of 1549 concludes Morning Prayer and Evening Prayer by the use of the Apostles' Creed, the Lord's Prayer, and the Suffrages, followed by three collects. In 1661 five additional prayers were inserted before the Benediction. The versicles (suffrages) are not from the Breviary, but from the "bidding of the bedes," according to the Sarum use, which was well known by the people.[17]

The Lutheran church made no change in the traditional conclusion of Matins and Vespers as found in the local breviaries in Germany and elsewhere. Luther in his German Mass specifically mentions only the following—"Lord's Prayer, collects and *Benedicamus Domino,*" but the fuller forms were regularly used. The Common Liturgy provides that Matins regularly be concluded with prayers as follows: Kyrie, Lord's Prayer, the Collect for the day, other collects concluding with the Collect for Grace, with which a versicle may be used, and the Benedicamus. The provision for Vespers is the same except that the Collect for Peace is substituted for the Collect for Grace. An important additional provision is given in the Common Liturgy (p. 276), where it is stated: "Instead of the Prayer appointed, the General Suffrages, the Morning [Evening] Suffrages, the Litany or other Prayers may be said." Complete texts of these prayer forms are supplied. The General Suffrages are arranged from the breviary prayers for Lauds and Vespers. The Morning Suffrages are the responsive prayers for Prime. Evening Suffrages are from similar forms for Compline.

THE CANTICLE

This is a general term describing certain hymnlike passages from Holy Scripture (not psalms), which, together with the Te Deum and the Benedicite (non-scriptural), are appointed to be sung at Matins and Vespers after the responsory. The ancient breviary use provided canticles for Lauds, Vespers, and Compline to be used every day. The Te Deum is appointed for Sundays and festivals, but is not specifically

---

[16] Cabrol, *Liturgical Prayer*, "Forms of Prayer used in Antiquity." Quotations from pp. 34-35. See Procter and Frere, *A New History of the Book of Common Prayer*, p. 392.

[17] The origin of the five additional prayers is discussed in Leighton Pullan, *The History of the Book of Common Prayer*, p. 163.

called a canticle. Seven Old Testament canticles are assigned to Lauds, one for each day of the week. These are regarded as taking the place of the fourth psalm. Three New Testament canticles, the Benedictus, the Magnificat and the Nunc Dimittis, are appointed for use at Lauds, Vespers, and Compline specifically. Each of these is provided with an antiphon, and they are all sung antiphonally to the psalm tones.

Closely resembling the psalms in inspiration and poetic form, the canticles were early accorded a special place in the liturgy, and are found near the psalms in the manuscripts.[18] The Mozarabic and the Benedictine breviaries and the French diocesan breviaries of the seventeenth and eighteenth centuries contain a much larger number of canticles. The three New Testament canticles and the Te Deum have been elevated above the others into distinct prominence in every liturgy.

As we have seen, the Reformation in England discarded the responsory as such. The Prayer Book, however, appointed the Te Deum (or the Benedicite) to be sung as a response after the first lesson at Morning Prayer. It provided the Benedictus (or Psalm 100) as a choral chant after the second lesson. Similarly at Evensong it appointed the Magnificat (or Psalm 98) to be sung after the first lesson, and the Nunc Dimittis (or Psalm 67) after the second lesson.[19] Thus, while losing their proper dignity as distinct canticles, the most important of the ancient series have been retained in the Anglican Prayer Books as chant forms alternating with the lessons somewhat after the manner of the responsory. This is a unique feature of the Anglican Liturgy.[20]

The Lutheran church orders and cantionales generally retained the historic canticles and the Te Deum. The Te Deum was usually given both in German and Latin, the texts being set to the ancient plain-song melodies.[21] The Common Service gave the three New Testament canticles and the Te Deum. *The Common Service Book* of the United Lutheran Church gave eight additional canticles. The Common Liturgy gives, in addition to the New Testament canticles and the Te Deum, five additional texts. These are: the Benedicite, or Song of the Three Children; the Song of Miriam and Moses (Exod. 15); the Prayer of Habakkuk (Chap. 3); the Prophet's Song (Isa. 12); and the Song of Hannah (I Sam. 2).

[18] Interesting testimony to this early use is given by the Codex Alexandrinus manuscript of the Scriptures (fifth century) in the British Museum, which gives the canticles at the end of the Psalter.

[19] The American *Book of Common Prayer* adds another alternative built up from portions of Psalm 103.

[20] See the discussion in Clarke and Harris, *Liturgy and Worship*, pp. 269ff.

[21] Lossius' *Psalmodia* gives the three New Testament canticles to each of the eight Gregorian tones. Spangenberg, the *Nürnberg Officium Sacrum*, etc., also give the full series.

CHAPTER XXIV

MATINS IN DETAIL

The name matins, which properly means "of the morning," was anciently attached to the office now known as Lauds, and said at dawn. Later "Matins" was applied to the night office which developed as the continuation of the ancient vigils (*Vigiliae,* the nocturnal "watches" of the soldiers). In the early church these were regularly held on Saturdays and other nights preceding festivals, on the anniversaries of martyrs, etc. They were immediately followed by the Eucharist. Thus in its origin Matins represents the most ancient public service of the church apart from the Eucharist itself. Eventually the night office was largely restricted to the monasteries where the daily discipline or rule appointed lengthy services to be read in common (*in choro*). The Reformation simplified this night office, preserving its essential structure, and made of it an early morning service.[1]

In the scheme of the hour services in the Roman Breviary, Matins is easily, by reason of length, variety, and richness of forms, the most important office of the day. It begins, as does no other, with an invitatory psalm. On Sundays there are three nocturns, corresponding to the ancient Roman division of the night into three "watches." Each nocturn has its own appointments of psalms, lessons, responsories, etc. Thus Sunday Matins has no less than eighteen psalms, nine lessons, eight responsories, and the Te Deum. In length this office almost equals all the other offices of the day combined. The weekday office is simpler. The psalms at Matins are chosen from the first two-thirds of the Psalter (Ps. 1-109). The lessons are much longer than those in any other hour, comprising extracts from all the books of the Bible to be read during the year.

---

[1] A full and interesting description of the earliest use of Matins is contained in *The Pilgrimage of Etheria*. Etheria (or Sylvia) was a Spanish abbess who traveled in the East and reported her impressions of Christian services in Jerusalem, etc., at the end of the fourth century. See Duchesne, *Christian Worship*, pp. 541-71 for complete text.

This length and complexity led to many efforts at simplification. Among others, the Franciscan monks greatly reduced the length of lessons, but added many festivals and special features. Cardinal Quignon's revision was important. Eventually the concluding part of Matins became a separate office (Lauds), which was said at dawn. Its psalms refer to the morning light and to the Resurrection, and its general character is that of praise. The canticle Benedictus, which also contains an allusion to the "Dayspring from on high," concludes this office, which in monastic practice generally follows Matins immediately.

Just before the Reformation, Matins, like Vespers, was frequently a public service in churches connected with monasteries or in larger parish churches, and attended by at least some of the laity. Luther wished to retain both Matins and Vespers, though he desired the simplification of Matins particularly. His suggestions retained the historic outline and provided for consecutive readings of the entire Scriptures with vernacular expositions on Sunday. The church orders generally retained Matins, usually in simplified form. On weekdays the services were in Latin, "that the boys may learn the language." On Sundays and festivals they were often in German.

While Matins practically disappeared from congregational use in the Lutheran church except for early services on Christmas, Easter, and Pentecost, the nineteenth-century revival of church life restored them to the deaconess institutions and a few other places in Europe. The Common Liturgy provides complete minor appointments including antiphons, responsories, etc., and Matins is increasingly used throughout the Lutheran church in America in daily chapel services of schools, seminaries, etc., for the daily devotional services of conferences, synods, and general bodies, and by congregations for early services on festivals. The Matin order is admirably adapted to all these uses because from beginning to end it is pervaded by the spirit of worship.

The significant quality of Matins, as distinguished from Vespers, is that of praise. Its petitions seek grace, guidance, and strength for the duties of the day.

The Reformation in England retained a simplified form of Matins, and then developed it. Taking the earlier German Lutheran forms as models, Cranmer and his associates incorporated in these a systematic division of the Psalms over the period of a month, and a plan of daily lessons similar to that suggested by Quignon. The Second Prayer Book of 1552 prefixed to Morning Prayer the penitential opening sentences, exhortation, confession, and absolution. Additional prayers were provided after the third collect in 1661. Certain features were drawn from the old office of Lauds and Prime and combined with the material from the ancient Matins.[2]

The office begins with a hymn, which may be a hymn to the Holy Spirit, a morning hymn, a hymn of praise, or of the season.

☩

In our use today Matins, like Vespers, is a congregational service rather than a choir office. It is generally conducted at the altar. Historic considerations, however, justify the practice, where local conditions permit, of the minister's reading these services from a prayer desk or clergy stall in the chancel. When this is done the minister goes to the altar for the final prayers and the benediction.

The minister may follow the choir or he may enter the chancel from the sacristy as the first stanza of the opening hymn is sung. He pauses for silent prayer at the foot of the altar steps and then proceeds to the altar (or to the prayer desk).

On festivals the hymn may be sung in procession. On other days the choir may enter the church in procession and go to the stalls without singing. The organist plays softly until the choir is in place and the minister in the chancel.

The congregation rises when the choir enters the church and remains standing until the end of the Venite.

At the end of the hymn the organist modulates into the key of the service before the minister begins the Versicles.

¶ *The Versicles with the Gloria Patri shall be sung or said, the Congregation standing until the end of the Venite.*

¶ *The Alleluia shall be omitted in Lent.*

THE VERSICLES

O Lord, open thou my lips.
℟. And my mouth shall show forth thy praise.
Make haste, O God, to deliver me.
℟. Make haste to help me, O Lord.
Glory be to the Father, and to the Son, and to the Holy Ghost:
℟. As it was in the beginning, is now, and ever shall be, world without end. Amen.

(Omit during Lent.)

Alleluia.

The Versicles are introductory psalm passages in the spirit of prayer. They conclude with the Gloria Patri, an act of praise. This liturgical introduction has been a part of the office of Matins since the sixth

[2] For details see Pullan, *History of the Book of Common Prayer,* pp. 160ff.

century. At first the text was sung throughout by the entire group and not in the form of versicles and responses.

The first versicle (Ps. 51:15) is particularly appropriate for the first service of the day. It is a petition for divine aid in offering praise as the first act in the entire series of the day's services. It was anciently used only in Matins.

The second versicle is from Psalm 70:1. This looks forward to the duties of the day and seeks divine help. Originally in monastic use the entire psalm, of which this is the first verse, was repeated on waking, or while going from the dormitory to the chapel. The use of these opening versicles in Matins today is therefore a fragmentary survival of this ancient custom.[3]

The Gloria Patri concludes the Versicles as it concludes every complete psalm when used in Christian worship.

"Alleluia" is a Hebrew expression used in the great psalms of praise, particularly Psalms 113-18. It is omitted during Lent. The English Prayer Book of 1549 gave the English equivalent, "Praise ye the Lord." In 1661 the response, "The Lord's Name be praised," was added.

✠

If the minister is conducting the service at the altar, he faces the altar for the Versicles.

✠

The *Service Book* contains only one musical setting for Matins and Vespers. This consists chiefly of Anglican chants.

The first rubric should be noted. It states that "intonations provided for the Minister's parts of the Services represent a permissive use. They are not to be considered directive."

The music of the Versicles and the Gloria Patri is a traditional setting based upon the ancient plain song and harmonized by Thomas Tallis for the English *Book of Common Prayer*. It was not published until 1641, though Tallis died in 1585.

The responses should be sung in modern volume and tempo with distinct enunciation of the words.

---

[3] An interesting provision is found in the Schleswig-Holstein Order of 1542 (pp. 161-62), where Bugenhagen gives two forms of Matins. The first is for the Latin schools. The second, a quite elaborate form, is for the canons of cathedrals and others. An unusual feature is the omission of the historic versicles. The reason given for this charges the Romanists with not using these forms "in the sense in which they were written by the Holy Spirit." The curious argument concludes with the statement: "If we were to sing everything that is good, there would be no end to the singing. Therefore, be content with the correct use of Scripture, that our prayer, rising out of faith, may be purer."

¶ *Then may follow the Invitatory with the Venite.*

THE INVITATORY

O come, let us worship the Lord.
℟.   For he is our Maker.

VENITE EXULTEMUS

O come, let us sing unto the Lord: let us make a joyful noise to the Rock of
our salvation.

Let us come before his presence with thanksgiving: and make a joyful noise
unto him with psalms.

For the Lord is a great God: and a great King above all gods.

In his hand are the deep places of the earth: the strength of the hills is his
also.

The sea is his and he made it: and his hands formed the dry land.

O come let us worship, and bow down: let us kneel before the Lord our
Maker.

For he is our God: and we are the people of his pasture and the sheep of
his hand.

Glory be to the Father: and to the Son and to the Holy Ghost;

As it was in the beginning, is now, and ever shall be, world without end.
Amen.

This extended invitation to worship fittingly continues the opening
call to praise in responsive fashion. It is a characteristic feature of
Matins as the first service of the day.

The Invitatory is a brief versicle and response, the first part of which
is a summons to worship, the latter part supplying the reason. It may
be thought of as the antiphon of the Venite. It may have come into the
liturgy from the custom of the early monks whose duty called them to
wake their brethren for the night office. This they did by intoning
passages of Scripture appropriate to the day or season as they made their
way through the dormitory.

Ordinarily the "common invitatory" given in the text of the service is
used and is not repeated after the Venite. Proper invitatories, however,
are provided for the different festivals and seasons. These all conform
to type, the first part sounding a call to worship and the second part
stating a characteristic fact of each season as the motive. The *Book of
Common Prayer* lost the invitatory in 1549, though the Proposed Book
of 1928 provided for its restoration.

The Invitatory, like the antiphons to the psalms, may be repeated after
the Venite.

The Venite (Ps. 95) is an invariable invitatory psalm sung or said
before the regular psalmody of the day. The King's Primer in England
(1545) called it "a song stirring to the praise of God." Originally solo

voices sang the psalm while the full choir sang the Invitatory and repeated it entire or in part after each verse of the psalm.[4]

The text of the English *Book of Common Prayer* includes the entire psalm. The American Episcopal Book, like the Lutheran Common Liturgy, omits the last four verses as unsuitable. The Episcopal Book, however, substitutes for them verses 9 to 13 of Psalm 96.

The Prayer Book omits the Venite on the nineteenth day of the month, when Psalm 95 is read in course. The Lutheran use retains the Venite as an invariable feature of Matins, but to avoid duplication directs that Psalm 95 shall not be read in course in the regular use of the Psalter at Matins (*Service Book*, p. 275).[5]

The Invitatory as an antiphon preceding the Venite partakes of the character of that which it introduces, even though the text of the Invitatory by itself suggests a sacramental interpretation. Its real character is established by the larger element to which it belongs, as in the case of the versicles and responses which precede collects. Both the Invitatory and the Venite therefore are sacrificial, and the minister faces the altar while they are read or sung.

The chant to the Invitatory is the traditional melody to the words "Praise ye the Lord" with their response "The Lord's Name be praised," which is the Prayer Book substitute for the Latin "alleluia" immediately following the opening versicles in both Morning and Evening Prayer.

The Venite is set to three modern Anglican chants. The text should be chanted clearly throughout with the easy rhythm of the words themselves. A slight pause should be made at the end of the psalm before the Gloria Patri in order to preserve the distinction between the two. The Gloria should be sung deliberately with clear enunciation of each syllable.

¶ *Then shall be sung the Hymn.*

THE HYMN

The principal hymn of Matins, the so-called "office hymn," comes before the psalm instead of before the canticle as in Vespers. This is in order to mark a separation between the invitatory psalm (the Venite) and the other psalms.

For discussion of hymnody in general see pp. 396-99.

If the minister is reading Matins at the altar he will leave the latter at the conclusion of the Venite and go to his stall for the hymn.

---

[4] Illustrated in Dowden, *The Workmanship of the Prayer Book*, pp. 61f.
[5] See the discussion in Philip Freeman, *The Principles of Divine Service* (Oxford: Parker, 1855-56), 330 ff.

The organist should modulate without any break from the key of the Venite into the key of the hymn tune, establishing the new tonality fully before giving out the tune.

The choir remains standing while the organist plays the hymn tune.

¶ *Then, all standing, shall be sung or said one or more Psalms.*

THE PSALM

For psalmody in general see pp. 393-96.

One or more psalms are read or chanted. Where daily services are held the Psalter may be read consecutively; in general congregational use a selection is made on the basis of propriety. (See the table of proper Psalms in the *Service Book,* pp. 282 f.)

If the psalms are chanted, an antiphon may be sung by a solo voice before each psalm and repeated by the choir after the Gloria Patri. Good reading, though, is to be preferred to poor chanting.

¶ *At the end of each Psalm, the Congregation shall sing or say the Gloria Patri.*

GLORIA PATRI

Glory be to the Father:
  and to the Son and to the Holy Ghost;

As it was in the beginning,
  is now, and ever shall be, world without end. Amen.

The Gloria Patri is a formula which combines doctrinal and devotional values. It is a brief but clear profession of faith in the Holy Trinity. As such it gives an impressive and truly Christian conclusion to the Old Testament psalms whenever they are used in Christian worship. "The psalms are thus sealed with the sign of Christian baptism—the confession of faith in the Father, Son, and Holy Ghost".[6]

The earliest form of the Gloria Patri was "Glory be to the Father, and to the Son, and to the Holy Ghost, world without end." The Arian heresy denied the eternity of the Son and used the form "Glory be to the Father *in* the Son and the Holy Ghost." To meet this error the orthodox party insisted upon the original form and added the clause, "As it was in the beginning, is now, and ever shall be." In the Middle Ages, particularly in Germany, the sign of the cross was made at the beginning of the Gloria Patri in recognition of its significance as a profession of faith. Ever since the fourth century the church has borne this repeated testimony to its faith in its use of the Gloria Patri. It continues to do so today as a protest against current errors.

[6] Cabrol, *Liturgical Prayer,* p. 176.

The minister, choir, and congregation stand for the Psalm. If it is chanted, the minister may remain at the clergy stall. If the Psalm is read responsively, the minister may read his part from his stall or at the altar.

While certain psalms, or portions of psalms, are definitely sacramental in character, psalmody as a whole, like hymnody, is a devotional or sacrificial element in the service. The minister faces the altar. Those who face the congregation justify their action by the traditional monastic practice according to which two groups faced each other as they recited the Psalter antiphonally. It would seem that this should have less weight in determining the position of the minister today than the evident sacrificial character of psalmody in general.

If chanted, the first half of each psalm verse may be sung by the choir, the congregation joining in the second half. This same division of the psalm verse into halves at the colon is usual in Lutheran congregations when the psalm is read. This has its origin in the chants of the monasteries. The meaning of the text, however, is probably more readily grasped when whole verses instead of half-verses are read responsively, though the half-verse style seems to have been the original Hebrew use.

If the Psalm is read responsively, the Gloria Patri may be sung to one of the Anglican chants given in the *Service Book*. There is a special chant for Lent (No. III) by Harold W. Gilbert. If the psalm is chanted, the music of the chant may be continued in the Gloria Patri.

THE LESSON

¶ *The Lessons shall then be read. After each Lesson shall be sung or said the Response.*

O Lord, have mercy upon us.
℟. Thanks be to God.

(For discussion of the Lesson in Matins and Vespers see pp. 399ff.)

From one to three lessons may be read. On Sundays and festivals two are prescribed, one from the Epistles and one from the Gospels. The stated lesson from the Old Testament may be read as a first lesson.

(For the prescribed lesson, see the *Service Book,* pp. 280f.)

Valuable suggestions for the choice of daily lessons will be found in another table, in the word edition only. This table seeks to include Scripture appropriate for public reading not contained in the Gospels and Epistles of the church year. It has less value for a single weekly service.

✠

The response to the Lesson is a significant and impressive conclusion

413

to the reading of Scripture. In the Roman rite it is said only in the little hours, Terce, Sext and None. Lutheran use in the Reformation period prescribed it at the end of each lesson at Matins and Vespers. It voices our constant need for mercy and our thankfulness that in God's Word, as nowhere else, we are assured of it.

The Latin and the German texts (*Tu autem, Domine, miserere nobis,* and *Du aber, O Herr, erbarme dich unser*) indicate a strong contrast of feeling. Upon hearing God's Word our first thought is how poorly we have kept and done it—"but thou, O Lord, have mercy upon us." Our second thought is of God's mercy and forgiveness—"Thanks be to God."

✠

The minister should pause before announcing the Lesson until assured that the congregation is seated and prepared to give quiet attention.

The Lesson should be announced and concluded precisely as indicated in the rubrics (*Service Book,* p. 275). Miscellaneous introductions and conclusions are incongruous and disturbing.

The reading of Holy Scripture should be invested with significance and dignity. The text of the lessons should be separated from everything else. A slight pause may well be made before the reader says, "Here endeth the Lesson," and again before "O Lord, have mercy upon us."

The minister at the lectern faces the congregation and makes a slight inclination as he says the response. The congregation's reply should be prompt and joyous.

THE RESPONSORY

¶ *After the Lesson a Responsory or a Hymn may be sung.*

(Advent)

BEHOLD, the days come, saith the Lord, that I will raise unto David a righteous Branch, and a King shall reign and prosper, and shall execute judgment and justice in the earth.
And this is his name whereby he shall be called, The Lord our Righteousness.
V. In his days shall Judah be saved, and Israel shall dwell safely.
And this is his name whereby he shall be called, The Lord our Righteousness.
Glory be to the Father, and to the Son, and to the Holy Ghost.
And this is his name whereby he shall be called, The Lord our Righteousness.

(For general discussion of the Responsory, see pp. 401-03.)

This is one of the oldest and most beautiful parts of the service. Its form is individual and its function significant. Liturgical and musical effectiveness is secured by having the single voice of the reader of the lesson followed immediately by a choral response; and by the fact that the text of this response relates the Lesson to the fundamental and far-reaching thought of the festival or season.

Because of its liturgical and musical interest the Responsory should be much more generally used than is the case.

The rubrics permit the substitution of a hymn in place of the Responsory. This substitution of congregational hymns for historic choral features such as the Introit and the Gradual in the Service, and the responsory in Matins and Vespers, results in liturgical and musical impoverishment. The congregation should be taught to appreciate the full content of the liturgy and its music. The choir should be taught to appreciate these characteristic and beautiful choral elements and to devote its first energies to the mastery of them, rather than to the sole study of anthems, many of which are intruders in the services, liturgically and artistically.[7]

THE SERMON OR ADDRESS

¶ *A brief Sermon or Address may then follow.*

The liturgical content of Matins with its large provision of hymns, Psalms, lessons, responsories, canticles and prayers, provides an adequate service of praise and prayer even without an address. Upon occasion a sermon or address is appropriate, and even necessary. It is well, however, to note the permissive form of the rubric concerning it.

The question as to the place of the sermon or address—whether after the lesson or at the end of the service—was not determined by the church orders. It may follow the lesson, or it may follow the Benedicamus. In the latter case a hymn, collect, and benediction will conclude the service. This latter arrangement is generally preferable for regular parish services and particularly for occasions when special exercises such as commencements, musical programs, discussions, or presentations of miscellaneous nature, etc., are held. By taking the Matin order through to the Benedicamus, the unity and continuity of the service itself are preserved, larger freedom is given the address or special feature of the day, and the entire service is brought to a prompt conclusion after the address.

THE CANTICLE

¶ *The Congregation shall rise and sing or say the Canticle.*

In the Canticle the congregation lifts its heart and voice to God in an exalted response to the message of his Word as given in the lessons,

---

[7] Adequate settings to the responsories are provided in a series by the eminent German musician, Max Reger; also in a series by J. F. Ohl. See p. 403, n. 15.

Responsory, and Address. The Canticle also serves as a transition to the closing prayers. (For general discussion of the Canticle see pp. 404-05.)

The Te Deum and the Benedictus are the canticles regularly appointed for Matins. Anciently the Benedictus was used in the office of Lauds, which followed Matins. Instead of either of these, other canticles may be used. (*Service Book and Hymnal,* pp. 215ff.)

TE DEUM LAUDAMUS

We praise thee O God: We acknowledge thee to be the Lord.
All the earth doth worship thee: The Father everlasting.
To thee all angels cry aloud: The heavens and all the powers therein.
To thee Cherubim and Seraphim: Continually do cry:
Holy, holy holy: Lord God of Sabaoth;
Heaven and earth are full of the Majesty: Of thy glory.
The glorious company of the Apostles praise thee:
   The goodly fellowship of the Prophets praise thee:
The noble army of Martyrs: Praise thee.
The holy Church throughout all the world doth acknowledge thee:
   The Father of an infinite Majesty:
Thine adorable true and only Son,
   Also the Holy Ghost the Comforter.
Thou art the King of Glory O Christ;
   Thou art the everlasting Son of the Father.
When thou tookest upon thee to deliver man:
   Thou didst humble thyself to be born of a Virgin.
When thou hadst overcome the sharpness of death:
   Thou didst open the kingdom of heaven to all believers.
Thou sittest at the right hand of God:
   In the glory of the Father.
We believe that thou shalt come to be our Judge.
We therefore pray thee help thy servants
   Whom thou hast redeemed with thy precious Blood
Make them to be numbered with thy saints
   In glory everlasting.
O Lord, save thy people and bless thine heritage.
   Govern them and lift them up forever.
Day by day we magnify thee;
   And we worship thy Name ever world without end.
Vouchsafe, O Lord:
   To keep us this day without sin.
O Lord, have mercy upon us:
   Have mercy upon us:
O Lord, let thy mercy be upon us:
   As our trust is in thee.
O Lord, in thee have I trusted:
   Let me never be confounded.

The Te Deum is one of the noblest hymns of the Western church and one of the greatest confessions of faith in song. It combines praise and prayer in exalted strains of rhythmic prose. Its affirmations, almost creedal in form (particularly vss. 10-19) constitute a basis for petitions of universal significance. Some of its phrases are reminiscent of prefaces in the Gallican liturgies.[8]

The earliest explicit reference to the liturgical use of the Te Deum occurs about A.D. 500. It was commonly known throughout the Western church by the time of Benedict, whose rule (A.D. 530) prescribes its use at the end of the night office. A medieval legend, current since the eighth century, credited its joint authorship to Ambrose and Augustine upon the occasion of the baptism of the latter by the former. Modern scholars generally accept the suggestion, first advanced by Dom Morin in 1894, that Niceta, missionary bishop of Remesiana in Dacia (A.D. 335-414), was the author or at least the compiler of the hymn.[9]

The text of the Te Deum can best be studied in its terse rhythmic Latin form. In structural outline it resembles the Gloria in Excelsis, which, indeed, may have influenced its form. There are three clear divisions—two principal parts and an appendix. The first part (vss. 1-13), somewhat analogous to the Preface and the Sanctus, sounds forth the praise of God the Father (vss. 1-6), and then, in full chorus, of the Holy Trinity (vss. 7-13). The second part (vss. 14-21), again like the liturgy, commemorates Christ's redemptive work, and upon the basis of this implores divine aid.[10]

The hymn in the beginning most likely ended with the words "in glory everlasting." The third part (vs. 22-29) was probably added from one of the suffrages in the form of versicle and response, which anciently concluded certain hymns, in this case the suffrages which followed the Gloria in Excelsis in the Eastern Office. The Gloria has had its place as a morning hymn in the Greek Office since the fourth century. When it was transferred to the Mass in the Western church the Te Deum may have been inserted in the vacant place at Matins. In this manner the last eight verses may have become attached to the original text. They are chiefly from the psalms and lack unity. Many of the early manuscripts do not contain them. When found, they are in Jerome's version of the psalms which we know was introduced into Gaul no sooner than the very end of the fourth century.[11]

---

[8] See Andrew Burn, *Introduction to the Creeds and to the Deum* (London: Methuen, 1899), pp. 265ff; and Dowden, *The Workmanship of the Prayer Book,* Ch. VII.

[9] For reasons, see the article "Te Deum" by H. T. Henry, in the *Catholic Encyclopedia*, XIV, 468ff.

[10] See particularly Fernand Cabrol, *Liturgical Prayer,* Chap. XII.

[11] The late addition of vss. 22-29 is confirmed by the ancient plain-song melody, which changes character at this point in the text. See Julian, *Dictionary of Hymnology*, pp. 1119ff., which discusses fully the text, translations, and music. Note especially p. 1131.

Luther translated the Te Deum into German in 1529, in a free version of fifty-two lines (*Herr Gott, dich loben wir*), arranged for antiphonal singing. This is found in Spangenberg's *Kirchengesenge* (1545) and in many other church orders and cantionales.

The English translation in the *Service Book* is practically that of the King's Primer (1545), one of the pre-Reformation vernacular service books in England. It is characterized by good rhythm but is not particularly accurate. It incorporates several changes first made in the American *Book of Common Prayer,* e.g., verse 12, "adorable" for "honorable"; verse 16, "Thou didst humble thyself to be born of a Virgin," for "Thou didst not abhor the Virgin's womb" (Bishop White's suggestion); and 28, "Let thy mercy be upon us" for "lighten upon us."

The historic plain-song melody of the Te Deum is clearly related to the ancient preface melodies. In Italy the peasants as well as the city folk sing it with enthusiasm at services of solemn thanksgiving. Palestrina, Anerio, Handel, and other composers used it as the *cantus firmus* for fine polyphonic compositions. It is given in Lossius, Eler, Keuchenthal, and other Lutheran cantionales of the sixteenth century. Merbecke simplified it greatly for use in connection with the first Prayer Book.[12]

The Te Deum is a morning hymn, as the petition "Vouchsafe, O Lord: to keep us this day without sin," clearly indicates. The rubrics (p. 276), in accordance with precedent, appoint it for Matins on all festivals (and during their seasons) and on all Sundays except in Advent and from Septuagesima to Palm Sunday. There is also ample authority for its use at Matins on ferial days during Eastertide, and as a hymn of thanksgiving at the Service on special occasions such as church anniversaries, national days, the declaration of peace after war, etc. Upon such occasions it may be sung between the Gospel and Epistle in place of the Gradual; it may take the place of the Gloria in Excelsis if there be no communion; or perhaps best of all, it may be sung at the end of the liturgy as a special act of thanksgiving.

The Gloria Patri is not used with the Te Deum; no antiphons are sung before or after it; and it is sung straight through and not antiphonally.

✠

The Minister may remain in his stall while the Canticle is sung if he also recites the Psalm from this place. Otherwise, and upon all festivals and special occasions of thanksgiving, he will stand at the altar facing

---

[12] This historic melody is set to the English text of the Common Liturgy, with harmonies by Joseph Hanisch, in the *Choral Service Book* by Archer and Reed, p. 182.

it while the Canticle is sung or read responsively. The congregation stands.

✠

The general use of the Te Deum in connection with solemn services of thanksgiving has led to the composition of innumerable polyphonic settings for choirs. English composers from Purcell to the present have produced many such anthem settings. Some are of great merit and others are hopelessly mediocre.

The congregation should join with the choir in singing the Te Deum.

The *Service Book* provides two virile Anglican chants by the eminent church musician Sir Sydney H. Nicholson. In each of these the threefold division of the text noted above is clearly indicated by changes in melody and harmony. These strong melodies are very effective sung in unison, though they may be sung, entire or in part, in four-part harmony.

BENEDICTUS

Blessed be the Lord God of Israel:
  for he hath visited and redeemed his people;
And hath raised up an horn of salvation for us:
  in the house of his servant David;
As he spake by the mouth of his holy prophets:
  which have been since the world began:
That we should be saved from our enemies:
  and from the hand of all that hate us;
To perform the mercy promised to our fathers:
  and to remember his holy covenant;
The oath which he sware:
  to our father Abraham,
That he would grant unto us, that we, being delivered out of the hand of our
    enemies:
  might serve him without fear,
In holiness and righteousness before him,
  all the days of our life.
And thou, child, shalt be called the prophet of the Highest:
  for thou shalt go before the face of the Lord to prepare his ways;
To give knowledge of salvation unto his people by the remission of their sins:
  through the tender mercy of our God;
Whereby the Dayspring from on high hath visited us:
  to give light to them that sit in darkness and in the shadow of death, to guide
  our feet into the way of peace.
Glory be to the Father:
  and to the Son and to the Holy Ghost;
As it was in the beginning,
  is now and ever shall be world without end. Amen.

The Benedictus is one of the three New Testament canticles which commemorate the Incarnation. The other two are the Magnificat and the Nunc Dimittis. All are found in the first two chapters of Luke's Gospel.

As early as the middle of the fourth century we find them appended to the Psalter, the hymnbook of the early church.

The Benedictus is Zacharias' song of thanksgiving at the birth of his son, John the Baptist (Luke 1:68-79). The text is cast in Jewish form, though the sentiment is truly Christian.[13] The first part (vss. 1-8) reminds us of the hope of the Messiah so long cherished by the Jewish people, but points out that the deliverance he has brought is a spiritual deliverance—to the end that we "might serve him without fear, in holiness and righteousness before him," etc. The second part (vs. 9-12) is addressed to the child John, whose birth not only fulfilled the ancient prophecy, "The voice of him that crieth in the wilderness, prepare ye the way of the Lord" (Isa. 40:3), but who, as the great forerunner of the Highest was called by the Master himself one of the greatest of the prophets.

In the Western Office the Benedictus was sung every morning following the Chapter (lesson) at Lauds. It was probably chosen for the hour —which was said at dawn—not only because of its thanksgiving for the coming of the Redeemer, but also because of its allusion to the light— "the Dayspring from on high." It is a Western feature not found in the Eastern or Mozarabic rites. In the Ambrosian Lauds the Benedictus was said immediately after the opening versicles. It came into the Lutheran Matins, as also into the Anglican Morning Prayer, at the time of the Reformation as an alternate canticle to the Te Deum.

The Benedictus is proper on all Sundays in Advent, and from Septuagesima to Palm Sunday, and also for daily use at any time. It is thus the proper alternative for the Te Deum.

✠

Anciently the Benedictus was sung to the psalm tones. It is now generally sung either to simple chants or in more elaborate anthem forms by the choir. The setting in the *Service Book* is to double Anglican chants by J. Turle and H. S. Keats, respectively. An antiphon may be used with the Benedictus as with the psalms.

THE PRAYER

This is a general heading for all that follows. We have had psalmody and Scripture, the Responsory, hymnody, and the Canticle. Now we have the final element of prayer, including everything from the Kyrie to the Collect for Grace.

Instead of the prayers appointed in the order, the Litany, the Gen-

[13] For discussion of Jewish parallels see Warren, *The Liturgy of the Ante-Nicene Church,* Chap. IV.

Instead of the prayers appointed in the order, the Litany, the General Suffrages, or the Morning Suffrages may be used. In the interest of variety and richness these other prayers should be used frequently.

¶ *Then shall be said the Prayers.*

THE KYRIE

¶ *The Minister shall sing or say:*

Lord, have mercy upon us.

¶ *Congregation.*

Lord, have mercy upon us.
Christ, have mercy upon us.
Lord, have mercy upon us.

The Kyrie, sometimes called the lesser litany, is a Christian version of a synagogue prayer based upon Psalm 51:1. The full phrase *Kyrie eleison* is the Greek equivalent of "Lord, have mercy." The Greek form persisted in the Latin Liturgy for centuries, a reminder of the fact that Greek was the original language of the liturgy as well as of the New Testament. The Greek form is still found in the German liturgies. The English liturgy retains the first word only as a title.

Scriptural parallels to this liturgical invocation are Isaiah 33:2; Matthew 15:22; 20:30; and Luke 16:24, though they were probably not its source (see above, p. 255). In every case we find here the cry of those in need and distress imploring divine mercy and help. In the ancient breviary offices the Kyrie at this place expanded into lengthy litany forms of prayer and intercession. As used here the Kyrie is a prelude to the supplications which follow, just as the Gloria at the end of the opening versicle in the office is a prelude to praise. The Kyrie thus regularly precedes the Lord's Prayer not only here and in Vespers, but in the Litany, the Suffrages, and the burial service.

☩

The minister goes to the altar, if he has not already done so for the Canticle. He faces the altar with joined hands and reads the prayers from the service book on the missal stand.

It will be noted that in Matins and Vespers the minister says the first petition only and the congregation sings and says the first three petitions in a continuous response. This is in accordance with the use of the early church and of the Eastern church today. The different arrangement in the alternate Kyrie in the Service corresponds to the Latin use.[14]

[14] See letter of Gregory the Great to John, bishop of Syracuse, quoted in J. A. Jungmann, *The Mass of the Roman Rite*, I, 338, n. 30; English translation in Bishop, *Liturgica Historica*, p. 123.

The first musical setting is from Tallis with the principal melody in the tenor. The second setting is a melody adapted by Merbecke from a longer Kyrie in a plain-song mass in the Sarum Missal. The melody in this case is in the soprano. Its form, with the first notes of the second and third petitions successively higher than the opening phrase, suggests increasing intensity with a diminishing conclusion.

Whichever setting is used, the music should be rendered softly but without dragging. Each petition should be phrased. The volume may be built up gradually until the word "mercy" in the final petition, after which the tone should diminish to a soft conclusion. At the end the organ accompaniment may be dropped entirely, the voices alone prolonging the final syllables.

THE LORD'S PRAYER

¶ *Then shall all say the Lord's Prayer.*

OUR Father, who art in heaven, Hallowed be thy Name, Thy kingdom come, Thy will be done, on earth as it is in heaven. Give us this day our daily bread; And forgive us our trespasses, as we forgive those who trespass against us; And lead us not into temptation But deliver us from evil. For thine is the kingdom, and the power, and the glory, for ever and ever. Amen.

This prayer, commonly known as the "Our Father" (*Pater noster*), expresses our deepest personal needs and the fundamental needs of humanity. Used as a common form by the congregation, its comprehensive petitions enable the individual worshipers to include such personal intercessions and requests as their own devotion may suggest. It also serves as a model for our private prayers.

The text of the Lord's Prayer used in the Common Liturgy may be said to follow the ancient liturgical and popular use rather than any single translation of Scripture as a whole. This explains the use of the word "trespasses," not found in the Authorized Version of Matthew (6:12) or Luke (11:4). It also explains the inclusion of the doxology, "For thine is the kingdom," etc., which is not in the best manuscripts. This is clearly a liturgical interpolation, though found as early as the *Didache* (A.D. 110), whose text incorporates Matthew's form. It is common in the Greek liturgies, but is not in the Roman. "For ever and ever" is a Hebraism carried over into early Christian services (Gal. 1:5, Heb. 13:21; Rev. 1:6).

The rubric, "Then shall *all* say the Lord's Prayer," contrasts with the medieval use, which was continued in some of the church orders for a time, according to which the priest said the entire prayer in Matins and Vespers, silently until the petition, "Lead us not into temptation," which he said aloud, the people joining in the last phrase, "But deliver us from evil."

The punctuation of the first two lines of the prayer has been changed from that in the Common Service to indicate that the phrase "on earth as it is heaven" is related to each of the first petitions and not only to the third petition.

✠

The minister faces the altar and says the prayer with hands joined.

✠

The Lord's Prayer at this place should be said and not sung. The use of chant forms here is not to be encouraged. There should be no organ accompaniment to cloud the clear and devout offering of its petitions.

THE SALUTATION

¶ *Then may be sung or said:*

The Lord be with you.

℞. And with thy spirit.

The origin of the Salutation and its response is to be found among the Hebrews, who employed the word "Emmanuel" (God with us), as a form of greeting (Ruth 2:4). We also find the expression under slightly different forms in the New Testament (Luke 1:28; Rom. 16:20; etc.). The formula was used by early Christian bishops upon entering the church. It soon found a place in the liturgy, where it introduced specific prayers such as the collects in the Mass and the Divine Office, the Preface, etc. It also introduced such sacramental elements as the reading of the Gospel, the Benediction, etc.

✠

The minister turns by his right and faces the congregation. He may slightly extend his parted hands in a gesture of greeting as he gives the Salutation, after which he joins them again. He may make a slight inclination in recognition of the response of the people.

✠

The response should be sung softly but without dragging.

THE OREMUS

Minister

Let us pray.

This brief invitation to pray is the remaining fragment of an earlier and longer use. We associate the *Oremus* with the collect which immediately follows. Anciently it was an invitation to private prayer with which specific directions were coupled, such as "Let us pray for Holy Church," etc. After a period of silent prayer the officiant collected and expressed the petitions of all in a brief prayer *(Collectio),* said aloud. In the Eastern Rite frequently the form was briefly imperative: "Pray"; or, as in the Byzantine Rite and the Kyrie of the Service, "In peace let us pray to the Lord." The fact that the *Oremus* originally introduced the perior of silent prayer rather than the collect, the latter serving merely as the conclusion of the silent prayer, may explain the brevity of many of the older collects.

¶ Then shall be said the Collect for the Day.

THE COLLECT FOR THE DAY

Stir up, we beseech thee, thy power, O Lord, and come; that by thy protection we may be rescued from the threatening perils of our sins, and saved by thy mighty deliverance; who livest and reignest with the Father and the Holy Ghost, one God, world without end.

Congregation

Amen.

This is the Collect appointed before the Epistle (or Lesson) in the Service on a particular Sunday or festival. It is repeated in Matins and in Vespers at this place throughout the week. If a festival falls within the week the proper collect of the festival becomes the Collect for the day and is read first. The Collect for the preceding Sunday may be read next.

As explained above, the ancient hour services, particularly in the Gallican Rite, provided an opportunity after each psalm for private silent prayer upon subjects announced in a bid. These silent prayers were finally summed up by the officiant in one brief collect. When desire for further brevity led to the discontinuance of the silent prayers, the fixed collect was borrowed from the Eucharistic Service of the day to conclude the office; or it was added to the series of versicles *(suffrages)* which, with the Lord's Prayer, concluded the office.

The use of the Collect for the day in Matins and in Vespers throughout the week links these services with the services of the preceding Sunday or festival and reminds us of its specific teaching. In recognition of its special function and dignity it is the first collect read, and receives the full liturgical conclusion as in the Service itself.

On the Collect, see also pp. 278ff.

The minister, having turned to the altar by the right (Epistle) side after the *Oremus,* prays the Collect with hands joined; or, if he prefers, he may hold his hands slightly uplifted with palms extended and facing each other at shoulder height. At the conclusion of each collect the hands should be joined.

The Collect is a very brief and often very sententious form of prayer. Its thought will not be grasped unless it is read deliberately and distinctly.

✠

The Amen after each collect and the response to the versicle should be sung promptly but in the mood of prayer.

¶ *Other Collects may then be said, and after them this Collect for Grace, with which a Versicle may be used.*

Let my mouth be filled with thy praise.

℟.   And with thy honor all the day.

THE COLLECT FOR GRACE

O Lord, our heavenly Father, Almighty and everlasting God, who hast safely brought us to the beginning of this day: Defend us in the same with thy mighty power; and grant that this day we fall into no sin, neither run into any kind of danger; but that all our doings, being ordered by thy governance, may be righteous in thy sight; through Jesus Christ, thy Son, our Lord, who liveth and reigneth with thee and the Holy Ghost, one God, world without end.

Congregation

Amen.

The final collect at Matins is the concluding prayer in the ferial (daily) office of Prime. The text, somewhat simplified, is found in the Gelasian Sacramentary. It was probably fashioned from two prayers of St. Basil attached to the Eastern office of Prime, and based chiefly upon the psalms appointed for that hour.[15] The translation is that of the American *Book of Common Prayer* from the Sarum Breviary text, which differs somewhat from the Roman.

It is difficult to conceive of a more beautiful or appropriate prayer for the beginning of day. Acknowledging divine providence in the past and looking forward to the trials and temptations of the day, it invokes the divine defence and governance.

The versicle and response which precede this collect (Ps. 71:8) were selected by the committee which prepared the *Common Service*

[15] Freeman, *The Principles of Divine Service,* I, 222.

Book in 1917 from the versicles anciently used in the Greek office of Prime.

☩

The minister remains facing the altar, not turning to the congregation for the versicle. This simply introduces the collect and shares its sacrificial character.

☩

The music of the response and of the Amen after the collect should express the mood of prayer.

THE BENEDICAMUS

¶ *Then may be sung or said the Benedicamus.*

Bless we the Lord.

℟.   Thanks be to God.

This liturgical conclusion and dismissal is a feature found in the Roman and the Lutheran liturgies, but not in the Anglican. In the pre-Reformation Office every hour was concluded in this manner. The Lutheran orders retained the Benedicamus, and, when no minister was present, this concluded the service.

The versicle is a summons to the congregation to thanksgiving. Its inspiration is found in the doxologies which conclude the first four books of the Psalter. (Pss. 41:13; 72:18; 89:52; 106:48. See also above, pp. 393-96.) The response *(Deo gratias),* is a prompt and terse reply in which thanks are given to God for grace received (I Cor. 15:57).

☩

The minister turns by his right and faces the congregation with joined hands.

☩

The response is sung by choir and congregation with fulness and breadth of musical tone.

The Benediction

¶ *Then shall the Minister sing or say the Benediction.*

The Grace of our Lord Jesus Christ, and the Love of God, and the Communion of the Holy Ghost, be with you all.

Congregation

Amen.

The New Testament benediction (II Cor. 13:14), sometimes called "the Grace," is found in the early Greek liturgies as an introduction to the Sursum Corda ("Lift up your hearts"). It was not used in the hour services of the pre-Reformation church. It appeared after the Reformation as the conclusion of the English Litany of 1559, and later was incorporated in the Prayer Book. In the Anglican use it is a prayer: "be with *us* all." In the Lutheran use it is a benediction: "be with *you* all."

The Benediction is a sacramental act. It is pronounced by the minister, facing the congregation with uplifted hand or hands. It should not be interpreted as a prayer. The text as given in the liturgy should be used without variation. (See also pp. 384-87.)

✠

The minister may lift and extend his right hand at more than shoulder height, the left being held flat upon his breast. He may partially draw the third and fourth fingers back into the palm, thus representing the trinitarian character of the Benediction by his extended fingers and thumb. If he desire, he may make the sign of the cross.

Instead of this traditional form, he may extend both hands fully open to make with his body the form of a cross. This procedure is, however, historically associated with the Old Testament benediction rather than with the New.

During the Amen the minister turns to the altar and offers his final personal devotions, which may include the Gloria or a prayer of thanksgiving. He may then retire directly to the sacristy. Or, he may follow the choir as it leaves the church in silent procession, or, upon festivals, singing a final hymn.

✠

The Amen after the Benediction is to be sung firmly but softly, with each note solemnly prolonged.

The congregation remains standing until the minister and the choir have left the church. It then bows or kneels in silent prayer which is brought to a close by a fuller volume of organ tone.

427

CHAPTER XXV

VESPERS IN DETAIL

Vespers (*vespera*—evening) is the historic name for the early evening service of the pre-Reformation church and of the Lutheran church since the Reformation. Corresponding names in Anglican usage are Evensong (1549) and Evening Prayer (1552).

This evening office from the earliest times has been invested with deep sentiment and poetic feeling. Man feels his kinship with all nature. The sun and the winds have done their work, the day draws to its close, the shadows lengthen, a peaceful calm descends upon the earth. So men feel a sense of duty done, the satisfaction that springs from honest toil in proper mood. Many seek change in worldly pleasure, and for some the hours of dark are the hours of frivolity and sin. The Christian, too, is not free from temptation. Isolation and weariness or evil companionship and example may lead him astray. There is grace and strength to be found in Christian fellowship and prayer, and a lively sense of God's providence may well lead the Christian, as opportunity affords, to recount the mercies of the day with thankful heart, and ask divine protection for the coming night.

The early church maintained an evening service called the Office of Lights *(Lucernarium),* at which candles were lighted for practical as well as symbolical purposes. In many respects this was reminiscent of the Jewish evening sacrifice with its incense and lights. Sylvia (Etheria) describes such an office in the Church of the Holy Sepulchre at Jerusalem in the fourth century. Cassian shortly afterward reports similar services of the monks in Egypt at which twelve psalms were recited as at Matins, each psalm followed by brief prayer. There were lessons from the Old and the New Testaments, and incense was used. Allusions in the earliest fathers—Clement of Rome, Ignatius, Tertullian, Hippolytus, and Cyprian, and references by Augustine, Ambrose, and Basil—testify to the general observance of the *Lucernarium.* Psalm 141 generally began this evening service, which included the Agnus and the Nunc Dimittis.

In the fifth century the Kyrie displaced the Agnus. The sixth century saw the introduction of responsories.

Benedict prepared his scheme of daily offices for religious communities in the West about A.D. 530. This was most likely an adaptation to monastic needs of the system in use at Rome, which in turn was probably largely influenced by Jerusalem. Benedict's order introduced the additional office of Compline to be said just before retiring. This deprived the ancient *Lucernarium* of some of its importance and symbolism. A new name, *Vespera,* was given the Office of Lights, which was advanced to a time between 4 and 6 P.M., when artificial light was not required. The ancient name *Lucernarium,* however, long continued in the Gallican, Mozarabic, and Milanese liturgies.

Thus Vespers, originally a congregational service, became, with Matins, the most important of the daily Hours observed by monastic communities. It never lost its hold, however, upon the imagination of the people. From earliest times to the present the faithful have resorted to their churches for this evening service, particularly on Sundays and festivals. The other offices, as a general rule, were observed only by the "religious." But Vespers has always been a popular service. The Roman church has consistently endeavored to give it particular solemnity, and provision is frequently made for a sermon. Certain dioceses have decreed that "complete Vespers be sung on Sundays and feasts in all churches," and efforts are constantly made to discourage the use of inferior music.

Luther's appreciation of Vespers led him to seek to retain and develop it for congregational as well as school use. He said that this devotion contained nothing but the Word of God, hymnody, and prayer. He provided consecutive readings of large portions of Scripture with vernacular expositions in place of the greatly abbreviated "little chapters" of the Roman Breviary.

The spirit of Lutheran worship did not favor the perpetuation of the entire system of hour services, but it sought to retain the essential features of Matins, particularly for schools, and of Vespers for congregational observance. The following Orders appointed both Matins and Vespers with particular fulness: Schleswig-Holstein (1542); Brunswick-Wolfenbüttel (1543); Waldeck (1565); Austria (1571); Saxony (1585); Pomerania (1690); Nuremberg (1691). Many other orders also include these offices in simplified form. German hymns were introduced in place of the Latin office hymns. The ancient melodies of the Psalms, antiphons, responsories, canticles, etc., from the Roman *Antiphonarium,* were adapted for use in the Lutheran services by Lucas Lossius, Spangenberg, Eler, and others, who edited "Cantionales" for

429

choir use. Some of the Orders provided that church bells (*kleine glocken*) should be rung an hour before Vespers, particularly on Sundays, and on Saturdays and other days before festivals. Parts of the service were retained in Latin, but the lessons and the hymns were in German. The confessional service was often incorporated. From this developed a particular form of *Beichtvesper* which substituted the Litany for the Magnificat and the usual prayers.

The later decline in the use of Vespers is to be attributed largely to continued use of the Latin language for many parts of the service. No prompt effort was made to translate the entire service into the vernacular as was done in England. German hymns were gradually substituted for particular parts of the ancient order, and the service thus lost the characteristic Vesper structure. Freedom was also permitted the choir in the introduction of special musical numbers. Thus this ancient and beautiful service, rich in devotional and esthetic elements, was eventually supplanted by more or less "free services" often of nondescript character. The nineteenth-century revival of church life in Germany under the leadership of Loehe, Schoeberlein, Armknecht, and others, sought to restore the ancient Vespers to congregational use. This was not generally successful, though deaconess institutions revived the observance of the office.

The Common Service restored Vespers and developed general congregational appreciation and use of this service throughout the Lutheran church in America. Schools and seminaries regularly use the order of Vespers for their daily chapel services, and conferences, synods and districts increasingly employ it for their devotional services. Congregations find this ancient office most acceptable for their regular Sunday evening services because of its interesting and balanced structure and its fine devotional spirit.

The Reformation in England, following the early Lutheran procedure in Germany, retained the Vesper outline for its order of Evening Prayer. Every parish priest "being at home and not otherwise reasonably hindered" was required to say Vespers (Evensong) in the church with the bell rung in advance so that "the people may come to hear God's Word and to pray with him." Considerable changes were made in the historic structure of the office, the complete text of which was provided at once in English. A new division of the Psalter was made; a plan of extensive Scripture reading was provided; penitential opening sentences and a confession were prefixed to the order (in 1552); and certain features from the office of Compline were incorporated. The provisions of the American *Book of Common Prayer* for this office have differed considerably from those of the English book ever since 1789.

Vespers is the "evening office of the church." As generally employed, it marks the consecration of the end of the day, though according to traditional practice Vespers of the day before actually begins the celebration of every day or feast in the calendar. Its significant quality, as distinguished from Matins, is contemplation, thanksgiving, and prayer. Its spirit is perhaps better expressed by the early English and the Swedish "Evensong" than by "Evening Prayer." It looks backward in thankfulness for the mercies of the day and invokes divine protection against all foes, and the gift of that peace which the world cannot give. The element of praise (e.g., in the Magnificat) is not lacking, but, generally speaking, God is praised in Vespers chiefly for his spiritual mercies.[1] The offices are similar, but there are significant differences. The Invitatory and the Venite, so appropriate in the first service of the day, are absent in Vespers. The order of parts differs in that the psalm immediately follows the opening versicles and the office hymn is connected with the Canticle rather than with the Psalm. The hymns naturally include the thought of the evening. The Canticle is the Magnificat or the Nunc Dimittis, the latter borrowed from Compline. The final Collect is the Collect for Peace.

Since Matins and Vespers are almost identical in structure, directions and suggestions for one apply almost equally to the other. Inasmuch as this book is in the nature of a study or reference work, it has been thought best to repeat for Vespers some of the material given for Matins.

The office begins with a hymn to the Holy Spirit, a hymn of the season, an evening hymn or a hymn of praise.

✠

In congregational use, Vespers is generally conducted at the altar. Historic considerations, however, justify the practice, where local conditions permit, of the minister reading this service from a prayer desk or a clergy stall in the chancel. In this case he will go to the altar for the final prayers and the Benediction. When small parish groups meet without organist or choir, Vespers may be used as a said office.

The minister may follow the choir or he may enter the chancel from the sacristy as the first stanza of the opening hymn is sung. He pauses for silent prayer at the foot of the altar steps and then proceeds to the altar (or to the prayer desk).

---

[1] The traditional Vesper hymns of the Roman Breviary, which may date from the sixth century, are hymns of praise related to the different days of creation. At Sunday Vespers the reference is to the creation of light; on Monday, to the separation of the earth and the waters; on Tuesday, the creation of the plants, etc. The Saturday hymn, because of the close connection with the office of Sunday, refers to the Holy Trinity.

On festivals the hymn may be sung in procession. On other days the choir may enter the church in procession and go to the stalls without singing. The organist plays softly until the choir is in place and the minister in the chancel.

The congregation rises when the choir enters the church and remains standing until the end of the Psalm.

At the end of the hymn the organist modulates into the key of the service before the minister begins the Versicles.

¶ *The Versicles with the Gloria Patri shall be sung or said, the Congregation standing until the end of the Psalm.*

¶ *The Alleluia shall be omitted in Lent.*

THE VERSICLES

O Lord, open thou my lips:
℞. And my mouth shall show forth thy praise.

Make haste, O God, to deliver me:
℞. Make haste to help me, O Lord.

Glory be to the Father, and to the Son, and to the Holy Ghost:
℞. As it was in the beginning, is now, and ever shall be, world without end. Amen.

(Omit during Lent.)

Alleluia

Vespers, like Matins, begins with a group of versicles followed by the Gloria. The versicles are introductory psalm passages in the spirit of prayer. They conclude with the Gloria Patri, an act of praise. Together they serve as a liturgical introduction to the major elements which follow—psalmody, hymnody, Scripture lessons, the Canticle, and prayer.

The first versicle (Ps. 51:15) was used in the pre-Reformation church only at Matins, where, at the first service of the day, it was particularly suitable. The Common Service (1888), omitted this versicle in Vespers. The *Common Service Book* (1917), recognizing its appropriateness for congregational use, included it in the Vesper order, and it has been retained in the Common Liturgy.

The second versicle (Ps. 70:1) began every hour service except Matins, before the Reformation. In early times the entire psalm was said while going from the dormitory to the chapel. This versicle, therefore, is the partial survival of an interesting ancient use. It invokes the divine aid and inspiration in all that follows. It is not in the American *Book of*

432

Common Prayer, though it is in the English and Scottish Prayer Books as well as in the Roman and Lutheran uses, generally.[2]

The Gloria Patri in responsive form concludes the versicles, as it concludes every psalm when used in Christian worship.

Alleluia is a Hebrew expression used in the great psalms of praise, particularly Psalms 113-118. It is omitted during Lent. The English Prayer Book of 1549 gave the English equivalent, "Praise ye the Lord." In 1661 the response "The Lord's Name be praised" was added.

✠

If the minister is conducting the service at the altar he faces the altar for the versicles.

✠

The very first rubric should be noted. This states that "intonations provided for the Minister's parts of the Services represent a permissive use. They are not to be considered directive."

The music of the versicles and the Gloria Patri is a traditional setting based upon the ancient plain song and harmonized by Thomas Tallis for the English *Book of Common Prayer.* It was not published until 1641, though Tallis died in 1585.

The responses should be sung in moderate volume and tempo with distinct enunciation of the words.

¶ *Then shall be sung or said one or more Psalms.*

THE PSALM

(For psalmody in general, see pp. 393-96.)

One or more psalms are read or chanted. Where daily services are held, the Psalter may be read consecutively; in general congregational use a selection is made on the basis of propriety. (See the table of Psalms, *Service Book,* pp. 282 f.)

If the psalms are chanted an antiphon may be sung by a solo voice before each psalm and repeated by the choir after the Gloria Patri. Good reading, however, is to be preferred to poor chanting.

¶ *At the end of each Psalm the Congregation shall sing or say the Gloria Patri.*

GLORIA PATRI

Glory be to the Father: and to the Son and to the Holy Ghost;
As it was in the beginning, is now and ever shall be, world without end. Amen.

The Gloria Patri is a formula which combines doctrinal and devotional values. It is a brief but clear profession of faith in the Holy

[2] See "Matins in Detail," above, p. 409, n. 3.

Trinity. As such it gives an impressive and truly Christian conclusion to the Old Testament Psalms whenever these are used in Christian worship. "The Psalms are thus sealed with the sign of Christian Baptism —the confession of faith in the Father, Son and Holy Ghost."[3] See also above p. 264.

The earliest form of the Gloria Patri was "Glory be to the Father, and to the Son, and to the Holy Ghost, world without end." The Arian heresy denied the eternity of the Son and used the form, "Glory be to the Father *in* the Son and the Holy Ghost." To meet this error the orthodox party insisted upon the original form and added the clause, "As it was in the beginning, is now, and ever shall be." In the Middle Ages, particularly in Germany, the sign of the cross was made at the beginning of the Gloria Patri in recognition of its significance as a profession of faith. Thus ever since the fourth century the church has borne this repeated testimony to the Holy Trinity in its use of the Gloria Patri. It continues to do so today as a protest against current errors.

✠

The minister, choir, and congregation stand for the Psalm. If it is chanted the minister may remain at the clergy stall. If the Psalm is read responsively, the minister may read his part from his stall or at the altar.

While certain psalms, or portions of psalms, are definitely sacramental in character, psalmody as a whole, like hymnody, is a devotional or sacrificial element in the service. The minister faces the altar. Those who face the congregation justify their action by the traditional monastic practice according to which the groups faced each other as they recited the Psalter antiphonally. It would seem, though, that this should have less weight in determining the position of the minister today than the evident sacrificial character of psalmody in general.

✠

If chanted, the first half of each psalm verse may be sung by the choir, the congregation joining in the second half. This same division of the psalm verse into halves at the colon is usual in Lutheran congregations when the Psalm is read. The meaning of the text, however, is probably more readily grasped when whole verses instead of half verses are read responsively.

If the Psalm is read responsively, the Gloria Patri may be sung to one of the Anglican chants given in the *Service Book*. There is a special chant for Lent (No. III) by Harold W. Gilbert.

[3] Cabrol, *Liturgical Prayer*, p. 176.

THE LESSON

¶ The Lessons shall then be read. After each Lesson shall be sung or said the Response.

O Lord, have mercy upon us.
℞.   Thanks be to God.

(For discussion of the Lesson in Matins and Vespers see p. 399.)

From one to three lessons may be read. On Sundays and festivals two are prescribed, one from the Epistles and one from the Gospels (*Service Book,* pp. 280f). The stated lesson from the Old Testament may be read as a first lesson.

Valuable suggestions for the choice of daily lessons will be found in a table in the word edition of the *Service Book.* This table seeks to include Scripture appropriate for public reading not contained in the Gospels and Epistles of the church year. It has less value for a single weekly service.

✠

The response here is a significant and impressive conclusion to the reading of Scripture. In the Roman use it is said only in the little hours, Terce, Sext, and None. Lutheran use in the Reformation period prescribed it at the end of each lesson at Matins and Vespers. It voices our constant need for mercy and our thankfulness that in God's Word, as nowhere else, we are assured of it.

The Latin and the German texts (*Tu autem, Domine, miserere nobis,* and *Du aber, O Herr, erbarme dich unser*) indicate a strong contrast of feeling. Upon hearing God's Word our first thought is how poorly we have kept and done it—"but thou, O Lord, have mercy upon us." Our second thought is of God's mercy and forgiveness—"Thanks be to God."

The minister at the lectern faces the congregation and makes a slight inclination as he says the response. The congregational reply should be prompt and joyous.

✠

The minister should pause before announcing the lesson until assured that the congregation is seated and prepared to give quiet attention.

The lesson should be announced and concluded precisely as indicated in the rubrics (*Service Book,* p. 275). Miscellaneous introductions and conclusions are incongruous and disturbing.

The reading of Holy Scripture should be invested with significance and dignity. The text of the lessons should be separated from everything else. A slight pause may well be made before the reader says,

"Here endeth the Lesson," and again before the response, "O Lord have mercy upon us."

¶ *After the Lesson a Responsory or a Hymn may be sung.*

THE RESPONSORY

Behold, the days come, saith the Lord, that I will raise unto David a righteous Branch, and a King shall reign and prosper, and shall execute judgment and justice in the earth.
And this is his name whereby he shall be called, The Lord our Righteousness.
In his days shall Judah be saved, and Israel shall dwell safely.
And this is his name whereby he shall be called, The Lord our Righteousness.
Glory be to the Father, and to the Son, and to the Holy Ghost.
And this is his name whereby he shall be called, The Lord our Righteousness.

(For general discussion of the Responsory see pp. 401-03.)

This is one of the oldest and most beautiful parts of the service. Its form is individual and its function significant. Liturgical and musical effectiveness is secured by having the single voice of the reader of the lesson immediately followed by a choral response, and by the fact that the text of this response relates the lesson to the fundamental and far-reaching thought of the festival or season.

Because of its liturgical and musical interest, the Responsory should be much more generally used than is the case.

The rubrics permit the substitution of a hymn in place of the responsory. This substitution of congregational hymns for historic choral features such as the Introit and the Gradual in the Service, and the Responsory in Matins and Vespers, results in liturgical and musical impoverishment. The congregation should be taught to appreciate the full content of the liturgy and its music. The choir should be taught to appreciate these characteristic and beautiful choral elements and to devote its first energies to the mastery of them rather than to the sole study of anthems, many of which are intruders in the services, liturgically and artistically.[4]

¶ *A Sermon or a brief Address may then follow.*

THE SERMON OR ADDRESS

The liturgical content of Vespers, with its large provision of hymns, psalms, lessons, responsories, canticles, and prayers, provides an adequate service of praise and prayer even without an address. Upon occasion a sermon or address is appropriate and even necessary. It is well, however, to note the permissive form of the rubric concerning it.

[4] Adequate settings to the responsories are provided by the eminent German musician, Max Reger (1914); and by Dr. J. F. Ohl in 1909. Both series may be secured from the United Lutheran Publication House, Philadelphia.

The question as to the place of the Sermon or Address, whether after the lesson or at the end of the service, was not determined by the church orders. It may follow the lesson, or it may follow the Benedicamus. In the latter case a hymn, Collect and benediction will conclude the service.

The latter arrangement is preferred by many for parish services and is particularly appropriate for occasions when special exercises such as commencements, musical programs, or discussions are held.

¶ *The Offering may then be received and placed upon the Altar.*

THE OFFERING

The minister may remain at the altar, facing it, or he may go to his stall while the offering is being received.

¶ *Then shall be sung the Hymn.*

THE HYMN

In Vespers the principal hymn, the so-called "office hymn," is connected with the Canticle instead of with the Psalm as in Matins. (See also pp. 396-99.)

The minister remains in the clergy stall for the hymn.

The organist modulates without any break from the key of the organ number or the offertory anthem into the key of the hymn tune. He must establish the new tonality fully before giving out the tune.

THE CANTICLE

¶ *The Congregation shall rise and sing or say the Canticle.*

¶ *A Versicle shall be used with the Canticle.*

℣. Let my prayer be set forth before thee as incense.

℟. And the lifting up of my hands as the evening sacrifice.

In the Canticle the congregation lifts its heart and voice to God in an exalted response to the message of his Word as given in the lessons, Responsory, and Address. It also serves as a transition to the closing prayers. (For general discussion see pp. 404-05.)

The Magnificat and the Nunc Dimittis are the canticles regularly appointed for Vespers. The Nunc Dimittis anciently was used in the final office of Compline. The Magnificat is proper on all festivals and may also be used at other times. The Nunc Dimittis may be used at any time except on the greater festivals. It is particularly appropriate during Advent, Lent, and the Trinity season. Instead of these, other canticles may be used. (*Service Book,* pp. 215ff.)

The minister may remain in his stall while the Canticle is sung if he also recites the Psalm from this place. Otherwise, and upon all festivals and special occasions of thanksgiving, he will stand at the altar facing the latter for the Versicle as well as for the Canticle. The congregation stands.

The Canticle is introduced by an appropriate versicle, which reminds us of the evening sacrifice in the Jewish temple. The response should be sung with moderate volume in prayerful mood.

THE MAGNIFICAT

My soul doth magnify the Lord,
    and my spirit hath rejoiced in God my Saviour.
For he hath regarded
    the low estate of his handmaiden.
For behold from henceforth
    all generations shall call me blessed.
For he that is mighty hath done to me great things;
    and holy is his Name.
And his mercy is on them that fear him
    from generation to generation.
He hath shewed strength with his arm;
    he hath scattered the proud in the imagination of their hearts.
He hath put down the mighty from their seats,
    and exalted them of low degree.
He hath filled the hungry with good things;
    and the rich he hath sent empty away.
He hath holpen his servant Israel, in remembrance of his mercy;
    as he spake to our fathers, to Abraham and to his seed forever.
Glory be to the Father:
    and to the Son and to the Holy Ghost;
As it was in the beginning,
    is now and ever shall be world without end. Amen.

The Magnificat or "Song of Mary" (Luke 1:46-55) derives its name from the initial words of the Latin text, *Magnificat anima mea Dominum.* It is known as the "Song of Mary" or more formally as "the Canticle of the Blessed Virgin." It is supposed to have been uttered by the mother of our Lord upon the occasion of her visit to her cousin Elisabeth (Luke 1:46-55). Some modern scholars believe that the Magnificat was really the song of Elisabeth and not of Mary. All the Greek and most of the Latin manuscripts, and many ancient witnesses, however, regard it as the Song of Mary. In some of the most ancient antiphonaries it is called the "Gospel of Mary."

The Magnificat shows a similarity to the Song of Hannah (I Sam. 2:1-10).[5] There are also echoes of the psalms in it. While steeped in Old

---

[5] See the interesting textual comparison in A. Harnack, *Luke the Physician,* trans. J. R. Wilkinson (New York: Putnam, 1907), pp. 203ff.

Testament phraseology, it combines, in a way peculiar to itself, exalted thought and utterance with great humility of spirit. It points to the fulfilment of ancient prophecy and it prophesies anew in declaring "from henceforth all generations shall call me blessed."

The text falls into four strophes, "advancing from the subjective to the objective, in order to return to the subjective, though in a higher form" (Harnack). In our use of it as a canticle, we regard Mary as a type of the whole church. In her song we too give thanks to God for the mystery of the Incarnation and affirm our belief in his mercy which is "on them that fear him from generation to generation."

The Christian emphasis also appears in the use of the Gloria Patri at the end of the Canticle. This specifically recognizes the fact that he who lives and reigns with the Father and the Spirit for ever and ever is our Mediator and that, as Paul says, it is right for us to give thanks "always for all things unto God and the Father in the name of our Lord Jesus Christ" (Eph. 5:20). The use of the Gloria Patri here thus incorporates Mary's specific thanksgiving into a more general thanksgiving.

The Magnificat has been sung at Vespers in the Western church since the sixth century at least. In the Eastern church it is a morning canticle. Durandus gives no less than six reasons for the use of the Magnificat at Vespers, the first of which is that "the world was saved in its eventide by the assent of Mary to the divine plan of redemption." Another quaint reason suggested is that it was "toward evening when Our Lady arrived at the home of St. Elisabeth."[6] Impressive ceremonies, including the use of incense, elaborate musical settings, etc., were traditionally connected with the chanting of the Magnificat at solemn Vespers.

In the Roman church the Magnificat is chanted to all of the Gregorian psalm tones. Eminent composers have set the text to elaborate contrapuntal compositions. Palestrina has no less than two settings in each of the eight modes. There are fifty known settings by Orlando di Lasso. César Franck planned one hundred settings and completed sixty-three. There are famous settings by Morales, Anerio, Vittoria, and others.

The Lutheran orders often referred to the Magnificat as "an excellent hymn of praise." It was frequently retained in Latin because of the music associated with this text. Many orders give the German text as an alternate with the prescription that this should be used at least once a month because the people attended Vespers and loved to sing this Song of Mary. The most frequently used congregational setting was to the Tonus Peregrinus (Pilgrim Tone). The Wittenberg Order of 1533 prescribed that "before a particular feast and after the sermon (in the

---

[6] *Rationale divinorum officiorum* (Venice: Valentinus, 1589), f. 162.

afternoon) they shall sing the German Magnificat as usual, with a German versicle." This points to a use which was quite general for a time, according to which each verse of the German (or the Latin) text was followed by a German hymn strophe which elaborated the thought.

In course of time elaborate choir settings by Lutheran composers pushed the congregational use of the Canticle into the background. Among such were the choral motets by Dietrich, Hassler, Vulpius, Crüger, and an elaborate five-part setting by Bach.

English translations of the Magnificat were current as early as the fourteenth century. The text in the Common Liturgy is that of the Authorized Version, preferable to that in the Anglican Prayer Books.

The position of the Magnificat was not so well assured in the Anglican service as in the Roman and the Lutheran liturgies. In 1552 the second *Book of Common Prayer* introduced psalms as alternatives to the Magnificat and the Nunc Dimittis in Evening Prayer. This was done in order to satisfy the Reformed party, which disliked the ancient canticles because of their use in the pre-Reformation services. Both the Magnificat and the Nunc Dimittis dropped entirely out of the American *Book of Common Prayer* for more than a hundred years (1789-1892). They were restored, though with the possible use of psalms as alternatives, in 1892.

The *Service Book* provides two fine double Anglican chants by distinguished composers for congregational use. An antiphon may be sung with the Canticle. On festivals the choir may sing a more elaborate choral setting, the congregation standing throughout.

THE NUNC DIMITTIS

Lord now lettest thou thy servant depart in peace,
   according to thy word;
For mine eyes have seen thy salvation,
   which thou hast prepared before the face of all people;
A light to lighten the Gentiles,
   and the glory of thy people Israel.

Glory be to the Father,
   and to the Son and to the Holy Ghost;
As it was in the beginning,
   is now and ever shall be, world without end. Amen.

This is the last of the three New Testament or evangelical canticles. The name is derived from the first words of the Latin text. It is known also as the "Song of Simeon." When Mary and Joseph brought the infant Jesus to the temple for the purification according to the law of Moses, Simeon, an aged man who looked for the redemption of Israel and the coming of the Messiah, took Jesus in his arms, and being filled with the

Holy Spirit, gave utterance to the words recorded in Luke 2:29-32.

There is a fine appropriateness in the use of this canticle for Vespers. Bright morning hymns and the jubilant Te Deum belong to Matins. The quieter evening hymns, and this, the shortest and tenderest of the canticles, belong to the close of the day. It is a hymn of parting and a prayer for peace and rest, in view of the end of the day and the close of life, sleep being a type of death. Its opening words suggest the figure of a sentinel who seeks permission to depart after a long vigil; or, more agreeable with oriental use, the figure of a guest departing after a visit. Like the Magnificat, it contains allusions to the Old Testament (Isa. 52:10; Ps. 98:2; Isa. 42:6). In our use of it, we, like Simeon, appropriate God's salvation in Christ and affirm our belief that God's promises in him are meant for the whole world. Philip Freeman refers to the connection between the Incarnation, the Holy Communion, and the evening office as suggested by the use of the Nunc Dimittis: "It originally occurred in an office (the Eastern Vespers) in which the True Light had symbolically been brought in, in the form of the Gospels; the summary of the Eucharistic Epistle read; and other features of the great Rite imitated or paralleled. It was a thanksgiving, therefore, not for the Incarnation only . . . but for the Eucharistic consummation . . . and for the Apostolic announcement to all nations . . . of the finished work of salvation. . . . These great topics then, associated with the eventide of the world and of the day, may well be in our thoughts in using this Canticle."[7]

This passage from Luke's Gospel probably was a canticle in the ancient Office of Lights (*Lucernarium*). It is mentioned in the *Apostolic Constitutions* of the fourth century (Book VII, 48). Though used in the Eastern Office at Vespers, it eventually came into the Roman, though not the Benedictine, Office of Compline. It was sung with much solemnity on the Feast of the Purification (Candlemas), February 2.

When the Lutheran orders simplified the ancient Vespers they introduced this canticle from Compline and appointed it as an alternate for the Magnificat. Frequently it was given as an additional canticle to be sung at the close of Vespers in connection with an evening hymn. The Nunc Dimittis doubtless came into the Anglican Prayer Book of 1549 from Lutheran sources, as it is not found in Archbishop Cranmer's second draft for his proposed reform of the breviary.

The Nunc Dimittis is set to two simple chants by Sir John Goss and C. H. Stewart. It should be sung devotionally but without dragging. The Gloria Patri introduces a brighter tone.

[7] *The Principles of Divine Service*, I, 358f.

THE PRAYER

This is a general heading for all that follows. We have had psalmody and Scripture, with their related features, hymnody and the Canticle. Now we have the final element of prayer, including everything from the Kyrie to the Collect for Peace.

Instead of the prayers appointed in the order, the general rubrics permit the use of the Litany, the Suffrages, or other prayers. In the interest of variety and richness these other prayers should be used frequently.

¶ *Then shall be said the Prayer.*

THE KYRIE

¶ *The Minister shall sing or say:*

Lord, have mercy upon us.
Congregation
Lord, have mercy upon us.
Christ, have mercy upon us.
Lord, have mercy upon us.

The Kyrie, sometimes called the lesser litany, is a Christian version of the synagogue prayer based upon Psalm 51:1. The full phrase *Kyrie eleison* is the Greek equivalent of "Lord, have mercy." The Greek form persisted in the Latin Liturgy for centuries, a reminder of the fact that Greek was the original language of the Liturgy as well as of the New Testament. The Greek form is still found in the German liturgies. The English Liturgy retains the first word only as a title.

Scriptural parallels to this liturgical invocation are Isaiah 33:2; Matthew 15:22; 20:30, and Luke 16:24. In every case we find here the cry of those in need and distress imploring divine mercy and help. The Kyrie is a strong, simple, natural cry of the heart. "It belongs to the intensity and the freshness of primal and spontaneous emotion. . . . Its accents are the tearful pleadings of a child with a merciful Father" (Bishop Dowden). In the ancient breviary offices the Kyrie at this place expanded into lengthy litany forms of prayer and intercession.

As used here the Kyrie is a prelude to the supplications which follow, just as the Gloria at the end of the opening versicle in the office is a prelude to praise. The Kyrie thus regularly precedes the Lord's Prayer not only here and in Matins, but in the Litany, the Suffrages, and the burial service.

✠

The minister goes to the altar, if he has not already done so for the Canticle. He faces the altar with joined hands, and reads the prayers from the service book on the missal stand.

It will be noted that in Matins and Vespers the minister says the first petition only and the congregation sings and says the first three petitions in a continuous response. This is in accordance with the use of the early church and of the Eastern church today. The different arrangement in the alternate Kyrie of the Service corresponds to the Latin use.[8]

✝

The first musical setting is from Tallis with the principal melody in the tenor. The second setting is a melody adapted by Merbecke from a longer Kyrie in a plain-song mass in the Sarum Missal. The melody in this case is in the soprano. Its form, with the first notes of the second and third petitions successively higher than the opening phrase, suggests increasing intensity with diminishing conclusion.

Whichever setting is used, the music should be rendered softly but without dragging. Each petition should be phrased. The volume may be built up gradually until the word "mercy" in the final petition, after which the tone should diminish to a soft conclusion. At the end the organ accompaniment may be dropped entirely.

THE LORD'S PRAYER

¶ *Then shall all say the Lord's Prayer.*

Our Father . . .

This prayer, commonly known as the "Our Father" (*Pater noster*), expresses our deepest personal needs and the fundamental needs of humanity. Used as a common form by the congregation, its comprehensive petitions enable the individual worshipers to include such personal intercessions and requests as their own devotion may suggest.

The text used throughout the Common Liturgy first appeared in the King's Book of 1543. This supplanted various English translations previously in use and gained universal recognition among English-speaking peoples. One petition was later changed. The text of 1543 read: "Let us not be led into temptation" a rendering to be preferred to the form we now have. This text of the King's Book, with the exception just noted, maintained its hold in English services even after the Authorized Version appeared in 1611. Our text of the Lord's Prayer, therefore, may be said to follow the ancient liturgical and popular use rather than any single translation of the Scriptures as a whole. This explains the use of the word "trespasses," not found in the Authorized Version of Matthew (6:12)

---

[8] See letter of Gregory the Great to John, Bishop of Syracuse, quoted in Jungmann, *The Mass of the Roman Rite,* I, 338, n. 30. English translations in Bishop, *Liturgica Historica,* p. 123.

or Luke (11:4). It also explains the inclusion of the doxology, "For thine is the kingdom," etc., which is not in the best manuscripts. This is clearly a liturgical interpolation, though found as early as the *Didache* (A.D. 110), whose text incorporates Matthew's form. It is common in the Greek liturgies, but is not in the Roman. "For ever and ever" is a Hebraism carried over into early Christian services (Gal. 1:5; Heb. 13:21; Rev. 1:6).

The Lord's Prayer is said only once in Matins and in Vespers in the Common Liturgy. Both the Roman and the Anglican liturgies give it more frequently. There is a gain in reverence and impressiveness in the restriction of its use.

The rubric, "Then shall *all* say the Lord's Prayer," contrasts with the medieval use, which was continued in some of the church orders for a time, according to which the priest said the entire prayer silently until the petition "Lead us not into temptation," which he said aloud, the people joining in the last phrase "But deliver us from evil."

The punctuation of the first two lines of the prayer has been changed to indicate that the phrase, "on earth as it is in heaven," is related to each of the first three petitions, and not only to the third petition.

✟

The minister faces the altar and says the prayer with hands joined.

✟

The Lord's Prayer should be said and not sung in Vespers. The use of chant forms here is not to be encouraged. There should be no organ accompaniment to cloud the clear and devout offering of the petitions.

THE SALUTATION

¶ *Then may be sung or said:*

The Lord be with you.
℟. And with thy spirit.

The origin of the Salutation and its response is to be found among the Hebrews, who employed the word "Emmanuel" (God with us) as a form of greeting (Ruth 2:4). We also find the expression under slightly different forms in the New Testament (Luke 1:28; Rom. 16:20; etc.) The formula was used by early Christian bishops upon entering the church. It soon found a place in the liturgy, where it introduced specific prayers such as the Collects in the Mass and the Divine Office, the Preface, etc. It also introduced such sacramental elements as the reading of the Gospel, the Benediction, etc.

444

The minister turns by his right and faces the congregation. He may slightly extend his parted hands in a gesture of greeting as he gives the Salutation, after which he joins them again. He may make a slight inclination in recognition of the response of the people.

✠

The response should be sung softly but without dragging.

The Oremus

Minister

Let us pray.

This brief invitation to prayer is the remaining fragment of an earlier and longer use. We associate the *Oremus* with the Collect which immediately follows. Anciently it was an invitation to private prayer with which specific directions were coupled, such as "Let us pray for Holy Church," etc. After a period of silent prayer the officiant collected and expressed the petitions of all in a brief prayer (*Collectio*), said aloud. In the Eastern Rite frequently the form was briefly imperative: "Pray"; or, as in the Byzantine Rite or in the Kyrie of the Service, "In peace let us pray to the Lord." The fact that the *Oremus* originally introduced the period of silent prayer rather than the Collect, the latter serving merely as the conclusion of the silent prayer, may explain the brevity of many of the older collects.

¶ *Then shall be said the Collect for the Day.*

THE COLLECT FOR THE DAY

Stir up, we beseech thee, thy power, O Lord, and come; that by thy protection we may be rescued from the threatening perils of our sins, and saved by thy mighty deliverance; who livest and reignest with the Father and the Holy Ghost, one God, world without end.

Congregation

Amen.

This is the Collect appointed before the Epistle (or Lesson) in the Service on a particular Sunday or festival. It is repeated in Matins and in Vespers at this place throughout the week. If a festival falls within the week, the proper Collect of the festival becomes the Collect for the day and is read first. The Collect for the preceding Sunday may be read next.

As explained above, the ancient Hour services, particularly in the Gallican Rite, provided an opportunity after each psalm for private silent prayer upon subjects announced in a bid. These silent prayers were finally summed up by the officiant in one brief Collect. When desire for further brevity led to the discontinuance of the silent prayers, the fixed Collect was borrowed from the Eucharistic Service of the day to conclude the office; or it was added to the series of versicles (suffrages) which, with the Lord's Prayer, concluded the office.

The use of the Collect for the day in Matins and in Vespers throughout the week links these services with the services of the preceding Sunday or festival and reminds us of its specific teaching. In recognition of its special function and dignity it is the first Collect read, and receives the full liturgical conclusion as in the Service itself.

The Lutheran Liturgy, differing in this respect from the Roman and the Anglican, permits the use of other Collects or prayers after the Collect of the day. These have the short termination: "Through Jesus Christ, thy Son, our Lord."

Traditionally the entire group of Collects should be uneven in number and not exceed seven. The final Collect for Peace again has the full termination.

In the earliest times the services of the Lord's Day and other festivals began with vigils on the night preceding. A survival of this is found in the Vespers of Saturday and other days immediately preceding a festival, such as Christmas Eve. These Vespers take on the character of the approaching festival. The rubrics prescribe that the Collect for the following Sunday or festival shall be used on these days.

On the Collect, see also pp. 278-87.

✠

The minister, having turned to the altar by the right (Epistle) side after the Oremus, prays the Collect with hands joined: or, if he prefers, he may hold his hands slightly uplifted, the palms extended and facing each other at shoulder height. At the conclusion of each Collect the hands should be joined.

The Collect is a very brief, and often very sententious form of prayer. Its thought will not be grasped unless it is read deliberately and distinctly.

✠

The Amen after each collect and the response to the Versicle should be sung promptly but in the mood of prayer.

¶ *Other Collects may then be said, and after them this Collect for Peace, with which a Versicle may be used.*

> The Lord will give strength unto his people.
> ℟. The Lord will bless his people with peace.

THE COLLECT FOR PEACE

O God, from whom all holy desires, all good counsels, and all just works do proceed: Give unto thy servants that peace which the world cannot give; that our hearts may be set to obey thy commandments, and also that by thee, we, being defended from the fear of our enemies, may pass our time in rest and quietness; through the merits of Jesus Christ our Saviour, who liveth and reigneth with thee and the Holy Ghost, one God, world without end.

Amen.

The Collect for Peace is one of the most ancient prayers of the church, being found in the Gelasian Sacramentary. It is unsurpassed in beauty and spiritual appeal. In the Latin pre-Reformation services it was used in the Mass for Peace as well as at Lauds, Vespers, and in the Litany. Because of its great popularity it was translated into many languages. It is found in many of the Lutheran orders.[9] There is an *English Prymer* version of the fourteenth century which is very quaint:

God, of whom ben hooli desiris, rizt councels and iust werkis: zyue to thi seruauntis pees that the world may not zeue, that in oure hertis zouun to thi commandementis, and the drede of enemyes puttawei, oure tymes be pesible thurz thi defendying.[10]

This collect is rich in historic associations. We cannot but think of the troublous times in the latter half of the fifth century when it was composed—"when sieges and barbaric invasions made men's hearts fail for fear, when Rome but narrowly escaped the Huns and did not escape the Vandals; when the Western Empire itself passed away before Odoacer, and Odoacer was overthrown by Theodoric" (Canon Bright). Then, if ever, it seemed as if the church and Christianity itself might perish in the general ruin.

Unhappily humanity has scarcely known a decade when, in some lands if not in many, wars and rumors of wars have not made this prayer appropriate. But beyond this, its deep spiritual significance expresses the longing of Christians everywhere in all ages, for peace within and without. The "fear of our enemies" is a constant experience, whether we think of threatened social upheavals, or whether we look into the depths of our own spirit and find tumult and temptations there.

As we use this collect in Vespers it also looks backward over the experiences of the day, and catching up the tone of the Nunc Dimittis ere it dies away, prolongs it in this petition for "that peace which the world cannot give."

The text in the Common Liturgy is that of the American *Book of Common Prayer,* which differs slightly from that of the English book. Beautiful as the translation is, the prayer is still more beautiful in its original Latin form.

[9] Paul Drews, *Beiträge zu Luthers liturgischen Reformen,* p. 97; *PE* 6, 358.
[10] William Maskell, *Monumenta Ritualis Ecclesiae Anglicanae,* III, 38.

The versicle and response which introduce this collect are from Psalm 29:11. This thought lays a solid foundation for the petition which follows.

Probably because of the strong sacramental character of these ancient versicles, Luther selected many from the storehouse of Latin service books and prefixed them to the collects which he translated or composed. The constant use of such pregnant passages of Scripture in responsive form in introducing collects has ever been a rich and characteristic feature of the Lutheran Liturgy, while it has dropped out of Anglican usage completely.

✠

The minister remains facing the altar, not turning to the congregation for the versicle. This simply introduces the Collect and shares its sacrificial character.

Inasmuch as the Collect is a very brief form of prayer, its thought will not be grasped unless it is read deliberately and distinctly.

✠

The music of the response and of the Amen after the Collect should express the mood of prayer.

THE BENEDICAMUS

¶ *Then may be sung or said the Benedicamus.*

Bless we the Lord.
℞. **Thanks** be to God.

This liturgical conclusion and dismissal is a feature found in the Roman and the Lutheran liturgies, but not in the Anglican. In the pre-Reformation Office every Hour was concluded in this manner. The Lutheran Orders retained the Benedicamus and, when no minister was present, this concluded the service.

The versicle is a summons to the congregation to thanksgiving. Its inspiration is found in the doxologies which conclude the first four books of the Psalter (Ps. 41:13; 72:18; 89:52; 106:48). The response (*Deo gratias*) is a prompt and terse reply in which thanks are given to God for grace received (I Cor. 15:57).

✠

The minister turns by his right and faces the congregation with joined hands.

✠

The response is sung by choir and congregation with fulness and breadth of musical tone.

THE BENEDICTION

¶ *Then shall the Minister sing or say the Benediction.*

The Grace of our Lord Jesus Christ, and the Love of God, and the Communion of the Holy Ghost, be with you all.

Amen.

The New Testament benediction (II Cor. 13:14), sometimes called "The Grace," is found in the early Greek liturgies as an introduction to the Sursum Corda (Lift up your hearts). It was not used in the hour services of the pre-Reformation church. It appeared after the Reformation as the conclusion of the English Litany of 1559, and later was incorporated in the Prayer Book. In the Anglican use it is a prayer: "be with *us* all." In the Lutheran use it is a benediction: "be yith *you* all."

The benediction is a sacramental act. It is pronounced by the minister, facing the congregation with uplifted hand or hands. It should not be interpreted as a prayer. The text as given in the Liturgy should be used without variation. (See also above, pp. 384-87.)

✠

The minister may lift and extend his right hand at more than shoulder height, the left being held flat upon his breast. He may partially draw the third and fourth fingers back into the palm, thus representing the Trinitarian character of the benediction by his extended fingers and thumb. If he wishes he may make the sign of the cross.

Instead of this traditional form he may extend both hands fully open to make with his arms and body the form of a cross. This procedure, however, is historically associated with the Old Testament benediction rather than with the New.

During the Amen the minister turns to the altar and offers his final personal devotions, which may include the Gloria or a prayer of thanksgiving. He may then retire directly to the sacristy, or he may follow the choir as it leaves the church in silent procession, or, upon festivals, singing a final hymn.

✠

The Amen after the Benediction is to be sung firmly but softly, with each note solemnly prolonged.

The congregation remains standing until the minister and the choir have left the church. It then bows or kneels in silent prayer which is brought to a close by a fuller volume of organ tone.

CHAPTER XXVI

THE PROPERS

The liturgical propers are an essential and characteristic feature of all Western liturgies. These liturgies, unlike the so-called "worship programs" prepared for a single service, provide complete and varied material for all the services of the ecclesiastical year. There is a fixed, invariable framework which is repeated every service. Into this are fitted variable "propers" pertinent to the particular service or festival.

These propers contribute more than variety, color, and interest. Their content focuses attention upon the specific message of each Sunday and determines the thought and mood underlying the celebration of the festivals. Taken as a whole they present the entire body of the church's teaching during the cycle of the year.

THE PROPERS AND THE CHRISTIAN YEAR

Early Christian worship was very simple. Scripture readings from the Old Testament, the Epistles, and later the Gospels were at first all *lectio continua,* that is, continuous readings of entire books. Weekly celebration of the Lord's Day and annual commemorations of Good Friday and Easter, and later on of other events in Christ's life and the life of the church, led to the development of the Christian year. This has two great divisions—the half year of our Lord and the half year of the church *(semester Domini* and *semester ecclesiae).* Saints' days and other minor festivals are distributed throughout both divisions. This system of corporate worship was born not of scientific exactness but of spiritual experience. It developed against a background of historic depth and consciousness with annually repeated commemorations of scriptural facts and persons. The Christian year and the Christian liturgy together constitute an effective and beautiful way of preserving and presenting the whole body of fundamental Christian truths in devotional form. Together they embrace the whole gospel, "the things most surely believed among us," the way of salvation, the rule of life. This regular and universal review of Christian essentials is theologically adequate, devotionally inspiring, and pedagogically sound. It also protects ministers and people against the intrusion of social and secular themes and personal preferences or prejudices into the services of worship.

The propers have unity and variety. They give direction, movement, and even dramatic intensity to the services for each day or festival They were not logically or psychologically planned. Their content, however, gives ample evidence of theological insight and liturgical skill. It would be difficult to conceive of more pertinent, harmonious, or beautiful selections than those for the Epiphany, Ash Wednesday, the Last Sunday after Trinity, and All Saints' Day, to mention but a few examples. Wisdom born of experience and knowledge of human nature are evident in the appointments for the fourth Sunday in Lent and for Holy Thursday, which afford relief from the rigors of Lent and the emotional strain of Holy Week, respectively.

We do not understand the reasons for some selections. Time has brought dislocations and changes. The historic series nevertheless remains today a significant and well-organized body of devotional material with Introits, Graduals, and Collects, as well as lessons, thoroughly scriptural in content and tone.

UNITY AND VARIETY IN THE THREE WESTERN LITURGIES

There are nine such propers in the Roman Liturgy. Each Mass has its own Introit, Collect, Epistle, Gradual, Gospel, Offertory, Secret, Communio, and Post-Communio. The Lutheran Liturgy retained the first five of these. The Anglican Liturgy dropped the Gradual in 1549 and the Introit in 1552, and ever since has had only the Collect, the Epistle, and Gospel. The Proper Prefaces which each of the three Western liturgies provide are also to be included among the liturgical propers.

The Lutheran, and the somewhat later Anglican, reforms of this complex medieval system were conservative, and yet critical and constructive. The two churches practically agreed in the festivals and saints' days to be retained in the calendar and in the retention or rejection of collect texts. While there was this general agreement in attitude and procedure, there were numerous differences in details as the two churches developed their vernacular services on the continent and in England respectively. Thus, the Lutheran Liturgy retained the historic Advent Collects while the Anglican Prayer Book substituted new compositions. Both churches rejected the Collect for the First Sunday in Lent as unevangelical. The Lutheran Liturgy substituted another Collect from the Gregorian

Sacramentary, while the Prayer Book introduced an original Collect based upon the Gospel. In the case of the Palm Sunday Gospel, which in the Roman Liturgy consists of two entire chapters of Matthew, the Prayer Book (1661) reduced this to fifty-four verses of Chapter 27. The Lutheran Liturgy departs entirely from the Passion narrative and gives the triumphal entry into Jerusalem, transferring this Gospel from the preliminary office of the Blessing of the Palms. A further illustration of the discriminating and constructive spirit of the Lutheran reform is found in the formulation of an entirely new set of propers for the last three Sundays after Trinity and in the introduction of such new festivals as Harvest and Reformation Day.

The critical and constructive spirit of Anglican reform is further shown in the lengthening, and occasionally the shortening, of many Epistles and Gospels, in the substitution of different Epistles and Gospels, and particularly in the free translations and expansions of the Collects and the composition of many new and beautiful collects such as those for Advent, Quinquagesima, Ash Wednesday, All Saints' Day, and many apostles' days.

THE INTROITS AND THE GRADUALS

The Introit and the Gradual are two of the historic propers retained in the Lutheran Liturgy. The church orders generally referred to them approvingly. They are given with Latin texts and the traditional plainsong settings in the Lutheran cantionales—Spangenberg, Lossius, Eler, etc.—and even in the seventeenth-century (1664) Nuremberg *Officium Sacrum*. As time went on they were partially translated into the vernacular. The Common Service gave a series of English texts of the Introits. The *Common Service Book* reintroduced the Graduals. The Common Liturgy expands both series. The Anglican Prayer Book does not have these propers.

The Introit and the Gradual are two of the three psalm selections in the Liturgy, the other being the Offertory. Occasionally New Testament and liturgical phrases are interspersed, as for example in Holy Week, when New Testament passages are used, and on Whitsunday, when extracts from the Book of Wisdom and the sequence *Veni Sancte Spiritus* are introduced.

Skill and taste of high order are evident in the choice of texts. The Introit sounds the theme of the day, especially on festivals. The Gradual is a song of passage, a liturgical transition from the Epistle to the Gospel. Both are choral elements which should be cultivated by organists and choirmasters in preference to the nondescript, irrelevant, and frequently incongruous anthems, solos, etc., which so often intrude in the services and mar their unity. Excellent settings, some plain song and others in anthem form, are available. Still more are in preparation. (See pp. 266 above.)

THE LITURGICAL LESSONS

The liturgical lessons are the core of the propers. The Introits, Collects and Graduals take their character and color from the lessons. In the early church certain books of the Bible were read through continuously. This *lectio continua* was interrupted by Easter and the later festivals, each of which had its own appropriate lessons. It was not until the fifth century in Gaul that a complete series of selected lessons for all the Sundays and festivals gained general acceptance.

The word "pericopes" as applied to the series of Gospels and Epistles which, with some differences, is appointed in the Roman, Lutheran, and Anglican liturgies, is of sixteenth-century Lutheran origin. (Brenz, *Pericopae Evangeliorum Expositae* [1566]). The basis for this series is the usage at Rome, perhaps in the time of Gregory the Great (A.D. 590-604). This was contained in the so-called *Comes* ("Companion" to the sacramentary). The earliest *Comes* has been ascribed to Jerome but is probably later than his time. Alcuin corrected the series of lessons for Charlemagne and the latter made it the basis for the homilies which he caused to be prepared for the clergy in his realm. Many changes were made during the following centuries. Isidore of Seville influenced the selection of Advent lessons. Other changes were made in Rome and other centers. The Roman Church finally unified and stabilized its use at the Council of Trent. The Lutheran and the Anglican liturgies, with few exceptions, follow the older use of Charlemagne's time and later, which had come to prevail throughout Germany, Scandinavia, and England (see the Preface to the Common Service [1888]).

The pericopes originated and continued in use largely because of homiletical considerations. In medieval times the lessons themselves were read only in Latin. The Hussites sought permission to use them, together with the Creed, in the vernacular. The church, however, permitted only the Sermon in the vernacular. This usually was a paraphrase or an interpretation of one of the lessons.

The Reformers took various attitudes towards the pericopes. The Reformed, beginning with Münzer [1523] and the Swiss leaders—Zwingli, Bullinger, etc.—abolished them. Calvin saw only homiletical values in them and substituted a *lectio continua*. The Lutherans, on the other hand, defended and kept the system, though admitting weaknesses.

Luther was one of the first to propose vernacular lessons, and it has been suggested that this idea may have influenced the preparation of his German Bible. He objected to some of the Epistles, those from James in particular. In general he favored a moderate revision of the lessons to be read in the services, but he kept the historic series, with few changes, as the basis for sermons. He and Bugenhagen and others published "Postils" on the series as an aid to preachers, quite as the homilies of Charlemagne had been prepared by Paul the Deacon for reading in monasteries and cathedral churches. The church orders generally established the series in Lutheran use, though a few prescribed the *lectio continua* and a few others gave a modified series.

At various times during the past two centuries the historic pericopes have met criticism at the hands of Lutheran scholars—Mosheim, Herder, Schleiermacher, and others. The Rationalists generally attacked them, claiming that some of the selections fostered superstition and violated good taste. Alternate systems were proposed by the Eisenach Conference, by Thomasius, and in the Hanoverian and the Swedish liturgies.

The considerations which have continued the pericopes in Lutheran use to the present are chiefly their popular appeal, the fact that preaching should deal with essentials, and the further fact that the series is Christocentric and better than any scheme which would encourage preaching on large portions of the Old Testament or on whole books of the Bible. The pedagogical values in repetition are also recognized, as is the fact that the series well defines and sustains the mood of the church's festivals and seasons.

Even the most earnest advocates of the historic series, however, must admit imperfections. Some of the great parables are missing, though the Lutheran Liturgy has introduced the parable of the Prodigal Son for its Day of Humiliation and Prayer. Some of the lessons for Lent represent medieval rather than evangelical ideas. The Gospel for Easter, and the Collect and the Epistle as well, are inadequate for this great festival. The former presents only the empty tomb and not the risen Christ. The Gospel for Trinity Sunday in the Common Service (John 3:1-15) was the historical and appropriate Gospel for the octave of Pentecost. It is not specifically trinitarian. The framers of the Common Liturgy decided to substitute the Roman appointment (Matt. 28:18-20) for this festival. The unique Lutheran provision of eschatological lessons for Trinity XXV and XXVI, while devotionally satisfying in connecting the end of life and the end of the world with the close of the ecclesiastical year, may be criticized from the practical point of view of giving a somber, lifeless tone to the season when congregational life normally swings into vigorous activity after the lassitude of the summer.

The mature judgment of the church recognizes the worth of the pericopes as a whole and approves their retention. As indicated above, the Lutheran and the Anglican liturgies have the lessons of the *Comes* and of Charlemagne's *Homilarium* with a few Reformation and post-Reformation developments. The Roman use, established by the Council of Trent, includes numerous variations occasioned by the multiplication of the feasts of Mary and of the martyrs, and by other later innovations.

From another point of view, we must recognize three types of lectionaries: (1) those of the early Middle Ages, before the general recognition of the Festival of the Holy Trinity; (2) those of a later period, from the thirteenth to the fifteenth centuries; (3) the sixteenth-century lectionaries of the Lutheran church orders, the Anglican *Book of Common Prayer,* and the Roman Missal. The lectionaries of the second period accepted the Festival of the Holy Trinity, and this, instead of the festivals of Pentecost and of a few important saints (Peter, Paul, Lawrence, Michael, etc.), soon came to dominate the final half of the ecclesiastical year, though the Roman church still continued to number these Sundays "after Pentecost." The Lutheran church, though in general keeping to the most ancient use, climaxed the process of development by establishing propers for all the Sundays that may occur in the Trinitytide.

A comparative study of the pericopes for this half of the church year in the medieval missals and in the modern Roman, Lutheran, and Anglican liturgies, shows that with the possible exception of the Epistle and the Gospel for Trinity III, no particular combination of Epistle and Gospel has been absolutely maintained throughout these centuries. The late Roman use discarded the traditional Gospel for the octave of Pentecost (Nicodemus and the necessity of regeneration), and substituted Matthew 28:18-20 (the divine commission in the Name of the Trinity) which was adopted by the Commission on the Liturgy. For the First and Second Sundays after Trinity it drew back the traditional lessons for Trinity II and III respectively. For Trinity III it appointed the old Epistle for Trinity IV and the Gospel for Trinity V. From this point to the end of the Trinity season the Roman Epistles are one Sunday behind and the Gospels are two Sundays behind the Carolingian lessons retained in the Lutheran and the Anglican liturgies.[1]

[1] For discussion of this and of other changes in Lent and Advent, see E. C. Achelis, *Lehrbuch der Praktischen Theologie* (3d ed.; Leipzig: Hinrichs, 1911), I, 361ff. Also Adolph Spaeth, "The Pericopes," in *Memoirs of the Lutheran Liturgical Association,* IV, 47-62. For the pericopes in general see also above, pp. 453ff.

The Lutheran church, on the whole, followed the Carolingian lectionary more closely than did the Anglican church. However, it established several new features, the most important of which were the appointment of the Festival of the Transfiguration, or its pericopes, on Epiphany VI, or, as in the *Common Service Book,* on the last Sunday after Epiphany; the permissive use of the History of the Passion instead of the traditional lessons for the days in Holy Week; and the establishment of an entirely new set of propers for Trinity XXIV—XXVII. The Anglican Liturgy was freer than the Lutheran in changing the length of the lessons. It advantageously lengthened a number and introduced several new Epistles and Gospels.

THE REVISED LECTIONARY OF THE COMMON LITURGY

The Joint Commission at first accepted without particular examination the traditional series of Epistles and Gospels which the Common Service of 1888 had taken without change from the *Church Book* of 1868. The entire subject had received no particular study by the American church for ninety years. As the work proceeded it became increasingly clear that some of the unsatisfactory features of the traditional system should be remedied. The commission also became aware of the thoroughgoing study of this subject in recent decades by liturgical scholars in Europe, and of the remarkable agreement reached by them in the matter of changes that should or might be made. The transfer in the Common Liturgy of nine Epistles to the list of Old Testament Lessons and the necessity of providing new Epistles to take their places, and also the necessity of providing Epistles and Gospels for additional days in the calendar, also focused attention upon this subject.

The "study group" of the commission (Horn, Seaman, Seltzer, Reed) examined the work of scholars in Germany, Sweden, England, Scotland, and the United States and the latest official books of European Lutheran, Anglican, and Scottish Presbyterian churches. The findings of the group were laid before the entire Joint Editorial Committee, which spent days in reviewing them and preparing the report which the entire commission discussed at length, modified slightly, and finally adopted.

The commission recognized the fundamental importance of this particular subject. In all its discussions, as in its final decisions, there never was any thought of abandoning the pattern of the lessons or of changing the emphases of the traditional system. The sole purpose was to improve the historic series, secure better balance, avoid duplication, introduce important passages of Scripture not found in the older series, and lengthen or shorten some selections.

The reason for lengthening or abbreviating certain selections by a verse or two stems from the fact that the verse numbers in the old Latin and German Bibles occasionally differ from the numbers in the English Authorized Version. The editors of the *Church Book* in 1868 probably followed the verse numbers in the older books without too careful examination of the text in every case. Now after ninety years all texts have been checked and necessary or desirable changes made.

The changes in appointments for the eighty-five days in the calendar as finally adopted may be summarized as follows:

Nine new Epistles were chosen for the festivals and days which, in the old series, had selections from the Old Testament as Epistle lessons.

Five Epistles and five Gospels were appointed for days in the calendar not previously supplied—St. Stephen, St. John, Holy Innocents, Saturday in Holy Week, and a second service for Easter Day.

Fifteen Epistles were substituted for selections in the old series (several transfers in this list).

Five alternate Epistles were introduced.

Five new Gospels and five alternate Gospels were appointed.

Twelve Epistles and sixteen Gospels were lengthened or shortened, in most instances by a verse or two.

Detailed comment upon these changes will be found in the following chapters.

THE OLD TESTAMENT LESSON

The desirability of including Old Testament Lessons has been frequently expressed. The rubrics in the Common Service and the *Common Service Book* permitted an Old Testament Lesson to be read before the Epistle, but this was rarely done. The readings from Scripture, on the average, consume but a small portion of the service hour. The commission believed that the reintroduction of an Old Testament series to precede the Epistle would not only be a return to a fine practice of the early church, but would be liturgically enriching and spiritually edifying as well.

The use of an Old Testament Lesson before the Epistle was universal in the early Christian church in both the East and the West. It may be well at this point to discuss precedents and sources for the reintroduction of this feature in the Common Liturgy, particularly as the Lutheran church everywhere else up to the present has followed the later Roman procedure in providing only an Epistle and a Gospel in the Service.

Rome's abandonment of the Old Testament Lesson was most likely part of an effort to shorten the services at various points so as to provide for much fuller material in connection with the ever increasing emphasis upon the consecration—lengthy prayers at the Offertory and in the Canon, etc. The Byzantine Liturgy in the East retained the Old Testament Lesson, as did many Gallican liturgies for many years in the West until the Roman use became dominant in the eighth and ninth centuries. Even then the massive power of Rome was not able to destroy this ancient custom in certain areas, notably northern Italy and Spain. The Ambrosian Rite in the diocese of Milan and the Mozarabic Rite in Spain have continued to provide an Old Testament Lesson in the Mass to this very day.

The non-Roman rites of the West are collectively called Gallican, though, in a restricted sense, the term "Gallican" applies specifically to what Joseph A. Jungmann calls "the magnificently independent and exclusive" liturgy (especially the *Missale Gothicum*) which prevailed in the Frankish realm of France and Germany until it yielded to Roman power in the eighth century and later. More loosely, the relatively minor rites—Ambrosian, Mozarabic, and Celtic (Scotland and Ireland)—are regarded as subdivisions of the Gallican family. We are concerned particularly with the Ambrosian and the Mozarabic liturgies because they are living rites, and because among other features they have retained to this day the ancient custom of reading an Old Testament Lesson before the Epistle.

THE AMBROSIAN OR MILANESE RITE

Milan in the fourth century was as powerful a center as Rome. The emperors resided there. It was the great northern metropolis of Italy, with commercial and cultural connections as far west as Spain. The towering personality of Ambrose, bishop of Milan A.D. 374-97, saved Italy from the Arian heresy and projected the influence of his city and diocese throughout the Western world. The liturgy of the Milanese church undoubtedly received extensive development from the East, particularly from Antioch, both before and after the time of Ambrose. The Cappodocian Auxentius (A.D. 355-374) was one of the bishops who came to Milan from the East, and others came later. At all events, a rite developed in Milan and spread throughout the Gallican areas, a rite which contains many features older than the Roman Mass and shows close similarities with corresponding features in the liturgies of the East.[2]

Charlemagne, seeking to unify his vast domains, attempted to suppress the Milanese Rite and substitute the Roman. He failed, though he did destroy all the Ambrosian liturgical books his agents could find. Various popes, as late as Gregory VII (A.D. 1073-1085), attempted the same thing

[2] See especially Jungmann, *The Mass of the Roman Rite;* Duchesne, *Christian Worship,* especially Chapter VII; and Fernand Cabrol, *Origines liturgiques* (Paris: 1906).

and also failed. There was a riot in the streets of Milan in 1440 because a papal legate said a Roman Mass in the city. The Ambrosian Rite was never certain of survival until the Council of Trent in the sixteenth century, in an effort to unify the entire Roman church to meet the shock of the Reformation, promulgated the rule which permitted the continuance of rites which could show an unbroken history of two hundred years or more. This saved the Ambrosian and the Mozarabic rites as independent liturgical systems within Roman jurisdiction.

The Ambrosian Rite, modified by Roman features, penetrated many areas in the Gallican West. There are traces of its use in Regensburg, Prague, and Augsburg well into the fourteenth and fifteenth centuries. It still survives in the province of Milan, in other parts of northern Italy and in parts of Italian-speaking Switzerland. Some of the characteristic features, chiefly of oriental origin, which distinguish the Ambrosian Rite in its divergence from the Roman use, are the reading of an Old Testament Lesson before the Epistle; the offertory procession; the invocation of the Holy Spirit (epiclesis); a period of six weeks in Advent; a great variety of Proper Prefaces and different melodies for the same; many rhetorical collects instead of simpler unified prayers. In addition, many ceremonial differences are to be noted.

THE MOZARABIC RITE

By the Mozarabic Rite we understand the earliest liturgy used in Spain and what is now Portugal. This liturgy is older than the present Roman Rite, though in later times it incorporated many Roman features. It survives today in the services of certain chapels in Toledo and Salamanca.

The name suggests Arab influence, though there was none of this. The rite was observed under Christian and under Moorish rule (after A.D. 711) until the eleventh century, when the Roman Rite gradually supplanted it except for the limited use in the chapels noted above. The supremacy of the Roman Rite was not easily established. Popes urged uniformity, but the Spanish kings and clergy opposed changes in the ancient forms. At one time, in accordance with medieval custom, two knights engaged in battle to determine which rite should prevail. At other times and places trials by fire were held to decide the issue. When the Roman Rite was finally generally accepted, Cardinal Ximenes, eminent as a theologian, philosopher, and astronomer, persuaded Pope Julius II (1503-1513) to authorize this Mozarabic Rite for six parish churches in Toledo and for a chapel in Salamanca. This secured the perpetuation of the rite.

The compilation known as the *Missale Mixtum,* and other well-preserved manuscripts, give us a good idea of the special features of the rite, and particularly of many agreements with the Ambrosian or Milanese Rite in differing from the Roman use. Our interest at this point centers in the use of an Old Testament lesson before the Epistle. Among other distinctive features may be noted: different saints listed in the calendar; differences in the liturgical lessons; a longer season of Lent; a lengthy post-Sanctus leading to the recital of the Dominical Words; greatly extended prayers for all occasions; the retention of the Epiclesis in at least fifteen masses; many differences in ceremonial; a special emphasis upon splendor, etc. Adrian Fortescue gives an admirable summary of the special features of the non-Roman rites and of the points in which they influenced the final Roman Liturgy. He speaks of the simplicity, austerity, and plainness of the pure Roman Rite where "nothing was done except for some reason of practical utility," and where the prayers were "short, dignified, . . . but almost bald compared with the exuberant rhetoric of the East" which strongly pervaded the Gallican rites.[3]

After the Joint Commission had decided to reintroduce a series of Old Testament Lessons in the Common Liturgy, a subcommittee (Drs. H. C. Leupold, E. T. Horn, and G. R. Seltzer) made a careful study of the Ambrosian and the Mozarabic lectionaries, the Eisenach series, the lectionaries of the Church of Hanover and the Church of Sweden, the privately published lists of Thomasius, Bishop Stählin, etc., as well as the lectionaries of the Anglican churches, the Church of Scotland, and the Roman Breviary. The committee's proposal of a table of Old Testament Lessons was finally adopted, with slight amendment, by the commission.

The lectionary of the Common Service (1888) appointed selections from the Old Testament as the Epistles for nine important days in the calendar—Christmas Day, the Epiphany, Ash Wednesday, Monday, Tuesday, and Wednesday in Holy Week, Good Friday, the Presentation of Christ, the Annunciation, St. John the Baptist, and the Visitation. The Common Liturgy, in each case, transfers these lessons to the Old Testament series, and appoints new Epistles in their places. It completes the entire Old Testament series with appropriate selections for the remaining festivals and days of the Christian year.

FORMATIVE FACTORS

A century ago Ernest Ranke undertook a critical study of the pericopes and concluded that many of the present selections are fragments of earlier and longer lessons, and that in many instances the occasion or reason for the selection of certain lessons has long since been forgotten. More recently the scholarly investigations of Stephen Beissel, Walter Howard Frere, Hartmann Grisar, Leonhard Fendt, Cardinal Ildefonso Schuster, and others have brought many of these occasions and reasons

[3] *The Mass,* pp. 173-84.

to light. The results of these exhaustive studies, with selected illustrations, may be summarized briefly as follows:

a. Ecclesiastical Festivals and Seasons

The lessons for festival days usually present the historic facts and the theological considerations which underlie these occasions. On Christmas we have the story of the Nativity and the doctrine of the Incarnation; on Easter the fact of the Resurrection and the implications of this doctrine; on Whitsunday the descent of the Holy Spirit, the functions of the Spirit, etc. The preparatory and penitential moods of Advent and Lent are fully brought out in the lessons of these seasons.

b. Survivals of the *Lectio continua*

Partial survivals of the early system of continuous reading from the different books of the Bible are found in the Epistles for Epiphany I-IV, where the lessons from Romans have but little reference to the season; in the Sundays from Easter to Trinity V, which, with few exceptions, have Epistles from the Catholic Epistles; and in Trinity VI to XXVI (except XVIII), which have Epistles from the books of the New Testament in their proper order.

c. Cycles which Present Specific Teaching

Four such cycles are evident in the Trinitytide. The division points originally seem to have been determined by the festivals of St. Peter and St. Paul on June 29; St. Lawrence's Day, August 10; and St. Michael's Day, September 29. As embodied in our present system these cycles are: Trinity I-V, the call to the kingdom of grace; Trinity VI-XI, the righteousness of the kingdom; Trinity XII-XVIII, aspects of the new life of righteousness; Trinity XIX-Advent, the consummation of the kingdom.

d. References to Catechumens, Baptism, Confirmation

These are particularly evident in the lessons for Sundays before and after Easter, as for example Lent I, II, III, and the first Sunday after Easter.

e. Commemoration of Apostles, Martyrs, etc.

The Epistles for Trinity III and V are probably related to the Feast of St. Peter and St. Paul; the Gospel and Epistle for Trinity XII reflect the proximity of St. Lawrence's Day. The lessons for apostles' days, evangelists' days, and All Saints' Day are definitely commemorative.

f. Significance of Station Churches

There were no less than forty-five different churches in Rome known as "stations," at which the pope or his representative regularly conducted services on eighty-nine specified days of the year (see p. 451). On

461

Sexagesima St. Paul-Without-the-Walls was the station church, and the lessons as well as the Collect specifically commemorate the great apostle in whose honor the basilica had been erected. The station church for the Fourth Sunday in Lent was the Basilica of the Holy Cross in Jerusalem, and references to Jerusalem are contained in the Introit as well as in the Epistle and the Gospel. The station church for the third Sunday in Lent was the Basilica of St. Lawrence, and Schuster even seems to suggest, quite fancifully, one may believe, that the Epistle ("Ye were sometimes darkness, but now are ye light in the Lord") may have some reference to alterations in the basilica which Pope Pelagius II (A.D. 579-90) made and which permitted more light to enter the older part of the building.[4]

g. Times of the Natural Year

The Gospels for Septuagesima (the Vineyard) and Sexagesima (the Sower) were originally appointed for early spring, when the farmers prepared their vineyards and fields. The later lengthening of Lent pushed these selections back so that they now normally come at the end of winter. The Epistle for Trinity XX ("Be not drunk with wine") may have some reference to the fact that this Sunday normally comes in Italy about the time when the new wine is drawn off (Schuster).

h. National and Local Conditions

The Introits and the Collects for Septuagesima, Sexagesima, and Quinquagesima reflect the great anxiety felt in Italy before and during the Lombard invasions. The Epistle and the Collect for Trinity IV probably refer to the disasters suffered by the Roman Empire. The Gospel for Trinity X may possibly have been selected in view of the fact that the date of the destruction of Jerusalem (August 10) usually falls about this time in the church year.

i. Influence of the Breviary Lessons

Dom Gaspar Lefebvre attempts to show how the general scheme of the pericopes for the period Septuagesima—Lent IV parallels the thought of the Old Testament Lessons in the Breviary (*The Saint Andrew Daily Missal*, p. 235); and how the Gospels for Trinity I-XI parallel the daily readings in the Breviary (*Ibid*. p. 754). The Epistles for Epiphany II-IV also parallel the lessons in the Breviary offices.

THE COLLECTS

The Collects, which have maintained their unique prayer form through more than 1200 years of unbroken history, have always been in close

---

[4] Card. Ildefonso Schuster, *The Sacramentary* (London: Burns, Oates and Washbourne, 1924-30), II, 95, 96.

relationship with the lessons. At the time of the Reformation the Lutherans and the Anglicans retained the Collects, while the Reformed churches discarded them. With relatively few exceptions, the same historic Collects for Sundays and festivals are in use today in the Roman, Lutheran, and Anglican churches (see p. 279).

The propers of the Common Liturgy present a more complete series of Collects than is to be found in most of the church orders or in modern European Lutheran service books. This series also keeps closer to the traditional body of Collects than does the series in the Anglican Prayer Book. Thus on three Sundays in Advent, Christmas Day, and Quinquagesima, the Lutheran Liturgy retains the historic Collects while the Prayer Book gives new or different ones.

The references to sources in the next two chapters will give the earliest known appearances of the Collects for the day and will also demonstrate the fact that this entire series of Collects had been incorporated in the pre-Reformation missals of Germany, Scandinavia, England, and other lands particularly affected by the Reformation. A careful study of the Nuremberg Missal (1484); the Bamberg Missal (1498); the Constance Missal (1505), and the Sarum Missal (J. Wickham Legg's collation of three early manuscripts) shows that of the seventy-five Collects for the day in the *Service Book* whose Latin originals have been identified, sixty-seven are found in all four of these missals, six others in three, one in two, and one in only one of the four Missals. In our use of these Collects today, therefore, we are continuing a use universally established throughout Western Christendom long before the Protestant Reformation.[5]

The English Reformers rendered a great service to the whole English-speaking world by their admirable translations, often free and expansive, of the historic Collects for the day and by their composition of new collects in the spirit and form of the ancient prayers, thoroughly evangelical in content. Usually these new Collects were developed from the thought of the Epistles. (Thus the Collects for Advent I, II, and III, Quinquagesima, Easter II, etc.). Occasionally these new Collects are based upon the thought of the Gospels, as for example the first Sunday in Lent, St. Thomas' Day, and other apostles' days.

[5] The three German missals are in the Krauth Memorial Library of the Lutheran Theological Seminary at Philadelphia. J. Wickham Legg's collation of three early manuscripts has supplied the Sarum texts. The author has not been able to consult a Swedish pre-Reformation missal except for the few scattered leaves of the Aboe, Strengnas, and Uppsala missals in the Pierpont Morgan Library, New York City. These fragments, however, and particularly the critical work of Gustaf Lindberg (*Die Schwedischen Missalien des Mittelalters*) make it clear that the entire system of propers found in the German and English pre-Reformation missals was also found with identical texts in the Swedish missals.

The Common Service generally accepted the classic translations of Latin originals prepared at the time of the Reformation for the English Prayer Book. Occasionally critical judgment was expressed in altered forms. The Common Service series also contained some original collects composed by the English Reformers and some original collects not found in the Roman or the Anglican services. Among the latter are the Collects for New Year, Trinity XXVI, Reformation Day, and Luther's Post-Communion Collect.

A careful appraisal of the translations and expansions made by the English Reformers and incorporated in the *Common Service Book* (1917) pronounces many of them real improvements upon the originals, as for example the collects for Epiphany II and V, Sexagesima, Whitsunday, Trinity V, XI.

On the other hand, some of the translations are inadequate, though in most instances only minor details are involved. In this group are the Collects for the Epiphany, Epiphany I and IV, Lent II, Tuesday in Holy Week, Easter III, the Festival of the Holy Trinity, Trinity XV, XVII. The Commission on the Liturgy, for the most part, accepted the series of Collects for the day as they stood in the *Common Service Book,* making only a few significant changes.

The liturgical propers, together with the liturgy and the church year, of which they are an indispensable part, constitute an important factor in the church's program of worship, edification, and education. Their liturgical, homiletical, musical, and practical values call for constant and careful study on the part of every minister, organist, and choirmaster. The minister will also do well to share some of the fruits of his studies in this field with his people. Catechumens can be given simple explanations of the propers and encouraged to follow the texts at every service. Bible classes and older groups may be led to an appreciation of what Professor Moffatt has called "the thrill of tradition" as they study the propers in connection with the history and the teaching of the church. Young and old will thus come to realize from their own experience the beauty and the worth of the Liturgy as a medium of devotion and an instrument of grace in the corporate worship of the church.

CHAPTER XXVII

THE PROPERS IN DETAIL:
ADVENT TO WHITSUNDAY

THE FIRST SUNDAY IN ADVENT

	Service Book	Roman Missal	American Book of Common Prayer
Lesson	Jer. 31:31-34		
Epistle	Rom. 13:11-14	Rom. 13:11-14a	Rom. 13:8-14
Gospel	Matt. 21:1-9	Luke 21:25-33	Matt. 21:1-13
	or		
	Luke 3:1-6		
Introit	Ps. 25:1-3a, 4	*Ibid.*	
Gradual	Ps. 25:3a, 4; 85:7	*Ibid.*	

Color: Violet. Creed: Nicene. Preface: Advent.

Collect

Service Book	Original
Stir up, we beseech thee, thy power, O Lord, and come; that by thy protection we may be rescued from the threatening perils of our sins, and saved by thy mighty deliverance; Who livest and reignest with the Father and the Holy Ghost, one God, world without end.	Excita, Domine, quaesumus, potentiam tuam et ueni. ut ab iminentibus peccatorum nostrorum periculis. te mereamur protegente eripi. te liberante saluari. qui uiuis et regnas cum deo patre in unitate spiritus sancti deus per omnia saecula saeculorum. *Gregorian*, 113. *B.C.N.S. missals.*[1]

Advent as a season of preparation for the Nativity originated in France. Its observance was general by the time of the second Council of Tours, 567. In some places six or seven Sundays were included. When Rome accepted this Gallican innovation, she limited the period

[1] These italicized notes on the originals of the collects are to be interpreted as follows (see p. 463):
B—Bamberg Missal, 1498
C—Constance Missal, 1505
N—Nuremberg Missal, 1484
S—Sarum Missal (Legg's collection)
Numbers following the names of the three sacramentaries (e.g., Gregorian, 113) indicate the locations in the corresponding editions of Feltoe and Wilson (see pp. 47-48).

to four Sundays. It was probably not until the thirteenth century that Advent was universally recognized as beginning the Christian year, which up to that time had begun with the Festival of the Annunciation in March or, in some places, with Christmas. While Advent never attained the severely penitential character of Lent, it has always been regarded as a season of solemn anticipation and of spiritual preparation and purification. Lossius, the friend of Melanchthon and the editor of a famous Reformation cantionale, speaks of a threefold advent—his coming in the flesh, his return to judgment, and his daily coming in the ministrations of the Word and the Sacraments. The seasonal color is violet.

The four Sundays in Advent are all festivals. The Nicene Creed is preferred, and when there is a Communion the Proper Preface for Advent is used all four weeks.

The Lutheran and the Anglican churches agree in the choice of lessons following the ancient *Comes* and the Lectionary of Charlemagne. The Roman Church later pushed back the Gospels for the second, third, and fourth Sundays and interchanged the Epistles for the third and fourth Sundays. In the latter case this was done to establish a parallel between the Third Sunday in Advent and the Fourth Sunday in Lent. The Lutheran and the Roman churches have the same Collects, while the Prayer Book has a series composed at the time of the Reformation.

The Gospel for the first Sunday recalls the word of prophecy, "thy King cometh," and its fulfilment in our Lord's entrance into Jerusalem on his way to the cross, whose centrality in God's plan of redemption is thus recognized at the very beginning of the Christian year. The Prayer Book advantageously lengthens the Gospel by four verses and the Epistle by three verses. The Epistle strikes the note of time and exhorts to preparation. The Collect voices the longing appeal of the church in the single word "Come," which is addressed directly to Christ. This form of address, while unusual in Collects, is particularly appropriate as we begin another "year of our Lord." The Common Liturgy retains the historic Collect but gives a free translation which avoids the unevangelical implications in the Latin word *mereamur* ("we may deserve"). The Anglican Reformers (1549), as in many other instances, prepared a new Collect based upon the thought of the Epistle. The Introit strikes the note of devotion to the coming King and consecration to his way.

In order to meet the objection that the traditional gospel for the first Sunday is the same as that for Palmarum, Luke 3:1-6 is proposed as an alternative. This introduces the Advent figure of St. John the Baptist, long foretold by Isaiah, and now come to cry, "Prepare ye the way of the Lord."

The Old Testament Lesson is Jeremiah's promise of God's "new covenant with the house of Israel," with his law not graven on tables of stone but "written in the hearts of his people." The collective character of the address makes the Lesson particularly appropriate as a message to the church of the New Testament.

THE SECOND SUNDAY IN ADVENT

	Service Book	Roman Missal	American Book of Common Prayer
Lesson	Mal. 4:1-6		
Epistle	Rom. 15:4-13	*Ibid.*	*Ibid.*
Gospel	Luke 21:25-33	Matt. 11:2-10	Luke 21:25-33
Introit	Isa. 62:11a; 30:30a, 29a	*Ibid.*	
	Ps. 80:1a		
Gradual	Ps. 50:2-3a, 5; 122:1-2	*Ibid.*	

Color: Violet.   Creed: Nicene.   Preface: Advent.

Collect

Stir up our hearts, O Lord, to make ready the way of thine only-begotten Son, so that by his coming we may be enabled to serve thee with pure minds; through the same thy Son, Jesus Christ our Lord, who liveth. . . .

Excita, Domine, quaesumus, corda nostra ad praeparandas Unigeniti tui vias; ut per eius adventum purificatis tibi servire mentibus mereamur. Per. *Gelasian*, 215. *B.C.N.S. missals.*

Again the propers are not in full agreement, as the Missal gives the story of St. John the Baptist for the Gospel (appointed for Advent III in the Common Liturgy) while the Common Liturgy and the Prayer Book give our Lord's account of the Second Coming. The Common Liturgy expands this as the leading thought of the day and provides its own translation of the historic Collect. The Anglican Reformers (1549) prepared an entirely new Collect based on the Epistle. This shifted the emphasis from the thought of the Second Coming to the significance of the Holy Scriptures ("Bible Sunday"). The Epistle is not closely related to the Gospel and probably was carried over from a *lectio continua* reading of Romans. The Introit voices the hopes of the post-Exilic age of restoration which harmonizes with the day's dominant theme.

The Gospel ends with the strong assertion of vs. 33, "But my words shall not pass away," the usual ending (MR, VEKD, LLKD, BCP).[2]

[2] Further abbreviations in this and the following chapter are as follows: MR, the Roman Missal; BCP, *The Book of Common Prayer* of the Anglican communion as a whole; BCPE, The English Book; BCPA, The American Book; BCPS, The Scottish Book, etc. SW, the Church of Sweden; VEKD, LLKD, RH, recent German Lutheran lectionaries; SC, Church of Scotland.

The Lesson is the stern final chapter of the prophet Malachi which speaks of "the coming of the great and dreadful day of the Lord," but also promises that the Sun of Righteousness shall "arise with healing in his wings."

THE THIRD SUNDAY IN ADVENT

	Service Book	Roman Missal	American Book of Common Prayer
Lesson	Isa. 40:1-8		
Epistle	I Cor. 4:1-5	Phil. 4:4-7	I Cor. 4:1-5
Gospel	Matt. 11:2-10	John 1:19b-28	Matt. 11:2-10
Introit	Phil. 4:4-6; Ps. 85:1	*Ibid.*	
Gradual	Ps. 80:1b, 2b, 1a, 2b	*Ibid.*	

Color: Violet. Creed: Nicene. Preface: Advent.

Collect

Lord, we beseech thee, give ear to our prayers, and lighten the darkness of our hearts by thy gracious visitation; who livest and reignest with the Father and the Holy Ghost, one God, world without end.

Aurem tuam quaesumus domine precibis nostris accomoda. et mentis nostrae tenebras. gratia tuae uisitationis inlustra. per. *Gregorian,* 114. *B.N.S. missals.*

The Gospel introduces the Advent figure of St. John the Baptist, the great forerunner who was "more than a prophet." The Missal gives the account in John 1:19-28 which the Common Liturgy and the Prayer Book reserve for Advent IV. The Epistle strikes a clear Advent note in vs. 5. The reference to "the ministers of Christ" and their work of preparing men for the Second Advent made it an appropriate selection for the Embertide ordinations.

The Collect is a typical example of the ancient Latin prayers which compressed spiritual thought of large significance in clear and terse phrase. The first Prayer Book (1549) retained this Collect. Bishop Cosin in the revision of 1662 introduced a new Collect based on the Epistle which again shifts the emphasis on this Sunday in the Anglican communion, here to the holy ministry. The Introit anticipates the pre-Reformation (Roman) Epistle, Philippians 4:4-7.

The Lesson is the opening passage in the second major section of the prophecies of Isaiah, the section of which Franz Delitzsch says, "In regard to language, there is nothing in the Old Testament more finished, nothing more splendid," and "in regard to content, this trilogy of prophetic discourses is still more incomparable." Jerusalem is comforted, for "her iniquity is pardoned." The rest of the Lesson points forward to St. John the Baptist, whose story is told in the Gospel.

THE FOURTH SUNDAY IN ADVENT

	Service Book	Roman Missal	American Book of Common Prayer
Lesson	Deut. 18:15-19 or Isa. 40:9-11		
Epistle	Phil. 4:4-7	I Cor. 4:1-5	Phil. 4:4-7
Gospel	John 1:19-28	Luke 3:1-6	John 1:19-28
Introit	Isa. 45:8a; Ps. 19:1	*Ibid.*	
Gradual	Pss. 145:18, 21; 40:17b	Ps. 145:18, 21; Veni, Domine	

Color: Violet. Creed: Nicene. Preface: Advent.

Collect

Stir up, O Lord, we beseech thee, thy power, and come, and with great might succor us, that by the help of thy grace whatsoever is hindered by our sins may be speedily accomplished through thy mercy and satisfaction; who livest and reignest with the Father and the Holy Ghost, one God, world without end.

Excita, Domine, potentiam tuam, et veni, et magna nobis virtute succurre, ut per auxilium gloriae tuae quod nostra peccata praepediunt, indulgentia tuae propitiationis acceleret. Per. *Gelasian,* 214. *B.N.S. missals.*

This last Sunday in Advent has been particularly designated as the *Praeparatio* in anticipation of Christmas rather than the Second Coming. There is a sense of immediacy in the lessons: "The Lord is at hand," "Make straight the way of the Lord." There is power in the very first word of this and other Advent Collects. Only four of the nearly one hundred proper Collects thus address the Second Person of the Trinity. In this instance we owe this address to Christ to a change made by Gregory the Great.

The thought of the Collect is quite similar to that in the Collect for Advent I. The Prayer Book (1549) has a free translation of the historic Collect which returned to the earlier Gelasian address to God the Father. The expansion of this prayer in 1662 caused it to differ further from the Roman and the Lutheran uses. The Introit, as on the second Sunday from the second part of Isaiah, again establishes a connection between the Old Testament hope of restoration and the New Testament Advent.

Alternate Old Testament lessons are appointed. The first, Deuteronomy 18:15-19, speaks of the prophet whom God will raise up. The Gospel records the statement of St. John the Baptist that he is not that prophet, but that "there standeth one among you whom ye know not." St. Peter and St. Stephen definitely apply this prophecy to Christ (Acts 3:22; 7:37).

The alternate Lesson, Isaiah 40:9-11, points to the triumphant approach of the Lord God, bringing back his redeemed people, coming "with a strong hand," but yet "feeding his flock like a shepherd."

Other Collects for Advent

O Lord, mercifully hear the prayers of thy people, that as they rejoice in the advent of thine only-begotten Son according to the flesh, so when he cometh a second time in his Majesty, they may receive the reward of eternal life; through the same thy Son, Jesus Christ our Lord.

Preces populi tui, quaesumus, Domine, clementer exaudi; ut qui de adventu Unigeniti tui secundum carnem laetantur, in secundo, cum venerit in maiestate sua, praemium aeternae vitae percipiant. Per. *Gelasian, 219.*

Most merciful God, who hast given thine eternal Word to be made incarnate of the pure Virgin: Grant unto thy people grace to put away fleshly lusts, that so they may be ready for thy visitation; through the same thy Son, Jesus Christ our Lord.

O milder Gott, der du dein ewiges wort der menschen natur hast lassen an sich nemen vom unvorruckten leybe der junkfrawen Marie, vorley deinen auserwelten, urlob zu geben, den fleyschlichen lusten, auf das sie all deiner heymsuchung stat geben, durch den selbigen Jesum Christum . . . *Thomas Münzer, 1524.* (Probably a Latin collect, translated.)

O Lord, we beseech thee, mercifully to hear the prayers of thy people, that we, who for our sins are justly afflicted, may be consoled by thy visitation; who livest . . . .

Preces populi tui, quaesumus, Deus, clementer exaudi; ut qui iuste pro peccatis nostris affligimur pietatis tuae visitatione consolemur. Per. *Gelasian, 222. B.C.N.S. missals.*

CHRISTMAS DAY. THE NATIVITY OF OUR LORD

I. FOR THE EARLY SERVICE

	Service Book	Roman Missal	American Book of Common Prayer
Lesson	Isa. 9:2-7		
Epistle	Titus 2:11-14 or I John 4:7-16	Titus 2:11-15a	Titus 2:11-15
Gospel	Luke 2:1-14	*Ibid.*	*Ibid.*
Introit	Pss. 2:7; 93:1	Ps. 2:7, 1	
Gradual	Pss. 110:3a, 1; 2:7	*Ibid.*	

Color: White.   Creed: Nicene.   Preface: Christmas.

Collect

O God, who hast made this most holy night to shine with the brightness of the true Light: Grant, we beseech thee, that as we have known on earth the mysteries of that Light, we may also come to the fulness of his joys in heaven; who liveth and reigneth with thee and the Holy Ghost, one God, world without end.

Deus, qui hanc sacratissiman noctem veri luminis fecisti illustratione clarescere, da, quaesumus, ut cuius lucis mysterium in terra cognovimus, eius quoque gaudiis in caelo perfruamur. Per. *Gelasian, 2. B.N.S. missals.*

II. FOR THE LATER SERVICE

	Service Book	*Roman Missal*	*American Book of Common Prayer*
Lesson	Isa. 45:1-8		
Epistle	Heb. 1:1-12	*Ibid.*	*Ibid.*
Gospel	John 1:1-14	*Ibid.*	*Ibid.*
Introit	Isa. 9:6; Ps. 98:1a	Isa. 9:6a, b; Ps. 98:1a	
Gradual	Pss. 98:3b-4a, 2; 95:1a, 6a	Ps. 98:3b-4a, 2; Dies sanctificatus	

Color: White.   Creed: Nicene.   Preface: Christmas.

Collect

Grant, we beseech thee, Almighty God, that the new birth of thine only-begotten Son in the flesh may set us free who are held in the old bondage under the yoke of sin; through the same Jesus Christ, thy Son, our Lord, who liveth . . . .

Concede, quaesumus, omnipotens Deus, ut Unigeniti tui nova per carnem nativitas liberet quos sub peccati iugo vetusta servitus tenet. Per. *Gelasian*, 2. *B.N.S. missals.*

III. AT VESPERS: LESSON. LUKE

The Christmas festival is of later observance than the festivals of Easter and Whitsunday. We do not know the date of our Lord's birth. The admittedly inexact calculations of Hippolytus (*c.* A.D. 220) determined March 25 as the date of the crucifixion. On an unfounded assumption that our Lord's earthly life must have included an exact number of years, fractions being imperfections, Hippolytus named December 25 as the date of the Nativity. By the fourth century this date was generally accepted and observed in the West. In the East the calculations of the Montanist sect fixed January 6 as the date of Christ's birth and this date was observed as a feast, celebrating both the birth and the baptism of our Lord.

In pagan Rome, December 25 was celebrated as a festival of the Sun and in recognition of the winter solstice. Church leaders took advantage of this deeply rooted observance and gave it Christian direction by celebrating the birth of the Sun of Righteousness on this date.

Christmas and Easter are the only days for which more than one service with complete propers is appointed. The Missal has three Christmas masses—at midnight, at dawn, and later in the morning. The Common Liturgy and the American Prayer Book provide two services. In the Common Liturgy the propers of the early service agree with those of the medieval midnight mass, except that the latter part of the Introit (Ps. 93:1) appears to be an innovation. It is not found in the medieval missals.

The propers of the later service are from the third mass for the day. The Introit is unusual again in its beginning with a passage from Isaiah. All of the Christmas lessons reflect the early church's thought of the Nativity as an epiphany, a manifestation of the nature and purpose of Christ, which thought is continued throughout Epiphanytide. The Gospel is often called the "last gospel," as it is read at the conclusion of mass in the Roman Church. Its opening words, "In the beginning," probably led to its being chosen as the Gospel for Easter in the Eastern Church, which begins its church year with the Resurrection festival.

The Prayer Book agrees with the Missal and the Common Liturgy selection of lessons, but it appoints different Collects. The one for the early service is the ancient Gelasian Collect for the vigil; the Anglican Collect for the later service is a composition of the Reformers in the first Prayer Book (1549).

The appointment of Old Testament lessons necessitated one change in the propers. In the early service, the former second Epistle becomes the Lesson, and the fine passage I John 4:7-16 is appointed as an alternate Epistle. In the later service, the strong passage Isaiah 45:1-8 is chosen as the Lesson.

An additional lesson is appointed for Vespers: Luke 2:15-20.

The entire Christmas season is festive. The Nicene Creed is used. The Proper Preface is that for Christmas, except on December 26, 27, and 28, when the Proper Preface is that for All Saints.

ST. STEPHEN, MARTYR

December 26

	Service Book	Roman Missal	American Book of Common Prayer
Lesson	II Chron. 24:17-22		
Epistle	Acts 7:54-60 or Acts 6:8—7:60	Acts 6:8-10; 7:54-60	Acts 7:55-60
Gospel	Matt. 23:34-39	*Ibid.*	*Ibid.*
Introit	Ps. 119:23a, 95a, 22b, 1	*Ibid.*	
Gradual	Matt. 5:10; Rev. 2:10b; Acts 7:56	Pss. 119:23a, 95a; 6:4; Acts 7:56	

Color: Red.   Creed: Nicene.   Preface: All Saints.

Collect

Grant us grace, O Lord, that like St. Stephen we may learn to love even our enemies, and seek forgiveness for those who desire our hurt; through thy Son, Jesus Christ our Lord, who liveth . . . .

Da nobis quaesumus domine imitari quod colimus. ut discamus et inimicos diligere. quia eius natalicia celebramus qui nouit etiam pro persecutoribus exorare. per dominum. *Gregorian, 13.*

The Lutheran church, generally speaking, is unique in recognizing December 26 as Second Christmas Day as well as St. Stephen's Day, and in places appointing a full set of propers for both feasts. The extension of the celebration of the Nativity to include the day following was, doubtless, the church's most ancient use, but the appointment of December 26 as a festival in honor of St. Stephen, the first martyr, was also very early. The Roman and the Anglican churches recognize only St. Stephen's Day.

In our present-day American church life there is practically no observance of Second Christmas Day, and the Common Liturgy recognizes this ' day as St. Stephen's Day, and December 28 as the day of the Holy Innocents. This restores the historical *tridium* of festivals which was established very early in Christian history in immediate connection with the festival of our Lord's Nativity.

Relieved of persecution, but still grieving over the death of thousands who had given their lives for their faith, the Western church of the fourth and fifth centuries established three festivals of martyrs. The bold witness of St. Stephen and his tragic death profoundly impressed the church. He was one of the seven deacons chosen by the disciples to oversee the work of the church in Jerusalem, and later St. Paul was a consenting witness at his stoning to death.

The festival honors St. Stephen as the "proto-martyr." Augustine in his *City of God* notes that many churches were named in his honor (Book XXII, Chap. 8). St. John was commemorated because of his special nearness to our Lord. The slaughter of the Innocents, in point of time so close to the birth of the Savior, dramatically illustrated the constant fact that "in the midst of life we are in death."

Medieval commentators suggest that these three festivals reveal a triple kind of martyrdom endured by the faithful: St. Stephen, martyrdom in will and deed; St. John, martyrdom in will but not in deed; the Holy Innocents, martyrdom in deed but not in will.

The Introit is the Missal text. The Gradual is composite, with two sentences from Matthew and the Revelation, and the final sentence, the Missal text from Acts. The Lesson recounts the stoning of the prophet Zechariah at the command of King Joash.

The Collect is a free translation of the original Gregorian, quite similar to the translation in the first English Prayer Book of 1549. The Prayer Book of 1662 made a wordy and none-too-happy expansion of this, introducing thoughts from the Epistle and addressing the prayer itself to Christ and not to the Father.

The Epistle is either the original lengthy selection giving the entire speech of St. Stephen or part of the abbreviated form of the Missal. The Gospel is the same everywhere.

ST. JOHN, APOSTLE, EVANGELIST
December 27

	Service Book	Roman Missal	American Book of Common Prayer
Lesson	Hosea 14:1-9 or 11:1-4		
Epistle	I John 1:1-10	Ecclus. 15:1-6	I John 1:1-10
Gospel	John 21:19b-24	*Ibid.*	*Ibid.*
Introit	For Introit and Gradual see Apostles' Days	Ecclus. 15:5; Ps. 92:1	
Gradual		John 21:23, 19b, 24	

Color: White. Creed: Nicene. Preface: All Saints.

Collect

Merciful Lord, we beseech thee to cast the bright beams of thy light upon thy Church; that it, being instructed by the doctrine of thy blessed Apostle and Evangelist St. John, may so walk in the light of thy truth, that it may at length attain to the light of everlasting life; through thy Son, Jesus Christ our Lord, who liveth . . . .

Ecclesiam tuam Dne benignus inlustra ut apostolicis beati Iohannis evangelistae inluminata doctrinis ad dona perveniat quae de tua fidelibus retributione promisit. Per. *Leonine,* 166. *B. S. missals.*

Persecution probably sent St. John to Ephesus in Asia Minor, and from there he was banished by the Emperor Domitian to Patmos, a lonely island in the Greek archipelago where he worked among the criminals in the mines. After the assassination of Domitian, his successor, the Emperor Nerva, allowed St. John to return to Ephesus where he died, according to tradition, at the advanced age of 94, probably the only disciple to die a natural death. His Gospel supplements the writings of the Synoptists (Matthew, Mark, and Luke), and vigorously proclaims the divinity of Christ in opposition to the heresies of the time. Many churches throughout the world bear his name. Christian iconography represents him as an eagle because the writings ascribed to him soar to sublime heights.

The Lesson records Hosea's call to Israel to forsake idols and return to the true God who promises forgiveness. The Epistle, as given in the Common Liturgy and the English Prayer Book, is a substitute for the Missal's passage from Ecclesiasticus in the Apocrypha. It is related to the Gospel for Christmas: "God is light; in him is no darkness at all."

"The man whose name was John came to bear witness to the light." The Gospel is the same in all churches.

The Collect is one of the few collects in the Common Liturgy from the earliest Roman Sacramentary, the Leonine. It was somewhat shortened, an unusual procedure, in the later Gregorian Sacramentary. The Prayer Book (1662) added a phrase. The metaphors of "light," "truth," and "life" which glow throughout the Collect, as well as in the Epistle and the Gospel, are characteristic of all the writing ascribed, perhaps none too accurately, to St. John. As Massey H. Shepherd says, they "describe not only the nature of Christian experience, but also the nature of God himself." It is interesting to note that the modern Roman Collect is more evangelical in tone than is the form we have inherited from the Prayer Book.

THE HOLY INNOCENTS, MARTYRS

December 28

	Service Book	Roman Missal	American Book of Common Prayer
Lesson	Jer. 31:15-17		
Epistle	Rev. 14:1-5	*Ibid.*	*Ibid.*
Gospel	Matt. 2:13-18	*Ibid.*	*Ibid.*
Introit	Ps. 8:2a, 1a	*Ibid.*	
Gradual	Pss. 124:7, 8; 113; 1b	*Ibid.*	

Color: Red. Creed: Nicene. Preface: All Saints.

Collect

O God our Father, who by the birth and infancy of thy Son didst sanctify and bless childhood: We commend to thy love all children, and beseech thee to protect them from every hurt and harm, and to lead them to the knowledge of thyself and the obedience of thy will; through the same Jesus Christ our Lord, who liveth . . . .

This festival appears everywhere in Greek, Roman, and Anglican calendars. It reminds us of the slaughter of children in Bethlehem by King Herod. Their sufferings led the church to regard them as martyrs for Christ. The careful Scottish scholar A. Allan McArthur believes that the Spanish abbess Etheria described a celebration of this festival in her account of a fourth-century service in Bethlehem.[3] By the end of the fifth century, the festival was observed everywhere in the Western church.

[3] *The Evolution of the Christian Year* (London: SCM, 1953), p. 155.

In Germany, France, and England the day was turned into a popular holiday known as the Feast of Fools (*Narrenfest*). A boy bishop elected on St. Nicholas' Day (December 6) officiated, sitting in the bishop's chair while choirboys sat in the canons' stalls. Evil-smelling incense was used and the liturgy was parodied. This scandalous performance was not checked until the Synod of Toledo of 1473 forbade it.

In England the day was known as Childermas, and children were playfully beaten to remind them of the fate of the Innocents. The horror attached to the meaning of the day fed the superstition that it was unlucky. Men refrained from business ventures, marriages were not solemnized. Many Lutheran church orders extended their observance of Christmas and dropped Holy Innocents from their calendars, though retaining the Gospel on the first or second Sunday after Christmas. The ancient Mozarabic (Spanish) Rite, with greater chronological consistency, observes the day after the Feast of the Epiphany which features the visit of the Wise Men.

The color for the day is red; the Proper Preface is that of All Saints. Our Collect differs from the one in the Roman and the Anglican service books. Its origin is uncertain, and in its thought it fails to capture any of the tragedy of the Gospel or the glory of the Epistle.

THE FIRST SUNDAY AFTER CHRISTMAS

	Service Book	Roman Missal	American Book of Common Prayer
Lesson	Isa. 63:7-16		
Epistle	Gal. 4:1-7	*Ibid.*	*Ibid.*
Gospel	Luke 2:33-40	*Ibid.*	Matt. 1:18-25
Introit	Ps. 93:5, 2, 1a	Bk. Wisd. 18:14: 15a; Ps. 93:1a	
Gradual	Pss. 45:2a, 1; 93:1a	*Ibid.*	

Color: White.   Creed: Nicene or Apostles'.   Preface: Christmas.

Collect

Almighty and everlasting God, direct our actions according to thy good pleasure, that in the Name of thy beloved Son, we may be made to abound in good works; through the same thy Son, Jesus Christ our Lord, who liveth . . . .

Omnipotens sempiterne deus. dirige actus nostros in beneplacito tuo. ut in nomine dilecti filii tui mereamur bonis operibus habundare. Per eundem. *Gregorian*, 16. *B.C.N.S. missals.*

If Christmas Day falls upon a Sunday, its octave will be the Festival of the Circumcision (New Year's Day), and this "First Sunday after Christmas" will not be observed as such. Nor will it be observed if it falls on the three days immediately following Christmas—St. Stephen's

Day, St. John's Day, or Holy Innocents' Day. When it is observed, its Epistle links the Gospel for the day with the Gospel of the Nativity. The thought of the Collect may stem from the "good works" of Anna and Simeon and the "good pleasure" of the Father in the human development of the child Jesus. The Common Liturgy has the historic propers throughout, except that it omits from the Introit a passage from the apocryphal Book of Wisdom and substitutes verses from Psalm 93. The Prayer Book departs from the Roman and the Lutheran uses and appoints Matthew 1:18-25 as the Gospel and repeats the 1549 Collect for Christmas Day. The Lesson speaks of the Lord God as "our father, our redeemer." The Epistle declares that "ye are sons," and "no more a servant."

THE CIRCUMCISION AND THE NAME OF JESUS

[NEW YEAR'S DAY]

	Service Book	Roman Missal	American Book of Common Prayer
Lesson	Josh. 24:14-24		
Epistle	Gal. 3:23-29	Titus 2:11-15a	Phil. 2:9-13
Gospel	Luke 2:21	*Ibid.*	Luke 2:15-21
Introit	Ps. 8:1, 4;	Isa. 9:6a;	
	Isa. 63:16b	Ps. 98:1a	
Gradual	Ps. 98:3b, 4a, 2;	*Ibid.*	
	Heb. 1:1, 2a		

Color: White. Creed: Nicene. Preface: Christmas.

Collect

O LORD God, who, for our sakes, hast made thy blessed Son our Saviour subject to the Law, and caused him to endure the circumcision of the flesh: Grant us the true circumcision of the spirit, that our hearts may be pure from all sinful desires and lusts; through the same thy Son, Jesus Christ our Lord, who liveth . . . .

Omnipotens deus. cuius unigenitus hodierna die ne legem solueret quam adimplere uenerat. corporalem suscepit circumcisionem. spiritali circumcisione mentes uestras ab omnibus uitiorum incentiuis expurget. et suam in uos infundat benedictionem. *Gregorian,* 304.

This concludes the Christmas octave. It was first observed only as the octave of the Nativity. Later (perhaps as late as A.D. 1100) it became the Feast of the Circumcision. The Reformers happily retained the idea of the Name of Jesus. (The Roman Missal appoints the second Sunday after Christmas as the Feast of the Holy Name.) The Common Liturgy has the Epistle and Gospel of the ancient *Comes.* The Missal and the Prayer Book have other Epistles. The Prayer Book extends the uniquely short Gospel of one verse to seven. The Common Liturgy and the Missal have the same Gradual but entirely different Introits. The Missal repeats the Introit for the Later Christmas Service. The Common Liturgy introduces a passage from Isaiah for the Psalm verse.

The Missal Collect centers in the thought of the intercession of the Blessed Virgin Mary. The Common Liturgy Collect is a free translation of a benediction for this feast in the Gregorian Sacramentary. This differs considerably from the original translation of the text by Cranmer in the Prayer Book of 1549. The Prayer Book Collect retains to this day an awkward interpolation of the printers "who did not understand the grammar of the sentence."[4] The Lesson records Joshua's exhortation to Israel: "Fear the Lord, and serve him in sincerity and truth."

Collect for New Year

Almighty and everlasting God, from whom cometh down every good and perfect gift: We give thee thanks for all thy benefits, temporal and spiritual, bestowed upon us in the year past, and we beseech thee of thy goodness, grant us a favorable and joyful year, defend us from all dangers and adversities, and send upon us the fulness of thy blessing; through thy Son, Jesus Christ our Lord, who liveth . . . .

Allmächtiger, ewiger Gott, von dem alle gute und alle vollkommene Gabe herabkommt, wir danken dir für deine Wohlthat die du uns in vergangenem beides geistlich und leiblich hast erzeiget; und bitten deine Barmherzigkeit, du wollest uns nun wiederum ein glückseliges und freudenreiches neues Jahr bescheren, vor Unglück und Gefahr uns gnädiglich behüten, und mit deinem göttlichen Segen erfüllen. *Ober-Lausitz Agende*, 1695.

The Collect for New Year is peculiar to the Lutheran Rite. Nothing like this is found in the Missal or the American Prayer Book. The Proposed Book of 1928 in England provides a somewhat similar Collect. The Common Liturgy Collect is an admirable prayer and a close translation from the *Ober-Lausitz Agende* (1695). The German text is in all probability a condensation of a very florid original in Austria (1571). The present translation first appears in the *Church Book* (1878).

THE SECOND SUNDAY AFTER CHRISTMAS

	Service Book	Roman Missal	American Book of Common Prayer
Lesson	I Sam. 2:1-10		
Epistle	Titus 3:4-7	Acts 4:8-12	Isa. 61:1-3
Gospel	John 1:14-18	Luke 2:21	Matt. 2:19-23
Introit	The same as for the First Sunday after Christmas	Phil. 2:10-11; Ps. 8:1a	
Gradual	The same as for the First Sunday after Christmas	Ps. 106:47; Isa. 63:16b; Ps. 145:21	

Color: White.   Creed: Nicene or Apostles'.   Preface: none.

[4] *Prayer Book Dictionary*, p. 213.

Collect

The Collect is the same as for the First Sunday after Christmas. The Common Liturgy repeats the Introit and the Gradual for the First Sunday after Christmas while the Missal provides other texts. The Missal Collect refers to the Name of Jesus; the Prayer Book Collect anticipates the thought of the Epiphany; and the Common Liturgy repeats the Collect for the First Sunday after Christmas.

The Roman, Lutheran, and Anglican liturgies appoint three different Epistles. The Common Liturgy appoints the Epistle formerly read on Second Christmas Day. The *Service Book* Gospel is the same as SC. and all the Prayer Books, except the American. The Missal appoints a Gospel from St. Luke.

THE EPIPHANY OF OUR LORD

	Service Book	Roman Missal	American Book of Common Prayer
Lesson	Isa. 60:1-6		
Epistle	Col. 1:23-27 or Eph. 3:1-12	Isa. 60:1-6	Eph. 3:1-12
Gospel	Matt. 2:1-12	*Ibid.*	*Ibid.*
Introit	Ecce advenit Dominator; Ps. 72:1	*Ibid.*	
Gradual	Isa. 60:6b, 1; Matt. 2:2b	*Ibid.*	

Color: White.   Creed: Nicene.   Preface: Epiphany.

Collect

O GOD, who on this day by the leading of a star didst reveal thine only-begotten Son to the Gentiles: Mercifully grant that we, who know thee now by faith, may be brought to contemplate the beauty of thy Majesty; through the same thy Son, Jesus Christ our Lord, who liveth . . . .

Deus qui hodierna die unigenitum tuum gentibus stella duce revelasti. concede propitius ut qui iam te ex fide cognouimus. usque ad contemplandam speciem tuae cel[e]studinis perducamur. Per eundem. *Gregorian,* 17. *B.C.N.S. missals.*

This festival, known in the West as "Twelfth Day," closes the Christmas cycle. Its origin is to be found in the Eastern Church, which celebrates both the birth and the baptism of our Lord on this day which it calls the "Day of Light." After the Western church had chosen December 25 for its celebration of the Nativity, it stressed the visit of the Magi as the high point of the Festival of the Epiphany. The Epiphany is one of the oldest festivals in the church's year. Modern scholars believe that it was celebrated in Asia Minor and Egypt in the second century. Like Christmas, it owes its date to a pagan solstice festival which it replaced in Christian use.

The transfer in the Middle Ages of the supposed relics of the Magi from Milan to Cologne Cathedral heightened the importance of the festival throughout Germany and the West. The Lutheran church orders of the sixteenth century regard it as a major festival. Henry Melchior Muhlenberg, a year after his arrival in America, writes that he celebrated the Epiphany in Providence (Trappe) and "preached to the congregation again in the barn."[5] This is the more remarkable since in that year (1743) Epiphany was on a weekday, and also because with pioneer conditions still prevailing, the church building had not yet been started.

In view of the festival's importance, particularly as commemorating the baptism of our Lord, and also because of its wide observance throughout the centuries, it is regrettable that under modern conditions in our own church life, it generally receives but slight attention unless, as occurs once every seven years, its date happens to fall upon a Sunday.

There is a general agreement in the rites concerning the Propers, except that the introduction of an Old Testament Lesson necessitated the transfer of the former Epistle to that series, and the substitution of new alternate Epistles, one of which (Eph. 3:1-12) is appointed in all the Anglican Prayer Books. The Introit (antiphon) is either apocryphal or a liturgical composition, imitating the doxology of the Lord's Prayer. The psalm verse harmonizes with the Gospel.

The Collect is a fine example of the collect form and of a natural and beautiful harmony with the lessons. The traditional translation from the first Prayer Book (1549) has been improved to bring out the antithesis between faith and sight which the original contains. The suggestion of a parallel with the leading of the Wise Men, which the Lation *perducamur* ("that we may be led on") offers, is not evident.

THE FIRST SUNDAY AFTER THE EPIPHANY

	Service Book	Roman Missal	American Book of Common Prayer
Lesson	Eccles. 12:1-7		
Epistle	Rom. 12:1-5	*Ibid.*	*Ibid.*
Gospel	Luke 2:41-52	Luke 2:4z-ɔ̇2	Luke 2:41-52
Introit	Isa. 6:1b; Rev. 19:6; Ps. 100:1-2a	Rev. 4:2b, 11:15; Ps. 100:1-2	
Gradual	Pss. 72:18-19a, 3; 100:1-2a	Pss. 72:18, 3; 100:1-2a	

Color: White.   Creed: Nicene or Apostles'.   Preface: Epiphany.

[5] *The Journals of Henry Melchior Muhlenberg,* I, 84.

Collect

O Lord, we beseech thee mercifully to receive the prayers of thy people who call upon thee; and grant that they may both perceive and know what things they ought to do, and also may have grace and power faithfully to fulfil the same; through thy Son, Jesus Christ our Lord, who liveth . . . .

Vota quaesumus domine supplicantis populi caelesti pietate prosequere. ut et quae agenda sunt uideant. et ad implenda quae uiderint conualescant. Per dominum. *Gregorian*, 16. *B.C.N.S. missals.*

The propers for this Sunday are the same in the three rites, except that the Common Liturgy has substituted sentences from Isaiah and the Revelation for a scriptural paraphrase in the Introit of the Roman Missal. The Gospel gives us our only account of the boyhood of our Lord. The story records his appearance in the temple and his devotion to his "Father's business." The Collect and the Epistle carry out this thought in a practical way in emphasizing our "reasonable service" and our need of divine grace and power. The Introit extends it to the biblical theophanies granted the young Isaiah and the aged St. John and the universal praise evoked by the psalmist.

The Lesson has affinities with the Gospel: "Remember now thy Creator in the days of thy youth," following this in highly poetic fashion with descriptions of the impotence of old age.

The Epistle is the first of four selections from the concluding hortatory chapters of Romans. These selections have little reference to the season and are evidently survivals of a *lectio continua* in the early church. The fifth and sixth Sundays, which occur irregularly, have unrelated selections.

The original of the Collect is of such excellence that Dr. Horn was moved to say, "Such a collect makes one wish that we always said our prayers in Latin." The translators have not preserved the terseness and crispness of its balanced phraseology, though they have contributed smoothness.

THE SECOND SUNDAY AFTER THE EPIPHANY

	Service Book	Roman Missal	American Book of Common Prayer
Lesson	Isa. 61:1-6		
Epistle	Rom. 12:6-16a	*Ibid.*	*Ibid.*
Gospel	John 2:1-11	*Ibid.*	Mark 1:1-11
Introit	Ps. 66:4, 1-2	*Ibid.*	
Gradual	Pss. 107:20-21; 148:2	*Ibid.*	

Color: White.   Creed: Nicene or Apostles'.   Preface: Epiphany.

Collect

ALMIGHTY and everlasting God, who dost govern all things in heaven and earth: Mercifully hear the supplications of thy people, and grant us thy peace all the days of our life; through thy Son, Jesus Christ our Lord, who liveth . . . .

Omnipotens sempiterne deus qui celesti simul et terrena moderaris. supplicationes populi tui clementer exaudi. et pacem tuam nostris concede temporibus. Per dominum. *Gregorian,* 164. *B.C.N.S. missals.*

There is entire agreement in the propers except that the American Prayer Book (1928) appoints the Baptism of Jesus (Mark 1:1-11) instead of John's account of "the beginning of miracles" as the Gospel. The choice of Epistles for this and the next two Sundays from Romans parallels the procedure in the breviary offices during this season where the lessons are from this same Epistle of the great Apostle to the Gentiles.

The Collect is from the Gregorian Sacramentary. Archbishop Cranmer's translation (1549), is a freer rendering which from a literary point of view improves the last phrase of the original by reading: "all of the days of our life" instead of "in our times," though the latter would be very pertinent in the living present. For the Introit, see Epiphany III.

The Lesson anticipates the Epistle in giving Isaiah's call "to preach good tidings" and in showing what is expected of "the ministers of our God."

THE THIRD SUNDAY AFTER THE EPIPHANY

	Service Book	Roman Missal	American Book of Common Prayer
Lesson	II Kings 5:1-15		
Epistle	Rom. 12:16b-21	*Ibid.*	*Ibid.*
Gospel	Matt. 8:1-13	Matt. 8:1-13	John 2:1-11
	or		
	John 1:29-34		
Introit	Ps. 97:7b, 8, 1	Ps. 97:7b, 8a, b, 1	
Gradual	Pss. 102:15-16; 97:1	*Ibid.*	

Color: White.   Creed: Nicene or Apostles'.   Preface: Epiphany.

Collect

ALMIGHTY and everlasting God, mercifully look upon our infirmities, and in all our dangers and necessities stretch forth the right hand of thy Majesty to help and defend us; through thy Son, Jesus Christ our Lord, who liveth . . . .

Omnipotens sempiterne deus infirmitatem nostram propitius respice. atque ad protegendum nos. dexteram tuae maiestatis extende. Per. *Gregorian,* 165. *B.C.N.S. missals.*

There is agreement in the propers except that the American Prayer Book (not the English) departs from the Roman and the Lutheran uses again in appointing a different Gospel, the marriage in Cana, which was the Gospel for the Second Sunday after Epiphany in the other churches. The Gospels for this and the remaining Sundays after Epiphany are from Matthew and testify to our Lord's miraculous power and great glory. The alternate Gospel records the Baptism of our Lord, originally appointed for Epiphany and later abandoned at that point for the account of the Wise Men. This restoration would have pleased Luther, who regretted the absence of the account of the Baptism of Christ from the Western lectionaries. The Introits and Graduals for the remaining Sundays (except in the Lutheran use for the Sixth Sunday) are the same as for this Third Sunday. They proclaim throughout Epiphanytide the kingship of Christ and call all to worship him.

The immediate relation of the Collect to the Gospel is shown in the petition "stretch forth the right hand of thy Majesty" with its obvious reference to the healing touch of the Savior in the case of the leper. The Collect is a slight expansion of the terse Latin original. The Prayer Book gives simply "thy right hand," omitting the phrase "of thy Majesty." This same phrase is used in the similar collect for Lent III.

The Lesson records the story of Naaman the Syrian and the cure of his leprosy, and thus connects with the Gospel.

THE FOURTH SUNDAY AFTER THE EPIPHANY

	Service Book	*Roman Missal*	*American Book of Common Prayer*
Lesson	Exod. 14:21-31		
Epistle	Rom. 13:8-10	*Ibid.*	Rom. 13:1-7
Gospel	Matt. 8:23-27	*Ibid.*	Matt. 8:1-13
Introit	The same as for the Third Sunday after Epiphany	*Ibid.*	
Gradual	The same as for the Third Sunday after Epiphany	*Ibid.*	

Color: White.   Creed: Nicene or Apostles'.   Preface: Epiphany.

Collect

ALMIGHTY God, who knowest us to be set in the midst of so many and great dangers, that by reason of the frailty of our nature we cannot always stand upright: Grant to us such strength and protection as may support us in all dangers, and carry us through all temptations; through thy Son, Jesus Christ our Lord, who liveth . . . .

Deus qui nos in tantis periculis constitutos. pro humana scis fragilitate non posse subsistere. da nobis salutem mentis et corporis. ut ea quae pro peccatis nostris patimur te adiuuante uincamus. Per dominum. *Gregorian*, 165. *B.C.N.S. missals.*

The Common Liturgy and the Missal have the same propers. The Prayer Book has chosen passages immediately preceding the selections in the Roman and the Lutheran uses for its Epistle and Gospel, the Gospel being the story of the leper and the centurion which the other churches assign to the Third Sunday after Epiphany. The Gospel tells our Lord's manifestation of power over the elements. The Epistle speaks of the moral and spiritual dangers which surround us and of the power of love in the kingdom of Christ.

Archbishop Cranmer substituted Romans 13:1-7 as the Epistle in the first Prayer Book (1549), possibly because he may have desired to support the principle of royal supremacy over the church in England by introducing this passage concerning obedience to civil authority.[6] The American Prayer Book omits the historic Gospel entirely.

The Collect enforces this spiritual note as the church's special teaching for the day. It is the Prayer Book translation (1549) of a Gregorian original, considerably altered in Queen Elizabeth's revision of 1558. The original accurately states that without divine strength and protection "we cannot at any time stand upright." The translation inserts the questionable word "always." This Collect appears in Luther's German Litany (1529) and in many Lutheran church orders. The Lesson in its account of the children of Israel passing safely through the Red Sea, connects with the Gospel.

THE FIFTH SUNDAY AFTER THE EPIPHANY

	Service Book	Roman Missal	American Book of Common Prayer
Lesson	Ezek. 33:10-16		
Epistle	Col. 3:12-17	*Ibid.*	*Ibid.*
Gospel	Matt. 13:24-30	*Ibid.*	*Ibid.*
Introit	The same as for the Third Sunday after Epiphany	*Ibid.*	
Gradual	The same as for the Third Sunday after Epiphany	*Ibid.*	

Color: White.   Creed: Nicene or Apostles'.   Preface: Epiphany.

Collect

O LORD, we beseech thee to keep thy Church and household continually in thy true religion; that they who do lean only upon the hope of thy heavenly grace may evermore be defended by thy mighty power; through thy Son, Jesus Christ our Lord, who liveth . . . .

Familiam tuam quaesumus domine continua pietate custodi. ut quae in sola spe gratiae caelestis innititur. tua semper protectione muniatur. Per dominum. *Gregorian, 165. B.C.N.S. missals.*

[6] Massey H. Shepherd, *The Oxford American Prayer Book Commentary,* p. 114.

484

There is agreement in the propers. The lessons for this Sunday manifest Christ's power and glory in the government of his "Church and household," and in the fruits of the "good seed of the Gospel," namely, the "Word of Christ" as it "dwells richly" in the hearts of believers. The Collect is a free but beautiful translation (1549) which introduces several ideas not in the Gregorian original. The first petition in the original is identical with that of the Collect for Trinity XXI, though the translations differ. The Lesson records Ezekiel's call to the house of Israel: "Turn ye from your evil ways . . . and live."

THE SIXTH SUNDAY AFTER THE EPIPHANY

The Propers for this Sunday may be used on The Last Sunday after the Epiphany, except when there is only one Sunday after the Epiphany.

	Service Book	Roman Missal	American Book of Common Prayer
Lesson	Exod. 34:29-35		
Epistle	II Pet. 1:16-21	I. Thess. 1:2-10	I John 3:1-8
Gospel	Matt. 17:1-9	Matt. 13:31-35	Matt. 24:23-31
Introit	Pss. 77:18b; 84:1-2a	The same as for the Third Sunday after Epiphany	
Gradual	Pss. 45:2a, b; 110:1; 96:2-3	The same as for the Third Sunday after Epiphany	

Color: White.   Creed: Nicene or Apostles'.   Preface: Epiphany.

Collect

O GOD, who in the glorious Transfiguration of thy only-begotten Son, hast confirmed the mysteries of the faith by the testimony of the Fathers, and who, in the voice that came from the bright cloud, didst in a wonderful manner foreshow the adoption of sons: Mercifully vouchsafe to make us co-heirs with the King of his glory and bring us to the enjoyment of the same; through the same thy Son, Jesus Christ our Lord, who liveth . . . .

Deus, qui fidei sacramenta in Unigeniti tui gloriosa Transfiguratione patrum testimonio roborasti, et adoptionem filiorum perfectam voce delapsa in nube lucida mirabiliter praesignasti: concede propitius; ut ipsius Regis gloriae nos coheredes efficias, et ejusdem gloriae tribuas esse consortes. Per eumdem Dominum nostrum. *15th century (?) MR. Bm.*

The Transfiguration, which was observed in the East as early as the sixth century but which was accepted only slowly in the West, is observed in the Roman and Anglican communions on August 6. This was the date on which in the year 1456 Pope Calixtus III announced the victory of Belgrade where Hunyady's army overcame the forces of Islam. The following year the pope extended the observance of the Feast of the Transfiguration to the whole church.

485

Since this feast received only limited observance on August 6, usually a weekday; and since it seemed appropriate as a climax to the Epiphany season, the reformers Bugenhagen and Veit Dietrich chose it as the theme for sermons on the Sixth Sunday after Epiphany. Eventually this became the general Lutheran use. The *Common Service Book* (not the Common Service), remembering that our Lord after descending from the mount "set his face to go to Jerusalem," appointed the Transfiguration for the last Sunday after the Epiphany in every year "except when there is only one Sunday after the Epiphany," and dropped the August 6 date altogether. The Common Liturgy has effected a compromise, replacing the festival on August 6 where it had been retained in early Lutheran use, but also following Reformation use in assigning its propers to Epiphany VI.

For this day the Roman and the Lutheran churches have different Introits, the Roman using that for Epiphany III, but having this Introit for the Transfiguration on August 6. The Transfiguration Introit used here is chosen with apt reference to the event and the disciples' instinctive reaction to the heavenly vision. The three churches have Peter's eyewitness account as the Epistle for the feast. The Prayer Book (American only and that since 1892) differs from the Roman and the Lutheran Transfiguration uses in giving Luke's account for the Gospel. The Roman and the Lutheran Rites have the same fine Collect, which indeed may have been composed by Pope Calixtus for this feast. Its unusual length and complicated structure, with double antecedent clauses and parallel construction throughout, indicate that it is not an early Latin composition. The American Prayer Book has a different Collect. The Lesson is the account of Moses on Mt. Sinai.

If Easter comes late enough to permit a sixth Sunday after Epiphany the day is observed as such by the Roman and the Anglican churches with appointed propers. These differ with respect to Epistles, Gospels, and Collects. The Prayer Book has a fine Collect of Bishop Cosin, one of the four original Collects added to the Prayer Book in 1662.

SEPTUAGESIMA SUNDAY

	Service Book	*Roman Missal*	*American Book of Common Prayer*
Lesson	Jer. 9:23-24		
Epistle	I Cor. 9:24—10:5	I Cor. 9:24—10:5a	I Cor. 9:24-27
Gospel	Matt. 20:1-16	*Ibid.*	*Ibid.*
Introit	Ps. 18:4a, 5a, 6a	*Ibid.*	
Gradual	Pss. 9:9-10, 18-19a; 130:1-2a	Pss. 9:9b-10, 18-19a; 130:1-4a, 5	

Color: Green.   Creed: Nicene.   Preface: none.

Collect

O LORD, we beseech thee favorably to hear the prayers of thy people: that we, who are justly punished for our offences, may be mercifully delivered by thy goodness, for the glory of thy Name; through thy Son, Jesus Christ our Lord, who liveth . . . .

Preces populi tui quaesumus domine clementer exaudi. ut qui iuste pro peccatis nostris affligimur. pro tui nominis gloria misericorditer liberemur. per dominum. *Gregorian,* 25. *B.C.N.S. missals.*

The names Septuagesima, Sexagesima, and Quinquagesima point forward to Easter, these Sundays falling within the seventh and the sixth decades and upon the fiftieth day before that great feast. The propers of the three Sundays provide a transition from the joyousness of the Christmas and Epiphany cycles to the stern penitential season of Lent. Momentous historic events originally led to the choice of the lessons and the composition of the Collects for these days. This accounts for the strongly individual character of these Sundays.

In 568 Pope John III appointed these Sundays as days of supplication in view of the perils threatened by the invading Lombards. Fear of impending disaster and trust in God are alternately expressed in the Introits and Graduals and in the earnest petitions of the Collects for these Sundays. The prayers and other propers were retained in the liturgy after the long-continued threats of invasion had ended, and have now received a spiritual interpretation.

The propers are practically the same in the three rites except that the Prayer Book has greatly abbreviated the lengthy Epistles for Septuagesima and Sexagesima. Modern European Lutheran lectionaries have done likewise. The general scheme of these propers and for those of the first four Sundays in Lent parallels the thought of the Old Testament Lessons for these same days in the Breviary.[7] The Gospels for Septuagesima (the vineyard) and for Sexagesima (the sower) were originally chosen for early spring when the farmers prepared their vineyards and fields. The later extension of Lent pushed these selections back so that they now normally come at the end of winter.

These Sundays have marked individuality and a Lent-like intensity of spirit. This is announced thematically in the Collects for Septuagesima and Sexagesima, which speak of being "mercifully delivered" and "defended against all adversity." The Epistle and the Gospel sound the warning that although many be called, few are chosen. The Gospel extols God's goodness, but the Epistle exhorts us to self-discipline and endeavor, an intimation of the approaching Lententide. In keeping

---

[7] See *The St. Andrew Daily Missal* by Dom Gaspar Lefebvre, 1940 ed.

with this, the alleluias of the Graduals are replaced, beginning with this Sunday, by "tracts," which continue in use throughout Lent. The Collect is a 1549 translation of a Gregorian original with the addition of the phrase "by thy goodness." The Lesson connects with the Gospel. It admonishes the wise man "not to glory in his wisdom," but to understand that the Lord "exercises lovingkindness, judgment, and righteousness in the earth."

SEXAGESIMA SUNDAY

	Service Book	Roman Missal	American Book of Common Prayer
Lesson	Amos 8:11-12		
Epistle	II Cor. 11:19—12:9	*Ibid.*	**II Cor.** 11:19-31
Gospel	Luke 8:4-15	Ps. 44:23-24, 25a, 26a, 1a, b	Ps. 44:23-24, 25b, 26a, 1a
Gradual	Pss. 83:18, 13; 60:4	Pss. 83:18, 13; 60:2, 5a	

Color: Green. Creed: Nicene. Preface: none.

Collect

O LORD God, who seest that we put not our trust in anything that we do: Mercifully grant that by thy power we may be defended against all adversity; through thy Son, Jesus Christ our Lord, who liveth . . . .

Deus qui conspicis quia ex nulla nostra actione confidimus. concede propitius. ut contra aduersa omnia. doctoris gentium protectione muniamur. per. *Gregorian, 25. B.C.N.S. missals.*

The Apostle to the Gentiles is specially honored in the propers for this day. The Epistle (the longest in all the Christian year) recounts St. Paul's labors and persecutions. The Gospel may indirectly point to him as the greatest of all missionaries, who sowed the seed of the Word everywhere. The Collect in its original form invokes his protection in the phrase *doctoris gentium protectione* (cf. I Tim. 2:7; II Tim. 1:11). This special reference to St. Paul possibly was related to the fact that the basilica of St. Paul-Without-the-Walls in Rome was the "station church" for Sexagesima Sunday. There are eighty-six days in the year "with station" at forty-five different churches in Rome. Anciently the pope or his representative celebrated a solemn high mass "of the city and the world" at these churches. The faithful assembled beforehand in another church "of the *collecta*" or assembly, and went in procession to the station church singing psalms and the Litany. The Anglican Reformers in 1549 omitted the reference in the Collect to St. Paul and substituted the phrase "by thy power," thus eliminating the unscriptural request for defense "by the protection of the teacher of the Gentiles" and directing all thought to the efficacy of God's power alone. The Lesson records the solemn warning of the prophet Amos: "The Lord God will send a famine in the land, not a famine of bread . . . but of hearing the words of the Lord."

QUINQUAGESIMA SUNDAY

	Service Book	Roman Missal	American Book of Common Prayer
Lesson	Jer. 8:4-9		
Epistle	I Cor. 13:1-13	*Ibid.*	*Ibid.*
Gospel	Luke 18:31-43	*Ibid.*	*Ibid.*
Introit	Ps. 31:2b-3, 1	*Ibid.*	
Gradual	Pss. 77:14-15; 100:1-2a	Pss. 77:14-15; 100:1-3	

Color: Green. Creed: Nicene. Preface: none.

Collect

O LORD, we beseech thee mercifully hear our prayers, and, having set us free from the bonds of sin, defend us from all evil; through thy Son, Jesus Christ our Lord, who liveth . . .

Preces nostras quaesumus domine clementer exaudi. atque a peccatorum uinculis absolutos. ab omni nos aduersitate custodi. per dominum. *Gregorian, 26. B.C.N.S. missals.*

This Sunday, actually fifty days before Easter, as the name indicates, marks the gateway to the Passion with our Lord's word in the Gospel, "Behold, we go up to Jerusalem." The propers combine to enforce the significance of love as the church's teaching for the day. This is exemplified in Christ's sacrificial journey to Calvary and in his compassionate ministry of healing on the way.

We might have expected St. John to voice this sublime panegyric of love in the Epistle, but it is St. Paul, whose zealous endeavors we have considered in previous Epistles, who shows us that all discipline and endeavor are unavailing unless accomplished in the spirit of love. The psalmist in the Introit psalm (31) supports this in a prayer peculiarly fitted to the coming Passiontide, quoted in our Lord's last Word from the Cross (vs. 5) and concluding, "O love the Lord, all ye his saints" (vs. 23).

The Collect, perhaps with remembrance of the freedom from infirmity granted Bartimaeus, centers its petitions upon freedom "from the bonds of sin" and reminds us of the general practice of confession and absolution (especially on "Shrove Tuesday") in preparation for Lent. The Anglican Reformers rejected the historic Collect—perhaps because of its limited scope and its repetition of the thought in the

Sexagesima Collect—and, as in other cases, composed a fine and entirely new collect based upon the thought of the Epistle.

The Lesson is Jeremiah's lament that "my people know not the judgment of the Lord."

ASH WEDNESDAY. THE FIRST DAY OF LENT

	Service Book	Roman Missal	American Book of Common Prayer
Lesson	Joel 2:12-19		
Epistle	I John 1:5-9 or Phil. 3:7-12	Joel 2:12-19	Joel 2:12-17
Gospel	Matt. 6:16-21	*Ibid.*	*Ibid.*
Introit	Ps. 57:2, 1b, 1a	Bk. Wisd. 11:24a, 25a, 24c, 27; Ps. 57:1a	
Gradual	Pss. 57:1a, 3a; 103:10; 79:9a	Pss. 57:1a, 3a; 103:10, 79:8-9	

Color: Violet. Creed: Nicene. Preface: Lent.

Collect

ALMIGHTY and everlasting God, who hatest nothing that thou hast made, and dost forgive the sins of all those who are penitent: Create and make in us new and contrite hearts, that we, worthily lamenting our sins, and acknowledging our wretchedness, may obtain of thee, the God of all mercy, perfect remission and forgiveness; through thy Son, Jesus Christ our Lord, who liveth . . . .

ALMIGHTIE and euerlastyng God, which hatest nothing that thou haste made, and doest forgeue the sinnes of all them that be penitente: Creat and make in vs newe and contrite heartes, that wee worthely lamentyng oure synnes, and knowlegyng our wretchednes, maye obtaine of thee, the God of al mercye, perfect remission and forgeuenes, thorough Jesus Christ. *BCP*, 1549.

The name Lent is probably derived from the Anglo-Saxon word meaning spring, the time when the days lengthen. The early Christians remembered with special devotions the forty hours during which our Savior lay in the tomb. The period of commemoration was later extended to two weeks (the Passiontide), and eventually, in recognition of the forty days of our Lord's temptation, to forty days. Since Sundays were never fast days, being in Lent but not of Lent, four weekdays were added to the six weeks and this (probably in the time of Gregory the Great) finally fixed the season as forty fasting days (the Quadragesima).[8]

---

[8] There is a good discussion in A. Allan McArthur, *The Evolution of the Christian Year;* also in Edward T. Horn, III, *The Christian Year* (Philadelphia: Muhlenberg, 1957).

The medieval observance of Lent with its rigors and efforts at appeasement was a tragic relapse from the joy of the early Christians in completed redemption to the fear and uncertainty of pre-Christian thought. Much of this is felt in the propers of the Sundays. Some of these seem to have been chosen in line with the medieval conception of fasting, penitence, and good works in the spirit of work-righteousness and the hope of acquiring "merit" before God.

However, even with the heavy medieval atmosphere still pervading it, the season of Lent has demonstrated positive values for the post-Reformation church. In the Lutheran church, Bugenhagen prepared a popular mosaic account of the Passion of our Lord as recorded in the Four Gospels. The idea did not originate with him. The Mozarabic Rite and the uses of various medieval dioceses had similar conflations.[9] It would be well if the use of the "History of the Passion" were restricted to Holy Week. Its use throughout the entire season of Lent restricts thought to contemplation of the sufferings and death of our Lord, to the exclusion of practically all other ideas. By the time Holy Week is reached, the mind of the church has been so saturated with morbidity that pastors and people find it wearisome and unrewarding to repeat the same lugubrious details. Lent should prepare us for Easter, not for Good Friday.

Whether we fully realize it or not, the church has made a major shift in emphasis from the sense of joy and triumph felt by the early Christians in the long celebration of Eastertide to the somber contemplation of Christ's sufferings and death and the subjective stress upon personal penitence and self-discipline which pervade the lengthy observance of Lententide. In this, as in other matters, we might well discard the garments of mourning and put on again the robes of victory and rejoicing worn by the pre-Roman church.

The Lutheran observance of Lent is commemorative and emulative as well as penitential. It regards the season as a time of special spiritual opportunity to contemplate the Passion of Christ as an incentive for self-examination, repentance, and growth in faith and grace.

The significance of the name "Ash Wednesday" is found in the medieval custom of penitents coming to the church on this day in sackcloth and with naked feet. After finishing their prayers, they threw ashes, made from palms blessed the previous Palm Sunday, over their heads.

In the Introit, verses from Psalm 57 are substituted for passages from the Book of Wisdom in the Missal. The Epistle and the Gospel both

[9] See E. T. Horn, III, *The Christian Year,* pp. 113, 114.

strike a thoroughly evangelical note with their call to "rend your hearts and not your garments" in the spirit of repentance toward the "Father which seeth in secret." The Roman Collect is saturated with the "venerable solemnity of fasting" and the English Reformers (1549), composed a prayer of rare beauty and balance for this day, a prayer which is one of the gems of collect literature. The opening phrase is drawn from a medieval benediction of ashes in the Sarum (Salisbury) Use, which in turn rests upon the Book of Wisdom 11:24. The petitions themselves are a development of Psalm 51:10, 17. The American Prayer Book prescribes this Collect "every day in Lent, after the Collect appointed for the day, until Palm Sunday."

The traditional Epistle from Joel now takes its place among the Old Testament Lessons. New alternate Epistles are provided; I John 1:5-9, which is a call to confess our sins; or Philippians 3:7-12, which is St. Paul's prayer "that I may know him, and the power of his resurrection, and the fellowship of his sufferings."

INVOCABIT. THE FIRST SUNDAY IN LENT

	Service Book	Roman Missal	American Book of Common Prayer
Lesson	Gen. 22:1-14		
Epistle	II Cor. 6:1-10	Ibid.	Ibid.
Gospel	Matt. 4:1-11	Ibid.	Ibid.
Introit	Ps. 91:15a, c, 16, 1	Ps. 91:15a, c, 16a, 1	
Gradual	Ps. 91:11-12, 1	Ps. 91:11-12, 1-7, 11-16	

Color: Violet. Creed: Nicene. Preface: Lent.

Collect

O LORD, mercifully hear our prayer, and stretch forth the right hand of thy Majesty to defend us from them that rise up against us; through thy Son, Jesus Christ our Lord, who liveth . . . .

Preces nostras quaesumus domine clementer exaudi. et contra cuncta nobis aduersantia dexteram tuae maiestatis extende. per. *Gregorian, 29. B.C.N. missals.*

The Sundays in Lent are known by the first words of their Latin Introits. The Introit and the Gradual are from Psalm 91, whose spirit is well caught by the Epistle. The latter probably had reference originally to the catechumens who were being instructed for baptism at Easter, and also to the fact that ordinations to the ministry were regularly appointed at the Lenten Ember season which began the following Saturday. As this Sunday anciently marked the beginning of the Quadragesima, the choice of our Lord's temptation as the Gospel was most appropriate. The Epistle is closely related to the Epistle for Sexagesima.

The Roman Collect is full of the idea of "good works." The Prayer Book (1549) has a Collect based on the Gospel, which is doubtless by Cranmer, though something of the same thought is expressed in an earlier Collect in the Ambrosian Missal. The Common Liturgy has a Gregorian Collect. The English translation appears in the *Church Book* (1879).

The Lesson prefigures the temptation of our Lord, as recorded in the Gospel, by its story of the testing of Abraham's faith and obedience in the sacrifice of his only son Isaac.

REMINISCERE. THE SECOND SUNDAY IN LENT

	Service Book	*Roman Missal*	*American Book of Common Prayer*
Lesson	Exod. 33:12-23		
Epistle	I Thess. 4:1-7	*Ibid.*	I Thess. 4:1-8
Gospel	Matt. 15:21-28	Matt. 17:1-9	Matt. 15:21-28
Introit	Ps. 25:6, 2b, 22, 1-2a	*Ibid.*	
Gradual	Pss. 25:17-18; 106:1b, c	Pss. 25:17-18; 106:1b-4	

Color: Violet. Creed: Nicene. Preface: Lent.

Collect

O GOD, who seest that of ourselves we have no strength: Keep us both outwardly and inwardly; that we may be defended from all adversities which may happen to the body, and from all evil thoughts which may assault and hurt the soul; through thy Son, Jesus Christ our Lord, who liveth . . . .

Deus qui conspicis omni nos uirtute destitui. interius exteriusque custodi. ut et ab omnibus aduersitatibus muniamur in corpore. et a prauis cogitationibus mundemur in mente. per dominum. *Gregorian, 32. B.C.N.S. missals.*

This Sunday is called *Reminiscere* ("remember"), the first word of the Latin Introit. The propers of the three rites are in agreement except that while the Common Liturgy and the Prayer Book follow the ancient *Comes* and give the account of the woman of Canaan and her daughter as the Gospel, the Missal appoints the story of the Transfiguration. The lessons as we have them for this Sunday and for the next Sunday probably had special reference to the catechumens in the early church, adults, it should be remembered, who were being instructed.

The Collect combines the Epistle's admonitions concerning purity and the thoughts of the soul and the Gospel story of the bodily adversity suffered by the daughter of the woman of Canaan. The Latin original has the strength of sharp antithesis tersely put in a verbal parallel: *Muniamur in corpore . . . mundemur in mente:* "defended in body . . . cleansed in mind." The Prayer Book translation (1549), loses some of this but gains smoothness and extension of thought in its longer form. The Common Service altered several redundant phrases, "no power of ourselves to help ourselves," and "outwardly in our bodies," etc.

The Lesson seems rather obscure, but it has affinities with the Gospel. The Lord tells Moses, "I will make all my goodness pass before thee. . . . I will show mercy on whom I will show mercy."

OCULI. THE THIRD SUNDAY IN LENT

	Service Book	Roman Missal	American Book of Common Prayer
Lesson	Jer. 26:1-15		
Epistle	Eph. 5:1-9	*Ibid.*	Eph. 5:1-14
Gospel	Luke 11:14-28	*Ibid.*	*Ibid.*
Introit	Ps. 25:15-16, 1-2a	*Ibid.*	
Gradual	Pss. 9:19, 3;	Pss. 9:19, 3;	
	123:1, 3a	123:1, 3a	

Color: Violet. Creed: Nicene. Preface: Lent.

Collect

WE beseech thee, Almighty God, look upon the hearty desires of thy humble servants, and stretch forth the right hand of thy Majesty to be our defence against all our enemies: through thy Son, Jesus Christ our Lord, who liveth . . . .

Quaesumus omnipotens deus uota humilium respice. atque ad defensionem nostram. dexteram tuae maiestatis extende. per. *Gregorian, 35. B.C.N.S. missals.*

This Sunday is call *Oculi* ("eyes") again from the first word of the Latin Introit. There is agreement in the propers except for the addition of five verses in the Prayer Book Epistle and one psalm verse in the Roman Gradual. The propers were chosen before the season of Lent, as we know and observe it, had developed. They are clearly related to the observance of this day and week in the early church, when the preliminary "scrutiny" or examination of catechumens was held followed by a public renunciation of the devil and all his works and ways and the pronouncement of the formula of exorcism. The Epistle shows how Christians must "walk in love" as "followers of God." The Gospel warns of the never-ending conflict with evil which calls for vigilance and the divine protection which is sought in the collect and trustfully awaited in the Introit. The Collect in its original form is one of the shortest in the church's use and does not have the concluding phrase: "Against all our enemies."

The Lesson records Jeremiah's stirring admonition to the city of Jerusalem and the prince of Judah: "Amend your ways and your doings, and obey the voice of the Lord your God." Though exorcism and belief in demoniacal possession have practically disappeared from the church's thought and practice, there has been no move to provide another Gospel. The traditional one is still found everywhere.

LAETARE. THE FOURTH SUNDAY IN LENT

	Service Book	*Roman Missal*	*American Book of Common Prayer*
Lesson	Isa. 55:1-7		
Epistle	Gal. 4:21—5:1a	Gal. 4:22-31, 5:1a	Gal. 4:21-31
Gospel	John 6:1-15	*Ibid.*	John 6:1-14
Introit	Isa. 66:10; Ps. 122:1	Isa. 66:10-11a; Ps. 122:1	
Gradual	Pss. 122:1, 7; 125:1	Pss. 122:1, 7; 125:1-2	

Color: Violet. Creed: Nicene. Preface: Lent.

Collect

GRANT, we beseech thee, Almighty God, that we, who for our evil deeds do worthily deserve to be punished, by the comfort of thy grace may mercifully be relieved; through thy Son, Jesus Christ our Lord, who liveth . . .

Concede quaesumus omnipotens deus. ut qui ex merito nostrae actionis affligimur. tuae gratiae consolatione respiremus. Per. *Gregorian, 39. B.C.N.S. missals.*

This Sunday, too, receives its name *Laetare* ("rejoice") from the first word of the Latin Introit. The day is popularly called "Rejoicing Sunday" because of the occurrence of this word in the Epistle as well as the Introit; or "Refreshment Sunday" in allusion to the miracle recorded in the Gospel; or simply "Mid-Lent." Anciently the "station" for this day was the "Basilica of the Holy Cross in Jerusalem" (actually the church is in Rome), and it will be noted that the Introit, Epistle, and Gospel all have reference to Jerusalem. The shortening of the Epistle in early times involved the loss of a magnificent climax in Galatians 5:1, a climax which has been restored in the Common Liturgy, and by paraphrase in the Missal. The propers seem definitely to have been chosen with the thought of relieving the austerities of the Lenten season. The observance of Lent in the early centuries began the following day, and the lessons for this Sunday may reflect something of a pre-Lenten carnival spirit. Anciently the pope distributed bread to the poor on this day. Later rose-colored vestments were worn and (sixteenth century) a golden rose, symbolic of our Lord, the Rose of Sharon, was solemnly blessed by the pope and sent as a gift to some king, queen, or other high dignitary in recognition of service rendered the church. This supplies the historic precedent for the annual award of the Laetare

Medal by Notre Dame University to an outstanding Roman Catholic.

The Collect is a Prayer Book translation of 1549, slightly altered in 1662, and somewhat resembles the Collect for Septuagesima. It provides the one stern note which, too, is softened by the reference to "the comfort of thy grace." Anciently, the catechumens were advanced a step on this day, and permitted to remain a bit longer with the faithful in order to hear the Gospel read and explained. On this day they were also taught the Creed and the Lord's Prayer. The rejoicing of the catechumens is reflected in the Introit and in the Gradual: "I was glad when they said unto me: let us go into the house of the Lord."

The Lesson connects with the Gospel, which records the miraculous feeding of the five thousand. Isaiah's invitation speaks of spiritual food: "Ho, every one that thirsteth, come ye to the waters . . . buy wine and milk without money and without price."

JUDICA. PASSION SUNDAY

	Service Book	*Roman Missal*	*American Book of Common Prayer*
Lesson	Num. 21:4-9		
Epistle	Heb. 9:11-15	*Ibid.*	*Ibid.*
Gospel	John 8:46-59	John 8:46-59a	*Ibid.*
Introit	Ps. 43:1-2a, 3a, b	Ps. 43:1-2a, 3	
Gradual	Pss. 143:9a, 10a;	Pss. 143:9a, 10a;	
	18:48; 129:1-2	18:48; 129:1-4	

Color: Violet.   Creed: Nicene.   Preface: Lent.

Collect

WE beseech thee, Almighty God, mercifully to look upon thy people, that by thy great goodness they may be governed and preserved evermore, both in body and soul; through thy Son, Jesus Christ our Lord, who liveth . . . .

Quaesumus omnipotens deus familiam tuam propitius respice. ut te largiente regatur in corpore. et te seruante custodiatur in mente. Per dominum. *Gregorian,* 42. *B.C.N.S. missals.*

The remote preparation for Easter began with Septuagesima. The spirit of preparation has been intensified throughout Lent up to this point. The preparation is now immediate as we enter upon the final two weeks, the Passiontide. This period of fourteen days was the earliest extended commemoration of our Lord's Passion. It vividly recalls his persecutions and sufferings, and this Sunday is popularly known as Passion Sunday. The term Passion Week is no older than the nineteenth century and originated in Anglican circles. The liturgical name for this Sunday is *Judica* ("Judge"), from the first word of the Latin Introit.

The Propers of the three rites are in agreement. The enmity of the "ungodly nation" of the Introit leads to the final declaration of hostilities in the Gospel, while the Epistle gives a terse but complete presentation of the Passion. The Collect, a 1549 translation of the Gregorian original, presents the petitions of the faithful, the household of God, "[We,] thy people." In general it is quite reminiscent of the Collect for the Second Sunday in Lent.

The Lesson presents the figure of a standard in the wilderness, with a brazen serpent upon it. The Epistle refers to the cross of Christ upon which our Lord "offered himself without blemish unto God."

PALMARUM. THE SIXTH SUNDAY IN LENT

	Service Book	*Roman Missal*	*American Book of Common Prayer*
Lesson	Zech. 9:9-12		
Epistle	Phil. 2:5-11	*Ibid.*	*Ibid.*
Gospel	Matt. 21:1-9 or Matt. 26:1—27:66	Matt. 26:1—27:66	Matt. 27:1-54
Introit	Ps. 22:19, 21, 1a	Ps. 22:19, 21, 1	
Gradual	Pss. 73:23b-24, 1; 22:1, 4a, 5a	Pss. 73:23b, 24, 1-3; 22:2-8, 17b, 18, 21, 23, 30b, 31	

Color: Violet.   Creed: Nicene.   Preface: Lent.

Collect

ALMIGHTY and everlasting God, who hast sent thy Son, our Saviour Jesus Christ, to take upon him our flesh, and to suffer death upon the Cross, that all mankind should follow the example of his great humility: Mercifully grant that we may both follow the example of his patience, and also be made partakers of his Resurrection; through the same thy Son, Jesus Christ our Lord, who liveth . . . .

Deus, qui humano generi ad imitandum humilitatis exemplum, Salvatorem nostrum et carnem sumere et crucem subire fecisti, concede propitius ut et patientiae eius habere documentum et resurrectionis eius consortia mereamur, Christi Domini nostri. Qui tecum vivit et regnat Deus in unitate Spiritus sancti, per. *Gelasian,* 60. *B.C.N. missals.*

This Sunday begins the "Holy Week," or the "Great Week," the latter name being explained by Chrysostom as referring to "the great things wrought at this time by the Lord."

Palm Sunday owes its name to fourth-century observances in Jerusalem, where on this day the faithful assembled on the Mount of Olives and from there went in procession to the city, carrying palm and olive branches and singing, while the bishop rode in their midst sitting on a donkey. Similarly, other events in the days preceding the crucifixion were dramatized in the later services of Holy Week. It was not until the sixth century that services in the West included a procession with palms. The present lengthy Roman office of blessing the palms which precedes the Mass for the day dates only from the ninth century. In the early church the candidates for baptism and confirmation were again taught the Creed. This fact gives some justification for the administration of confirmation on this day, though too frequently now this feature dominates the service almost to the exclusion of its deeper significance.

The propers differ. The Introit in the Missal and the Common Liturgy, with our Lord's cry of anguish from the cross, sound the note of solemnity which this and the later services of Holy Week should maintain. The Roman Gradual with its Trach is very lengthy. The Roman Gospel is the "Matthew Passion" (the entire chapter 26 and 27). The Prayer Book appoints fifty-four verses of Matthew 27, a reduction dating from 1661. The Lutheran church is unique in departing from the Passion history and giving the Gospel of the triumphal entry into Jerusalem, which historically is the Gospel for the preliminary office of the blessing of the palms. The three rites agree in appointing Philippians 2:5-11 as the Epistle, a passage describing "the mind of Christ" which is generally regarded as a quotation from an early Christian hymn. The Common Liturgy restores the historic straight readings of the Passion narrative from the Four Gospels in its alternate Gospels for Palm Sunday, and for Tuesday, Wednesday, and Friday in Holy Week. (As LLKD, BCP, MR.)

The Gelasian Collect is a noble and beautiful prayer which perfectly summarizes the divine plan of redemption. The Prayer Book translation (1549) expanded the invocation by adding "of thy tender love toward mankind," a phrase which Bishop Dowden says "suffuses the whole prayer with its flush of emotion." The Common Liturgy has not accepted this clause. The Reformers also avoided the unevangelical thought in the Latin word *mereamur* ("that we may deserve to have") by the alteration: "that we may follow" the example, etc.

The Lesson is Zechariah's prophecy exhorting the "daughter of Jerusalem" to rejoice "for behold, thy King cometh unto thee."

MONDAY IN HOLY WEEK

	Service Book	*Roman Missal*	*American Book of Common Prayer*
Lesson	Isa. 50:5-10		
Epistle	I Pet. 2:21-24	Isa. 50:5-10	Isa. 63:1-19
Gospel	John 12:1-36	John 12:1-9	Mark 14:1-72
Introit	Ps. 35:1-3	*Ibid.*	
Gradual	Pss. 35:23, 3a; 79:9	Pss. 35:23, 3a; 103:10; 79:8-9	

Color: Violet.   Creed: Nicene.   Preface: Lent.

Collect

GRANT, we beseech thee, Almighty God, that we, who amid so many adversities do fail through our own infirmities, may be restored through the Passion and Intercession of thine only-begotten Son, who liveth . . . .

Da quaesumus omnipotens deus. ut qui in tot aduersis ex nostra infirmitate deficimus. intercedente unigeniti filii tui passione respiremus. Per eundem. *Gregorian,* 46. *B.C.N.S. missals.*

Every day in Holy Week is given a full set of propers. The Introit for Monday anticipates the thought of the Savior's sufferings as prophetically described in Isaiah 50, a section of which is traditionally appointed as the Epistle. In the Common Liturgy this becomes the Lesson. The Epistle is St. Peter's call to all Christians to follow the steps of "Christ, who suffered for us, leaving us an example." The Gospel relates the incidents of the last days, and has been extended to verse 36. The Collect is Gregorian. The American Prayer Book has an entirely different Epistle, Collect, and Gospel. The English Prayer Book repeats the Collect for Palm Sunday every day until Good Friday.

TUESDAY IN HOLY WEEK

	Service Book	Roman Missal	American Book of Common Prayer
Lesson	Jer. 11:18-20		
Epistle	I Tim. 6:12-14	Jer. 11:18-20	Isa. 50:5-11
Gospel	John 12:37-50 or Mark 14:1—15:46	Mark 14:1—15:46	Mark 15:1-39
Introit	Gal. 6:14a; In quo est salus; Ps. 67:1	*Ibid.*	
Gradual	Ps. 35:13 b, c, 1a, 2	Ps. 35:13, 1-2	

Color: Violet.   Creed: Nicene.   Preface: Lent.

Collect

ALMIGHTY and everlasting God, grant us grace so to contemplate the Passion of our Lord, that we may find therein forgiveness for our sins; through the same thy Son, Jesus Christ our Lord, who liveth . . . .

Omnipotens sempiterne deus. da nobis ita dominicae passionis sacramenta peragere. ut indulgentiam percipere mereamur. per. *Gregorian,* 47. *B.C.N.S. missals.*

The Introits for this and the following days in Holy Week point definitely to the cross and its significance. They are unusual in containing passages from the New Testament and verses which are liturgical interpolations, not actually from Scripture but thoroughly scriptural in tone. The traditional Epistle is a messianic prophecy from Jeremiah, and now becomes the Lesson. The new Epistle is St. Paul's exhortation to Timothy to "fight the good fight of faith." The Prayer Book Epistle is from Isaiah. The Gospel is a passage from John 12, a continuation of Monday's Gospel, which speaks of the corn of wheat which falls into the ground and dies and brings forth much fruit. The Roman Gospel comprises Mark 14-15, which is the original liturgical Gospel for the day and is given as an alternate in the Common Liturgy. The Prayer Book gives Chapter 15. The Collect is Gregorian and in the terse Latin of the original has more strength and meaning than the colorless English translation indicates. The latter, however, avoids the objectionable *mereamur* of the Latin.

WEDNESDAY IN HOLY WEEK

	Service Book	Roman Missal	American Book of Common Prayer
Lesson	Isa. 62:11—63:7 or Isa. 52:13—53:3	Isa. 62:11b; 63:1-7a	
Epistle	Rev. 1:5b-7	Isa. 53:1-12	Heb. 9:16-28
Gospel	Luke 22:1—23:53	*Ibid.*	Luke 22:1-71
Introit	Phil. 2:10, 8b, 11b; Ps. 102:1	*Ibid.*	
Gradual	Pss. 69:17, 1-2a; 102:1, 13	Pss. 69:17, 1-2a; 102:1-4, 13	

Color: Violet.   Creed: Nicene.   Preface: Lent.

Collect

GRANT, we beseech thee, Almighty God, that we, who for our evil deeds are continually afflicted, may mercifully be relieved by the Passion of thine only-begotten Son, who liveth . . . .

Praesta quaesumus, omnipotens Deus, ut qui nostris excessibus incessanter affligimur, per unigeniti tui passionem liberemur, qui tecum. *Gregorian,* 47. *B.C.N.S. missals.*

The Introit again contains verses from the New Testament and sings of victory beyond the grave. The Lesson in the *Service Book* and the Missal is the former Lutheran Epistle, a passage from Isaiah, whose accurate foretelling of the Savior's sufferings has led some to call him the "fifth evangelist." The Prayer Book chooses its Epistle from Hebrews 9, and the Missal from Isaiah 53, this being one of the very few days on which there are three lessons in the Roman use. All three rites agree in appointing Luke 22 as the Gospel, though the Prayer Book includes a shorter section than the others. The Collect is Gregorian and the translation would be improved by the substitution of the word "freed" for "relieved."

The fact that the Gospel records the treacherous covenant between Judas and the chief priests has given the name "Spy Wednesday" to the day. In the Roman Church the Office of Tenebrae ("darkness") begins and continues over the next day and Good Friday. The story of the Passion interspersed with psalms is chanted and candles (fifteen in all) are extinguished one by one until the church is in darkness except for a single candle hidden behind the altar to represent Christ in the tomb.

THURSDAY IN HOLY WEEK

	Service Book	Roman Missal	American Book of Common Prayer
Lesson	Exod. 12:1-14		
Epistle	I Cor. 11:20-32	Ibid.	I Cor. 11:23-26
Gospel	John 13:1-15	John 13:1-15	Luke 23:1-49
	or		or
	John 6:28-37		John 13:1-15
Introit	The same as for Tuesday	Ibid.	
Gradual	Phil. 2:8b-9	Ibid.	

Color: Violet. Creed: Nicene. Preface: Lent.

Collect

O LORD God, who hast left unto us in a wonderful Sacrament a memorial of thy Passion: Grant, we beseech thee, that we may so partake of this Sacrament of thy Body and Blood, that the fruits of thy redemption may continually be manifest in us; who livest . . . .

Deus qui nobis sub Sacramento mirabili passionis tuae memoriam reliquisti: tribue, quaesumus, ita nos Corporis et Sanguinis tui sacra mysteria venerari; ut redemptionis tuae fructum in nobis jugiter sentiamus: Qui vivis . . . *Thomas Aquinas, B.C.N. missals.*

This day has always had high significance, chiefly because it commemorates the institution of the Lord's Supper. This fact has given it various names: *Dies Coenae Domini* ("Day of the Lord's Supper"); *Dies Natalis Calicis* ("Birthday of the Chalice"); *Dies Mysteriorum* ("Day of the Mysteries"). The name by which it is most commonly known, "Maundy Thursday" (*Dies Mandati,* "Day of the Commandment"), has particular reference to the injunctions to humility and love in connection with the account of the feet-washing given in the Gospel, (cf. also John 13:34); while we also must not forget the command of the Institution, "This do in remembrance of me." The reconciliation of penitents, which the ancient church observed particularly on this day, is commemorated in the German name *Gründonnerstag.* Remembering Luke 23:31, the ceremony of reconciliation brought the withered branches (sinners) back to the fellowship of the church.

Anciently three masses were appointed: for the reconciliation of penitents; for the consecration of the holy oils; and for the special commemoration of the institution of the Holy Eucharist. The first two have been dropped. The third mass, however, is celebrated with ancient ceremonies in every Roman cathedral, where the bishop, attended by twelve priests, seven deacons, and seven subdeacons, blesses the oils to be used at the service of baptism and confirmation at Eastertide and for the consecration of bishops, the dedication of churches, altar, bells, etc., at other times. Everywhere the note of sorrow is stilled and the institution of the Holy Supper is celebrated with rejoicing. The priest consecrates two hosts, one of which is reserved for consumption on Good Friday when the "Mass of the Pre-Sanctified" is held without consecration. Until very recently Maundy Thursday was the only day on which Mass might be celebrated in the evening. In 1952 the Roman Church relaxed its regulations on this point.

Dr. Edward T. Horn, III, has the following interesting paragraph in his comments on this day:

> In the later Middle Ages—from the fifteenth century on—the papal bull *In Coena Domini* was read. This was a general excommunication of all heretics. By the sixteenth century it included Hussites, Wyclifites, Lutherans, Zwinglians, Calvinists, Huguenots, Anabaptists, Antitrinitarians, and all apostates in general. Of it Luther remarked in his *Table Talk:* "At Rome they wait all year for Maundy Thursday, when Christ instituted the Holy Supper, to damn the heretics, of whom I, Martin Luther, am first and foremost. This happens on the very day when men should be thanking God for his great goodness in the Lord's Supper and his suffering and death. But there sits the pope on high; the cardinals light the torch and all the banned are consigned to hell. I have been in hell for twenty-eight years —since 1518—and I'm still quite hearty in spite of it."[10]

Neither doctrinal errors and abuses noted in parts of the church nor the vigorous remarks of the great Reformer in the intimacy of his Table Talk should divert us from recognizing the true character and importance of the day for us and for all Christians. Maundy Thursday takes its place beside Good Friday as one of the great days of the Christian year, a day charged with profound spiritual significance.

The Introit is the same as for Tuesday. The Gradual is unique in being entirely from the New Testament. The Gospel is John's account of the feet-washing. The alternate Gospel is from the sixth chapter of John: "I am the bread of life." The Prayer Book gives Luke's account of the crucifixion, with the traditional Gospel as an alternate. The Collect is not the historic Collect for this day but was composed by

[10] *The Christian Year,* p. 122. Luther's statement is quoted in Heinrich Alt, *Das Kirchenjahr,* p. 357f.

St. Thomas Aquinas in 1264 for the then newly authorized Feast of Corpus Christi which was observed on the Thursday following Trinity Sunday. This feast celebrated the Roman conception of the Sacrament and it soon became the most popular of all feasts. The host was carried through the streets in a procession which included not only ecclesiastical and civil authorities but craftsmen's guilds and all kinds of organizations.

This feast was most offensive to the Reformers, who unanimously denounced it. Their opposition, however, did not prevent the Lutherans, at least, from retaining this marvelously beautiful Collect and appointing it for the service on Holy Thursday or, as in a number of instances, as an alternate to Luther's Post-Communion Collect (Duke Henry of Saxony [1539], Spangenberg [1545], Austria [1571], etc.). The address to our Lord himself is unusual and appropriate, and the content of the prayer is thoroughly evangelical and satisfying, though the emphasis has been changed from contemplation to reception. The Collects in the Missal and the American Prayer Book are both inferior to this Collect of St. Thomas.

GOOD FRIDAY

	Service Book	Roman Missal	American Book of Common Prayer
Lesson	Isa. 53:4-12 or Hos. 6:1-6	Hos. 6:1-6	
Epistle	Rev. 5:1-14	Exod. 12:1-11	Heb. 10:1-25
Gospel	John 18:1—19:42	*Ibid.*	John 19:1-37
Introit	Isa. 53:4a, 5a, 6a, c; Ps. 102:1		
Gradual	Isa. 53:5, 11a		

Color: Black.   Creed: Nicene.   Preface: Lent.

Collect

ALMIGHTY God, we beseech thee graciously to behold this thy family, for which our Lord Jesus Christ was contented to be betrayed and given up into the hands of wicked men, and to suffer death upon the Cross; through the same thy Son, Jesus Christ our Lord, who liveth . . . .

Respice domine quaesumus super hanc familiam tuam. pro qua dominus noster iesus christus non dubitauit manibus tradi nocentium. et crucis subire tormentum. qui tecum uiuit. *Gregorian,* 48. *B.C.N. missals.*

The earliest name for this day, "Parasceve," means "Preparation." Other names were "Day of the Lord's Passion," "Day of the Absolution," and "Day of the Cross." The name "Good Friday" is a peculiarly English expression. It reflects the joy of completed redemption and protests against superstitious notions that all Fridays are "unlucky" and that this particular Friday must be shrouded in funereal gloom. Its original meaning may have been "God's Friday."

The Roman Church invests this day with the spirit of desolation and mourning. The altars are bare, organs and bells and all glorias are stilled, and there are no lights or incense. A "Mass of the Catechumens" with lessons from Isaiah and Exodus, lengthy tracts, and the Passion according to John are followed by the "solemn prayers, a series of eight intercessions in collect form (see the Bidding Prayer, pp. 651ff). Then follows the adoration of the cross, during which the "reproaches" and hymns of the Passion are sung. The Mass of the Pre-Sanctified follows. For this there are no Propers as such. The host, which had been consecrated the previous day, and the chalice are brought from the altar of repose and the priest communicates himself and recites the final prayers. Thus nothing is reserved over the two days of the tomb.

The Lutheran and the Anglican churches provide normal services with the usual propers. The Lutheran church especially gives this service the character of solemn, restrained praise. The Introit and Gradual are from Isaiah. The Epistle, new with the Common Liturgy, is from Revelation. The Gospel is the Johannine account of the crucifixion. Hymns of Lutheran origin do not bewail the sufferings of Christ but rather solemnly rejoice that "with his stripes we are healed." The Prayer Book abbreviates the Gospel and takes its Epistle from Hebrews. The Collect is Gregorian and in the Roman use is the prayer *super populum* for Wednesday before Easter.

Other Collects For Good Friday

Merciful and everlasting God, who hast not spared thine only Son, but delivered him up for us all, that he might bear our sins upon the Cross: Grant that our hearts may be so fixed with steadfast faith in him that we may not fear the power of any adversaries; through the same thy Son, Jesus Christ our Lord.

Barmhertiziger ewiger Gott, der du deines einigen Sons nicht verschonet hast, sondern fur uns alle dahin gegeben, das er unser sünde am creutz tragen solte, Verleihe uns, das unser hertz in solchem glauben nimermehr erschrecke noch verzage, Durch den selbigen etc. *Sax. 1540.*

Almighty and everlasting God, who hast willed that thy Son should bear for us the pains of the Cross, that thou mightest remove from us the power of the adversary: Help us so to remember and give thanks for our Lord's Passion that we may obtain remission of sin and redemption from everlasting death; through the same Jesus Christ, our Lord.

Deus qui pro nobis filium tuum crucis patibulum subire uoluisti. ut inimici a nobis expelleres potestatem. concede nobis famulis tuis ut resurrectionis gratiam consequamur. per eundem. *Gregorian, 47.*

SATURDAY IN HOLY WEEK—EASTER EVE

	Service Book	Roman Missal	American Book of Common Prayer
Lesson	Exod. 13:17-22		
Epistle	I Pet. 3:17-22	Col. 3:1-4	I Pet. 3:17-22
Gospel	Matt. 27:57-66	Mat. 28:1-7	Matt. 27:57-66
Introit	Ps. 130:6a, 5, 1-2a		
Gradual	Pss. 16:9b-10a; 31:5, 1a		

Color: Violet. (White in evening). Creed: Nicene.

Preface: Lent (Easter in evening).

Collect

O GOD, who didst enlighten this most holy night with the glory of the Lord's Resurrection: Preserve in all thy people the spirit of adoption which thou hast given, so that renewed in body and soul they may perform unto thee a pure service; through thy Son, Jesus Christ our Lord, who liveth . . . .

Deus qui hanc sacratissimam noctem gloria Dominicae resurrectionis illustras, conserva in nova familiae tuae progenie adoptionis spiritum quem dedisti, ut corpore et mente renovati puram tibi exhibeant servitutem. Per Dominum. *Gelasian*, 88. *B.C.N. missals.*

The early church held no service on Holy Saturday. Later the Roman Church developed a series of ceremonies which included the blessing of the new fire and the Paschal candle; chanting of prophecies (twelve in number); and blessing of the font and the Litany of the Saints. The mass which follows has a full set of propers. Since the ancient propers were displaced by the baptismal and new fire ceremonies, the Lutheran and Anglican churches had to provide propers on their own accounts. The Prayer Book appoints an Epistle, Collect, and Gospel. The Collect, introduced in 1662, is an adaptation of the Collect in the Scottish Prayer Book (1637). The Common Liturgy appoints only the historic Collect which anticipates Easter dawn and recalls the custom of the early church in baptising catechumens on this day. The opening words may possibly contain an allusion to the custom in the early church of lighting lamps and torches in churches and homes on Easter Eve. The "new fire" is still lighted on this day in many places.

The Lesson recalls the hope and expectation of the children of Israel as they were led through the wilderness. The Epistle recalls Christ's preaching "unto the spirits in prison," and the figure of baptism saving us "by the resurrection of Jesus Christ." The Gospel is the request of Joseph of Arimathea for the body of the Lord and the sealing of the sepulchre.

EASTER DAY. THE RESURRECTION OF OUR LORD
I. FOR AN EARLY SERVICE

	Service Book	*Roman Missal*	*American Book of Common Prayer*
Lesson	Isa. 25:6-9 or Dan. 3:8-25		
Epistle	I Pet. 1:3-9		I Cor. 5:6b-8
Gospel	John 20:1-18		Mark 16:1-8
Introit	Luke 24:6a, 5b, 6b, 7a, c		
Gradual	Ps. 118:24, 29; I Cor. 5:7b, 8a, 8c		

Color: White. Creed: Nicene. Preface: Easter.

Collect

O God, who for our redemption didst give thine only-begotten Son, Jesus Christ, to suffer death upon the Cross, and by his glorious Resurrection hast delivered us from the power of the enemy: Grant us so to die daily unto sin, that we may evermore live with him who died and rose again for us; through the same Jesus Christ our Lord, who liveth . . . .

Deus qui pro nobis filium tuum crucis patibulum subire uoluisti. ut inimici a nobis expelleres potestatem. concede nobis famulis tuis ut resurrectionis gratiam consequamur. Per eundem. *Gregorian, 47.*

II. FOR THE SERVICE

	Service Book	*Roman Missal*	*American Book of Common Prayer*
Lesson	Dan. 3:8-25 or Isa. 25:6-9		
Epistle	I Cor. 5:7-8 or I Cor. 15:20-26	I Cor. 5:7-8	I Cor. 5:7-8
Gospel	Mark 16:1-7	*Ibid.*	John 20:1-10
Introit	Ps. 139:18b, 5b, 6, 1, 2a	Ps. 139:18b, 5b, 6a, 1, 2a	
Gradual	Ps. 118:24, 1; I Cor. 5:7b, 8a, c	Ps. 118:24, 1; I Cor. 5:7b; Sequence: Victimae paschali	

Color: White. Creed: Nicene. Preface: Easter.

Collect

Almighty God, who through thine only-begotten Son Jesus Christ hast overcome death, and opened unto us the gate of everlasting life: We humbly beseech thee, that as thou dost put into our minds good desires, so by thy continual help we may bring the same to good effect; through the same, Jesus Christ our Lord, who liveth . . . .

Deus qui hodierna die per unigenitum tuum aeternitatis nobis aditum deuicta morte reserasti. uota nostra quae praeueniendo adspiras. etiam adiuuando prosequere. per eundem dominum nostrum. *Gregorian, 59. B.C.N.S. missals.*

III. AT VESPERS. LESSON: LUKE 24:13-35

Easter, the queen of festivals, was the first feast observed by the Christians who really kept the entire "pentecost" of fifty days from Easter to Whitsunday as a time of rejoicing. There were no days of fasting, and standing in prayer was enjoined instead of kneeling. This continued observance of Easter, together with the weekly commemoration in the services of the Lord's day, combined to make the fact of the Resurrection a dominant note in the life and thought of the early church and gave a joyful though reverent character to early Christianity. The medieval church, with its insistence upon the Friday fast, its development of the lengthy and rigorously penitential season of Lent, and its cultivation of an all-pervasive atmosphere of fear and uncertainty, lost this mood of the early church. It remained for the Reformation to recapture at least some of it.

The church's Alleluia rings out again after nine weeks' absence in the Introit and the Gradual. The Common Liturgy provides a second Introit (Cf. Schoeberlein and Loehe), chiefly from the New Testament, in addition to the traditional one. The Gradual also includes a New Testament passage.

The historic Gospel in the Later Service omits vs. 8, which the Prayer Book retains (MR, LLKD, and VEKD also omit). This gives a stronger conclusion, but even so the Gospel is inadequate in that it describes only the empty tomb and does not include an appearance of the risen Christ. This is explained historically by the fact that the ancient use carried the account of the Resurrection through the services held every day in Easter week. In consequence of this, the Gospel for Easter Day itself presented only the preliminary section of the Easter narrative. The Common Liturgy provides for a service on Easter Monday, and the Gospel for this day gives the account of our Lord's appearance on the way to Emmaus.

The American Prayer Book (1892) revived the provisions of 1549 and appointed propers for two services on Easter Day. The Collect in the Common Liturgy for the early service was originally appointed in the Gregorian Sacramentary for the Wednesday before Easter. As Professor Shepherd observes, this association "with the Holy Week observance makes it a fitting transition from the thoughts of the Passion to those of the Resurrection."[11] The Collect for the later service is in classic form and begins by establishing the historic fact of the Resurrection as the basis for its petition. The original is Gregorian, expanded

---

[11] *Oxford American Prayer Book Commentary,* p. 165.

in the Prayer Book translation. The Common Liturgy omits the awkward phrase of 1549, "by thy special grace preventing us." We agree that the petition of this Collect "has the merit of associating a consistent Christian life with the Resurrection, but seems inadequate to the greatest festival of the Christian year."[12]

OTHER EASTER COLLECTS

GRANT, we beseech thee, Almighty God, that we who celebrate thy Paschal Feast, kindled with heavenly desires, may ever thirst for the fountain of life, Jesus Christ our Lord, who liveth . . . .

Concede quaesumus omnipotens deus. ut qui festa paschalia agimus. caelestibus desideriis accensi. fontem uitae sitiamus. per dominum nostrum. *Gregorian, 55.*

GRANT, we beseech thee, Almighty God, that we who celebrate the solemnities of the Lord's Resurrection, may by the renewal of thy Holy Spirit rise again from the death of the soul; through the same Jesus Christ our Lord.

Concede quaesumus omnipotens deus. ut qui resurrectionis dominicae solemnia colimus. innouatione tui spiritus. a morte animae resurgamus. per dominum nostrum iesum christum. *Gregorian, 60.*

MONDAY AFTER EASTER

	Service Book	Roman Missal	American Book of Common Prayer
Lesson	Exod. 15:1-18		
Epistle	Acts. 10:34-43	Acts 10:37-43	Acts 10:34-43
Gospel	Luke 24:13-35	*Ibid.*	*Ibid.*
Introit	The same as for the [Later] Service on Easter Day	Exod. 13:5b, 9b; Ps. 105:1	
Gradual	The same as for the [Later] Service on Easter Day	Ps. 118:24, 2; Matt. 28:2b	

Color: White.   Creed: Nicene.   Preface: Easter.

The Missal provides propers for every day in Easter week; the Prayer Book for Monday and Tuesday; the Common Liturgy for Monday only. For the Monday service, the Missal appoints a proper Introit and Gradual. The Common Liturgy repeats the texts for Easter Day. There is agreement in the Epistle and the Gospel except that the Prayer Book shortens the Epistle by two verses. The Common Liturgy repeats the Collect for Easter Day. The Missal and the Prayer Book each appoint different Collects.

[12] Charles Neill and J. M. Willoughby, *The Tutorial Prayer Book* (London: Harrison Trust, 1913), p. 173.

508

QUASI MODO GENITI. THE FIRST SUNDAY AFTER EASTER

	Service Book	*Roman Missal*	*American Book of Common Prayer*
Lesson	Gen. 32:22-30		
Epistle	I John 5:4-12	I John 5:4-10a	I John 5:4-12
Gospel	John 20:19-31	*Ibid.*	John 20:19-23
Introit	I Pet. 2:2a;	I Pet. 2:2a;	
	Ps. 81:8, 1	Ps. 81:1	
Gradual	Matt. 28:2b;	Matt. 28:7b	
	John 20:26a, c	John 20:26a, c	

Color: White. Creed: Nicene. Preface: Easter.

Collect

GRANT, we beseech thee, Almighty God, that we who have celebrated the solemnities of the Lord's Resurrection may, by the help of thy grace, bring forth the fruits thereof in our life and conversation; through the same thy Son, Jesus Christ our Lord, who liveth . . . .

Praesta quaesumus omnipotens deus. ut qui paschalia festa peregimus. haec te largiente moribus et uita teneamus. per. *Gregorian,* 65. *B.C.N.S. missals.*

The ecclesiastical name for this Sunday is derived from the opening words of the Latin Introit, *Quasi modo geniti,* "as newborn babies." It is also called *Dominica in albis (post albas depositas),* "The Lord's Day in White," because those who had been baptized at Easter now received their first communion and then laid aside the white robes which they had worn throughout the week. Long before the Reformation, confirmation was observed on this Sunday in Germany, a time to be preferred to Palm Sunday. The name Low Sunday for this octave of the Resurrection marks the contrast with the great feast celebrated the week before, or it is in recognition of the fact that in many places it was customary to repeat some of the Easter solemnities.

The propers are in substantial agreement. The *Service Book* has restored three historic alleluias to the Introit. The Gradual is unusual, being a combination of New Testament passages. The Epistle is the last of the "baptismal" sections. It is well adapted to further instruction in the Christian life. The Epistles for all of Eastertide are non-Pauline, and Schuster interestingly suggests that the fact that St. Paul was not converted until after Pentecost may have determined the plan of selection of these Epistles. The Gospel reports two of the first reappearances of our Lord. The Prayer Book in abbreviating the Gospel loses the story of the appearance of our Lord "after eight days" and the incredulity of Thomas. The Missal and the Common Liturgy have the traditional Col-

509

lect, which fits perfectly with the thought of the Epistle. The Prayer Book has a different Collect. The Lesson is the story of Jacob's wrestling with a man "until the breaking of the day," and of his prevailing. Note the Epistle: "This is the victory that overcometh the world, even our faith"; and the Gospel with its account of Thomas and his lack of faith.

MISERICORDIA DOMINI: THE SECOND SUNDAY AFTER EASTER

	Service Book	Roman Missal	American Book of Common Prayer
Lesson	Ezek. 34:11-16		
Epistle	I Pet. 2:21b-25	*Ibid.*	I Pet. 2:19-25
Gospel	John 10:11-16	*Ibid.*	*Ibid.*
Introit	Ps. 33:5b, 6a, 1	*Ibid.*	
Gradual	Luke 24:35b;	*Ibid.*	
	John 10:14		

Color: White.   Creed: Nicene.   Preface: Easter.

Collect

GOD, who, by the humiliation of thy Son, didst raise up the fallen world: Grant unto thy faithful ones perpetual gladness, and those whom thou hast delivered from the danger of everlasting death, do thou make partakers of eternal joys; through the same thy Son, Jesus Christ our Lord, who liveth . . . .

Deus, qui in Filii tui humilitate iacentem mundum erexisti, laetitiam concede fidelibus tuis; ut quos perpetuae mortis eripuisti casibus, gaudiis facias sempiternis perfrui. Per. *Gelasian,* 102. *B.C.N.S. missals.*

The name *Misericordia Domini,* "Goodness of the Lord," is derived from the phrase in the first verse of the Latin Introit. The popular name "Good Shepherd Sunday" refers directly to the Gospel, Epistle, and Gradual. The propers in the three rites are in agreement except that the Prayer Book has advantageously lengthened the Epistle by two verses and has substituted for the historic Collect an admirable new prayer composed in 1549 and based upon a passage in the Epistle.

There is no clear reason for the choice of the Gospel for this particular Sunday. It may represent a survival of a favorite passage from early continuous reading of the Scriptures. Similarly the fact that the Epistles during Eastertide and, with a few exceptions, until the Fifth Sunday after Trinity, are all from the Catholic Epistles, may also indicate the survival of a primitive section of continuous reading. The abrupt address in the Collect—"God"—is unique. The Lesson from Ezekiel promises that the Lord God will "both search my sheep" and "will feed them in a good pasture."

JUBILATE. THE THIRD SUNDAY AFTER EASTER

	Service Book	*Roman Missal*	*American Book of Common Prayer*
Lesson	Isa. 40:25-31		
Epistle	I Pet. 2:11-20	I Pet. 2:11-19a	I Pet. 2:11-17
Gospel	John 16:16-22	*Ibid.*	*Ibid.*
Introit	Ps. 66:1, 2, 3	*Ibid.*	
Gradual	Ps. 111:9a;	*Ibid.*	
	Luke 24:46b, 26b		

Color: White.   Creed: Nicene.   Preface: Easter.

Collect

ALMIGHTY God, who showest to them that be in error the light of thy truth, to the intent that they may return into the way of righteousness: Grant unto all them that are admitted into the fellowship of Christ's religion that they may eschew those things that are contrary to their profession, and follow all such things as are agreeable to the same; through thy Son, Jesus Christ our Lord, who liveth . . . .

Dͩ errantes in via posse redire veritatis lumen ostendis da cunctis qui Christiana professione censentur et illa respuere quae huic inimica sunt nomini et ea quae sunt apta sectari. Per. *Leonine, 9. B.C.N.S. missals.*

The name *Jubilate,* "Rejoice," comes from the first word of the Latin Introit. The Propers are in agreement except as to length. The Epistle and particularly the Collect vividly recall the Easter baptisms and confirmations and point all who have been "admitted into the fellowship of Christ's religion" to the Christian way of life.

The earliest Collect text (Leonine Sacramentary) says simply "return into the Way," an obvious reference to the designation by the early Christians of their faith and manner of life as the "Way." The phrase "of righteousness" restricts the thought, and its insertion probably indicates that the full significance of the original *via* had been forgotten. The Latin word for "eschew" (*respuere*) is very forceful: "to eject from the mouth" (cf. Rev. 3:16). The softened form "eschew" in the Common Liturgy is further weakened in the translation "avoid" given in the American Prayer Book. The Gospel looks forward and anticipates the Ascension. Actually the text is part of the discourse of our Lord before his crucifixion.

The Lesson is general, a great passage from Isaiah concerning the majesty and might of "the everlasting God."

511

CANTATE. THE FOURTH SUNDAY AFTER EASTER

	Service Book	*Roman Missal*	*American Book of Common Prayer*
Lesson	Isa. 29:9-14		
Epistle	James 1:17-21	*Ibid.*	*Ibid.*
Gospel	John 16:4b-15	John 16:5-14	John 16:5-15
Introit	Ps. 98:1a, 2, 1b	Ps. 98:1a, 2b, 1b	
Gradual	Ps. 118:16; Rom. 6:9	*Ibid.*	

Color: White.   Creed: Nicene.   Preface: Easter.

Collect

O GOD, who makest the minds of the faithful to be of one will: Grant unto thy people that they may love what thou commandest, and desire what thou dost promise; that, among the manifold changes of this world, our hearts may there be fixed where true joys are to be found; through thy Son, Jesus Christ our Lord, who liveth . . .

Deus, qui fidelium mentes unius efficis voluntatis, da populis tuis, id amare quod praecipis, id desiderare quod promittis, ut inter mundanas varietates ibi nostra fixa sint corda ubi vera sunt gaudia. Per. *Gelasian,* 103. *B.C.N.S. missals.*

The name *Cantate,* "Sing ye," again comes from the first word of the Latin Introit. The propers agree in the three rites. The Introit reminds us that we are still in Eastertide. The Epistle begins with vs. 17 (as MR, VEKD, LLKD, Rh, SW, etc.). The Gospel looks ahead to the Ascension and to Whitsunday. There is no close connection between the Epistle and the Gospel, though we may think of the Holy Spirit as the supremely "good and perfect gift from above." The Gospel has been improved by having it begin with vs. 4b.

The Collect, whose thought can readily be related to the Epistle and the Gospel, is a 1549 translation of a Gelasian original. The Prayer Book in 1662 altered the antecedent clause to "who alone canst order the unruly wills and affections of sinful men," thereby making the ground of the petition more obvious, but losing entirely the important idea of unity. The *Tutorial Prayer Book* (p. 176) offers this interesting comment: "This more sad opening may be an intentional reflection of the divided state of English Christianity at the time." The Common Liturgy, as in many other instances, adheres to the original text.

The Lesson is related to the Gospel: the "wisdom of their wise men shall perish," but "when he, the Spirit of truth, is come, he will guide you into all truth."

ROGATE. THE FIFTH SUNDAY AFTER EASTER

	Service Book	*Roman Missal*	*American Book of* *Common Prayer*
Lesson	Isa. 55:6-11		
Epistle	Jas. 1:22-27	*Ibid.*	*Ibid.*
Gospel	John 16:23b-30	*Ibid.*	John 16:23-33
Introit	Isa. 48:20b; Ps. 66:1-2	*Ibid.*	
Gradual	Luke 24:46b, 26b; John 16:28	Surrexit Christus; John 16:28	

Color: White.   Creed: Nicene.   Preface: Easter.

Collect

O God, from whom all good things do come: Grant to us thy humble servants, that by thy holy inspiration we may think those things that be right, and by thy merciful guiding may perform the same; through thy Son, Jesus Christ our Lord, who liveth . . . .

Deus, a quo bona cuncta procedunt, largire supplicibus ut cogitemus, te inspirante, quae recta sunt, et te gubernante, eadem faciamus. Per. *Gelasian,* 104. *B.C.N.S. missals.*

The name *Rogate,* "Pray ye," is derived not from the Introit but from our Lord's assurance concerning prayer in the Gospel. This Sunday came to be known as Rogation Sunday, and the days following, which were observed as a prolonged vigil of the Ascension, were known as "Rogation days" ("Days of Asking"). In a normal season these days came when the seed in the fields was springing to life. The custom arose in Gaul in the fifth century, after a siege of devastating earthquakes, pestilence, and famine, of having the faithful meet in the churches and then go in processions through the countryside chanting litanies which invoked God's blessings upon the fruits of the earth, the husbandmen, etc. These "lesser litanies" were not introduced in Rome until the ninth century.

The propers agree, except that the Prayer Book extends the Gospel by three verses. The Gospel stresses prayer; the Epistle exhorts to action; the Introit begins with a passage from Isaiah. The Psalm verse celebrates a triumph which anticipates that of the ascended Lord. Alleluias emphasize the festal note. The Collect is a 1549 translation of a Gelasian original which can readily be related to both the Epistle and the Gospel. The Prayer Book again substitutes a word of wider significance, viz., "good" for "right," in the phrase, "those things that be right." The Lesson is a fine general passage which calls men to repentance and promises God's forgiveness.

THE ASCENSION OF OUR LORD

	Service Book	Roman Missal	American Book of Common Prayer
Lesson	II Kings 2:9-15 or		
Epistle	Gen. 5:21-24		
Gospel	Acts 1:1-11	*Ibid.*	*Ibid.*
Introit	Mark 16:14-20	*Ibid.*	Luke 24:49-53
	Acts 1:11; Ps. 47:1	*Ibid.*	
Gradual	Pss. 47:5; 68:18a	Pss. 47:5; 68:17b-18a	

Color: White. Creed: Nicene. Preface: Ascension.

Collect

GRANT, we beseech thee, Almighty God, that like as we do believe thy only-begotten Son, our Lord Jesus Christ, to have ascended into the heavens; so may we also in heart and mind thither ascend, and with him continually dwell; who liveth . . . .

Concede quaesumus omnipotens deus. ut qui hodierna die unigenitum tuum redemptorem nostrum ad caelos ascendisse credimus. ipsi quoque mente in caelestibus habitemus. Per eundem. *Gregorian, 74. B.C.N.S. missals.*

or

O KING of Glory, Lord of Hosts, who didst this day ascend in triumph far above all heavens: We beseech thee leave us not comfortless, but send to us the Spirit of Truth, promised of the Father; who livest . . . .

O rex gloriae, Domine virtutum, qui triumphator hodie super omnes coelos ascendisti, ne derelinquas nos orphanos; sed mitte promissum Patris in nos spiritum veritatis, alleluia. *Liber Responsalis.*

The Festival of the Ascension was observed at least as early as the fourth century and always in the spirit of joy as commemorating the completion of Christ's redemptive work. The Roman Church employs a symbolic ceremony. After the reading of the Gospel, a Paschal candle, whose light during the forty days had represented the presence of our Lord in the midst of his disciples, is extinguished. The three rites agree in the propers except that the Prayer Book gives Luke's brief account for the Gospel instead of Mark's longer form. All the Propers are related to the historic event.

The Introit begins by quoting the final verses of the Epistle for the day. The Proper Collect is Gregorian, 1549 translation. The second Collect is a 1549 adaptation of the beautiful Antiphon addressed to God the Son at the Magnificat in Second Vespers, which the Venerable Bede is said to have repeated on his deathbed. This combines verses from Psalm 24:10, Ephesians 4:10, John 14:18, and Luke 24:49. The Collect begins by proclaiming the triumph of the ascended Lord and concludes with a prayer for the coming of the Spirit. This Collect is appointed in the Prayer Book for the Sunday after the Ascension.

514

EXAUDI. THE SUNDAY AFTER THE ASCENSION

	Service Book	*Roman Missal*	*American Book of Common Prayer*
Lesson	Isa. 32:14-20		
Epistle	I Pet. 4:7b-11	*Ibid.*	I Pet. 4:7-11
Gospel	John 15:26—16:4a	*Ibid.*	*Ibid.*
Introit	Ps. 27:7a, 8-9a, 1a	*Ibid.*	
Gradual	Ps. 47:8; John 14:18a; 16:22b	*Ibid.*	

Color: White. Creed: Nicene. Preface: Ascension.

Collect

ALMIGHTY, everlasting God, make us to have always a devout will towards thee, and to serve thy Majesty with a pure heart; through thy Son, Jesus Christ our Lord, who liveth . . . .

Omnipotens sempiterne deus, fac nos tibi semper et devotam gerere voluntatem, et maiestati tuae sincero corde servire. Per. *Gelasian*, 105. *B.C.N.S.* *missals.*

The name *Exaudi,* "Hear," comes from the first word of the Latin Introit. The thought of the day turns definitely from the Ascension to Whitsunday, and the day is sometimes called "Expectation Sunday." The propers are in agreement, except that the Prayer Book substitutes for the historic Collect an altered and expanded translation of the Antiphon for Vespers on Ascension Day which the Common Liturgy gives in its original form, as addressed to Christ himself, as the second Collect for Ascension Day. The Alleluias in the Introits for this Sunday and for Pentecost respond to those of Easter and Rogate.

THE DAY OF PENTECOST. WHITSUNDAY

	Service Book	*Roman Missal*	*American Book of Common Prayer*
Lesson	Joel 2:28-32		
Epistle	Acts 2:1-11	*Ibid.*	*Ibid.*
Gospel	John 14:23-31a	*Ibid.*	John 14:15-31a
Introit	Bk. Wisd. 1:7a; Ps. 68:3, 1	Bk. Wisd. 1:7 Ps. 68:1	
Gradual	Ps. 104:30; Veni Sancte Spiritus	*Ibid.*; also Sequence: Veni Sancte Spiritus	

Color: Red. Creed: Nicene. Preface: Pentecost.

Collect

O GOD, who didst teach the hearts of thy faithful people, by sending to them the light of thy Holy Spirit: Grant us by the same Spirit to have a right judgment in all things, and evermore to rejoice in his holy comfort; through thy Son, Jesus Christ our Lord, who liveth . . . .

Deus qui hodierna die corda fidelium sancti spiritus inlustratione docuisti. da nobis in eodem spiritu recta sapere. et de eius semper consolatione gaudere. Per dominum. *Gregorian*, 78. *B.C.N.S.* *missals.*

AT VESPERS: LESSON: ACTS 2:14-21

This is the third great festival of the Christian year. The name *Pentecost* (fifty days) is a Greek word. As used in the Septuagint it refers to the second great Jewish festival which followed the Passover after fifty days. As at first observed by the Jews, it was a festival of the wheat harvest. Later it commemorated the giving of the law and the establishment of the Jewish church.

The Christian observance is very early (Hippolytus, *c.* 217, knew of it) and the Christian significance of the festival as a celebration of the outpouring of the Holy Spirit is better expressed by the English word Whitsunday. This has reference to the white garments worn by the newly baptized or to the gift of wisdom (early Anglo-Saxon "wit") by the Holy Spirit. The first explanation is favored because of the history of the word in medieval documents, Icelandic and Welsh use of the term "White Sunday," and the analogy of Saxon words in which the syllable "Whit" means "white."

This festival, coming at the end of fifty days of rejoicing, ranked with Easter itself in the thought of the early church and shared the popularity of that feast as a proper time for baptism. This was particularly true of the northern churches even in later times, for considerations of climate led them to prefer Pentecost to Easter as the great season for baptism. Whitsunday became in fact their *Dominica in Albis* (see p. 509). The medieval church developed many customs in connection with this festival. Among these were the lavish use of roses and the employment of trumpets in the service. The liturgical color for the day is red, a reminder of the tongues of fire and also of the blood of the martyrs, "the seed of the church."

The propers are in agreement, except that the Prayer Book (1552) expanded the Gospel to include the text for the vigil as well as that for the feast, and that the American Book (1928) provides an additional set of propers for an early service. The Introit and the Gradual are unusual in introducing passages from the Book of Wisdom and the sequence Veni Sancte Spiritus, respectively. The psalm (68) is one of the most majestic hymns of the Old Testament church. The Epistle (from Acts, not strictly an Epistle) recounts the historic event which the day commemorates. The Gospel recalls our Lord's words concerning the work of the Holy Spirit.

The Collect is a 1549 translation of a Gregorian original with two additions which improve its thought and rhythm: "in all things" and "holy." A regrettable loss in the Common Liturgy is the omission of the phrase at the beginning which specifically relates the prayer to the day (*hodierna die,* in the Missal; "as at this time," in the Prayer Book).

The Lesson from Joel, promises: "I will pour out my spirit upon all flesh."

MONDAY AFTER PENTECOST

	Service Book	Roman Missal	American Book of Common Prayer
Lesson	Isa. 57:15-21		
Epistle	Acts 10:42-48a	Acts 10:34a, 42-48	Acts 10:34-48a
Gospel	John 3:16-21	*Ibid.*	*Ibid.*
Introit	The same as for Pentecost	Ps. 81:16, 1	
Gradual	The same as for Pentecost	Acts 2:4; Veni Sancte Spiritus; Sequence: Veni Sancte Spiritus	

Color: Red.   Creed: Nicene.   Preface: Pentecost.

Collect

O GOD, who didst give thy Holy Spirit to thine Apostles: Grant unto thy people the performance of their petitions, so that on us to whom thou has given faith, thou mayest also bestow peace; through thy Son, Jesus Christ our Lord, who liveth . . . .

Deus qui apostolis tuis sanctum dedisti spiritum. concede plebi tuae piae petitionis effectum. ut quibus dedisti fidem largiaris et pacem. per dominum nostrum in unitate eiusdem. *Gregorian, 79. B.C.N.S. missals.*

The Missal provides propers for every day in Whitsun-week; the Prayer Book for Monday and Tuesday; the Common Liturgy for Monday only. The Introits and the Graduals for Whitsunday are repeated. The Epistle, a continuation of the Epistle for Easter Monday, establishes a connection between the two great festivals. Anglican usage actually combines these two sections in one lengthy Epistle for Whitmonday. The Missal and the Common Liturgy have the historic Gregorian Collect. The American Prayer Book has an entirely different Collect. The Lesson records the divine promise to "revive the spirit of the humble," though "there is no peace . . . to the wicked."

CHAPTER XXVIII

THE PROPERS IN DETAIL:
THE TRINITYTIDE, SAINTS' DAYS, ETC.

TRINITY SUNDAY
[THE OCTAVE OF PENTECOST]

	Service Book	Roman Missal	American Book of Common Prayer
Lesson	Isa. 6:1-8		
Epistle	Rom. 11:33-36	Ibid.	Rev. 4:1-11
Gospel	Matt. 28:18-20 or John 3:1-15	Matt. 28:18-20	John 3:1-15
Introit	Benedicta sit; Tob. 12:6b; Ps. 8:1a or Isa. 6:3a; Rom. 11:36a; Ps. 8:1a	Benedicta sit; Tob. 12:6b; Ps. 8:1a Ibid.	
Gradual	Song of the Three Children 32a, 34, 29		

Color: White. Creed: Nicene. Preface: Trinity.

Collect

ALMIGHTY and everlasting God, who hast given unto us thy servants grace, by the confession of a true faith, to acknowledge the glory of the eternal Trinity, and in the power of the Divine Majesty to worship the Unity: We beseech thee, that thou wouldest keep us steadfast in this faith, and evermore defend us from all adversities; who livest and reignest, . . .

Omnipotens sempiterne Deus, qui dedisti famulis tuis in confessione verae fidei, aeternae Trinitatis gloriam agnoscere, et in potentia maiestatis adorare unitatem: quaesumus; ut ejusdem fidei firmitate, ab omnibus muniamur adversis. Per. *Late Gregorian, B.C.N.S. missals.*

This Sunday is unique in character and position. The preceding Sundays in the first half of the year have recalled events in the life of our Lord. Whitsunday concluded these historic commemorations.

The early medieval centuries witnessed local diocesan celebrations, particularly throughout the West, in honor of the Holy Trinity. Popes Alexander II in the eleventh century and Alexander III in the twelfth century regarded this as unnecessary, and discouraged the observance, contending that the Holy Trinity was acclaimed in every day's worship. Pope John XXII (d. 1334) ordered this festival observed by the universal church, and on this Sunday.

Coming at the conclusion of the historic celebrations, Trinity Sunday, the octave of Pentecost, provides a fitting climax to the first half of the year and lends a dogmatic foundation for the Sundays in the second half with their messages concerning the teaching of our Lord as exemplified in the life of the church. It thus has a central position, concluding the half year of our Lord and beginning the half year of the church. The vestments are white in recognition of the holiness and glory of the Godhead.

The propers by their disunity reflect the late date and the provincial origins of the festival. The Introit, Collect, Gradual and Epistle, though differing as to texts, all sound the note of adoration and praise. The Gospel in the Prayer Book and the alternate Gospel in the Common Liturgy is the story of Nicodemus and our Lord's teaching concerning regeneration. This is the traditional Gospel for the Sunday after Pentecost and its relation to that festival is evident. The local dioceses in Germany and England retained this Gospel even after the first Sunday after Pentecost was no longer observed as the octave of that feast. Rome appointed a different Gospel (the divine commission in the Name of the Trinity—Matt. 28:18-20) for the new Festival of the Holy Trinity, and this is now given as the first of the alternate Gospels in the Common Liturgy (as also LLKD, VEKD, SW). The Epistle in the Missal and the Common Liturgy suggests the mystery of the doctrine of the Trinity. The Prayer Book Epistle more appropriately sounds the note of adoration. The Proper Preface is a late composition, full of involved phraseology. It is used only on this Sunday and its octave.

The Collect appears in the late Gregorian manuscripts but its involved dogmatic phraseology indicates that it is a later insertion, and also makes it one of the least admirable of all the Collects in the church's use. The translation is Prayer Book (1549) with the unfortunate alteration of 1662 which replaces the much-to-be-preferred original: "Through the steadfastness of this faith we may evermore be defended from all adversity." It is also regrettable that the Latin preposition *in,* which is used in both clauses of the text, should have been translated "by" in one instance and "in" in another. "By the confession

... by the power" would not only preserve the native balance of the Collect, but would clarify its meaning. The Lesson is Isaiah's vision of the Lord and the seraphim.

THE FIRST SUNDAY AFTER TRINITY

[THE SECOND SUNDAY AFTER PENTECOST]

	Service Book	*Roman Missal*	*American Book of Common Prayer*
Lesson	Deut. 6:4-13		
Epistle	I John 4:16b-21	I John 3:13-18	I John 4:7-21
Gospel	Luke 16:19-31	Luke 14:16-24	Luke 16:19-31
Introit	Ps. 13:5-6, 1	Ps. 18:18b-19, 1-2a	
Gradual	Pss. 41:4, 1; 7:1	Pss. 120:1-2; 7:1	

Color: White.   Creed: Nicene.   Preface: Trinity.

Collect

O GOD, the strength of all them that put their trust in thee: Mercifully accept our prayers; and because through the weakness of our mortal nature we can do no good thing without thee, grant us the help of thy grace, that in keeping thy commandments we may please thee, both in will and deed; through thy Son, Jesus Christ our Lord, who liveth . . . .

Deus, in te sperantium fortitudo, adesto propitius invocationibus nostris; et quia sine te nihil potest mortalis infirmitas, praesta auxilium gratiae tuae, ut in exequendis mandatis tuis et voluntate tibi et actione placeamus. Per Dominum. *Gelasian*, 106. *B.C.N.S. missals.*

With this Sunday we enter upon the half year of the church. The preceding half year of our Lord had a chronological sequence which is lacking from this point on. In some instances historical or other considerations influenced the choice of the propers. In general, however, the most we can say is that each Sunday the church presents edifying selections from the Scriptures and appropriate prayers which together comprise a fine body of devotion and instruction. In its totality this material illustrates the practical life of Christianity as it develops from truths presented in the first half of the year.

An ancient scheme of four cycles, or groupings of material, is still evident after the many substitutions and dislocations which the propers in this half of the year have suffered. These cycles are (1) from Pentecost to the Feast of St. Peter and St. Paul, June 29, (2) from this date to St. Lawrence's Day, August 10, (3) from this date to St. Michael's Day, September 29, (4) from this date to Advent. The propers for a particular day frequently exhibit a natural harmony, but in other cases the effort to demonstrate this would be forced and artificial.

Originally all these Sundays were counted Sundays after Pentecost. When the Festival of the Holy Trinity was introduced, it was particularly acclaimed in northern Europe, where it was accorded the dignity of a vigil and a full octave. In these areas the Sundays following were then numbered "after Trinity," while the use at Rome and in the southern churches (as well as in the Greek church) continued to count them "after Pentecost." The introduction of the octave of Trinity Sunday led to some confusion in the northern section of the church, and changes and dislocations made in Rome and not introduced in the distant dioceses of Germany, Scandinavia, and England were responsible for the discrepancies which now exist between the Lutheran and the Anglican lectionaires, on the one hand, and the Roman lectionary, on the other (see pp. 288-92).

The Common Liturgy has retained the north European numbering of Sundays "after Trinity," though giving "after Pentecost" in brackets, a reading much to be preferred. "After Trinity" is inaccurate. The reading should be "After Trinity Sunday," and the further question remains as to whether it is proper to name Sundays after such a theological concept as the Holy Trinity.

In general, the Epistles for Sundays VI to XXVII are a remnant of early continuous reading, with the books of the New Testament themselves in their correct order. The Gospels, for the first to the eleventh Sundays particularly, parallel the daily readings in the Breviary.

For the First Sunday after Trinity the Common Liturgy and the Prayer Book agree in the Epistle, Gospel and Collect, the Prayer Book having advantageously lengthened the Epistle. The theme of the day is the love of God and the love of man. The Missal appoints our Epistle and Gospel for Pentecost III and assigns our Gospel to the third Thursday in Lent. In the Roman use, though Trinity Sunday has displaced the First Sunday after Pentecost, the latter Sunday is still kept in the calendar and the proper Mass for that day is celebrated on one of the three weekdays before Corpus Christi.

The Collect in the Common Liturgy and the Prayer Book is Gelasian, and the phrase "through the weakness of our mortal nature" reminds us of Pope Gelasius' defense of the faith against Pelagianism. This Collect is also a "commemoration" in the Missal for Pentecost I. The translation (1549) would be more literal if "hope" were substituted for "trust."

[1] See *The St. Andrew Daily Missal* (1940), p. 754.

The Lesson admonishes Israel to "love the Lord thy God with all thine heart," etc.

THE SECOND SUNDAY AFTER TRINITY

[THE THIRD SUNDAY AFTER PENTECOST]

	Service Book	Roman Missal	American Book of Common Prayer
Lesson	Prov. 9:1-10		
Epistle	I John 3:13-18	I Pet. 5:6-11	I John 3:13-24
Gospel	Luke 14:15-24	Luke 15:1-10	Luke 14:16-24
Introit	Ps. 18:18b-19, 1-2a	Ps. 25:16, 18, 1-2a	
Gradual	Pss. 120:1-2; 7:17	Pss. 55:22a, 17b, c, 18b; 7:11	

Color: Green.   Creed: Nicene or Apostles'.   Preface: none.

Collect

O LORD, who never failest to help and govern those whom thou dost bring up in thy steadfast fear and love: Make us to have a perpetual fear and love of thy holy Name; through thy Son, Jesus Christ our Lord, who liveth . . . .

Sancti nominis tui, Domine, timorem pariter et amorem fac nos habere perpetuum; quia nunquam tua gubernatione destituis quos in soliditate tuae dilectionis instituis. Per. *Gelasian,* 109. *B.C.N.S. missals.*

The Common Liturgy, in agreement with modern paragraphing, begins the Gospel with vs. 15. The *Service Book* and the Prayer Book have the same Epistle and Gospel, both of which, in the spirit of Whitsuntide, present manifestations of love actively at work. The Introit suggests the basis for this in the love of God. From another aspect, both suggest the choice which comes to all men: the things of the world or the things of Christ.

The Collect in the 1549 translation gave a literal version of the forthright Gelasian original, which was not in true Collect form but which went directly into the petition: "Lord, make vs to haue a perpetuall feare and loue of thy holy name." The present altered form dates from 1662. The Missal appoints the Introit, Epistle and Gospel which the Common Liturgy and the Prayer Book give for Trinity III.

The Lesson speaks of Wisdom's having "furnished her table" and of her cry: "Come, eat of my bread," etc.

From this Sunday to the end of Trinity season, the color of the paraments on Sundays is green, signifying growth in the Christian life. There is no Proper Preface. Saints' days, of course, have their own individual appointments.

THE THIRD SUNDAY AFTER TRINITY

[THE FOURTH SUNDAY AFTER PENTECOST]

	Service Book	*Roman Missal*	*American Book of Common Prayer*
Lesson	Isa. 12:1-6		
Epistle	I Pet. 5:6-11	Rom. 8:18-23	I Pet. 5:5b-11
Gospel	Luke 15:1-10	Luke 5:1-11	Luke 15:1-10
Introit	Ps. 25:16, 18; 1-2a	Ps. 27:1-2a, 2c-3a	
Gradual	Pss. 55:22a, 16, 18a; 18:1-2a	Ps. 79:9b, 10a, 9a	

Color: Green.   Creed: Nicene or Apostles'.   Preface: none.

Collect

O GOD, the protector of all that trust in thee, without whom nothing is strong, nothing is holy: Increase and multiply upon us thy mercy; that, thou being our ruler and guide, we may so pass through things temporal, that we finally lose not the things eternal; through thy Son, Jesus Christ our Lord, who liveth . . . .

Protector in te sperantium deus sine quo nihil est ualidum. nihil sanctum. multiplica super nos misericordiam tuam. ut te rectore. te duce. sic transeamus per bona temporalia. ut non ammittamus aeterna. per dominum. *Late Gregorian, 169. B.C.N.S. missals.*

The Common Liturgy and the Prayer Book have the same Epistle and Gospel, and these lections, together with the Introit and Collect, teach God's loving care for "all that trust" (better, "hope") in him, whether those who suffer affliction (Introit and Epistle) or those who for a time wander away and are "lost" (Gospel). The Epistles for this day and for Trinity V, both from I Peter, may have reference to the approaching Festival of St. Peter and St. Paul.

The fine Collect is a Gregorian original in a free translation of 1549. This Collect is appointed in the Missal for Pentecost III and in the Prayer Book for Trinity IV. A different Collect is used for this Sunday (Trinity III) in both the Missal and the Prayer Book. The Missal appoints the Introit and Epistle which the Common Liturgy and the Prayer Book give for Trinity IV, and the Gospel which they give for Trinity V.

The Lesson again is a general one: "Behold, God is my salvation . . . ," etc.

THE FOURTH SUNDAY AFTER TRINITY

[THE FIFTH SUNDAY AFTER PENTECOST]

	Service Book	Roman Missal	American Book of Common Prayer
Lesson	Num. 6:22-27		
Epistle	Rom. 8:18-23	I Pet. 3:8-15a	Rom. 8:18-23
Gospel	Luke 6:36-42	Matt. 5:20-24	Luke 6:36-42
Introit	Ps. 27:1-2a, 2c-3a	Ps. 27:7a, 9b, 1a	
Gradual	Pss. 79:9b, 10a, 9a; 21:1	Pss. 84:9, 8a; 21:1	

Color: Green. Creed: Nicene or Apostles'. Preface: none.

Collect

GRANT, O Lord, we beseech thee, that the course of this world may be so peaceably ordered by thy governance, that thy Church may joyfully serve thee in all godly quietness; through thy Son, Jesus Christ our Lord, who liveth . . . .

Da nobis, Dñe Dš noster ut et mundi cursus pacifico nobis tuo ordine dirigatur et ecclesia tua tranquilla devotione laetetur Per. *Leonine,* 80. *B.C.N.S. missals.*

The Common Liturgy and the Prayer Book have the same Epistle and Gospel. These lessons were originally chosen with reference to the Embertide and they present the duties (Gospel) and the patience and hope (Epistle) required of Christian leaders. The Gospel is appointed in the Missal for Pentecost I and the Missal gives Matthew 5:20-24 and I Peter 3:8-15a as the Gospel and Epistle for Trinity IV (Pentecost V).

The Collect (1549 translation) is one of the most ancient in the church's use. As Canon Bright remarks, "It seems to have been suggested . . . by the disasters of the dying Western Empire."[2] The word *nobis* in the original text "may be peaceably ordered *for us,*" would seem to bear out this conjecture. The Reformers widened the scope of the petition by omitting this and stressing the idea that the church's opportunities of service are enhanced in a world at peace. The Introit breathes the same air of confident trust. The connection of the Introit and the Collect with the Epistle is evident. This Introit and Collect are given in the Missal on Pentecost IV and in the Prayer Book on Trinity V.

The Lesson is the Lord's blessing of Israel in the words of the "Old Testament benediction."

[2] William Bright, *Ancient Collects and Other Prayers* (4th ed.; Oxford: Parker, 1869), p. 208.

THE FIFTH SUNDAY AFTER TRINITY

[THE SIXTH SUNDAY AFTER PENTECOST]

	Service Book	Roman Missal	American Book of Common Prayer
Lesson	Lam. 3:22-33		
Epistle	I Pet. 3:8-15a	Rom. 6:3-11	I Pet. 3:8-15a
Gospel	Luke 5:1-11	Mark 8:1-9	Luke 5:1-11
Introit	Ps. 27:7a, 9b, 1a	Ps. 28:8, 9a, c, 1	
Gradual	Pss. 84:9, 8a; 31:1	Pss. 90:13, 1; 31:1-2a	

Color: Green.   Creed: Nicene or Apostles'.   Preface: none.

Collect

O GOD, who hast prepared for them that love thee such good things as pass man's understanding: Pour into our hearts such love toward thee, that we, loving thee above all things, may obtain thy promises, which exceed all that we can desire; through thy Son, Jesus Christ our Lord, who liveth . . . .

Deus, qui diligentibus te bona invisibilia praeparasti, infunde cordibus nostris tui amoris affectum, ut te in omnibus et super omnia diligentes, promissiones tuas, quae omne desiderium superant, consequamur. Per dominum nostrum. *Gelasian, 224. B.C.N.S. missals.*

This Sunday marks the close of the first cycle in the Trinity season, a period of five Sundays which emphasizes the call to the kingdom of grace. The Common Liturgy and the Prayer Book have the ancient lessons which were originally appointed for the Sunday immediately before the Festival of St. Peter and St. Paul, June 29. The Gospel is the story of the great draught of fishes and the call of Peter; the Epistle is a section of St. Peter's foremost Epistle. The festival is a joint one, but St. Peter is the featured character. Later changes in the Missal assigned our Epistle to Pentecost V and the Gospel to Pentecost IV, and appointed for this Sunday the Epistle which the Common Liturgy and the Prayer Book give on Trinity VI and the Gospel which they give on Trinity VII.

The Collect is one of the finest in the church's use, a prayer of rare spiritual beauty, perfect form, and fine diction. The original is Gelasian. The invocation is based upon I Corinthians 2:9: "Eye hath not seen, nor ear heard, neither have entered into the heart of man," etc. The original chose the phrase, "The things which eye hath not seen" (*invisibilia*); the 1549 translation, "The things which have not entered into man's heart"; and the final form incorporated the phrase in Philippians 4:7, "which passeth all understanding," and became "such good things as pass man's understanding." The opening phrase "for them that love thee" brings to mind our Lord's question addressed to Peter:

"Lovest thou me?" The Prayer Book appoints this Collect for Trinity VI; the Missal appoints it for Pentecost V.

The Lesson speaks of the Lord's mercies and how "his compassions fail not."

THE SIXTH SUNDAY AFTER TRINITY

[THE SEVENTH SUNDAY AFTER PENTECOST]

	Service Book	Roman Missal	American Book of Common Prayer
Lesson	Ruth 1:1-18		
Epistle	Rom. 6:3-11	Rom. 6:19-23	Rom. 6:3-11
Gospel	Matt. 5:20-26	Matt. 7:15-21	Matt. 5:20-26
Introit	Ps. 28:8-9, 1	Ps. 47:1-2	
Gradual	Pss. 90:13, 1; 47:1	Pss. 34:11, 5; 47:1	

Color: Green.   Creed: Nicene or Apostles'.   Preface: none.

Collect

LORD of all power and might, who art the author and giver of all good things: Graft in our hearts the love of thy Name, increase in us true religion, nourish us with all goodness, and of thy great mercy keep us in the same; through thy Son, Jesus Christ our Lord, who liveth . . . .

Deus virtutum, cuius est totum quod est optimum, insere pectoribus nostris amorem tui nominis, et praesta ut in nobis religionis augmento quae sunt bona nutrias; ac vigilanti, studio quae sunt nutrita custodias. Per. *Gelasian,* 225. *B.C.N.S. missals.*

This Sunday begins the second Trinity cycle, which runs from St. Peter's and St. Paul's Day, June 29, to St. Lawrence's Day, August 10, a period of six Sundays. The general theme of the Propers for this day and for the entire cycle is newness of life and righteousness as marks of those who are in the kingdom of grace and "alive unto God." This is the "true religion" of which the Collect speaks.

The Introits of this series continue to select from the Psalms in numerical order. The selections from Trinity Sunday through this Sunday are from the first book (Pss. 1-41); beginning with the Seventh Sunday after Trinity, from the second book (Pss. 42-72). The Roman series really marks the distinction, however, by starting the second cycle on this Sunday.

The Common Liturgy and the Prayer Book have the same lessons. The Epistles for the Sundays Trinity VI to Trinity XXV (except Trinity XVIII, when there is a dislocation due to Embertide) are all from St. Paul's Epistles in their proper order. The Missal appoints for this Sunday the Epistle which the Common Liturgy and the Prayer Book give on Trinity VII and the Gospel which they give on Trinity VIII. This Collect is a meaningful and forceful prayer from the Gelasian Sacramentary which the English Reformers materially enriched by their free translation in 1549. The Missal and the Prayer Book each give a different Collect for this Sunday, the former appointing the Collect which the Common Liturgy gives for Trinity VIII and the latter the Collect which the Common Liturgy gives for Trinity V.

The Lesson is the story of Ruth and Naomi.

THE SEVENTH SUNDAY AFTER TRINITY

[THE EIGHTH SUNDAY AFTER PENTECOST]

	Service Book	Roman Missal	American Book of Common Prayer
Lesson	Isa. 62:6-12		
Epistle	Rom. 6:19-23	Rom. 8:12-17a	Rom. 6:19-23
Gospel	Mark 8:1-9	Luke 16:1-9	Mark 8:1-9
Introit	Ps. 47:1, 3	Ps. 48:9-10, 1	
Gradual	Pss. 34:11, 5: 59:1	Pss. 31:2b, 1a; 48:1	

Color: Green. Creed: Nicene or Apostles'. Preface: none.

Collect

O GOD, whose never-failing providence ordereth all things both in heaven and earth: We humbly beseech thee to put away from us all hurtful things, and to give us those things which be profitable for us; through thy Son, Jesus Christ our Lord, who liveth . . . .

Deus, cuius providentia in sui dispositione non fallitur, te supplices exoramus, ut noxia cuncta submoveas, et omnia nobis profutura concedas. Per. *Gelasian, 225. B.C.N.S. missals.*

The Common Liturgy and the Prayer Book again have the same Epistle and Gospel. The Missal appoints for this day our Epistle for Trinity VIII and our Gospel for Trinity IX. Each of the three Rites has a different Collect. The theme of the propers is the providence of God as shown in his gifts of grace and the kind of lives we should live as "free from sin" and "servants of God."

Psalm 47 (the Introit) celebrates the providential deliverance of Jerusalem from the Assyrians (701 B.C.). The fine Collect (Prayer Book Trinity VIII, Missal Pentecost VII), is Gelasian. The inadequate 1549 translation of the invocation, "God, whose providence is never deceived," was greatly improved (1662) by the present happy paraphrase, though this still falls short of the full significance of the original, "whose providence is not deceived in the management of its own."

The Lesson records God's promise of food and drink and of salvation for Jerusalem.

THE EIGHTH SUNDAY AFTER TRINITY

[THE NINTH SUNDAY AFTER PENTECOST]

	Service Book	Roman Missal	American Book of Common Prayer
Lesson	Jer. 23:16-29		
Epistle	Rom. 8:12-17	I Cor. 10:6b-13	Rom. 8:12-17
Gospel	Matt. 7:15-21	Luke 19:41-47a	Matt. 7:15-21
Introit	Ps. 48:9-10, 1	Ps. 54:4-5, 1	
Gradual	Pss. 31:2b, 1a; 1:6	Pss. 8:1; 59:1	

Color: Green.   Creed: Nicene or Apostles'.   Preface: none.

Collect

GRANT to us, Lord, we beseech thee, the spirit to think and do always such things as are right; that we, who cannot do anything that is good without thee, may by thee be enabled to live according to thy will; through thy Son, Jesus Christ our Lord, who liveth . . . .

Largire nobis Dñe quaesumus spm cogitandi quae bona sunt promptius et agendi ut qui sine te esse non possumus secundum te vivere valeamus. Per. *Leonine*, 131. *B.C.N.S. missals.*

The Common Liturgy and the Prayer Book have the same Epistle and the same Gospel. The Missal appoints for this day our Epistle for Trinity IX and our Gospel for Trinity X. The Collect in the three rites again differs due to shifting of liturgical material in the medieval dioceses. This slight dislocation of the propers continues throughout Trinitytide, the same Epistles, Gospels, Collects, etc., being found in the same general areas in the three rites, and the same Introits in the Roman and Lutheran uses, but frequently a Sunday or two apart.

The teaching of the propers for this Sunday is the gift of the Spirit of God and the tests of life which demonstrate whether we "live after the flesh" or whether we are truly "led by the Spirit of God." In the Introit (Ps. 48) the church of the Old Testament exemplifies the life of grace. The Collect is an early Leonine original of the fifth century which exhibits a fine balance of phraseology which it is almost impossible to preserve in translation: *ut qui sine te esse non possumus secundum te vivere valeamus.* The 1549 translation "that we, which cannot be without thee" was changed to its present improved form in 1662. The Gospel has been shortened by omitting the last two verses (as MR, BCP, VEKD, LLKD, Rh). The Lesson connects with the Gospel in that it gives Jeremiah's denunciation of false prophets.

THE NINTH SUNDAY AFTER TRINITY

[THE TENTH SUNDAY AFTER PENTECOST]

	Service Book	Roman Missal	American Book of Common Prayer
Lesson	Prov. 16:1-9		
Epistle	I Cor. 10:1-13	I Cor. 12:2-11	I Cor. 10:1-13
Gospel	Luke 16:1-9	Luke 18:9-14	Luke 15:11-32
	or		
	Luke 15:11-32	Ps. 55:16a, 17b, 18b,	
Introit	Ps. 54:4-5, 1	19a, 22a, 1-2a	
Gradual	Pss. 8:1, 78:1	Ps. 17:8, 2; 65:1	

Color: Green.　Creed: Nicene or Apostles'.　Preface: none.

Collect

LET thy merciful ears, O Lord, be open to the prayers of thy humble servants; and, that they may obtain their petitions, make them to ask such things as shall please thee; through thy Son, Jesus Christ our Lord, who liveth . . . .

Pateant aures misericordiae, Domine, precibus supplicantium; et ut petentibus desiderata concedas, fac tibi eos, quaesumus, placita postulare. Per. *Gelasian,* 227. *B.C.N.S. missals.*

The Common Liturgy has lengthened the Epistle of the Common Service by beginning the section five verses earlier. This explains what "our examples" were. VEKD, LLKD, Rh, and BCP do the same. The Missal appoints for this Sunday our Epistle for Trinity X and our Gospel for Trinity XI. The American Prayer Book (1928), introduces a new Gospel in the story of the Prodigal Son, which the Scottish Prayer Book gives as an alternate Gospel. The Common Liturgy also gives this as an alternate Gospel. There is no agreement in the Collects.

The general theme of the propers is the admonition to all believers to be on guard against divers temptations and to use their talents in the cause of righteousness, in which God is our helper (Introit). The Collect, an exhortation to the right kind of prayer, is very ancient, actually appearing first in the Gelasian Sacramentary, but closely related to a similar Collect in the earlier Leonine Sacramentary. The 1549 translation was made from the later version. The Missal appoints this Collect for Pentecost IX and the Prayer Book for Trinity X.

The Lesson connects with the traditional Gospel: "Better is a little with righteousness than great revenues without right."

THE TENTH SUNDAY AFTER TRINITY
[THE ELEVENTH SUNDAY AFTER PENTECOST]

	Service Book	Roman Missal	American Book of Common Prayer
Lesson	Jer. 7:1-11		
Epistle	I Cor. 12:1-11	I Cor. 15:1-10a	I Cor. 12:1-11
Gospel	Luke 19:41-47a	Mark 7:31-37a, 37c	Luke 19:41-47a
Introit	Ps. 55:16a, 17b, 18a, 19a, 22a, 1	Ps. 68:5b, 6a, 35b, 1	
Gradual	Pss. 17:8, 2; 59:1	Pss. 28:7b, c, 1a; 81:1, 2a, c	

Color: Green.   Creed: Nicene or Apostles'.   Preface: none.

Collect

O GOD, who declarest thine almighty power chiefly in showing mercy and pity: Mercifully grant unto us such a measure of thy grace, that we, running the way of thy commandments, may obtain thy gracious promises, and be made partakers of thy heavenly treasure; through thy Son, Jesus Christ our Lord, who liveth . . . .

Deus, qui omnipotentiam tuam parcendo maxime et miserando manifestas, multiplica super nos gratiam tuam; ut ad tua promissa currentes caelestium honorum facias esse consortes. Per. *Gelasian*, 227. *B.C.N.S. missals.*

The Epistle and the Gospel are the same in the Common Liturgy and the Prayer Book. The Missal gives for this Sunday our Epistle for Trinity XI and our Gospel for Trinity XII. There is the usual dislocation of a Sunday or two in the Introits and the Collects. There is probably little to substantiate the oft-expressed idea that the choice of the destruction of Jerusalem as the Gospel for Trinity X was determined by the fact that this city was twice destroyed on August 10, about this very time in a normal church year. The message of the propers is rather an intensification of the teaching of the Sunday just past—the diversity of spiritual gifts and the consequences of failure to recognize our privileges and opportunities, "the time of our visitation." The Gospel has been shortened a verse and a half from the Common Service (as MR, SW, BCP).

The Collect (which is appointed in the Missal for Pentecost X and in the Prayer Book for Trinity XI) is in harmony with the Epistle and the Gospel in appealing for "such a measure of thy grace that . . . we may obtain . . . be made partakers," etc. The Collect is Gelasian. The 1549 translation was expanded by the revisers of the Prayer Book of 1662, and this has given us our present text.

The Lesson connects with the Gospel: "Is this house, which is called by my name, become a den of robbers?"

THE ELEVENTH SUNDAY AFTER TRINITY

[THE TWELFTH SUNDAY AFTER PENTECOST]

	Service Book	Roman Missal	American Book of Common Prayer
Lesson	Dan. 9:15-19		
Epistle	I Cor. 15:1-10	II Cor. 3:4-9	I Cor. 15:1-11
Gospel	Luke 18:9-14	Luke 10:23-37	Luke 18:9-14
Introit	Ps. 68:5b-6a, 35b, 1	Ps. 70:1-2	
Gradual	Pss. 28:7b, c, 1a, 2a; 65:1	Pss. 34:1-2; 88:1	

Color: Green.   Creed: Nicene or Apostles'.   Preface: none.

Collect

ALMIGHTY and everlasting God, who art always more ready to hear than we to pray, and art wont to give more than either we desire or deserve: Pour down upon us the abundance of thy mercy, forgiving us those things whereof our conscience is afraid, and giving us those good things which we are not worthy to ask, but through the merits and mediation of Jesus Christ, thy Son, our Lord, who liveth . . . .

Omnipotens sempiterne Deus, qui abundantia pietatis tuae et merita supplicum excedis et vota, effunde super nos misericordiam tuam, ut dimittas quae conscientia metuit, et adiicias quod oratio non praesumit. Per. *Gelasian*, 228. *B.C.N.S. missals.*

The Epistle and the Gospel are the same in the Common Liturgy and the Prayer Book. The Missal has the usual dislocation, and appoints our Introit and Epistle for one week ahead (Trinity X) and our Gospel for Trinity IX. There is also the usual discrepancy in the Collect, the *Service Book* Collect for this day being the one for Pentecost XI in the Missal and for Trinity XII in the Prayer Book. For this Sunday the Missal appoints our Collect for Trinity XII, the Prayer Book our Collect for Trinity X.

This Sunday concludes the second cycle of the Trinity season, whose teaching has concerned itself with aspects of the new life of righteousness. The Introit employs the great Pentecost Psalm (68), though the Missal appointment concludes the series from Book II of the Psalter. The lessons reveal, in sharp contrast, the story of the Pharisee and the publican, and also the story of the two Pharisees—the one traditionally proud and boastful, and the other the converted Pharisee who became an apostle, and who "by the grace of God which was with me" "labored more abundantly than they all," but in that spirit of humility which the publican exemplified.

The remarkably fine Collect, with its reference to prayer, conscience, and the spirit of humility, is in harmony with both the Epistle and the

Gospel. The germ of this Collect is Leonine. The later Gelasian form added the clause "forgiving us those things whereof our conscience is afraid," and the Prayer Book (1549) added to the invocation the phrase "who art always more ready to hear than we to pray." Bishop Cosin in 1662 further changed the conclusion from "giving unto us that that our prayer dare not ask" to the present full form.

The Lesson is Daniel's prayer for the city and the people.

THE TWELFTH SUNDAY AFTER TRINITY

[THE THIRTEENTH SUNDAY AFTER PENTECOST]

	Service Book	Roman Missal	American Book of Common Prayer
Lesson	Isa. 29:17-21		
Epistle	II Cor. 3:4-9	Gal. 3:16-22	II Cor. 3:4-9
Gospel	Mark 7:31-37	Luke 17:11-19	Mark 7:31-37
Introit	Ps. 70:1-2	Ps. 74:20a, 19b, 22a, 23a, 1	
Gradual	Pss. 34:1-2; 81:1	Pss. 74:20a, 19b, 22; 90:1	

Color: Green.   Creed: Nicene or Apostles'.   Preface: none.

Collect

ALMIGHTY and merciful God, of whose only gift it cometh that thy faithful people do unto thee true and laudable service: Grant, we beseech thee, that we may so faithfully serve thee in this life, that we fail not finally to attain thy heavenly promises; through thy Son, Jesus Christ our Lord, who liveth
. . . .

Omp̄ et misericors D̄s de cuius munere venit ut tibi a fidelibus tuis digne et laudabiliter serviatur tribue ut ad promissiones tuas sine offensione curramus per. *Leonine, 74, B.C.N.S. missals.*

The Epistle and the Gospel are the same in the Common Liturgy and the Prayer Book. The latter, which frequently lengthens the Epistle, has in this case shortened it by two verses. MR, VEKD, LLKD, and SW are in agreement with this, and the Common Liturgy lection has been abbreviated accordingly. The Missal, as generally in these Sundays, is one Sunday ahead (Trinity XIII) with its Introit and Epistle, and two Sundays ahead (Trinity XIV) with its Gospel.

This Sunday begins the third cycle within the Trinity season, a cycle which extends to Trinity XVIII. The first cycle (Trinity I-V) presented the call to the kingdom of grace; the second (Trinity VI-XI) the righteousness of the kingdom; and the third, from St. Lawrence's Day to St. Michael's Day, discusses practical aspects of Christian faith and life as manifested in works of love and service. The Missal Introits (and

532

ours after this Sunday) are from Book III (Pss. 73-89) of the Psalter, until Trinity XVI.

The lessons for this Sunday were undoubtedly chosen because of the proximity of St. Lawrence's Day, August 10. Lawrence was a famous deacon and preacher in Rome, "an able minister of the New Testament" (Epistle). The psalmist's prayer in this Introit almost seems an anticipation of his martyrdom. The "true and laudable service" which all God's "faithful people" (Collect) may render is indicated in the Gospel which tells of the ministrations of those who "brought" a sufferer to Christ; "besought" his aid and "published" the story abroad.

The Collect (Trinity XIII in the Prayer Book; Pentecost XII in the Missal) is a somewhat expanded form of the Leonine original. The insertion of the word "only" before "gift" is a quaint and suggestive addition. The substitution of "true" for "worthy" (*digne*) is in line with evangelical belief, which seeks genuineness but cannot claim "worthiness." The 1549 translation also had a more literal rendering of the petition: "that we may so runne to thy heauenly promises, that we faile not finally to attayne the same." In 1662 the prayer was changed to its present form with the addition of the final phrase, "through the merits of Jesus Christ our Lord," an addition which the Common Liturgy has not accepted.

The Lesson connects with the Gospel: "In that day shall the deaf hear the words of the book."

THE THIRTEENTH SUNDAY AFTER TRINITY
[THE FOURTEENTH SUNDAY AFTER PENTECOST]

	Service Book	Roman Missal	American Book of Common Prayer
Lesson	Zech. 7:4-10		
Epistle	Gal. 3:16-22	Gal. 5:16-24	Gal. 3:16-22
Gospel	Luke 10:23-37	Matt. 6:24-33	Luke 10:23-37
Introit	Ps. 74:20a, 21a, 22a, 23a, 1	Ps. 84:9-10a, 1-2a	
Gradual	Pss. 74:20a, 21a, 22a, 23a; 88:1	Pss. 118:8-9, 95:1	

Color: Green. Creed: Nicene or Apostles'. Preface: none.

Collect

ALMIGHTY and everlasting God, give unto us the increase of faith, hope, and charity; and that we may obtain that which thou dost promise, make us to love that which thou dost command; through thy Son, Jesus Christ our Lord, who liveth . . . .

Omp̄ semp̄ Dš da nobis fidei spei et caritatis augmentum et ut mereamur adsequi quod promittis fac nos amare quod praecipis per. *Leonine, 76. B.C.N.S. missals.*

The Common Liturgy and the Prayer book agree in the Epistle and the Gospel. The Missal is again one Sunday ahead with its Introit and Epistle and two Sundays ahead with its Gospel. The three rites differ in the Collects. The Introit sounds the theme of the day, "have respect to the covenant." The Epistle discusses the old covenant which could not give life. The Gospel answers the lawyer's question in the parable of the Good Samaritan with its message of serving love, which is the fulfilment of the law and the practical manifestation of that "increase of faith, hope, and charity" for which we pray in the Collect. The latter, a Leonine original in briefest form, is in the translation of 1549. It is well related to both the Epistle and the Gospel and is, of course, reminiscent of I Corinthians 13. The Latin has *ut mereamur adsequi:* "that we may deserve to obtain." By the simple omission of "deserve to" in this and similar instances, the Reformers recognized and rejected one of the major doctrinal errors of the medieval (and modern Roman) church. The Lesson is the Lord's word to Zechariah: "Show mercy and compassions every man to his brother."

THE FOURTEENTH SUNDAY AFTER TRINITY
[THE FIFTEENTH SUNDAY AFTER PENTECOST]

	Service Book	Roman Missal	American Book of Common Prayer
Lesson	Prov. 4:10-23		
Epistle	Gal. 5:16-24	Gal. 5:25—6:10	Gal. 5:16-24
Gospel	Luke 17:11-19	Luke 7:11b-16	Luke 17:11-19
Introit	Ps. 84:9-10a, 1-2a	Ps. 86:1a, 2b-4	
Gradual	Pss. 118:8-9; 90:1	Pss. 92:1-2; 95-3	

Color: Green.   Creed: Nicene or Apostles'.   Preface: none.

Collect

KEEP, we beseech thee, O Lord, thy Church with thy perpetual mercy; and, because the frailty of man without thee cannot but fall, keep us ever by thy help from all things hurtful, and lead us to all things profitable to our salvation; through thy Son, Jesus Christ our Lord, who liveth . . . .

Custodi, Domine, quaesumus, ecclesiam tuam propitiatione perpetua; et, quia sine te labitur humana mortalitas, tuis semper auxiliis et abstrahatur a noxiis et ad salutaria dirigatur. Per. *Gelasian, 229. B.C.N.S. missals.*

The Epistle and the Gospel are the same in the Common Liturgy and the Prayer Book. The Missal, as usual, is one and two Sundays ahead respectively in its lections. The three rites appoint the Collect for different Sundays in this area (Missal, Pentecost XIV; Prayer Book, Trinity XV). The theme is an exhortation to practical Christian living

—the realization in our own daily lives of "the fruit of the Spirit" as over against "the works of the flesh" (Epistle). The Introit psalm (84) is a model for this realization, by its transition from the blessedness of the worshiper to that of the man of true faith and moral power (cf. Ps. 84:4, 5, 12).

The Gospel adds another fruit of the Spirit in stressing the faith and gratitude of the Samaritan who was cleansed of leprosy, always the symbol of sin. The commendation of the thankful Samaritan in this day's Gospel and of the Good Samaritan of the past Sunday's Gospel pointedly suggests that more is required of us than a merely formal church connection, and that those who have not enjoyed our privileges may excel us in spiritual gifts and graces.

The Collect is a Gelasian prayer for the preservation of the church. Its form is unusual in that its very first word voices its petition, before the usual invocation. The original *propitiatione perpetua,* "by thy perpetual atonement," is suggestive of a possible reference to the sacrifice of the Mass, and the Reformers substituted "by thy perpetual mercy." On the other hand, the original "without thee human mortality falls" is more forthright in its warning that danger to the church constantly arises from the "frailty of man" than is the 1549 translation.

The Lesson connects with the Epistle: "The path of the just is as the shining light."

THE FIFTEENTH SUNDAY AFTER TRINITY

[THE SIXTEENTH SUNDAY AFTER PENTECOST]

	Service Book	Roman Missal	American Book of Common Prayer
Lesson	I Kings 17:8-16		
Epistle	Gal. 5:25—6:10	Eph. 3:13-21	Gal. 6:11-18
Gospel	Matt. 6:24-34	Luke 14:1-11	Matt. 6:24-34
Introit	Ps. 86:1a, 2b-4	Ps. 86:3, 5, 1	
Gradual	Pss. 92:1-2; 108:1	Pss. 102:15-16; 98:1a	

Color: Green. Creed: Nicene or Apostles'. Preface: none.

Collect

O LORD, we beseech thee, let thy continual pity cleanse and defend thy Church; and because it cannot continue in safety without thy succor, preserve it evermore by thy help and goodness; through thy Son, Jesus Christ our Lord, who liveth . . . .

Ecclesiam tuam, Domine, miseratio continuata mundet et muniat; et quia sine te non potest salva consistere, tuo semper munere gubernetur. Per. *Gelasian,* 230. *B.C.N.S. missals.*

There is great diversity in the propers, the one agreement being between the Common Liturgy and the Prayer Book in the matter of the Gospel. The three rites have three different Epistles and three different Collects. The Missal is, as usual, one Sunday ahead with its Introit and Epistle and two Sundays ahead with its Gospel. The Prayer Book at the time of the Reformation appointed an Epistle (Gal. 6:11-18) which is not found in either of the other lectionaries.

The theme of the day is living and walking in the Spirit in singleness of heart, in trust and contentment, ever seeking to "do good unto all men" (Epistle) as a "servant of the Lord." (Introit). The Collect is Gelasian, and is another prayer for the church, this time for its cleansing and defense. The Prayer Book translation (1549) has not been able to preserve the triple play on the Latin words *mundet, muniat,* and *munere,* which the original provides. The substitution of "govern" for "preserve" in the final petition would be nearer the original thought. The translation of 1549, with its petition "clense and defende thy congregacion" (changed to "church" in 1662) reminds us of Luther's frequent use of "Gemeine" for *ecclesia.*

The Lesson is the story of Elijah and the widow's "barrel of meal" and "cruse of oil."

THE SIXTEENTH SUNDAY AFTER TRINITY
[THE SEVENTEENTH SUNDAY AFTER PENTECOST]

	Service Book	Roman Missal	American Book of Common Prayer
Lesson	Job 5:17-26		
Epistle	Eph. 3:13-21	Eph. 4:1-6	Eph. 3:13-21
Gospel	Luke 7:11-16	Matt. 22:34a, 34c-46	Luke 7:11-17
Introit	Ps. 86:3, 5, 1	Ps. 119:137, 124a, 1	
Gradual	Pss. 102:15-16; 98:1a	Pss. 33:12, 6; 102:1	

Color: Green.   Creed: Nicene or Apostles'.   Preface: none.

Collect

LORD, we pray thee, that thy grace may always go before and follow after us, and make us continually to be given to all good works; through thy Son, Jesus Christ our Lord, who liveth . . . .

Tua nos domine quaesumus gratia semper et preueniat et sequatur. ac bonis operibus iugiter prestet esse intentos. per. *Gregorian,* 174. *C.N.S. missals.*

The Common Liturgy and the Prayer Book appoint the same Epistle and the same Gospel. The Missal, as usual, is one Sunday ahead with its Introit and Epistle and two Sundays ahead with its Gospel. There is no agreement in the Collect. The theme of the Propers is the power of God and the love of Christ, which make it possible for believers to be "strengthened with might by his Spirit in the inner man," to meet the doubts, sufferings, and sorrows of this present life. This the psalmist found (Introit) in forgiveness and mercy in his time of need. The Gospel omits the final anticlimactic verse in the former lection (as MR, VEKD, LLKD, Rh).

The Collect (Prayer Book Trinity XVII) which might perhaps more properly have been appointed for last Sunday (Trinity XV) is a Gregorian prayer for grace, whose thought is quite similar to that of the Collect, "Direct us, O Lord, in all our doings," etc. (*Service Book,* p. 233, Collect No. 113). The translation is Prayer Book (1549) except that "go before" has been substituted for the archaic expression "prevent" which anciently had the same meaning, as is indicated in the theological term "prevenient grace."

The Lesson ties in with the Gospel: "He woundeth, and his hands make whole."

THE SEVENTEENTH SUNDAY AFTER TRINITY

[THE EIGHTEENTH SUNDAY AFTER PENTECOST]

	Service Book	Roman Missal	American Book of Common Prayer
Lesson	Prov. 25:6-14		
Epistle	Eph. 4:1-6	I Cor. 1:4-8	Eph. 4:1-6
Gospel	Luke 14:1-11	Matt. 9:1-8	Luke 14:1-11
Introit	Ps. 119:137, 124a, 1	Ecclus. 36:16, 17a; Ps. 122:1	
Gradual	Pss. 33:12, 6; 116:1	Pss. 122:1, 7; 102:15	

Color: Green.   Creed: Nicene or Apostles'.   Preface: none.

Collect

LORD, we beseech thee, grant thy people grace to withstand the temptations of the devil, and with pure hearts and minds to follow thee, the only God; through thy Son, Jesus Christ our Lord, who liveth . . . .

Da, quaesumus, Domine, populo tuo diabolica vitare contagia, et te solum Dominum puro corde sectari. Per. *Gelasian,* 231. B.C.N.S. missals.

Again the Common Liturgy and the Prayer Book have the same Epistle and the same Gospel, and the Missal is one Sunday ahead with its Introit and Epistle (Pentecost XIX), and two Sundays ahead (Pentecost XX) with its Gospel. There is no agreement in the Collect, the usual separation of a Sunday or two prevailing. The theme of the propers is a life "worthy of the vocation wherewith ye are called" (Epistle), "walking in the law of the Lord" (Introit) with special emphasis upon the virtue of humility (Gospel).

The Collect is Gelasian. The Prayer Book translation (1549) in its more literal rendering, "to auoyde the infeccions of the Deuil" preserved the antithesis of the original Latin *diabolica contagia* and *puro corde*. This was lost in the later (1662) amended form "to withstand the temptations of the world, the flesh, and the devil." This recognized the fact that infections (contacts) may be avoided but that temptations must be withstood. The Common Liturgy omits "the world" and "the flesh."

The Lesson, like the Gospel, stresses the virtue of humility.

THE EIGHTEENTH SUNDAY AFTER TRINITY
[THE NINETEENTH SUNDAY AFTER PENTECOST]

	Service Book	Roman Missal	American Book of Common Prayer
Lesson	II Chron. 1:7-12		
Epistle	I Cor. 1:4-9	Eph. 4:23-28	I Cor. 1:4-8
Gospel	Matt. 22:34-46	Matt. 22:1-14	Matt. 22:34-46
Introit	Ecclus. 36:16-17a; Ps. 122:1	Salus populi; Ps. 78:1	
Gradual	Pss. 122:1, 7; 117:1	Pss. 141:2; 105:1	

Color: Green.   Creed: Nicene or Apostles'.   Preface: none.

Collect

O GOD, forasmuch as without thee we are not able to please thee: Mercifully grant, that thy Holy Spirit may in all things direct and rule our hearts; through thy Son, Jesus Christ our Lord, who liveth . . . .

Dirigat corda nostra, Domine, quaesumus, tua miserationis operatio, quia tibi sine te placere non possumus. Per. *Gelasian*, 232. *B.C.N.S. missals.*

The Epistle and the Gospel are the same in the Common Liturgy and the Prayer Book. The Missal, as usual, gives here our Epistle for next Sunday (Trinity XIX) and the Gospel for two Sundays ahead (Trinity XX). There is the usual dislocation of the Collect. This Sunday concludes the third cycle of Sundays within the Trinity Season, a cycle which began with Trinity XII and which has stressed practical aspects of Christian faith and life as revealed in works of love and service. The Introits from Book III of the Psalter, however, were already interrupted at Trinity XVI (Missal) or XVII (*Service Book*).

The teaching of the day contemplates with thanksgiving the gift of the grace of God which enriches Christian fellowship "in all utterance, and in all knowledge" (Epistle), and stresses the two great commandments and the acknowledgment of Christ as Lord (Gospel) as fundamental, under the constant guidance of the Holy Spirit (Collect) to the life and growth of believers. The Collect is Gelasian, probably earlier. The Latin text is unusual in that it begins directly with the petition. The 1549 translation conformed to the usual collect pattern and began with the "antecedent reason." Its petition, "Graunte that the workyng of thy mercie, maye in all thynges," etc., was a literal translation of the terse original. The reference to the Holy Spirit came in with the revision of 1662, which also retained the idea of mercy by inserting the word "mercifully" before "grant."

The Lesson is Solomon's prayer for "wisdom and knowledge," which connects with the Epistle.

THE NINETEENTH SUNDAY AFTER TRINITY

[THE TWENTIETH SUNDAY AFTER PENTECOST]

	Service Book	Roman Missal	American Book of Common Prayer
Lesson	Gen. 28:10-17		
Epistle	Eph. 4:17-28	Eph. 5:15-21	Eph. 4:17-32
Gospel	Matt. 9:1-8	John 4:46b-53	Matt. 9:1-8
Introit	Pss. 35:3b; 34:17; 48:14a; 78:1	Song of the Three Children 8a, c, 6, 20b, 19b; Ps. 119:1	
Gradual	Pss. 141:2; 118:16	Pss. 145:15, 16; 108:1	

Color: Green.   Creed: Nicene or Apostles'.   Preface: none.

Collect

O ALMIGHTY and most merciful God, of thy bountiful goodness keep us, we beseech thee, from all things that may hurt us; that we, being ready, both in body and soul, may cheerfully accomplish those things that thou wouldest have done; through thy Son, Jesus Christ our Lord, who liveth . . . .

Omnipotens et misericors Deus, universa nobis adversantia propitiatus exclude; ut, mente et corpore pariter expediti, quae tua sunt liberis mentibus exequamur. Per. *Gelasian, 232. B.C.N.S. missals.*

The Common Liturgy and the Prayer Book have the same Epistle and the same Gospel. The Prayer Book lengthened the Epistle. The Common Liturgy has added five verses to the former lection. The Missal has the usual dislocation and appoints for this day our Epistle for Trinity XX and our Gospel for Trinity XXI.

539

This Sunday begins the fourth and final cycle within the Trinity season, extending from St. Michael's Day, September 29, to Advent. The general theme of its teaching is the consummation of the kingdom, which, according to the propers of this day, requires that we "be renewed in the spirit of our mind" and "put on the new man" (Epistle), while it assures us of Christ's purpose and power to heal the ravages of sin (Gospel) and to make us "ready both in body and soul" (Collect) for life here and for the consummation of all things, since the Lord is our "God for ever and ever" (Introit).

The Collect is Gelasian. The translation, Prayer Book (1549), slightly altered (1662), has numerous but unimportant variations from the original. We may regret the word "cheerfully" of 1662 as an inadequate substitute for the quality of spiritual freedom expressed in *liberis mentibus* or "with free heartes" (1549).

The Lesson is the story of Jacob's dream of a ladder at Bethel.

THE TWENTIETH SUNDAY AFTER TRINITY
[THE TWENTY-FIRST SUNDAY AFTER PENTECOST]

	Service Book	Roman Missal	American Book of Common Prayer
Lesson	Prov. 2:1-9		
Epistle	Eph. 5:15-21	Eph. 6:10-17	Eph. 5:15-21
Gospel	Matt. 22:1-14	Matt. 18:23-35	Matt. 22:2-14
Introit	Dan. 9:14b; Pss. 115:1b; 69:16b; 48:1	Esther 13:9b, d, 10-11a; Ps. 119:1	
Gradual	Pss. 145:15-16; 105:1	Pss. 90:1-2; 114:1	

Color: Green. Creed: Nicene or Apostles'. Preface: none.

Collect

GRANT, we beseech thee, merciful Lord, to thy faithful people pardon and peace, that they may be cleansed from all their sins, and serve thee with a quiet mind; through thy Son, Jesus Christ our Lord, who liveth . . . .

Largire, quaesumus, Domine, fidelibus tuis indulgentiam placatus et pacem; ut pariter ab omnibus mundentur offensis, et secura tibi mente deserviant. Per. *Gelasian*, 233. *B.C.N.S. missals.*

The Common Liturgy and the Prayer Book agree as usual in the lections. The Missal is again one Sunday ahead with the Introit and Epistle and two Sundays ahead with the Gospel. The Collect differs in the three rites. The teaching of the propers is the necessity of right living and of "understanding what the will of the Lord is" (Epistle), because God not only provides bountifully for our needs and our pleasure but will judge and condemn those who "make light" of his goodness and grace (Gospel). Schuster, in commenting on the Epistle ("be not drunk with wine"), calls attention to the fact that this Sunday normally comes in Italy about the time when the new wine is drawn off.

The Collect, a brief but beautiful prayer, which would seem to have been particularly appropriate for Trinity XIX, is a Gelasian original in a none-too-literal Prayer Book (1549) translation.

The Lesson connects with the Epistle in its call for "wisdom and understanding."

THE TWENTY-FIRST SUNDAY AFTER TRINITY
[THE TWENTY-SECOND SUNDAY AFTER PENTECOST]

	Service Book	Roman Missal	American Book of Common Prayer
Lesson	II Sam. 7:18-29		
Epistle	Eph. 6:10-17	Phil. 1:6-11	Eph. 6:10-20
Gospel	John 4:46b-53	Matt. 22:15-21	John 4:46b-54
Introit	Esther 13:9b, d, 10-11a; Ps. 119:1	Ps. 130:3-4a, 1-2a	
Gradual	Pss. 90:1-2; 125:1	Pss. 133:1-2a; 115:11	

Color: Green.   Creed: Nicene or Apostles'.   Preface: none.

Collect

LORD, we beseech thee to keep thy household, the Church, in continual godliness; that through thy protection it may be free from all adversities, and devoutly given to serve thee in good works, to the glory of thy Name; through thy Son, Jesus Christ our Lord, who liveth . . . .

Familiam tuam quaesumus domine continua pietate custodi. ut a cunctis aduersitatibus te protegente sit libera. et in bonis actibus tuo nomini sit deuota. per dominum. *Gregorian, 176. B.C.N.S. missals.*

The lections are the same in the Common Liturgy and the Prayer Book. The Epistle in the Prayer Book is lengthened by three verses and the Gospel by one. The interjection of the lesson from John's Gospel in the sequence of lessons from Matthew's Gospel is to be noted, though there is no explanation for it.

The Missal again is one Sunday ahead with its Introit and Epistle and two Sundays ahead with its Gospel. The Introit is taken from an apocryphal chapter of Esther. There is the usual dislocation of Collects. The theme of the propers is the Christian warfare and the necessity of taking "the whole armor of God, that ye may be able to withstand in the evil day" (Epistle). The "shield of faith" makes an easy connection with the Gospel. The Introit sings of God's omnipotence and the Collect invokes his protection and maintenance of the church in all adversities. The Collect is a late Gregorian original in a Prayer Book (1549) translation. It is similar in content to the Collect for Epiphany V. Indeed, in the Latin the first portion is exactly the same.

The Lesson speaks of God's blessing upon the house of David, thus connecting with Christ's blessing of the nobleman's house in the Gospel.

THE TWENTY-SECOND SUNDAY AFTER TRINITY
[THE TWENTY-THIRD SUNDAY AFTER PENTECOST]

	Service Book	Roman Missal	American Book of Common Prayer
Lesson	Prov. 3:11-20		
Epistle	Phil. 1:3-11	Phil. 3:17—4:3	Phil. 1:3-11
Gospel	Matt. 18:21-35	Matt. 9:18-26	Matt. 18:21-35
Introit	Ps. 130:3-4, 1-2a	Jer. 29:11b, 12 a, c, 14b, d; Ps. 85:1	
Gradual	Pss. 133:1, 3b; 146:1b, 2a, b	Pss. 44:7-8; 130:1-2a	

Color: Green.   Creed: Nicene or Apostles'.   Preface: none.

Collect

O GOD, our refuge and strength, who art the author of all godliness: Be ready, we beseech thee, to hear the devout prayers of thy Church; and grant that those things which we ask faithfully, we may obtain effectually; through thy Son, Jesus Christ our Lord, who liveth ....

Deus refugium nostrum et uirtus. adesto piis ecclesiae tuae precibus. auctor ipse pietatis. et presta ut quod fideliter petimus. efficaciter consequamur. per dominum. *Gregorian, 176. B.C.N.S. missals.*

The usual arrangement of the propers prevails. The Common Liturgy and the Prayer Book have the same Epistle and the same Gospel; the Missal gives our Introit and Epistle and our Collect on Trinity XXIII and our Gospel on Trinity XXIV. The Prayer Book appoints the Collect we used the past Sunday (Trinity XXI).

The theme of the propers is growth in grace on the part of the "fellowship in the Gospel" (Epistle), with special reference to exercising the spirit of forgiveness illustrated in the Gospel and proclaimed in the Introit. There is possibly the suggestion of an eschatological note in the phrase "until the day of Jesus Christ." The Collect, a fine Gregorian original in the Prayer Book (1549) translation, reinforces the social significance of the day's teaching by its reference to "the devout prayers of thy Church." It has not been possible to retain in translation the play upon *piis* and *pietatis* in the original, although Goulburn suggests the possibility of "godly" and "godliness," or of "devout" and "devotion."

The Lesson says of Wisdom that "length of days is in her right hand," and "all her paths are peace."

THE TWENTY-THIRD SUNDAY AFTER TRINITY
[THE TWENTY-FOURTH SUNDAY AFTER PENTECOST]

	Service Book	Roman Missal	American Book of Common Prayer
Lesson	Prov. 8:11-22		
Epistle	Phil. 3:17-21	Epiphanytide lessons repeated.	Phil. 3:17-21
Gospel	Matt. 22:15-22	Epiphanytide lessons repeated.	Matt. 22:15-22
Introit	Jer. 29:11a, b, 12, 14b	Trinity XXII repeated.	
Gradual	Pss. 44:7-8; 115-11	Trinity XXII repeated.	

Color: Green.　Creed: Nicene or Apostles'.　Preface: none.

Collect

ABSOLVE, we beseech thee, O Lord, thy people from their offences; that from the bonds of our sins which, by reason of our frailty, we have brought upon us, we may be delivered by thy bountiful goodness; through thy Son, Jesus Christ our Lord, who liveth . . . .

Absolue quaesumus domine tuorum delicta populorum. et a peccatorum nostrorum nexibus quae pro nostra fragilitate contraximus. tua benignitate liberemur. per. *Gregorian*, 103. *C.N.S. missals*.

Again the Common Liturgy and the Prayer Book have the same Epistle and the same Gospel. The Missal reverts to the unused lections from Epiphanytide. While the Missal thus has new lessons today, it has no new Introit. It repeats the Introit for last Sunday and so comes into line again with our more ancient use. The usual dislocation of Collects prevails, the Missal appointing for this day the Epiphanytide Collect, and the Prayer Book appointing our Collect for Trinity XXII.

For this Sunday and those following (except the Last Sunday after Trinity) the medieval and modern Roman missals make no separate appointments. As the movable portion of the church year shifts, any increase in the number of Sundays after Trinity will be compensated for by a decrease in the number after the Epiphany. The Roman Rite thus appoints the extra Collects and lessons from Epiphanytide for use here, while repeating the Introit and Gradual for Trinity XXII. The

Prayer Book makes appointments for this Sunday and next, then repeats Epiphany VI or V and VI, as required. The Common Liturgy makes full appointments (with some repetition) for all possible Sundays after Trinity.

The theme of this day's teaching is our heavenly citizenship, which requires standards of life and conduct worthy of that high estate but which does not free us from meeting the normal obligations of our earthly citizenship. The Collect is Gregorian, Prayer Book (1549) translation. This Collect is the same as that given to be used "the last Sunday after Trinity of each year," and it is well adapted to this requirement. Its thought encompasses the year which is closing and which calls for the confession of our sins and an appeal for the absolution which alone can give peace and deliverance "from the bonds of our sins" in accordance with the divine word announced in the Introit. The American Prayer Book has reconstructed the text of the Collect with resulting smoothness.

The Lesson, connecting with the Gospel, proclaims wisdom to be "better than rubies."

THE TWENTY-FOURTH SUNDAY AFTER TRINITY
[THE TWENTY-FIFTH SUNDAY AFTER PENTECOST]

	Service Book	*Roman Missal*	*American Book of Common Prayer*
Lesson	I Kings 17:17-24		
Epistle	Col. 1:9-14	Epiphanytide lessons repeated.	Col. 1:3-12
Gospel	Matt. 9:18-26	Epiphanytide lessons repeated.	Matt. 9:18-26
Introit	Ps. 95:6-7, 1	Trinity XXII repeated.	
Gradual	Pss. 1:1a, 2; 91:15a, 16	Trinity XXII repeated.	

Color: Green.   Creed: Nicene or Apostles'.   Preface: none.

Collect

STIR up, we beseech thee, O Lord, the wills of thy faithful people; that they, plenteously bringing forth the fruit of good works, may of thee be plenteously rewarded; through thy Son, Jesus Christ our Lord, who liveth . . . .

Excita domine quaesumus tuorum fidelium uoluntates. ut diuini operis fructum propensius exsequentes. pietatis tuae remedia maiora percipiant. per dominum. *Gregorian, 177.*

The Lutheran Liturgy is unique in providing Propers for twenty-seven Sundays after Trinity. When there are more than twenty-three Sundays, the Roman use repeats the Introit and the Gradual for Trinity XXII each Sunday except the last. It supplies Collects, Epistles, and Gospels from the Sundays after Epiphany that were passed over that year. It always uses the propers appointed for that day on the Sunday before Advent.

The Prayer Book provides Collects, Epistles, and Gospels for twenty-five Sundays, those for the last Sunday always being used on "the Sunday next before Advent." If there are twenty-six or twenty-seven Sundays the Propers for Epiphany VI and V are used as required. Though providing Propers for twenty-seven Sundays, the Common Liturgy agrees with the Missal and the Prayer Book in always using the same Propers (Trinity XXVII) on the last Sunday of the Trinity season.

The Common Liturgy and the Prayer Book have the same Epistle and Gospel, except that the Epistle is lengthened in the Prayer Book. The Common Liturgy Introit first appears in Lutheran sources (Nuremberg *Officium Sacrum* [1664] and probably earlier). The Collect is Gregorian in a very free English translation of 1549. The Prayer Book gives this Collect on Trinity XXV. Its first word *Excita,* "stir up," anticipates the characteristic cry of the Advent Collects. There is no significant unity observable in the propers, though the necessary relation of "the wills of the faithful" (Collect) to "the knowledge of his will" (Epistle) will not escape the homiletician.

The Lesson is Elijah's prayer for the widow's son.

THE TWENTY-FIFTH SUNDAY AFTER TRINITY
[THE TWENTY-SIXTH SUNDAY AFTER PENTECOST]

	Service Book	Roman Missal	American Book of Common Prayer
Lesson	Job. 14:1-6		
Epistle	I Thess. 4:13-18	Epiphanytide lessons repeated.	See comment, Trinity XXIV.
Gospel	Matt. 24:15-28	Epiphanytide lessons repeated.	See comment, Trinity XXIV.
Introit	Ps. 31:9a, 15b, 17a, 1a	Trinity XXII repeated.	
Gradual	Ps. 91:2, 4b, 1	Trinity XXII repeated.	

Color: Green. Creed: Nicene or Apostles'. Preface: none.

Collect

ALMIGHTY God, we beseech thee, show thy mercy unto thy humble servants; that we, who put no trust in our own merits, may not be dealt with after the severity of thy judgment, but according to thy mercy; through thy Son, Jesus Christ our Lord, who liveth . . . .

Omnipotens sempiterne deus misericordiam tuam ostende supplicibus. ut qui de meritorum qualitate diffidimus. non iudicium tuum, sed indulgentiam sentiamus. Per. *Gregorian, 105.*

The Roman Missal appointed no propers beyond Trinity XXII, as explained in the comment on Trinity XXIII. Luther in his *Kirchenpostille* chose lessons referring to the Lord's second coming for Trinity XXV and XXVI, stating that there were very few references to this event in the lessons throughout the year, while it was of great importance to the believer. These selections soon established themselves as a Lutheran use. Their appropriateness is also generally recognized because it seems natural that we should consider eschatological themes on the closing Sundays of the Christian year as a culmination and final focus of all the church's teaching throughout the year.

The Epistle is rich in assurance and comfort for the believer. The Gospel sounds a solemn warning to all. The Introit and the Gradual sing of the church's confidence and trust in God's mercy and protection. The Introit first appears here in Lutheran sources, though it is the same as that given by the Missal for the Friday after Passion Sunday. The Nuremberg *Officium Sacrum* (1664) adds the final phrase, "Deliver me in thy righteousness." The Collect is Gregorian, and appears in its present English form in the *Church Book* (1868). It, too, voices an appeal for divine mercy.

The Lesson is Job's cheerless observation that "man is of few days, and full of trouble."

THE TWENTY-SIXTH SUNDAY AFTER TRINITY
[TWENTY-SEVENTH SUNDAY AFTER PENTECOST]

	Service Book	Roman Missal	American Book of Common Prayer
Lesson	Dan. 7:9-14		
Epistle	I Thess. 5:1-11	Epiphanytide lessons repeated.	See comment, Trinity XXIV.
Gospel	Matt. 25:31-46	Epiphanytide lessons repeated.	See comment, Trinity XXIV.
Introit	Ps. 54:1-2, 5	Trinity XXII repeated.	
Gradual	Ps. 24:3-4a, 5a Isa. 43:1b	Trinity XXII repeated.	

Color: Green.　Creed: Nicene or Apostles'.　Preface: none.

Collect

O GOD, so rule and govern our hearts and minds by thy Holy Spirit, that being ever mindful of the end of all things and the day of thy just judgment, we may be stirred up to holiness of living here, and dwell with thee forever hereafter; through thy Son, Jesus Christ our Lord, who liveth . . . .

O Herre Gudh reqera tu så vår Hierta och Tanckar med tinom Helga Anda, at wij altidh tänckia på ändan, och tin rättwijsa Dom; och ther af upwäckias altijd, at Gudeliga lefwa medtig ewinnerliga. Genom tin son Jesus Christum ec. *Een fullkomligh Psalm-Book*, 1677. (Swedish.)

546

This day is seldom observed, as there are rarely twenty-seven Sundays after Trinity, which would be necessary if the appointments for Trinity XXVI were to be used. The theme of the day is definitely our Lord's return and judgment. All the propers point to this. The Introit first appears in Lutheran sources. The Nuremberg *Officium Sacrum* (1664) omits the second half of the second verse. The Introit and the Gradual sing of the Christian assurance of salvation. The Epistle has been transferred from Trinity XXVII. The Gospel describes the final judgment.

The Collect is unique as coming from a Swedish source. It first appeared in the *Evangeliebok* of the Church of Sweden (1639). The Swedish text given above is the earliest available form, that of the *Psalm-Book* (1677). It appears in the present English form in the *Church Book* (1868).

The Lesson is Daniel's vision of the Son of Man's coming "with the clouds of heaven."

THE LAST SUNDAY AFTER TRINITY
[THE LAST SUNDAY AFTER PENTECOST]

The Introit, Collect, Lesson, Epistle, Gradual, and Gospel here following shall be used on the Last Sunday after Trinity of each year.

	Service Book	*Roman Missal*	*American Book of Common Prayer*
Lesson	Isa. 35:3-10		
Epistle	II Pet. 3:8-14	Col. 1:9b-14	Jer. 23:5-8
Gospel	Matt. 25:1-13	Matt. 24:15-35	John 6:5-14
Introit	Rev. 1:8; 21:3b, c	Jer. 29:11b, 12a, c,	
	Ps. 85:1	14b, d; Ps. 85:1	
Gradual	John 8:12b;	Pss. 44:7-8;	
	Rev. 22:17a-c, 20b	130:1-2a	

Color: Green.   Creed: Nicene or Apostles'.   Preface: none.

Collect

ABSOLVE, we beseech thee, O Lord, thy people from their offences; that from the bonds of our sins which, by reason of our frailty, we have brought upon us, we may be delivered by thy bountiful goodness; through thy Son, Jesus Christ our Lord, who liveth . . . .

Absolue quaesumus domine tuorum delicta populorum. et a peccatorum nostrorum nexibus quae pro nostra fragilitate contraximus. tua benignitate liberemur. per. *Gregorian,* 103. *C.N.S. missals.*

Each of the three rites makes definite liturgical provision for the Last Sunday after Trinity. These appointments differ throughout. The Lutheran use presents a beautiful mosaic. The Introit and the Gradual mingle the figures of the light and the wedding suggested by the Gospel and sound the note of triumphant welcome to the church's Bridegroom and King. The Epistle and the Gospel urge preparation and vigilance, the former in direct admonition and the latter in a parable. Luther suggested the Gospel for All Saints' Day (Matt. 5:1-12, the Beatitudes) for this Sunday, but the story of the ten virgins, first found in this connection in T. H. Hesshusen of Helmstadt (1580) eventually became the accepted Gospel. The Collect (Trinity XXIII repeated) is a final confession and plea for absolution, without the assurance of which there can be no freedom "from the bonds of our sins" and no hope of heaven. These propers are to be used "on the Last Sunday after Trinity of each year."

The Roman Missal simply repeats the Introit and Gradual of Trinity XXII with new lessons. The Prayer Book appoints a passage from Jeremiah for the Epistle and repeats the Gospel for the fourth Sunday in Lent. In contrast, the rich and beautiful appointments of the Lutheran Liturgy for this and the two preceding Sundays bring the liturgical year to an impressive conclusion in a mood that is dramatic yet wholly devotional.

The Lesson is Isaiah's promise that "the ransomed of the Lord shall return . . . with songs and everlasting joy."

APOSTLES' DAYS

	Service Book	*Roman Missal*	*American Book of Common Prayer*
Introit	II Tim. 1:12b; 4:8a; Ps. 139:1-2a		
Gradual	Ps. 19:4a, 1; John 15:16a		

The Roman calendar contains hundreds of saints' days. Practically every day in the year is assigned to at least one apostle, martyr, confessor, saint, pope, or doctor of the church. The most important days have a full set of propers. The others have a Collect or a lesson specially appointed while the other required texts are found in a section of the Missal called the Common of Saints.

The Lutheran reform as a rule rejected almost all saints' days except those which could be justified by Scripture. Of the nonscriptural, the feasts of St. Lawrence, St. Martin (of Tours, after whom Martin Luther was named, being born on November 11, St. Martin's Day), St. Catharine, and St. Nicholas in particular have tended to remain in use among

European Lutherans. In course of time four other days of different character (and differing merit) were introduced: the Festival of the Reformation, the Festival of Harvest, a Day of Humiliation and Prayer, and (in America) a Day of General or Special Thanksgiving.

The later Anglican reform was along almost identical lines. The Prayer Book observes all the days in the Lutheran calendar except the Visitation, the Festival of the Reformation, the Festival of Harvest, and a Day of Humiliation and Prayer. It adds to the Lutheran list, St. Barnabas and (in America) Independence Day.

The Lutheran calendar might properly welcome again some important nonscriptural observances, though the problem of judicious selection and common agreement is fully recognized. Some of the saints in our present calendar, for example, St. Simon or St. Matthias, are obscure characters of whom nothing is known. In contrast, the examples of St. Ambrose, St. Augustine, or St. Francis are well known, inspiring, and worthy of emulation. Our inclusion of the festivals of Reformation, Harvest, and of Thanksgiving (Thanksgiving Day) shattered the principle of including scriptural days, only. The emptiness of our calendar from the first century to the sixteenth and thereafter to the twentieth encourages the ignorant and false idea that these unrecognized centuries were devoid of importance or even interest. This vacuum in Protestant thought also strongly supports the Roman contention that Protestantism is not the church purified, but rather a new and human institution sprung in 1517 from the brain of an Augustinian heretic. This situation presents a challenge which our church is scarcely prepared to meet in the present hour. The future may offer a solution. Meanwhile we shall do well to ponder this paragraph in Dr. Edward T. Horn's recent book:

> The lives of the saints continually remind us of the great host of witnesses in the faith who have gone before us and who, we believe, are still our examples and our encouragement in the Christian life. They are also a reminder of the continuing existence of the body of Christ—the Church—and of the fact that whether it be militant on earth or triumphant and in the joy of its Lord in heaven, it is one, holy catholic church, timeless and composed of God's people of every age."[3]

Each day in the Lutheran calendar has its own Lesson, Collect, Epistle, and Gospel. The Common Liturgy provides a common Introit and a common Gradual for apostles' days, and makes similar provision for evangelists' days. The common Introit for apostles' days is the historic one for the Conversion of St. Paul with the addition of the pas-

---

[3] E. T. Horn, III, *The Christian Year,* p. 183. For concise discussion of "Saints' Days and Holy Days," see pp. 177ff.

sage II Timothy 4:8a. The common Gradual is the text for St. Luke's Day. Many of the Collects appointed for these days are the work of the English Reformers who composed a dozen or more Collects as substitutes for the unevangelical medieval Collects for saints' days which generally invoked the intercession of the saints.

EVANGELISTS' DAYS

	Service Book
Introit	Mark 16:15; Pss. 19:4a; 119:105
Gradual	Ps. 19:4a, 1; John 15:16a

The Common Liturgy provides a common Introit and Gradual. Portions of both texts are found in the Missal text of the Gradual for St. Luke's Day.

ST. ANDREW, APOSTLE
November 30

	Service Book	*Roman Missal*	*American Book of Common Prayer*
Lesson	Ezek. 3:16-21		
Epistle	Rom. 10:10-18	*Ibid.*	Rom. 10:9-21
Gospel	Matt. 4:18-22	*Ibid.*	*Ibid.*
Introit	See Apostles' Days.	Ps. 139:17, 1-2a	
Gradual	See Apostles' Days.	Ps. 45:16b, 17a, 16a, 17b; Dilexit Andream Dominus . . .	

Color: Red. Creed: Nicene. Preface: All Saints.

Collect

ALMIGHTY God, who didst give such grace unto thy holy Apostle Saint Andrew, that he readily obeyed the calling of thy Son Jesus Christ, and followed him without delay: Grant unto us all, that we, being called by thy holy Word, may forthwith give up ourselves obediently to fulfil thy holy commandments; through the same, thy Son, Jesus Christ our Lord, who liveth . . . .

Almightie god which didst geue such grace vnto thy holy Apostle Saincte Andrewe, that he redily obeyed the callyng of thy sōne Iesus Christ, and folowed hym without delaye: Graunt vnto vs all, that we being called by the holy worde, maye furthwith geue ouer our selfes, obediently to folow thy holy commaūdements: through thesame Iesus Chryste our Lorde. *BCP, 1552.*

This feast was observed in the fourth century by the Eastern church and in the sixth century in Rome and elsewhere. Andrew and John were the first apostles to follow Christ (John 1:35-40), and the former's name always appears next to the first three in the lists of the apostles. After Pentecost he is supposed to have preached in Palestine, Scythia,

Epirus, and Thrace, and the Greek church particularly holds him in high honor. Tradition states that he was martyred November 30 on a special kind of cross which has ever since borne his name, and that his body, together with that of St. Luke, was taken to the Church of the Holy Apostles, Constantinople (A.D. 357), and later removed (A.D. 1210) to Amalfi in Italy. Quite early, certain of his relics were taken to St. Andrew's Church, Fife, and Andrew thus became the patron saint of Scotland.

The three liturgies have the same lesson (Prayer Book lengthened) and liturgical unity is found in the missionary theme which pervades them. The Gospel records St. Andrew's second call (with Simon Peter, his brother). The Roman Collect seeks St. Andrew's intercession. The present Collect is by the English Reformers, the only original Collect (though there were translations) prepared for the second Prayer Book (1552). The Common Liturgy refers to the Common of Apostles' Days for the Introit and Gradual.

The Lesson is Ezekiel's statement: "I have made thee a watchman . . . to give them warning from me."

ST. THOMAS, APOSTLE
December 21

	Service Book	Roman Missal	American Book of Common Prayer
Lesson	Judg. 6:36-40		
Epistle	Eph. 1:3-6	Eph. 2:19-22	Heb. 10:35—11:1
Gospel	John 20:24-29	*Ibid.*	John 20:24-31
Introit	See Apostles' Days.	Ps. 139:17, 1-2a	
Gradual	See Apostles' Days.	Pss. 139:17-18a; 33:1	

Color: Red.   Creed: Nicene.   Preface: All Saints.

Collect

ALMIGHTY and everliving God, who hast given to them that believe exceeding great and precious promises: Grant us so perfectly, and without all doubt, to believe in thy Son Jesus Christ, that our faith in thy sight may never be reproved; through the same, thy Son, Jesus Christ our Lord, who liveth . . . .

Almightie euerliuing God, whiche for the more confyrmacion of the fayth, didst suffer thy holy Apostle Thomas, to bee doubtfull in thy sonnes resurreccyon: Graunt vs so perfectly, and without all doubt to beleue in thy sonne Jesus Christe, that our fayth in thy syghte neuer be reproued: heare vs, O Lorde, through the same Jesus Christe . . . *BCP*, 1549.

Not much is known of "Thomas, which is called Didymus" (Greek for "a twin"). There are only four references to him in the New Testament. Later legend associates him with Bartholomew, Matthew, Simon, and Jude, the five "apostles of the East," and states that his labors extended as far as India. A church body called "The Christians of St. Thomas" still exists at Malabar. The Eastern churches were the first to commemorate him (sixth century). The Roman observance dates from the ninth century. It is strange that the story of his doubts concerning the Savior's resurrection (Gospel) should not have placed his feast in the Easter season.

The Roman, Lutheran, and Anglican liturgies give the same Gospel, but have different Epistles. The Common Liturgy appoints Ephesians 1:3-6. The American Prayer Book (1928) gives Hebrews 10:35—11:1; the English Prayer Book retains the Missal selection (Eph. 2:19-22). The Roman Collect invokes "the patronage" of St. Thomas, and the English Reformers (1549) composed a new Collect based upon the Gospel. This Collect had its inspiration in a homily of Gregory the Great, in the breviary office of Matins on St. Thomas' Day.

The Lesson is Gideon's sign of the fleece.

ST. STEPHEN, MARTYR
December 26

ST. JOHN, APOSTLE, EVANGELIST
December 27

THE HOLY INNOCENTS, MARTYRS
December 28

The proper appointments for these days are given in the proper of the season, above, pp. 472-76.

THE CONVERSION OF ST. PAUL
January 25

	Service Book	Roman Missal	American Book of Common Prayer
Lesson	Jer. 1:4-10		
Epistle	Acts 9:1-22	*Ibid.*	*Ibid.*
Gospel	Matt. 19:27-29	*Ibid.*	Matt. 19:27-30
Introit	See Apostles' Days.	II Tim. 1:12b; Ps. 139:1-2a	
Gradual	See Apostles' Days.	Gal. 2:8,9a; I Cor. 15:10b; Sed gratia, Magnus Sanctus, Paulus . . . or Gal. 2:8, 9a; I Cor. 15: 10b; Sed gratia; Tu es vas electionis . . .	

Color: Red.   Creed: Nicene.   Preface: All Saints.

Collect

O GOD, who didst teach the multitude of the Gentiles by the preaching of blessed Paul the Apostle: Grant us grace, that we, who this day recall his conversion, may by his example be led to thee; through thy Son, Jesus Christ our Lord, who liveth . . . .

Deus qui uniuersum mundum beati pauli apostoli praedicatione docuisti da nobis quaesumus ut qui eius [h]odie conuersionem colimus per eius ad te exempla gradiamur. Per. *Gregorian, 319 BC.N.S. missals.*

This was a fourth-century feast in Rome, which when introduced in western Europe much later laid special emphasis upon the conversion. Kellner suggests that the removal ("translation") of the relics from the catacombs to the basilica of St. Paul, in the reign of Constantine, may have determined the date, though the apostle's conversion became the dominant idea as the observance of the feast spread.[4] The diocese of Worms adopted it A.D. 1198; Cologne in A.D. 1260. The chief commemoration of Paul was in association with Peter on June 29, though his martyrdom was also commemorated June 30.

The dramatic and miraculous elements in St. Paul's conversion seem to have had a particular appeal for the Western church in medieval times. The Greek church has no observance.

All three rites appoint the same Epistle and Gospel. The Common Liturgy refers to the Common of Apostles for the Introit and Gradual. The Collect is late Gregorian. The first phrase of the translation, however, is from an earlier Gelasian Collect for the martyrdom of St. Paul.

The Lesson is the call of Jeremiah to be "a prophet unto the nations."

THE PRESENTATION OF OUR LORD
February 2

	Service Book	Roman Missal	American Book of Common Prayer
Lesson	Hag. 2:6-9		
Epistle	I Cor. 1:26-31	Mal. 3:1-4	Mal. 3:1-5
Gospel	Luke 2:22-32	Ibid.	Luke 2:22-40
Introit	Ps. 48:9-10, 1	Ibid.	
Gradual	Ps. 48:9-10a	Ps. 48:9-10a, 8	
	Isa. 11:12a, c	a Senex Puerum;	
		or	
		Ps. 48:9-10a, 8a;	
		Luke 2:29-32	

Color: White. Creed: Nicene. Preface: Christmas.

[4] K. A. Heinrich Kellner, *Heortology; a History of the Christian Festivals from their Origin to the Present Day,* English ed. (London: Kegan Paul, 1908), p. 288.

Collect

ALMIGHTY and everliving God, we humbly beseech thy Majesty, that as thine only-begotten Son was this day presented in the temple in substance of our flesh, so we may be presented unto thee with pure and clean hearts; through the same thy Son, Jesus Christ our Lord, who liveth . . . .

Omnipotens sempiterne deus maiestatem tuam supplices exoramus. ut sicut unigenitus filius tuus hodierna die cum nostrae carnis substantia in templo est praesentatus. ita nos facias purificatis tibi mentibus praesentari. per eundem. *Gregorian, 22. B.S. missals.*

Etheria mentions this feast as observed in Jerusalem at the end of the fourth century. Justinian introduced it in Constantinople in the sixth century. Its earliest name was *Hypapante* (Greek for "Meeting"), and the reference was to the meeting of our Lord with Simeon. Thus the feast was one of our Lord rather than of the Virgin. The historic Collect for the day, as well as the prayer for the blessing of the candles, stresses the thought of presentation and not that of purification.

After the ninth century the expanding cult of Mary established the title, "The Purification of the Virgin," which is strikingly incongruous with the later dogma of her immaculate conception. The Lutheran and the Anglican churches have retained the feast as a festival of Christ. The date, forty days after Christmas, is in recognition of the requirement of the Mosaic law that every mother should go to Jerusalem and offer a sacrifice forty days after the birth of her child.

In the Middle Ages the feast was popularly known as Candlemas, in reference to the blessing and use of an unusual number of candles in the services of this day. This was originally a feature of a pagan festival anciently held in Rome on February 2, which under Christian direction became a penitential procession. The Feast of the Presentation later displaced this but incorporated this particular custom within its own order, possibly because of Luke 2:32, "a light to lighten the Gentiles."

The propers are in agreement throughout, except that the Common Liturgy appoints an Epistle from the New Testament. The Collect is Gregorian, translated for the Prayer Book (1549) and revised 1662. The use in the Prayer Book of "by" instead of "through" at the close is unique in collect literature. It adds a new idea by associating our final presentation by Christ (Eph. 5:27; Col. 1:22; Jude 24) with his presentation in the temple.

The Lesson is Haggai's promise of the Lord: "I will shake all nations. . . . I will fill this house with glory."

ST. MATTHIAS, APOSTLE
February 24

	Service Book	Roman Missal	American Book of Common Prayer
Lesson	Isa. 66:1-2		
Epistle	Acts 1:15-26	*Ibid.*	*Ibid.*
Gospel	Matt. 11:25-30	*Ibid.*	*Ibid.*
Introit	See Apostles' Days.	Ps. 139:17, 1-2a	
Gradual	See Apostles' Days.	Pss. 139:17-18a; 21:2-3	

Color: Red.   Creed: Nicene.   Preface: All Saints.

Collect

ALMIGHTY God, who didst number thy servant Matthias among the twelve Apostles: Grant that thy Church may ever be instructed and guided by faithful and true pastors; through thy Son, Jesus Christ our Lord, who liveth . . . .

Almyghtye God, whiche in the place of the traytor Judas, didst chose thy faythfull seruaunte Mathie, to be of the number of thy twelue Apostles: Graunt that thy churche being always preserued from false Apostles, may be ordred and guided by faythfull and true pastors: through Jesus Christ our Lorde. *BCP, 1549.*

Scripture is silent concerning the subsequent history of the apostle who was chosen to take the place of Judas. Tradition also has nothing positive to offer, though an interesting surmise repeatedly appears, viz., that the election of Matthias was premature and that in fact Paul was our Lord's selection. The feast is not found in the early sacramentaries and probably was not observed before A.D. 1000.

All rites have the same lessons. The Epistle recounts the story of the "giving of the lots." Names were written on wood or parchment and placed in a bowl which was shaken until one fell out. In this instance the lot literally "fell" upon Matthias. The Gospel is a general one with possible reference to Judas in the phrase "the wise and prudent." The Latin Collect was unacceptable, and the Prayer Book (1549) has a new composition. The Common Liturgy refers to the Common of Apostles for the Introit and Gradual.

The Lesson affirms that the Lord will look upon "him that is poor and of a contrite spirit."

555

THE ANNUNCIATION
March 25

	Service Book	Roman Missal	American Book of Common Prayer
Lesson	Mic. 5:2-4		
Epistle	Phil. 4:4-9	Isa. 7:10-15	*Ibid.*
Gospel	Luke 1:26-38	Luke 1:26-38a	Luke 1:26-38
Introit	Ps. 45:12b, 14, 15a, 1a	Ps. 45:12b, 14b-15a, 1a	
Gradual	Ps. 45:2b, 7a, b; Isa. 7:14b	Ps. 45:2b, 4b, c, 10a, 11a, 12b-13a, 14b-15 or Luke 1:28b; Num. 17:8b; Virgo Deum	

Color: White.   Creed: Nicene.   Preface: Christmas.

Collect

WE beseech thee, O Lord, pour thy grace into our hearts; that as we have known the Incarnation of thy Son Jesus Christ by the message of an angel, so by his Cross and Passion we may be brought unto the glory of his Resurrection; through the same thy Son, Jesus Christ our Lord, who liveth . . . .

Gratiam tuam domine mentibus nostris infunde. ut que angelo nuntiante christi filii tui incarnationem cognouimus. per passionem eius et crucem. ad resurrectionis gloriam perducamur. per eundem. *Gregorian, 25.*

This festival, popularly known as "Lady Day," originated in Constantinople and was accepted in Rome about A.D. 600, along with the Feast of the Presentation. The fact that the dates of both these festivals are determined by Christmas places them in the calendar without relationship to their respective seasons. Thus the Annunciation frequently comes in Lent and sometimes close to Good Friday. This may be one reason why some Eastern churches do not observe it. Marking the first moment of the Incarnation, it is a feast of Christ rather than of Mary, as the ancient prayers for the day fully attest.

The Bamberg Missal (also Spangenberg and Lossius among Lutheran authorities) prescribes the Introit for Advent IV. The Nuremberg Missal appoints Advent I. The Common Liturgy and the Roman Missal have the same Introit, and the Lutheran, Anglican, and Roman liturgies agree in the other propers, except that the Lutheran Epistle differs. The Gospel is Luke's account of the angel Gabriel's announcement.

The Collect is Gregorian, in a 1549 translation. The original is not properly the Collect of the day but a Post-Communion Collect. The feast has its place in the calendar between Christmas and Easter, and the Collect embraces both the Incarnation and the Resurrection.

The Lesson declares that out of Bethlehem shall come one who "is to be ruler in Israel."

ST. MARK, EVANGELIST
April 25

	Service Book	Roman Missal	American Book of Common Prayer
Lesson	Isa. 55:1-5		
Epistle	Eph. 4:7-16	Ezek. 1:10-14	Eph. 4:7-16
Gospel	John 15:1-11	Luke 10:1-9	John 15:1-11
Introit	See Evangelists' Days.	Ps. 64:2, 1	
Gradual	See Evangelists' Days.	Pss. 89:5; 21:3b	

Color: Red.   Creed: Nicene.   Preface: All Saints.

Collect

O ALMIGTHY God, who hast instructed thy holy Church with the heavenly doctrine of thy Evangelists: Give us grace, that being not like children carried away with every blast of vain doctrine, we may be established in the truth of thy holy Gospel; through thy Son, Jesus Christ our Lord, who liveth . . . .

Almyghtie God, whiche haste instructed thy holy Church, with the heauenly doctrine of thy Euangelist Sainct Marke: geue vs grace so to be established by thy holy Gospell, that we be not, lyke chyldren, caried away with euery blast of vaine Doctrine: Through Jesus Christ our Lorde. *BCP*, 1549.

Mark, though not one of the twelve, was the friend and companion of several of the apostles. After breaking an early association with Paul (Acts 12:25; 13:13; 15:37, 38) he became the close companion of Peter, a successful missionary, and the writer of the earliest Gospel. Unconfirmed tradition connects him with Alexandria, where his opposition to the worship of Serapis led to his martyrdom, and Venice, to which city his body is supposed to have been removed (A.D. 829) and where the Cathedral of St. Mark was later erected in his honor. In this cathedral on Easter, the liturgical Gospel is announced as being recorded "in the sixteenth chapter of the Gospel according to *him*," the reader dramatically pointing to the high altar under which the bones of Mark are supposed to rest. The late observance of his festival in Rome (*c.* 1200) may be explained, as Schuster suggests, by the fact that his body was not buried there.

The Common Liturgy and the Prayer Book have the same Collect, Epistle, and Gospel, the latter being one of the medieval "common" Gospels for saints' days. The Collect is the Prayer Book (1549) Collect for this day, an original composition of the English Reformers with a transposition of clauses made, perhaps not too happily, in 1662. The petition is based upon Ephesians 4:14, a part of the Epistle. In view of Mark's fine record as a missionary and evangelist, it is unfortunate that this Collect should contain what seems a disparaging reference to his desertion of Paul.

The Lesson says: "Ho, every one that thirsteth, come ye to the waters."

ST. PHILIP AND ST. JAMES, APOSTLES
May 1

	Service Book	Roman Missal	American Book of Common Prayer
Lesson	Mal. 3:16-18		
Epistle	Eph. 2:19-22	Bk. Wisd. 5:1-5	Jas. 1:1-12
Gospel	John 14:1-13a	*Ibid.*	John 14:1-14
Introit	See Apostles' Days.	Neh. 9:27a; Ps. 33:1	
Gradual	See Apostles' Days.	Ps. 89:5; John 14:9a	

Color: Red.   Creed: Nicene.   Preface: All Saints.

Collect

O ALMIGHTY God, whom to know is everlasting life: Grant us perfectly to know thy Son Jesus Christ to be the way, the truth, and the life; that following his steps we may steadfastly walk in the way that leadeth to eternal life, through the same thy Son, Jesus Christ our Lord, who liveth . . . .

Almightie God, whome truely to knowe is euerlasting lyfe: Graunte vs perfectly to knowe thy sonne Jesus Christe, to bee the way, the trueth, and the lyfe, as thou has taught sainct **Philip** and other the Apostles: Through Jesus Christ our Lorde. *BCP, 1549.*

This combined feast is Roman in origin. The Greek Rite, as well as the Mozarabic and other Gallican liturgies, commemorates the two apostles separately. The combination and the date seem to have been determined by the fact that the Church of the Holy Apostles in Rome, built A.D. 350, was rebuilt in the sixth century and rededicated May 1, 561, on which occasion the relics of the two apostles were transferred to this church, which was rededicated in their honor.

Philip, like Peter and Andrew, was of Bethsaida in Galilee. Through him "certain Greeks" sought to see Jesus (John 12:21). Like Thomas, he wished "to be shown," and the Gospel for the day records his dialogue with the Lord. Later tradition confuses him with Philip the evangelist. He is supposed to have died on a cross, even as did Peter and Andrew, somewhere in Phrygia. James is traditionally known as "James the Less" and identified with James "the brother of the Lord," though in all probability the latter was an entirely different person.

The Epistle refers to the church as being "built upon the foundation of the apostles and prophets, Jesus Christ himself being the chief corner stone," a passage which led the medieval church to give apostles' days equal honor with Sundays. The Collect was composed for the first Prayer Book and expanded in the revision of 1662. The uncertainty as to which James was meant may explain the omission of his name in the 1549 Collect. John 17:13 is the basis for the invocation and John 14:6 for the petition. The latter passage is from our Lord's discourse with Thomas.

The Lesson promises "and they shall be mine . . . in that day when I make up my jewels."

THE NATIVITY OF ST. JOHN, THE BAPTIST
June 24

	Service Book	Roman Missal	American Book of Common Prayer
Lesson	Mal. 4:4-6		
Epistle	I John 1:1-4	Isa. 49:1-3	Isa. 40:1-11
Gospel	Luke 1:57-80	Luke 1:57-68	Luke 1:57-80
Introit	Isa. 40:3, 5a; Ps. 92:1	Isa. 49:1b, 2a, b; Ps. 92:1	
Gradual	Luke 1:76; John 1:15, 29b	Jer. 1:5a, b, 9a; Luke 1:76	

Color: Red. Creed: Nicene. Preface: All Saints.

Collect

O LORD God, heavenly Father, who, through thy servant John the Baptist, didst bear witness that Jesus Christ is the Lamb of God which taketh away the sin of the world, and that all who believe in him shall inherit eternal life: We humbly pray thee to enlighten us by thy Holy Spirit that we may at all times find comfort and joy in this witness, continue steadfast in the true faith, and at last with all believers attain unto eternal life; through the same thy Son, Jesus Christ our Lord, who liveth . . . .

Herr Gott, himmlischer Vater, der Du durch den heiligen Teuffer Johannem uns allen zu Trost hast bezeugen lassen, dass Jesus Christus das ware unschüldige Lemblin were, welcher der gantzen Welt Sünde tragen solte, in welchem auch alle gleubingen das ewige Leben überkomen werden: wir bitten Dich von Herzen, Du wollest uns durch Deinen heiligen Geist erleuchten, dass wir uns allezeit solcher gezeugnis von unserem Heiland Jesu Christo trösten und erfrewen, in rechtem Glauben darinne bestendig beharren und entlichen mit Johanne dem Teuffer und allen Gleubigen die ewige Seligkeit überkome mögen, durch Denselben Deinen Sohn. *Lüneburg, 1564.*

The story of John the Baptist greatly influenced the literature, the worship, and the art of both the early and the medieval church. The Nativity of St. John the Baptist and the Nativity of our Lord are the two feasts in the calendar which commemorate actual birthdays and not days of death (called "birthdays" in the heavenly kingdom).

This festival is of Western origin and of very early observance. Augustine refers to it in the fourth century and cites the agreement between John 3:30 ("He must increase, but I must decrease") and the astronomical fact that after this midsummer feast the days become shorter while after Christmas they become longer. The Benedictine monk, Guy of Arezzo, in the thirteenth century called attention to the fact that the notes set to the first syllables in each line of Paul the Deacon's hymn in honor of the Baptist (*ut queant laxis, resonare fibris,* etc.) constituted a sequence of the first six degrees of the musical scale. His naming of each degree by the corresponding syllable established the "Ut (Do), Re, Mi, Fa, So, La, Si" scale to help master musical intervals.

The three rites have the same Gospel, advantageously lengthened in the Lutheran and the Anglican liturgies. The Epistle has been changed from Isaiah to I John. Each of the three liturgies has a different Collect. The Prayer Book Collect (1549) stresses repentance; the Lutheran Collect, faith. The latter is found in the Lüneburg Order (1564) and, in somewhat different translation, in the *Church Book* (1868).

The Lesson says: "Behold, I will send you Elijah the prophet."

ST. PETER AND ST. PAUL, APOSTLES
June 29

	Service Book	Roman Missal	American Book of Common Prayer
Lesson	Jer. 26:12-16 or Isa. 22:20-23		
Epistle	Acts 12:1-11 or Gal. 1:11-20	Acts 12:1-11	*Ibid.*
Gospel	Matt. 16:13-19	*Ibid.*	*Ibid.*
Introit	See Apostles' Days.	Acts 12:11b; Ps. 139:1-2a	
Gradual	See Apostles' Days.	Ps. 45:16b, 17a, 16a, 17b; Matt. 16:18a	

Color: Red.   Creed: Nicene.   Preface: All Saints.

Collect

O ALMIGHTY God, who by thy Son Jesus Christ didst give to thy holy Apostles many excellent gifts, and commandedst them earnestly to feed thy flock: Make, we beseech thee, all pastors diligently to preach thy holy word, and the people obediently to follow the same, that they may receive the crown of everlasting glory; through thy Son, Jesus Christ our Lord, who liveth . . . .

Almightie God, whiche by thy sonne Jesus Christe haste geuen to thy Apostle saincte Peter many excellente giftes, and commaundedste him earnestly to feede thy flocke: make wee beseche thee, all bishops and pastors diligently to preache thy holy worde, and the people obediently to folowe thesame, that they maye receiue the croune of euerlasting glory, through Jesus Christ our Lord. *BCP,* 1549.

This is one of the oldest saints' days, its observance beginning early in the fourth century. In ancient Rome it was regarded as the greatest feast of the year except Christmas, and three masses were appointed, one in honor of Peter, another for Paul, and the third in commemoration of all the apostles. The two great apostles have been associated in Christian thought and worship from earliest times. Their apostleships embraced the church's complete ministry to both the Jewish and the Gentile worlds. There also was a tradition that they were martyred on the same day, though in different years, and that their bodies were removed to the catacombs on June 29, in the year 258, during the Valerian persecution. This established the date of the combined feast. Later in Rome, when two great basilicas were erected in honor of these apostles, Peter particularly was commemorated on June 29 and Paul on June 30. At the time of the Reformation the Church of England retained only the name of Peter on June 29 and the Prayer Book is without any special commemoration of the martyrdom of Paul. The Lutheran calendars retained the traditional combination.

All rites have the same lessons, and these refer exclusively to Peter. The Epistle records his deliverance from prison; the Gospel, his confession of our Lord's divinity. The Common Liturgy provides an alternate Lesson and an alternate Epistle. The Collect is from the Prayer Book (1549), which Collect, however, refers only to St. Peter.

In the first Lesson, Jeremiah foresaw possible martyrdom, the fate which befell the two apostles. The alternate Lesson and the Gospel speak of "the key of the house of David" and "the keys of the kingdom of heaven." The alternate Epistle notes the conference of Peter and Paul in Jerusalem.

THE VISITATION
July 2

	Service Book	Roman Missal	American Book of Common Prayer
Lesson	Judg. 13:2-7 or Song of Sol. 2:8-14	Song of Sol. 2:8-14	
Epistle	I Pet. 3:1-5a	*Ibid.*	
Gospel	Luke 1:39-47	Salva sancta Parens	
Introit	See the Annunciation.	(*by* Sedulius); Ps. 45:1a	
Gradual	See the Annunciation.	Benedicta et venerabilis es	

Color: White.   Creed: Nicene.   Preface: Christmas.

Collect

ALMIGHTY God, who hast dealt wonderfully with thy handmaiden the Virgin Mary, and hast chosen her to be the mother of thy Son, and hast graciously made known that thou regardest the poor and the lowly and the despised: Grant us grace in all humility and meekness to receive thy word with hearty faith, and so to be made one with thy dear Son, who liveth . . . .

The Visitation is a minor festival which presumably was retained in Lutheran church orders because it was based upon an incident recorded in Scripture. Its observance as a universal feast does not antedate A.D. 1389 when Urban VI established it as part of an effort to heal the great Western schism. The English Reformers did not include it in the calendar of the Prayer Book.

The Gospel recounts the visit of Mary to her cousin Elisabeth and the latter's joy at the coming of "the mother of my Lord." It concludes with Mary's utterance of the Magnificat. The Epistle is a passage from I Peter which is an improvement upon the Missal selection from the Song of Solomon, the alternate Lesson in the Common Liturgy.

The Collect is first found in the earliest German church order, the vernacular Mass of Theobald Schwartz (Nigri) in Strasbourg (1524).

ST. JAMES THE ELDER, APOSTLE
July 25

	Service Book	*Roman Missal*	*American Book of Common Prayer*
Lesson	I Kings 19:9-18		
Epistle	I Cor. 4:9-15	*Ibid.*	Acts 11:27——12:3a
Gospel	Matt. 20:20-28	Matt. 20:20-23	Matt. 20:20-28
Introit	See Apostles' Days.	Ps. 139:17, 1-2a	
Gradual	See Apostles' Days.	Ps. 45:16b, 17a, 16a, 17b; John 15:16a	

Color: Red.   Creed: Nicene.   Preface: All Saints.

Collect

O ALMIGHTY God, who has built thy Church upon the foundation of the Apostles and Prophets, Jesus Christ himself being the head cornerstone: Grant us so to be joined together in unity of spirit by their doctrine, that we may be made a holy temple acceptable unto thee; through the same thy Son, Jesus Christ our Lord, who liveth . . . .

Almightie God, whiche hast builded the congregacion vpon the foundacion of the Apostles and prophetes, Jesu Christ himselfe beyng the head corner stone: graunte vs so to bee ioyned together in vnitie of spirit by their doctrine, that we maye be made an holye temple acceptable to thee: throughe Jesu Christe oure Lorde. *BCP, 1549.*

James, the son of Zebedee and the brother of John, is called the Elder (Greater), possibly because of his association with Peter and John as intimates of our Lord. He is the only one of the apostles whose death is recorded in Scripture. Herod Agrippa, willing to please the Jews, had him beheaded in Jerusalem just before the Passover, A.D. 42 (Acts 12:1ff). The date of the feast, July 25, can have no reference to this, but presumably recalls the later "translation" of his body, because of fear of the Arabs, to Campostella in Spain, which country, according to tradition, James had visited before his martyrdom. The feast does not antedate the eighth or ninth century.

The three rites have the same Gospel (differing in length) and different Epistles. The Lutheran Epistle has been changed to I Corinthians 4:9-15, as in MR. For the Introit and Gradual the reference is to the Common of Apostles' Days.

This Collect is again one of the prayers composed for the Prayer Book of 1549. It is a substitute for the Collect in the Missal for St. Simon's and St. Jude's Day (October 28), which was unacceptable. The scriptural source is Ephesians 2:20-22 (cf. also Isa. 28:16). The only change in text was the substitution in 1662 of "Church" for "congregacion."

The Lesson is the story of Elijah at Horeb.

THE TRANSFIGURATION OF OUR LORD
August 6

	Service Book	Roman Missal	American Book of Common Prayer
Lesson	Exod. 34:29-35		
Epistle	II Pet. 1:16-21	II Pet. 1:16-19	II Pet. 1:13-18
Gospel	Matt. 17:1-9	Ibid.	Luke 9:28-36
Introit	Pss. 77:18b; 84:1-2a	Ibid.	
Gradual	Pss. 45:2a, b; 110:1; 96:2-3	Ps. 45:2a, 1a Bk. Wisd. 7:26	

Color: White.   Creed: Nicene.   Preface: Epiphany.

Collect

O GOD, who in the glorious Transfiguration of thy only-begotten Son, hast confirmed the mysteries of the faith by the testimony of the Fathers, and who, in the voice that came from the bright cloud, didst in a wonderful manner foreshow the adoption of sons: Mercifully vouchsafe to make us co-heirs with the King of his glory, and bring us to the enjoyment of the same; through the same thy Son, Jesus Christ our Lord, who liveth . . . .

Deus, qui fidei sacramenta in Unigeniti tui gloriosa Transfiguratione patrum testimonio roborasti, et adoptionem filiorum perfectam voce delapsa in nube lucida mirabiliter praesignasti: concede propitius; ut ipsius Regis gloriae nos coheredes efficias, et ejusdem gloriae tribuas esse consortes. Per eumdem Dominum nostrum. *15th century* (?) MR, B. Missal.

For comment, see pp. 485-86 (Sixth Sunday after the Epiphany), for which day these same propers are appointed in the Common Liturgy.

ST. BARTHOLOMEW, APOSTLE
August 24

	Service Book	Roman Missal	American Book of Common Prayer
Lesson	Prov. 3:1-7		
Epistle	I Cor. 12:27-31a	*Ibid.*	Acts 5:12-16
Gospel	Luke 22:24-30	Luke 6:12-19	Luke 22:24-30
Introit	See Apostles' Days.	Ps. 139:17, 1-2a	
Gradual	See Apostles' Days.	Ps. 45:16b, 17a, 16a, 17b; Te gloriosus Apostolorum (*from* Te Deum)	

Color: Red. Creed: Nicene. Preface: All Saints.

Collect

ALMIGHTY God, who hast made the remembrance of thine apostles days of gladness and joy to thy Church: Grant that we may ever love thee whom they loved, and set forth the doctrine which they taught; through thy Son, Jesus Christ our Lord, who liveth . . . .

Composite, *Service Book, 1958.*

This is an Eastern feast introduced in the West about the eighth century. The date, August 24, is supposed to recall the removal by the Emperor Anastasius of the saint's relics to Daros on the borders of Mesopotamia (A.D. 500). Eastern tradition identifies Bartholomew with Nathanael, whom Philip brought to our Lord (John 1:45-49). This has never been fully accepted by the Western church. Eusebius refers to Bartholomew's successful preaching, presumably in Arabia where he is said to have suffered martyrdom.

The Lutheran and Anglican liturgies have the same Gospel, a selection which may reflect the early tradition that Bartholomew was of noble birth and that this occasioned the "strife" (vs. 24). The Missal has a different Gospel. The Epistle has been changed to I Corinthians 12:27-31a (as MR, VEKD, LLKD, etc.). The Prayer Book Collect is partly new (1549) and partly a translation of the Missal collect, altered in 1662.

The Lesson is an exhortation to "trust in the Lord."

ST. MATTHEW, APOSTLE, EVANGELIST
September 21

	Service Book	Roman Missal	American Book of Common Prayer
Lesson	Ezek. 1:4-14 or Prov. 30:7-9	Ezek. 1:10-14	
Epistle	Eph. 4:7-16	*Ibid.*	II Cor. 4:1-6
Gospel	Matt. 9:9-13	Ps. 37:30-31a, 1	*Ibid.*
Introit	See Apostles' Days.	Ps. 112:1b-2;	
Gradual	See Apostles' Days.	Te gloriosus Apostolorum	

Color: Red.   Creed: Nicene.   Preface: All Saints.

Collect

O ALMIGHTY God, who by thy blessed Son didst call Matthew from the receipt of custom to be an Apostle and Evangelist: Grant us grace to forsake all covetous desires and inordinate love of riches, and to follow the same thy Son Jesus Christ, who liveth . . . .

Almightie God, whiche by thy blessed sonne dyddest call Mathewe from the receipte of custome to be an Apostle and Euangelist: Graunt vs grace to forsake all couetous desires and inordinate loue of riches, and to folowe thy sayed sonne Jesus Christ: who lyueth . . . . *BCP*, 1549.

This is another feast of Eastern origin. It is not found in the early Roman sacramentaries, though it is in the Ambrosian, Mozarabic, and other Gallican calendars. The Greek church observes it November 16. Little is known of Matthew apart from his Gospel, in which he records what is thought to be his call from the receipt of custom to follow the Lord. He is supposed to have preached in Palestine and Ethiopia and to have been martyred in the latter country.

The three liturgies have the same Gospel, the story of Matthew's call. For the Epistle, the Common Liturgy gives a selection of general application (the diversity of spiritual gifts); the Prayer Book gives Paul's eulogy of "the glorious gospel of Christ"; and the Missal appoints a selection which records the vision of Ezekiel, with its description of the animal types of the four evangelists, Matthew's symbol being a man since he more fully than the others records the human genealogy of our Lord. The Collect is from the *Book of Common Prayer* (1549).

The first Lesson is the Missal text of the Epistle lengthened.

ST. MICHAEL AND ALL ANGELS
September 29

	Service Book	*Roman Missal*	*American Book of Common Prayer*
Lesson	II Kings 6:8-17		
Epistle	Rev. 12:7-12	Rev. 1:1-5	Rev. 12:7-12
Gospel	Matt. 18:1-10	*Ibid.*	*Ibid.*
Introit	Ps. 103:20-21, 1	Ps. 103:20, 1	
Gradual	Pss. 103:20, 1;	Ps. 103:20a, b, 1;	
	91:11; Rev. 4:8	Sancte Michael	
		Archangele	

Color: White. Creed: Nicene. Preface: All Saints.

Collect

O Everlasting God, who hast or-dained and constituted the services of angels and men in a wonderful order: Mercifully grant, that as thy holy angels always do thee service in heaven, so by thy appointment they may succor and defend us on earth; through thy Son, Jesus Christ our Lord, who liveth . . . .

Deus qui miro ordine angelorum min-isteria hominumque dispensas. concede propitius. ut a quibus tibi ministrantibus in caelo semper assistitur. ab his in terra. nostra uita muniatur. per. *Gregorian*, 105. *B. S. missals.*

Feasts in honor of angels developed particularly in the East. After the time of Constantine many churches were dedicated in honor of Michael, the only archangel named in Scripture (Daniel and Revelation). Gabriel is the only other angel mentioned by name in Scripture proper, though Raphael and Uriel are named in the Apocrypha. September 29 was the date of the dedication, in the fifth century, of a small basilica on the Via Salaria, six miles from Rome, the first church in Italy dedicated in honor of Michael.

The feast which commemorates this event, and in which the church eventually regarded Michael as representative of all angels, gradually spread throughout the West. The Council of Mainz introduced it in A.D. 813, and the popularity of the "warrior saint" in Teutonic lands is shown by the large number of churches which bear his name. King Ethelred established the feast in England in A.D. 1019. The term "all angels" is an Anglican addition at the time of the Reformation.

There is agreement in the propers except that the Epistle in the Common Liturgy and in the Prayer Book is a Reformation substitute for the selection in the Missal. The Collect is a Gregorian original, 1549 translation, slightly altered 1662.

The Lesson is the story of Elisha and the "chariots of fire" that surrounded him.

ST. LUKE, EVANGELIST
October 18

	Service Book	Roman Missal	American Book of Common Prayer
Lesson	Isa. 35:5-8		
Epistle	II Tim. 4:5-11	II Cor. 8:16-24	II Tim. 4:5-15
Gospel	Luke 10:1-9	*Ibid.*	Luke 10:1-7a
Introit	See Evangelists' Days.	Ps. 139:17, 1-2a.	
Gradual	See Evangelists' Days.	Ps. 194:4a, 1; John 15:16a	

Color: Red.   Creed: Nicene.   Preface: All Saints.

Collect

ALMIGHTY God, who didst call Saint Luke the Physician, whose praise is in the Gospel, to be an evangelist and physician of the soul: Strengthen thy Church, we beseech thee, in a like vocation, that men may learn the message of thy love, and receive healing for their souls and bodies; through the merits of thy Son, Jesus Christ our Lord, who liveth . . . .

Almightie God whiche calledst Luke the phisicion, whose prayse is in the gospell, to be a phisicion of the soule: it may please thee by thy holsome medicines of his doctryne, to heale all the diseases of oure soules, through thy sonne Jesus Christe our Lorde. *BCP,* 1549.

Luke, the "beloved physician," is supposed to have been one of the seventy and possibly the unnamed companion of Cleopas on the walk to Emmaus (Luke 24:18). He was originally a pagan and was born, according to tradition, in Antioch in Syria. He became the close friend and companion of Paul and his Gospel is spoken of as Pauline, as the Gospel of Mark is referred to as Petrine. He was apparently talented and well educated. Tradition states that he was a painter. His Gospel with its large number of parables and its poetic imagery certainly reveals an unusual appreciation of beauty.

Luke was commemorated first in the East. He was the last of the evangelists to be honored with a festival in Rome, and this was not until the tenth century. The propers are in agreement except that the Lutheran and the Anglican liturgies have substituted an Epistle which differs from the selection in the Missal. The Prayer Book Collect was new in 1549. Its form in the Common Liturgy is an expansion of the original, which was based upon the second lesson for Matins of St. Luke's Day in the Sarum Use. The idea of "church" in the Collect is from the revision in the American Prayer Book.

The Lesson is Isaiah's promise of healing for the blind, the deaf, the lame, and the dumb.

ST. SIMON AND ST. JUDE, APOSTLES
October 28

	Service Book	Roman Missal	American Book of Common Prayer
Lesson	Jer. 26:16-19		
Epistle	I Pet. 1:3-9	Eph. 4:7-13	Eph. 2:19-22
Gospel	John 15:17-25	*Ibid.*	John 15:17-27
Introit	See Apostles' Days.	Ps. 139:17, 1, 2a	
Gradual	See Apostles' Days.	Pss. 45:16b, 17a, 16a, 17b; 139:17	

Color: Red.   Creed: Nicene.   Preface: All Saints.

Collect

O ALMIGHTY God, who has built thy Church upon the foundation of the Apostles and Prophets, Jesus Christ himself being the head cornerstone: Grant us so to be joined together in unity of spirit by their doctrine, that we may be made a holy temple acceptable unto thee; through the same thy Son, Jesus Christ our Lord, who liveth . . . .

Almightie God, whiche hast builded the congregacion vpon the foundacion of the Apostles and prophetes, Jesu Christ himselfe beyng the head corner stone: Graunt vs so to bee ioyned together in vnitie of spirite by their doctrine, that we maye be made an holye temple acceptable to thee: throughe Jesu Christe oure Lorde. *BCP, 1549.*

The association of these two apostles may be due to nothing more than their immediate connection in the lists of the apostles in Luke and Acts. There is a tradition, however, that Simon the Zealot (extreme nationalist) and Jude (identical with Thaddaeus) labored together in Persia and were martyred there on the same day. The festival is of late (ninth century) origin.

The Lutheran, Roman, and Anglican liturgies have the same Gospel. The fact that they all have different Epistles and that none of these is from the Epistle of Jude probably reflects the opinion of scholars that the apostle Jude himself did not write the brief Epistle ascribed to him.

The Lesson is the arraignment and acquittal of the prophet Jeremiah.

REFORMATION DAY
October 31

	Service Book	Roman Missal	American Book of Common Prayer
Lesson	I. Sam. 3:19—4:1a		
Epistle	Rom. 3:21-28		
Gospel	John 8:31-36		
Introit	Ps. 46:7, 2, 1		
Gradual	Ps. 48:1, 12a, c, 13-14		

Color: Red.   Creed: Nicene.   Preface: All Saints.

Collect

O LORD God, heavenly Father, pour out, we beseech thee, thy Holy Spirit upon thy faithful people, keep them steadfast in thy grace and truth, protect and comfort them in all temptation, defend them against all enemies of thy Word, and bestow upon Christ's Church militant thy saving peace; through the same thy Son, Jesus Christ our Lord, who liveth . . . .

Herr gott himlischer vater, wir bitten dich, du woltest deinen heiligen geist in unsere herzen geben, uns in deiner gnade ewig zu erhalten, und in aller anfechtung zu behüten, wöllest auch allen feinden deines worts umb deines namens ehre willen wehren und deine arme christenheit allenthalben gnedig befrieden, durch Jesum Christum deinen lieben son unsern herrn. *Saxony (Duke Henry)*, 1539.

Or,

Almighty God, who through the preaching of thy servants, the blessed Reformers, hast caused the light of the Gospel to shine forth: Grant, we beseech thee, that, knowing its saving power, we may faithfully guard and defend it against all enemies, and joyfully proclaim it, to the salvation of souls and the glory of thy holy Name; through thy Son, Jesus Christ our Lord, who liveth . . . .

The Lutheran Liturgy is unique among the churches of the world in appointing a Festival of the Reformation. This festival, which the Common Liturgy regards as of major rank, may be traced back to the annual commemoration in domestic circles of the translation of the Bible into the German language, or to the annual thanksgiving service commemorating the introduction of the Reformation in specific districts which Bugenhagen appointed in several of his church orders (Brunswick [1528], Hamburg [1529], Lübeck [1531]). Similar services of thanksgiving were instituted by the Elector Joachim in 1563, and in the Pomeranian Church Order (1568). In some places services were held on the eve of Luther's birthday (Nov. 10) or on the anniversary of his death. In Württemberg and Baden the festival was observed on the Sunday following June 25, the date of the delivery of the Augsburg Confession.

The Thirty Years' War obliterated these observances, but in 1667 Elector John George II of Saxony reestablished the festival, appointing it for October 31. This date, or the Sunday preceding or the Sunday following, came to be generally accepted in practically all German-speaking and other Lutheran lands, where the festival itself rapidly gained general observance. The use of the Sunday following, however, practically eliminates the equally important All Saints' Day. For this reason, the Common Liturgy sets the *preceding* Sunday as Reformation Sunday in every case, leaving the following Sunday for the solemnities of the universal festival of All Saints.

The Introit and the Gradual are from Psalms 46 and 48, usually associated with the Reformation. The Epistle features the doctrine of justification by faith and the Gospel speaks of the freedom which the truth of the Gospel assures. The first Collect is found in the Saxon (Duke Henry) Church Order (1539-40). The Lüneburg (1564) form specifically mentions the pope and the Turk among the "enemies of thy Word." The English translation first appears in the *Church Book* (1878, not in 1868). The second Collect first appears in the *Common Service Book* (1917).

The Lesson speaks of the "word of the Lord" being revealed by the "word of Samuel."

ALL SAINTS' DAY
November 1

	Service Book	*Roman Missal*	*American Book of Common Prayer*
Lesson	Deut. 33:1-3		
Epistle	Rev. 7:2-17	Rev. 7:2-12	Rev. 7:2-17
Gospel	Matt. 5:1-12	Matt. 5:1-12a	Matt. 5:1-12
Introit	Rev. 7:14b-15a; Ps. 33:1	Guadeamus omnes in Domino; Ps. 33:1	
Gradual	Ps. 34:9, 10b; Matt. 11:28	*Ibid.*	

Color: Red.   Creed: Nicene.   Preface: All Saints.

Collect

O ALMIGHTY God, who hast knit together thine elect in one communion and fellowship in the mystical body of thy Son, Christ our Lord: Grant us grace so to follow thy blessed Saints in all virtuous and godly living, that we may come to those unspeakable joys which thou hast prepared for those who unfeignedly love thee; through the same Jesus Christ our Lord, who liveth . . . .

Almightie God whiche haste knitte together thy electe in one Communion and felowship in the misticall body of thy sonne Christe our Lord: graunt vs grace so to folow thy holy Saynctes in all vertues and godly liuyng, that we maye come to those vnspeakeable ioyes, whiche thou hast prepared for all them that vnfaynedly loue thee, through Jesus Christe. *BCP, 1549.*

The Feast of All Saints has had an interesting development. Strictly speaking, it dates from the ninth century. Its beginnings, however, are to be found in a very early festival in honor of all martyrs which originated in Syria, A.D. 360. In Rome the Pantheon, which had been dedicated in 27 B.C. to all the gods of the seven planets, was rededicated by Boniface IV in A.D. 610 as a Christian basilica in honor of Mary and the martyrs, and the remains of many of the early martyrs were "translated" from the catacombs to the church. Another feast in commemoration of all saints (confessors as well as martyrs) was appointed for November 1 by Pope Gregory IV in A.D. 835. Gregory VII later transferred the anniversary of the dedication of the Pantheon to this date and confirmed the title of the feast as All Saints instead of All Martyrs.

The feast, therefore, recalls the memories of all the faithful departed and the triumph of Christ over all false gods. At the very end of the tenth century an additional feast of All Souls (November 2) was initiated at Cluny and officially accepted by the Roman church in the fourteenth century. This met the situation created by acceptance of the doctrine of purgatory by establishing a day commemorating those souls in purgatory and not technically regarded as saints.

All Saints' Day through the centuries became exceedingly popular with pilgrims. After the Reformation the Lutherans (in many parts of Germany and generally in Scandinavia) and the Anglicans continued to observe All Saints' Day, but rejected All Souls' Day because of its unscriptural implications.

The propers, in point of harmony, depth of sentiment, and poetic beauty, are unsurpassed by any series in the church's calendar. They reflect the church's early emphasis in this feast upon the martyrs of the first three centuries. The Gospel depicts ideal qualities of "the blessed" in this world; the Epistle is a glorious passage which gives a vision of them in the heavenly world; the Collect in superlatively beautiful language unites the faithful of both worlds in the communion of saints, the church of Christ. The lessons are the same in the three liturgies. The Collect is by the English Reformers (1549). Brightman[5] suggests a Leonine Collect as a basis, but the text is not convincing.

The Common Liturgy rubrics permit All Saints to be celebrated on the Sunday following November 1. Thus proper provision is made for the commemoration each year, at a regular Sunday service, of those who have died in the parish. In the past, some have used All Saints' Day for this observance, but perhaps more have used the Last Sunday after Trinity. Though the latter is at the end of the church year, and its propers deal with the Second Coming, still they are not particularly suited to commemoration. It is hoped that the provision of a particular Sunday each year, the Sunday after November 1, will encourage a

[5] *The English Rite*, II. 633.

regular and perhaps less doleful remembrance of those who, after all, have entered not death, but life.

The Lesson records the blessing of Moses upon Israel, and describes the coming of the Lord "with ten thousands of saints."

THE FESTIVAL OF HARVEST

	Service Book	Roman Missal	American Book of Common Prayer
Lesson	Deut. 11:8-21		
Epistle	Acts 14:11-18		
Gospel	Luke 12:15-34		
Introit	Ps. 65:11, 9a, 10d, 1		
Gradual	Pss. 145:15-16; 103:1-2		

Color: Red.   Creed: Nicene or Apostles'.   Preface: none.

Collect

ALMIGHTY God, most merciful Father, who openest thine hand, and satisfiest the desire of every living thing: We give thee most humble and hearty thanks that thou hast crowned the fields with thy blessing, and hast permitted us once more to gather in the fruits of the earth; and we beseech thee to bless and protect the living seed of thy word sown in our hearts, that in the plenteous fruits of righteousness we may always present to thee an acceptable thank-offering; through thy Son, Jesus Christ our Lord, who liveth . . . .

Church Book, 1868.

The Festival of Harvest is another unique day in the Lutheran calendar. The Roman church observes three Rogation days—Monday, Tuesday, and Wednesday before Ascension Day (and after Rogate Sunday) —with penitential processional litanies followed by a mass for which special propers are appointed which implore God's forgiveness and invoke his blessings upon the fruits of the earth. The American Prayer Book (not the English) also recognizes these Rogation days, eliminating the penitential features, and appoints proper lessons and a special Collect.

The Lutheran festival has a different character. It is definitely a thanksgiving for the fruits of the earth and is observed according to local appointment, usually on a Sunday, after the harvests have been gathered. Many sixteenth-century Lutheran orders (Calenberg [1642]; Osnabrück [1543]; Hildesheim [1544]; Prussia [1558]) combine the

572

Festival of Harvest with the Feast of St. Michael (September 29). Other orders specify the Sunday before or the Sunday after St. Michael's Day. Others, again, simply direct that such a harvest festival be held annually, without specifying the date.

The Introit and the Gradual sing of God's bounty and of our thanksgiving. The Epistle speaks of the "living God's" gift of "rain from heaven, and fruitful seasons." The Gospel warns against covetousness and exhorts everyone to be "rich toward God" and not to "lay up treasure for himself." The Collect combines phrases from the Introit and the Gradual and leads to the thought of spiritual gifts, the "living seed of thy word" and "plenteous fruits of righteousness." It appears in the *Church Book* (1868), and, in German, in Loehe's *Agende* (1884).

The Lesson is a call to remembrance and thanksgiving for God's providence in nature.

A DAY OF HUMILIATION AND PRAYER

	Service Book	Roman Missal	American Book of Common Prayer
Lesson	I Sam. 7:3-12		
Epistle	Acts 3:12-19a		
Gospel	Matt. 7:6-12		
Introit	Isa. 1:2, 4b;		
	Ps. 130:3		
Gradual	Isa. 55:6-7		

Color: Black.   Creed: Nicene or Apostles'.   Preface: none.

Collect

ALMIGHTY and most merciful God, our heavenly Father, of whose compassion there is no end; who art long-suffering, gracious, and plenteous in goodness and truth; forgiving iniquity, transgression and sin: We have sinned and done perversely, we have sinned and grievously offended thee; against thee, thee only, have we sinned and done evil in thy sight; but, we beseech thee, O Lord, remember not against us former iniquities; let thy tender mercies speedily prevent us, for we are brought very low; help us, O God of our salvation, and purge away our sins, for the glory of thy holy Name, and for the sake of thy dear Son, Jesus Christ, our Saviour, who liveth . . . .

O Allmächtiger Barmherziger HERR und Himmlischer Vatter! desz Barmherzigkeit kein Ende ist/der Du langmütig/gnädig/und von grosser Güte und Treue bist/und vergibst die Missethat/-Ubertrettung und Sünden/wir haben miszhandelt und sind gottlos gewesen/-und Dich oft erzürnet/Dir allein haben wir gesündiget/und übel für Dir gethan/aber HErr gedenke nicht an unsere vorige Missethat/lasz bald deine Barmherzigkeit über uns grösser seyn/dañ wir sind fast elend worden/hilff uns GOTT unsers Heils/errette uns/und vergib uns unsere Sünden/um der Ehren willen deines heiligen Namens/und von wegen deines lieben, Sohns unsers Heilandes JEsu Christi/ *Nuremberg, 1691.*

The Common Liturgy provides proper appointments for a Day of Humiliation and Prayer without naming any specific date. This accords with sixteenth-century Lutheran practice generally. Later in many sections, particularly after the Thirty Years' War, a fixed date was established for annual observance, frequently on or near the ancient Rogation days (the Sunday after Ascension Day, for example). Where Reformed influence was strong (Cassel, Hesse, Württemberg, etc.), quarterly and even monthly penitential days were appointed. After 1893 most Lutheran areas in central and northern Germany observed Wednesday before the last Sunday after Trinity as such a day.

The Introit and the Gradual of the *Service Book* give passages from the prophet Isaiah and the penitential Psalm 130. The Epistle is St. Peter's call to repentance and conversion. The Gospel is our Lord's encouragement to "asking, seeing and knocking," as given in the Sermon on the Mount. The Collect is from the Nuremberg *Agend-Buchlein* (1691). The translation first appears in the *Church Book* (1878, not in 1868).

The Lesson records Samuel's crying "unto the Lord for Israel," and the latter's deliverance.

A DAY OF GENERAL OR SPECIAL THANKSGIVING

	Service Book	Roman Missal	American Book of Common Prayer
Lesson	Deut. 8:1-20 or Isa. 61:10-11		
Epistle	I Tim. 2:1-8 or Acts 14:8-18		Jas. 1:16-27
Gospel	Matt. 6:25-33		Matt. 6:25-34
Introit	Ps. 150:6, 2, 1		
Gradual	Pss. 145:15-16; 103:1-2		

Color: Red.   Creed: Nicene or Apostles'.   Preface: none.

Collect

ALMIGHTY God, our heavenly Father, whose mercies are new unto us every morning, and who, though we have in no wise deserved thy goodness, dost abundantly provide for all our wants of body and soul: Give us, we pray thee, thy Holy Spirit, that we may heartily acknowledge thy merciful goodness toward us, give thanks for all thy benefits, and serve thee in willing obedience; through thy Son, Jesus Christ our Lord, who liveth . . . .

Church Book, 1878.

574

Thanksgiving Day is a uniquely American day established by the proclamations of governors of states and the President of the nation. The Pilgrims proclaimed a day of thanksgiving at Plymouth in 1621 after their first harvest. By 1680 this had become an annual festival in the Massachusetts Bay Colony. In 1789 after the adoption of the Constitution, George Washington proclaimed Thursday, November 26, a day of thanksgiving. Again in 1795 he appointed a day of thanksgiving and prayer for the benefits and welfare of the nation. President Madison did the same after the end of the War of 1812. By 1858 no less than twenty-five governors of the states annually appointed such days. In 1863 President Lincoln appointed a national day of thanksgiving and each President since has followed his example, the date now being the fourth Thursday in November.

The Lutheran and the Episcopal churches provide liturgical appointments. The *Common Service Book* states that "the proper service for this Day is the Order for Matins." The Common Liturgy appoints propers for the Service, which may be used if desired. The Introit is a selection from Psalm 150; the Gradual is the same as for the Festival of Harvest; three lessons are provided. The Collect appears in the *Church Book* (1878, not in 1868) and, in German, in Loehe's *Agende* (1884).

The Lesson rejoices in the providence of God in nature and grace.

INVITATORIES, ANTIPHONS, AND RESPONSES

These minor Propers for Matins and Vespers (*Service Book,* pp. 149-152) are an imporant and characteristic feature of the Lutheran Liturgy. They provide a rich collection of variable material for all festivals and seasons. The items are all historic, being found in the pre-Reformation breviaries, in the Lutheran cantionales of the sixteenth century—Spangenberg (1545); Lossius (1553); Eler (1588), etc.— and in many church orders—Rhein Pfalz (1570), Nuremberg *Officium Sacrum* (1664), etc.

Limitations of space prevent discussion of this material at this point. Attention may be called to comment on pp. 393-403.

COLLECTS AND PRAYERS

The author's indebtedness to his friend, Mr. James P. Berg, for valuable help, has already been acknowledged in the foreword to this edition. Mention should be made at this point that the author entrusted the revision of this entire chapter (XXIX) to him. To start with, Mr. Berg had the author's listing (in the first edition of *The Lutheran Liturgy*) of sources of the fifty-five Collects and prayers carried over from the *Common Service Book*. In addition, he had the author's references to immediate sources of most of the other hundred new Collects in the *Service Book*. Mr. Berg's further researches led him to libraries in Washington, Philadelphia, Princeton, New York, Boston and Rock Island, Illinois, and to microscopic study of material in six languages— Latin, Greek, German, French, and Swedish, as well as English. In many cases, he carried the author's references back to earlier sources. In other instances he uncovered early originals not previously known or even suspected.

The supplementary collection of Collects represents the fastest changing and fastest growing portion of our service books. The Common Service of 1888 provided seventy-seven Collects. In 1917 this number was expanded in the *Common Service Book* to eighty-four. As a result of World War I, the list in the word edition was expanded to one hundred one, twelve of these new additions being written especially for the book. The *Service Book and Hymnal* has a total of one hundred thirty-eight Collects in this section, of which less than half (fifty-five) were carried over from the *Common Service Book*.

These Collects and prayers supplement the Collects for the day, and are intended chiefly for use at Matins and Vespers. They may also be used for the special supplications, intercessions, and thanksgivings which will be added to the Prayer of the Church from time to time as special needs arise in the churches.

When the Commission on the Common Liturgy resolved to revise and enlarge this collection of prayers, Dr. Paul Z. Strodach was asked to present recommendations. He submitted a preliminary report which was modified and approved. Upon Dr. Strodach's death shortly afterwards, Dr. George R. Seltzer was requested to make a fresh study of the entire collection with the purpose of introducing material of recent composition and special relevance to contemporary needs and situations. His recommendations were finally adopted as given in the *Service Book,* pp. 218-36.

These Collects and prayers constitute a rich collection drawn from many sources, ancient and modern. No less than nineteen are from the earliest prayer collections of the Western church, the Leonine, Gelasian, and Gregorian sacramentaries of the sixth to the ninth centuries. There are four translations from the Eastern liturgies, and six from the Mozarabic, Roman, and Sarum liturgies. Twenty-seven are compositions of the Reformation era, eleven of these appearing first in the Lutheran church orders in German and ten in the *Book of Common Prayer* of the Church of England. The number of Collects from more modern sources has increased from twenty-three in the *Common Service Book* to eighty in the *Service Book and Hymnal.* Of these twenty-nine are Lutheran, thirty-nine Anglican, ten Presbyterian, one Methodist, and one Congregational. At least fifty-seven were written during the twentieth century, though only four appear here for the first time. The origin of one Collect is unknown. Thus, in content and in form, the collection is well within the great liturgical tradition of the church, yet makes full provision for the peculiar needs of our own day.

The ancient Latin originals are for the most part terse, sententious prayers with simple strong thought cast in traditional collect form. One of these in our collection (No. 86) says what it has to say in just eleven words. Many of these Latin Collects were translated into German in the church orders a decade or two before they appeared in English in the first *Book of Common Prayer* in 1549. In accordance with general Gallican practice, the tendency in both the Lutheran and Anglican churches was to expand the Latin material, or to combine the thought of several Collects in one new and longer vernacular form. In Cranmer's case, the lengthening is often particularly auspicious, for he seems to have realized that much of the power of the Latin forms rested in their strong rhythm, and to have created such a rhythm in the English by careful expansion. Thus it is that in nearly every case where early Latin prayers are found in both the German church orders and in the English *Book of Common Prayer,* the translations in the latter have been accepted in recognition of the literary grace and liturgical feeling so

577

beautifully expressed in the work of Cranmer and his associates.

Many of the original Collects in the German church orders reflect the concern of the time for purity of doctrine and wholehearted acceptance of God's Word. Others stress a sense of unworthiness and of divine chastisement in times of national distress (No. 15). A number of their wordy and constantly repeated expressions have been pruned in translation. The original Collects taken from the *Book of Common Prayer* are for the most part post-Communion collects and collects for apostles' days, the latter adapted for more general use by the framers of the Common Service in 1888 (*e.g.,* nos. 103, 106, Per. Dev. No. 13).

The earliest original German Collect is No. 97, found in Döber's Mass for the Hospital Church, in Nuremberg (1525), an early Lutheran vernacular service which appeared a full year before Luther's *Deutsche Messe.* The simple, lucid form of the Collect suggests a Latin original, but none has been found. The process of emendation and amplification is illustrated by the fact that when this Collect was inserted five years later in the Riga Church Order (1530), it had already undergone change and expansion.

The church owes a real debt to the many translators, known and unknown, who have made these prayers available for our use today. In many instances they have added to the originals the gifts of their own genius and left us richer for it. Such was the case with Cranmer and his associates, who were in large part successful because their work was free and not literal. In some cases, however, important thoughts have been lost in the translation from one language to another. In collect No. 119, for example, the phrase "whose service is perfect freedom," while excellent in itself, introduces a new idea and omits the stronger thought of the original *cui servire regnare est,* retained by the German of Brandenburg-Nuremberg (1533), *wer dir dienet der regieret.* The manuscript studies of Drs. Beale M. Schmucker, Charles Porterfield Krauth, F. W. Geissenhainer, and Edward T. Horn[1] show how painstaking is the task of producing clear thought and felicitous expression in translation. Dr. Schmucker's work was particularly important for the collection of Collects in the *Church Book* of the General Council (1868), some of which passed unchanged into the Common Service of 1888. In the *Common Service Book* collection, the greatest number of new translations (four), and eight original Collects, were provided by Dr. Paul Zeller Strodach, an active member, until his death in 1947, of the Joint Commissions preparing the *Service Book and*

---

[1] Preserved in the Krauth Memorial Library, Philadelphia Lutheran Theological Seminary.

Hymnal. His total of original Collects in the new collection is eleven.

These prayer forms, like the Service itself, represent the discriminating thought and devotional experience of the church throughout the centuries. The survival and unbroken use, for over a thousand years, of many of these forms, is in itself a testimony to their spiritual worth and vitality. In content and form they have satisfied millions of worshipers in the past. They serve admirably as vehicles of our corporate devotion today.

The collection as a whole, however, is the most flexible part of the official service book of the Lutheran church. It is the one part of the book which must respond most rapidly to new conditions and express the living faith and work of the church in each successive age. As such it can never be complete or final. Every successive revision of the service book will require thorough reworking of this material.[2] This to some extent explains the extremely large number of modern prayers in the *Service Book and Hymnal*. Prayers for industrial prosperity (No. 73), the unemployed (No. 76) or labor-management relations (No. 72) are of recent origin and current need. Nothing taken from the Leonine Sacramentary will quite fit.

The increase in the number of prayers taken from Anglican and other non-Lutheran sources is due largely to the fact that the Lutheran church in America is an English-speaking church. It is both more natural and, considering the difficulties of translation, more prudent to take prayers composed in English than to translate them. But even more important is the fact that, as English-speaking people, we tend to think in the same manner and be concerned with the same problems as other English-speaking men and women more than we tend to think along denominational lines, especially in areas of public life and concern. In this we are indeed fortunate, for the English language has been used, ever since the Reformation, to create a truly great literature of devotion.

The following notes give the fullest information as to sources in the possession of the author at this time. Further research will doubtless disclose earlier sources for some items, particularly those for which reference is made simply to a modern collection. For the most part, no attempt has been made to indicate more than the earliest known appearance of individual Collects, though many appear in several

---

[2] So rapid is this change that the United Lutheran Church in America, after the *Common Service Book* had been in use for less than twenty years, felt constrained to issue a collection of four hundred thirty-one Collects and prayers prepared by its *Common Service Book* Committee, under the title *Collects and Prayers for Use in Church* (Philadelphia: U.L.P.H., 1935).

different collections, often with considerable variation in text.

Quotations from the German church orders are mostly from original editions, in a few instances from Sehling, etc. Modern prayers are taken from the original editions, except as noted. In the case of the sacramentaries, references, with the exception of a single Collect from the eighteenth-century edition of Muratori, are to the modern editions of Feltoe and Wilson.

THE CHURCH

ORIGINAL

Deus, incommutabilis virtus, lumen aeternum, respice propitius ad totius ecclesiae tuae mirabile sacramentum, et opus salutis humanae perpetuae dispositionis affectu tranquillus operare, totusque mundus experiatur et videat deiecta erigi, inveterata novari, et per ipsum redire omnia in integrum, a quo sumpsere principium. Per.

Gelasian (Wilson, p. 82). Holy Saturday.
From a translation by William Bright, *Ancient Collects,* p. 92.

O Almechtiger güttiger Got vnd Vater vnsers Herrn Jesu Christi/ Der du vns ernstlich befolhen hast/ das wir dich bitten sollen vmb arbeyter in deiner erndten/ das ist vmb rechtgeschaffne prediger deins worts Wir bitten dein grundlose barmhertzigkeyt/ Du wöllest vns rechtgeschaffne lerer vnd diener deines Götlichen worts zuschicken/ vnd denselben dein haylsams wort in das hertz vnd in den mund geben/ Das sie deinen befelch treülich aussrichten vnd nichts predigen/ das deinem heyligen wort entgegen sey/ Auff das wir durch dein hymlisch ewigs wort ermanet/ geleret/ gespeyst/ getrost vnd gesterckt werden/ thun was dir gefellig vnd vns fruchtbarlich ist/ Gib Herr deiner gemain deinen gayst vnd Götliche weyssheyt/ Das dein wort vnter vns lauffe vnd wachse/ vnnd mit aller fraidigkeit wie sichs gepürt gepredigt/ vnd dein heylige Christenliche

SERVICE BOOK AND HYMNAL

1. *For the Church*

O God of unchangeable power and eternal light, look favorably on thy whole Church, that wonderful and sacred mystery; and, by the tranquil operation of thy perpetual Providence, carry out the work of man's salvation; and let the whole world feel and see that things which were cast down are being raised up, that things which had grown old are being made new, and that all things are returning to perfection through him from whom they took their origin, even thy Son, Jesus Christ our Lord.

2. *For the Church*

Grant, we beseech thee, Almighty God, unto thy Church, thy Holy Spirit, and the wisdom which cometh down from above; that thy word, as becometh it, may not be bound, but have free course and be preached to the joy and edifying of Christ's holy people; that in steadfast faith we may serve thee, and in the confession of thy Name abide unto the end; through Jesus Christ, thy Son, our Lord.

gemain dadurch gepessert werde/ auff das wir mit bestendigem glauben dir dienen/ vnd in bekantnuss dienes namens biss an das ende verharren/ Durch vnsern Herrn ec.

Brandenburg-Nuremberg (1533).
Translated in the *Church Book* (1868).

Ecclesiae tuae Dñe voces placatus admitte ut destructis adversantibus universis secura tibi serviat libertate per.

Leonine (Feltoe, p. 56). *Cf.* Gelasian (Wilson, p. 277).

Gracious Father, I humbly beseech thee, for thy holy Catholick Church, fill it with all truth; in all truth with all peace. Where it is corrupt, purge it: where it is in error, direct it: where it is superstitious, rectifie it: where any thing is amiss, reform it: where it is right, strengthen and confirm it: where it is in want, furnish it: where it is divided and rent asunder, make up the breaches of it, O thou holy one of Israel.

Abp. William Laud, *A Summarie of Devotions* (Oxford, 1667), p. 192.

National Day of Prayer (England), March 23, 1941. Text in F. A. Iremonger, *Each Returning Day* (London, 1944), p. 21.

O heauenly father/ the father of all wisedom/ understandinge/ and true strengthe/ I beseche thee for thy onli sonne our sauiour Christes sake/ looke mercifulli vpon me wretched creature/ and sende thine holye spirite into my breaste/ that not only I maye vnder-

3. *For the Church*

O Lord, favorably receive the prayers of thy Church; that, being delivered from all adversity and error, it may serve thee in safety and freedom; and grant us thy peace in our time; through Jesus Christ, thy Son, our Lord.

4. *For the Church*

Most gracious Father, we humbly beseech thee for thy holy catholic Church. Fill it with all truth, in all peace. Where it is corrupt, purify it; where it is in error, direct it; where anything is amiss, reform it; where it is right, strengthen and confirm it; where it is in want, provide for it; where it is divided and rent asunder, heal the breaches thereof, O thou Holy One of Israel; through Jesus Christ our Lord.

5. *For the Church*

O Most Holy Spirit of God, from whom alone floweth the fulness of wisdom and life: Come in thine everlasting power and glory, we beseech thee, upon thy Church and into the hearts of men; to bring to the world a new birth of holiness, new interpretations of truth, and new unity in love; through Jesus Christ our Lord, who with the Father and thee liveth and reigneth, one God, world without end.

6. *For the Church Militant*

Heavenly Father, the author of all wisdom, understanding, and true strength: We beseech thee to look mercifully upon thy servants and send thy Holy Spirit into their hearts; that when they must join to fight in the field for the glory of thy holy Name,

581

stande according to thy wisedome/ how this pestilent and deadly dart is to be borne of/ and with what answere it is to be beaten backe/ but also when I must ioyne to fight in the fielde for the glorye of thy name/ that then I being strengthened with the defence of thy right hande/ maie manfully stande in the confession of thy faieth/ and of thy trueth/ and continue in the same vnto the ende of my life/ through the same our Lorde Jesus Christ.

Nicholas Ridley (d. 1555), Bishop of London. *Certain Godly, Learned, Comfortable Conferences . . .* (1556). Parker Society, XL, 142.

Jacobite Liturgy of St. Dionysius of Athens, "first prayer before the pax." Translated by William Bright, *Ancient Collects,* p. 81. This abbreviated version from Paul Zeller Strodach, *Oremus* (Philadelphia, 1925), p. 72.

Edwin James Palmer, Bishop of Bombay, *Our Hope and Strength,* p. 20.

then they, being strengthened with the defense of thy right hand, may manfully stand in the confession of thy faith and of thy truth, and continue in the same unto the end of their lives; through Jesus Christ our Lord.

7. *For Church Unity*

O God our Father, good beyond all that is good, fair beyond all that is fair, in whom is calmness and peace: Do thou make up the dissensions which divide us from each other, and bring us back into a unity of love, which may bear some likeness to thy sublime Nature; grant that we may be spiritually one, as well in ourselves as in each other; through that peace of thine which maketh all things peaceful, and through the grace, mercy and compassion of thy Son, Jesus Christ, our Lord.

8. *For Church Unity*

O God, the physician of men and nations, the restorer of the years that have been destroyed: Look upon the distractions of the world, and be pleased to complete the work of thy healing hand; draw all men unto thee and one to another by the bands of thy love; make thy Church one, and fill it with thy Spirit, that by thy power it may unite the world in a sacred brotherhood of nations, wherein justice, mercy and faith, truth and freedom may flourish, and thou mayest be ever glorified through Jesus Christ our Lord.

9. *For the Parish*

Almighty and everlasting God, Who dost govern all things in heaven and earth, mercifully hear our prayers, and

Almighty and everlasting God, who dost govern all things in heaven and earth: Mercifully hear our supplica-

grant to this parish all things that are needful for its spiritual welfare: strengthen and confirm the faithful; visit and relieve the sick; turn and soften the wicked; arouse the careless; recover the fallen; restore the penitent; remove all hindrances to the advancement of Thy truth and bring all to be of one heart and mind within the fold of Thy holy Church; to the honour and glory of Thy ever-blessed Name, through Jesus Christ our Lord.

William J. Butler, Dean of Lincoln, in R. M. Benson, *The Manual of Intercessory Prayer* (London, 1914), p. 24. From an office used at meetings of special intercession at St. Barnabas', Pimlico.

Increase, O God, the faith and the zeal of all Thy people, that they may more earnestly desire, and more diligently seek, the salvation of their fellow-men, through the message of Thy love in Jesus Christ our Lord. Send forth a mighty call unto Thy servants to preach Thy Word, and multiply the number of those who labour in the Gospel; granting unto them a heart of love, sincerity of speech, and the power of the Holy Ghost, that they may be able to persuade men to forsake sin and turn unto Thee. And so bless and favour the work of Thine evangelists, that multitudes may be brought from the kingdom of evil into the kingdom of Thy dear Son, our Saviour Jesus Christ.

Book of Common Worship (Presbyterian Church, U. S. A.) (1906), p 133.

Church of Scotland, *Book of Common Order* (1940), p. 268.

tions, and grant unto this parish all things that are needful for its spiritual welfare. Strengthen and increase the faithful; visit and relieve the sick; rouse the careless; restore the fallen and penitent; remove all hindrances to the advancement of thy truth; and bring all to be of one heart and mind within the fold of thy holy Church, to the honor and glory of thy holy Name; through Jesus Christ our Lord.

10. *For the Spread of the Gospel* *(Evangelistic Work)*

Increase, O God, the faith and the zeal of all thy people, that they may more earnestly desire, and more diligently seek, the salvation of their fellow-men, through the message of thy love in Jesus Christ our Lord. Send forth a mighty call unto all thy servants, granting unto them hearts of love, sincerity of speech, and the power of the Holy Spirit, that they may be able to persuade men to forsake sin and return unto thee. And so bless and favor the work of thine evangelists, that multitudes may be brought from the bondage of evil into the kingdom of thy dear Son; through the same Jesus Christ our Lord.

11. *For the Anniversary of a Church Building*

O God, who hast promised to be present with thy Church even unto the end of the world: We thank thee for this House builded to thine honor and glory. For the faith and life and worship for which it has witnessed, for the love which thou hast manifested to thy people here (from age to age), for the blessing which thou hast vouchsafed to

583

them in worship and in work, and for all who in this place have testified to things unseen and eternal and handed on the light of truth from generation to generation: Glory be to thee, O Lord, most High.

Guide and bless thy people still, we beseech thee; increase in them the spirit of faith and love, make them worthy of the heritage they have received, knit them together in the communion of thy saints, and grant that this place may be unto all who worship here none other than the House of God and the Gate of Heaven; through Jesus Christ, thy Son, our Lord.

Deus qui nobis per singulos annos. huius sancti templi tui consecrationis reparas diem. et sacris semper mysteriis representas incolomes. exaudi preces populi tui. et praesta ut quisquis hoc templum beneficia petiturus ingreditur. cuncta se impertrasse laetetur. per dominum.

Gregorian (Wilson, p. 185).
Collects and Prayers for Use in Church
p. 50.

12. *A Church Anniversary*

O God, who year after year dost return to us the day of the founding of this congregation, and ever dost bring us again into the presence of thy holy mysteries: Hear the prayers of thy people, and grant that whosoever shall enter this temple to seek blessing may rejoice in his desires wholly fulfilled; through Jesus Christ our Lord.

13. *For Synods of the Church*

¶ *The following prayer may be said in churches on the Sunday, or during the week, before the meeting of a Synod or other ecclesiastical body, or during its sessions.*

Common Service Book, 1919. Order for the Opening of Synods.

O Lord, the only Source of true wisdom: We invoke thy blessing upon the ——————— about to assemble (*or,* now assembled) in thy Name to deliberate upon those things which make for the well-being and extension of thy holy Church among us throughout the world; and as thou hast promised to send thy Holy Spirit to lead thy people into all truth, so guide the representatives of thy Church that they may seek only thy glory and the welfare of those whom thou hast redeemed by the death of thy Son; through the same thy Son, Jesus Christ our Lord.

O Lord Jesus Christ, Who didst establish Thy Church on earth, and didst command Thy disciples to be thy witnesses among all nations: Grant unto Thy faithful people, amid the labors and distresses of this present time, boldness to confess Thy Name; enable them, by Thy Holy Spirit, to be among their fellowmen as those who serve, turning the hearts of men to Thee, uplifting the weak, comforting the sorrowing, and speaking peace to the desolate and afflicted; Thou Who livest . . . .

Luther Dotterer Reed, 1917. *Common Service Book* (Word Edition. 1919).

O Almechtiger ewiger Got/ Der du wilt das allen menschen geholffen werde vnd zu erkantnuss/ deiner Götlichen warheyt kumen/ Wir bitten dein Götliche mayestat/ durch Jesum Christum deinen aynigen Sune vnsern Herren vnd haylandt/ Du wöllest dein Götliche gnad hilffvnd gayst mittaylen/ aller ordenlichen Oberkeyt/ das sie fridlich vnd wol regieren/ Allen Christenlichen dienern deines heyligen worts/ das sie recht vnd fruchtbarlich leren/ Und wöllest durch deinen allmechtigen gewalt vnd vnerforschliche weyssheit widerstandt thun/ allen denen die dein heylig wort hassen/ vnd mit falscher lere vnd vnordenlichem gewalt verfolgen/ sie erleuchten/ vnd zu erkantnuss deiner herrligkeyt füren/ Auff das wir alle in einem stillen gerüigen vnstrefflichen lebẽ/ die reychtumber deiner Götlichen gnaden/ durch einen raynen glauben erlernen/ vñ dir aynigem waren Gott vnd Herrn aller Herrn/ in heyligkeyt vnd gerechtigkeyt/ die dir gefellig ist/ dienen mögen/ Durch vnzern Herrn.

Brandenburg-Nuremberg (1533).
Translation from the *Church Book* (1868), condensed, 1878.

Omnipotens sempiterne Deus, qui ecclesiam tuam nova semper prole

14. *For the Church in Time of War or Distress*

O God, who dost will that thy Church bear witness to thee among all nations: Grant unto thy faithful people, amid the labors and distresses of this present time, boldness to confess thy Name; enable them, by thy Holy Spirit, to be among their fellow men as those who serve, turning the hearts of men to thee, uplifting the weak, comforting the sorrowing, and speaking peace to the desolate and afflicted; through Jesus Christ our Lord, who liveth and reigneth with thee and the Holy Ghost, one God, world without end.

15. *For the Protection and Peace of the Church*

Almighty God, who wilt have all men to be saved and come to the knowledge of the truth: Impart, we beseech thee, the grace of thy Holy Spirit to thy ministers, so that they may teach thy truth to the saving of men. Bring to naught the counsels of the enemies of thy word, who by corrupt teaching or with violent hands would destroy it; and enlighten them with its saving power. Increase and enrich our faith, and lead us in the way of quietness and peace; through Jesus Christ, thy Son, our Lord.

16. *For Catechumens*

Almighty and everlasting God, who dost always multiply thy Church, and

585

fecundas, auge fidem et intellectum catechumenis nostris, ut renati fonte baptismatis, adoptionis tuae filiis aggregentur. Per.

Gelasian (Wilson, p. 76). (Good Friday).

with thy light and grace dost strengthen the hearts of those whom thou hast regenerated, confirming unto them thy covenant and faithfulness: Grant unto our Catechumens increase both of faith and knowledge, that they may rejoice in their Baptism and really and heartily renew their covenant with thee; through Jesus Christ, thy Son, our Lord.

Allmächtiger ewiger Gott/ dieweil dein Wille nicht ist/ dass jemand aus diesen geringsten verlohren werde/ sondern hast deinen einigen Sohn gesandt/ das verlohrne selig zu machen/ und durch desselben Mund befohlen/ wir sollen die Kinder zu dir bringen/ dann solcher sey das Himmelreich/ Wir bitten dich hertzlich du wollest diese unsere Jugend mit deinem heiligen Geist segnen und regieren/ dass sie in deinem Wort heilig wachsen und zunehmen/ und durch den Schutz deiner Engel/ wider alle Gefählhgkeit/ beschützen und bewahren/ umb Jesu Christi/ deines lieben Sohnes/ unsers Herren willen/ Amen.

Saxe-Coburg (1626). Translated by Paul Zeller Strodach, Common Service Book.

New. George Rise Seltzer.

17. *For the Children of the Church*

Almighty and everlasting God, who hast sent thine only Son to seek and to save that which was lost, and through him hast said, Suffer the little children to come unto me, and forbid them not, for of such is the kingdom of God: Most heartily we beseech thee so to bless and govern the children of thy Church, by thy Holy Spirit, that they may grow in grace and in the knowledge of thy word; protect and defend them against all danger and harm, and give thy holy angels charge over them; through the same Jesus Christ, thy Son, our Lord.

18. *For a Conference of Christian People*

O God, whose beloved Son ministered to men in the market place and in the country, by the hearth and in thy holy House: We beseech thee to bless us who are gathered in thy Name. Help us to learn and to do thy will. Guide us by thy Spirit; comfort us with the sense of thy presence and let our life and fellowship be to the praise of thy Name and the advancement of thy kingdom; through the same Jesus Christ, our Lord.

THE MINISTRY

Omnipotens sempiterne Deus, qui facis mirabilia magna solus, praetende super famulos tuos spiritum gratiae

19. *For the Ministry*

Almighty and everlasting God, who alone doest great wonders: Send down upon thy Ministers and upon the Con-

salutaris; et ut in veritate tibi complaceant, perpetuum eis rorem tuae benedictionis infunde. Per.

Gelasian (Wilson, p. 263). Translated in Cranmer's English Litany (1544).

O Lord, we beseech Thee to raise up for the work of the ministry faithful and able men, counting it all joy to spend and be spent for the sake of Thy dear Son, and for the souls for which He shed His most precious blood upon the cross; and we pray Thee to fit them for their holy function by Thy bountiful grace and heavenly benediction, through Jesus Christ our Lord, who liveth and reigneth . . .

Archbishop Edward White Benson, *Prayers Public and Private,* p. 36. For a matriculation service at the theological school at Lincoln.

O Almighty God, look mercifully upon the world, redeemed by the blood of Thy dear Son, and send forth many more to do the work of the ministry, that perishing souls may be rescued, and Thy glorious triumph may be hastened by the perfecting of Thine elect; through the same Thy Son Jesus Christ our Lord.

Richard Meux Benson, *The Manual of Intercessory Prayer,* p. 44.

O God who, through thy Holy Spirit, dost illuminate the minds and sanctify the lives of those whom thou dost call to the work of pastors and teachers; Look with thy favour upon all colleges for the instruction and discipline of those who are to serve in the sacred ministry of thy Church; bless those who teach and those who learn, that they may apply themselves with such diligence to the knowledge which is able to make men wise unto salvation, and submit themselves with such ready obedience to the law of thy Son our Saviour,

gregations committed to their charge, the healthful Spirit of thy grace; and, that they may truly please thee, pour upon them the continual dew of thy blessing; through Jesus Christ, thy Son, our Lord.

20. *For the Ministry*

O Lord, we beseech thee to raise up for the work of the Ministry faithful and able men, who shall count it all joy to spend and be spent for the sake of thy dear Son, and for the souls for whom he shed his most precious Blood upon the Cross; and fit them, we pray thee, for their holy office by thy bountiful grace and heavenly benediction; through the same Jesus Christ our Lord.

21. *For the Increase of the Ministry*

O Almighty God, look mercifully upon the world, which thou hast redeemed by the Blood of thy dear Son, and incline the hearts of many to offer themselves for the sacred Ministry of thy Church; so that by their labors thy light may shine in the darkness, and the coming of thy kingdom may be hastened by the perfecting of thine elect; through the same thy Son, Jesus Christ our Lord.

22. *For Theological Seminaries*

O God, who through thy Holy Spirit dost illuminate the minds and sanctify the lives of those whom thou dost call to the work of pastors and teachers: Look with thy favor upon all seminaries for the instruction and discipline of those who are to serve in the sacred Ministry of thy Church; bless those who teach and those who learn, that they may apply themselves with such diligence to the knowledge which is able to make men wise unto salvation, and submit themselves with such ready obedience to the law of thy Son our Saviour, that they may fulfil their ministry with joy; through the same Jesus Christ our Lord.

Book of Common Prayer (Scotland) (1912), p. 57.

that they may fulfill their ministry with joy; through the same Jesus Christ, our Lord.

MISSIONS

Protector noster aspice, Deus, et respice in faciem Christi tui: qui dedit redemptionem semetipsum pro omnibus, et fac, ut ab ortu solus usque ad occasum magnificetur nomen tuum in gentibus, ac in omni loco sacrificetur et offeratur nomini tui oblatio munda. Per eumdem.

Missale Romanum (Secret, Mass for the Propagation of the Faith). (*Cf.* Mal. 1:11)

23. *For Missions*
O God our Protector, behold, and look upon the face of thine Anointed, who hath given himself for the redemption of all, and grant that, from the rising of the sun to the going down thereof, thy Name may be great among the Gentiles; and that in every place, sacrifice and a pure offering may be made unto thy Name; through the same Jesus Christ, thy Son, our Lord.

24. *For Missions*
Almighty God, who hast called the Church out of the world that she might bring the world to thee: Make her faithful, we beseech thee, in the work thou hast entrusted to her hands. Stir up the hearts of thy people here and everywhere, that by their prayers, gifts, and labors, they may have due part in the spreading of thy Gospel over all the earth; and hasten the time when all the ends of the world shall remember and turn unto the Lord, and all the kindreds of the nations shall worship before thee; through Jesus Christ our Lord.

Almighty God, who hast called the Church out of the world that she might bring the world to Thee, make her faithful, we beseech Thee, in the work Thou hast entrusted to her hands. Bless and uphold Thy servants who are gone forth in her name to preach the Gospel in distant lands; be with them in all perils by land or by water, in weariness and painfulness, in discouragement and persecution; endue them with power from on high; and so prosper their labours by Thy Holy Spirit, that the fullness of the Gentiles may be gathered in, and that all Israel may be saved. Stir up the hearts of Thy people here and everywhere, that by their prayers, their gifts, and their labours, they may have part in the spreading of The Gospel over all the earth; and hasten the time when all the ends of the world shall remember and turn unto the Lord, and all the kindreds of the nations shall worship before Thee; through Jesus Christ our Lord.

Church of Scotland, *Prayers for Divine Service* (2d. ed., 1929), p. 239.

Dieu Eternel & tout puissant, qui as fait le salut & la redemptiō du genre humain par vne façon admirable en enuoyant to Fils vinq pour accomplir les promesses faites aux peres: manifeste de pl° en plus la cognoissance de ce salut, & qu'il n'y ait lieu sur la terre, ou ta puissance & verité ne soit cogneuë, afin que toutes nations te chantent louange, t'honorent & glorifient, par iceluy Iesus Christ nostre Seigneur, Amen.

Augustin Marlorat, in *Les Pseaumes de David, avec . . . une oraison a la fin d'un chacun Pseaume* (Geneva, 1577), prayer on Psalm 98.[3]

Henry Eyster Jacobs, 1917, in Common Service Book (Word Edition, 1919).

25. *For Missionary Work*

Almighty and everlasting God, who hast wrought the redemption of man after a miraculous manner, in sending thine only Son to fulfill the promises made unto our fathers: Open up more and more the knowledge of that salvation, that in all places of the earth thy truth and power may be made known, to the intent that all nations may praise, honor, and glorify thee; through the same thy Son, Jesus Christ our Lord.

26. *For Missions*

O God, who didst so love the world as to give thine only-begotten Son, that whosoever believeth in him should not perish, but have everlasting life: Look with compassion upon the heathen who know thee not, and on the multitudes that are scattered as sheep having no shepherd; and so bestow upon us thy grace, that we, with all thy believing people, may be the messengers of thy Gospel, seek them that are lost, and restore them unto thee; that they, being gathered out of all places whither they have wandered, may be strengthened, nurtured, protected and guided by the true Shepherd and Bishop of souls, Jesus Christ our Lord; to whom, with thee and the Holy Ghost be honor and power, dominion and glory, world without end.

[3] This Collect has an interesting history. The French Huguenot Psalter appeared in several editions. The Collects appended to the Psalms were translated into English in the Scottish Psalter of 1595, but were dropped from subsequent editions. This one was then picked up by the editors of the *Book of Common Order* of Canada's United Church in 1950, and from the Canadian book was selected for use in the *Service Book and Hymnal*. The text of this "prayer vpon the xcviii Psalme" in the 1595 *Psalms of David in Metre . . . According as they are sung in the Kirk of Scotland* is as follows:

Almightie and euerlasting God, that hes vvroght the Redemption of man, after ane meruelous maner, in sending thy only Sonne, for fulfilling of the promises made vnto our Fatheris. Oppin vp mair & mair the knavvledge of that saluatioun, that in all places of the earth, thy truth and puissance may be made known: to the intent, that all Nations may praise, honour, and glorifie the, through the self same Sonne, Iesus Christ, So be it.

(These texts courtesy of the National Library of Scotland.)

Henry Eyster Jacobs, in Common Service Book (Word Edition, 1919).

27. For the Maintenance of the Gospel

Almighty God, our heavenly Father, who givest us our daily bread in answer to our prayers: Withhold not from us, nor from our children's children, nor from our land, nor from the people of any nation of the earth, the Bread of Life; but grant that the living seed of thy word may everywhere be sown plenteously, and that the fruits thereof may abound by thy grace unto life everlasting; through the same Jesus Christ, thy Son, our Lord.

28. For the Coming of the Kingdom

O God, who hast made of one blood all nations of men for to dwell on the face of the earth, and didst send thy blessed Son to preach peace to them that are afar off and to them that are nigh; grant that the people of this land may feel after thee and find thee, and hasten, O heavenly Father, the fulfilment of thy promise to pour out thy Spirit upon all flesh through Jesus Christ our Saviour.

O God, who didst send thy blessed Son Jesus Christ to preach peace to them that are afar off, and to them that are nigh: Grant that all the peoples of the world may feel after thee and find thee; and hasten, O God, the fulfillment of thy promise to pour out thy Spirit upon all flesh through Jesus Christ our Lord.

Bishop Cotton of Calcutta, about 1861. The shortened form appears in the 1916 *Report of the Joint Commission on the Book of Common Prayer Appointed by the General Convention of 1913* [American], p. 31.

Henry Eyster Jacobs, in Common Service Book.

29. For Missionary Work

Almighty God, heavenly Father, who through thy Son Jesus Christ hast given commandment unto thy people to go into all the world and preach the Gospel to every creature: Grant us a ready will to obey thy word; and as we have entered into the labors of other men, help us to serve thee, that others may enter into our labors; and that we with them, and they with us, may attain unto everlasting life; through the same Jesus Christ, thy Son, our Lord.

30. For the Heathen

Aeterne Deus omnium rerum Creator, memento infidelium animas te solum creasse, quas ad imaginem et similitudinem tuam fecisti. Ecce domine in opprobrium tuum eis ipsis implentur inferni. Memento, domine, IESV Christi filij tui, qui sanguinem suum tam

O God of all the nations of the earth, remember the multitudes of the heathen, who, though created in thine image, are ignorant of thy love; and according to the propitiation of thy Son Jesus Christ grant that by the prayers and labors of thy holy Church,

liberaliter effundens, pro illis passus est. Ne permittas domine eundem filium tuum dominum nostrum a paganis amplius contemni, sed precibus sanctorum electorum tuorum et Ecclesiae beatissimae eiusdem filij tuae sponsae placatus, recordare misericordiae tuae, et oblitus idolatriae et infidelitatis eorum, fac vt ipsi quoque agnoscant quem misisti IESVM Christum filium tuum dominum nostrum, qui est salus, vita et resurrectio nostra, per quem saluati et liberati sumus, cui sit gloria per infinita saeculorum saecula.

St. Francis Xavier. Written at Goa, *ca.* 1548. Text in *Epistolae*, t. I (*Monumenta historica Societatis Iesu*, Vol. 67), pp. 460-62.

O God, the God of Abraham, look upon Thine everlasting covenant; cause the captivity of Judah and of Israel to return. They were Thy people; O be Thou their Saviour! and may all who love Jerusalem and mourn for her, rejoice with her, for Jesus Christ's sake, their Saviour and ours.

Bishop Thomas Wilson, *Sacra Privata*. (Based on Gen. 17:7; Isa. 46:11).

Almighty God, our heavenly Father, who in thy goodness hast caused the light of the Gospel to shine in our land; Extend thy mercy, we beseech thee, to the nations of the world that still walk in darkness. Enlighten the Moslems with the knowledge of thy truth; and grant that the Gospel of salvation may be made known in all lands, that the heart of the peoples may be turned unto thee, through Jesus Christ our Lord.

Book of Common Prayer (Scotland) 1912, p. 51.

New. Paul Zeller Strodach. Based on the Mozarabic (*See* Bright, *Ancient Collects*, p. 19).

they may be delivered from all superstition and unbelief, and brought to worship thee; through him whom thou hast sent to be our salvation, the Resurrection and the Life of all the faithful, the same thy Son, Jesus Christ our Lord.

31. *For the Jews*

O God, the God of Abraham, look upon thine everlasting covenant, and cause the captivity of Judah and Israel to return. They are thy people; O be thou their Saviour, that all who love Jerusalem and mourn for her may rejoice with her, for Jesus Christ's sake, their Saviour and ours.

32. *For Islam*

Almighty God, our heavenly Father, who in thy goodness hast caused the light of the Gospel to shine in our land: Extend thy mercy, we beseech thee, to the nations of the world that still walk in darkness. Enlighten the Moslems with the knowledge of thy truth; and grant that the Gospel of salvation may be made known in every land, that the hearts of all people may be turned unto thee; through Jesus Christ our Lord.

33. *For the Consummation*

O Lord Jesus Christ, who wilt come again in glory and bring in thine eternal reign: Establish us in the Faith, and by thy might defend us amid the

591

temptations and cares of this life; that in steadfast devotion we may look for the consummation of thy glorious kingdom; who livest and reignest with the Father and the Holy Ghost, one God, world without end.

INTERCESSIONS

Pareillement, O Dieu de toute consolation, nous te recommandons tous ceux que tu visite et chastie, par croix et tribulation, soit par paouvreté, ou prison, ou maladie, ou banissement, ou autre calamité de corps, ou affliction d'esprit, que tu leur vueille faire congnoistre et entendre ton affection paternelle, qui est de les chastier pour leur amendement afin que de tout leur coeur ilz se convertissent a toy, et enstans convertis receoyvent entiere consolation, et soyent delivrez de tous maulx.

John Calvin, from the Great Prayer in his *La manyere de faire prieres aux eglises francoyses . . .* (1542). The prayer is based on Bucer's *Psalme vnd geystliche Lieder . . .* Strasbourg (1537). The translation is that of *The Book of Common Worship* (Presbyterian Church U.S.A.) (1906).

Omnipotens sempiterne Deus, moestorum consolatio, laborantium fortitudo, perveniant ad te preces de quacumque tribulatione clamantium, ut omnes sibi in necessitatibus suis misericordiam tuam gaudeant adfuisse. Per Dominum.

Gelasian (Wilson, p. 76) (Good Friday).

Translated by Eric Milner-White, *The Occasional Prayers in the 1928 Book Reconsidered* (London, 1930), p. 25. The last sentence of the translation is from the Liturgy of St. Mark.

Respice domine de celo & vide &

34. *For Those in Affliction and Sorrow*

God of all comfort, we commend to thy mercy all those upon whom any cross or tribulation is laid : the nations which are afflicted with famine, pestilence, or war; those of our brethren who suffer persecution for the sake of the Gospel; all such as are in danger by sea or land or in the air; and all persons oppressed with poverty, sickness, or any infirmity of body or sorrow of mind. We pray particularly for the sick and afflicted members of this church, and for those who desire to be remembered in our prayers (and for any such known to ourselves, whom we name in our hearts before thee). May it please thee to show them thy fatherly kindness, chastening them for their good, that their hearts may turn unto thee, and receive perfect consolation, and deliverance from all their troubles; for the sake of Christ our Lord.

35. *For Those in Affliction*

Almighty and everlasting God, the comfort of the sad, the strength of them that suffer: Let the prayers of thy children who cry out of any tribulation come unto thee; and unto every soul that is distressed grant thou mercy, grant relief, grant refreshment; through Jesus Christ, our Lord.

36. *For Those in Affliction*

O Lord, look down from heaven, be-

visita hunc famulum tuum N . . . Respice super eum domine oculis misericordie tue: & reple eum omni gaudio & letitia et timore tuo. Expelle ab eo omnes inimici insidias: et mitte angelum pacis qui eum custodiat & domum istam in pace perpetua. Per dominum nostrum.

Sarum. Translated in the *Book of Common Prayer* (1549), (The Order for the visitacion of the sicke, and the Communion of the same).

Omnipotens sempiterne Deus, salus aeterna credentium, exaudi nos pro famulis tuis *Illis,* pro quibus misericordiae tuae imploramus auxilium; ut reddita sibi sanitate gratiarum tibi in ecclesia tua referant actionem. Per.

Gelasian (Wilson, p. 282). Translation from the *Church Book* (1878).

Deus qui caritatis dona per gratiam sancti spiritus. tuorum cordibus fidelium infudisti. da famulis tuis pro quibus tuam deprecamur clementiam. salutem mentis et corporis. ut te tota uirtute diligant. et que tibi pracita sunt. tota dilectione perficiant. per.

Gregorian (Wilson, p. 193)
Translation from Common Service (1888).

O God, our heavenly Father, who hast set the solitary in families: look in favour, we beseech Thee, upon the homes of Thy people. Defend them against all evil, and supply all their needs according to the riches of Thy grace. Make them sanctuaries of purity and peace, love and joy. Bless all dear to us wheresoever they are, and grant that they and we may follow Thee at every step of our daily life, that, though our paths may lead us far from one another, we may all abide within the safe shelter of Thy love; through Jesus Christ our Lord.

Church of Scotland, *Book of Common Order* (1940), p. 300.

hold, visit and relieve thy servants, for whom we offer our supplications; look upon them with the eyes of thy mercy; give them comfort and sure confidence in thee; defend them from the danger of the enemy, and keep them in perpetual peace and safety; through Jesus Christ, thy Son, our Lord.

37. *For the Sick*
Almighty, everlasting God, the eternal Salvation of them that believe: Hear our prayers in behalf of thy servants who are sick, for whom we implore the aid of thy mercy; that being restored to health, they may render thanks to thee in thy Church; through Jesus Christ, thy Son, our Lord.

38. *For Friends*
O God, who through the grace of the Holy Spirit, dost pour the gifts of thy love into the hearts of the faithful: Grant unto all our friends, for whom we entreat thy clemency, health of mind and body; so that they may love thee with all their strength, and in gladness accomplish all things pleasing unto thee; through Jesus Christ, thy Son, our Lord.

39. *For Home and Kindred*
O God, our heavenly Father, look in favor, we beseech thee, upon the homes of thy people defend them against all evil, and supply all their needs according to the riches of thy grace; make them sanctuaries of purity and peace, love and joy. Bless all dear to us wheresoever they are, and grant that they and we may follow thee at every step of our daily life; that, though our paths may lead us far from one another, we may all abide within the safe shelter of thy love through Jesus Christ, thy Son, our Lord.

Eric Milner-White, *The Occasional Prayers in the 1928 Book Reconsidered,* p. 15.

40. *For Children*

O Heavenly Father, who long ago didst watch thy Son on earth grow as in stature so in wisdom and in perfect love of thee: Teach, by the wondrous tale of Jesus and his Church, the children whom thou watchest now; that they may grow into his likeness, loving thee, obedient to thy will, and happy in thy House; through the same Jesus Christ our Lord.

Heavenly Father, from whom all fatherhood in heaven and earth is named: bless, we beseech thee, all children, and give to their parents, and to all in whose charge they may be, thy Spirit of wisdom and love; so that the home in which they grow up may be to them an image of thy Kingdom, and the care of their parents a likeness of thy love.

41. *For Our Children*

Heavenly Father, from whom all fatherhood in heaven and earth is named: Bless, we beseech thee, all children, and give to their fathers and mothers the spirit of wisdom and love; so that the homes in which they grow up may be to them an image of thy kingdom, and the care of their parents a likeness of thy love; through our Lord Jesus Christ.

Leslie Stannard Hunter, bishop of Sheffield, in *New Every Morning* (London: British Broadcasting Corporation, 1936), p. 42.

New. Paul Zeller Strodach

42. *For the Sanctity of Marriage*

O Lord God, who didst institute matrimony in Eden: Preserve in our land the sanctity of the marriage bond; that those who enter therein may in honor and fidelity to each other be enriched with thy blessing; through Jesus Christ, thy Son, our Lord.

Church of Scotland, *Book of Common Order* (1940), p. 59.

43. *Thanksgiving for the Faithful Departed*

With reverence and affection we remember before thee, O everlasting God, all our friends and kindred who have passed within the veil. Keep us in union with them here, through faith and love towards thee, that hereafter we may enter into thy blessed presence, and be numbered with those who serve thee and behold thy face, in glory everlasting; through Jesus Christ our Lord, unto whom with thee and the Holy Spirit, be glory and praise, now and forevermore.

O God, Who hast brought us near to an innumerable company of Angels, and to the spirits of just men made perfect; grant us during our pilgrimage to abide in their fellowship, and in our Country to become partakers of their joy; through Jesus Christ our Lord.

William Bright, *Ancient Collects,* p. 236.

44. *For the Fellowship of Saints*

O God, who hast brought us near to an innumerable company of angels, and to the spirits of just men made perfect: Grant us during our earthly pilgrimage to abide in their fellowship and in our heavenly country to become partakers of their joy; through Jesus Christ our Lord.

NATION AND WORLD

45. *For the Nation*

O God, Who in this land hast made the people the ministers of Thy just rule: So turn their hearts unto Thee, that holding their citizenship as a trust from Thee, they may guard, defend and use it according to Thy will, and that, serving Thee with willing, joyful and obedient hearts, they may cherish their freedom as a blessing of Thy Gospel, and strive to bring it unto all peoples; through Jesus Christ, Thy Son, our Lord.

O God, who in this land hast made the people the ministers of thy just rule: So turn their hearts unto thee that, holding their citizenship as a sacred trust, they may guard, defend and use it according to thy will; and that, serving thee with willing, joyful and obedient hearts, they may cherish their freedom as a blessing of thy Gospel, and strive to bring it unto all peoples through Jesus Christ, thy Son, our Lord.

Henry Eyster Jacobs, 1917, in Common Service Book (Word Edition, 1919).

Paul Zeller Strodach, 1917, in Common Service **Book.**

46. *For Our Nation*

O God, who by thy Providence didst lead our forefathers to this land wherein they found refuge from oppression and freedom to worship thee: We beseech thee ever to guide our Nation in the way of thy truth and peace, so that we may never fail in the blessing which thou hast promised to that people whose God is the Lord; through Jesus Christ our Lord.

47. *For Our Country*

Henry Eyster Jacobs, 1917, in Common Service **Book.**

Almighty God, who hast given us a land wherein we are free to read and hear thy word, to confess thy Name, and to labor together for the extension of thy kingdom: Grant, we beseech thee, that the liberty vouchsafed unto us may be continued to our children, and our children's children; and that the power of the Gospel may here abound to the blessing of all the nations of the earth, and to thine eternal glory; through Jesus Christ our Lord.

Almighty and Everlasting God, we humbly implore Thee graciously to regard the President of the United States, his counsellors, and all others in authority over us, that, guided by Thy Holy Spirit, they may be high in purpose, wise in counsel, unwavering in duty, and in the administration of their solemn charge may wholly serve Thy will, uphold the honor of our Nation, secure the protection of our people, and bring victory to our righteous cause; through Jesus Christ, Thy Son, our Lord.

Paul Zeller Strodach, in Common Service Book (Word Edition, 1919).

Henry Eyster Jacobs, 1917, in Common Service Book (Word Edition, 1919).

Luther Dotterer Reed, in *Collects and Prayers for Use in Church,* p. 141.

48. *For the President and Those in Authority*

Almighty and everlasting God, we humbly implore thee graciously to regard the President of the United States, his counselors, and all others in authority over us; that, guided by thy Holy Spirit, they may be high in purpose, wise in counsel, and unwavering in duty; and in the administration of their solemn charge may wholly serve thy will, uphold the honor of our Nation, secure the protection of our people, and set forward every righteous cause; through Jesus Christ, thy Son, our Lord.

49. *For Those in Our Country's Service in Time of War*

Almighty God, our heavenly Father, let thy protection be upon all those who are in the service of our Country; guard them from all harm and danger of body and soul; sustain and comfort those at home, especially in their hours of loneliness, anxiety, and sorrow; prepare the dying for death and the living for thy service; give success to our arms on land and sea and in the air; and grant unto us and all nations a speedy, just and lasting peace, to the glory of thy Name and the coming of thy kingdom; through Jesus Christ our Lord.

50. *For the Armed Forces of the Nation (For Those in the Service)*

Almighty and everlasting God, whose Providence hath given us as a people this great land stored with treasure and around it hath cast like a mantle the sea: Bless, we pray thee, the officers and men of our armed forces as they perform the duties of their calling; give them not only true love of Country, but also love of thee, and understanding of thy love for all mankind; so that, relying upon thine almighty aid, they may promote righteousness, honor, and unity among our people in time of peace, and be a means of fostering mutual respect and understanding among the peoples of the world; through Jesus Christ our Lord.

O eternall Lord God, who alone spreadest out the Heavens, and rulest the raging of the Sea; who hast compassed the waters with bounds vntill day and night come to an end: be pleased to receive into thy Almighty and most gracious protection, the persons of vs thy servants, and the Fleet in which we serve: Preserve vs from the dangers of the sea, and from the violence of the enemy, that we may be a safeguard vnto our most gracious Soveraigne Lord King Charles, and his kingdoms, and a security for such as pass on the seas vpon their lawfull occasions. That the Inhabitants of our Island may in peace and quietness serve thee our God, and that we may return in safety to enjoy the blessings of the Land, with the fruits of our labours: and with a thankfull remembrance of thy mercies, to praise and glorifie thy holy name through Jesus Christ our Lord.

Book of Common Prayer (1662), Forms of Prayer to be Used at Sea. Possibly by Bishop Sanderson, 1661. Present form from the revision of 1928, Eric Milner-White substituting for the long conclusion a single sentence from Jeremy Taylor's *Devotions for Several Occasions.*

51. *For Seafarers*
O Eternal Lord God, who alone spreadest out the heavens and rulest the raging of the sea: Be pleased to receive into thy protection all those who go down to the sea in ships and do business in great waters. Make thou their voyages safe to their persons and their goods (especially in this present storm); and be thyself their way and light till journeying shall end; through Jesus Christ our Lord.

52. *For Chaplains and Those Who Minister to the Sick and Wounded*
O Most merciful Father, who dost commit to our love and care our fellow men in their necessities: Graciously be with and prosper all those who are seeking and ministering to the sick and wounded; let their ministry be abundantly blessed in bringing ease to the suffering, comfort to the sorrowing, and peace to the dying; and let them know that inasmuch as they do it unto the least of these, Christ's brethren, they do it unto him, who liveth and reigneth with thee and the Holy Ghost, one God, world without end.

O Most Merciful Father, Who dost commit to our love and care our fellowmen in their necessities: Graciously be with and prosper all those who are seeking and ministering to the sick and wounded; let their ministry be abundantly blessed in bringing ease to the suffering, comfort to the sorrowing, and peace to the dying, knowing that inasmuch as they do it unto the least of these, Christ's brethren, they do it unto Him, Who liveth and reigneth with Thee and the Holy Ghost, ever One God, world without end.

597

Paul Zeller Strodach, 1917, in Common Service Book (Word Edition, 1919).

William Bellars.

O God, our Refuge and Strength, our very present help in trouble: Protect and prosper, we beseech Thee, our beloved Country in this time of war; make us, by Thy grace, a people worthy to be entrusted with victory; and so use, direct and bless our Army and Navy that they may be Thy chosen instruments in overcoming wrong and establishing liberty, truth and righteousness in the earth; through Jesus Christ, Thy Son, our Lord.

Luther Dotterer Reed, 1917, in common Service Book (Word Edition, 1919).

O Almighty Lord God, who alone riddest away the tyrants of this world by thine everlasting determination, and stillest the noise and tumult of the people; Stir up thy great strength, we beseech thee, and come and help us, and by the breath of thy vengeance scatter the counsels of them that secretly devise mischief, and bring thou their violent dealings to naught; that the land may have rest before thee, and that all the people may praise thee, O God, who only hast been our Deliverer, and only canst be our Help and our Shield, both now and evermore.

Book of Common Prayer as amended by the Westminster Divines (1661), ed. Charles W. Shields (1864), p. 347. Latter portion amended from the shortened form in *The Book of Common Worship* (1906), p. 127.

53. *For the Bereaved*

Have compassion, O Lord, upon all who mourn and upon all who are lonely and desolate; be thou their Comforter and Friend; give them such earthly solace as thou seekest to be best for them; bring them to fuller knowledge of thy love, and wipe away all their tears; for the sake of Jesus Christ our Lord.

54. *For Victory*

O God, our refuge and strength, our very present help in trouble: Protect and prosper, we beseech thee, our beloved Country in this time of war; make of us, by thy grace, a people worthy to be entrusted with victory; and so use, direct and bless our armed forces that they may be thy servants in overcoming wrong and establishing liberty, truth and righteousness in the earth; through Jesus Christ, thy Son, our Lord.

55. *Against Evildoers*

O Lord God Almighty, who alone riddest away tyrants and stillest the noise and tumult of the people: Scatter, we beseech thee, the counsels of them that secretly devise mischief, and bring the dealings of the violent to naught; cast down the unjust from high places and cause the unruly to cease from troubling; put down all envious and malicious passions and subdue the haters and evil-doers, that the whole world may have rest before thee, and that all nations may serve thee; through Jesus Christ our Lord.

O Almechtiger Herr Gott hymlischer Vater/ von dem wir on vnterlass allerlay guts ganz vberflüssig empfahen/ vnd täglich vor allem vbel statlich vnd gnedigklich behütet werden/ Wir bitten dich/ gib vns durch deinen gayst/ sollichs alles mit gantzem hertzen in rechtem glauben zuerkennen/ auff das wir deiner milten gütte vnd barmhertzigkeyt/ hie vnd dort ewigklich dancken vnd dich loben/ Durch . . .

Brandenburg-Nuremberg (1533), XLIV, b.

Eric Milner-White, *Memorials upon Several Occasions* (London, 1933), No. 7b.

56. *National Thanksgiving*

Almighty God, our heavenly Father, whose mercies are new unto us every morning, and who, though we have in no wise deserved thy goodness, dost abundantly provide for all our wants of body and soul: Give us, we pray thee, thy Holy Spirit, that we may heartily acknowledge thy merciful goodness toward us, give thanks for all thy benefits, and serve thee in willing obedience; through Jesus Christ, thy Son, our Lord.

57. *For Peace*

O God, who wouldst fold both heaven and earth in a single peace: Let the design of thy great love lighten upon the waste of our wraths and sorrows; and give peace to thy Church, peace among nations, peace in our dwellings, and peace in our hearts; through thy Son, our Saviour, Jesus Christ.

Emil E. Fischer, in *Collects and Prayers for Use in Church*, p. 143.

58. *For Peace*

O God, the Father in heaven: Grant thy mighty aid to the efforts of men to establish peace among the nations of the world. Give strength of purpose to those who lead; enlighten those who sit in council; and so transform the hearts of men everywhere by thy gracious Gospel, that they may exalt peace above war, service above gain, and righteousness above glory; through Jesus Christ our Lord.

59. *For Peace*

Eternal Father, Who in the sending of Thy Son, Jesus Christ, our Lord, didst speak Peace to the world, and in the Blood of His Cross hast opened to all mankind the Way to peace with Thee: Turn all men to the Cross, and fire every heart with Thy Holy Spirit that all may accept in Christ the way of life, that following His holy example and burning with His zeal of service, all men may become one brotherhood in Him, and Thy peace possess every heart and rule in all the nations of the world; through the same Jesus Christ, Thy Son, our Lord.

Eternal Father, who in the sending of thy Son didst speak peace to the world, and in the Blood of his Cross hast opened to all mankind the way to peace with thee: Turn all men to the Cross, that, following his holy example and burning with his zeal of service, they may become one brotherhood in him, and his peace possess every heart and rule in all the nations of the world; through the same Jesus Christ, thy Son, our Lord.

Paul Zeller Strodach, in Common Service Book (Word Edition, 1919).

O God, who hast made man in Thine own likeness and who dost love all whom Thou hast made, teach us the unity of Thy family and the breadth of Thy love. By the example of Thy Son, Jesus our Saviour, enable us, while loving and serving our own, to enter into the fellowship of the whole human family; and forbid that, from pride of race or hardness of heart, we should despise any for whom Christ died, or injure any in whom He lives.

Mornay Williams (d. 1926), American attorney, in *Book of Common Worship Revised* (Presbyterian U.S.A.) (1932), p. 182.

60. *For Brotherhood*

O God, who hast made man in thine own likeness, and who dost love all whom thou hast made: Teach us the unity of thy family and the breadth of thy love. By the example of thy Son, Jesus Christ our Saviour, enable us, while loving and serving our own, to enter into the fellowship of the whole human family; and forbid that, from pride of race or hardness of heart, we should despise any for whom he died, or injure any in whom he lives; through the same Jesus Christ our Lord. *Amen.*

Almighty Father, Who has so formed man for Thyself that his heart is restless until it finds rest in Thee: By the ministry of Thy Church and the lives of those who humbly love and follow Thee daily, convince the world that Thou art the sure refuge of all who are weary and distressed in mind and life, the safe Harbor to all who are restlessly seeking certainty and peace of heart, and the eternal Salvation of every burdened soul; so that coming to Thee they may find and possess that peace which Thou givest in Thy Son, our Saviour, Jesus Christ.

Paul Zeller Strodach, in *Collects and Prayers for Use in Church*, p. 17.

61. *For the Church and the World*

Almighty Father, who hast so formed man for thyself that his heart is restless till it find rest in thee: By the ministry of thy Church and the lives of those who humbly love and follow thee, convince the world that thou art the sure refuge of all who are weary and distressed in mind and body, the safe harbor for all who seek certainty and peace of heart, and the eternal salvation of every burdened soul; through Jesus Christ our Lord

SOCIETY AND COMMUNITY

O Father of men, who hast promised that the kingdom of this world shall become the Kingdom of thy Son: purge the nations of error and corruption; overthrow the power of sin, and establish the Kingdom of grace in every land. Incline the hearts of all rulers and

62. *For All People*

O God our Father, who hast promised that the kingdoms of this world shall become the kingdom of thy Son: Purge the nations of error and corruption; overthrow the power of sin, and establish the kingdom of grace in every land; incline the hearts of all peoples to the Lord of lords and King of glory, that he may enter into their cities, churches, and homes, to dwell there, and govern all things by his Word and Spirit.

New Every Morning (1936), p. 85.

O heavenly Father: we thank thee for those who, out of the bitter memories of strife and loss, are seeking a more excellent way for the nations of the world, whereby justice and order may be maintained and the differences of peoples be resolved in equity. We pray thee to establish their purpose on sure foundations and to prosper their labours, that thy will may be done; for the sake of Jesus Christ our Lord.

New Every Morning (1936), p. 113 Present version from F. A. Iremonger, *Each Returning Day,* p. 10.

O Lord, who hast set before us the great hope that thy kingdom shall come, and hast taught us to pray for its coming: give us grace to discern the signs of its dawning, and to work for the perfect day when thy will shall be done on earth as it is in heaven; through Jesus Christ our Lord.

Canon Percy Dearmer (*See* Frederick B. Macnutt, *The Prayer Manual* [London, 1951], p. 168).

Eric Milner-White, *A Cambridge Bede Book* (London, 1936), p. 27.

O God, at Whose Word chaos became an ordered creation: Brood over this troubled world, as once Thy Spirit brooded o'er the face of the deep, and create in the nations, by the grace of Thy Son, that love for Thee and for

rulers and peoples to the Lord of lords and King of glory, that he may enter into their cities, churches and homes, to dwell there and govern all things by his word and Holy Spirit; through Jesus Christ our Lord.

63. *For Those Who Seek Peace*

O Heavenly Father, we thank thee for all those who, even at this time of strife and loss, are seeking a more excellent way for the nations of the world, whereby justice and order may be established and the differences of peoples be resolved in equity. We pray thee to set their purpose on sure foundations and to prosper their labors, that thy will may be done; for the sake of Jesus Christ our Lord.

64. *For the Kingdom*

O Lord, who hast set before us a great hope that thy kingdom shall come on earth, and hast taught us to pray for its coming: Make us ever ready to thank thee for the signs of its dawning, and to pray and work for the perfect day when thy will shall be done, on earth as it is in heaven; who livest and reignest with the Father and the Holy Ghost, one God, world without end.

65. *For World Peace*

We beseech thee, O Lord our God, to set the peace of heaven within the hearts of men, that it may bind the nations also in a covenant which cannot be broken; through Jesus Christ our Lord.

66. *For the New World*

O God, at whose word chaos became an ordered creation: Brood over this troubled world as once thy Spirit moved upon the face of the waters, and create in the nations such love for thee and for each other, that this

601

each other, which will make this world a new creation in righteousness and peace and joy, in brotherhood and mutual service; through the saving merit of the same Thy Son, Jesus Christ, our Lord.

Paul Zeller Strodach, in *Collects and Prayers for Use in Church,* p. 143.

O God, Who through the gift of Thy Holy Spirit hast established the Church in this community: Grant unto all who have been converted unto Thee such a knowledge of Thy will and trust in Thy grace that they may truly exemplify the life that they profess, and by their good works enable men to glorify Thee, the only true God; through Jesus Christ, our Lord.

Emil E. Fischer, in *Collects and Prayers for Use in Church,* p. 18.

Book of Common Prayer (American, 1928), p. 43. By Bishop E. L. Parsons of California (?)

O eternal God, the Father of our Lord Jesus Christ, who didst call Phoebe and Dorcas into the service of thy Church, look upon *these thy servants* who *are* now to be set apart to the office of Deaconess, and grant *them* thy Holy Spirit, that *they* may worthily discharge the work committed to *them,* to the blessing of mankind and the praise of thy Christ, our adorable Saviour.

world may be a new creation in righteousness, peace and brotherhood: through thy Son, Jesus Christ our Lord.

67. *The Church and the Community*

O God, who through the gift of thy Holy Spirit hast established the Church in this place: Grant unto all who have been converted unto thee such a knowledge of thy will and trust in thy grace that they may truly exemplify the life they profess, and by their good works enable men to glorify thee, the only true God; through Jesus Christ our Lord.

68. *Christian Service (Social Missions)*

O Lord, our heavenly Father, whose blessed Son came not to be ministered unto, but to minister: We beseech thee to bless all who, following in his steps, give themselves to the service of their fellow men. Endue them with wisdom, patience, and courage to strengthen the weak and raise up those who fall; that, being inspired by thy love, they may worthily minister in thy Name to the suffering, the friendless, and the needy; for the sake of him who laid down his life for us, thy Son our Saviour, Jesus Christ.

69. *For Deaconesses*

O God, the Father of Jesus Christ our Lord, who in olden time didst call holy women to the service of thy Church: Let thy blessing rest upon all who are set apart for the work of serving love; grant them knowledge of thy Gospel, sincerity of purpose, true diligence in service, and beauty of life in Christ; that many souls may rise up to bless them, and that thy holy Name may be glorified; through the same thy Son, Jesus Christ our Lord.

The Ritual of the Methodist Episcopal Church, 1916, Order for the Consecration of Deaconesses, p. 129; based on a prayer mentioning Old Testament women in the 1908 Ritual. Latter portion expanded to nearly present form in the *Book of Worship,* 1944, p. 452.

70. *For Compassion (For a Social Conscience)*

O God, our King, who hast called us through Jesus Christ to be kings and priests unto thee: teach us to bear one another's burdens and the burdens of the commonwealth. Open the eyes of us all to see the woes of our land, the despair in the lives of many of our fellow-citizens, the deep and shameful wrongs that cry to be put right. Give to us also a vision of our land as thou wouldest have it be, and as thou alone canst remake it. Take us, we humbly beseech thee, to be thy servants, giving us no rest or discharge until thou hast wrought this work of pity, that generations yet unborn may praise thy name.

O God our King, who hast called us through Jesus Christ to be kings and priests unto thee: Teach us to bear one another's burdens and the burdens of the commonwealth. Open our eyes to see the woes of our land, the despair in the lives of many, and the deep and shameful wrongs that cry to be put right. Give to us also a vision of our land as thou wouldst have it be, and as thou alone canst fashion it. Make us thy servants, giving us no rest or discharge until thou hast wrought this work of compassion, that generations yet unborn may praise thy Name. We ask this for Jesus Christ's sake.

New Every Morning (1936), p. 46.

71. *For the Relations of Men to One Another*

O God, the King of righteousness, lead us, we pray thee, in the ways of justice and of peace; inspire us to break down all tyranny and oppression, to gain for every man his due reward, and from every man his due service; that each may live for all, and all may care for each, in the name of Jesus Christ our Lord.

O God, the King of righteousness, lead us, we pray thee, in the ways of justice and of peace; inspire us to break down all oppression and wrong, to gain for every man his due reward, and from every man his due service; that each may live for all, and all may care for each; in the Name of Jesus Christ our Lord.

William Temple, in *Life and Liberty:* a *Call to Prayer* (London, 1918), p. 13. Present form from E. Milner-White, *The Occasional Prayers in the 1928 Book Reconsidered.*

72. *For Industrial Peace*

O God, who in thy providence hast appointed to every man his work; Assuage, we humbly beseech thee, all strife and contention between those who are engaged in the labours of industry and those who employ their

O God, who in thy providence dost appoint to every man his work: We humbly beseech thee to still all strife and contention amongst those who are engaged in industry (*especially those who are now at variance*); defend them

603

labour; deliver both masters and workmen from all greed and covetousness; and grant that they, seeking only that which is just and equal, may live and work together in brotherly union and concord, to their own well-being, and the prosperity of this realm; through Jesus Christ our Lord.

Bishop John Dowden, in *Book of Common Prayer* (Scotland, 1912), p. 60. Present form based on that of *Book of Common Prayer* (Canada, 1918).

Prosper our industries, we pray thee, God most high, that our land may be full with all manner of store, and there be no complaining in our streets: and, as thy glorious Son our Lord plied tool and trade on earth, so give to all that labour pride in their work, a just reward, and joy both in supplying need and serving thee; through the same Jesus Christ our Lord.

Eric Milner-White, *The Occasional Prayers in the 1928 Book Reconsidered,* p. 22.

O God, who in thy love hast bestowed upon us gifts such as our fathers never knew nor dreamed of: Mercifully grant that we be not so occupied with material things that we forget the things which are spiritual; lest, having gained the whole world, we lose our own soul; for thy mercy's sake.

Eric Milner-White, *Daily Prayer* (London, 1941), p. 75.
(Phil. 3:19; Mark 8:36)

O Jesus Christ, Son of the Highest, Who camest to give light to all that are in darkness; fill us with Thine own infinite love for men; and, since Thou hast entrusted to us both the knowledge of Thy truth and the gifts of Thy bounty, help us to use them as good stewards, giving liberally, praying instantly, and working diligently, that we may be sharers in bringing all men to

from all greed and covetousness, and grant that they, seeking only that which is just, may live and work together in brotherly unity and concord, to their own well-being, and the prosperity of this land; through Jesus Christ our Lord.

73. *For the Labors of Men*
Prosper our industries, we pray thee, God most high, that our land may be full with all manner of store, and there be no complaining in our streets; and, as thy Son our Lord plied tools on earth, so give to all that labor pride in their work, a just reward, and joy both in supplying need and serving thee; through the same Jesus Christ our Lord.

74. *The Perils of Abundance*
O God, who in thy love hast bestowed upon us gifts such as our fathers neither knew nor dreamed of: Mercifully grant that we be not so occupied with material things that we forget the things which are spiritual; lest, having gained the whole world, we lose our own soul; for thy mercy's sake.

75. *For the Right Use of Wealth*
O God, who in thine infinite love hast entrusted to us both the knowledge of thy truth and the gifts of thy bounty: Help us to use them as good stewards, giving liberally, praying instantly, and working diligently, that we may share in bringing all men to thy truth and in hastening the coming of thy kingdom; through Jesus Christ our Lord.

Thy light and hastening the coming of Thy kingdom; Who with the Father, in the unity of the Spirit, livest and reignest, God, for ever and ever.

Church of Scotland, *Prayers for the Christian Year* (Oxford, 1935), p. 12. A Collect for the Epiphany.

O Lord and heavenly Father, we commend to Thy care and protection the men and women of this land who are suffering distress and anxiety through lack of work. Strengthen and support them, we beseech Thee; and so prosper the counsels of those who govern and direct our industries, that Thy people may be set free from want and fear to work in peace and security, for the relief of their necessities and the well-being of this realm; through Jesus Christ our Lord.

Industrial Christian Fellowship (*See* F. B. Macnutt, *The Prayer Manual,* p. 198).

Almighty God, who hast blessed the earth that it should be fruitful and bring forth abundantly whatsoever is needful for the life of man: bless us in all our labours, and grant us such seasonable weather that we may gather in the fruits of the earth, and ever rejoice in thy goodness, to the praise of thy holy Name; through Jesus Christ our Lord.

Prayer Book Commissioners of 1689, the Collect proposed for Easter V. Used in *Book of Common Prayer* (American, 1885), dropped 1928.

O Almighty God, who hast created the earth for man, and man for thy glory: Mercifully hear the supplications of thy people, and be mindful of thy covenant; that both the earth may yield her increase, and the good seed of thy word may bring forth abundantly, to the glory of thy holy Name; through Jesus Christ our Lord.

Bishop John Dowden, in *Book of Common Prayer* (Scotland, 1912), p. 50.

76. *For the Unemployed*

O Lord, our heavenly Father, we commend to thy protecting care and compassion the men and women of our land now suffering distress and anxiety through lack of work. Support and strengthen them, we beseech thee; and so prosper the counsels of those who order our common life, that thy people may be set free from want and fear, and be enabled to work in security and peace, for the relief of their necessities, and for the well-being of our land; through Jesus Christ our Lord.

77. *For the Fruits of the Earth*

Almighty God, who hast blessed the earth that it should be fruitful and bring forth abundantly whatsoever is needful for the life of man: Prosper, we beseech thee, the labors of the husbandman, and grant such seasonable weather that we may gather in the fruits of the earth, and ever rejoice in thy goodness, to the praise of thy holy Name; through Jesus Christ our Lord.

78. *For the Fruits of the Earth*

O Almighty God, who hast created the earth for man, and man for thy glory: Mercifully hear the supplications of thy people, and be mindful of thy covenant; that the earth may yield her increase, and the good seed bring forth abundantly, to the glory of thy holy Name; through Jesus Christ our Lord.

MORNING AND EVENING

Eric Milner-White, *The Occasonal Prayers in the 1928 Book Reconsidered,* p. 11.

79. *For the Right Use of the Lord's Day*

Lord, who dost ask of thy people love for love, and worship in return for life: Assist us to keep holy, week by week, the day of thy Son's mighty rising from the dead, and bless us in the breaking of the bread and the prayers; that other thy children who behold our joy may seek thy lovingkindness in the midst of thy temple through the same Jesus Christ our Lord.

80. *Morning*

Grant us, O Lord, to pass this day in gladness and peace, without stumbling and without stain, that reaching the eventide victorious over all temptation through thy ever present aid, we may praise thee, the eternal God, who dost govern all things and art blessed for evermore; through Jesus Christ, thy Son, our Lord.

Manè, Dómine, orátio nostra pervéniat ad te. Quia suscepísti confractiônem fragilitâtis nostrae, concêde nobis diem istum jocúndum, pacíficum sine scándalo, sine mácula: sine ulla tentatiône adveniéntes ad vésperam, te collaudâmus regem aetérnum.

Mozarabic Breviary, first Collect of Lauds, Advent I (Migne, *PL,* t. LXXXVI, col. 58).
Translation based on Bright, *Ancient Collects,* p. 8.

81. *Morning*

O Lord, King of heaven and earth, may it please thee this day to order and hallow, to rule and govern our hearts and bodies, our thoughts, words and works, according to thy commandments; through Jesus Christ, thy Son, our Lord.

Dirigere et sanctificare, regere et gubernare dignare, Domine Deus, Rex caeli et terrae, hodie corda et corpora nostra, sensus, sermones et actus nostros in lege tua, et in operibus mandatorum tuorum: ut hic, et in aeternum, te auxiliante, salvi et liberi esse mereamur, Salvator mundi: Qui vivis et regnas in saecula saeculorum.

Breviarium Romanum (at Prime). Compare No. 105.

82. *Morning*

O God, Lord of all power and might, preserver of all thy creatures: Keep us this day in health of body and soundness of mind, in purity of heart and cheerfulness of spirit, in contentment with our lot and charity with our neighbor; and further all our lawful undertakings with thy blessing. In our labor strengthen us; in our pleasure purify us; in our difficulties direct us; in our perils defend us; in our troubles comfort us; and supply all our needs, ac-

O God, most holy, wise, and powerful Preserver and Governor of all Thy creatures and all their actions; Keep us this day in health of body and soundness of mind, in purity of heart and cheerfulness of spirit, in contentment with our lot and charity with our neighbour; and further all our lawful undertakings with Thy blessing. In our labour strengthen us: in our pleasure purify us: in our difficulties direct us: in our perils defend us: in our troubles comfort us: and supply all our needs, according to the riches of Thy grace in Christ Jesus our Lord.

Henry Van Dyke, chairman of the preparing committee, in *Book of Common Worship* (Presbyterian U.S.A., 1906), p. 22.
Based on Question 11, Shorter Catechism, Westminster Confession.
Present version is that of the *Book of Common Order* of the United Church of Canada (1932), p. 38.

O Lord God, in whose presence there is no darkness, for thou dwellest in unapproachable light, Keep and defend us and all thy saints, in soul and body, during the coming night, and in all the darkness of this mortal life.

May we rest in the assurance of thy favour; in the peace of a good conscience; in the hope of a better life; in the faith of thy providence and protection; and in the love of thy Spirit.

May we rise up again to be diligent in our several callings, working the work of God while the day lasts, remembering that the night cometh in which no man can work. And whether we wake or sleep, may we live together with Christ.

Dr. Robert Lee, *The Order for Public Worship* (1865) (written for the church of Greyfriars), p. 52.
Almost present form appears in the Church Service Society's *Euchologion* by 1890 (*See* 6th ed., p. 190).

O God, who hast drawn over weary day the restful veil of night, wrap our consciences in heavenly peace. Lift from our hands our tasks, and all through the night bear in Thy bosom the full weight of our burdens and sorrows, that in untroubled slumber we may press our weakness close to Thy strength, and win new power for the morrow's duty from Thee who givest Thy beloved sleep.

Charles H. Brent, Episcopal bishop of the Philippines, 1904. Published in his *With God in Prayer* (Philadelphia, 1907), p. 52.

cording to the riches of thy grace in Christ Jesus our Lord.

83. *Evening*

O God, with whom there is no darkness, but the night shineth as the day: Keep and defend us and all thy children, in soul and body, during the coming night. Make us to rest in the peace of a good conscience, in the hope of a better life, in the faith of thy providence, and in the comfort of thy love; through Jesus Christ our Lord.

84. *Evening*

O God, who hast drawn over weary day the restful veil of night, enfold us in thy heavenly peace. Lift from our hands our tasks, and bear in thy bosom the weight of our burdens and sorrows; that in untroubled slumber we may press our weariness close to thy strength, and win from thee new power for the morrow's labors; through Jesus Christ our Lord.

St. Augustine(?)

85. *Evening*

Watch thou, dear Lord, with those who wake, or watch, or weep tonight, and give thine angels charge over those who sleep. Tend thy sick ones, O Lord. Rest thy weary ones. Bless thy dying ones. Soothe thy suffering ones. Pity thine afflicted ones. Shield thy joyous ones. And grant all, for thy love's sake, in Jesus Christ our Lord.

Illumina, quaesumus, Domine, tenebras nostras, et totius noctis insidias repelle propitius. Per.

Gelasian (Wilson, p. 292). Translated in the *Book of Common Prayer* (1549), from Compline of the Sarum Breviary.

86. *Evening*

Lighten our darkness, we beseech thee, O Lord; and by thy great mercy defend us from all perils and dangers of this night; for the love of thy only Son, our Saviour, Jesus Christ, who liveth and reigneth with thee and the Holy Ghost, one God, world without end.

May he support us all the day long, till the shades lengthen and the evening comes, and the busy world is hushed, and the fever of life is over, and our work is done. Then in his mercy may he give us a safe lodging, and a holy rest, and peace at the last.

John Henry Newman, *Sermons on the Subjects of the Day,* No. XX, Feb. 19, 1843. Cast as a prayer by George W. Douglas, c. 1876.

87. *For Divine Protection*

O Lord, support us all the day long of this troublous life, until the shadows lengthen, and the evening comes, and the busy world is hushed, and the fever of life is over, and our work is done. Then in thy mercy, grant us a safe lodging and a holy rest, and peace at the last; through Jesus Christ our Lord.

SPIRITUAL GIFTS

O Herr Gott, himmlischer Vater, der Du Deinen eingebornen Sohn um unsrer Sünden willen dahingegeben und uns zur Gerechtigkeit wieder auferweckt hast: wir bitten Deine Barmherzigkeit, Du wollest unsere erstorbenen Herzen durch Deinen Geist zum neuen Leben erwecken und dort mit Christo ewig lebendig machen durch die Kraft der Auferstehung Deines Sohnes unsers Herrn Jesu Christi, der mit Dir in Einigkeit des heiligen Geistes, wahrer Gott, lebet und herrschet immer und ewiglich.

88. *For Spiritual Renewal*

O Lord God, heavenly Father, who hast given thine only Son to die for our sins, and to rise again for our justification: Quicken us, we beseech thee, by thy Holy Spirit, unto newness of life, that, through the power of his Resurrection, we may dwell with Christ forever; who liveth and reigneth with thee and the Holy Ghost, one God, world without end.

Loehe, *Agende,* 1853 (Easter). First part from Austria (1571) (CXL b), also in the *Book of Common Prayer* (1662).

89. *For Spiritual Renewal*

Almyghtye God whiche haste geuen vs thy onlye begotten sonne to take our nature vpon him, and this daye to bee borne of a pure vyrgyn: Graunte that we beying regenerate and made thy children by adoption and grace, maye dailye be renued by thy holy spirite, through thesame our Lorde Jesus Christe, who lyueth and reygneth, etc.

Almighty God, who hast given us thine only-begotten Son to take our nature upon him: Grant that we, being regenerate and made thy children by adoption and grace, may daily be renewed by thy Holy Spirit; through the same Jesus Christ, thy Son, our Lord.

Book of Common Prayer (1549) (Christmas, 2d. celebration).
Based on the Gelasian, which see above (p. 471).

90. *For the Holy Spirit*

Allmectiger Ewiger Gott/ der du durch deinen Sohn/ vergebung der Sünden/ Gerechtigkeit und Ewiges Leben uns hast verheissen/ Wir bitten dich/ du wöllest durch deinen heiligen Geist/ unsere Hertzen also führen und erwecken/ dass wir solche hülff durch täglichs Gebet/ und sonderlich in aller Anfechtung/ bey ihm suchen/ und durch ein rechten festen Glauben/ auff seine Zusagung und Wort/ gewiss finden und erlangen/ durch denselben deinen Sohn/ unsern Herrn Jesum Christum/ der mit dir/ und dem heiligen Geist/ lebet und regieret in Ewigkeit/.

Almighty and everlasting God, who of thy great mercy in Jesus Christ thy Son dost grant us forgiveness of sin, and all things pertaining to life and godliness: Grant us, we beseech thee, thy Holy Spirit, that we may strive to mortify the flesh and overcome the world; and, serving thee in holiness and pureness of living, may give thee continual thanks for all thy goodness; through the same Jesus Christ, thy Son, our Lord.

Brandenburg-Calenberg (1569), p. 136.

91. *For the Holy Spirit*

Herr Jhesu Christe/ du Son des almechtigen Gottes/ Wir bitten dich/ du wollest durch dein Wort/ deinen heiligen Geist in vnser hertze geben/ das derselbige vns regiere vnd füre/ nach deinem willen/ vns in allerley Anfechtung vnd Vnglück tröste/ in deiner Warheit wider allen Irthumb leite vnd erhalte/ auff das wir im glauben fest bestehen mügen/ in der liebe vnnd guten wercken zunemen/ vnnd durch eine gewisse hoffnung/ deiner erworbenen vnd geschenckten Gnaden/ ewig

Send, we beseech thee, Almighty God, thy Holy Spirit into our hearts, that he may rule and direct us according to thy will, comfort us in all our temptations and afflictions, defend us from all error, and lead us into all truth; that we, being steadfast in the faith, may increase in love and in all good works, and in the end obtain everlasting life; through Jesus Christ, thy Son, our Lord.

selig werden/ der du mit dem Vater/ vnd heiligen Geist regierest/ von ewigkeit zu ewigeit/

Brunswick-Lüneburg (1564) (Pentecost).

Mentes nostras, Domine, Spiritus Paraclitus qui a te procedit illuminet et inducat in omnem, sicut tuus promisit Filius, veritatem. Per.

Gelasian (Wilson, p. 124). (Vespers within the octave of Pentecost).

Blessed lord, which hast caused al holy scriptures to bee written for our learnyng: graunte vs that we maye in suche wise heare them, read, marke, learne, and inwardly digeste them: that by pacience and coumfort of thy holy woorde, we may embrace and euer holde fast the blessed hope of euerlasting life, which thou hast geuen vs in our sauiour Jesus Christe.

Book of Common Prayer (1549) (Advent II).

Omnipotens & misericors Deus, Pater coelestis, qui solus in nobis efficis, ut velimus ac perficiamus, quae tibi placita sunt . . . . paternam manum tuam semper fore super eos extentam, Spiritum sanctum tuum . . . nūquam defuturum . . . in Ecclesia tua agnitione & obedientia Euangelii tui semper proficientes . . . per Dominum nostrum Iesum Christum.

Hermann's Ref. of Cologne (1543) (Confirmation). Translated and condensed, *Book of Common Prayer* (1549) (Confirmation).

O God, by Whom the meek are guided in judgment, and light riseth up in darkness for the godly; grant us, in all our doubts and uncertainties, the grace to ask what Thou wouldest have us to do; that the Spirit of wisdom may save us from all false choices, and that

92. *For Guidance into Truth*
Enlighten our minds, we beseech thee, O God, by the Spirit who proceedeth from thee; that, as thy Son hath promised, we may be led into all truth; through the same Jesus Christ our Lord.

93. *For Grace to Receive the Word*
Blessed Lord, who hast caused all Holy Scriptures to be written for our learning: Grant that we may in such wise hear them, read, mark, learn, and inwardly digest them, that by patience and comfort of thy holy word, we may embrace, and ever hold fast the blessed hope of everlasting life, which thou hast given us in our Saviour Jesus Christ, who liveth and reigneth with thee and the Holy Ghost, one God, world without end.

94. *For Guidance*
Almighty and everlasting God, who makest us both to will and to do those things which are good, and acceptable unto thy Divine Majesty: Let thy fatherly hand, we beseech thee, ever be over us; let thy Holy Spirit ever be with us; and so lead us in the knowledge and obedience of thy word, that in the end we may obtain everlasting life; through Jesus Christ, thy Son, our Lord. *Amen.*

95. *For Guidance*
O God, by whom the meek are guided in judgment, and light riseth up for the godly: Grant us in all our doubts and uncertainties the grace to ask what thou wouldst have us do; that the spirit of wisdom may save us from false choices, and that in thy light we

610

in Thy light we may see light, and in Thy straight path may not stumble; through Jesus Christ our Lord.

William Bright, *Ancient Collects,* p. 234.

O Lord God, who hast called thy servants to ventures of which we cannot see the ending, by paths as yet untrodden, through perils unknown: Give us faith to go out with a good courage, not knowing whither we go, but only that thy hand is leading us, and thy love supporting us; to the glory of thy Name.

Eric Milner-White, *Daily Prayer,* p. 14.

O Got vatter, verleyhe uns eynen bestendigen glauben in Christum, eyn unerschrockene hoffnung in dein barmherzigkeit wider alle blötigkeit unsers süntlichen gewissens, eyn gruntgütige lyeb zu dir und allen menschen.
Döbers Mass, Nuremberg (1525) (Smend, *Die evangelischen deutschen Messen . . . .* p. 165).

Deus qui caritatis dona per gratiam sancti spiritus. tuorum cordibus fidelium infudisti. da famulis tuis pro quibus tuam deprecamur clementiam. salutem mentis et corporis. ut te tota uirtute diligant. et quae tibi placita sunt. tota dilectione perficiant. per.

Gregorian (Wilson, p. 193).

God, whiche haste prepared to them that loue thee, suche good thynges as passe all mannes vnderstanding: Powre into our hartes such loue toward thee, that we louyng thee in al thinges, may obteine thy promises, whiche excede all that we canne desyre: Through Jesus Christe our Lorde.

Book of Common Prayer (1549) (Trinity VI). Our Trinity V, this is a Gelasian Collect (For Latin text, see above, p. 525).

---

may see light and in thy straight path may not stumble; through our Lord and Saviour Jesus Christ.

96. *For Guidance*
O Lord God, who hast called us thy servants to ventures of which we cannot see the ending, by paths as yet untrodden and through perils unknown: Give us faith to go out with good courage, not knowing whither we go, but only that thy hand is leading us and thy love supporting us; through Jesus Christ our Lord.

97. *For Faith, Hope and Love*
Grant us, we beseech thee, Almighty God, a steadfast faith in Jesus Christ, a cheerful hope in thy mercy, and a sincere love to thee and to all our fellow men; through the same Jesus Christ, thy Son, our Lord.

98. *For Love to God*
O God, who through the grace of thy Holy Spirit dost pour the gifts of charity into the hearts of thy faithful people: Grant unto thy servants health both of mind and body, that they may love thee with their whole strength, and with their whole heart perform those things which are pleasing unto thee; through Jesus Christ, thy Son, our Lord.

99. *For Love of God*
O God, who hast prepared for them that love thee such good things as pass man's understanding: Pour into our hearts such love toward thee, that we, loving thee above all things, may obtain thy promises, which exceed all that we can desire; through Jesus Christ, thy Son, our Lord.

O Lorde whiche doeste teache vs, that all our doynges without charitie are nothyng woorthe: sende thy holy ghost and powre into our heartes that most excellent gyft of charitie, the very bond of peace and al vertues, without the whiche whosoeuer lyueth is counted dead before thee: Graunte this, for thy onlye sonne Jesus Christes sake.

Book of Common Prayer (1549) (Quinquagesima).

Almyghtye God, geue vs grace, that we may cast awaye the workes of darknes, and put vpon vs the armour of light, now in the tyme of this mortall lyfe (in the whiche thy sonne Jesus Christe came to visite vs in great humilitie:) that in the last day when he shal come again in his glorious maie-stye to iudge bothe the quicke and the dead: we maye ryse to the lyfe im-mortal, through him, who liueth and reigneth with thee and the holy ghoste, now and euer.

Book of Common Prayer (1549) (Advent I).

William Bright, *Ancient Collects,* p. 234.

Almightie euerliuing God, whiche for the more confyrmacion of the fayth, didst suffer thy holy Apostle Thomas, to bee doubtfull in thy sonnes resur-reccyon: graunte vs so perfectly, and without all doubt to beleue in thy sonne Jesus Christe, that our fayth in thy syghte neuer be reproued: heare vs, O Lorde, through the same Jesus Christe,

100. *For Charity*

O Lord, who hast taught us that all our doings without charity are nothing worth: Send thy Holy Ghost, and pour into our hearts that most excellent gift of charity, the very bond of peace and of all virtues, without which whosoever liveth is counted dead before thee; grant this for thine only Son Jesus Christ's sake.

101. *For Grace to Do God's Will*

Almighty God, give us grace that we may cast away the works of darkness, and put upon us the armor of light, now in the time of this mortal life, in which thy Son Jesus Christ came to visit us in great humility; that in the last day, when he shall come again in his glorious Majesty to judge both the quick and the dead, we may rise to the life immortal; through the same Jesus Christ, thy Son, our Lord.

102. *For Faith*

O most loving Father, who willest us to give thanks for all things, and to dread nothing but the loss of thee, and to cast all our care upon thee who carest for us: Preserve us from faith-less fears and worldly anxieties; and grant that no clouds of this mortal life may hide from us the light of that love which is immortal, and which thou hast manifested unto us in thy Son, Jesus Christ our Lord.

103. *For Faith*

Almighty and everliving God, who hast given to them that believe exceed-ing great and precious promises: Grant us so perfectly, and without all doubt, to believe in thy Son Jesus Christ, that our faith in thy sight may never be re-proved. Hear us, O Lord, through the same, our Saviour Jesus Christ.

to whome with thee and the holy goste be al honour. etc.

Book of Common Prayer (1549) (St. Thomas' Day).

William Bright, *Ancient Collects,* p. 235.

104. *For Zeal*

O God, the sovereign good of the soul, who requireth the hearts of all thy children: Deliver us from all sloth in thy work and all coldness in thy cause; and grant us by looking unto thee to rekindle our love, and by waiting upon thee to renew our strength; through Jesus Christ our Lord.

105. *Consecration*

O almighty and everlasting God, vouchsafe, we beseech thee, to direct, sanctify and govern both our hearts and bodies in the ways of thy laws, and in the works of thy commandments; that, through thy most mighty protection, both here and ever, we may be preserved in body and soul; through Jesus Christ, thy Son, our Lord.

Dirigere & sanctificare et regere dignare domine deus quesumus corda et corpora nostra in lege tua: & in operibus mandatorum tuorum vt hic & in eternum te auxiliante sani et salui esse mereamur. Per.

Sarum Breviary (Prime). Translation in *Book of Common Prayer* (1549) (Post-Communion).
(Compare No. 81 above).

106. *For Grace to Use Our Gifts*

O Lord God Almighty, who dost endue thy servants with singular gifts of the Holy Ghost: Leave us not, we beseech thee, destitute of thy manifold gifts, nor yet of grace to use them alway to thy honor and glory; through Jesus Christ, thy Son, our Lord.

Lorde almightie, wniche hast indued thy holy Apostle Barnabas, with singuler giftes of thy holy goste: let vs not be destytute of thy manyfolde giftes, nor yet of grace to vse them alway to thy honour and glory: Through Jesus Christ our Lorde.

Book of Common Prayer (1549) (St. Barnabas' Day).

107. *For Grace to Follow Christ*

Almighty God, who hast given thine only Son to be unto us both a sacrifice for sin and also an ensample of godly life: Give us grace that we may always most thankfully receive that his inestimable benefit, and also daily endeavor ourselves to follow the blessed steps of his most holy life; through the same Jesus Christ, thy Son, our Lord.

Almightie God, whiche haste geuen thy holy sonne to bee vnto vs, bothe a sacrifice for synne, and also an example of Godly life: Geue vs the grace that we maie alwaies moste thankfully receiue, that his inestimable benefite, and als dayely indeuor our selfes, to folow the blessed steppes of his moste holy lyfe.

Book of Common Prayer (1549) (Easter II).
An alternate Post-Communion Collect in the Common Liturgy (See above pp. 380-81).

Deus, qui Unigeniti tui patientia antiqui hostis contrivisti superbiam: da nobis, quaesumus, quae idem pie pro nobis pertulit, digne recolere; sicque exemplo ejus, nobis adversantia aequanimiter tolerare. Per eundem Dominum.

Missale Romanum (Orationes diversae 28, ad postulandam patientiam). Translated in the *Church Book* (1878).

New. Paul Zeller Strodach.

All machtiger Gott unser lieber unnd Himmlischer Vatter/ Der du die Vöglein speysest/ und alle Blümlein kleidest/ und sorgest für uns/ wie ein Vatter für seine Kinder. Wir bitten deine milde Gütte/ du wöllest uns vor Misstrawen und eiteler vergebener Sorgfältigkeit behütten/ und uns durch deinen Geist nach deines Namens Heiligung/ und dienem Reich und Willen leben lassen/ dass wir all unzer Sorge unnd Anligen in starckem Glauben auff dich werffen/ und dir befelhen könen/ Durch denselben dienen lieben Son Jesum Christum unsern Herren.

Austria (1571) (CXLIX). Translated by Paul Zeller Strodach, *Common Service Book.*

Barmhertziger/ ewiger Gott/ der du wilt/ dass wir zuvor mit Christo leyden und sterben sollen/ ehe dan wir mit ihm zur Herrligkeit erhoben werde/ Verleihe uns gnediglich/ dass wir uns allzeit in deinen willen ergeben/ und im rechte Glauben biss an unser Ende bestendig bleiben/ und uns der zukünfftigen Aufferstehung und Herrligkeit

108. *For Patience*

O God, who by the meek endurance of thine only-begotten Son didst beat down the pride of the old enemy: Help us, we beseech thee, rightly to treasure in our hearts what our Lord hath of his goodness borne for our sakes; that after his example we may bear with patience whatsoever things are adverse to us; through the same Jesus Christ, thy Son, our Lord.

109. *For Meekness and Gentleness of Heart*

O God our Father, whose chastenings are for our purification and strengthening; Teach us, by the things we suffer, both meekness of heart and gentleness of spirit; that we may endure all things manfully, and enduring, conquer for thy Name's sake; through Jesus Christ, thy Son, our Lord.

110. *For Contentment*

Almighty God, our heavenly Father, who dost feed the birds and clothe the flowers, and who carest for us as a father for his children: Guard us against distrust and anxiety; and help us, through thy Holy Spirit, to live to the hallowing of thy Name, the coming of thy kingdom, and the doings of thy will; so that in unwavering faith we may cast all our care upon thee; through Jesus Christ our Lord.

111. *For Steadfastness in Affliction*

Almighty and most merciful God, who hast appointed us to endure sufferings and death with our Lord Jesus Christ before we enter with him into eternal glory: Grant us grace at all times to subject ourselves to thy holy will, and to continue steadfast in the true faith unto the end of our lives, and at all times to find peace and joy

614

trösten und frewen mögen/ durch Jsum Christum unsern Herren/

Saxe-Coburg (1626), p. 86. (Burial).

Deus, cui omne cor patet, & omnis voluntas loquitur, & nullum latet secretum: purifica per infusionem Sancti Spiritus cogitationes cordis nostri, ut perfecte te diligere & digne laudare mereamur. Per &c.

Late Gregorian (Muratori, *Liturgia Romana vetus* t. II, p. 383, Missa de Spiritu Sancto).
Translated in Book of Common Prayer (1549).
(Holy Communion, first Collect).

Actiones nostras quaesumus domine et aspirando praeueni. et adiuuando prosequere. ut cuncta nostra operatio. et a te semper incipiat. et per te coepta finiatur. per dominum.

Gregorian (Wilson, p. 32)
(Ember Saturday in Lent).
Translated in Book of Common Prayer (1549).
("Prevent us").

Herr gott himlischer vater, wir danken dir deiner grossen gnade und barmherzigkeit das du dein eingebornen son in unser fleisch kommen und durch in uns von sünden und ewigen tod gnediglich hast helfen lassen, und bitten dich erleuchte unsere herzen durch deinen heiligen geist, das wir vor solche deine gnade dir dankbar sein und derselben in allen nöten und anfechtung uns trösten, durch denselben.

Saxony (Duke Henry) (1539) (Sehling, *Die evangelischen Kirchenordnungen* . . . I, 278).
A Christmas Collect in many German orders.

in the blessed hope of the resurrection of the dead, and of the glory of the world to come; through Jesus Christ, thy Son, our Lord.

112. *For Purity*

Almighty God, unto whom all hearts are open, all desires known, and from whom no secrets are hid: Cleanse the thoughts of our hearts by the inspiration of thy Holy Spirit, that we may perfectly love thee, and worthily magnify thy holy Name; through Jesus Christ, thy Son, our Lord.

113. *For Divine Assistance*

Direct us, O Lord, in all our doings, with thy most gracious favor, and further us with thy continual help; that in all our works begun, continued, and ended in thee, we may glorify thy holy Name; and finally, by thy mercy, obtain everlasting life; through Jesus Christ, thy Son, our Lord.

114. *For the Blessings of Redemption*

O Lord God, heavenly Father, we give thee thanks, that of thy great goodness and mercy, thou didst suffer thine only-begotten Son to become incarnate, and to redeem us from sin and everlasting death; and we beseech thee, enlighten our hearts by thy Holy Spirit, that we may evermore yield thee unfeigned thanks for this thy grace, and therein find comfort in time of tribulation and distress; through the same Jesus Christ, thy Son, our Lord.

115. *For the Blessings of Redemption*

O Lord, who art God from eternity, yet man for our sakes: Grant us, thine unworthy servants, what thou hast promised to all alike; that thy Passion may be our deliverance, thy wounds our healing, thy Cross our redemption, thy death our life; and that, as thou wast raised upon the Cross, so by thy Cross we may be lifted up to thy Father, with whom thou livest and reignest in the unity of the Spirit, one God.

Charles M. Jacobs, in *Collects and Prayers for use in Church,* p. 40.

116. *For Increase in the Knowledge of God*

O God, who didst send thy Son to live with men that, through him, they might know thee truly, love thee purely, and worship thee aright: Remove far from us all the wrong desires that cloud our vision when we look on him; and bestow upon us the aid of thy Holy Spirit, that, knowing Christ, we may come to an ever truer knowledge of thyself; through the same, thy Son, Jesus Christ our Lord.

Memento Dñe quod es operatus in nobis et non quid mereamur sed conlati gratiam tui muneris intuere ut sicut me sacris altaribus tua dignatio pontificali servire praecipit officio, ita dignum praestet et merito per.

Leonine (Feltoe, p. 126)
(In natale episcoporum).
Translated by J. Armitage Robinson.

117. *Vocation*

Remember O God, what thou hast wrought in us, and not what we deserve; and, as thou hast called us to thy service, make us worthy of our calling; through Jesus Christ our Lord.

Church Book (1878).

118. *For the Blessedness of Heaven*

Almighty, everlasting God, who didst give thine only Son to be a High Priest of good things to come: Hereafter grant unto us, thine unworthy servants, to have our share in the company of the blessed; through the same Jesus Christ, thy Son, our Lord.

Deus, auctor pacis et amator, quem nosse vivere, cui servire regnare est, protege ab omnibus impugnationibus supplices tuos; ut qui defensione tua fidimus, nullius hostilitatis arma timeamus. Per.

Gelasian (Wilson, p. 272). Brandenburg-Nuremberg (1533). *Book of Common Prayer* (1549).

119. *For Inner Peace*

O God, who art the author of peace and lover of concord, in knowledge of whom standeth our eternal life, whose service is perfect freedom: Defend us, thy humble servants, in all assaults of our enemies; that we, surely trusting in thy defense, may not fear the power of any adversaries; through Jesus Christ, thy Son, our Lord.

William Bright, *Ancient Collects,* p. 233.

Ὁ τὰς κοινὰς ταύτας καὶ συμφώνους ἡμῖν
χαρισάμενος προσευχάς, ὁ καὶ δύο καὶ τρισὶ συμ-
φωνοῦσιν ἐπὶ τῷ ὀνόματί σου τὰς αἰτήσεις παρ-
έχειν ἐπαγγειλάμενος· αὐτὸς καὶ νῦν τῶν δούλων
σου τὰ αἰτήματα πρὸς τὸ συμφέρον πλήρωσον
χορηγῶν ἡμῖν ἐν τῷ παρόντι αἰῶνι τὴν ἐπίγνω-
σιν τῆς σῆς ἀληθείας καὶ ἐν τῷ μέλλοντι ζωὴν
αἰώνιον χαριζόμενος.

Liturgy of St. John Chrysostom.
(Prayer of the third antiphon).
Translated in Cranmer's English Litany,
1544.

Almightie God, the fountayn of all
wisdome, which knowest our necessities
beefore we aske, and our ignoraunce in
asking: we beseche thee to haue compassion vpon our infirmities, and those
thynges whiche for our vnwoorthines
we dare not, and for our blindnes we
can not aske, vouchsaue to geue vs for
the woorthines of thy sonne Jesu Christ
our Lorde.

Book of Common Prayer (1549) (Post-
Communion).

Almightie god, which hast promised
to heare the peticions of them that aske
in thy sonnes name, we beseche thee
mercifully to inclyne thyne eares to vs
that haue made nowe our prayers and
supplicacions vnto thee, and graunte
that those thynges whiche we haue
faythfullye asked according to thy will,
maye effectually bee obteyned to the
reliefe of oure necessitye, and to the
settyng foorth of thy glorye: Through
Jesus Christ our Lorde.

Book of Common Prayer (1549)
(Post-Communion).

120. *For the Spirit of Prayer*

O almighty God, from whom every
good prayer cometh, and who pourest
out on all who desire it the spirit of
grace and supplication: Deliver us,
when we draw nigh to thee, from coldness of heart and wanderings of mind;
that with steadfast thoughts and
kindled affections we may worship thee
in spirit and in truth; through Jesus
Christ our Lord.

121. *For Answer to Prayer*

Almighty God, who hast given us
grace at this time with one accord to
make our common supplications unto
thee; and dost promise that when two
or three are gathered together in thy
Name, thou wilt grant their requests:
Fulfill now, O Lord, the desires and
petitions of thy servants as may be
most expedient for them; granting us
in this world knowledge of thy truth,
and in the world to come life everlasting.

122. *For Answer to Prayer*

Almighty God, the fountain of all
wisdom, who knowest our necessities
before we ask and our ignorance in
asking: We beseech thee to have compassion upon our infirmities, and those
things which for our unworthiness we
dare not, and for our blindness we
cannot ask, vouchsafe to give us, for
the worthiness of Jesus Christ, thy Son,
our Lord.

123. *For Answer to Prayer*

Almighty God, who hast promised
to hear the petitions of those who ask
in thy Son's Name: We beseech thee
mercifully to incline thine ear to us
who have now made our prayers and
supplications unto thee; and grant that
those things which we have faithfully
asked according to thy will, may effectually be obtained, to the relief of
our necessity and to the setting forth
of thy glory; through Jesus Christ our
Lord.

COLLECTS AND PRAYERS

PRIVATE DEVOTION

Paul Zeller Strodach, *Collects and Prayers for Use in Church,* p. 41.

Multiplices Dñe incursus quos mundus ingerit tu repelle ut haec dona caelestia tranquillis cogitationibus capere valeamus per.

Leonine (Feltoe, p. 112). Translated and emended by Willard L. Sperry, *Prayers for Private Devotion in Wartime* (New York, 1943), p. 3.

Ὁ Θεὸς ὁ παντοκράτωρ, ὁ μεγαλώνυμος Κύριος, ὁ δοὺς ἡμῖν εἴσοδον εἰς τὰ ἅγια τῶν ἁγίων, διὰ τῆς ἐπιδημίας τοῦ μονογενοῦς σου Τίου, Κυρίου δὲ καὶ Θεοῦ καὶ Σωτῆρος ἡμῶν Ἰησοῦ Χριστοῦ, ἱκετεύομεν καὶ παρακαλοῦμεν τὴν σὴν ἀγαθότητα, ἐπειδὴ ἔμφωβοι καὶ ἔντρομοί ἐσμεν, μέλλοντες παρεστάναι τῷ ἁγίῳ σου θυσιαστηρίῳ, ἐξαπόστειλον ἐφ᾽ ἡμᾶς ὁ Θεὸς τὴν χάριν σου τὴν αγαθήν, καὶ ἁγίασον ἡμῶν τὰς ψυχὰς καὶ τὰ σώματα καὶ τὰ πνεύματα, καὶ ἀλλοίωσον τὰ φρονήματα ἡμῶν πρὸς εὐσέβειαν, ἵνα ἐν καθαρῷ συνειδότι προσφερώμεν σοι δῶρα, δόματα, καρπώματα, εἰς ἀθέτησιν τῶν ἡμετέρων πλημμελημάτων, καὶ εἰς ἱλασμὸν παντὸς τοῦ λαοῦ σου, χάριτι καὶ οἰκτιρμοῖς καὶ φιλανθροπίᾳ τοῦ μονογενοῦς σου Τίου μεθ᾽ οὗ εὐλογητὸς εἶ εἰς τοὺς αἰῶνας τῶν αἰώνων.

Liturgy of St. James (Jerusalem)
(Prayer at the Entrance.)
Translated by Paul Zeller Strodach.

O God, whose goodness is great, and the multitudes of thy mercies innumerable; we have sinned against thee, and done evil in thy sight, yet because thou art the God of mercy and the Fountain of eternal purity we present unto thee the sacrifice of a troubled spirit, beseeching thee to let the fire of thy love cleanse our sins and purify our souls. Make us clean hearts, O God; though our sins be as scarlet, yet make them like wool; though they be as purple,

1. *Before Service*
Bless me, O God, with a reverent sense of thy Presence, that I may be still and adore thee: through Jesus Christ our Lord.

2. *Before Service*
Dispel for this hour, O Lord, the manifold distractions of the world; that we may be able with quiet minds to receive the promptings of thy still small voice; through Jesus Christ our Lord.

3. *Before Service*
Send forth, O God, thy good grace, and sanctify our souls, bodies, and spirits; turn our thoughts to holiness, so that with pure conscience we may offer to thee the sacrifice of praise; through the mercy and compassion of thine only-begotten Son, with whom thou art blessed, together with thy Holy, and Good, and Quickening Spirit, now and always.

4. *Penitence, Confession*
(Before Worship)
O God, whose goodness is great, and the multitudes of thy mercies without number; we have sinned against thee, and done evil in thy sight; yet, since thou art the God of mercy and the Fountain of eternal purity, we present unto thee the sacrifice of a troubled spirit, beseeching thee to let the fire of thy love consume our sins and purify our souls. Make clean our hearts, O God; though our sins be as scarlet, yet make them like wool, though they be

618

yet make them white as snow. Restore the voice of joy and gladness to us; give us the comforts of thy help again, and let thy free Spirit establish us in the liberty of the sons of God: so shall we sing of thy righteousness, and our lips shall give thee praise in the congregation of thy redeemed, now, henceforth, and for ever.

A Free Church Book of Common Prayer (London, 1929), p. 202. Attributed to Jeremy Taylor.

Armenian Liturgy (prayer at the commingling).
Translated by William Bright, *Ancient Collects,* p. 136.

Caelesti lumine, quaesumus, Domine, semper et ubique nos praeveni, ut mysterium cuius nos participes esse voluisti et puro cernamus intuitu et digno percipiamus effectu. Per.

Gelasian (Wilson, p. 12).
Translated by Paul Zeller Strodach, *Collects and Prayers for Use in Church,* p. 41.

We do not presume to come to this thy table (O mercifull lord) trusting in our owne righteousnes, but in thy manifold and great mercies: we be not woorthie so much as to gather vp the cromes vnder thy table, but thou art the same lorde whose propertie is alwayes to haue mercie: Graunt vs therfore (gracious lorde) so to eate the fleshe of thy dere sonne Jesus Christ, and to drynke his blood in these holy Misteries, that we may continuallye dwell in hym, and he in vs, that oure synfull bodyes may bee made cleane by his body, and our soules washed through hys most precious bloud.

as crimson, yet make them white as snow. Restore to us the voice of joy and gladness; give us the comforts of thy Presence again, and let thy free Spirit establish us in the liberty of the sons of God; so shall we sing of thy righteousness, and our lips shall give thee praise in the congregation of thy redeemed, now, henceforth, and forever. *Amen.*

5. *Before Holy Communion*

O Lord our God, who from the Name of thine only-begotten Son hast called us to be Christians, and hast given us the Baptism of the new birth for the remission of sins: Make us, we beseech thee, worthy now to receive this Communion for the forgiveness of all our sins, and to give thanks with grateful hearts, as to thee so to the Son and to the Holy Ghost, now and forever.

6. *Before Holy Communion*

Direct and control us, O Lord, always and everywhere with heavenly light; that we may both discern with clear vision and share with worthy effect that mystery of which thou hast willed us to partake; through Jesus Christ our Lord.

7. *Before Holy Communion*

We do not presume to come to this thy Table, O merciful Lord, trusting in our own righteousness, but in thy manifold and great mercies: We are not worthy so much as to gather up the crumbs under thy Table; but thou art the same Lord whose property is always to have mercy. Grant us therefore, gracious Lord, so to eat the Flesh of thy dear Son, and to drink his Blood in these holy mysteries, that we may continually dwell in him and he in us, that our sinful bodies may be made clean by his Body, and our souls washed through his most precious Blood.

Book of Common Prayer (1549)
(Based on Liturgy of St. Basil; Mark
7:28; John 6:56; *Summa Theologica*
III, 74 §1).

Custodi intra nos Domine gloriae
tuae munus, ut aduersus omnia prae-
sentis et futuri seculi mala eucharistiae,
quā percepimus uiribus et uirtute muniamur, qui uiuis, etc.

Missal published by Matthias Flaccus
Illyricus, 1557, p. 67.
Translated by William Bright, *Ancient
Collects,* p. 156.

Paul Zeller Strodach, *Collects and
Prayers for Use in Church,* p. 45.

Almighty God, who hast given to thy
people the true Bread who cometh
down from heaven, even thy Son Jesus
Christ; grant that our souls may be
so fed by him who giveth health unto
the world, that we may abide in him
and he in us, and thy Church be filled
with the power of his deathless life;
through the same Jesus Christ our Lord.

*The Kingdom, the Power and the
Glory (The Grey Book,* Part III)
(3rd ed.; London, 1925), p. 69.

We give thanks to thee, Almighty
God, that thou hast vouchsafed to us
this memorial of thy love and of thy
great gift, even Jesus Christ our Lord;
and we beseech thee to strengthen in
us our faith in thee and to increase in
us our love toward one another;
through Jesus Christ our Lord.

8. *After Holy Communion*

Preserve in us, O Lord, the gift of
thy grace, that, by the power and virtue
of the Eucharist which we have received, we may be fortified against all
evils now and evermore; through Jesus
Christ our Lord.

9. *After Holy Communion*

O merciful Father, we render thee
thanks and praise that thou hast
vouchsafed to feed us, thine unworthy
servants, with the precious Body and
Blood of thy dear Son; and we pray
that by thy grace we may walk worthy
of our holy calling, and learn to adorn
the doctrine of God our Saviour in all
things; through the same Jesus Christ,
thy Son, our Lord.

10. *After Holy Communion*

Almighty God, who givest the true
Bread which cometh down from heaven,
even thy Son, Jesus Christ our Lord:
Grant, we beseech thee, that we who
have received the Sacrament of his
Body and Blood may abide in him, and
he in us, that we may be filled with the
power of his endless life; who liveth
and reigneth with thee and the Holy
Ghost, one God, world without end.

11. *After Holy Communion*

We give thanks to thee, Almighty
God, that thou hast refreshed us with
this Sacrament of thy love, and hast
granted to us the presence of thy Son,
even Jesus Christ our Lord; and we
beseech thee to strengthen our faith in
thee and to increase our love toward
one another; through the same thy Son,
Jesus Christ our Lord.

620

The Pilgrim Hymnal (1931) (Communion order). Modified in *Common Worship* (Congregational) (1948).

Allmechtiger ewiger gott, der du durch deinen son vergebung unser sünden gerechtigkeit und ewiges legen uns hast verheissen, wir bitten dich, du wöllest durch deinen heiligen geist unsere herzen also füren und erwecken, das wir solche hülfe durch tegliches gebet und sonderlich in aller anfechtung bei im suchen und durch ein rechten festen glauben auf sein zusagung und wort gewis finden und erlangen, durch denselben deinen son, unsern herren Jesum Christum, der mit dir und dem heiligen geist lebet und regiert in ewigkeit.

Saxony (Duke Henry) (1539) (Sehling, I, 276).

Mercyful father geue vs grace, that we neuer presume to synne thorough the example of any creature, but if it shall chaunce vs at any tyme to offende thy diuine maiestie: that then we may truely repent and lament thesame, after the example of Mary Magdalene, and by lyuely fayth obtaine remission of all our sinnes, through the only merites of thy sonne our sauiour Christ.

Book of Common Prayer (1549) (St. Mary Magdalene's Day).

Thou knowest, Lord, the deep places through which our lives must go; help us, when we enter them, to lift our hearts to Thee; help us to be patient when we are afflicted, to be humble when we are in distress; and grant that the hope of Thy mercy may never fail us and the consciousness of Thy loving kindness never be clouded or hidden from our eyes; through Jesus Christ, our Lord.

Charles M. Jacobs, *Helps on the Road* (Philadelphia, 1933), p. 98.

12. *For Aid in Temptation*

O God, who by thy Son, our Saviour, hast promised us forgiveness of sins and everlasting life: Lead us by thy Spirit to seek help from Christ in our daily need, especially in times of temptation; that by faith we may obtain thy promises and live as thy children; through the same Jesus Christ our L⸱⸱⸱

13. *For Repentance*

Merciful Father, give us grace that we may never presume to sin; but if at any time we offend thy Divine Majesty, may we truly repent and lament our offence, and by a lively faith obtain remission of all our sins; solely through the merits of Jesus Christ, thy Son, our Lord.

14. *In Time of Affliction*

Lord, who knowest the deep places through which our lives must go: Help us, when we enter them, to lift our hearts to thee, to be patient when we are afflicted, to be humble when we are in distress; and grant that the hope of thy mercy may never fail us, and the consciousness of thy lovingkindness may never be clouded nor hidden from our eyes; through Jesus Christ, thy Son, our Lord.

WAka öffuer oss käre himmelske Fadher, och bewara oss för then listighe Frestaren, som altijdh omkring gåår, sökiandes hwem han vpsluka kan, giff oss nådhena, at wij måghe honom medh een stadigh troo manligha emoot stå, och i thenna natt vnder titt beskerm trygge hwilas, Genom tin Son JEsum CHristum wår HERRA.

Church of Sweden, *Handbook, ther vthi är författadt, huruledes Gudztiensten* . . . (1614), fol. LXXXVI-LXXX-VII (ad Completorium) Translated by Paul Zeller Strodach, *Oremus,* p. 113.[4]

15. Evening: Personal Prayer

Watch over us, O Lord, our heavenly Father. Preserve us from all evil, and grant that we may this night rest secure beneath thy care. Bless thy Church and our government. Remember the sick and those who are in need or in peril. Have mercy upon all men. And when our last evening shall come, grant us to fall asleep in thy peace and to awake in thy glory; through Jesus Christ, thy Son, our Lord.

[4] This prayer has undergone many revisions. Changes of wording were made in 1799 and 1809. In the *Förslag* (Proposals) of 1854 it appears in a lengthened form, probably influenced by Loehe's *Agende* and Thiele's *Kirchenbuch.* The 1854 form, with some emendations, occurs in the American *Försök till Fullständig Kyrko Handbok* of 1885, and in the Swedish *Handbok* of 1894. The translation is from this 1894 version, now discarded in favor of a compromise form first appearing in that year. The full 1894 version is as follows:
Vaka öfver oss, Herre, Himmelske Fader, och bevara oss för allt ondt både till kropp och själ! Gif oss nåd att i denna natt tryggt hvila under ditt beskärm! Beskydda och välsigna din kyrka och församling samt vår älskade öfverhet! Tänk i nåd och förbarmande på dem, som äro stadda i sjukdom, nöd farlighet! Förbarma Dig öfver alla människor! Och när omsider vår sista afton kommer, låt oss då få insomna i din frid, att vi må uppvakna till din härlighet.

CHAPTER XXX

THE LITANY

The Litany is a responsive prayer of the church, penitential in character but unselfish in its intercessions for all human need and mighty in its grasp of the grounds for divine compassion. It is the most ancient of the services of the church except the Holy Communion. In form and content it is a people's prayer. The Te Deum scales the heights, and the Litany plumbs the depths of our common humanity.

The Litany is unique. It expresses the fundamental needs of all people tersely, energetically, and yet with pathos. It provides opportunity for individual concentration and for corporate action. It requires no accompanying ceremonial and can even dispense with the necessity of service books.

The text of the Litany is given pp. 635-38.

A few appreciations may be of interest. Luther regarded the Litany as "next to the holy Lord's Prayer the very best that has come to earth."[1] Lucas Lossius, the church musician and friend of Melanchthon, spoke of it as *"explicatio orationis dominicae,"* or "exposition of the Lord's Prayer." Wilhelm Loehe, the nineteenth-century liturgical scholar, says that the Litany is a glorious creation of ancient times whose power lies in the incessant stroke upon stroke of intonation and response. "Beginning with adoration, confessing Christ in its heart, it ends in the lovely Agnus . . . how evangelical, how entirely agreeable to our church and to its temper."[2]

Among older English commentators Bishop Hooker spoke of its "absolute (i.e., finished) perfection." Bishop Gore says it is "among the noblest and most searching instruments of devotion to be found . . . in the whole range of liturgical literature." The regular use of such a model is in itself a "deep and thorough schooling in the divine art of prayer."[3]

[1] Christian Gerber, *Historie der Kirchenceremonien in Sachsen* (Dresden: Sauressig, 1732), p. 268.
[2] *Agende* (3. Aufl., 1884), p. 159.
[3] Charles Gore, *Reflections on the Litany* (London: Mowbray, 1932), pp. 1, 97.

Professor Bayard H. Jones says, "Ancient faiths cried for mercy to gods whom they feared. . . . Their despairing petitions contained none of the trust in the prevailing goodness of God's providence which inspires the Litany. On the other hand, popular modern cults attempt to evade and ignore suffering. . . . Christianity alone accepts the fact of suffering as enshrined in the heart of God himself, lifts it up in sacrifice to him, and nails it to the Cross of Christ."[4] Canon Dearmer somewhere notes that the Lutheran and the Anglican litanies, "with so much in common and yet so different, stand together in a place apart from the tedious repetition of the Roman Litany with its despairing appeal to the compassionate intercession of numberless saints on the one hand and from the sentimental and selfishly limited utterances of many modern devotions on the other." In using the Litany "we can turn to the whole world, Christian and otherwise, and say, 'This is how we pray, this is how we are taught to think of life and death, of God and man.' "[5]

The name "litany" is of Greek extraction ($\lambda\iota\tau\alpha\nu\epsilon\iota\alpha$—prayer, entreaty). Its Latin equivalent *rogatio* survives in the special prayers appointed for Rogation days, the three days before Ascension Day. The liturgy in Rome in the earliest times began with a litany. The ninefold Kyrie of the Roman Mass is a surviving fragment of this early use. Practically all Eastern and Gallican liturgies have such a prayer after the Sermon and before the Mass of the Faithful at the place of the Lutheran and the Anglican Prayer of the Church.

While the so-called Eucharistic Litany disappeared very early from Western services, the litany form received independent development in connection with processions. These were first held out-of-doors and later were brought into the church building itself in services distinct from the Eucharist. The early use of processional litanies included supplications for divine blessing upon the fields and the fruits of the earth, or prayers for divine aid against enemies or impending calamity. The litany book came to be called the "Processional," and the Litany "the Procession" even when sung in church by the people kneeling. There is an account of such procedure after the battle of Pinkie in 1547, when "all the parish churches of London 'kept a solemn procession on their knees in English.' "[6]

These processions, with their chanted responses, gave the people a voice. They proved so popular that the penitential prayers which formed their substance were repeated in the regular processions on festivals and

[4] Parsons and Jones, *The American Prayer Book*, p. 136.
[5] For further thoughts on the Litany, see Dearmer's *Everyman's History of the Prayer Book* (1912), p. 173, and his book, *The Story of the Prayer Book*, p. 174.
[6] Dearmer, *The Story of the Prayer Book*, p. 174.

in the special processions appointed for church dedications, coronations, and other occasions. To the "stationary dialogue" of the earliest Eastern litanies was added the processional feature of the West. Thus, the ancient Eucharistic Litany and the later Processional Litany combined to produce the medieval forms which lie immediately back of our purified and simplified litany text.

"David's litany" (Psalm 51), the humble prayer of the publican (Luke 18:13), the cry "Spare thy people, O Lord" (Joel 2:17), and the form of responsorial psalmody in Psalm 136 are scriptural instances of a type of prayer which came to fuller congregational expression in the Deacon's Litany of the *Apostolic Constitutions*. Just before the catechumens were dismissed, the deacon, "ascending some high place," read the bids in this prayer, which contained petitions for different groups in the church—catechumens, energumens, the recently baptized, penitents, the faithful, etc. Each petition was followed by a fixed congregational response: "Lord, have mercy," one of the very few liturgical responses borrowed by the early church from the pagan world.

Early Syrian litanies concluded by invoking the intercessions of saints.[7] These invocations were multiplied in the later litanies of Western Europe and were placed before the supplications. Rome, with greater conservatism, held to simpler forms for a time but eventually yielded to the general trend, and the invocation of saints and the veneration of relics became accepted features of medieval processions and litanies. These have been retained in Roman use to the present without material change.

Scholars believe that the earliest litany forms originated in Antioch during the second half of the fourth century.[8] The pagans in Rome observed a festival of the God Robigus, April 25. He was credited with preserving the crops from mildew. The Christians, in line with their practice of observing a pagan holiday but giving it Christian significance, followed the pagan procession over the same route, but after crossing the Milvian Bridge, proceeded to St. Peter's praying as they went, thus joining litany to procession. Duchesne compares pagan and Christian processions and prayers and describes the worship of Syrian congregations as they fell upon the ground toward the east and followed the deacon as he said the petitions of the litanies.[9]

An earthquake and other calamities which befell the city of Vienne in Gaul led Mamertus, the archbishop in 470, when the people had fled in panic leaving him kneeling alone before the altar, to organize litanies on the three days before Ascension Day. These Rogation days were extended to the whole

---

[7] Parsons and Jones, *The American Prayer Book*, p. 131, where references are given to texts in Brightman, *Liturgies Eastern and Western*. See also Warren, *The Liturgy and Ritual of the Celtic Church*, pp. 226-38, esp. p. 238.

[8] Clarke and Harris, *Liturgy and Worship*, p. 282; Underhill, *Worship*, pp. 100f; Brightman, *Liturgies Eastern and Western*, pp. 4, 471, 521, give ancient forms which were commonly called *Ektene* ("stretched out"), i.e., earnest prayer.

[9] *Christian Worship*, p. 59. See also Schuster, *The Sacramentary*, II, 355ff. Duchesne, *Christian Worship*, 198-201; and Warren, *Celtic Church*, pp. 229f.; for early forms.

of Frankish Gaul in A.D. 511. For the most part, however, early Western processional litanies invoked the divine blessing upon the fruits of the earth.

Later the first three days in November were also observed as litany days, coinciding with the time for the sowing of the seed. Leo III in 799 ordered the Litany to be used in Rome, reorganizing the spring Rogations according to Gallican usage. The church in Milan also appointed it for Monday, Tuesday, and Wednesday after Ascension. The Synod of Mainz (813) ordered the Litany to be sung. In the Stowe Missal the Litany is placed between the Epistle and the Gospel, and its form resembles that of the *Apostolic Constitutions*. Duchesne (p. 199) gives the text of the Milanese Litany for Lent. Maskell gives English versions of the fourteenth century.[10]

E. C. Ratcliff believes that the *deprecatio* which Pope Gelasius in the fifth century appointed to be sung "on behalf of the church throughout the world" probably determined the form of subsequent litanies in Latin.[11] The eminent Roman scholar, Edmund Bishop, suggests that the ultimate source of the Litany of All Saints was a Greek litany which came to England from Rome during the pontificate of Sergius I, a Greek-speaking pope (A.D. 687-701). From England this litany passed to Ireland, where it appeared in the Stowe Missal. From thence it passed to Germany and Gaul and finally, with additions, back to Rome again.[12]

Anciently only classes of saints were invoked; then individual names were added, and in many places local saints.[13] Martene and Muratori give litany forms invoking nearly one hundred saints.

Thus, before the Reformation, a Rogation or processional litany was the common form of supplication. There were processions about the church introductory to high mass on Sundays and festivals. The recitation of these litanies gained indulgences of hundreds of days and the people superstitiously regarded the litanies as miracle-working measures, especially when they were connected with the veneration of relics.

At the beginning of the seventeenth century there were at least eighty different forms of litany in use in the Roman Church. To simplify this and to establish order, Clement VIII in 1601 forbade the use of any litany except that of All Saints and that of Loretto. The Congregation of Sacred Rites in 1860 allowed the private use of litanies sanctioned by the Ordinary, and in 1862 it sanctioned the Litany of the Holy Name of Jesus, and in 1899 the Litany of the Sacred Heart.[14] Since that time the number of litanies has grown rapidly.

All the Reformers protested against abuses connected with processions. The radicals abandoned all litany types of prayer, and under Karlstadt's influence the litany form disappeared from church life in Wittenberg after

[10] William Maskell, *Monumenta ritualia ecclesiae Anglicanae*, III, 227ff.

[11] In his article, "The Choir Offices," in Clarke and Harris, *Liturgy and Worship*, p. 284.

[12] *Liturgica Historica*, pp. 144ff.

[13] Daniel Rock and W. H. J. Weale, *Hierurgia*, I, 326-32; also D. Rock, G. W. Hart, and W. H. Frere, *The Church of Our Fathers* (2d ed.; London: Murray, 1905), III, 182ff.

[14] See *The Catholic Encyclopedia* for commentary on all the saints invoked.

1521.[15] Luther and Cranmer alone appreciated its spiritual values and preserved it for future generations by purifying its text and enlarging its petitions in an evangelical spirit. Luther's litany is simple, direct, and less ornate than Cranmer's with its more stately phrases.

Luther revised the Litany of All Saints (the "Great Litany") in 1529, first in Latin and later in a briefer German text. The latter at once became immensely popular throughout Germany and Scandinavia. Cranmer leaned heavily upon Luther in the preparation of his English Litany in 1544, a work which marked the beginning of liturgical reform in the Church of England. Cranmer's Litany is recognized as one of the masterpieces of English devotional literature.

Pietism and the later Rationalism in Lutheran lands could not understand the corporate and objective character of the Litany or the broad sweep of its intercessions, and it passed out of church use. Modern Lutheran liturgical scholars everywhere seek its reintroduction, and the whole church is coming to a fuller appreciation of its worth as a true people's prayer and an effective instrument of corporate devotion.

The Moravians have made special use of litany forms of prayer, and the "Church Litany" and the "Litany of the Life, Passion and Death of Jesus Christ" are regularly in their use today. Litany hymns have appeared in great numbers during the past century, particularly among the Moravians and also as a product of the Oxford Movement in England. Litanies of private composition are found also in many books of devotion.[16] Abandoning completely the traditional antagonism of Calvinism to the Litany and other responsive forms of prayer, leaders in the non-liturgical churches are now producing and using novel and individual "litanies," most of which fall far short of historic forms in scope, depth, and sobriety.

Luther disapproved of invoking the saints and of other superstitious observances connected with medieval processions, but when the high tide of the Turkish invasion reached the gates of Vienna in 1528, he published a pamphlet on "The War Against the Turks" in which he urged earnest and fervent prayer by all Christians and suggested that "the Litany be sung or read in the churches, especially by the young folks; this might be done at mass, at Vespers, or after the sermon." Toward the end of this year he revised and expanded the Litany of All

---

[15] Its popularity and adaptability as a prayer form are attested, however, by the curious litany for Luther's cause, entitled "Litany for the Germans," which Dr. Henry E. Jacobs describes in his *Lutheran Movement in England*, pp. 232f., and which is given in full in Walch's edition of Luther's works, Bd. XV, col. 2174ff. For text and comment on Luther's litanies, see *WA* 30^{III}, 1ff.

[16] Dr. Seiss published three litanies in his *Golden Altar* (1882). Dr. Strodach included several in his *Oremus* (1925).

Saints. His immediate purpose may have been to arouse the church to prayer against the Turk, but his fuller thought certainly was to separate the Litany from the processions, to purify and enlarge it, and to make of it a vernacular prayer of the congregation in connection with the latter's normal services of worship. His litany thus became part of his larger effort to provide the people with the purified historic liturgy, the Holy Scriptures, and a body of hymns and prayers for corporate use in their own language.

Luther's revision and enlargement of the Litany was not a casual performance, but a careful and thoroughgoing study. His personal preference for Latin as the traditional liturgical use had led him to prepare his Latin Mass in 1523 to be followed by his German Mass in 1526. Similarly he worked on his Latin Litany first and followed this with a slightly briefer litany in German.[17] Loehe thinks of these as children of a common mother, yet differing from her and from each other. Both are fuller, more beautiful, and more developed than the Roman; and with obvious reference to the Parthenon, he describes the two forms together as being "like a stately structure of the ancient world."[18]

Luther retained the general form and order and much of the contents of the Litany with which he was familiar in the use of the Augustinian Order. Both his Latin and his German litanies omit the invocation of the saints, the intercessions for the pope and the departed, a dozen suffrages, and the Psalm. He changed the order of some of the petitions and introduced twenty-five new ones.[19] Both in criticism and new construction, he displayed a marvelous grasp of the spirit of this ancient church prayer. His version is not only evangelical but churchly and never sentimental.

These new suffrages of Luther are much more concise and specific than the pre-Reformation forms. They testify not only to the Reformer's independence and originality but also to his spiritual insight and warmheartedness. Archbishop Cranmer later incorporated nearly all of them in his English Litany, recognizing the worth of Luther's modifications.

The new petitions of Luther include prayers for deliverance from all error; from pestilence and famine; from war and bloodshed; from sedition and rebellion. Also, the phrases, "in all time of our tribulation; in all time of our prosperity and in the hour of death." Also, prayers that God would

[17] Luther wrote to his friend Hausmann on February 12, 1529, saying, "We are singing litanies in our church [Wittenberg] in Latin and in German" (*WA* Br 5, 17f, No. 1381). Exactly one month later he sent the vernacular edition with a statement that he had found it helpful (*WA* Br 5, 37f, No. 1395).

[18] *Agende* (3. Aufl.), p. 159.

[19] *WA* 30[III], 11. See also comparative table in Appendix, pp. 736-50. Also Drews, *Studien zur Geschichte des Gottesdienstes . . .* IV, 24-32.

"preserve all bishops, pastors and ministers; put an end to schisms and causes of offense; bring into the way of truth all such as have erred, etc.; beat down Satan under our feet; send faithful laborers into his harvest; accompany his word with his Spirit and grace; raise up them that fall and strengthen such as do stand; comfort and help the weak-hearted and the distressed."

Luther's final group of petitions include the prayer that God would "behold and succor all who are in danger, necessity and tribulation; strengthen and keep all sick persons and young children; free all who are innocently imprisoned; defend and provide for all fatherless children and widows; have mercy upon all men; forgive our enemies, persecutors and slanderers and turn their hearts; and give and preserve to our use the fruits of the earth."

Luther followed tradition in providing a series of collects at the end, which according to the original meaning of the Gallican term *collectio,* assemble the accumulated thought and secret "intentions" of the worshipers in a generalized conclusion. These collects, each of which had its own versicle and response, differed from the traditional Roman series.[20]

Luther's German Litany was instantly accepted in wide circles. It spread from Wittenberg and Magdeburg to Leipzig, Erfurt, Lübeck, Rostock, Austria, and Scandinavia. Brenz and Bucer especially commended it. There was far less deviation from Luther's text of the Litany as it appeared in hymn books, church orders, and cantionales than from his Latin or German masses.

The penitential character of the Litany was especially emphasized in South Germany. The church orders appointed it for Fridays, Wednesdays and Fridays, or Saturday Vespers in place of the Magnificat. In towns and villages it was used on Sundays before the Service, after the Epistle, or following the Sermon when there were no communicants.

The Litany of the Church of England was prepared to meet a national emergency quite as Luther's Litany had been called forth by the threat of war with the Turks. In 1543 the crops were threatened by excessive rains, and on August 20 King Henry directed Archbishop Cranmer to see to it that "general Rogations and processions be made incontinently." The Archbishop appointed a series of "Latin supplications and suffrages" for Wednesdays and Fridays. The following year England was at war with Scotland and with France. On June 11, the eve of his projected invasion of France, the King wrote Archbishop Cranmer—as Brightman suggests, the letter probably being penned by the Archbishop himself—calling attention to "the miserable state of all Christendom . . . plagued with most cruel wars, hatreds and dissensions." Desire was expressed for "general processions to be said and sung with such reverence and devotion as appertaineth," and the letter expressly referred to "godly prayers and suffrages in our native English tongue."

June 18 of this year, 1544, Cranmer issued a mandate to the bishop

[20] See *WA* 30[III], 35-36, 41-42. Drews, *Studien,* IV, 24-32; and Brightman, *The English Rite,* I, xxx.

of London, enclosing with it the royal letter and a copy of a litany which the archbishop had prepared, together with a plain-song notation. A later letter of October 7 from Cranmer to the King explains what he has done and expresses the hope that "it will much excitate and stir the hearts of all men unto devotion and godliness." He also modestly says, "Nevertheless they that be cunning in singing can make a much more solemn note thereto. I made them only for a proof, to see how English would do in song."[21]

Dr. Henry E. Jacobs first revealed the extent to which Archbishop Cranmer was indebted to Luther's Litany of 1529. He showed that William Marshall, an English bookseller, in his *Goodly Primer* of 1535 had reproduced in English large portions of Luther's Latin Litany along with his expositions of the Ten Commandments, the Creed, and the Lord's Prayer.[22]

Anglican scholars now fully recognize the Lutheran influence in the preparation of their Prayer Book. Bishop Dowden says "it is beyond question that many of the most beautiful, affecting and precious of the suffrages of our English Litany are due to Luther." They came in "by a direct transfer from a German source." He lists no less than twelve examples, and also credits the direction to say the Litany on Wednesdays and Fridays to suggestions from German church orders, notably Saxony (1539) and Calenburg (1542). Luther's influence is also revealed in the order of the concluding versicles, responses, and prayers. Dr. F. E. Brightman and Bishop Frere make similar acknowledgements.[23]

Cranmer's Litany of 1544 was really the beginning of the English *Book of Common Prayer*. The first Prayer Book of 1549 did not actually include the Litany but had a rubric directing that it be sung on Wednesdays and Fridays and that it be followed by at least the ante-Communion service. Later editions of the Prayer Book incorporated the Litany following the Communion. In 1661 it was ordered to be sung after Morning Prayer. The Puritans violently opposed the Litany, not appreciating its essential character and worth. They desired to expand the form of the ancient Collects, so they

[21] For fuller description, see particularly Brightman, *The English* Rite, I, lviii-lxviii; Dowden, *The Workmanship of the Prayer Book,* pp. 140ff.

[22] See H. E. Jacobs, *The Lutheran Movement in England,* pp. 230ff. For a description of the *Goodly Primer,* see Charles C. Butterworth, *The English Primers 1529-1545* (Philadelphia: Univ. of Pa. Pr., 1953), pp. 104ff.

[23] See Dowden's *The Workmanship of the Prayer Book,* pp. 254f., 263; Procter and Frere, *A New History of the Book of Common Prayer,* pp. 414ff; Brightman, *The English Rite,* I, lxv ff. Also Clarke and Harris, *Liturgy and Worship,* p. 148, and *The Prayer Book Dictionary,* article "Foreign Influences," pp. 353f.

suggested changing the Litany so that "the particulars thereof may be composed into one solemn prayer to be offered by the ministers."[24]

Cranmer's Litany of 1544 retained an invocation of St. Mary, one of All Holy Angels and Archangels, and one of All Holy Patriarchs and Prophets. It also included a curious prayer for the Queen, "giving her increase of all godliness, honour and children." Tension between England and Rome was reflected in a petition for deliverance "from the Bishop of Rome and all his detestable enormities." Queen Elizabeth, in an effort at conciliation in 1559, removed this last petition. The invocations had disappeared before the 1549 edition. When the Catholic Queen Mary prohibited the use of the English Prayer Book in 1553 and re-introduced the Roman Mass, she made an exception in favor of the English Litany and permitted its continued use.

Archbishop Cranmer was particularly fitted for the task of liturgical criticism and construction. As Brightman says, "He was not original, but, as the Litany is enough to prove, he had an extraordinary power of absorbing and improving other people's work."[25] He used as his sources the Roman Litany, the Sarum Processional Litany, and in full measure Luther's Latin Litany. Minor details were also drawn from the uses of York and Hereford and the Byzantine Liturgy of Constantinople. He introduced a new rhythm by grouping together many of the ancient brief petitions and enriching them with descriptive phrases concluding each group with a single response.

The Litany contains sixty-one separate petitions and prayerful phrases and twenty-three responses. As the Lord's Prayer itself teaches us to do, the Litany establishes the mood of adoration at the very beginning with an introductory Kyrie and an invocation of the Holy Trinity. It concludes with the Agnus Dei followed by the Lord's Prayer and Collects. The body of the Litany is definitely a prayer to Christ, the first example of which we find in the cry of the martyr Stephen.

This central part of the Litany consists of deprecations, obsecrations, supplications, and intercessions. The long history of the church and the profound experiences of great spirits are reflected in the petitions of these four groups. In them we hear an echo of the persecutions of the early centuries and of the distress of nations in the medieval age when, as a Gallican Collect reminds us, all Christians heard "the crash of a falling world" and when, as Bishop Hooker truly said, "Rogations or Litanies were then the very strength, stay, and comfort of God's Church."[26] In them, too, we share the deep spiritual experience of Luther and others in the age of the Reformation. Yet so universal and timeless are these petitions that they express our truest needs today.

[24] Edward Cardwell, *A History of Conferences and Other Proceedings Connected with the Revision of the Book of Common Prayer, from the Year 1558 to the Year 1690* (2nd ed.; Oxford: The Univ. Pr., 1841), p. 306.

[25] *The English Rite,* I, lxvii.

[26] Canon Bright in John Henry Blunt's *The Annotated Book of Common Prayer* (London: Rivingtons, 1866), p. 46.

The deprecations (from *deprecari,* to avert by prayer) against evils and dangers begin with the words "From all sin" and conclude with the words "everlasting death." The response in every case is "Good Lord, deliver us." This section is more extended in the Roman and the Anglican than in the Lutheran form. "Crafts and assaults" remind us of the secret as well as the open attacks of Satan. "Sudden death" is more properly unprepared or unforeseen death. We may recall Canon Bright's reference to the aversion to this deprecation oft expressed by the parliamentary general Lord Brooke (Robert Greville) who himself met "sudden death" March 2, 1643, when his forces besieged Lichfield. Having compelled the governor to retire into the Minster close, Greville led the attack, but was struck in the eye and killed instantly by a bullet fired from the cathedral spire.[27]

The obsecrations (from *obsecrare,* to ask on religious grounds) lead us into the "mysteries" of the redemptive work of Christ and the sanctifying power of the Spirit. They begin with the words "by the mystery of thy holy Incarnation" and have the response "Help us, good Lord." These sentences recall the entire redemptive cycle of events in Christ's life, the "whole drama of his earthly obedience."

Like the "antecedent reason" in the collects, they lay the foundation for our confident appeal for divine aid. Canon Bright gives this helpful thought: "Every several act of our Lord's Mediatorial life has its appropriate saving energy; . . . virtue goes out of each, because each is the act of a Divine Person."[28] Or, as St. Leo suggested: All of Christ's acts are sacramental as well as exemplary. We plead each of these acts as mystically effective in the whole scheme of providence and redemption.[29]

The supplications, or prayers for ourselves, are remarkably few and brief. This small proportion in relation to the large number of intercessions, reveals the broad and unselfish spirit of the Litany itself. The supplications include only the phrases "in all time of our tribulation . . . our prosperity . . . the hour of death . . . the day of judgment" with the response "Help us, good Lord"; and the two concluding petitions, "to give and preserve to our use the fruits of the earth" and "graciously to hear our prayers."

The intercessions, or entreaties in behalf of others, constitute the largest group of petitions. They include first of all prayers for the church. These are followed by prayers for the nation and for our fellow men. All are introduced by a confession of our sinfulness: "We poor sinners do beseech thee" and the response to all petitions "We beseech thee to hear us, good Lord." "Thy holy Christian Church" is "thy holy catholic Church" in Luther's Latin Litany and "thy holy Church Universal" in the English Prayer Book. Luther's introduction of the petitions concerning "schisms and causes of offense" and "such as have erred and are deceived" reflects his concern for purity of doctrine. His petition "to beat down Satan under our feet" is a clear reference to Romans 16:20. His "excellent and moving petitions" (Bishop Gore) "to raise up them

---

[27] *Ibid.,* p. 51.

[28] *Ibid.*

[29] Every student of the deeper meanings of the Litany will particularly appreciate Canon Bright's fine study in Blunt's *Annotated Book of Common Prayer,* and also Bishop Gore's discerning *Reflections on the Litany.* Among German writers, Loehe is particularly to be noted (see his *Agende* [3. Aufl.; 1884], pp. 157-69).

that fall and to strengthen such as do stand" must be thought of as a part of the group relating to the church and as an expression of concern for the spiritual welfare of believers, especially the timid or those who are referred to in Marshall's *Goodly Primer* (1535), as "weak in virtue and soon overcome in temptation."[30]

The intercessions for the nation remind us of I Timothy 2:2 and of petitions in early Christian liturgies. The early church in praying for pagan rulers was praying for its persecutors as well as for its own peace. We are praying for the church's defenders and these petitions express our obligations as citizens. The petition in the Common Service "to give to our nation perpetual victory over all its enemies" was not to be limited to foreign foes. It certainly included the thought that our enemies may be within as well as without and that the nation's worst foes may conceivably be some of its own citizens or officials or the sins of the people as a whole.[31]

Notwithstanding this wider understanding, it was thought best to omit this petition from the text in the Common Liturgy. The final Kyrie was also omitted as repetitious. "Air" was added to the petition for travelers "by land or water," and at the very beginning the invocation "O Holy Trinity" was restored, as in the pre-Reformation texts.

The intercessions for all sufferers are by Luther, though there are reminiscences of early church prayers such as the following from the Greek Liturgy of St. Basil: "Sail thou with the voyagers, travel with the travellers, stand forth for the widows, shield the orphans, deliver the captives, heal the sick, remember all who are affliction or necessity." Luther does not give a special petition for travelers. The petition "to set free all who are innocently imprisoned" reminds us of the prayer in the *Apostolic Constitutions* for those in bonds "for the name of the Lord" which the Middle Ages adapted to the needs of those who in travel and commerce found themselves in peril from pirates, highwaymen, and slavers.

The Litany concludes with the Lord's Prayer followed by six Collects, each introduced by a versicle. The versicles emphasize the congregational character of the Litany and introduce the theme of the Collects which follow. Luther's Latin Litany had five versicles and five Collects; his German, six versicles and four Collects. The first five Collects in our Litany are found in either or both of Luther's litanies. Drews speaks of them as re-workings of Latin originals, "Frei, aber vortrefflich."

The first Collect in the Litany of the Common Liturgy is the third in Luther's Latin and the second in his German Litany. Its Latin form can be traced as far back as the Leonine Sacramentary. It is given in Brandenburg-Nuremberg (1533), Mark Brandenburg (1540), Riga (1537), Mecklenburg (1552), Saxony (1539), Reformation of Cologne (1543), and others.

The second Collect is the second in Luther's Latin Liturgy and the fourth in his German (after 1530). It is Gelasian in origin and appears in the Milan, Roman, Bamberg, Nuremberg, and Sarum missals and in Saxony

---

[30] Bishop Gore calls attention to the fact that "the prayers in the New Testament are not to any considerable extent prayers for the conversion of those outside or of wilful sinners. They are prayers for the perfecting of the faithful." *Reflections on the Litany*, p. 73.

[31] The Nuremberg *Officium sacrum* (1664) has the phrase "over all *thine* enemies" (*contra hostes tuos*).

633

(1539), Mecklenburg (1552), Pfalz-Zweibrücken (1557), Wittenberg (1559), Spangenberg (1545), Lüneburg (1564), Austria (1571), and other church orders.

The third is the first in Luther's Latin and German litanies. It is in the Bamberg Missal (1499) (ccxcii, col. 2, *missa pro tribulatio*) and in the Sarum Missal (Legg, 408), *missa pro tribulacione cordis*. It is in Brandenburg-Nuremberg (1533), Saxony (1539), Schwäbisch-Hall (1543), Reformation of Cologne (1543), Mecklenburg (1552), Brunswick-Lüneburg (1544), and other church orders.

The fourth is the fourth in Luther's Latin and the third in his German litanies. It is Gregorian in origin and is the Proper Collect in the Roman Missal for the Fourth Sunday after Epiphany. It is also in the Bamberg, Nuremberg, Constance, and Sarum pre-Reformation missals, and in Brandenburg-Nuremberg (1533), Cassel (1539), Riga (1537), Reformation of Cologne (1543), Lüneburg (1564), Austria (1571), and other church orders.

The fifth is the fifth in Luther's Latin Litany.

The sixth Collect in the Common Service form is not in Luther's litanies but appears in his hymns in 1533. It is the Proper Collect of the Roman *Missa pro pace*.[32] It is Gelasian in origin and is found in the Roman, Milan, Sarum, and other missals, and in many church orders. It is the final Collect in Vespers. The Common Liturgy has given as an alternate for this Collect the Matins Collect for use in the morning. (For further discussion of these, see above, pp. 425, 446-47.)

The Litany has remained practically as the Reformers revised it four hundred years ago. New petitions might well be added in view of modern conditions. The church is more conscious of world needs and of its own world mission than it was four centuries ago, and there might well be petitions for missions and missionaries and for the spread of Christ's Spirit among all peoples. The needs of special groups in our modern social structure might be remembered. A prayer for Christian unity would be in harmony with the basic character of the Litany itself.

Luther provided musical settings for both his Latin and his German litanies. His plan called for two choirs. The first choir, a group of two to six singers, sang the first half of each clause or petition, and the congregation joined the second choir or group in the response. When such full choral arrangement was not possible, the pastor sang or read the petition and the choir and congregation sang or repeated the response. Both choirs joined in the final Kyrie and Amen.

[32] For the sources of Luther's litanies including versicles and Collects see Paul Zeller Strodach's critical notes in *PE* 6, 319ff. Also Drew's *Studien zur Geschichte des Gottesdiensts*, Parts IV and V; and his introduction and notes in *WA* 30^{III}, 1-42, where the musical settings are given and discussed. See also Paul Althaus, *Zur Einführung in die Quellengeschichte der kirchlichen Kollekten in den lutherischen Agenden des 16. Jahrhunderts*, a valuable study which asserts (p. 12), that Luther in translating the old litany Collects followed the version in the *Psalmorum Liber* of Andreas Crantander (Basel, 1524) which showed variations from the originals.

Various composers including Orlando di Lasso, Palestrina, etc., have provided polyphonic settings for the three approved litanies of the Roman church.[33]

Professor Drews believes that while Luther's text was in large part a rearrangement of earlier material, the music of his litanies was of his own composition.[34]

Luther's *Latina litania correcta* and its melody appears in Lossius and the Pomeranian Order but had no wide usage. Many orders and cantionales give Luther's German text with the melody composed for it—Spangenberg, Lossius, Keuchenthal, Eler, Pomerania, Rhein Pfalz, and others. This melody has been universally associated with Luther's German Litany since the Reformation. All modern editors give it—Schoeberlein, Mecklenburg Cantionale, Bavaria, Prussia, Loehe, Herold, Endlich, Saxony, Sweden, etc. Archer and Reed first arranged these melodies to the English text in the *Choral Service Book* (1901), and this was incorporated in the *Common Service Book* in 1917. Schoeberlein gives two four-part settings by Praetorius and one of five and six parts by Vulpius in his *Schatz des liturgischen Chor- und Gemeindegesangs*, I, 731-49. Notwithstanding its general use in Lutheran circles, this setting is dull and heavy. The Common Liturgy provides a more attractive melody adapted from traditional Latin forms.

Lutheran usage has generally recognized that the Litany is more than a penitential prayer. Its grasp of the whole gospel and way of salvation and its wide and deep understanding of human need give it independent value. It is appointed for use as a general prayer in the Service on Sundays except on festivals or when there is a Communion. It may also be used at Matins and Vespers, except on festivals; and as a special office at any time. When used as a special office it is preceded by the Invocation, a psalm, a lesson, and a hymn. A benediction follows the last Collect and concludes the office.

THE LITANY

¶ *The Litany may be used at The Service on Sundays in place of the Prayer of the Church, except on Festivals or when there is a Communion.*

¶ *It may be used at Matins and Vespers, except on Festivals.*

¶ *When used at Matins or Vespers, it shall immediately follow the Canticle, and after it shall be said the Benedicamus and the Benediction.*

¶ *It may be used alone on Days of Humiliation and Prayer, or as a Penitential Office, or at specially appointed times; the ancient litany days being Wednesday and Friday.*

¶ *When used as a special Office, the Order shall be: The Minister shall say:* In the Name of the Father, and of the Son, and of the Holy Ghost. ℞ Amen. *Then shall be said one or more of the Psalms with the Gloria Patri. A brief*

---

[33] Proske gives ten such polyphonic settings, *Musica Divina* IV: pp. 319-78. (A rare work available in the Boston Public Library.)

[33] For discussion of the melodies which Luther appointed, see *WA* 30^III, 21ff, where questions concerning Luther's authorship are discussed.

*Lesson with the Response and a Hymn may follow. Then shall the Litany
follow, and after the last Collect shall follow this Benediction:* The Blessing
of Almighty God, the Father, the Son, and the Holy Ghost, be with you all.
℟. Amen.

¶ *The Responses shall be sung or said by the Congregation.*

Lord, have mercy upon us.
 ℟. Lord, have mercy upon us.
Christ, have mercy upon us.
 ℟. Christ, have mercy upon us.
Lord, have mercy upon us.
 ℟. Lord, have mercy upon us.

O Christ, hear us.
 ℟. O Christ, hear us.

O God, the Father in heaven:
 ℟. Have mercy upon us.
O God, the Son, Redeemer of the world:
 ℟. Have mercy upon us.
O God the Holy Ghost:
 ℟. Have mercy upon us.
O Holy Trinity, One God:
 ℟. Have mercy upon us.
Be gracious unto us.
 ℟. Spare us, good Lord.
Be gracious unto us.
 ℟. Help us, good Lord.
From all sin; from all error; from all evil:
 ℟. Good Lord, deliver us.

From the crafts and assaults of the devil;
From sudden and evil death;
From pestilence and famine;
From war and bloodshed;
From sedition and rebellion;
From lightning and tempest;
From all calamity by fire and water;
And from everlasting death:
℟. Good Lord, deliver us.

By the mystery of thy holy Incarnation;
By thy holy Nativity;
By thy Baptism, Fasting, and Temptation;
By thine Agony and bloody Sweat;
By thy Cross and Passion;
By thy precious Death and Burial;
By thy glorious Resurrection and Ascension;
And by the coming of the Holy Ghost, the Comforter:
 ℟. Help us, good Lord.

In all time of our tribulation;
In all time of our prosperity;
In the hour of death;
And in the day of judgment:
 ℟. Help us, good Lord.

We poor sinners do beseech thee;

℟. To hear us, O Lord God.

And to rule and govern thy holy Christian Church;
To preserve all pastors and ministers of thy Church in the true knowledge
and understanding of thy Word, and in holiness of life;
To put an end to all schisms and causes of offence;
To bring into the way of truth all such as have erred, and are deceived;
To beat down Satan under our feet;
To send faithful laborers into thy harvest;
To accompany thy Word with thy Spirit and grace;
To raise up them that fall, and to strengthen such as do stand;
And to comfort and help the weak-hearted and the distressed:

℟. We beseech thee to hear us, good Lord.

To give to all nations peace and concord;
To preserve our country from discord and contention;
To direct and defend our President (*or,* our gracious Sovereign), and all in
authority;
And to bless and keep our magistrates, and all our people:

℟. We beseech thee to hear us, good Lord.

To behold and succor all who are in danger, necessity and tribulation;
To protect all who travel by land, air or water;
To preserve all women in the perils of childbirth;
To strengthen and keep all sick persons and young children;
To set free all who are innocently imprisoned;
To defend and provide for all fatherless children and widows;
And to have mercy upon all men:

℟. We beseech thee to hear us, good Lord.

To forgive our enemies, persecutors, and slanderers, and to turn their hearts;
To give and preserve to our use the fruits of the earth;
And graciously to hear our prayers:

℟. We beseech thee to hear us, good Lord.

O Lord Jesus Christ, Son of God;

℟. We beseech thee to hear us.

O Lamb of God, that takest away the sin of the world;
℟. Have mercy upon us.
O Lamb of God, that takest away the sin of the world;
℟. Have mercy upon us.
O Lamb of God, that takest away the sin of the world;
℟. Grant us thy peace.

¶ *Then shall the Minister, and the Congregation with him, say the Lord's Prayer.*
Our Father, who art in heaven . . .

¶ *Then shall the Minister say the Collect for the Day, except when The Litany
is used at The Service. Then may be said one or more of the Litany Collects
here following.*

1

℣. O Lord, deal not with us after our sins.
℟. Neither reward us according to our iniquities.

ALMIGHTY God, our heavenly Father, who desirest not the death of a sinner, but rather that he should turn from his evil way and live: We beseech thee graciously to turn from us those punishments which we by our sins have deserved, and to grant us grace ever hereafter to serve thee in holiness and pureness of living; through Jesus Christ, thy Son, our Lord. *Amen.*

2

℣. Help us, O God of our salvation, for the glory of thy Name.
℟. Deliver us, and purge away our sins, for thy Name's sake.

ALMIGHTY and everlasting God, who by thy Holy Spirit dost govern and sanctify the whole Christian Church: Hear our prayers for all members of the same, and mercifully grant, that by thy grace they may serve thee in true faith; through Jesus Christ, thy Son, our Lord. *Amen.*

3

℣. O Lord, deal not with us after our sins.
℟. Neither reward us according to our iniquities.

O GOD, merciful Father, who despisest not the sighing of a contrite heart, nor the desire of such as are sorrowful: Mercifully assist our prayers which we make before thee in all our troubles and adversities, whensoever they oppress us; and graciously hear us, that those evils which the craft and subtilty of the devil or man worketh against us, may, by thy good providence, be brought to naught; that we thy servants, being hurt by no persecutions, may evermore give thanks unto thee in thy holy Church; through Jesus Christ, thy Son, our Lord. *Amen.*

4

℣. O Lord, enter not into judgment with thy servant.
℟. For in thy sight shall no man living be justified.

ALMIGHTY God, who knowest us to be set in the midst of so many and great dangers, that by reason of the frailty of our nature we cannot always stand upright: Grant us such strength and protection, as may support us in all dangers, and carry us through all temptations; through Jesus Christ, thy Son, our Lord. *Amen.*

5

℣. Call upon me in the day of trouble.
℟. I will deliver thee, and thou shalt glorify me.

SPARE us, O Lord, and mercifully forgive us our sins, and though by our continual transgressions we have merited thy punishments, be gracious unto us, and grant that all those evils which we have deserved may be turned from us, and overruled to our everlasting good; through Jesus Christ, thy Son, our Lord. *Amen.*

¶ *In the Morning the final Collect shall be the Collect for Grace with its Versicle* (p. 139).

¶ *In the Evening the final Collect shall be the Collect for Peace with its Versicle* (p. 147).

CHAPTER XXXI

THE SUFFRAGES; THE BIDDING PRAYER; ALTERNATE GENERAL PRAYERS

THE SUFFRAGES

The suffrages (from *suffragium,* a prayer of intercession) are a series of versicles and responses, chiefly from the Psalms, arranged to constitute a complete prayer much in the spirit and form of a litany, but more objective and poetic in character than the Litany itself.

The name "preces" was given quite early to suffrages or supplications in the form of versicles and responses. Cyprian speaks of the preces as a "litany." This prayer form recognizes the importance of the active participation of the congregation in responsive worship, "an holy priesthood, to offer up spiritual sacrifice" of which St. Peter speaks (I Pet. 2:5).

Possibly both the *missa catechumenorum* and the *missa fidelium* began with an intercessory prayer (*preces*) from which the Bidding Prayer after the Gospel or after the Offertory later developed.[1] The early Gallican church concluded the offices with a developed litany of responsive character which later included the Kyrie, Lord's Prayer, and Creed. The early Roman Rite had no suffrages of this kind but finally accepted the Gallican forms, some of which were quite lengthy. The late medieval pattern of suffrages containing the Kyrie, Lord's Prayer, versicles and responses, and a collect, gained acceptance throughout the entire church. At all events the practice of following the psalms in the offices by the preces had been continuous since the time of Charlemagne.[2]

In the Anglican communion, the term "preces" is applied somewhat

[1] Scudamore, *Notitia Eucharistica,* p. 304.

[2] The Benedictine Suitbert Bäumer, in his *Geschichte des Breviers* (Freiburg: Herder, 1895), p. 611-13, gives an interesting preces from the ninth century codex of the diocese of Rheims, now in the library of Corpus Christi College, Cambridge. This dates from the year A.D. 885 and is a much more complicated form than the later Roman texts.

differently to the opening versicles of Morning Prayer and Evening Prayer ("O Lord, open thou our lips," etc., with the concluding Gloria Patri) and also to the abbreviated series of two versicles with their responses following the Creed in Morning Prayer and the six versicles with their responses in Evening Prayer. These portions of the ancient preces are beautiful and impressive, notwithstanding their fragmentary character.[3] They have been furnished with musical settings by some of the most eminent Anglican composers, e.g., "The Preces and Responses" by Thomas Tallis and "The First and Second Preces" by Orlando Gibbons, as well as similar works by modern composers.[4]

The suffrages (*preces feriales*) doubtless were used in Latin in Matins and Vespers in Lutheran services in the sixteenth century, though there probably were no vernacular versions for the people. The cantionales provide no musical settings for them. Loehe's *Agende* of 1844, originally prepared for the use of German Lutheran congregations in the American Middle West, contained not only the Litany and the Bidding Prayer, but the General Suffrages and the Morning Suffrages and Evening Suffrages as well. The *Church Book* of the General Council (1868) first provided the English text of the General Suffrages. The Common Service of 1888 added the English texts of the Morning Suffrages and the Evening Suffrages. The *Common Service Book* of 1917 made possible the use of any of these forms as a special office by rubrical provisions for an opening invocation, a psalm, lesson, hymn, and concluding benediction. The suffrages have been carried over into the Common Liturgy. They provide admirable forms for congregational worship or for the devotional services of colleges, seminaries, synods, conferences, and other assemblies.

As Loehe states, Matins and Vespers are rich in hymns, psalms, and Scripture readings, but they in themselves provide little opportunity for supplications or for far-reaching intercessions in behalf of others. This concern for others, and for the general interests of the church and the world, may well be cultivated by the use of the Suffrages in connection with Matins and Vespers or as a special office. So used, they will be found a vital, quickening introduction to the Collects which conclude the service. Their responsive character is an attractive and arresting

[3] Maskell, *Monumenta ritualia ecclesiae Anglicanae,* III, 400ff., gives a "Form of Bidding the Bedes, anciently used in the Cathedral Church of the Diocese of Salisbury," which contains a form of preces which may have influenced the selection of material in the Prayer Book.

[4] See John Jebb, *Choral Service of the United Church of England and Ireland* (1843), and *The Choral Responses and Litanies of the United Church of England and Ireland,* 2 vols. (London: Bell, 1847-77).

form of prayer and a devotional recognition of common belief, fellowship, and work.

The text of the Suffrages is derived, without material change, from the prayers appointed in the Roman Breviary. The *preces feriales* in varying forms are said on weekdays at all hours except Matins. Our Morning Suffrages and our Evening Suffrages are taken from these ferial preces of Prime and Compline respectively. The Creed finds a place in both these suffrages. The General Suffrages are the preces at Lauds and Vespers, with the omission of petitions for the pope, the bishop, benefactors, and the departed, which the Roman Church inserts among the Psalm verses.

The text of the General Suffrages conforms to ancient usage in assigning the Lord's Prayer to the minister alone, with the final petition, "But deliver us from evil," as a response by the congregation. The doxology, "For thine is the kingdom," is also omitted. The Morning Suffrages and the Evening Suffrages include the doxology and give the entire Lord's Prayer to the congregation, because this is followed immediately by the Creed. These services conclude with the "Prayers for Morning and Evening" from Luther's Small Catechism. These fine prayers unquestionably are expansions of the Collects which concluded the offices of Prime and Compline respectively. In the ancient services, the Collect for Grace ("O Lord our heavenly Father, Almighty and everlasting God, who hast safely brought us to the beginning of this day") followed the preces and concluded the office of Prime. The resemblance between this Collect and the longer Collect which Luther provided is apparent. The resemblance in the case of the prayer for evening is even more striking, as is shown in the comparison of texts. In all his Collects and prayers, Luther kept within the great Christian tradition. There was no striving for originality. On the other hand, there is every evidence of church consciousness, respect for historical continuity, and liturgical restraint. With these principles in view, Luther treated the ancient forms freely, infusing into them a warmth peculiarly his own, yet ever retaining the hard core of these expressions of centuries of Christian experience.

THE GENERAL SUFFRAGES

Breviarium Romanum	*Common Liturgy*
	¶ *The General Suffrages may be said at Matins or Vespers immediately following the Canticle.*
Kyrie, eléison.	Lord, have mercy upon us.
	℞. Lord, have mercy upon us.

Christe, eléison.

Christ, have mercy upon us.
   R̷. Christ, have mercy upon us.

Kyrie, eléison.

Lord, have mercy upon us.
   R̷. Lord, have mercy upon us.

Pater noster,
  quod dicitur a solo Hebdomadario totum clara voce, usque ad:

¶ Then shall the Minister say:
Our Father, who art in heaven, Hallowed by thy Name, Thy kingdom come, Thy will be done, on earth as it is in heaven. Give us this day our daily bread; And forgive us our trespasses, as we forgive those who trespass against us; And lead us not into temptation:

Et ne nos indúcas in tentatiónem.
   R̷. Sed líbera nos a malo.

Ego dixi: Dómine, miserére mei.
   R̷. Sana ánimam meam, quia peccávi tibi. (Ps. 41:4.)

I said, O Lord, be merciful unto me:
   R̷. Heal my soul; for I have sinned against thee.

Convértere, Dómine, úsquequo?
   R̷. Et deprecábilis esto super servos tuos. (Ps. 90:13.)

Return, O Lord, how long?
   R̷. And let it repent thee concerning thy servants.

Fiat misericórdia tua, Dómine, super nos.

Let thy mercy, O Lord, be upon us:
   R̷. According as we hope in thee.

   R̷. Quemádmodum sperávimus in te. (Ps. 33:22.)

Sacerdótes tui induántur justítiam.
   R̷. Et sancti tui exsúltent. (Ps. 132:9.)

Let thy priests be clothed with righteousness:
   R̷. And let thy saints shout for joy.

Orémus pro beatíssimo Papa nostro *N.*
   R̷. Dóminus consérvet eum, et vivíficet eum, et beátum fáciat eum in terra, et non tradat eum in ánimam inimicórum ejus.
Orémus et pro Antístite nostro *N.*
   R̷. Stet et pascat in fortitúdine tua, Dómine, in sublimitáte nóminis tui.

Dómine, salvum fac regem.
   R̷. Et exáudi nos in die, qua invocavérimus te. (Ps. 20:9.)

O Lord, save our rulers:
   R̷. Let the King hear us when we call.

Salvum fac pópulum tuum, **Dómine,** et bénedic hereditáti tuae.
   R̷. Et rege eos, et extólle illos usque in aetérnum. (Ps. 28:9.)

Save thy people, and bless thine inheritance:
   R̷. Feed them also, and lift them up for ever.

Meménto Congregatiónis tuae.
℟. Quam possedísti ab inítio.
(Ps. 74:2.)

Remember thy congregation:
℟. Which thou hast purchased of old.

Fiat pax in virtúte tua.
℟. Et abundántia in túrribus tuis.
(Ps. 122:7.)

Peace be within thy walls:
℟. And prosperity within thy palaces.

Orémus pro benefactóribus nostris.
℟. Retribúere dignáre, Dómine, ómnibus nobis bona faciéntibus propter nomen tuum, vitam aetérnam. Amen.

Orémus pro fidélibus defúnctis.
℟. Réquiem aetérnam dona eis, Dómine, et lux perpétua lúceat eis.

Requiéscant in pace.
℟. Amen.

Pro frátribus nostris abséntibus.
℟. Salvos fac servos tuos, Deus meus, sperántes in te. (Ps. 86:2.)

Let us pray for our absent brethren:
℟. O thou our God, save thy servants that trust in thee.

Pro afflíctis et captívis.
℟. Líbera eos, Deus Israël, ex ómnibus tribulatiónibus suis. (Ps. 25:22.)

Let us pray for the broken-hearted and the captives:
℟. Redeem Israel, O God, out of all his troubles.

Mitte eis, Dómine, auxílium de sancto.
℟. Et de Sion tuére eos. (Ps. 20:2.)

Send them help from the sanctuary:
℟. And strengthen them out of Zion.

Hear my prayer, O Lord;
℟. And let my cry come unto thee.

¶ *At Matins may then be said responsively the Psalm (130), De profundis; and at Vespers may be said the Psalm (51), Miserere mei, Deus, secundum.*
¶ *Then shall be said:*

Dómine, Deus virtútum, convérte nos.
℟. Et osténde fáciem tuam, et salvi érimus. (Ps. 80:7.)

Turn us again, O God of hosts:
℟. Cause thy face to shine, and we shall be saved.

Exsúrge, Christe, ádjuva nos.
℟. Et líbera nos propter nomen tuum. (Ps. 44:26.)

Arise, O Christ, for our help:
℟. And redeem us, for thy mercy's sake.

643

Dómine, exáudi oratiónem meam.
R̷. Et clamor meus ad te véniat.
(Ps. 102:1.)

Hear my prayer, O Lord:
R̷. And let my cry come unto thee.

Dóminus vobíscum.
R̷. Et cum spíritu tuo.

The Lord be with you.
R̷. And with thy spirit.

Orémus.

Let us pray.

Oratio—Et dicitur Oratio conveniens. Postea fiunt Commemorationes, si occurrant.

¶ Then shall the Minister say the Collect for the Day, after which he may say any other suitable Collects, ending with this Collect for Peace.

Fiat pax in virtúte tua.
R̷. Et abundántia in túrribus tuis.

O Lord, let there be peace in thy strength:
R̷. And abundance in thy towers.

O God, from whom all holy desires, all good counsels, and all just works do proceed: Give unto thy servants that peace, which the world cannot give; that our hearts may be set to obey thy commandments, and also that by thee, we, being defended from the fear of our enemies, may pass our time in rest and quietness; through the merits of Jesus Christ our Saviour, who liveth and reigneth with thee and the Holy Ghost, one God, world without end. *Amen.*

Post ultiman Orationem additur:

¶ Then may be said the Benedicamus.

Benedicamus Domino.
R̷. Deo grátias.
or
Fidélium ánimae per misericordiam Dei requiéscant in pace.
R̷. Amen.

Bless we the Lord.
R̷. Thanks be to God.

Pater noster (totum secreto). Dóminus det nobis suam pacem.
R̷. Et vitam aetérnam. Amen.

Divínum auxílium máneat semper nobíscum.
R̷. Amen.

¶ Then shall be said the Benediction.
The Grace of our Lord Jesus Christ, and the Love of God, and the Communion of the Holy Ghost, be with you all. *Amen.*

THE MORNING SUFFRAGES

Breviarum Romanum

Common Liturgy

¶ *The Morning Suffrages may be said at Matins, or in the Morning Prayer of the Household, or alone as a brief Office.*

¶ *When said at Matins, the Morning Suffrages shall immediately follow the Canticle.*

¶ *When used as a special Office, the Morning Suffrages shall begin:*

In the Name of the Father, and of the Son, and of the Holy Ghost. ℟. Amen.

Kyrie, eléison.

Lord, have mercy upon us.
℟. Lord, have mercy upon us.

Christe, eléison.

Christ, have mercy upon us.
℟. Christ, have mercy upon us.

Kyrie, eléison.

Lord, have mercy upon us.
℟. Lord, have mercy upon us.

¶ *Then shall all say the Lord's Prayer and the Apostles' Creed.*

Pater noster (*secreto usque ad*).

Our Father, who are in heaven . . .

Et ne nos indúcas in tentatiónem.

℟. Sed líbera nos a malo.

Credo in Deum *secreto usque ad.*

I believe . . .

Carnis resurrectiónem.
℟. Vitam aetérnam. Amen.

¶ *When the Morning Suffrages are used as a Special Office, here shall follow the Psalm, the Lesson, and the Hymn.*

¶ *Then shall the Minister say:*

Et ego ad te, Dómine, clamávi.
℟. Et mane orátio mea praevéniet te. (Ps. 88:13.)

Unto thee have I cried, O Lord:
℟. And in the morning shall my prayer come before thee.

Repleátur os meum laude.
℟. Ut cantem glóriam tuam, tota die magnitúdinem tuam. (Ps. 71:8.)

Let my mouth be filled with thy praise:
℟. And with thy honor all the day.

645

Dómine, avérte fáciem tuam a peccátis meis.
℟. Et omnes iniquitátes meas dele. (Ps. 51:9.)

O Lord, hide thy face from my sins:
℟. And blot out all mine iniquities.

Cor mundum crea in me, Deus.
℟. Et spíritum rectum innova in viscéribus meis. (Ps. 51:10.)

Create in me a clean heart, O God:
℟. And renew a right spirit within me.

Ne projícias me a fácie tua.
℟. Et spiritum sanctum tuum ne áuferas a me. (Ps. 51:11.)

Cast me not away from thy presence:
℟. And take not thy Holy Spirit from me.

Redde mihi laetítiam salutáris tui.

Restore unto me the joy of thy salvation:

℟. Et spíritu principáli confírma me. (Ps. 51:12.)

℟. And uphold me with thy free Spirit.

In Precibus ferialibus tantum.
Eripe me, Dómine, ab hómine malo.
℟. A viro iníquo éripe me. (Ps. 140:1.)
Eripe me de inimícis meis, Deus meus.
℟. Et ab insurgéntibus in me líbera me. (Ps. 59:1.)

Eripe me de operántibus iniquitátem.
℟. Et de viris sánguinum salva me. (Ps. 59:2.)

Sic psalmum dicam nómini tuo in sáeculum sáeculi.
℟. Ut reddam vota mea de die in diem. (Ps. 145:2.)

Exáudi nos, Deus, salutáris noster.
℟. Spes ómnium fínium terrae, et in mari longe. (Ps. 65:5.)

Deus, in adjutórium meum inténde.
℟. Dómine, ad adjuvándum me festína. (Ps. 70:1.)

Sanctus Deus, Sanctus fortis, Sanctus immortális.

Bénedic, ánima mea, Dómino.
℟. Et ómnia, quae intra me sunt, nómini sancto ejus. (Ps. 103:1.)

Bénedic, ánima mea, Dómino.
℞. Et noli oblivísci omnes retributiónes ejus. (Ps. 103:2.)

Qui propitiátur ómnibus iniquitátibus tuis.
℞. Qui sanat omnes infirmitates tuas. (Ps. 103:3.)

Qui rédimit le intéritu vitam tuam.
℞. Qui corónat te in misericórdia et miseratiónibus. (Ps. 103:4.)

Qui replet in bonis desidérium tuum.
℞. Renovabitur ut aquilae juventus tua. (Ps. 103:5.)

In Precibus dominicalibus et ferialibus

Adjutórium nostrum in nómine Dómini.
℞. Qui fecit caelum et terram. (Ps. 124:8.)

Confíteor.

Misereátur.

Indulgéntiam.

Dignáre, Dómine, die isto. ℞. Sine peccáto nos custodíre.	Vouchsafe, O Lord, this day: ℞. To keep us without sin.
Miserére nostri, Dómine. ℞. Miserére nostri.	Have mercy upon us, O Lord: ℞. Have mercy upon us.
Fiat misericórdia tua, Dómine, super nos. ℞. Quemádmodum sperávimus in te.	O Lord, let thy mercy be upon us: ℞. As our trust is in thee.
Dómine, exáudi oratiónem meam. ℞. Et clamor meus ad te véniat. (Ps. 102:1.)	Hear my prayer, O Lord: ℞. And let my cry come unto thee.

Dóminus vobíscum.   The Lord be with you.
℞. Et cum spíritu tuo.   ℞. And with thy spirit.

Orémus.   Let us pray.

Oratio

¶ *Then shall be said the Collect for the Day, and any other suitable Collects; after which may be said the Prayer here following:*

Dómine, Deus omnípotens, qui ad princípium hujus diéi nos perveníre fecísti: tua nos hódie salva virtúte; ut in hac die ad nullum declinémus peccátum, sed semper ad tuam justítiam faciéndam nostra procédant elóquia, dirigántur cogitatiónes et ópera. Per Dóminum.
℟. Amen.

We give thanks to thee, heavenly Father, through Jesus Christ, thy dear Son, that thou hast protected us through the night from all danger and harm; and we beseech thee to preserve and keep us, this day also, from all sin and evil; that in all our thoughts, words and deeds, we may serve and please thee. Into thy hands we commend our bodies and souls, and all that is ours. Let thy holy angel have charge concerning us, that the wicked one have no power over us. *Amen.*

Dóminus vobíscum.
℟. Et cum spíritu tuo.

¶ *Then may be said the Benedicamus.*

Benedicámus Dómino.
℟. Deo grátias.

Bless we the Lord.
℟. Thanks be to God.

¶ *When the Morning Suffrages are said as a special Office, the following Blessing may be said.*

May the Lord Almighty dispose our days and our deeds in his peace. *Amen.*

¶ *At Matins shall be said this Benediction.*

The Grace of our Lord Jesus Christ, and the Love of God, and the Communion of the Holy Ghost, be with you all. *Amen.*

THE EVENING SUFFRAGES

Breviarium Romanum

Common Liturgy

¶ *The Evening Suffrages may be said at Vespers, or in the Evening Prayer of the Household, or alone as a brief Office.*
¶ *When said at Vespers, the Evening Suffrages shall immediately follow the Canticle.*

648

¶ *When used as a special Office, the Evening Suffrages shall begin:* ℣. In the Name of the Father, and of the Son, and of the Holy Ghost.
℟. Amen.

Kyrie, eléison.

Lord, have mercy upon us.
℟. Lord, have mercy upon us.

Christe, eléison.

Christ, have mercy upon us.
℟. Christ, have mercy upon us.

Kyrie, eléison.

Lord, have mercy upon us.
℟. Lord, have mercy upon us.

¶ *Then shall all say the Lord's Prayer and the Apostles' Creed.*

Pater noster
secreto usque ad

Our Father, who are in heaven . . .

Et ne nos indúcas in tentatiónem.
℟. Sed líbera nos a malo.

Credo in Deum
secreto usque ad

I believe . . .

Carnis resurrectiónem.
℟. Vitam aetérnam. Amen.

¶ *When the Evening Suffrages are used as a Special Office, here shall follow the Psalm, the Lesson, and the Hymn.*

¶ *Then shall the Minister say:*

Benedíctus es, Dómine, Deus patrum nostrórum.
℟. Et laudábilis et gloriósus in sáecula. (Benedicite.)

Blessed art thou, O Lord God of our fathers:
℟. And greatly to be praised and glorified forever.

Benedicámus Patrem et Fílium cum Sancto Spíritu.
℟. Laudémus, et superexaltémus eum in sáecula. (Benedicite)

Bless we the Father, and the Son, and the Holy Ghost:
℟. We praise and magnify him forever.

Benedíctus es, Dómine, in firmaménto caeli.
℟. Et laudábilis, et gloriósus, et superexaltátus in sáecula. (Benedicite.)

Blessed art thou, O Lord, in the firmament of heaven:
℟. And greatly to be praised, and glorified, and highly exalted forever.

649

Benedícat et custódiat nos omnípotens et miséricors Dóminus.
℟. Amen.

The Almighty and merciful Lord, bless and preserve us.
℟. Amen.

Dignáre, Dómine, nocte ista.
℟. Sine peccáto nos custodíre.

Vouchsafe, O Lord, this night:
℟. To keep us without sin.

Miserére nostri, Dómine.
℟. Miserére nostri.

O Lord, have mercy upon us:
℟. Have mercy upon us.

Fiat misericórdia tua, Dómine, super nos.
℟. Quemádmodum sperávimus in te. (Ps. 33:22.)

O Lord, let thy mercy be upon us:
℟. As our trust is in thee.

Dómine, exáudi oratiónem meam.
℟. Et clamor meus ad te véniat. (Ps. 102:1.)

Hear my prayer, O Lord:
℟. And let my cry come unto thee.

Dóminus vobíscum.
℟. Et cum spíritu tuo.
Orémus.

The Lord be with you.
℟. And with thy spirit.
Let us pray.

¶ Then shall be said the Collect for the Day, and any other suitable Collects; after which may be said the Prayer here following:

Oratio

Vísita, quáesumus, Dómine, habitatiónem istam, et omnes insídias inimíci ab ea longe repélle: Angeli tui sancti hábitent in ea, qui nos in pace custódiant; et benedíctio tua sit super nos semper. Per Dóminum.

We give thanks unto thee, heavenly Father, through Jesus Christ, thy dear Son, that thou hast this day so graciously protected us; and we beseech thee to forgive us all our sins, and the wrong which we have done, and by thy great mercy defend us from all the perils and dangers of this night. Into thy hands we commend our bodies and souls, and all that is ours. Let thy holy angel have charge concerning us, that the wicked one have no power over us. *Amen.*

℟. Amen.

Dóminus vobíscum.
℟. Et cum spíritu tuo.

¶ Then may be said the Benedicamus.

Benedicámus Dómino.
℟. Deo Grátias.

Bless we the Lord.
℟. Thanks be to God.

650

¶ *When the Evening Suffrages are said as a special Office, the following Blessing may be said.*

May the Almighty and Merciful Lord, the Father, the Son, and the Holy Ghost, bless and preserve us. *Amen.*

¶ *At Vespers shall be said this Benediction.*

The Grace of our Lord Jesus Christ, and the Love of God, and the Communion of the Holy Ghost, be with you all. *Amen.*

THE BIDDING PRAYER

The germ of the Bidding Prayer may be found in the worship of the Jewish synagogue, where, after the lessons, prayers were offered for members of the Jewish community and its needs. The early Christians expanded this idea. Justin Martyr in the second century speaks of a primitive litany which was recited after the Gospel, and the Eastern liturgies early developed and still have a so-called "deacon's litany" at this place in the liturgy. The deacon reads the lengthy prayer, and after each petition the congregation and the choir respond, "Lord, have mercy"; or the deacon announces the content of each petition, the priest reads the prayer itself, and the congregation responds "Amen" or "Kyrie eleison."

The early Roman liturgy contained such a deacon's litany, known also as the Prayer of the Faithful. About the time of Gregory the Great, this dropped out of all ordinary masses except for a meaningless *Dominus vobiscum* and *Oremus,* which remained in the text of the Mass without any prayer following. The Prayer of the Faithful, however, was retained in full in the solemn service of Good Friday, which in other respects also conforms to the most ancient rite of the church, e.g., in having the mass without an Introit but with two Old Testament lessons. Immediately following the Gospel, John's narrative of the Passion (John 18-19), is the Deacon's Litany or Bidding Prayer. The prayer is read in the following manner: the priest announces the thought of each petition and exhorts to unite in prayer, closing with the *Oremus.* The deacon calls out: "Let us kneel." After a few moments of private prayer the subdeacon says "Arise" and the priest offers the Collect. This procedure is repeated with each group of petitions.

651

The text of the Bidding Prayer in the Roman Mass probably dates from the time of Leo the Great in the fifth century. This is evident from the terms employed for the officers of the church and the religious; from the references to the Roman Empire as the one regularly constituted temporal power (a favorite tenet of Leo which has only now been partly erased in the revisions of the Holy Week Office by Pius XII in 1956); from the references to the catechumenate still in force; and from the indications of a confused and turbulent society torn by heresies, plagued by pestilence and famine, with innocent men kept in prison and slavery a recognized institution. All of these reflect conditions in Rome in the fifth century.

Many church orders, especially in south and southwestern Germany (Schwäbisch Hall [1543]; Pfalz Neuburg [1543]; Baden [1556]; Württemberg [1582]; Ulm [1656], etc.) retained the Bidding Prayer, modifying it to meet evangelical points of view and broadening it to include wider areas of human needs and concluding the entire prayer with the Lord's Prayer.

The Bidding Prayer, like some other features of the historic liturgy, has never found a place in the Prayer Books of the Anglican communion, though the name is given to a prayer of quite different nature.

The Common Service followed the *Church Book* in giving the ancient Bidding Prayer, omitting features peculiar to the Roman church and adopting some of the features from the church orders. A few minor changes in text and arrangement have been made in the Common Liturgy. This will be evident from comparison of the following texts from the new Roman Holy Week order (1956), the Schwäbisch-Hall Order of 1543, and the Common Liturgy.

We recognize in this ancient Bidding Prayer a true general prayer, whose unusual form quickens interest and encourages active participation, and whose thought unites us with martyrs and confessors of every age. In use, the "bids" should preferably be read by someone other than the officiating minister (another clergyman or a capable layman). After each bid there is a brief pause for silent prayer before the minister reads the Collect.

Common Liturgy

¶ *By ancient usage this Prayer was specially appointed for Good Friday. It may also be used on Wednesdays and Fridays in Lent and at other times.*

¶ *When this Prayer is said, a quiet moment should be kept after each bid, during which the people may make their silent petitions. The Collect, said by the Minister, is followed by the response, Amen, said by the people.*

Let us pray, dearly beloved, for the *holy Church of God*, that our Lord God would grant it peace and unity, and preserve it throughout the world, keeping it perpetually upon the true foundation, Jesus Christ.

Almighty and everlasting God, who hast revealed thy glory to all nations in Jesus Christ and the word of his truth: Keep in safety, we beseech thee, the works of thy mercy, that thy Church, spread throughout all nations, may serve thee in truth faith, and persevere in the confession of thy Name; through Jesus Christ, thy Son, our Lord. *Amen.*

Let us pray for the *chief pastor of the Church*, that the Lord God who called him

Von dem Gemeinem Gebeet

Hierauff/lassent uns bitten/für die gmein Christlich Kirch vnd für jre diener/das sie vnser Herr Gott beschütze/ wider alle anleuff vnd versuchung des bösen feinds/ vnd erhalte sie bestendiglich auff dem rechten felsen/vnsern Herrn Jesu Christo.

Bettent also:

Allmechtiger ewiger Gott/der du hast allen Völckern dein genad durch Jesum Christum/vnd sein Euangelion offenbaret/ erhalt Herr das volck deiner barmhertzigkeit/das dein Kirch/sampt jren dienern/ inn der gantzen welt zerstrewet/dir mit rechtem glauben diene/vnd inn bekantnus deines namens bestande.

Oratio Fidelium

1. Pro Sancta Ecclesia

Orémus, dilectíssimi nobis, pro Ecclésia sancta Dei: ut eam Deus et Dóminus noster pacificáre, adunáre et custodíre dignétur toto orbe terrárum: subíiciens ei principátus et potestates: detque nobis quiétam et tranquíllam vitam degéntibus, glorificáre Deum Patrem omnipoténtem.

Orémus

Omnípotens sempiterne Deus, qui glóriam tuam omnibus in Christo géntibus revelásti: custódi ópera misericórdiae tuae; ut Ecclésia tua, toto orbe diffúsa, stábili fide in confessióne tui nóminis persevéret. Per éundem Dóminum. ℟. Amen.

2. Pro Summo Pontifice

Orémus et pro beatíssimo Papa nostro N . . . : ut Deus et Dóminus noster, qui

to his office, may keep him in health and safety, for the good of the holy Church and the leadership of the people of God.

Almighty and everlasting God, by whose will all things are established: Mercifully hear our prayer, and of thy goodness preserve him whom thou hast called as our chief pastor, that under his guidance the Christian people, subject to thy rule, may grow in faith and in all good works; through Jesus Christ, thy Son, our Lord. *Amen.*

Let us pray for *all estates of men in the holy Church*, for pastors and ministers, for missionaries and deaconesses, for all faithful laymen, and for all the people of God.

Almighty and everlasting God, by whose Spirit the whole body of the Church is governed and sanctified: Receive our supplications and prayers for all estates of men in thy holy Church, that every member of the same, in his vocation and ministry, may faithfully serve thee; through Jesus Christ, thy Son, our Lord. *Amen.*

elégit eum in órdine episcopátus, salvum atque incólumem custódiat Ecclésiae suae sanctae, ad regéndum pópulum sanctum Dei.

Orémus

Omnípotens sempitérne Deus, cuius iudício univérsa fundántur: réspice propitius ad preces nostras, et eléctum nobis Antístitem tua pietáte consérva; ut christiána plebs, quae te gubernátur auctóre, sub tanto pontífice, credulitátis suae méritis augeátur. Per Dóminum.

3. Pro Omnibus Ordinibus Gradibusque Fidelium

Orémus et pro ómnibus epíscopis, presbýteris, diacónibus, subdiacónibus, acólythis, exorcístis, lectóribus, ostiáriis, confessóribus, virgínibus, víduis: et pro omni pópuli sancto Dei.

Orémus

Omnípotens sempitérne Deus, cuius spíritu totum corpus Ecclésiae sanctificátur et régitur: exáudi nos pro univérsis ordínibus supplicántes; ut grátiae tuae múnere ab ómnibus tibi grádibus fidéliter serviátur. Per Dóminum.
℟. Amen.

[The following two prayers are reversed in the Roman order.]

5. Pro Catechúmenis

Orémus et pro catechúmenis nostris: ut Deus et Dóminus noster adapériat aures praecordiórum ipsórum, ianuámque misericórdiae; ut, per lavácrum regeneratiónis accépta remissióne ómnium peccatórum, et ipsi inveniántur in Christo Iesu Dómino nostro.

Orémus

Omnípotens sempitérne Deus, qui Ecclésiam tuam nova semper prole foecúndas: auge fidem et intelléctum catechúmenis nostris; ut, renáti fonte baptísmatis, adoptiónis tuae filiis aggregéntur. Per Dóminum.

℟. Amen.

(Before 1956)

Orémus et pro Christianíssimo Imperatóre nostro N. ut Deus et Dóminus noster súbditas illi fáciat omnes bárbaras natiónes, ad nostram perpétuam pacem.

Let us pray for our *Catechumens*, that our Lord God would open their hearts and the door of his mercy, that having received the remission of all their sins by the washing of regeneration, they may be mindful of their baptismal covenant, and evermore be found in Christ Jesus our Lord.

O Almighty and eternal God, who dost always provide new children for thy Church: Increase the faith and understanding of our catechumens, that, being born again in the waters of baptism, they may be numbered among thine adopted children and daily renew their covenant with thee; through Jesus Christ, thy Son, our Lord. *Amen.*

Let us pray for *all in authority*, and especially for the Government (*of the United States*, or, *or the Dominion of Canada*), that we may lead a quiet and peaceable life in all godliness and honesty.

Lassent vns bitten/ für die weltlich Oberkeit/für vnsere Herrn/die Römischen Keyser vnd König/ für alle Christliche herschafft/sonderlich für ein Erbarn Rath diser Stadt/dat wire ein gerüwigs vnd stils leben/in allem Götlichem gehorsam füren mögen.

(After 1956)

4. Pro Res Publicas Moderantibus

Orémus et pro ómnibus res públicas moderántibus, eorúmque ministériis et potestátibus: ut Deus et Dóminus noster mentes et corda eórum secúndum voluntátem suam dírigat ad nostrum perpétuam pacem.

(Before 1956)

Orémus

Omnípotens sempitérne Deus, in cujus manu sunt ómnium potestátes, et ómnium jura regnórum: réspice ad Románum benignus Impérium; ut gentes, quae in sua feritáte confídunt, poténtiae tuae déxtera comprimántur. Per Dóminum.

℞. Amen.

(After 1956)

Orémus

Omnípotens sempitérne Deus, in cuius manu sunt ómnium potestátes et ómnium iura populórum: réspice benignus ad eos, qui nos in potestáte regunt; ut ubíque terrárum, déxtera tua protegénte, et religiónis intégritas, et pátriae secúritas indesinénter consístat. Per Dóminum.

℞. Amen.

Bittent also:

Barmhertziger Himelischer Vater/ in welches hand bestehet aller menschen gwalt/vnd Oberkeit/von dir gesetzt/zur straff der bösen/vnd wolfart der frummen/ inn welches hand auch stehn alle Recht vñ Gesetz aller Reich auff Erden. Wir bitten dich sihe gnediglich auff vnsere Herrn/ die Römischen Keyser vnnd König als vnsere öbriste weltliche häupter/vnd andere ordenliche Christliche Oberkeit/sonderlich auff vnsere herschafft ein Erbarn Rath der Stadt Schwebischen Hall/das sie weltlich Schwerdt/ jnen von dir beuolhen/ nach deinem beuelch füren mögen.

O merciful Father in heaven, of whom is all earthly rule and authority: Graciously regard thy servants, the President of the United States, (*or*, Her Majesty the Queen), and those who serve in public office, that under their direction this people may walk in the ways of thy commandments and be blessed with thy continued favor; through Jesus Christ, thy Son, our Lord. *Amen.*

6. Pro Fidelium Necessitatibus

Orémus. Orémus, dilectíssimi nobis, Deum Patrem omnipoténtem, ut cunctis mundum purget erróribus: morbos áuferat: famem depéllat: apériat cárceres: víncula dissólvat: peregrinántibus réditum: infirmántibus sanitátem: navigántibus portum salútis indúlgeat.

Orémus

Omnípotens sempitérne Deus, maestórum consolátio, laborántium fortitúdo: pervéniant ad te preces de quacúmque tribulatióne clamántium; ut omnes sibi in necessitátibus suis misericórdiam tuam gáudeant affuisse. Per Dóminum.

℞. Amen.

7. Pro Unitate Ecclesiae

Orémus et pro haeréticis, et schismáticis: ut Deus et Dóminus noster éruat eos ab erróribus univérsis; et ad sanctam matrem Ecclésiam, Cathólicam, atque Apostólicam revocáre dignétur.

Orémus

Omnípotens sempitérne Deus, qui salvas omnes, et néminem vis períre: réspice ad ánimas diabólica fraude decéptas; ut, omni haerética pravitáte depósita, errántium corda resipiscant, et ad veritátis tuae rédeant unitátem. Per Dóminum.

℞. Amen.

Lassent vns bitten/das Gott vns gnediglich erlöse/von allem jrthumb/kranckheit/tewrung/gfengnus/pestilentz/vnd von aller widerwertigkeit/so der böss feind vns zur verderbnus zu füget.

Bittent also:

Allmechtiger ewiger Gott/ein trost der traurigen/ein stercke der schwachen/las für dein angesicht kommen/die bitt aller derē die in bekümmernus vnd anfechtung zu dir seufftzen/das sie dein gnedig hilff inn aller jrer not entpfinden/durch vnsern Herrn Jesum Christ./

Let us pray our Lord God Almighty that he would deliver the world from all *error*, take away *disease*, ward off *famine*, set free *those in bondage*, grant health to the *sick*, and a safe passage to *all travellers*.

Almighty and everlasting God, the consolation of the sorrowful and the strength of the weak: May the prayers of them that in any tribulation or distress cry unto thee graciously come before thee, so that in all their necessities they may mark and receive thy manifold help and comfort; through Jesus Christ, thy Son, our Lord. *Amen.*

Let us pray for *all who are without the Church*, that our Lord God would be pleased to deliver them from all their errors, call them to faith in the true and living God and his only Son, Jesus Christ our Lord, and gather them into his holy family, the Church.

Almighty and everlasting God, who seekest not the death but the life of all mankind: Hear our prayers for all those who have no right knowledge of thee; free them from their errors, and for the glory of thy Name bring them into the fellowship of thy holy Church; through Jesus Christ, thy Son, our Lord. *Amen.*

Here may be said Collects 30, 31, and 32 / *Collects and Prayers, pp. 222, 223.*

8. Pro Conversione Iudaeorum

Orémus et pro pérfidis Iudáeis; ut Deus et Dóminus noster áuferat velámen de córdibus eórum; ut et ipsi agnóscant Iesum Christum Dóminum nostrum.

Orémus

Omnípotens sempitérne Deus, qui étiam Iudáicam perfídiam a tua misericórdia non repéllis: exáudi preces nostras, quas pro illíus pópuli obcaecatióne deférimus; ut, ágnita veritátis tuae luce, quae Christus est, a suis ténebris eruántur. Per eúndem Dóminum.

℟. Amen.

9. Pro Conversione Infidelium

Orémus et pro pagánis: ut Deus omnípotens áuferat iniquitátem a córdibus eeórum; ut relíctis idólis suis, convertántur ad Deum vivum et verum, et únicum Fílium eius Iesum Christum, Deum et Dóminum nostrum.

Orémus

Omnípotens sempitérne Deus, qui non mortem peccatórum, sed vitam semper inquíris: súscipe propítius oratiónem nostram, et líbera eos ab idolórum cultúra; et ággrega Ecclésiae tuae sanctae, ad laudem et glóriam nóminis tui. Per Dóminum.

℟. Amen.

(*Ordo Hebdomadae Sanctae* . . . . Marietta: no pub., 1956, pp. 63-68.)

Let us pray for *peace throughout the world*, and for the guidance of God's Spirit in the councils of men.

Almighty and everlasting God, King of Glory, and Lord of heaven and earth, by whose Spirit all things are governed: Bestow thy heavenly peace and concord upon the nations of the earth, that all men may serve thee in true fear, to the praise and glory of thy holy Name; through Jesus Christ, thy Son, our Lord. *Amen.*

Let us pray for our *enemies*, that God would remember them in mercy, and graciously vouchsafe unto them such things as are both needful for them and profitable unto their salvation.

O Almighty, everlasting God, who, through thine only Son, our blessed Lord, has commanded us to love our enemies, to do good to them that hate us, and to pray for them that persecute us: We earnestly beseech thee, that by thy gracious visitation all our enemies may have the same love, and be of one accord and of one mind and heart, with us and with thy whole Christian Church; through the same Jesus Christ, thy Son, our Lord. *Amen.*

Lassent uns auch bitten vmb ein gemeinen friden/das wir Gottis wort mögen lernen/vnd inn einem erbarlichen Christlichem leben wandeln.

Allmechtiger ewiger Got/ein Herr Himmels vnd der Erden/durch welches Geist alle ding regirt/durch welches fürsehung alle ding geordnet werden/der du bist ein Gott des friedens/Wir bitten dich/du wollest vns mit deinem Gotlichen friden vnd einigkeit begnaden/das wir dir/in rechter forcht/zu lob vñ preiss deiner namens dienen.

Lassent vns auch bitten/ für vnsere feinde/das Gott sie mit gnaden bedencke/ vnd jnen/ was zu jrem heil nutzlich vñ notdürfftig ist/gnediglich verleyhe.

Bittent also:

Allmechtiger ewiger Gott/ der du vns beuolhen hast/ das wir vnser feind lieb haben sollen/ denen die vns beleidigen guts thun/vnd für vnsere verfolger bitten. Wir schreien ernstlich zu dir/das du alle vnsere feind wöllest gnediglich heimsuchen/jnen ware rewjrer sünden verleihen/ auch mit vns/vnd der gantzen Christenheit ein freundtliches Gotsförchtigs einhelligs gemüt vnd hertz geben/durch vnsern Herrn Jesum Christ/

Lassent vns auch bitten für alle schwangere Weiber/das Gott sie gnediglich von Kindsbande erlösen wöl.

Bittent also:

Allmechtiger ewiger Gott vnd Vater/ einschöpfer aller ding/ der du Man vnd Weib gnediglich gesegnet/ vñ dem Weib jren kummer im geberen/zu einem heiligen Creutz durch vnsern Herrn Jesum Christum geweyhet hast. Wir bitten dich Herre Gott/ du wöllest die frucht jres leibs/dein eigen geschöpff/erhalten/vnd bewaren/vnd vnter dem Creutz inn der bekümmerlichen geburt/ nicht verderben lassen/ sonder gnediglich vnd mit freuden entpinden/

Lassent vns auch bittē für die frücht der Erden/das sie Gott wöl gesegnen/vnd vns die selben/inn seinem gehorsam zugniessen/gnediglich verleihen.

Bittent also:

Allmechtiger ewiger Gott der du durch dein wort alle ding erschaffest vnd gesegnest. Wir bitten dich/das du dein Wort/ vnsern Herrn Jesum Christ inn vnser hertz pflantzest/dardurch an vns gesegnet werde/ mit fruchtbarer wachsung/vnd Götlichem gebrauch/alles was vns zur leiblichen notdurfft dienet.

Lassent vns auch sonst bitten für alles/ so vnser Herr gebeeten sein wil/sprechent/ Vater vnser u.

(Ordnung der Kirchen inn eins Erbarn Raths zu Schwäbischen Hall oberkeit und gepiet gelegen [1543]. Fol. XLIIII-XLVII.)

Let us pray for the *Fruits of the earth*, that God would send down his blessing upon them, and graciously dispose our hearts to enjoy them in obedience to his holy will.

O Lord, Father Almighty, who by thy Word has created and dost bless and uphold all things: We pray thee so to reveal unto us thy Word, our Lord Jesus Christ, that he dwelling in our hearts, we may by thy grace be made meet to receive thy blessing on all the fruits of the earth, and whatsoever pertains to our bodily need; through the same Jesus Christ, thy Son, our Lord. *Amen.*

Finally, let us pray for all those things which our Lord would have us ask, saying: Our Father, ...

ALTERNATE GENERAL PRAYERS

The Lutheran Liturgy is unique in providing a certain flexibility in its Prayer of the Church. The Roman Mass, since the loss of the Prayer of the Faithful, is without a true "general prayer," though invariable intercessions for the living and the departed are scattered throughout its Offertory and Canon. The Anglican *Book of Common Prayer* has its Prayer for the Church, which also is an invariable form used at every celebration of the Holy Communion. The Lutheran church orders, whether wisely or not, provided a variety of forms of general prayer and permitted the minister at his discretion to choose any of them or to use the Litany, the Suffrages, the Bidding Prayer, or a selection of Collects. The true idea of a general prayer was definitely guarded, but freedom was permitted in the matter of its form.

The Common Liturgy, in addition to the new text of the Prayer of the Church (*Service Book,* p. 6; discussion in this volume pp. 312-20), provides four alternate general prayers. (*Service Book and Hymnal,* pp. 238-41.) It also permits the use of the Litany "or any other suitable Prayer."

The four alternate prayers are excellent examples of a true Prayer of the Church, broad in scope, unselfish in spirit, revealing concern for the universal church, the world, and all sorts and conditions of men, and free from artificiality or sentimentality. They come from an interesting variety of sources—Greek, Anglican, German Lutheran, and Scotch Presbyterian respectively.

The first, "O Lord our God, who has bidden the light . . ." is a condensation and adaptation of one of the prayers said at Matins, and before the Holy Door, in the services of the Orthodox-Catholic Apostolic Church. Its origin is shrouded in the dim light of the early Christian centuries.[1]

The second prayer, "Almighty God, our heavenly Father, we thine unworthy servants . . ." is a conflation of texts in four separate prayers in the Anglican *Book of Common Prayer.* Dr. Massey Hamilton Shepherd, Jr., states that the original suggestion for the phrasing of the first paragraph "appears to have been a private prayer of Queen Elizabeth issued in 1546."[2] Its present form as a "General Thanksgiving" in the Prayer Book of 1662 is attributed to Bishop Edward Reynolds, the moderate Anglican who became a Puritan but "conformed" at the Restoration and was rewarded with the bishopric of Norwich. It happily pro-

---

[1] Isabel Florence Hapgood, *Service Book of the Holy Orthodox-Catholic Apostolic Church* (New York: Houghton, Mifflin, 1906), p. 21.

[2] *The Oxford American Prayer Book Commentary,* p. 19.

vided theological content with biblical allusions, in simple and practical form. It thankfully recalls God's gracious gifts and mercies and dutifully relates them all to daily Christian living. Its excellence has carried it beyond the bounds of Anglican devotion into the service books of many other communions. Rubrical permission for the congregation to join with the minister in the general thanksgiving first appeared in the Irish Prayer Book of 1878. This is now a general practice.

The third prayer, "Almighty and everlasting God, who art worthy to be had in reverence . . . ," first appeared in the *Church Book* of the General Council (1868). It may have been translated or adapted from German sources by Dr. Joseph A. Seiss.

The fourth prayer, "Almighty and most merciful Father . . . ," is an abbreviation, with two changes in "bids," of a bidding prayer in the 1940 *Book of Common Order* of the Church of Scotland (Presbyterian) (pp. 32ff.). It is part of the fourth order of morning service.

The Service Book and Hymnal did not include as an alternate the earliest of all Lutheran general prayers in the English language, and one with an interesting history. Beginning "Merciful God, heavenly Father, who has commanded us to meet together . . . ," this prayer had its original English source in *A Simple and Religious Consultation* of 1548. This was an English translation of a prayer in the Reformation of Cologne, the church order Melanchthon and Bucer prepared for Archbishop Hermann in 1543. This Lutheran order, which may have been translated into English by Archbishop Cranmer himself, exerted a great influence upon the first English Prayer Book of 1549. Dr. Joseph A. Seiss in his manuscript autobiography states that he "translated this prayer from the German" for the *Church Book* of the General Council, from which it came into the *Common Service Book* (p. 159). The omission of this prayer, an excellent condensation of historical material, is to be regretted.[3]

---

[3] The quaint English text of 1548 was reproduced in full in the first edition of *The Lutheran Liturgy* (1947), pp. 578-79. It is possible that this, the earliest example in the English language of a Lutheran general prayer, may have influenced the content, if not the form, of the prayer "for the whole State of Christes Churche" in the first English Prayer Book of 1549.

APPENDIX

I. THE GREEK LITURGY OF ST. JOHN CHRYSOSTOM

Taken from Three Liturgies of the Eastern Orthodox Church, *trans. Bishop Fan Stylian Noli (Boston: Albanian Orthodox Church in America, 1955), pp. 149-209. The liturgy begins with a lengthy preparatory office in which the priest and deacon prepare the holy elements behind the closed doors of the iconostasis. This finished, the liturgy itself begins as follows:*

The Deacon, holding his Orarion with three fingers, says:

Deacon: Arise and bless, O Master.

The congregation rises. The Priest, standing in front of the Holy Altar, elevates the Holy Gospel Book with both hands, makes the sign of the Cross therewith over the Antimens, and says:

Priest: Blessed is the kingdom of Father, Son, and Holy Spirit, always, both now and forever, and for ages to come.

Choir: Amen.

The congregation sits down.

PEACE LITANY

Deacon: In peace, let us pray to the Lord.

Choir: Lord our God, have mercy.

Deacon: For the peace from above, and for the salvation of our souls, let us pray to the Lord.

Choir: Lord our God, have mercy.

Deacon: For the peace of the whole world, for the welfare of the holy churches of God, and for the union of all, let us pray to the Lord.

Choir: Lord our God, have mercy.

Deacon: For this holy temple, and for those who with faith, devotion, and fear of God enter therein, let us pray to the Lord.

Choir: Lord our God, have mercy.

Deacon: For our Archbishop Theophan, for the honorable Presbytery, for the Diaconate in Christ, for all the clergy and the laity, let us pray to the Lord.

Choir: Lord our God, have mercy.

Deacon: For the President of the United States of America, for the armed forces of the nation, and for the American people, let us pray to the Lord.

Choir: Lord our God, have mercy.

Deacon: For their triumph over all foes and adversaries, let us pray to the Lord.

Choir: Lord our God, have mercy.

Deacon: For this city, for every city and country, and for the faithful dwelling therein, let us pray to the Lord.

Choir: Lord our God, have mercy.

Deacon: For propitious weather, for abundance of the fruits of the earth, and for peaceful times, let us pray to the Lord.

Choir: Lord our God, have mercy.

Deacon: For travelers by sea, by land, and by air, for the sick, for the suffering, for those in captivity, and for their salvation, let us pray to the Lord.

Choir: Lord our God, have mercy.

Deacon: For our deliverance from all tribulation, wrath, danger, and necessity, let us pray to the Lord.

Choir: Lord our God, have mercy.

Deacon: Help us, save us, have mercy on us, and protect us, O God, by thy grace.

Choir: Lord our God, have mercy.

Deacon: Commemorating our most holy, immaculate, blessed, and glorious Lady, the Mother of God and ever-virgin Mary, with all the Saints, let us commend ourselves, and one another, and all our life unto Christ our God.

Choir: To thee, Lord our God.

Priest: For unto thee are due all glory, honor, and worship, Father, Son, and Holy Spirit, always, both now and forever, and for ages to come.

Choir: Amen.

FIRST ANTIPHON

Choir. O bless the Lord and worship him, O my Soul; forever blessed art thou, O Lord. O bless the Lord and worship him, O my soul; O my heart and all within me, praise ye his holy name. O bless the Lord and worship him, O my soul; praise him and forget not all his benefits; who forgiveth every sin and iniquity of thine; and who healeth every wound and illness of thine; and who graciously doth redeem thee from destruction, and crowneth thy life with goodness and mercy and tenderness. O bless the Lord and worship him, O my soul; O my heart and all within me, praise ye his holy name. Forever blessed art thou, O Lord.

In some Churches of the East the entire Psalm 103 is read or sung:
Psalm 103

Bless the Lord, O my soul; and all that is within me, bless his holy name. Bless the Lord, O my soul, and forget not all his benefits;

He forgives all thy iniquities; he heals all thy diseases; he redeems thy life from destruction; he crowns thee with loving-kindness and tender mercies;

He satisfies thy mouth with good things; so that thy youth is renewed like the eagle's.

The Lord executes righteousness and judgment for all the oppressed.

He made known his ways unto Moses, his acts unto the children of Israel.

The Lord is merciful and gracious, slow to anger, and plenteous in mercy.

He will not always chide, neither will he keep his anger forever.

He has not dealt with us after our sins, nor rewarded us according to our iniquities.

For as the heaven is high above the earth, so great is his mercy toward those who fear him.

As far as the east is from the west, so far has he removed our transgressions from us.

As a father pities his children, so the Lord pities those who fear him.

For he knows our frame; he remembers that we are dust.

Man's days are as grass; as a flower of the field, so he flourishes.

For the wind passes over it, and it is gone; and the place thereof shall know it no more.

But the mercy of the Lord is forever and ever upon those who fear him and his righteousness unto children's children;

To those who keep his covenant, and to those who remember his commandments to do them.

The Lord has prepared his throne in the heavens; and his kingdom rules over all.

Bless the Lord, all his angels, mighty in strength, who do his commandments, hearkening unto the voice of his word.

Bless the Lord, all his hosts, his servants who do his will.

Bless the Lord, all his works in all place of his dominion; bless the Lord, O my soul.

Glory to Father, Son, and Holy Spirit, always.

Both now and forever, and for ages to come. Amen.

Bless the Lord, O my soul, and all that is within me, bless his holy name. Blessed art thou, O Lord.

Instead of the preceding Psalm, especially on Feast Days, the following Antiphonal Refrain is sung with the proper verses:

Choir: Through the intercession of thy Holy Mother, Savior save us. *(Thrice.)*

In the meantime, the Priest prays secretly:

FIRST ANTIPHON PRAYER

Priest: O Lord our God, whose power is incomparable, whose glory is inconceivable, whose mercy is immeasurable, and whose lovingkindness is ineffable; do thou, O Master, look down upon us and upon this holy temple with compassion, and bestow thy rich mercies and blessings upon us and upon our fellow-worshippers.

The Deacon makes a reverence, goes in front of the Icon of Christ holding his Orarion with three fingers, and says:

FIRST SHORT LITANY

Deacon: Again and again, in peace let us pray to the Lord.

Choir: Lord our God, have mercy.

Deacon: Help us, save us, have mercy on us, and protect us, O God, by thy grace.

Choir: Lord our God, have mercy.

Deacon: Commemorating our most holy, immaculate, blessed, and glorious Lady, the Mother of God and ever-virgin Mary, with all the Saints, let us commend ourselves, and one another, and all our life unto Christ our God.

Choir: To thee, Lord our God.

Priest: For thine is the majesty, and thine is the kingdom, and the power, and the glory, Father, Son, and Holy Spirit, always, both now and forever, and for ages to come.

Choir: Amen.

SECOND ANTIPHON

Psalm 146

Praise the Lord, O my soul. I will praise the Lord while I live; I will sing unto my God while I have any being.

Put not your trust in princes, nor in the son of man, in whom there is no help.

When his spirit departs, he returns to dust; and in that very day all his plans shall perish.

Happy is he that has the God of Jacob for his help, and who hopes in the Lord our God.

He made heaven and earth; the sea, and all that is therein, and he remains true forever.

He renders justice to the oppressed; he gives food to the hungry; he releases the prisoners.

The Lord opens the eyes of the blind; the Lord raises up those who are bowed down; the Lord loves the righteous.

The Lord protects the strangers; he supports the orphans and the widows; but he turns upside down the ways of the wicked.

The Lord shall reign forever, even thy God, O Zion, unto all generations.

Instead of the preceding, especially on Feast Days, the following Anthems are sung:

Choir: O Son of God, O save us, O Lord who art risen, we sing unto thee, Alleluia. *(Thrice.)*

ONLY-BEGOTTEN

Glory to Father, Son, and Holy Spirit, always, both now and forever, and for ages to come. Amen.

Only-begotten Son and our Lord immortal and Word of God, thou hast deigned for our eternal salvation in heaven to assume our flesh from the holy and immaculate and ever-virgin Saint Mary, thou wast made man for us unalterably, wast crucified, O Christ our God, death by thy death subduing, art one of the Holy Trinity, and art glorified with Father and Holy Spirit, O save us, O save us.

In the meantime, the Priest prays secretly:

SECOND ANTIPHON PRAYER

Priest: O gracious Lord, who hast given us these common prayers, and hast promised that when two or three are gathered in thy name thou wilt grant their requests; fulfill now the petitions of thy servants as may be most expedient for them; and bestow upon us knowledge of thy truth in this world, and life everlasting in the world to come.

At the end of the Second Antiphon, the Deacon makes a reverence, returns to his accustomed place in front of the Holy Doors, and holding the tip of his Orarion with three fingers, says:

SECOND SHORT LITANY

Deacon: Again and again, in peace let us pray to the Lord.

Choir: Lord our God, have mercy.

Deacon: Help us, save us, have mercy on us, and protect us, O God, by thy grace.

Choir: Lord our God, have mercy.

Deacon: Commemorating our most holy, immaculate, blessed, and glorious Lady, the Mother of God and ever-virgin Mary, with all the Saints, let us commend ourselves, and one another, and all our life unto Christ our God.

Choir: To thee, Lord our God.

Priest: For thou art a gracious and merciful God, and unto thee we ascribe glory, Father, Son, and Holy Spirit, both now and forever, and for ages to come.

Thereupon the Deacon goes into the Sanctuary through the south door.

THIRD ANTIPHON

Choir: In thy kingdom remember us, O Lord, when thou comest into thy kingdom.

Blessed are the poor in spirit; for theirs is the kingdom of heaven.

Blessed are those who mourn; for they shall be comforted.

Blessed are the meek; for they shall inherit the earth.

Blessed are those who hunger and thirst after righteousness; for they shall be filled.

Blessed are the merciful; for they shall obtain mercy

Blessed are the pure in heart; for they shall see God.

Blessed are the peacemakers; for they shall be called the children of God.

Blessed are those who are persecuted for righteousness' sake; for theirs is the kingdom of heaven.

Blessed are ye, when men shall revile you, and persecute you, and shall say all manner of evil against you falsely for my sake.

Rejoice, and be glad; for great is your reward in heaven.

In some Churches of the East the Beatitude Anthems are sung in the proper Tone with the preceding Verses. Instead of them, the Dismissal Anthem of the Tone or of the Feast is sung thrice. In the meantime, the Priest prays secretly;

PROCESSION PRAYER

Priest: O Master, Lord our God, who hast appointed orders and hosts for the service of thy glory in heaven: make our ceremony a procession of Angels and Archangels, ministering with us and praising thy goodness. For unto thee are due all glory, honor, and worship, Father, Son, and

Holy Spirit, always, both now and forever, and for ages to come. Amen.
The Congregation rises.

GOSPEL PROCESSION

The Priest and the Deacon make three reverences in front of the Altar, then the Priest takes up the Gospel Book and gives it to the Deacon. Then they pass behind the Altar, and go out through the north door, preceded by a Taper-bearer, and stand in front of the Holy Doors. Here Archdeacons, Archpriests, and Archimandrites are promoted. Then the Deacon, holding his Stole with three fingers, points therewith toward the east, and says in a low voice:

Deacon: Bless the holy entrance, O Master.

The Priest blesses it crosswise, and says:

Priest: Blessed is the entrance of thy Sanctuary, always, both now and forever, and for ages to come.

Deacon: Amen.

The Deacon goes in front of the Priest, who kisses the Gospel Book. Then the Deacon, standing in front of the Holy Doors, elevates the Gospel Book, and exclaims:

Deacon: Wisdom, arise.

Then he makes a reverence, enters the Sanctuary, followed by the Priest, and places the Gospel Book on the Altar.

PROCESSIONAL

Choir: Let us pray and let us worship, and let us kneel before Christ. O Son of God, O Save us, O Lord who art risen, we sing unto thee, Alleluia.

The Congregation sits down after the Gospel Procession. Then the Dismissal Anthem of the Patron Saint of the Church and the proper Collect Anthem are sung.

THRICE-HOLY HYMN

Deacon: Let us pray to the Lord.

Choir: Lord our God, have mercy.

Priest: For holy art thou, O Lord our God, and unto thee we ascribe glory, Father, Son, and Holy Spirit, always, both now and forever.

Deacon: And for ages to come.

Choir: Amen. O thrice-holy, O Lord mighty, O God immortal, have mercy on us. *(Thrice.)*

Glory to Father, Son, and Holy Spirit, always, both now and forever, and for ages to come. Amen. O God immortal, have mercy on us.

O thrice-holy, O Lord mighty, O God immortal, have mercy on us.

Here Bishops are consecrated. On Easter, Pentecost, Christmas, Epiphany, Saturday of Saint Lazarus, and Holy Saturday, the following substitute for the Thrice-holy Hymn is sung:

AS MANY

Choir: As many as have been baptized in Christ have put on Jesus Christ our Lord. Alleluia. *(Thrice.)*

Glory to Father, Son, and Holy Spirit, always, both now and forever, and for ages to come. Amen. Have put on Jesus Christ our Lord. Alleluia.

As many as have been baptized in Christ have put on Jesus Christ our Lord. Alleluia.

On September 14, on the Third Sunday of the Easter Lent, and on August First:

WE BOW DOWN

Choir: We bow down in worship before thy Cross, O Master, and we praise thy Resurrection from the dead, O Lord.

In the meantime the Priest prays secretly:

THRICE-HOLY PRAYER

Priest: O holy Lord, who sittest on thy holy throne; who art hailed by the Seraphim with thrice-holy greetings; who art glorified by the Cherubim; who art worshipped by all the Angelic hosts; who hast created the universe out of nothing; who hast fashioned man in thy own image and likeness, and hast adorned him with all thy gifts; who givest wisdom and understanding to him who seeks them; who dost not neglect the sinner, but has appointed repentance for his salvation; who hast vouchsafed unto us, thy humble and unworthy servants, to stand before the glory of thy Holy Altar at this hour, and to offer the praise and adoration due unto thee; thou, O Master, accept the Thrice-holy Hymn from our sinful mouths, and visit us in thy goodness; forgive us all trespasses both voluntary and involuntary; sanctify both our souls and bodies; and enable us to worship thee in holiness all the days of our life; through the intercession of the blessed Mother of God, Saint Mary, and of all the Saints, who have been well-pleasing unto three throughout the ages. For holy art thou, O Lord our God, and unto thee we ascribe glory, Father, Son, and Holy Spirit, always, both now and forever, and for ages to come. Amen.

Then the Deacon says to the Priest in a low voice:

Deacon: Command, O Master.

Priest: Blessed is he who comes in the name of the Lord.

Deacon: Bless the throne, O Master.

The Priest blesses crosswise the throne behind the Altar.

Priest: Blessed art thou, O Lord, who sittest on the glorious throne of thy kingdom, surrounded by the Cherubim, always, both now and forever, and for ages to come.

Deacon: Amen.

LESSON FROM EPISTLE

At the end of the Thrice-holy Hymn, the Deacon faces the congregation, and exclaims from the Altar:

Deacon: Let us attend.

The Priest turns to the congregation, blesses them crosswise, and says:

Priest: Peace unto all.

Choir: And with thee may it be.

The Reader announces the Epistle Gradual.

Deacon: Wisdom.

The Reader announces the Title of the Epistle.

Reader: The Lesson from the Epistle of Saint N.
Deacon: Let us attend.

The Reader recites the Epistle Lesson. In the meantime the Deacon censes the Altar, the Icon-screen, and the people. The Priest prays secretly.

GOSPEL PRAYER

Priest: O merciful Master, kindle in our hearts the brilliant light of thy divine revelation, and open the eyes of our mind to the understanding of thy Evangelistic doctrine; instill in our souls the fear of thy blessed commandments; enable us to suppress all sensual desires and lead a spiritual life by professing and practicing whatever is pleasing unto thee. For thou art the illumination of our souls and bodies, O Christ our God, and unto thee we ascribe glory, together with thy eternal Father, and thy most holy, gracious, and life-giving Spirit, always, both now and forever, and for ages to come. Amen.

At the end of the Epistle Lesson the Choir sings:

Choir: Alleluia, alleluia, alleluia.

In the meantime the Priest blesses the Reader crosswise, and says in a low voice:

Priest: Peace unto thee, O Reader.
Reader: And with thee may it be.

LESSON FROM GOSPEL

The Deacon approaches the Priest, bows to him, and says in a low voice:

Deacon: Bless, O Master, the reader of the Lesson from the Gospel of the Holy Apostle and Evangelist N.

Priest: May God enable thee to proclaim the Gospel of his beloved Son, our Lord Jesus Christ, through the intercession of the Holy Apostle and Evangelist N.

The Deacon makes a reverence, takes the Gospel Book, and goes out through the Holy Doors, preceded by a Taper-bearer, and stands on the Tribune; the congregation rises; the Priest faces the congregation, and proclaims from the Altar:

Priest: Wisdom, arise! Let us listen to the Holy Gospel. Peace unto all.

The Priest blesses the congregation crosswise.

Choir: And with thee may it be.
Deacon: The lesson from the Holy Gospel according to Saint N.
Priest: Let us attend.
Choir: Glory to thee, Lord our God, glory to thee.

The Deacon reads the Gospel. At the end of the Lesson the Choir sings:

Choir: Glory to thee, Lord our God, glory to thee.

The Deacon goes to the Holy Doors, and gives the Gospel Book to the Priest, who places it on the Altar behind the Antimens. The Deacon, standing in his accustomed place, says:

MERCY LITANY

Deacon: Let us pray with all our soul and with all our mind, let us pray.
Choir: Lord our God, have mercy. *(Thrice.)*
Deacon: O Lord Almighty, God of our fathers, we pray unto thee, hearken and have mercy. *(Thrice.)*
Choir: Lord our God, have mercy. *(Thrice.)*
Deacon: Have mercy on us, O God, according to thy great mercy, hearken and have mercy.
Choir: Lord our God, have mercy. *(Thrice.)*
Deacon: Furthermore we pray for all pious and Orthodox Christians, we pray unto thee, hearken and have mercy.
Choir: Lord our God, have mercy. *(Thrice.)*
Deacon: Furthermore we pray for our Archbishop Theophan, and for all our Brotherhood in Christ, we pray unto thee, hearken and have mercy.
Choir: Lord our God, have mercy. *(Thrice.)*
Deacon: Furthermore we pray for the President of the United States of America, for the armed forces of the nation, and for the American people, we pray unto thee, hearken and have mercy.
Choire: Lord our God, have mercy. *(Thrice.)*
Deacon: Furthermore we pray for the blessed and ever-memorable founders of this holy temple, for all our fathers, brothers and sisters, and for all the Orthodox believers, who have gone before us to their rest and who are asleep in the Lord here and in all the world, we pray unto thee, hearken and have mercy.
Choir: Lord our God, have mercy. *(Thrice.)*
Deacon: Furthermore we pray for mercy, peace, life, health, salvation, and remission of sins of thy servants, N., we pray unto thee, hearken and have mercy.
Choir: Lord our God, have mercy. *(Thrice.)*
Deacon: Furthermore we pray for those who bear fruit and do good works in this holy temple, for those who labor in its service, for the singers, and for the people here present who wait to receive thy great and rich mercies, we pray unto thee, hearken and have mercy.
Choir: Lord our God, have mercy. *(Thrice.)*

In the meantime, the Priest prays secretly:

MERCY LITANY PRAYER

Priest: O Lord our God, accept this devout supplication from thy servants; be gracious unto us according to thy infinite loving-kindness; and send down thy bounties upon us and upon all thy people who are expecting thy rich blessings from thee.

The Priest unfolds all the Antimens except the upper part, and exclaims:
Priest: For thou art a gracious and merciful God, and unto thee we ascribe

glory, Father, Son, and Holy Spirit, always, both now and forever, and for ages to come.

Choir: Amen.

If there is a Memorial Service, the following Litany is inserted:

MEMORIAL LITANY

Deacon: Have mercy on us, O God, according to thy great mercy, we pray unto thee, hearken and have mercy.

Choir: Lord our God, have mercy. *(Thrice.)*

Deacon: Furthermore we pray for the repose of the souls of thy departed servants, N., and for the forgiveness of all their sins both voluntary and involuntary, we pray unto thee, hearken and have mercy.

Choir: Lord our God, have mercy. *(Thrice.)*

Deacon: That their souls may be established where the just repose, we pray unto thee, hearken and have mercy.

Choir: Lord our God, have mercy. *(Thrice.)*

Deacon: That the Lord may grant them his mercy, the kingdom of heaven, and the remission of their sins, let us beseech of Christ, our immortal King and our God.

Choir: We pray, grant, O Lord.

Deacon: Let us pray to the Lord.

Choir: Lord our God, have mercy.

Priest: O God of spirit and all flesh, who hast trampled down Death, and overthrown the Devil, and given life unto thy world; do thou, O Lord, give rest to the souls of thy departed servants, N., in a place of light, in a place of green pastures, in a place of repose, whence all pain and sorrow and grief have fled away. O thou gracious and merciful God, pardon every sin which they have committed, whether by word, or deed, or thought, because there is no man who lives and sins not; for thou alone art without sin; for thy righteousness is to all eternity, and thy word is truth.

For thou art the resurrection, and the life, and the repose of thy departed servants, N., and unto thee we ascribe glory, together with thy eternal Father and thy most holy, and gracious, and life-giving Spirit, always, both now and forever, and for ages to come.

Choir: Amen.

LITANY OF THE LEARNERS

Deacon: O ye Learners, pray to the Lord.

Choir: Lord our God, have mercy.

Deacon: O ye faithful, let us pray to the Lord for the Learners, that the Lord may have mercy on them.

Choir: Lord our God, have mercy.

Deacon: That he may teach them the word of truth.

Choir: Lord our God, have mercy.

Deacon: That he may reveal to them the Gospel of Righteousness.

Choir: Lord our God, have mercy.

Deacon: That he may unite them to his Holy, Universal, and Apostolic Church.

Choir: Lord our God, have mercy.

Deacon: Save them, have mercy on them, help them, and protect them, O God, by thy grace.

Choir: Lord our God, have mercy.

Deacon: O ye learners, bow your heads unto the Lord.

Choir: To thee, Lord our God.

In the meantime the Priest prays secretly:

PRAYER OF THE LEARNERS

Priest: O Lord our God, who dwellest on high and regardest below; who hast sent thy only-begotten Son and God, our Lord Jesus Christ, for the salvation of mankind; look down upon thy servants, the Learners, who bow their heads unto thee; make them worthy at the proper time to receive the laver of regeneration, the remission of sins, and the garment of purity; unite them with thy Holy, Universal, and Apostolic Church; and number them with the flock of thy elect.

Then the Priest unfolds the upper part of the Antimens, and exclaims:

Priest: That with us they may also glorify thy most honorable and majestic name, Father, Son, and Holy Spirit, always, both now and forever, and for ages to come.

Choir: Amen.

The Priest makes the sign of the cross over the Antimens with the Sponge, which he kisses and lays on the Altar.

Deacon: Depart, all ye Learners, depart. All ye Learners, depart. Let no Learner remain. Let only the Faithful remain.

Choir: Lord our God, have mercy.

FIRST LITANY OF THE FAITHFUL

Deacon: O ye Faithful, again and again, in peace let us pray to the Lord.

Choir: Lord our God, have mercy.

Deacon: Help us, save us, have mercy on us, and protect us, O God, by thy grace.

Choir: Lord our God, have mercy.

In the meantime the Priest prays secretly:

FIRST PRAYER OF THE FAITHFUL

Priest: We give thanks unto thee, O God, Lord of hosts, for thou hast allowed us again to kneel before thy Holy Altar and to beseech thy mercy for our sins. O Lord, accept our prayers, for thou hast appointed us for this ministry through the grace of thy Holy Spirit; make us worthy to offer unbloody sacrifices for the trespasses of all thy people; enable us to call upon thee in every time and place, blamelessly and fearlessly, in purity of heart and conscience. Hear us, O Lord, and be gracious unto us in thy infinite goodness.

Then the Deacon exclaims:

Deacon: Wisdom!

Priest: For unto thee are due all glory, honor, and worship, Father, Son,

673

and Holy Spirit, always, both now and forever, and for ages to come.
Choir: Amen.

SECOND LITANY OF THE FAITHFUL

Deacon: Again and again, in peace let us pray to the Lord.
Choir: Lord our God, have mercy.
Deacon: For the peace from above, and for the salvation of our souls, let us pray to the Lord.
Choir: Lord our God, have mercy.
Deacon: For the peace of the world, for the welfare of the holy churches of God, and for the union of all, let us pray to the Lord.
Choir: Lord our God, have mercy.
Deacon: For our deliverance from all tribulation, wrath, danger, and necessity, let us pray to the Lord.
Choir: Lord our God, have mercy.
Deacon: Help us, save us, have mercy on us, and protect us, O God, by thy grace.
Choir: Lord our God, have mercy.

In the meantime the Priest prays secretly:

SECOND PRAYER OF THE FAITHFUL

Priest: Over and over again we beseech thee, O gracious and merciful Lord: Accept our prayers; purify our souls and bodies of every sinful blemish; allow us to approach thy Holy Altar freely and deservedly; grant unto us and unto all our fellow worshippers a prosperous life, a pure faith, and spiritual understanding; and enable us, O Lord, to receive thy Holy Sacrament and inherit thy heavenly kingdom.

In Greek use all the Litanies and secret Prayers after the Lesson of the Gospel are usually omitted. In Russian use only the Second Litany of the Faithful is sometimes omitted.

Deacon: Wisdom!
Priest: That, always protected by thy might, we may ascribe glory to thee, Father, Son, and Holy Spirit, always, both now and forever, and for ages to come.
Choir: Amen.

CHERUBIMIC HYMN

Choir: We are symbolizing mystic choirs of Cherubim, and to the life-giving Trinity the Thrice-holy Hymn we are chanting here. Let us now cast far away from us every care of our earthly life.

In the meantime the Priest prays secretly:

CHERUBIMIC PRAYER

Priest: None of those enslaved by sensual desires and pleasures is worthy to come unto thee, or to approach thee, or to minister unto thee, O King of Glory; for to serve thee is a great and awesome responsibility even for the Angelic Hosts; nevertheless, for the sake of thy ineffable and infinite mercy, thou wast made man unalterably and inalienably; thou hast officiated as our High Priest; and thou hast delivered unto us the Sacrament of this liturgical and unbloody sacrifice as the Master of the universe; for thou alone, O Lord our God, art reigning over heaven and earth; thou art riding on the wings of Cherubim; thou art the Lord of Seraphim; thou art the King of Israel; thou art holy and sitting on the holy throne of heaven; thou alone art good and ready to listen. Therefore, I beseech thee; Look down upon me, thy wayward and helpless attendant; purge my soul and my heart from an evil conscience; enable me through the power of thy Holy Spirit, which has invested me with the grace of thy priesthood, to stand before thy Holy Altar and perform the sacred ceremony of thy immaculate Body and precious Blood; for unto thee I come, before thee I bow my head, and unto thee I pray: Turn not away thy face from me, nor reject me from thy children, but condescend to accept these gifts from me, thy sinful and unworthy servant; for thou art the offerer and the offered, the receiver and the received. O Christ our God, and unto thee we ascribe glory, together with thy eternal Father, and thy most holy, gracious, and life-giving Spirit, always, both now and forever, and for ages to come. Amen.

The Deacon censes the Altar round about, the Icon-screen, the congregation, and again the Altar. Then the Priest and the Deacon stand before the Altar, raise their hands, and say thrice in a low voice:

Priest: We are symbolizing mystic choirs of Cherubim, and to the life-giving Trinity the Thrice-holy Hymn we are chanting here. Let us now cast far away from us every care of our earthly life.

Deacon: For the King of all we shall welcome. Angels and Saints invisibly escort him down from heaven. Alleluia, alleluia, alleluia.

They make three reverences, kiss the Antimens and the Altar, turn toward the congregation, bow to them, and go to the Oblation Table, which the Priest censes. Then the Deacon says to the Priest in a low voice:

Deacon: Lift up, O Master.

The Priest, taking the Great Veil, places it on the Deacon's left shoulder, and says:

Priest: Lift up your hands unto heaven and bless the Lord.

EUCHARIST PROCESSION

The Priest takes the Paten and sets it on the Deacon's head; the latter holds the Paten with one hand and the Censer with the other. Then the Priest takes the Chalice and both go out through the north door, preceded by a Taper-bearer, and stand facing the people. The congregation rises. The Deacon exclaims:

Deacon: All of us may the Lord remember in his kingdom, always, both now and forever, and for ages to come.

Choir: Amen.

Priest: Our Archbishop Theophan may the Lord remember in his kingdom always, both now and forever, and for ages to come.

Choir: Amen.

Priest: The President of the United States of America, the armed forces of the nation, and the American people; the founders, the trustees, the members and the supporters of this holy temple; all the Orthodox Christians who have gone before us to their rest, and who are asleep in the Lord; and the souls of the departed servants of God, N., may the Lord remember in his kingdom always, both now and forever, and for ages to come.

Choir: Amen. For the King of all we shall welcome. Angels and Saints invisibly escort him down from heaven. Alleluia, alleluia, alleluia.

The Deacon enters through the Holy Doors, stands on the right, and says to the Priest, who enters after him, in a low voice:

Deacon: May the Lord remember thy Priesthood in his kingdom.

Priest: May the Lord remember thy Diaconate in his kingdom.

The Priest places the Chalice upon the Altar to the right, then he takes the Paten from the Deacon's head, places it upon the Altar to the left, and says in a low voice:

Priest: Joseph, the noble and brave friend, took down from the Cross thy sacred remains, wrapped them up in fine linen, full of myrrh, musk, and perfumes, and wailing laid thee with tears in a grave.

In the tomb physically, in Hades spiritually, in Paradise with the sinner, and on the throne with the Father and the Holy Spirit, hast thou been, O Christ our God, omnipresent and omnipotent.

Lovelier than Paradise, and richer than a royal palace is thy life-giving tomb, the fountain of our resurrection, O Christ our God.

In the meantime the Priest takes the Veils from the Paten and the Chalice, and places them on one side of the Altar; then he takes the Great Veil from the Deacon's shoulder, censes it, covers therewith both the Chalice and the Paten, and says in a low voice:

Priest: Joseph, the noble and brave friend, took down from the Cross thy most sacred remains, wrapped them up in linen, full of myrrh, musk, and perfumes, and wailing laid these with tears in a grave.

Then he takes the Censer from the Deacon's hands, censes the Holy Gifts, and says in a low voice:

Priest: Exalt thou Zion in thy good pleasure; build thou the walls of Jerusalem. Then shalt thou be pleased with the sacrifice of righteousness, with oblations, and whole burnt offerings; then shall they offer bullocks upon thy altar.

Then he gives the Censer to the Deacon, bows his head, and says in a low voice:

Priest: Remember me, O brother and fellow-minister.

Deacon: May the Lord remember thy Priesthood in his kingdom. Pray for me, O Master.

Priest: May the Holy Spirit come upon thee, and the power of the Most High overshadow thee.

Deacon: Remember me, O Master.

Priest: May the Lord remember thee in his kingdom, always, both now and forever, and for ages to come.

Deacon: Amen.

The congregation sits down. Here Priests are ordained. Then the Deacon kisses the Priest's hand, goes out through the north door, stands in his customary place in front of the Holy Doors, and says:

FIRST SUPPLICATION LITANY

Deacon: Let us complete our prayer to the Lord.

Choir: Lord our God, have mercy.

Deacon: For this holy temple, and for those who with faith, devotion, and fear of God enter therein, let us pray to the Lord.

Choir: Lord our God, have mercy.

Deacon: For our deliverance from all tribulation, wrath, danger, and necessity, let us pray to the Lord.

Choir: Lord our God, have mercy.

Deacon: Help us, save us, have mercy on us, and protect us, O God, by thy grace.

Choir: Lord our God, have mercy.

Deacon: A perfect, holy, peaceful, and sinless day, let us beseech of the Lord.

Choir: We pray, grant, O Lord.

Deacon: An angel of peace, a faithful guide, and a guardian of our souls and bodies, let us beseech of the Lord.

Choir: We pray, grant, O Lord.

Deacon: Pardon and remission of our sins and trespasses, let us beseech of the Lord.

Choir: We pray, grant, O Lord.

Deacon: All things beneficial and salutary to our souls, and peace for the world, let us beseech of the Lord.

Choir: We pray, grant, O Lord.

Deacon: That we may spend the rest of our life in peace and repentance, let us beseech of the Lord.

Choir: We pray, grant, O Lord.

Deacon: A Christian ending to our life, painless, blameless, peaceful, and a good defense before the awesome tribunal of Christ, let us beseech of the Lord.

Choir: We pray, grant, O Lord.

Deacon: Commemorating our most holy immaculate, blessed and glorious Lady, the Mother of God and ever-virgin Mary, with all the Saints, let us commend ourselves, and one another, and all our life unto Christ our God.

In the meantime the Priest prays secretly:

OBLATION PRAYER

Priest: Almighty Lord our God, who alone art holy, who dost receive sacrifice of praise from those calling upon thee with all their heart; accept our prayer of sinners, and elevate it to thy heavenly Altar; enable us to offer oblations and spiritual sacrifices for our sins and for the errors of the people; make us worthy of thy favor; welcome our sacrifice; and send down the grace of thy Holy Spirit upon us, upon the Gifts here set forth, and upon all thy people.

Then the Priest exclaims:

Priest: Through the bounties of thy only-begotten Son, with whom thou art blessed, together with thy most holy, and gracious, and life-giving Spirit, always, both now and forever, and for ages to come.

Choir: Amen.

The Priest turns to the congregation, blesses them crosswise, and says:

Priest: Peace unto all.

Choir: And with thee may it be.

Deacon: Let us love one another that we may unanimously confess.

Choir: One Father, Son, and Holy Spirit, always, Trinity both consubstantial and indivisible.

The Priest makes three reverences and kisses the Holy Gifts, covered as they are, first the Paten, then the Chalice, then the edge of the Altar to the right, saying each time in a low voice:

Priest: I will love thee, O Lord, my strength: the Lord is my fortress and my refuge.

KISS OF PEACE

If there are several Priests, they all kiss the Holy Gifts and the Altar in the order of their ranks, and they exchange the Kiss of Peace as follows: They clasp their right hands, kiss each other on both shoulders and the right hand, saying in a low voice.

Priest I. Christ is in our midst.

Priest II: He is and shall be always.

The Deacon likewise makes three reverences in his accustomed place, and kisses the Cross upon his Orarion. If there are several Deacons, they do likewise and exchange the Kiss of Peace as the Priests do. Then the Deacon exclaims:

Deacon: The doors, the doors. In wisdom let us attend.

The congregation kneels. The Priest elevates the Great Veil and fans the Holy Gifts therewith until the passage of the Creed: "And ascended into heaven." Then he kisses the Veil and lays it aside on the Altar.

THE CREED

Choir: I believe in one God, the Father Almighty, maker of heaven and earth, and of all things visible and invisible. And in one Lord, Jesus Christ, the only-begotten Son of God, born of the Father before all ages, light of light, very God of very God, begotten not made, consubstantial with the Father, through whom all things were made; who for us men and for our salvation came down from heaven, and was incarnate of the Holy Spirit and the Virgin Mary and was made man; and was crucified for us under Pontius Pilate, and suffered and was buried; and the third day he rose according to the Scriptures; and ascended into heaven, and sitteth at the right hand of the Father, and he shall come again with glory to judge the quick and the dead, and his kingdom shall have no end. And I believe in the Holy Spirit, the Lord and life-giver, who proceedeth from the Father, who with the Father and Son is worshipped and glorified, who spake by the Prophets. I believe in one Holy, Universal, and Apostolic Church. I confess one Baptism for the remission of sins. I look for the resurrection of the dead and the life of the world to come. Amen.

The congregation sits down.

PEACE AND MERCY

Deacon: Let us stand reverently, let us stand with awe, let us attend, that we may offer the Holy Oblation in peace.
Choir: Peace and mercy, glory of sacrifice.
The Priest turns to the congregation, blesses them crosswise, and says:
Priest: The grace of our Lord Jesus Christ, and the love of God the Father, and the communion of the Holy Spirit, be with you all.
Choir: And with thee may it be.
Priest: Let us lift up our hearts.
Choir: Up we lift them to the Lord.
Priest: Let us give thanks unto the Lord.
Choir: Praiseworthy and rightful it is to adore and worship always Father, Son, and Holy Spirit, Trinity both consubstantial and indivisible.

In the meantime the Priest prays secretly:

THANKSGIVING PRAYER

Priest: Praiseworthy and rightful it is to sing of thee, to bless thee, to praise thee, to give thanks unto thee, and to worship thee in every place of thy dominion. For thou art God ineffable, incomprehensible, invisible, inconceivable, eternal, and unchangeable, thou and thy only-begotten Son and thy Holy Spirit. Thou hast created us out of nothing; thou hast raised us up when we had fallen; and thou hast left nothing undone to bring us to thy future kingdom. We give thanks unto thee, and to thy only-begotten Son, and to thy Holy Spirit for all these favors, for all the other benefits, known and unknown, public and secret. We give thanks unto thee also for this Liturgy, which thou has condescended to accept from our hands, even though beside thee thousands of Archangels and tens of thousands of Angels, the Cherubim and the Seraphim, six-winged, many-eyed, soaring and flying,—

Then the Priest exclaims:

Priest: Sing the triumphal hymn, shout, exclaim, and say:
Choir: O thrice-holy Lord Sabaoth, behold, all the universe praises thee and shouts Hosanna on high; forever blest is he who comes in the Lord's name, hosanna on high.

The congregation rises. The Deacon takes the Star-cover, makes the sign of the cross over the Paten therewith, and lays it aside on the Altar. Then he takes up the Sacramental Fan, and waves it gently over the Holy Gifts, while the Priest prays secretly:

PRE-EUCHARISTIC PRAYER

Priest: With these heavenly powers, O merciful Master, we also cry and say: Holy and most holy art thou, and thy only-begotten Son, and thy

Holy Spirit. Holy and most holy art thou in thy glorious majesty; for thou hast loved men so dearly that thou hast given away thy only-begotten Son in order to save them from perdition, and bestow eternal life upon those who believe in him. He fulfilled his mission in our behalf; and in the night in which he was betrayed, nay in which he gave himself up for the salvation of mankind, he took bread in his holy, flawless, and immaculate hands; he gave thanks, he blessed it, he consecrated it, he broke it, he gave it to his holy disciples and Apostles saying:

The Deacon points out the Paten to the Priest, holding his Orarion with three fingers, and the Priest exclaims:

Priest: Take, eat; this is my Body, which is broken for you, for the remission of sins.

Choir: Amen.

The Priest says in a low voice:

Priest: Likewise he consecrated the Cup after the Supper saying:

The Deacon points out the Chalice to the Priest, holding his Orarion with three fingers, and the Priest exclaims:

Priest: Drink of it, all of you; this is my Blood of the New Testament, which is shed for you, and for many, for the remission of sins.

Choir: Amen.

The congregation kneels. The Priest says secretly:

Priest: Therefore, bearing in mind this command of our Savior and the Passion he endured for our sake, the Crucifixion, the Burial, the Resurrection after three days, the Ascension into heaven, the Enthronement at the right hand of the Father, the second and glorious Advent:

The Deacon takes the Paten in his right hand, and the Chalice in his left crosswise, with his right hand over the left, elevates them and makes the sign of the cross over the Antimens therewith. The Priest exclaims:

Priest: Thine from thine own we offer unto thee, in all and for all.

Choir: To thee we sing, to thee we offer praise, to thee we render thanks, Lord our God; we pray unto thee, Lord our God.

CONSECRATION OF HOLY EUCHARIST

The Priest prays secretly:

Priest: Furthermore we offer unto thee this spiritual and unbloody sacrifice, and we pray, and beseech, and implore thee: Send down thy Holy Spirit upon us and upon these Gifts here presented.

Then the Priest and the Deacon make three reverences, lift up their hands, and look upward, while the Priest says in a low voice:

Priest: O gracious Lord, take not away from us thy most Holy Spirit, whom thou hast sent unto thy Holy Apostles at the third hour, but renew him in the hearts of thy servants, who pray unto thee.

Deacon: Create in me a clean heart, O Lord, and renew in me a righteous Spirit.

Priest: O gracious Lord, take not away . . .

Deacon: Cast me not away from thy presence, and take not away from me thy Holy Spirit.

Priest: O gracious Lord, take not away . . .

The Deacon points out the Paten to the Priest, holding his Orarion with three fingers, and says in a low voice:

Deacon: Consecrate the Holy Bread, O Master.

The Priest makes the sign of the cross over the Holy Bread and says:

Priest: And make this Bread the precious Body of thy Christ.

The Deacon points out the Holy Chalice to the Priest likewise, and says:

Deacon: Consecrate the Holy Chalice, O Master.

The Priest makes the sign of the cross over the Holy Chalice, and says.

Priest: And make what is in this Chalice the precious Blood of thy Christ.

The Deacon points out both Paten and Chalice to the Priest likewise, and says:

Deacon: Consecrate them both, O Master.

The Priest makes the sign of the cross over both Paten and Chalice, and says:

Priest: By changing them through thy Holy Spirit.

Deacon: Amen, Amen, Amen.

They both kneel, and the Priest prays secretly:

Priest: May they bestow upon the communicants purification of soul; remission of sins; the fellowship of thy Holy Spirit; the inheritance of the Kingdom of Heaven; the privilege of approaching thee blamelessly and fearlessly; let them not lead us to judgment or condemnation; but let them help us to obtain mercy and grace with the Saints, who have been well-pleasing unto thee through the ages, namely our Forefathers, Fathers, Patriarchs, Prophets, Apostles, Preachers, Evangelists, Martyrs, Confessors, Ascetics, and all the souls of the righteous departed in the faith.

The Deacon bows his head to the Priest, and says in a low voice:

Deacon: Remember me, O Master.

Priest: May the Lord remember thee in his kingdom, always, both now and forever, and for ages to come.

Deacon: Amen.

The congregation sits down. The Deacon censes the Holy Gifts, and the Priest exclaims:

Priest: Especially let us commemorate our most holy, immaculate, blessed, and glorious Lady, the Mother of God and ever-virgin Mary.

PRAISEWORTHY

Choir: Praiseworthy 'tis humbly and piously to sing the glories thou dost deserve, thou ever blessed one, holy and immaculate and gracious Mother of our Lord, more honored than Cherubim, more glorious beyond all measure than Seraphim, thou in mystery God the Word hast borne for us; Mother of God thou art indeed, we magnify thee.

The Deacon brings a tray containing small pieces of Altar-bread to the Priest, who makes the sign of the cross over the Holy Gifts therewith, and then prays secretly:

COMMEMORATION PRAYER

Priest: Let us commemorate the holy Prophet and Forerunner, Saint John the Baptist; the holy, glorious, and renowned Apostles; the Saint of this day, N., whose memory we celebrate; and all thy Saints. Look down upon us, O Lord, through their intercession; remember, O Lord, all the Orthodox believers who have fallen asleep in the hope of a resurrection to everlasting life; remember, O Lord, the souls of thy departed servants, N., and give them rest in Paradise where the light of thy countenance is shining; remember, O Lord, the Holy, Universal, and Apostolic Church; remember, O Lord, all the Orthodox Bishops, Priests, Deacons, Friars and Nuns; remember, O Lord, the President of the United States of America and the American people, and grant them peace, prosperity, and piety; remember, O Lord, this city, every city and country, and the faithful dwelling therein; remember, O Lord, those traveling by land, by sea, and by air, the sick, the suffering, and those in captivity; remember, O Lord, those who bear fruit and do good works in thy Churches, those who care for the poor; and send down thy mercies upon all of us.

From Easter Sunday to the Feast of Ascension the following substitute is sung:

SEEING MARY

Choir: Seeing Mary full of grace, the Angel greeted her saying, Hail all hail, and once again I say, All hail, thy Son is risen from the grave in three days, and granted life to all the dead. Shout and rejoice, all ye people. Shine, O shine with radiance, New Jerusalem of heaven, for our Savior's glory upon thee dawns again. O dance thou now, leap and be merry, O Zion. Thou immaculate and Holy Mother of our Lord, celebrate the Easter Day of thy Son.

Priest: Among the first remember, O Lord, our Archbishop Theophan, and grant that he may rightly administer unto thy holy churches the word of thy truth in peace, safety, health, honor, and length of days.

Choir: And all mankind.

Deacon: And all whom each has in mind, both men and women.

Choir: Amen.

Priest: And grant us with one voice and one heart to glorify and exalt thy most blessed and majestic name, Father, Son, and Holy Spirit, always, both now and forever, and for ages to come.

Choir: Amen.

Priest: And may the mercy of our Almighty God and Savior Jesus Christ be with you all.

Choir: And with thee may it be.

Here Deacons are ordained. Then the Deacon stands in his accustomed place in front of the Holy Doors, and says:

SECOND SUPPLICATION LITANY

Deacon: Commemorating all the Saints, again and again, in peace let us pray to the Lord.

Choir: Lord our God, have mercy.

Deacon: For the Holy Gifts now offered and consecrated, let us pray to the Lord.

Choir: Lord our God, have mercy.

Deacon: That our merciful God, who has received them upon his holy, heavenly, and mystical Altar as the fragrance of spiritual perfume, will send down upon us in return the divine grace and the gift of the Holy Spirit, let us pray to the Lord.

Choir: Lord our God, have mercy.

Deacon: Help us, save us, have mercy on us, and protect us, O God, by thy grace.

Choir: Lord our God, have mercy.

Deacon: A perfect, holy, peaceful, and sinless day, let us beseech of the Lord.

Choir: We pray, grant, O Lord.

Deacon: An angel of peace, a faithful guide, and a guardian of our souls and bodies, let us beseech of the Lord.

Choir: We pray, grant, O Lord.

Deacon: Pardon and remission of our sins and trespasses, let us beseech of the Lord.

Choir: We pray, grant, O Lord.

Deacon: All things beneficial and salutary to our souls, and peace for the world, let us beseech of the Lord.

Choir: We pray, grant, O Lord.

Deacon: That we may spend the rest of our life in peace and repentance, let us beseech of the Lord.

Choir: We pray, grant, O Lord.

Deacon: A Christian ending to our life, painless, blameless, peaceful, and a good defense before the awesome tribunal of Christ, let us beseech of the Lord.

Choir: We pray, grant, O Lord.

Deacon: Beseeching the Lord for unity in faith and for the communion of the Holy Spirit, let us commend ourselves, and one another, and all our life unto Christ our God.

Choir: To thee, Lord our God.

In Greek use, the Second Supplication Litany is usually omitted. While the Deacon recites it, the Priest prays secretly.

FIRST SUPPLICATION PRAYER

Priest: To thee, O Merciful Master, we commit all our life and our hope; and we pray, and beseech, and implore thee: Make us worthy to partake of thy heavenly and awesome Sacraments from this holy and spiritual Altar with a clear conscience, for the remission of sins, for the forgiveness of trespasses, for the fellowship of the Holy Spirit, for the inheritance of the kingdom of heaven, for the privilege of approaching thee blamelessly and fearlessly.

The congregation kneels. The Deacon girds his Stole about him crosswise, and the Priest exclaims:

Priest: And enable us, O Lord, freely and deservedly to invoke thee, God the heavenly Father, and to say:

THE LORD'S PRAYER

Choir: Our Father, who art in heaven; hallowed be thy name; thy kingdom come; thy will be done on earth as it is in heaven; give us this day our daily bread; and forgive us our trespasses as we forgive those who trespass against us; and lead us not into temptation; but deliver us from evil.

Priest: For thine is the kingdom, and the power and the glory, Father, Son, and Holy Spirit, always, both now and forever, and for ages to come.

Choir: Amen.

The congregation sits down. The Priest faces the congregation, blesses it crosswise, and says:

Priest: Peace unto all.

Choir: And with thee may it be.

Deacon: Let us bow our heads unto the Lord.

Choir: To thee, Lord our God.

The Priest prays secretly:

SECOND SUPPLICATION PRAYER

Priest: We give thanks unto thee, O invisible King, who in thy boundless power and infinite mercy hast created the universe out of nothing; do thou look down from heaven upon those who have bowed their heads, not before flesh and blood, but before thee, Almighty God; do thou therefore administer these offerings for our benefit according to the special need of every one of us; sail with the sailors; travel with the wayfarers; heal the sick, O Physician of our souls and bodies.

Then the Priest exclaims:

Priest: Through the bounties, grace, and mercy of thy only-begotten Son, with whom thou art blessed, together with thy most holy, and gracious, and life-giving Spirit, always, both now and forever, and for ages to come.

Choir: Amen.

The Priest prays secretly:

THIRD SUPPLICATION PRAYER

Priest: Hearken, O Lord Jesus Christ our God, from thy holy habitation and from the glorious throne of thy kingdom; come and sanctify us, thou who sittest with the Father in heaven, and art here invisibly present with us; and vouchsafe by thy mighty hand to impart unto us thy sacred Body and thy precious Blood, and through us to all the people.

The Priest before the Altar and the Deacon before the Holy Doors, make three reverences, saying in a low voice:

Priest and Deacon: O Lord, be gracious and merciful unto me a sinner.

The Deacon exclaims:

ELEVATION

Deacon: Let us attend.

The Priest elevates the Holy Bread, and says:

Priest: The Sacraments for the Saints.

The Holy Doors are closed, and the curtain is drawn.

Choir: One is blest and one is Lord, Savior Jesus Christ, the Son and glory of God. Amen.

COMMUNION HYMN

O praise ye God, the Lord of hosts, O praise him in the highest. Alleluia, alleluia, alleluia.

COMMUNION OF CLERGY

In the meantime the Deacon goes into the Sancutary, stands at the right hand of the Priest, and says in a low voice:

Deacon: Break the Holy Bread, O Master.

The Priest breaks the Holy Bread into four pieces, and says:

Priest: The Lamb of God is broken and distributed; always broken and never divided; always eaten and never exhausted; it consecrates its communicants.

The Priest arranges the pieces of Holy Bread in the Paten in the form of a cross, as follows:

I C

N I   K A

X C

The Deacon, holding his Orarion with three fingers, points out the Chalice to the Priest, and says in a low voice:

Deacon: Fill the Holy Chalice, O Master.

The Priest takes the piece marked I C, makes the sign of the cross over the Chalice therewith, drops it in, and says:

Priest: The fullness of the Holy Spirit.
Deacon: Amen.

The Deacon gives the boiling water to the Priest, and says:

Deacon: Bless the boiling water, O Master.

The Priest blesses it crosswise, and says:

Priest: Blessed is the fervor of thy Saints, always, both now and forever, and for ages to come.
Deacon: Amen.

The Deacon pours the boiling water into the Chalice crosswise, and says:

Deacon: The fervor of faith, full of the Holy Spirit. Amen.

The Priest and the Deacon pray secretly:

Priest and Deacon: I believe, O Lord, and I confess that thou art verily the Christ, the Son of the living God, who hast come into the world to save the sinners, of whom I am the worst one. I also believe that this is thy sacred Body and this is thy precious Blood. Therefore I pray thee, have mercy upon me and forgive my trespasses, both voluntary and involuntary, whether by word or deed, whether wittingly or unwittingly, and enable me to partake of thy Holy Sacraments for the remission of my sins and for everlasting life. Amen.

Let me, O Son of God, Savior Christ, share at thy Altar thy mystical Supper this day. I shall not tell to foes thy Mystery, nor shall I give thee a kiss like that of Judas, but like the poor sinner shall I pray unto thee: Lord my God, remember me forever in thy realm.

Let the Communion of thy Holy Sacraments, O Lord, bring me neither judgment nor punishment, but let it heal my soul and my body.

Forgive me, O brother and fellow-minister.

The Priest breaks the piece of Holy Bread marked X C into as many particles as there are clergymen participating in the Liturgy, and says:

Priest: Behold, I approach Christ, our immortal King and God. I, the unworthy Priest, N., partake of the holy and precious Body of our Lord, and God, and Savior, Jesus Christ, for the remission of my sins and for everlasting life.

He partakes of the Holy Bread, and says:

Priest: This has touched my lips, and shall take away my iniquities, and it shall purge my sins.

Then he takes the Sponge, wipes his hands, kisses the Sponge, lays it aside, and says:

Priest: Deacon, approach.

The Deacon apporaches, makes a reverence, and says:

Deacon: Behold, I approach Christ, our immortal King and God. Impart unto me, O Master, the holy and precious Body of our Lord, and God, and Savior, Jesus Christ, for the remission of my sins and for everlasting life.

The Priest gives him a particle of the Holy Bread, and says:

Priest: This has touched thy lips, and it shall take away thy iniquities, and it shall purge thy sins.

The Priest takes the Chalice, partakes of the Holy Wine thrice, and says:

Priest: Behold, again I approach Christ, our immortal King and God. I, the unworthy Priest, N., partake of the holy, precious, and life-giving Blood of our Lord, and God, and Savior, Jesus Christ, for the remission of my sins and for everlasting life, in the name of Father, Son, and Holy Spirit. Amen.

The Priest wipes his lips with the Veil, kisses the Chalice, and says:

Priest: This has touched my lips, and it shall take away my iniquities, and it shall purge my sins.

Then the Priest says:

Priest: Deacon, approach again.

The Deacon makes a reverence, and says:

Deacon: Behold, again I approach Christ, our immortal King and God. Impart unto me, O Master, the holy, precious, and life-giving Blood of our Lord, and God, and Savior, Jesus Christ, for the remission of my sins and for everlasting life.

The Priest gives him the Chalice, and says:

Priest: The servant of God, Deacon N., partakes of the holy, precious, and life-giving Blood of our Lord, and God, and Savior, Jesus Christ, for the remission of his sins and for everlasting life, in the name of Father, Son, and Holy Spirit. Amen.

The Deacon partakes of the Holy Wine thrice, wipes his lips with the Veil, and kisses the Chalice and the hand of the Priest, who says:

Priest: This has touched thy lips, and it shall take away thy iniquities, and shall purge thy sins.

The Priest divides the pieces of the Holy Bread marked N I and K A into small particles for the lay communicants, and places them in the Holy Chalice, which he covers with the Veil. Likewise he places the Star-cover over the Paten, and covers the latter with the Veil. Then he prays secretly:

POST-COMMUNION PRAYER

Priest: We thank thee, O merciful Master, benefactor of our souls, for thou hast vouchsafed this day to impart unto us thy heavenly and immortal Sacraments; direct us into the right way; strengthen all of us in thy faith; protect our life; guard our steps; through the prayers and supplications of the glorious Mother of God and ever-virgin Saint Mary, and of all the Saints.

In the meantime the Deacon recites secretly:

EASTER ANTHEMS

Deacon: Now that we have seen the resurrection of Christ, let us bow before the Holy Lord Jesus who alone is sinless. We worship thy Cross, O Christ, and we praise and glorify thy Resurrection; for thou art our God, and we know no other beside thee, and we call upon thy name. Come, all ye faithful, let us worship the holy Resurrection of Christ. For lo, through the Cross is joy come into all the world. Ever blessing the Lord, let us praise his Resurrection, for he has endured crucifixion and has destroyed death by his death.

Shine, O shine with radiance, New Jerusalem of heaven, for our Savior's glory upon thee dawns again. O dance thou now, leap and be merry, O Zion; thou immaculate and Holy Mother of our Lord, celebrate the Easter Day of thy son.

O Easter most blessed, O Savior Christ our gracious Lord; light and wisdom supernal, Word of God ineffable; grant unto us to rejoice with thee when thou shalt come with glory and power to reign over us eternally.

Then the Holy Doors are opened. The congregation rises. The Deacon takes the Chalice from the Priest, elevates it, faces the congregation, and says:

Deacon: With fear of God, faith, and charity, approach.

Choir: Praised and blest is he that comes in the Lord's name. God the Lord is revealed to us.

In the meantime the Deacon returns to the Altar and places the Chalice thereon.

COMMUNION OF PEOPLE

Those who desire to communicate approach. The Priest reads aloud the Communion Prayer: "I believe, O Lord, and I confess . . ." Then he imparts the Holy Communion from the Chalice to each one, and says:

Priest: The servant of God, N., partakes of the Holy Communion for the remission of his sins and for everlasting life.

Choir: Come and receive the Bread of Heaven, and taste the Wine of the immortal fountain. Alleluia, alleluia, alleluia.

Let me, O Son of God, Savior Christ, share at thy Altar thy mystical Supper this day. I shall not tell to foes thy Mystery, nor shall I give thee a kiss like that of Judas, but like the poor sinner shall I pray unto thee: Lord my God, remember me forever in thy realm.

Then the Priest places the Chalice on the Altar, faces the congregation, blesses it crosswise, and says:

Priest: O Lord, save thy people, and bless thy inheritance.

Choir: We have seen the very light, received the heavenly Spirit now, we have found the truthful faith of the Lord, by adoring Trinity, which forever saved us.

The Priest takes the Sponge, wipes therewith the remaining particles of Altar-bread on the Paten into the Chalice, and says in a low voice:

Priest: Wash away, O Lord, the sins of all those who are commemorated in thy precious Blood through the prayers of thy Saints.

Deacon: Amen.

The Priest covers the Chalice, places the Star-cover, the Paten-veil, and the folded Great Veil, upon the Paten, censes the Chalice thrice, and says in a low voice:

Priest: Blessed is our God.

Then the Priest exclaims:

Priest: Always, both now and forever, and for ages to come.

The congregation sits down.

LET OUR MOUTHS

Choir: Amen. Let our mouths be always filled with hymns and eulogies for thee, O Lord our God, so that we may sing praises to thee, for thou hast granted unto us to partake today of thy immortal Sacraments, bestowing life eternal and salvation; sanctify us with thy grace and mercy this day and forever, O Lord, in thy truth. Alleluia, alleluia, alleluia.

In the meantime the Priest places the Chalice upon the Oblation Table. The Deacon goes out through the north door, stands in his accustomed place before the Holy Doors, and says:

POST-COMMUNION LITANY

Deacon: Arise! Having partaken of the divine, holy, immaculate, immortal, heavenly, life-giving, and awesome Sacraments of Christ, let us worthily give thanks unto the Lord.

Choir: Lord our God, have mercy.

Deacon: Help us, save us, have mercy on us, and protect us, O God, by thy grace.

Choir: Lord our God, have mercy.

Deacon: Beseeching a perfect, holy, peaceful, and sinless day, let us commend ourselves, and one another, and all our life unto Christ our God.

Choir: To thee, Lord our God.

The Priest folds the Antimens, makes the sign of the cross over it with the Gospel Book, and says:

Priest: For thou art our sanctification, and unto thee we ascribe glory, Father, Son, and Holy Spirit, always, both now and forever, and for ages to come.

Choir: Amen.

Priest: Let us depart in peace.

Choir: In peace, in the Lord's name.

Deacon: Let us pray to the Lord.

Choir: Lord our God, have mercy.

The Priest goes out through the Holy Doors, stands before the Icon of Christ, accompanied by the Deacon, and recites aloud:

TRIBUNE PRAYER

Priest: O Lord, who blessest those who bless thee and sanctifiest those who trust in thee; save thy people and bless thy inheritance. Preserve the fullness of thy church; sanctify those who love the beauty of thy house; glorify them in recompense with thy divine power, and forsake us not who rely on thee. Give peace to mankind, to thy churches, to thy priests, to the American people, and to all the peoples of the world. For every good and perfect gift is from above, and comes from thee, the Father of lights, and unto thee we ascribe glory, Father, Son, and Holy Spirit, always, both now and forever, and for ages to come.

Choir: Amen. May the Lord's name be blessed for generations, for ages, and forever. *(Thrice.)*

In the meantime the Priest returns into the Altar through the Holy Doors, goes to the Oblation Table, and prays secretly:

CONCLUDING PRAYER

Priest: O Christ our God, who art thyself the consummation of the Law and the Prophets, and hast fulfilled the plan of the Father for our salvation, do thou fill our hearts with joy and gladness, always, both now and forever, and for ages to come. Amen.

Deacon: Let us pray to the Lord.

Choir: Lord our God, have mercy.

The Priest blesses the congregation crosswise, and says:

Priest: May the blessing of the Lord, his mercy and grace be upon you, always, both now and forever, and for ages to come.

Choir: Amen.

Priest: Glory to thee, O Christ, our God and our hope, glory to thee.

Choir: Glory to Father, Son, and Holy Spirit, always, both now and forever, and for ages to come. Amen. Lord our God, have mercy; Lord our God, have mercy; Lord our God, have mercy. Bless, O Master.

The Priest blesses the congregation crosswise, and says:

BENEDICTION

Priest: May our gracious and merciful Lord, Jesus Christ, our true God, who rose from the dead, through the intercession of his most blessed, holy, and immaculate Mother, Saint Mary; through the might of the holy and life-giving Cross; through the protection of the holy and heavenly Angelic Powers; of the holy and glorious Prophet and Forerunner; Saint John the Baptist; of the holy, glorious, and renowned Apostles; of our holy Father, Saint John Chrysostom; of the holy, righteous, and divine ancestors, Saint Joachim and Saint Ann; of the Patron Saint, N., of the Church; of Saint N., whose memory we celebrate today; and of all the Saints; have mercy upon us and save us.

Through the prayers of our Holy Fathers, O Lord Jesus Christ, our God, have mercy upon us and save us.

The Priest stands on the lowest step of the stairs before the Holy Doors with the Cross in his left hand, distributes the Altar-bread to the congregation, and says:

Priest: The Lord's blessing and mercy be with you.

The worshippers kiss the Cross, receive the Altar-bread, and leave the Church. In the meantime the Deacon goes to the Oblation Table, consumes the Holy Gifts, wipes the Chalice, places the Holy Vessels in their accustomed place, and covers them with the Great Veil. Then the Priest and the Deacon pray:

POST-LITURGIC PRAYER

Priest: O Christ, our God and Master, king of heaven, and creator of the universe, we thank thee for all the blessings thou hast bestowed upon us, and for thy holy and life-giving Sacraments which thou hast imparted unto us. Therefore, we pray thee, O gracious and merciful Lord: Keep us under thy protection, under the shelter of thy wings; and grant that even unto our last breath we may worthily and with a pure conscience receive thy Holy Communion for the remission of our sins and for everlasting life. For thou art the Bread of Life, the fountain of consecration, the donor of heavenly gifts, and unto thee we ascribe glory, Father, Son, and Holy Spirit, always, both now and forever, and for ages to come. Amen.

Now dismiss, O Lord my God, thy servant in peace and mercy, for thy word has been fulfilled this day, for my eyes have beheld thy redemption, thy salvation now, which thou hast granted to all repentant people on earth, light of revelation unto Gentiles, and glory forever unto Israel.

Deacon: O thrice-holy, O Lord mighty, O God immortal, have mercy on us. *(Thrice.)*

Glory to Father, Son, and Holy Spirit, always, both now and forever, and for ages to come. Amen.

O Holy Trinity, have mercy on us. O Lord, forgive our sins. O Master, pardon our trespasses. O Holy One, visit and heal our infirmities for thy name's sake.

Lord our God, have mercy. *(Thrice.)*

Glory to Father, Son, and Holy Spirit, always, both now and forever, and for ages to come. Amen.

Our Father, who art in heaven, hallowed be thy name, thy kingdom come; thy will be done on earth as it is in heaven; give us this day our

daily bread; and forgive us our trespasses as we forgive those who tres-
pass against us; and lead us not into temptation; but deliver us from evil.
Priest: For thine is the kingdom, and the power, and the glory, Father,
Son, and Holy Spirit, always, both now and forever, and for ages to come.
Deacon: Amen.
Priest: Thy graceful sermon, shining like a torch-light, enlightened all the
Churches of the world, enriched mankind with Christian virtues, Teacher
and Father, St. John Chrysostom, intercede with Christ our God for the
salvation of our souls.
Priest: O ever-present protector of Christians and unfailing mediator be-
fore the Creator, despise not the prayers of sinners, but extend thy kind
assistance to us, who call with faith upon thee. Hasten to intercede, O
Mother of God, for all those who honor thee.
Deacon: More honored than Cherubim, more glorious beyond all measure
than Seraphim, thou in mystery God the Word hast borne for us, Mother
of God thou art indeed, we magnify thee.
Priest: Glory to thee, O Christ, our God and our hope, glory to thee.
Deacon: Glory to Father, Son, and Holy Spirit, always, both now and
forever, and for ages to come, Amen. Lord our God, have mercy; Lord
our God, have mercy; Lord our God, have mercy. Bless, O Master.
Priest: May our gracious and merciful Lord Jesus Christ, our true God,
who rose from the dead, through the intercession of his most blessed
Mother, Saint Mary, and of all the Saints, have mercy on us and save us.
Deacon: Amen.

*The Priest and the Deacon remove their vestments, wash their hands, kiss
the Altar, and leave the Church.*

II. COMPARATIVE STUDY OF THE ROMAN, LUTHERAN, AND ANGLICAN LITURGIES

The following study shows the way in which the Lutheran and the Anglican
churches purified and simplified the text of the Roman Mass, and restored
or introduced various features in accordance with the genius of each communion.

Simplifications of ceremonial—the use of vestments, incense, lights, posture
—were also important. They are not indicated, as diversity in these matters
generally prevails. The text of the liturgy, however, is definitely prescribed,
and this is given entire, although in simplest possible form and with the
fewest possible rubrics.

The official text of the Roman liturgy is the Latin text of the *Missale
Romanum*. The English translation here given is from the approved *Saint
Andrew Daily Missal* edited by Dom Gaspar Lefebvre.[1]

The text of the Lutheran Liturgy is that of the *Service Book and Hymnal*
of the Lutheran Church in America (1958).

The text of the Anglican liturgy is that of the *Book of Common Prayer* of
the Protestant Episcopal Church (1928). This differs in minor details from
earlier editions of the American Book, and also from the English, the

---

[1] American ed. (St. Paul: Lohmann, 1940). Later editions have somewhat
modernized the translation. Alternates and additions for high mass are omitted.

Scottish, the Canadian, and other Books of Common Prayer of the various churches of the Anglican communion.

Psalms and lessons occasionally are indicated and not printed in full. Other liturgical texts (Gloria in Excelsis, Creed, etc.) in which there are no important differences are also indicated. The propers are of the First Sunday in Advent.

Important differences in the use of these services by the three communions should be noted. The Mass, in its entirety, is the normal service of Roman Catholic congregations on Sundays and festivals. The present liturgical movement in this communion provides vernacular texts of all masses throughout the year, and urges the faithful to participate in the responses. At the principal mass, at least on Sundays, a sermon usually follows the Gospel.

The Lutheran church for the most part was faithful to the great Christian tradition of the Holy Communion on Sundays and festivals throughout the sixteenth and seventeenth centuries. There was a marked development of the sermon, but the purified and simplified liturgy was used in its entirety, and the Sacrament was administered every Sunday in cities and towns to all who desired it. The disruption of church life occasioned by the Thirty Years' War, the influence of Calvinism in certain areas, and the unchurchly methods of Pietism combined to reduce the normal Sunday service to a "half mass" which was practically the Service of the Catechumens of the early church. The complete service (the ancient Service of the Faithful) was held less and less frequently. Rationalism, with entire concentration upon the sermon, reduced even the Liturgy of the Catechumens to pitiful proportions, and limited the administration of the Holy Communion to four times or fewer a year. The liturgical movement of the last three-quarters of a century has restored the historic liturgy in its entirety to Lutheran congregations. Many churches today celebrate the Holy Communion frequently. It is particularly to be noted that even when there is no communion, Lutheran congregations have the first half of the historic liturgy on Sundays and festivals, and thus regularly use the historic Introits, Collects, Epistles, Graduals, and Gospels for the day.

The Anglican Church at the time of the Reformation revised and emphasized the use of Matins and Vespers, with the result that Morning Prayer with sermon became the principal congregational service on Sundays and festivals. The Holy Communion was usually celebrated monthly, either immediately following Morning Prayer, or at an earlier hour. Developments in the Anglican communion have greatly increased the frequency of Communion. The additional Communion services, however, are generally restricted to small groups, and are held at an early hour, without sermon or music.

In normal experience, therefore, Anglican congregations on Sundays and festivals use the order of Morning Prayer, with its appointed lessons. This is given first place in the Prayer Book. The historic Gospels and Epistles for the liturgical year are not regularly read to the congregations, as they are in the Roman and the Lutheran churches. The omission of the historic Introits and Graduals has also further weakened the hold of the Anglican communion upon the great choral and liturgical tradition of the church. This is a loss for which the development of the anthem has not provided adequate compensation.

The Roman Mass

At the foot of the Altar.
In the Name of the Father, ✝ and of the Son, and of the Holy Ghost. Amen.

℣. I will go in unto the altar of God.
℟. Unto God, who giveth joy to my youth.

(Psalm 43)
Priest. Judge me, O God, and distinguish my cause against an ungodly nation: deliver me from the unjust and deceitful man.
℟. For Thou, O God, art my strength: why hast Thou cast me from Thee, and why go I sorrowful while the enemy afflicteth me?
P. O send out Thy light and Thy truth: they have led me and brought me unto Thy holy hill, even unto Thy tabernacles.
℟. Then will I go unto the altar of God, unto God, who giveth joy to my youth.

The Service of the Lutheran Church

¶ *The Congregation shall rise. The Minister shall sing or say:*
In the Name of the Father, and of the Son, and of the Holy Ghost.
¶ *The Congregation shall sing or say:* Amen.

The Order for Holy Communion of the Protestant Episcopal Church

(Optional)
Our Father, who art in heaven, Hallowed be thy Name. Thy kingdom come. Thy will be done, On earth as it is in heaven. Give us this day our daily bread. And forgive us our trespasses, As we forgive those who trespass against us. And lead us not into temptation, But deliver us from evil. Amen.

The Collect
Almighty God, unto whom all hearts are open, all desires known, and from whom no secrets are hid; Cleanse the thoughts of our hearts by the inspiration of thy Holy Spirit, that we may perfectly love thee, and worthily magnify thy holy Name; through Christ our Lord. *Amen.*

THE DECALOGUE
¶ *... The Priest may omit that part of the Commandment which is inset.*
¶ *The Decalogue may be omitted, provided it be said at least one Sunday in each month. But Note, That whenever it is*

P. I will praise Thee upon the harp, O God, my God; why art thou cast down, O my soul? and why art thou disquiet within me?

R. Hope thou in God: for yet will I praise Him, who is the health of my countenance, and my God.

P. Glory be to the Father, and to the Son, and to the Holy Ghost.

R. As it was in the beginning, is now and ever shall be, world without end. Amen.

*Ant.....*V. I will go in unto the altar of God.

R. Unto God, who giveth joy to my youth.

THE CONFESSION

V. Our help ✠ is in the name of the Lord.

R. Who hath made heaven and earth.

THE CONFESSION OF SINS

¶ *The Minister shall say:*

Beloved in the Lord! Let us draw near with a true heart, and confess our sins unto God our Father, beseeching him, in the Name of our Lord Jesus Christ, to grant us forgiveness.

¶ *The Minister and Congregation may kneel.*

¶ *They shall sing or say:*

Our help is in the Name of the Lord.

Response. Who made heaven and earth.

I said, I will confess my transgressions unto the Lord.

R. And thou forgavest the iniquity of my sin.

omitted, the Priest shall say the Summary of the Law, beginning,

Hear what our Lord Jesus Christ saith.

The Decalogue

God spake these words, and said:

I am the Lord thy God; Thou shalt have none other gods but me.

Lord, have mercy upon us, and incline our hearts to keep this law.

Thou shalt not make to thyself any graven image, nor the likeness of any thing that is in heaven above, or in the earth beneath, or in the water under the earth; thou shalt not bow down to them, nor worship them;

for I the Lord thy God am a jealous God, and visit the sins of the fathers upon the children, unto the third and fourth generation of them that hate **me;** and show mercy unto thousands in them that love me and keep my commandments.

Lord, have mercy upon us, and incline our hearts to keep this law.

Thou shalt not take the Name of the Lord thy God in vain;

for the Lord will not hold him guiltless, that taketh his Name in vain.

Lord, have mercy upon us, and incline our hearts to keep this law.

Remember that thou keep holy the Sabbath-day.

Six days shalt thou labour, and do all that thou hast to do; but the seventh day is the Sabbath of the Lord thy God. In it thou shalt do no manner of work; thou, and thy son, and thy daughter, thy man-servant, and thy maid-servant, thy cattle, and the stranger that is within thy gates. For in six days the Lord made heaven and earth, the sea, and all that in them is, and rested the seventh day: wherefore the Lord blessed the seventh day, and hallowed it.

Lord, have mercy upon us, and incline our hearts to keep this law.

Honour thy father and thy mother; that thy days may be long in the land which the Lord thy God giveth thee.

Lord, have mercy upon us, and incline our hearts to keep this law.

Thou shalt do no murder.

Lord, have mercy upon us, and incline our hearts to keep this law.

Thou shalt not commit adultery.

Lord, have mercy upon us, and incline

¶ *Then shall the Minister say:*

Almighty God, our Maker and Redeemer, we poor sinners confess unto thee, that we are by nature sinful and unclean, and that we have sinned against thee by thought, word, and deed. Wherefore we flee for refuge to thine infinite mercy, seeking and imploring thy grace, for the sake of our Lord Jesus Christ.

¶ *The Congregation shall say with the Minister:*

O most merciful God, who hast given thine only-begotten Son to die for us, have mercy upon us, and for his sake grant us remission of all our sins: and by thy Holy Spirit increase in us true knowledge of thee and of thy will, and true obedience to thy Word, that by thy grace we may come to everlasting life; through Jesus Christ our Lord. Amen.

¶ *Then the Minister, standing and facing the Congregation, shall say:*

Almighty God, our heavenly Father, hath had mercy upon us, and hath given his only Son to die for us, and for his sake forgiveth us all our sins. To them that be-

By the Priest

P. I confess to almighty God, etc. (*as below*)

℟. May almighty God have mercy upon thee, forgive thee thy sins, and bring thee to life everlasting.

P. Amen.

By the assisting minister, acolytes, etc.

I confess
to almighty God,
to blessed Mary ever Virgin,
to blessed Michael the archangel,
to blessed John the Baptist,
to the holy apostles Peter and Paul,
to all the saints,
and to you, Father,
that I have sinned exceedingly in thought, word and deed,
through my fault,
through my fault, through my most grievous fault.

Therefore I beseech
blessed Mary ever Virgin,
blessed Michael the archangel,
blessed John the Baptist,
the holy apostles Peter and Paul,
all the saints,
and you, Father,
to pray to the Lord our God for me.

P. May almighty God have mercy upon you, forgive you your sins, and bring you to life everlasting.

℟. Amen.

℣. May the almighty and merciful Lord grant us pardon, ✠ absolution, and remission of our sins. ℟. Amen.

---

our hearts to keep this law.

Thou shalt not steal.

Lord, have mercy upon us, and incline our hearts to keep this law.

Thou shalt not bear false witness against thy neighbour.

Lord, have mercy upon us, and incline our hearts to keep this law.

Thou shalt not covet thy neighbour's house, thou shalt not covet thy neighbour's wife, nor his servant, nor his maid, nor his ox, nor his ass, nor any thing that is his.

Lord, have mercy upon us, and write all these thy laws in our heart, we beseech thee.

¶ *Then may the Priest say,*

Hear what our Lord Jesus Christ saith.

Thou shalt love the Lord thy God with all thy heart, and with all thy soul, and with all thy mind. This is the first and great commandment. And the second is like unto it; Thou shalt love thy neighbour as thyself. On these two commandments hang all the Law and the Prophets.

---

lieve on his name, he giveth power to become the sons of God, and bestoweth upon them his Holy Spirit. He that believeth, and is baptized, shall be saved. Grant this, O Lord, unto us all.

¶ *Or, he may say:*

The Almighty and merciful God grant unto you, being penitent, pardon and remission of all your sins, time for amendment of life, and the grace and comfort of his Holy Spirit.

¶ *The Congregation shall sing or say:* Amen.

¶ *A brief silence may be kept before the Introit for the Day.*

℣. Thou wilt turn, O God, and bring us to life.

℟. And Thy people shall rejoice in Thee.

℣. Show us, O Lord, Thy mercy.

℟. And grant us Thy salvation.

℣. O Lord, hear my prayer.

℟. And let my cry come unto Thee.

℣. The Lord be with you.

℟. And with thy spirit.

Let us pray.

Ascending to the Altar;

Take away from us our iniquities, we beseech Thee, O Lord, that, with pure minds, we may worthily enter into the Holy of Holies, through Christ our Lord. Amen.

We beseech Thee, O Lord, by the merits of Thy saints, whose relics are here, and of all the saints, that Thou wouldst vouchsafe to forgive me all my sins. Amen.

THE INTROIT

To Thee have I lifted up my soul: in Thee, O my God, I put my trust, let me not be ashamed: neither let my enemies laugh at me: for none of them that wait on Thee shall be confounded. Ps. Show me, O Lord, Thy ways: and teach me thy paths. ℣. Glory be to the Father, and to the Son, and to the Holy Ghost. As it was in the beginning, is now, and ever shall be, world without end. Amen. To Thee have I lifted, etc.

THE KYRIE

¶ The Introit for the Day with the Gloria Patri shall be sung or said.

THE INTROIT

Unto thee, O Lord, do I lift up my soul: O my God, I trust in thee; let me not be ashamed; let not mine enemies triumph over me; yea, let none that wait on thee: be ashamed. Psalm. Show me thy ways, O Lord: teach me thy paths. Glory be to the Father. . . .

(Antiphon may be repeated.)

KYRIE

In peace let us pray to the Lord.
℟. Lord, have mercy.

For the peace that is from above, and for the salvation of our souls, let us pray to the Lord.
℟. Lord, have mercy.

For the peace of the whole world, for the well-being of the churches of God, and for the unity of all, let us pray to the Lord.
℟. Lord, have mercy.

For this holy house, and for them that in faith, piety and fear of God offer here

697

their worship and praise, let us pray to the Lord.

℟. Lord, have mercy.

Help, save, pity, and defend us, O God, by thy grace.

℟. Amen.

¶ *In place of the foregoing, the following Kyrie may be sung or said:*

KYRIE

Lord, have mercy upon us.
℟. Lord, have mercy upon us.

Christ, have mercy upon us.
℟. Christ, have mercy upon us.

Lord, have mercy upon us.
℟. Lord, have mercy upon us.

Lord, have mercy on us.
Lord, have mercy on us.
Lord, have mercy on us.

Christ, have mercy on us.
Christ, have mercy on us.
Christ, have mercy on us.

Lord, have mercy on us.
Lord, have mercy on us.
Lord, have mercy on us.

¶ *Here, if the Decalogue hath been omitted, shall be said:*

Lord, have mercy upon us.

Christ, have mercy upon us.

Lord, have mercy upon us.

¶ *Then the Priest may say,*
O almighty Lord, and everlasting God, vouchsafe, we beseech thee, to direct, sanctify, and govern, both our hearts and bodies, in the ways of thy laws, and in the works of thy commandments; that, through thy most mighty protection, both here and ever, we may be preserved in body and soul; through our Lord and Saviour Jesus Christ. *Amen.*

THE GLORIA IN EXCELSIS

(Omitted during Advent, pre-Lent and Lent, and on weekdays except during Eastertide.)

Glory to God in the highest....

℣. The Lord be with you.
℟. And with thy Spirit.

Let us pray.

THE COLLECTS

Stir up Thy power, we beseech Thee, O Lord, and come: that from the threatening dangers of our sins, by Thy protection we may deserve to be rescued, and be saved by Thy deliverance: who livest and reignest with God the Father, in the unity of the Holy Ghost, God, world without end. Amen.

O God, who hast willed that Thy Word should take flesh, at the message of an angel, in the womb of the blessed Virgin Mary: grant to us Thy servants, that we who believe her to be truly the Mother of God may be helped by her intercession with Thee. Through...

We beseech Thee, O Lord, mercifully to receive the prayers of Thy Church: that, all adversity and error being destroyed, she may serve Thee in security and freedom. Through...

GLORIA IN EXCELSIS

¶ *The Minister shall sing or say:*
Glory be to God on high!
¶ *The Congregation shall sing or say:*
And on earth peace, etc.
¶ *Then shall the Minister sing or say*
The Lord be with you.
℟. And with thy spirit.
¶ *The Minister shall say:*
Let us pray.
¶ *Then shall the Minister say the Collect for the Day.*

COLLECT

Stir up, we beseech thee, thy power, O Lord, and come; that by thy protection we may be rescued from the threatening perils of our sins, and saved by thy mighty deliverance; who livest and reignest with the Father and the Holy Ghost, one God, world without end. *Amen.*

¶ *Here shall be said,*
The Lord be with you.
Answer. And with thy spirit.
Minister. Let us pray.
¶ *Then shall the Priest say the Collect of the Day...*

THE COLLECT

Almighty God, give us grace that we may cast away the works of darkness, and put upon us the armour of light, now in the time of this mortal life, in which thy Son Jesus Christ came to visit us in great humility; that in the last day, when he shall come again in his glorious majesty to judge both the quick and the dead, we may rise to the life immortal, through him who liveth and reigneth with thee and the Holy Ghost, now and ever. *Amen.*

¶ *This Collect is to be repeated every day, after the other Collects in Advent, until Christmas Day.*

¶ Here the Minister may read the appointed Lesson from the Old Testament, saying:
The Lesson is written in the . . . Chapter of . . . , beginning at the . . . Verse.
¶ The Lesson ended, he shall say,
Here endeth the Lesson.

THE LESSON

Lesson. Jeremiah 31:31-34.
Behold, the days come, saith the Lord, etc.

¶ Then may be sung a Psalm or a hymn version of a Psalm.

¶ Then shall the Minister announce the Epistle for the Day, saying:
The Epistle for (*here he shall name the Festival or Day*) is written in the . . . Chapter of . . . , beginning at the . . . Verse.

THE EPISTLE

Romans 13:11-14.
Brethren, ye know the time, that now it is high time to awake out of sleep; etc.

¶ The Epistle ended, the Minister shall say:
Here endeth the Epistle for the Day.

¶ Then may the Gradual for the Day be sung.

THE GRADUAL

¶ When the Gradual for the Day is omitted, the Alleluia or the Gradual for the Season may be sung.

¶ . . . And after the Collect the Minister appointed shall read the Epistle, first saying,
The Epistle is written in the . . . Chapter of . . . , beginning at the . . . Verse.

THE EPISTLE

Romans iii. 8.
Owe no man any thing, but to love one another: for he that loveth another hath fulfilled the law, etc.

¶ The Epistle ended, he shall say,
Here endeth the Epistle.

¶ Here may be sung a Hymn or an Anthem.

THE EPISTLE

Romans 13:11-14. Brethren, knowing that it is now the hour, etc.

℟. Thanks be to God.

THE GRADUAL

All they, that wait on Thee, shall not be confounded, O Lord.

℣. Show, O Lord, Thy ways to me: and teach me Thy paths.

Alleluia, alleluia. ℣. Show us, O Lord, Thy mercy: and grant us Thy salvation. Alleluia.

(Alleluia omitted pre-Lent, Lent, week-days in Advent, etc.)

Let none that wait on thee: be ashamed. Verse. Show me thy ways, O Lord: teach me thy paths.

Alleluia, Alleluia. ℣. Show us thy mercy, O Lord: and grant us thy salvation. Alleluia.

THE ALLELUIA
Alleluia

¶ *In Lent this Sentence shall be sung instead of the Alleluia.*

Christ hath humbled himself, etc.

(Before the Gospel)

Cleanse my heart and my lips, O almighty God, who didst cleanse the lips of the prophet Isaias with a burning coal: vouchsafe through Thy gracious mercy so to cleanse me that I may worthily proclaim Thy holy Gospel. Through Christ our Lord. Amen.

Pray, Lord, a blessing. May the Lord be in my heart and on my lips, that I may worthily and fitly proclaim His Gospel. Amen.

℣. The Lord be with you.
℟. And with thy spirit.

℣. The beginning (or continuation) of the holy Gospel according to N. ....

¶ *Then shall the Minister announce the Gospel for the Day, saying:*

The Holy Gospel is written in the . . . Chapter of . . . , beginning at the . . . Verse.

¶ *Then, all the People standing the Minister appointed shall read the Gospel, first saying,*

The Holy Gospel is written in the . . . Chapter of . . . , beginning at the . . . Verse.

℟. Glory be to Thee, O Lord.

THE GOSPEL

Luke 21:25-33. At that time Jesus said to His disciples: There shall be signs, etc.

℟. Praise be to Thee, O Christ.

By the words of the Gospel may our sins be blotted out.

¶ *The Congregation shall rise and sing or say:*

Glory be to thee, O Lord.

THE GOSPEL

Matthew 21:1-9. And when they drew nigh unto Jerusalem, and were come to Bethphage, etc. *or,* Luke 3:1-6.

¶ *The Gospel ended, the Minister shall say:* Here endeth the Gospel for the Day.

¶ *The Congregation shall sing or say:* Praise be to thee, O Christ.

¶ *Here shall be said,*

Glory be to thee, O Lord.

THE GOSPEL

St. Matthew xxi. 1. When they drew nigh, etc.

¶ *And after the Gospel may be said,* Praise be to thee, O Christ.

¶ *Then shall be said or sung the Creed.*
THE CREED

¶ *The Nicene Creed shall be said or sung on all Festivals and whenever there is a Communion.*

THE NICENE CREED

I believe in one God, etc.

(or)

THE APOSTLES' CREED

I believe in God, etc.

¶ *Then shall be said the Creed commonly called the Nicene, or else the Apostles' Creed: but the Creed may be omitted, if it hath been said immediately before in Morning Prayer; Provided, That the Nicene Creed shall be said on Christmas Day, Easter Day, Ascension Day, Whitsunday, and Trinity Sunday.*

I believe in one God the Father Almighty, etc.

¶ *Then shall be declared unto the People what Holy Days, or Fasting Days, are in the week following to be observed; and (if occasion be) shall Notice be given of the Communion, and of the Banns of Matrimony, and of other matters to be published.*

THE SERMON

THE NICENE CREED

I believe in one God, etc.

THE OFFERTORY

The Lord be with you.
R̷. And with thy spirit.
Let us pray.

(Taking the paten with the Host)

Receive, O holy Father, almighty and eternal God, this spotless host, which I Thy unworthy servant, offer unto Thee, my living and true God, for mine own

---

¶ *Then shall be sung the Hymn.*

THE HYMN

¶ *Then shall follow the Sermon.*

THE SERMON

¶ *The Sermon being ended, the Congregation shall rise and the Minister shall then say:*

The Peace of God, which passeth all understanding, keep your hearts and minds through Christ Jesus.
R̷. Amen.

THE OFFERING

¶ *Then shall follow the Offertory, the Congregation standing meanwhile. One of the Offertories here following, or any other suitable Offertory, may be sung or said.*

THE OFFERTORY

I

The sacrifices of God are a broken spirit: a broken and a contrite heart, O God, thou wilt not despise.

Do good in thy good pleasure unto Zion: build thou the walls of Jerusalem.

Then shalt thou be pleased with the sacrifices of righteousness: with burnt-of-

---

¶ *Here, or immediately after the Creed, may be said the Bidding Prayer, or other authorized prayers and intercessions.*

¶ *Then followeth the Sermon . . .*
THE SERMON

THE OFFERTORY SENTENCES

¶ *. . . the Priest, when there is a Communion, shall return to the Holy Table, and begin the Offertory, saying one or more of these Sentences following, as he thinketh most convenient.*

Remember the words of the Lord Jesus, how he said, It is more blessed to give than to receive. *Acts* xx. 35.

Let your light so shine before men, that

they may see your good works, and glorify your Father which is in heaven. *St. Matt.* v. 16.

Lay not up for yourselves treasures upon earth, where moth and rust doth corrupt, and where thieves break through and steal: but lay up for yourselves treasures in heaven, where neither moth nor rust doth corrupt, and where thieves do not break through nor steal. *St. Matt.* vi. 19, 20.

Not every one that saith unto me, Lord, Lord, shall enter into the kingdom of heaven; but he that doeth the will of my Father which is in heaven. *St. Matt.* vii. 21.

He that soweth little shall reap little; and he that soweth plenteously shall reap plenteously. Let every man do according as he is disposed in his heart, not grudgingly, or of necessity; for God loveth a cheerful giver. 2 *Cor.* ix. 6, 7.

While we have time, let us do good unto all men; and especially unto them that are of the household of faith. *Gal.* vi. 10.

God is not unrighteous, that he will forget your works, and labour that proceedeth of love; which love ye have showed for his Name's sake, who have ministered unto the saints, and yet do minister. *Heb.* vi. 10.

To do good, and to distribute, forget not; for with such sacrifices God is well pleased. *Heb.* xiii. 16.

Whoso hath this world's good, and seeth his brother have need, and shutteth up his

fering and whole burnt-offering.

II

What shall I render unto the Lord: for all his benefits toward me?

I will offer to thee the sacrifice of thanksgiving: and will call upon the Name of the Lord.

I will take the cup of salvation: and call upon the Name of the Lord.

I will pay my vows unto the Lord now in the presence of all his people: in the courts of the Lord's house, in the midst of thee, O Jerusalem.

III

Create in me a clean heart, O God: and renew a right spirit within me.

Cast me not away from thy presence: and take not thy Holy Spirit from me.

Restore unto me the joy of thy salvation: and uphold me with thy free Spirit.

countless sins, offenses and negligences, and for all here present; as also for all faithful Christians living and dead, that it may avail both for my own and their salvation unto life eternal. Amen.

Pouring wine and water into the chalice, the priest says:

O God, who in a wonderful manner didst create and ennoble human nature, and still more wonderfully hast renewed it; grant that, by the mystery of this water and wine, we may be made partakers of His divinity who vouchsafed to become partaker of our humanity. Jesus Christ Thy Son, our Lord: who liveth and reigneth with Thee in the unity of the Holy Ghost, one God, world without end. Amen.

Offering up the chalice, he says:

We offer unto Thee, O Lord, the chalice of salvation, beseeching Thy clemency that it may ascend in the sight of Thy divine majesty with a sweet savor, for our own salvation and for that of the whole world. Amen.

In the spirit of humility and with a contrite heart receive us, O Lord, and grant that the sacrifice which we offer this day in Thy sight may be pleasing unto Thee, O Lord God.

Come, O Sanctifier, almighty and eternal God and bless ✛ this sacrifice prepared for Thy holy name.

THE INCENSING OF THE OFFERINGS
AND OF THE FAITHFUL

Through the intercession of blessed Michael the Archangel standing at the right hand of the altar of incense, and of all His elect, may the Lord vouchsafe to bless ✠ this incense, and to receive it in the odor of sweetness. Through Christ our Lord. Amen.

May this incense which Thou hast blessed, O Lord, ascend to Thee, and may Thy mercy descend upon us.

Let my prayer, O Lord, be directed as incense in Thy sight; the lifting up of my hands as an evening sacrifice.

Set a watch, O Lord, before my mouth, and a door round about my lips:

That my heart may not incline to evil words, and seek excuses in sins.

May the Lord kindle within us the fire of His love and flame of everlasting charity. Amen.

Washing his fingers, the priest says:
I will wash my hands among the innocent and will encompass Thy Altar, O Lord.

That I may hear the voice of Thy praise and tell of all Thy wondrous works.

I have loved, O Lord, the beauty of Thy house, and the place where Thy glory dwelleth.

Take not away my soul, O God, with compassion from him, how dwelleth the love of God in him? I *St. John* iii. 17.

Be merciful after thy power. If thou hast much, give plenteously; if thou hast little, do thy diligence gladly to give of that little: for so gatherest thou thyself a good reward in the day of necessity. *Tobit* iv. 8, 9.

And the King shall answer and say unto them, Verily I say unto you, Inasmuch as ye have done it unto one of the least of these my brethren, ye have done it unto me. *St. Matt.* xxv. 40.

How then shall they call on him in whom they have not believed? and how shall they believe in him of whom they have not heard? and how shall they hear without a preacher? and how shall they preach, except they be sent? *Rom.* x. 14, 15.

Jesus said unto them, The harvest truly is plenteous, but the labourers are few: pray ye therefore the Lord of the harvest, than he send forth labourers into his harvest. *St. Luke* x. 2.

Ye shall not appear before the Lord empty; every man shall give as he is able, according to the blessing of the Lord thy God which he hath given thee. *Deut.* xvi. 16, 17.

Thine, O Lord, is the greatness, and the power, and the glory, and the victory, and the majesty: for all that is in the heaven and in the earth is thine; thine is the kingdom, O Lord, and thou art exalted as head above all. I *Chron.* xxix. 11.

All things come of thee, O Lord, and of thine own have we given thee. I *Chron.* xxix. 4.

¶ *The Deacons, Church-wardens, or other fit persons appointed for that purpose, shall receive the Alms for the Poor, and other Offerings of the People, in a decent Basin to be provided by the Parish; and reverently bring it to the Priest, who shall humbly present and place it upon the Holy Table.*

¶ *And the Priest shall then offer, and shall place upon the Holy Table, the Bread and the Wine.*

¶ *And when the Alms and Oblations are being received and presented, there may be sung a Hymn, or an Offertory Anthem in the words of Holy Scripture or of the Book of Common Prayer, under the direction of the Priest.*

the wicked nor my life with men of blood. In whose hands are iniquities: their right hand is filled with gifts.

But as for me, I have walked in my innocence: redeem me and have mercy on me.

My foot hath stood in the direct way: in the churches I will bless Thee, O Lord.

Glory be to the Father, and to the Son, ✠ and to the Holy Ghost, as it was in the beginning, is now, and ever shall be, world without end. Amen.

Prayer to the Most Holy Trinity.

Receive, O Holy Trinity, this oblation which we make to Thee in remembrance of the Passion, Resurrection and Ascension of our Lord Jesus Christ, and in honour of blessed Mary ever Virgin, of blessed John the Baptist, the holy apostles Peter and Paul, of these (the martyrs whose relics are contained in the altar stone) and of all the saints, that it may avail to their honour and our salvation: and that they may vouchsafe to intercede for us in heaven, whose memory we now keep on earth. Through the same Christ our Lord. Amen.

Brethren, pray that my sacrifice and yours may be acceptable to God the Father almighty.

℟. May the Lord receive the sacrifice

at thy hands, to the praise and glory of His name, to our own benefit, and to that of all His holy Church.

The priest alone says:
Amen.

The Secret (Variable).
May these holy Mysteries, O Lord, cleanse us by their powerful efficacy, and

¶ *Then shall follow the Prayer of the Church.*

THE PRAYER OF THE CHURCH

¶ *The indented paragraphs in the Prayer of the Church may be omitted, at the discretion of the Minister.*

¶ *If special prayers are desired by or for members of the Church, the Minister may make mention of them before beginning the Prayer of the Church, as occasion may require, or as follows:*

Intercessions: The prayers of the Church are asked for the following brethren who are sick (*or*, in adversity, *or*, in suffering, *or*, in need): N. N.

Thanksgivings: N. N. desires to return thanks to God, for special blessings (*or*, for restoration from illness, *or*, for gifts of grace), and asks the prayers of the Church.

Commemorations: Let us remember with thanksgiving before God our brethren who have departed his life with the sign of faith: N. N. (*or*, our *brother* N. N., who has departed this life.)

Let us pray.

Almighty God, the Father of our Lord Jesus Christ: We give thee praise and

¶ *Here the Priest may ask the secret intercessions of the Congregation for any who have desired the prayers of the Church.*

Then shall the Priest say:
Let us pray for the whole state of Christ's Church.

We beseech thee to hear us, good Lord.

enable us to come with greater purity to Him who is their foundation. Through our Lord....

We beseech Thee, O Lord, to strengthen in our minds the mysteries of the true faith: that we who confess Him, Who was conceived of the Virgin, to be true God and man, may be the power of His saving resurrection merit to attain eternal joy. Through the same....

Protect us, O Lord, who assist at Thy mysteries: that, fixed upon things divine, we may serve Thee in both body and mind. Through....

Aloud: World without end.
Ry. Amen.

hearty thanks for all thy goodness and tender mercies. We bless thee for the love which hath created and doth sustain us from day to day. We praise thee for the gift of thy Son, our Saviour, through whom thou hast made known thy will and grace. We thank thee for the Holy Ghost, the Comforter; for thy holy Church, for the Means of Grace, for the lives of all faithful and godly men, and for the hope of the life to come. Help us to treasure in our hearts all that our Lord hath done for us; and enable us to show our thankfulness by lives that are given wholly to thy service;

Ry. We beseech thee to hear us, good Lord.

Save and defend thy Church Universal, purchased with the precious Blood of Christ. Give it pastors and ministers according to thy Spirit, and strengthen it through the Word and the holy Sacraments. Make it perfect in love and in all good works, and establish it in the faith delivered to the saints. Sanctify and unite thy people in all the world, that one holy Church may bear witness to thee, the God and Father of all;

Ry. We beseech thee to hear us, good Lord.

Upon all in any holy office in thy Church

Almighty and everliving God, who by thy holy Apostle hast taught us to make prayers, and supplications, and to give thanks for all men; We humbly beseech thee most mercifully to accept our [*alms and*] oblations, and to receive these our prayers, which we offer unto thy Divine Majesty; beseeching thee to inspire continually the Universal Church with the spirit of truth, unity, and concord: And grant that all those who do confess thy holy Name may agree in the truth of thy holy Word, and live in unity and godly love.

We beseech thee also, so to direct and dispose the hearts of all Christian Rulers, that they may truly and impartially administer justice, to the punishment of wickedness and vice, and to maintenance of thy true religion, and virtue.

Give grace, O heavenly Father, to all Bishops and other Ministers, that they may, both by their life and doctrine, set forth thy true and lively Word, and rightly and duly administer thy holy Sacraments.

And to all thy People give thy heavenly grace; and especially to this congregation here present; that, with meek heart and due reverence, they may hear, and receive thy holy Word; truly serving thee in holiness and righteousness all the days of their life.

And we most humbly beseech thee, of thy goodness, O Lord, to comfort and succour all those who, in this transitory life, are in trouble, sorrow, need, sickness, or any other adversity.

And we also bless thy holy Name for all thy servants departed this life in thy faith and fear; beseeching thee to grant them continual growth in thy love and service, and to give us grace so to follow their good examples, that with them we may be partakers of thy heavenly kingdom. Grant this, O Father, for Jesus Christ's sake, our only Mediator and Advocate. *Amen.*

bestow thy wisdom and heavenly grace, and enable them to fulfill their duties in thy fear and in purity of heart. Let thy gracious benediction rest upon our clergy and people, and upon all who are set over us in the Lord; that faith may abound, and thy kingdom increase;

℟. We beseech thee to hear us, good Lord.

Send forth thy light and truth into all the earth, O Lord. Raise up, we pray thee, faithful servants of Christ to labor in the Gospel at home and in distant lands;

℟. We beseech thee to hear us, good Lord.

According to thy merciful goodness, O God, extend thy saving health and strength to the younger Churches. Grant that they may rejoice in a rich harvest of souls for thy kingdom. Support them in times of trial and weakness, and make them steadfast, abounding in the work of the Lord;

℟. We beseech thee to hear us, good Lord.

Preserve our Nation in righteousness and honor, and continue thy blessings to us as a people, that we may lead a quiet and peaceable life, in all godliness and honesty. Grant health and favor to all who bear office in our land (especially to the President and the Congress, the Governor and Legislature of this State),* and help them to acknowledge and obey thy holy will:

℟. We beseech thee to hear us, good Lord.

Give to all men the mind of Christ, and dispose our days in thy peace, O God. Take from us all hatred and prejudice, and whatever may hinder unity of spirit and concord. Prosper the labors of those who take counsel for the nations of the world, that mutual understanding and common endeavor may be increased among all peoples;

℟. We beseech thee to hear us, good Lord.

Bless, we pray thee, the schools of the Church, universities and centers of research, all institutions of learning, and those who exercise the care of souls therein. Withhold not, we pray thee, thy Word and Wisdom, but bestow it in such measure

* In Canadian Churches the following may be said: especially to Her Gracious Majesty the Queen, the Prime Minister and the Parliament, and all Provincial Authorities.

that men may serve thee in Church and
State, and our common life be brought
under the rule of thy truth and righteousness;

℞. We beseech thee to hear us, good
Lord.

We pray thee especially, heavenly Father,
to sanctify our homes with thy light and
joy. Keep our children in the covenant of
their baptism, and enable their parents to
rear them in a life of faith and godliness.
By the spirit of affection and service unite
the members of all Christian families, that
they may show forth thy praise in our land
and in all the world;

℞. We beseech thee to hear us, good
Lord.

God of mercies, we pray thee to comfort
with the grace of thy Holy Spirit all who
are in sorrow or need, sickness or adversity. Remember those who suffer persecution for the faith. Have mercy upon those
to whom death draws near. Bring consolation to those in sorrow or mourning. And
to all grant a measure of thy love, taking
them into thy tender care;

℞. We beseech thee to hear us, good
Lord.

Let thy blessing rest upon the seed-time
and harvest, the commerce and industry,

711

the leisure and rest, and the arts and culture of our people. Take under thy special protection those whose toil is difficult or dangerous, and be with all who lay their hands to any useful task. Give them just rewards for their labor, and the knowledge that their work is good in thy sight, who art the Maker and Sustainer of all things;

℟. We beseech thee to hear us, good Lord.

We remember with thanksgiving those who have loved and served thee in thy Church on earth, who now rest from their labors (especially those most dear to us, whom we name in our hearts before thee). Keep us in fellowship with all thy saints, and bring us at length to the joy of thy heavenly kingdom;

℟. We beseech thee to hear us, good Lord.

¶ *Here special Supplications, Intercessions, and Thanksgivings may be made.*

All these things, and whatever else thou seest that we need, grant us, O Father, for his sake who died and rose again, and now liveth and reigneth with thee in the unity of thy Holy Ghost, one God, world without end.

℟. Amen.

¶ *If there be no Communion the Minister and Congregation shall say the Lord's Prayer.*

Our Father, who art in heaven . . .

¶ *A Hymn may then be sung.*
¶ *Then the Minister, standing at the Altar, shall sing or say the Benediction.*

The Lord bless thee, and keep thee. The Lord make his face shine upon thee, and be gracious unto thee. The Lord lift up his countenance upon thee, and give thee peace:
In the Name of the Father, and of the Son, and of the Holy Ghost.

¶ *The Congregation shall sing or say:*
Amen.

¶ *Then shall the Priest say to those who come to receive the Holy Communion,*

Ye, who do truly and earnestly repent you of your sins, and are in love and charity with your neighbours, and intend to lead a new life, following the commandments of God, and walking from henceforth in his holy ways; Draw near with faith, and take this holy Sacrament to your comfort; and make your humble confession to Almighty God, devoutly kneeling.

¶ *Then shall this General Confession be*

made, by the Priest and all those who are minded to receive the Holy Communion, humbly kneeling.

Almighty God, Father of our Lord Jesus Christ, Maker of all things, Judge of all men; We acknowledge and bewail our manifold sins and wickedness, Which we, from time to time, most grievously have committed, By thought, word, and deed, Against thy Divine Majesty, Provoking most justly thy wrath and indignation against us. We do earnestly repent, And are heartily sorry for these our misdoings; The remembrance of them is grievous unto us; The burden of them is intolerable. Have mercy upon us, Have mercy upon us, most merciful Father; For thy Son our Lord Jesus Christ's sake, Forgive us all that past; And grant that we may ever hereafter Serve and please thee In newness of life, To the honour and glory of thy Name; Through Jesus Christ our Lord. Amen.

¶ *Then shall the Priest (the Bishop if he be present) stand up, and turning to the People, say,*

Almighty God, our heavenly Father, who of his great mercy hath promised forgiveness of sins to all those who with hearty repentance and true faith turn unto him; Have mercy upon you; pardon and deliver you from all your sins; confirm and strengthen you in all goodness; and bring you to everlasting life; through Jesus Christ our Lord. *Amen.*

714

¶ *Then shall the Priest say,*

Hear what comfortable words our Saviour Christ saith unto all who truly turn to him.

Come unto me, all ye that travail and are heavy laden, and I will refresh you. *St. Matt.* xi. 28.

So God loved the world, that he gave his only-begotten Son, to the end that all that believe in him should not perish, but have everlasting life. *St. John* iii. 16.

Hear also what Saint Paul saith.

This is a true saying, and worthy of all men to be received, That Christ Jesus came into the world to save sinners. I *Tim.* i. 15.

Hear also what Saint John saith.

If any man sin, we have an Advocate with the Father, Jesus Christ the righteous; and he is the Propitiation for our sins. I *St. John* ii. 1, 2.

THE THANKSGIVING

¶ *A Hymn shall be sung.*
¶ *The Congregation shall rise at the beginning of the Preface.*

THE PREFACE

¶ *The Minister and Congregation shall sing or say:*

The Lord be with you.
℟. And with thy spirit.
Lift up your hearts.
℟. We lift them up unto the Lord.

¶ *After which the Priest shall proceed, saying,*

Lift up your hearts.
Answer. We lift them up unto the Lord.

THE PREFACE

℣. The Lord be with you.
℟. And with thy spirit.
℣. Lift up your hearts.
℟. We lift them up unto the Lord.

715

V̸. Let us give thanks to the Lord our God.

R̸. It is meet and right.

It is truly meet and just, right and availing unto salvation, that we should at all times and in all places give thanks unto Thee, O holy Lord, Father almighty and everlasting God,

For Christmas

Because by the mystery of the Word made flesh the light of Thy glory hath shone anew upon the eyes of our mind: that while we acknowledge Him to be God seen by men, we may be drawn by Him to the love of things unseen. And

---

Let us give thanks unto the Lord our God.

R̸. It is meet and right so to do.

¶ *Then shall the Minister turn to the Altar and sing or say:*

It is truly meet, right, and salutary, that we should at all times, and in all places, give thanks unto thee, O Lord, Holy Father, Almighty everlasting God:

¶ *Here shall follow the **Proper Preface** for the Day or Season. If there be none especially appointed, then shall follow immediately, Therefore with Angels, etc.*

For Advent

Who didst comfort thy people with the promise of the Redeemer, through whom thou wilt also make all things new in the day when he shall come again to judge the world in righteousness. Therefore with Angels, etc.

For Christmas

For in the mystery of the Word made flesh, thou hast given us a new revelation of thy glory; that seeing thee in the person of thy Son, we may be drawn to the love of those things which are not seen. Therefore with Angels, etc.

Priest. Let us give thanks unto our Lord God.

Answer. It is meet and right so to do.

¶ *Then shall the Priest turn to the Holy Table, and say,*

It is very meet, right, and our bounden duty, that we should at all times, and in all places, give thanks unto thee, O Lord, Holy Father, Almighty, Everlasting God.

¶ *Here shall follow the **Proper Preface**, according to the time, if there be any specially appointed; or else immediately shall be said or sung by the Priest,* Therefore with Angels, etc.

Christmas

¶ *Upon Christmas Day, and seven days after.*

Because thou didst give Jesus Christ, thine only Son, to be born as at this time for us; who, by the operation of the Holy Ghost, was made very man, of the substance of Virgin Mary his mother; and that without spot of sin, to make us clean

therefore with angels and archangels, with thrones and dominions, and with all the heavenly hosts, we sing a hymn to Thy glory, saying without ceasing:

For Epiphany

For when Thine only-begotten Son showed Himself in the substance of our mortal nature, He restored us by the new light of His own immortality. And therefore with angels and archangels, with thrones and dominions, and with all the heavenly hosts, we sing a hymn to Thy glory, saying without ceasing:

For Lent

Who by the fasting of the body dost curb our vices, elevate our minds and bestow virtue and reward; through Christ our Lord, through whom the angels praise Thy majesty, the dominions worship it, and the powers stand in awe. The heavens and the heavenly hosts, with the blessed

For Epiphany

And now do we praise thee, that thou didst send unto us thine only-begotten Son, and that in him, being found in fashion as a man, thou didst reveal the fullness of thy glory. Therefore with angels, etc.

For Lent

Who on the Tree of the Cross didst give salvation unto mankind; that whence death rose, thence life also might arise again; and that he who by a tree once overcame, might likewise by a Tree be overcome, through Christ our Lord; through whom with Angels, etc.

from all sin.
Therefore with Angels, etc.

Epiphany
¶ *Upon the Epiphany, and seven days after.*

Through Jesus Christ our Lord; who, in substance of our mortal flesh, manifested forth his glory; that he might bring us out of darkness into his own glorious light.

Therefore with Angels, etc.

Purification, Annunciation, and Transfiguration
¶ *Upon the Feasts of the Purification, Annunciation, and Transfiguration.*

Because in the Mystery of the Word made flesh, thou hast caused a new light to shine in our hearts, to give the knowledge of thy glory in the face of thy Son Jesus Christ our Lord.

Therefore with Angels, etc.

seraphim, join together in celebrating their joy. With these we pray Thee join our voices also, while we say with lowly praise:

In Passiontide

Who didst set the salvation of mankind upon the tree of the Cross, so that whence death, thence also life might rise again, and that he who overcame by the tree might also be overcome on the tree: through Christ our Lord, through whom the angels praise, etc.

For Easter

It is truly meet and just, right and availing unto salvation, that at all times, but more especially on this day (especially at this season) we should extol Thy glory, O Lord, when Christ our Pasch was sacrificed. For He is the true Lamb that hath taken away the sins of the world. Who by dying hath overcome our death, and by rising again hath restored our life. Therefore . . .

For the Ascension

Through Christ our Lord, Who after His resurrection appeared and showed Himself to all His disciples; and while they beheld Him, was lifted into heaven, so that He might make us partakers of

Easter

¶ *Upon Easter Day, and seven days after.*

But chiefly are we bound to praise thee for the glorious Resurrection of thy Son Jesus Christ our Lord: for he is the very Paschal Lamb, which was offered for us, and hath taken away the sin of the world; who by his death hath destroyed death, and by his rising to life again hath restored to us everlasting life.

Therefore with Angels, etc.

For Easter

But chiefly are we bound to praise thee for the glorious Resurrection of thy Son, Jesus Christ, our Lord: for he is the very Paschal Lamb, which was offered for us, and hath taken away the sin of the world; who by his death hath destroyed death, and by his rising to life again hath restored to us everlasting life. Therefore with Angels, etc.

For the Ascension of our Lord

Through Jesus Christ our Lord, who, after his Resurrection, appeared openly to all his disciples, and in their sight was taken up into heaven, that he might make

Ascension

¶ *Upon Ascension Day, and seven days after.*

Through thy most dearly beloved Son Jesus Christ our Lord; who, after his most glorious Resurrection, manifestly appeared to all his Apostles, and in their sight ascended up into heaven, to pre-

His Godhead. And therefore with angels and archangels, with thrones and dominions, and with all the heavenly hosts, we sing a hymn to Thy glory, saying without ceasing:

For Pentecost

Through Christ our Lord, Who ascending above all the heavens, and sitting at Thy right hand, (on this day) sent forth the Holy Ghost, as He had promised, on the children of adoption. Wherefore does the whole world rejoice with exceeding great joy; the hosts above and also the angelic powers join in singing the hymn to Thy glory saying without ceasing:

For the Most Holy Trinity

Who with Thine only-begotten Son and the Holy Ghost art one God, one Lord; not in the oneness of a single person, but in the Trinity of one substance. For that which we believe from Thy revelation concerning Thy glory, that same we believe also of Thy Son, and of the Holy Ghost, without difference or separation. So that in confessing the true and everlasting Godhead, we shall adore distinction in persons, oneness in being, and equality

us partakers of his divine Nature. Therefore with Angels, etc.

For the Day of Pentecost

Through Jesus Christ our Lord, who, ascending above the heavens and sitting at thy right hand, poured out on this day the Holy Spirit, as he had promised, upon the chosen disciples; whereat the whole earth rejoices with exceeding joy. Therefore with Angels, etc.

For Trinity Sunday

Who with thine only-begotten Son, and the Holy Ghost, art one God, one Lord. And in the confession of the only true God, we worship the Trinity in Person, and the Unity in Substance, of Majesty co-equal. Therefore with Angels, etc.

pare a place for us; that where he is, thither we might also ascend, and reign with him in glory.
Therefore with Angels, etc.

Whitsuntide
¶ *Upon Whitsunday, and six days after.*
Through Jesus Christ our Lord; according to whose most true promise, the Holy Ghost came down as at this time from heaven, lighting upon the disciples, to teach them, and to lead them into all truth; giving them boldness with fervent zeal constantly to preach the Gospel unto all nations; whereby we have been brought out of darkness and error into the clear light and true knowledge of thee, and of thy son Jesus Christ.
Therefore with Angels, etc.

Trinity Sunday
¶ *Upon the Feast of Trinity only.*
Who, with thine only-begotten Son, and the Holy Ghost, art one God, one Lord, in Trinity of Persons and in Unity of Substance. For that which we believe of thy glory, O Father, the same we believe of the Son, and of the Holy Ghost, without any difference of inequality.
Therefore with Angels, etc.

Or this
For the precious death and merits of

719

in majesty. Which the angels and arch-angels, the cherubim also and the sera-phim do praise, nor cease to cry out as with one voice:

For Christ the King

Who with the oil of gladness hast anointed Thine only-begotten Son, our Lord Jesus Christ, as eternal High Priest and universal King; that offering Himself on the altar of the Cross as an immaculate host and peace-offering, He might com-plete the mysteries of human redemption; and all creation being made subject to His dominion, He might deliver into the hands of Thine infinite Majesty a kingdom eter-nal and universal, a kingdom of holiness and grace, a kingdom of justice, love and peace. And therefore . . .

In Masses for the Dead

Through Christ our Lord, in whom the hope of a blessed resurrection hath shone upon us, that those whom the certainty of dying afflicteth, may be consoled by the promise of future immortality. For unto Thy faithful, O Lord, life is changed, not taken away: and the abode of this earthly sojourn being dissolved, an eternal dwelling is prepared in heaven. And therefore . . .

(Also proper prefaces for the Sacred Heart; the Blessed Virgin Mary; feasts of St. Joseph; and feasts of the Apostles.)

720

thy Son Jesus Christ our Lord, and for the sending to us of the Holy Ghost, the Comforter; who are one with thee in thy Eternal Godhead.

Therefore with Angels, etc.

For All Saints' Day (or at any time when the faithful departed are remembered)

Through Jesus Christ our Lord, who in the blessedness of thy saints hath given us a glorious pledge of the hope of our call-ing; that, following their example and be-ing strengthened by their fellowship, we may exult in thee for thy mercy, even as they rejoice with thee in glory. Therefore with Angels, etc.

All Saints

¶ *Upon All Saints' Day and seven days after.*

Who, in the multitude of thy Saints, hast compassed us about with so great a cloud of witnesses that we, rejoicing in their fellowship, may run with patience the race that is set before us, and, together with them, may receive the crown of glory that fadeth not away.

(through Christ our Lord. Through whom) the angels praise Thy majesty, the dominions worship it, the powers stand in awe. The heavens, and the heavenly hosts, and the blessed seraphim join together in celebrating their joy. With whom we pray Thee join our voices also, while we say with lowly praise:

THE SANCTUS

Holy, holy, holy, Lord God of hosts. Heaven and earth are full of Thy glory. Hosanna in the highest.

Blessed is He that cometh in the name of the Lord. Hosanna in the highest.

THE CANON OR RULE OF CONSECRATION

(Said silently until the Lord's Prayer)

We therefore humbly pray and beseech Thee, O most merciful Father, through Jesus Christ Thy Son, our Lord, that Thou wouldst vouchsafe to receive and bless ✚ these gifts, these ✚ offerings, these holy and unblemished sacrifices.

Which in the first place, we offer up to Thee for Thy holy Catholic Church, that it may please Thee to grant her peace, to protect, unite and govern her throughout the world, together with Thy servant *N.*

¶ *After the Preface shall follow immediately:*

Therefore with Angels and Archangels, and with all the company of heaven, we laud and magnify thy glorious Name; evermore praising thee, and saying:

¶ *Then shall be sung or said the Sanctus.*

THE SANCTUS

Holy, holy, holy, Lord God of Sabaoth; Heaven and earth are full of thy glory; Hosanna in the highest.

Blessed is he that cometh in the Name of the Lord; Hosanna in the highest.

Therefore with Angels and Archangels, and with all the company of heaven, we laud and magnify thy glorious Name; evermore praising thee, and saying,

¶ *Priest and people.*

Holy, Holy, Holy, Lord God of hosts, Heaven and earth are full of thy glory: Glory be to thee, O Lord Most High. Amen.

our Pope, *N.* our Bishop, and all true believers and professors of the Catholic and Apostolic Faith.

COMMEMORATION OF THE LIVING

Be mindful, O Lord, of Thy servants and handmaids *N.* and *N.* *(the priest calls to mind the living he wants to pray for)* and of all here present, whose faith and devotion are known to Thee, for whom we offer, or who offer up to Thee this sacrifice of praise for themselves and all those dear to them, for the redemption of their souls, the hope of their safety and salvation: who now pay their vows to Thee, the eternal, living and true God.

In communion with, and venerating the memory in the first place of the glorious ever Virgin Mary Mother of our God and Lord Jesus Christ; *(or, instead of the above, the proper Communicantes, always ending:)* also of Thy blessed Apostles and Martyrs.

Peter and Paul, Andrew, James, John, Thomas, James, Philip, Bartholomew, Matthew, Simon and Thaddeus, Linus, Cletus, Clement, Sixtus, Cornelius, Cyprian, Laurence, Chrysogonus, John and Paul, Cosmas and Damian, and of all Thy saints; by whose merits and prayers grant that we may be defended in all things by the help of Thy protection. Through the same Christ our Lord. Amen.

This oblation, therefore, of our service and that of Thy whole family, we beseech Thee, O Lord, graciously to accept, and to order our days in Thy peace and bid us to be delivered from eternal damnation and numbered among the flock of Thy elect. Through Christ our Lord. Amen.

Which oblation do Thou, O God, vouchsafe in all things to bless ✠, approve ✠, ratify ✠, make worthy and acceptable; that it may become for us the Body ✠ and Blood ✠ of Thy most beloved Son our Lord Jesus Christ.

723

¶ *Then may the Congregation kneel.*
¶ *The Minister standing before the Altar, and facing it, shall say the Prayer of Thanksgiving.*

THE PRAYER OF THANKSGIVING

Holy art thou, Almighty and Merciful God. Holy art thou, and great is the Majesty of thy glory.

Thou didst so love the world as to give thine only-begotten Son, that whosoever believeth in him might not perish, but have everlasting life; Who, having come into the world to fulfill for us thy holy will and to accomplish all things for our salvation,

¶ *When the Priest, standing before the Holy Table, hath so ordered the Bread and Wine, that he may with the more readiness and decency break the Bread before the People, and take the Cup into his hands, he shall say the Prayer of Consecration, as followeth.*

All glory be to thee, Almighty God, our heavenly Father, for that thou, of thy tender mercy, didst give thine only Son Jesus Christ to suffer death upon the Cross for our redemption; who made there (by his one oblation of himself once offered) a full, perfect, and sufficient sacrifice, oblation, and satisfaction, for the sins of the whole world; and did institute, and in his holy Gospel command us to continue, a perpetual memory of that his precious death and sacrifice until his coming again:

Who the day before He suffered took bread into His holy and venerable hands, and with His eyes lifted up to heaven, unto Thee, God, His almighty Father, giving thanks to Thee, He blessed ✠, broke and gave it to His disciples, saying: Take and eat ye all of this, for this is My Body.

(Adoration of the Sacred Host and the Elevation)

In like manner, after He had supped, taking also this excellent chalice into His holy and venerable hands, and giving thanks to Thee, He blessed ✠ and gave it to His disciples, saying: Take and drink ye all of this, for this is the Chalice of My Blood, of the new and eternal testament: the mystery of faith: which shall be shed for you and for many unto the remission of sins.

As often as ye shall do these things, ye shall do them in remembrance of me.

(The Adoration and the Elevation of the Chalice)

In the night in which he was betrayed, ᵃtook bread; and, when he had given thanks, he brake it and gave it to his disciples, saying, Take, eat; this is my Body, which is given for you; this do in remembrance of me.
(a) *Here he shall take the Bread in his hand.*

After the same manner also, he ᵇtook the cup, when he had supped, and, when he had given thanks, he gave it to them, saying, Drink ye all of it; this cup is the New Testament in my Blood, which is shed for you, and for many, for the remission of sins; this do, as oft as ye drink it, in remembrance of me.

(b) *Here he shall take the Cup in his hand.*

For in the night in which he was betrayed, (*a*) he took Bread; and when he had given thanks, (*b*) he brake it, and gave it to his disciples, saying, Take, eat, (*c*) this is my Body, which is given for you; Do this in remembrance of me.

Likewise, after supper, (*d*) he took the Cup; and when he had given thanks, he gave it to them, saying, Drink ye all of this; for (*e*) this is my Blood of the New Testament, which is shed for you, and for many, for the remission of sins; Do this, as oft as ye shall drink it, in remembrance of me.

(a) *Here the Priest is to take the Paten into his hands.*
(b) *And here to break the Bread.*
(c) *And here to lay his hand upon all the Bread.*
(d) *Here he is to take the Cup into his hands.*
(e) *And here he is to lay his hand upon every vessel in which there is any Wine to be consecrated.*

724

Wherefore, O Lord, we Thy servants, and likewise Thy holy people, calling to mind the blessed Passion of the same Christ, Thy Son our Lord, and also His glorious Resurrection from hell and also his glorious Ascension into heaven, offer unto Thy most excellent Majesty, of Thy gifts and presents, a pure ✝ Victim, a holy ✝ Victim, a spotless ✝ Victim, the holy ✝ Bread of eternal life, and the Chalice ✝ of everlasting salvation.

Upon which vouchsafe to look with a propitious and serene countenance, and to accept them as Thou were pleased to accept the gifts of Thy just servant Abel, and the sacrifice of our Patriarch Abraham, and that which Thy high priest Melchisedech offered to Thee, a holy sacrifice, a spotless Victim.

We most humbly beseech Thee, almighty God, command these things to be carried up by the hands of Thy holy angels, to Thine altar on high, in the sight of Thy divine majesty, that as many of us who, by participation at this altar, shall receive the most sacred Body ✝ and Blood ✝ of Thy Son may be filled with every heavenly blessing and grace. Through the same Christ our Lord. Amen.

Commemoration of the Departed

Be mindful also, O Lord, of Thy servants and handmaids N. and N. who

Remembering, therefore, his salutary precept, his life-giving Passion and Death, his glorious Resurrection and Ascension and the promise of his coming again, we give thanks to thee, O Lord God Almighty, not as we ought, but as we are able; and we beseech thee mercifully to accept our praise and thanksgiving, and with thy Word and Holy Spirit to bless us, thy servants, and these thine own gifts of bread and wine, so that we and all who partake thereof may be filled with heavenly benediction and grace, and, receiving the remission of sins, be sanctified in soul and body, and have our portion with all thy saints.

And unto thee, O God, Father, Son, and Holy Spirit, be all honor and glory in thy holy Church, world without end. Amen.

THE OBLATION

Wherefore, O Lord and heavenly Father, according to the institution of thy dearly beloved Son our Saviour Jesus Christ, we, thy humble servants, do celebrate and make here before thy Divine Majesty, with these thy holy gifts, which we now offer unto thee, the memorial thy Son hath commanded us to make; having in remembrance his blessed passion and precious death, his mighty resurrection and glorious ascension; rendering unto thee most hearty thanks for the innumerable benefits procured unto us by the same.

THE INVOCATION

And we most humbly beseech thee, O merciful Father, to hear us; and, of thy almighty goodness, vouchsafe to bless and sanctify, with thy Word and Holy Spirit, these thy gifts and creatures of bread and wine; that we, receiving them according to thy Son our Saviour Jesus Christ's holy institution, in remembrance of his death and passion, may be partakers of his most blessed Body and Blood.

And we earnestly desire thy fatherly goodness, mercifully to accept this our sacrifice of praise and thanksgiving; most humbly beseeching thee to grant that, by the merits and death of thy Son Jesus Christ, and through faith in his blood, we, and all thy whole Church, may obtain remission of our sins, and all other benefits

are gone before us with the sign of faith and repose in the sleep of peace.

To these, O Lord, and to all that rest in Christ, grant, we beseech Thee, a place of refreshment, light and peace. Through the same Christ our Lord. Amen.

And to us sinners also, Thy servants hoping in the multitude of Thy mercies, vouchsafe to grant some part and fellowship with Thy holy apostles and martyrs; with John, Stephen, Mathias, Barnabas, Ignatius, Alexander, Marcellinus, Peter, Felicitas, Perpetua, Agatha, Lucy, Agnes, Cecilia, Anastasia, and with all Thy saints; into whose company admit us, we beseech Thee, not considering our merits, but pardoning our offenses, through Christ our Lord.

Through whom, O Lord, Thou dost always create, sanctify ✠, quicken ✠, bless ✠, and bestow upon us all these Thy gifts.

Through ✠ Him, and with ✠ Him, and in ✠ Him, be unto Thee, O God the Father ✠ almighty, in the unity of the Holy ✠ Ghost, all honor and glory, world without end.

Let us pray.

Taught by Thy saving precepts and guided by the divine institution, we make bold to say:

of his passion. And here we offer and present unto thee, O Lord, our selves, our souls and bodies, to be a reasonable, holy, and living sacrifice unto thee; humbly beseeching thee, that we, and all others who shall be partakers of this Holy Communion, may worthily receive the most precious Body and Blood of thy Son Jesus Christ, be filled with thy grace and heavenly benediction, and made one body with him, that he may dwell in us, and we in him. And although we are unworthy, through our manifold sins, to offer unto thee any sacrifice; yet we beseech thee to accept this our bounden duty and service; not weighing our merits, but pardoning our offences, through Jesus Christ our Lord; by whom, and with whom, in the unity of the Holy Ghost, all honour and glory be unto thee, O Father Almighty, world without end. *Amen.*

And now, as our Saviour Christ hath taught us, we are bold to say,

Our Father, who art in heaven, hallowed be Thy name; Thy kingdom come; Thy will be done on earth as it is in heaven. Give us this day our daily bread; and forgive us our trespasses, as we forgive those who trespass against us. And lead us not into temptation.

R̃. But deliver us from evil. Amen.

Deliver us, we beseech Thee, O Lord, from all evils, past present and to come, and by the intercession of the blessed and glorious ever Virgin Mary, Mother of God, together with Thy blessed apostles Peter and Paul, and Andrew, and all the saints, mercifully grant peace in our days: that through the bounteous help of Thy mercy we may be always free from sin

¶ *Then shall the minister sing or say:*
Our Father, who art in heaven, Hallowed be thy Name, Thy kingdom come, Thy will be done, on earth as it is in heaven. Give us this day our daily bread; And forgive us our trespasses, as we forgive those who trespass against us; And lead us not into temptation, But deliver us from evil.

¶ *The congregation shall sing or say:*
For thine is the kingdom, and the power and the glory, for ever and ever. Amen.

¶ *Or, instead of the above Prayer of Thanksgiving, "Holy art thou, Almighty and Merciful God," the Minister may say the Words of Institution, followed by the Lord's Prayer*

Our Father, who art in heaven, Hallowed be thy Name. Thy kingdom come. Thy will be done, On earth as it is in heaven. Give us this day our daily bread. And forgive us our trespasses, As we forgive those who trespass against us. And lead us not into temptation, But deliver us from evil.

For thine is the kingdom, and the power and the glory, for ever and ever. Amen.

¶ *Then shall the Priest, kneeling down at the Lord's Table, say, in the name of all those who shall receive the Communion, this Prayer following.*

We do not presume to come to this thy Table, O merciful Lord, trusting in our own righteousness, but in thy manifold and great mercies. We are not worthy so much as to gather up the crumbs under thy Table. But thou art the same Lord, whose property is always to have mercy: Grant us therefore, gracious Lord, so to eat the flesh of thy dear Son Jesus Christ,

and secure from all disturbance. Through the same Jesus Christ Thy Son our Lord, who liveth and reigneth with Thee and the Holy Ghost, one God,

Said aloud

world without end.

℣. The peace ✠ of the Lord be always ✠ with you.

℟. And with thy spirit.

May this mingling and consecration of thy Body and Blood of our Lord Jesus Christ be to us who receive it effectual to life everlasting. Amen.

THE AGNUS DEI
Lamb of God, who takest, etc.

O Lord Jesus Christ, who saidst to Thy Apostles. Peace I leave with you. My peace I give unto you; look not upon my sins, but upon the faith of Thy church; and vouchsafe to grant her peace and

¶ *Then shall the Minister turn to the Congregation and sing or say:*
The peace of the Lord be with you alway.
¶ *The Congregation shall sing or say:*
And with thy spirit.

¶ *Then, the Congregation standing, shall be sung or said the Agnus Dei.*
AGNUS DEI
O Christ, Thou Lamb of God, that takest away the sin of the world, have mercy upon us.
O Christ, Thou Lamb of God, that takest away the sin of the world, have mercy upon us.
O Christ, Thou Lamb of God, that takest away the sin of the world, grant us Thy peace. Amen.

and to drink his blood, that our sinful bodies may be made clean by his body, and our souls washed through his most precious blood, and that we may evermore dwell in him, and he in us. *Amen.*

¶ *Here may be sung a Hymn.*

unity according to Thy will: O God, who livest and reignest world without end. Amen.

O Lord Jesus Christ, Son of the living God, who according to the will of the Father, through the co-operation of the Holy Ghost, hast by Thy death given life to the world: deliver me by this Thy most holy Body and Blood from all my transgressions and from all evils; make me always adhere to Thy commandments and never suffer me to be separated from Thee; who with the same God the Father and the Holy Ghost livest and reignest, God, for ever and ever. Amen.

Let not the partaking of Thy Body, O Lord Jesus Christ, which I, though unworthy, presume to receive, turn to my judgment and condemnation; but through Thy goodness may it be unto me a safeguard and a healing remedy both of soul and body; who livest and reignest with God the Father in the unity of the Holy Ghost, God, world without end. Amen.

I will take the bread of heaven, and call upon the Name of the Lord,

Lord, I am not worthy that Thou shouldst enter under my roof; say but the word and my soul shall be healed.

May the Body of our Lord Jesus Christ preserve my soul to live everlasting. Amen.

What shall I render to the Lord for all the things that He hath rendered to me? I will take the chalice of salvation, and I will call upon the name of the Lord.

Praising, I will call upon the Lord, and I shall be saved from my enemies.

May the Blood of our Lord Jesus Christ preserve my soul to live everlasting. Amen.

(*If there are communicants they approach the Sanctuary and the server says the Confiteor.*
I confess, etc.
The priest pronounces the Absolution:
May almighty God have mercy, etc.

Elevating a particle of the Blessed Sacrament the priest says:)
Behold the Lamb of God, behold Him who taketh away the sins of the world.
Lord I am not worthy that Thou shouldst enter under my roof; say but the word and my soul shall be healed.

730

¶ *Then shall the Communicants present themselves before the Altar and receive the Holy Sacrament.*

THE COMMUNION

¶ *Then shall the Priest first receive the Holy Communion in both kinds himself, and proceed to deliver the same to the Bishops, Priests, and Deacons, in like manner, (if any be present,) and, after that, to the People also in order, into their hands, all devoutly kneeling. And sufficient opportunity shall be given to those present to communicate. And when he delivereth the Bread, he shall say,*

The Body of our Lord Jesus Christ, which was given for thee, preserve thy body and soul unto everlasting life. Take and eat this in remembrance that Christ died for thee, and feed on him in thy heart by faith, with thanksgiving.

¶ *And the Minister who delivereth the Cup shall say,*

The Blood of our Lord Jesus Christ, which was shed for thee, preserve thy body and soul unto everlasting life. Drink this in remembrance that Christ's Blood was shed for thee, and be thankful.

¶ *When the Minister giveth the Bread he shall say:*

The Body of Christ, given for thee.

May the Body of our Lord Jesus Christ preserve Thy soul to life everlasting. Amen.

¶ *When he giveth the Cup he shall say:*

The Blood of Christ, shed for thee.

¶ *The Communicant may say Amen after each Element has been received.*

¶ *After he hath given the Bread and the Cup, or after all have been communicated, the Minister shall say:*

The Body of our Lord Jesus Christ and his precious Blood strengthen and preserve you unto eternal life.

THE POST-COMMUNION

¶ *Then shall the Congregation rise, and the Nunc Dimittis may be sung or said.*

NUNC DIMITTIS

Lord, now lettest thou thy servant depart in peace: according to thy word;

THE POST-COMMUNION

For mine eyes have seen thy salvation: which thou hast prepared before the face of all people;

A light to lighten the Gentiles: and the glory of thy people Israel.

Glory be to the Father, etc.

¶ *Then shall be said the Prayer.*

THE PRAYER

¶ *The Minister shall say one of the following Prayers; or he may say the Collect for Thursday in Holy Week.*

Grant, O Lord, that what we have taken with our mouth, we may receive with a pure mind: and that from a temporal gift it may become for us an eternal remedy.

May Thy Body, O Lord, which I have received, and Thy Blood which I have drunk, cleave to my inmost parts, and grant that no stain of sin may remain in me, whom these pure and holy sacraments have refreshed. Who livest and reignest world without end. Amen.

(The proper Communio. Advent I)

The Lord will give goodness: and our earth shall yield her fruit.

O give thanks unto the Lord, for he is good.

¶ *Then shall the Priest say,*

Let us pray.

Almighty and everlasting God, we most heartily thank thee, for that thou dost vouchsafe to feed us who have duly received these holy mysteries, with the spiritual food of the most precious Body and Blood of thy Son our Saviour Jesus Christ; and dost assure us thereby of thy favour and goodness towards us; and that we are very members incorporate in the mystical body of thy Son, which is the blessed company of all faithful people; and are also heirs through hope of thy everlasting kingdom, by the merits of his most precious death and passion. And we humbly beseech thee, O heavenly Father, so to assist us with thy grace, that we may continue in that holy fellowship, and do all such good works as thou hast prepared for us to walk in; through Jesus Christ our Lord, to whom, with thee and the Holy Ghost, be all honour and glory,

℣. The Lord be with you.
℟. And with thy spirit.

(The proper Postcommunio)

May we receive Thy mercy, O Lord, in the midst of Thy temple: that we may with becoming honor prepare for the approaching solemnities of our redemption. Through our Lord.

℟. And his mercy endureth for ever.

We give thanks to thee, Almighty God, that thou hast refreshed us with this thy salutary gift; and we beseech thee, of thy mercy, to strengthen us through the same gift, in faith towards thee and in fervent love toward one another; through Jesus Christ, thy dear Son, our Lord, who liveth and reigneth with thee and the Holy Ghost, one God, world without end.

Or,

Pour forth upon us, O Lord, the spirit of thy love, that by thy mercy thou mayest make of one will those whom thou hast fed with one heavenly food; through thy Son, Jesus Christ our Lord, who liveth and reigneth with thee and the Holy Ghost, one God, world without end.

Or,

Almighty God, who givest the true Bread which cometh down from heaven, even thy Son, Jesus Christ our Lord: Grant, we beseech thee, that we who have received the Sacrament of his Body and Blood may abide in him, and he in us, that we may be filled with the power of his endless life; who liveth and reigneth with thee and the Holy Ghost, one God, world without end.

Or,

Almighty God, who hast given thine only Son to be unto us both a sacrifice for sin and also an ensample of godly

world without end. *Amen.*

733

life: Give us grace that we may always most thankfully receive that his inestimable benefit, and also daily endeavor ourselves to follow the blessed steps of his most holy life; through the same Jesus Christ our Lord, who liveth and reigneth with thee and the Holy Ghost, one God, world without end.
Amen.

¶ *The Congregation shall sing or say:*
Amen.

¶ *Then may be sung or said the Salutation and the Benedicamus.*
The Lord be with you.
℟. And with thy spirit.

Bless we the Lord.
℟. Thanks be to God.

¶ *Then shall be said the Gloria in excelsis, all standing, or some proper Hymn.*
Glory be to God on high, etc.

℣. Go, you are dismissed.
℟. Thanks be to God.

(*or if there be no Gloria*)
℣. Bless we the Lord.
℟. Thanks be to God.

May the homage of my bounden duty be pleasing to Thee, O Holy Trinity; and grant that the sacrifice which I, though unworthy, have offered in the sight of Thy majesty may be acceptable to Thee, and through Thy mercy be a propitiation for me and for all those for whom I have offered it. Through Christ our Lord. Amen.

¶ Then the Minister, standing at the Altar, shall sing or say the Benediction.

THE BENEDICTION

The Lord bless thee, and keep thee. The Lord make his face shine upon thee, and be gracious unto thee.

The Lord lift up his countenance upon thee, and give thee peace: In the Name of the Father, and of the Son, and of the Holy Ghost.

¶ The Congregation shall sing or say:
Amen.

¶ Then, the People kneeling, the Priest (the Bishop if he be present) shall let them depart with this Blessing.

The Peace of God, which passeth all understanding, keep your hearts and minds in the knowledge and love of God, and of his Son Jesus Christ our Lord: And the Blessing of God Almighty, the Father, the Son, and the Holy Ghost, be amongst you, and remain with you always Amen.

May almighty God bless you, the Father, the Son and the Holy Ghost. ℟. Amen

THE LAST GOSPEL
John 1:1-14. In the beginning was the word, etc.

THE LEONINE PRAYERS

735

III. COMPARATIVE STUDY OF THE ROMAN, LUTHERAN, AND ANGLICAN LITANIES

This comparison of texts has been made upon the basis of similar but less complete tables in Prof. Drews' *Studien zur Geschichte des Gottesdiensts,* etc., Bd. IV-V, *Beiträge zu Luthers liturgischen Reformen, 24-32;* and in Dr. P. Z. Strodach's introduction to Luther's litanies in *PE* 6, 249-61.

The pre-Reformation texts have been assembled in one column which shows the principal source to have been the breviary of the Augustinian Eremites. Material from contemporary sources is indicated as follows: that from the Magdeburg Breviary as supplied by Prof. Drews is marked (M.B.), that from the Augsbury Breviary as supplied by Dr. Strodach is marked (A.B.). The Lutheran text is that of the Common Liturgy. The Anglican text is from the American *Book of Common Prayer.*

For discussion of the concluding collects and versicles, see pp. 633-34.

Pre-Reformation Breviary Augustinian Eremites	Luther's Latina Litania Correcta	Luther's Deutsche Litanei	Common Liturgy	American Book of Common Prayer
Kyrieleison	Kyrie Eleison	Kyrie Eleison	Lord, have mercy upon us. R̥. Lord, have mercy upon us.	
Christe eleyson	Christe Eleison	Christe Eleison	Christ, have mercy upon us. R̥. Christ, have mercy upon us.	
Kyrie Eleison (A.B.)	Kyrie Eleison	Kyrie Eleison	Lord, have mercy upon us. R̥. Lord, have mercy upon us.	
Christe audi nos Christe exaudi nos	Christi exaudi nos	Christe Erhöre uns	O Christ, hear us. R̥. O Christ, hear us.	
Pater de coelis deus miserere nobis	Pater de coelis deus Miserere nobis	Her Got vater ym himmel Erbarm dich vber vns	O God, the Father in heaven: R̥. Have mercy upon us.	O God the Father, Creator of heaven and earth; *Have mercy upon us.*
Fili redemptor mundi deus miserere nobis	Fili redemptor mundi deus Miserere nobis	Her Got son der welt heiland Erbarm dich vber vns	O God, the Son, Redeemer of the world: R̥. Have mercy upon us.	O God the Son, Redeemer of the world; *Have mercy upon us.*
Spiritus sancte deus miserere nobis	Spiritus sancte deus Miserere nobis	Her Gott heiliger geist Erbarm dich vber vns	O God the Holy Ghost: R̥. Have mercy upon us.	O God the Holy Ghost, Sanctifier of the faithful; *Have mercy upon us.*
Sancta trinitas unus Deus miserere nobis (A.B.) (Nomina Sanctorum et Sanctarum)			O Holy Trinity, One God: R̥. Have mercy upon us.	O holy, blessed, and glorious Trinity, one God; *Have mercy upon us.*

Pre-Reformation Breviary Augustinian Eremites	Luther's Latina Litania Correcta	Luther's Deutsche Litanei	Common Liturgy	American Book of Common Prayer
Propitius esto:parce nobis domine Propitius esto Exaudi nos domine A peccatis nostris: libera nos domine (M.B.) (*Repeated after each prex.*)	Propitius esto:parce nobis domine Propitius esto: Libera nos domine (*Repeated after each prex.*)	Sey uns gnedig Verschon vnser lieber herre got Sey uns gnedig: hilff vns lieber Herre Gott	Be gracious unto us. ℟. Spare us, good Lord. Be gracious unto us. ℟. Help us, good Lord.	Remember not, Lord, our offences, nor the offences of our forefathers; neither take thou vengeance of our sins: Spare us, good Lord, spare thy people, whom thou hast redeemed with thy most precious blood, and be not angry with us for ever. *Spare us, good Lord.*
Ab omni malo	Ab omni peccato:	Für allen sünden Behüt vns lieber Herre Gott (*after each prex.*)	From all sin;	
Ab omni peccato				
Ab ira tua	Ab omni errore Ab omni malo	Für allem yrsal Für allem vbel	from all error; from all evil: ℟. Good Lord, deliver us.	From all evil and mischief; from sin; from the crafts and assaults of the devil; from thy wrath, and from everlasting damnation, *Good Lord, deliver us.* From all blindness of heart; from pride, vainglory, and hypocrisy; from envy, hatred, and malice, and all uncharitableness, *Good Lord, deliver us.*
(*See below*)	Ab insidiis diaboli	Für des teuffels trug vnd list	From the crafts and assaults of the devil;	

Pre-Reformation Breviary Augustinian Eremites	*Luther's Latina Litania Correcta*	*Luther's Deutsche Litanei*	*Common Liturgy*	*American Book of Common Prayer*
Ab subitanea et improvisa morte	Ab subitanea et improvisa morte	Für bösem schnellen tod	From sudden and evil death;	From all inordinate and sinful affections; and from all the deceits of the world, the flesh, and the devil, *Good Lord, deliver us.*
Ab insidiis diaboli	*(See above)*	*(See above)*	*(See above)*	*(See above)*
(See below)	*(See below)*	*(See below)*	*(See below)*	From lightning and tempest; from earthquake, fire, and flood; from plague, pestilence, and famine; from battle and murder, and from sudden death, *Good Lord, deliver us.*
(See above)	A peste et fame	Für pestilentz vnd tewer zeit	From pestilence and famine;	*(See above)*
Ab ira et odio et omni mala voluntate	A bello et caede	Für krieg vnd blut	From war and bloodshed;	*(See above)*
A spiritu fornicatoris	*(See above)*	*(See above)*	*(See above)*	*(See above)*
	A seditione et simultate	Für auffrhur vnd zwitracht	From sedition and rebellion;	From all sedition, privy conspiracy, and rebellion;
A fulgure et tempestate	A fulgure et tempestatibus	Für hagel vnd vngewitter	From lightning and tempest;	*(See above)*
			From all calamity by fire and water;	*(See above)*
A morte perpetua	A morte perpetua	Für dem ewigen Tod	And from everlasting death:	*(See above)*
Ab omni malo (M.B.)	*(See above)*	*(See above)*	*(See above)*	*(See above)*

Pre-Reformation Breviary Augustinian Eremites	Luther's Latina Litania Correcta	Luther's Deutsche Litanei	Common Liturgy	American Book of Common Prayer
			℞. Good Lord, deliver us. (*See above*)	from all false doctrine, heresy, and schism; from hardness of heart, and contempt of thy Word and Commandment. *Good Lord, deliver us.*
Per mysterium sanctae incarnationis tuae	Per mysterium sanctae incarnationis tuae		By the mystery of thy holy Incarnation;	By the mystery of thy holy Incarnation;
Per adventum tuum				
Per nativitatem tuam	Per sanctam nativitatem tuam	Durch dein heilig geburt	By thy holy Nativity;	by thy holy Nativity and Circumcision;
Per baptismum et sanctum jejunium tuum	Per baptismum, jejunium et tentationes tuas		By thy Baptism, Fasting, and Temptation;	by thy Baptism, Fasting, and Temptation; *Good Lord, deliver us.*
	Per agoniam et sudorem tuum sanguineum	Durch dein todkampff vnd blutigen schweiss	By thine Agony and Bloody Sweat;	By thine Agony and Bloody Sweat;
Per crucem et passionem tuam	Per crucem et passionem tuam	Durch dein Creutze vnd tod	By thy Cross and Passion;	by thy Cross and Passion;
Per mortem et sepulturam tuam	Per mortem et sepulturam tuam		By thy Precious Death and Burial;	by thy precious Death and Burial;
Per sanctam resurrectionem tuam Per admirabilem ascensionem tuam	Per resurrectionem et ascensionem tuam	Durch dein heiliges aufferstehn und hymelfart	By thy glorious Resurrection and Ascension;	by thy glorious Resurrection and Ascension;

740

Pre-Reformation Breviary Augustinian Eremites	Luther's Latina Litania Correcta	Luther's Deutsche Litanei	Common Liturgy	American Book of Common Prayer
Per adventum spiritus sancti paracliti	Per adventum spiritus sancti paracliti		And by the coming of the Holy Ghost, the Com-forter: ℟. Help us, good Lord.	and by the Coming of the Holy Ghost, *Good Lord, deliver us.*
	In omni tempore tribula-tionis nostrae / In omni tempore facilita-tis nostrae		In all time of our tribu-lation; / In all time of our pros-perity;	In all time of our tribu-lation; / in all time of our pros-perity;
In die judicii	In hora mortis / In die judicii	Inn vnser letzsten stund / Am jüngsten gericht	In the hour of death; / And in the day of judg-ment: ℟. Help us, good Lord.	in the hour of death, / and in the day of judg-ment; *Good Lord, deliver us.*
Peccatores te rogamus audi nos	Peccatores te rogamus audi nos	Wir armen sünder bitten / Du wollest vns hören / lieber **herre Gott**	We poor sinners do be-seech thee: ℟. To hear us, O Lord God.	We sinners do beseech thee to hear us, O Lord God;
(Te rogamus, etc. *follows each prex*) / Ut nobis parcas / Ut nobis indulgeas / Ut ad veram poenitentiam nos perducere digneris / Ut dominum apostolicum et omnes ecclesiasticos ordines in sancta reli-gione conservare dig-neris	(Te rogamus, etc. *follows each prex*)			

Pre-Reformation Breviary Augustinian Eremites	Luther's Latina Litania Correcta	Luther's Deutsche Litanei	Common Liturgy	American Book of Common Prayer
Ut inimicos sanctae ecclesiae humiliare digneris Ut ecclesiam tuam sanctam regere et conservare digneris	Ut ecclesiam tuam sanctam catholicam regere et gubernare digneris	Vnd deine heilige Christliche Kirche regieren und füren	And to rule and govern thy holy Christian Church;	and that it may please thee to rule and govern thy holy Church universal in the right way; *We beseech thee to hear us, good Lord.* (See below)
	Ut cunctos Episcopos, Pastores et ministros ecclesiae in sancto verbo et sancta vita servare digneris	Alle bischoff, pfarrherr, vnd kirchendiener ynn heilsamen wort vnd heiligen leben behalten	To preserve all pastors and ministers of thy Church in the true knowledge and understanding of thy Word, and in holiness of life;	(See below)
	Ut sectas et omnia scandala tollere digneris	Allen rotten und ergernissen wehren	To put an end to all schisms and causes of offence;	
	Ut errantes et seductos reducere in viam veritatis digneris	All yrrigen vnd verfürten wider bringen	To bring into the way of truth all such as have erred, and are deceived;	(See below)
	Ut Satanam sub pedibus nostris conterere digneris	Den Satan vnter unser füsze treten	To beat down Satan under our feet;	(See below)
	Ut operarios fideles in messem tuam mittere digneris	Trew arbeiter ynn deine erndte senden	To send faithful laborers into thy harvest;	(See below)

Pre-Reformation Breviary Augustinian Eremites	Luther's Latina Litania Correcta	Luther's Deutsche Litanei	Common Liturgy	American Book of Common Prayer
	Ut incrementum verbi et fructum spiritus cunctis audientibus donare digneris	Deinen geist vnd krafft zum wort geben	To accompany thy Word with thy Spirit and grace;	*(See below)*
	Ut lapsos erigere et stantes confortare digneris		To raise up them that fall, and to strengthen such as do stand;	*(See below)*
	Ut pusillanimes et tentatos consolari et adiuvare digneris	Allen betrübten vnd blöden helffen vnd trösten	And to comfort and help the weak-hearted and the distressed; R⃫. We beseech thee to hear us, good Lord.	*(See below)*
Ut regibus et principibus christianis pacem et veram concordiam largiri (donare) digneris	Ut regibus et principibus cunctis pacem et concordiam donare digneris	Allen königen vnd fürsten frid vnd eintracht geben	To give to all nations peace and concord;	*(See below)*
			To preserve our country from discord and contention;	
	Ut Caesari nostro perpetuam victoriam contra hostes suos donare digneris	Unsern Kaiser stet sieg widder seine feinde gönnen		
Ut antistitem nostrum cum omnibus sibi commissis in sancta (vera) religione conservare digneris (M.B.)	Ut principem nostrum cum suis praesidibus dirigere et tueri digneris	Unsern Landherrn mit allen seinen gewaltigen leiten und schützen	To direct and defend our President (or, our gracious Sovereign), and all in authority;	That it may please thee so to rule the heart of thy servant, The President of the United States, that he may above all things seek

Pre-Reformation Breviary Augustinian Eremites	Luther's Latina Litania Correcta	Luther's Deutsche Litanei	Common Liturgy	American Book of Common Prayer
				thy honour and glory; *We beseech thee to hear us, good Lord.*
Ut cuncto populo christiano pacem et unitatem largiri digneris				
Ut nos metipsos in tuo sancto servitio confortare et conservare digneris				
Ut cunctum populum christianum percioso sanguine tuo redemptum conservare digneris (M.B.)				
Ut mentes nostras ad coelestia desideria erigas				
Ut omnibus benefactoribus nostris sempiterna bona retribuas				
Ut animas nostras fratrum propinquorum et benefactorum nostrorum ab aeterna damnatione eripias	Ut magistratum et plebem nostram benedicere et costodire digneris	Vnsern Rat vnd gemeine segnen und behüten	And to bless and keep our magistrates, and all our people: R̨. We beseech thee to hear us, good Lord.	That it may please thee to bless and preserve all Christian Rulers and Magistrates, giving them grace to execute justice, and to maintain truth; *We beseech thee to hear us, good Lord.*

Pre-Reformation Breviary Augustinian Eremites	Luther's Latina Litania Correcta	Luther's Deutsche Litanei	Common Liturgy	American Book of Common Prayer
(See above)	*(See above)*	*(See above)*	*(See above)*	That it may please thee to illuminate all Bishops, Priests, and Deacons, with true knowledge and understanding of thy Word; and that both by their preaching and living they may set it forth, and show it accordingly; *We beseech thee to hear us, good Lord.*
	(See above)	*(See above)*	*(See above)*	That it may please thee to send forth labourers into thy harvest; *We beseech thee to hear us, good Lord.*
(See above)	*(See above)*	*(See above)*	*(See above)*	That it may please thee to bless and keep all thy people; *We beseech thee to hear us, good Lord.*
(See above)	*(See above)*	*(See above)*	*(See above)*	That it may please thee to give to all nations unity, peace, and concord; *We beseech thee to hear us, good Lord.*
	(See above)	*(See above)*	*(See above)*	That it may please thee to give us an heart to love

Pre-Reformation Breviary Augustinian Eremites	Luther's Latina Litania Correcta	Luther's Deutsche Litanei	Common Liturgy	American Book of Common Prayer
				and fear thee, and diligently to live after thy commandments; *We beseech thee to hear us, good Lord.*
	(See above)	*(See above)*	*(See above)*	That it may please thee to give to all thy people increase of grace to hear meekly thy Word, and to receive it with pure affection, and to bring forth the fruits of the Spirit; *We beseech thee to hear us, good Lord.*
	(See above)		*(See above)*	That it may please thee to bring into the way of truth all such as have erred, and are deceived; *We beseech thee to hear us, good Lord.*
	(See above)	*(See above)*	*(See above)*	That it may please thee to strengthen such as do stand; and to comfort and help the weak-hearted; and to raise up those who fall; and finally to beat down Satan under our feet; *We beseech thee to hear us, good Lord.*

Pre-Reformation Breviary Augustinian Eremites	Luther's Latina Litania Correcta	Luther's Deutsche Litanei	Common Liturgy	American Book of Common Prayer
	Ut afflictos et periclitantes respicere et salvare digneris	Allen, so yn not vnd far sind, mit hülff erscheinen	To behold and succor all who are in danger, necessity and tribulation;	That it may please thee to succour, help, and comfort, all who are in danger, necessity, and tribulation; *We beseech thee to hear us, good Lord.*
			To protect all who travel by land, air or water;	That it may please thee to preserve all who travel by land, by water, or by air,
	Ut praegnantibus et lactentibus felicem partum et incrementum largiri digneris	Allen schwangern vnd seugern, fröliche frücht vnd gedeyen geben	To preserve all women in the perils of childbirth;	all women in child-birth,
	Ut infantes et aegrotos fovere et custodire digneris	Alle kinder vnd kranken pflegen vnd warten	To strengthen and keep all sick persons and young children;	all sick persons, and young children;
	Ut captivos liberare digneris	Alle gefangene los vnd ledig lassen	To set free all who are innocently imprisoned;	and to show thy pity upon all prisoners and captives; *We beseech thee to hear us, good Lord.*
	Ut pupillos et viduas protegere et providere digneris	Alle witwen vnd waisen verteydigen vnd versorgen	To defend and provide for all fatherless children and widows;	That it may please thee to defend, and provide for, the fatherless children, and widows, and all who are desolate and oppressed; *We beseech thee to hear us, good Lord.*

Pre-Reformation Breviary Augustinian Eremites	Luther's Latina Litania Correcta	Luther's Deutsche Litanei	Common Liturgy	American Book of Common Prayer
	Ut cunctis hominibus miserere digneris	Aller menschen dich erbarmen	And to have mercy upon all men: ℞. We beseech thee to hear us, good Lord.	That it may please thee to have mercy upon all men; *We beseech thee to hear us, good Lord.*
	Ut hostibus, persecutoribus, et calumniatoribus nostris ignoscere et eos convertere digneris	Unsern feinden, verfolgern vnd lestern vergeben vnd sie bekeren	To forgive our enemies, persecutors, and slanderers, and to turn their hearts;	That it may please thee to forgive our enemies, persecutors, and slanderers, and to turn their hearts; *We beseech thee to hear us, good Lord.*
Ut fructus terrae dare et conservare digneris	Ut fruges terrae dare et conservare digneris	Die frücht auff dem lande geben und bewaren	To give and preserve to our use the fruits of the earth;	That it may please thee to give and preserve to our use the kindly fruits of the earth, so that in due time we may enjoy them; *We beseech thee to hear us, good Lord.*
Ut omnibus fidelibus defunctis requiem aeternam donare digneris				That it may please thee to give us true repentance; to forgive us all our sins, negligences, and ignorances; and to endue us with the grace of thy

Pre-Reformation Breviary Augustinian Eremites	Luther's Latina Litania Correcta	Luther's Deutsche Litanei	Common Liturgy	American Book of Common Prayer
Ut nos exaudire digneris	Ut nos exaudire digneris	Vnd vns gnediglich erhören	And graciously to hear our prayers: ℞. We beseech thee to hear us, good Lord.	Holy Spirit to amend our lives according to thy holy Word; *We beseech thee to hear us, good Lord.*
Fili dei Te rogamus audi nos	Fili dei Te rogamus audi nos	O Jhesu Christ Gottes son Erhöre vns lieber herre gott	O Lord Jesus Christ, Son of God; ℞. We beseech thee to hear us.	Son of God, we beseech thee to hear us. *Son of God, we beseech thee to hear us.*
Agnus dei qui tollis peccata mundi parce nobis domine miserere nobis (M.B.)	Agne dei qui tollis peccata mundi miserere nobis	O du Gottes lam das der welt sünde tregt Erbarm dich vber vns	O Lamb of God, that takest away the sin of the world; ℞. Have mercy upon us.	O Lamb of God, who takest away the sins of the world; *Grant us thy peace.*
Agnus dei qui tollis peccata mundi parce nobis domine miserere nobis (M.B.)	Agne dei qui tollis peccata mundi miserere nobis	O du Gottes lam der welt sünde tregt Erbarm dich vber vns	O Lamb of God, that takest away the sin of the world; ℞. Have mercy upon us.	O Lamb of God, who takest away the sins of the world; *Have mercy upon us.*
Agnus dei qui tollis peccata mundi miserere nobis. (M.B.) dona nobis pacem	Agne dei qui tollis peccata mundi da nobis pacem	O du Gottes lam der welt sünde tregt Verley vns steten frid	O Lamb of God, that takest away the sin of the world; ℞. Grant us thy peace. Amen.	

Pre-Reformation Breviary Augustinian Eremites	Luther's Latina Litania Correcta	Luther's Deutsche Litanei	Common Liturgy	American Book of Common Prayer
Christe audi nos	Christe exaudi nos	Christe		O Christ, hear us.
Christe exaudi nos		Erhöre vns		O Christ, hear us.
Kyrieleyson	Kyrie eleison	Kyrie eleison		Lord, have mercy upon us,
				Lord, have mercy upon us.
Christeleison	Christe eleison	Christe eleison		Christ, have mercy upon us.
				Christ, have mercy upon us.
Kyrieleison	Kyrie eleison	Kyrie eleison		Lord, have mercy upon us.
		Amen		Lord, have mercy upon us.
Pater noster	Pater noster		Our Father, who art in heaven ...	Our Father, who art in heaven ...

IV. EXTRACTS FROM EUCHARISTIC PRAYERS

A. THE TEACHING OF THE TWELVE APOSTLES (A.D. C. 100)

Now as regards the Eucharist (the Thank-offering), give thanks after this manner:
First for the cup:
> "We give thanks to Thee, our Father, for the holy vine of David Thy servant, which Thou hast made known to us through Jesus, Thy servant: to Thee be the glory for ever."

And for the broken bread:
> "We give thanks to Thee, our Father, for the life and knowledge which Thou hast made known to us through Jesus, Thy servant: to Thee be the glory for ever. As this broken bread was scattered upon the mountains and gathered together became one, so let Thy church be gathered together from the ends of the earth into Thy kingdom, for Thine is the glory and the power through Jesus Christ for ever."

But let no one eat or drink of your Eucharist, except those baptized into the name of the Lord; for as regards this also the Lord has said: "Give not that which is holy to the dogs."

Now after being filled, give thanks after this manner:
> "We thank Thee, Holy Father, for Thy holy Name, which Thou hast caused to dwell (tabernacle) in our hearts, and for the knowledge and faith and immortality which Thou hast made known to us through Jesus Thy Servant; to Thee be the glory for ever.

> "Thou, O Almighty Sovereign, didst make all things for Thy Name's sake; Thou gavest food and drink to men for enjoyment that they might give thanks to Thee; but to us Thou didst freely give spiritual food and drink and eternal life through Thy servant.

> "Before all things we give thanks to Thee that Thou art mighty; to Thee be the glory for ever.

> "Remember, O Lord, Thy Church, to deliver her from all evil and to perfect her in Thy love; and gather her together from the four winds, sanctified for Thy kingdom which Thou didst prepare for her; for Thine is the power and the glory for ever.

> "Let grace come, and let this world pass away. Hosanna to the God (Son) of David. If any one is holy let him come, if any one is not holy let him repent. Maranatha. Amen."

(Philip Schaff, *The Teaching of the Twelve Apostles.* [3d ed., 1889] pp. 190 ff.)

B. APOSTOLIC TRADITION OF HIPPOLYTUS (*c.*A.D. 215)

"And when he is made bishop, all shall offer him the kiss of peace, for he has been made worthy. To him then the deacons shall bring the offering, and he, laying his hand upon it, with all the presbytery, shall say as the thanksgiving:
> The Lord be with you.

And all shall say:

751

And with thy spirit.
Lift up your hearts.
We lift them up unto the Lord.
Let us give thanks to the Lord.
It is meet and right.

And then he shall proceed immediately:

We give thee thanks, O God, through thy beloved Servant Jesus Christ, whom at the end of time thou didst send to us a Saviour and Redeemer and the Messenger of thy counsel. Who is thy Word, inseparable from thee; through whom thou didst make all things and in whom thou art well pleased. Whom thou didst send from heaven into the womb of the Virgin, and who dwelling within her, was made flesh, and was manifested as thy Son, being born of [the] Holy Spirit and the Virgin. Who, fulfilling thy will, and winning for himself a holy people, spread out his hands when he came to suffer, that by his death he might set free them who believed on thee. Who, when he was betrayed to his willing death, that he might bring to nought death, and break the bonds of the devil, and tread hell under foot, and give light to the righteous, and set up a boundary post, and manifest his resurrection, taking bread and giving thanks to thee, said: Take, eat: this is my body, which is broken for you. And likewise also the cup, saying: This is my blood, which is shed for you. As often as ye perform this, perform my memorial.

Having in memory, therefore, his death and resurrection, we offer to thee the bread and the cup, yielding thee thanks, because thou hast counted us worthy to stand before thee and to minister to thee.

And we pray thee that thou wouldest send thy Holy Spirit upon the offerings of thy holy church; that thou, gathering them into one, wouldest grant to all thy saints who partake to be filled with [the] Holy Spirit, that their faith may be confirmed in truth, that we may praise and glorify thee. Through thy Servant Jesus Christ, through whom be to thee glory and honour, with [the] Holy Spirit in the holy church, both now and always and world without end. Amen."

(Burton Scott Easton, *The Apostolic Tradition of Hippolytus.* pp. 35-36.)

C. THE LITURGY OF ST. JOHN CHRYSOSTOM
(GREEK ORTHODOX CHURCH)

We also with these (blessed) powers, O Master, Lover of men, cry aloud, and say: Holy art Thou and All-Holy, Thou and Thine Only-Begotten Son and Thine Holy Spirit. Holy art Thou and All-Holy, and Great is the Majesty of Thy glory; Who didst so love the world as to give Thine Only-Begotten Son, that whoso believeth in Him might not perish but have everlasting life: Who having come and having fulfilled for us the dispensation, in the night wherein He (was given up, or rather,) gave Himself up (for the life of the world), took bread in His holy and pure and spotless hands, and gave thanks, and blessed, (and hallowed) and brake, and gave to His holy disciples and apostles, saying: Take, eat: this is My Body which is (broken) for you (for the remission of sins). (Amen.) Likewise after supper, He took the cup, saying: Drink ye all of it: this is My Blood of the new covenant, which is shed for you and for many for the remission of sins. (Amen.)

We, therefore, remembering this salutary precept, and all that happened for us: the Cross, the tomb, the resurrection on the third day, the ascension into Heaven, the session on the right hand, the second and glorious coming again; in relation to all and through all, we offer to Thee Thine Own of Thine Own. (*Choir:* We hymn Thee, we bless Thee, we give thanks to Thee, O Lord, and pray of Thee, Our God.) Moreover, we offer to Thee this reasonable and unbloody sacrifice; we beseech Thee and pray and supplicate; send down Thy Holy Spirit upon us and upon these gifts lying before Thee. (*Deacon:* Sir, Bless the Holy Bread.) And make this bread the Precious Body of Thy Christ. (Amen.) (*Deacon:* Sir, Bless the Holy Cup.) And that which is in this cup, the Precious Blood of Thy Christ. (Amen.) (*Deacon:* Sir, Bless them both.) Changing them by Thy Holy Spirit. (Amen, Amen, Amen.) (*Deacon:* Holy Sir, remember me, a sinner.) So that they may be to those who partake for purification of soul, forgiveness of sins, communion of the Holy Spirit, fulfillment of the Kingdom (of Heaven), and boldness towards Thee, and not to judgment nor to condemnation. And moreover we offer to Thee this reasonable service, etc.

(*Here follow the Intercessions.*)

And send forth on us all Thy mercies, and grant us with one mouth and one heart to glorify and praise Thy glorious and majestic Name of Father, Son, and Holy Spirit, now and ever and to the ages of the ages. Amen.

(Arthur Linton, *Twenty-five Consecration Prayers* [New York, Macmillan, 1921], pp. 56 ff.) The passages in parentheses, except those which indicate interruptions by the deacon or the choir, are missing from the ninth-century manuscript, and apparently have been added since that time.

D. PFALZ-NEUBURG CHURCH ORDER, 1543

O Lord Jesus Christ, thou only true Son of the living God, who hast given thy body unto bitter death for us all, and hast shed thy blood for the forgiveness of our sins, and hast bidden all thy disciples to eat that same thy body and to drink thy blood whereby to remember thy death; we bring before thy divine Majesty these thy gifts of bread and wine and beseech thee to hallow and bless the same by thy divine grace, goodness and power and ordain (*schaffen*) that this bread and wine may be (*sei*) thy body and blood, even unto eternal life to all who eat and drink thereof; who livest and reignest. . . .

(*Kirchen Ordnung . . . Otthainrichen pfaltzgrauen bey Rhein . . . fürstenthumb gehalten wirt.* Nuremberg [1543], Bd. II, fol. 26.)

The *Liturgie und Agende* of the Ministerium of Pennsylvania, the Ministerium of New York, and the Synod of Ohio (1855) repeated the above prayer with the addition of a few words, e·g., "eternal high priest" after the address; "according to thy Word" after "hallow and bless"; and "with contrite hearts" after "to all who." Following the Amen by the communicants is this prayer of the officiant: "O Holy Spirit, sanctify us and cleanse my heart and lips so that in the Name of the Lord and in the power of his Word I may worthily administer the holy Testament." (2d ed., p. 284.)

E. KING JOHN'S LITURGY, SWEDEN, 1576
(Intercession and Epiclesis)

We therefore humbly pray thee, and desire, most merciful Father, through

thy Son Jesus Christ our Lord, that thou wilt suffer our prayers to be pleasing
to thee, and graciously hear that which we bring before thee for thy holy
universal Christian church, that thou wouldest vouchsafe to grant it peace, to
preserve, unite, and govern it throughout the world, together with all government, spiritual and worldly, of whatsoever dignity, loftiness, and name it
may be, so likewise all true Christians, that love and confess the true
universal and Apostolic faith.

O Lord God, who willest that thy Son's holy and most worthy Supper
should be unto us a pledge and assurance of thy mercy: awaken our heart,
that we who celebrate the same his Supper may have a salutary remembrance
of thy benefits, and humbly give thee true and bounden thanks, glory,
honour, and praise for evermore. Help us thy servants and thy people that
we may herewith remember the holy, pure, stainless, and blessed offering
of thy son, which he made upon the cross for us, and worthily celebrate the
mystery of the new testament and eternal covenant. Bless and sanctify with
the power of thy holy Spirit that which is prepared and set apart for this
holy use, bread and wine, that rightly used it may be unto us the body and
blood of thy Son, the food of eternal life, which we may desire and seek
with greatest longing. Through the same thy Son Jesus Christ our Lord,
who with thee and the holy Spirit liveth and reigneth in one godhead from
everlasting to everlasting. Amen. (E. E. Yelverton, *The Mass in Sweden,*
pp. 101-03.)

F. THE FIRST PRAYER BOOK OF KING EDWARD VI, 1549

O God heauenly father, which of thy tender mercie, diddest geue thine
only sonne Jesu Christ to suffre death vpon the crosse for our redempcion,
who made there (by his one oblacion once offered) a full, perfect, and
sufficient sacrifice, oblacion, and satysfacyon, for the sinnes of the whole
worlde, and did institute, and in his holy Gospell commaund vs, to celebrate
a perpetuall memory, of that his precious death, vntyll his comming again:
Heare vs (O merciful father) we besech thee: and with thy holy spirite and
worde, vouchsafe to bl✚esse and sanc✚tifie these thy gyftes, and creatures
of bread and wyne, that they maie be vnto vs the bodye and bloude of thy
moste derely beloued sonne Jesus Christe. Who in thesame nyght that he
was betrayed: tooke breade, and when he had blessed, and geuen thankes:
he brake it, and gaue it to his disciples, saiyng: Take, eate, this is my bodye
which is geuen for you, do this in remembraunce of me.

Likewyse after supper he toke the cuppe, and when he had geuen thankes,
he gaue it to them, saiyng: drynk ye all of this, for this is my bloude of the
newe Testament, whyche is shed for you and for many, for remission of
synnes: do this as oft as you shall drinke it in remembraunce of me.

Wherefore, O Lorde and heauenly father, according to the Instytucyon of
thy derely beloued sonne, our sauiour Jesu Christ, we thy humble seruauntes
do celebrate, and make here before thy diuine Maiestie, with these thy holy
giftes, the memoryall whyche thy sonne hath wylled vs to make, hauyng in
remembraunce his blessed passion, mightie resurreccyon, and gloryous ascen-
cion, renderyng vnto thee most hartie thankes, for the innumerable benefites
procured vnto vs by thesame, entierly desiryng thy fatherly goodnes, mercifully to accepte this our Sacrifice of praise and thankes geuing: most humbly

beseching thee to graunt, that by the merites and death of thy sone Jesus Christ, and through faith in his bloud, we and al thy whole church, may obteigne remission of our sinnes, and all other benefites of hys passyon. And here wee offre and present vnto thee (O Lorde) our selfe, oure soules, and bodies, to be a reasonable, holy, and liuely sacrifice vnto thee: humbly besechyng thee, that whosoeuer shalbee partakers of thys holy Communion, maye worthely receiue the moste precious body and bloude of thy sonne Jesus Christe: and bee fulfilled with thy grace and heauenly bene-diccion, and made one bodye with thy sonne Jesu Christe, that he maye dwell in them, and they in hym. And although we be vnworthy (through our manyfolde synnes) to offre vnto thee any Sacryfice: Yet we besche thee to accepte thys our bounden duetie and seruice, and commaunde these our prayers and supplicacions, by the Ministery of thy holy Angels, to be brought vp into thy holy Tabernacle before the syght of thy dyuine maiestie: not waiyng our merites, but pardonyng our offences, through Christe our Lorde, by whome, and with whome, in the vnitie of the holy Ghost: all honour and glory, be vnto thee, O father almightie, world without ende. Amen.

Let us praye.

As our sauiour Christe hath commaunded and taught vs, we are bolde to saye. Our father whyche art in heauen, halowed be thy name. Thy Kyngdome come. Thy wyll be doen in yearth, as it is in heauen. Geue vs this daye our dayly breade. And forgeue vs our trespaces, as wee forgeue them that tres-passe agaynst vs. And leade vs not into temptacion.

The aunswere. But deliuer vs from euill. Amen. (*The First Prayer Book of King Edward VI* [facsimile]. [London: De La Mon, 1903], pp. 281-283.)

G. AGENDA OF THE LUTHERAN CHURCH IN BAVARIA, 1879, AND LITURGY OF THE JOINT SYNOD OF OHIO

The Bavarian Liturgy gives three prayers, one of which is to be used following the Sanctus and before the Words of Institution. The first of these prayers in English translation is incorporated in the Liturgy of the Joint Synod of Ohio as follows:

Glory be to Thee, O Lord Jesus Christ, Thou almighty and everlasting Son of the Father, that by the sacrifice of Thyself upon the cross, offered up once for all, Thou didst perfect them that are sanctified, and ordain, as a memorial and seal thereof, Thy Holy Supper, in which Thou givest us Thy body to eat, and Thy blood to drink, that being in Thee, even as Thou art in us, we may have eternal life, and be raised up at the last day. Most merciful and exalted Redeemer, we humbly confess that we are not worthy of all the mercies, and of all the truth, which Thou hast shown unto us, and that, by reason of our sins, we are too impure and weak worthily to receive Thy saving gifts. Sanctify us, therefore, we beseech Thee, in our bodies and souls, by Thy Holy Spirit, and thus fit and prepare us to come to Thy Supper, to the glory of Thy grace, and to our own eternal good. And in whatsoever, through weakness, we do fail and come short, in true re-pentance and sorrow on account of our sins, in living faith and trust in Thy merits, and in an earnest purpose to amend our sinful lives, do Thou graciously supply and grant, out of the fulness of the merits of Thy bitter sufferings and death; to the end that we, who even in this present world desire to enjoy Thee, our only comfort and Savior, in the Holy Sacrament, may at last see Thee face to face in Thy heavenly kingdom, and dwell with Thee, and with all Thy saints, for ever and ever. Amen.

(*A Liturgy for the Use of Evangelical Lutheran Pastors* [Columbus, Ohio: Lutheran Book Concern, 1912], pp. 49-50.)

In the Ohio Synod Liturgy this prayer is followed by the Lord's Prayer and the Words of Institution, after which is said this prayer for Sanctification:

Praise, and honor, and glory, be unto Thee, O Christ! The bread which we bless is the communion of Thy holy body, and the cup which we bless is the communion of Thy holy blood. O Thou everlasting Son of the Father, sanctify us by Thy Holy Spirit, and make us worthy partakers of Thy sacred body and blood, that we may be cleansed from sin and made one with all the members of Thy Church in heaven and on earth. Lord Jesus! Thou hast bought us: to Thee will we live, to Thee will we die, and Thine we will be forever. Amen.

H. BOOK OF WORSHIP OF THE LUTHERAN CHURCHES IN INDIA, GUNTUR, 1936

(This text was originally proposed by Dr. Paul Z. Strodach and was later adopted, with some changes, by the Indian churches. It consists entirely of extracts from the following liturgies: St. James, St. Chrysostom, St. Basil, the Gallican, and the first Prayer Book of Edward VI.)

After the Sanctus, the following prayer:

We also with this blessed host cry aloud and say:

Holy art Thou, O God, Thou and Thine Only-begotten Son and Thy Holy Spirit; Holy art Thou, and great is the Majesty of Thy glory, O Father and Lover of men, Who didst so love the world as to give Thine Only-begotten Son, that whosoever believeth in Him might not perish, but have everlasting life.

Who having come into the world and having fulfilled for us Thy holy will, and being obedient unto the end,

In the night in which He was betrayed took bread; and when He had given thanks, He break [*sic*] it and gave it to His disciples, saying:

Take, eat; this is My Body, which is given for you; this do in remembrance of Me.✚

After the same manner also, when He had supped, He took the cup, and when He had given thanks, He gave it to them, saying:

Drink ye all of it; this cup is the new testament in My Blood, which is shed for you and for many, for the remission of sins; this do, as oft as ye drink it, in remembrance of Me.✚

Therefore remembering His salutary precept, and all that He endured for us: His passion and death, His resurrection and ascension, His session on the right hand, and His glorious coming again, we give thanks to Thee, O Lord God Almighty, not as we ought, but as we are able; and we bring before Thee, according to His institution, these Thy gifts of bread and wine, giving thanks to Thee through Him, that Thou hast deemed us worthy to stand before Thee, celebrating and making the Memorial which Thy Son hath willed us to make;

And we beseech Thee: Send down Thy Holy Spirit upon us and upon these gifts here before Thee, that according to the Word of Thy Dear Son they may be sanctified and blessed; that in this bread and wine we may worthily receive the Body of Christ and His precious Blood; that in true faith and with contrite hearts we may eat and drink thereof to the remission of sins, and be sanctified in soul and body; that we may be one body and one spirit, and may have our portion with all Thy saints who have been well-pleasing unto Thee; through Christ our Lord;

Taught by Whose salutary precepts and following Whose Divine command, we make bold to say:

Our Father, Who art in heaven; Hallowed be Thy Name; Thy kingdom come; Thy will be done on earth, as it is in heaven; Give us this day our daily bread; And forgive us our trespasses, as we forgive those who trespass against us; And lead us not into temptation; But deliver us from evil; *Amen.*

Deliver us, O Lord, from all evil, both the present and that which may come; grant us gracious peace in our days, that in all things Thy Holy Name may be hallowed, praised and blessed, for to Thee is due all glory, worship and adoration, O Father, Son and Holy Ghost, now and evermore. *Amen.* (Book of Worship . . . , p. 21-23.)

I. BOOK OF COMMON ORDER OF THE CHURCH OF SCOTLAND, 1940

Verily holy, verily blessed, art Thou, Almighty and Merciful God, who didst so love the world that Thou gavest Thine only-begotten Son, that whosoever believeth in Him should not perish but have everlasting life.

Not as we ought, but as we are able, do we bless thee for His holy incarnation, for His perfect life on earth, for His precious sufferings and death upon the Cross, for His glorious resurrection and ascension, for His continual intercession and rule at Thy right hand, for the promise of His coming again, and for His gift of the Holy Spirit.

Wherefore, having in remembrance the work and passion of our Saviour Christ, and pleading His eternal sacrifice, we Thy servants do set forth this memorial, which He hath commanded us to make; and we most humbly beseech Thee to send down Thy Holy Spirit to sanctify both us and these Thine own gifts of bread and wine which we set before Thee, that the bread which we break may be the Communion of the body of Christ, and the cup of blessing which we bless the Communion of the blood of Christ; that we, receiving them, may by faith be made partakers of His body and blood, with all His benefits, to our spiritual nourishment and growth in grace, and to the glory of Thy most holy name.

And here we offer and present unto Thee ourselves, our souls and bodies, to be a reasonable, holy, and living sacrifice; and we beseech Thee mercifully to accept this our sacrifice of praise and thanksgiving, as, in fellowship with all the faithful in heaven and on earth, we pray Thee to fulfill in us, and in all men, the purpose of Thy redeeming love; through Jesus Christ our Lord, by whom, and with whom, in the unity of the Holy Spirit, all honour and glory be unto Thee, O Father Almighty, world without end. Amen.

And now, as our Saviour Christ hath taught us, we humbly pray, Our Father . . .

Then the Minister shall say:

According to the holy institution, example, and command of our Lord

757

Jesus Christ, and for a memorial of Him, we do this: who, the same night in which He was betrayed, took bread
and when He had blessed, and given thanks, He brake it
and said,
Take, eat; this is My Body, which is broken for you: this do in remembrance of Me.
After the same manner also, He took the cup,
saying:
This cup is the new Covenant in My Blood: this do ye, as oft as ye drink it, in remembrance of Me. (Pp. 119-20.)
The Presbyterian Church in the United States of America has a form in close agreement with the above text of the Church of Scotland. (*Book of Common Worship*, 1946.)

J. LITURGY OF THE CHURCH OF SWEDEN, 1942
Praise be unto Thee, Lord of heaven and earth, that Thou hast had compassion upon the children of men and hast given Thine only-begotten Son that whosoever believeth on Him should not perish but have everlasting life. We thank Thee for the salvation which Thou hast prepared for us through Jesus Christ. Send Thy Spirit into our hearts, that He may kindle in us a living faith and prepare us truly to remember our Saviour and to receive Him as He comes to us in His Holy Supper.
This prayer of "humble access," is followed by the Words of Institution and the Lord's Prayer. (*Missale för Svenska Kyrkan . . .*, C. W. K. Gleerups Forlag, 1942, p. 24.)

K. LUTHERISCHE AGENDE, BERLIN, 1955
Gelobet seist du, Herr des Himmels und der Erde, dasz du dich über deine Geschöpfe erbarmt und deinen eingebornen Sohn in unser Fleisch gesandt hast. Wir danken dir für die Erlösung, die du uns bereitet hast durch das heilige allgenugsame Opfer seines Leibes und Blutes am Stamms des Kreuzes.
In seinem Namen und zu seinem Gedächtnis versammelt, bitten wir dich, Herr: sende herab auf uns den Heiligen Geist, heilige und erneuere uns nach Leib und Seele und gib, dasz wir unter diesem Brot und Wein deines Sohnes wahren Leib und Blut im rechtem Glauben zu unserem Heil empfangen, da wir jetzt nach seinem Befehl sein eigen Testament also handeln und brauchen.
(Here follow the Words of Institution.)
Also gedenken wir, Herr, himmlischer Vater, des heilbringinden Leidens und Sterbens deines lieben Sohnes, Jesu Christi. Wir preisen seine sieghafte Auferstehung von den Toten und getrüsten uns seiner Auffahrt in dein himmlisches Heiligtum, da er, unser Hohepriester, uns immerdar vor dir vertritt. Und wie wir alle durch die Gemeinschaft seines Leibes und Blutes ein Leib sind in Christo, so bringe zusammen deine Gemeinde von den Enden der Erde, auf dasz wir mit allem Gläubingen das Hochzeitsmahl des Lammes feiern mögen in seinem Reich. Durch ihn, u.s.w. *(After this the* Vaterunser *and the* Friedensgruss.)
(Agende für evangelisch-lutherische Kirchen und Gemeinden [Berlin: Lutherisches Verlagshaus, 1955], Bd. I, pp. 70-74.)

GLOSSARY

LITURGICAL AND MUSICAL TERMS

A CAPPELLA: choral music sung without accompaniment.

ACOLYTE: 1) an assistant to the minister in the public services of the church, usually a young layman; his duties are, generally, to kindle and extinguish the altar-lights, to care for the alms-basons, to serve at the offertory, and to perform other duties which may be assigned to him; 2) an acolyte is also one of the "minor orders" in the old system of grades of the ministry. The acolyte is vested in cassock and cotta.

AGAPE: the primitive Christian social meal ("love-feast") which was observed preceding the Eucharist; as early as the second century it was observed separately; it was discontinued generally in the fourth century.

AGENDA, AGENDE: books containing the services and offices of the church, primarily for the use of the clergyman; the word is Latin or German; in English, the word is most generally used to signify the "order of business" in a meeting.

AGNUS DEI ("Lamb of God"): the canticle, or liturgical hymn, sung before the administration of the Sacrament in the Service; it is also said at the end of the Litany; it is based upon the words of the Baptist about our Lord in John's Gospel.

ALB: the long white vestment of linen anciently worn at the celebration of the Holy Communion, and still retained in Lutheran use, chiefly in Scandinavia; it has long narrow sleeves, reaches to the feet, and is secured at the waist by a cincture; it is worn over a cassock; over it are placed the stole, chasuble, etc.; at "choir services" a cope may be worn over the alb on festivals.

ALLELUIA (Hebrew, Hallelu-jah): "Praise ye the Lord"; an ascription to God, from the Hebrew liturgy; in the Service, it is used between Epistle and Gospel, except during Lent; in Matins and Vespers, it is used at the end of the Gloria Patri which concludes the opening versicles (again omitted during Lent).

ALLOCUTION: an address, or brief "charge"; an example is the address to the sponsors after the administration of baptism, "and now I admonish you . . ."; in the Swedish Liturgy of 1811 the opening address is called "The Allocution."

ANAMNESIS: "recollection"; the liturgical commemoration of the whole life and work of Christ in the Eastern liturgies: his incarnation, teaching, passion, death, resurrection, and ascension; it is the corporate obedience of the church, in a liturgical way, to our Lord's command, "Remember me."

Especially prominent in all Eastern liturgies, it is now found in the service books of many Western churches.

ANAPHORA: a Greek word which means "offering" or "oblation," hence, the prayer of consecration in the liturgy; "pro-anaphora" and "anaphora" correspond to "the Mass of the Catechumens" and "the Mass of the Faithful."

ANTE-COMMUNION: that part of the Service which precedes the Preface of the communion office; an alternate term for the ancient "Missa catechumenorum"; "the Service" when the Holy Communion is not celebrated.

ANTIPHON: the brief verse of Psalmody or other Holy Scripture which is sung or said before and after the Psalms, or portions of the Psalms, such as the Introits.

ANTIPHONAL: a method of singing: between two parts of the choir; or, between the clergyman and the choir; or, between the choir and the congregation, each part taking alternate phrases or verses of a Psalm, canticle, etc.

APSE: 1) in a basilica: the semicircular space at end of the nave; 2) in a Gothic church: the semicircular or polygonal end of the choir ("chancel") or end of an aisle or transept; cf. with the square-ended choir in English Gothic churches.

ATRIUM: the court before a basilica, in the center of which there was a fountain for ritual purification; it was often arcaded or "cloistered" on four sides, and was reserved for the use of catechumens, penitents, etc.

BAPTISTRY: the place containing the font, where baptism is administered; it is often built near the entrance of churches in a separate bay or apse which is below the level of the church itself; in Italy particularly some of the churches have separate buildings as baptistries.

BASILICA: the early type of Christian church derived from the Roman hall used for legal or business purposes; the basilica is rectangular, with an apse at one end, columns extending the length of the nave, and a narthex, or arcaded porch, at the other end.

BEMA: the "holy place" or sanctuary in Eastern Orthodox churches; it is a raised platform at the eastern end of the church; in the later Greek churches it is enclosed by the "iconostasis" or screen which is ornamented with icons of the saints.

BENEDICITE ("praise ye"): the great canticle of the praise of God by all nature; "the Song of the Three Holy Children," vss. 35-65 of the deuterocanonical book of the same name; Canticle No. 5 in the *Service Book·*

BENEDICTION: "The putting of the Name of God upon the people of God by the priest of God," cf. Numbers 6. In Lutheran churches the "Aaronic" or "O. T." benediction is used at the Service, either alone, or, as in the Common Liturgy, ending with, "In the Name of the Father, and of the Son, and of the Holy Ghost. *Amen.*" Other benedictions commonly used are II Cor. 13:14, Hebrews 13:20-21, and the liturgical form, "The Blessing of Almighty God. . . ."

BENEDICTUS ("Blessed"): the alternate canticle at Matins, from Luke 1: 68-79, the Song of Zacharias, father of St. John the Baptist. Originally used at Lauds.

BENEDICTUS QUI VENIT ("Blessed who cometh"): the concluding verse of the Sanctus in the Communion order; it is based on Matt. 21:9; at the

Reformation it was retained in the Lutheran orders, but dropped from the *Book of Common Prayer* in 1552; its omission has been a contentious question since that time in the Church of England.

BIDDING PRAYER: 1) a special form of liturgical prayer which consists of a series of petitions, each of which is composed of (a) an invitation to pray for a special object; (b) a silence, for private prayers; (c) a collect to sum up the prayers of the congregation, said by the minister, concluded with an Amen by the people. 2) A special prayer for Good Friday, of the above form.

BREVIARY: the book (or books) containing the Divine Office or "canonical hours" (q. v.). The Roman Breviary is divided into four parts, corresponding to the four seasons of the year; the principal elements in the breviary are the calendar, the *Psalterium,* the *Propria de tempore,* and the *Propria de sanctis.*

CANON: "the rule," *i.e.,* for the consecration of the "gifts" or elements in the Mass. In the Roman Mass the Canon comes between the Sanctus and the Lord's Prayer; it includes the prayers and actions beginning with the *Te igitur* and concluding with the commemoration of the departed. In one of the earliest extant anaphorae, the *Apostolic Tradition* of Hippolytus (c.217), the consecration consists of the following: the bringing forward of the offering, which is blessed by the bishop; salutation, Sursum corda, and Vere dignum; the prayer, consisting of an extended thanksgiving for the incarnation, life, death and resurrection of Christ (embodying the "Words of Institution"); offering of the bread and the cup with thanks, and the invocation of the Holy Spirit. It will be seen that here the essential parts are the anamnesis, the oblation, and the epiclesis. The later Roman Canon included highly objectionable features; it was eliminated by the Reformers, who retained only the "Words of Institution." This drew increased attention to the "moment" of consecration, and in this respect heightened the "Roman" effect; see also "Eucharistic Prayer."

CANONICAL HOURS, CHOIR SERVICES, DIVINE OFFICE: the "prayer services" of the church contained in the breviary and recited daily by the clergy and "religious." Also called "choir services" (as distinguished from the "altar-service," which is the Eucharist). The entire series consists of Matins, Lauds, Prime, Terce, Sext, Nones, Vespers, and Compline; the hours were accounted "seven," inasmuch as Matins and Lauds were said together; collectively they are known as the Divine Office (as distinguished from the Divine Liturgy or Eucharist). Matins and Vespers are preserved in Lutheran use with parts of Lauds, Prime, and Compline retained in the Suffrages.

CANTIONALES: books of Lutheran service-music; for the altar-song of the clergyman, the chant of the choir, and the hymns of the congregation; first prepared in the sixteenth century; two famous ones are those of J. Spangenberg (1545) and L. Lossius (1561).

CAPITULUM: "little chapter"; the verse or brief passage of Holy Scripture read at certain canonical hours.

CATHEDRAL (from *cathedra,* L., chair): the seat of a bishop; hence the principal church of a diocese; not simply a large church.

CENSER: the vessel in which incense is burned during the services of the church, or out of service-time; the other name for it is "thurible"; cf. Rev. 8:3-5, where incense is symbolic of the "prayers of the saints."

CEREMONIAL (n): the prescribed action(s) or movement(s) which accompany a rite or a part of the liturgy; or, the total actions which accompany the service.

CHALICE: the liturgical cup used in the celebration of the Holy Communion; where small cups are used for giving communion to the people, there ought always to be a chalice on the altar for the consecration of the Sacrament; for the communion of the people there should also be a chalice with a pouring lip.

CHANTRY: a chapel or altar which has been endowed "for the maintenance of priests who shall perform services"; a small chapel annexed to a church.

CHAPTER: 1) a short lesson read at some of the breviary offices; 2) the body of men, consisting of the dean and the canons, of a collegiate or cathedral church; 3) the meeting of the canons of a cathedral or collegiate church, at which the dean presides.

CHASUBLE: the principal vestment traditionally worn at the celebration of the Holy Communion; worn over alb and stole; it is usually made of silk or brocade in the color of the day or season, and is ornamented with orphreys; retained in Lutheran use in Scandinavia and other parts of Europe, and used elsewhere in Lutheran churches.

CHOIR: 1) the place in the church before the sanctuary, where are places for the clergy and singers: the "chancel"; 2) the body of singers in a church.

CHOIR OFFICES: Matins and Vespers, and other "prayer services," which may be said from the stalls in the chancel of the church; they are contrasted with the Service (the Communion), which is the altar service in a special sense, always celebrated at the altar. (See "Canonical Hours.")

CHORALE: a form of melody for the support of hymns used in the worship of the church; its greatest development occurred in the Lutheran churches of Europe in the sixteenth century and following centuries; its greatest and most artistic contrapuntal enrichment was made by J. S. Bach (1685-1750) and other composers in the church cantatas and in choral preludes, etc., for the organ.

CHURCH ORDER: 1) in the ancient church: the order of the Eucharist, ordination, baptism, and other ecclesiastical offices: e.g., "The Egyptian Church Order"; "The Didache," etc. 2) one of the provincial Lutheran books of the sixteenth century; these contained doctrinal discussions, forms of service, as well as rules for the church, the school, and the works of Christian beneficence.

CIBORIUM: 1) the honorific architectural covering of an altar in a church, consisting of columns and a dome or other covering; 2) the vessel used to contain the altar breads, either for storage, or for use in the administration.

COLLECT: the brief, highly stylized prayer used after the Gloria in Excelsis in the liturgy and also in the Divine Office of the Western church; it is a Latin form which gains its effect by the economy and compression of the language; the English Collects of the *Service Book* are generally closer to the Latin originals than are those of the *Book of Common Prayer,* which are often extended and wordy.

COLLEGIA PIETATIS: the pietistic circles of church members developed by Spener and Francke in the eighteenth century for the cultivation of the Christian life.

COMPLINE (Latin, *completorium*): the last of the canonical hours, which completes the day; in the Evening Suffrages of the *Service Book* are the preces of Compline.

CONCURRENCE: the falling of two festivals on successive days. Ordinarily, the propers of a festival are used beginning with Vespers of the preceding day; in case of a concurrence, the propers of the more important day prevail. Thus Vespers on Christmas Day use the propers of Christmas rather than those for St. Stephen.

CONIFITEOR (Latin, I confess): the first part, or "preparation" of the Mass or the Service, conducted "at the foot of the altar"; anciently, the Confiteor was conducted by the celebrant and his ministers in the sacristy of the church, before the beginning of mass.

COPE: the liturgical cloak, of silk or damask, ornamented with orphreys, and a morse to join it in front; around the neck, at the rear, is the "hood"; it is worn at Vespers on Sundays and festivals; in some Lutheran countries it is used especially by bishops; the cope is worn over the alb (or surplice) and stole; it is made in the liturgical colors.

CORPUS CHRISTI: literally, "The body of Christ"; 1) in the New Testament, and in theology, a term for the holy church. "Ye are the body of Christ"— St. Paul; 2) a feast of the Roman Church observed on the Thursday after Trinity Sunday; it is a feast in honor of the Blessed Sacrament; unfortunately it also celebrates the doctrine of transubstantiation; Thomas Aquinas composed the propers of the feast·

COUNTERPOINT: a system of musical composition in which two or more (4, 8, or 12) independent melodies are related to each other in a way which is agreeable; *"punctum contra punctum";* it is the predecessor and the basis of much modern ecclesiastical music.

CREDENCE (Italian, *credenza*): a side-table placed at the south wall of the chancel, or at the east wall on the south side; it is used for the elements of the Holy Communion, and for the offerings of the church; it should be covered with a linen cloth.

CROSIER: the pastoral staff or crook of a bishop or abbot; originally the word signified the bearer of the episcopal cross; later, it has come to signify the staff itself; the crosier is still used by the bishops of Sweden.

CRUET: a small vessel or vial of crystal or glass, used to contain wine or water for the celebration of the Eucharist.

CURATE: a clergyman who serves as an assistant in a parish, under the direction of the pastor or rector; usually his appointment is limited (*Vide* also "vicar"); one who has the care or "cure" of souls.

DAY HOURS: those of the canonical hours said in the daytime; i.e., Prime (6 A.M.); Terce (9 A.M.); Sext (noon); Nones (3 P.M.); Vespers (6 P.M.); and Compline (8 P.M.).

DAY OFFICES: a term denoting Matins and Evensong in the Church of England, where their daily recitation is incumbent upon the clergy; by analogy, Matins and Vespers of the *Service Book.*

DEACON: 1) Liturgical: the principal assistant to the celebrant at a liturgical function; his ministerial grade may be the same as his liturgical office, or, as is more generally the case, he may be of the grade of presbyter or fully-ordained clergyman; 2) a member of the vestry or church council in a local church; 3) in Europe: a lay-servant of the church, engaged in merciful work; analogous to a deaconess.

DEPRECATION: prayer that evil may be removed or turned away from us.

DESCANT: a melody which is complementary to the principal melody in plain chant or other forms of music; some of the more familiar hymn tunes are occasionally performed with a descant (also spelled "discant").

DIPTYCH: 1) the wax tablets on which were written the names of those faithful departed who were to be commemorated in the liturgy of the Eucharist (in the early church); 2) lists of names for intercession or commemoration.

DISCIPLINA ARCANI: the custom of the early church by which catechumens were acquainted with the "mysteries of the faith" during their course of instruction; the Lord's Prayer and the Rule of Faith (Creed) were not committed to writing, but were imparted secretly at several stages of the course of preparation.

DIVINE OFFICE: the inclusive name for the services of the breviary; *vide* also "canonical hours" and "Matins," etc.

DOXOLOGY: means "blessing"; the Gloria Patri is a liturgical doxology; another form is the final stanza of a hymn, in which the praises of the persons of the Blessed Trinity are recited.

ELEVATION: the action in the celebration of the Eucharist in which the celebrant raises the Sacrament before his and the people's eyes after the consecration of the bread and the wine; Luther retained this action in the forms of the Mass which he issued; *vide* his *Formula Missae* of 1523, and the *Deutsche Messe* of 1526.

EMBOLISM: the liturgical expansion of the last petition of the Lord's Prayer in the Mass: e.g., "Deliver us from all evils, O Lord, past, present, and to come; and . . . mercifully grant peace in our days . . ." the embolism follows the Amen said after the last petition of the Lord's Prayer. (Used in the Roman Rite.)

EPICLESIS: a Greek word, "invocation"; used of the prayer in the Divine Liturgy of the Orthodox Church in which the Holy Spirit of God is invoked upon the elements "that they may become the body of the Lord and his precious blood." It is by the epiclesis, rather than by the recitation of the Verba, that the consecration is supposed to be effected, although the Orthodox do not like to point to any one time of consecration; they prefer to ascribe this to the whole action of the Divine Liturgy.

EUCHARIST: a Greek word, "thanksgiving"; the most ancient and venerable name for the celebration of the Holy Communion, after the age of the apostles; the name attaches especially to the words of the Preface ("It is truly meet, right, and salutary) and of the Proper Prefaces; the celebration of the Holy Communion is a great act of thanksgiving on the part of the church for the incarnation and teaching, the passion and death, the resurrection and ascension, and the other deeds of the church's Lord and Saviour.

EUCHARISTIC PRAYER: in the Lutheran use, the Prayer of Thanksgiving in the Holy Communion. The early developed form of the Eucharistic Prayer contained: salutation and exhortation, with responses; Preface, Sanctus, thanksgiving for creation and redemption; narrative of institution of the Sacrament (part of the prayer); anamnesis and oblation; epiclesis; intercession for living and departed. See also "Canon."

EVENSONG: the name for Vespers in the church books of the Church of Sweden, and the *Book of Common Prayer* of the Church of England.

EXORCISM: one of the ceremonies in the pre-Reformation baptismal serv·ice; it is the act of "casting out of the unclean spirit" from the candidate for baptism, by the use of prayer and the sign of the cross; Luther retained this ceremony in his baptismal service of 1526, but omitted it in 1529.

EXPOSITION: 1) Liturgical: a characteristic ceremony of the Roman Catholic Church, in which the reserved Sacrament is exhibited for the adoration of the faithful; the exposition is performed by placing the sacred host in a liturgical vessel, richly ornamented, which is called the "ostensorium" or "monstrance"; 2) the method of explaining passages of Holy Scripture or other texts.

FAITHFUL, PRAYER OF THE: in the Oriental church, the great prayer of intercession said after the dismissal of the catechumens; the General Prayer in the Lutheran Rite is analogous.

FARSED: a method of expanding liturgical texts, generally in connection with the musical settings of the same; e.g., instead of the usual *"Kyrie, eleison,"* the farsed form might be *"Kyrie, pater coelestis, eleison,"* or, *"Kyrie, fons bonitatis, eleison";* other standard liturgical texts also suffered this treatment.

FIXED FESTIVALS: the immovable days attached to calendar dates, in contrast to those festivals which are movable (Easter and Pentecost); Christmas and Epiphany are examples of fixed festivals; so are the saints' days.

FRACTION: The ceremonial breaking of the bread, in imitation of our Lord's action at the Last Supper, at the Holy Communion; it has regrettably disappeared from Lutheran services.

FRONTAL-SUPERFRONTAL: frontal: the altar cloth, in the color of the season, which completely covers the front of the altar; super-frontal; a narrower altar cloth or parament, extending across the front of the altar, just below the *mensa altaris;* it may be used singly, or with a frontal; in the latter case it is hung outside of the frontal; the frontal and/or superfrontal are generally made of silk or damask; the ornament may be embroidery, symbols, or orphreys made of rich galloons.

GALLICAN: 1) pertaining to the Gallican Liturgy, i.e., the other great liturgy which existed for centuries with the Roman, in the Western church; 2) pertaining to the use of the church of France.

GRADUAL: the liturgical anthem, consisting of verses of Psalms arranged in a special form, which is sung between the Epistle and Gospel; the Gradual is the liturgical vestige of the complete Psalms which were anciently sung at this place in the liturgy.

GRADUALE: one of the service books of the Latin church, which contains the proper music for the choir at mass; the *Graduale Romanum* provides for the Sundays and feasts the following musical settings, in plain song: Introit, Gradual (in Lent, the tract), the Offertory, and the "communion" of the Mass.

GREAT INTERCESSION: another name for the Prayer of the Faithful (q. v.); in the *Service Book,* the Prayer of the Church.

GREGORIAN TONES: melodies of recognized form, used in the chanting of the Psalms; there are eight Gregorian tones, and the *"tonus peregrinus,"* the latter sung to Psalms 114 and 115, which are taken together.

HAGIOLATRY: a Greek word which means "the cult of the saints," or "the idolatrous worship of the saints"; the word is not without the odor of opprobrium (cf., e.g., "bibliolatry"; *vide* "mariolatry" *infra*), especially when it is incorrectly used for the veneration of the saints.

HARMONY: that system of musical composition by which simultaneous musical tones are arranged and related to form chords which are "consonant" (contrasted with melody and counterpoint).

HIGH MASS: *missa solemnis*: i.e., a mass celebrated with (1) a deacon and subdeacon (in orders) to assist the celebrant; (2) music for the responses; (3) additional lights on the altar (six); and (4) the use of incense. The term was and is common in Scandinavian Lutheran churches, either for the Holy Communion, or for the ante-communion service (i.e., service without the communion).

HOUR SERVICES: the "canonical hours" or breviary offices, which together form the "Divine Office" (q. v.); they are Matins and Lauds, Prime, Terce, Sext, Nones, Vespers, and Compline.

HUMANISM: the movement which began in the Renaissance, which idealized the culture and civilization of the ancient Greeks, and strove to recapture it by rediscovery of the ancient classics; Erasmus, Reuchlin, and even Melanchthon were representatives of the movement; in modern times there has been a revival of humanism, new style, which magnifies the ethical and intellectual elements in Christianity at the expense of the supernatural elements. This is now being transformed.

ILLUMINATION: the art of adorning the texts of manuscripts in colors and drawings; initial-letters were the special subjects for this kind of treatment; full-page representations were also made in rich colors with the use of gold-leaf.

INDULGENCE: a "remission of the punishment which is still due to sin after its guilt has been taken away by the Sacrament of Penance; this remission is made by applying to the repentant sinner's soul the 'treasure of merit' which the church possesses" (Sullivan, *The Externals of the Catholic Church*, p. 295); at the time of the Reformation grave abuses arose in connection with the granting of indulgences; it was against these that Luther protested; also against the atomistic view of sins, and against the idea of a "treasury of merit" of Christ and the saints.

INTINCTION: a method of administering the Holy Communion, by dipping the host into the chalice, and administering it to the communicant; at present it is chiefly used in clinical cases (hospitals), and in army camps.

INTROIT: the liturgical anthem at the beginning of the Service, composed of an antiphon, Psalm-verse, Gloria Patri, and antiphon repeated; it is the "entrance" hymn of the service, and, like the Gradual, is vestigial in its present form.

INVOCATION: "a calling upon" God; 1) "In the Name of the Father . . ." at the beginning of the Service or the Mass; 2) a prayer in the Holy Communion, calling upon God to consecrate and bless the elements of the Eucharist.

JUS LITURGICUM (Latin, "the liturgical law"): whereby a bishop has the right and duty to oversee and order the services and prayers of the church in his diocese; the phrase is also used to cover the bishop's privilege of composing and setting forth special prayers for the church over which he presides; in a derived sense, the right of the church to provide service books for the clergy and the faithful.

766

KYRIE ELEISON ("Lord, have mercy"): a Greek response at the litanies which occur in the Divine Liturgy of the Eastern Church; in the West, the litanies were abbreviated; as a result the Church of Rome has a ninefold Kyrie; the Lutheran Church a sixfold Kyrie (except for the Eastern form in the Common Liturgy); and the Church of England a threefold Kyrie, in the Mass.

LAUDS: the second of the "canonical hours"; it was frequently said with Matins, forming one office.

LECTION: a lesson or reading from Holy Scripture, appointed for the services of the church; the lections are indicated in the lectionaries.

LECTIONARY: the table of lessons from Holy Scripture for the Sundays and festivals of the church year.

LITANY: an ancient form of general intercession; it is a highly organized form with marked responsive character; the Litany of the *Service Book* is a translation of Luther's *Litania Latina Correcta,* which was a revision of the great Roman Litany of the Saints; Luther esteemed the Litany the "best prayer on earth after our Lord's Prayer"; in congregational use the Litany may be sung or said; the Litany is to be forever distinguished from the never-ceasing flow of "litanies" which are being produced at the present time, which can never compare with it.

LITTLE HOURS: another name for three of the canonical hours (q. v.), Terce, Sext, and Nones; the name derives from the brevity of these prayer-services.

LITURGY (Greek, "a public work"): 1) the whole system of services, seasons, ceremonies, etc., of a church; 2) the book containing the church-services; 3) the service of the Eucharist; the "Divine Liturgy," the Mass (this might easily be counted No. 1).

MANUAL ACTS: the actions indicated in the rubrics at the Words of Institution in the Communion service.

MARIOLATRY: the cult of the Blessed Virgin Mary in the Roman Catholic and Eastern Orthodox churches, *cf. supra,* "Hagiolatry"; in general use, a term of opprobrium, referring to the worship of Mary as "Mother of God," worship which properly belongs only to Jesus Christ.

MARTYROLOGY: one of the books of the Roman Rite; it contains the names of saints and martyrs whose days are to be observed, with the dates of their commemorations.

MASS: the central service of the Christian Church; the liturgy of the Eucharist or the Holy Communion; it is thought that the name derives from words sometimes used at the end of Mass, *Ite, missa est,* "Go, it is ended"; Luther retained the name; many Lutherans all over the world still use it to designate "the principal divine service" of the church. (Luther's fulminations against "the abominations of the Mass" were not directed at the name, but at grievous doctrinal and devotional abuses which had entered into the church's services.)

MATINS: the first of the "canonical hours"—it includes the "nocturns" said during the hours of darkness; in the reformed service books "Matins" denotes the morning service of prayer; it has elements from the old Matins, and from Lauds (q. v.).

MINSTER: an English name for a church, derived from the word "monastery"; it may be applied to an abbey church or a collegiate church.

767

MISSA CATECHUMENORUM: the first part of the Service or the Mass; the "Office of the Word," including the lessons and the sermon or homily; after the sermon, in the early church, the catechumens were dismissed.

MISSA FIDELIUM: the "Service of the Faithful"; the "Office of Communion"; in the early church only the faithful were allowed to remain for the "holy mysteries" of the Eucharist; catechumens, penitents, those under discipline were excluded; all the faithful remained and received the Sacrament; and to the absent it was taken by the deacons after the mass ended.

MISSAL: 1) the Roman service book containing the Ordinary and the Canon of the Mass and the propers of the time and of the saints; 2) in modern use, a large edition of the service book, well bound, intended for use at the altar.

MISSAL STAND: the desk of metal or wood upon which the service book rests on the altar in time of public worship.

MITRE: the ceremonial headdress of the bishop—made of silk, richly ornamented; two lappets depend from the rear and hang down on the shoulders.

MIXED CHALICE: this term signifies the ceremonial addition of a small quantity of water to the wine at the time the chalice is prepared for the celebration of the Holy Communion; it is supposed to root in the ancient sumptuary custom with respect to the use of wine; symbolically, it is thought to represent the "water and the blood" which flowed from the Saviour's side on the cross.

MODE: analogous to a "key" in modern music; "mode" indicates the intervals and the compass of the "scales" in plain song; melodies were arranged in one or another of the "modes," as a modern melody is arranged in a certain "key."

MOSAICS: artistic representations (picture or geometrical pattern) made by cementing together small pieces of colored stone, glass, etc., on a flat surface; an ancient art form employed in the ornamentation of Christian churches.

MOTET: a sacred choral composition in contrapuntal style; the text is biblical prose; at first the texts were in Latin; later composers employed vernacular biblical texts; the motet is sung unaccompanied (*a cappella*); the motet generally treats the text with respect, and with a minimum of senseless repetition.

NAVE: from the Latin word for "ship," referring to the ark of salvation; hence, the body of the church building, where the faithful are during the public liturgy; approaching the church from the entrance the divisions are: narthex, nave, choir, and sanctuary.

NEUMES: a system of musical signs employed before the invention of notation; the signs vaguely, but not exactly, indicated the direction and the duration of the notes; the pitch was only generally indicated; the neumes were perhaps more mnemonic suggestions for the performance of the music than a precise "notation."

NOCTURN: One of the three divisions of Matins, the night or nocturnal office and one of the canonical hours.

NONE: one of the canonical hours, associated with the hour of three o'clock in the afternoon ("after-none"). The time was reckoned from six o'clock in the morning and None was the ninth hour.

OBLATION: means "offering"; the word is applied in the early church to the whole liturgy of the Eucharist; next, to the offerings of bread and wine, from which the sacramental elements were taken; another meaning of the word refers to the offering of the Christian's life and powers in the service of God, in thanksgiving for God's gifts in Jesus Christ. *Vide* also "anaphora."

OBSECRATION: a fervent petition; more particularly, a calling upon God to grant a request because of a divine action, attribute, or revelation; in the Litany, the petitions beginning with "by" are obsecrations; e.g., "by thy Cross and Passion."

OCCURRENCE: the falling of two festivals on the same day. In this case the greater festival prevails; the lesser is postponed to the next "free" day.

OCTAVE: the period of eight days following the great feasts, e.g., Easter and Pentecost; the word is specially used for the last day of the week after the festival, which falls on the same day as the feast; e.g., Trinity Sunday is the octave of Pentecost.

OFFERTORY: 1) in the Service, the verses of the Psalms which are sung after the Offering and before the General Prayer; they may vary like other propers; 2) the name for the offerings of bread and wine, the fruits of the earth, and other gifts of the faithful, at the Eucharist; (in Protestantism, incorrectly limited to offerings); 3) the action in the liturgy of bringing to the altar the elements of bread and wine (and water) for the consecration and administration of the communion.

ORARION: the wide stole of the deacon in the Greek Church.

ORDINARY: 1) the bishop or other ruler of a diocese; 2) the invariable parts of the liturgy.

ORGANUM: in music, the earliest attempt at complementary melody or polyphony; made by adding to a given melody another one which followed it at an interval of a fourth or a fifth above or below the given melody; this kind of "harmony" has been not inappropriately called "excruciating" to modern ears.

ORIENTATION: 1) the practice of locating churches in such a way as to have the altar in the eastern position; 2) the liturgical custom of facing the altar for all parts of the service which are not directly addressed to the people; also called "the eastward position."

ORPHREY: an ornamental band or border of a vestment or parament.

ORTHODOXY: 1) in Lutheranism, a period of theological scholasticism, regularity, and, some would say, sterility, during the seventeenth century; 2) the general name for the churches and peoples and way of life of the Eastern Orthodox Church; 3) correctness of belief; 4) in the Orthodox churches, "the right giving of glory (to God)."

PAX: 1) name for the salutation after the Words of Institution in the Eucharist, "The Peace of the Lord be with you alway" 2) the ceremonial kiss of peace in the early liturgies.

PENITENTIAL PSALMS: those Psalms of a penitential spirit: 6, 32, 38, 51, 102, 130, 143; they are specially appointed for use in Lent, and at other times of penitence.

PENTECOST: (fiftieth day): the major festival which commemorates the descent of the Holy Spirit upon the church; the seventh Lord's day after Easter; another name for Pentecost is Whitsunday; Pentecost corresponds to a Jewish feast of the same name, as Easter does to the Passover.

PERICOPES: 1) a Greek word which means lessons of Holy Scripture appointed for reading in public worship; 2) more specifically, the ancient system of Epistles and Gospels for the Service on the Sundays and festivals of the ecclesiastical year.

PERISTYLE (architecture): a row of columns surrounding a temple or a court; when the range of columns is attached to the front of a building it (with its entablature) is known as the portico; the peristyle is a complete colonnade; the portico is partial.

PIETISM: a system of Christian life which flourished in the eighteenth century in the Lutheran Church in Europe under Spener and Francke; these men sought to revive and quicken the personal religious life, which had languished under a desiccated orthodoxy (q. v.); the methods they employed were the *collegia pietatis* (q. v.), Bible-study, and works of mercy; the weaknesses of pietism were subjectivism, emotionalism, and a tendency to be separatistic as far as the church was concerned; the reaction to Pietism came in the form of Rationalism.

PLAIN SONG: also called plain chant; this denotes the unisonous choral music of the church. It is purely melodic, unmeasured, the length of the notes being determined by the length of the syllables of the words to which they are sung, and unaccompanied. Plain song is really a system of musical recitation of liturgical texts by a choir in unison; in plain song the text achieves greater importance, clarity, and significance, than in most other forms of choral music. Plain song melodies also are modal, i.e., in the "church modes" and not in the modern "scales."

POLYPHONY: the system of musical composition in which two or more independent melodies are combined in an agreeable and "harmonious" (but not according to rules of harmony) progression; counterpoint; polyphony is contrasted with homophony and harmony.

PONTIFICAL: pertaining to services conducted by a bishop, e.g., pontifical mass, pontifical vespers; or services reserved to bishops, e.g., ordination, dedication of churches, etc.

PONTIFICALE: the Roman Catholic liturgical book which contains the episcopal offices, i.e., sacraments, services, and benedictions reserved to bishops, e.g., ordinations, consecration of churches, pontifical blessings, etc.

PRAYER OF THE CHURCH: The great prayer following the Offering and the Offertory; commonly called the "General Prayer."

PRECES: prayers in the form of versicles and responses, as seen in the Morning Suffrages, Evening Suffrages, etc.

PREFACE: the solemn series of versicles, responses, special prefaces, conclusion, and the Sanctus, which begins the anaphora or Communion Office; it is one of the most ancient elements in the Christian liturgy, and is set to almost equally venerable melodies.

PRE-RAPHAELITES: the school of painters formed in England in the nineteenth century to emulate the spirit of painters before the time of Raphael; the school was called the Pre-Raphaelite Brotherhood, and numbered among its more prominent representatives such men as Millais, D. G. Rossetti, and Holman Hunt.

PRIME: one of the canonical hours; it follows Lauds.

PRIMER: a type of devotional manual or book of prayers used by the laity shortly before the Reformation, and for some time after it; this type of book generally contained the Lord's Prayer, Creed, Ave Maria, Decalogue, prayers

770

and Psalms, and other devotional material, sometimes with an exposition.

PRO-ANAPHORA: the part of the Service before the anaphora (i.e., the Preface)—another name for the ante-communion or the Mass of the Catechumens.

PRONE: a form of general intercession, conducted by the priest or preacher from the pulpit, before or (more generally) after the sermon, in medieval times; it was partly a bidding prayer, partly a general intercession; frequently common prayers (such as the Pater noster) were used with it; the prone was a vernacular office used at high mass on Sundays and feasts in connection with the sermon.

PROPRIA—PROPERS: the variable parts of the Liturgy of the Eucharist; Introit, Collect, Lesson, Epistle, Gradual (or Tract), Gospel (Offertory), and Proper Preface. In the Roman Rite, also the proper Communio and Post-communio.

RATIONALISM: a philosophical school which came to great prominence in the eighteenth century, which emphasized reason as the only source of knowledge.

RECITATIVE: musical term, a type of declamatory singing which arose in opera about the year 1700; a recitative is sung *ad libitum* by the singer; it may be supported only at intervals by chords or arpeggios; or, it may have a more sustained and continuous accompaniment.

REGULARS: clergymen who are members of a monastic order and hence follow a rule (*regula*) and are under an abbot, contrasted with seculars, who are under a bishop; in the monastic order there were priests and lay-brothers; it was these priests who belonged to the "regular clergy."

"RELIGIOUS": a member of one of the monastic, mendicant, missionary, or teaching orders of the Roman Church, i.e., a nun, sister, monk, or "brother."

RELIQUARY: vessel or ornamental container designed to hold the relic of a saint; a reliquary might be made in many different forms; a relic deposited in an altar is placed in an oblong metal box, a reliquary; a relic displayed to the faithful may be exhibited in a vessel somewhat like the monstrance used in benediction or exposition of the host. (*Vide* "Exposition".)

REREDOS: the architectural screen erected at the rear of an altar, usually built of marble or other stone; it may be enriched with sculptured figures or architectural ornament.

RITES AND CEREMONIES: RITE: the body of customs, habits, practices, and liturgies of the church in a defined place, e.g., the Roman Rite, the Ambrosian Rite, the Sarum Rite; CEREMONY: an external sacred act or observance; the term may be employed generally, e.g., the ceremony of Blessing of Psalms; or, more specially, the ceremony of kindling lights at the reading of the Gospel.

RITUAL (RITUALE): the book containing the occasional services and sacraments which may be performed by the parochial clergy; the "occasional services" are the "ritual" of the Lutheran Church.

ROOD SCREEN: also called rood-loft: a gallery built over the entrance to the chancel; on it stood a cross or rood (a cross flanked by figures of St. Mary and St. John); portions of the service were read from this loft; later the rood screen became mainly a decorative feature in the church, and the gallery feature was omitted; it was simply an ornamental and symbolical screen which separated the nave and the choir.

ROSARY: a form of nonliturgical, vernacular prayer used in the Roman Catholic Church; its features are repeated prayers and meditations centering around the "joyful," "sorrowful," and "glorious" mysteries of our Saviour's life; and, the use of graded strings of beads to regulate the prayers and to remind the user of his place in the round of devotions.

RUBRICS: directions for the conduct of the services of the church; the name comes from the red ink which was used for these directions, as contrasted with the text of the services, which was written in black ink.

SACRAMENTAL AND SACRIFICIAL: terms employed to denote the manward (sacramental) and Godward (sacrificial) "movements" of the parts of the public services of the church; correlative terms are objective and subjective.

SACRAMENTARY: the ancient collection of prayers and other offices of the Western church for the use of the celebrant at Mass: at first these books were called *Libri sacramentorum;* later, *Sacramentarium;* the *Sacramentarium* later also contained not only prayers at the Eucharist, but also the prayers and benedictions used at other sacramental rites: baptism, ordination, etc.; the three best known collections are those attributed to Leo the Great, Gelasius I, and Gregory the Great.

SALUTATION: the liturgical greeting, "The Lord be with you, ℞. And with thy spirit," which precedes prayers, benedictions, and other parts of the liturgy.

SECULARS: members of the clergy who were not members of a monastic or other religious order; the ordinary parochial clergy, who were subject to the bishop of the diocese.

SEQUENCE: the metrical hymn sung on the great feasts between the Epistle and Gospel; at the time of the Counter-Reformation their number was greatly reduced in the Roman Missal; in the Lutheran Church several continue in use in the hymnal, notably those of Easter and Pentecost.

SEXT: the noon-day office in the breviary.

STATION DAYS: 1) the times at which the Christian people of Rome gathered for a public service at one of the designated basilicas, called therefrom, "the stational church" for that day; 2) the fast-days, Wednesday and Friday. (*Shepherd of Hermas,* Tertullian, etc.).

STOLE: the scarf of silk or other material worn around the neck, hanging from the shoulders in front of the wearer; it is usually ornamented with crosses or other symbols, and is made in the colors of the church's seasons; it is the peculiar vestment of the ministry and is worn over the alb or surplice.

SURSUM CORDA: "Lift up your hearts"—the name for the versicle, and for the series of versicles, which stand at the beginning of the communion Office; it is of the greatest antiquity, and probably goes back to the middle of the second century.

TERCE: one of the canonical hours; it is associated with the hour of nine o'clock in the morning.

TRANSUBSTANTIATION: the doctrine of the Roman Catholic Church which defines the method of the change in the elements at the consecration in the Mass: the substance of the bread and wine is changed into the substance of the body and blood of Christ—and thereafter only the "accidents" remain; the doctrine is specially repugnant to Protestant Christians.

UNISONAL: type of singing done in one voice or melody, without harmony or accompaniment; this was the manner of performing the Gregorian chant and plain song melodies.

USE: 1) the particular body of ceremonies, customs, and usages employed in the church in one place; e.g., the use of the church of Toledo, Salisbury, etc. 2) a particular custom which prevails in a certain place.

VERBA (*Verba institutionis*): the Words of Institution used at the consecration in Holy Communion; also called the "Dominical Words."

VERSICLES: brief responsive verses from the Psalms, employed in public services; a typical feature of churchly worship.

VESPERS: the service for the late afternoon; at the Reformation, Vespers was made the daily evening prayer-service; it now has some features from Compline (e.g., Nunc Dimittis, when used as a canticle).

VICAR (deputy): 1) the clergyman in charge of a parish in place of the rector; 2) the incumbent of a parish in which the tithes are otherwise assigned; 3) in European Lutheran churches the term is frequently applied to the assistant minister, or curate, of a parish; one who serves under the pastor.

VIGIL: 1) the "eve" of a festival or greater holy day; 2) the service held on the eve of a festival, which concluded with the Holy Communion: e.g., the service on Christmas Eve.

BIBLIOGRAPHY

The following select bibliography has been chosen from the vast number of published sources and discussions in the liturgical and musical fields. It includes the more important works referred to in preceding pages and other material of value. Significant articles in periodicals and similar special studies are included in the list.

Many older titles of importance are not mentioned, since their soundest discussions and conclusions are for the most part referred to in later works. In the case of the sixteenth-century church orders, only those are included which have figured prominently in this present volume.

When a work is published abroad and also in this country, the name of the American publisher is given. When the publishing house has more than one name the first significant word is used.

In case of rare books pagination is given in capital Roman numerals. Where "ff" appears, unnumbered pages following these numerals are indicated.

The note "n.d." indicates no date of publication; "c" refers to the copyright date; "unp." indicates unpaged; "n.p.n.p." means no place and no publisher.

I. WORSHIP AND THE LITURGY

1. GENERAL WORKS

ALTMANN, ULRICH. *Hilfsbuch zur Geschichte des christlichen Kultus.* 3 vols. Berlin: Töpelmann, 1941-47.

ASMUSSEN, HANS. *Die Lehre vom Gottesdienst.* München: Chr. Kaiser, 1937. 294 pp.

BAUMSTARK, ANTON. *Vom geschichtlichen Werden der Liturgie.* Freiburg: Herder, 1923. 159 pp.

BENOIT, JEAN DANIEL. *Liturgical Renewal: Studies in Catholic and Protestant Developments on the Continent.* Translated by Edwin Hudson. London: S.C.M. Pr., 1958. 112 pp.

BOGLER, THEODOR. *Liturgische Erneuerung in aller Welt.* Maria Laach: Verlag Ars Liturgica, 1950. 174 pp.

BRENNER, SCOTT FRANCIS. *The Way of Worship: A Study in Ecumenical Recovery.* New York: Macmillan, 1944. 200 pp.

BRILIOTH, YNGVE. *Eucharistic Faith and Practice, Evangelical and Catholic.* Translated by A. G. HEBERT. New York: Macmillan, 1930. 295 pp.

BRUNNER, HEINRICH EMIL. *The Word and the World.* New York: Scribner, 1931. 127 pp.

BURBIDGE, EDWARD. *Liturgies and Offices of the Church for the Use of English Readers, in Illustration of the Book of Common Prayer.* London: Bell, 1885. 361 pp.

CABROL, FERNAND. *The Year's Liturgy, the Sundays, Feriae and Feasts of the Liturgical Year.* 2 vols. London: Burns, 1938-40.

CABROL, FERNAND, and H. LECLERCQ. *Dictionnaire d'archéologie chrétienne et de liturgie.* Paris: Letouzey, 1907–. Vols. 1-15 so far published.

The Catholic Encyclopedia. 17 vols. New York: Appleton, c1907-22.

DEARMER, PERCY. *Art and Religion.* London: S.C.M. Pr., 1924. 87 pp.

——. *The Art of Public Worship.* Milwaukee: Morehouse, 1919. 213 pp.

——. *The Church at Prayer and the World Outside.* London: Clarke, 1923. 256 pp.

DOWDEN, JOHN. *The Church Year and Kalendar.* Cambridge: The Univ. Pr., 1910. 160 pp.

DUCHESNE, LOUIS, M. O. *Christian Worship: its Origin and Evolution. A Study of the Latin Liturgy Up to the Time of Charlemagne.* Translated by M. L. MCCLURE (5th ed.). New York: Macmillan, 1931. 593 pp.

FAIRBAIRN, ANDREW M. *Catholicism: Roman and Anglican.* (4th ed.). New York: Scribner, 1900. 481 pp.

FENDT, LEONARD. *Einführung in die Liturgiewissenschaft.* Berlin: Töpelmann, 1958. 287 pp.

FISKE, GEORGE W. *The Recovery of Worship: a Study of the Crucial Problem of the Protestant Churches.* New York: Macmillan, 1931. 269 pp.

FREEMAN, PHILIP. *The Principles of Divine Service.* 2 vols. in 3. London: Henry, 1855-62. 2d ed. Parker, 1866.

HARDMAN, OSCAR. *A History of Christian Worship.* Nashville: Cokesbury, 1937. 263 pp.

HEBERT, ARTHUR G. *Liturgy and Society.* London: Faber, 1935. 267 pp.

HEILER, FRIEDRICH. *Prayer; a Study in the History and Psychology of Religion.* Translated by SAMUEL MCCOMB, ed., & J. EDGAR PARK. 2d ed. New York: Oxford, 1938. 376 pp.

——. *The Spirit of Worship, Its Forms and Manifestations in the Christian Churches* . . . . Translated by W. MONTGOMERY. London: Hodder, 1926. 214 pp.

HENNIG, LIEMAR (ed.). *Theologie und Liturgie; eine Gesamtschau der gegenwärtigen Forschung in Einzeldarstellungen.* Kassel: J. Stauda, 1952. 354 pp.

HERZOG, JOHANN J. (ed.). *Realencyklopädie für protestantische Theologie und Kirche* (3d ed.). Herausgegeben von ALBERT HAUCK. 24 vols. Leipzig: Hinrichs, 1896-1913.

HISLOP, DAVID H. *Our Heritage in Public Worship.* New York: Scribner, 1935. 342 pp.

HORN, EDWARD TRAILL. *Outlines of Liturgics.* 2d rev. ed. Philadelphia: Lutheran Publication Society, c1912. 162 pp.

JACOBS, HENRY EYSTER, and J. A. W. HAAS. *The Lutheran Cyclopedia.* New York: Scribner, 1899.

JACOBY, HERMANN. *Die Liturgik der Reformatoren.* 2 vols. Gotha: Perthes, 1871-76.

JAKOB, G. *Die Kunst im Dienste der Kirche*. 5th ed. Landshut: Thomann, 1901. 535 pp.

JAMES, EDWIN OLIVER. *Christian Myth and Ritual; A Historical Study*. London: Murray, 1933. 345 pp.

JUNGMANN, JOSEF ANDREAS. *Public Worship*. Translated by CLIFFORD HOWELL. London: Challoner, 1957. 249 pp.

KELLNER, KARL ADAM HEINRICH. *Heortology; a History of the Christian Festivals from their Origin to the Present Day*. Translated from 2d German ed. London: Paul, 1908. 466 pp.

KING, ARCHDALE A. *Liturgies of the Primatial Sees*. Milwaukee: Bruce, 1957. 656 pp.

KIRK, KENNETH ESCOTT (ed.). *The Study of Theology*. London: Hodder, 1939. 484 pp.

————. *The Vision of God: The Christian Doctrine of the Summum Bonum*. New York: Longmans, 1931. 583 pp.

LOEHE, WILHELM. *Three Books Concerning the Church*. Translated by EDWARD T. HORN. Reading, Pa.: Pilger, 1908. 202 pp.

MAXWELL, WILLIAM D. *An Outline of Christian Worship, its Development and Forms*. London: Oxford Univ. Pr., 1936. 199 pp.

MELAND, BERNARD E. *Modern Man's Worship; a Search for Reality in Religion*. New York: Harper, 1934. 317 pp.

MICKLEM, EDWARD R. *Our Approach to God; a Study in Public Worship*. London: Hodder, 1934. 271 pp.

MICKLEM, NATHANIEL (ed.). *Christian Worship, Studies in its History and Meaning*. Oxford: Clarendon, 1936. 259 pp.

Monatschrift für Gottesdienst und kirchliche Kunst, begründet von FRIEDRICH SPITTA und JULIUS SMEND, Gottingen: Vandenhoeck, 1896—June, 1941. Vols. 1-46.

MULLER, KARL FERDINAND (ed.). *Leiturgia; Handbuch des evangelischen Gottesdienstes*. Herausgegeben von KARL FERDINAND MULLER und WALTER BLANKENBURG. 3 vols. to date. Kassel: J. Stauda, 1954—. (A collection of articles by specialists.)

NEALE, JOHN MASON. *Essays on Liturgiology and Church History*. London: Saunders, 1863. 527 pp.

OTTO, RUDOLF. *The Idea of the Holy; an Inquiry into the Non-Rational Factor in the Idea of the Divine and its Relation to the Rational*. Translated by JOHN W. HARVEY. New York: Oxford, 1923. 228 pp. (Rev. ed., 1936).

PAQUIER, RICHARD. *Traité de Liturgique*. Paris: Delachaux & Niestlé S. A., 1954. 224 pp.

RATCLIFF, EDWARD C. "Christian Worship and Liturgy." In K. E. KIRK, *The Study of Theology,* pp. 407-80.

REED, LUTHER DOTTERER. *Worship: A Study of Corporate Devotion*. Philadelphia: Muhlenberg, 1959. 437 pp.

————. "Church Art." *Lutheran Church Review,* XXIX (1910), 765-88.

RICHARD, JAMES WILLIAM, and F. V. N. PAINTER. *Christian Worship: Its Principles and Forms*. 2d ed. Philadelphia: Lutheran Publication Society, c1908. 368 pp.

SCUDAMORE, WILLIAM E. *Notitia Eucharistica, a Commentary, Explanatory, Doctrinal, and Historical, on the Order for the Administration of the*

Lord's Supper or Holy Communion According to the Use of the Church of England. 2d ed. rev. and enl. London: Rivingtons, 1876. 1055 pp.

SHEPHERD, MASSEY HAMILTON, JR. (ed.). *The Liturgical Renewal of the Church.* New York: Oxford, 1960. 160 pp.

Siona. Monatschrift für Liturgie und Kirchenmusik (Vols. 1-45). Herausgegeben von MAX HEROLD. Gütersloh: Bertelsmann, 1876-1920.

SMITH, WILLIAM and S. CHEETHAM. *A Dictionary of Christian Antiquities.* 2 vols. Hartford: Burr, 1880.

SPENGLER, OSWALD. *The Decline of the West.* Translated with notes by C. F. ATKINSON. 2 vols. New York; Knopf, 1926-28.

SPERRY, WILLARD L. *Reality in Worship; a Study of Public Worship and Private Religion.* New York: Macmillan, 1925. 346 pp.

STREETER, BURNETT H. *Reality; a New Correlation of Science and Religion.* New York: Macmillan, 1926. 350 pp.

TAYLOR, HENRY OSBORN. *The Mediaeval Mind.* 2 vols. 4th ed. Cambridge: Harvard Univ. Pr., 1949.

TEMPLE, WILLIAM. *Basic Convictions.* New York: Harper, 1936. 81 pp.

UNDERHILL, EVELYN. *Worship.* New York: Harper, 1937. 350 pp.

VOGT, VON OGDEN, *Modern Worship.* New Haven: Yale Univ. Pr., 1927. 153 pp.

WALKER, WILLISTON. *A History of the Christian Church.* New York: Scribner, 1918. 624 pp.

WARD, A. W., *et al.* (eds.). *The Cambridge Modern History.* 13 vols. and atlas. New York: Macmillan, 1902-12.

WEBBER, FREDERICK R. *Studies in the Liturgy.* Erie, Pa.: Ashby, 1938. 231 pp.

WEDGWOOD, CICELY V. *The Thirty Years' War.* New Haven: Yale Univ. Pr., 1959. 544 pp.

WILL, ROBERT. *Le culte; étude d'histoire et de philosophie religieuses . . .* 3 vols. Paris: Istra, 1924-35.

WILLIAMS, NORMAN P., and C. HARRIS. (eds.). *Northern Catholicism; Centenary Studies in the Oxford and Parallel Movements.* New York: Macmillan, 1933. 555 pp.

WORDSWORTH, JOHN. *The Ministry of Grace: Studies in Early Church History with Reference to Present Problems.* 2d ed. rev. New York: Longmans, 1901. 488 pp.

2. TEXTS AND COMMENT

a. Early Church

BRIGHTMAN, FRANK EDWARD. *Liturgies Eastern and Western. See* C. E. HAMMOND.

CABROL, FERNAND. *The Prayer of the Early Christians.* Translated by ERNEST GRAF. London: Burns, 1930. 175 pp.

CULLMANN, OSCAR. *Early Christian Worship.* Translated by A. STEWART TODD and JAMES B. TORRANCE. ("Studies in Biblical Theology," No. 10.) Chicago: Regnery, 1953. 124 pp.

FORTESCUE, ADRIAN. *The Orthodox Eastern Church.* Re-issue. London: Catholic Truth Society, 1916. 451 pp.

GAVIN, FRANK S. *The Jewish Antecedents of the Christian Sacraments.* New York: Macmillan, 1928. 120 pp.

HAMMOND, CHARLES EDWARD. *Liturgies Eastern and Western, Being the Texts, Original or Translated, of the Principal Liturgies of the Church* ed. F. E. BRIGHTMAN. Vol. I only. Oxford: Clarendon, 1896.

HIGGINS, ANGUS J. *The Lord's Supper in the New Testament.* ("Studies in Biblical Theology," No. 6.) Chicago: Regnery, 1952. 96 pp.

HIPPOLYTUS. *The Apostolic Tradition of Hippolytus.* Translated by BURTON SCOTT EASTON. Cambridge: The Univ. Pr., 1934. 112 pp.

————. *The Treatise on the Apostolic Tradition of St. Hippolytus of Rome . . .* ed. GREGORY DIX. Vol. I only. New York: Macmillan, 1937.

HOLLOWAY, HENRY. *A Study of the Byzantine Liturgy.* London: Mitre, 1933. 267 pp.

JACOBS, CHARLES MICHAEL. "Christian Worship in the Apostolic Age." *Memoirs of the Lutheran Liturgical Association,* VI, 41-64.

————. "Christian Worship in the First Post-Apostolic Age." *Memoirs of the Lutheran Liturgical Association,* VII, 49-74.

JEREMIAS, JOACHIM. *The Eucharistic Words of Jesus.* Translated by ARNOLD EHRHARDT from the 2d German ed. New York: Macmillan, 1955. 195 pp.

LIETZMANN, HANS. *Mass and Lord's Supper; a Study in the History of the Liturgy.* Translated by DOROTHEA H. G. REEVE. Leiden: Brill, 1953— (Translation of the following item.)

————. *. . . Messe und Herrenmahl, eine Studie zur Geschichte der Liturgie.* Bonn: Marcus, 1926. 263 pp.

McCLURE, M. L. and C. L. FELTOE (eds.). *The Pilgrimage of Etheria.* New York: Macmillan, 1919. 103 pp.

MacDONALD, ALEXANDER B. *Christian Worship in the Primitive Church.* Edinburgh: Clark, 1934. 230 pp.

MACGREGOR, GEORGE H. C. *Eucharistic Origins: A Survey of the New Testament Evidence.* London: Clarke, 1929. 256 pp.

MACLEAN, ARTHUR J. *The Ancient Church Orders.* Cambridge: The Univ. Pr., 1910. 181 pp.

NIELEN, JOSEF M. *The Earliest Christian Liturgy.* Translated by PATRICK CUMMINS. St. Louis: Herder, 1941. 416 pp.

OESTERLEY, WILLIAM O. E. *The Jewish Background of the Christian Liturgy.* Oxford: Clarendon, 1925. 243 pp.

ROBERTS, ALEXANDER, and JAMES DONALDSON (eds·). *The Ante-Nicene Fathers. Translations of the Writings of the Fathers down to A.D. 325.* Revised by A. CLEVELAND COXE. 10 vols. Buffalo: Christian Literature Pub. Co., 1885-96.

SALAVILLE, SEVERIN. *An Introduction to the Study of Eastern Liturgies.* Translated by JOHN M. T. BARTON. London: Sands, 1938. 226 pp.

SCHAFF, PHILIP (ed.). *The Teaching of the Twelve Apostles . . . or, The Oldest Church Manual, the Didache and Kindred Documents in the Original with Translations and Discussions of Post-Apostolic Teaching, Baptism, Worship and Discipline. . . .* 3d ed. rev. and enl. New York: Funk, 1890. 325 pp.

SERAPION. *Bishop Serapion's Prayer-Book, an Egyptian Sacramentary.* Edited by JOHN WORDSWORTH. 2d. rev. ed. New York: Macmillan, 1915. 104 pp.

Service Book of the Holy Orthodox-Catholic Apostolic (Greco-Russian) Church. Compiled, translated, and arranged by ISABEL FLORENCE HAP-GOOD. Rev. ed. Boston: Houghton, 1922. 615 pp.

SRAWLEY, JAMES HERBERT. *The Early History of the Liturgy.* Cambridge: The Univ. Pr., 1913. 251 pp.

WARREN, FREDERICK E. *The Liturgy and Ritual of the Ante-Nicene Church.* 2d rev. ed. New York: Gorham, 1912. 317 pp.

WOOLLEY, REGINALD M. *The Liturgy of the Primitive Church.* Cambridge: The Univ. Pr., 1910. 182 pp.

b. Pre-Reformation and Roman

ATCHLEY, EDWARD G. C. F. (ed. & trans.). *The Ambrosian Liturgy.* London: Cope, 1909. 108 pp.

————. *Ordo Romanus Primus.* London: Moring, 1905. 199 pp.

BATIFFOL, PIERRE. *History of the Roman Breviary.* Translated by A. M. Y. BAYLAY from 3rd French ed. New York: Longmans, 1912. 341 pp.

BAUDOT, JULIUS L. *The Breviary, Its History and Contents.* Translated by the Benedictines of Stanbrook. St. Louis: Herder, 1929. 160 pp.

BAUMER, SUITBERT. *Geschichte des Breviers.* Freiburg: Herder, 1895. 637 pp.

BISHOP, EDMUND. *Liturgica Historica; Papers on the Liturgy and Religious Life of the Western Church.* Oxford: Clarendon, 1918. 506 pp.

BISHOP, WILLIAM C. *The Mozarabic and Ambrosian Rites; Four Essays in Comparative Liturgiology,* ed. C. L. FELTOE. Milwaukee: Morehouse, 1924. 135 pp.

BOUYER, LOUIS. *Liturgical Piety.* Notre Dame, Ind.: Univ. of Notre Dame Pr., 1955. 284 pp.

Breviarium romanum, ex decreto sacrosancti Concilii tridentini restitutum ... 4 vols. Boston: Benzinger, 1946-47.

CABROL, FERNAND. *The Books of the Latin Liturgy.* Translated by the Benedictines of Stanbrook. St. Louis: Herder, 1932. 166 pp.

————. *Liturgical Prayer, its History & Spirit.* Translated by a Benedictine of Stanbrook. New York: Kenedy, 1922. 382 pp.

————. *The Mass of the Western Rites.* Translated by C. M. ANTONY [*pseud.*]. St. Louis: Herder, 1934. 241 pp.

DREWS, PAUL G. *Zur Entstehungsgeschichte des Kanons in der römischen Messe.* ("Studien zur Geschichte des Gottesdienstes und des gottesdienst-lichen Lebens," I.) Tübingen: Mohr, 1902. 39 pp.

EBNER, ADALBERT. *Quellen und Forschungen zur Geschichte und Kunst-geschichte des Missale Romanum im Mittelalter. Iter Italicum.* St. Louis: Herder, 1896. 487 pp.

EISENHOFER, LUDWIG. *See* Valentin Thalhofer.

ELLARD, GERALD. *Christian Life and Worship.* Rev. & enl. ed. Milwaukee: Bruce, c1940. 420 pp.

————. *The Mass in Transition.* Milwaukee: Bruce, 1956. 387 pp.

————. *Men at Work at Worship: America Joins the Liturgical Move-ment.* New York: Longmans, 1940. 307 pp.

FELTOE, CHARLES L. (ed.). *Sacramentarium Leonianum.* Cambridge: The Univ. Pr., 1896. 244 pp.

FORTESCUE, ADRIAN. *The Ceremonies of the Roman Rite Described.* New ed., rev. by J. B. O'Connell. London: Burns, 1930. 469 pp.

————. *The Mass, a Study of the Roman Liturgy.* New York: Longmans, 1937. 433 pp.

FRERE, WALTER HOWARD. *Studies in Early Roman Liturgy.* 3 vols. London: Oxford Univ. Pr., 1930-35.

GERBERT, MARTIN. *Monumenta veteris liturgiae Alemannicae.* 2 vols. [St. Blasii in Hyrcinia monast.] Typis San-Blasianis, 1777-79.

HERWEGEN, ILDEFONS. *The Art-Principle of the Liturgy.* Translated by WILLIAM BUSCH. Collegeville, Minn.: Liturgical Pr., 1931. 42 pp.

JENNER, HENRY. "Ambrosian Liturgy and Rite," *Catholic Encyclopedia,* I, 394-403.

JUNGMANN, JOSEF A. *The Mass of the Roman Rite: Its Origins and Development (Missarum Solemnia).* 2 vols. Translated by FRANCIS A. BRUNNER. New York: Benziger, 1951-55.

KING, ARCHDALE A. *Notes on the Catholic Liturgies.* New York: Longmans, 1930. 544 pp.

KLAUSER, THEODOR. *The Western Liturgy and its History; Some Reflections on Recent Studies.* Translated by F. L. CROSS, New York: Morehouse, 1952. 63 pp.

KOENKER, ERNEST B. *The Liturgical Renaissance in the Roman Catholic Church.* Chicago: Univ. of Chicago Pr., 1954. 271 pp.

LEFEBVRE, GASPAR (ed.). *Saint Andrew Daily Missal.* St. Paul (Minn.): E. M. Lohmann, 1940. 1852 pp. (Later editions vary considerably.)

LEGG, JOHN WICKMAN (ed.). *The Sarum Missal; ed. from three early manuscripts.* Oxford: Clarendon, 1916. 612 pp.

LINDBERG, GUSTAF. *Die schwedischen Missalien des Mittelalters.* Vol. I only. Uppsala: Almquist, 1923. 439 pp.

MASKELL, WILLIAM (ed.). *Monumenta ritualia ecclesiae Anglicanae, or Occasional Offices of the Church of England According to the Ancient Use of Salisbury, the Prymer in English, and other Prayers and Forms with Dissertations and Notes.* 3 vols. 2d. ed. Oxford: Clarendon, 1882.

MESSENGER, ERNEST C. *The Reformation, the Mass and the Priesthood; A Documented History with Special Reference to the Question of Anglican Orders.* 2 vols. New York: Longmans, 1936-37.

Missale Bambergense. Bamberg: Johann Pfeyl, 1499. 321 leaves.

Missale Constantiniense. Augsburg: Erhard Ratdolt, 1504. 272 leaves.

Missale romanum (i.e., *Nurembergense*). Nuremberg: Georgius Stuchs de Sultzbach, 1484. 255 leaves.

Missale romanum ex decreto S. S. Concilii tridentini restitutem summorum pontificum cura recognitum. Editio XXX post typicam. Radisbonae: F. Pustet, 1956.

O'CONNELL, J. B. *The Celebration of Mass; a Study of the Rubrics of the Roman Missal.* 3 vols. Milwaukee: Bruce, 1940-41.

Ordo Hebdomadae Sanctae instauratus. Editio Taurinensis iuxta typicam. Torino: Marietti, 1956. 108 pp.

PARSCH, PIUS. *The Liturgy of the Mass.* Translated by H. E. WINSTONE. 3d ed. St. Louis: Herder, 1957. 344 pp.

Rituale romanum Pauli V pontificis maximi . . . . Editio juxta typicam Vaticanam. New York: Benziger, 1944. 580+16+38 pp.

Rock, Daniel. *The Church of Our Fathers, as Seen in St. Osmund's Rite for the Cathedral of Salisbury, with Dissertations on the Belief and Ritual in England before and after the Coming of the Normans.* New ed. edited by G. W. Hart and W. H. Frere. 4 vols. London: Murray, 1905.

————. *Hierurgia; or, the Holy Sacrifice of the Mass. With Notes and Dissertations Elucidating its Doctrines and Ceremonies.* . . . . Revised by W. H. James Weale. 2 vols. 4th ed. London: Baker, 1900.

Schuster, Ildefonso. *The Sacramentary (Liber sacramentorum): Historical & Liturgical Notes on the Roman Missal.* Translated by Arthur Levelis-Marke, from the Italian; completed by Mrs. W. Fairfax-Cholmeley. 5 vols. London: Burns, 1924-30.

The Small Missal (7th ed.). London: Burns, 1934. 442 pp.

Sullivan, John F. *The Externals of the Catholic Church; a Handbook of Catholic Usage.* Revised by J. C. O'Leary, New York: Kenedy, 1951. 403 pp.

Swete, Henry B. *Church Services and Service-Books before the Reformation.* New ed. Revised by Arthur John Maclean. New York: Macmillan, 1930. 182 pp.

Thalhofer, Valentin. *Handbuch der katholischen Liturgik.* 3d ed. edited by Ludwig Eisenhofer. 2 vols. Freiburg: Herder, 1932-33.

Warren, Frederick E. (tr.). *The Sarum Missal in English.* 2 vols. London: Moring, 1911.

Weale, William H. J. *Bibliographia liturgica. Catalogus missalium ritus latini, ab anno M. CCCC. LXXV. impressorum.* London: Quaritch, 1886. 296 pp.

Wilson, Henry A. (ed.). *The Gelasian Sacramentary. Liber sacramentorum Romanae ecclesiae.* Oxford: Clarendon, 1894. 400 pp.

———— (ed.). *The Gregorian Sacramentary under Charles the Great.* (Henry Bradshaw Society Publications XLIX). London: Harrison, 1915. 360 pp.

c. Lutheran

Agende für die Evangelisch-Lutherische Landeskirche des Königreichs Sachsen. 2 vols. in 1. 2. aufl. Leipzig: Pöschel, 1906.

Agende für evangelisch-lutherische Kirchen und Gemeinden. Vol. I, III, IV pub. to date. Berlin: Lutherisches Verlaghaus, 1952–.

Alt, Heinrch. *Der Christliche Cultus.* 2 vols. 2. verm. aufl. Berlin: Müller, 1847-60.

American Lutheran Hymnal (music ed.). Columbus, Ohio: Lutheran Book Concern, c1930. 227+585 pp.

Bergendoff, Conrad J. I. *Olavus Petri and the Ecclesiastical Transformation in Sweden (1521-1552).* New York: Macmillan, 1928. 264 pp.

The Book of Worship; see United Synod of the Evangelical Lutheran Church in the South.

Book of Worship with Hymns; see General Synod of the Evangelical Lutheran Church in the United States.

Christliche Kirchen Agenda. Wie die bey den zweyen Ständen der Herrn und Ritterschafft in Ertzhertzogthumb Oesterreich unter der Enns gebraucht wirdt. n.p.n.p., 1571. CCXIIII leaves.

781

*Christliche Kirchen Ordnung, Ceremonien und Gesenge, für Arme Unge-
schickte Pfarrherrn gestelt und in den Druck gegeben.* Calenberg &
Göttingen: 1542.

Church Book for the Use of Evangelical Lutheran Congregations. See General Council of the Evangelical Lutheran Church in North America.

Common Service. See *Standard Manuscript.*

Common Service Book of the Lutheran Church. See United Lutheran Church
in America.

COOPER, FREDERICK E. *et al. An Explanation of the Common Service, with
appendices on Christian Hymnody and Liturgical Colors and a Glossary
of Liturgical Terms.* 6th ed. rev. and enl. Philadelphia: U.L.P.H., c1941.
123 pp.

DREWS, PAUL G. *Beiträge zu Luthers liturgischen Reformen.* 2 vols. Tübingen: Mohr, 1910. ("Studien zur Geschichte des Gottesdienstes und des
gottesdienstlichen Lebens," IV-V.)

Ekklesia; eine Sammlung von Selbstdarstellungen der christlichen Kirchen;
Herausgegeben von FRIEDRICH SIEGMUND-SCHULTZE. Gotha: Klotz,
1934-41. Bd. II: Die Skandinavischen Länder. 4 parts. 1935-38.

*Der Erbarn Stadt Brunswig Christlike ordeninge, to denste dem hilgen
Euangelio, Christliker leue, tucht, frede unde eynicheit. Ock dar under
vele Christlike lere vor de Borere. Dorch Joannem Bugenhagen Pomern
bescreuen.* 1528.

EVANGELICAL LUTHERAN AUGUSTANA SYNOD. *The Hymnal and Order of
Service.* Rock Island, Ill.: Augustana Book Concern, 1926. 1134 pp.

FENDT, LEONHARD. *Der lutherische Gottesdienst des 16. Jahrhunderts; sein
Werden und sein Wachsen.* München: Reinhardt, 1923. 386 pp.

GENERAL COUNCIL OF THE EVANGELICAL LUTHERAN CHURCH IN NORTH
AMERICA. *Church Book for the Use of Evangelical Lutheran Congregations.* Philadelphia: Lutheran Book Store, 1868. 127+58+464 pp.

————. *Church Book, for the Use of Evangelical Lutheran Congregations.*
. . . With music, arranged . . . by Harriet R. Krauth. Philadelphia: J. K.
Schryock, 1893. 244+498 pp.

GENERAL SYNOD OF THE EVANGELICAL LUTHERAN CHURCH IN THE UNITED
STATES OF AMERICA. *Book of Worship, with Hymns.* Philadelphia: Lutheran Publication Society, 1899. 1008 pp.

*Geschichte der Auflösung der alten gottesdienstlichen Formen in der evan-
gelischen Kirche Deutschlands.* 2 vols. Göttingen: Vandenhoeck, 1937-39.
(Bd. I-2. Aufl.)

HERMANN V, VON WIED (ed.). *Von Gottes genadē unser Hermans/ Ertzbischoffs zu Cöln vñ Churfürstē einfältigs bedencken/ warauff/ ein
Christliche/ inn dem wort Gottes gegrünte Reformation/ an Lehr/
brauch der Heiligen Sacramenten und Ceremonien/ Seelsorge/ vnd anderem Kirchen dienst/ bis auff eines freyen Christlichenn/ Gemeinen/
oder Nationals Concili; oder des Reichs Teutscher Nation Stende/ im
Heiligen Geist versamlet/ verbesserung/ bei denen so vnserer Seelsorge
befolhenn/ auzurichten seye.* Bonn: Von der Mülen, 1544. CCXCIIII
leaves. (1st German edition, Bonn, 1543; Latin translation, Bonn, 1545;
English translation, *Simple and Religious Consultation.* . . . 2 vols. London: Daye, 1548.)

HEROLD, MAX. *Alt-Nürnberg in Seinen Gottesdiensten; ein Beitrag zur Geschichte der Sitte und des Kultus.* Gütersloh: Bertelsmann, 1890. 333 pp.

————. *Vesperale; Nachmittags- und Abendgottesdienste mit und ohne Chor.* 3 vols. in 2. Gütersloh: Bertelsmann, 1893-1907. (Vol. I, 3. aufl., 1907; Vol. II, 2. aufl., 1893.)

HÖFLING, JOHANN W. F. *Liturgisches Urkundenbuch enthaltend die Akte der Communion, der Ordination und Introduction, und der Trauung.* Herausgegeben von THOMASIUS und HARNACK. Leipzig: Teubner, 1854. 244 pp.

HORN, EDWARD TRAIL. "Liturgy," *Lutheran Cyclopedia* (1899), pp. 278-83).

————. "Luther on the Principles and Order of Christian Worship," *Lutheran Church Review,* X (1891), 217-56.

————. "The Lutheran Sources of the Common Service," *Lutheran Quarterly,* XXI (1891), 239-68.

JACOBS, HENRY EYSTER. *Memoirs.* (Manuscript in Krauth Memorial Library, Philadelphia.)

————. "Archbishop Hermann of Cologne and his Consultation." *Lutheran Church Review,* XI (1892), 301-44.

————. *A History of the Evangelical Lutheran Church in the United States.* New York: Christian Literature Co., 1893. 539 pp. ("American Church History Series," IV.) 2d ed. New York: Scribner, 1899).

————. "The Making of the Church Book." *Lutheran Church Review,* XXXI (1912), 597-622.

Kirchen-agende der Evangelisch-Lutherischen Vereinigten Gemeinen in Nord-America. Philadelphia: Steiner, 1786. 58 pp.

Kirchenagende, herausgegeben in Auftrage der liturgischen Ausschüsse von Rheinland und Westfalen u.s.w. von JOACHIM BECKMANN, PETER BRUNNER, HANS LUDWIG KUPP, und WALTER REINDELL. 3 vols. Gütersloh: C. Bertelsmann, 1948-57.

Kirchen-Ordnung für die Stadt Wittenberg. 1533.

Kirchen Ordnung im Churfürstenthum der Marcken zu Brandemburg/ wie man siche beide mit der Leer vnd Ceremonien halten sol. Berlin: Weis, 1540. unp.

Kirchen Ordnung/ in meiner gnedigen Herrn der Marggrauen zue Brandenburg/ vnd eins erbern Rats der Stat Nürmberg Oberkeyt vnd Gepieten/ wie man sich bayde mit der Leer vnd Ceremonien halten solle. [Nürmberg: Gutknecht] 1533. LVII leaves, [159] p.

Kirchenordnung, wie es inn des durchleuchtigen/ hochgebornen fürsten vnd herrn/ herren Wolffgangs/ pfaltzgrauen bey Rhein/ herzogen in Bayern/ grauens zu Veldentz vnnd Sponhaim rc fürstenthumben vnnd landen/ biss anhero mit der christlichen lehr/ raichung der heiligen sacramenten/ ordination der diener des euangelij/ vnd ordenlichen ceremonien/ erhaltung christlicher schulen vnd studien/ auch anderer der kirchen notwendigen stücken/ rc. gehalten worden . . . Nürmberg: Gerlatz, 1570. 16 p. +CLXXVIII+CXIX+5 leaves.

Kirchenordnung: Wie es mit christlicher Lere, Reichung der Sacrament, Ordination der Diener des Euangelii, ordenlichen Ceremonien in den Kirche, Visitation, Consistoria vnd Schulen im Hertzogthumb zu Meckelnburg etc. gehalten wird. Witteberg: [Lufft], 1552. 136 leaves.

Kirchen/ ordnunge zum anfang/ fur die Pfarherrn in Hertzog Heinrichs zu Sachsen. v.g.h. Furstenthumb. Wittemberg; Lufft, 1539. [43 pp.] (verm. Ausg. 1540, 1555, 1564.)

KLIEFOTH, THEODOR F. D. *Liturgische Abhandlungen.* 8 vols. Schwerin: Stiller, 1854-61.

―――――. *Theorie des Kultus der evangelischen Kirche.* Parchim: Hinstorff, 1844. 256 pp.

―――――. *Die ursprüngliche Gottesdienst-Ordnung in den deutschen Kirchen lutherischen Bekentnisses, ihre Destruction und Reformation.* 2. Aufl. Schwerin: Stiller, 1859-61. 5 vols. in 2. (liturgische Abhandlungen, Bd. IV-VIII.)

KRETZMANN, PAUL E. *Christian Art in the Place and in the Form of Lutheran Worship.* St. Louis: Concordia, 1921. 415 pp.

LOCHNER, FRIEDRICH. *Der Hauptgottesdienst der evangelisch-lutherischen Kirche.* St. Louis: Concordia, 1895. 294 pp.

LOEHE, WILHELM (ed.) *Agende für christliche Gemeinden des lutherischen Bekenntnisses.* Nördlingen: Beck, 1844. 252 pp. 3. Aufl., 2 vols. in 1, 1884. (English tr. *Liturgy for Christian Congregations of the Lutheran Faith* [Newport, Ky., 1902].)

LUTHER, MARTIN. *Briefwechsel;* begründet von ERNST LUDWIG ENDERS. 19 vols. Frankfort am Main: Evangel. Verein, 1884-1932.

―――――. *D. Martin Luthers Werke;* kritische gesammtausgabe. Weimar: Böhlau, 1883–. (86 vols. in 97 to date, plus index.)

―――――. *Works of Martin Luther,* ed. CHARLES M. JACOBS et al. 6 vols. Philadelphia: Holman, 1915-32.

The Lutheran Hymnal, authorized by the synods constituting the Evangelical Lutheran Synodical Conference of North America. St. Louis: Concordia, c1941. 852 pp.

The Lutheran Hymnary; see Norwegian Lutheran Church.

Memoirs of the Lutheran Liturgical Association, ed. LUTHER D. REED. 7 vols. in 1. Pittsburgh: The Association, 1906. (Out of print.)

MUHLENBERG, HEINRICH MELCHIOR. *The Journals of Henry Melchior Muhlenberg.* Translated by T. G. TAPPERT and JOHN W. DOBERSTEIN. 3 vols Philadelphia: Evangelical Lutheran Ministerium of Pa. and Muhlenberg Pr. 1942-58.

NORWEGIAN LUTHERAN CHURCH OF AMERICA (E.L.C.). *The Lutheran Hymnary; Including the Symbols of the Evangelical Lutheran Church* (rev. ed.). Minneapolis: Augsburg, c1935. 679 pp.

Officium Sacrum quod in Aede D. Sebaldi Norimbergensium primariā, singulis anni diebus exhiberi solet; cum Introitibus, Tractibus, Responsoriis & Antiphonis; accessit Ordo Officii Sacri, S. Aedi Laurentianae consuetus; cum hymnis Ecclesiasticis. Norimbergae: Michael Endter, 1664. 312 pp.

QUENSEL, OSCAR. *Bidrag till svenska liturgiens historia.* 2 vols. Uppsala: Lundequistska bokhandlung, 1890-93.

REED, LUTHER DOTTERER. "Historical Sketch of the Common Service," *Lutheran Church Review,* XXXVI (1917), 501-19.

―――――. "The Character and the Claims of the Church Book," *Lutheran Church Review,* XXVI (1907), 689-700.

————. "The Common Service in the Life of the Church," *Lutheran Church Quarterly*, XII (1939), 3-25.

————. "The Standard Manuscript of the Common Service, and Variata Editions," *Lutheran Church Review*, XX (1901), 459-73.

RENDTORFF, FRANZ M. *Die Geschichte des christlichen Gottesdienstes unter dem Gesichtspunkt der liturgischen Erbfolge.* Giessen: Töpelmann, 1914. 51 pp.

RICHARD, JAMES WILLIAM. "The Liturgical Question," *Lutheran Quarterly*, XX (1890), 103-85.

RICHTER, AEMILIUS L. (ed.). *Die evangelischen Kirchenordnungen des sechzehnten Jahrhunderts: Urkunden und Regesten zur Geschichte des Rechts und der Verfassung der evangelischen Kirche in Deutschland.* 2 vols. in 1. Weimar: Land-industriecomptoir, 1846. (2. Aufl. Leipzig: Günther, 1871.)

RIETSCHEL, GEORG. *Lehrbuch der Liturgik.* 2 vols. Berlin: Reuther, 1899-1908.

RODHE, EDVARD MAGNUS. *Svenskt gudstjänstliv. Historisk belysning av den svenska kyrkohandboken.* Stockholm: Diakonistyr, 1923. 513 pp.

The Sacraments. The Meeting of the Joint Theological Commission of the Church of South India and the Federation of Evangelical Lutheran Churches in India, 1955. Madras (Park Town): Christian Lit. Soc., 1956. 166 pp.

SCHMIEDER, PAUL H. C. "The Church Orders of the Sixteenth Century," *Lutheran Church Review*, XXXII (1913), 361-72; XXXVII (1918), 195-99, 450-56.

SCHMUCKER, BEALE M. "The First Pennsylvania Liturgy, Adopted in 1748," *Lutheran Church Review*, I (1882), 16-27, 161-72.

SEHLING, EMIL (ed.). *Die evangelischen Kirchenordnungen des XVI. Jahrhunderts.* I-V, Leipzig: Reisland, 1902-13. VI–, Tbingen: Mohr, 1955–.

SEISS, JOSEPH AUGUSTUS. Notes on My Life. 11 vols. (Unpublished manuscript, in Krauth Memorial Library, Philadelphia.)

Service Book and Hymnal of the Lutheran Church in America (Music ed.). Minneapolis (etc.): Augsburg (etc.), 1958. 1012 pp.

SMEND, JULIUS. *Der evangelische Gottesdienst. Ein Liturgik nach evangelischen Grundsätzen.* . . . Göttingen: Vandenhoeck, 1904. 203 pp.

————. *Die evangelischen deutschen Messen bis zu Luthers deutscher Messe.* Göttingen: Vandenhoeck, 1896. 283 pp.

SMITH, ROBERT MORRIS, *et al.* "Liturgical Development within the Evangelical Church in the United States." *Lutheran Church Review*, XXXVI (1917), 469-500.

SPAETH, ADOLPH. "History of the Liturgical Development of the Ministerium of Pennsylvania." *Lutheran Church Review*, XVII (1898), 93-119.

SPAETH, MRS. HARRIET REYNOLDS (Krauth) (ed.). *Church Book with Music, See* General Council, *Church Book* (1893).

The Standard Manuscript of the Common Service, with minutes of the Joint Committee, 1884-88, and comments by Edward T. Horn, secretary. Ms., 1889. (In Krauth Memorial Library, Philadelphia.)

STRODACH, PAUL ZELLER. *A Manual on Worship: Venite adoremus.* Philadelphia: U.L.P.H., c1930. 237 pp. (Rev. ed., 1946. 379 pp.).

UNITED LUTHERAN CHURCH IN AMERICA. *Common Service Book of the Lutheran Church.* Philadelphia: The Board of Publication of the United Lutheran Church in America, 1919. 495 pp. (1st ed., 1917; music ed., 1918, 310+631 pp.)

————. *Collects and Prayers for Use in Church.* Philadelphia: The Board of Publication of the United Lutheran Church in America, 1935. 265 pp.

————. *The Occasional Services, from the Common Service Book of the Lutheran Church.* Philadelphia: The Board of Publication of the United Lutheran Church in America, 1918. 99 pp.

UNITED SYNOD OF THE EVANGELICAL LUTHERAN CHURCH IN THE SOUTH. *The Book of Worship.* Columbia, S. C.: W. J. Duffie, 1888. 326+229 to 574 pp. (Contains the standard text of the Common Service.)

VARRENTRAPP, CONRAD. *Hermann von Wied und sein Reformationsversuch in Köln,* 2 vols. in 1. Leipzig: Duncker, 1878.

WADDAMS, HERBERT M. *The Swedish Church.* London: S.P.C.K., 1946. 70 pp.

WENNER, GEORGE U. "An Answer to the Liturgical Question," *Lutheran Quarterly,* XX (1890), 299-342.

WENTZ, ABDEL ROSS. *A Basic History of Lutheranism in America.* Philadelphia: Muhlenberg, 1955. 430 pp.

WORDSWORTH, JOHN. *The National Church of Sweden.* Milwaukee: Young Churchman Co., 1911. 459 pp.

YELVERTON, ERIC E. (ed. and tr.). *The Mass in Sweden. Its Development from the Latin Rite from 1531 to 1917.* London: Harrison, 1920. 189 pp.

————. (ed.). *The Swedish Rite; a translation of "Handbok för Svenska Kyrkan."* New York: Macmillan, 1921. 159 pp.

————. *An Archbishop of the Reformation.* London: Epworth, 1958. 154 pp.

d. Anglican

ADDLESHAW, GEORGE W. O. *The High Church Tradition; a Study in the Liturgical Thought of the Seventeenth Century.* London: Faber, 1941. 204 pp.

ARMITAGE, WILLIAM J. *The Story of the Canadian Revision of the Prayer Book.* Cambridge: The Univ Pr., 1922. 442 pp.

BLUNT, JOHN H. *The Annotated Book of Common Prayer. See* Church of England.

BRIGHTMAN, FRANK E. *The English Rite. Being a Synopsis of the Sources and Revisions of the Book of Common Prayer with an Introduction and an Appendix.* 2 vols. London: Rivingtons, 1915.

BRILIOTH, YNGVE. *The Anglican Revival, Studies in the Oxford Movement.* New York: Longmans, 1925. 357 pp.

CHURCH, RICHARD W. *The Oxford Movement, Twelve Years, 1833-1845.* 3d ed. New York: Macmillan, 1904. 416 pp.

CHURCH OF ENGLAND. *The Annotated Book of Common Prayer, Forming a Concise Commentary on the Devotional System of the Church of England,* ed. JOHN HENRY BLUNT. Rev. and enl. ed. New York: Dutton, 1899. 732 pp.

————. *The Book of Common Prayer and Administration of the Sacrament & other Rites and Ceremonies of the Church, According to the Use of the Church of England, Together with the Form and Manner of Making, Ordaining, and Consecrating of Bishops, Priests, and Deacons; the Book of 1662 with Additions & Deviations Approved in 1927.* London: Eyre and Spottiswoode, 1927. 447 pp.

————. *The Book of Common Prayer with the Additions and Deviations Proposed in 1928.* London: Oxford Univ. Pr., 1928. 506 pp. (Another ed., S.P.C.K., 699 pp.)

————. *The First Prayer Book of King Edward VI.* London: De La More, 1903. 372 pp. (Reprint of the edition of Whitechurch, March, 1549.)

————. LITURGICAL COMMISSION. *Prayer Book Revision in the Church of England.* London: S.P.C.K., 1917. 55 pp.

CHURCH OF INDIA, PAKISTAN, BURMA, AND CEYLON. *Principles of Prayer Book Revision; the Report of a Select Committee of the Church of India, Pakistan, Burma and Ceylon.* London: S.P.C.K., 1957. 105 pp.

CLARKE, WILLIAM KEMP LOWTHER, and CHARLES HARRIS (eds.). *Liturgy and Worship; a Companion to the Prayer Books of the Anglican Communion.* New York: Macmillan, 1932. 868 pp.

————. *The Prayer Book of 1928 Reconsidered.* London: S.P.C.K., 1943. 87 pp.

DEARMER, PERCY. *Everyman's History of the Prayer Book.* New American ed. Milwaukee: Morehouse, 1931. 268 pp.

————. *The Parson's Handbook.* New York: Oxford, 1931. 496 pp. (First publ. 1899.)

————. *The Story of the Prayer Book in the Old and New World and Throughout the Anglican Church.* London: Oxford Univ. Pr., 1933. 269 pp.

DIX, GREGORY. *The Shape of the Liturgy.* London: Dacre, 1945. 764 pp.

DOWDEN, JOHN. *Further Studies in the Prayer Book.* London: Methuen, 1908. 362 pp.

————. *The Workmanship of the Prayer Book in Its Literary and Liturgical Aspects.* 2d ed., rev. and enl. London: Methuen, 1902. 270 pp.

EPISCOPAL CHURCH IN SCOTLAND. *The Scottish Book of Common Prayer, and Administration of the Sacraments and Other Rites and Ceremonies of the Church. . . .* Edinburgh: Cambridge Univ. Pr., 1929. 406 pp.

GARRETT, THOMAS S. *Worship in the Church of South India.* Richmond: John Knox Pr., 1958. 62 pp.

GASQUET, FRANCIS A., and EDMUND BISHOP. *Edward VI and the Book of Common Prayer. An Examination into its Origin and Early History with an Appendix of Unpublished Documents.* 2d ed. London: Hodges, 1891. 466 pp.

GRISBROOKE, WILLIAM JARDINE. *Anglican Liturgies of the Seventeenth and Eighteenth Centuries.* London: S.P.C.K., 1958. 390 pp.

HARFORD, G., M. STEVENSON and J. W. TYRER (eds.). *The Prayer Book Dictionary.* New York: Pitman, 1925. 832 pp. (First issued 1912.)

HERBERT, ARTHUR G. (ed.). *The Parish Communion, a Book of Essays.* New York: Macmillan, 1937. 311 pp.

787

JACOBS, HENRY E. *The Lutheran Movement in England During the Reigns of Henry VIII and Edward VI, and its Literary Monuments.* Rev. ed. Philadelphia: Frederick, 1892. 376 pp.

JONES, BAYARD HALE (ed.). *Prayer Book Studies by the Standing Liturgical Commission of the Protestant Episcopal Church.* New York: Church Pension Fund, 1950—. Parts I-XI to date.

LADD, WILLIAM PALMER. *Prayer Book Interleaves.* Greenwich, Conn.: Seabury, 1957. 188 pp. (First publ. 1942.)

LOWRIE, WALTER. *Action in the Liturgy, Essential and Unessential.* New York: Philosophical Library, 1953. 303 pp.

————. *The Lord's Supper and the Liturgy.* New York: Longmans, 1943. 184 pp.

MAXWELL, WILLIAM D. *The Book of Common Prayer and the Worship of the Non-Anglican Churches.* London: Oxford Univ. Pr., 1950. 36 pp.

MORISON, STANLEY. *English Prayer Books; an Introduction to the Literature of Christian Public Worship.* Cambridge: The Univ. Pr., 1943. 143 pp.

MUSS-ARNOLT, WILLIAM. *The Book of Common Prayer Among the Nations of the World, a History of the Translations of the Prayer Book of the Church of England and of the Protestant Episcopal Church of America.* New York: Gorham, 1914. 473 pp.

NEIL, CHARLES, and J. M. WILLOUGHBY (eds.). *The Tutorial Prayer Book.* London: Harrison Trust, 1913. 669 pp.

PALMER, WILLIAM. *Origines liturgicae, or Antiquities of the English Ritual, and a Dissertation on Primitive Liturgies.* 2 vols. 4th ed. London: Rivingtons, 1845.

PARSONS, EDWARD L., and BAYARD H. JONES. *The American Prayer Book; its Orgins and Principles.* New York: Scribner, 1937. 340 pp.

PERRY, WILLIAM. *The Scottish Prayer Book; its Value and History.* Cambridge: The Univ. Pr., 1929. 142 pp.

PROCTER, FRANCIS, and W. H. FRERE (eds.) *A New History of the Book of Common Prayer, with a Rationale of its Offices;* revised and rewritten. New York: Macmillan, 1902. 699 pp. (First ed. 1855.)

PROTESTANT EPISCOPAL CHURCH IN THE U.S.A. *The Book of Common Prayer and Other Rites and Ceremonies of the Church According to the Use of the Protestant Episcopal Church in the United States of America: Together with the Psalter or Psalms of David.* Printed for the Commission, 1928. Boston: Merrymount, 1930. 611 pp. (Other editions by Harper, Oxford, etc.)

PULLAN, LEIGHTON. *The History of the Book of Common Prayer.* 3d ed. New York: Longmans, 1909. 330 pp. (Later issue, 1929.)

SHEPHERD, MASSEY HAMILTON, JR. *The Living Liturgy.* New York: Oxford, 1946. 139 pp.

————. *The Oxford American Prayer Book Commentary.* New York: Oxford, 1951. 611 pp.

STONE, DARWELL (ed.). *The Deposited Prayer Book,* by a group of priests. London: Allan, 1927. 152 pp.

WHEATLEY, CHARLES. *A Rational Illustration of the Book of Common Prayer of the Church of England: Being the Substance of Every Thing Liturgical in Bishop Sparrow, Mr. L'Estrange, Dr. Comber, Dr. Nichols, and All*

Former Ritualists, Commentators, and Others, Upon the Same Subject.
London: Bell, 1890. 532 pp. (First ed. 1710.)

e. Presbyterian

CHURCH OF SCOTLAND. *The Book of Common Order of the Church of Scotland;* by authority of the General Assembly. New York: Oxford, 1940. 338 pp.

KNOX, JOHN. *John Knox's Genevan Service Book, 1556. The Liturgical Portions of the Genevan Service Book Used by John Knox while a Minister of the English Congregation of Marian Exiles at Geneva, 1556-1559,* ed. WILLIAM D. MAXWELL. London: Oliver, 1931. 222 pp.

MAXWELL, WILLIAM D. *A History of Worship in the Church of Scotland.* New York: Oxford, 1955. 190 pp.

MCMILLAN, WILLIAM. *The Worship of the Scottish Reformed Church, 1550-1638.* London: Clarke, 1931. 383 pp.

PRESBYTERIAN CHURCH IN THE U.S.A. *The Book of Common Worship.* [Ed. HENRY VAN DYKE.] Philadelphia: Presbyterian Board of Publication and Sabbath School Work, 1906. 263 pp. (Rev. ed. 1932.)

_____. *The Book of Common Worship.* Philadelphia: Publication Division of the Board of Christian Education of the Presbyterian Church in the U.S.A., 1946. 388 pp.

3. SPECIAL STUDIES

ADAMS, HENRY. *Mont-Saint-Michel and Chartres.* Boston: Houghton, c1904; pub. 1913; re-issue 1936. 397 pp.

ALT, HEINRICH. *Das Kirchenjahr des christlichen Morgen- und Abendlandes, mit seinen Festen, Fasten und Bibellectionen historisch dargestellt.* ("Der Christliche Cultus . . ." II.) Berlin: Müller, 1860. 570 pp.

ALTHAUS, PAUL. *Zur Einführung in die Quellengeschichte der kirchlichen Kollekten in den lutherischen Agenden des 16. Jahrhunderts.* Leipzig: Edelmann, 1919. 74 pp.

ATCHLEY, EDWARD G. C. F. *On the Epiclesis of the Eucharistic Liturgy and in the Consecration of the Font.* London: Milford, 1935. 210 pp.

BEISSEL, STEPHAN. *Entstehung der Perikopen des römischen Messbuches. Zur Geschichte der Evangelienbücher in der ersten Hälfte des Mittelalters.* St. Louis: Herder, 1907. 220 pp.

BLOMFIELD, JOHN. *The Eucharistic Canon.* London: S.P.C.K., 1930. 183 pp.

BRIGHT, WILLIAM (comp.). *Ancient Collects and other Prayers Selected for Devotional Use from Various Rituals.* 4th ed. London: Parker, 1869. 238 pp. (First ed., 1859; later issue, 1887.)

_____. "On the Collects," *Prayer Book Commentary* (q. v.), pp. 83-96.

BROWN, WILLIAM ADAMS. *The Life of Prayer in a World of Science.* New York: Scribner, 1927. 194 pp.

DRURY, T. W. *Elevation in the Eucharist: Its History and Rationale.* Cambridge: The Univ. Pr., 1907. 204 pp.

DUGMORE, CLIFFORD W. *The Influence of the Synagogue upon the Divine Office.* London: Oxford Univ. Pr., 1944. 151 pp.

EASTON, BURTON SCOTT and H. C. ROBBINS. *The Eternal Word in the Modern World; Expository Preaching on the Gospels and Epistles for the Church Year.* New York: Scribner, 1937. 321 pp.

FENDT, LEONHARD. *Die alten Perikopen, für die theologische Praxis erläutert.* Tübingen: Mohr, 1931. 232 pp.

FRERE, WALTER HOWARD. *The Anaphora; or, Great Eucharistic Prayer; an Eirenical Study in Liturgical History.* New York: Macmillan, 1938. 212 pp.

GORE, CHARLES. *Reflections on the Litany.* 2 vols. Milwaukee: Morehouse, 1932.

GOULBURN, EDWARD M. *The Collects of the Day.* 2 vols. New ed. New York: Young, 1892.

GRISAR, HARTMANN. *Das Missale im Lichte römischer Stadtgeschichte; Stationen, Perikopen, Gebräuche.* Freiburg: Herder, 1925. 120 pp.

GUMMEY, HENRY R., JR. *The Consecration of the Eucharist; a Study of the Prayer of Consecration in the Communion Office from the Point of View of the Alterations and Amendments Established Therein by the Revisers of 1789.* Philadelphia: Anners, 1908. 459 pp.

HEADLAM, A. C., and RODERIC DUNKERLEY (eds.). *The Ministry and the Sacraments.* A publication of the Faith and Order Movement. London: S.C.M. Pr., 1937. 560 pp.

HERERT, ARTHUR G. *The Meaning of the Epiclesis.* London: S.P.C.K., 1933. 15 pp.

HORN, EDWARD TRAILL. *The Christian Year.* Philadelphia: The Lutheran Book Store, 1876. 95 pp.

————. "The Significance of Liturgical Reform," *Memoirs of the Lutheran Liturgical Association,* I, 19-39.

HORN, EDWARD TRAILL, III. *Altar and Pew: The Devotional Life of the Pastor and his People.* Philadelphia: Muhlenberg, 1951. 111 pp.

————. *The Christian Year.* Philadelphia: Muhlenberg, 1957. 243 pp.

HUBERT, FRIEDRICH. *Die Strassburger liturgischen Ordnungen im Zitalter der Reformation, nebst einer Bibliographie der Strassburger Gesangbücher.* Göttingen: Vandenhoeck, 1900. lxxxiv+154 pp.

KRETZMANN, PAUL E. *The Liturgical Element in the Earliest Forms of the Medieval Drama, with Special Reference to the English and German Plays.* Minneapolis: Univ. of Minnesota, 1916. 170 pp.

KUNZE, GERHARD. *Die gottesdienstliche Schriftlesung.* (Veröffentlichungen der evangelischen Gesellschaft für Liturgieforschung," I.) Göttingen: Vandenhoeck, 1947. I. Stand und Aufgaben der Perikopenforschung. 224 pp.

LINTON, ARTHUR (ed.). *Twenty-five Consecration Prayers, with Notes and Introduction.* New York: Macmillan, 1921. 145 pp.

MALE, EMILE. *Religious Art in France, XIII Century; a Study in Mediaeval Iconography and its Sources of Inspiration.* Translated, revised and enlarged by Dora Nussey from the 3d ed. New York: Dutton, 1913. 415 pp.

MILNER-WHITE, ERIC. *After the Third Collect.* 4th ed. London: Mowbray, 1952. 141 pp.

————. *A Cambridge Bede Book.* New York: Longmans, 1936. 143 pp.

_____, and GEORGE WALLACE BRIGGS. *Daily Prayer.* London: Oxford Univ. Pr., 1941. 188 pp.

MUETHEL, JULIUS. *Ein wunder Punkt in der lutherischen Liturgie.* Leipzig: Hartmann, 1895. 140 pp.

_____. *Nochmals Sätze über unser lutherische Consecrations-Liturgie im Abendmahls-Akte.* Leipzig: Deicher, 1896. 108 pp.

NEBE, AUGUST. *Die evangelischen und epistolischen Perikopen des Kirchenjahres* . . . · 6 vols. 2. aufl. Philadelphia: Schaefer, 1874-76.

RITSCHL, ALBRECHT B. *Geschichte des Pietismus.* 3 vols. Bonn: Marcus, 1880-86.

SACHSSE, EUGEN. *Ursprung und Wesen des Pietismus* . . . . Philadelphia: Schäfer, 1884. 382 pp.

SHORT, ERNEST H. *The House of God; a History of Religious Architecture and Symbolism.* New York: Macmillan, 1926. 342 pp. Also new and revised edition entitled: *A History of Religious Architecture.* New York: Macmillan, 1936. 304 pp.

STONE, DARWELL. *A History of the Doctrine of the Holy Eucharist.* 2 vols. New York: Longmans, 1909.

STRODACH, PAUL ZELLER. *The Church Year; Studies in the Introits, Collects, Epistles and Gospels.* Philadelphia: U.L.P.H., 1924. 265 pp.

_____. "The Collect: a Study," *Lutheran Church Review,* XLIV (1925), 34-42.

_____. *The Collect for the Day.* Philadelphia: U.L.P.H., c1939. 263 pp.

_____. "The Collects in the Church Book," *Lutheran Church Review,* XXXV (1916), 401-25; XXXVI (1917), 105-36.

_____. "The Collects in the Common Service Book," *Lutheran Church Review,* XL (1921), 57-74, 242-66.

_____. *Oremus: Collects, Devotions, Litanies, from Ancient and Modern Sources.* Philadelphia: U.L.P.H., 1925. 213 pp.

TYRER, JOHN W. *The Eucharistic Epiclesis.* New York: Longmans, 1917. 72 pp.

UNDERHILL, EVELYN. *Eucharistic Prayers from the Ancient Liturgies.* New York: Longmans, 1939. 127 pp.

VAJTA, VILMOS. *Die Theologie des Gottesdienstes bei Luther.* Stockholm: Diakonistyr, 1952. 375 pp. English trans. *Luther on Worship, an Interpretation.* Translated and condensed by U. S. LEUPOLD. Philadelphia: Muhlenberg, 1958. 200 pp.

VOGT, VON OGDEN. *Art and Religion.* New Haven: Yale Univ. Pr., 1921. 265 pp.

WEBBER, FREDERICK R. *The Small Church; How to Build and Furnish it, with some Account of the Improvement of Existing Buildings.* Rev. ed. Cleveland, O.: Jansen, 1939. 324 pp.

II. LITURGICAL MUSIC

1. GENERAL WORKS

AUDSLEY, GEORGE A. *The Art of Organ-Building.* 2 vols. New York: Dodd, 1905.

BARNES, WILLIAM HARRISON. *The Contemporary American Organ, its Evo-*

lution, Design and Construction. 3d ed. New York: Fischer, 1937. 366 pp.

DAVIES, HENRY WALFORD, and HARVEY GRACE. *Music and Worship.* New York: Gray, 1935. 255 pp.

DAVISON, ARCHIBALD T. *Protestant Church Music in America.* Boston: Schirmer, c1933. 182 pp.

DICKINSON, EDWARD. *Music in the History of the Western Church.* New York: Scribner, 1902. 426 pp.

DOUGLAS, CHARLES WINFRED. *Church Music in History and Practice; Studies in the Praise of God.* New York: Scribner, 1937. 311 pp.

ELLINWOOD, LEONARD W. *The History of American Church Music.* New York: Morehouse-Gorham, 1953. 274 pp.

GROVE, GEORGE (ed.). *Grove's Dictionary of Music and Musicians.* 9 vols. 5th ed. edited by ERIC BLOM. New York: St. Martin's, 1954.

KUMMERLE, SALOMON. *Encyklopädie der evangelischen Kirchenmusick.* 4 vols. Gütersloh: Bertelsmann, 1888-95.

LUTKIN, PETER CHRISTIAN. *Music in the Church.* Milwaukee: Young Churchman Co., 1910. 274 pp.

MOSER, HANS JOACHIM. *Die evangelische Kirchenmusik in Deutschland.* 12 vols. in 8. Berlin: Merseburger, 1953-54. 545 pp.

New Oxford History of Music. New York: Oxford, 1954–. 2 vols. to date.

NICHOLSON, SYDNEY H. *Quires and Places Where They Sing.* London: Bell, 1932. 280 pp.

The Oxford History of Music. 8 vols. Oxford: Clarendon, 1901-34.

PRATT, WALDO SELDEN. *The History of Music.* Rev. ed. New York: Schirmer, 1935. 713+36 pp.

REED, LUTHER DOTTERER. *Worship: A Study of Corporate Devotion.* Philadelphia: Muhlenberg, 1959. 437 pp.

ROUTLEY, ERIK. *The Church and Music; an Enquiry into the History, the Nature and the Scope of Christian Judgment on Music.* London: Duckworth, 1950. 255 pp.

SCEATS, GODFREY. *The Liturgical Use of the Organ.* London: "Musical Opinion," 1922. 47 pp.

SCHOLES, PERCY A. *The Oxford Companion to Music. . . .* 9th ed. New York: Oxford, 1955. 1195 pp.

SKINNER, ERNEST M. *The Modern Organ.* New York: Gray, c1917. 48 pp.

WIBBERLEY, BRIAN. *Music and Religion, a Historical and Philosophical Survey.* London: Epworth, 1934. 317 pp.

2. OFFICE BOOKS, COLLECTIONS, COMMENT, ETC.

a. Roman

Graduale sacrosanctae romanae ecclesiae de tempore et de sanctis SS. D. N. Pii X. pontificis maximi. Iussu restitutum et ed. ad exemplar editionis typicae concinnatum et rhythmicis signis a Solesmensibus monachis. Paris: Desclée, 1956. Various pagings.

A Grammar of Plainsong, by a Benedictine of Stanbrook. 2d ed. Worcester: Stanbrook Abbey, 1926. 128 pp.

HABERL, FRANZ XAVER. *Magister Choralis; A Theoretical and Practical*

Manual of Gregorian Chant for the Use of the Clergy, Seminarists, Organists, Choir-Masters, Choristers, &c. 2d [English] ed. Translated by Most Rev. Dr. DONNELLY from 9th German ed. New York: Pustet, 1892. 212 pp.

HUME, PAUL. *Catholic Church Music.* New York: Dodd, Mead, 1956. 259 pp.

JOHNER, DOMINICUS. *A New School of Gregorian Chant;* 3d English ed. based on 5th German ed. by HERMANN ERPF and MAX FERRARS. New York: Pustet, 1925. 363 pp.

_____. *The Chants of the Vatican Gradual.* Translated by monks of St. John's Abbey. Collegeville (Minn.): St. John's Abbey Pr., 1940. 500 pp.

The Liber Usualis, with introduction and rubrics in English. eds. the Benedictines of Solesmes. Tournai (Belgium): Society of St. John the Evangelist. Desclée & Co., 1952. 121+45 pp.

TERRY, SIR RICHARD RUNCIMAN. *The Music of the Roman Rite, a Manual for Choirmasters in English-Speaking Countries.* London: Burns, 1931. 293 pp.

b. Lutheran

ARCHER, HARRY G., and LUTHER D. REED (eds.) *The Choral Service Book; Containing the Authentic Plain Song Intonations and Responses . . . of the Common Service . . .*2d ed. Philadelphia: General Council Publication Board, 1901 (Out of print).

_____. *The Psalter and Canticles Pointed for Chanting to the Gregorian Psalm Tones.* New York: Christian Literature Co., 1897; Philadelphia: General Council Publication Board, 1901. 450 pp. (out of print).

BACHMANN, FRANZ. *Grundlagen und Grundfragen zur evangelischen Kirchenmusik.* Gütersloh: Bertelsmann, 1899. 186 pp.

Cantionale für die evangelisch-lutherischen Kirchen im Grossherzogthum Mecklenburg-Schwerin. 2 vols. in 4. Schwerin: Sandmeyer, 1868-87.

CHRISTENSEN, ALBERT O. and H. E. SCHUNEMAN. *The Proper of the Service.* New York: Gray, 1947. 56 pp.

ELER, FRANZ. *Cantica sacra, partim ex sacris literis desumta, partim ab orthodoxis patribus, et piis ecclesiae doctoribus composita, et in usum ecclesiae et iuventutis scholasticae Hamburgensis collecta, atque ad durodecim modos ex doctrina Glareani accomodata et edita.* (Second part has title: *Psalmi D. Martini Lutheri et aliorum ejus saeculi Psalmistarum, itidem modis applicati.*) Hamburg: Wolff, 1588. CCLXII leaves.

Libellus continens antiphona, responsoria, introitus, sequent . hymnos, versicul . et officia missae, germanicae, quae ad singulas dominicas et festa praecipua, ac vigilias eorundem in ecclesia Onoltzbacensi et Heilsbronnensi decantatur. Noribergae: Sartorii, 1627. 237 leaves.

LIEMOHN, EDWIN. *The Chorale Through Four Hundred Years of Musical Development as a Congregational Hymn.* Philadelphia: Muhlenberg, 1953. 170 pp.

LILIENCRON, ROCHUS W.T.H.F. *Chorordnung für die Sonn- und Festtage des evangelischen Kirchenjahres.* Gütersloh: Bertelsmann, 1900. 264 pp.

_____. *Liturgisch-musikalische Geschichte der evangelischen Gottesdienste vom 1523 bis 1700.* Schleswig: Bergas, 1893. 171 pp.

LINDEMANN, HERBERT F. *The Psalter of the Authorized Version of the Scriptures; set to the Gregorian Psalm Tones and supplied with Proper Antiphons.* Minneapolis: Augsburg, 1940. 201 pp.

LOSSIUS, LUCAS. *Psalmodia; hoc est, Cantica Sacra Veteris Ecclesiae Selecta. Quo ordine, & Melodiis per totius anni curriculum cantati visitate solent in templis* . . . Cum Praefatione Philippi Melanchthonis. Noribergae: Hayn: 1553. (Also pub. 1561, 1569, 1579, 1595.)

LYRA, JUSTUS W. D. M. *Luthers Deutsche Messe und Ordnung des Gottesdienstes in ihren liturgischen und musikalischen Bestandteilen nach der Wittenberger Original—Ausgabe von 1526 erlautert aus dem System des Gregorianischen Gesanges.* Herausgegeben von MAX HEROLD. Gütersloh: Bertelsmann, 1904. 192 pp.

MATTHEWS, HARRY ALEXANDER (composer). *The Introits and Graduals of the Church Year;* introduction by Luther D. Reed. 2 vols. Philadelphia: U.L.P.H., 1924-26.

Musiken till svenska mässan stadfäst af Konungen 1897. Högmässan och litianian. Lund: Gleerup, 1898, 140 pp.

NETTL, PAUL. *Luther and Music.* Translated by FRIDA BEST and RALPH WOOD. Philadelphia: Muhlenberg, 1948. 174 pp.

OHL, JEREMIAH F. (ed.). *School and Parish Hymnal with Tunes; School and Parish Service-Book with Music.* 2 vols. in 1. Philadelphia: Frederick, 1892.

PARRY, CHARLES H. H. *Johann Sebastian Bach; the Story of the Development of a Great Personality.* Rev. ed. New York: Putnam, 1934. 584 pp.

PREUSS, HANS. *Martin Luther, der Künstler.* Gutersloh: Bertelsmann, 1931. 319 pp.

RIETSCHEL, CHRISTIAN GEORG. *Die aufgabe der Orgel im Gottesdienste bis in das 18. Jahrhundert geschichtlich dargelegt.* Leipzig: Dürr, 1893. 72 pp.

SCHOEBERLEIN, LUDWIG. *Schatz des liturgischen Chor- und Gemeindegesangs nebst den Altarweisen in der deutschen evangelischen Kirche; aus den Quellen vornehmlich des 16. and 17. Jahrhunderts geschöpft mit den nöthigen geschichtlichen und praktischen Erläuterungen versehen und unter den musikalischen Redaktion von Friedrich Riegel . . . für den Gebrauch in Stadt- und Landkirchen hrsg.* 2 vols. in 3. Göttingen: Vandenhoeck, 1865-72.

SCHREMS, THEOBALD. *Die Geschichte des Gregorianischen Gesanges in den protestantischen Gottesdiensten.* Freiburg (Schweiz): St. Paulus, 1930. 163 pp.

SCHWEITZER, ALBERT. *J. S. Bach.* Translated by Ernest Newman. 2 vols. New York: Breitkopf, 1911.

SEISS, JOSEPH A., and C. P. ENGELMANN. *Church Song.* 2d ed. 2 pts. in 1. Philadelphia: Lutheran Book Store, 1875; General Council Publication Board, 1898, 1917.

Service Book and Hymnal of the Lutheran Church in America. Authorized by the churches co-operating in the Commission on the Liturgy and the Commission on the Hymnal. Music ed. Minneapolis (etc.): Augsburg (etc.), 1958. 1012 pp.

SPANGENBERG, JOHANN (ed.). *Cantiones ecclesiasticae Latinae, dominicis et festis diebus, in commemoratione Cenae Domini, per totius anni circulum cantandae, Per I. Spangenbergum . . . collectae & in ordinem redactae . . . Kirchengesenge Deutsch, auff die Sontage und fürnemliche Feste, durchs ganze Jar, auffs kurtzest durch J. Spangenberg verfasset.* Magdeburg: Lotther, 1545. CLX+CXCIX Leaves.

TERRY, CHARLES S. *Bach; a Biography.* London: Oxford Univ. Pr. 1928. 292 pp.+76 pl.

————. *Bach's Chorals.* 3 vols. Cambridge: The Univ. Pr., 1915-21.

ZAHN, JOHANNES. *Die Melodien der deutschen evangelischen Kirchenlieder, aus den Quellen geschöpft und mitgeteilt.* 6 vols. Gütersloh: Bertelsmann, 1889-93.

For other musical settings to Lutheran liturgies and hymnals in the United States, see texts noted above under I: 2c (pp. 781-86).

c. Anglican

BROWN, RAY F. (ed.). *The Oxford American Psalter; the Psalms and Canticles According to the Use of the Protestant Episcopal Church in the United States of America; Pointed and Set to Anglican Chants.* New York: Oxford, 1949. 242 pp.

BUMPUS, JOHN S. *A History of English Cathedral Music, 1549-1889.* 2 vols. New York: Pott, 1908.

CHURCH OF ENGLAND: ARCHBISHOPS' COMMITTEE ON MUSIC IN WORSHIP. *Report.* London: S.P.C.K., n.d 55 pp.

GARDINER, GEORGE L. H., and SYDNEY H. NICHOLSON (eds.). *A Manual of English Church Music.* New York: Macmillan, 1923. 232 pp. (Reprint, 1936. 247 pp.)

JEBB, JOHN. *The Choral Responses and Litanies of the United Church of England and Ireland.* 2 vols. London: Bell, 1847-57.

MARBECK, JOHN (ed.). *The Booke of Common Praier Noted.* London: Grafton, 1550. [68] leaves. (Reprinted by Novello, 1845.)

PROTESTANT EPISCOPAL CHURCH IN THE U.S.A. *The American Psalter; the Psalms and Canticles According to the Use of the Protestant Episcopal Church, pointed and set to Anglican Chants, Together with the Choral Service.* New York: Gray, 1930. 256 pp.

3. HYMNODY

BENSON, LOUIS F. *The English Hymn; its Development and Use in Worship.* Philadelphia: Presbyterian Board of Publication; New York: Doran, 1915. 624 pp.

BIRD, FREDERIC M. "Lutheran Hymnology." *Evangelical Quarterly Review,* XVI (1865), 23-46, 193-225, 218-51.

DEARMER, PERCY (comp.). *Songs of Praise Discussed; a Handbook to the Best-Known Hymns and to Others Recently Introduced;* with notes on the music by ARCHIBALD JACOB. New York. Oxford, 1933. 560 pp. (Companion volume to his *Songs of Praise.*)

HAEUSSLER, ARMIN. *The Story of our Hymns; the Handbook to the Hymnal of the Evangelical and Reformed Church.* St. Louis: Eden Publishing House, 1952. 1088 pp.

Hymns Ancient and Modern for Use in the Services of the Church, with Accompanying Tunes. Historical edition with notes on the origin of both hymns and tunes and a general historical introduction. . . . London: Clowes, 1909. 911 pp. (First ed., 1861; latest, 1950.)

Jahrbuch für Liturgik und Hymnologie. Herausgegeben von KONRAD AMEIN, CHRISTARD MAHRENHOLZ, KARL FERDININD MULLER. Vol. I–. Kassel: J. Stauda, 1955–.

JULIAN, JOHN. *A Dictionary of Hymnology.* . . . 2 vols. New York: Dover, 1957. 1768 pp. (Re-issue of the revision of 1925.)

MCCUTCHAN, ROBERT GUY. *Hymn Tune Names: their Sources and Significance.* Nashville: Abingdon, 1957. 206 pp.

MESSENGER, RUTH ELLIS. *The Medieval Latin Hymn.* Washington: Capital, 1953. 138 pp.

NELLE, WILHELM. *Unsere Kirchenliederdichter; Lebens- und Charakterbilder.* Hamburg: Schloessmann, 1905. 654 pp.

PARRY, KENNETH L. (ed.). *Companion to Congregational Praise.* With notes on the music by ERIK ROUTLEY. London: Independent Pr. 1953. 580 pp.

PATRICK, MILLAR. *Four Centuries of Scottish Psalmody.* New York: Oxford, 1949. 234 pp.

POCKNEE, CYRIL E. *The French Diocesan Hymns and their Melodies.* New York: Morehouse-Gorman, 1954. 162 pp.

PROTESTANT EPISCOPAL CHURCH IN THE U.S.A. *The Hymnal 1940 Companion.* New York: Church Pension Fund, 1949. 732 pp. (Another ed. 1951.)

RABY, FREDERICK J. E. *A History of Christian-Latin Poetry, from the Beginnings to the Close of the Middle Ages.* Oxford: Clarendon, 1927. 491 pp.

REED, LUTHER DOTTERER· *Luther and Congregational Song.* ("Papers of the Hymn Society of America," No. 12.) New York: Hymn Society of America, 1947.

RYDEN, ERNEST EDWIN. *The Story of Christian Hymnody.* Rock Island: Augustana Pr., 1959. 670 pp.

INDEX

COMPILED BY WILLIAM S. AVERY

797

parative forms, 652ff.
Billing, Einar, 124, 230
Bilney, Thomas, 133
Bingham, Joseph, 374
Bird, Frederick M., 173, 178, 180
Bishop, 32, 39
Bishop, Edmund, 32, 39, 56, 80, 130, 135, 270, 279, 339, 360, 382, 421, 443, 626
Bishop's Book of 1537, 134
Björkquist, Manfred, 124
Blackwelder, Oscar, 206
Blessing: of the font, 505; of the new fire, 505; of the palms, 452, 498; of the paschal candle, 505
Blunt, John, H., 286, 631-32
Boeckh church order, C. F. von, 153
Bogatsky, Karl von, 145
Bohemian Brethren, 272
Böhme, Jacob, 143
Bona, cardinal, 280, 340, 370, 376
Boniface IV, pope, 51, 571
Book of Common Order: of Canada, 607; of Scotland, 214, 335, 357, 362, 583, 593-94, 662, 757
Book of Common Prayer, xi, 4, 56, 75, 85, 97, 123, 128ff., 132, 137ff., 155, 168, 193, 195, 214, 236, 291, 318-19, 328, 343ff., 360, 381, 392, 395, 401, 405, 411, 433, 449, 455, 577, 598, 603, 606, 609, 661; comparisons of litany with Lutheran and Roman, 737ff., comparison of liturgy with Lutheran and Roman, 691ff.; differences from Lutheran, 131ff.; in the propers, 467-575 *passim*
Book of Common Prayer, American, 139, 259, 303, 328, 345, 362, 369, 379, 387, 401, 405, 411, 418, 425, 430, 432, 440, 447, 605; comparisons of lessons with Lutheran and Roman, 465-575 *passim*; in the propers, 467-575 *passim*
Book of Common Prayer, Canadian, 138, 401
Book of Common Prayer, First (1549), 134ff., 195, 237, 263, 271, 283, 296, 316, 328, 333, 340, 344, 357, 367, 369, 374, 379, 382-83, 386, 390-91, 398, 401, 404, 409-10, 433, 441, 593, 608ff., 612-13, 615ff., 620-21, 662, 754; differences in texts, 189; influences on Lutheran, 129-30; Lutheran influences on, 135
Book of Common Prayer, Fourth

(1604), 137
Book of Common Prayer, Free church, 619
Book of Common Prayer, Indian, 138
Book of Common Prayer, Irish, 662
Book of Common Prayer, Proposed (1928), 214, 270, 345, 362, 367, 410
Book of Common Prayer, Scottish, 137-38, 259, 299, 329, 333, 345, 362, 367, 369, 279, 401, 433, 588, 591, 604-05; in the propers, 467-575 *passim*
Book of Common Prayer, Second (1552), 345, 362, 367, 369-70, 374, 376, 379, 382, 407, 440; Calvinistic influence on, 136; description, 136ff.; Puritan influence on, 135ff.; restoration, 136
Book of Common Prayer, South African, 138, 329, 346, 362, 379
Book of Worship: of Evangelical and Reformed Church, 346; of General Synod, 193; of General Synod, South, 176, 198; of Indian church, 176, 183, 237, 603, 756-57; of Presbyterian church, 363, 583, 600, 607; of United Synod in South, 193
Borthwick, Jane, 180
Bostrom, 211, 218
Brandenburg church order, *see* Church orders
Brandenburg-Calenberg church order; *see* Church orders
Brandenburg-Lüneberg church order; *see* Church orders
Brandenburg-Nuremberg church order; *see* Church orders
Breaking of bread, 369
Bread, unleavened, 53
Bremen church order, *see* Church orders
Brent, Charles H., 607
Brenz church order; *see* Church orders
Brenz, John 89-90, 96, 134, 193, 453, 629
Bretschneider, C. G., 103
Breviary, 61, 143, 279, 283, 390, 397, 402, 421, 442, 761; Ambrosian, 57, 397; Augsburg, 736-50 *passim*; Augustinian Eremites, 736ff.; Benedictine, 57, 61, 405; Cluniac, 397; Cranmer's, 441; French, 405; lessons, formative factor in lectionaries, 462; Magdeburg, 736-50 *passim*; Mozarabic, 57, 397, 405, 606; Paris, 397,

Sarum, 422, 443, 463, 577, 634, in propers, 465-575, *passim*; stand, 229, 768; Stowe, 626; Strengas, 112, 463; Swedish, 114; Tridentine of Pope Pius V, 257, 273; Uppsala, 112, 463
Missal, Roman (*Missale Romanum*), 214, 264, 328, 357, 382, 588, 614, 634; based on Gregorian Sacramentary, 48; in the propers compared to *Service Book* and *American Book of Common Prayer*, 465-575 *passim*; influence on Munzer, 75; issuance of, 56
Missale Gothicum, 458
Missale mixtum, 326, 459-60
Missale plenarium, 48
Missouri Synod, 176, 197, 206-07; invitation to participate in Common Liturgy, 208-09; declined, 208
Mithras, mysteries of, 31
Mitre, 768
Mixed chalice, 34, 159, 768
Mode, 768
Modern collects, 577
Mohammedans, 322
Mohldenke, 179
Monasticism, 46, 66; cultivated art, 14
Mone, 471
Monk, 297
Montanists, 471
Morales, 439
Moravians, 145, 162, 627
Morin, Dom, 417
Morison, Stanley, 154
Morning Prayer, 391-92, 394, 407, 420, 640, 692
Morning Suffrages; *see* Suffrages
Morris, J. G., 171
Morrison, A. J. W., 142
Mosaics, 768
Mosheim, Johann, 147, 454
Motet, 649
Mozart, Wolfgang, 269, 330, 370
Muethel, Julius, 352-53
Muhlenberg, Henry Melchoir, vii, 125, 130, 144-45, 162ff., 168ff., 182, 196, 258, 385, 480
Muhlenberg, Peter, 168
Muilenburg, J., 29
Münzer, Thomas, 75-76, 242, 340, 343, 349, 361, 453; church order, 91
Muratori, 626
Music, church, xii, 80, 84ff., 126, 108, 136, 155, 224, 229, 255, 329, 333, 371, 377, 383-84, 386, 402, 414, 419,

422, 433, 440-41, 443, 448, 635, 640; congregational character of Lutheran, 248; contrapuntal, 64-65; development of, 15, 62-63; Cranmer's contribution, 263; evaluation, 248ff.; forbidden by Zwingli, 86; German, 87; Gregorian, *see* Plain song; historical character, 248-49; in early church, 48-49; influence of Pietism, 146; instrumental encouraged in West, forbidden in East, 48; introduction of, 63-64; limited to psalm singing, 83; liturgical, 63, 223, 389; in Common Liturgy, 218ff.; in Eastern church, 41-42; loss of musical culture, 141; Luther's contribution, 82ff.; Luther's regard for, 84; medieval, 62ff.; Netherlands school, 64; of the fifteenth-sixteenth centuries, 63; of the Service, 248ff.; scale, origin of, 560; settings for Matins and Vespers, 403, 409; polyphonic, 63-64; rationalistic, 148-49; revival, 154; Roman school, 64; supplied by cantionales, 85; traditional, 84; Venetian school, 64
Myconius, 89, 166; church order, 89
Mystery in liturgy, 240ff.; in early church, 241; in medieval church, 241f.; in Sacrament 240-41
Mysticism, 70, 76, 241
Nassau church order; *see* Church orders
National and local conditions, formative factor in lectionaries, 462
National Lutheran Council, 205-06
Natural year, times of, formative factor in liturgies, 362
Naumburg church order; *see* Church orders
Nave, 768
Neale, John Mason, 26, 160, 180, 398
Neill, Charles, 508
Nelle, 154
Nelson, Clifford A., 127
Nerva, emporer, 474
Netherlands school, 64
Neumark, George, 86
Neumes, 768
New Testament, worship in, 26-27
New Year, collect for, unique in Lutheranism, 478
Newman, John Henry, 157, 180, 398, 608
Newton, John, 157
New York Synod, 172ff.; hymnal of 1814, 171; liturgy of 1833, 174

Type used in this book

Body: 10 on 12, 9 on 10, 8 on 9 Times Roman and 8 on 9 Garamond Bold
Display: Caledonia and Times Roman
Paper: White Glatfelten E. F. Book with Titanium

824